T. S. ELIOT
COLLECTED PROSE

By T. S. Eliot

THE POEMS OF T. S. ELIOT
Volume 1: Collected and Uncollected Poems
Volume 2: Practical Cats and Further Verses
edited by Christopher Ricks and Jim McCue

COLLECTED POEMS 1909–1962
PRUFROCK AND OTHER OBSERVATIONS
THE WASTE LAND AND OTHER POEMS
FOUR QUARTETS
SELECTED POEMS
THE WASTE LAND:
A Facsimile and Transcript of the Original Drafts
edited by Valerie Eliot
INVENTIONS OF THE MARCH HARE:
Poems 1909–1917
edited by Christopher Ricks
THE ARIEL POEMS
THE WASTE LAND
ANNIVERSARY EDITION
OLD POSSUM'S BOOK OF PRACTICAL CATS
THE COMPLETE POEMS AND PLAYS

plays
MURDER IN THE CATHEDRAL
THE FAMILY REUNION
THE COCKTAIL PARTY
THE CONFIDENTIAL CLERK
THE ELDER STATESMAN

literary criticism
THE SACRED WOOD
SELECTED ESSAYS
THE USE OF POETRY AND THE USE OF CRITICISM
THE VARIETIES OF METAPHYSICAL POETRY
edited by Ronald Schuchard
TO CRITICIZE THE CRITIC
ON POETRY AND POETS
FOR LANCELOT ANDREWES
SELECTED PROSE OF T. S. ELIOT
edited by Frank Kermode

social criticism
THE IDEA OF A CHRISTIAN SOCIETY
NOTES TOWARDS THE DEFINITION OF CULTURE

letters
THE LETTERS OF T. S. ELIOT
Volume 1: 1898–1922; Volume 2: 1923–1925
edited by Valerie Eliot and Hugh Haughton
Volume 3: 1926–1927; Volume 4: 1928–1929;
Volume 5: 1930–1931; Volume 6: 1932–1933;
Volume 7: 1934–1935; Volume 8: 1936–1938;
Volume 9: 1939–1941
edited by Valerie Eliot and John Haffenden

prose
T. S. ELIOT COLLECTED PROSE
Volume 1: 1905–1928; Volume 2: 1929–1934;
Volume 3: 1935–1950; Volume 4: 1951–1966
edited by Archie Burnett

T. S. Eliot
COLLECTED PROSE

EDITED BY
ARCHIE BURNETT

VOLUME 4
1951–1966

faber

First published in 2024
by Faber & Faber Ltd, The Bindery,
51 Hatton Garden,
London, EC1N 8HN

Typeset by Donald Sommerville
Printed in Poland

All rights reserved

All writings by T. S. Eliot,
© Set Copyrights Limited 2024

The moral right of Archie Burnett to be identified
as editor of this work has been asserted in accordance with
Section 77 of the Copyright, Designs and Patents Act 1988

A CIP record for this book is available from the British Library

ISBN 978–0–571–29554–8

2 4 6 8 10 9 7 5 3 1

Contents

Guide to Using This Edition — xi
Abbreviations — xiii

THE PROSE

1951

The Three Provincialities (1922) — 3
Poetry and Film — 6
Poetry and Drama — 8
Foreword — 9
Preface — 10
Poetry and Drama — 12
The Spoken Word — 12
The Aims of Education. 2. The Interrelation of Aims — 16
The Aims of Education. 3. The Conflict between Aims — 17
[A Comment on James Thurber] — 17
Preface — 17
The Aims of Education. 4. The Issue of Religion — 18
Preface — 18
Vergil and the Christian World — 19
The Value and Use of Cathedrals in England To-Day — 19
'Those Who need Privacy and Those Whose Need is Company' — 27

1952

[Message from T. S. Eliot] — 30
Introduction By T. S. Eliot — 31
Scylla and Charybdis — 35
Preface — 48
Dossier on *Murder in the Cathedral* — 54
Foreword — 56
Découverte de Paris — 60
Some Thoughts on Braille — 60
An Address — 63

[Tribute to Luigi Pirandello]	68
The Publishing of Poetry	68

1953

L'amitié Franco-Britannique	74
[Greeting to the Asociacíon de Artistas Aficionados]	76
Foreword to the English Edition	76
[American Literature and the American Language]	78
Reflections on the Unity of European Culture (II)	79
Thomas Stearns Eliot Gratulation	79
Literature	79
The Three Voices of Poetry	82

1954

Introduction	83
A Message	88
Comments by T. S. Eliot	90
A Tribute	91
Preface	92
A note on *Monstre Gai* by Wyndham Lewis	93
[Books of the Year]	97
Mrs Runcie's Pudding	98

1955

[*The Women of Trachis*: A Symposium]	99
[The Saddest Word]	99
'Le salut de trois grands poètes: Londres: T. S. Eliot'	100
[Contribution to journal on 'Das Theater ist unersetzlich' ('The theatre is irreplaceable')]	100
A Note on *In Parenthesis* and *The Anathemata*	101
Gordon Craig's Socratic Dialogues	103
The Literature of Politics	107
'Goethe as the Sage'	115
[To Ezra Pound on his Seventieth Birthday]	115

1956

Fr Cheetham Retires from Gloucester Road	116
[To Ezra Pound on his Seventieth Birthday]	118
[Tribute to Artur Lundkvist]	118
The Frontiers of Criticism	119
[Brief über Ernst Robert Curtius]	119
Essays on Elizabethan Drama	121

Foreword	121
Poetry and the Schools	124

1957

Das schöpferische Recht des Regisseurs (The creative right of directors)	125
Homage to Wyndham Lewis 1884–1957	126
The Importance of Wyndham Lewis	126
Wyndham Lewis	127
[Tribute to John Davidson]	130
[Speech to the BBC Governors]	131
On Poetry and Poets	134
Preface	134
I. On Poetry	135
The Social Function of Poetry	135
The Music of Poetry	145
What Is Minor Poetry?	158
What is a Classic?	172
Poetry and Drama	189
The Three Voices of Poetry	208
The Frontiers of Criticism	221
II. On Poets	236
Virgil and the Christian World	236
Sir John Davies	247
Milton I	252
Milton II	259
Johnson as Critic and Poet	277
Byron	305
Goethe as the Sage	319
Rudyard Kipling	339
Yeats	362
Preface	373

1958

[A special message about Ezra Pound]	375
[Report on Obscene Publications]	376
Introduction	384
[Lady Margaret Rhondda]	395
T. S. Eliot Talks about his Poetry	396
Bishop Bell	400
The Very Revd F. P. Harton	401
[Salutation]	401

Television is not Friendly Enough	402
[Eliot's choice of Books of the Year]	402

1959

[Edwin Muir]	404
Rudyard Kipling	405
The Art of Poetry I	413
Foreword	432
The Unfading Genius of Rudyard Kipling	435
[Statement about *The New Leader*]	440
The Panegyric by Mr T. S. Eliot	440
[Mr Ashley Dukes]	443
[Address]	444
Preface	448
A Note	451
Countess Nora Wydenbruck	452
[Greeting to the Staatstheater Kassel]	452
[Address at Mary Institute]	453

1960

Foreword	458
The Influence of Landscape upon the Poet	460
On Teaching the Appreciation of Poetry	463
Thomas Stearns Eliot	471
[Tribute to Giuseppe Ungaretti]	474
[On the production of *The Confidential Clerk*]	475

1961

Bruce Lyttelton Richmond	476
Preface	478
Obituary	479
Preface	482
Geoffrey Faber	483
Talking Freely: T. S. Eliot and Tom Greenwell	486
Preface	494
Miss Harriet Weaver	496
Mögen Sie Picasso?	496
A Note of Introduction	497

1962

[Interview]	499
Miss Harriet Weaver	501

Notes Towards the Definition of Culture	502
Preface to the 1962 Edition	502
[Memorial Tribute for Mrs Violet Schiff]	503
[Interview with T. S. Eliot]	504
[Tribute to Victoria Ocampo]	509
[Memorial Tribute for Sylvia Beach]	510
George Herbert	511
I	511
II	519
III	528
George Herbert A Select Bibliography	535
[The Common Market]	538
T. S. Eliot on the Language of *The New English Bible*	538

1963

[The Festival of Poetry]	544
[*The Tower* by Hugo von Hofmannsthal]	545
[Obituary Notice for Louis MacNeice]	546
[Anti-Semitism in Russia]	547
Elizabethan Dramatists	548
Preface	548

1964

Ulysses, Order, and Myth	551
Knowledge and Experience in the Philosophy of F. H. Bradley	555
Preface	555
Chapter I: On Our Knowledge of Immediate Experience	557
Chapter II: On the Distinction of 'Real' and 'Ideal'	570
Chapter III: The Psychologist's Treatment of Knowledge	591
Chapter IV: The Epistemologist's Theory of Knowledge	612
Chapter V: The Epistemologist's Theory of Knowledge *continued*	635
Chapter VI: Solipsism	657
Chapter VII: Conclusion	667
Appendix I: The Development of Leibniz's Monadism	680
Appendix II: Leibniz's Monads and Bradley's Finite Centres	697
[A Tribute to Wilfred Owen]	705
A Note on Translation	705
Edwin Muir: 1887–1959	706
[Tribute to Georg Svensson on his 60th Birthday]	706
A Conversation with T. S. Eliot	707

1965

[Eliot interviewed by T. S. Matthews]	716
Thomas Stearns Eliot	718
Preface	719
[Tribute to Aldous Huxley]	721
To Criticize the Critic and other writings	723
Note	723
To Criticize the Critic	724
From Poe to Valéry	736
American Literature and the American Language	736
The Aims of Education 1	751
The Aims of Education 2	764
The Aims of Education 3	777
The Aims of Education 4	789
What Dante Means to Me	802
The Literature of Politics	802
The Classics and the Man of Letters	803
Ezra Pound: His Metric and Poetry	816
Reflections on Vers Libre	816
[Memoir of Richard Aldington]	817

1966

A Tribute To Mario Praz	818
A Note on *The Criterion* By T. S. Eliot	818
Index of Article Titles	821

Guide to Using This Edition

This is a text-only edition, with the prose arranged in a single chronological sequence. However, the chronology has to be handled carefully in view of the fact that it was Eliot's practice to revise his work. (It is a shortcoming of Donald Gallup's indispensable 1969 bibliography that he does not always note that a reprinted text has also undergone revision: this means that all versions must be scrutinised for variants.) Where Eliot revised wording, even slightly, the latest revised version is printed at the point at which it appeared, and variants in wording are recorded there from the earlier version(s). An example: 'Tradition and the Individual Talent' was originally published in two parts in *The Egoist* in September and November/December 1919; both parts were combined and revised in *The Sacred Wood* (November 1920); and the text was further revised in *Selected Essays* (September 1932). Readers will find the text under *Selected Essays*, together with a record of the changes Eliot made at each stage. The earlier versions are recorded at the point at which they appeared, with an indication that they would undergo revision.

Even where revision involves merely putting a word in italics or quotation marks to introduce a new emphasis or attitude, this is regarded as a substantive change. In the few cases where revision also involves translation from French into English, variants are not recorded: translation itself constitutes a form of variation, and it would be difficult to decide, on the basis of often very slight differences of idiom and nuance, which variants are to be recorded and which not. Both the French and the English versions are printed in full, however. Textual variants are recorded below the latest revised text and variants are recorded by paragraph. Thus, '4 vast energy] energy' records that in paragraph 4, where the revised text has 'vast energy', the previously published text has 'energy'. Where the text was revised more than once, each variant is labelled. This edition aims to provide the most complete record available of Eliot's revisions to his authorised prose.

For the first time, page numbers in the text chosen for printing are inserted in a different font in editorial square brackets – for example [76], for convenience of reference to the original publications.

The conventions of all publications are regularised to Faber's house style. Block quotations are given in roman, single-spaced, and indented, and quotation marks at the beginning and end are not reproduced. Inconsistent punctuation for introducing block quotations (':—' as well as ':') is regularised to a colon. American spellings, when used, have been retained.

The numbers of volumes and issues of periodicals are given in arabic. Thus '2. 3' means 'volume 2, number 3'.

Obvious misprints, such as 'desert' for 'dessert', or 'writed' for 'writer', or beginning a sentence with 'they' instead of 'They', are silently corrected. It is not always possible to distinguish a misprint from an authorial error, but the following have been routinely corrected: passages in French (almost always a question of accents: Eliot's French was good, and it is hard to believe that in an article such as 'Marivaux' (Gallup C73), for instance, 'Corbiere' is followed within a few lines by 'Corbière', and hardly a single French accent is rendered correctly); names of persons ('Rubenstein' to 'Rubinstein', 'Weckerlin' to 'Weckherlin', the poet [Thomas] 'Grey' to 'Gray', [Sybil] 'Thorndyke' to 'Thorndike'); and titles of books (*Dorian Grey* to *Dorian Gray*, *Biographia Litteraria* to *Biographia Literaria*).

Eliot's misquotations, both of literature and of passages from books under review, are left uncorrected, in the interests of preserving what Eliot thought he was commenting on. Eliot on occasion makes use of terminology that will be offensive to contemporary readers, but has been retained in the text as originally published.

I have supplied or changed punctuation only where necessary, and have placed missing punctuation, as well as words, in editorial square brackets. One unusual practice in Eliot's punctuation has been highlighted by Jayme Stayer:[1] a comma inserted between subject and predicate:

What the poet has to say about poetry, will often be most valuable . . .

Even those of us who are not addressed, can agree that all 'sane' people are for peace.

Professor Stayer plausibly suggests that Eliot may be marking his sense of how a sentence should be delivered orally. It is often found when the grammatical subject is long. It causes no problems of comprehension, however, and I have therefore let such punctuation stand.

Archie Burnett
The Editorial Institute
Boston University

---

[1] 'Of Commas and Facts: Editing Volume 5 of *The Complete Prose*,' *T. S. Eliot Studies Annual*, 2 (2018), 121–8.

Abbreviations

A.	*The Athenaeum* (see also *N&A*)
A&L	*Art and Letters*
ASG	*After Strange Gods* (London: Faber & Faber, 1934)
C.	*The Criterion*
CT	*The Church Times*
EAAM	T. S. Eliot, *Essays Ancient & Modern* (London: Faber & Faber, 1936)
ED	*Elizabethan Dramatists* (London: Faber & Faber, 1934)
EE	T. S. Eliot, *Elizabethan Essays* (London: Faber & Faber, 1934)
ER	*The English Review*
FLA	T. S. Eliot, *For Lancelot Andrewes: Essays on Style and Order* (London: Faber & Gwyer, 1928)
Gallup	*T. S. Eliot: A Bibliography*, by Donald Gallup (London: Faber & Faber, 1969)
HA	*The Harvard Advocate*
HJD	T. S. Eliot, *Homage to John Dryden: Three Essays on the Poetry of the Seventeenth Century* (London: The Hogarth Press, 1924)
HR	*The Hudson Review*
ICS	*The Idea of a Christian Society* (London: Faber & Faber, 1939)
IJE	*International Journal of Ethics*
JDPDC	*John Dryden The Poet the Dramatist the Critic* (London: Faber & Faber, 1932)
KEPB	T. S. Eliot, *Knowledge and Experience in the Philosophy of F. H. Bradley* (London: Faber & Faber, 1964)
King's	King's College Library, Cambridge
KR	*The Kenyon Review*
LM	*The London Magazine*
MG	*The Manchester Guardian* newspaper
N.	*The Nation*
N&A	*The Nation & Athenaeum*
NC	*The New Criterion*
NER	*New English Review*

NEW	*The New English Weekly*
NRF	*La Nouvelle Revue Française*
NS	*The New Statesman and Nation*
NTDC	*Notes Towards the Definition of Culture*
OPAP	T. S. Eliot, *On Poetry and Poets* (London: Faber & Faber, 1957; New York: Farrar, Straus & Cudahy, 1957)
SE	T. S. Eliot, *Selected Essays: 1917–1932* (London: Faber & Faber, 1932; 3rd UK edn: Faber & Faber, 1951, with supplementary material)
Spectator	*The Spectator*
SR	*The Sewanee Review*
SW	T. S. Eliot, *The Sacred Wood: Essays on Poetry and Criticism* (London: Methuen & Co., 1920)
T&T	*Time and Tide*
TCTC	T. S. Eliot, *To Criticize the Critic* (London: Faber & Faber, 1965; New York: Farrar, Straus & Giroux, 1965)
TES	*The Times Educational Supplement*
TLR	*The Little Review*
TLS	*The Times Literary Supplement* [London]
UPUC	T. S. Eliot, *The Use of Poetry and the Use of Criticism: Studies in the Relation of Criticism to Poetry in England* (London: Faber & Faber, 1933)

COLLECTED PROSE
1951–1966

1951

The Three Provincialities (1922)
With a Postscript (1950)
Essays in Criticism, 1. 1 (Jan. 1951), 38–41. Gallup C559; also C129, 1922 version.

['The Three Provincialities' was originally published in the second (and last) number of *The Tyro: A Review of the Arts of Painting Sculpture and Design* – an Egoist Press venture which was edited by Wyndham Lewis. It is reprinted here with Mr Lewis's consent. – Editor]

It has been perceptible for several years that not one but three English literatures exist: that written by Irishmen, that written by Americans and that composed by the English themselves. Thirty years ago Irish and English literature were in a state of partial amalgamation. That is to say, the literary movement in England was very largely sustained by Irishmen; for some years, otherwise on the whole rather barren years, the depleted English ranks were filled by Irishmen. English literature lacked the vitality to assimilate this foreign matter; and, more recently, in accord with political tendencies, Irish writers (mostly of minor importance) have reassembled in Dublin. There remain, as a permanent part of English literature, some of the poetry of Yeats, and more doubtfully the plays of Synge (probably too local for permanence). As for the future, it may be predicted that the work of Mr Joyce should arrest the separate Irish current, for the reason that it is the first Irish work since that of Swift to possess absolute European significance. Mr Joyce has used what is racial and national and transmuted it into something of international value; so that future Irish writers, measured by the standard he has given, must choose either to pursue the same ideal or to confess that they write solely for an Irish, not for a European public. No more comic peasants, epic heroes, banshees, little people, Deirdres; Mr Joyce has shown them up. Mr James Stephens (I think it was) in a recent number of the *Outlook* advocated that Irish writers should return to the Irish language. In that case, there will be no further need to discuss Irish literature at all.

[39] American literature, in contrast to Irish, has not yet received this death blow from a native hand. Owing to the fact that America possesses a much greater number (even making full allowance for the difference of population) of able second order writers than England, its 'national literature' is extremely flourishing. If it has produced nothing of European importance it nevertheless counts a considerable number of intelligent writers; has several literary critics more alert and open-minded than any of their generation in this country; and some of its poets and novelists at least admire respectable ideals, and tend towards the light. The advance of 'American literature' has been accelerated by the complete collapse of literary effort in England. One may even say that the present situation here has now become a scandal impossible to conceal from foreign nations; that literature is chiefly in the hands of persons who may be interested in almost anything else; that literature presents the appearance of a garden unmulched, untrimmed, unweeded, and choked by vegetation sprung only from the chance germination of the seed of last year's plants.

It is a sign of the poverty and blindness of our criticism that in all three countries a mistaken attitude toward nationality has unconsciously arisen or has been consciously adopted. The point is this: literature is not primarily a matter of nationality, but of language; the traditions of the language, not the traditions of the nation or the race, are what first concern the writer. The Irish radicals are commendable in so far as they mark the necessity for a choice. Ireland must either employ a language of its own or submit to international standards. It is immaterial, from my point of view, whether English literature be written in London, in New York, in Dublin, in Indianapolis, or in Trieste. In fifty years' time it may all make its appearance in Paris or in New York. But so far as it is literature of the first order, not merely an entertaining slideshow, it will be English literature. Should America in time develop a superior language (as Ireland may try to revert to a more barbarous one) there would be a separate American literature – contingent, probably, upon the disappearance or sufficient degeneration of the English language in England.

Every literature has two sides; it has that which is essential [40] to it as literature, which can be appreciated by everyone with adequate knowledge of the language, and on the other hand it has that which can only be enjoyed by a particular group of people inhabiting a particular portion of the earth. As in the end *adequate* knowledge of the language means *complete* knowledge, and as *no* person can ever have the opportunity to acquire complete knowledge of any language but his own, it is easy to confuse the two appreciations. For those who have the best opportunity for knowing the language are precisely this particular group in a particular portion of the earth. The critic is the person who has the power to distinguish between the two points of view in himself; and to discern what, in any work of literary art, takes its place, through its expression of the genius of its own language, in European literature, and what is of purely local importance. (In the case of such a writer as Dickens, for example, this dissociation remains to be performed.)

English literature at the present time suffers as much, I think, as that written in America, from this pleasant provinciality. (How much contemporary verse, for instance, appeals rather to the Englishman's love of English rustic scenery than to a universal perception of Nature, such as Wordsworth *rarely* attained.) And how tardy, and still how deficient, has been the English appreciation of one of the greatest and least local: Edgar Poe. The lesson of language, therefore, is one to be learned on both sides of the Atlantic. (The statement of this fact places the author, as M. Cocteau might say, in the position of Calchas in *Troilus and Cressida*.) Whatever words a writer employs, he benefits by knowing as much as possible of the history of these words, of the *uses to which they have already been applied*. Such knowledge facilitates his task of giving to the word a new life and to the language a new idiom. The essential of tradition is in this; in getting as much as possible of the whole weight of the history of the language behind his word. Not every good writer need be conscious of this – I do not know to what extent Mr Wyndham Lewis has studied Elizabethan prose – Mr Joyce at least has not only the tradition but the consciousness of it. The best writers will always produce work which will not be American or Irish or English, [41] but which will take its predestined place in 'English literature'. It is a pity, however, that the second-best writers, for want of a little critical breadth of view, should insist, out of national vanity or mere unconscious complacency, on what will render them only completely insupportable to posterity. The British writer, who shrinks from working overtime or at weekends, will not find these ideas congenial. Nor, for other reasons, will all American critics.

POSTSCRIPT 1950. I had completely forgotten 'The Three Provincialities', and re-read it, as I re-read any prose piece that I wrote many years ago, with a good deal of misgiving and apprehension. Its republication does not embarrass me, however, so much as I expected. I seem to have made a rash prediction about the influence of Joyce; and when I find that I said that America at that time at which I was writing possessed a much greater number of able second-order writers than England, I now wonder what writers I could have been thinking of. The author of 'The

Three Provincialities' appears to have been unduly sanguine about the prospects of American literature, and perhaps a little more pessimistic about England than was, at that moment, strictly justified. I am glad to find him asserting that literature is not primarily a matter of nationality but of language; and that true literature has in it something which can be appreciated by intelligent foreigners who have a reading knowledge of the language, and also something which can only be understood by the particular people living in the same place as the author. I am also glad to find the affirmation, that it is a good thing for a writer to take an interest in the history of the words that he uses. I detect a slightly aggressive tone which now gives a mild amusement; and I cannot regard the article as a whole as anything but a very small literary curio.

Poetry and Film
MR T. S. ELIOT'S VIEWS

CT, 134. 4591 (2 Feb. 1951), 78. Eliot delivered the address on 19 Jan. 1951. Not in Gallup, but would be C560a.

The following is the text of Mr T. S. Eliot's address at the opening of the exhibition of dresses and settings for the film Murder in the Cathedral. *We produced a very brief summary of his speech last week.*

The subject 'Poetry and Film' comprehends two questions. The first is: Of what use can the film be to poetry? The second: Of what use can poetry be to the film? The first question is obviously the more appropriate for me; the second is that on which you would perhaps be more interested to hear what the film producer would have to say.

We cannot go into the general question of the *pros* and *cons* of recorded speech and direct readings: that can be considered sufficiently in relation to gramophone records. We are concerned, furthermore, only with dramatic poetry, which, in the widest sense, means poetry which is merely a part of a total work of art. In non-dramatic poetry, the visual imagery is to be supplied by the reader's imagination; and it is the function of the poet to stimulate the imagination of each individual reader to the utmost of its capacity.

In dramatic poetry, the scene, human beings in action, must be provided by the co-operation of producer, actor and designer. The precedence of the author is due primarily to the fact that the play starts with him, and secondarily, to the fact that any play of permanent value must be susceptible of an indefinite variety of interpretations by different producers and actors, and by successive generations of producers and actors.

When we try to strike a balance between the respective advantages of stage and screen for the drama, we must keep in mind that there are three kinds of plays: those which are suitable only for the stage, those which are possible only on the screen, and those which can be adapted for either. It is convenient to confine ourselves here to the last, considering the fact that we assume that *Murder in the Cathedral* belongs to this category.

I have in the course of work on this firm, made two observations. The first is pretty obvious, and was brought to our notice several years ago by Sir Laurence Olivier's *Henry V*: the pleasure that we get from the complete audibility of every word in every part of the house. This, of course, is of particularly great value with a verse play, in which every word and phrase is important, and in which any inaccuracy on the part of the actor, or any inaudibility to the audience, is a much more serious blemish than for a play in prose.

Directing Eyes –

The second observation is more tentative, and perhaps more open to dispute. But anyone who has viewed films with critical attention, must be aware that in a film we are constantly, and without knowing it, being directed what to look at. In a stage play you may be looking at one moment at the actor who is speaking; at another moment watching the face of the person addressed, or observing the behaviour of other characters on the stage. If you go repeatedly to the same play, you may choose to look at different actors in a different order, for you certainly cannot observe everybody and everything simultaneously. But in a film, the lens of the camera is constantly telling you what to look at – it may be a close-up of the actor's hand, by the movement of which he betrays the emotion not visible in his face.

Now Mr Hoellering (the producer and director of the film, *Murder in the Cathedral*) recently made a very interesting documentary film employing this power of the camera. It took one through an exhibition of works of sculpture; it decided for you the order in which you looked at the figures, and pointed contrasts between them; the camera took you round a statue, showing the masses and planes from different angles. The camera directed by the producer was in fact making the observer look at the object with the eye of a particular critic; it was supplying the ordinary onlooker, to a surprising degree, with the trained vision of the critic.

– and Ears

It has struck me, since seeing this film, that the technique of the film can do with the spoken word, and probably will do, something of the same thing to direct the audience's ears, that we have seen it do for the audience's eyes. I remembered then, several years later, that one or two speeches from *Henry V* to which I had never given special attention in reading or at stage performances, emerged with a fresh and startling beauty and importance. In other words, the producer has it within his power to teach the audience how to listen, as well as to teach it how to see. This is of especial importance for poetic drama, and places indefinite possibilities within the reach of the intelligent and conscious producer.

Of the value of poetry to the film I shall say little, because from my point of view it is a corollary to the proposition that poetry has still a function on the stage, and this proposition I have already defended on several occasions. The question of poetry on the screen, therefore, is to my mind simply a question of whether the higher possibilities of the cinema are to be realised, or whether it is to sink to the lowest level of what the greatest number of empty-headed people are willing to look at. I will only add this: I know that a poet who turns to the theatre, after years of practice in other kinds of poetry, has to be willing to submit himself to an arduous and painful discipline. But film technique is not stage technique; and if he is to proceed to write for the screen, he will see that he has a great deal still to learn.

Poetry and Drama

The first Theodore Spencer Memorial Lecture, delivered at Harvard on 21 Nov. 1950, was publ. in *Atlantic Monthly*, 187. 2 (Feb. 1951), 30–7. 'By T. S. Eliot'. Gallup C560. Revised in *OPAP. See below*, pp. 189–207.

Foreword

Foreword to *D. H. Lawrence and Human Existence* by Father William Tiverton, [vii–viii]. Subheaded '*by* T. S. ELIOT', and signed 'T. S. ELIOT' at the end. Publ. 16 Feb. 1951. Gallup B61.

The author of this book is a priest of an Anglican religious order, whom I know. If he has chosen to publish his book under the name of William Tiverton, it is only to make the point that his views are personal. The common reader, especially if he knows nothing of the monastic life, is apt to presume that the member of an order can be only a spokesman for his community. This author writes with the full knowledge and approval of his superiors, but speaks only for himself.

My reason for contributing a preface is not the fact that I know the author. It is that I think this is a serious piece of criticism of Lawrence, of a kind for which the time is now due. We have had a number of books about Lawrence by people who knew him; we need books about him by critics who know him only through his works. To have been associated with Lawrence was, evidently, for those who were attracted, or alternately attracted and repelled, by that dominating, cross-grained and extreme personality, a very important part of their lives, an experience which had to be recorded in print. But perhaps one of the reasons why Lawrence's books are now less read by young people than they were twenty and thirty years ago, is that the books about him give the impression that he is a man to read about, rather than an author to read: a Johnson surrounded by a shoal of Boswells, some of them less tender towards the great man than was Johnson's biographer.

This is not the only reason why Lawrence's work needs to be examined from a new perspective. He was an impatient and [viii] impulsive man (or so I imagine him to have been; for, like the author of this book, I never knew him). He was a man of fitful and profound insights, rather than of ratiocinative powers; and therefore he was an impatient man: he expressed some of his insights in the form least likely to make them acceptable to most of his contemporaries, and sometimes in a form which almost wilfully encouraged misunderstanding. If the foolish or the ill-disposed chose to regard him as a blasphemer, a 'fascist', or a pornographer, Lawrence would not put himself out to persuade them. Wrong he often was (I think) from ignorance, prejudice, or drawing the wrong conclusions in his conscious mind from the insights which came to him from below consciousness: and it will take time to dissociate the superficial error from the fundamental truth. To me, also, he seems often to write very badly; but to be a writer who had to write often badly in order to write sometimes well. After being misunderstood, he is in danger of being ignored. As for his religious attitude (of the development of which the author of this book has something to say) we can now begin to see better how much was ignorance, rather than hostility; for Lawrence was an ignorant man in the sense that he was unaware of how much he did not know. His strictures upon Christianity (and indeed upon Buddhism) are often ill-informed; at other times they go straight to the heart of the matter; and no Christian ought to feel sure that he is religious-minded enough, to ignore the criticism of a man who, without being a Christian, was primarily and always religious.

Preface

Preface to *Thoughts for Meditation: A Way to Recovery from Within*, an anthology selected and arranged by N. Gangulee, 11–14. Publ. 9 Mar. 1951. Signed 'T. S. Eliot'. Gallup B62.

If I had thought that this anthology was suitable only for readers who had already entered upon the spiritual life, I should not have had the audacity to introduce it; and if it were only a collection of morsels for nibblers I should not wish to do so. The author, in calling this book *Thoughts for Meditation*, means what he says. These are selections from among many extracts from his reading over many years; and they are passages which have borne his test of repeated meditation. They are intended for everyone who is curious about those emotions, and states of soul, which are to be found, so to speak, only beyond the limit of the visible spectrum of human feeling, and which can be experienced only in moments of illumination, or by the development of another organ or perception than that of everyday vision. But they can be of service to the reader only on one hard condition – that he is willing to try to learn to read.

Very few people, I suspect, know how to read – in the sense of being able to read for a variety of motives and to read a variety of books each in the appropriate way. We all read for diversion, or in order to satisfy a temporary curiosity; most of us read also under the necessity of acquiring information or a grasp of the contents of some book for an immediate end. For many workers, it is difficult to read a book unless it has some bearing on their own work; a professional reviewer may come to find it [12] difficult to read a book except for the purpose of reviewing it; and a publisher may come to find it difficult to read a book except as a manuscript to be accepted or rejected. Philosophy is difficult, unless we discipline our minds for it; the full appreciation of poetry is difficult for those who have not trained their sensibility by years of attentive reading. But devotional reading is the most difficult of all, because it requires an application, not only of the mind, not only of the sensibility, but of the whole being.

Thoughts for Meditation is a book of which, after the first examination – that in which one runs through a book to get a general view of the contents and a grasp of the design – I myself should not choose to read very much at a time. To read two or three passages (at first, choosing passages in the same section), to attend closely to every word, to ponder on the quotations read for a little while and try to fix them in my mind, so that they may continue to affect me while my attention is engrossed with the affairs of the day: that is enough for me in twenty-four hours, and enough, I imagine, even for those more practised in meditation than I.

I do not suggest that it is wholly unprofitable to acquaint oneself with some mystical literature without attempting to penetrate the world of the authors. To be wholly ignorant of this literature, to be unacquainted with examples of it from several languages and civilisations, is to lack some vital information about Man; just as much, as if we read only those historical works which ignore the action of religion upon history. But to learn from these writers needs something more than mere acquaintance. We have to abandon some of our usual motives for reading. We must surrender the Love of Power – whether over others, or over ourselves, or over the material world. We must abandon even the Love of [13] Knowledge. We must not be distracted by interest in the personality of particular authors, or by delight in the phrases in which they have expressed their insights. What these writers aim at, in their various idioms, in whatever language or in the terms of whatever religion, is the Love of God. They gave their lives to this: and their destination is not one which we can reach any quicker than they did, or without the same tireless activity and tireless passivity.

There are some readers who, attracted perhaps by curiosity about 'the occult', regard Asiatic literature as the sole repository or religious understanding; there are others who, perhaps under the prejudice that mysticism is something morbid and perverse, refuse to venture further than a narrow Christian tradition. For both kinds of reader, it is salutary to learn that the Truth is not 'occult', and that it is not wholly confined to their own religious tradition, or on the other hand to an alien culture and religion which they regard with superstitious awe; and to learn how frequently contemplatives of religions and civilisations remote from each other are saying the same thing. I am aware also that there are readers who persuade themselves that there is an 'essence' in all religions which is the same, and that this essence can be conveniently distilled and preserved, while every particular religion is rejected. Such readers may perhaps be reminded that no man has ever climbed to the higher stages of the spiritual life, who has not been a believer in a particular religion or at least a particular philosophy; and that the authors who are represented in this volume, would all have repudiated the suggestion that their religion or philosophy did not matter. It was only in relation to his own religion that the insights of any one of these men had its significance to him, and what they say can only reveal its meaning to the reader [14] who has his own religion of dogma and doctrine in which he believes. With these thoughts in mind, I attach a special value to an anthology which places side by side passages from Christian, Jewish, Moslem, Hindu and Buddhist scriptures and devotional writings.

Poetry and Drama

The Theodore Spencer Memorial Lecture

Publ. by Harvard University Press on 15 Mar. 1951: Gallup A57. Revised in the edn publ. by Faber on 28 Sept. 1951 (Gallup A57), and further revised in *OPAP*. *See below*, pp. 189–207.

The Spoken Word

Festival of Britain 1951 London Season of the Arts Official Souvenir Programme, 6–9. Subheaded '*T. S. Eliot, O.M.*' Published for the Arts Council of Great Britain in the last week of Apr. 1951. Gallup B63.

Few of those few people in any generation who care for poetry need to be told that poetry must be understood through the ear and not merely taken in by the eye. It is a common experience that a poem found difficult when read to oneself, is suddenly elucidated when read aloud by someone who has understood it. And in Great Britain nowadays there is ample opportunity to learn how poetry should sound. The poetry readings regularly broadcast by the B.B.C., the reproduction of verse by gramophone records, and public recitals of poetry, enable us to familiarise ourselves through the ear with the poetry of the past; and when the reader is a living poet reading his own verse, we can hear modern poetry as nearly as possible as the author hears it. I find, for my own part, that

I prefer to read a new poem by a contemporary author before I hear it; but that the hearing of it can send me back to re-read it with fuller understanding. It is thus that the music lover acquaints himself with a new composition: if he has read the score he is better prepared for the first audition; and after he has heard the piece interpreted, he can return to the score with greater understanding.

To say that poetry must be heard is a commonplace. What is perhaps less commonplace is to make the point that the poet is at the same time in a relation of dependence upon, and responsibility towards, the language in which he writes; and that the English language has peculiar resources of enrichment and revitalisation available to its poets. It will be admitted, even in our time, that some languages are 'greater' than others; but that among the 'great' languages there is diversity of gifts, such that one language may be more expressive for some purposes and another language for some other purposes; and that therefore we cannot say of two languages, such as English and French, that one is 'greater' than the other. But the English language has, as I have just said, certain peculiar advantages for the poet; and the English poets, by availing themselves of these advantages, have played, and should continue to play, a most important part in the development and renovation of the language.

[7] English owes a great deal, in the first place, to her ballads. We think first of the 'border ballads' – those which were composed, during a certain period of time, in the closely related speech of the people living on both sides of the frontier between England and Scotland. At the stage of what is called (having regard to its anonymity of authorship) 'folk poetry' the language of verse and the language of common speech are almost identical – and both are nearer to song than in more highly developed stages of language. But we must remember that the development from folk poetry to more sophisticated poetry is not in a simple way chronological. Behind the language of the border ballads is the Anglo-Saxon language, which at the end of the Norman conquest had arrived at such a point of sophistication that the practice of verse was an art of exacting rules. On the other hand, the popular ballad, in town and country, was a living form up to the twentieth century, and preserved the relation between poetry and common speech. Samuel Johnson, commonly regarded as a representative of the period of the most artificial verse, expressed in strong terms his admiration for the 'Ballad of Johnny Armstrong'.

In the history of English poetry we can observe two alternating and almost periodic movements. One is toward elaboration, the other a reaction towards simplification. In the first phase, poets refine, complicate, achieve the more subtle or the more decorative; they tend to borrow words and idioms from Latin and Greek and from other more highly developed modern languages. They depart from the common speech of their day. This is naturally the first in time, because it happens when the language is still in the awkward age, when poets recognise the crudity of their language compared to those of the ancients or to that of some contemporary people. The reverse, the return to simplicity – or rather, the conscious effort towards simplification – occurs later, because it springs from a more sophisticated consciousness. Poets try to return to common speech: not, of course, to the common speech of earlier times, because that is already obsolete and quaint, but to a common speech contemporary with themselves, a speech which has undergone many changes. In the history of these changes of language, Geoffrey Chaucer occupies a unique position. For he enriched and exercised the English language by his study of French models, at a time when the French language was more advanced than the English; yet he also listened to the homely talk of his own people, so that in spite of his innovations we hear in his poetry the voice of a cultivated English gentleman of his day, speaking not only to courtiers but to all his fellow-countrymen.

After Chaucer there was little development until the sixteenth century. The impact of the Renaissance upon England brought about a more widespread and enthusiastic study of the classics, and especially of the pre-Christian Latin writers. Prose writing became heavily latinised, and many new words were coined out of Latin metal. New words were very much needed, if English civilisation was to catch up with that of France or Italy; out of the new currency of words some have proved valueless and sound pedantic or uncouth to modern ears; others have become part of the small change of our everyday transactions. At the same time, in the sixteenth and well into the seventeenth century, the influence of the Italian poetry of the Renaissance was very strong. A revolution took place in English prosody. Then were shaped the verse forms – on Latin, Italian and French models – which are now called 'traditional English verse'. What is now called 'modern verse' is partly a return to older forms of English versification – to the stress, to 'sprung rhythm', to alliteration – the apparent irregularity and lawlessness of which is due to its being [8] based on the musical bar instead of the foot, and to its refusal to admit that some syllables of the English language are *always* long and others *always* short, instead of their being longer or shorter according to their position.

The man who brought order out of the innovations and borrowings of the sixteenth century – a great innovator himself, and with a sensitiveness to words almost equal to that of Chaucer – was Edmund Spenser. He was an elaborator, and he elaborated to excess. If his influence was immensely for good, instead of leading merely to further excesses ending in decadence, it was, I think, because of what appears to have been a happy accident. The great poets who underwent and transmitted his teaching, happened to be dramatic poets. First of his disciples was Christopher Marlowe. A dramatic poet, a poet who is writing for the theatre, who is dependent for his livelihood upon immediate success with a popular audience, cannot afford to depart too far from common speech. In the work of Marlowe, as in the work of Shakespeare (who owed much to his precocious contemporary), we can observe that as they became more experienced in the theatre their characters speak more naturally – and that the *poetry* gains, in concentration, in economy, in force and in intensity, in the process. The disciplinary value of the theatre, not for poetic drama only, but for the whole of English poetry during the last three hundred years, has not received its due attention.

The non-dramatic poetry at the turn of the sixteenth century might, however, have gone the way of Euphuism, becoming more and more alienated from common speech, but for the appearance of John Donne. It was he who taught lyric verse to speak again with a tone and in an idiom of polite conversation. On the other hand, his verse owes much to his living in an age in which lyric poetry was closely allied to music, the age in which Thomas Campion wrote both the words and the music of his songs. But the naturalness of the style of Donne contained the seeds of a new artificiality. After him George Herbert, and less steadily, Thomas Vaughan, write in a natural style; but after them, the lyrical tradition becomes more and more artificial in the work of poets – of genuine talent – such as Cleveland, Benlowes and Cowley. The return to common speech is chiefly associated with the name of John Dryden. Not only in his satirical and polemical poems, but also in his rhymed heroic drama, we hear the tones of the speech of good society in his time. And the same tones are heard a generation later in the incomparable octosyllabic couplets of Swift.

I shall not attempt to follow in detail the history of the swing of the pendulum between elaboration and simplification, between the artificial and the natural. The next great revolution was that initiated by Wordsworth, in revolt against the debased style of the eighteenth century imitators of Spenser, Milton, and Pope. In the *Preface* to his early poems – a poetic manifesto of great importance – he affirmed the poetic potentiality of the speech of common people. The history of poetry through the nineteenth century can be viewed as an elaboration of the idiom used by Wordsworth and his contemporaries. There are partial exceptions, notably in the poetry of Browning, whose weakness was that in his attempt to find a more conversational style he tended to lapse into a style peculiar to Browning himself; and in a few single poems or lines by lesser men, such as Ernest Dowson and John Davidson.

The effort of the first half of the twentieth century has been towards another revolution, towards finding a new idiom by exploring the poetic possibilities of the speech of our own time. It has been a revolt against the poetic diction, and also against the limited subject matter, of the 'Victorians'. I have no doubt that the [9] idiom and versification which we now call 'modern' contain, like those of every previous period, the seeds of a new artificiality, and will end in verse as remote from the speech of its time as that of any earlier period of decline; but – if we continue to produce poets – I have also no doubt that the resources of the English language will be adequate for a new revolution.

The English language has had two great advantages which lead one to believe that it will continue to hold its own in literature. One is the complexity of its formation, the strands of different languages – each introducing different poetic rhythms – out of which it is woven. The other is the fact that so many of its poets have had (and still have) the ambition to write for the theatre. That most of them have had but little, or only ephemeral success on the stage, and that their plays are among the least read parts of their work, is irrelevant to this point. Addison, Johnson, Wordsworth, Coleridge, Byron, Shelley, Keats, Tennyson and Browning, Swinburne and Matthew Arnold, all wrote plays which have never been and never will be successful in the theatre. But a poet who has tried to write for the stage, even one who has merely cherished the desire to do so, has before his eyes this criterion of writing; that poetry must be written to be spoken, that it must be capable of being spoken by other voices than that of the author, that it must *hold the attention* of those who hear it, and that it must not be written in a language remote from that which its contemporary audience speaks.

The Aims of Education.
2. The Interrelation of Aims

Publ. in *Measure*, 2. 2 (Spring 1951), [191]–203: Gallup C561.
Revised in *TCTC*. *See below*, pp. 764–76.

The Aims of Education.
3. The Conflict between Aims

Publ. in Measure, *2. 3 (Summer 1951), [285]-97.*
Revised in TCTC. *See below, pp. 777-89.*

[A Comment on James Thurber]

Time, 58.2 (9 July 1951), 88. Quoted as 'said last year' by Eliot.
It has the air of an official statement. Gallup C562a.

It is a form of humour which is also a way of saying something serious. There is a criticism of life at the bottom of it. It is serious and even sombre. Unlike so much humour, it is not merely a criticism of manners – that is, of the superficial aspects of society at a given moment – but something more profound. His writings and also his illustrations are capable of surviving the immediate environment and time out of which they spring. To some extent, they will be a document of the age they belong to.

Preface

Preface to T. S. Eliot Murder in the Cathedral: A Screenplay, *1.*
Signed 'T. S. Eliot'. Publ. 28 July 1951. Gallup B64.

This is, I believe, the first attempt that has been made to adapt a modern verse play to the screen. It was, at any rate, an experiment both from the point of view of the producer and that of the author of the text. The question of the suitability of poetry in the cinema is one I leave to others to answer. My own curiosity extended primarily to the question of the suitability of the cinema for poetry. The designing of a film in which the visual element must support the words, without distracting attention from them, without subordinating words to pictures, and without imposing upon the spectator a double effort of attention, presents new problems for the producer. That these problems have been solved, I judge from my own satisfaction in the result. Contrary to my apprehensions, I find that my words gain, rather than lose, by this presentation.

There is the first obvious advantage of clarity. In the film, every word can be audible to every member of the audience. The advantages are still more evident in dialogue than in monologue, and yet more apparent in the choral passages. And when the eye is, at every moment, made to fix itself on the particular aspect of the scene that will best correspond to the words that are spoken, the advantages for interpretation are very great.

Such an experiment, to be wholly successful, demands close co-operation between the creator of the film and the author of the verse to be spoken. I hope that this film may have the result of attracting poets to the possibilities of the film, and of persuading film directors to turn their attention to the possibilities of poetry. For the benefit of the poets, I should like to add one admonition as a result of my experience during the creation of the film of *Murder in the Cathedral*: that even if they have already had some practice in writing for the theatre, they will have a great deal to learn about another art; and that the cinema has its own laws which are not those of the stage.

The Aims of Education.
4. The Issue of Religion

Publ. in *Measure*, 2. 4 (Fall 1951), [362]–75: Gallup C564. Revised in *TCTC*.
See below, pp. 789–802.

Preface

Preface to *SE* (1951), 7. Publ. 3 Sept. 1951. Gallup A21.
The new preface had appeared in the 2nd American edn, Oct. 1950: Gallup A21d.

I have expanded the original volume of *Selected Essays: 1917-1932* by including a few essays from the now superfluous *Essays Ancient and Modern*. There remain several [8] uncollected papers which I am disposed to preserve, as well as a number of unpublished lectures, on matters connected with the art of poetry, which await their final form. But *Selected Essays* is already bulky enough; and any literary essays which are not to be found in it must abide their collection into another book.

On reviewing the contents of this book, I find myself at times inclined to quarrel with my own judgements, and more often to criticise the way in which they were expressed. For myself, this book is a kind of historical record of my interests and opinions. As one grows older one may become less dogmatic and pragmatical; but there is no assurance that one becomes wiser; and it is even likely that one becomes less sensitive. And where I have adhered to the same opinions, many readers may prefer them in the form in which they were first expressed.

T. S. E.
London: April, 1951.

Vergil and the Christian World

Publ. in *Listener*, 46. 1176 (13 Sept. 1951), 411–12, 423–4: Gallup C565. Repr., revised, in *SR*, 61. 1 (Jan./Mar. 1953), [1]–14, in *Selected Prose* (1953), and in *OPAP. See below*, pp. 236–46.

The Value and Use of Cathedrals in England To-Day

(*An Address delivered to the Friends of Chichester Cathedral on June 16th, 1951.*)

Friends of Chichester Cathedral Annual Report (1950/51), 1–16. (Gallup gives the pagination wrongly as '17–27'.) Gallup C566.

My subject this afternoon is one that was suggested to me: I admit that I was attracted by the opportunity of putting into order thoughts which I had never fully articulated: but I should not have ventured on my own initiative to do so on a public occasion and especially before an audience in a cathedral. And even with the encouragement to do so, I have felt more and more that I committed myself to an act of temerity. To come to a cathedral city, to stand before Dean and Chapter and before an audience of Friends of the Cathedral, and put forward my own notions of the value and use of cathedrals in England to-day, has come to strike me more and more as an impertinence. Yet I did not face this conclusion until it was too late to propose some other subject.

I should like at least to make clear at the start, that I propose to avoid all consideration of what is and is not practical. I do not pretend to any knowledge of cathedral administration and finance; [2] I am not myself expert in any form of finance; and I am completely incompetent in what are called ways and means. I say this to anticipate objections which are likely to occur to your minds long before I have finished. Otherwise, you are likely to say, in so far as you approve my ideas at all: this is all very fine, but how are these things to be done without money, and where is the money to come from? But I hold that the proper order in which to consider these matters, is to draw as clear a picture as we can, of what we should like if we could get it; and only in the second place, to consider how nearly we can approach to this ideal with the means at our disposal. Obviously, our several aims must then be arranged in order of prior necessity and of importance, so that we may not neglect the fabric of any scheme in attending to the decorations. I shall not attempt to set forth, in these brief and random notes, any order of importance; any more than I am prepared to attempt to defend my suggestions against the charge that they are impracticable. I would only suggest, that if we keep before our eyes what is desirable, even when it appears impossible of realisation, we may find that it is not all so impossible as it seems; for things sometimes become more possible if we want them enough. And that, on the other hand, if we limit our desires to what can be easily had, we are likely to sink further into mediocrity. But I would remind you again, that the question of where the money and [3] the men are to be found is one which I leave to those who are qualified to struggle with it.

So much is merely preamble. At this point I must raise the question: what do we mean by the *use* of a cathedral? For the word *use* can be a very dangerous one to use. This, no doubt, will strike some people as hair-splitting, and others as merely a tedious way of coming to an already accepted conclusion. I am afraid I can't help that: it is the way in which my mind works, and I cannot escape from it. There are different criteria of usefulness in different contexts. We are certainly likely to have something different in mind, when we speak of the 'usefulness' of a cathedral and when we speak of the 'usefulness' of a parish church. Now I don't suppose that anyone present holds the view that cathedrals should be done away with on the ground that they are obsolete in the modern world, and that the money spent to keep them going were better devoted to other public purposes. There are, I am sure, people outside the Church who would gladly see them preserved simply as ancient monuments of historical and artistic interest with turnstiles and admission charges; who would not approve of the actual destruction of the older cathedrals, though they would grudge the money spent on building new ones in new dioceses. The edifice has some use for nearly everybody, even if it is only the use of attracting tourist traffic. So we do not question the assertion that a particular [4] cathedral has *some* use. But there is a legitimate sense in which we may ask about the usefulness of a particular parish church. I have always held that the amalgamation of country parishes is at best a deplorable necessity; and with regard to the City churches of

London, that all of which even the shell remains should be preserved and used as churches. The closing of any church is a disaster. But with shifts of population it is sometimes justified; and where there are two churches near each other, in a neighbourhood that needs only one, it is better that one Church should be properly kept up and staffed than that both should be half-empty and half-derelict. The question of whether a particular church is 'useful' is the question whether the funds and the clergy would not be better employed, for the glory of God and the salvation of souls, elsewhere. And even if there was no lack of either there might still be something unedifying in there being two churches in near proximity, both very poorly attended.

Clearly, we can never say that a cathedral could, in this way, become superfluous, except in the unlikely event of a whole diocese becoming completely uninhabited. Nor is my contrast between the cathedral and the churches of a diocese – only between the cathedral and any one parish church. But while there is sometimes a good reason for closing a church, there is one reason which could never be a good one. To some people at least, brought up outside of the Church, it can seem less [5] reasonable for a small cathedral city to have parish churches as well, than for it to have several small cinemas as well as a grand one. For at least the small cinema will be showing an older film, at a lower price of admission; whereas at a small church, they will only be getting the same ceremony which they could see in the cathedral where it will probably be more grandly done, and certainly at the same price. And I have known even church members, who worshipped regularly at their cathedral, but almost never went near their parish church. It is not my duty – indeed it would be an impertinence – to lecture people on the obligation to support in every way, and primarily by attendance, their parish church, or at least the nearest church that suits them. I only make this point to proceed to the differences in the meaning of 'usefulness' as applied to cathedrals and churches. The purpose of both is the worship of God according to the rites of the Church. But a church needs a congregation, in a sense in which a cathedral does not.

The 'use' of the cathedral is for the performance of the complete liturgy of the Church for the Christian Year. The numbers of lay people attending services seems to me of quite minor importance. I should feel no misgivings even were there no congregation at all, so long as I believed that people who weren't there were all attending a service in a parish church instead. A cathedral is doing its proper work even when [6] no one is present except celebrant, deacons and servers; and if it omitted a single service because no one attended it, then it would be failing in its proper work. This work is the continuity and completeness of the liturgy and the continuous prayer and worship by its clergy. A cathedral is a kind of monastic institution open to the public: and the attendance of the public is only important, if important at all, when there is some ceremony which concerns the whole diocese or the whole province or perhaps the whole nation.

On the other hand – I am proceeding to my next point – a cathedral in doing this would be relieving the burdens of many parish churches. I do not want to confuse my plea with matters on which there is difference of taste and opinion. I like a full liturgy myself, and what I call a full liturgy may be fuller than some people like, though I should not care to be called a 'ritualist'. But whatever our views, most of us can, I hope, agree that there are some services which are better left by the churches to the cathedral. Under present conditions, certainly, it becomes more and more of a burden upon parish churches to illustrate the full beauty of the Christian Year. Conscientious clergy are heavily tried by their pastoral duties; and the church finances are usually strained. To perform all the proper services of Holy Week, for example, is a very heavy tax, physically and spiritually, upon a vicar who is fortunate if he has one curate to help him. The increasingly popular [7] midnight corporate communion at Christmas – if it is to be observed at all – is more fittingly performed in a cathedral. In short, whereas a poor parish church must struggle to perform faithfully the minimum essential, a cathedral should be able to perform the maximum possible.

I proceed to a point which follows very naturally from what I have been saying. As it is the function of the cathedral to maintain the highest liturgical standards, it is also its function to maintain the highest standards of religious art and music. With respect to the former, most cathedrals, like many churches, are handicapped by the monumental piety of the nineteenth and even earlier centuries – a piety which was sometimes nicely divided between religious zeal and family pride; but it is in any case better to put up with what we have inherited, rather than turn a cathedral inside out to suit the taste of each period in turn. But while I am conservative in the matter of doing away with what is old, I deplore excessive conservatism where there is new work to be done; and I had rather take the risk of a great modern artist, when we have one, than employ a man who can be depended on to produce a close imitation of the devotional art of an earlier age. Of course, by far the greater work of our cathedrals must be work of restoration, i.e. the work and expense to maintain the cathedral and its identity. And by restoration, I mean the replacement of what was there before as exactly as possible. The opportun-[8]ities and occasions and needs for new work – for work which is not merely to supply something lost or decayed but which is an addition – the opportunities for these are relatively few and far between. But for such new work the Church ought to be prepared to make use of the best modern artists; and that is good for the artists too.

I should explain at this point that by the Church making use of the best modern artists, I am not contemplating a central board or committee to sit in London and issue recommendations to dioceses as to what sort of work they may or may not do; or even to give them a list of artists whom they are at liberty to use. I am always apprehensive of the dangers of centralisation in the patronage of art, because what begins in the spirit of encouragement may easily become repressive and controlling; indeed, from the point of view of an artist one thing we ought to maintain and increase is a de-centralisation of patronage; and here I have particularly in mind the plea that every cathedral should retain its autonomy in these matters, as well as in others. It certainly seems to be better that sometimes work should fall below the best standards and taste than that it should all be controlled by a Central Committee – but that is an aside.

But I am not primarily concerned with the cathedral as a patron of art: its effect upon artists and upon the general standards of art is incidental. [9] That should be a by-product. What is important is that the perfection of service is a religious obligation, and that the artistic decorum is a part of the worship. I do not want cathedrals to be turned into art museums, whether of medieval or of modern art. For painting, sculpture and music should all be considered as ancillary to worship: they should never distract from it. I know that the first effect of a piece of church furniture by a living artist may be, to many worshippers, distracting. It is a form of art to which they are not accustomed; it is in a style with which they have no religious associations. If it is second-rate it may always remain an intruder. But when it is really good, it seems to me that work by modern artists quickens devotional feeling. When people are used to ecclesiastical ornament only of a particular historical period – and I have known people habituated to Gothic, who found baroque architecture unfavourable to devotion – it may be that their religious life and their daily life are too far from each other. To feel in a devotional mood, they have to be surrounded by reminders of some particular past, and, as they think, more pious age. Surely it is the great task of the religious artist, musician, and even the creative writer, to realise religious feeling in the terms of his own time.

For this reason, the Church – and, for the reasons I have given, especially the cathedral – needs the living artist. I would not have you infer that I [10] should give any preference to modern music in the services, but I think it ought to be represented. At least we ought to give it a trial from time to time; and even commission religious music from modern composers. But in matters of music I am still less qualified than in those of the visual arts. It is sufficient for my purpose to make the point that it is a function of the cathedral to have the best church music and the best performance of it; and that this is necessary as a part of its worship, whether anybody comes to hear it or not. But that, as far as people do come, the cathedral has the responsibility of satisfying the best taste, correcting the imperfect, and educating that which is unformed and setting the standard in these matters for churches.

I now come to a few observations on the most delicate matter of all. I mean the value and use of the Dean and Chapter. This is really, I believe, a logical inference from what I have said about the functions of the cathedral, in remarking that, in distinction to a parish church, the important thing was that the service and prayer should go on all the time, whether any congregation attended or not. That is itself a commonplace, but quite contrary to most people's habits of thought. Similarly, I should say that the first obligation of Dean and Chapter was not in any direct relation to the faithful, still less to the general public, but to the cathedral itself. This is also a commonplace but revolutionary idea. Nobody ought to expect [11] of deans and canons that they should undertake anything that interfered with this. And it seems to me that whatever else they are deprived of, they ought to have leisure: which means not having to account for one's time in terms of public activity. In my schooldays we were given to understand that, before the Reformation, England was groaning under the burden of supporting innumerable idle monks; and that Henry VIII sent them all packing, except a small number of the least incorrigible, whom he turned into deans and canons. I suspect that some of the reputation of the lazy monks has attached itself to their successors: for there lingers a belief among the unenlightened, that canons have nothing to do. I am not proposing to spring to their defence at this opportunity, simply because, not knowing all the members of all the chapters in the country, I have not the statistics with which to support my defence. But I have known canons who struck me as having too much to do: partly perhaps for the very reason that they were assumed to have time for odd jobs, especially that of preaching a good deal about their diocese and elsewhere. Now, in the world in which we live the possession and enjoyment of leisure has become a very rare privilege, and is visited with strong moral condemnation. It is taken for granted that anyone with leisure is certain to abuse it; and that if anyone is found to have any, he must be loaded with work to fill up his spare time. I think that [12] this is a very serious error. I think that civilisation depends upon the right people having the right leisure; and that the Church should set the example for the rest of the world in this respect as well as in others. It is now fairly well recognised, I hope, that a Bishop has no leisure, because he is doing the work of a permanent head of a Department of State, or of several heads at once, without a fraction of the staff which such a civil servant would consider essential. Most people know that a conscientious parish priest has no time to read or think, and hardly time for his private devotions. Where is the thinking of the Church to be done? There are our Professors of Divinity in the universities, and we have several of great intellectual distinction: but a professor in a university nowadays holds no sinecure, and is thinking under difficulties and primarily for the benefit of his students. Some of our best theological thinking is done in the religious communities, but these are also very busy places. Furthermore, a man may have a genuine vocation for the religious life and yet not be gifted with powers of original thought; and on the other hand, there are those with intellectual abilities who should be more in the world and not in communities. It is in the cathedrals that we ought to affirm the last stronghold of leisure, for the sake of scholarship and theology. The fruits of leisure seem to me so important, that it is worth while to accept the abuse of leisure by those who are negligent of their opportunity, in order to [13] obtain the benefits of the work of those who employ it profitably.

May I, at the risk of appearing self-centred, support this opinion by enlarging the generalisation from my own experience? For I do not think that the position of the philosopher and the theologian, and that of the writer of works of imagination, differ fundamentally in this respect of leisure. What I have found desirable to enable me to go on writing, is a life in which part of my time is spent in a definite paid job which I believe to be useful – in my case, concerning myself with the publication of other people's books – and only part in writing those books which I write simply because I want to write them. What people who only see one's published writings do not know, is, the difficulty of maintaining the conviction that something one is writing simply because one wants to write it, and not because anybody wants it – because until it is written they can't know whether they want it, as they don't know what it is going to be – that such a work is worth while. While I am engaged on any piece of writing that I set about in this way, I am always haunted by the fear that it is not worth doing, that it is a waste of time, that I am attempting something foolhardy and beyond my capacities. Well, I can with equanimity risk wasting a part of my time, but not all of my time. Everything I have done which has permanent value – if I have written anything of permanent value – has been written on this gamble. [14] But to do that I need to feel that the rest of my time is spent in activities which other people recognise *a priori* as useful. The things I do because I want to do them are only worth doing if I succeed; but I couldn't do them at all if I did not have other activities which are worth doing by a standard which I know I can satisfy.

On the basis of my own experience and observation of others, I hazard a rough division of people into three kinds, in respect of occupation and leisure. There are those whose occupation and means of livelihood so engross their attention that their 'leisure' is required only for recreation. At the other extreme, there are those whose individual activity, that which they pursue for its own sake, is so engrossing that they too need no 'leisure' except for recreation: these persons either have independent means to enable them to pursue their bent, or else their bent is such that in pursuing it they obtain also a livelihood. For these also leisure may mean merely recreation. The two extremes may thus have a great deal in common, and in some cases may even be indistinguishable. A successful novelist or playwright, who earns his living by doing the only work that he most wants to do, may easily find himself in a position in which he has, from financial pressure, to write a novel or a play when he doesn't want to, or when he has nothing to say; he may even find himself forced into writing what the public wants, instead of what his conscience tells him he ought to write. [15] The third class of persons consists of those who wish to devote themselves to some kind of original work, of scholarship, of thought, of imagination, but who do not want to devote the whole of their time to it, for one of the reasons I have already hinted at. It may be wholly unremunerative work, or they may be apprehensive of the dangers to the quality of the work itself of depending upon it for a livelihood. Or, if they have independent means, they may have a kind of social conscience which compels them also to some activity the usefulness of which, to God and to their fellow men, may be modest but is assured. In this way, the work that they do in their 'spare time' may often be meagre, but it represents the use of leisure in the full meaning. It has in it an element of disinterestedness which relates it to contemplation; and contemplation, we need to remind ourselves often, is the highest form of human activity.

I may have seemed to you to have strayed from the subject of cathedrals to talking about myself; and from talking about myself to a subject more general but equally irrelevant. But I launched upon this part of my discourse by way of expressing my sympathy with canons. At least, with some canons, for I don't mean to suggest that they should all be of one type. There must be different kinds of canon, and there must be different kinds of author; and I am quite aware that some writers much greater than myself have worked in a very different way from mine. But I do think that the [16] necessity of leisure, and a right understanding of the meaning of leisure, need to be constantly brought to our attention in the modern world. And in particular, I think that it is necessary to defend leisure in the Church, in an age in which everyone is expected to be perpetually busy in ways which can be understood and approved by the meanest intelligence; and that the increasing lack of leisure, in the sense in which I take it, for everyone from bishop to curate, is a matter of most serious concern. All I can do is to talk about it: but I apologise if my interest in the point has caused my discourse to be different from what my title may have led you to expect.

'Those Who need Privacy and Those Whose Need is Company'

Cecil Houses (Incorporated) 23rd Report (1950–51), 15–17. 'A report, with some omissions, from shorthand notes': Gallup. Signed '*T. S. Eliot, O.M.*' Gallup C567. The address was delivered at a public meeting in His Majesty's Theatre, London, on 5 June 1951.

I must apologise first for arriving on the stage so obviously prepared with very full notes. The fact simply is that I have unfortunately not had the time to prepare an extempore address. The unpremeditated flash of wit or pathos which is so appropriate on such occasions costs me so much labour to think out, to say nothing of the labour of memorising it, that I must fall back, having been very busy lately, on my usual style and method, which, as is fairly well known, are rather heavy and very dry. If, however, I add that it is very rare that I speak in public for good causes and charitable enterprises, I am not mentioning that as a further excuse for myself, but merely to point out that one does not do something which one knows one does rather badly unless one is sure that it is a very good cause indeed. It is only on this occasion, when I have some first-hand knowledge and some complete convictions, that I go through this ordeal for this reason.

I have just used the phrase 'charitable enterprises', but in relation to Cecil Houses I think I should correct that. They are certainly in the widest sense charitable in that they are fulfilling a public need through private enterprise. But the fact that it is only the capital expenditure for which appeal is made to individual generosity, and that the aim is always that the running expenses to be provided should be contributed by the beneficiaries, makes a particular appeal to me, as you will see. But I shall not talk about Cecil Houses directly – I shall leave that to those better qualified.

I thought the best contribution I could make would be to put before you a general observation or two, and indicate briefly my [16] application of those observations to this undertaking. This cause for which we are assembled today is the setting up of a residential house for elderly women. My experience of old people is that they are divisible into two kinds in one respect and are identical in another respect. In the respect in which they differ I should say that the old people who need help are of two species: those who primarily need privacy at the end of their lives and those whose primary need is company. But the resemblance, which is more important for my purpose, is that they all want to some extent to be independent. This desire for independence which touches at the roots of self-respect is equally strong irrespective of class or economic status.

I have some knowledge of old ladies, and I have always been very fond of old ladies, and in the course of my life have collected in my memory some very choice specimens indeed. But today I am thinking particularly of one whom I knew for a number of years. She insisted on living alone and caring entirely for herself in one room up to a very advanced age, and would probably have gone on doing so up to the end, for she was otherwise strong and sound, but for increasing blindness. The fact that she had outlived all her relatives who might have looked after her necessitated her eventual removal to a public institution. I think it was only after she had burned herself rather badly fumbling with her gas ring that she consented to do so. I visited her several times, and while I am sure that she was well looked after I know that she pined as a result of being merely an inmate instead of a paying guest, and of having no further control over her own tiny pension. But what hurt her most was the curious fact that she had to be registered in this institution under her maiden name, although she had been for sixty years a genuine and *bona fide* widow. This was for the following reason. The synagogue at which she had been married a great many years before had been destroyed in the blitz, together with all its records. As the public authorities had no documentary evidence of her wedlock, they were obliged to register her as a spinster. Indeed, the first time I went there I had some difficulty in finding her, because the attendants all seemed to know her as Miss X instead of Mrs Y. Her last wish in this world was one to which I am happy to say we were able to give effect. She wanted to be buried under her married name in the grave of her family. Whether this represented a craving for privacy or a craving for company perhaps is a matter of opinion, but I am inclined to think that it implies something of both.

Independence is a relative term, and probably self-respect is a more comprehensive way of putting what I mean. It is purely accidental, but I think it is appropriate, in relation to an undertaking associated with the name of Chesterton, that what I have to say occurs to me in the form of a paradox. I suppose it is one of the benevolent motives of the Welfare State to cherish people's self-[17]respect by giving them what they need and calling it, not 'charity' but a 'public service' to which they are entitled. The interesting point is that the effect can so easily be exactly the opposite; and this is one of several good reasons for maintaining private charities. For the effect of the State looking after everybody can be that everybody comes to feel himself to be nobody, to be merely an indifferent unit in a series; one may feel no longer of any personal interest to any individual, to any one person. One can become merely the object of occasional attention from a harassed official who is dealing with a great many similar cases, about none of which he has time to learn very much, in every hour of every working day. Of course, this is unfortunate also for the soul of the official, who instead of a vocation has only found a salaried post. But with him or her I am not here concerned. I wish to make the point simply that the sense of self-respect which everyone needs and has the right to is not necessarily preserved by abolishing 'charity' in favour of 'social service'. You are offering perhaps a more flattering name, but the improvement may be only verbal while the deterioration in status may be real. What matters for the preservation of self-respect, as it seems to me, is the relation between the person who gives and the person who receives; and it may be better to be looked after by people who care about us as individuals than by a State which does not.

My particular interest in Cecil Houses, and in this particular house, is that for one thing they are not so big as to be impersonal. We need more of them rather than bigger ones. Every resident – I say resident, you notice, and not inmate, a word I dislike – of the new house for old ladies will, I am sure, always be the subject of personal interest to those who administer it, and will feel also that she is free to come or go, and will have the pride of feeling that she pays for what she receives. So it is only in contrast to State care and guardianship that we call this a charity, in that it appeals to the conscience and the charitable feelings of individual supporters, but in relation to those who will benefit by it, it certainly is not.

1952

[Message from T. S. Eliot]

Four paragraphs from a message sent by Eliot to the fifth annual conference of the Union of Christian Democrats of Europe *held at Bad Ems in Sept. 1951.*
The Frontier, *3. 1 (Jan. 1952), 14. Gallup C569.*

Introduced by: 'After observing that he did not want to add to what he had said in his broadcast talks to Germany on the general question of *The Unity of European Culture*, Mr. Eliot offered the following observations "as testimony of goodwill".'

On the one hand, I distinguish sharply between the field of action with which, as I understand the terms of reference, we are concerned, and that of political action. The primary concern of political leaders must be the immediate future. They must defer to popular feeling, yield to circumstance and take advantage of expedients. Their decisions must often be taken in the light of considerations of which most of us remain in ignorance. They take the form of pacts and plans which can be judged only by experts and by results. Politicians must appeal to obvious and pressing interests and often to the desire to avoid misfortune rather than to enthusiasm for a more distant goal.

Those who concern themselves with the cultural unity of Europe do not aim at the return to some earlier phase of society before the appearance of nations – or to restore the Holy Roman Empire. Nor do they wish to fabricate a new unity by a complete break with the past and the present. They wish rather to bring to light, to make patent to the eyes of more and more people, what we inherit and hold in common, the culture which we still share.

It is necessary to distinguish our task clearly from that of the politicians and the heads and representatives of governments. Otherwise we risk the loss of our own ideals. Ours is a long-term struggle towards a distant goal which cannot be, and should not be, too clearly visualised.

Nevertheless, our work is concerned, so to speak, with the cultivation of the soil out of which the political ideas of the future must grow. How to conserve and nourish the spiritual life of Europe, how to cultivate in each region and amongst those of each race and language, the sense of a *vocation* in relation to each other. So that the glory of each people should be measured, not in material power and wealth, but by its contribution to the spiritual well-being of all the others. We do not aim merely to persuade people to accept a policy, or pay lip-service to some magniloquent verbal creed, but to awaken their consciousness and their conscience.

Introduction By T. S. Eliot

Introduction to Josef Pieper, *Leisure as the Basis of Culture*,
translated by Alexander Dru, 11–17. Publ. 25 Jan. 1952. Signed 'T. S. Eliot'.
Gallup B65.

The complaint is frequently heard that our time has little to boast of in the way of philosophy. Whether this deficiency is due to some ailment of philosophy itself, or to the diversion of able philosophical minds towards other studies, or simply to a shortage of philosophers, is never made clear: these are divisions of the question which are apt to become confused. Certainly, 'Where are the great philosophers?' is a rhetorical question often asked by those who pursued their philosophical studies forty or fifty years ago. Allowing for the possibility that the great figures of our youth have become magnified by the passage of time, and for the probability that most of those who ask the question have not followed modern philosophical developments very closely, there remains some justification of the lament. It may be merely a longing for the appearance of a philosopher whose writings, lectures and personality will arouse the imagination as Bergson, for instance, aroused it forty years ago; but it may be also the expression of a need for philosophy in an older meaning of the word – the need for new authority to express *insight* and *wisdom*.

To those who pine for philosophy in this ampler sense, logical positivism is the most conspicuous object [12] of censure. Certainly, logical positivism is not a very nourishing diet for more than the small minority which has been conditioned to it. When the time of its exhaustion arrives, it will probably appear, in retrospect, to have been for our age the counterpart of surrealism: for as surrealism seemed to provide a method of producing works of art without imagination so logical positivism seems to provide a method of philosophising without insight and wisdom. The attraction which it thus offers to the immature mind may have unfortunate results for some of those who pursue their undergraduate studies under its influence. Yet I believe that in the longer view, logical positivism will have proved of service by explorations of thought which we shall, in future, be unable to ignore; and even if some of its avenues turn out to be blind alleys, it is, after all, worth while exploring a blind alley, if only to discover that it *is* blind. And, what is more important for my theme, I believe that the sickness of philosophy, an obscure recognition of which moves those who complain of its decline, has been present too long to be attributable to any particular contemporary school of thought.

At the time when I myself was a student of philosophy – I speak of a period some thirty-five to forty years ago – the philosopher was beginning to suffer from a feeling of inferiority to the exact scientist. It was felt that the mathematician was the man best qualified to philosophise. Those students of philosophy [13] who had not come to philosophy from mathematics did their best (at least, in the university in which my studies were conducted) to try to become imitation mathematicians – at least to the extent of acquainting themselves with the paraphernalia of symbolic logic. (I remember one enthusiastic contemporary who devised a Symbolic Ethics, for which he had to invent several symbols not found in the *Principia Mathematica*.) Beyond this, some familiarity with contemporary physics and with contemporary biology was also prized: a philosophical argument supported by illustrations from one of these sciences was more respectable than one which lacked them – even if the supporting evidence was sometimes irrelevant. Now I am quite aware that to the philosopher no field of knowledge should come amiss. The ideal philosopher would be at ease with every science, with every branch of art, with every language, and with the whole of human history. Such encyclopedic knowledge might preserve him from excessive awe of those disciplines in which he was untrained, and excessive bias towards those in which he was well exercised. But in an age in which every branch of study becomes more subdivided and more specialised, the ideal of omniscience is more and more remote from realisation. Yet only omniscience is enough, once the philosopher begins to rely upon science. No one today, I imagine, would follow the example of Bosanquet, who in his *Logic* leant so heavily upon illustrations drawn from Linnaean Botany. But while the [14] philosopher's exploitation of science is now likely to meet with severe criticism, we are perhaps too ready to accept the conclusions of the scientist when he philosophises.

One effect of this striving of philosophy towards the condition of the exact sciences was that it produced the illusion of a progress of philosophy, of a kind to which philosophy should not pretend. It turned out philosophical pedagogues ignorant, not merely of history in the general sense, but of the history of philosophy itself. If our attitude towards philosophy is influenced by an admiration for the exact sciences, then the philosophy of the past is something that has been superseded. It is punctuated by individual philosophers, some of whom had moments of understanding, but whose work as a whole comes to be regarded as quaint and primitive. For the philosophy of the present, from this point of view, is altogether better than that of the past, when science was in its infancy; and the philosophy of the future will proceed from the discoveries of our own age. It is true that the history of philosophy is now admitted as a branch of study in itself, and that there are specialists in this subject: but I suspect that in the opinion of a philosopher of the modern school, the historian of philosophy is rather an historian than a philosopher.

The root cause of the vagaries of modern philosophy – and perhaps, though I was unconscious of it, the reason for my dissatisfaction with philosophy as a [15] *profession* – I now believe to lie in the divorce of philosophy from theology. It is very necessary to anticipate the resistance to such an affirmation: a resistance springing from an immediate emotional response, and expressed by saying that any dependence of philosophy upon theology would be a limitation of the freedom of thought of the philosopher. It is necessary to make clear what one means by the necessary relation between philosophy and theology, and the implication in philosophy of some religious faith. This I shall not attempt, because it is done very much better by Josef Pieper: I desire only to call attention to this central point in his thought. He is himself a Catholic philosopher, grounded on Plato, Aristotle and the scholastics: and he makes his position quite clear to his readers. But his writings do not constitute a Christian *apologetic* – that, in his view, is a task for the theologian. For him, a philosophy related to the theology of some other communion than that of Rome, or to that of some other religion than Christianity, would still be a genuine philosophy. It is significant that he pays a passing word of approval to the existentialism of Sartre, on the ground that he finds in it religious presuppositions – utterly different as they are from those which Dr Pieper holds himself.

The establishment of a right relation between philosophy and theology, which will leave the philosopher quite autonomous in his own area, is I think one of the most important lines of investigation which Dr Pieper [16] has pursued. In a more general way, his influence should be in the direction of restoring philosophy to a place of importance for every educated person who thinks, instead of confining it to esoteric activities which can affect the public only indirectly, insidiously and often in a distorted form. He restores to their position in philosophy what common sense obstinately tells us ought to be found there: *insight* and *wisdom*. By affirming the dependence of philosophy upon revelation, and a proper respect for 'the wisdom of the ancients', he puts the philosopher himself in a proper relation to other philosophers dead and living. Two dangers to philosophy are thus averted. One is the conscious or unconscious imitation of exact science, the assumption that philosophers should be organised as teams of workers, like scientists in their laboratories, investigating various parts of a problem which is conceived as soluble in the same way as a problem in physics. The opposite error is that of an older and more romantic attitude, which produced what I may call the 'one-man' philosophy: that is to say, a world view which was the projection of the personality of its author, a disguised imposition of his own temperament with all its emotional bias, upon the reader. I do not wish to diminish the grandeur or the value of the greatest one-man philosophies. When such a philosophy is done superbly well, as by Spinoza, it retains a permanent importance for humanity: for an acquaintance with Spinoza, and a temporary submission to his influence, [17] is an experience of great value. On the other hand, the colossal and grotesque achievement of Hegel may continue in concealed or derivative forms to exercise a fascination upon many minds. I would mention also the work of such a writer as F. H. Bradley, which owes its persuasiveness to a masterly prose style. The charm of the author's personality stimulates an agreeable state of feeling: and such books will continue to be read as literature, for the enlargement of our experience through a contact with powerful and individual minds.

Dr Pieper also has style: however difficult his thought may sometimes be, his sentences are admirably constructed, his ideas expressed with the maximum clarity. But his mind is submissive to what he believes to be great, the main tradition of European thought; his originality is subdued and unostentatious. And as he is a philosopher who accepts explicitly a dogmatic theology, his presuppositions are in full view, instead of being, as with some philosophers who profess complete detachment, concealed from both author and reader. The attitude towards philosophy which he maintains, and which distinguishes him from most of our contemporaries, is enough to account for his preference for expression in brief and concentrated essays rather than in constructions of greater bulk. Of such essays he has already published an impressive list: the two here presented are those which the author, translator and publishers agreed upon as the most suitable introduction to his thought.

Scylla and Charybdis

This lecture is dated 'February 1952' at the end and is designated 'Copyright Valerie Eliot'. It was publ. in Agenda, *23. 1–2 (1985), 5–21, in a 'T. S. Eliot Special Issue: including Scylla and Charybdis, a Hitherto Unpublished Lecture', ed. William Cookson and Peter Dale, and issued by Black Swan Books. Not in Gallup, but would be [C569a].*

My writings, in prose and verse, may or may not have surprised other people: but I know that they always, on first sight, surprise myself. I have often found that my most interesting or original ideas, when put into words and marshalled in final order, were ideas which I had not been aware of holding. It is ordinarily supposed that a writer knows exactly what he wants to say, before he sits down at his desk; and that his subsequent labours are merely a matter of a better choice of words, a neater turn of phrase, and a more orderly arrangement. Yet I have always discovered that anything I have written – anything at least which pleased me – was a different thing from the composition which I had thought I was going to write. Perhaps I never quite know what I am saying until I have said it. Whether I have undertaken the particular task spontaneously, or whether it is a task set for me by circumstances, the element of the unexpected always plays a great part.

Hence the importance, at an early stage, of the title. One begins by choosing a title, in order to assure oneself that one has a subject: for a title is a kind of substitute or shadow of a subject. Now the relation of title to subject, and of both to the final composition, is, in the case of this address which I am at the moment delivering, a peculiar one. I am, as you may already have noted with impatience, curious about the process by which anything gets written: I am the more tempted to indulge this curiosity on the present occasion, because the Centre Meditérranéen is so closely associated in my mind with the name of the great explorer of thought, feeling and language who was Paul Valéry. So, in the first place, I will reveal that the title of this lecture not only preceded the subject, but was itself due to a misunderstanding. In correspondence with your President, M. Émile Henriot, I complained of the difficulties of deciding on what to talk about to an unknown audience; and I added, in a parenthetical and ejaculatory way: 'Scylla and Charybdis! to avoid both frivolity and dullness!' Your [6] President, under the impression that I was offering this remark as a subject, replied at once that he thought it a happy idea, and that this title would be announced. I did not immediately correct him, because I wanted to wait until I had thought of something else. And then I said to myself: 'Why not?' The title is in itself a good one. The myth belongs to that Mediterranean world from which our culture springs; it refers to a well-known episode in Mediterranean pre-history; like other myths in the story of Ulysses it is what I believe Professor Jung would call a universal archetype of human experience. It responds to some of the deepest desires, and terrors of all human beings: it is the experience of life itself. It is applicable to almost any subject one can discuss. So, having had the title thrust upon me, I launched with zest into the exploration of my own mind, curious to discover what I might find there.

I turned then to consider the significance of Scylla and Charybdis in poetry; for it is my experience that to enlist the attention of an audience it is best to begin from what one is generally supposed to know something about. It struck me at once that while trying to write a poem I am frequently in the position of the Homeric navigator in that particular difficulty. It is supposed that the poet, if anybody, is one engaged in perpetual pursuit of *the right word*. My own experience would be more accurately described as the attempt to avoid the wrong word. For as to the right word, I am not convinced it is anything but a mirage. I will try to justify this opinion.

To take the problem first in its simplest form. The word which is the right word in one respect may be the wrong word in another. The *poetic* value, the poetic *meaning* I may say, of a passage of verse, depends upon three things: the literal meaning of the word, the associations of the word, and the sound of the word. The word with the exact meaning you want may be very far from euphonious in the context of the words among which it must be fitted. The word which has the right sound in that place may not mean quite what you want it to mean. Either choice means shipwreck. If the word makes the wrong noise, the surface of the poem is defaced; if it has the wrong meaning, the poem will not stand examination. In neither case, is the result poetry.

To illustrate this simple dilemma to you briefly and [7] cogently, I should have to find instances in French. But few persons, and certainly not myself, know any language but their own intimately enough to be sure of themselves in choosing illustrations. So perhaps an insoluble problem which I encountered in the course of my own work, may suffice, as I do not need to quote the English line of verse. In one of my poems, *The Dry Salvages*, I had occasion to describe the sort of debris found on a sea beach, and among it the shells of a particular kind of crab. On re-reading the poem some time after the final text had been published, I was horrified to find that I had referred to the wrong kind of crab – the *hermit* crab which has no shell of its own, but takes for a habitation the shell of some other deceased crustacean. The hermit crab, having no shell of its own, could hardly be identified by a shell on the beach; and indeed, I am not sure that I have ever seen a hermit crab. The crab I had in mind was the *horseshoe* crab. I knew the difference perfectly well: how was it that after spending months in re-writing and revising that poem, I had failed to notice that I continue to associate the name of one kind of crab with the mental picture of another? Simply because the sound of the word *hermit* fitted perfectly for my line, and the sound of *horseshoe* was harsh. In such a dilemma, there was only one choice: to put in the right crab, and sacrifice the right sound.

In another situation, it might be desirable to take the other course and sacrifice sense to sound. Such dilemmas are frequent in the choice of words. Sometimes there is no one word which will do. The line of verse would be very much more effective if there was that word, but in its absence you must sacrifice concision and have recourse to a phrase or a periphrasis. In another poem, for instance, I found myself in great difficulties for a word to express *twilight before dawn*, as distinct and different from *twilight before night*. The word *dusk*, in English, means either: but its immediate denotation, to every English speaking person, is the evening. I suppose that is simply due to the fact that everybody is about in the evening, and only a minority of people are out of doors before dawn. (I have chosen this instance because I believe that *crépuscule* presents the same difficulty as *dusk*.) I believe that I could have found one word meaning the dusk of morning, [8] in one or more English country dialects, because country people are more likely to need such a word than townsfolk. But a dialect word – apart from the fact that its obscurity would probably have required a footnote – would have aroused the wrong associations. The scene I was describing was in a London street; the personages in the scene were not people who would express themselves in country dialect; and any dialect word would have been most unsuitable. So, after giving up the hope of finding one word, I had to try to find two words. The substantive could only be *dusk*; there would have to be an adjective to indicate *which* dusk I meant; and if necessary I should have to support it with some other indication of the time of day. I first hit upon a word which seemed to me, for a short time, to be a real *trouvaille*: the adjective *antelucan* 'before the light'; in the great Oxford dictionary it is defined as: 'of or pertaining to the hours just before dawn'. Its meaning was exactly what I required, and I was much taken by the *sound* of the word. It is a word of Latin origin which appears to have been adapted to the English language during the Sixteenth Century, when a great many new English words – many of which have since been abandoned – were coined by scholars directly from Latin. As I do not find it in *Littré*, it does not appear to have been adopted into French. But here was a word with the right meaning and a very agreeable sound which nevertheless would not do. It is a rare word. Though its meaning is clear enough, such a word is appropriate only for an *ornate* style; and the passage into which I wished to insert it was in a very deliberately *plain* style: the word would have attracted attention to itself, and away from the task it had to perform. It might have been a suitable word if I had been writing in the style of Milton; but in my context it would have had the incongruity of a spectator appearing in full evening dress at a football match. So I had in the end to put 'waning dusk'. It was not what I wanted: but it was, I believe, the best that the English language could do for me.

I hope I have not taxed your attention too long with what may seem problems of interest only to those of the *métier*; because these reflections on the verbal difficulties of the poet lead up to problems of wider interest. My point is that [9] the perpetual compromise with words, the necessity for vigilant attention to the literal meaning, the associations and the sound, has a bearing on the process of development of the original idea. In avoiding the several dangers of navigation, the poet cannot be too much concerned with the choice of the port which he hopes eventually to reach. It is necessary certainly, in a poem of any length, to have a plan, to lay a course. But the final work will be another work than that which the author set out to write; and will, as I have already suggested, be something of a surprise to the author himself. For the *idea* behind a poem will always be less than the *meaning* of a poem: the meaning depends upon the musical structure as well as upon the intellectual structure. In a poem, one does not altogether know what it is that one has to say, until one has said it; for what one intends to say is altered in the course of making poetry of it.

All this has a bearing upon the endlessly discussed problem of form and content, of *la poésie pure*, and of what is nowadays called *engagement*. The problem of Scylla and Charybdis is now appearing in the following form: should we regard poetry as a vehicle for the expression of our ideas, beliefs, emotions, observations and experiences, or should we consider these ideas, beliefs, emotions, observations and experiences simply as the material out of which we make a poem?

It is obvious that there are here two problems: that of the poet himself, and that of the reader of poetry. The poet may consciously intend to do one thing, and unconsciously achieve something else: the result may be something either better or worse than what he set out to do. In either event, he is judged by the achievement rather than the intention. The reader, however, who enjoys a poem under the impression that it is something different from what it is, is hardly to be congratulated upon his capacity for appreciation. Let us turn our attention, then, to the poem.

Here one would like to be able to give illustrations of bad poetry; and this is always difficult to do effectively. If the bad poetry one cites is unknown to the audience, the reference is ineffective. But the bad poetry of the past is soon forgotten by all but a few curious scholars; and to cite bad poetry of the present would be unkind to living authors. So I will ask you to [10] accept my assurance that I have gained in the course of my life a very extensive acquaintance with bad and indifferent verse. It comes to me daily, from all quarters of the world; chiefly, of course, in English; but in other languages too, and even in languages wholly unknown to me – for the last, I can only guess at its quality from the laws of probability. The worst, of course, is that in which the authors have nothing to say, and do not know how to say it. But the rest is divisible into two kinds: that in which the author has something to say, but does not make poetry of it; and that in which the author has nothing to say, but says it rather charmingly. At these two extremes we are exasperated or bored by the result: at the one, we are annoyed with the author who appears to be merely making use of verse, and exploiting its resources, for purposes of exposition or persuasion; at the other we feel that the author has been wasting our time with something trivial. In either case an imposture, conscious or unconscious, has been attempted: either to deceive us into believing that an idea has been transmuted into poetry, or into believing that a melodious arrangement of words contains an idea.

Between the extremes of two kinds of bad poetry, however, there is a range in which good poetry can differ widely. With some good poetry, we are, in reading it, more attentive to what the author is saying; with other good poetry, more attentive to the way in which he says it. For me, the poet who can make a fine poem with the minimum of the poetic, and at the other end of the scale the poet who can make a fine poem with the minimum of content, are always the subject of particular interest. At the one extreme, we might point to the *Divine Comedy* of Dante, and the poems of St John of the Cross; at the other to some of the lyrics in Shakespeare's plays – notably those in *The Tempest*. But in choosing these illustrations I must make an important qualification. Dante may give the impression of being concerned with what he has to say, rather than with the way in which he says it: but we know perfectly well that no poet has ever given closer attention than did he to the technical problems of versification and language, or has ever attained a greater mastery of the *craft*. And as for Shakespeare's songs, though they are magical even when extracted from their context, they [11] have a dramatic value also, which means that for their author they were a necessary detail in the structure of the scene in which they occur: their significance is due to the context in which we find them.

Let us try to find some other illustration, therefore, than Shakespeare's songs, of genuine poetry with the minimum of content. And here I must make a distinction. There are poems in which the content appears unimportant because the poem is a perfect and individual expression of commonplaces; there are others in which the content appears unimportant because we do not know what it is, and yet can enjoy and appreciate the poem without the necessity of knowing what it is. In my own enjoyment of poetry, at least, these are two distinct experiences. For the perfect and final expression of the commonplace, I can think of no better example than Gray's *Elegy in a Country Churchyard*. For those who do not know the poem, I will say briefly that it is, naturally, a meditation on mortality. The poet remarks that the graves are those of humble peasants who were once living and are now dead. In death we are all equal, and it does not matter very much whether we have an impressive monument or a plain stone. This leads to the conjecture that one or two of the obscure people buried here may have had gifts which would have brought them to fame and power had circumstances favoured such success. He ends with a rather improbable epitaph upon a young man, dead before his prime, who, one infers, might in other circumstances have become a distinguished poet.

I have alluded to this particular poem because it is a good example of a beautiful poem which is nearly all platitude. Such poems are untranslatable: they can only be paraphrased by another poet of genius who can clothe the same international platitudes in the beauties of his own language. '*Rien n'est plus beau que le lieu commun*' says Baudelaire somewhere. From Homer to our own day, poetry has depended upon it. And we should be mistaken if we said that a poem like this, containing no strikingly original idea, was poetry of form rather than content. The content is never negligible. But we may say, I think, that the *idea* of a poem, or the ideas in it, so far as they can be expressed in words other than those of the poem itself, *must* be platitude, or rather, must belong to [12] a genus of which what we call platitude or the 'commonplace' is a species.

Within this genus I include *The Divine Comedy*. What is the difference, with regard to the content of idea, between *The Divine Comedy* and Gray's *Elegy*? There is not merely a much greater number and variety of ideas, or a much more complex structure. The ideas themselves are much more philosophic: that is, they are commonplaces for a much smaller number of people than the commonplaces of Gray's poem. That is the difference. The commonplaces of Gray are known to everybody and accepted by everybody: no mental effort is necessary to apprehend them. The commonplace is a matter of degree. It is when the statement is familiar to everyone – as, for instance, the statement that all men are mortal – that we say that it is the form and not the content that makes that poem.

It is not only, however, the immediate accessibility and simplicity of the idea that makes us attend to form rather than content. The same thing happens in an antithetical case: when the idea is inaccessible. When a poem is so obscure that we do not know what the meaning is, or even what it is about, but when nevertheless it gives us enduring delight in a high degree, then also we are inclined to say that it is the form and not the content that matters. I pass from Gray to Mallarmé: no two poets, surely, could be more different. I have read, or attempted to read, a number of treatises written to explain the meaning of Mallarmé's poems. I am not prepared to deny the value of such investigation of origins; but I have never found that they enhanced my enjoyment of the poem. On the contrary, I have sometimes been tempted to say: 'if that is all there is to the poem, apart from a felicitous arrangement of syllables, it is not so fine a poem as I thought it was – perhaps I was mistaken.' But my mind obstinately refuses to believe this: I return to the poem, and I still enjoy it, after forgetting the explanation. Some of the 'explanations', indeed, set forth no more than certain accidents of circumstance which made the poem germinate in the poet's mind: these seem to me curious, but irrelevant. Others – especially when it comes to 'Un coup de dès' or 'Igitur' – profess to set forth an underlying philosophy: but the philosophy, as expounded by the interpreter, never seems to me quite worthy of the poem. [13] Yet I do not draw the conclusion, from the lack of concurrence between the interpretation of the poem and my enjoyment of it, either that Mallarmé's poems are meaningless, and consequently that it is not necessary for a great poem to mean anything, or even that I myself can enjoy a poem knowing that it has no meaning. A poem that means nothing must be trivial – and therefore cannot be genuinely a poem. It has merely given us a momentary illusion; but I am sure that, the moment we perceived an absence of meaning, we should all reject it. Mallarmé's poem is for me therefore at the opposite extreme from *The Divine Comedy*, only within these limits: that I can enjoy a canto of Dante while paying conscious attention only to what he is saying, and a sonnet of Mallarmé while paying conscious attention only to the way in which he says it. But this does not mean that the verbal genius and technical mastery of Dante, or the meaning of Mallarmé's sonnet, are not essential to my enjoyment of the poem.

I have held the view, and expressed it here and there in essays for many years past, that a poet does better to take over his 'philosophy' from the philosophers, than to invent his own. This comes down to a simple division of function: the genius for conceptual formulation and abstraction, which the greatest philosophers possess, and the genius for transmuting a philosophy into poetry, were in my opinion quite distinct:

it would be a miracle, and almost a monstrosity, for the two gifts, to the point of genius, to co-exist within the same mind. On this ground, I exalted the poems of Lucretius and Dante at the expense of the philosophical books of Blake; and I even went so far as to maintain that an inferior, fragmentary or chaotic philosophy could serve a great poet, in certain circumstances, as well as a more dignified one; for otherwise we should be obliged, for this reason alone, to admit the inferiority of Shakespeare to Dante.

I now believe that I have seen a little farther into the matter. I am inclined to think that we may mean two quite different things, when we speak of the 'philosophy' of a poet: first, a philosophy which he either takes over, or has attempted to devise for himself in the *language of philosophy*, and another 'philosophy' which can only be expressed in *the [14] language of poetry*, and which is, in the truest sense, the poet's own contribution. Certain observations of Professor Pieper of Muenster, on the relation of the philosophic to the poetic activity, have encouraged me in this view. When we study the Aristotelian and Thomist metaphysic, for the purpose of understanding Dante better, we are increasing our knowledge, certainly, but it is knowledge of *origins*, of the material which went to form the poem. But the philosophy of Dante *qua* poet is a different matter from his philosophy *qua* student of the philosophers. If for instance we read certain of the more philosophical passages of the *Purgatorio*, translating them back into the terms of the *De Anima* of Aristotle, we may simply marvel that the poet has been able to make poetry of such austere and refractory matter. But the fact that it has been transmuted into poetry means that we are no longer in the same world of discourse as that of Dante's philosophical masters. On the other hand, this view of the matter explains to me my disappointment in the interpretations of Mallarmé. The philosophy of a poet cannot be translated into conceptual terms. What we do, when we make this attempt with Dante, is to shift our attention from Dante to Aristotle and Thomas, and to give Dante the credit which belongs to the latter. What we do, when we apply the attempt to Mallarmé, is to reduce his poetic philosophy to an inferior conceptual philosophy. In neither case are we estimating the intellectual achievement of the poet.

By this statement, I do not mean to suggest, either that Mallarmé is as great a poet as Dante, which he certainly is not; or that it is worth while to discuss the work of every poet with reference to his 'philosophy'. It may be that I am risking confusion, in my own mind as well as in yours, by using the word 'philosophy' in two senses. In the ordinary sense, when we ask 'what is the philosophy of so and so?' – mentioning a poet, we expect the answer to be in terms of some philosopher or school of philosophers. If the poet in question is Dante, we answer 'Aristotle and Aquinas'; if Lucretius, we reply glibly 'the Epicurean philosophy'. Or, in the case of Goethe, we have to use a great many more words: we have to consult all of Goethe's writings, his letters, the reports of his conversation, trace the origin of all his ideas, [15] and attempt to constitute them into an intelligent and coherent whole. But in either case, we are replying as we should to the same question when asked about any person with whom we are acquainted. When asked 'what does so and so believe?' we are usually satisfied if we are informed whether he is Catholic, Protestant, Spiritualist, Theosophist or Rationalist, and at the same time are given the name of some political party to which he adheres. We are usually satisfied if we are told what the man *professes* to believe. If there is an evident contradiction between his profession of belief and his behaviour, we are reduced to conjecture. If we suspect the man of hypocrisy, we may make a likely guess; but if we suspect that his own mind is confused, and that he has not put his beliefs into order, we may say 'he doesn't know what he believes'. And in a few human beings do we find a complete consistency of belief and behaviour; nor, in the greater part of life, is such consistency to be demanded: in one aspect, our beliefs are those ideas and principles which we maintain consciously throughout our lives, and on the other hand, our belief at any particular moment is the *way in which we behave that moment*. Only, perhaps, in facing and accepting martyrdom, is a man's religious belief completely realised and authenticated.

The difference may be made a little clearer if I cite specifically religious or *devotional* poetry (Dante escapes from this category). In such poetry the commonest failure occurs when the author's conceptual philosophy is one which he *wants* to believe, but to which his intellectual assent is not complete. That is the most usual reason for the failure of would-be religious poets. Among the writers of good devotional poetry are those whose belief is genuine and passionate, but in whose work the personality of the author is essential: we share his feelings, we experience our exaltation through him. Of such is George Herbert. In another and higher category I should put St John of the Cross, in whose poems the emotion is so directly the consequence of the idea that the personality of the author is, somehow, annihilated: in experiencing his poems we seem to be in direct relation with what he saw, without any mediation through the personality of the author himself.

[16] It would perhaps be best to speak of the 'philosophy of the author' when we mean the philosophy which he either adopted from philosophers, or devised for himself *qua* philosopher; and the 'philosophy of the poem' when we mean only what is found in the poem itself and cannot

be translated into concepts. It might be helpful if I recalled our point of departure. We started from the ordinary distinction of *content* and *form*, and noted that in common terms we may find ourselves enjoying one poem for what the poet is saying, and another poem because of the way in which it says it. In the one case we are inclined to consider the form of expression merely as *means*, in the other to consider the content merely as *material*. This is a matter of experience. At the one extreme, we have to ask, 'why is this a poem, and not versified prose?' and at the other 'why is this not nonsense?' I am not here concerned with the limiting cases; but with the question: 'what is the relation between the value of a poem and the value of the ideas out of which it is composed?' And I ask this question because of my own experience, specifically as an instance with the poetry of Mallarmé. I do not feel, in reading Mallarmé's poems, that I am enjoying them because of their 'form' only: I find the content important. But I feel no impulse to try to explain to myself what a poem of Mallarmé is about; and, as I have said, when I have read explanations of their meaning, I have always felt cheated. The Interpreter may be right, on his own plane of discourse; but what I am offered is something different from what I want. In the case of Dante it is something highly respectable in its own kind, a recognisable philosophy; in the case of Mallarmé it is something comparatively trivial. That is the only difference. And I feel that the poet has given me something which has caused in me an enjoyment which I cannot call simply sensuous: he has given me an intellectual exercise and an intellectual delight, which is different from that given me by the prose explanation.

Whether I am justified in referring to the cause of this intellectual pleasure as 'the philosophy of the poem' can only be judged by the reception of the phrase by my public – which is, first of all, yourselves: for, as I have warned you, these reflections have only come to me as the result of meditating [17] upon my title, 'Scylla and Charybdis'. Obviously, the phrase 'the philosophy of the poem' is not equally applicable to every kind of poem. It is most relevant to the poems of those poets who, if they had not been poets, might have been philosophers. That includes poets who, if they had turned to philosophy instead of to poetry, might have achieved only a very modest place as philosophers. Among these latter, I do not disguise the fact that I include myself. (For I take it as inevitable, that when a poet theorises about poetry, the kind of poetry upon which his attention is centred is his own kind of poetry. And, as Valéry has said, '*il n'est pas de théorie qui ne soit un fragment, soigneusement préparé de quelque autobiographie*'.)

When I speak of 'the philosophy of a poem', then, I have in mind primarily a poem by a poet who has pursued philosophic studies, and who has even elaborated philosophic theories of his own. These have played an important part in his formation, and will make their appearance in his poetry, but in a form in which they are no longer maintained as theories, but presented as something experienced, and go to compose, together with his experience of life of all other kinds, the material of his poem. Different philosophies, or opposed philosophical opinions which cannot in the philosophical area of discourse be maintained at once, may thus be united and poetically reconciled. I should say, furthermore, that in this operation there is an intellectual work of organisation, which is analogous to the work of the conceptual philosopher. And I should maintain that the experience of the sensitive reader, in assimilating such a poem, is analogous in kind to his experience in assimilating the work of a philosopher. Only, *understanding*, with a philosophic work and with a poem, is a very different thing. It is owing to the misunderstanding of the fact that there is more than one kind of *understanding*, that we have inflicted upon us so many false explanations of philosophical poetry: those in fact, which reduce the philosophy of a poem to conceptual terms: whether of the poet's philosophical masters, or to his own thought when he was philosophising and not writing a poem.

With regard to the conceptual philosophy which a poet borrows from philosophers, or invents for himself *qua* philo-[18]sopher, there are reservations to be made. The considerations I have been discussing are not, of course, equally applicable to every type of poetry, nor are they equally important in every poem of the same type. They are applicable to the degree in which philosophical ideas have contributed to forming the poet's mind and have been digested into (we might say *composted* into) that profound *couche* of experience which constitutes the soil in which the germs of his poetry are nourished. They are peculiarly applicable when the matter of a poem, rich with philosophical ingredients, is *organised* into a structural design. But neither the presence of such elements, nor their organisation, is a universal condition for *all* poetry. The *value* we assign to the poem in which they are found has no direct relation to our valuation of the original ideas in their conceptual forms: it is possible not only to make a bad poem out of the greatest philosophy, but a very fine poem out of a philosophy which, put abstractly, is almost negligible. Otherwise, we should have to assert, if we are Christians, that Dante is a greater poet than Homer or Virgil, Racine a greater dramatist than Sophocles; which would be manifestly absurd. The greatness of any particular poetry depends upon many things; among others upon the greatness of the language in which the poet writes; depends, therefore, upon the other poets who have previously written in the same language. It is hard, but I believe true, that some poet of limited gifts, who has the advantage of a great language, may be more important for the world than another poet, more richly endowed by nature, who has had to work in a language in itself of lower status in the world at large.

I come at last to a particular case of poetry which, in the sense which I have been trying to indicate, may be called philosophical. When I alluded, a little while ago, to Gray's *Elegy in a Country Churchyard*, that was not only for its illustrative value in that context, but with a view to a comparison I am about to draw. I cannot recall ever having read a comparative analysis of Gray's *Elegy* and *Le Cimetière Marin*, although I should be very surprised to learn that no one had yet drawn the parallel. An English poet of the Eighteenth Century, and a French poet of the Twentieth, have both written poems of meditation in a cemetery – each, [19] the finest poem on this subject in the language. Each is a poem which anyone must know, who has any pretension to acquaintance with the poetry of that language. The comparison is peculiarly interesting in the present context.

Gray's poem is, of course, the perfection of an idiom and a versification which was a common style of poets of his time, and which had been brought to that point of excellence by a century of practice. Valéry's poem, on the other hand, is striking, from the first reading, by the triumphant boldness of its technical originality. I speak with diffidence, but I should suppose that in this poem of Valéry there is to be found a refreshment of French metric from Italian sources. I have spoken of Gray's *Elegy* as the distinguished expression of the commonplace. In Valéry's poem there are commonplaces – in what great poem are there not? – but there is a great difference between a poem in which commonplaces occur, and a poem based on the commonplace. Such a line as

  La larve file où se formaient des pleurs

or even

  Tout va sous terre et rentre dans le jeu

has all the force of the commonplace thought expressed in words which no one has found before: as with lines of Gray, I feel a kind of wonder and admiration as at a miracle of resuscitation of the dead. There are interesting differences on the same plane:

  The breezy call of incense-breathing Morn

and

  Les cris aigus des filles chatouillées –

there is more difference here than the difference between the Eighteenth and the Twentieth centuries, or even between what can be said in the two languages. But is there any important difference of type between the two poems?

The difference is fundamental. The content of Gray's poem, as I have said, consists chiefly of ideas which have occurred to all men in all languages at all times. Hence its structure is merely the plausible sequence by which one such thought leads to another. Valéry's poem has what I call the [20] philosophic structure: an organisation, not merely of successive responses to the situation, but of further responses to his own responses. He has put more of himself into the poem – to that point at which the surrendering of the maximum of one's being to the poem ends by arriving at the maximum of impersonality.

Valéry solved the problem of Scylla and Charybdis in his own way, and because of his own peculiar combination of gifts. I cannot think of any other poet who could so certainly, if he had taken that course, have distinguished himself as a philosopher in the non-poetic sense. I can easily imagine him, had he made that choice in early life, as pursuing a course which would have led him to the Collège de France and such audiences as flocked, forty years ago, to the lectures of Henri Bergson. His parentage with Mallarmé seems to me exaggerated, or at least to be sometimes regarded as if he had no other lines of descent. His mind, in my opinion, was far more philosophical than that of Mallarmé, or than that of Edgar Poe to whom both poets have paid such generous tribute. Having turned to poetry, he achieved the miracle of writing poetry in which the approximation between the two modes of philosophising which I have tried to determine, the conceptual and the poetic, comes closer than in the work of any other poet. He remains a poet, because the translation of the content of any of his poems into conceptual terms converts it into something else – and *something else of less value*.

In remarking this unique character of Valéry's poetry I am not implying that he reached, or came nearer towards some goal towards which all poetry ought to strive, than anyone else. I have said nothing about his relative *greatness* compared to other poets. I only say of him that he explored what no one else has explored: and if a poet gives us a few poems (for I rate 'La Jeune Parque' and 'Le Cimetière Marin' as his triumphs) in which he has realised some potentiality of poetry as no one else has done or is likely to do, that, in itself, is glory.

Let me return to my two marine monsters. If a poet gives us the impression that he is employing his gifts to persuade us to accept a particular theory, or if on the other hand he seems to be exploiting, irresponsibly, a theory or a belief [21] as material to make poetry out of, he will equally suffer shipwreck and destruction. The philosopher tries to make us *see* one aspect of reality; the poet tries to make us *see* another. These are two modes of contemplation: persuasion and propaganda belong to quite another universe of discourse. And yet there is one reservation to be made. Scylla and Charybdis cannot be escaped merely by having a good chart of the channel. Not all poets are equally conscious of what they are doing: and it may happen sometimes, that a poet succeeds in writing a fine poem with the wrong intentions. If his compass is in error, he may even, in laying his course directly for Scylla or directly for Charybdis, have the good fortune to pass triumphantly between them.

I should have liked to embark upon an examination of the Scylla and Charybdis of the dramatist – or even to proceed into more dangerous seas, and consider the Scylla and Charybdis of the politician which may be named *ideology* and *expediency*. But I must leave you to your own reflections on these matters, for I have, as lecturer, my own Scylla and Charybdis to avoid. I have escaped the Scylla of brevity, but I am in danger of the Charybdis of tedium.

Preface

Preface to Simone Weil, *The Need for Roots: Prelude to a Declaration of Duties towards Mankind*, v–xii. Signed 'T. S. ELIOT'. Publ. 7 Mar. 1952. Gallup B66.

The only kind of introduction which could merit permanent association with a book by Simone Weil would be – like that provided by M. Gustave Thibon to *Gravity and Grace*[1] – an introduction by someone who knew her. The reader of her work finds himself confronted by a difficult, violent, and complex personality; and the assistance of those who had the advantage of long discussions or correspondence with her, especially those who knew her under the peculiar conditions of the last five years of her life, will be of permanent value in the future. I lack these qualifications. My aims in writing this preface are, first, to affirm my belief in the importance of the author and of this particular book; second, to warn the reader against premature judgement and summary classification – to persuade him to hold in check his own prejudices and at the same time to be patient with those of Simone Weil. Once her work is known and accepted, such a preface as this should become superfluous.

1. *La Pésanteur et la Grâce*.

All of Simone Weil's work is posthumous. *Gravity and Grace* – the selection from her voluminous notebooks made by M. Thibon, and the first volume to appear in France – is admirable in its contents, but somewhat deceptive in its form. The comparison with Pascal (a writer of whom Simone Weil sometimes spoke with asperity) may be pressed too far. The fragmentariness of the extracts elicits the profound insights and the startling originality, but suggests that hers was a mind of occasional flashes of [vi] inspiration. After reading *Waiting for God*[1] and the present volume I saw that I must try to understand the personality of the author; and that the reading and rereading of all of her work was necessary for this slow process of understanding. In trying to understand her, we must not be distracted – as is only too likely to happen on a first reading – by considering how far, and at what points, we agree or disagree. We must simply expose ourselves to the personality of a woman of genius, of a kind of genius akin to that of the saints.

Perhaps 'genius' is not the right word. The only priest with whom she ever discussed her belief and her doubts has said, '*Je crois que son âme est incomparablement plus haute que son génie.*' That is another way of indicating that our first experience of Simone Weil should not be expressible in terms of approval or dissent. I cannot conceive of anybody's agreeing with all of her views, or not disagreeing violently with some of them. But agreement and rejection are secondary: what matters is to make contact with a great soul. Simone Weil was one who might have become a saint. Like some who have achieved this state, she had greater obstacles to overcome, as well as greater strength for overcoming them, than the rest of us. A potential saint can be a very difficult person: I suspect that Simone Weil could be at times insupportable. One is struck, here and there, by a contrast between an almost superhuman humility and what appears to be an almost outrageous arrogance. There is a significant sentence by the French priest whom I have already quoted. He reports that he does not remember 'ever having heard Simone Weil, in spite of her virtuous desire for objectivity, give way in the course of a discussion.' This comment throws light on much of her published work. I do not believe that she was ever animated by delight in her own forensic skill – a self-indulgence to which I [vii] suspect Pascal came dangerously near, in the *Letters* – the display of power in overcoming others in controversy. It was rather that all her thought was so intensely lived, that the abandonment of any opinion required modifications in her whole being: a process which could not take place painlessly, or in the course of a conversation. And – especially in the young, and in those like Simone Weil in whom one

1. *Attente de Dieu.*

detects no sense of humour – egotism and selflessness can resemble each other so closely that we may mistake the one for the other.

The statement that Simone Weil's 'soul was incomparably superior to her genius' will, however, be misunderstood if it gives the impression of depreciating her intellect. Certainly she could be unfair and intemperate; certainly she committed some astonishing aberrations and exaggerations. But those immoderate affirmations which tax the patience of the reader spring not from any flaw in her intellect but from excess of temperament. She came of a family with no lack of intellectual endowment – her brother is a distinguished mathematician; and as for her own mind, it was worthy of the soul which employed it. But the intellect, especially when bent upon such problems as those which harassed Simone Weil, can come to maturity only slowly; and we must not forget that Simone Weil died at the age of thirty-three. I think that in *The Need for Roots* especially, the maturity of her social and political thought is very remarkable. But she had a very great soul to grow up to; and we should not criticise her philosophy at thirty-three as if it were that of a person twenty or thirty years older.

In the work of such a writer we must expect to encounter paradox. Simone Weil was three things in the highest degree: French, Jewish, and Christian. She was a patriot who would gladly have been sent back to France to suffer and die for her compatriots; she had to die – partly, it would seem, as the result of self-mortification, in refusing to take more food than the official [viii] rations of ordinary people in France – in 1943 in a sanatorium at Ashford, Kent.

She was also a patriot who saw clearly, as this book shows, the faults and the spiritual weakness of contemporary France. She was a Christian with an intense devotion to Our Lord in the Sacrament of the Altar, yet she refused baptism, and much of her writing constitutes a formidable criticism of the Church. She was intensely Jewish, suffering torments in the affliction of the Jews in Germany; yet she castigated Israel[1] with all the severity of a Hebrew Prophet. Prophets, we are told, were stoned in Jerusalem: but Simone Weil is exposed to lapidation from several quarters. And in her political thinking she appears as a stern critic of both Right and Left; at the same time more truly a lover of order and hierarchy than most of those who call themselves Conservative, and more truly a lover of the people than most of those who call themselves Socialist.

As for her attitude toward the Church of Rome and her attitude toward Israel I wish, in the space of a preface, to make only one observation.

---

1. I use the term 'Israel' as she used it, and not, of course, with reference to the modern State.

The two attitudes are not only compatible but coherent, and should be considered as one. It was in fact her rejection of Israel that made her a very heterodox Christian. In her repudiation of all but a few parts of the Old Testament (and in what she accepted she discerned traces of Chaldean or Egyptian influence) she falls into something very like the Marcionite heresy. In denying the divine mission of Israel she is also rejecting the foundation of the Christian Church. Hence the difficulties that caused her so much agony of spirit. I must affirm that there is no trace of the Protestant in her composition: for her, the Christian Church could only be the Church of Rome. In the Church there is much to which she is blind, or about which she is strangely silent: she seems to give no thought to the Blessed Virgin; and as for the Saints, she is concerned only with those [ix] who attract her interest through their writings – such as St Thomas Aquinas (whom she dislikes, perhaps on insufficient acquaintance) and St John of the Cross (whom she admires because of his profound knowledge of spiritual method).

In one respect she has, at first sight, something in common with those intellectuals of the present day (mostly with a vague liberal Protestant background) who can find their way toward the religious life only through the mysticism of the East. Her enthusiasm for everything Greek (including the mysteries) was unbounded. For her, there was no revelation to Israel, but a good deal of revelation to the Chaldeans, the Egyptians, and the Hindus. Her attitude may appear to be dangerously close to that of those universalists who maintain that the ultimate and esoteric truth is one, that all religions show some traces of it, and that it is a matter of indifference to which one of the great religions we adhere. Yet she is saved from this error – and this is a matter for admiration and thankfulness – by her devotion to the person of Our Lord.

In her criticism of the Jewish and the Christian faiths, I think that we have to try to make for ourselves a threefold distinction, asking ourselves: How much is just? How much is serious objection that must be rebutted? And how much, in the way of error, can be extenuated on the ground of the immaturity of a superior and passionate personality? Our analyses may differ widely, but we must ask and answer these questions for ourselves.

I do not know how good a Greek scholar she was. I do not know how well read she was in the history of the civilisations of the Eastern Mediterranean. I do not know whether she could read the Upanishads in Sanskrit; or, if so, how great was her mastery of what is not only a very highly developed language but a way of thought, the difficulties of which only become more formidable to a European student the more diligently he applies himself to it. But I do not think that she shows, in this field, the [x] mind of a historian. In her adulation of Greece, and of the 'wisdom of the East', as in her disparagement of Rome and Israel, she seems to me almost wilful. In one quarter she sees only what she can admire; in another, she repudiates without discrimination. Because she dislikes the Roman Empire, she dislikes Virgil. Her admirations, when not motivated by her dislikes, seem to be at least intensified by them. One may sympathise with her horror at the brutalities of expanding or imperialistic peoples (as the Romans in Europe and the Spanish in America) in crushing local civilisations. But when, in order to enhance her denunciation of the Romans, she attempts to make out a case for the culture of the Druids, we do not feel that our meagre knowledge of that vanished society gives any ground for her conjectures. We can share her revulsion from the atrocities committed in the suppression of the Albigensian heresy, and yet speculate whether the peculiar civilisation of Provence had not come to the end of its productivity. Would the world be a better place today if there were half a dozen different cultures flourishing between the English Channel and the Mediterranean, instead of the one which we know as France? Simone Weil begins with an insight; but the logic of her emotions can lead her to make generalisations so large as to be meaningless. We may protest that we are completely in the dark as to what the world would be like now if events had taken a different course, that such a question as that whether the latinisation of Western Europe by Roman conquest was a good thing or bad thing is unanswerable. Her flights of fancy of this kind must not, however, be taken as invalidating her fundamental concept of *rootedness*, and her warnings against the evils of an overcentralised society.

This book was written during the last year or so of Simone Weil's life, during her employment at French Headquarters in London; and it issues, I understand, from memoranda which she submitted in connection with the policy to be pursued after the [xi] Liberation. The problems of the moment led her to much larger considerations; but even those pages in which she is concerned with the programme to be followed by the Free French during the war and immediately after the Liberation show such foresight and maturity of judgement that they are of permanent value. This is, I think, among those works of hers already published, the one which approximates most closely to the form in which she might herself have chosen to release it.

I have dwelt chiefly upon certain ideas which are to be met with in all her writings, with some emphasis upon her errors and exaggerations. I have taken this course in the belief that many readers, coming for the first time upon some assertion likely to arouse intellectual incredulity or emotional antagonism, might be deterred from improving their acquaintance with a great soul and a brilliant mind. Simone Weil needs patience from her readers, as she doubtless needed patience from the friends who most admired and appreciated her. But in spite of the violence of her affections and antipathies, in spite of such unjustified generalisations as I have instanced, I find in the present book especially a balanced judgement, a wisdom in avoiding extremes, astonishing in anyone so young. It may be that in her conversations with Gustave Thibon she profited more than she knew from contact with that wise and well-balanced mind.

As a political thinker, as in everything else, Simone Weil is not to be classified. The paradoxicality of her sympathies is a contributing cause of the equilibrium. On the one hand she was a passionate champion of the common people and especially of the oppressed – those oppressed by the wickedness and selfishness of men and those oppressed by the anonymous forces of modern society. She had worked in the Renault factory, she had worked as a field labourer, in order to share the life of people of town and country. On the other hand, she was by nature a solitary and an individualist, with a profound horror of what she called the [xii] *collectivity* – the monster created by modern totalitarianism. What she cared about was human souls. Her study of human rights and human obligations exposes the falsity of some of the verbiage still current which was used during the war to serve as a moral stimulant. Not the least striking example of her shrewdness, balance, and good sense is her examination of the principle of monarchy; and her short review of the political history of France is at once a condemnation of the French Revolution and a powerful argument against the possibility of a restoration of the kingship. She cannot be classified either as a reactionary or as a socialist.

This book belongs in that category of prolegomena to politics which politicians seldom read, and which most of them would be unlikely to understand or to know how to apply. Such books do not influence the contemporary conduct of affairs: for the men and women already engaged in this career and committed to the jargon of the market place, they always come too late. This is one of those books which ought to be studied by the young before their leisure has been lost and their capacity for thought destroyed in the life of the hustings and the legislative assembly; books the effect of which, we can only hope, will become apparent in the attitude of mind of another generation.

Dossier on *Murder in the Cathedral*
PLAYWRIGHT PRESENTS BOTH AN EVALUATION AND APPRECIATION OF THE FILM VERSION
New York Times, 23 Mar. 1952, 5. Not in Gallup, but would be C570a.

So many years have passed since the idea of making a film of my play, *Murder in the Cathedral*, was conceived in the brain of George Hoellering that I cannot remember when our conversations on the subject began. It was in the middle of the war, in 1941 or 1942, that we were brought together by a mutual friend.

Hoellering's first problem was how to convert me to believing that his idea was realisable and worth realising – and even then I said to myself: 'I don't believe that it can be satisfactorily done; but unless I agree to make this experiment I shall never know whether it is possible.' Besides, I wanted to find out how films were made. So I should not regret the experience, even were the film, which has resulted, not the masterpiece which I believe it to be.

I expected the first discussions to be concerned with casting; instead, I found that my director postponed that problem to a very late stage. Instead, he began by fabricating on hand-looms (which had to be constructed for the purpose) the material for costumes, such as were used in the twelfth century.

Meticulous

I was, and still am, amazed by the infinite pains he took for historical accuracy in costume, furniture and setting. This was the first difference to strike me: on the stage minor anachronisms can be ignored or forgiven – but not in a film. In other words, the picture, though it can also produce effects or fantasy impossible on the stage, is also very much more realistic. When it introduces fantasy, it is a realistic fantasy.

Again, I had expected that much of the photographing would be done on location at Canterbury Cathedral (for which the permission of the Dean and Chapter had been given), using the crypt and any other parts of the cathedral where Norman architecture remained. I now see that even the original Norman parts of the cathedral would have been anachronistic. The cathedral had to look as it did in 1170, when it was still new. Stone-work after nearly 800 years shows signs of wear and tear. And I believe that some electric lighting had been installed, which even the most ignorant film-goer could hardly have accepted as twelfth-century work. It was much more satisfactory to fabricate sets inside a disused war-damaged church in London.

Hoellering imposed two tasks upon me. (Indeed, in spite of my very secondary role in the creation of the film, I found myself, first and last, doing a great deal more work than I had bargained for.) The first was to write the preliminary scenes, especially that of the 'trial' at Northampton. Here, he met with a great deal of resistance. I was used to the shape of my play, and didn't want to change it. I agreed rather grudgingly, thinking that I was being asked to make a concession to that part of the film audience that didn't know the historical story.

New Material

I came to see that these additional scenes are necessary for any audience; that it is not a question of film audience being different from stage audience, but rather a question of the same audience under the different conditions of stage and screen. On the screen, much more has to be explained. Plot, and form, are different things for stage and screen.

My second important task – I think both of these were performed in the bitter winter of 1945–46 – was to record the whole play (including the new additions) in my own voice. This, Hoellering explained, was to serve as a guide to his actors, not for dramatic expression, but for pronunciation and preservation of the verse rhythms. Only Mr Hoellering himself can say how useful this recording proved. But if this was useful for the film, it strikes me that such recordings might prove helpful also to producers of stage plays in verse. One consequence, unexpected to me, of this recording, was that it suggested to him the use of my voice for the Invisible Tempter. I may observe that my being cast for the Invisible Tempter constituted my third task and that by no means the least arduous.

Now, there is one question to which I think there is no answer. It is the question: Do I think that *Murder in the Cathedral* is better as a play or as a film? I don't think the question has any meaning. But there are two other questions to which I can give answers. First, in what way, if any, is the text of the film an improvement on that of the play? And, in what ways has the film an advantage, for this play, over the stage?

Improvement

In the first place, the film assures, what the stage cannot, maximal clarity of diction and complete audibility throughout the house. In the second place, it opens up much larger possibilities for variation in the use of the chorus at the same time more realistic and more nightmarish. It is evident in the film, as not always in the theatre, that the chorus is not a Greek chorus of commentators, but is much more closely implicated in the action. Thirdly, the film gains, I think, by being played straight through without the intermission which is inevitable in the theatre.

Finally, there was the difficult problem of the Knight's speeches. These speeches were of course designed to be addressed to the audience: if they were addressed to a stage crowd, they would become completely pointless. But, even if such long harangues to the audience could be provided with suitable photography, they would, in a film, take us away from the scene of the murder far too long, and would break the illusion of being eye-witnesses of the actual event, which it is the business of the camera to create. The speeches therefore had to be considerably abbreviated and modified, to be addressed to the twelfth century crowd, and the moment of address to the audience (and without this address to the audience the play loses its whole point) had to be made as brief, as concentrated, and of as violent an impact as possible.

I think that this is an improvement, in that the meaning is made clear beyond a shadow of doubt. And I think that if I were to rewrite the play (but nothing is less likely) I should here follow the lines which Hoellering and the film medium itself imposed upon me, rather than retain the original speeches.

It is generally assumed that in the film, the only value of the words you hear is that they should help you to understand what you see. That is to say, that the spoken word in the film is merely an improvement upon the captions of the silent film. In this film I find that my words gain, instead of losing value.

Hoellering understands poetic drama from the author's point of view, and that is an exceptional good fortune for me. I have, I believe, made some progress in understanding and appreciating the possibilities of poetic drama from the film director's point of view. We survived these years of preparation without any violent quarrels. My only complaint is that he has been so scrupulous to avoid doing anything I didn't like, that he has made me do much more work myself than I would have been obliged to do for anyone else.

Foreword

Foreword to Joseph Chiari, *Contemporary French Poetry*, vii–xi.
Subheaded *'by* | T. S. ELIOT' and signed 'T. S. ELIOT' at the end.
Publ. 18 Apr. 1952. Gallup B67.

A critical introduction to contemporary poetry may take one of two forms, according to the degree of knowledge of the material that may be attributed to the audience addressed. If the poets to be discussed are almost unknown, the critic's chief service is to bring their work to the notice of readers who are likely to appreciate them; and his critical acumen will be most appropriately exhibited by copious and well-chosen quotation. His main task is to persuade his readers that his poets deserve their attention, and to send them eagerly to the poetry itself. If, however, the authors are already known, his aim may be to help readers who have some acquaintance with their work to read more intelligently and analytically, to modify their earlier opinions, and to perceive more accurately the virtues and defects of writers already accepted as important.

The area which Mr Chiari has chosen to cover obliges him to employ both of these methods. Two of his poets, Valéry and Claudel, authors of an older generation, are already famous in this country as they are in France: there exist a number of translations of both the verse and the prose of Valéry, and at least two of Claudel's plays have been presented to London audiences. Two of his poets belong to a middle generation – Supervielle and Perse – but their work is not yet so widely known in this country as it should be. The work of a still younger generation – that of such men as Eluard, Emmanuel, and Michaux – is known only to those readers of poetry in England who endeavour to [viii] acquaint themselves with new French verse while the poets' reputations are still in the making at home.

I am tempted to draw a comparison here between the task which Mr Chiari has set himself, and that undertaken half a century ago by Arthur Symons in *The Symbolist Movement in French Literature*. Symons did perform the function of bringing important poets to the attention of English readers; and for that reason his book will remain a landmark. As criticism I cannot say that Symons's book stands the test of time. He omitted one or two poets of the first importance – notably Tristan Corbière; he included one or two writers – Maeterlinck and Villiers de l'Isle Adam – whose reputation is now somewhat diminished; and even when he admired the right authors, one cannot say that it was always for the right reason. My reason for mentioning Symons's book, however, is to point a difference between the poetry of the epoch which he treated, and that considered by Mr Chiari: a difference which renders the task of the latter much the more difficult.

With all the abundance and variety of the French poetry of the period to which we attach the phrase 'the Symbolist movement' – and the difference of aim, technique and idiom between such poets as Corbière, Laforgue, Mallarmé, and Rimbaud is amazing – there is a certain unity which makes it manageable as a whole. It is not so easy to say in what the unity consists: for the more closely we examine the meaning of the term

'Symbolism' the more it comes to seem merely a convenient label, and not a defining term. In part, the unity is due to a common derivation from Baudelaire: but the poets whom I have named were anything but epigoni, and what is interesting is not so much what they got from Baudelaire, but what they made of it. The unity is, in any case, felt; and the contrast makes us more aware of our own period – that which Mr Chiari has under review – as one in which common directions have been lacking.

Whereas, therefore, Arthur Symons could treat certain [ix] poets as forming, between them, the outline of a period, so that he had no need to refer to a number of admirable poets much of whose work has permanent value (I mention in passing only the names of Verhaeren, Jammes, Samain, Tailhade, Kahn, Regnier, Viélé-Griffin), Mr Chiari cannot assign to any of his poets the same representative function. He has, I think rightly, made no attempt to discuss all the poets of the last forty years; he has omitted some of great distinction. His selection has had to be of those poets whose work he finds most sympathetic; and, as a personal choice, it omits a number of names one or another of which the informed reader will miss. But to have been otherwise, his book would have had to be conceived on a much larger scale; it might have become only one of those comprehensive scholarly chronicles which seem to exist only to preserve dull writers from complete oblivion. Had he attempted to perform this task, I do not think that I should have been much interested in the result. I therefore cannot repine at the absence of, for instance, Henri Franck, whose poems deserve a greater fame than they have ever enjoyed. In the same way I only mention the absence of Guillaume Apollinaire (in some ways the most representative poet of one type); and the absence of several significant figures of the twenties – Cocteau, André Salmon, and Max Jacob. I could wish that more space had been given to St John Perse, not only for the intrinsic value of his poems, but because I think he will prove to have had a greater influence upon Anglo-American verse than is yet recognised. And there are, as Mr Chiari admits in his preface, other younger poets besides Eluard and Michaux who deserve a place. But I mention such omissions only in support of my contention that the nature of the period with which Mr Chiari is concerned is such as to compel, in any treatment of this kind, a selection which may appear somewhat arbitrary.

For the period itself is one which, until it can be reviewed in a much longer perspective, must be left unexplained: it cannot be exposed to the reader in a neat and intelligible [x] order. Even if we consider the only two eldest and most famous of the poets whose work Mr Chiari examines, it is difficult to think of Paul Valéry and Paul Claudel as contemporaries. Their technique, their aims, their view of life are in striking contrast.

Even their comparative chronology is paradoxical. In 1910, when I had my first introduction to literary Paris, Claudel was already a great poet in the eyes of a younger generation – my own generation. He had published *Connaissance de l'Est, Art poétique*, and those plays which appeared in one volume under the general title of *L'Arbre*: and I am not sure that these three books do not constitute his strongest claim to immortality. Paul Valéry, if known at all, was known only as a minor, late Symbolist poet whose work was represented in the standard anthology of Symbolist verse, *Poètes d'Aujourd'hui* of Van Bever and Léautaud. It was only in 1917, after the publication of *La Jeune Parque*, that his name was suddenly illuminated with glory; yet curiously enough, while Claudel still remained known only to a few readers in England, the fame of Valéry spread as quickly as that of Proust. Finally, when Valéry died, in 1945, his death seemed to mark the end of an age, with greater definitiveness and solemnity than that of any other European author of his generation could have done. What Valéry represented, in his total *oeuvre* – for his poetry and his critical and speculative prose form one inseparable whole – was the perfection, the culmination of a type of civilised mind which becomes, to the post-war world, increasingly alien. While the work of Claudel remains, for better or worse, closer to the state of mind of the beginning of the second half of the twentieth century.

When we turn to the representatives of the middle generation, we find equally little relation between the two poets whom Mr Chiari has chosen, Jules Supervielle and St John Perse. And neither of them can be associated with either of their great predecessors. I am very glad that Mr Chiari chose these two poets, for there are no two poets of their generation in France of whose permanence I feel more [xi] assured. But what generalisations can we make, from the work of Valéry, Claudel, Supervielle, and Perse, together with the younger writers such as Emmanuel and Michaux and half a dozen others who were worthy of inclusion, about the place and function of poetry today? It would be impossible to erect an *art poétique* of the achievements of French poetry in the twentieth century. Perhaps it is as imprudent to attempt to define the condition of poetry today in any one language as it would be to generalise about the condition of poetry everywhere. But at least, when we confine our attention to the poetry of one language, we can speak of it in the more manageable terms of the technical problem. Confining ourselves to these terms, we can I think speak of the present situation of French poetry as corresponding to a *crisis of prosody*. It is a period in which each poet is engaged in his own private experiments and explorations in the endeavour to find the right vehicle, the right vocabulary, and the right versification. Eventually, out of these struggles – and only the poet himself knows how arduous, agonising, and solitary such effort must be in our time – a common style may emerge in the poetry of a generation to come. Meanwhile, the struggle itself is of the greatest significance for all those readers, in other countries and of other languages, who know that without poetry civilisation cannot flourish.

Découverte de Paris

Les Nouvelles Littéraires, 1286 (24 Apr. 1952), [1].
Not in Gallup, but would be C570b.

Je vins à Paris pour la première fois en 1910, après mes études à l'université de Harvard, aux États-Unis, à l'âge de 21 ans. J'en avais eu le désir depuis plusieurs années.

Ma dette envers Paris est incalculable. Je dois beaucoup aux conférences et aux cours que j'ai suivis à la Sorbonne et au Collège de France; mais ma dette est surtout envers la ville elle-même. Cette dette est plus grande qu'aucune de celles que j'ai envers les autres villes du monde. Mon année à Paris, à cet âge, à bien des égards, la plus importante de ma vie.

Le stimulus de Paris était d'ordre intellectuel, artistique et profondément émotionnel. Ce n'était pas simplement telle ou telle influence en particulier, mais tout un genre de vie, le plus riche, le plus développé et civilisé qu'un jeune homme ait pour avoir le privilège d'expérimenter.

Some Thoughts on Braille

An address delivered on 25 June 1952 to the National Book League and the National Institute for the Blind in support of the Braille Centenary Fund.

Books, The Journal of the National Book League, 272 (Sept. 1952), 75–6.
Revised from 'National Book League Celebrates Braille Centenary',
The New Beacon, 36. 428 (15 Aug. 1952), 176–7. Gallup C571.

1 The name of Louis Braille has been conspicuous in the Press, and his native country has just paid him the highest posthumous honour within its power to give. But funerary honours are quickly forgotten: tombs are soon unfrequented; and as for statues, the more publicly they are situated the more completely they become ignored – after a little while few pause to look at them, fewer still to decipher their inscriptions. Perhaps the most enduring honour to the memory of Louis Braille is the half-conscious honour we pay him by applying his name to the script he

invented – and, in this country, adapting the pronunciation of his name to our own language. We honour Braille whenever we speak of *braille*. His memory has in this way a security firmer than that of the memories of many men more famous in their day. And his is a name which we are all under obligation to honour, in perpetuity, in the most practical way: by carrying on the work for the blind that he initiated.

2 There are several ways in which we may contribute to make the lives of the blind happier, fuller and more useful. But it is appropriate that we should turn our minds to-night especially to the problem of the provision of literature for the blind. We are the guests of the National Book League, formed to promote the reading of books; Lord Normanby is to address you on the subject on which no one is so well qualified to speak – the National Library for the Blind; and I presume that it is as a man of letters – for I have no other qualification – that I was invited to take the chair at this meeting. That is certainly the reason why I accepted: or rather, it is the reason for my interest in the subject.

3 May I make some observations from the point of view of a writer – a writer who has also been connected for many years with the publishing of books, and who, incidentally, both in writing and in publishing, has had to read books written by other people? At times a grievous burden: but in this dual capacity, no demand gives me more pleasure than the request for permission to print one of my works in braille. It is a request any author should regard as a signal compliment. From the point of view of the publisher, the arrangement has a simplicity, an absence of complications, which is all too rare in his business negotiations. There can be no hesitation in accepting; a simple exchange of letters; and author and publisher have done their part. I regret, however, that I am ignorant of what follows. I do not know by what process the books are produced. I have never seen one of my own books in braille, and – what is more important – I do not know whether anybody reads them. I infer, from the fact that I have received this welcome request more than once, that the interest in a previous book has been enough to justify the production of another; but whether my works in braille are well-thumbed, or remain on the shelf, I have never discovered. Perhaps I shall now obtain this information.

4 I am interested in braille, however, for a personal reason. I do not know whether the thought of possible blindness haunts other writers, but I know that it has always haunted me. And this, without any physical premonition: my sight I am thankful to say is as reliable as most people's. For a writer, blindness need not be, of course, the end of his activity, as it must be for a painter: but it involves readjustments so great as to frighten

me. It happens that two great writers of my own generation, both friends of mine, came to suffer from this affliction, and I know something of their difficulties. It is easy to speak of the resource of dictation, for those who have never had to dictate more than their business correspondence. At one time I made the experiment, for a short while, of trying to dictate essays and lectures. I had the advantage of being able to read what I had dictated, to correct and alter – and a great deal of correction and alteration proved necessary. Even so, I found that [76] dictation changed my style of writing, and that the mental effort involved, if I was to escape diffuseness and repetition, was immense. Nowadays, the dictaphone, when available, has facilitated the work of the blind author; but even with this aid the labour of correction and improvement of what one has dictated must be prodigious.

5 It is not, however, so much the difficulties of composition that appal me, as the impossibility of reading: for, as I have hinted, if a writer has not constant access to what other people have written, his own work may come to suffer from undernourishment. It is often said, of poetry, that its primary appeal should be to the ear; that it is meant to be heard rather than seen. This is true, but it is only a half-truth. Only at early stages of history has poetry been purely auditory, memorised by the bard and passed on by word of mouth; and for centuries we have been accustomed to the printed book.

6 Poetry is meant to be heard *and* read: and this is true even of dramatic verse: think how incomplete would be our appreciation of Shakespeare if, however many times we had seen and heard performances, we had never had access to the printed text! It is excellent that poetry should be read to us by skilled readers: it is a common experience to find that a poem which seemed dull or incomprehensible when we have read it to ourselves became living and meaningful when we heard it well read. But then, I think, after this experience, we want to open the book and read the poem to ourselves. We want the interpreter – but the interpreter is also, inevitably, another personality interposed between ourselves and the author. I like to hear poetry well read. But I depend still more on reading it to myself. And if, on the one hand, a good reader can help us to understand a poem which had meant nothing when we read it to ourselves, I find also that when my first acquaintance with a poem is by hearing it read, I do not altogether take it in. What the good reader can do, is to provoke in me the *desire* to read it to myself. So I find that I need both to hear and to read. If I were completely dependent upon readers I should never feel that I had attained complete intimacy with the poem itself, and with its author.

7 That is why, if I were suddenly blinded, or if I found the world slowly dimming before my eyes, I should be thankful for the invention of braille. Whether at my age I could master it, I do not know; but the hope of mastering it would sustain me. For without being able to read, independent of others to read to me, I do not believe that I could write – or, in so far as I could write, I should be chiefly dependent upon my past reading during my years of vision. That is why I want the blind to be able to read for themselves, as well as to be read to.

Variants from 15 Aug. 1952:
Title NATIONAL BOOK LEAGUE CELEBRATES BRAILLE CENTENARY
1 invented – and] invented and
2 speak – the National Library] speak, of the National Library
[Between 'why I accepted' and 'May I make':] . I had outer forms of compulsion laid upon me, but I had also an inner compulsion to attend, for are books not more necessary to the blind than to others?
3 grievous burden:] grievous burden,
braille] Braille [*passim*]
4 affliction] great handicap
6 performances] the performance
became] becomes
heard] hear

An Address
to
Members of the London Library
by T. S. Eliot O.M.

On the occasion of his assuming the office of President of the Library. Delivered at the Annual General Meeting of Members in the Reading Room, 22 July 1952.

<sub>The Book Collector, 1. 3 (Autumn 1952), 139–44. Gallup C572.
Repr. in Sept. 1952 as *An Address to Members of the London Library By T. S. Eliot O.M.* (Gallup A59).</sub>

On my first appearance before you as President, it has seemed to me proper, and a sign of due respect to my audience, that I should offer an address more formally prepared than might be desirable on later occasions; and that the content of this address should be a kind of testament of faith in the London Library.

First of all, I should like to say something of my personal debt to this

Library. It is a great many years ago that – under the sponsorship of the late Sir Sydney Waterlow, one of his many kindnesses to me – I was admitted to membership. I was then employed in a bank in the City, and had little time to spend in libraries. I was also writing for various literary periodicals, notably *The Athenaeum* and *The Times Literary Supplement*. As a conscientious reviewer, I needed to consult standard works and works of scholarship. There was the British Museum: but I had only my Saturday afternoons free – three Saturday afternoons out of four, as the fourth, at one period of my modest career as a financier, was spent in Cornhill dealing with an obscure operation called 'the clearing'. I am not ungrateful to the British Museum: but when I installed myself there after lunch on a Saturday, it often happened that I had hardly opened the essential volume for which I had been waiting, when there sounded the familiar warning which corresponds to the phrase 'Hurry up, please, it's time'. At this juncture, it was the London Library that made my literary journalism possible. I could go there at my leisure, after lunch on Saturday, [140] rummage the stacks, and emerge with nine or ten volumes to take home with me. Without the London Library, many of my early essays could never have been written.

This personal record, however, is parenthetical, and has no direct bearing upon my main theme, which is: What is the value of such an institution as the London Library to-day, and why is its preservation worth fighting for? The question has a double pertinence. First, in relation to the financial perplexities of the Library, of which we are all aware; and second, in relation to current tendencies of opinion. Sooner or later a cry may be raised, to put us on the horns of a dilemma. It will say, either that the London Library is superfluous, and should therefore be abolished; or else that it is too valuable to be reserved, and should therefore be taken over by some public authority and thrown open to everybody. So we have to answer two questions: can such a library, limited to members and supported by subscriptions, survive? And, *ought* it to survive? Our answer to the first question will depend partly on our answer to the second. Now, I should not be here, unless I believed that the London Library, in its present form, ought to be preserved. And when I say this, I am not thinking primarily of its august tradition of service, of all that it has done for letters and scholarship in the last hundred years. The maintenance of an institution cannot be defended on the ground of its usefulness in the past: only on the ground of its value for the present and the future. I am not even thinking primarily of its services to its members – though I *am* thinking of the services so many of its members have performed which they could not have performed so well without the London Library. I am thinking of the Library as itself performing a service to English civilisation. And as for the future, I shall endeavor to give grounds for my belief, that the London Library, instead of diminishing in value, is becoming more necessary than ever before.

Consider, then, whether there is any other type of library which could replace ours. Certainly, not the great National Libraries. These foundations have their own problems: have you ever reflected on their nightmare future, the world over? Publishers have sometimes complained of the compulsion they are under, to send [141] a copy of every book they publish to the so-called copyright libraries. But what of the other side of the picture? These libraries have the awful burden of having to accept every book that is sent to them – file it, catalogue it, and preserve it until the time of holocaust. Their problem, like the traffic problem, is insoluble: nothing but the exhaustion of fuel supplies can solve the traffic problem, and nothing but the exhaustion of paper supplies can solve the National Library problem. And indeed, in some great modern libraries there is a traffic problem too: I have visited a great new library building in America, in which I was shown, with pride, the system of directions which had been elaborated to prevent the possibility of readers getting lost in the interminable maze of stacks. True, all libraries suffer to some degree from the same complaint: it is in the nature of things that until the day of doom every library must grow and grow. All libraries bear this burden of Atlas (and indeed the burden of Atlas was less, for it remained constant, of the same size and weight): but some libraries are at least free to dispose quietly, after a decent space of time, of those books which nobody wants at all, and of those which no one wants except the few who want them so much that they are prepared to go to a national or a university library to consult them.

I say nothing of the circulating libraries which perform a different function, and serve on the whole a different public, from ours: though they have nowadays a subscription quandary not dissimilar to ours. It is rather to the municipal and borough libraries that our critics will point, those who will say that *if* the London Library is not superfluous, then, on moral grounds, it ought to be thrown open to everyone, because to exclude people from something they cannot pay for is contrary to social justice. At this point, I do not propose to enlarge my subject to include any general affirmations about liberty, equality and privilege: a region of discourse in which passionate prejudice obfuscates counsel and eclipses reason. I am only concerning myself with the special case of libraries. I recognize, of course, the important function which only the local public library can perform. But I hold that the London Library is unique, of essential service just [142] because it *is* restricted to members. If this is 'privilege', then it is privilege which I defend with complete conviction:

only adding that amongst the 'privileged', for the London Library, should be included as many as possible of those individuals whom the Committee recognises as suitable and desirable members, but who cannot afford the subscription. The members of the Library should in general be such people as are prepared to make some sacrifice, to economise in any reasonable way, in order to pay their subscription. But beyond that point there are many readers who deserve the 'privilege', who are amongst those best qualified to profit by it, and who nowadays cannot afford the subscription at all. Hence the imperative need for the Carlyle Trust, and for benefactions to enable it to carry out its functions.

Here is the great difference between the London Library and the public library: the London Library has always had a certain homogeneity of membership. In what this homogeneity consists, would be hard to define: but with great diversity of interests, our membership has always represented the high level of culture and of what I may call serious readership. And without such a membership, the assembling of this collection of books would have been impossible. The Committee, when they buy a book, know, in a sense, for whom they are buying it. I do not believe that there is another library of this size which contains so many of the books which I *might* want, and so few of the books which I cannot imagine anyone wanting; and in saying this I believe that I am speaking simply as a representative member. A public library, however judicious it may be in the selection of books, and however desirous to improve the taste of its readers, has to consider the interests of that great, vague, unknown entity called 'the public'. It may be easy to build up a public library for specialised or technical books: it would be impossible to build up a public library, of the size of the London Library, equally suitable for the type of reader represented by our members.

The optimum number of members of the London Library seems to me contingent upon this consideration, as well as upon our limitations of size, and the limitations of physical endurance of the staff. It should, from this point of view, be the largest number of [143] members of the right kind, of men and women of general culture as well as special interests. I do not think we need fear that there will ever be too many such potential members at our doors, suing for entrance. I only say that the unique character of the London Library which, with the aid of the Carlyle Trust, we hope to preserve, has been due, not only to the wisdom, scholarship, taste and administrative ability of successive Librarians and Committees, but to the quality of our membership: and this is an advantage which no *public* library can enjoy.

I have suggested that, whatever social changes come about, the disappearance of the London Library would be a disaster to civilisation. But

I also hinted that some of the transformations which we have witnessed in our lifetime render this library more essential than ever. I was thinking of the disappearance of what used to be called 'the gentleman's library'; the decline of those already formed, and the impossibility to-day of forming a new one. There are three kinds of private collections of books. There is the collection of the collector: the man who collects valuable and rare editions, usually of some one author or of some one type or period, and who, when he really knows what he is about, is a bibliographer. Such collections have great value: but, so far as they are not dispersed on the death of the collector, but preserved intact in some public institution where they will be accessible to those worthy to examine them, we need not repine at their passage from private hands. There is what I called 'the gentleman's library', a library of the best editions of such books as a person of general education and culture would wish to have at hand. And finally, there is the private library which is merely a haphazard accumulation. The last is the most frequently found to-day, and it is the kind that I own myself. Mine includes, for instance, books which I reviewed years ago and have never consulted since (some of them still containing the label for returning them to *The Times* after the review was written); it includes books which I have bought to read and have never opened; it includes books presented by their authors – which I keep, some in the hope of reading them, some out of personal regard for the author, and some out of politeness or prudence. It includes some books which ought to [144] have found their way to Foyle's outdoor bin years ago. I have an accumulation of books so various, so recalcitrant of order, that when I want to consult some book I know I possess, I cannot find it, and have to borrow it from the London Library.

Very few people, nowadays, do possess a collection of books which deserves to be called 'a library'. Very few of us have the space. We all suffer from claustrophobia, from living in boxes too tight for us. Just as, sitting in the vast smoking room of some large club, I can imagine myself the proprietor of a palace, so when I come here, I have a better library than the library I should like to own myself. Here are so many of the books I should like to own. Complete editions, for example, of the works of minor Elizabethan dramatists. Even if I could get them (and some are very difficult to obtain) I have no room for them. Nobody can give house room to the complete works of voluminous authors; yet no one, I hold, is well educated unless he knows the *complete* works of several great authors and a few favourite minor ones.

The great private libraries have had their day, and are gone. Even the more modest private library is a rarity. And under these conditions the London Library takes its place: this is the private library of each one of its members. This is a very important function indeed; and I am convinced that if this library disappeared, it would be a disaster to the world of letters, and would leave a vacancy that no other form of library would fill.

[Tribute to Luigi Pirandello]

Sipario, 7. 80 (Dec. 1952), 66. Signed 'T. S. ELIOT'.
Not in Gallup but would be C573a.

Pirandello is a dramatist to whom all serious dramatists, of my generation and the next, must recognise a debt of gratitude. He has taught us something about what our problems are, and indicated directions in which their solution may be sought. He has shown us by his example that the escape from the confinement of naturalistic realism in the theatre, need not be sought in the artificially 'poetic' or in the fantasies of a play of bloodless ideas and epigrams. He has had the courage and the imagination which have made it possible to penetrate 'realism' and arrive at reality.

The Publishing of Poetry

The Bookseller, 2450 (6 Dec. 1952), 1568–70. Gallup C574.
Headnote: 'The following article reproduces the substance of a talk which Mr. Eliot gave to the Society of Young Publishers last month.'

I felt flattered by the invitation to address the Society of Young Publishers: it struck me that at last I had achieved the honour of being recognised as an Old Publisher. I am accustomed to being regarded, by other publishers, as a member of that tiresome, inferior but necessary class of beings known as Authors. I expect to be treated as a Publisher only by my own Authors – who do not necessarily always regard me as a *good* Publisher. Yet, if I am not qualified to address you on this subject – the *publishing* of poetry – I am not qualified to talk to people on any subject whatever. For I have had twenty-five years' experience of this branch of publishing. What I propose to offer you this evening is a selection of the small fruit of my experience, picked in a somewhat haphazard manner.

The first point I have to make will appear so simple as to be almost a glimpse of the obvious. It is this: that the most important difference between poetry and any other department of publishing is, that whereas with most categories of books you are aiming to make as much money as possible, with poetry you are aiming to lose as little as possible. And I maintain that it takes as much canniness to achieve this result with your poetry as it does to make comfortable profits from some other kinds. I admit that publishers do bring out now and then books, in other categories, on which they expect to lose money: I am only suggesting that poetry is the only whole department in which you expect to lose money.

Two Necessary Conditions

If the only thing one had in view was to lose the minimum, the answer would be plain: don't publish poetry at all. This is the way in which many publishers solve the problem. There must be some other reason impelling some publishers to undertake this unprofitable activity. The word which springs immediately to every lip is 'prestige'. But this word prestige needs looking at. We use it rather freely: sometimes it is a consolation prize which publishers award themselves for a book which hasn't done as well as they had hoped. It is curious that we should attach so much value to prestige: we are not quite sure what it is, we are never quite sure that we have got it, and we are never sure how much it is worth when we have it. I shall say something more on this subject of prestige presently. But one thing I am sure of is, that if you publish poetry solely in order to get prestige, you are unlikely to get it, and you will probably waste money instead of merely losing it. You have to have some better reason. I think that for publishing poetry two conditions are necessary.

The first is, that the director of directors in a firm publishing general literature must be convinced that English poetry has been one of the glories, perhaps the chief glory, of our literature in the past; and that, in consequence, it is a responsibility towards society that such a firm should do something for English poetry, by publishing the best poetry, written in our time, that it can get hold of. And the second essential is, that there should be somebody in the firm who can give a good deal of time to this department: someone, preferably, with a flair for recognising at an early stage poets who will be publicly recognised in ten or fifteen years' time.

'Prestige' Only a By-Product

If these two conditions are fulfilled, you may be able to build up a list which in due course will contribute to the firm's prestige. But the prestige must come as a by-product: what you are aiming at is to publish some of the best poetry being written in your time. You won't get prestige – not the right kind – merely by taking over poets who have already established their reputation: the firm itself must have had something to do with building up that reputation. You must be known to have backed the right authors long before they became famous.

This raises another interesting point about the kind of prestige with which I am concerned. After you have acquired it, you can't sit back and relax. You have got to go on earning more, if you are to keep what you have earned. If you close your list, and simply go on publishing the work of the same successful poets, people will begin to say 'What a good firm that used to be: now all the life seems to have gone out of it.' So prestige has two parts: (1) having picked the right authors in the past; (2) going on guessing about the younger generation.

With this combination it is obvious that your prestige for what you have done up to date will help to establish your newer authors. That is, your imprint on a book of verse will be an initial advantage: it will, at least, ensure some attention from editors and reviewers when the new books reach them. I don't know how much difference the imprint makes to the buying public, which depends for poetry on reviews and on recommendations in conversation. And, incidentally, I don't think that advertising makes much difference: all you can do is to announce that a new book of verse has been published. The more famous authors will sell just as well, and the younger ones just as meagrely, on the minimum of advertising matter.

Three Classes of Poets

My next point is that I think we can divide the poets on a good, well-balanced poetry list into three classes, roughly speaking. My three classes do not bear any necessary relation to the relative importance [1569] of the poets – this is a classification only into sales. It is of course to be expected that, other things being equal, the better-selling poets will be the older and the poor sellers the younger ones.

First, there are the poets who actually make some money, for themselves and for their publisher. Not much money, compared with some lines of merchandise, but still a cosy little sum. Any poet whose new book can be expected to sell 3,000 within a year of publication belongs in this class: which has a very, very small number of members indeed! This class can be counted on to provide good property for a back list. In the course of time, the Collected Poetical Works and a few volumes of Selected Poems of various sizes and prices should go on selling throughout the term of copyright, sufficiently to make it worth while to keep them in print, for profit as well as prestige.

The second class consists of poets who have proved their worth, who consistently get fully reviewed and noticed, who are always mentioned in lists of the best poets of their generation. Incidentally, it is when a poet is not merely reviewed but constantly referred to, that I begin to have confidence in his success. When the reviewer of the new poets X, Y and Z gives his readers to understand that they ought to be familiar with the work of A, B and C – then I feel happy about A, B and C. This second class ought not to show more than a small deficit on a book at the end of twelve months. You are not making money, but your losses are negligible. Some of these will get into the first class in time, others will stay where they are.

Third, there are the poets on whom you are losing money. They are the young ones who may – or may not – get into the second class in a few years' time. You are still testing them out, for a promising start may be deceptive: you don't know about their staying power. Yet they are a necessary part of your list: otherwise you will be thought to have lagged behind. And I believe that if the Poetry Editor is himself convinced of the exceptional merit of a poet he should stick to him through thick and thin however disappointing the response of reviewers and readers.

This leads me immediately to my next point. I look at a good many poetry scripts every week. Of the great majority, I may say that there is no part of my work which costs [1570] me less time and trouble. That is the thing about verse: you can judge from a very small quantity whether the author has any possibilities or not: you can often say, 'The man who can write as bad a line as that simply hasn't got it in him.' The rarest experience is to come across a new poet who strikes you as so good that you don't need anybody's judgement but your own. There remain a small number of scripts by new authors about which you cannot make up your mind at once. I usually keep such scripts for a long time, to take them up again at intervals, to read them in a different mood, at a different time of day. When one is tired, and has been looking at a number of bad scripts, it is very easy to deceive oneself into thinking that a collection of poems is better than it is, merely because it is better than the others.

Also, there is a time span beyond which one has less confidence in one's own judgement. With volumes by new poets more than twenty years younger than myself – and the majority of new poets now are much younger than that! – I do not altogether trust my own reactions. It becomes necessary to have a few younger friends, themselves in touch with what is happening among the young, whose opinion one can take. I don't say that I always accept their valuations, but they are always helpful. And if a new poet seems to me meritorious, but I don't feel that at the moment our own list ought to have an addition, I consider that I ought to commend him to some other firm.

The Importance of the 'Little' Publisher

It is exceptional when a new poet of merit turns up, without my having heard or seen his name before. He has usually appeared from time to time in one or more of the little reviews and poetry journals. I consider these periodicals – most of which do not survive for long – of great value in general: to the young poets, because it is helpful to see one's work in print, and because they get known in this way to each other; to the editorial departments of publishers, as they enable us to keep an eye on the development of the younger writers without having to commit ourselves. But equally important are what I call the 'little publishers'.

What I mean by a 'little publisher' is something like this. Somebody, very likely a lady with some means and great enthusiasm, starts a small business for publishing poetry, and is prepared to lose money by it. It is firms like this which can publish small booklets by young poets. For a large firm, the overheads on such little books are so excessive in proportion to the possible benefits to either publisher or author that their publication is out of the question; and a small specialised firm can often handle them more successfully. A 'little publisher' can also afford to publish such little poetry books in a series. For the large firm, a series of new poets is undesirable. A series is likely to conform to a sort of Gresham's Law: it is judged and remembered, not by the few good poets who are launched by it, but by the much higher proportion of mediocre verse in that series. Furthermore, the 'little publisher' incurs no great responsibility: he can drop a poet without that poet suffering any loss of reputation; and he knows that his more successful poets will eventually be taken on by some larger firm of general publishers anyway. But the general business firm cannot afford to be constantly publishing single volumes by poets whose later work they must decline. It doesn't look well, and is not fair to the poets themselves, or to the other poets established on one's list.

Publisher-Poet Relationship

Finally, when we get to the stage of taking on a new poet, there is often much work to be done in preparing his first volume. With such a book, I have to read every poem several times and make tactful suggestions of detail. Then I may have to make a selection from among the poems offered, for a young poet does not always know which are his good poems and which are not. The order in which the poems are to be placed in the volume is important, and the editorial expert ought to know better than the author what the best order will be: the order in which they should meet the reviewer's eye. Then a good title has to be found for the book – often the title of one of the poems: but which one? And finally, the blurb. Everyone engaged in publishing knows what a difficult art blurb-writing is; every publisher who is also an author considers this form of composition more arduous than any other that he practises. But nobody knows the utmost difficulty until he has to write blurbs for poetry: especially when several are to appear in the same catalogue. If you praise highly, the reviewer may devote a paragraph to ridiculing the publisher's pretensions: if you try understatement, the reviewer may remark that even the publisher doesn't seem to think much of the book. I have had both experiences.

As for the publisher's relation with the poets, he has two chief troubles. The first is to dissuade a poet from wanting to publish too soon: before he has *enough* good poems for a volume without putting in inferior poems. The other is to prevent a poet from wanting to publish too often. The saturation point of the market for poetry, for poetry even by a very well known poet, is low. It does even a good poet harm to bring out his volumes in rapid succession. It is sometimes the poet's literary agent who has failed to grasp this elementary market principle.

Monopoly a Bad Thing

One final question – which I put last because I don't know the answer: indeed, I am not sure there is one. How large should your poetry list be, in relation to the total output of books of your firm? I believe there must be an optimum somewhere, because I believe that an excessively swollen poetry list is a disadvantage to the poets on it, as well as to the publisher's balance sheet. But on the one hand the poets already on your list go on writing and turning in new books; and these poets must certainly have priority – except when they produce something lamentably below their level, which isn't often. And on the other hand, as I have said before, you have to add new poets from time to time, in order to keep up to date. The only answer I can find – not, perhaps, a final answer – is that I wish that there were more publishers who considered it worth their while to have a poetry list. A monopoly would be a very bad thing, not only for poets themselves and for society itself, but for the poetry publisher who was the monopolist. I am sure that the other publishers who do publish verse will agree with me in wishing that we might see the publication of verse more widely diffused.

1953

L'amitié Franco-Britannique

T. S. ELIOT

Answers to questions about literature and franco-britannic friendship.
Les Nouvelles Littéraires, 1326 (29 Jan. 1953), [1], 5. Not in Gallup, but would be C575a.

C'est dans son bureau d'éditeur, au-dessus des arbres de Russell Square, que T. S. Eliot me reçoit. Sa haute taille légèrement voûtée lui donne une allure de grand seigneur. De ce prince de l'esprit et du langage rayonne une humanité si chaude que toute contrainte disparaît en l'approchant.

– À votre première question posée en termes si généraux, me dit-il, il est difficile de répondre. Parmi les écrivains dont l'influence se fait sentir dans un pays étranger, il faut distinguer ceux qui délibérément, par amour du pays voisin, essaient de l'atteindre; ceux qui, malgré eux, par la nature même de leur talent, influencent les écrivains d'autres pays, et ce son ceux-ci les plus grands. Sans le chercher ils atteignent plus profondément et, par le moyen des traductions, rendent la compréhension plus facile, resserrent les liens entre les deux pays. Il faut avant tout qu'un écrivain soit honnête avec lui-même, que son oeuvre soit conforme à sa nature.

– Parmi ces deux catégories d'écrivains y en a-t-il qui vous paraissent particulièrement importants?

[5] – Certaines oeuvres semblent faites pour l'exportation, parce que plus facilement accessibles. Moins marquées par leur pays, elles sont en quelque sorte d'un attrait mondial. D'autres, et parmi celles-ci peuvent se trouver les chefs-d'oeuvre les plus rares, sont si marquées par leur origine qu'elles restent nationales, locales et ne sont accessibles qu'à un nombre restreint.

Il y a deux façons de resserrer les liens entre la France et l'Angleterre: soit qu'un écrivain entreprenne de faire connaître son propre pays au pays voisin, et c'est je crois la manière la plus difficile – elle n'est réalisable que dans la mesure où il connaît admirablement le peuple voisin – soit qu'il tente d'expliquer ce peuple à ses compatriotes, et c'est ainsi qu'il a le plus de chances de réussite.

Le mode de pénétration idéale c'est qu'une oeuvre exerce une influence dans le pays voisin en dehors même de la volonté de son créateur et sans que le lecteur en ait conscience. C'est ainsi que les différences, les antagonismes s'aplanissent. Mais ce n'est pas la tâche d'un écrivain d'exercer délibérément une influence ni de faire de la politique. Sa tâche est de parfaire son oeuvre au maximum de ses possibilités.

– Les Anglais considèrent, je crois, que la littérature française est trop imprégnée de politique?

– Oui, ceci n'existe presque pas ici. Mais il est essentiel pour tout écrivain anglais de connaître la littérature française.

– La proposition peut être renversée.

– Il ne m'appartient pas d'en juger. Mais en Angleterre c'est dans le texte même que l'élite doit apprendre à connaître votre littérature.

– Vous semble-t-il qu'il y ait en ce moment de grands courants d'idées communs à la France et à l'Angleterre?

– Nous sommes trop proches pour en décider. Mais il me semble par exemple que l'existentialisme français n'a suscité ici qu'un intérêt de curiosité.

– Ne croyez-vous pas qu'il y a dans nos deux pays une espèce de renaissance religieuse dans le domaine littéraire?

– Je n'aime pas cette expression de *religious revival* qui peut faire croire à une nouvelle forme de foi. On peut parler de renaissance religieuse dans la mesure où les écrivains dont l'oeuvre repose sur la religion sont pris au sérieux, plus qu'il y a vingt-cinq ans, si bien que le public ignorant de la religion s'intéresse et discute des oeuvres de Graham Greene auxquelles il n'existe pourtant que les réponses théologiques.

– Il en est même en France de l'oeuvre de Bernanos. Les *Diologues des carmélites* ont été un des plus grands succès de la saison.

– Oui, le public accepte tout sermon, à condition qu'il ne soit pas prononcé en chaire. La religion est redevenue respectable du point de vue intellectuel. Scepticisme religieux et littérature ne sont plus synonymes.

– Du point de vue pratique quelle serait la meilleure façon de rapprocher les deux peuples?

– Les voyages d'un pays à l'autre sont excellents. Les conditions matérielles les rendent très difficiles et c'est là que les nombreux congrès littéraires trouvent leur utilité, non point pour leurs discussions à la tribune mais pour les sympathies spontanées qui jaillissent, les liens personnels qui se créent. Les écrivains peuvent ainsi discuter entre eux, sans la contrainte de la tribune, de problèmes artistiques. C'est le hasard de ces rencontres amicales qui suscite les conversations les plus captivantes et donne naissance à des idées nouvelles.

[Greeting to the Asociacíon de Artistas Aficionados]

Printed in *Revista programa: Ciclo de orígines del teatro, invierno, 1953*,
by the Academia de Arte Dramático de la Asociacíon de Artistas Aficianados (Lima).
Not in Gallup, but would be C575b.

Estimados señores:

He recibido su carta del 15 de enero, y estoy escribiendo simplemente para expresar mi simpatía y admiracíon a su ambicioso esfuerzo al aspirar presentar en un año, tantas obras maestras de la antigüedad clásica. Como ustedes bien lo pueden suponer, soy un convencido admirador de los dramaturgos griegos, y desearía que nosotros pudiéramos ver in este país, algunas de las obras que Lima va a gozar durante la dos próximas estaciones.

Con todos mis mejores deseos.
T. S. ELIOT

Foreword to the English Edition

Foreword to Henri Fluchère, *Shakespeare*, [v]–vii. Publ. 13 Apr. 1953.
Signed 'T. S. Eliot'. Gallup B68.

In the penultimate para. a dash has been inserted
after 'specialised investigations'.

In writing *Shakespeare: dramaturge élisabéthain* the author had no thought of addressing himself to an English-speaking audience. As he tells us in his preface, the book emerged out of his lectures to his pupils at the University of Aix-en-Provence during the years of the occupation; and his modest intention, as he told me at the time of its publication in France, was to introduce French students of Shakespeare to the development of Shakespeare criticism in England during the previous quarter of a century. For such a task M. Fluchère was exceptionally well qualified. He had pursued his English studies for several years at Cambridge University; he had become bilingual; his knowledge of English literature was exact and comprehensive; he not only knew all the more recent English contributions to Shakespeare criticism, but was personally acquainted with some of their authors. His experience as a translator (he had translated *Everyman* and my own *Murder in the Cathedral* into French) had given him an understanding of the correspondences and what I may call the *reciprocal inadequacies* of the two languages, which cannot be acquired in any other way. As one of the authors whose work he has translated, I feel qualified to pronounce this encomium.

My purpose in writing this preface, however, is not to praise M. Fluchère as an interpreter of English literature to French readers, but to affirm the value of his book for English-speaking readers and students of Shakespeare. Its author's qualities, as scholar and critic, far exceed the requirements of his original purpose. I am not acquainted with any recent English work which serves the same need as this of M. Fluchère – not only giving us a conspectus of Shakespeare's drama as a whole, but exhibiting that drama in its relation to the other masterpieces of the Elizabethan theatre, and taking account of recent studies by English critics. Even had he done no more than summarise the conclusions of English criticism in the last twenty-five years, he would have written a book useful to English readers. But he has [vi] done much more: his book commends itself to us because of the value of the author's own ideas, which are supported by his combination of scholarship and understanding and experience of the theatre.

At the present stage of Shakespeare criticism, the critic who would give a well-balanced interpretation of Shakespeare's total work needs a number of qualifications not commonly found together. The ideal Shakespeare critic should be a scholar, with knowledge not of Shakespeare in isolation, but of Shakespeare in relation to the Elizabethan Theatre in which he is only one, though very much the greatest, of the masters, and of that Theatre in relation to the social, political, economic and religious conditions of its time. He should also be a poet; and he should be a 'man of the theatre'. And he should have a philosophic mind. Shakespeare criticism cannot be written by a committee consisting of a number of specialised scholars, a dramatist, a producer, an actor, a poet and a philosopher: each of them would be incompetent without sharing some of the knowledge and capacities of the others. Certainly, to be a poet or a philosopher is not enough. A poet is not a qualified interpreter, unless he understands the particular technique of *dramatic* verse. In order to understand dramatic verse he must needs have had some success in writing it; and if his dramatic verse is to be really dramatic he must acquire also the point of view of the producer, the actor and the audience. To understand Shakespeare he must understand the theatre of his own time – but also the differences between the theatre of his own time and that of Shakespeare's time; he should know the latter, not merely as an antiquary, but from the point of view of the producer, the actor and the audience of Shakespeare's time. For such understanding, both scholarship and imagination are required. Nor is the philosophic critic, without the other qualifications, in better case than the poet. The philosopher needs to understand the nature of poetry, if he is to avoid the danger of confusing the philosophical ideas which can be elicited from a poem with a system of philosophical belief which can be attributed to the author. And it follows from what I have said above that he needs to understand the special conditions of the stage, the peculiar kind of reality manifested by those personages of the stage who strike us as most 'real', if he is to avoid the error of analysing dramatic characters [vii] as if they were living men and women, or figures from the historical past.

Our demands upon the Shakespeare critic have, in our time, become exacting. The number of important specialised investigations – historical, social, linguistic, and studies of imagery and symbolism in Shakespeare – have to be taken into account by the critic who aims to consider the work of Shakespeare in all its aspects. But perhaps more than any other single writer, Mr Harley Granville-Barker by his Prefaces, illuminating the plays with the understanding of the producer, has suggested the need for a synthesis of the several points of view from which Shakespeare can be studied.

The reader will judge for himself of the proportions in which M. Fluchère possesses all the qualifications I have named: but I am convinced that M. Fluchère has been able, to an exceptional degree, to put himself at one after another of these points of view. In passing from one section to another of his book, I have been struck by his comprehension of all the problems involved – whether of the conditions of the theatre, of the particular conditions and aims of the Elizabethan theatre, of the nature of dramatic poetry, or of the development of Shakespeare's style from first to last. And, incidentally, I have noted with admiration his penetrating remarks upon the works of Shakespeare's contemporaries, notably Ben Jonson and Beaumont and Fletcher.

[American Literature and the American Language]

An Address Delivered at Washington University on June 9, 1953, was publ. as Washington University Studies – New Series – Language and Literature – No. 23, in June 1953. Slightly revised in *TCTC*. *See below*, pp. 736–51.

Reflections on the Unity of European Culture (II)

Adam, 14. 159/60 (June/July 1946), 1–3, was revised under the title 'THE CRITERION', omitting three paragraphs (not two, as Gallup states), in *Adam*, 21. 234 (1953), 20–1: Gallup C517. Further revised in *NTDC* (1948; *see* Vol. 3, pp. 710–14 in the present edition) and repr. in *NTDC* 1962.

Thomas Stearns Eliot
Gratulation

Tribute to Rudolf Kassner. *Rudolf Kassner zum achtzigsten Geburtstag Gedenskbuch* (A. Cl. Kensik und D. Bodmer), 58. Publ. 9 Sept. 1953. Signed 'T. S. Eliot'. Gallup B70.

To contribute to the chorus of praise and thanks which should greet Rudolf Kassner on his eightieth birthday, is a privilege which confers greater honour on the contributor than on the recipient. I am happy to have the opportunity on this occasion to salute and pay homage to so distinguished an author and so great a European who has every reason to look back with pride upon his life-work.

Literature

The Unity of European Culture, A Series of Broadcasts given over the B.B.C. Foreign Service July to October 1953, 19–21. Subheaded '*talk by* T. S. Eliot'. Publ. Dec. 1953. Gallup B71.

We can approach the question of the unity of European literature from two different points of view. It is from the historian of literature that we learn the meaning of the phrase 'unity of European literature' in the *past*. Or, we may start from the point of view of the contemporary man of letters, whose centre of interest is the literature of the *present and immediate future*. My own starting point is the latter: I speak, not as a scholar, but simply as a man of letters. As a writer, I recognise my own immense debt to other authors not only of my own language but of other European languages, ancient and modern. I am aware that but for what I leave learned from poets and prose-writers of other languages than my own, I might never have had anything to say, and certainly should never have found out how to say it; and I have, throughout my life, tried to keep in touch with what was happening, in the world of letters, in other countries of Europe. For seventeen years I edited a literary review, whose main *raison d'être* was to stimulate the circulation of ideas, to arouse attention to whatever new and significant, in poetry and prose, was coming into existence in other countries as well as my own. To me, the unity of European literature has always seemed a self-evident *necessity*; to me, the rapid circulation throughout Europe of the best that was being thought and written in each country of Europe has seemed as essential for the continued life of literature as is the function of breathing for the life of a human being.

I point the difference between these two lines of approach – that of the scholar and that of the man of letters – only to affirm that they are *complementary*. It is from the study of history that we learn what we are now: by learning *how* we have come to be what we are, we acquire understanding of *what* we are. And I find that my own faith in the unity of European literature, derived from experience, is confirmed by what I [20] have learnt from scholars about the history of European literature from its earliest beginnings. I refer you to a great and monumental book, by Professor Ernst Robert Curtius of Bonn: *Europaeische Literatur und Lateinisches Mittelalter* – a book that ought to be perused by every European man of letters. Dr Curtius, indeed, is both scholar and in my sense 'man of letters'; he has made important contributions to the literary criticism of our time, and to the criticism of modern French and English authors in particular. He brings the light of his organised learning to bear on our situation today. I am happy to find that the conclusions to which he is led, are in accord with those which I have held instinctively or reached empirically.

Obviously, if the unity of European literature were merely an historical fact with no bearing upon the future, it would be of only limited interest. But the unity in the past is the strongest reason for believing that unity is necessary in the future. If, that is, our several literatures are to survive – if we are to hope, in any country of Europe, to continue to produce imaginative and philosophical work of the first order. Dr Curtius holds that the literature of Europe can be understood only if considered as a whole, from Homer to Goethe. I agree: and I would add that for the future, European literature must continue to exist as one organism, if literature is to be written in any of the countries which constitute Europe.

When I say that the literature of Europe is an organic whole, I am not dissimulating, but rather emphasising, the differences between the literature of one country and that of another. It is because of these varieties of region and language, and the divergent paths of development, as well as because of more primitive differences between the Nordic, Celtic, Latin and Slavonic languages, that there is *significant* unity – unity, not uniformity. And the testimony of medieval scholars like Dr Curtius is supported by all we know of later periods. Sometimes one country, sometimes another, has taken the lead: at one time or another, powerful influences have swept Europe coming from Italy, Spain, France, England or Germany in turn. And what modern writer has not been deeply affected by the work of the great Russian novelists? I have mentioned only the larger nations of Europe; but we must not forget that a single man of genius in one of the smaller nations, from time to time, has exercised immense power over minds everywhere. Such, in our own time, have been Kierkegaard in Denmark, and Ibsen in Norway. I am sure, for my own part, that dramatic literature will always be something different from whatever it might have been, if Ibsen had never appeared.

There is another way of stating the reason for our unity in the past, and I trust, in the present, which should have an immediate appeal. We do not need to consult the works of historians of literature, to know that the literature of every country of Europe has been nourished from the same three sources: the literature of the Bible, and the literatures of the Greeks and Romans. We have origins in Israel, Greece and Rome. These literatures are the common heritage of Gentile and Jew, Catholic and Protestant. I am not speaking of the common religious formation: I am speaking of the *poetry* of the Old and the New Testament and the Apocrypha, and the *poetry* of Greece and Rome: for, apart from sharing a common religion, it is by sharing the poetry of great civilisations of the past that a common sensibility is formed. Theodor Haecker gave to his masterly essay on Virgil a significant title: *Vergil Vater des Abendlandes*. For many centuries, we have all been indebted to these three sources of our own poetry. For many centuries, our poets have been educated by Israel, Greece and Rome. Without these literatures we should become unable to understand, not only the great literature of other languages, but the great literature of our own.

Every literature, if it is to thrive, needs constant refreshment from two sources: from its own past, and from contemporary writing abroad, as well as from the classics of foreign literatures. I do not ignore the value of literary influences from the other side of the world: I myself owe much to ancient India, and other writers have enriched literature by seeking influence still further afield, from Persia, China, Japan, and even from less highly developed societies. But because of our inextricable common history, and because of our closer cultural kinship, Europeans must continue to owe their largest debts to each other, and to those three ancient civilisations of which we are all the heirs.

Finally, I ask two questions: Is this unity threatened today? And, why should it be worth preserving? First, it is threatened by immoderate censorship and direction: most, when men of letters are told, not only what they may not say, but also what they *must* say. Second, it is threatened by modern and erroneous conceptions of the Nature of Man – what we call ideologies. And finally, it is threatened by ignorance – by increasing indifference to the humanist element in education, the element that (religion excepted) most helps to bind us together. As for why it is worth preserving, my answer is one that you may have anticipated. The health of the literature of each language of Europe depends upon that of the others. If, through the laceration of civil war, from oppression or control by a government, or from some more obscure cause, the literature of any one area of Europe languishes, so much the worse for the rest of Europe. If there were no such thing as European literature, there would be no French or German or English or any other local literature within Europe. In losing our kinsmen, we should find ourselves severed also from our ancestors, and from our own literatures that patriotism holds dear. So, if you think it desirable that your own country should continue to produce great works of literature, and that it should continue to appreciate its writers of the past, you must agree that we all have a common interest at stake.

The Three Voices of Poetry

Eliot's lecture to the National Book League, delivered on 19 Nov. 1953, was publ. on 11 Dec. 1953: Gallup A63. Revised in *OPAP*. *See below*, pp. 208–20.

1954

Introduction

Introduction (ix–xv) to *The Literary Essays of Ezra Pound*, Edited with an Introduction by T. S. Eliot (Faber & Faber, publ. 22 Jan. 1954). Signed 'T. S. Eliot'. Gallup B72.

The editor of this volume is alone responsible for the choice of essays and reviews included; and he is therefore called upon to give account of his principles of selection. I have not aimed at including everything, in the area of literary criticism, that seemed to me worth preserving: there is enough material for another volume. Limitation of size has imposed the exclusion of much; so I have tried only to give a representative choice from Ezra Pound's literary criticism over a period of some thirty years. Being a retrospective selection, this book differs from the four books of critical papers from which the bulk of the material has been taken, and to the publishers of which I make acknowledgement: *Pavannes and Divisions* (A. A. Knopf, New York, 1918), *Instigations* (Boni & Liveright, New York, 1920), *Make It New* (Faber & Faber, London, and the Yale University Press, 1934) and *Polite Essays* (Faber & Faber, London, 1937). These collections were assembled in a form which does not seem to me permanently satisfactory: they have served their purpose in prolonging the effect at which the various papers were aimed on their original publication in periodicals. The books themselves have become more difficult to obtain; and there is furthermore some overlapping of contents between the American and the English collections. I have included also shorter pieces rescued from the files of periodicals: amongst such, I have made selections from photostats from American magazines, supplied to me by Mr James Laughlin. There must be other uncollected writings which have escaped our notice: Pound has contributed indefatigably to little magazines. There remain two books from which I have taken nothing: *Guide to Kulchur* (Faber & Faber, 1938) and the early but very important *The Spirit of Romance* (Dent, London, 1910). Both these books have been out of print, but have recently been republished by New Directions: they should both be read entire.

    The present book is designed differently from any previous collection of Pound's essays; so I believe there is justification for its having been entrusted to another hand than that of the author. The [x] author – like any author – would make a somewhat different choice from that of his editor; he has, in fact, expressed regret at certain omissions, and deprecated the inclusion of several items which appear to the editor to be of more lasting value than they do to him. But Mr Pound has never valued his literary criticism except in terms of its immediate impact; the editor, on the other hand, wished to regard the material in historical perspective, to put a new generation of readers, into whose hands the earlier collections and scattered essays did not come when they were new, into a position to appreciate the central importance of Pound's critical writing in the development of poetry during the first half of the twentieth century.

I hope, furthermore, that this volume will demonstrate that Pound's literary criticism is the most important contemporary criticism of its kind. Of a very important kind – perhaps the kind that we can least afford to do without: what the kind is I shall have to consider presently. If this selection succeeds in its purpose, it will show (1) that Pound has said much about the art of writing and of writing poetry in particular, that is permanently valuable and useful. Very few critics have done that. It will show (2) that he said much that was peculiarly pertinent to the needs of the time at which it was written; (3) that he forced upon our attention not only individual authors, but whole areas of poetry, which no future criticism can afford to ignore. And finally (what will matter less to *him* than any of the foregoing achievements) that he has shown a more immediate and generous appreciation of authors whose work one would not expect him to find sympathetic, than is generally known. It is for this last reason that I have included the early reviews of poems by Robert Frost and D. H. Lawrence. For this reason also I have included the early essay on Lionel Johnson, otherwise unobtainable: the edition of Lionel Johnson's poems of which this essay formed the Introduction was withdrawn immediately after publication. Mr Pound tells me that his Introduction aroused hostility: it is difficult for me, and I think it will be difficult for other readers now, to understand why. This essay is of interest, not only for what Pound says about Johnson, but for Johnson's own opinions, there quoted, about his contemporaries – judgements to which, by the fact of quoting them, Pound seems to have given implicit assent.

To appreciate any retrospective collection of literary opinions and judgements, it is necessary to pay attention to the dates at which [xi] they were written. I have tried to establish as nearly as possible, the dates of all the pieces included; and here must make acknowledgement of invaluable help from Mr Hugh Kenner[1] of the University of California,

---

1. Mr Kenner is the author of *The Poetry of Ezra Pound* (Faber & Faber, London; and New Directions, New York: both 1951).

and from Mr Norman Holmes Pearson of Yale University. Such dating is essential. Malevolent critics have two well-known resources: to quote and collate isolated sentences torn from their context, and to quote what a writer said twenty or thirty years ago as if it was something he had said yesterday. Every collection of statements written at different times and in different contexts must be protected as far as possible against such misrepresentation. The views of any writer, if his mind develops and matures, will change or will be modified by events; a statement may lose the validity which it had when it was written; but if it was valid for its place and time, it may still have permanent value. Much of the *permanence* of Mr Pound's criticism is due simply to his having seen so clearly what needed to be said at a particular time; his occupation with his own moment and its needs has led him to say many things which are of permanent value, but the value of which may not be immediately appreciated by later readers who lack the sense of historical situation.

Inevitably, after the passage of time, such a critic as Mr Pound (who has never been afraid of his own insights) will appear to have exaggerated the importance of some principles, or of some authors, and to have unjustly depreciated others. He has enlarged criticism by his interpretation of neglected authors and literatures, and by his rehabilitation of misesteemed authors. As for the reputations that he has attacked, we must recall the reaction against the Augustan Age initiated by the Lake Poets. Any pioneer of a revolution in poetry – and Mr Pound is more responsible for the XXth Century revolution in poetry than is any other individual – is sure to attack some venerated names. For the real point of attack is the idolatry of a great artist by unintelligent critics, and his imitation by uninspired practitioners. A great writer can have, at a particular time, a pernicious or merely deadening influence; and this influence can be most effectively attacked by pointing out those faults which ought not to be copied, and those virtues any emulation of which is anachronistic. Pound's disparagement of Milton, for instance, was, I am convinced, [xii] most salutary twenty and thirty years ago; I still agree with him against the academic admirers of Milton; though to me it seems that the situation has changed.

It is necessary to consider Pound's literary pronouncements in the light of the circumstances in which they were written, both in order to grasp the extent of the revolution of taste and practice which he has brought about, and in order to understand the particular kind of critic of which he is so eminent an example. He has always been, first and foremost, a teacher and a campaigner. He has always been impelled, not merely to find out for himself how poetry should be written, but to pass on the benefit of his discoveries to others; not simply to make these benefits available, but to insist upon their being received. He would cajole, and almost coerce, other men into writing well: so that he often presents the appearance of a man trying to convey to a very deaf person the fact that the house is on fire. Every change he has advocated has always struck him as being of instant urgency. This is not only the temperament of the teacher: it represents also, with Pound, a passionate desire, not merely to write well himself, but to live in a period in which he could be surrounded by equally intelligent and creative minds. Hence his impatience. For him, to discover a new writer of genius is as satisfying an experience, as it is for a lesser man to believe that he has written a great work of genius himself. He has cared deeply that his contemporaries and juniors should write well; he has cared less for his personal achievement than for the life of letters and art. One of the lessons to be learnt from his critical prose and from his correspondence is the lesson to care unselfishly for the art one serves.

Pound's criticism is always addressed, implicitly, first of all to his fellow craftsmen; to all those who write the English language, though his especial concern and care has been for his fellow craftsmen in America. But it is precisely this address to *writers* that gives Pound's criticism a special and permanent value for *readers*. One learns from him appreciation of literature by learning to understand the preparation, study and training to which the writer should submit himself. Whether Pound is giving his attention to the enunciation of general principles, or to the reassessment of neglected authors and to expounding neglected literatures, or whether he is advertising the merits of new writers (corresponding to the three sections into which I have divided this book) the motive is fundamentally [xiii] the same: the refreshment, revitalisation, and 'making new' of literature in our own time.

It is something, but not much, for the classification of Pound's criticism, to place it with the other notable contributions of poets to criticism: the essays and prefaces of Dryden, the two prefaces of Wordsworth, the *Biographia Literaria* of Coleridge: all of whom were concerned with 'making new' in their own time. (I should like to add, to please myself, Samuel Johnson; and, to please Pound, Walter Savage Landor.) But none of these was so consistently concerned with teaching others how to write. And of no other poet can it be more important to say, that his criticism and his poetry, his precept and his practice, compose a single *oeuvre*. It is necessary to read Pound's poetry to understand his criticism, and to read his criticism to understand his poetry. I am not interested – it is inessential to my purpose – to assert that one kind of criticism is of higher value than another. What does seem to me true, and necessary to say, is that Pound's critical writings, scattered and occasional as they have been, form the *least dispensable* body of critical writing in our time. They began at a moment when they were very much needed: the situation of poetry in 1909 or 1910 was stagnant to a degree difficult for any young poet of to-day to imagine. Pound himself had a long way to go: and he has gone it. Comparison of his earliest with his latest verse should give ample evidence of how much he himself has learnt from his own critical meditations and from study of the authors about whom he has written.

To say that any kind of criticism has its limitations is not to belittle it, but to contribute towards its definition and understanding. The limitation of Pound's kind is in its concentration upon the craft of letters, and of poetry especially. (The fact that he ignores consideration of dramatic verse, which he regards, quite rightly, as a distinct form of application of verse, and which is a form or application in which he is not interested, is a deliberate limitation worth noting, but not otherwise important.) On the one hand, this very limitation gives him a wider range: Pound's contribution, by calling attention to the merits of poetry of remote or alien societies – Anglo-Saxon, Provençal, early Italian, Chinese and Japanese, to say nothing of his beneficial, though irritating and sometimes disputable knocking about of accepted valuations in Latin and Greek literature – is immense. But when we want to try to understand what a foreign [xiv] literature means, or meant, to the people to whom it belongs, when we want to acquaint ourselves with the spirit of a whole civilisation through the whole of its literature, we must go elsewhere. With some literatures, as the Provençal, that literature may, for aught I know, be comprehensively exhibited by the specimens of it which Pound recommends for study by the contemporary writer of English. For those literatures whose summits have been mostly in the drama, the exclusion of drama is serious; but Pound has never yet written about a form of verse which he would not care to practise. And (to take the foreign literature which I know best) Pound performed a great service (especially in *The Spirit of Romance*) for the English-speaking reader in emphasising the greatness of Villon. He was quick to appreciate the originality of Laforgue and Corbière. He showed a discriminating taste among the minor poets of the 'Symbolist Movement'. But he ignores Mallarmé; he is uninterested in Baudelaire; and to his interests such poets as Malherbe and La Fontaine are irrelevant. In Elizabethan literature, apart from the drama, and apart from the songs about which he has spoken well, what about poetry such as that of Jonson and Chapman? I mention these omissions, not as cautious reservations in my admiration for Pound's criticism, but the better to praise it for what it is. You can't ask everything of anybody; and it is an illusion fostered by academic authorities on literature, that there is only one kind of criticism, the kind that is delivered on academic foundations, to be printed afterwards in the 'proceedings' or as a brochure in a series.

I must add a word about footnotes. I have tried to avoid notes (with the exception of one modest correction bearing my initials) except to supply dates. Any notes newly contributed by Mr Pound are initialled E. P. Notes with no such indication are the author's notes to the text as originally published.

Mr Pound regrets the omission (for which the editor is responsible) of an essay on René Crevel; he regrets that he has not yet written a study of the work of Jean Cocteau, and that he has not produced a more recent and comprehensive study of the work of Wyndham Lewis. And I gather that he has recently been giving thought to Sophocles – an excursion into new territory, the fruits of which should be interesting. Other papers which he would have liked me to include struck me as being outside the frame of a volume entitled 'Literary Essays'.

[xv] I should add that amongst the papers excluded from this volume of literary essays, are those on music, painting and sculpture, with two exceptions: the notes on Dolmetsch and Brancusi which I have appended as a reminder to the reader of all the other essays on the arts, which fall outside the scope of the present volume.

A Message

LM, 1. 1 (Feb. 1954), 15–16. Gallup C581.

A message of good will, from an elderly man of letters, on the appearance of a new literary periodical, may easily be regarded as a mere act of courtesy towards a venture in which he bears no responsibility. In order, therefore, to make it evident that this is something more than a perfunctory gesture of benediction, I wish to produce my credentials and explain why I am interested in the success of *The London Magazine*.

In the first place, I am interested because I myself edited a Literary Review for seventeen years. I am far from wishing that *The London Magazine* should be cut on the pattern of *The Criterion*: for one thing, it must be shaped according to very different conditions; and, equally important, it must be shaped according to the mind of the editor. But my own years of editorship have given me some understanding of the essential functions of a Literary Review at any time, as well as some experience of the difficulties which it has always to confront. And that experience, in spite of and because of my own mistakes, should qualify me, to some degree, to appraise the editorial direction of a new periodical of the same kind. I am confident that the Editor and Board of *The London Magazine* will produce a periodical in which I shall continue to be interested.

My belief in the value of Literary Reviews has not waned: indeed, it has only been strengthened by awareness of the vacuum of the recent post-war years. It is undoubtedly a scandal, that we have had, in London, since the end of the War, no literary magazines to compare with those which have sprung up in other countries. There are half a dozen, on the Continent, for which we have no equivalent. As for America, I am aware of a common Anglo-American danger of abandoning the central position for those of two extremes: the Academic and the Popular Educational. The type of magazine from the lack of which we suffer is neither that which provides a vehicle of expression for critics occupying university posts nor that which [16] endeavours to elevate the Public Taste. What we need is the magazine which will boldly assume the existence of a public interested in serious literature, and eager to be kept in touch with current literature and with criticism of that literature by the most exacting standards.

But will that public give its support? In England, there are far too many people, professing to be lovers of literature, who are ready to say either 'this magazine lacks support, and therefore there is no point in my supporting it'; or else 'this magazine is substantially backed, and therefore can do without my support'. Too many of the people who ought to *subscribe* to a literary magazine say 'I haven't time to read it regularly, but I shall buy a copy when there is something that I ought to read.' Such people most frequently overlook the number containing something they ought to have read. They say then that they are sorry they missed it. During seventeen years, I knew which lovers of literature, amongst those who could afford to pay the subscription, were subscribers, and which were not.

The first function of a literary magazine, surely, is to introduce the work of new or little known writers of talent. The second is to provide critical valuation of the work of living authors, both famous and unknown. The third is to be in the best sense *international*. The magazine must be aware of what is happening in other countries and of what is being written in other languages; and must keep its readers informed of what is happening – but never, I would say emphatically, merely in the way of 'news' or gossip. The readers must be encouraged to read books, not merely to talk about books they have not read. But the most important international aspect of any literary magazine is that it should be read by, and should command the respect of, the editors and collaborators of similar magazines in other countries. And the new writers, whose work it introduces, should be writers who deserve the attention of writers and of readers of literary magazines in other countries.

I am addressing myself, however, primarily to those English readers, at home and overseas, who profess to take an interest in literature. It is their duty to take out a subscription to *The London Magazine*. Without literary magazines the vitality of the world of contemporary letters is very gravely reduced. If our society cannot provide for such a magazine, a circulation large enough to justify its existence – and a subscription, it must be remembered, is not merely an act of financial support but a declaration of *moral* support – then the outlook for our civilisation is all the more sombre.

Comments by T. S. Eliot

Eliot's answers to questions concerning *The Confidential Clerk*. *New York Herald Tribune*, 7 Feb. 1954, Section 4, p. [1]. Gallup C583.

On his progress from *The Cocktail Party* to *The Confidential Clerk* in his experiments on prosody in verse:
I can only say that I feel more at home with it. I wear it more easily; and that has contributed to my greater satisfaction with the play *as drama*.

On the meaning of *The Confidential Clerk*:
Now let's see, I mustn't say too much about this play, as I want the audience to make up its own mind. If I say I intended such-and-such, then people will say they have to find just that in it. But, really, if a play is any good it ought to have a great deal in it that its author doesn't completely understand.

On whether *The Confidential Clerk* is comedy or tragedy:
Since no one is murdered or dies violently in *The Confidential Clerk* I am letting the audience call it what they like. It can be regarded as either.

On the improvement of his technique as a dramatist:
In *The Cocktail Party* only four of the seven characters are characters in the true sense. The psychiatrist and his two assistants are outside the action of the play. They interfere, but there is no character development in these three. They just perform a job. I think that the audience may have been mystified by this. So, in *The Confidential Clerk*, all seven in the cast are characters in their own right with none being outside the action.

On what Eliot thought of the comment that the last act of *The Cocktail Party* was actually an epilogue, and how he improves on this in *The Confidential Clerk*:
It was a necessary epilogue, but these critics were right in the sense that the dramatic action was all over. In my new play, I've tried to keep things happening up to the end. To tell you the truth I think psychiatry had a lot to do with the success of *The Cocktail Party*. It made it very fashionable.

On the classical sources for his work:
The idea for *The Confidential Clerk* came to me out of a classical story, just as *The Cocktail Party* started out with my wondering about *Alcestis*. I was interested in what happened at the point Euripides leaves off. What was it going to be like when the wife is brought back? . . . I wasn't trying to be smart-alecky and suggest that the dramatic critics were damn fools not to notice the parallel. After all, it's the dramatic critic's business to say if a play is good theatre, and not to record these other things. I was merely amused that the people who came along afterwards, with months to study the play and who found all sorts of hidden meanings that I never dreamt of in it, didn't come across the one thing that stimulated me into writing it.

On not revealing the source of *The Confidential Clerk*:
Why I don't let this very small cat out of the bag is that if you say that such and such a parallel exists it will lead people up the garden path.

Of the characters in relation to the author of *The Confidential Clerk*:
I was more concerned with getting the reactions of the people to each other right than I was with the deductions to be drawn from these reactions.

On the poet in the theatre:
The poet has a hell of a lot to learn in the theatre. You can't get along with good verse and bad theatrical technique.

A Tribute

Tribute to Wallace Stevens. *Trinity Review*, 8. 3 (May 1954), 9.
Signed 'T. S. Eliot'. Gallup C587.

When I received a letter from Mr Morse inviting my co-operation in an issue of the *Review* in honour of the seventy-fifth birthday of Wallace Stevens, I replied at once to explain why I could do nothing that would be adequate to the occasion. I was at the moment engaged on a task which would take me through most of November. The contributors to the *Review* were allowed until February 2nd; but I could allow myself only until Christmas, having arranged to take a long voyage from which I should not be returning until March. Having given these explanations, I asked whether a paragraph, a sentence or a phrase might serve as a token, so that my name at least should not be absent from the chorus.

I write not only as an admirer, but with the special responsibility of a Director of the Firm who publish Wallace Stevens in England. I am not boasting of that: in fact I am rather ashamed of the fact that Stevens has not been published in London before. I had taken for granted that some other firm had published his work, and wondered at their incompetence in taking so little trouble to make the fact known; it was one of my fellow directors who first called my attention to the fact that Stevens, although his name and some of his poems were very well known to the élite who really know, had had no book to himself. Now, his reputation is beginning to spread to the people who don't know. There is no compliment on my own work that gives me more pleasure than that of the man who says 'I didn't know anything about this chap, but I picked up a volume of his the other day – and found I *liked* it.' I have heard that said lately several times, about the book of Wallace Stevens.

If I was writing a critical article, I should have to try to explain *why* I like the poems of Wallace Stevens so much: and the explaining why is always what takes the time. But I am only writing in order to get my name into this *Festschrift*; and I hope that the Editor will see that my name is printed so that no one can miss it.

Preface

Preface to *Zabójstwo w katerdze*, a Polish translation of *Murder in the Cathedral*; trns. Zofia Ilińska. Tipped-in in Tunbridge Wells: Oficnya Poetów i Malarzy na emigracji w Anglii (1954).

Not in Gallup, but would be B72a.

My ignorance of the Polish language disqualifies me from praising this translation of *Murder in the Cathedral* as I have no doubt it deserves. But to spend ten years polishing a translation which, alas, has now no prospect of being presented in the Polish theatre, and which now can reach only a limited number of readers, is surely a labour of love. For this labour I wish to thank my translator. At the same time I take the opportunity of expressing my sympathy for all Poles in exile: and my recognition of our debt to those who died in action in the War – may they rest in peace.

A note on *Monstre Gai* by Wyndham Lewis

HR, 7. 4 (Winter [1954/]1955), [522]–6. Gallup C591.

Monstre Gai is a sequel, or continuation of *The Childermass*, and *Monstre Gai* also is to have a sequel. This much is common knowledge. But many people will read *Monstre Gai* who will not have read *The Childermass*, which was published in 1928 and has been for some years out of print: for a younger generation, certainly for those who do not live near a library containing a copy of the book, *The Childermass* is only a name, the name of a lost work known only in critical citations. While awaiting republication we do not, fortunately, need to have read *The Childermass* in order to understand what *Monstre Gai* is about. We need to know that it is a work not only of imagination but of fantasy, like the romances of Rabelais and Swift, to which it will in due course be compared, though with little relevance. For Mr Lewis has set himself a much more difficult feat to carry out than that of either of these authors. If, for instance, one chooses to deposit a human being among a race of people very much bigger or very much smaller than himself, or if one chooses to depict the adventures of a colossus or a midget among human beings, the *mechanics* of the story is not very difficult. The author has only to take care to have everything to scale; and the imaginative genius consists in making us feel what it would be like to be a giant among ordinary human beings, or an ordinary human being among giants. But Mr Lewis has chosen to take his human beings – Pullman and his ex-fag Satterthwaite, who first make their appearance in *The Childermass*, and continue their adventures in *Monstre Gai* – to the world beyond the grave; and not as excursionists like Dante, but as denizens. They are not only among the dead but are ghosts themselves; so that, unlike Dante and Rabelais and Swift, Mr Lewis has to do without the normal standards of consistency. This makes the mechanism of the story much more difficult to construct. Mr Lewis has, I believe, come as near as possible to triumphing over such difficulties; and when we consider how [523] numerous these difficulties are, our respect for what he has actually done will be all the greater.

At the opening of *The Childermass* Pullman and Satterthwaite (usually known as Pulley and Satters) whose paths have hardly crossed since schooldays, find themselves in 'the Camp' – a kind of Transit Camp where the newly dead sojourn for a time, before being drafted off to other destinations – on the hither bank of a river analogous to that which Virgil and Dante had to cross. At the point at which *Monstre Gai* begins, the pair of them have succeeded in smuggling themselves across the river, and are discovered just outside the Magnetic City to which they seek to gain admittance. For the hope of admission, they depend upon attaching themselves to the retinue of an ambiguous figure, a personage of authority, called the Bailiff. This Bailiff played an important part in *The Childermass*, and plays a still more important part in *Monstre Gai*, for he is in fact himself the *monstre gai*. And that, really, is all the new reader who has not read *The Childermass* needs to know about *Monstre Gai* before he opens the book.

I hope that after *Monstre Gai* and its successor (for we are promised a third volume of this vast supernatural saga) have been assimilated, *The Childermass* may be re-published without further delay. I write 'after' with some emphasis; having re-read *The Childermass* after reading *Monstre Gai*, I believe the sequel to be a better introduction to its forerunner, than the other way about. For *Monstre Gai* is, I am convinced, a much better piece of construction. *The Childermass* strikes me – now that I have its sequel to compare it with – as a brilliant, a long, an interminable opening chapter or first scene, a first scene which breaks off abruptly at the end of a dialogue – or is the dialogue really ended? At the end, we still do not know enough about the characters to be quite sure what the author is up to. The reader's attention is held by the power of the style, the vividness of the pictures, (the *peons*, as a detail, are unforgettable) and the brilliance of the debate. And yet, at the end, we have begun to be a bit impatient at being kept waiting so long, we know not for what. *Monstre Gai*, on the other hand, tells a story, and is filled with what it is an understatement to call exciting episodes – in a more serious dimension than that of 'Space Fiction'.

The story gets moving at once, and it moves in a definite direc-[524]tion. And beyond the structural improvement, the much greater skill at plain story-telling. I think I find a more important difference still: there is, it seems to me, as in other of Mr Lewis's recent writing (*Rotting Hill, The Writer and the Absolute, Self Condemned*), a gain in *maturity*. I do not mean that *The Childermass*, or any of the author's earlier published writings, could strike any reader as immature. The comparison reflects no discredit on earlier work. *Troilus and Cressida*, *Antony and Cleopatra*, or *Coriolanus*, any of these is a more mature work than *Hamlet* – to say nothing of *Romeo and Juliet*: but one does not wish the earlier plays to be other than what they are, or for this reason adjudge them to be imperfect. *Self Condemned* is a much more mature work than *Tarr*, and at the age at which I now find myself I prefer the later book: yet it is not so startlingly original, not in the same way 'epoch-making' (no artist can make more than one epoch, after all, however many surprises he springs). And the difference in maturity between *The Childermass* and *Monstre Gai* is not merely that the philosophy is riper or more explicit or more coherent: there is, I believe, also a development in humanity. In the first part of *The Childermass* one is too often and too irritatingly reminded that Pulley and Satters belong to Mr Lewis's puppet-gallery.[1] It is not that their creator *failed* to make them real – it is that he *denied* them more than a measure of reality. Just as one of them seemed about to behave like a human being, instead of like a caricature (though a caricature which only Lewis could have drawn) the author would give a little twitch of the string (and how often, and how tiresomely, we are reminded that Pulley is a 'little' man) to put him in his place: 'if you are going to try to behave like human beings, I'll slap you back into your puppet box.'

In *Monstre Gai* the puppets begin to get the better of the puppet-master, and to become human beings – or we may say, in their less substantial but yet not indestructible new world, ex-human beings. There is even a moment suggestive of the high tragedy of *Self Condemned* (a book of almost unbearable spiritual agony) when Pulley suspects that in his behaviour during his stay in the Magnetic City he has been repeating the pattern of the life he had chosen on earth – only here the supernatural reveals [525] itself, and Good and Evil can no longer be disguised, now that the choice has been irrevocably made.

The reference to *Self Condemned* leads me to another point. Mr Lewis's eminence as both painter and writer has tended to mask the variety of his work in both arts. I mean that while recognising his gifts in both painting and writing, people may overlook the variety of his achievement as a painter and the variety of his achievement as a writer. As a painter and draughtsman Mr Lewis, unlike Picasso, Dior or other fashionable designers, has never been concerned with finding a new style for next spring. In his pictures, and in his prose, he has sought all his life to explore the possibilities of a number of different forms of expression: it is his strict awareness of the limitations of each of the several forms he has employed, that has driven him to make use of the others. But none of these forms represents a 'phase', none is ever finally abandoned: the painter, draughtsman or writer would return to any of them when

1. See Hugh Kenner's excellent study *Wyndham Lewis* (New Directions).

it suited his purpose. Such a range of powers has its penalties. It is easily belittled: it is easily dismissed as virtuosity (implying a shallow slickness) or as amateurism – implying that a man who does several things must do all of them badly. (Goethe, by the way, was certainly an 'amateur' in the theatre.) And even the admirers of such a man may be selective in their admiration. But you can't treat Wyndham Lewis like that, any more than you can Goethe or Leonardo. (As for Leonardo, that formidable and unpleasant personality, the simpering madonnas and epicene saints of his famous canvases are obviously phantasms of the same brain that conceived the flying machine, the submarine, and other subversive contraptions.) When you read one kind of prose work by Mr Lewis (let us say, *Time and Western Man*, or *The Apes of God*, or *The Revenge for Love*, as instances of different *genres*) you should remind yourself that the author has chosen this particular *genre* as the best for the purpose in hand, but that he can do a number of other things quite as well, and that the mind which conceives and executes them all is one. As for 'the novel', it is well known that I am not a novel reader, that there are notable novelists with whose work I have only a partial acquaintance, and others with whose work I have no expectation of acquainting myself at all; so I can only *suspect* that Mr Lewis is the most [526] distinguished living novelist. With Mr Lewis's critical opinions, on contemporary society, art and letters and philosophy, I usually expect to find myself in agreement. As for his own philosophy (and theology – for I cannot accept his affirmation of the stupidity of Angels) he does make me think. There are some writers who please me because they seem to hold the same views as myself, others who annoy me by maintaining opinions that seem to me manifestly silly, but very few who can set my sluggish brain in motion, and for that I am always grateful. The opinion to which I do not hesitate to commit myself, is that Mr Lewis is the greatest prose master of style of my generation – perhaps the only one to have invented a new style. And by 'style' I do not mean 'craftsmanship' nor do I impute impeccability. (James Joyce was the greatest *non*-stylist, the master of the vacuum of personal style into which all things rush.) I have observed that Mr Lewis has this in common with Henry James: that when people write sympathetically or appreciatively about him, they tend to mimic his style. I detect traces of this mimicry – more properly, *magnetism* – in the recent book by Mr Hugh Kenner. I detect traces in this piece that I have just written: you may have noticed that it is not quite in my *Times-Literary-Supplement*-leading-article manner.

[Books of the Year]

The Times, 26 Dec. 1954, 6. Headed 'From T. S. ELIOT, O.M.'
Gallup C592.

I am naturally precluded from mentioning any book published by the firm of which I am a director; and for other reasons as well I exclude poetry from my list. Observing these limitations, I have no doubt in my mind about three books of recent date which I have read during 1954. The first is Paul Tillich's *Systematic Theology*, Vol. 1 (Nisbet). Whether one comes to agree with the author, or whether one accepts all of his conclusions, is a matter of secondary importance: what is of first importance is that the reader gains a deeper understanding of the problems. To read this book is to learn new ways of thinking, and illumination even of subjects apparently remote from those with which the author is concerned.

The second book is *The Heresy of Democracy*, by Lord Percy of Newcastle (Eyre and Spottiswoode). To his experience of public life Lord Percy adds humane learning and sage reflection. The word 'democracy' has been the unexamined term in so many propositions, has become so sacrosanct and so evacuated of meaning, that this book should be studied by any reader who combines an interest in social and political affairs with a scrupulosity in the use of words with strong emotional appeal.

My third book is a novel, *Self Condemned* by Wyndham Lewis (Methuen). This is a painful, indeed an agonising book. In that respect, perhaps, it does not differ from many contemporary novels: the difference lies in the fact that the agony approximates to that of high tragedy, and in consequence is neither brutal nor sordid. This is, furthermore, a compassionate book.

The only factor common to these three books, so far as I am aware, is that the authors are all men of great originality of mind and independence of character. These also seem to me to be, each in its kind, books which contain wisdom and reveal courage. There are also, of course, reasons for admiring each book which do not apply to the others.

Mrs Runcie's Pudding

Symphony of Cooking, compiled under the direction of Mrs J. Eldred Newton, cover by Rudolph Czufin, illustrations by Aurelia Gerhard and Ganz Propper, Women's Association of the St Louis Symphony Society, 419. Publ. Dec. 1954. Signed 'T. S. Eliot | London, England'. Gallup B73.

This recipe is taken from a book called *Wishful Cooking*, published by Faber and Faber, but as a friend of the authors, I have partaken of Mrs Runcie's pudding many times. I understand that Mrs Runcie of Prestwick kept a kind of select boarding house for gentlemen who came to Prestwick to play golf, and this pudding appears to have been very successful as a gentlemen's pudding.

- 1 teacup breadcrumbs
- 1 tablespoon sherry
- 1 teacup milk
- 1/2 lb. strawberry jam
- 2 eggs
- 1/4 lb. castor sugar
- 1 tablespoon brown sugar

Boil milk and breadcrumbs until firm; lay aside till cool. Beat the yolks of eggs with brown sugar and sherry. Mix with the bread and milk. Put in a pudding dish and bake till a skin forms. Take out of the oven and cover top with jam. Put back into oven and bake for another 1/4 hour. Beat the whites of the eggs very stiff with castor sugar and lay on the top of the pudding. Brown slightly and serve.

1955

[*The Women of Trachis*: A Symposium]

Pound Newsletter, 5 (Jan. 1955), 3. Introduced as a statement from 'Mr. T. S. Eliot, poet and publisher, critic and playwright, friend of Ezra Pound'. Gallup C593.

I have read the text of Mr Pound's *Women of Trachis*, and I also heard the excellent production of the play in the Third Programme of the B.B.C. I can say with complete assurance that I do not think Pound has lost any of his skill. His handling of the verse, especially in the choruses of this play, seems to me masterly. His ear is as faultless as ever. Furthermore, he is attempting something that he has never attempted before – that is to say, the translation of a Greek play involves handling a different form from that of any of his previous work – and doing it extremely well. My only criticism of the play is one of personal taste – that I am at a loss to understand how Mr Pound justifies the introduction of so much English and American slang, some of which is already out of date. If there was any Attic slang in the original, it would be a different matter, but I think that some of the phrases will take a great deal of explaining if Mr Pound ever meets Sophocles in person!

[The Saddest Word]

Response to a survey conducted by Norman J. Zierold asking for 'The Saddest Word in the English Language'. *Reader's Digest*, 66. 394 (Feb. 1955), 107. Not in Gallup, but would be C593a.

Also quoted in Ralph J. Kaplan's column 'Watch Your Language', *Los Angeles Times* (29 Apr. 1955), A5.

The saddest word in the English language is, of course, 'saddest'.

'Le salut de trois grands poètes: Londres: T. S. Eliot'

One of three tributes to Paul Claudel occasioned by his death.
The other two were from W. H. Auden and Giuseppe Ungaretti.
Le Figaro Littéraire, 10. 463 (5 Mar. 1955), [1]. Gallup C596.

Il y a quarante-cinq ans Alain-Fournier mettait entre mes mains *L'Arbre et Connaissance de L'Est*. L'impression que ces deux courages, les essais en prose et les cinq pièces, fit alors sur mon esprit est encore très claire dans ma mémoire. Je pense que Claudel n'a jamais surpassé l'oeuvre de cette première période. D'autre part, je ne crois pas que rien qu'il écrivit ensuite soit indigne de l'objectif qu'il s'était alors assigné: avoir maintenu ce niveau pendant une si longue vie est on soi quelque preuve de grandeur. Paul Claudel n'est pas un des écrivains dont j'aie moi-même appris: son pense dramatique est très différent de tout ce á quoi j'ai visé. Cet ultime hommage que je lui rends, comme au plus grand poète dramatique du siècle, étant ainsi désintéressé, sera, je l'espère, d'autant plus convaincant pour cette raison.

[Contribution to journal on 'Das Theater ist unersetzlich' ('The theatre is irreplaceable')]

Blätter des Burgtheaters (Vienna, 3 Mar. 1955), 2. Signed 'T. S. ELIOT'.
Preceded by a translation into German. Not in Gallup, but would be C595b.

If theatre should eventually be wholly superseded by the moving picture, or by the newer medium of television which stands half-way between the living drama and the moving picture, this would be brought about by economic and social causes similar to those which favour mass-production of every kind. I mean, the attraction of the cheap and perishable article, within the means of everyone and acceptable to everyone: in the theatrical sphere, an inferior quality of entertainment for a large, uncritical and standardised public. What reasons have we for protesting that the living theatre – by which I mean a performance by dramatic artists of a work of dramatic art, in the presence of an audience – can never be satisfactorily replaced by these mechanised forms of entertainment; and that, on the contrary, the disappearance of the theatre as we have known it in the past would be a disaster for civilisation?

In answer, we need only (in a Christian country) point to the analogy between the drama and the liturgy of the Church. It is not irrelevant that the drama should have had religious origins, that it should have been, in the beginning, a kind of *extra-liturgical service*. So let us suppose that, instead of having High Mass celebrated on Sundays and Holy Days in every church in the country, a decision were taken to rationalise divine worship and effect economies by centralisation. Instead of a High Altar, then, a television screen; instead of a local celebration, one of the same celebration to be witnessed by the faithful throughout the land. What manifest advantages! The smallest village would have the same benefits as the metropolitan cathedral: the demand for equality should be satisfied. The numbers of the Clergy could be reduced: the complaint of extravagance would be silenced. And yet, I am sure that not even the simplest-minded and least reflective Christian would believe that he had participated in an act of worship.

I hope this analogy will not seem to you irreverent: I only use it to call attention to a likeness between Liturgy and Drama that has always been recognised. To have the genuine experience of the theatre – and I maintain, this experience is something that human beings crave for – two conditions are necessary: first, that each performance should be unique; second, that the performers and the audience should be in direct contact, and there should be *participation*. The television performance fails to satisfy the second condition; the cinematograph violates both. And both conditions must be fulfilled if the audience is to *be* an audience. It is the taking part in the life of the personages in the play, as lived by the artists who have assumed those roles, that *unites* the members of the audience to each other, that creates an *audience* out of a miscellaneous collection of human beings. And it is an analogous relationship that creates in a church a congregation, that gives meaning to the phrase *corporate* worship.

Anything more that I adduced in support of the thesis that the theatre is irreplaceable would be merely an expansion of what I said above.

A Note on *In Parenthesis* and *The Anathemata*

Dock Leaves, 6. 16 (Spring 1955), 21–3. 'T. S. Eliot, O.M.' is identified as the author below the title. On p. 22 'culture-phrases' has been emended to 'culture-phases'.
Gallup C594.

There are two questions which people are given to asking, often in a peremptory tone, about certain modern works of literature. The first is: 'Is this poetry or prose? – with the implication that it is neither. The second question is: 'What is this book about?' – with the implication that it is not really about anything. A good deal of time, which one would prefer to spend otherwise, can be devoted to trying to explain to such people that the questions are unimportant, even if not meaningless. These questions were asked about David Jones's *In Parenthesis*.

But people like to classify: and *In Parenthesis* was not so difficult to classify as his second book, *The Anathemata*. *In Parenthesis* could be regarded as a 'war book', a book about the first world war; even though the author had said 'I did not intend this as a "War Book" – it happens to be concerned with war.' The distinction is important. But if *In Parenthesis* was a 'War Book', then, people could say, it was probably intended to be prose, even though you could not take the typography as a reliable guide. But as for *The Anathemata*, it is certainly not a 'War Book', so what *is* it about? Now, Mr David Jones is exceptional amongst [22] writers of works of imagination, in writing for his own books introductions which do introduce, which explain to the reader what he is doing – if the reader is prepared to study them carefully and to believe that the author means what he says. *The Anathemata*, he says, is 'about one's own thing, which *res* is unavoidably part and parcel of the Western Christian *res*, as inherited by a person whose perceptions are totally conditioned and limited by and dependent upon his being indigenous to this Island'.

Now that the first generation of 'obscure' writers, those who survive, is approaching old age, the accusation of 'obscurity' can no longer be employed so effectively for dismissing the work of younger men. And it might at last be worth while for some critic to ask whether there may not have been some cause of obscurity other than wilfulness or charlatanism. My own belief is that we, including David Jones, have all been desperately anxious to communicate, and maddened by the difficulty of finding a common language. May not the malady perhaps be in the reader, rather than in the writer, unless it is a malady of the world to-day from which we all suffer? In the preface to *The Anathemata* David Jones shows himself aware of this problem. 'There have been culture-phases,' he says, 'in which the maker and the society in which he lived shared an enclosed and common background, where the terms of reference were common to all. It would be an affectation to pretend that such was our situation to-day.'

He is, in this context, justifying his Notes. *The Anathemata* is unusual, in my experience of long poems with notes, in having notes which really do give useful information. I recommend reading the book three times: first, rapidly without reading the notes; second, slowly and reading the notes with great care; third, at a normal pace, having become so familiar with the notes as hardly to look at them. I am aware that very few books are worth so much trouble, and that very few readers are capable of taking so much trouble. There may still be, however, even amongst readers capable of such mental exertion, some who will say:

'I don't think this book is meant for *me*; there's too much that's Welsh and too much that's Catholic – but I dare say it would mean a lot to a Welsh Roman Catholic!' Well, if I thought that the book was only for Welsh Roman Catholics, I should not [23] have the impudence to talk about it. The book is, as the author says, about his own *thing*. Every author of works of imagination is trying to tell us about the world as he sees it. Nowadays, the more such a writer has to communicate, the more difficulty he may have in communicating it. So he must endeavour to convey a sense of his own private world – the world *he* lives in – *the* world as he has experienced it: he must turn that world inside out for you to look at, as if he was emptying his pockets on the table in front of you. Would you be annoyed to find that the contents of his pocket differed from yours? I am thinking of several other writers of major importance, besides David Jones. It seems to me that if we approach these authors in the right way we shall find that in coming to understand the different worlds in which each of them lives, we shall, each of us, come to know more about his own. And this is, at least, a surcease of solitude.

Gordon Craig's Socratic Dialogues

Drama, NS 36 (Spring 1955), 16–21. Subheaded 'By T. S. ELIOT', followed by a headnote: *'The year 1955 marks the Fiftieth Anniversary | of the publication of Gordon Craig's First Dialogue "The Art of the Theatre".'*
Repr. in *Center, A Magazine of the Performing Arts*, 2. 3 (June 1955), 2–5. Gallup C595.

Of Gordon Craig's two dialogues which are included in *On the Art of the Theatre*, the first appeared in 1903; the second is dated 1910. I am confident that I read the first dialogue while I was an undergraduate at Harvard – probably in 1907 or 1908. Other discoveries of the same period were Manet and Monet, Japanese prints, the plays of Maeterlinck, the music of Debussy and above all the combination of Maeterlinck and Debussy in *Pelleas and Mélisande*. I mention these facts, in themselves of trivial autobiographical interest, to place my first acquaintance with the work of Gordon Craig, and to indicate the sort of background of associated memories against which, a short time ago, I re-read those two dialogues.

To assess the achievement of Gordon Craig could be the task only of those who have followed the course of the drama and the stage in Europe and America during the past fifty years. It may well be that the influence of Gordon Craig on modern production in this country is much greater than I am aware of. His views appear to have been taken most seriously on the Continent, particularly in Germany. It may be that his influence upon production in England is unrecognised by persons like myself, simply because of its having been indirect: it may be that our theatre has been influenced by Continental practice which has itself been influenced directly by Craig's art and Craig's writing. Furthermore, I have little recollection of what the theatre was like fifty years ago, either here or in America. But if I am not equipped to do justice to Craig, I can at least try to avoid doing him injustice; and make clear that I can only consider these two dialogues in relation to the theatrical situation as I know it to-day.

The art of the theatre is a mixed or composite art; from one point of view, more composite in the production of drama than in the production of opera. For in opera, after all, the music, the concurrence of instrument and voice, is the main thing. The situation, the plot, must be expressed in music: the words have only to accord with orchestra and singing notes; and the mechanics of Fafner are less important than the mechanics of the crocodile in *Peter Pan*. We can all get pleasure from reading a play of Shakespeare or Ibsen – a pleasure different from that of seeing and hearing the play, and equally valuable as experience; but few of us have the training that would enable us to derive as much pleasure from reading the score of an opera as from hearing it on the stage. It is the voice of a great singer, rather than his skill as an actor, that we most clearly remember. But in a great production of a great play what is it that we are enjoying? Is it the words which we know very well already, and could enjoy at home; is it the actor's elocution of the words, or is it the other arts of movement, gesture and expression? How much is owing [17] to the actor and how much to his director and producer? And what difference has the setting and lighting made to our enjoyment?

It seems to me that Gordon Craig, in his first dialogue, follows a course that we all tend to follow. That is to say, all of us taking part in a production pay a handsome tribute to the contributions of our colleagues, and then we all tend to relapse into thinking our own contribution the most important. We [18] can't help it: and I dare say we do our work all the better in this belief. Craig starts by saying:

> The Art of the Theatre is neither acting nor the play, it is not scene nor (*sic*) dance, but it consists of all the elements of which these things are composed: action, which is the very spirit of acting; words, which are the body of the play; line and colour, which are the very heart of the scene; rhythm, which is the very essence of dance.

We can all agree. Perfect concord reigns. But very soon we begin to magnify our own claims, and to regard the claims of other participants as exaggerated. Craig's first step, in wading through seas of theatrical blood to grasp his own crown, is to dismiss the poet:

> A dramatic poem is to be read. A drama is not to be read, but to be seen upon the stage.

One wonders at this point where the work of Shakespeare belongs. It would seem that there are two Shakespeares: the poet, whose works are in libraries, and the dramatist, whose works only exist during a performance. Some of the illustrations in *The Art of the Theatre* are designs for Shakespeare plays; and a little later in this same dialogue Craig is telling us how *Romeo and Juliet* should be played. Only, by this time, the poet having been put in his place, it is the actor whom he has to subdue. The relevant passages are too long to quote, but if you will read the dialogues for yourself, I think you will find that what Craig says about the subordination of actor to producer can be taken in two ways: either as asserting only the authority without which the producer could not produce at all – as an affirmation of the obvious law that the man who is responsible for the *total effect* must be able to over-rule the actor who is responsible only for his own part; or on the other hand it can be read as establishing a kind of dictatorship. I wonder whether the relation of a producer to his cast will not vary according to the personality of each member of the cast. But that (I am happy to say) is none of my business. I only remark that what Craig says could either be taken as claiming only the minimum control for the producer, or as claiming something more than the maximum.

Similarly, with Gordon Craig's ideas for stage sets. It seems to me quite likely that the influence of Gordon Craig was exercised beneficially in the way of eliminating a great deal of rubbish and superfluous gear from the English stage. But when I inspect his designs they look as if they would overpower both play and cast by a cyclopean simplicity so extreme as to be fiercely aggressive. And it does seem to me possible that simplification, in its utmost perfection of balance of lights, planes and masses, can commit exactly the same mistakes as the elaboration against which it reacts – i.e. by calling attention to itself. Instead of a stage set, it might give us a picture. For a stage set is, to my mind, something on which the attention of the audience should be focused only when it is empty, or before the action starts. It should, certainly, be designed with a view to reinforcing the mood, the meaning of the play, though the ways in which it is to do so, the symbolism, abstraction or realism, elaboration or simplification, the style, the personality of the designer, may be as various as the varieties of drama itself. But ordinarily, the set should only be the conscious centre of attention for the audience for a few seconds after the curtain is raised. After that, its impression should be unconsciously received. It is difficult to tell, merely from looking at Craig's sketches, and without seeing them as the background for a play directed according to his principles, whether his sets would support the play or distract attention from it.

It has seemed to me at moments, while reading the two dialogues, as if Craig's ideal for the drama was that of a kind of wordless ballet. ('The father of the dramatist was the dancer.') In any case, his emphasis upon action is perhaps outdated by the development [19] of the cinema – development both in the mechanism and in the technique of production – during the last fifty years. I cannot but think that the development of the screen-play will prove to have influenced, imperceptibly perhaps but profoundly, the stage of our day and of to-morrow. Just as photography has influenced the art of portrait painting, in that the aim of the modern portrait painter is directed to what *the photographer cannot do*, so the people of the theatre – from author to actor – are likely to concentrate on what *the screen cannot do*.[1] Now the animated picture – successor of the *zoetrope* which captured my fancy as a child – is essentially visual action. On the stage, you can present action as an interruption of stillness: on the screen, you can present stillness only as an interruption of action. On the screen the words, however important and however beautiful (as in a screen-play by William Shakespeare), can only complete the message conveyed by the picture: on the stage, accordingly, it should be permissible and acceptable that the picture – the total scene, the movement, posture and gesture of each member of the cast – should be calculated with a view to completing the [20] message conveyed by the words.[2] Hence it would seem to suggest itself, that every statement about the theatre (from Aristotle to Gordon Craig and in the future) is limited by conditions of the critic's time and place. He cannot foresee changes to come in the world, or the relevance of such changes to the theatre. Aristotle was not legislating for Shakespeare or Racine; and I do not think that we can regard Gordon Craig as legislating for the theatre of the Picture Palace age.

There remain two very strong commendations which I must pay to Gordon Craig. The first is that there are incidental remarks in the dialogues which seem to me as true to-day as ever. For instance, Gordon

---

1. I am fearful of pronouncing judgement where I am incompetent. So I wish that one of those actors of our time who have achieved eminence both on stage and on screen – one who was also highly conscious and articulate – would write us an essay on the difference between the two media from the actor's point of view.

2. And when I say *words* I mean the words in action – that is, the words as written by that author and as spoken by those interpreters.

Craig advises the producer to ignore the author's stage directions: I have always felt that stage directions were an interference by the author in the domain of the producer, and that every stage direction that I found myself obliged to insert, was an admission of some flaw in the play.[1] Speaking as an author I heartily applaud Craig's advice to the producer to ignore the author's stage directions.

[21] My second commendation can be prefaced by a sentence of Heraclitus:

Πόλεμος πάντων μὲν πατήρ ἐστι

which, as Sir Winston Churchill is wont to say, may be translated for the benefit of our Wykehamist friends as *War is the father of all things*. I am grateful to Gordon Craig for the things he says that infuriate me; they give me something to kick against. Who is the most important person in the theatre is a question that will never be finally settled: the fight must go on. Sometimes the author, sometimes the producer, sometimes the actor-manager, sometimes the star will be top-dog; it depends too on the type of play, on the conditions of the time, on what the critics will approve and what the public will pay for. And I hope there will always be iconoclasts and malcontents and stirrers-up of strife (as well as experimenters in every direction) and someone like Gordon Craig (who, if he *is* like Gordon Craig, will probably disagree with Craig and with everyone else) in every generation or two. Not least, to keep us in touch with the Continent and prevent the English stage lapsing, as it will always tend to do, into insularity.

The Literature of Politics

A lecture delivered at a Conservative Political Centre Literary Luncheon on 19 Apr. 1955 at the Overseas League, London. Publ. in June 1955 (pp. 9–22), with a Foreword by the Rt. Hon. Sir Anthony Eden. Repr. in *TCTC*. Gallup A67.

Not today, for the first time, but for some time past, have I been aware how very rash it was of me to accept your invitation to address this Literary Luncheon: my acceptance is only one more illustration of a truth that I

---

1. That is an exaggeration. But at this point, I was just about to express regret that the late Bernard Shaw had not observed Craig's prescription. And then I thought No! It is true that Shaw's stage directions limit and date the plays, but the plays will date anyway – John Tanner will not survive the Fabian Society of which he is a foundation member. Possibly it is the prefaces and the stage directions that will preserve Shaw's plays, like flies in amber. But this is an exception of the kind that proves the rule.

should have learned from experience, that one can face nearly any danger intrepidly, and even court it wantonly, so long as it is far enough off. My foolhardiness, on this occasion, was twofold. While I do not suppose that everyone in this room is an accomplished public speaker, I take it for granted that those who are not, are at least seasoned listeners, with pretty high standards of what they expect in the way of oratory. And a man of letters, far from being thereby licensed to the platform and the rostrum, is more likely than not to be a poor speaker, relatively at ease – but only relatively – when he has prepared, as I have today, not only his thoughts but his words. Second, I was rash in consenting to appear in an unfamiliar role and [10] context. That, of course, may have increased the size of my audience: you are, very likely, at this moment experiencing the thrill of a crowd gathered to watch a man take a very high dive, when the rumour has been put about that he does not know how to swim. I hope you will be disappointed: but I do not know myself whether or not, after the splash has subsided, my head will emerge from the water.

Some excitement and misunderstanding may have arisen from the title originally advertised, which led a columnist in a daily newspaper to exclaim: 'Mr Eliot, who writes his plays in verse, is turning to politics. He has kept well away from them up to now.' Well, I intend to be just as political, and not a jot more so, than I have been in some of my prose writings which perhaps the writer, so appreciative of my plays, has overlooked.

The title first given is one which I suggested as a good subject for somebody – without specifying myself. Rather late in the day I realized that the title had come home to roost and that I must push it off the roost. I am reminded of an experience some years ago when I agreed to give a lecture in Nice. In correspondence with the President of the society which I was to address, I remarked that, not knowing which of two kinds of audience to expect, I found myself, for the choice of a subject, between Scylla and Charybdis. Before I had made up my mind what to talk about, it was [11] announced in Nice that I was to speak on the subject of Scylla and Charybdis. After a moment's consternation I thought – And why not? Almost any topic can be dealt with under that heading. *Scylla and Charybdis* is delightfully general, and arouses curiosity by its vagueness. *The Relation of Political Philosophy to the Practice of Politics*, on the other hand, was alarmingly precise. It is a subject to demand all the learning, profundity and torrential eloquence of such a philosopher as Mr Isaiah Berlin. As for me, I am not competing with such authorities. I am merely a man of letters who believes that the questions he raises may sometimes be of interest, even if the answers he can give are negligible. And as a man of letters, I have never taken any part in politics other than that of a voter – a walking-on part, and that of a reader – a sitting-down part.

* * *

So let me approach my subject by asking: what is the literature of Conservatism? That is to say, what are the 'classic' writings in the English language, with which any thoughtful Conservative is presumed to have some familiarity, writings by authors whose work is supposed to yield some understanding of what Conservatism is? There are four names which we could all, without any prompting, repeat in chorus, for they constantly turn up together. They lead off in the bibliographical note to that admirable little book [12] *Conservatism* written by Lord Hugh Cecil, as he was then, in 1912 for the Home University Library. They are, of course, the names of Bolingbroke, Burke, Coleridge and Disraeli.

Now, could one assemble four men, in one field of thought, more dissimilar to each other than these? The one thing they obviously have in common is that each in his own way was a master of prose, whose work can no more be ignored by the student of English literature than by the student of politics. Each of these men had a sense of style – and that is something more than merely a trick of knowing how to write. This is all to the good, that the Conservative tradition should be also a tradition of good writing; but it may seem irrelevant. When we consider Bolingbroke, he is hardly an example of that devotion to Christian belief and Christian morals that Lord Hugh Cecil quite rightly called for. Burke is certainly a Christian thinker; Coleridge was a distinguished theologian as well as philosopher; Disraeli also deserves a pass degree, though churchmanship is the one point on which I feel more sympathy with Mr Gladstone. As for their politics, the situations in which the three who practised politics found themselves, were very different. Bolingbroke, in fact, is pre-Conservative, if we agree with those who derive Conservatism itself only from a fusion of Tory and Whig elements, due largely to the effect of the French Revolution upon the mind of [13] Burke. Burke, as has often been observed, uttered his most important statements of Conservative doctrine in the course of current controversy; Disraeli delivered himself through his novels as well as in Parliament. As for Coleridge, he was rather a man of my own type, differing from myself chiefly in being immensely more learned, more industrious, and endowed with a more powerful and subtle mind.

So we remark that, with three of these writers, their philosophy was nourished on their political experience. The fourth was a philosopher with no political experience. What are we to make of this diversity, and what common principles can be elicited from the work of such different men, writing under such different conditions? I am inclined to believe it a good thing that we should find the question difficult to answer. If, in my attempt to give grounds for my belief, you find me descending to platitude and commonplace, I hope you will attribute it to my simplicity and inexperience; if, on the other hand, you convict me of uttering nonsense, I ask for no quarter at all.

* * *

I venture to put forward the suggestion that political thinking, that is, thinking that concerns itself with the permanent principles, if any, underlying a party name, can follow two contrasted lines of development. At the beginning may be a body of doctrine, perhaps a [14] canonical work; and a band of devoted people set out to disseminate and popularise this doctrine through its emotional appeal to the interested and the disinterested; and then, as a political party, endeavour to realise a programme based on the doctrine. Before arriving at the position of governing, they have envisaged some final state of society of which their doctrines give the outline. The theory has altogether preceded the practice.

But political ideas may come into being by an opposite process. A political party may find that it has had a history, before it is fully aware or agreed upon its own permanent tenets; it may have arrived at its actual formation through a succession of metamorphoses and adaptations, during which some issues have been superannuated and new issues have arisen. What its fundamental tenets are, will probably be found only by careful examination of its behaviour throughout its history and by examination of what its more thoughtful and philosophic minds have said on its behalf; and only accurate historical knowledge and judicious analysis will be able to discriminate between the permanent and the transitory; between those doctrines and principles which it must ever, and in all circumstances, maintain, or manifest itself a fraud, and those called forth by special circumstances, which are only intelligible and justifiable in the light of those circumstances.

[15] Of the two, the latter type seems to me the more likely to correspond to that preference of the organic over the mechanical that Burke maintained: but each has its peculiar dangers.

I do not propose to plunge into the controversies of historical determinism. Determinism has a strong emotional appeal: curiously enough, it can appeal to the same type of mind as that which believes in the unlimited possibilities of planning. Determinism seems to give great encouragement, and at times access of force, to those who can convince themselves that what they want to happen is going to happen anyway, and to those who like to feel that they are going with the tide: and we have all heard, now and again, that freedom is to be found only in the acceptance of necessity – though it is also natural to the human mind to suspect that there is a catch in this somewhere. But it should also be obvious to everyone from his personal experience, that there is no formula for infallible prediction; that everything we do will have some unforeseen consequences; that often our best justified ventures end in disaster, and that sometimes our most irrational blunders have the most happy results; that every reform leads to new abuses which could not have been predicted but which do not necessarily justify us in saying that the reform should not have been carried out; that we must constantly adapt ourselves to the new and unexpected; and that we move always, if not [16] in the dark, in a twilight, with imperfect vision, constantly mistaking one object for another, imagining distant obstacles where none exists, and unaware of some fatal menace close at hand. This is Frederick Scott Oliver's *Endless Adventure*.

When a party committed to an unalterable doctrine finds itself in a position of power, two things may happen. Leaders who have learnt from experience will exercise their ingenuity in discovering reasons for postponing the part of their programme that they see to be impracticable, or in proving that what appears to be a change is a logical development: in the East, I believe, it is assumed that Marx would have approved, and Lenin acted upon, whatever is done – until the contrary policy is officially adopted. The alternative to such suppleness is the Jacobinism of the obstinate doctrinaire, ready to ruin all rather than modify theory in the face of fact.

Whereas the point of view I have just mentioned, is subject to the alternative dangers of inadaptability, or of adaptation by subterfuge, having committed itself to tenets which it cannot renounce, the danger of the other point of view is equally great: that is the danger of becoming so protean, so endlessly and obligingly adaptable to changing circumstances, that it discredits itself by its indifference to principle. To know what to surrender, and what to hold firm, and indeed to recognise the situation of critical choice when it arises, is an [17] art requiring such resources of experience, wisdom and insight, that I cannot envy those public men, of whatever party, who may at any moment be called upon to make grave decisions, and who may in due course be censured by posterity, either as fanatics or as opportunists. And just as politics of the one type has need constantly to review its tenets and accepted ideas in the light of experience, for otherwise it is in danger of acting on principles that have been discredited, so the politics of the other type needs from time to time to re-open the inquiry as to what are its permanent principles, and review its actions in the light of these principles. For the permanent and the transitory have to be distinguished afresh by each generation.

*   *   *

In an article which I read recently, on the subject of Conservatism in America, the author made the point, which struck me forcibly, that the true conservatives in that country in recent times had none of them been political figures: they had been the philosophic observers and moralists, often in academic positions; and the names he cited were nearly all of men I had known, or with whose work I was acquainted; such men as Paul More and Irving Babbitt in the last generation, and amongst those living, Canon B. I. Bell, and Professor Nisbet of California. If the writer, himself an American, is right, this is not a very healthy state of [18] affairs, unless the views of such writers become more widely diffused and translated, modified, adapted, even adulterated, into action. It seems to me that in a healthy society, there will be a gradation of types between thought and action; at one extreme the detached contemplative, the critical mind which is concerned with the discovery of truth, not with its promulgation and still less with its translation into action, and at the other extreme, the N.C.O. of politics, the man who in spite of relative indifference to general ideas, is equipped with native good sense, right feeling and character, supported by discipline and education. Between these two extremes there is room for several varieties and several kinds of political thinking; but there should be no breach of continuity between them.

At the same time, it is as well that everyone who thinks about politics at all, should recognise his own abilities and limitations, and should not engage in every kind of activity, of those which range from what we call philosophic thought to what we call action. Yet we all understand our own function in society the better for mixing with men of different functions from ours, and the man whose business is merely to think and write, will do his job much better if he has some frequentation of the society of those whose business is to direct policy and make decisions; just as the legislator should be able to put himself at the point of view [19] of those who have to carry out his legislation, and at the point of view of those who have to endure it. There are obviously dangers for society when functions are so sharply divided that men of one profession can no longer understand the mind and temperament of men of another. And to go more directly to the point, a political tradition in which the doctrinaire dominates the man of action, and a tradition in which political philosophy is formulated or re-codified to suit the requirements and justify the conduct of a ruling clique, may be equally disastrous.

*   *   *

I have been making the point that there should be no complete separation of function between men of thought and men of action, and I have maintained that men of different activities, or of political interests, in whom the proportions of the speculative or theoretic and the active were differently mixed, should be able to understand and learn from each other. I have also suggested that it is here, as generally in life, everyone's concern to find out what he ought to meddle with and what he ought to leave alone.

On this last point, I think of a man whom I held in respect and admiration, although some of his views were exasperating and some deplorable – but a great writer, a genuine lover of his country, and a man who deserved a better fate than that which he had in the [20] end to meet. I know that it is easy to criticise a man for not being another man than the man he was; and we should be particularly reserved in criticism of a man whose political setting was that of another country from our own. But with the reservations compelled by this awareness, I have sometimes thought that if Charles Maurras had confined himself to literature, and to the literature of political theory, and had never attempted to found a political party, a *movement* – engaging in, and increasing the acrimony of the political struggle – if he had not given his support to the restoration of the Monarchy in such a way as to strengthen instead of reducing animosities – then those of his ideas which were sound and strong might have spread more widely, and penetrated more deeply, and affected more sensibly the contemporary mind.

But how, in the end, does the work of a mere writer affect political life? One is sometimes tempted to answer that the profounder and *wiser* the man, the less likely is his influence to be discernible. This, of course, is to take a very short view; and at the other extreme, in considering the thought of the very greatest, we can hardly speak of their 'influence' at all: it becomes ridiculous to ask whether the influence of Plato or Aristotle has been good or bad, for we cannot conceive what the history of the European mind would have been without them. Yet the immediate influence of – shall we say – Mr Bernard Shaw in the period of his [21] most potent influence, I suppose, at the beginning of this century, must have been more appreciable, and more widely diffused, than that of much finer minds: and one is compelled to admire a man of such verbal agility as not only to conceal from his readers and audiences the shallowness of his own thought, but to persuade them that in admiring his work they were giving evidence of their own intelligence as well. I do not say that Shaw could have succeeded alone, without the more plodding and laborious minds with which he associated himself; but by persuading low-brows that they were high-brows, and that high-brows must be socialists, he contributed greatly to the prestige of socialism. But between the influence of a Bernard Shaw or an H. G. Wells, and the influence of a Coleridge or a Newman, I can conceive no common scale of measurement.

* * *

I confess, however, that I am not myself very much concerned with the question of influence, or with those publicists who have impressed their names upon the public by catching the morning tide, and rowing very fast in the direction in which the current was flowing; but rather that there should always be a few writers preoccupied in penetrating to the core of the matter, in trying to arrive at the truth and to set it forth, without too much hope, without ambition to alter the [22] immediate course of affairs, and without being downcast or defeated when nothing appears to ensue.

The proper area for such men is what may be called, not the political, but the *pre-political* area. I borrow the term from Canon Demant, the Regius Professor of Theology at Oxford; and I am thinking of work such as his, and Mr Christopher Dawson's, and that of Professor Reinhold Niebuhr in America. It is in this area also that my own much slighter talents have been employed. But we can look still further for literary influence, not only philosophical, but imaginative, upon politics. Disraeli gained much from his early association with Smythe and Manners, who owed a good deal to Walter Scott. And my defence of the importance of the *pre-political* is simply this, that it is the stratum down to which any sound political thinking must push its roots, and from which it must derive its nourishment. It is also, if you don't mind my changing the metaphor so abruptly, the land in which dwell the Gods of the Copy Book Headings; and, abandoning figurative language altogether, it is the domain of ethics – in the end, the domain of theology. For the question of questions, which no political philosophy can escape, and by the right answer to which all political thinking must in the end be judged, is simply this: What is Man? what are his limitations? what is his misery and what his greatness? and what, finally, his destiny?

'Goethe as the Sage'

'Goethe as the Sage Address by T. S. Eliot Hamburg, 1955' was publ. in *Gedenkschrift zur Verleihung des Hansishcen Goethe-Preises 1954 der gemeinnützigen Stiftung F.V.S. zu Hamburg durch die Universität Hamburg an Thomas Stearns Eliot* (Aug. 1955), 49–71: Gallup B74. Revised in *OPAP. See below*, pp. 319–39.

[To Ezra Pound on his Seventieth Birthday]

Pound Newsletter, 8 (Oct. 1955), 7. Introduced with '*From London . . .*' and signed '. . . T. S. Eliot'. Gallup C601.

It is very right that every periodical devoted to poetry should pay homage to Ezra Pound on his seventieth birthday. It is especially right that the *Newsletter* should assemble testimony to his achievement; and I wish that my tribute could be at greater length. But I have in various places and at various times expressed my opinion that Mr Pound – in so far as we can pass such a judgement on a contemporary – is a great poet; and I have tried to make clear the grounds for my conviction. I cannot enlarge upon what I have already said in his praise; and I should not wish on such an occasion to risk the appearance of diminishing that praise by referring to any of the vital matters upon which I take issue with him. For me at such a moment, what matters is the poetry and not the ingredients which have entered into its composition: I venture to express the hope that the readers of the *Newsletter* also will not, in their concern with the sources, lose their appreciation of the end-product.

I offer this as a token.

1956

Fr Cheetham Retires from Gloucester Road

CT, 139. 4856 (9 Mar. 1956), 12. Subheaded '*By T. S. Eliot*'. Gallup C603.
Eliot wrote more fully about Fr Cheetham in 'The Panegyric',
S. Stephen's Magazine (May 1959), [5–7] (Gallup C633). *See below*, pp. 440–3.

On February 29 there took effect the resignation of the Rev. Eric Samuel Cheetham, Prebendary of St Paul's from the living of St Stephen's, Gloucester-road, in the sixty-fourth year of his age and the thirty-ninth year of his service in that parish.

In 1917, Fr Cheetham was appointed to a curacy under the Rev. Lord Victor Seymour; in 1929, he succeeded Lord Victor as Vicar. Ill-health, resulting in a peremptory ultimatum from medical advisers, is the reason for his resignation before the normal time of retirement. Yet, though his incumbency has thus been cut short, St Stephen's has had, in over half a century, only two Vicars. In the current number of his parish magazine, reviewing his own career, Fr Cheetham pays tribute to his predecessor. 'I am more grateful to Lord Victor than I can express,' he says. 'He would be described to-day as one of "the old school", a great fighter for the faith, and the very priest to train a nature like mine.'

It is this continuity of tradition, from the Vicar to the curate who became Vicar after him, that has given St Stephen's the place it occupies and the influence it has exerted. A long incumbency, even of one of the most important Catholic parishes of London, does not in itself call for special notice, except by the congregation deprived of the pastoral care to which it has become accustomed. St Stephen's, under Cheetham, however, will always have a very strong hold on the memory of a far larger number than its congregation at any one moment, and it is not likely to be forgotten even by those whose worship in that church has been infrequent, or whose connection with it has been brief.

A PRIEST'S GIFTS

A parish priest possessing *all* the gifts useful in the exercise of his vocation is a person who perhaps has never existed; and the more one knows of the divers tasks and functions which a parish priest may be called upon to perform, the less is one able even to conceive the possibility of such a paragon. But a layman who has occupied, for twenty-two years, a position behind the scenes – in the vestry or in the presbytery – could not fail to be impressed by the number of things that Fr Cheetham could do and did well. (I speak in the past tense; for although his gifts remain with him, the physical capacity of fully exercising them has, alas! been withdrawn.)

To begin with the least important (though more important than most people realise): the parish magazine, which he edited and a great part of which he wrote himself – individual, somewhat eccentric, but always readable and always worth reading. Second, his great skill in entertainment and in pageantry – in the confecting of pageants he had a talent for invention and for improvisation which enabled him, in that area of activity, sometimes to make bricks without straw. And his gifts as producer and stage-manager contributed to making the sequence of the Christian year at St Stephen's an achievement of great impressiveness. With the precision, the discipline, the taste of the good theatrical *régisseur*, Fr Cheetham has never exercised these gifts for their own sake, but to the glory of God; and the beauty of art, ritual and music was always the handmaid of the beauty of holiness.

INDIVIDUAL SERMONS

He was gifted as a preacher: and his mode of delivery must have convinced every listener that his sermons had been prepared for that particular occasion and was addressed to that particular congregation. Nor did he allow the exercise of the gifts already enumerated to distract him from his pastoral duties – not only the normal pastoral duties, but those arising from the crises great and small in which humanity, sometimes blindly, turns to a priest for help.

While Fr Cheetham has never thought of himself as possessing any business ability, he showed long ago a foresight for which the parish council must always be grateful. When he came to St Stephen's it was a rich parish, but with no endowment. Foreseeing a day when the wealth would have vanished from Kensington, he started an endowment fund which – now that St Stephen's has become a poor parish – assures at least a stipend for the incumbent.

The achievement of Fr Cheetham at St Stephen's may be summed up by saying that he made it a centre of Evangelical Catholicism: truly Catholic and truly wholly Anglican.

[To Ezra Pound on his Seventieth Birthday]

Ezra Pound at Seventy, [5–6]. Publ. after Mar. 1956. Gallup B75.

Prefatory statement: 'To mark Ezra Pound's seventieth year New Directions wrote to a number of persons and here publishes the statements they sent about him . . .' Eliot's statement is headed 't. s. eliot'.

I believe that I have in the past made clear enough my personal debt to Ezra Pound during the years 1915–22. I have also expressed in several ways my opinion of his rank as a poet, as a critic, [6] as impresario of other writers, and as pioneer of metric and poetic language. His 70th birthday is not a moment for qualifying one's praise, but merely for recognition of those services to literature for which he will deserve the gratitude of posterity, and for appreciation of those achievements which even his severest critics must acknowledge.

[Tribute to Artur Lundkvist]

As printed in *Artur Lundkvist 3 Mars 1956* (1956), 101.
Not in Gallup, but would be B75b.

2 December 1955

Dear Mr Artur Lundkvist,

I am honoured by the privilege of being numbered with the friends who will greet you on your attaining what seems to me the very youthful age of 50. We have met several times, you paid me the compliment of translating one of my poems as long ago as 1942; and I know by reliable witness of your achievements as author and as linguist. I rejoice in your reputation; and I regret only that my ignorance of Swedish disqualifies me from the full tribute. Would that I were the linguist that you are! Nevertheless, I greet you fraternally on this occasion, and express my good wishes (you are only 50: the best years of creative activity are still before you!) as from one European man of letters to another.

Salve.
T. S. ELIOT

The Frontiers of Criticism

The Gideon D. Seymour Memorial Lecture, delivered at the University of Minnesota on 30 Apr. 1956, was publ. and distributed gratis beginning on 13 Aug. 1956. It was not publ. in Britain. Revised in *OPAP*. *See below*, pp. 221–36.

[Brief über Ernst Robert Curtius]

Freundesgabe für Ernst Robert Curtius zum 14. April 1956, ed. Max Rychner and Walter Boehlich (1956), 25–7. Gallup Bl15.

Dear Dr Rychner,

    I regret deeply that I have no original contribution worthy of inclusion in the Festschrift for Ernst Robert Curtius, but I should be very grieved not to have my name appear amongst those who wish to pay honour to him on the occasion of his 70th birthday. So I send you the following greeting to him:

    Time is an important element in friendship – much more important, in my experience, than frequency of meeting. Is it twice, in the last thirty-five years, that I have met Ernst Curtius face to face? It need not have been more than once: I count him nevertheless among my old friends. In one sense, it is as if I had always known him, for the beginning of our acquaintance coincides, very nearly, with what seems to me the beginning of my adult life: the period in my life which is marked by *The Waste Land*, and the foundation of *The Criterion*, and the development of relations with men of letters in the several countries of Europe.

    It is true of many of my friendships that I cannot remember how they began. I cannot remember whether I first discovered Curtius, or whether he first discovered me. Was it in 1922? Did he first come across *The Criterion*, and there read *The Waste Land*, about which he was to write, and which he was to translate? Certainly, in common with other English and French writers, I owe him a great debt, and perhaps I owe him more than does any other: for it was he who first brought my work to the notice of the German public. On the other hand, it may be that somehow my attention was drawn to *Literarische Wegbereiter des neuen Frankreichs*, and that I asked him to contribute to my recently founded review. I do not know.

    At the time when *The Criterion* was founded, it must have appeared to any reasonable person an act of folly on my part, for the task of editing a magazine had to be the evening occupation of a man fully occupied as a bank clerk in the day time. At that time, *The Criterion* seemed destined to put an end to my original activity, for it left me little time for my own writing. In the end, it altered the whole course of my life, and led to greater freedom for original work; and I must be grateful to the first Viscountess Rothermere, who provided the funds by which the printers and publishers and contributors were paid during the first years of the periodical's existence. But what I had chiefly to be grateful for, at the time – the most definite immediate benefit to myself as editor – was the opportunity *The Criterion* opened up to me, as I have said above, of establishing relations with men of letters in other European countries.

[26] The years immediately following the War of 1914–18 were, as I have said in other contexts, a hopeful period in the world of letters. *The Criterion* was only one of a number of reviews similar in character and in purpose, in France, Germany, Switzerland, Italy, Spain and elsewhere; and my own interest in making my contemporaries in other countries known in England, responded to the interests of the editors and contributors of these other reviews. No ideological differences poisoned our intercourse; no political oppression limited freedom of communication. Of the men whose acquaintance I made at this time – some directly, others only by exchange of correspondence – I think of Valery Larbaud, of Charles du Bois, of Ortega y Gasset, among others (and yourself, Dr Rychner!). But no name stands, in my memory, with more distinction in this international activity, no name is more representatively that of the *European* man of letters, than the name of Ernst Robert Curtius.

I have, as I have said, my own personal debt of gratitude to acknowledge to Curtius, for translating, and introducing, *The Waste Land*. Curtius was also, I think, the first critic in Germany to recognise the importance of James Joyce. And when it is a question of other writers than myself, and especially when we consider his essays on French contemporaries, and his *Balzac*, and his *Proust*, I am at liberty to praise Curtius as a critic. A generous enthusiast, with no great critical ability, might succeed in communicating his enthusiasm for some foreign author to his fellow-countrymen; but only a critic of scholarship, discrimination and intellect could perform the services that Curtius has performed. For his critical studies are contributions to the study of the authors criticised, which must be reckoned with by those authors' compatriots. *We cannot determine the true status and significance of the significant writers in our own language, without the aid of foreign critics with a European point of view.* For it is only such critics who can tell us, whether an author is of European importance. And of such critics in our own time, Curtius is one of the most illustrious.

[27] There were years when communication was interrupted. After the seizure of power by Adolf Hitler, we feared for the author of *Deutscher Geist in Gefahr*; after the outbreak of war, we heard a rumour that he had been removed to a concentration camp. Happily this was not true; and there eventually appeared that masterly work, *Europäische Literatur und Lateinisches Mittelalter*, on which he had been at work during the years when freedom of speech and freedom of travel were suspended. It bears testimony to his integrity and indomitable spirit. Ernst Robert Curtius deserves, in his life and in his work, the gratitude and admiration of his fellow writers of every European nation.

Yours sincerely,
T. S. ELIOT

Essays on Elizabethan Drama

This revised American reprint of *Elizabethan Essays* (1934) was publ. on 14 Sept. 1956. It was reprinted with the title *Elizabethan Dramatists* by Faber & Faber on 13 Dec. 1963: Gallup A27.

Variants from the 1956 dedication page and Preface are recorded under the 1963 edn. *See below*, pp. 548–50.

Foreword

Foreword to Joseph Chiari, *Symbolisme from Poe to Mallarmé*, v–viii. Subheaded 'By T. S. ELIOT' and signed 'T. S. Eliot' at the end. Publ. Dec. 1956. Gallup B76.

This is a book about the poet Mallarmé, but the author has done well to entitle it '. . . from Poe to Mallarmé': for a book about Mallarmé must also be a book about Poe and about Baudelaire, and must not ignore Mallarmé's most illustrious disciple, Paul Valéry. It must be a book about a movement – the most important 'movement' in the world of poetry since that of Wordsworth and Coleridge – and about the aesthetics of that movement.

I must surround the term 'movement' with safeguards of several kinds. To say that this is the most important poetic movement since Wordsworth and Coleridge is not to exaggerate the individual importance of the poets involved in it, or to place them higher than other poets, in France, England, and other countries, who are outside of it. Nor can the term here have any of its popular associations. We usually think of a literary movement as a group of young enthusiastic writers who issue a manifesto; who have or who pretend to have certain principles in common; whose work is likely to show a family resemblance; and who are banded together in championship of a common cause, or for sociability and mutual comfort, or at worst for purposes of collective self-advertisement. We think of a 'movement' as a phenomenon of youth, and we expect that the sturdier members will in time leave the group as they develop their individual styles, and that the weaker members will disappear into oblivion. By 'movement', here, I mean a continuity of admiration: Baudelaire [vi] admired Poe, Mallarmé admired Poe and Baudelaire, Valéry admired Poe and Baudelaire and Mallarmé – and a continuity of development of poetic theory. Valéry was the disciple of Mallarmé: but there was no personal association among the rest. Mallarmé, I have been told, came to Paris because Baudelaire was there: he once saw Baudelaire at a bookstall on a quay, but had not the courage to address him. And of course Baudelaire never met Poe. And, as Mr Chiari points out, although each of these French poets in turn found Poe intensely stimulating, there is no evidence of imitation or even of borrowing from Poe in their work.

How far Baudelaire would have been Baudelaire, or Mallarmé Mallarmé, without the stimulus provided by Poe, is a question to which the answer can never be more than conjecture; but Mr Chiari is right to raise the question, and leave it in our minds. To Anglo-Saxon readers it must seem that this paradoxical 'movement', in which the poets from generation to generation were not greatly influenced by each other's poetry, but deeply influenced by each other's attitude towards poetry, was largely propelled by an initial misunderstanding. It is difficult for us to see how three French poets, all men of exceptional intellectual gifts, could have taken Poe so seriously as a philosopher – for it is Poe's theories about poetry, rather than his poems, that meant most to them. How good a poet was Poe? There is no poet whose status is more disputed. And as a philosopher? It is difficult for an English or American reader to regard as anything but extravagant the praise which Valéry lavishes upon *Eureka*. We suspect, indeed, that if the French poets had known the English language better they could not have rated Poe so high as a stylist; and that if they had known English literature better they might have based their aesthetics not on that of Poe but on that of Coleridge.

No matter: if the influence of Poe upon Baudelaire, Mallarmé and Valéry was based upon misunderstanding, it was a fecund and significant misunderstanding, for the aesthetic which they [vii] erected upon this dubious foundation remains valid for their own work. The time had come for a new attitude towards poetry, on the part of poets first, to be accepted by readers afterwards. It does not matter whether Poe's account of the composition of 'The Raven' was a conscious hoax, or whether Poe was hoaxing himself; what it suggested to the French poets was an aesthetic which might have come into existence in some other way, if Poe had never written or if Baudelaire had never read Poe.

Any good poet, of course, can be enjoyed without our having previously informed ourselves about his relation to other poets, and without our knowing anything about his theory of poetry – if he has one. Indeed, if this were not so, we might doubt whether what he had written was poetry at all. What we get from a study of these French poets in relation to Poe, is an understanding of their aesthetic which enlarges our understanding of their poetry. And by 'aesthetic' here I do not mean merely an abstract theory of what poetry should be; I mean an attitude to poetry, by poets of great critical capacity, which has affected indirectly a good deal of poetry written since and which has also affected the attitude of readers towards their poetry. What the reader of poetry has come to expect of modern poetry, and the way in which he is prepared to enjoy it, are partly due to the attitude of these French poets to their own work. Without this aesthetic I do not think that the work of some other modern writers would be quite what it is (I am thinking of Rilke, for example, and of some of my own later work) or that, if it was the same, it would find a public prepared for it.

This, of course, is not the whole story. Baudelaire would have been a great poet in any case, a greater than Poe; and much more became possible because of Baudelaire – I am thinking of Laforgue, Corbière and Rimbaud – than is found in the poetic current examined in this book. But this poetic current represents a peculiar development of self-consciousness [viii] in the poetry of the last hundred years. Mr Chiari, who is at home in both languages and with both literatures, English and French, and who has examined the voluminous critical literature of his subject in French, has performed a useful service in giving us the first book in English on Mallarmé and his art of poetry.

Poetry and the Schools

Remarks at a press conference of the Poetry Book Society after its second Annual General Meeting, 10 Apr. 1956. Issued as a promotional broadside by the Poetry Book Society and distributed from late Dec. 1956.

Gallup designates it C599 and places it in 1955, but in view of the date of the address (10 Apr. 1956) and its distribution date it should be in 1956 and would be C607b.

I have never been very much in favour of introducing the work of living authors into school curricula of the study of English literature, for two reasons. First, I think that schoolboys and girls should be given a background of the classic authors of our language whose work is part of history and can be taught as such. Second, I think that all growing boys and girls should have an area of literature which they're not taught anything about, on which they don't have to pass any examinations, in which they can make their own discoveries, their own errors, and learn for themselves. If every secondary school in the country joined the Poetry Book Society and had a shelf in its library exhibiting the books of new poetry, this year and last year and several years, and just left them there for the boys and girls in the upper forms to discover for themselves and find out what they liked, we would be doing a very great service, because it is in the years between 14 and 18 if ever that people become readers of poetry and lovers of poetry, and also amongst those readers will be the poets of that generation. I think every poet has been a reader of poetry before he has been inflamed with the desire to become a writer of poetry, and it is a good thing also that boys and girls of that age should learn to think of poetry as a living art, as something which is still being written and which will be written in their own generation. I have always held firmly that a nation which ceases to produce poetry will in the long run cease to be able to enjoy and even understand the poetry of its own past.

1957

Das schöpferische Recht des Regisseurs
(The creative right of directors)

Maske und Kothurn: Vierteljahrsschrift für Theaterwissenschaft, 3 (Jan./Mar. 1957), 10. Gallup C608.

T. S. ELIOT (London): It seems to me that the question of the limits of the stage manager's rights of interfering with the text and stage directions of the dramatist is not one which can be answered in the abstract: it depends on the particular stage manager and the particular dramatist. There will always be instances where the stage manager will exceed his province, and there will always be instances where the dramatist will make difficulties on matters where the stage manager knows best. I should say that when the dramatist is a living dramatist, he should always be consulted with regard to any changes in the text, and to any changes in presentation from his own directions. I should myself be very much annoyed with any stage manager or producer who cut out lines from my verse plays without having consulted me first. On the other hand if, as has sometimes happened, the stage manager or producer has given good reason for omitting lines, I have always been ready to fall in with his wishes.

I think that in works of the past which are already well known, greater liberties are permitted than in works by living authors. If they are famous works of drama or opera, the more intelligent part of the audience may be assumed to be acquainted with other productions, and to be quite aware of any contrast between a traditional form of production and that offered by some enterprising producer.

I do hold the view – this is not altogether beside the point – that an author is well advised to keep his stage directions to the very minimum and leave the maximum possible to the imagination and originality of future producers. For instance, it seems to me that some of Bernard Shaw's stage directions overweight the play, and if followed exactly can sometimes result only in the play appearing as a kind of period piece which will show the ideas, as well as the manners, as being out of date.

Homage to Wyndham Lewis 1884–1957

Spectrum, 1. 29 (Spring/Summer 1957), [45]. Gallup C609.

Since Wyndham Lewis's death I have twice written about him elsewhere. Nevertheless I should not like my name to be absent from any collection of tributes. Wyndham Lewis was in my opinion one of the few men of letters in my generation whom I should call, without qualification, men of genius. It is for other painters and draughtsmen to praise his genius as a painter and draughtsman. I would like to repeat what I have said several times before, that Lewis was the most versatile prose-writer of my time and had the most interesting style. I would also like to pay a special tribute to the work he did after he became completely blind. In *Self Condemned*, he seems to me to have written a novel greater than *Tarr* or *The Revenge for Love*; in *Monstre Gai* a sequel to *The Childermass* more remarkable than *The Childermass* itself. It is a great artist and one of the most intelligent men of my age who is dead.

The Importance of Wyndham Lewis

Sunday Times (10 Mar. 1957), 10. Gallup C611.

I first met Wyndham Lewis early in the year 1915, at the flat of Ezra Pound, whose acquaintance I had made only a few days before. Pound had already shown me Lewis's *Timon of Athens* drawings: this was in the days of Vorticism and *Blast*, before Lewis had gone to the war as a gunner.

I do not remember that Lewis had much to say on that occasion, but I recall that in those early years and in general company he could be a brilliantly amusing talker, his conversation having much of the wit and original phrasing of his prose. Six years later Lewis and I were in Paris, and again through an arrangement with Ezra Pound together made the acquaintance of James Joyce. Lewis himself has recorded in a most humorous way both of these meetings, which are landmarks in the history of my association with three men, very different in every way from each other – and from myself.

I have always thought of Lewis as a very great draughtsman who also painted some masterly portraits. But as I have no standing in the world of art criticism it is of his prose that I prefer to speak.

* * *

His versatility, variety, and vitality in both arts were prodigious. His writings are of several distinct kinds. To mention only those writings which I know well: first, the criticism of ideas, *Time and Western Man*, *The Art of Being Ruled*, and *The Lion and the Fox*; more recently, *The Writer and the Absolute*.

Second, works of satire and extravagant imagination – the trilogy of *The Childermass*, *Monstre Gai* and *Malign Fiesta*, with a slighter though bulky work *The Apes of God*. His first novel, *Tarr*, is primarily satiric; his later, and to my mind, greater novels, *The Revenge for Love* and *Self Condemned*, have moments of pathos and poignancy which the satirist had not led us to expect.

There are volumes of short stories, *The Wild Body*, *Rotting Hill*; there is *Blasting and Bombardiering* in the category of memoirs; and there is miscellaneous work, from *The Caliph's Design* to *The Demon of Progress in the Arts*, which can only be described as pamphleteering.

The output was outstanding. The views expressed were independent and unpopular. In everything Lewis wrote there was evidence of a powerful critical intelligence or of an astonishing visual imagination.

Finally, there is, in everything he wrote, style. I would even affirm that Wyndham Lewis was the only one among my contemporaries to create a new, an original, prose style. Most prose of my time, indeed, seems to me, when compared with that of Lewis, lifeless. A great intellect is gone, a great modern writer is dead.

Wyndham Lewis

HR, 10. 2 (Summer 1957), [167]–70. Gallup C612.

Of my first meeting with Wyndham Lewis, which took place in Ezra Pound's rooms early in 1915, Lewis himself wrote so amusingly, and with so precise a painter's memory for visual detail, in his contribution to a volume published in my honour in 1948, that I can have nothing further to say. Pound had previously showed me some of Lewis's drawings – I possessed myself of a copy of the *Timon* portfolio, which mysteriously vanished from my library some years ago; I had also seen the first number of *Blast*; and Pound had, I think, mentioned a remarkable novel called *Tarr* which was to be serialised in *The Egoist*. I was then doing some post-graduate work at Oxford, and my early meetings with Pound and Lewis took place during the Christmas vacation. I dined one evening with Lewis at a restaurant in Charlotte Street which I still frequent, and visited him in his rooms in Fitzroy Street on some occasion on which he was at home to the artists with whom he was then associated. I remember Bomberg, Etchells, Roberts, Wadsworth, Miss Sanders and Miss Dismorr being present.

Later in that same year Lewis appeared in the khaki brassard, decorated with the royal crown in red, which was the badge of those who had volunteered and were in due course to be called up. During the rest of the 1914–18 War I saw him but rarely, even during the period when he, with a number of other artists, had been withdrawn from the Front (Lewis, of course, was an artilleryman, and ended the war as a subaltern) to render their impressions of the battlefield on canvas. It was not until 1921 that I began to see much of him, beginning with an expedition which Lewis himself has mentioned, but of which I have some supplementary memories worth recording.

In the summer of that year, 1921, Lewis and I made an excursion down the Loire to Nantes and the Morbihan, ending with a few days in Paris. Whether we were away for two or three weeks I cannot remember: it was my summer holiday when I was working [168] in Lloyds Bank in the City. It was on this visit that we both first made the acquaintance of James Joyce. Our first meeting with Joyce on this visit has been described by Lewis, in a book of reminiscences, not only with great humour and verbal felicity, but with an accuracy to which I can bear witness. I had almost forgotten that episode, until my memory was revived by Lewis's account, but my memory thus aroused confirmed every detail of his story of that first meeting, at which we presented a parcel of unknown contents confided to us for delivery to Joyce by Pound.

My memory is a feeble one, whether for scenes or for conversation, and I envy Lewis's ability to conjure up pictures from the past. While we were on the Loire I provided myself with a sketch book; and under Lewis's critical eye, and guided by his tuition, made a number of sketches, which, feeble as they were, served to fix some of the landscape and domestic architecture in my mind. But one scene, which I had no opportunity of sketching, remains very clear in my mind. At Saumur Lewis and I hired bicycles for the day, with the intention of riding over to Chinon. It was Lewis's bicycle that caused all the trouble. We had hardly got out of the town when the chain came off; efforts to get it in place proved fruitless, and I think we returned to the bicycle shop for repairs. On our second start we got further on the way, indeed rather too far; for we were speeding along at a great pace, well beyond the town, when suddenly Lewis's handlebars snapped off, and he was precipitated violently on to the road. He was rather badly shaken, one trouser was torn and his knee badly bruised. There was an inn not far off; I managed to lead

Lewis to a bench outside the door; and after some difficulty persuaded a rather unsympathetic hostess to provide brandy. Leaving Lewis on the bench, with his battered cycle beside him, I hastened back to Saumur and chartered an open barouche, which I led to the scene of the accident. The driver and I got Lewis into the barouche, hoisted his cycle behind, and returned to Saumur. As might be expected, a violent altercation with the bicycle-shop proprietor ensued: Lewis very angry at having been given so unreliable a machine, and the owner insistent that Lewis should pay for the damage to the bicycle. The dispute was terminated, in a hostile atmosphere, without any money changing hands.

The incident in itself is, up to this point, purely comic. But a good deal of dirt from the road had got into the wound on Lewis's [169] knee, and he was firmly persuaded that there might have been some contamination which would lead to lockjaw. So much did this thought prey upon his mind, that he saw a doctor in Paris as well as a local practitioner in Saumur; and I do not think that his fears were appeased until the lapse of time, with no symptoms, proved them to have been vain. This fear of tetanus, which surprised me, was, I came to think, indicative of Lewis's temperament. Many people have thought of Lewis as 'tough' and aggressive, with a tendency to persecution mania. He was rather, it now seems to me, a highly strung, nervous man, who was conscious of his own abilities, and sensitive to slight or neglect. To what extent, I still wonder, was the aggressiveness self-protective? His work was persistently ignored, or depreciated, throughout his life, by persons of influence in the world of art and letters who did not find him congenial. Those who dislike such a man call him 'neurotic'; but I do not think he was any more neurotic than other men of genius. He was independent, outspoken, and difficult. Temperament and circumstances combined to make him a great satirist: satire can be the defence of the sensitive.

I remember Lewis, at the time when I first knew him, and for some years thereafter, as incomparably witty and amusing in company, with the same gift of phrase in conversation as is found in his writings. Later I saw less of him; and on his return from Canada and America he was already a sick man, with the danger of blindness imminent. After the blindness had put an end to painting, and he was obliged to confine himself to writing, his conversation lost its brilliance, but its temper, I thought, was somewhat mellowed. (His essay describing the approach of blindness, printed in *The Listener* of May 10th, 1951, is a terrifying masterpiece of calm and detached self-observation.) Yet at no time do I remember his wit as having any savour of malice. His criticism was impartial. He had been a frank and merciless critic even of his friends, to whom indeed he devoted more attention than to his foes – witness his comments, in *Time and Western Man*, on Joyce and Pound, and elsewhere on myself.

It may be that the very variety of Lewis's achievement, and the fact that so much of it just falls short of perfection, obscure his excellence in each kind. But the point I should like to make is that some of his best work was done after blindness had overtaken him, when the difficulties of composition might [170] have been, for another man, insuperable. I think of *Rotting Hill*, *The Writer and the Absolute*; but chiefly of *Self Condemned* and *Monstre Gai*. His last published book, *The Red Priest*, is I think inferior: not, however, because of failing powers, but because of a mistaken choice of subject-matter (his Anglo-Catholic priest is quite preposterous). And in the best of his late work, *Self Condemned* and *Monstre Gai*, there is a seriousness absent from *Tarr*. *Tarr* is a not altogether satisfactory composite of satire and tragedy; in *The Revenge for Love* the tragedy and pathos begin to dominate and give greater significance to the satire; in *Self Condemned* Lewis wrote a novel of almost unbearable poignancy.

There is enough of Lewis's best work as painter, as draughtsman and as novelist to content us: what we miss most, I think, is Lewis the Gadfly and inspired pamphleteer. We have no critic of the contemporary world at once so fearless, so honest, so intelligent, and possessed of so brilliant a prose style.

I dined with Lewis and his wife in December: he was obviously a very sick man. I never saw him again. Early in January I went abroad with my wife. On our return I was very busy, and then succumbed to bronchitis. While I was confined to bed I had a message from Ashley Dukes to say that Lewis had been taken to hospital and was unconscious; and a few days later another message to say that Wyndham Lewis was dead.

[Tribute to John Davidson]

Saltire Review, 4. 11 (Summer 1957), 57. Gallup C613.

Quoted in Maurice Lindsay's 'John Davidson – The Man Forbid', 64–71, as 'a recorded tribute for radio' by T. S. Eliot. Repr. in part in the preface to Lindsay's *John Davidson: A Selection of his Poems* (1961), 8–9.

I read John Davidson's poems first – I can't remember whether it was towards the end of my school days or in my first year or two at Harvard University. But I read them at a time when I was reading the poets of the 'nineties, who were the only poets – most of them were dead, of course – who at that period of history seemed to have anything to offer me as a beginner. What I wanted, I think, from the poets of the 'nineties was what they did not have in common with the Pre-Raphaelites, but what was new and original in their work. And I remember three poets in particular, one of whom was John Davidson. One was Arthur Symons, some of his poems; another was Ernest Dowson, again one or two poems; and the third was Davidson, in his *Thirty Bob a Week*. From these men I got the idea that one could write poetry in English such as one would speak oneself. A colloquial idiom. There was a spoken rhythm in some of their poems. Now, I admire other poems of Davidson very much indeed. I think they should be read again and again; but it is *Thirty Bob a Week* which made a terrific impact on me. I think that poem one of the great poems of the end of the nineteenth century. And with some of those by the other men I've mentioned, I think it prepared me for initiation into the work of some of the French symbolists, such as Laforgue, whom I came across shortly after. But *Thirty Bob a Week* has a very important place in the development of my own poetic technique.

[Speech to the BBC Governors]

LM, 4. 9 (Sept. 1957), 54–6. Gallup C616.

I should like to remark first, that I had no hand in preparing the statement about Talks to be issued by the Society, but I have read it and am in cordial agreement with it. I think it would be a waste of time for me to attempt to go over quite the same ground which is there so thoroughly covered: I shall assume that the Governors present will give it their careful consideration.

What is at issue is, as the Sound Broadcasting Society affirms, the future, not only of the Third Programme but of the whole BBC. That is not for me to demonstrate: I am to speak to the point of *Talks*. I am not quite sure where 'Drama' ends and 'Talks' begin, for there are feature items which partake of the nature of both; there are also dialogues and discussions, sometimes on philosophical, scientific or religious topics, which disseminate ideas or stimulate thought by a quasi-dramatic appeal. But even the most abstract or abstruse subject is given dramatic aid by the voice of the author of the talk. I mention this point because I have heard the suggestion that a great deal of the more serious matter of talks is better read than heard and therefore should not be broadcast at all. Now, I know that not every author has the gift of putting his ideas across on the air. I have indeed heard Talks which I found well worth reading, but which were boring as Talks because the speaker had failed to learn – perhaps had not tried to learn – how to write for broadcast delivery – how to simplify his vocabulary and sentence structure; or had not learned how to read so as to give to his listeners the effect of spontaneity and keen interest. But, to mention one example, Sir Isaiah Berlin is a brilliant broadcaster who has something to give us when we hear him, over and above the value of his ideas in cold print, great as that is. So had the late Desmond McCarthy, in a lighter vein. There is an excitement of interest in listening to the voice of a good broadcaster which the printed word cannot arouse. Any argument against the broadcasting of talks on the ground [55] that they ought to be read, is indeed an argument against all lectures from a full script.

The argument that serious talks could be dispensed with because the listener would gain more by reading them, is similar to the argument that the Third Programme can be dispensed with because the Third Programme public is precisely that which does not need a third programme. It is, admittedly, a minority public: therefore it is assumed, perhaps, to be the public which knows its way about the world of music, art, drama, poetry, the highest class of fiction, and ideas. But why should this assumption be made? Has the BBC, the Third Programme, no educative function? I think that there must be many people in this country to whom the Third Programme is important because they are isolated and do not know how to inform themselves; because their education has been inadequate and they wish to supply its deficiencies; or because opportunities for hearing the best music, seeing the best drama, and listening to the highest authorities on various subjects are not otherwise available to them.

I was highly alarmed when I read Sir Alexander Cadogan's letter in *The Times* of May 3: I am always alarmed when I read a public statement, by anyone in authority, the sense of which I fail utterly to grasp. I should be glad, however, if keener intelligence than mine could be applied to the elucidation of Sir Alexander's use of the terms 'minority' and 'minority interest'. Sir Alexander concedes that the Third Programme provides service for 'a highly important minority'. Later, he tells us that Network Three, which is to occupy the two hours deducted from the Third Programme, will with these two hours 'cater for many other minority interests, including further education'. I am sorry, as are other people, that 'further education' is no longer to be conducted on the Light or the Home, but is to be segregated in a sort of isolation ward; but what are the other 'minority interests' which are to be recognised on the same footing as the 'minority interest' of the listeners to the Third Programme? I would plead with the Governors of the BBC to tell the public something more about Network Three and those 'minority interests' which have hitherto been mute and inglorious. I can only think of hobbies: stamp collecting, building model yachts, etc. I submit that the term 'minority' is used in Sir Alexander's letter in two different senses: one is the 'minority' which is the more serious-minded part of the nation, that which consists of those who wish to educate their taste or discipline their intellect – that is one kind of minority. The minorities which have specialised interests such as those I have mentioned, or even more serious interests, constitute a different kind of minority. There is no [56] parallel to be drawn between the interests of the two kinds.

I find myself hampered, in speaking to my point, by two impediments: the absence, so far, of any argument in *favour* of diminishing the Third Programme, and the mystery which appears to surround Network Three; I should like to be given the opportunity to examine a specimen programme. I should like to ask questions, but the Governors, I understand, are not here to answer questions. I should like, in closing, to protest against one word in Sir Alexander's letter: the fact that the Sound Broadcasting Society is not implicated in any object on which I raise emboldens me. He wrote: 'there was contained in the recent letter by fifteen distinguished signatories an innuendo that the competitive situation in television has shaken the Corporation's resolve to be much more than a provider of mass entertainment'. The word against which I protest is the word 'innuendo'. For this word itself is capable of containing an innuendo, and the innuendo which it may convey is *willing to wound and yet afraid to strike*. Speaking for myself, I should wish to disclaim any resemblance to Atticus. I find this explanation – which Sir Alexander deprecates – of the Corporation's new policy a plausible one; for I cannot think of any other reason for reasonable men adopting this policy. If this explanation is untrue, then I hope that the Corporation will not be content with a denial, but will provide a better explanation, and issue a statement to the public in simple language that persons like myself can understand, which will dispel the fear that the BBC is preparing a catastrophic abdication of its responsibilities, lowering the standards of culture at home and lowering the prestige of Britain abroad.

134 • 1957

On Poetry and Poets

On Poetry and Poets was publ. on 13 Sept. 1957. Gallup A69.

Contents: Preface; I. ON POETRY 'The Social Function of Poetry' (1945); 'The Music of Poetry' (1942); 'What is Minor Poetry' (1944); 'What is a Classic?' (1944); 'Poetry and Drama' (1951); 'The Three Voices of Poetry' (1953); 'The Frontiers of Criticism' (1956). II. ON POETS 'Virgil and the Christian World' (1951); 'Sir John Davies' (1926); 'Milton I' (1936); 'Milton II' (1947); 'Johnson as Critic and Poet' (1944), 'Byron' (1937); 'Goethe as the Sage' (1955); 'Rudyard Kipling' (1941); 'Yeats' (1940).]

Preface

OPAP, 11.

With one exception[1] all the essays included in this book are subsequent to those included in my *Selected Essays*. Most of them were written within the last sixteen years. My *Selected Essays* was a miscellaneous collection; this book, as the title indicates, is limited to essays concerned with poets or with poetry.

The present collection differs from my *Selected Essays* in another respect. Only one essay in that book – the paper on Charles Whibley – was written for delivery to an audience; the rest were all written for publication in periodicals. Of the sixteen essays which make up the present book, ten were originally addressed directly to audiences; an eleventh essay, that on Virgil, was a broadcast talk. In publishing these addresses now, I have not attempted to transform them into what they might have been if originally designed for the eye instead of the ear; nor have I made alterations beyond omitting the prefatory remarks to *Poetry and Drama*, and also some of those preambular remarks and incidental pleasantries which, having been intended to seduce the listener, might merely irritate the reader. Nor did it seem to me right, in preparing for publication in one volume papers which were written at different times and for various occasions, either to remove passages which repeat statements made elsewhere, or to try to suppress inconsistencies and reconcile contradictions. Each item is substantially the same as on the date of its delivery or first publication.

Some papers or addresses, qualified by date and subject matter for inclusion, I have rejected, on re-reading after some lapse of time, as not good enough. I wish that I could have found worthy of inclusion two lectures delivered at Edinburgh University [12] before the War, on *The*

---

1. The paper on Sir John Davies which appeared in *The Times Literary Supplement* in 1926; it was rescued from oblivion, and recommended for inclusion here by Mr John Hayward.

Development of Shakespeare's Verse; for what I was trying to say still seems to me worth saying. But the lectures struck me as badly written, and in need of thorough revision – a task to be deferred to some indefinite future. I regret the omission the less, however, as I had pillaged this set of lectures of one of its best passages – an analysis of the first scene of *Hamlet* – to incorporate in another address, *Poetry and Drama*. So, having already robbed one lecture for the benefit of another, I now append to *Poetry and Drama* another brief extract from the same Edinburgh lecture, a note on the balcony scene in *Romeo and Juliet*.

My acknowledgements appear in the form of footnotes to the several essays. They do not convey my grateful memories of hospitality in several cities – in Glasgow, Swansea, Minneapolis, Bangor (N. Wales) and Dublin. The debts of gratitude are too numerous to particularise; but as my essay on *Goethe as the Sage* was delivered on the occasion of my receiving the Hanseatic Goethe Prize, I should like to express my appreciation of the hospitality of the Stiftung F.V.S. (the foundation which awards the prize), the Rector of the University, and the Burgomaster and Senate of the City of Hamburg.

October 1956   T. S. E.

I. On Poetry

The Social Function of Poetry[1]

OPAP, 15–25.

The title of this essay is so likely to suggest different things to different people, that I may be excused for explaining first what I do not mean by it before going on to try to explain what I do mean. When we speak of the 'function' of anything we are likely to be thinking of what that thing *ought* to do rather than of what it does do or has done. That is an important distinction, because I do not intend to talk about what I think poetry *ought* to do. People who tell us what poetry ought to do, especially if they are poets themselves, usually have in mind the particular kind of poetry that they would like to write. It is always possible, of course, that poetry may have a different task in the future from what it has had in the past; but even if that is so, it is worth while to decide first what function it has had in the past, both at one time or another in one language or another, and universally. I could easily write about what I do with poetry

[1]. An address delivered at the British-Norwegian Institute in 1943 and subsequently developed for delivery to an audience in Paris in 1945. It later appeared in *The Adelphi*.

myself, or what I should like to do, and then try to persuade you that this is exactly what all good poets have tried to do, or ought to have done, in the past – only they have not succeeded completely, but perhaps that is not their fault. But it seems to me probable that if poetry – and I mean *all* great poetry – has had no social function in the past, it is not likely to have any in the future.

When I say *all* great poetry I mean to avoid another way in which I might treat the subject. One might take up the various kinds of poetry, one after another, and discuss the social function of each kind in turn without reaching the general question of what is the function of poetry as poetry. I want to distinguish between the general and particular functions, so that we shall know what we are not talking about. Poetry may have a deliberate, conscious [16] social purpose. In its more primitive forms this purpose is often quite clear. There are, for example, early runes and chants, some of which had very practical magical purposes – to avert the evil eye, to cure some disease, or to propitiate some demon. Poetry is early used in religious ritual, and when we sing a hymn we are still using poetry for a particular social purpose. The early forms of epic and saga may have transmitted what was held to be history before surviving for communal entertainment only; and before the use of written language a regular verse form must have been extremely helpful to the memory – and the memory of primitive bards, story-tellers and scholars must have been prodigious. In more advanced societies, such as that of ancient Greece, the recognised social functions of poetry are also very conspicuous. The Greek drama develops out of religious rites, and remains a formal public ceremony associated with traditional religious celebrations; the pindaric ode develops in relation to a particular social occasion. Certainly, these definite uses of poetry gave poetry a framework which made possible the attainment of perfection in particular kinds.

In more modern poetry some of these forms remain, such as that of the religious hymn which I have mentioned. The meaning of the term *didactic* poetry has undergone some change. *Didactic* may mean 'conveying information', or it may mean 'giving moral instruction', or it may mean something which comprehends both. Virgil's *Georgics*, for instance, are very beautiful poetry, and contain some very sound information about good farming. But it would seem impossible, at the present day, to write an up-to-date book about farming which should also be fine poetry: for one thing the subject itself has become much more complicated and scientific; and for another, it can be handled more readily in prose. Nor should we, as the Romans did, write astronomical and cosmological treatises in verse. The poem, the ostensible aim of which is to convey information, has been superseded by prose. Didactic poetry has gradually become limited to poetry of moral exhortation, or poetry which aims to *persuade* the reader to the author's point of view about something. It therefore includes a great deal of what can be called *satire*, though satire overlaps with burlesque and parody, the purpose of which is primarily to cause mirth. Some of Dryden's poems, in the seventeenth century, are satires in the sense that they aim to ridicule the objects against which they are directed, and also didactic in the aim to persuade [17] the reader to a particular political or religious point of view; and in doing this they also make use of the allegorical method of disguising reality as fiction: *The Hind and the Panther*, which aims to persuade the reader that right was on the side of the Church of Rome against the Church of England, is his most remarkable poem in this kind. In the nineteenth century a good deal of the poetry of Shelley is inspired by a zeal for social and political reforms.

As for *dramatic* poetry, that has a social function of a kind now peculiar to itself. For whereas most poetry to-day is written to be read in solitude, or to be read aloud in a small company, dramatic verse alone has as its function the making an immediate, collective impression upon a large number of people gathered together to look at an imaginary episode acted upon a stage. Dramatic poetry is different from any other, but as its special laws are those of the drama its function is merged into that of the drama in general, and I am not here concerned with the special social function of the drama.

As for the special function of philosophical poetry, that would involve an analysis and an historical account of some length. I have, I think, already mentioned enough kinds of poetry to make clear that the special function of each is related to some other function: of dramatic poetry to drama, of didactic poetry of information to the function of its subject-matter, of didactic poetry of philosophy or religion or politics or morals to the function of these subjects. We might consider the function of any of these kinds of poetry and still leave untouched the question of the function of *poetry*. For all these things can be dealt with in prose.

But before proceeding I want to dismiss one objection that may be raised. People sometimes are suspicious of any poetry that has a particular purpose: poetry in which the poet is advocating social, moral, political or religious views. And they are much more inclined to say that it isn't poetry when they dislike the particular views; just as other people often think that something is real poetry because it happens to express a point of view which they like. I should say that the question of whether the poet is using his poetry to advocate or attack a social attitude does not matter. Bad verse may have a transient vogue when the poet is reflecting a popular attitude of the moment; but real poetry survives not only a change of popular opinion but the complete extinction of interest in the issues with which the poet was passionately con-[18]cerned. Lucretius' poem remains a great poem, though his notions of physics and astronomy are discredited; Dryden's, though the political quarrels of the seventeenth century no longer concern us; just as a great poem of the past may still give great pleasure, though its subject-matter is one which we should now treat in prose.

Now if we are to find the essential social function of poetry we must look first at its more obvious functions, those which it must perform if it is to perform any. The first, I think, that we can be sure about is that poetry has to give pleasure. If you ask what kind of pleasure then I can only answer, the kind of pleasure that poetry gives: simply because any other answer would take us far afield into aesthetics, and the general question of the nature of art.

I suppose it will be agreed that every good poet, whether he be a great poet or not, has something to give us besides pleasure: for if it were only pleasure, the pleasure itself could not be of the highest kind. Beyond any specific intention which poetry may have, such as I have already instanced in the various kinds of poetry, there is always the communication of some new experience, or some fresh understanding of the familiar, or the expression of something we have experienced but have no words for, which enlarges our consciousness or refines our sensibility. But it is not with such individual benefit from poetry, any more than it is with the quality of individual pleasure, that this paper is concerned. We all understand, I think, both the kind of pleasure which poetry can give, and the kind of difference, beyond the pleasure, which it makes to our lives. Without producing these two effects it simply is not poetry. We may acknowledge this, but at the same time overlook something which it does for us collectively, as a society. And I mean that in the widest sense. For I think it is important that every people should have its own poetry, not simply for those who enjoy poetry – such people could always learn other languages and enjoy their poetry – but because it actually makes a difference to the society as a whole, and that means to people who do not enjoy poetry. I include even those who do not know the names of their own national poets. That is the real subject of this paper.

We observe that poetry differs from every other art in having a value for the people of the poet's race and language, which it can have for no other. It is true that even music and painting have a local and racial character: but certainly the difficulties of appreciation in these arts, for a foreigner, are much less. It is true on the other hand that prose writings have significance in their own lan-[19]guage which is lost in translation; but we all feel that we lose much less in reading a novel in translation than in reading a poem; and in a translation of some kinds of scientific work the loss may be virtually nil. That poetry is much more local than prose can be seen in the history of European languages. Through the Middle Ages to within a few hundred years ago Latin remained the language for philosophy, theology, and science. The impulse towards the literary use of the languages of the peoples began with poetry. And this appears perfectly natural when we realise that poetry has primarily to do with the expression of feeling and emotion; and that feeling and emotion are particular, whereas thought is general. It is easier to think in a foreign language than it is to feel in it. Therefore no art is more stubbornly national than poetry. A people may have its language taken away from it, suppressed, and another language compelled upon the schools; but unless you teach that people to *feel* in a new language, you have not eradicated the old one, and it will reappear in poetry, which is the vehicle of feeling. I have just said 'feel in a new language', and I mean something more than merely 'express their feelings in a new language'. A thought expressed in a different language may be practically the same thought, but a feeling or emotion expressed in a different language is not the same feeling or emotion. One of the reasons for learning at least one foreign language well is that we acquire a kind of supplementary personality; one of the reasons for not acquiring a new language *instead* of our own is that most of us do not want to become a different person. A superior language can seldom be exterminated except by the extermination of the people who speak it. When one language supersedes another it is usually because that language has advantages which commend it, and which offer not merely a difference but a wider and more refined range, not only for thinking but for feeling, than the more primitive language.

Emotion and feeling, then[,] are best expressed in the common language of the people – that is, in the language common to all classes: the structure, the rhythm, the sound, the idiom of a language, express the personality of the people which speaks it. When I say that it is poetry rather than prose that is concerned with the expression of emotion and feeling, I do not mean that poetry need have no intellectual content or meaning, or that great poetry does not contain more of such meaning than lesser poetry. But to develop this investigation would take me away from my immediate [20] purpose. I will take it as agreed that people find the most conscious expression of their deepest feelings in the poetry of their own language rather than in any other art or in the poetry of other languages. This does not mean, of course, that true poetry is limited to feelings which everyone can recognise and understand; we must not limit poetry to *popular* poetry. It is enough that in a homogenous people the feelings of the most refined and complex have something in common with those of the most crude and simple, which they have not in common with those of people of their own level speaking another language. And, when a civilisation is healthy, the great poet will have something to say to his fellow countrymen at every level of education.

We may say that the duty of the poet, as poet, is only indirectly to his people: his direct duty is to his *language*, first to preserve, and second to extend and improve. In expressing what other people feel he is also changing the feeling by making it more conscious; he is making people more aware of what they feel already, and therefore teaching them something about themselves. But he is not merely a more conscious person than the others; he is also individually different from other people, and from other poets too, and can make his readers share consciously in new feelings which they had not experienced before. That is the difference between the writer who is merely eccentric or mad and the genuine poet. The former may have feelings which are unique but which cannot be shared, and are therefore useless; the latter discovers new variations of sensibility which can be appropriated by others. And in expressing them he is developing and enriching the language which he speaks.

I have said quite enough about the impalpable differences of feeling between one people and another, differences which are affirmed in, and developed by, their different languages. But people do not only experience the world differently in different places, they experience it differently at different times. In fact, our sensibility is constantly changing, as the world about us changes: ours is not the same as that of the Chinese or Hindu, but also it is not the same as that of our ancestors several hundred years ago. It is not the same as that of our fathers; and finally, we ourselves are not quite the same persons that we were a year ago. This is obvious; but what is not so obvious is that this is the reason why we cannot afford to *stop* writing poetry. Most educated people take a certain pride in the great authors of their language, though [21] they may never read them, just as they are proud of any other distinction of their country: a few authors even become celebrated enough to be mentioned occasionally in political speeches. But most people do not realise that this is not enough; that unless they go on producing great authors, and especially great poets, their language will deteriorate, their culture will deteriorate and perhaps become absorbed in a stronger one.

One point is, of course, that if we have no living literature we shall become more and more alienated from the literature of the past; unless we keep up continuity, our literature of the past will become more and more remote from us until it is as strange to us as the literature of a foreign people. For our language goes on changing; our way of life changes, under the pressure of material changes in our environment in all sorts of ways; and unless we have those few men who combine an exceptional sensibility with an exceptional power over words, our own ability, not merely to express, but even to feel any but the crudest emotions, will degenerate.

It matters little whether a poet had a large audience in his own time. What matters is that there should always be at least a small audience for him in every generation. Yet what I have just said suggests that his importance is for his own time, or that dead poets cease to be of any use to us unless we have living poets as well. I would even press my first point and say that if a poet gets a large audience very quickly, that is a rather suspicious circumstance: for it leads us to fear that he is not really doing anything new, that he is only giving people what they are already used to, and therefore what they have already had from the poets of the previous generation. But that a poet should have the right, small audience in his own time *is* important. There should always be a small vanguard of people, appreciative of poetry, who are independent and somewhat in advance of their time or ready to assimilate novelty more quickly. The development of culture does not mean bringing everybody up to the front, which amounts to no more than making everyone keep step: it means the maintenance of such an *élite*, with the main, and more passive body of readers not lagging more than a generation or so behind. The changes and developments of sensibility which appear first in a few will work themselves into the language gradually, through their influence on other, and more readily popular authors; and by the time they have become well established, a new advance will be called for. It is, moreover, [22] through the living authors that the dead remain alive. A poet like Shakespeare has influenced the English language very deeply, not only by his influence on his immediate successors. For the greatest poets have aspects which do not come to light at once; and by exercising a direct influence on other poets centuries later, they continue to affect the living language. Indeed, if an English poet is to learn how to use words in our time, he must devote close study to those who have used them best in *their* time; to those who, in their own day, have made the language new.

So far I have only suggested the final point to which I think the influence of poetry may be said to extend; and that can be put best by the assertion that, in the long run, it makes a difference to the speech, to the sensibility, to the lives of all the members of a society, to all the members of the community, to the whole people, whether they read and enjoy poetry or not: even, in fact, whether they know the names of their greatest poets or not. The influence of poetry, at the furthest periphery, is of course very diffused, very indirect, and very difficult to prove. It is like following the course of a bird or an aeroplane in a clear sky: if you have seen it when it was quite near, and kept your eye on it as it flew farther and farther away, you can still see it at a great distance, a distance at which the eye of another person, to whom you try to point it out, will be unable to find it. So, if you follow the influence of poetry, through those readers who are most affected by it, to those people who never read at all, you will find it present everywhere. At least you will find it if the national culture is living and healthy, for in a healthy society there is a continuous reciprocal influence and interaction of each part upon the others. And this is what I mean by the social function of poetry in its largest sense: that it does, in proportion to its excellence and vigour, affect the speech and the sensibility of the whole nation.

You must not imagine me to be saying that the language which we speak is determined exclusively by our poets. The structure of culture is much more complex than that. Indeed it will equally be true that the quality of our poetry is dependent upon the way in which the people use their language: for a poet must take as his material his own language as it is actually spoken around him. If it is improving, he will profit; if it is deteriorating, he must make the best of it. Poetry can to some extent preserve, and even restore, the beauty of a language; it can and should also help it to develop, to be just as subtle and precise in the more complicated conditions [23] and for the changing purposes of modern life, as it was in and for a simpler age. But poetry, like every other single element in that mysterious social personality which we call our 'culture', must be dependent upon a great many circumstances which are beyond its control.

This leads me to a few after-thoughts of a more general nature. My emphasis to this point has been upon the national and local function of poetry; and this must be qualified. I do not wish to leave the impression that the function of poetry is to divide people from people, for I do not believe that the cultures of the several peoples of Europe can flourish in isolation from each other. There have been, no doubt, in the past, high civilisations producing great art, thought and literature, which have developed in isolation. Of that I cannot speak with assurance, for some of them may not have been so isolated as at first appears. But in the history of Europe this has not been so. Even Ancient Greece owed much to Egypt, and something to the Asiatic frontiers; and in the relations of the Greek states to each other, with their different dialects and different manners, we may find a reciprocal influence and stimulus analogous to that of the countries of Europe upon each other. But the history of European literature will not show that any has been independent of the others; rather that there has been a constant give and take, and that each has in turn, from time to time, been revitalised by stimulation from outside. A general *autarky* in culture simply will not work: the hope of perpetuating the culture of any country lies in communication with others. But if separation of cultures within the unity of Europe is a danger, so also would be a unification which led to uniformity. The variety is as essential as the unity. For instance, there is much to be said, for certain limited purposes, for a universal *lingua franca* such as Esperanto or Basic English. But supposing that all communication between nations was carried on in such an artificial language, how imperfect it would be! Or rather, it would be wholly adequate in some respects, and there would be a complete lack of communication in others. Poetry is a constant reminder of all the things that can only be said in one language, and are untranslatable. The *spiritual* communication between people and people cannot be carried on without the individuals who take the trouble to learn at least one foreign language as well as one can learn any language but one's own, and who consequently are able, to a greater or less degree, to *feel* in another language as well as in their own. And one's under-[24]standing of another people, in this way, needs to be supplemented by the understanding of those individuals among that people who have gone to the pains to learn one's own language.

Incidentally, the study of another people's poetry is peculiarly instructive. I have said that there are qualities of the poetry of every language, which only those to whom the language is native can understand. But there is another side to this too. I have sometimes found, in trying to read a language which I did not know very well, that I did not understand a piece of prose until I understood it according to the standards of the school teacher: that is, I had to be sure of the meaning of every word, grasp the grammar and syntax, and then I could think the passage out in English. But I have also found sometimes that a piece of poetry, which I could not translate, containing many words unfamiliar to me, and sentences which I could not construe, conveyed something immediate and vivid, which was unique, different from anything in English – something which I could not put into words and yet felt that I understood. And on learning that language better I found that this impression was not an illusion, not something which I imagined to be in the poetry, but something that was really there. So in poetry you can, now and then, penetrate into another country, so to speak, before your passport has been issued or your ticket taken.

The whole question of the relation of countries of different language but related culture, within the ambit of Europe, is therefore one into which we are led, perhaps unexpectedly, by inquiring into the social function of poetry. I certainly do not intend to pass from this point into purely political questions; but I could wish that those who are concerned with political questions would more often cross the frontier into these which I have been considering. For these give the spiritual aspect of problems the material aspect of which is the concern of politics. On my side of the line one is concerned with living things which have their own laws of growth, which are not always reasonable, but must just be accepted by the reason: things which cannot be neatly planned and put into order any more than the winds and rain and the seasons can be disciplined.

If, finally, I am right in believing that poetry has a 'social function' for the whole of the people of the poet's language, whether they are aware of his existence or not, it follows that it matters to each people of Europe that the others should continue to have [25] poetry. I cannot read Norwegian poetry, but if I were told that no more poetry was being written in the Norwegian language I should feel an alarm which would be much more than generous sympathy. I should regard it as a spot of malady which was likely to spread over the whole Continent; the beginning of a decline which would mean that people everywhere would cease to be able to express, and consequently be able to feel, the emotions of civilised beings. This of course might happen. Much has been said everywhere about the decline of religious belief; not so much notice has been taken of the decline of religious sensibility. The trouble of the modern age is not merely the inability to believe certain things about God and man which our forefathers believed, but the inability to *feel* towards God and man as they did. A belief in which you no longer believe is something which to some extent you can still understand; but when religious feeling disappears, the words in which men have struggled to express it become meaningless. It is true that religious feeling varies naturally from country to country, and from age to age, just as poetic feeling does; the feeling varies, even when the belief, the doctrine, remains the same. But this is a condition of human life, and what I am apprehensive of is death. It is equally possible that the feeling for poetry, and the feelings which are the material of poetry, may disappear everywhere: which might perhaps help to facilitate that unification of the world which some people consider desirable for its own sake.

The Music of Poetry[1]

OPAP, 26–38.

Originally publ. as *The Music of Poetry*, The third W. P. Ker Memorial Lecture delivered in the University of Glasgow 24th February 1942 by T. S. Eliot . . . (30 Aug. 1942): Gallup A41. Repr. in *Partisan Review*, 9. 6 (Nov./Dec. 1942), 450–65: Gallup C482.

In para. 11 'Thompson' has been corrected to 'Thomson', and in para. 12 'had been called for' has been corrected to 'has been called for'.

1 The poet, when he talks or writes about poetry, has peculiar qualifications and peculiar limitations: if we allow for the latter we can better appreciate the former – a caution which I recommend to poets themselves as well as to the readers of what they say about poetry. I can never re-read any of my own prose writings without acute embarrassment: I shirk the task, and consequently may not take account of all the assertions to which I have at one time or another committed myself; I may often repeat what I have said before, and I may often contradict myself. But I believe that the critical writings of poets, of which in the past there have been some very distinguished examples, owe a great deal of their interest to the fact that the poet, at the back of his mind, if not as his ostensible purpose, is always trying to defend the kind of poetry he is writing, or to formulate the kind that he wants to write. Especially when he is young, and actively engaged in battling for the kind of poetry which he practises, he sees the poetry of the past in relation to his own: and his gratitude to those dead poets from whom he has learned, as well as his indifference to those whose aims have been alien to his own, may be exaggerated. He is not so much a judge as an advocate. His knowledge even is likely to be partial: for his studies will have led him to concentrate on certain authors to the neglect of others. When he theorises about poetic creation, he is likely to be generalising one type of experience; when he ventures into aesthetics, he is likely to be less, rather than more competent than the philosopher; and he may do best merely to report, for the information of the philosopher, the data of his own introspection. What he writes about poetry, in short, must be assessed in relation to the poetry he writes. We must return to the scholar for ascertainment of facts, and to the more detached critic for impartial judgement. [27] The critic, certainly, should be something of a scholar, and the scholar something of a critic. Ker, whose attention was devoted mainly to the literature of the past, and to problems of historical relationship, must be put in the category of scholars; but he had in a high degree the sense of value, the good

---

1. The third W. P. Ker Memorial Lecture, delivered at Glasgow University in 1942, and published by Glasgow University Press in the same year.

taste, the understanding of critical canons and the ability to apply them, without which the scholar's contribution can be only indirect.

2 There is another, more particular respect in which the scholar's and the practitioner's acquaintance with versification differ. Here, perhaps, I should be prudent to speak only of myself. I have never been able to retain the names of feet and metres, or to pay the proper respect to the accepted rules of scansion. At school, I enjoyed very much reciting Homer or Virgil – in my own fashion. Perhaps I had some instinctive suspicion that nobody really knew how Greek ought to be pronounced, or what interweaving of Greek and native rhythms the Roman ear might appreciate in Virgil; perhaps I had only an instinct of protective laziness. But certainly, when it came to applying rules of scansion to English verse, with its very different stresses and variable syllabic values, I wanted to know why one line was good and another bad; and this, scansion could not tell me. The only way to learn to manipulate any kind of English verse seemed to be by assimilation and imitation, by becoming so engrossed in the work of a particular poet that one could produce a recognisable derivative. This is not to say that I consider the analytical study of metric, of the abstract forms which sound so extraordinarily different when handled by different poets, to be an utter waste of time. It is only that a study of anatomy will not teach you how to make a hen lay eggs. I do not recommend any other way of beginning the study of Greek and Latin verse than with the aid of those rules of scansion which were established by grammarians after most of the poetry had been written; but if we could revive those languages sufficiently to be able to speak and hear them as the authors did, we could regard the rules with indifference. We have to learn a dead language by an artificial method, and we have to approach its versification by an artificial method, and our methods of teaching have to be applied to pupils most of whom have only a moderate gift for language. Even in approaching the poetry of our own language, we may find the classification of metres, of lines with different numbers of syllables and stresses in different places, useful at a preliminary stage, as a simplified map of a complicated territory: [28] but it is only the study, not of poetry but of poems, that can train our ear. It is not from rules, or by cold-blooded imitation of style, that we learn to write: we learn by imitation indeed, but by a deeper imitation than is achieved by analysis of style. When we imitated Shelley, it was not so much from a desire to write as he did, as from an invasion of the adolescent self by Shelley, which made Shelley's way, for the time, the only way in which to write.

3 The practice of English versification has, no doubt, been affected by awareness of the rules of prosody: it is a matter for the historical scholar

to determine the influence of Latin upon the innovators Wyatt and Surrey. The great grammarian Otto Jespersen has maintained that the structure of English grammar has been misunderstood in our attempts to make it conform to the categories of Latin – as in the supposed 'subjunctive'. In the history of versification, the question whether poets have misunderstood the rhythms of the language in imitating foreign models does not arise: we must accept the practices of great poets of the past, because they are practices upon which our ear has been trained and must be trained. I believe that a number of foreign influences have gone to enrich the range and variety of English verse. Some classical scholars hold the view – this is a matter beyond my competence – that the native measure of Latin poetry was accentual rather than syllabic, that it was overlaid by the influence of a very different language – Greek – and that it reverted to something approximating to its earlier form, in poems such as the *Pervigilium Veneris* and the early Christian hymns. If so, I cannot help suspecting that to the cultivated audience of the age of Virgil, part of the pleasure in the poetry arose from the presence in it of two metrical schemes in a kind of counterpoint: even though the audience may not necessarily have been able to analyse the experience. Similarly, it may be possible that the beauty of some English poetry is due to the presence of more than one metrical structure in it. Deliberate attempts to devise English metres on Latin models are usually very frigid. Among the most successful are a few exercises by Campion, in his brief but too little read treatise on metrics; among the most eminent failures, in my opinion, are the experiments of Robert Bridges – I would give all his ingenious inventions for his earlier and more traditional lyrics. But when a poet has so thoroughly absorbed Latin poetry that its movement informs his verse without deliberate artifice – as with Milton and in some of Tennyson's poems – the [29] result can be among the great triumphs of English versification.

4 What I think we have, in English poetry, is a kind of amalgam of systems of divers sources (though I do not like to use the word 'system', for it has a suggestion of conscious invention rather than growth): an amalgam like the amalgam of races, and indeed partly due to racial origins. The rhythms of Anglo-Saxon, Celtic, Norman French, of Middle English and Scots, have all made their mark upon English poetry, together with the rhythms of Latin, and, at various periods, of French, Italian and Spanish. As with human beings in a composite race, different strains may be dominant in different individuals, even in members of the same family, so one or another element in the poetic compound may be more congenial to one or another poet or to one or another period. The kind

of poetry we get is determined, from time to time, by the influence of one or another contemporary literature in a foreign language; or by circumstances which make one period of our own past more sympathetic than another; or by the prevailing emphasis in education. But there is one law of nature more powerful than any of these varying currents, or influences from abroad or from the past: the law that poetry must not stray too far from the ordinary everyday language which we use and hear. Whether poetry is accentual or syllabic, rhymed or rhymeless, formal or free, it cannot afford to lose its contact with the changing language of common intercourse.

5 It may appear strange, that when I profess to be talking about the 'music' of poetry, I put such emphasis upon conversation. But I would remind you, first, that the music of poetry is not something which exists apart from the meaning. Otherwise, we could have poetry of great musical beauty which made no sense, and I have never come across such poetry. The apparent exceptions only show a difference of degree: there are poems in which we are moved by the music and take the sense for granted, just as there are poems in which we attend to the sense and are moved by the music without noticing it. Take an apparently extreme example – the nonsense verse of Edward Lear. His non-sense is not vacuity of sense: it is a parody of sense, and that is the sense of it. 'The Jumblies' is a poem of adventure, and of nostalgia for the romance of foreign voyage and exploration; 'The Yongy-Bongy Bo' and 'The Dong with a Luminous Nose' are poems of unrequited passion – 'blues' in fact. We enjoy the music, which is of a high order, and we enjoy the feeling of irresponsibility towards the [30] sense. Or take a poem of another type, the 'Blue Closet' of William Morris. It is a delightful poem, though I cannot explain what it means and I doubt whether the author could have explained it. It has an effect somewhat like that of a rune or charm, but runes and charms are very practical formulae designed to produce definite results, such as getting a cow out of a bog. But its obvious intention (and I think the author succeeds) is to produce the effect of a dream. It is not necessary, in order to enjoy the poem, to know what the dream means; but human beings have an unshakeable belief that dreams mean something: they used to believe – and many still believe – that dreams disclose the secrets of the future; the orthodox modern faith is that they reveal the secrets – or at least the more horrid secrets – of the past. It is a commonplace to observe that the meaning of a poem may wholly escape paraphrase. It is not quite so commonplace to observe that the meaning of a poem may be something larger than its author's conscious purpose, and something remote from its origins. One of the more obscure of modern

poets was the French writer Stéphane Mallarmé, of whom the French sometimes say that his language is so peculiar that it can be understood only by foreigners. The late Roger Fry, and his friend Charles Mauron, published an English translation with notes to unriddle the meanings: when I learn that a difficult sonnet was inspired by seeing a painting on the ceiling reflected on the polished top of a table, or by seeing the light reflected from the foam on a glass of beer, I can only say that this may be a correct embryology, but it is not the meaning. If we are moved by a poem, it has meant something, perhaps something important, to us; if we are not moved, then it is, as poetry, meaningless. We can be deeply stirred by hearing the recitation of a poem in a language of which we understood no word; but if we are then told that the poem is gibberish and has no meaning, we shall consider that we have been deluded – this was no poem, it was merely an imitation of instrumental music. If, as we are aware, only a part of the meaning can be conveyed by paraphrase, that is because the poet is occupied with frontiers of consciousness beyond which words fail, though meanings still exist. A poem may appear to mean very different things to different readers, and all of these meanings may be different from what the author thought he meant. For instance, the author may have been writing some peculiar personal experience, which he saw quite unrelated to anything outside; yet for the reader the poem may become the expression of a general [31] situation, as well as of some private experience of his own. The reader's interpretation may differ from the author's and be equally valid – it may even be better. There may be much more in a poem than the author was aware of. The different interpretations may all be partial formulations of one thing; the ambiguities may be due to the fact that the poem means more, not less, than ordinary speech can communicate.

6 So, while poetry attempts to convey something beyond what can be conveyed in prose rhythms, it remains, all the same, one person talking to another; and this is just as true if you sing it, for singing is another way of talking. The immediacy of poetry to conversation is not a matter on which we can lay down exact laws. Every revolution in poetry is apt to be, and sometimes to announce itself to be a return to common speech. That is the revolution which Wordsworth announced in his prefaces, and he was right: but the same revolution had been carried out a century before by Oldham, Waller, Denham and Dryden; and the same revolution was due again something over a century later. The followers of a revolution develop the new poetic idiom in one direction or another; they polish or perfect it; meanwhile the spoken language goes on changing, and the poetic idiom goes out of date. Perhaps we do not realise how natural

the speech of Dryden must have sounded to the most sensitive of his contemporaries. No poetry, of course, is ever exactly the same speech that the poet talks and hears: but it has to be in such a relation to the speech of his time that the listener or reader can say 'that is how I should talk if I could talk poetry'. This is the reason why the best contemporary poetry can give us a feeling of excitement and a sense of fulfilment different from any sentiment aroused by even very much greater poetry of a past age.

7 The music of poetry, then, must be a music latent in the common speech of its time. And that means also that it must be latent in the common speech of the poet's *place*. It would not be to my present purpose to inveigh against the ubiquity of standardised, or 'B.B.C.' English. If we all came to talk alike there would no longer be any point in our not writing alike: but until that time comes – and I hope it may be long postponed – it is the poet's business to use the speech which he finds about him, that with which he is most familiar. I shall always remember the impression of W. B. Yeats reading poetry aloud. To hear him read his own works was to be made to recognise how much the Irish way of [32] speech is needed to bring out the beauties of Irish poetry: to hear Yeats reading William Blake was an experience of a different kind, more astonishing than satisfying. Of course, we do not want the poet merely to reproduce exactly the conversational idiom of himself, his family, his friends and his particular district: but what he finds there is the material out of which he must make his poetry. He must, like the sculptor, be faithful to the material in which he works; it is out of sounds that he has heard that he must make his melody and harmony.

8 It would be a mistake, however, to assume that all poetry ought to be melodious, or that melody is more than one of the components of the music of words. Some poetry is meant to be sung; most poetry, in modern times, is meant to be spoken – and there are many other things to be spoken of besides the murmur of innumerable bees or the moan of doves in immemorial elms. Dissonance, even cacophony, has its place: just as, in a poem of any length, there must be transitions between passages of greater and less intensity, to give a rhythm of fluctuating emotion essential to the musical structure of the whole; and the passages of less intensity will be, in relation to the level on which the total poem operates, prosaic – so that, in the sense implied by that context, it may be said that no poet can write a poem of amplitude unless he is a master of the prosaic.[1]

---

1. This is the complementary doctrine to that of the 'touchstone' line or passage of Matthew Arnold: this test of the greatness of a poet is the way he writes his less intense, but structurally vital, matter.

9 What matters, in short, is the whole poem: and if the whole poem need not be, and often should not be, wholly melodious, it follows that a poem is not made only out of 'beautiful words'. I doubt whether, from the point of view of *sound* alone, any word is more or less beautiful than another – within its own language, for the question whether some languages are not more beautiful than others is quite another question. The ugly words are the words not fitted for the company in which they find themselves; there are words which are ugly because of rawness or because of antiquation; there are words which are ugly because of foreignness or ill-breeding (e.g. *television*): but I do not believe that any word well-established in its own language is either beautiful or ugly. The music of a word is, so to speak, at a point of intersection: it arises from its relation first to the words immediately preceding and following it, and indefinitely to the rest of its context; and from another [33] relation, that of its immediate meaning in that context to all the other meanings which it has had in other contexts, to its greater or less wealth of association. Not all words, obviously, are equally rich and well-connected: it is part of the business of the poet to dispose the richer among the poorer, at the right points, and we cannot afford to load a poem too heavily with the former – for it is only at certain moments that a word can be made to insinuate the whole history of a language and a civilisation. This is an 'allusiveness' which is not the fashion or eccentricity of a peculiar type of poetry; but an allusiveness which is in the nature of words, and which is equally the concern of every kind of poet. My purpose here is to insist that a 'musical poem' is a poem which has a musical pattern of sound and a musical pattern of the secondary meanings of the words which compose it, and that these two patterns are indissoluble and one. And if you object that it is only the pure sound, apart from the sense, to which the adjective 'musical' can be rightly applied, I can only reaffirm my previous assertion that the sound of a poem is as much an abstraction from the poem as is the sense.

10 The history of blank verse illustrates two interesting and related points: the dependence upon speech and the striking difference, in what is prosodically the same form, between dramatic blank verse and blank verse employed for epical, philosophical, meditative and idyllic purposes. The dependence of verse upon speech is much more direct in dramatic poetry than in any other. In most kinds of poetry, the necessity for its reminding us of contemporary speech is reduced by the latitude allowed for personal idiosyncrasy: a poem by Gerard Hopkins, for instance, may sound pretty remote from the way in which you and I express ourselves – or rather, from the way in which our fathers and grandfathers expressed themselves: but Hopkins does give the impression that his poetry has

the necessary fidelity to his way of thinking and talking to himself. But in dramatic verse the poet is speaking in one character after another, through the medium of a company of actors trained by a producer, and of different actors and different producers at different times: his idiom must be comprehensive of all the voices, but present at a deeper level than is necessary when the poet speaks only for himself. Some of Shakespeare's later verse is very elaborate and peculiar: but it remains the language, not of one person, but of a world of persons. It is based upon the speech of three hundred years ago, yet when we hear it well rendered we [34] can forget the distance of time – as is brought home to us most patently in one of those plays, of which *Hamlet* is the chief, which can be fittingly produced in modern dress. By the time of Otway dramatic blank verse has become artificial and at best reminiscent; and when we get to the verse plays by nineteenth-century poets, of which the greatest is probably *The Cenci*, it is difficult to preserve any illusion of reality. Nearly all the greater poets of the last century tried their hands at verse plays. These plays, which few people read more than once, are treated with respect as fine poetry; and their insipidity is usually attributed to the fact that the authors, though great poets, were amateurs in the theatre. But even if the poets had had greater natural gifts for the theatre, or had toiled to acquire the craft, their plays would have been just as ineffective, unless their theatrical talent and experience had shown them the necessity for a different kind of versification. It is not primarily lack of plot, or lack of action and suspense, or imperfect realisation of character, or lack of anything of what is called 'theatre', that makes these plays so lifeless: it is primarily that their rhythm of speech is something that we cannot associate with any human being except a poetry reciter.

11 Even under the powerful manipulation of Dryden dramatic blank verse shows a grave deterioration. There are splendid passages in *All for Love*: yet Dryden's characters talk more naturally at times in the heroic plays which he wrote in rhymed couplets, than they do in what would seem the more natural form of blank verse – though less naturally than do the characters of Corneille and Racine in French. The causes for the rise and decline of any form of art are always complex, and we can trace a number of contributory causes, while there seems to remain some deeper cause incapable of formulation: I should not care to advance any one reason why prose came to supersede verse in the theatre. But I feel sure that one reason why blank verse cannot be employed now in the drama is that so much non-dramatic poetry, and great non-dramatic poetry, has been written in it in the last three hundred years. Our minds are saturated in these non-dramatic works in what is formally the same kind of verse.

If we can imagine, as a flight of fancy, Milton coming before Shakespeare, Shakespeare would have had to discover quite a different medium from that which he used and perfected. Milton handled blank verse in a way which no one has ever approached or ever will approach: and in so doing did more than anyone or [35] anything else to make it impossible for the drama: though we may also believe that dramatic blank verse had exhausted its resources, and had no future in any event. Indeed, Milton almost made blank verse impossible for any purpose for a couple of generations. It was the precursors of Wordsworth – Thomson, Young, Cowper – who made the first efforts to rescue it from the degradation to which the eighteenth-century imitators of Milton had reduced it. There is much, and varied, fine blank verse in the nineteenth century: the nearest to colloquial speech is that of Browning – but, significantly, in his monologues rather than in his plays.

12 To make a generalisation like this is not to imply any judgement of the relative stature of poets. It merely calls attention to the profound difference between dramatic and all other kinds of verse: a difference in the music, which is a difference in the relation to the current spoken language. It leads to my next point: which is that the task of the poet will differ, not only according to his personal constitution, but according to the period in which he finds himself. At some periods, the task is to explore the musical possibilities of an established convention of the relation of the idiom of verse to that of speech; at other periods, the task is to catch up with the changes in colloquial speech, which are fundamentally changes in thought and sensibility. This cyclical movement also has a very great influence upon our critical judgement. At a time like ours, when a refreshment of poetic diction similar to that brought about by Wordsworth has been called for (whether it has been satisfactorily accomplished or not) we are inclined, in our judgements upon the past, to exaggerate the importance of the innovators at the expense of the developers.

13 I have said enough, I think, to make clear that I do not believe that the task of the poet is primarily and always to effect a revolution in language. It would not be desirable, even if it were possible, to live in a state of perpetual revolution: the craving for continual novelty of diction and metric is as unwholesome as an obstinate adherence to the idiom of our grandfathers. There are times for exploration and times for the development of the territory acquired. The poet who did most for the English language is Shakespeare: and he carried out, in one short lifetime, the task of two poets. I can only say here, briefly, that the development of Shakespeare's verse can be roughly divided into two periods. During

the first, he was slowly adapting his form to colloquial speech: so that by the [36] time he wrote *Antony and Cleopatra* he had devised a medium in which everything that any dramatic character might have to say, whether high or low, 'poetical' or 'prosaic', could be said with naturalness and beauty. Having got to this point, he began to elaborate. The first period – of the poet who began with *Venus and Adonis*, but who had already, in *Love's Labour's Lost*, begun to see what he had to do – is from artificiality to simplicity, from stiffness to suppleness. The later plays move from simplicity towards elaboration. The late Shakespeare is occupied with the other task of the poet – that of experimenting to see how elaborate, how complicated, the music could be made without losing touch with colloquial speech altogether, and without his characters ceasing to be human beings. This is the poet of *Cymbeline*, *The Winter's Tale*, *Pericles*, and *The Tempest*. Of those whose exploration took them in this one direction only, Milton is the greatest master. We may think that Milton, in exploring the orchestral music of language, sometimes ceases to talk a social idiom at all; we may think that Wordsworth, in attempting to recover the social idiom, sometimes oversteps the mark and becomes pedestrian: but it is often true that only by going too far can we find out how far we can go; though one has to be a very great poet to justify such perilous adventures.

14 So far, I have spoken only of versification and not of poetic structure; and it is time for a reminder that the music of verse is not a line by line matter, but a question of the whole poem. Only with this in mind can we approach the vexed question of formal pattern and free verse. In the plays of Shakespeare a musical design can be discovered in particular scenes, and in his more perfect plays as wholes. It is a music of imagery as well as sound: Mr Wilson Knight has shown in his examination of several of the plays, how much the use of recurrent imagery and dominant imagery, throughout one play, has to do with the total effect. A play of Shakespeare is a very complex musical structure; the more easily grasped structure is that of forms such as the sonnet, the formal ode, the ballade, the villanelle, rondeau or sestina. It is sometimes assumed that modern poetry has done away with forms like these. I have seen signs of a return to them; and indeed I believe that the tendency to return to set, and even elaborate patterns is permanent, as permanent as the need for a refrain or a chorus to a popular song. Some forms are more appropriate to some languages than to others, and any form may be more appro-[37]priate to some periods than to others. At one stage the stanza is a right and natural formalisation of speech into pattern. But the stanza – and the more elaborate it is, the more rules to be observed in its proper execution, the more surely this happens – tends to become fixed to the idiom of the moment of its perfection. It quickly loses contact with the changing colloquial speech, being possessed by the mental outlook of a past generation; it becomes discredited when employed solely by those writers who, having no impulse to form within them, have recourse to pouring their liquid sentiment into a ready-made mould in which they vainly hope that it will set. In a perfect sonnet, what you admire is not so much the author's skill in adapting himself to the pattern as the skill and power with which he makes the pattern comply with what he has to say. Without this fitness, which is contingent upon period as well as individual genius, the rest is at best virtuosity: and where the musical element is the only element, that also vanishes. Elaborate forms return: but there have to be periods during which they are laid aside.

15 As for 'free verse', I expressed my view twenty-five years ago by saying that no verse is free for the man who wants to do a good job. No one has better cause to know than I, that a great deal of bad prose has been written under the name of free verse; though whether its authors wrote bad prose or bad verse, or bad verse in one style or in another, seems to me a matter of indifference. But only a bad poet could welcome free verse as a liberation from form. It was a revolt against dead form, and a preparation for new form or for the renewal of the old; it was an insistence upon the inner unity which is unique to every poem, against the outer unity which is typical. The poem comes before the form, in the sense that a form grows out of the attempt of somebody to say something; just as a system of prosody is only a formulation of the identities in the rhythms of a succession of poets influenced by each other.

16 Forms have to be broken and remade: but I believe that any language, so long as it remains the same language, imposes its laws and restrictions and permits its own licence, dictates its own speech rhythms and sound patterns. And a language is always changing; its developments in vocabulary, in syntax, pronunciation and intonation – even, in the long run, its deterioration – must be accepted by the poet and made the best of. He in turn has the privilege of contributing to the development and maintaining the quality, the capacity of the language to express a wide range, [38] and subtle gradation, of feeling and emotion; his task is both to respond to change and make it conscious, and to battle against degradation below the standards which he has learnt from the past. The liberties that he may take are for the sake of order.

17 At what stage contemporary verse now finds itself, I must leave you to judge for yourselves. I suppose that it will be agreed that if the work of the last twenty years is worthy of being classified at all, it is as belonging to a

period of search for a proper modern colloquial idiom. We have still a good way to go in the invention of a verse medium for the theatre, a medium in which we shall be able to hear the speech of contemporary human beings, in which dramatic characters can express the purest poetry without highfalutin and in which they can convey the most commonplace message without absurdity. But when we reach a point at which the poetic idiom can be stabilised, then a period of musical elaboration can follow. I think that a poet may gain much from the study of music: how much technical knowledge of musical form is desirable I do not know, for I have not that technical knowledge myself. But I believe that the properties in which music concerns the poet most nearly, are the sense of rhythm and the sense of structure. I think that it might be possible for a poet to work too closely to musical analogies: the result might be an effect of artificiality; but I know that a poem, or a passage of a poem, may tend to realise itself first as a particular rhythm before it reaches expression in words, and that this rhythm may bring to birth the idea and the image; and I do not believe that this is an experience peculiar to myself. The use of recurrent themes is as natural to poetry as to music. There are possibilities for verse which bear some analogy to the development of a theme by different groups of instruments; there are possibilities of transitions in a poem comparable to the different movements of a symphony or a quartet; there are possibilities of contrapuntal arrangement of subject matter. It is in the concert room, rather than in the opera house, that the germ of a poem may be quickened. More than this I cannot say, but must leave the matter here to those who have had a musical education. But I would remind you again of the two tasks of poetry, the two directions in which language must at different times be worked: so that however far it may go in musical elaboration, we must expect a time to come when poetry will have again to be recalled to speech. The same problems arise, and always in new forms; and poetry has always before it, as F. S. Oliver said of politics, an 'endless adventure'.

Variants from 1942:

[3 opening paras. not in *OPAP*:] I debated with myself for some time before electing, for this occasion, to talk about the subject the nature of which is vaguely indicated by my title. Circumstance and conscience conspire, in these times, to direct our attention to matters of a wider scope and perhaps of more general interest. It seems almost impertinent, even as a man of letters, to concern oneself with a purely literary subject: I find myself to the opposite impertinence of talking about matters beyond my range. Even within my own field, there seem to be questions of greater urgency and relevance: the place of literature in culture, the place of culture itself in the society of the future, and all the educational problems implicit in the cultivation of letters. There are many problems of literature and the arts which lead towards political, sociological and religious speculation; and the question which is in every mind – the question of the condition of society after the war, of its limitations, necessities and possibilities, of its inevitable or of its desirable change – this insistent question might suggest, as a more suitable subject for a formal address on a distinguished foundation, some discussion of the place of literature in a changing world.

If I have resisted this temptation, it is for two reasons, the second of which supports the first. At a time when everyone is interested in the phenomena of change, and when any reflexions on these phenomena, whether analytical or constructive, may command attention if only by stimulating controversy and eliciting contradictory opinion, there is a particular need to consider, now and then, problems which only seem unimportant, because they are no more important now than they always have been and always will be. The prime interest of a practitioner of verse like myself must be the immediate future; not that we regard the future with either hope or fear, or are moved by either the aspiration or despair of excelling dead masters, but simply because our first concern is always the perennial question, what is to be done next? what direction is unexplored? what is there to be done immediately before us, which has not been done already, once and for all, as well as it can be done? When absorbed in these investigations, the poet is no more concerned with the social consequences than is the scientist in his laboratory – though without the context of the use to society, neither the writer nor the scientist could have the conviction which sustains him. This concern with the future requires a concern with the past also: for in order to know what there is to be done we need a pretty accurate knowledge of what has been done already; and this again leads to the examination of those principles and conditions which hold good always, to distinguish them from those which only held good for one or another group of our predecessors.

If my subject is justifiable by its permanence, it is also the more fitting on a foundation designed to perpetuate the memory of W. P. Ker. I never met Ker: it is a cause of regret to me that I missed the one opportunity offered me, which came only a few weeks before his last journey to Switzerland. But I found myself asking the question: what would Ker prefer me to talk about, supposing that he could appraise my abilities and my limitations? Not a subject requiring a parade of learning, certainly; for he would be the first to detect, and the most qualified to denounce, such an imposture. I can think of no other great scholar who would have been more certain to perceive both the difference and the relation between his area and mine, and to condemn any trespass from one area to the other. He was a great scholar who was also a great humanist, who was always aware that the end of scholarship is understanding, and that the end of understanding poetry is enjoyment, and that this enjoyment is gusto disciplined by taste. He was remarkable, not only for the comprehensiveness and accuracy of his knowledge of medieval and modern European literature, a knowledge with a firm basis of Latin and Greek, but for his ability to enjoy the most diverse species of it, and for the intuition, fortified by a great memory, which enabled him to detect analogies or relationships which few other men, even as learned as he, would have noticed. Each compartment of his learning was at the disposal of every other: a line of modern verse would take him back to Iceland or Provence, or the rhythm of a popular Spanish ballad could evoke half a dozen modern comparisons. I recently read again the posthumous volume of lectures collected under the title of *Form and Style in Poetry* – mostly lecture notes, but Ker always wrote, and must have spoken, well. It is a book from which the poet, as much as the scholar and the general reader, can profit. I think it is worth while, before proceeding to conjectures of my own as to what we mean, or ought to mean, or can mean, when we say that a poem is musical or unmusical, to emphasise the difference between the approach of the scholar and that of the writer of verse.

1 often contradict] equally well contradict
the poet, at the back of his mind] at the back of the poet's mind
3 the innovators] the great innovators
4 emphasis] emphases
5 horrid secrets] horrid ones
6 announce itself to be] announce itself as,
9 [Between 'find themselves;' and 'there are words which are ugly because of foreignness':] there are words which are ugly because of rawness or because of antiquation;
11 can trace] can always trace
12 [After 'the developers' and before para. 13:] : which might account for what will seem surely, to a later age, our undue adulation of Donne and depreciation of Milton.
13 [Between 'two poets.' and 'I can only say here':] I have attempted to indicate his dual achievement elsewhere:
The late Shakespeare] He
[Between 'other task of the poet' and 'that of experimenting':] – doing the work of two poets in one lifetime –

What Is Minor Poetry?[1]

OPAP, 39–52.

The original address delivered on 26 Sept. 1944 was publ. in *Welsh Review*, 3. 4 (Dec. 1944), [256]–67, and repr. in *SR*, 54. 1 (Jan./Mar. 1946), 1–18: Gallup C504.

The misprint 'known' for 'know' in para. 13 has been corrected.

1 I do not propose to offer, either at the beginning or at the end, a definition of 'minor poetry'. The danger of such a definition would be, that it might lead us to expect that we could settle, once for all, who are the 'major' and who are the 'minor' poets. Then, if we tried to make out two lists, one of major and one of minor poets in English literature, we should find that we agreed about a few poets for each list, that there

---

1. An address delivered before the Association of Bookmen of Swansea and West Wales at Swansea in September 1944. Subsequently published in *The Sewanee Review*.

would be more about whom we should differ, and that no two people would produce quite the same lists: and what then would be the use of our definition? What I think we can do, however, is to take notice of the fact that when we speak of a poet as 'minor', we mean different things at different times; we can make our minds a little clearer about what these different meanings are, and so avoid confusion and misunderstanding. We shall certainly go on meaning several different things by the term, so we must, as with many other words, make the best of it, and not attempt to squeeze everything into one definition. What I am concerned to dispel is any derogatory association connected with the term 'minor poetry', together with the suggestion that minor poetry is easier to read, or less worth while to read, than 'major poetry'. The question is simply, what kinds of minor poetry are there, and why should we read it?

2 The most direct approach, I think, is by considering the several kinds of anthologies of poetry: because one association of the term 'minor poetry' makes it mean 'the kind of poems that we only read in anthologies'. And, incidentally, I am glad of an opportunity to say something about the uses of anthologies, because, if we understand their uses, we can also be guarded against their dangers – for there are poetry-lovers who can be called anthology-addicts, and cannot read poetry in any other way. Of course the primary [40] value of anthologies, as of all poetry, lies in their being able to give pleasure: but, beyond this, they should serve several purposes.

3 One kind of anthology, which stands by itself, is that which consists of poems by young poets, those who have not yet published volumes, or whose books are not yet widely known. Such collections have a particular value for both poets and readers, whether they represent the work of one group of poets, with certain principles in common, or whether the only unity of the contents is that given by the fact all the poets belong to the same literary generation. For the young poet, it is generally desirable to have several stages of publicity, before he arrives at the point of having a small book all to himself. First, the periodicals: not the well-known ones with a national circulation – the only advantage, to the young poet, of appearing in these, is the possible guinea (or guineas) that he may receive on publication – but the small magazines, devoted to contemporary verse, and edited by young editors. These small magazines often appear to circulate only among contributors and would-be contributors; their condition is usually precarious, they appear at irregular intervals, and their existence is brief, yet their collective importance is out of all proportion to the obscurity in which they struggle. Apart from the value they may have in giving experience to future literary editors – and good literary

editors have an important part to play in a healthy literature – they give the poet the advantage of seeing his work in print, of comparing it with that of his equally obscure, or slightly better known contemporaries, and of receiving the attention and criticism of those who are most likely to be in sympathy with his style of writing. For a poet must make a place for himself among other poets, and within his own generation, before he appeals to either a larger or an older public. To those people who are interested in publishing poetry, these small magazines also provide a means of keeping an eye on the beginners, and watching their progress. Next, a small group of young writers, with certain affinities or regional sympathies between them, may produce a volume together. Such groups frequently bind themselves together by formulating a set of principles or rules, to which usually nobody adheres; in course of time the group disintegrates, the feebler members vanish, and the stronger ones develop more individual styles. But the group, and the group anthology, serve a useful purpose: young poets do not ordinarily get, and indeed are better without, much attention from the general public, but they [41] need the support and criticism of each other, and of a few other people. And, last, there are the more comprehensive anthologies of new verse, preferably compiled by more detached young editors: these have the value of giving the poetry reader a notion of what is going on, a chance of studying the changes in subject-matter and style, without going through a great number of periodicals or separate volumes; and they serve to direct his further attention to the progress of a few poets who may seem to him of promise. But even these collections do not reach the general reader, who as a rule will not have heard of any of the poets until they have produced several volumes and consequently found inclusion in other anthologies covering a greater span of time. When he looks at one of these books, he is apt to judge it by standards which should not be applied: to judge promise as if it were mature performance, and to judge the anthology, not by the few best poems in it, but at best by the average.

4 The anthologies which have the widest circulation are of course those which, like the *Oxford Book of English Verse*, cover the whole of English literature up to the last generation; or those specialising in a particular period of the past; or those which cover the history of some part of poetry in English; or those which are limited to 'modern' poetry of the last two or three generations, including such living poets as have established some reputation. These last, of course, serve some of the purpose of the purely contemporary anthology as well. But, confining ourselves for convenience to those anthologies which include only the work of dead poets, let us ask what purposes they may be expected to serve their readers.

5 No doubt *The Golden Treasury*, or the *Oxford Book*, has given many people their introduction to Milton, to Wordsworth, or to Shelley (not to Shakespeare: but we don't expect to make our acquaintance with a dramatic poet through anthologies). But I should not say that anyone who had read, and enjoyed, these poets, or half a dozen others, in an anthology, and yet had not the curiosity and appetite to tackle their complete works, and at least look to see what else they might like – I should not say that any such person was a real poetry lover. The value of anthologies in introducing us to the work of the greatest poets, is soon over; and we do not go on reading anthologies for the selections from these poets, though they have to be there. The anthology also helps us to find out, whether there are not some lesser poets of whose work we [42] should like to know more – poets who do not figure so conspicuously in any history of literature, who may not have influenced the course of literature, poets whose work is not necessary for any abstract scheme of literary education, but who may have a strong *personal* appeal to certain readers. Indeed, I should be inclined to doubt the genuineness of the love of poetry of any reader who did not have one or more of these personal affections for the work of some poet of no great historical importance: I should suspect that the person who only liked the poets whom the history books agree to be the most important, was probably no more than a conscientious student, bringing very little of himself to his appreciations. This poet may not be very important, you should say defiantly, but his work is good for *me*. It is largely a matter of chance, whether and how one makes the acquaintance of such poetry. In a family library there may be a book which somebody bought at the time it was published, because it was highly spoken of, and which nobody read. It was in this way that I came across, as a boy, a poem for which I have preserved a warm affection, *The Light of Asia*, by Sir Edwin Arnold. It is a long epic poem on the life of Gautama Buddha: I must have had a latent sympathy for the subject-matter, for I read it through with gusto, and more than once. I have never had the curiosity to find out anything about the author but to this day it seems to me a good poem, and when I meet anyone else who has read and liked it, I feel drawn to that person. Now you don't, as a rule, come across extracts from forgotten epics in anthologies: nevertheless it is always possible that in an anthology you will be struck by some piece by an obscure author, which leads to a close acquaintance with the work of some poet whom nobody else seems to enjoy, or to have read.

6 Just as the anthology can introduce us to poets who are not very important, but whose work is what one happens to like, so a good

anthology can give us useful knowledge of other poets who are very important, but whom we don't like. There are only two reasons for reading the whole of *The Faery Queen* or of Wordsworth's *Prelude*. One is that you enjoy reading it: and to enjoy either of the poems is a very good mark. But if you don't enjoy it, the only reason is that you are going to set up as a teacher of literature, or as a literary critic, and have *got* to know these poems. Yet Spenser and Wordsworth are both so important in the history of English literature because of all the other poetry which you [43] understand better because of knowing them, that everybody ought to know something about them. There are not many anthologies which give substantial extracts from long poems – there is a very useful one, compiled by Charles Williams, who had the peculiar qualification of really enjoying all sorts of long poems which nobody else reads. But even a good anthology composed of short pieces, can give one some knowledge, which is worth having, of those poets whom we do not enjoy. And just as everybody must have his personal tastes for some poetry which other people set no store by, so everybody, I suspect, has a blind spot towards the work of one or more poets who must be acknowledged to be great.

7 The next use of the anthology is one which can only be served if the compiler is not only very well read, but a man of very sensitive taste. There are many poets who have been generally dull, but who have occasional flashes. Most of us have not time to read through the works of competent and distinguished dull poets, specially those of another epoch, to find out the good bits for ourselves: and it would seldom be worth while even if we could afford the time. A century ago or more, every poetry lover devoured a new book by Tom Moore as soon as it came out: who to-day has read the whole even of *Lalla Rookh*? Southey was Poet Laureate, and accordingly wrote epics: I do know one person who had *Thalaba*, if not *The Curse of Kehama*, read to her as a child, and retains something of the same affection for it that I have for *The Light of Asia*. I wonder whether many people ever read *Gebir*; and yet Landor, the author of that dignified long poem, was a very able poet indeed. There are many long poems, however, which seem to have been very readable when they first appeared, but which no one now reads – though I suspect that nowadays, when prose fiction supplies the need that was filled, for most readers, by the verse romances of Scott and Byron and Moore, few people read a very long poem even when it is new from the press. So anthologies, and volumes of selections, are useful; because no one has time to read everything, and because there are poems only parts of which remain alive.

8 The anthology can have another use which, following the train of thought I have been pursuing, we might overlook. It lies in the interest of comparison, of being able to get, in a short space, a conspectus of the progress of poetry: and if there is much that we can only learn by reading one poet entire, there is much to learn by [44] passing from one poet to another. To pass to and fro between a border ballad, an Elizabethan lyric, a lyric poem by Blake or Shelley, and a monologue by Browning, is to be able to get emotional experiences, as well as subjects for reflection, which concentration of attention on one poet cannot give. Just as in a well arranged dinner, what one enjoys is not a number of dishes by themselves but the combination of good things, so there are pleasures of poetry to be taken in the same way; and several very different poems, by authors of different temperaments and different ages, when read together, may each bring out the peculiar savour of each other, each having something that the others lack. To enjoy this pleasure we need a good anthology, and we need also some practice in the use of it.

9 I shall now return to the subject from which you may think that I have strayed. Though it is not only the minor poets who are represented in anthologies, we may think of the minor poets as those whom we only read in anthologies. I had to enter a *caveat* against this, in asserting that for every poetry reader there ought to be some minor poets whom it is worth while for *him* to read entire. But beyond this point we find more than one type of minor poet. There are of course poets who have written just one, or only a very few, good poems: so that there seems no reason for anybody going beyond the anthology. Such, for example, was Arthur O'Shaughnessy, whose poem beginning 'We are the music makers' is in any anthology which includes late nineteenth-century verse. Such, for some readers but not for all, will be Ernest Dowson, or John Davidson. But the number of poets of whom we can say that it holds true for all readers that they left only one or two particular poems worth reading, is actually very small: the chances are that if a poet has written one good poem, there will be something in the rest of his work which will be worth reading, for at least a few persons. Leaving these few out of account, we find that we often think of the minor poet as the poet who has only written short poems. But we may at times also speak of Southey, and Landor, and a host of writers in the seventeenth and eighteenth centuries, as minor poets also, although they left poems of the most monumental size: and I think that nowadays few, at least among younger readers, would think of Donne as a minor poet, even if he had never written satires of epistles, or of Blake as a minor poet, even if he had never written his Prophetic Books. So we must count as minor poets, in one sense, some poets whose

reputation, such as it [45] is, rests upon very long poems; and as major poets, some who wrote only short ones.

10 It might seem at first simpler to refer to the minor poets of epics as *secondary*, or still more harshly as *failed great* poets. They have failed, certainly, in the sense that no one reads their long poems now: they are secondary, in the sense that we judge long poems according to very high standards. We don't feel that a long poem is worth the trouble unless it is, in its kind, as good as *The Faery Queen*, or *Paradise Lost*, or *The Prelude*, or *Don Juan*, or *Hyperion*, and the other long poems which are in the first rank. Yet we have found that some of these secondary poems are worth reading, for some people. We notice further that we cannot simply divide long poems into a small number of masterpieces and a large number of those we needn't bother about. In between such poems as those I have just mentioned, and an estimable minor work like *The Light of Asia*, there are all sorts of long poems of different kinds and of every degree of importance, so that we cannot draw any definite line between the major and the minor. What about Thomson's *Seasons* and Cowper's *Task*? – these are long poems which, if one's interest lies in other directions, one may be content to know only by extracts; but I would not admit that they are minor poems, or that any part, of either of them, is as good as the whole. What about Mrs Browning's *Aurora Leigh*, which I have never read, or that long poem by George Eliot of which I don't remember the name?

11 If we have difficulty in separating the writers of long poems into major and minor poets, we have no easier decision with writers of short poems. One very interesting case is George Herbert. We all know a few of his poems, which appear again and again in anthologies; but when we read through his collected poems, we are surprised to find how many of the poems strike us as just as good as those we have met with in anthologies. But *The Temple* is something more than a number of religious poems by one author: it was, as the title is meant to imply, a book constructed according to a plan; and as we get to know Herbert's poems better, we come to find that there is something we get from the whole book, which is more than a sum of its parts. What has at first the appearance of a succession of beautiful but separate lyrics, comes to reveal itself as a continued religious meditation with an intellectual framework; and the book as a whole discloses to us the Anglican devotional spirit of the first half of the seventeenth century. What is more, [46] we get to understand Herbert better, and feel rewarded for the trouble, if we know something about the English theological writers of his time; if we know something about the English mystical writers of the fourteenth century; and if we

know something of certain other poets his contemporaries – Donne, Vaughan and Traherne, and come to perceive something in common between them in their Welsh origin and background; and finally, we learn something about Herbert by comparing the typical Anglican devotion which he expresses, with the more continental, and Roman, religious feeling of his contemporary Richard Crashaw. So in the end, I, for one cannot admit that Herbert can be called a 'minor' poet; for it is not of a few favourite poems that I am reminded when I think of him, but of the whole work.

12 Now compare Herbert with two other poets, one a little senior to him, and one of the previous generation, but both very distinguished writers of lyrics. From the poems of Robert Herrick, also an Anglican parson, but a man of very different temperament, we also get the feeling of a unifying personality, and we get to know this personality better by reading all of his poems, and for having read all of his poems we enjoy still better the ones we like best. But first, there is no such continuous conscious *purpose* about Herrick's poems; he is more the purely natural and un-selfconscious man, writing his poems as the fancy seizes him; and second, the personality expressed in them is less unusual – in fact, it is its honest *ordinariness* which gives the charm. Relatively, we get much more of him from one poem than we do of Herbert from one poem: still, there is *something* more in the whole than in the parts. Next, consider Thomas Campion, the Elizabethan writer of songs. I should say that within his limits there was no more accomplished craftsman in the whole of English poetry than Campion. I admit that to understand his poems fully there are some things one should know: Campion was a musician, and he wrote his songs to be sung. We appreciate his poems better if we have some acquaintance with Tudor music and with the instruments for which it was written; we like them better if we like this music; and we want not merely to read them, but to hear some of them sung, and sung to Campion's own setting. But we do not so much need to know any of the things that, in the case of George Herbert, help us to understand him better and enjoy him more; we need not concern ourselves with what he thought, or with what books he had read, or with his racial background or his personality. All we need is the [47] Elizabethan setting. What we get, when we proceed from those of his poems which we read in anthologies, to read his entire collection, is a repeated pleasure, the enjoyment of new beauties and new technical variations, but no such total impression. We cannot say, with him, that the whole is more than the sum of its parts.

13 I do not say that even this test – which, in any case, everyone must apply for himself, with various results – of whether the whole is more than the sum of its parts, is in itself a satisfactory criterion for distinguishing between a major and a minor poet. Nothing is so simple as that: and although we do not feel, after reading Campion, that we know the man Campion, as we do feel after reading Herrick, yet on other grounds, because he is so much the more remarkable craftsman, I should myself rate Campion as a more important poet than Herrick, though very much below Herbert. All I have affirmed is, that a work which consists of a number of short poems, even of poems which, taken individually, may appear rather slight, may, if it has a unity of underlying pattern, be the equivalent of a first-rate long poem in establishing an author's claim to be a 'major' poet. That claim may, of course, be established by *one* long poem, and when that long poem is good enough, when it has within itself the proper unity and variety, we do not need to know, or if we know we do not need to value highly, the poet's other works. I should myself regard Samuel Johnson as a major poet by the single testimony of *The Vanity of Human Wishes*, and Goldsmith by the testimony of *The Deserted Village*.

14 We seem, so far, to have arrived at the tentative conclusion that, whatever a minor poet may be, a major poet is one the whole of whose work we ought to read, in order to fully appreciate any part of it: but we have somewhat qualified this extreme assertion already by admitting any poet who has written even one long poem which combines enough variety in unity. But there are certainly very few poets in English of whose work one can say that the whole ought to be read. Shakespeare, certainly, and Milton: and as to Milton one can point out that his several long poems, *Paradise Lost*, *Paradise Regained*, and *Samson Agonistes*, not only should each be read entire, for its own sake – we need to read them all, just as we need to read *all* of the plays of Shakespeare, in order fully to understand any one of them; and unless we read Shakespeare's sonnets as well, and the minor poems of Milton, there is something lacking to our appreciation of what we have read. But the poets for whom one can make such a claim are very [48] few. One can get on very well in life without having read all the later poems of Browning or Swinburne; I would not affirm confidently that one ought to read everything by Dryden or Pope; and it is certainly not for *me* to say that there is no part of *The Prelude* or *The Excursion* which will not bear skipping. Very few people want to give much time to the early long poems of Shelley, *The Revolt of Islam* and *Queen Mab*, though the notes to the latter poem are certainly worth reading. So that we shall have to say that a major poet is one of

whose work we have to read a great deal, but not always the whole. And besides asking the question, 'Of which poets is it worth while to read the whole work?' we must also ask the question, 'Of which poets is it worth *my* while to read the whole?' The first question implies that we should always be trying to improve our taste. The second implies that we must be sincere about what taste we have. So, on the one hand, it is no use diligently going through even Shakespeare or Milton from cover to cover, unless you come across something there which you like at once: it is only this immediate pleasure which can give you either the motive power to read the whole, or the prospect of any benefit when you have done so. And there may be, indeed, there should be – as I have already said – some poets who mean enough to *you* to make you read the whole of their work, though they may not have that value for most other people. And this kind of liking does not only pertain to a stage in your development of taste which you will outgrow, but may indicate also some affinity between yourself and a particular author which will last a lifetime: it may even be that you are peculiarly qualified to appreciate a poet whom very few other people are able to enjoy.

15 I should say then that there is a kind of orthodoxy about the relative greatness and importance of our poets, though there are very few reputations which remain completely constant from one generation to another. No poetic reputation ever remains in exactly the same place: it is a stock market in constant fluctuation. There are the very great names which only fluctuate, so to speak, within a narrow range of points: whether Milton is up to 104 to-day and down to 97 1/4 to-morrow, does not matter. There are other reputations like that of Donne, or Tennyson, which vary much more widely, so that one has to judge their value by an average taken over a long time; there are others again which are very steady a long way below par, and remain good investments at that price. And there are some poets who are good investments for [49] *some* people, though no prices are quoted for them on the market, and the stock may be unsaleable – I am afraid that the comparison with the stock exchange rather fades out at this point. But I should say that although there is an objective ideal of orthodox taste in poetry, no one reader can be, or should try to be, quite orthodox. There are certainly some poets, whom so many generations of people of intelligence, sensibility and wide reading have liked, that (if we like any poetry) it is worth our while to try to find out why these people have liked them, and whether we cannot enjoy them too. Of the smaller poets, there are certainly some about whom, after sampling, we can pretty safely take the usual opinion that they are quite adequately represented by two or three poems: for, as I have said, nobody has time

to find out everything for himself, and we must accept some things on the assurance of others.

16 The majority of smaller poets, however – of those who preserve any reputation at all – are poets of whom every reader of poetry should know something, but only a few of whom any one reader will come to know well. Some appeal to us because of a peculiar congeniality of personality; some because of their subject-matter, some because of a particular quality, of wit or pathos for example. When we talk about Poetry, with a capital P, we are apt to think only of the more intense emotion or the more magical phrase: nevertheless there are a great many casements in poetry which are not magic, and which do not open on the foam of perilous seas, but are perfectly good windows for all that. I think that George Crabbe was a very good poet, but you do not go to him for magic: if you like realistic accounts of village life in Suffolk a hundred and twenty years ago, in verse so well written that it convinces you that the same thing could not be said in prose, you will like Crabbe. Crabbe is a poet who has to be read in large chunks, if at all; so if you find him dull you must just glance and pass by. But it is worth while to know of his existence, in case he might be to your liking, and also because that will tell you something about the people who do like him.

17 The chief points which I have tried so far to make are, I think, these: The difference between major and minor poets has nothing to do with whether they wrote long poems, or only short poems – though the *very* greatest poets, who are few in number, have all had something to say which could only be said in a long poem. The important difference is whether a knowledge of the whole, or [50] at least a very large part, of a poet's work, makes one enjoy more, because it makes one understand better, any one of his poems. That implies a significant unity in his whole work. On can't put this increased understanding altogether into words: I could not say just why I think I understand and enjoy *Comus* better for having read *Paradise Lost*, or *Paradise Lost* better for having read *Samson Agonistes*, but I am convinced that this is so. I cannot always say why, through knowing a person in a number of different situations, and observing his behaviour in a variety of circumstances, I feel that I understand better his behaviour or demeanour on a particular occasion: but we do believe that person is a unity, however inconsistent his conduct, and that acquaintance with him over a span of time makes him more intelligible. Finally, I have qualified this objective discrimination between major and minor poets by referring it back to the particular reader. For no two readers, perhaps, will any great poet have quite the same significance, however in accord they may be as to his eminence: all the more likely, then, that to no two people will the pattern of English poetry be quite the same. So that of two equally competent readers, a particular poet may be to one of major importance and to the other of minor.

18 There is a final reflection to be made, when we come to consider contemporary poetry. We sometimes find critics confidently asserting, on their first acquaintance with the work of a new poet, that this is 'major' or 'minor' poetry. Ignoring the possibility that what the critic is praising or placing may not be poetry at all (for sometimes one can say, '*If* this was poetry, it would be major poetry – but it isn't') I don't think it is advisable to make up one's mind so quickly. The most that I should venture to commit myself to, about the work of any living poet when I met it for the first time, is whether this is *genuine* poetry or not. Has this poet something to say, a little different from what anyone has said before, and has he found, not only a different way of saying it, but *the* different way of saying it which expresses the difference in what he is saying? Even when I commit myself thus far, I know that I may be taking a speculative risk. I may be impressed by what he is *trying* to say, and overlook the fact that he hasn't found the new way of saying it; or the new idiom of speech which at first gives the impression that the author has something of his own to say, may turn out to be only a trick or mannerism which conceals a wholly conventional vision. For anyone who reads, like myself, a good many manu-[51]scripts, and manuscripts of writers no work by whom he may have seen before, the pitfalls are more dangerous still: for one lot of poems may be so much better than any of the others I have just been looking at, that I may mistake my momentary feeling of relief for an awareness of distinguished talent. Many people content themselves either with looking at anthologies – and even when they are struck by a poem, they may not realise the fact, or if they do, they may not notice the name of the author – or with waiting until it becomes apparent that some poet, after producing several volumes (and that in itself is some assurance) has been accepted by the reviewers (and it is not what the reviewers say in writing about a poet, but their references to that poet when writing about some other poet, that impresses us most).

19 The first method does not get us very far; the second is not very safe. For one thing, we are all apt to be somewhat on the defensive about our own epoch. We like to feel that our own epoch can produce great art – all the more so because we may have a lurking suspicion that it can't: and we feel somehow that if we could believe that we had a great poet, that would in some way reassure us and give us self-confidence. This is a pathetic wish, but it also disturbs critical judgement, for we may jump to the conclusion that somebody is a great poet who is not; or we may quite

unfairly depreciate a good poet because he isn't a great one. And with our contemporaries, we oughtn't to be so busy enquiring whether they are great or not; we ought to stick to the question: 'Are they *genuine?*' and leave the question whether they are great to the only tribunal which can decide: *time.*

20 In our own time there is, in fact, a considerable public for contemporary poetry: there is, perhaps, more curiosity, and more expectation, about contemporary poetry than there was a generation ago. There is the danger, on the one hand, of developing a reading public which will know nothing about any poet earlier than say Gerard Manley Hopkins, and which will not have the background necessary for critical appreciation. There is also the danger that people will wait to read a poet until his contemporary reputation is established; and the anxiety, for those of us who are in the business, that after another generation has established its poets, we who are still contemporary will no longer be read. The danger for the reader is double: that he will never get anything *quite* fresh, and that he will never return to read what always remains fresh.

[52] 21 There is therefore a proportion to be observed between our reading of old and modern poetry. I should not trust the taste of anyone who never read any contemporary poetry, and I should certainly not trust the taste of anyone who read nothing else. But even many people who read contemporary poetry miss the pleasure, and the profit, of finding something out for themselves. When you read *new* poetry, poetry by somebody whose name is not yet widely known, someone whom the reviewers have not yet passed, you are exercising, or should be exercising, your *own* taste. There is nothing else to go by. The problem is not, as it appears to many readers, that of trying to like something you don't, but of leaving your sensibility free to react naturally. I find this hard enough, myself: for when you are reading a new poet with the deliberate purpose of coming to a decision, that purpose may interfere and obscure your awareness of what you feel. It is hard to ask the two questions, 'Is it good, whether I like it or not?' and 'Do I like this?' at the same time: and I often find that the best test is when some phrase, or image, or a line out of a new poem, recurs to my mind unsummoned. I find, too, that it is useful for me to look at the new poems in the poetry magazines, and at the selections from new poets in the contemporary anthologies: because in reading these I am not bothered by the question, 'Ought I to see that these poems are published?' I think it is similar to my experience, that when I go to hear a new piece of music for the first time, or to see a new exhibition of pictures, I prefer to go alone. For if I am alone, there is nobody to whom I am obliged to express an immediate opinion. It isn't that I need time to

make up my mind: I need time in order to know what I really felt at the moment. And that feeling is not a judgement of greatness or importance: it is an awareness of *genuineness*. So, we are not really concerned, in reading a contemporary poet, with whether he is a 'major' or a 'minor' poet. But if we read one poem, and respond to it, we should want to read more by the same author; and when we have read enough, we ought to be able to answer the question, 'Is this merely more of the same thing?' – is it, in other words, merely the same, or different, without adding up to anything, or is there a relation between the poems which makes us see a little more in each of them? That is why, with the same reservation as about the work of dead poets, we must read not only separate poems, as we get them in anthologies, but the work of a poet.

Variants from 1944:

3   guinea (or guineas)] guinea
    principles or rules] principles, or rules
4   those which, like . . . cover] those, like . . . which cover
5   to have read] have read
6   whose work is] are
    the poems] these poems
    compiled by Charles] compiled a few years ago by Mr. Charles
    who had] who has
8   [Between 'dinner' and 'what one enjoys':] (if I may be pardoned for reminding you of such pleasures nowadays),
9   Shaughnessy] Shaughnessey
12 like this music;] like this music,
13 the sum of its parts] its parts
14 the whole work] the whole
    about what taste] towards what taste
    the whole of their work] the whole
16 nevertheless there are] but there are
    George Crabbe] the Revd. George Crabbe
17 That implies] That means
18 thus far] this far
19 our own epoch] our own age
    We like] We should like
    epoch] age
    time] Time
21 Is it good] Is this good
    unsummoned] afterwards unsummoned

What is a Classic?[1]

OPAP, 53–71.
Revised from *What is a Classic?*, an address delivered before the Virgil Society on 16 October 1944, publ. by Faber & Faber, 1945: Gallup A45.

1 The subject which I have taken is simply the question: 'What is a classic?' It is not a new question. There is, for instance, a famous essay by Ste Beuve with this title. The pertinence of asking this question, with Virgil particularly in mind, is obvious: whatever the definition we arrive at, it cannot be one which excludes Virgil – we may say confidently that it must be one which will expressly reckon with him. But before I go farther, I should like to dispose of certain prejudices and anticipate certain misunderstandings. I do not aim to supersede, or to outlaw, any use of the word 'classic' which precedent has made permissible. The word has, and will continue to have, several meanings in several contexts: I am concerned with one meaning in one context. In defining the term in this way, I do not bind myself, for the future, not to use the term in any of the other ways in which it has been used. If, for instance, I am discovered on some future occasion, in writing, in public speech, or in conversation, to be using the word 'classic' merely to mean a 'standard author' in any language – using it merely as an indication of the greatness, or of the permanence and importance of a writer in his own field, as when we speak of *The Fifth Form at St Dominic's* as a classic of schoolboy fiction, or *Handley Cross* as a classic of the hunting field – no one should expect one to apologise. And there is a very interesting book called *A Guide to the Classics*, which tells you how to pick the Derby winner. On other occasions, I permit myself to mean by 'the classics', either Latin and Greek literature *in toto*, or the greatest authors of those languages, as the context indicates. And, finally, I think that the account of the classic which I propose to give here should remove it from the area of the antithesis between 'classic' and 'romantic' – a pair of terms belonging to literary politics, and therefore arousing [54] winds of passion which I ask Aeolus, on this occasion, to contain in the bag.

2 This leads me to my next point. By the terms of the classic-romantic controversy, to call any work of art 'classical', implies either the highest praise or the most contemptuous abuse, according to the party to which one belongs. It implies certain particular merits or faults: either the perfection of form, or the absolute zero of frigidity. But I want to define one kind of art, and am not concerned that it is absolutely and in every

---

1. The Presidential Address to the Virgil Society in 1944. Published by Faber & Faber 1945.

respect *better* or *worse* than another kind. I shall enumerate certain qualities which I should expect the classic to display. But I do not say that, if a literature is to be a great literature, it must have any one author, or any one period, in which all these qualities are manifested. If, as I think, they are all to be found in Virgil, that is not to assert that he is the greatest poet who ever wrote – such an assertion about any poet seems to me meaningless – and it is certainly not to assert that Latin literature is greater than any other literature. We need not consider it as a defect of any literature, if no one author, or no one period, is completely classical; or if, as is true of English literature, the period which most nearly fills the classical definition is not the greatest. I think that those literatures, of which English is one of the most eminent, in which the classical qualities are scattered between various authors and several periods, may well be the richer. Every language has its own resources, and its own limitations. The conditions of a language, and the conditions of the history of the people who speak it, may put out of question the expectation of a classical period, or a classical author. That is not in itself any more a matter for regret than it is for gratulation. It did happen that the history of Rome was such, the character of the Latin language was such, that at a certain moment a uniquely classical poet was possible: though we must remember that it needed that particular poet, and a lifetime of labour on the part of that poet, to make the classic out of his material. And, of course, Virgil couldn't know that *that* was what he was doing. He was, if any poet ever was, acutely aware of what he was trying to do: the one thing he couldn't aim at, or know that he was doing, was to compose a classic: for it is only by hindsight, and in historical perspective, that a classic can be known as such.

3 If there is one word on which we can fix, which will suggest the maximum of what I mean by the term 'a classic', it is the word [55] *maturity*. I shall distinguish between the universal classic, like Virgil, and the classic which is only such in relation to the other literature in its own language, or according to the view of life of a particular period. A classic can only occur when a civilisation is mature; when a language and a literature are mature; and it must be the work of a mature mind. It is the importance of that civilisation and of that language, as well as the comprehensiveness of the mind of the individual poet, which gives the universality. To define *maturity* without assuming that the hearer already knows what it means, is almost impossible: let us say then, that if we are properly mature, as well as educated persons, we can recognise maturity in a civilisation and in a literature, as we do in the other human beings whom we encounter. To make the meaning of maturity really

apprehensible – indeed, even to make it acceptable – to the immature, is perhaps impossible. But if we are mature we either recognise maturity immediately, or come to know it on more intimate acquaintance. No reader of Shakespeare, for instance, can fail to recognise, increasingly as he himself grows up, the gradual ripening of Shakespeare's mind: even a less developed reader can perceive the rapid development of Elizabethan literature and drama as a whole, from early Tudor crudity to the plays of Shakespeare, and perceive a decline in the work of Shakespeare's successors. We can also observe, upon a little conversance, that the plays of Christopher Marlowe exhibit a greater maturity of mind and of style, than the plays which Shakespeare wrote at the same age: it is interesting to speculate whether, if Marlowe had lived as long as Shakespeare, his development would have continued at the same pace. I doubt it: for we observe some minds maturing earlier than others, and we observe that those which mature very early do not always develop very far. I raise this point as a reminder, first that the value of maturity depends upon the value of that which matures, and second, that we should know when we are concerned with the maturity of individual writers, and when with the relative maturity of literary periods. A writer who individually has a more mature mind, may belong to a less mature period than another, so that in that respect his work will be less mature. The maturity of a literature is the reflection of that of the society in which it is produced: an individual author – notably Shakespeare and Virgil – can do much to develop his language: but he cannot bring that language to maturity unless the work of his predecessors has prepared it for his final touch. A [56] mature literature, therefore, has a history behind it: a history, that is not merely a chronicle, an accumulation of manuscripts and writings of this kind and that, but an ordered though unconscious progress of a language to realise its own potentialities within its own limitations.

4 It is to be observed, that a society, and a literature, like an individual human being, do not necessarily mature equally and concurrently in every respect. The precocious child is often, in some obvious ways, childish for his age in comparison with ordinary children. Is there any one period of English literature to which we can point as being fully mature, comprehensively and in equilibrium? I do not think so: and, as I shall repeat later, I hope it is not so. We cannot say that any individual poet in English has in the course of his life become a more mature man than Shakespeare: we cannot even say that any poet has done so much, to make the English language capable of expressing the most subtle thought or the most refined shades of feeling. Yet we cannot but feel that a play like Congreve's *Way of the World* is in some way more mature than any play

of Shakespeare's: but only in this respect, that it reflects a more mature society – that is, it reflects a greater maturity of *manners*. The society for which Congreve wrote was, from our point of view, coarse and brutal enough: yet it is nearer to ours than the society of the Tudors: perhaps for that reason we judge it the more severely. Nevertheless, it was a society more polished and less provincial: its mind was shallower, its sensibility more restricted; it has lost some promise of maturity but realised another. So to maturity of *mind* we must add maturity of *manners*.

5 The progress towards maturity of language is, I think, more easily recognised and more readily acknowledged in the development of prose, than in that of poetry. In considering prose we are less distracted by individual differences in greatness, and more inclined to demand approximation towards a common standard, a common vocabulary and a common sentence structure: it is often, in fact, the prose which departs the farthest from these common standards, which is individual to the extreme, that we are apt to denominate 'poetic prose'. At a time when England had already accomplished miracles in poetry, her prose was relatively immature, developed sufficiently for certain purposes but not for others: at that same time, when the French language had given little promise of poetry as great as that in English, French prose was much more [57] mature than English prose. You have only to compare any Tudor writer with Montaigne – and Montaigne himself, as a stylist, is only a precursor, his style not ripe enough to fulfil the French requirements for the classic. Our prose was ready for some tasks before it could cope with others: a Malory could come long before a Hooker, a Hooker before a Hobbes, and a Hobbes before an Addison. Whatever difficulties we have in applying this standard to poetry, it is possible to see that the development of a classic prose is the development towards a *common style*. By this I do not mean that the best writers are indistinguishable from each other. The essential and characteristic differences remain: it is not that the differences are less, but that they are more subtle and refined. To a sensitive palate the difference between the prose of Addison and that of Swift will be as marked as the difference between two vintage wines to a connoisseur. What we find, in a period of classic prose, is not a mere common convention of writing, like the common style of newspaper leader writers, but a community of taste. The age which precedes a classic age, may exhibit both eccentricity and monotony: monotony because the resources of the language have not yet been explored, and eccentricity because there is yet no generally accepted standard – if, indeed, that can be called eccentric where there is no centre. Its writing may be at the same time pedantic and licentious. The age following a classic age, may also

exhibit eccentricity and monotony: monotony because the resources of the language have, for the time at least, been exhausted, and eccentricity because originality comes to be more valued than correctness. But the age in which we find a common style, will be an age when society has achieved a moment of order and stability, of equilibrium and harmony; as the age which manifests the greatest extremes of individual style will be an age of immaturity or an age of senility.

6 Maturity of language may naturally be expected to accompany maturity of mind and manners. We may expect the language to approach maturity at the moment when men have a critical sense of the past, a confidence in the present, and no conscious doubt of the future. In literature, this means that the poet is aware of his predecessors, and that we are aware of the predecessors behind his work, as we may be aware of ancestral traits in a person who is at the same time individual and unique. The predecessors should be themselves great and honoured: but their accomplishment must be such as to suggest still undeveloped resources of the language, and [58] not such as to oppress the younger writers with the fear that everything that can be done has been done, in their language. The poet, certainly, in a mature age, may still obtain stimulus from the hope of doing something that his predecessors have not done; he may even be in revolt against them, as a promising adolescent may revolt against the beliefs, the habits and the manners of his parents; but, in retrospect, we can see that he is also the continuer of their traditions, that he preserves essential family characteristics, and that his difference of behaviour is a difference in the circumstances of another age. And, on the other hand, just as we sometimes observe men whose lives are overshadowed by the fame of a father or grandfather, men of whom any achievement of which they are capable appears comparatively insignificant, so a late age of poetry may be consciously impotent to compete with its distinguished ancestry. We meet poets of this kind at the end of any age, poets with a sense of the past only, or alternatively, poets whose hope of the future is founded upon the attempt to renounce the past. The persistence of literary creativeness in any people, accordingly, consists in the maintenance of an unconscious balance between tradition in the larger sense – the collective personality, so to speak, realised in the literature of the past – and the originality of the living generation.

7 We cannot call the literature of the Elizabethan period, great as it is, wholly mature: we cannot call it classical. No close parallel can be drawn between the development of Greek and Latin literature, for Latin had Greek behind it; still less can we draw a parallel between these and any modern literature, for modern literatures have both Latin and Greek

behind them. In the Renaissance there is an early semblance of maturity, which is borrowed from antiquity. We are aware of approaching nearer to maturity with Milton. Milton was in a better position to have a critical sense of the past – of a past in English literature – than his great predecessors. To read Milton is to be confirmed in respect for the genius of Spenser, and in gratitude to Spenser for having contributed towards making the verse of Milton possible. Yet the style of Milton is not a classic style: it is a style of a language still in formation, the style of a writer whose *masters* were not English, but Latin and to a less degree Greek. This, I think, is only saying what Johnson and in turn Landor said, when they complained of Milton's style not being quite English. Let us qualify this judgement by saying immediately that Milton did much to develop the language. One [59] of the signs of approach towards a classic style is a development towards greater complexity of sentence and period structure. Such development is apparent in the single work of Shakespeare, when we trace his style from the early to the late plays: we can even say that in his late plays he goes as far in the direction of complexity as is possible within the limits of dramatic verse, which are narrower than those of other kinds. But complexity for its own sake is not a proper goal: its purpose must be, first, the precise expression of finer shades of feeling and thought; second, the introduction of greater refinement and variety of music. When an author appears, in his love of the elaborate structure, to have lost the ability to say anything simply; when his addiction to pattern becomes such that he says things elaborately which should properly be said simply, and thus limits his range of expression, the process of complexity ceases to be quite healthy, and the writer is losing touch with the spoken language. Nevertheless, as verse develops, in the hands of one poet after another, it tends from monotony to variety, from simplicity to complexity; as it declines, it tends towards monotony again, though it may perpetuate the formal structure to which genius gave life and meaning. You will judge for yourselves how far this generalisation is applicable to the predecessors and followers of Virgil: we can all see this secondary monotony in the eighteenth-century imitators of Milton – who himself is never monotonous. There comes a time when a new simplicity, even a relative crudity, may be the only alternative.

8 You will have anticipated the conclusion towards which I have been drawing: that those qualities of the classic which I have so far mentioned – maturity of mind, maturity of manners, maturity of language and perfection of the common style – are most nearly to be illustrated, in English literature, in the eighteenth century; and, in poetry, most in the poetry of Pope. If that were all I had to say on the matter, it would

certainly not be new, and it would not be worth saying. That would be merely proposing a choice between two errors at which men have arrived before: one, that the eighteenth century is the finest period of English literature; and the other, that the classical idea should be wholly discredited. My own opinion is, that we have no classic age, and no classic poet, in English; that when we see why this is so, we have not the slightest reason for regret; but that, nevertheless, we must maintain the classic ideal before our eyes. Because we must main-[60]tain it, and because the English genius of language has had other things to do than to realise it, we cannot afford either to reject or to overrate the age of Pope; we cannot see English literature as a whole, or aim rightly in the future, without a critical appreciation of the degree to which the classical qualities are exemplified in the work of Pope: which means that unless we are able to enjoy the work of Pope, we cannot arrive at a full understanding of English poetry.

9 It is fairly obvious that the realisation of classical qualities by Pope was obtained at a high price – to the exclusion of some greater potentialities of English verse. Now, to some extent, the sacrifice of some potentialities in order to realise others, is a condition of artistic creation, as it is a condition of life in general. In life the man who refuses to sacrifice anything, to gain anything else, ends in mediocrity or failure; though, on the other hand, there is the specialist who has sacrificed too much for too little, or who has been born too completely the specialist to have had anything to sacrifice. But in the English eighteenth century, we have reason for feeling that too much was excluded. There was the mature mind: but it was a narrow one. English society and English letters were not provincial, in the sense that they were not isolated from, and not lingering behind, the best European society and letters. Yet the age itself was, in a manner of speaking, a provincial age. When one thinks of a Shakespeare, a Jeremy Taylor, a Milton, in England – of a Racine, a Molière, a Pascal, in France – in the seventeenth century, one is inclined to say that the eighteenth century had perfected its formal garden, only by restricting the area under cultivation. We feel that if the classic is really a worthy ideal, it must be capable of exhibiting an amplitude, a catholicity, to which the eighteenth century cannot lay claim; qualities which are present in some great authors, like Chaucer, who cannot be regarded in my sense as classics of English literature; and which are fully present in the medieval mind of Dante. For in the *Divine Comedy*, if anywhere, we find the classic in a modern European language. In the eighteenth century, we are oppressed by the limited range of sensibility, and especially in the scale of religious feeling. It is not that, in England

at least, the poetry is not Christian. It is not even that the poets were not devout Christians; for a pattern of orthodoxy of principle, and sincere piety of feeling, you may look long before you find a poet more genuine than Samuel Johnson. Yet there are evidences of a deeper [61] religious sensibility in the poetry of Shakespeare, whose belief and practice can be only a matter of conjecture. And this restriction of religious sensibility itself produces a kind of provinciality (though we must add that in this sense the nineteenth century was more provincial still): the provinciality which indicates the disintegration of Christendom, the decay of a common belief and a common culture. It would seem then, that our eighteenth century, in spite of its classical achievement – an achievement, I believe, which still has great importance as an example for the future – was lacking some condition which makes the creation of a true classic possible. What this condition is, we must return to Virgil to discover.

10 I should like first to rehearse the characteristics which I have already attributed to the classic, with special application to Virgil, to his language, his civilisation, and the particular moment in the history of that language and civilisation at which he arrived. Maturity of mind: this needs history, and the consciousness of history. Consciousness of history cannot be fully awake, except where there is other history than the history of the poet's own people: we need this in order to see our own place in history. There must be the knowledge of the history of at least one other highly civilised people, and of a people whose civilisation is sufficiently cognate to have influenced and entered into our own. This is a consciousness which the Romans had, and which the Greeks, however much more highly we may estimate their achievement – and indeed, we may respect it all the more on this account – could not possess. It was a consciousness, certainly, which Virgil himself did much to develop. From the beginning, Virgil, like his contemporaries and immediate predecessors, was constantly adapting and using the discoveries, traditions and inventions of Greek poetry: to make use of a foreign literature in this way marks a further stage of civilisation beyond making use only of the earlier stages of one's own – though I think we can say that no poet has ever shown a finer sense of proportion than Virgil, in the uses he made of Greek and of earlier Latin poetry. It is this development of one literature, or one civilisation, in relation to another, which gives a peculiar significance to the subject of Virgil's epic. In Homer, the conflict between the Greeks and the Trojans is hardly larger in scope than a feud between one Greek city-state and a coalition of other city-states: behind the story of Aeneas is the consciousness of a more radical distinction,

a distinction, which is [62] at the same time a statement of *relatedness*, between two great cultures, and, finally, of their reconciliation under an all-embracing destiny.

11 Virgil's maturity of mind, and the maturity of his age, are exhibited in this awareness of history. With maturity of mind I have associated maturity of manners and absence of provinciality. I suppose that, to a modern European suddenly precipitated into the past, the social behaviour of the Romans and the Athenians would seem indifferently coarse, barbarous and offensive. But if the poet can portray something superior to contemporary practice, it is not in the way of anticipating some later, and quite different code of behaviour, but by an insight into what the conduct of his own people at his own time might be, at its best. House parties of the wealthy, in Edwardian England, were not exactly what we read of in the pages of Henry James: but Mr James's society was an idealisation, of a kind, of *that* society, and not an anticipation of any other. I think that we are conscious, in Virgil more than in any other Latin poet – for Catullus and Propertius seem ruffians, and Horace somewhat plebeian, by comparison – of a refinement of manners springing from a delicate sensibility, and particularly in that test of manners, private and public conduct between the sexes. It is not for me, in a gathering of people, all of whom may be better scholars than I, to review the story of Aeneas and Dido. But I have always thought the meeting of Aeneas with the shade of Dido, in Book VI, not only one of the most poignant, but one of the most civilised passages in poetry. It is complex in meaning and economical in expression, for it not only tells us about the attitude of Dido – still more important is what it tells us about the attitude of Aeneas. Dido's behaviour appears almost as a projection of Aeneas's own conscience: this, we feel, is the way in which Aeneas's conscience would *expect* Dido to behave to him. The point, it seems to me, is not that Dido is unforgiving – though it is important that, instead of railing at him, she merely snubs him – perhaps the most telling snub in all poetry: what matters most is, that Aeneas does not forgive himself – and this, significantly, in spite of the fact of which he is well aware, that all that he has done has been in compliance with destiny, or in consequence of the machinations of gods who are themselves, we feel, only instruments of a greater inscrutable power. Here, what I chose as an instance of civilised manners, proceeds to testify to civilised consciousness and conscience: but all of the levels at which we may [63] consider a particular episode, belong to one whole. It will be observed, finally, that the behaviour of Virgil's characters (I might except Turnus, the man without a destiny) never appears to be according to some purely local or tribal code of

manners: it is in its time, both Roman and European. Virgil certainly, on the plane of manners, is not provincial.

12 To attempt to demonstrate the maturity of language and style of Virgil is, for the present occasion, a superfluous task: many of you could perform it better than I, and I think that we should all be in accord. But it is worth repeating that Virgil's style would not have been possible without a literature behind him, and without his having a very intimate knowledge of this literature: so that he was, in a sense, re-writing Latin poetry – as when he borrows a phrase or a device from a predecessor and improves upon it. He was a learned author, all of whose learning was relevant to his task; and he had, for his use, just enough literature behind him and not too much. As for maturity of style, I do not think that any poet has ever developed a greater command of the complex structure, both of sense and sound, without losing the resource of direct, brief and startling simplicity when the occasion required it. On this I need not dilate: but I think it is worth while to say a word more about the *common style*, because this is something which we cannot perfectly illustrate from English poetry, and to which we are apt to pay less than enough deference. In modern European literature, the closest approximations to the ideal of a common style, are probably to be found in Dante and Racine; the nearest we have to it in English poetry is Pope, and Pope's is a common style which, in comparison, is of a very narrow range. A common style is one which makes us exclaim, not 'this is a man of genius using the language' but 'this realises the genius of the language'. We do not say this when we read Pope, because we are too conscious of all the resources of the English speech upon which Pope does not draw; we can at most say 'this realises the genius of the English language of a particular epoch'. We do not say this when we read Shakespeare or Milton, because we are always conscious of the greatness of the man, and of the miracles that *he* is performing with the language; we come nearer perhaps with Chaucer – but that Chaucer is using a different, from our point of view a cruder speech. And Shakespeare and Milton, as later history shows, left open many possibilities of other uses of English in poetry: whereas, after Virgil, it is truer to say that no great develop-[64]ment was possible, until the Latin language became something different.

13 At this point I should like to return to a question which I have already suggested: the question whether the achievement of a classic, in the sense in which I have been using the term throughout, is, for the people and the language of its origin, altogether an unmixed blessing – even though it is unquestionably a ground for pride. To have this question raised in one's mind, it is almost enough simply to have contemplated Latin poetry

after Virgil, to have considered the extent to which later poets lived and worked under the shadow of his greatness: so that we praise or dispraise them, according to standards which he set – admiring them, sometimes, for discovering some variation which was new, or even for merely rearranging patterns of words so as to give a pleasing faint reminder of the remote original. But English poetry, and French poetry also, may be considered fortunate in this: that the greatest poets have exhausted only particular areas. We cannot say that, since the age of Shakespeare, and respectively since the time of Racine, there has been any really first-rate poetic drama in England or in France; since Milton, we have had no great epic poem, though there have been great long poems. It is true that every supreme poet, classic or not, tends to exhaust the ground he cultivates, so that it must, after yielding a diminishing crop, finally be left in fallow for some generations.

14 Here it may be objected that the effect on a literature which I am imputing to the classic, results not from the classic character of that work, but simply from its greatness: for I have denied to Shakespeare and to Milton the title of classics, in the sense in which I am employing the term throughout, and yet have admitted that no supremely great poetry of the same kind has been written since. That every great work of poetry tends to make impossible the production of equally great works of the same kind is indisputable. The reason may be stated partly in terms of conscious purpose: no first-rate poet would attempt to do again, what has already been done as well as it can be done in his language. It is only after the language – its cadence, still more than vocabulary and syntax – has, with time and social change, sufficiently altered, that another dramatic poet as great as Shakespeare, or another epic poet as great as Milton, can become possible. Not only every great poet, but every genuine, though lesser poet, fulfils once for all some possibility of the language, and so leaves one possibility [65] less for his successors. The vein that he has exhausted may be a very small one; or may represent some major form of poetry, the epic or dramatic. But what the great poet has exhausted is merely one form, and not the whole language. When the great poet is also a great classic poet, he exhausts, not a form only, but the language of his time; and the language of his time, as used by him, will be the language in its perfection. So that it is not the poet alone of whom we have to take account, but the language in which he writes: it is not merely that a classic poet exhausts the language, but that an exhaustible language is the kind which may produce a classic poet.

15 We may be inclined to ask, then, whether we are not fortunate in possessing a language which, instead of having produced a classic, can

boast a rich variety in the past, and the possibility of further novelty in the future? Now while we are *inside* a literature, while we speak the same language, and have fundamentally the same culture as that which produced the literature of the past, we want to maintain two things: a pride in what our literature has already accomplished, and a belief in what it may still accomplish in the future. If we cease to believe in the future, the past would cease to be fully *our* past: it would become the past of a dead civilisation. And this consideration must operate with particular cogency upon the minds of those who are engaged in the attempt to add to the store of English literature. There is no classic in English: therefore, any living poet can say, there is still hope that I – and those after me, for no one can face with equanimity, once he understands what is implied, the thought of being the *last* poet – may be able to write something which will be worth preserving. But from the aspect of eternity, such interest in the future has no meaning: when two languages are both dead languages, we cannot say that one is greater, because of the number and variety of its poets, or the other because its genius is more completely expressed in the work of one poet. What I wish to affirm, at one and the same time, is this: that, because English is a living language and the language in which we live, we may be glad that it has never completely realised itself in the work of one classic poet; but that, on the other hand, the classic criterion is of vital importance to us. We need it in order to judge our individual poets, though we refuse to judge our literature as a whole in comparison with one which has produced a classic. Whether a literature does culminate in a classic, is a matter of fortune. It is largely, I suspect, [66] a question of the degree of fusion of the elements within that language; so that the Latin languages can approximate more closely to the classic, not simply because they are Latin, but because they are more homogeneous than English, and therefore tend more naturally towards the *common style*: whereas English, being the most various of great languages in its constituents, tends to variety rather than perfection, needs a longer time to realise its potency, and still contains, perhaps, more unexplored possibilities. It has, perhaps, the greatest capacity for changing and yet remaining itself.

16 I am now approaching the distinction between the relative and the absolute classic, the distinction between the literature which can be called classic in relation to its own language, and that which is classic in relation to a number of other languages. But first I wish to record one more characteristic of the classic, beyond those I have enumerated, which will help to establish this distinction, and to mark the difference between such a classic as Pope and such a classic as Virgil. It is convenient to recapitulate certain assertions which I made earlier.

17 I suggested, at the beginning, that a frequent, if not universal feature of the maturing of individuals may be a process of selection (not altogether conscious), of the development of some potentialities to the exclusion of others; and that a similarity may be found in the development of language and literature. If this is so, we should expect to find that in a minor classic literature, such as our own of the late seventeenth and the eighteenth century, the elements excluded, to arrive at maturity, will be more numerous or more serious; and that satisfaction in the result, will always be qualified by our awareness of the possibilities of the language, revealed in the work of earlier authors, which have been ignored. The classic age of English literature is not representative of the total genius of the race: as I have intimated, we cannot say that that genius is wholly realised in any one period – with the result that we can still, by referring to one or another period of the past, envisage possibilities for the future. The English language is one which offers wide scope for legitimate divergencies of style; it seems to be such that no one age, and certainly no one writer, can establish a norm. The French language has seemed to be much more closely tethered to a normal style; yet, even in French, though the language appeared to have established itself, once for all, in the seventeenth century, there is an *esprit gaulois*, an [67] element of richness present in Rabelais and in Villon, the awareness of which may qualify our judgement of the *wholeness* of Racine or Molière, for we may feel that it is not only unrepresented but unreconciled. We may come to the conclusion, then, that the perfect classic must be one in which the whole genius of a people will be latent, if not all revealed; and that it can only appear in a language such that its whole genius can be present at once. We must accordingly add, to our list of characteristics of the classic, that of *comprehensiveness*. The classic must, within its formal limitations, express the maximum possible of the whole range of feeling which represents the character of the people who speak that language. It will represent this at its best, and it will also have the widest appeal: among the people to which it belongs, it will find its response among all classes and conditions of men.

18 When a work of literature has, beyond this comprehensiveness in relation to its own language, an equal significance in relation to a number of foreign literatures, we may say that it has also *universality*. We may for instance speak justly enough of the poetry of Goethe as constituting a classic, because of the place which it occupies in its own language and literature. Yet, because of its partiality, of the impermanence of some of its content, and the germanism of the sensibility; because Goethe appears, to a foreign eye, limited by his age, by his language, and by his culture, so

that he is unrepresentative of the whole European tradition, and, like our own nineteenth-century authors, a little provincial, we cannot call him a *universal* classic. He is a universal author, in the sense that he is an author with whose works every European ought to be acquainted: but that is a different thing. Nor, on one count or another, can we expect to find the proximate approach to the classic in *any* modern language. It is necessary to go to the two dead languages: it is important that they are dead, because through their death we have come into our inheritance – the fact that they are dead would in itself give them no value, apart from the fact that all the peoples of Europe are their beneficiaries. And of all the great poets of Greece and Rome, I think that it is to Virgil that we owe the most for our standard of the classic: which, I will repeat, is not the same thing as pretending that he is the greatest, or the one to whom we are in every way the most indebted – it is of a particular debt that I speak. His comprehensiveness, his peculiar kind of comprehensiveness, is due to the [68] unique position in our history of the Roman Empire and the Latin language: a position which may be said to conform to its *destiny*. This sense of destiny comes to consciousness in the *Aeneid*. Aeneas is himself, from first to last, a 'man in fate', a man who is neither an adventurer nor a schemer, neither a vagabond nor a careerist, a man fulfilling his destiny, not under compulsion or arbitrary decree, and certainly from no stimulus to glory, but by surrendering his will to a higher power behind the gods who would thwart or direct him. He would have preferred to stop in Troy, but he becomes an exile, and something greater and more significant than any exile; he is exiled for a purpose greater than he can know, but which he recognises; and he is not, in a human sense, a happy or successful man. But he is the symbol of Rome; and, as Aeneas is to Rome, so is ancient Rome to Europe. Thus Virgil acquires the centrality of the unique classic; he is at the centre of European civilisation, in a position which no other poet can share or usurp. The Roman Empire and the Latin language were not any empire and any language, but an empire and a language with a unique destiny in relation to ourselves; and the poet in whom that Empire and that language came to consciousness and expression is a poet of unique destiny.

19 If Virgil is thus the consciousness of Rome and the supreme voice of her language, he must have a significance for us which cannot be expressed wholly in terms of literary appreciation and criticism. Yet, adhering to the problems of literature, or to the terms of literature in dealing with life, we may be allowed to imply more than we state. The value of Virgil to us, in literary terms, is in providing us with a criterion. We may, as I have said, have reasons to rejoice that this criterion is provided by a poet writing in a different language from our own: but that is not a reason for rejecting the criterion. To preserve the classical standard, and to measure every individual work of literature by it, is to see that, while our literature as a whole may contain everything, every single work in it may be defective in something. This may be a necessary defect, a defect without which some quality present would be lacking: but we must see it as a defect, at the same time that we see it as a necessity. In the absence of this standard of which I speak, a standard we cannot keep clearly before us if we rely on our own literature alone, we tend, first to admire works of genius for the wrong reasons – as we extol Blake for his *philosophy*, and Hopkins for his *style*: and from this we proceed to greater error, to [69] giving the second-rate equal rank with the first-rate. In short, without the constant application of the classical measure, which we owe to Virgil more than to any other one poet, we tend to become provincial.

20 By 'provincial' I mean here something more than I find in the dictionary definitions. I mean more, for instance, than 'wanting the culture or polish of the capital', though, certainly, Virgil was of the Capital, to a degree which makes any later poet of equal stature look a little provincial; and I mean more than 'narrow in thought, in culture, in creed' – a slippery definition this, for, from a modern liberal point of view, Dante was 'narrow in thought, in culture, in creed', yet it may be the Broad Churchman, rather than the Narrow Churchman, who is the more provincial. I mean also a distortion of values, the exclusion of some, the exaggeration of others, which springs, not from lack of wide geographical perambulation, but from applying standards acquired within a limited area, to the whole of human experience; which confounds the contingent with the essential, the ephemeral with the permanent. In our age, when men seem more than ever prone to confuse wisdom with knowledge, and knowledge with information, and to try to solve problems of life in terms of engineering, there is coming into existence a new kind of provincialism which perhaps deserves a new name. It is a provincialism, not of space, but of time; one for which history is merely the chronicle of human devices which have served their turn and been scrapped, one for which the world is the property solely of the living, a property in which the dead hold no shares. The menace of this kind of provincialism is, that we can all, all the peoples on the globe, be provincials together; and those who are not content to be provincials, can only become hermits. If this kind of provincialism led to greater tolerance, in the sense of forbearance, there might be more to be said for it; but it seems more likely to lead to our becoming indifferent, in matters where we ought to maintain a distinctive dogma or standard, and to our becoming intolerant, in

matters which might be left to local or personal preference. We may have as many varieties of religion as we like, provided we all send our children to the same schools. But my concern here is only with the corrective to provincialism in literature. We need to remind ourselves that, as Europe is a whole (and still, in its progressive mutilation and disfigurement, the organism out of which any greater world harmony must develop), so European literature is a whole, the several members of which [70] cannot flourish, if the same blood-stream does not circulate throughout the whole body. The blood-stream of European literature is Latin and Greek – not as two systems of circulation, but one, for it is through Rome that our parentage in Greece must be traced. What common measure of excellence have we in literature, among our several languages, which is not the classical measure? What mutual intelligibility can we hope to preserve, except in our common heritage of thought and feeling in those two languages, for the understanding of which, no European people is in any position of advantage over any other? No modern language could aspire to the universality of Latin, even though it came to be spoken by millions more than ever spoke Latin, and even though it came to be the universal means of communication between peoples of all tongues and cultures. No modern language can hope to produce a classic, in the sense in which I have called Virgil a classic. Our classic, the classic of all Europe, is Virgil.

In our several literatures, we have much wealth of which to boast, to which Latin has nothing to compare; but each literature has its greatness, not in isolation, but because of its place in a larger pattern, a pattern set in Rome. I have spoken of the new seriousness – *gravity* I might say – the new insight into history, illustrated by the dedication of Aeneas to Rome, to a future far beyond his living achievement. *His* reward was hardly more than a narrow beachhead and a political marriage in a weary middle age: his youth interred, its shadow moving with the shades the other side of Cumae. And so, I said, one envisages the destiny of ancient Rome. So we may think of Roman literature: at first sight, a literature of limited scope, with a poor muster of great names, yet universal as no other literature can be; a literature unconsciously sacrificing, in compliance to its destiny in Europe, the opulence and variety of later tongues, to produce, for us, the classic. It is sufficient that this standard should have been established once for all; the task does not have to be done again. But the maintenance of the standard is the price of our freedom, the defence of freedom against chaos. We may remind ourselves of this obligation, by our annual observance of piety towards the great ghost who guided Dante's pilgrimage: who, as it was his function to lead Dante towards a vision he could never himself enjoy, led Europe towards the Christian culture which he could never know; and who, speaking his final words in the new Italian speech, said in farewell [71]

> il temporal foco e l'eterno
> veduto hai, figlio, e sei venuto in parte
> dov' io per me più oltre non discerno.

> Son, the temporal fire and the eternal, hast
> thou seen, and art come to a place where I,
> of myself, discern no further.

Variants from 1945:

[Para. before para. 1:] In the whole of European literature there is no poet who can furnish the texts for a more significant variety of discourse than Virgil. The fact that he symbolises so much in the history of Europe, and represents such central European values, is the justification for our founding a society to preserve his memory: the fact that he is so central and so comprehensive is my justification for this address. For if Virgil's poetry were a subject upon which only scholars should presume to speak, you would not have put me in this position, or have cared to listen to what I have to say. I am emboldened by the reflection, that no specialised knowledge or proficiency can confer the exclusive title to talk about Virgil. Speakers of the most diverse capacities, can bring his poetry to bear upon matters within their competence; can hope to contribute, from those studies to which they have given their minds, to the elucidation of his value; can try to offer, for the general use, the benefit of whatever wisdom Virgil may have helped them to acquire, in relation to their own experience of life. Each can give his testimony of Virgil in relation to those subjects which he knows best, or upon which he has most deeply reflected: that is what I meant by variety. In the end, we may all be saying the same thing in different ways: and that is what I meant by significant variety.

1 [Between 'with this title' and 'The pertinence':] : whether it is as misfortune or not, that – not having read it for some thirty-odd years – accidents of the present time have prevented me from re-reading it before preparing this address, I hope to find out as soon as libraries are more accessible and books more plentiful.
I am discovered] you find me
to be using] using
no one should expect one to apologise] you are not to expect an apology
I ask Aeolus, on this occasion] I should wish, on this occasion, Aeolus

2 absolute zero] absolute
5 monotony because the resources] monotony, because the resources
6 ancestry] paternity
7 modern literatures have] modern literatures had
8 drawing] approaching
eighteenth century is the finest] eighteenth century is (as it thought itself) the finest
11 still more important] what is still more important

12 to which we are apt to pay less than enough deference] we are therefore apt to pay not enough deference to it
approximations] approximation
are probably] is probably
13 [Between 'remote original.' and 'But English poetry, and French':] We may raise a rather different question, when we view Italian poetry after Dante: for the later Italian poets did not imitate Dante, and had this advantage, that they lived in a world which was more rapidly changing, so that there was obviously something different for them to do; they provoke no direct disastrous comparison.
14 it may be objected] you may object
[Between 'written since.' and 'That every great work':] You may or may not be disposed to accept the distinction which I shall make.
When the great poet is also a great classic poet, he] The classic poet, on the other hand,
and the language of his time, as used by him,] and when he is a wholly classic poet, the language of his time
15 a longer time] the longest time
changing and] changing, and
19 a criterion] a critical criterion
20 problems of life] problems of life,

Poetry and Drama[1]

OPAP, 72–88.

Originally publ. in *Atlantic Monthly*, 187. 2 (Feb. 1951), 30–7: Gallup C560. This followed Eliot's giving it as a lecture at Harvard on 21 November 1950. Publ. by Harvard University Press on 15 Mar. 1951 and by Faber & Faber on 28 Sept. 1951: Gallup A57.

I

1 Reviewing my critical output for the last thirty-odd years, I am surprised to find how constantly I have returned to the drama, whether by examining the work of the contemporaries of Shakespeare, or by reflecting on the possibilities of the future. It may even be that people are weary of hearing me on this subject. But, while I find that I have been composing variations on this theme all my life, my views have been continually modified and renewed by increasing experience; so that I am impelled to take stock of the situation afresh at every stage of my own experimentation.

2 As I have gradually learned more about the problems of poetic drama, and the conditions which it must fulfil if it is to justify itself, I have made a little clearer to myself, not only my own reasons for wanting to write

---

1. The first Theodore Spencer Memorial Lecture delivered at Harvard University and published by Faber & Faber and by the Harvard University Press in 1951.

in this form, but the more general reasons for wanting to see it restored to its place. And I think that if I say something about these problems and conditions, it should make clearer to other people whether and if so why poetic drama has anything potentially to offer the playgoer, that prose drama cannot. For I start with the assumption that if poetry is merely a decoration, an added embellishment, if it merely gives people of literary tastes the pleasure of listening to poetry at the same time that they are witnessing a play, then it is superfluous. It must justify itself dramatically, and not merely be fine poetry shaped into a dramatic form. From this it follows that no play should be written in verse for which prose is *dramatically* adequate. And from this it follows, again, that the audience, its attention held by the dramatic action, its emotions stirred by the situation between the characters, should be too intent upon the play to be wholly conscious of the medium.

3 Whether we use prose or verse on the stage, they are both but [73] means to an end. The difference, from one point of view, is not so great as we might think. In those prose plays which survive, which are read and produced on the stage by later generations, the prose in which the characters speak is as remote, for the best part, from the vocabulary, syntax, and rhythm of our ordinary speech – with its fumbling for words, its constant recourse to approximation, its disorder, and its unfinished sentences – as verse is. Like verse, it has been written, and rewritten. Our two greatest prose stylists in the drama – apart from Shakespeare and the other Elizabethans who mixed prose and verse in the same play – are, I believe, Congreve and Bernard Shaw. A speech by a character of Congreve or of Shaw has – however clearly the characters may be differentiated – that unmistakable personal rhythm which is the mark of a prose style, and of which only the most accomplished conversationalists – who are for that matter usually monologuists – show any trace in their talk. We have all heard (too often!) of Molière's character who expressed surprise when told that he spoke prose. But it was M. Jourdain who was right, and not his mentor or his creator: he did not speak prose – he only talked. For I mean to draw a triple distinction: between prose, and verse, and our ordinary speech which is mostly below the level of either verse or prose. So if you look at it in this way, it will appear that prose, on the stage, is as artificial as verse: or alternatively, that verse can be as natural as prose.

4 But while the sensitive member of the audience will appreciate, when he hears fine prose spoken in a play, that this is something better than ordinary conversation, he does not regard it as a wholly different language from that which he himself speaks, for that would interpose a

barrier between himself and the imaginary characters on the stage. Too many people, on the other hand, approach a play which they know to be in verse, with the consciousness of the difference. It is unfortunate when they are repelled by verse, but can also be deplorable when they are attracted by it – if that means that they are prepared to enjoy the play and the language of the play as two separate things. The chief effect of style and rhythm in dramatic speech, whether in prose or verse, should be unconscious.

5 From this it follows that a mixture of prose and verse in the same play is generally to be avoided: each transition makes the auditor aware, with a jolt, of the medium. It is, we may say, justifiable when the author wishes to produce this jolt: when, that is, he [74] wishes to transport the audience violently from one plane of reality to another. I suspect that this kind of transition was easily acceptable to an Elizabethan audience, to whose ears both prose and verse came naturally; who liked high-falutin and low comedy in the same play; and to whom it seemed perhaps proper that the more humble and rustic characters should speak in a homely language, and that those of more exalted rank should rant in verse. But even in the plays of Shakespeare some of the prose passages seem to be designed for an effect of contrast which, when achieved, is something that can never become old-fashioned. The knocking at the gate in *Macbeth* is an example that comes to everyone's mind; but it has long seemed to me that the alternation of scenes in prose with scenes in verse in *Henry IV* points an ironic contrast between the world of high politics and the world of common life. The audience probably thought they were getting their accustomed chronicle play garnished with amusing scenes of low life; yet the prose scenes of both Part I and Part II provide a sardonic comment upon the bustling ambitions of the chiefs of the parties in the insurrection of the Percys.

6 To-day, however, because of the handicap under which verse drama suffers, I believe that in verse drama prose should be used very sparingly indeed; that we should aim at a form of verse in which everything can be said that has to be said; and that when we find some situation which is intractable in verse, it is merely because our form of verse is inelastic. And if there prove to be scenes which we cannot put in verse, we must either develop our verse, or avoid having to introduce such scenes. For we have to accustom our audiences to verse to the point at which they will cease to be conscious of it; and to introduce prose dialogue would only be to distract their attention from the play itself to the medium of its expression. But if our verse is to have so wide a range that it can say anything that has to be said, it follows that it will not be 'poetry' all the

time. It will only be 'poetry' when the dramatic situation has reached such a point of intensity that poetry becomes the natural utterance, because then it is the only language in which the emotions can be expressed at all.

7 It is indeed necessary for any long poem, if it is to escape monotony, to be able to say homely things without bathos, as well as to take the highest flights without sounding exaggerated. And it is still more important in a play, especially if it is concerned with contemporary life. The reason for writing even the more pedestrian [75] parts of a verse play in verse instead of prose is, however, not only to avoid calling the audience's attention to the fact that it is at other moments listening to poetry. It is also that the verse rhythm should have its effect upon the hearers, without their being conscious of it. A brief analysis of one scene of Shakespeare's may illustrate this point. The opening scene of *Hamlet* – as well constructed an opening scene as that of any play ever written – has the advantage of being one that everybody knows.

8 What we do not notice, when we witness this scene in the theatre, is the great variation of style. Nothing is superfluous, and there is no line of poetry which is not justified by its dramatic value. The first twenty-two lines are built of the simplest words in the most homely idiom. Shakespeare had worked for a long time in the theatre, and written a good many plays, before reaching the point at which he could write those twenty-two lines. There is nothing quite so simplified and sure in his previous work. He first developed conversational, colloquial verse in the monologue of the character part – Faulconbridge in *King John*, and later the Nurse in *Romeo and Juliet*. It was a much further step to carry it unobtrusively into the dialogue of brief replies. No poet has begun to master dramatic verse until he can write lines which, like these in *Hamlet*, are *transparent*. You are consciously attending, not to the poetry, but to the meaning of the poetry. If you were hearing *Hamlet* for the first time, without knowing anything about the play, I do not think that it would occur to you to ask whether the speakers were speaking in verse or prose. The verse is having a different effect upon us from prose; but at the moment, what we are aware of is the frosty night, the officers keeping watch on the battlements, and the foreboding of a tragic action. I do not say that there is no place for the situation in which part of one's pleasure will be the enjoyment of hearing beautiful poetry – providing that the author gives it, in that place, dramatic inevitability. And of course, when we have both seen a play several times and read it between performances, we begin to analyse the means by which the author has produced his effects. But in the immediate impact of this scene we are unconscious of the medium of its expression.

I. ON POETRY – POETRY AND DRAMA

9 From the short, brusque ejaculations at the beginning, suitable to the situation and to the character of the guards – but not expressing more character than is required for their function in the play – the verse glides into a slower movement with the appearance of the courtiers Horatio and Marcellus. [76]

> Horatio says 'tis but our fantasy, . . .

and the movement changes again on the appearance of Royalty, the ghost of the King, into the solemn and sonorous

> What art thou, that usurp'st this time of night, . . .

(and note, by the way, this anticipation of the plot conveyed by the use of the verb *usurp*); and majesty is suggested in a reference reminding us whose ghost this is:

> So frown'd he once, when, in an angry parle,
> He smote the sledded Polacks on the ice.

There is an abrupt change to staccato in Horatio's words to the Ghost on its second appearance; this rhythm changes again with the words

> We do it wrong, being so majestical,
> To offer it the show of violence;
> For it is, as the air, invulnerable,
> And our vain blows malicious mockery.

The scene reaches a resolution with the words of Marcellus:

> It faded on the crowing of the cock.
> Some say that ever 'gainst that season comes
> Wherein our Saviour's birth is celebrated,
> The bird of dawning singeth all night long; . . .

and Horatio's answer:

> So have I heard and do in part believe it.
> But, look, the morn, in russet mantle clad,
> Walks o'er the dew of yon high eastern hill.
> Break we our watch up.

This is great poetry, and it is dramatic; but besides being poetic and dramatic, it is something more. There emerges, when we analyse it, a kind of musical design also which reinforces and is one with the dramatic movement. It has checked and accelerated the pulse of our emotion without our knowing it. Note that in these last words of Marcellus there is a deliberate brief emergence of the poetic into consciousness. When we hear the lines

> But, look, the morn, in russet mantle clad,
> Walks o'er the dew of yon high eastern hill,

[77] we are lifted for a moment beyond character, but with no sense of unfitness of the words coming, and at this moment, from the lips of Horatio. The transitions in the scene obey laws of the music of dramatic poetry. Note that the two lines of Horatio which I have quoted twice are preceded by a line of the simplest speech which might be either verse or prose:

> So have I heard and do in part believe it,

and that he follows them abruptly with a half line which is hardly more than a stage direction:

> Break we our watch up.

It would be interesting to pursue, by a similar analysis, this problem of the double pattern in great poetic drama – the pattern which may be examined from the point of view of stagecraft or from that of the music. But I think that the examination of this one scene is enough to show us that verse is not merely a formalisation, or an added decoration, but that it intensifies the drama. It should indicate also the importance of the unconscious effect of the verse upon us. And lastly, I do not think that this effect is felt only by those members of an audience who 'like poetry' but also by those who go for the play alone. By the people who do not like poetry, I mean those who cannot sit down with a book of poetry and enjoy reading it: these people also, when they go to a play in verse, should be affected by the poetry. And these are the audiences whom the writer of such a play ought to keep in mind.

10 At this point I might say a word about those plays which we call *poetic*, though they are written in prose. The plays of John Millington Synge form rather a special case, because they are based upon the idiom of a rural people whose speech is naturally poetic, both in imagery and in rhythm. I believe that he even incorporated phrases which he had heard from these country people of Ireland. The language of Synge is not available except for plays set among that same people. We can draw more general conclusions from the plays in prose (so much admired in my youth, and now hardly even read) by Maeterlinck. These plays are in a different way restricted in their subject matter; and to say that the characterisation in them is dim is an understatement. I do not deny

that they have some poetic quality. But in order to be poetic in prose, a dramatist has to be so consistently poetic that his scope is very limited. Synge wrote plays about characters whose originals [78] in life talked poetically, so he could make them talk poetry and remain real people. The poetic prose dramatist who has not this advantage, has to be too poetic. The poetic drama in prose is more limited by poetic convention or by our conventions as to what subject matter is poetic, than is the poetic drama in verse. A really dramatic verse can be employed, as Shakespeare employed it, to say the most matter-of-fact things.

11 Yeats is a very different case, from Maeterlinck or Synge. A study of his development as a dramatist would show, I think, the great distance he went, and the triumph of his last plays. In his first period, he wrote plays in verse about subjects conventionally accepted as suitable for verse, in a metric which – though even at that early stage having the personal Yeats rhythm – is not really a form of speech quite suitable for anybody except mythical kings and queens. His middle-period *Plays for Dancers* are very beautiful, but they do not solve any problem for the dramatist in verse: they are poetic prose plays with important interludes in verse. It was only in his last play *Purgatory* that he solved his problem of speech in verse, and laid all his successors under obligation to him.

II

12 Now, I am going to venture to make some observations based on my own experience, which will lead me to comment on my intentions, failures, and partial successes, in my own plays. I do this in the belief that any explorer or experimenter in new territory may, by putting on record a kind of journal of his explorations, say something of use to those who follow him into the same regions and who will perhaps go farther.

13 The first thing of any importance that I discovered, was that a writer who has worked for years, and achieved some success, in writing other kinds of verse, has to approach the writing of a verse play in a different frame of mind from that to which he has been accustomed in his previous work. In writing other verse, I think that one is writing, so to speak, in terms of one's own voice: the way it sounds when you read it to yourself is the test. For it is yourself speaking. The question of communication, of what the reader will get from it, is not paramount: if your poem is right to you, you can only hope that the readers will eventually come to accept it. The poem can wait a little while; the approval of a few sympathetic and judicious critics is enough to begin with; and it is [79] for future readers to meet the poet more than half way. But in the theatre, the problem of communication presents itself immediately. You are deliberately writing

verse for other voices, not for your own, and you do not know whose voices they will be. You are aiming to write lines which will have an immediate effect upon an unknown and unprepared audience, to be interpreted to that audience by unknown actors rehearsed by an unknown producer. And the unknown audience cannot be expected to show any indulgence towards the poet. The poet cannot afford to write his play merely for his admirers, those who know his non-dramatic work and are prepared to receive favourably anything he puts his name to. He must write with an audience in view which knows nothing and cares nothing, about any previous success he may have had before he ventured into the theatre. Hence one finds out that many of the things one likes to do, and knows how to do, are out of place; and that every line must be judged by a new law, that of dramatic relevance.

14 When I wrote *Murder in the Cathedral* I had the advantage for a beginner, of an occasion which called for a subject generally admitted to be suitable for verse. Verse plays, it has been generally held, should either take their subject matter from some mythology, or else should be about some remote historical period, far enough away from the present for the characters not to need to be recognisable as human beings, and therefore for them to be licensed to talk in verse. Picturesque period costume renders verse much more acceptable. Furthermore, my play was to be produced for a rather special kind of audience – an audience of those serious people who go to 'festivals' and expect to have to put up with poetry – though perhaps on this occasion some of them were not quite prepared for what they got. And finally it was a religious play, and people who go deliberately to a religious play at a religious festival expect to be patiently bored and to satisfy themselves with the feeling that they have done something meritorious. So the path was made easy.

15 It was only when I put my mind to thinking what sort of play I wanted to do next, that I realised that in *Murder in the Cathedral* I had not solved any general problem; but that from my point of view the play was a dead end. For one thing, the problem of language which that play had presented to me was a special problem. Fortunately, I did not have to write in the idiom of the twelfth century, because that idiom, even if I knew Norman French and [80] Anglo-Saxon, would have been unintelligible. But the vocabulary and style could not be exactly those of modern conversation – as in some modern French plays using the plot and personages of Greek drama – because I had to take my audience back to an historical event; and they could not afford to be archaic, first because archaism would only have suggested the wrong period, and second because I wanted to bring home to the audience the contemporary relevance of the situation.

The style therefore had to be *neutral*, committed neither to the present nor to the past. As for the versification, I was only aware at this stage that the essential was to avoid any echo of Shakespeare, for I was persuaded that the primary failure of nineteenth-century poets when they wrote for the theatre (and most of the greatest English poets had tried their hand at drama) was not in their theatrical technique, but in their dramatic language; and that this was due largely to their limitation to a strict blank verse which, after extensive use for non-dramatic poetry, had lost the flexibility which blank verse must have if it is to give the effect of conversation. The rhythm of regular blank verse had become too remote from the movement of modern speech. Therefore what I kept in mind was the versification of *Everyman*, hoping that anything unusual in the sound of it would be, on the whole, advantageous. An avoidance of too much iambic, some use of alliteration, and occasional unexpected rhyme, helped to distinguish the versification from that of the nineteenth century.

16 The versification of the dialogue in *Murder in the Cathedral* has therefore, in my opinion, only a *negative* merit: it succeeded in avoiding what had to be avoided, but it arrived at no positive novelty: in short, in so far as it solved the problem of speech in verse for writing to-day, it solved it for this play only, and provided me with no clue to the verse I should use in another kind of play. Here, then, were two problems left unsolved: that of the idiom and that of the metric (it is really one and the same problem), for general use in any play I might want to write in future. I next became aware of my reasons for depending, in that play, so heavily upon the assistance of the chorus. There were two reasons for this, which in the circumstances justified it. The first was that the essential action of the play – both the historical facts and the matter which I invented – was somewhat limited. A man comes home, foreseeing that he will be killed, and he is killed. I did not want to increase the number of characters, I did not want to write a chronicle of twelfth-century politics, nor did I want to tamper [81] unscrupulously with the meagre records as Tennyson did (in introducing Fair Rosamund, and in suggesting that Becket had been crossed in love in early youth). I wanted to concentrate on death and martyrdom. The introduction of a chorus of excited and sometimes hysterical women, reflecting in their emotion the significance of the action, helped wonderfully. The second reason was this: that a poet writing for the first time for the stage, is much more at home in choral verse than in dramatic dialogue. This, I felt sure, was something I could do, and perhaps the dramatic weaknesses would be somewhat covered up by the cries of the women. The use of a chorus strengthened the power, and concealed the defects of my theatrical technique. For this reason I

decided that next time I would try to integrate the chorus more closely into the play.

17 I wanted to find out also, whether I could learn to dispense altogether with the use of prose. The two prose passages in *Murder in the Cathedral* could not have been written in verse. Certainly, with the kind of dialogue verse which I used in that play, the audience would have been uncomfortably aware that it was verse they were hearing. A sermon cast in verse is too unusual an experience for even the most regular churchgoers: nobody could have responded to it as a sermon at all. And in the speeches of the knights, who are quite aware that they are addressing an audience of people living eight hundred years after they themselves are dead, the use of platform prose is intended of course to have a special effect: to shock the audience out of their complacency. But this is a kind of trick: that is, a device tolerable only in one play and of no use for any other. I may, for aught I know, have been slightly under the influence of *St Joan*.

18 I do not wish to give you the impression that I would rule out of dramatic poetry these three things: historical or mythological subject-matter, the chorus, and traditional blank verse. I do not wish to lay down any law that the only suitable characters and situations are those of modern life, or that a verse play should consist of dialogue only, or that a wholly new versification is necessary. I am only tracing out the route of exploration of one writer, and that one myself. If the poetic drama is to reconquer its place, it must, in my opinion, enter into overt competition with prose drama. As I have said, people are prepared to put up with verse from the lips of personages dressed in the fashion of some distant age; therefore they should be made to hear it from people dressed like ourselves, living in houses and apartments like ours, [82] and using telephones and motor cars and radio sets. Audiences are prepared to accept poetry recited by a chorus, for that is a kind of poetry recital, which it does them credit to enjoy. And audiences (those who go to a verse play because it is in verse) expect poetry to be in rhythms which have lost touch with colloquial speech. What we have to do is to bring poetry into the world in which the audience lives and to which it returns when it leaves the theatre; not to transport the audience into some imaginary world totally unlike its own, an unreal world in which poetry is tolerated. What I should hope might be achieved, by a generation of dramatists having the benefit of our experience, is that the audience should find, at the moment of awareness that it is hearing poetry, that it is saying to itself: 'I could talk in poetry too!' Then we should not be transported into an artificial world; on the contrary, our own sordid, dreary daily world would be suddenly illuminated and transfigured.

19 I was determined, therefore, in my next play to take a theme of contemporary life, with characters of our own time living in our own world. *The Family Reunion* was the result. Here my first concern was the problem of the versification, to find a rhythm close to contemporary speech, in which the stresses could be made to come wherever we should naturally put them, in uttering the particular phrase on the particular occasion. What I worked out is substantially what I have continued to employ: a line of varying length and varying number of syllables, with a caesura and three stresses. The caesura and the stresses may come at different places, almost anywhere in the line; the stresses may be close together or well separated by light syllables; the only rule being that there must be one stress on one side of the caesura and two on the other. In retrospect, I soon saw that I had given my attention to versification, at the expense of plot and character. I had, indeed, made some progress in dispensing with the chorus; but the device of using four of the minor personages, representing the Family, sometimes as individual character parts and sometimes collectively as chorus, does not seem to me very satisfactory. For one thing, the immediate transition from individual, characterised part to membership of a chorus is asking too much of the actors: it is a very difficult transition to accomplish. For another thing, it seemed to me another trick, one which, even if successful, could not have been applicable in another play. Furthermore, I had in two passages used the device of a lyrical duet further isolated from the [83] rest of the dialogue by being written in shorter lines with only two stresses. These passages are in a sense 'beyond character', the speakers have to be presented as falling into a kind of trance-like state in order to speak them. But they are so remote from the necessity of the action that they are hardly more than passages of poetry which might be spoken by anybody; they are too much like operatic arias. The member of the audience, if he enjoys this sort of thing, is putting up with a suspension of the action in order to enjoy a poetic fantasia: these passages are really less related to the action than are the choruses in *Murder in the Cathedral*.

20 I observed that when Shakespeare, in one of his mature plays, introduces what might seem a purely poetic line or passage, it never interrupts the action, or is out of character, but on the contrary, in some mysterious way supports both action and character. When Macbeth speaks his so often quoted words beginning

> To-morrow and to-morrow and to-morrow,

or when Othello, confronted at night with his angry father-in-law and friends, utters the beautiful line

Keep up your bright swords, for the dew will rust them,

we do not feel that Shakespeare has thought of lines which are beautiful poetry and wishes to fit them in somehow, or that he has for the moment come to the end of his dramatic inspiration and has turned to poetry to fill up with. The lines are surprising, and yet they fit in with the character; or else we are compelled to adjust our conception of the character in such a way that the lines will be appropriate to it. The lines spoken by Macbeth reveal the weariness of the weak man who had been forced by his wife to realise his own half-hearted desires and her ambitions, and who, with her death, is left without the motive to continue. The line of Othello expresses irony, dignity, and fearlessness; and incidentally reminds us of the time of night in which the scene takes place. Only poetry could do this; but it is *dramatic* poetry: that is, it does not interrupt but intensifies the dramatic situation.

21 It was not only because of the introduction of passages which called too much attention to themselves as poetry, and could not be dramatically justified, that I found *The Family Reunion* defective: there were two weaknesses which came to strike me as more serious still. The first was, that I had employed far too much of the strictly limited time allowed to a dramatist, in presenting a situa-[84]tion, and not left myself enough time, or provided myself with enough material, for developing it in action. I had written what was, on the whole, a good first act; except that for a first act it was much too long. When the curtain rises again, the audience is expecting, as it has a right to expect, that something is going to happen. Instead, it finds itself treated to a further exploration of the background: in other words, to what ought to have been given much earlier if at all. The beginning of the second act presents much the most difficult problem to producer and cast: for the audience's attention is beginning to wander. And then, after what must seem to the audience an interminable time of preparation, the conclusion comes so abruptly that we are, after all, unready for it. This was an elementary fault in mechanics.

22 But the deepest flaw of all, was in a failure of adjustment between the Greek story and the modern situation. I should either have stuck closer to Aeschylus or else taken a great deal more liberty with his myth. One evidence of this is the appearance of those ill-fated figures, the Furies. They must, in future, be omitted from the cast, and be understood to be visible only to certain of my characters, and not to the audience. We tried every possible manner of presenting them. We put them on the stage, and they looked like uninvited guests who had strayed in from a fancy dress ball. We concealed them behind gauze, and they suggested a still out of a Walt Disney film. We made them dimmer, and they looked like

shrubbery just outside the window. I have seen other expedients tried: I have seen them signalling from across the garden, or swarming on to the stage like a football team, and they are never right. They never succeed in being either Greek goddesses or modern spooks. But their failure is merely a symptom of the failure to adjust the ancient with the modern.

23 A more serious evidence is that we are left in a divided frame of mind, not knowing whether to consider the play the tragedy of the mother or the salvation of the son. The two situations are not reconciled. I find a confirmation of this in the fact that my sympathies now have come to be all with the mother, who seems to me, except perhaps for the chauffeur, the only complete human being in the play; and my hero now strikes me as an insufferable prig.

24 Well, I had made some progress in learning how to write the first act of a play, and I had – the one thing of which I felt sure – made a good deal of progress in finding a form of versification [85] and an idiom which would serve all my purposes, without recourse to prose, and be capable of unbroken transition between the most intense speech and the most relaxed dialogue. You will understand, after my making these criticisms of *The Family Reunion*, some of the errors that I endeavoured to avoid in designing *The Cocktail Party*. To begin with, no chorus, and no ghosts. I was still inclined to go to a Greek dramatist for my theme, but I was determined to do so merely as a point of departure, and to conceal the origins so well that nobody would identify them until I pointed them out myself. In this at least I have been successful; for no one of my acquaintance (and no dramatic critics) recognised the source of my story in the *Alcestis* of Euripides. In fact, I have had to go into detailed explanation to convince them – I mean, of course, those who were familiar with the plot of that play – of the genuineness of the inspiration. But those who were at first disturbed by the eccentric behaviour of my unknown guest, and his apparently intemperate habits and tendency to burst into song, have found some consolation in having their attention called to the behaviour of Heracles in Euripides' play.

25 In the second place, I laid down for myself the ascetic rule to avoid poetry which could not stand the test of strict dramatic utility: with such success, indeed, that it is perhaps an open question whether there is any poetry in the play at all. And finally, I tried to keep in mind that in a play, from time to time, something should happen; that the audience should be kept in the constant expectation that something is going to happen; and that, when it does happen, it should be different, but not too different, from what the audience had been led to expect.

26 I have not yet got to the end of my investigation of the weaknesses of this play, but I hope and expect to find more than those of which I am yet aware. I say 'hope' because while one can never repeat a success, and therefore must always try to find something different, even if less popular, to do, the desire to write something which will be free of the defects of one's last work is a very powerful and useful incentive. I am aware that the last act of my play only just escapes, if indeed it does escape, the accusation of being not a last act but an epilogue; and I am determined to do something different, if I can, in this respect. I also believe that while the self-education of a poet trying to write for the theatre seems to require a long period of disciplining his poetry, and putting it, so to speak, on a very thin diet in order to adapt it to the needs of [86] the stage he may find that later, when (and if) the understanding of theatrical technique has become second nature, he can dare to make more liberal use of poetry and take greater liberties with ordinary colloquial speech. I base this belief on the evolution of Shakespeare, and on some study of the language in his late plays.

27 In devoting so much time to an examination of my own plays, I have, I believe, been animated by a better motive than egotism. It seems to me that if we are to have a poetic drama, it is more likely to come from poets learning how to write plays, than from skilful prose dramatists learning to write poetry. That some poets can learn how to write plays, and write good ones, may be only a hope, but I believe a not unreasonable hope; but that a man who has started by writing successful prose plays should then learn how to write good poetry, seems to me extremely unlikely. And, under present-day conditions, and until the verse play is recognised by the larger public as a possible source of entertainment, the poet is likely to get his first opportunity to work for the stage only after making some sort of reputation for himself as the author of other kinds of verse. I have therefore wished to put on record, for what it may be worth to others, some account of the difficulties I have encountered, and the mistakes into which I have fallen, and the weaknesses I have had to try to overcome.

28 I should not like to close without attempting to set before you, though only a dim outline, the ideal towards which poetic drama should strive. It is an unattainable ideal: and that is why it interests me, for it provides an incentive towards further experiment and exploration, beyond any goal which there is prospect of attaining. It is a function of all art to give us some perception of an order in life, by imposing an order upon it. The painter works by selection, combination, and emphasis among the elements of the visible world; the musician in the world of sound. It seems to me that beyond the nameable, classifiable emotions and motives of

our conscious life when directed towards action – the part of life which prose drama is wholly adequate to express – there is a fringe of indefinite extent, of feeling which we can only detect, so to speak, out of the corner of the eye and can never completely focus; of feeling of which we are only aware in a kind of temporary detachment from action. There are great prose dramatists – such as Ibsen and Chekhov – who have at times done things of which I would not otherwise have supposed prose to be capable, but who seem to me, in spite of their success, to have been hampered in [87] expression by writing in prose. This peculiar range of sensibility can be expressed by dramatic poetry, at its moments of greatest intensity. At such moments, we touch the border of those feelings which only music can express. We can never emulate music, because to arrive at the condition of music would be the annihilation of poetry, and especially of dramatic poetry. Nevertheless, I have before my eyes a kind of mirage of the perfection of verse drama, which would be a design of human action and of words, such as to present at once the two aspects of dramatic and of musical order. It seems to me that Shakespeare achieved this at least in certain scenes – even rather early, for there is the balcony scene of *Romeo and Juliet* – and that this was what he was striving towards in his late plays. To go as far in this direction as it is possible to go, without losing that contact with the ordinary everyday world with which drama must come to terms, seems to me the proper aim of dramatic poetry. For it is ultimately the function of art, in imposing a credible order upon ordinary reality, and thereby eliciting some perception of an order *in* reality, to bring us to a condition of serenity, stillness, and reconciliation; and then leave us, as Virgil left Dante, to proceed toward a region where that guide can avail us no farther.

NOTE TO 'POETRY AND DRAMA'

29 As I explained in my Preface, the passage in this essay analysing the first scene of *Hamlet* was taken from a lecture delivered some years previously at Edinburgh University. From the same Edinburgh lecture I have extracted the following note on the balcony scene in *Romeo and Juliet*:

> In Romeo's beginning, there is still some artificiality:
>
>> Two of the fairest stars in all the heaven,
>> Having some business, do intreat her eyes
>> To twinkle in their spheres till they return.
>
> For it seems unlikely that a man standing below in the garden, even on a very bright moonlight night, would see the eyes of the lady above flashing

so brilliantly as to justify such a comparison. Yet one is aware, from the beginning of this scene, that there is a musical pattern coming, as surprising in its kind as that in the early work of Beethoven. The arrangement of voices – Juliet has three single lines, followed by Romeo's three, four and five, fol-[88]lowed by her longer speech – is very remarkable. In this pattern, one feels that it is Juliet's voice that has the leading part: to her voice is assigned the dominant phrase of the whole duet:

> My bounty is as boundless as the sea,
> My love as deep: the more I give to thee
> The more I have, for both are infinite.

And to Juliet is given the key-word 'lightning', which occurs again in the play, and is significant of the sudden and disastrous power of her passion, when she says

> 'Tis like the lightning, which doth cease to be
> Ere one can say 'it lightens'.

30 In this scene, Shakespeare achieves a perfection of verse which, being perfection, neither he nor anyone else could excel – for this particular purpose. The stiffness, the artificiality, the poetic decoration, of his early verse has finally given place to a simplification to the language of natural speech, and this language of conversation again raised to great poetry, and to great poetry which is essentially dramatic: for the scene has a structure of which each line is an essential part.

Variants from *Atlantic Monthly*, Harvard edn, 1951, and Faber edn, 1951:

[Before para. 1:] 1 *It is a customary act of respect that the lecturer on a foundation should begin by saying something about the man in whose name the lectureship was founded. The fact that between Theodore Spencer and myself there had been a long friendship terminated only by death, was I believe [(I believe): Faber edn] the primary reason for my being asked to inaugurate this series: as it was certainly my primary reason for accepting the honour. [Atlantic Monthly, Faber edn]*

[Between *'was founded.'* and *'The fact that'*, in *Harvard edn*, p. [3]:] On the present occasion there are two strong reasons why this reminder should be more than the ordinary formal tribute. This is the first of the lectures to be given annually in the name of Theodore Spencer, sometime Boylston professor of Rhetoric in Harvard University. In the second place,

[Between *'accepting the honour'* and *'Except when there has been'* in *Harvard edn*, pp. [3]–4:] If I speak of [4] him at greater length than is usual on such occasions, I feel sure that you will not only excuse but approve my doing so. There must be many of his friends and former pupils in this audience; much that I shall say of him will therefore be familiar knowledge; but I am sure that an act of homage to his personality, his work, and his influence will be welcome to all of you.
Except when there has been some accident to fix it in my memory, I find that I seldom

I. ON POETRY — POETRY AND DRAMA • 205

remember the occasion of my first meeting with anyone who has subsequently become an associate or friend. I am not now sure whether I first met Theodore Spencer when he was an undergraduate at Trinity College, Cambridge, or on some later visit that he paid to England – for he loved Cambridge and liked to return there. I had certainly met him in England, and probably several times, before I came to Harvard as Norton Professor in 1932. But it was during that year, when I saw him almost every day, at Eliot House, or in his own home, or in the company of mutual friends, that we were closely associated; and it was through this constant frequentation that I came to love and appreciate the man. He put his time most generously at my disposal; helped me at every juncture with a course of lectures to a small class which he himself had been instrumental in selecting; and there was no detail of daily life in which he was not ready to give aid, and no material need which he was not anxious to anticipate. And the day in which he did not drop in for a chat before lunch, was always a duller day than the others.

After 1933 I saw him, of course, only at intervals. He visited England several times – I remember that he was present, in Cambridge, at the Encaenia [Congregation: *Harvard edn*, p. 5] at which I received a doctor's degree, and I remember his pleasure in the event. Between visits, we carried on a desultory correspondence. In 1938, or perhaps early in 1939, the rumor reached us in England that economies were being effected, [No comma in *Harvard edn*, p. 5] which might be adverse to his promotion or security of tenure at Harvard [in this university; *Harvard edn*, p. 5], and I was a party to the maneuvers of some of his friends in Cambridge, England, toward obtaining for him a Lectureship there. In 1939 he was appointed [You know that he was in 1939 appointed: *Harvard edn*, p. 5] to a Lectureship at Cambridge University, but [but that,: *Harvard edn*, p. 6] owing to the outbreak of war, the immediate reduction in the numbers of students in the English Tripos [(for only those were left who were unfit for wartime service): *Harvard edn*, p. 6], and the consequent reduction in the number of tutors, it was deemed best that his appointment should be deferred. This was a great disappointment to his friends in England; but on the other hand, we had the pleasure of hearing of his reappointment to Harvard as "visiting lecturer from Cambridge University." It was not long before he received promotion.

I should like to add a note which I hope is not indiscreet. When the august position of Boylston Professor became vacant, Ted Spencer was not one to covet that post for himself. He wrote to me privately, to ask whether I would consider the position if my name were put forward. Well, there were several reasons, both private and public, why I would not regard myself as eligible: not the least of which was my lack of scholarship – I think I told him that I should have had to spend all my spare time reading the books I ought to have read, and would have no leisure left for writing. My delight and satisfaction were great when I read that he himself had received that distinguished appointment.

Though I do not remember our first meeting, I remember very clearly our last. It was in Cambridge, Massachusetts, just before my return to London, and only a few weeks before his death. He was full of enthusiasm for the work he was to undertake that year; he appeared in better health, and more radiantly happy, than I had ever seen him; and I thought that he had many years of both scholarly and creative work and of useful influence before him.

I do not need to remind those who knew him, or indeed those who were even slightly acquainted with him, of the charm of his personality, his interest in human beings, his *gaiety, sense of humour and conviviality – with a bearing such that he could put his pupils on terms of informal equality, without ever losing his dignity or their respect. He had several traits, in happy combination, which made him a good teacher. His standards of scholarship were high, and his view of English studies was humane; he mixed with men of letters in New York and London, as well as in the universities; and was perfectly at ease in society, whether intellectual society or not, so that he knew his students as human beings, not merely as candidates for degrees. He had a sensitive appreciation of the best in contemporary literature; and his own poetic gift was genuine. His poetry had developed, and would I believe have gone on to still greater strength after he had further assimilated and re-created the powerful influence of Yeats. But I have left to the last, mention of those characteristics which most endeared him as a friend: humility, charity, generosity, and what I can only call a fundamental goodness.*

In choosing a subject [for this lecture: *Harvard edn,* p. 8], *I have had in mind* [,first,: *Harvard edn,* p. 8] *that it should be a subject in some way related to Theodore Spencer's interests, and that it* [second, that it: *Harvard edn,* p. 8] *should be a subject on which he himself would have liked to hear me* [speak, and, third, that it should be a subject about which this audience might like to hear me speak: *Harvard edn,* p. 8]. *Faber edn*

[*Harvard edn,* between 'hear me speak.' and 'Reviewing my critical output', pp. 8–9:] Poetic drama was certainly something that Spencer cared about: I hardly need mention his studies of Shakespeare, or his fascinated interest in the [9] poetry of Shakespeare' contemporaries; but I should like to remind you of those performances of Elizabeth drama by the members of Eliot House which Spencer did so much to inspire and organise and in which he participated with so much zest (I remember in particular a performance of *The Shoemaker's Holiday* in which the late Master, Roger Merriman, played the part of the King with all the majesty appropriate to the Master of a Harvard House). As for myself, this is no new subject for me; in fact,

[Before 'Reviewing my critical output':] **2** *Atlantic Monthly,* Faber edn

1 [After 'my own experimentation.':] And I hope I have profited by this experience. *Harvard edn*

2 if so] , if so, *Harvard edn*

4 [No new para. in Harvard edn]
can also be deplorable] it can also be deplorable *Harvard edn*
attracted by it] attracted by verse *Harvard edn*
effect of style] effect and style *Harvard edn*

6 believe that in verse drama prose] believe that prose *Atlantic Monthly, Harvard edn, Faber edn*
because our form] that our form *Atlantic Monthly, Harvard edn, Faber edn*
prose dialogue] prose dialogue, *Atlantic Monthly, Faber edn*

8 a tragic action] an ominous action *Atlantic Monthly, Harvard edn, Faber edn*

10 this advantage,] this advantage *Harvard edn*
employed it] was able to employ it *Harvard edn*
[Before para. 12:] **3** *Atlantic Monthly, Faber edn*

13 cares nothing,] cares nothing *Harvard edn*

I. ON POETRY — POETRY AND DRAMA • 207

14 for a beginner,] for a beginner *Harvard edn*
16 first time for the stage,] first time for the stage *Harvard edn*
    strengthened the power,] strengthened the power *Harvard edn*
17 find out also,] find out, also, *Harvard edn*
    [Between 'the use of prose.' and 'The two prose passages':] I have already given the justification of this aim. *Harvard edn*
    churchgoers] churchgoer *Atlantic Monthly, Harvard edn, Faber edn*
18 therefore they should] they should *Atlantic Monthly, Harvard edn, Faber edn*
    unlike its own] unlike their own *Atlantic Monthly, Harvard edn*
    poetry is tolerated] poetry can be spoken *Atlantic Monthly, Harvard edn*
19 light syllables;] light syllables, *Harvard edn*
20 [No new para. in *Harvard edn*]
    but on the contrary,] but, on the contrary, *Harvard edn*
    irony, dignity,] irony, dignity *Harvard edn*
21 employed far too much] taken far too much *Atlantic* Monthly, *Harvard edn, Faber edn*
    allowed to a dramatist,] allowed to a dramatist *Harvard edn*
22 [No new para. in *Harvard edn*]
23 [No new para. in *Harvard edn*]
24 to do so] to take this *Atlantic Monthly, Harvard edn*
    in having their attention called] after I have called their attention *Atlantic Monthly, Faber edn*
25 [No new para. in *Harvard edn*]
26 the needs of the stage] the needs of the drama, *Harvard edn*
    he may find that later] there may be a later stage *Atlantic Monthly, Harvard edn, Faber edn*
    this belief] that belief *Atlantic Monthly, Harvard edn, Faber edn*
    [Between 'language in his late plays.' and 'In devoting':] But to give reason for this belief involves an examination and defence of Shakespeare's late plays as plays; and this obviously is the subject for a separate essay. *Harvard edn*
27 the mistakes into which I have fallen, and the weaknesses I have had to try to overcome] the weaknesses I have had to try to overcome, and the mistakes into which I have fallen *Atlantic Monthly, Harvard edn*
28 close without] close, however, without *Harvard edn*
    set before you, though only in dim outline,] set before myself, and, if I can, before you, though only in dim outline, *Harvard edn*]

[No 'Note to "Poetry and Drama"' in *Atlantic Monthly, Harvard edn, Faber edn*]

The Three Voices of Poetry[1]

OPAP, 89–102.

Revised from *The Three Voices of Poetry* (11 Dec. 1953), the eleventh Annual Lecture of the National Book League, which Eliot had delivered at the Central Hall, Westminster, on Thursday, 19 Nov. 1953: Gallup A63a.

1 The first voice is the voice of the poet talking to himself – or to nobody. The second is the voice of the poet addressing an audience, whether large or small. The third is the voice of the poet when he attempts to create a dramatic character speaking in verse; when he is saying, not what he would say in his own person, but only what he can say within the limits of one imaginary character addressing another imaginary character. The distinction between the first and the second voice, between the poet speaking to himself and the poet speaking to other people, points to the problem of poetic communication; the distinction between the poet addressing other people in either his own voice or an assumed voice, and the poet inventing speech in which imaginary characters address each other, points to the problem of the difference between dramatic, quasi-dramatic, and non-dramatic verse.

2 I wish to anticipate a question that some of you may well raise. Cannot a poem be written for the ear, or for the eye, of one person alone? You may say simply, 'Isn't love poetry at times a form of communication between one person and one other, with no thought of a further audience?'

3 There are at least two people who might have disagreed with me on this point: Mr and Mrs Robert Browning. In the poem 'One Word More', written as an epilogue to *Men and Women*, and addressed to Mrs Browning, the husband makes a striking value judgement:

> Rafael made a century of sonnets,
> Made and wrote them in a certain volume,
> Dinted with the silver-pointed pencil
> Else he only used to draw Madonnas:
> [90] These, the world might view – but one, the volume.
> Who that one, you ask? Your heart instructs you . . .
> You and I would rather read that volume . . .
> Would we not ? than wonder at Madonnas . . .
>
> Dante once prepared to paint an angel:
> Whom to please? You whisper 'Beatrice'. . .

---

1. The eleventh Annual Lecture of the National Book League, delivered in 1953 and published for the N.B.L. by the Cambridge University Press.

> You and I would rather see that angel,
> Painted by the tenderness of Dante,
> Would we not ? – than read a fresh *Inferno*.

I agree that one *Inferno*, even by Dante, is enough; and perhaps we need not too much regret the fact that Rafael did not multiply his Madonnas: but I can only say that I feel no curiosity whatever about Rafael's sonnets or Dante's angel. If Rafael wrote, or Dante painted, for the eyes of one person alone, let their privacy be respected. We know that Mr and Mrs Browning liked to write poems to each other, because they published them, and some of them are good poems. We know that Rossetti thought that he was writing his *House of Life* sonnets for one person, and that he was only persuaded by his friends to disinter them. Now, I do not deny that a poem may be addressed to one person: there is a well-known form, not always amatory in content, called The Epistle. We shall never have conclusive evidence: for the testimony of poets as to what they thought they were doing when they wrote a poem, cannot be taken altogether at its face value. But my opinion is, that a good love poem, though it may be addressed to one person, is always meant to be overheard by other people. Surely, the proper language of love – that is, of communication to the beloved and to no one else – is prose.

4 Having dismissed as an illusion the voice of the poet talking to one person only, I think that the best way for me to try to make my three voices audible, is to trace the genesis of the distinction in my own mind. The writer to whose mind the distinction is most likely to occur is probably the writer like myself, who has spent a good many years in writing poetry, before attempting to write for the stage at all. It may be, as I have read, that there is a dramatic element in much of my early work. It may be that from the beginning I aspired unconsciously to the theatre – or, unfriendly critics might say, to Shaftesbury Avenue and Broadway. I have, however, gradually come to the conclusion that in writing verse for the stage [91] both the process and the outcome are very different from what they are in writing verse to be read or recited. Twenty years ago I was commissioned to write a pageant play to be called *The Rock*. The invitation to write the words for this spectacle – the occasion of which was an appeal for funds for church-building in new housing areas – came at a moment when I seemed to myself to have exhausted my meagre poetic gifts, and to have nothing more to say. To be, at such a moment, commissioned to write something which, good or bad, must be delivered by a certain date, may have the effect that vigorous cranking sometimes has upon a motor car when the battery is run down. The task was clearly laid out: I had only to write the words of prose dialogue for scenes of the

usual historical pageant pattern, for which I had been given a scenario. I had also to provide a number of choral passages in verse, the content of which was left to my own devices: except for the reasonable stipulation that all the choruses were expected to have some relevance to the purpose of the pageant, and that each chorus was to occupy a precise number of minutes of stage time. But in carrying out this second part of my task, there was nothing to call my attention to the third, or dramatic voice: it was the second voice, that of myself addressing – indeed haranguing – an audience, that was most distinctly audible. Apart from the obvious fact that writing to order is not the same thing as writing to please oneself, I learnt only that verse to be spoken by a choir should be different from verse to be spoken by one person; and that the more voices you have in your choir, the simpler and more direct the vocabulary, the syntax, and the content of your lines must be. This chorus of *The Rock* was not a dramatic voice; though many lines were distributed, the personages were unindividuated. Its members were speaking for me, not uttering words that really represented any supposed character of their own.

5 The chorus in *Murder in the Cathedral* does, I think, represent some advance in dramatic development: that is to say, I set myself the task of writing lines, not for an anonymous chorus, but for a chorus of women of Canterbury – one might almost say, charwomen of Canterbury. I had to make some effort to identify myself with these women, instead of merely identifying them with myself. But as for the dialogue of the play, the plot had the drawback (from the point of view of my own dramatic education) of presenting only one dominant character; and what dramatic conflict there is takes place within the mind of that character. The third, or [92] dramatic voice, did not make itself audible to me until I first attacked the problem of presenting two (or more) characters, in some sort of conflict, misunderstanding, or attempt to understand each other, characters with each of whom I had to try to identify myself while writing the words for him or her to speak. You may remember that Mrs Cluppins, in the trial of the case of Bardell *v.* Pickwick, testified that 'the voices was very loud, sir, and forced themselves upon my ear'. 'Well, Mrs Cluppins,' said Sergeant Buzfuz, 'you were not listening, but you heard the voices.' It was in 1938, then, that the third voice began to force itself upon my ear.

6 At this point I can fancy the reader murmuring: 'I'm sure he has said all this before.' I will assist memory by supplying the reference. In a lecture on 'Poetry and Drama', delivered exactly three years ago and subsequently published, I said:

> In writing other verse (i.e. non-dramatic verse) I think that one is writing, so to speak, in terms of one's own voice: the way it sounds

when you read it to yourself is the test. For it is yourself speaking. The question of communication, of what the reader will get from it, is not paramount. . . .

7 There is some confusion of pronouns in this passage, but I think that the meaning is clear; so clear, as to be a glimpse of the obvious. At that stage, I noted only the difference between speaking for oneself, and speaking for an imaginary character; and I passed on to other considerations about the nature of poetic drama. I was beginning to be aware of the difference between the first and the third voice, but gave no attention to the second voice, of which I shall say more presently. I am now trying to penetrate a little further into the problem. So, before going on to consider the other voices, I want to pursue for a few moments the complexities of the third voice.

8 In a verse play, you will probably have to find words for several characters differing widely from each other in background, temperament, education, and intelligence. You cannot afford to identify one of these characters with yourself, and give him (or her) all the 'poetry' to speak. The poetry (I mean, the language at those dramatic moments when it reaches intensity) must be as widely distributed as characterisation permits; and each of your characters, when he has words to speak which are poetry and not merely verse, must be given lines appropriate to himself. When the poetry comes, the personage on the stage must not give the [93] impression of being merely a mouthpiece for the author. Hence the author is limited by the kind of poetry, and the degree of intensity in its kind, which can be plausibly attributed to each character in his play. And these lines of poetry must also justify themselves by their development of the situation in which they are spoken. Even if a burst of magnificent poetry is suitable enough for the character to which it is assigned, it must also convince us that it is necessary to the action; that it is helping to extract the utmost emotional intensity out of the situation. The poet writing for the theatre may, as I have found, make two mistakes: that of assigning to a personage lines of poetry not suitable to be spoken by that personage, and that of assigning lines which, however suitable to the personage, yet fail to forward the action of the play. There are, in some of the minor Elizabethan dramatists, passages of magnificent poetry which are in both respects out of place – fine enough to preserve the play for ever as literature, but yet so inappropriate as to prevent the play from being a dramatic masterpiece. The best-known instances occur in Marlowe's *Tamburlaine*.

9 How have the very great dramatic poets – Sophocles, or Shakespeare, or Racine – dealt with this difficulty? This is, of course, a problem which

concerns all imaginative fiction – novels and prose plays – in which the characters may be said to live. I can't see, myself, any way to make a character live except to have a profound sympathy with that character. Ideally, a dramatist, who has usually far fewer characters to manipulate than a novelist, and who has only two hours or so of life to allow them, should sympathise profoundly with all of his characters: but that is a counsel of perfection, because the plot of a play with even a very small cast may require the presence of one or more characters in whose reality, apart from their contribution to the action, we are uninterested. I wonder, however, whether it is possible to make completely real a wholly villainous character – one toward whom neither the author nor anyone else can feel anything but antipathy. We need an admixture of *weakness* with either heroic virtue or satanic villainy, to make character plausible. Iago frightens me more than Richard III; I am not sure that Parolles, in *All's Well That Ends Well*, does not disturb me more than Iago. (And I am quite sure that Rosamund Vincy, in *Middlemarch*, frightens me far more than Goneril or Regan.) It seems to me that what happens, when an author creates a vital character, is a sort of give-and-take. The author may put into that character, besides its other attributes, some trait of his own, some strength or weakness, some tendency to violence or to indecision, some eccentricity even, that he has found in himself. Something perhaps never realised in his own life, something of which those who know him best may be unaware, something not restricted in transmission to characters of the same temperament, the same age, and, least of all, of the same sex. Some bit of himself that the author gives to a character may be the germ from which the life of that character starts. On the other hand, a character which succeeds in interesting its author may elicit from the author latent potentialities of his own being. I believe that the author imparts something of himself to his characters, but I also believe that he is influenced by the characters he creates. It would be only too easy to lose oneself in a maze of speculation about the process by which an imaginary character can become as real for us as people we have known. I have penetrated into this maze so far only to indicate the difficulties, the limitations, the fascination, for a poet who is used to writing poetry in his own person, of the problem of making imaginary personages talk poetry. And the difference, the abyss, between writing for the first and for the third voice.

10 The peculiarity of my third voice, the voice of poetic drama, is brought out in another way by comparing it with the voice of the poet in non-dramatic poetry which has a dramatic element in it – and conspicuously in the dramatic monologue. Browning, in an uncritical moment, addressed

himself as 'Robert Browning, you writer of plays'. How many of us have read a play by Browning more than once; and, if we have read it more than once, was our motive the expectation of enjoyment? What personage, in a play by Browning, remains living in our mind? On the other hand, who can forget Fra Lippo Lippi, or Andrea del Sarto, or Bishop Blougram, or the other bishop who ordered his tomb? It would seem without further examination, from Browning's mastery of the dramatic monologue, and his very moderate achievement in the drama, that the two forms must be essentially different. Is there, perhaps, another voice which I have failed to hear, the voice of the dramatic poet whose dramatic gifts are best exercised outside of the theatre? And certainly, if any poetry, not of the stage, deserves to be characterized as 'dramatic', it is Browning's.

11 In a play, as I have said, an author must have divided loyalties; [95] he must sympathise with characters who may be in no way sympathetic to each other. And he must allocate the 'poetry' as widely as the limitations of each imaginary character permit. This necessity to divide the poetry implies some variation of the style of the poetry according to the character to whom it is given. The fact that a number of characters in a play have claims upon the author, for their allotment of poetic speech, compels him to try to extract the poetry from the character, rather than impose his poetry upon it. Now, in the dramatic monologue we have no such check. The author is just as likely to identify the character with himself, as himself with the character: for the check is missing that will prevent him from doing so – and that check is the necessity for identifying himself with some other character replying to the first. What we normally hear, in fact, in the dramatic monologue, is the voice of the poet, who has put on the costume and make-up either of some historical character, or of one out of fiction. His personage must be identified to us – as an individual, or at least as a type – before he begins to speak. If, as frequently with Browning, the poet is speaking in the role of an historical personage, like Lippo Lippi, or in the role of a known character of fiction, like Caliban, he has taken possession of that character. And the difference is most evident in his *Caliban upon Setebos*. In *The Tempest*, it is Caliban who speaks; in *Caliban upon Setebos*, it is Browning's voice that we hear, Browning talking aloud through Caliban. It was Browning's greatest disciple, Mr Ezra Pound, who adopted the term 'persona' to indicate the several historical characters through whom he spoke: and the term is just.

12 I risk the generalisation also, which may indeed be far too sweeping, that dramatic monologue cannot create a character. For character is created and made real only in an action, a communication between imaginary people. It is not irrelevant that when the dramatic monologue

is not put into the mouth of some character already known to the reader – from history or from fiction – we are likely to ask the question 'Who was the original?' About Bishop Blougram people have always been impelled to ask, how far was this intended to be a portrait of Cardinal Manning, or of some other ecclesiastic? The poet, speaking, as Browning does, in his own voice, cannot bring a character to life: he can only mimic a character otherwise known to us. And does not the point of mimicry lie in the recognition of the person mimicked, and in the incompleteness of the illusion? We have to be aware that the [96] mimic and the person mimicked are different people: if we are actually deceived, mimicry becomes impersonation. When we listen to a play by Shakespeare, we listen not to Shakespeare but to his characters; when we read a dramatic monologue by Browning, we cannot suppose that we are listening to any other voice than that of Browning himself.

13 In the dramatic monologue, then, it is surely the second voice, the voice of the poet talking to other people, that is dominant. The mere fact that he is assuming a role, that he is speaking through a mask, implies the presence of an audience: why should a man put on fancy dress and a mask only to talk to himself? The second voice is, in fact, the voice most often and most clearly heard in poetry that is not of the theatre: in all poetry, certainly, that has a conscious social purpose – poetry intended to amuse or to instruct, poetry that tells a story, poetry that preaches or points a moral, or satire which is a form of preaching. For what is the point of a story without an audience, or of a sermon without a congregation? The voice of the poet addressing other people is the dominant voice of epic, though not the only voice. In Homer, for instance, there is heard also, from time to time, the dramatic voice: there are moments when we hear, not Homer telling us what a hero said, but the voice of the hero himself. *The Divine Comedy* is not in the exact sense an epic, but here also we hear men and women speaking to us. And we have no reason to suppose that Milton's sympathy with Satan was so exclusive as to seal him of the Devil's Party. But the epic is essentially a tale told to an audience, while drama is essentially an action exhibited to an audience.

14 Now, what about the poetry of the first voice – that which is not primarily an attempt to communicate with anyone at all?

15 I must make the point that this poetry is not necessarily what we call loosely 'lyric poetry'. The term 'lyric' itself is unsatisfactory. We think first of verse intended to be sung – from the songs of Campion and Shakespeare and Burns, to the arias of W. S. Gilbert, or the words of the latest 'musical number'. But we apply it also to poetry that was never intended for a musical setting, or which we dissociate from its music: we speak of

the 'lyric verse' of the metaphysical poets, of Vaughan and Marvell as well as Donne and Herbert. The very definition of 'lyric', in the Oxford Dictionary, indicates that the word cannot be satisfactorily defined: [97]

> *Lyric*: Now the name for short poems, usually divided into stanzas or strophes, and directly expressing the poet's own thoughts and sentiments.

How short does a poem have to be, to be called a 'lyric'? The emphasis on brevity, and the suggestion of division into stanzas, seem residual from the association of the voice with music. But there is no necessary relation between brevity and the expression of the poet's own thoughts and feelings. 'Come unto these yellow sands' or 'Hark! hark! the lark' are lyrics – are they not? – but what sense is there in saying that they express directly the poet's own thoughts and sentiments? *London*, *The Vanity of Human Wishes*, and *The Deserted Village* are all poems which appear to express the poet's own thoughts and sentiments, but do we ever think of such poems as 'lyrical'? They are certainly not short. Between them, all the poems I have mentioned seem to fail to qualify as lyrics, just as Mr Daddy Longlegs and Mr Floppy Fly failed to qualify as courtiers:

> One never more can go to court,
> Because his legs have grown too short;
> The other cannot sing a song,
> Because his legs have grown too long!

16 It is obviously the lyric in the sense of a poem 'directly expressing the poet's own thoughts and sentiments', not in the quite unrelated sense of a short poem intended to be set to music, that is relevant to my first voice – the voice of the poet talking to himself – or to nobody. It is in this sense that the German poet Gottfried Benn, in a very interesting lecture entitled *Probleme der Lyrik*, thinks of lyric as the poetry of the first voice: he includes, I feel sure, such poems as Rilke's Duinese Elegies and Valéry's *La Jeune Parque*. Where he speaks of 'lyric poetry', then, I should prefer to say 'meditative verse'.

17 What, asks Herr Benn in this lecture, does the writer of such a poem, 'addressed to no one', start with? There is first, he says, an inert embryo or 'creative germ' (*ein dumpfer schöpferischer Keim*) and, on the other hand, the Language, the resources of the words at the poet's command. He has something germinating in him for which he must find words; but he cannot know what words he wants until he has found the words; he cannot identify this embryo until it has been transformed into an arrangement of the right words in the right order. When you have the words for it, the [98] 'thing' for which the words had to be found has

disappeared, replaced by a poem. What you start from is nothing so definite as an emotion, in any ordinary sense; it is still more certainly not an idea; it is – to adapt two lines of Beddoes to a different meaning – a

> bodiless childful of life in the gloom
> Crying with frog voice, 'what shall I be?'

I agree with Gottfried Benn, and I would go a little further. In a poem which is neither didactic nor narrative, and not animated by any other social purpose, the poet may be concerned solely with expressing in verse – using all his resources of words, with their history, their connotations, their music – this obscure impulse. He does not know what he has to say until he has said it; and in the effort to say it he is not concerned with making other people understand anything. He is not concerned, at this stage, with other people at all: only with finding the right words or, anyhow, the least wrong words. He is not concerned whether anybody else will ever listen to them or not, or whether anybody else will ever understand them if he does. He is oppressed by a burden which he must bring to birth in order to obtain relief. Or, to change the figure of speech, he is haunted by a demon, a demon against which he feels powerless, because in its first manifestation it has no face, no name, nothing; and the words, the poem he makes, are a kind of form of exorcism of this demon. In other words again, he is going to all that trouble, not in order to communicate with anyone, but to gain relief from acute discomfort; and when the words are finally arranged in the right way – or in what he comes to accept as the best arrangement he can find – he may experience a moment of exhaustion, of appeasement, of absolution, and of something very near annihilation, which is in itself indescribable. And then he can say to the poem: 'Go away! Find a place for your self in a book – and don't expect *me* to take any further interest in you.'

18 I don't believe that the relation of a poem to its origins is capable of being more clearly traced. You can read the essays of Paul Valéry, who studied the workings of his own mind in the composition of a poem more perseveringly than any other poet has done. But if, either on the basis of what poets try to tell you, or by biographical research, with or without the tools of the psychologist, you attempt to explain a poem, you will probably be getting [99] further and further away from the poem without arriving at any other destination. The attempt to explain the poem by tracing it back to its origins will distract attention from the poem, to direct it on to something else which, in the form in which it can be apprehended by the critic and his readers, has no relation to the poem and throws no light upon it. I should not like you to think that I am

trying to make the writing of a poem more of a mystery than it is. What I am maintaining is, that the first effort of the poet should be to achieve clarity for himself, to assure himself that the poem is the right outcome of the process that has taken place. The most bungling form of obscurity is that of the poet who has not been able to express himself *to* himself; the shoddiest form is found when the poet is trying to persuade himself that he has something to say when he hasn't.

19 So far I have been speaking, for the sake of simplicity, of the three voices as if they were mutually exclusive: as if the poet, in any particular poem, was speaking *either* to himself or to others, and as if neither of the first two voices was audible in good dramatic verse. And this indeed is the conclusion to which Herr Benn's argument appears to lead him: he speaks as if the poetry of the first voice – which he considers, moreover, to be on the whole a development of our own age – was a totally different kind of poetry from that of the poet addressing an audience. But for me the voices are most often found together – the first and second, I mean, in non-dramatic poetry; and together with the third in dramatic poetry too. Even though, as I have maintained, the author of a poem may have written it primarily without thought of an audience, he will also want to know what the poem which has satisfied *him* will have to say to other people. There are, first of all, those few friends to whose criticism he may wish to submit it before considering it completed. They can be very helpful, in suggesting a word or a phrase which the author has not been able to find for himself; though their greatest service perhaps is to say simply 'this passage won't do'– thus confirming a suspicion which the author had been suppressing from his own consciousness. But I am not thinking primarily of the few judicious friends whose opinion the author prizes, but of the larger and unknown audience – people to whom the author's name means only his poem which they have read. The final handing over, so to speak, of the poem to an unknown audience, for what that audience will make of it, seems to me the consummation of the process begun [100] in solitude and without thought of the audience, the long process of gestation of the poem, because it marks the final separation of the poem from the author. Let the author, at this point, rest in peace.

20 So much for the poem which is primarily a poem of the first voice. I think that in every poem, from the private meditation to the epic or the drama, there is more than one voice to be heard. If the author never spoke to himself, the result would not be poetry, though it might be magnificent rhetoric; and part of our enjoyment of great poetry is the enjoyment of *overhearing* words which are not addressed to us. But if the poem were exclusively for the author, it would be a poem in a private and unknown

language; and a poem which was a poem only for the author would not be a poem at all. And in poetic drama, I am inclined to believe that all three voices are audible. First, the voice of each character – an individual voice different from that of any other character: so that of each utterance we can say, that it could only have come from that character. There may be from time to time, and perhaps when we least notice it, the voices of the author and the character in unison, saying something appropriate to the character, but something which the author could say for himself also, though the words may not have quite the same meaning for both. That may be a very different thing from the ventriloquism which makes the character only a mouthpiece for the author's ideas or sentiments.

To-morrow and to-morrow and to-morrow . . .

Is not the perpetual shock and surprise of these hackneyed lines evidence that Shakespeare and Macbeth are uttering the words in unison, though perhaps with somewhat different meaning? And finally there are the lines, in plays by one of the supreme poetic dramatists, in which we hear a more impersonal voice still than that of either the character or the author.

Ripeness is all

or

Simply the thing I am
Shall make me live.

21 And now I should like to return for a moment to Gottfried Benn and his unknown, dark *psychic material* – we might say, the octopus or angel with which the poet struggles. I suggest that between the three kinds of poetry to which my three voices corre-[101]spond there is a certain difference of process. In the poem in which the first voice, that of the poet talking to himself, dominates, the 'psychic material' tends to create its own form – the eventual form will be to a greater or less degree the form for that one poem and for no other. It is misleading, of course, to speak of the material as creating or imposing its own form: what happens is a simultaneous development of form and material; for the form affects the material at every stage; and perhaps all the material does is to repeat 'not that! not that!' in the face of each unsuccessful attempt at formal organisation; and finally the material is identified with its form. But in poetry of the second and in that of the third voice, the form is already to some extent given. However much it may be *trans*formed before the poem is finished, it can be represented from the start by an outline or scenario. If I choose to tell a story, I must have some notion of the plot of

the story I propose to tell; if I undertake satire, moralising, or invective, there is already something given which I can recognise and which exists for others as well as myself. And if I set out to write a play, I start by an act of choice: I settle upon a particular emotional situation, out of which characters and a plot will emerge, and I can make a plain prose outline of the play in advance – however much that outline may be altered before the play is finished, by the way in which the characters develop. It is likely, of course, that it is in the beginning the pressure of some rude unknown *psychic material* that directs the poet to tell that particular story, to develop that particular situation. And on the other hand, the frame, once chosen, within which the author has elected to work, may itself evoke other psychic material; and then, lines of poetry may come into being, not from the original impulse, but from a secondary stimulation of the unconscious mind. All that matters is, that in the end the voices should be heard in harmony; and, as I have said, I doubt whether in any real poem only one voice is audible.

22 The reader may well, by now, have been asking himself what I have been up to in all these speculations. Have I been toiling to weave a laboured web of useless ingenuity? Well, I have been trying to talk, not to myself – as you may have been tempted to think – but to the reader of poetry. I should like to think that it might interest the reader of poetry to test my assertions in his own reading. Can you distinguish these voices in the poetry you read, or hear recited, or hear in the theatre? If you complain that a poet is obscure, and apparently ignoring you, the reader, or that [102] he is speaking only to a limited circle of initiates from which you are excluded – remember that what he may have been trying to do, was to put something into words which could not be said in any other way, and therefore in a language which may be worth the trouble of learning. If you complain that a poet is too rhetorical, and that he addresses you as if you were a public meeting, try to listen for the moments when he is not speaking to you, but merely allowing himself to be overheard: he may be a Dryden, a Pope, or a Byron. And if you have to listen to a verse play, take it first at its face value, as entertainment, for each character speaking for himself with whatever degree of reality his author has been able to endow him. Perhaps, if it is a great play, and you do not try too hard to hear them, you may discern the other voices too. For the work of a great poetic dramatist, like Shakespeare, constitutes a world. Each character speaks for himself, but no other poet could have found those words for him to speak. If you seek for Shakespeare, you will find him only in the characters he created; for the one thing in common between the characters is that no one but Shakespeare could have created

any of them. The world of a great poetic dramatist is a world in which the creator is everywhere present, and everywhere hidden.

Variants from 1953:

[Before para. 1:] There may be four voices. There may be, perhaps, only two. I say this to indicate the tentative nature of my enquiry. And I wish to explain at once why I have chosen, for such a serious occasion as the National Book League Annual Lecture, to propound a notion the validity of which is uncertain, and the value of which, even if true, may be questionable.

   In choosing a subject about which to speak on an occasion such as this, I have two preliminary aims in mind. One is, to avoid saying anything that I have said before; the other is, to avoid saying anything that somebody else has said before – and probably said better. These aims together are almost impossible of realisation. Most of us have very few original ideas, in the course of a lifetime; most of our original ideas come to us when we are young and inexperienced; and some of us devote our later years to trying the express the same ideas better, or to facing the fact that they are not nearly so original as they once seemed to be. Alas! if there is no truth that has not been discovered by our ancestors, then there is also no possible error by which they have not been deceived. Yet we go on, to the end of our lives, hoping to say something that we have never said before, that no one else has ever said before, something which is worth saying, something which is even *true*. And while we are under the illusion that we have found such a thing to say, it seems to us at the moment the best offering that we can possibly make to any audience.

   I shall explain at once what I mean by the "three voices".

1   The first voice is] The first is
3   on this point] on this point, after the lecture, if they could have been present
4   unfriendly critics might say, to Shaftesbury Avenue and Broadway.] critics might say with more asperity, to Shaftesbury Avenue.
    this second part of my task] this task
5   charwomen of Canterbury.] the charwomen of the Cathedral.
6   the reader murmuring] someone in the audience murmuring to a neighbour
7   [No new para.]
    [After 'the complexities of the third voice.':] I should not like to tarnish my reputation by giving any member of this audience cause to complain that I have made my discourse too intelligible.
22 The reader] You
    himself] yourselves

The Frontiers of Criticism[1]

OPAP, 103–18.

Revised from *The Frontiers of Criticism*, the Gideon D. Seymour Memorial Lecture, delivered at the University of Minnesota on 30 Apr. 1956 and distributed gratis beginning on 13 Aug. 1956: Gallup A68. It was not publ. in Britain.

In para. 15 'C. C. Jung' has been corrected to 'C. G. Jung', in para. 19 'F. E. Bateson' to 'F. W. Bateson'; and in para. 21 'Professors Richards' to 'Professor Richards'.

1 The thesis of this paper is that there are limits, exceeding which in one direction literary criticism ceases to be literary, and exceeding which in another it ceases to be criticism.

2 In 1923 I wrote an article entitled *The Function of Criticism*. I must have thought well of this essay ten years later, as I included it in my *Selected Essays*, where it is still to be found. On re-reading this essay recently, I was rather bewildered, wondering what all the fuss had been about – though I was glad to find nothing positively to contradict my present opinions. For, leaving aside a wrangle with Mr Middleton Murry about 'the inner voice' – a dispute in which I recognise the old *aporia* of Authority v. Individual Judgement – I found it impossible to recall to mind the background of my outburst. I had made a number of statements with assurance and considerable warmth; and it would seem that I must have had in mind one or more well-established critics senior to myself whose writings did not satisfy my requirements of what literary criticism should be. But I cannot recall a single book or essay, or the name of a single critic, as representative of the kind of impressionistic criticism which aroused my ire thirty-three years ago.

3 The only point in mentioning this essay now, is to call attention to the extent to which what I wrote on this subject in 1923 is 'dated'. Richards's *Principles of Literary Criticism* was published in 1925. A great deal has happened in literary criticism since this influential book came out; and my paper was written two years earlier. Criticism has developed and branched out in several directions. The term 'The New Criticism' is often employed by people without realising what a variety it comprehends; but its currency does, I think, recognise the fact that the more distinguished critics [104] of to-day, however widely they differ from each other, all differ in some significant way from the critics of a previous generation.

4 Many years ago I pointed out that every generation must provide its own literary criticism; for, as I said, 'each generation brings to the

---

1. The Gideon Seymour Lecture delivered at the University of Minnesota in 1956 and published by the University.

contemplation of art its own categories of appreciation, makes its own demands upon art, and has its own uses for art.' When I made this statement I am sure that I had in mind a good deal more than the changes of taste and fashion: I had in mind at least the fact that each generation, looking at masterpieces of the past in a different perspective, is affected in its attitude by a greater number of influences than those which bore upon the generation previous. But I doubt whether I had in mind the fact that an important work of literary criticism can alter and expand the content of the term 'literary criticism' itself. Some years ago I drew attention to the steady change in meaning of the word *education* from the sixteenth century to the present day, a change which had taken place owing to the fact that education not only comprised more and more subjects, but was being supplied for or imposed upon more and more of the population. If we could follow the evolution of the term *literary criticism* in the same way, we would find something similar happening. Compare a critical masterpiece like Johnson's *Lives of the Poets* with the next great critical work to follow it, Coleridge's *Biographia Literaria*. It is not merely that Johnson represents a literary tradition to the end of which he himself belongs, while Coleridge is defending the merits and criticising the weaknesses of a new style. The difference more pertinent to what I have been saying, is due to the scope and variety of the interests which Coleridge brought to bear on his discussion of poetry. He established the relevance of philosophy, aesthetics and psychology; and once Coleridge had introduced these disciplines into literary criticism, future critics could ignore them only at their own risk. To appreciate Johnson an effort of historical imagination is needed; a modern critic can find much in common with Coleridge. The criticism of to-day, indeed, may be said to be in direct descent from Coleridge, who would, I am sure, were he alive now, take the same interest in the social sciences and in the study of language and semantics, that he took in the sciences available to him.

5 The consideration of literature in the light of one or more of these studies, is one of the two main causes of the transformation of literary criticism in our time. The other cause has not been so [105] fully recognised. The increasing attention given to the study of English and American literature in our universities and indeed in our schools, has led to a situation in which many critics are teachers, and many teachers are critics. I am far from deploring this situation: most of the really interesting criticism to-day is the work of men of letters who have found their way into universities, and of scholars whose critical activity has been first exercised in the classroom. And nowadays, when serious literary

journalism is an inadequate, as well as precarious means of support for all but a very few, this is as it must be. Only, it means that the critic to-day may have a somewhat different contact with the world, and be writing for a somewhat different audience from that of his predecessors. I have the impression that serious criticism now is being written for a different, a more limited though not necessarily a smaller public than was that of the nineteenth century.

6 I was struck not long ago by an observation of Mr Aldous Huxley in a preface to the English translation of *The Supreme Wisdom*, a book by a French psychiatrist, Dr Hubert Benoit, on the psychology of Zen Buddhism. Mr Huxley's observation responded to the impression which I had myself received from that remarkable book when I read it in French. Huxley is comparing Western psychiatry with the discipline of the East as found in Tau and Zen:

> The aim of Western psychiatry (he says) is to help the troubled individual to adjust himself to the society of less troubled individuals – individuals who are observed to be well adjusted to one another and the local institutions, but about whose adjustment to the fundamental Order of Things no enquiry is made. . . . But there is another kind of normality – a normality of perfect functioning. . . . Even a man who is perfectly adjusted to a deranged society can prepare himself, if he so desires, to become adjusted to the Nature of Things.

7 The applicability of this to my present matter is not immediately obvious. But just as Western psychiatry, from a Zen Buddhist point of view, is confused or mistaken as to what healing is for, and its attitude needs really to be reversed, so I wonder whether the weakness of modern criticism is not an uncertainty as to what criticism is for? As to what benefit it is to bring, and to whom? Its very richness and variety have perhaps obscured its ultimate purpose. Every critic may have his eye on a definite goal, may be engaged on a task which needs no justification, and yet criticism [106] itself may be lost as to its aims. If so, this is not surprising: for is it not now a commonplace, that the sciences and even the humanities have reached a point in development at which there is so much to know about any speciality, that no student has the time to know much about anything else? And the search for a curriculum which shall combine specialised study with some general education has surely been one of the problems most discussed in our universities.

8 We cannot, of course, go back to the universe of Aristotle or of St Thomas Aquinas; and we cannot go back to the state of literary criticism before Coleridge. But perhaps we can do something to save ourselves from being

overwhelmed by our own critical activity, by continually asking such a question as: when is criticism not literary criticism but something else?

9 I have been somewhat bewildered to find, from time to time, that I am regarded as one of the ancestors of modern criticism, if too old to be a modern critic myself. Thus in a book which I read recently by an author who is certainly a modern critic, I find a reference to 'The New Criticism', by which, he says, 'I mean not only the American critics, but the whole critical movement that derives from T. S. Eliot.' I don't understand why the author should isolate me so sharply from the American critics; but on the other hand I fail to see any critical movement which can be said to derive from myself, though I hope that as an editor I gave the New Criticism, or some of it, encouragement and an exercise ground in *The Criterion*. However, I think that I should, to justify this apparent modesty, indicate what I consider my own contribution to literary criticism to have been, and what are its limitations. The best of my *literary criticism* – apart from a few notorious phrases which have had a truly embarrassing success in the world – consists of essays on poets and poetic dramatists who had influenced me. It is a byproduct of my private poetry-workshop; or a prolongation of the thinking that went into the formation of my own verse. In retrospect, I see that I wrote best about poets whose work had influenced my own, and with whose poetry I had become thoroughly familiar, long before I desired to write about them, or had found the occasion to do so. My criticism has this in common with that of Ezra Pound, that its merits and its limitations can be fully appreciated only when it is considered in relation to the poetry I have written myself. In Pound's criticism there is a more didactic motive: the reader he had in mind, I think, was primarily the young poet whose style [107] was still unformed. But it is the love of certain poets who had influenced him, and (as I said of myself) a prolongation of his thinking about his own work, that inspires an early book which remains one of the best of Pound's literary essays, *The Spirit of Romance*.

10 This kind of criticism of poetry by a poet, or what I have called workshop criticism, has one obvious limitation. What has no relation to the poet's own work, or what is antipathetic to him, is outside of his competence. Another limitation of workshop criticism is that the critic's judgement may be unsound outside of his own art. My valuations of poets have remained pretty constant throughout my life; in particular, my opinions about a number of living poets have remained unchanged. It is, however, not only for this reason, that what I have in mind, in talking as I am to-day about criticism, is the criticism of poetry. Poetry, as a matter of

fact, is what most critics in the past have had in mind when generalising about literature. The criticism of prose fiction is of comparatively recent institution, and I am not qualified to discuss it; but it seems to me to require a somewhat different set of weights and measures from poetry. It might, indeed, provide an interesting subject for some critic of criticism – one who was neither poet nor novelist – to consider the differences between the ways in which the critic must approach the various *genres* of literature, and between the kinds of equipment needed. But poetry is the most convenient object of criticism to have in mind, when talking about criticism, simply for the reason that its formal qualities lend themselves most readily to generalisation. In poetry, it might seem that style is everything. That is far from being true; but the illusion that in poetry we come nearer to a purely aesthetic experience makes poetry the most convenient *genre* of literature to keep in mind when we are discussing literary criticism itself.

11 A good deal of contemporary criticism, originating at that point at which criticism merges into scholarship, and at which scholarship merges into criticism, may be characterised as the criticism of explanation by origins. To make clear what I mean I shall mention two books which have had, in this connection, a rather bad influence. I do not mean that they are bad books. On the contrary: they are both books with which everyone should be acquainted. The first is John Livingston Lowes's *The Road to Xanadu* – a book which I recommend to every student of poetry who has not yet read it. The other is James Joyce's *Finnegans Wake* – a book [108] which I recommend every student of poetry to read – at least some pages of. Livingston Lowes was a fine scholar, a good teacher, a lovable man and a man to whom I for one have private reasons to feel very grateful. James Joyce was a man of genius, a personal friend, and my citation here of *Finnegans Wake* is neither in praise nor dispraise of a book which is certainly in the category of works that can be called *monumental*. But the only obvious common characteristic of *The Road to Xanadu* and *Finnegans Wake* is that we may say of each: one book like this is enough.

12 For those who have never read *The Road to Xanadu*, I will explain that it is a fascinating piece of detection. Lowes ferreted out all the books which Coleridge had read (and Coleridge was an omnivorous and insatiable reader) and from which he had borrowed images or phrases to be found in 'Kubla Khan' and *The Ancient Mariner*. The books that Coleridge read are many of them obscure and forgotten books – he read, for instance, every book of travels upon which he could lay his hands. And Lowes showed, once and for all, that poetic originality is largely an

original way of assembling the most disparate and unlikely material to make a new whole. The demonstration is quite convincing, as evidence of how material is digested and transformed by the poetic genius. No one, after reading this book, could suppose that he understood *The Ancient Mariner* any better; nor was it in the least Dr Lowes's intention to make the *poem* more intelligible as poetry. He was engaged on an investigation of process, an investigation which was, strictly speaking, beyond the frontier of literary criticism. How such material as those scraps of Coleridge's reading became transmuted into great poetry remains as much of a mystery as ever. Yet a number of hopeful scholars have seized upon the Lowes method as offering a clue to the understanding of any poem by any poet who gives evidence of having read anything. 'I wonder,' a gentleman from Indiana wrote to me a year or more ago, 'I wonder – it is possible that I am mad, of course' (this was his interjection, not mine; of course he was not in the least mad, merely slightly touched in one corner of his head from having read *The Road to Xanadu*) 'whether "the dead cats of civilization", "rotten hippo" and Mr Kurtz have some tenuous connection with "that corpse you planted last year in your garden"?' This sounds like raving, unless you recognise the allusions: it is merely an earnest seeker trying to establish some connection between *The Waste Land* and Joseph Conrad's *Heart of Darkness*. [109]

13 Now while Dr Lowes has fired such practitioners of hermeneutics with emulative zeal, *Finnegans Wake* has provided them with a model of what they would like all literary works to be. I must hasten to explain that I am not deriding or denigrating the labours of those exegetists who have set themselves to unravel all the threads and follow all the clues in that book. If *Finnegans Wake* is to be understood at all – and we cannot judge it without such labour – that kind of detection must be pursued; and Messrs Campbell and Robinson (to mention the authors of one such piece of work) have done an admirable job. My grievance if any is against James Joyce, the author of that monstrous masterpiece, for writing a book such that large stretches of it are, without elaborate explanation, merely beautiful nonsense (very beautiful indeed when recited by an Irish voice as lovely as that of the author – would that he had recorded more of it!) Perhaps Joyce did not realise how obscure his book is. Whatever the final judgement (and I am not going to attempt a judgement) of the place of *Finnegans Wake* may be, I do not think that most poetry (for it is a kind of vast prose poem) is written in that way or requires that sort of dissection for its enjoyment and understanding. But I suspect that the enigmas provided by *Finnegans Wake* have given support to the error, prevalent nowadays, of mistaking explanation for understanding. After

the production of my play *The Cocktail Party*, my mail was swollen for months with letters offering surprising solutions of what the writers believed to be the riddle of the play's meaning. And it was evident that the writers did not resent the puzzle they thought I had set them – they liked it. Indeed, though they were unconscious of the fact, they invented the puzzle for the pleasure of discovering the solution.

14 Here I must admit that I am, on one conspicuous occasion, not guiltless of having led critics into temptation. The notes to *The Waste Land*! I had at first intended only to put down all the references for my quotations, with a view to spiking the guns of critics of my earlier poems who had accused me of plagiarism. Then, when it came to print *The Waste Land* as a little book – for the poem on its first appearance in *The Dial* and in *The Criterion* had no notes whatever – it was discovered that the poem was inconveniently short, so I set to work to expand the notes, in order to provide a few more pages of printed matter, with the result that they became the remarkable exposition of bogus scholarship that is still on view to-day. I have sometimes [110] thought of getting rid of these notes; but now they can never be unstuck. They have had almost greater popularity than the poem itself – anyone who bought my book of poems, and found that the notes to *The Waste Land* were not in it, would demand his money back. But I don't think that these notes did any harm to other poets: certainly I cannot think of any good contemporary poet who has abused this same practice. (As for Miss Marianne Moore, *her* notes to poems are always pertinent, curious, conclusive, delightful and give no encouragement whatever to the researcher of origins.) No, it is not because of my bad example to other poets that I am penitent: it is because my notes stimulated the wrong kind of interest among the seekers of sources. It was just, no doubt, that I should pay my tribute to the work of Miss Jessie Weston; but I regret having sent so many enquirers off on a wild goose chase after Tarot cards and the Holy Grail.

15 While I was pondering this question of the attempt to understand a poem by explaining its origins, I came across a quotation from C. G. Jung which struck me as having some relevance. The passage was quoted by Fr Victor White, O.P. in his book *God and the Unconscious*. Fr White quotes it in the course of exposing a radical difference between the method of Freud and the method of Jung.

> It is a generally recognised truth (says Jung) that physical events can be looked at in two ways, that is from the mechanistic and from the energic standpoint. The mechanistic view is purely causal: from this standpoint an event is conceived as the result of a cause. . . . The energic viewpoint on the other hand is in essence final; the event is

traced from effect to cause on the assumption that energy forms the essential basis of changes in phenomena. . . .

16 The quotation is from the first essay in the volume *Contributions to Analytical Psychology*. I add another sentence, not quoted by Fr White, which opens the next paragraph: 'both viewpoints are indispensable for the comprehension of physical phenomena.'

17 I take this simply as a suggestive analogy. One can explain a poem by investigating what it is made of and the causes that brought it about; and explanation may be a necessary preparation for understanding. But to understand a poem it is also necessary, and I should say in most instances still more necessary, that we should endeavour to grasp what the poetry is aiming to be; one might say – though it is long since I have employed such terms with any assurance – endeavouring to grasp its entelechy.

[111] 18 Perhaps the form of criticism in which the danger of excessive reliance upon causal explanation is greatest is the critical biography, especially when the biographer supplements his knowledge of external facts with psychological conjectures about inner experience. I do not suggest that the personality and the private life of a dead poet constitute sacred ground on which the psychologist must not tread. The scientist must be at liberty to study such material as his curiosity leads him to investigate – so long as the victim is dead and the laws of libel cannot be invoked to stop him. Nor is there any reason why biographies of poets should not be written. Furthermore, the biographer of an author should possess some critical ability; he should be a man of taste and judgement, appreciative of the work of the man whose biography he undertakes. And on the other hand any critic seriously concerned with a man's work should be expected to know something about the man's life. But a critical biography of a writer is a delicate task in itself; and the critic or the biographer who, without being a trained and practising psychologist, brings to bear on his subject such analytical skill as he has acquired by reading books written by psychologists, may confuse the issues still further.

19 The question of how far information about the poet helps us to understand the poetry is not so simple as one might think. Each reader must answer it for himself, and must answer it not generally but in particular instances, for it may be more important in the case of one poet and less important in the case of another. For the enjoyment of poetry can be a complex experience in which several forms of satisfaction are mingled; and they may be mingled in different proportions for different readers. I will give an illustration. It is generally agreed that the greatest part of Wordsworth's best poetry was written within a brief span of years –

brief in itself, and brief in proportion to the whole span of Wordsworth's life. Various students of Wordsworth have propounded explanations to account for the mediocrity of his later output. Some years ago, Sir Herbert Read wrote a book on Wordsworth – an interesting book, though I think that his best appreciation of Wordsworth is found in a later essay in a volume entitled *A Coat of Many Colours* – in which he explained the rise and fall of Wordsworth's genius by the effects upon him of his affair with Annette Vallon, about which information had at that time come to light. More recently still, Mr F. W. Bateson has written a book about Wordsworth which is also of considerable interest (his chapter on 'The [112] Two Voices' does help to understand Wordsworth's style). In this book he maintains that Annette doesn't figure nearly so importantly as Sir Herbert Read had thought, and that the real secret was that Wordsworth fell in love with his sister Dorothy; that this explains, in particular, the Lucy poems, and explains why, after Wordsworth's marriage, his inspiration dried up. Well, he may be right: his argument is very plausible. But the real question, which every reader of Wordsworth must answer for himself, is: does it matter? does this account help me to understand the Lucy poems any better than I did before? For myself, I can only say that a knowledge of the springs which released a poem is not necessarily a help towards understanding the poem: too much information about the origins of the poem may even break my contact with it. I feel no need for any light upon the Lucy poems beyond the radiance shed by the poems themselves.

20 I am not maintaining that there is *no* context in which such information or conjecture as that of Sir Herbert Read and Mr Bateson may be relevant. It is relevant if we want to understand Wordsworth; but it is not directly relevant to our understanding of his poetry. Or rather, it is not relevant to our understanding of *the poetry as poetry*. I am even prepared to suggest that there is, in all great poetry, something which must remain unaccountable however complete might be our knowledge of the poet, and that that is what matters most. When the poem has been made, something new has happened, something that cannot be wholly explained by *anything that went before*. That, I believe, is what we mean by 'creation'.

21 The explanation of poetry by examination of its sources is not the method of all contemporary criticism by any means; but it is a method which responds to the desire of a good many readers that poetry should be explained to them in terms of something else: the chief part of the letters I receive from persons unknown to me, concerning my own poems, consists of requests for a kind of explanation that I cannot possibly

give. There are other tendencies such as that represented by Professor Richards's investigation of the problem of how the appreciation of poetry can be taught, or by the verbal subtleties of his distinguished pupil, Professor Empson. And I have recently noticed a development, which I suspect has its origin in the classroom methods of Professor Richards, which is, in its way, a healthy reaction against the diversion of attention from the poetry to the poet. It is found [113] in a book published not long ago, entitled *Interpretations*: a series of essays by twelve of the younger English critics, each analysing one poem of his own choice. The method is to take a well-known poem – each of the poems analysed in this book is a good one of its kind – without reference to the author or to his other work, analyse it stanza by stanza and line by line, and extract, squeeze, tease, press every drop of meaning out of it that one can. It might be called the lemon-squeezer school of criticism. As the poems range from the sixteenth century to the present day, as they differ a good deal from one another – the book begins with 'The Phoenix and the Turtle' and ends with 'Prufrock' and Yeats's 'Among School Children', and as each critic has his own procedure, the result is interesting and a little confusing – and, it must be admitted, to study twelve poems each analysed so painstakingly is a very tiring way of passing the time. I imagine that some of the poets (they are all dead except myself) would be surprised at learning what their poems mean: I had one or two minor surprises myself, as on learning that the fog, mentioned early in 'Prufrock', had somehow got into the drawing-room. But the analysis of 'Prufrock' was not an attempt to find origins, either in literature or in the darker recesses of my private life; it was an attempt to find out what the poem really meant – whether that was what I had meant it to mean or not. And for that I was grateful. There were several essays which struck me as good. But as every method has its own limitations and dangers, it is only reasonable to mention what seem to me the limitations and dangers of this one, dangers against which, if it were practised for what I suspect should be its chief use, that is, as an exercise for pupils, it would be the business of the teacher to warn his class.

22 The first danger is that of assuming that there must be just one interpretation of the poem as a whole, that must be right. There will be details of explanation, especially with poems written in another age than our own, matters of fact, historical allusions, the meaning of a certain word at a certain date, which can be established, and the teacher can see that his pupils get these right. But as for the meaning of the poem as a whole, it is not exhausted by any explanation, for the meaning is what the poem means to different sensitive readers. The second danger – a danger into

which I do not think any of the critics in the volume I have mentioned has fallen, but a danger to which the reader is exposed – is that of assuming that the interpretation of a poem, [114] if valid, is necessarily an account of what the author consciously or unconsciously was trying to do. For the tendency is so general, to believe that we understand a poem when we have identified its origins and traced the process to which the poet submitted his materials, that we may easily believe the converse – that any explanation of the poem is also an account of how it was written. The analysis of 'Prufrock' to which I have referred interested *me* because it helped *me* to see the poem through the eyes of an intelligent, sensitive and diligent reader. That is not at all to say that *he* saw the poem through my eyes, or that his account has anything to do with the experiences that led up to my writing it, or with anything I experienced in the process of writing it. And my third comment is, that I should, as a test, like to see the method applied to some new poem, some very good poem, and one that was previously unknown to me: because I should like to find out whether, after perusing the analysis, I should be able to enjoy the poem. For nearly all the poems in the volume were poems that I had known and loved for many years; and after reading the analyses, I found I was slow to recover my previous feeling about the poems. It was as if someone had taken a machine to pieces and left me with the task of reassembling the parts. I suspect, in fact, that a good deal of the value of an interpretation is – that it should be my own interpretation. There are many things, perhaps, to know about this poem, or that, many facts about which scholars can instruct me which will help me to avoid definite *mis*understanding; but a valid interpretation, I believe, must be at the same time an interpretation of my own feelings when I read it.

23 It has been no part of my purpose to give a comprehensive view of all the types of literary criticism practised in our time. I wished first to call attention to the transformation of literary criticism which we may say began with Coleridge but which has proceeded with greater acceleration during the last twenty-five years. This acceleration I took to be prompted by the relevance of the social sciences to criticism, and by the teaching of literature (including *contemporary* literature) in colleges and universities. I do not deplore the transformation, for it seems to me to have been inevitable. In an age of uncertainty, an age in which men are bewildered by new sciences, an age in which so little can be taken for granted as common beliefs, assumptions and background of all readers, no explorable area can be forbidden ground. But, among all this variety, we may ask, what is there, if anything, that [115] should be common to all literary criticism? Thirty years ago, I asserted that the essential

function of literary criticism was 'the elucidation of works of art and the correction of taste'. That phrase may sound somewhat pompous to our ears in 1956. Perhaps I could put it more simply, and more acceptably to the present age, by saying to 'promote the understanding and enjoyment of literature'. I would add that there is implied here also the negative task of pointing out what should not be enjoyed. For the critic may on occasion be called upon to condemn the second-rate and expose the fraudulent: though that duty is secondary to the duty of discriminating praise of what is praiseworthy. And I must stress the point that I do not think of *enjoyment* and *understanding* as distinct activities – one emotional and the other intellectual. By *understanding* I do not mean *explanation* though explanation of what can be explained may often be a necessary preliminary to understanding. To offer a very simple instance; to learn the unfamiliar words, and the unfamiliar forms of words, is a necessary preliminary to the understanding of Chaucer; it is explanation: but one could master the vocabulary, spelling, grammar and syntax of Chaucer – indeed, to carry the instance a stage further, one could be very well informed about the age of Chaucer, its social habits, its beliefs, its learning and its ignorance – and yet not *understand the poetry*. To understand a poem comes to the same thing as to enjoy it for the right reasons. One might say that it means getting from the poem such enjoyment as it is capable of giving: to enjoy a poem under a misunderstanding as to what it is, is to enjoy what is merely a projection of our own mind. So difficult a tool to handle, is language, that 'to enjoy' and 'to get enjoyment from' do not seem to mean quite the same thing: that to say that one 'gets enjoyment from' poetry does not sound quite the same as to say that one 'enjoys poetry'. And indeed, the very meaning of 'joy' varies with the object inspiring joy; different poems, even, yield different satisfactions. It is certain that we do not fully enjoy a poem unless we understand it; and on the other hand, it is equally true that we do not fully understand a poem unless we enjoy it. And that means, enjoying it to the right degree and in the right way, relative to other poems (it is in the relation of our enjoyment of a poem to our enjoyment of other poems that *taste* is shown). It should hardly be necessary to add that this implies that one *shouldn't* enjoy bad poems – unless their badness is of a sort that appeals to our sense of humour.

[116] **24** I have said that explanation may be a necessary preliminary to understanding. It seems to me, however, that I understand some poetry without explanation, for instance Shakespeare's

> Full fathom five thy father lies

I. ON POETRY – THE FRONTIERS OF CRITICISM • 233

or Shelley's

> Art thou pale for weariness
> Of climbing heaven and gazing on the earth

for here, and in a great deal of poetry, I see nothing to be explained – nothing, that is, that would help me to understand it better and therefore enjoy it more. And sometimes explanation, as I have already hinted, can distract us altogether from *the poem as poetry*, instead of leading us in the direction of understanding. My best reason, perhaps, for believing that I am not deluded in thinking that I understand such poetry as the lyrics by Shakespeare and Shelley which I have just cited, is that these two poems give me as keen a thrill when I repeat them to-day as they did fifty years ago.

25 The difference, then, between the literary critic, and the critic who has passed beyond the frontier of literary criticism, is not that the literary critic is 'purely' literary, or that he has no other interests. A critic who was interested in nothing but 'literature' would have very little to say to us, for his literature would be a pure abstraction. Poets have other interests beside poetry – otherwise their poetry would be very empty: they are poets because their dominant interest has been in turning their experience and their thought (and to experience and to think means to have interests beyond poetry) – in turning their experience and their thinking into poetry. The critic accordingly is a *literary* critic if his primary interest, in writing criticism, is to help his readers to *understand and enjoy*. But he must have other interests, just as much as the poet himself; for the literary critic is not merely a technical expert, who has learned the rules to be observed by the writers he criticises: the critic must be the whole man, a man with convictions and principles, and of knowledge and experience of life.

26 We can therefore ask, about any writing which is offered to us as literary criticism, is it aimed towards understanding and enjoyment? If it is not, it may still be a legitimate and useful activity; but it is to be judged as a contribution to psychology, or sociology, or logic, or pedagogy, or some other pursuit – and is to be judged [117] by specialists, not by men of letters. We must not identify biography with criticism: biography is ordinarily useful in providing explanation which may open the way to further understanding; but it may also, in directing our attention on the poet, lead us away from the poetry. We must not confuse knowledge – factual information – about a poet's period, the conditions of the society in which he lived, the ideas current in his time implicit in his writings, the state of the language in his period – with understanding his poetry. Such

knowledge, as I have said, may be a necessary preparation for understanding the poetry; furthermore, it has a value of its own, as history; but for the appreciation of the poetry, it can only lead us to the door: we must find our own way in. For the purpose of acquiring such knowledge, from the point of view taken throughout this paper, is not primarily that we should be able to project ourselves into a remote period, that we should be able to think and feel, when reading the poetry, as a contemporary of the poet might have thought and felt, though such experience has its own value; it is rather to divest ourselves of the limitations of our own age, and the poet, whose work we are reading, of the limitations of *his* age, in order to get the direct experience, the immediate contact with his poetry. What matters most, let us say, in reading an ode of Sappho, is not that I should imagine myself to be an island Greek of twenty-five hundred years ago; what matters is the experience which is the same for all human beings of different centuries and languages capable of enjoying poetry, the spark which can leap across those 2,500 years. So the critic to whom I am most grateful is the one who can make me look at something I have never looked at before, or looked at only with eyes clouded by prejudice, set me face to face with it and then leave me alone with it. From that point, I must rely upon my own sensibility, intelligence, and capacity for wisdom.

27 If in literary criticism, we place all the emphasis upon *understanding*, we are in danger of slipping from understanding to mere explanation. We are in danger even of pursuing criticism as if it was a science, which it never can be. If, on the other hand, we over-emphasise *enjoyment*, we will tend to fall into the subjective and impressionistic, and our enjoyment will profit us no more than mere amusement and pastime. Thirty-three years ago, it seems to have been the latter type of criticism, the impressionistic, that had caused the annoyance I felt when I wrote on 'the function of criticism'. To-day it seems to me that we need to be more on [118] guard against the purely explanatory. But I do not want to leave you with the impression that I wish to condemn the criticism of our time. These last thirty years have been, I think, a brilliant period in literary criticism in both Britain and America. It may even come to seem, in retrospect, too brilliant. Who knows?

Variants from 1956:
[Prefatory material:]

Gideon D. Seymour

A distinguished newsman and brilliant editor, Gideon Deming Seymour served during the final decade of his life (1944–1954) as vice president and executive editor of the Minneapolis *Star* and *Tribune*. At his passing, he was extolled by leaders in journalism throughout the country as 'one of America's great editors in the finest traditions of journalism' and 'a fearless guardian of a free press and a true exponent of the highest ethics of our profession.'

He covered the news in many parts of the world for the Associated Press before becoming editorial editor of the Minneapolis *Star* in 1939. Five years later he assumed executive editorial responsibilities for the *Star* and *Tribune*, directing news and editorial operations of the two newspapers.

An indefatigable worker in community betterment causes, Mr Seymour labored energetically to promote public welfare and to activate an enlightened interest in the major issues of the region, the nation, and the world. He died May 20, 1954, at fifty-two years of age.

[1] Introduction
by ALLEN TATE

I am guilty this evening of the presumption, and aware of the responsibility, of reversing a rule of scientific method, by which we arrive at the less familiar through previous knowledge of that which is better known. I should feel more comfortable and I think you would acknowledge a greater propriety if, on this occasion, the third lecturer in the Gideon Seymour Memorial Lecture Series were telling you who I am.

It is my privilege to introduce our speaker to what must surely be the largest audience ever assembled to hear a discourse on literary criticism. I have the honor to present to you an old friend whom I would acknowledge as my master, the most eminent man of letters in the world, the greatest living poet, and if I may alter a phrase of one of *his* masters, *maestro di color che scrivono*. I present to you Mr T. S. Eliot.

NOTE: Allen Tate, poet and critic, is himself an eminent man of letters, now a member of the Department of English at the University of Minnesota.

2 In 1923 I wrote an article entitled *The Function of Criticism*.] Having decided that this was what I wanted to talk to you about, I turned to see what I had said in an essay called *The Function of Criticism*, published in 1923.
   On re-reading this essay recently, I was rather bewildered, wondering what all the fuss had been about – though I was glad to find nothing positively to contradict my present opinions.] I did not, on re-reading, find it at all helpful, though on the other hand I was glad to find nothing positively to contradict my present opinions: I was merely rather bewildered, wondering what all the fuss was about.

3 Richards's *Principles of Literary Criticism* was published in 1925.] My copy of Richards's *Principles of Literary Criticism* is of the first edition, which was published in 1925.

6 French] the original edition

9 can be fully appreciated only] can only be fully appreciated

19 Mr F. W. Bateson] a Mr Bateson
   towards understanding] toward understanding

21 warn his class.] warn his class against.

22 be able to enjoy] ever be able to enjoy

24 as keen a thrill when] as keen a thrill, when

26 the same for all human beings of different centuries and languages capable of enjoying poetry] the same, for all human beings capable of enjoying poetry, of different centuries and languages

2,500] twenty-five hundred

27 Britain] England

II. On Poets

Virgil and the Christian World[1]

OPAP, 121–31.

Originally publ. in *Listener*, 46. 1176 (13 Sept. 1951), 411–12, 423–4. Revised in *SR*, 61. 1 (Jan./Mar. 1953), [1]–14, and repr. in *OPAP*.

1 The esteem in which Virgil has been held throughout Christian history may easily be made to appear, in a historical account of it, largely due to accidents, irrelevances, misunderstandings and superstitions. Such an account can tell you why Virgil's poems were prized so highly; but it may not give you any reason to infer that he deserved so high a place; still less might it persuade you that his work has any value for the world to-day or tomorrow or forever. What interests me here are those characteristics of Virgil which render him peculiarly sympathetic to the Christian mind. To assert this is not to accord him any exaggerated value as a poet, or even as a moralist, above that of all other poets Greek or Roman.

2 There is however one 'accident', or 'misunderstanding', which has played such a part in history that to ignore it would appear an evasion. This is of course the fourth *Eclogue*, in which Virgil, on the occasion of the birth or the expectation of a son to his friend Pollio, recently named consul, speaks in highflown language in what purports to be a mere letter of congratulation to the happy father.

> Now is come the last age of the song of Cumae; the great line of the centuries begins anew. Now the Virgin returns, the reign of Saturn returns....
>
> He shall have the gift of divine life, shall see heroes mingled with gods, and shall himself be seen of them, and shall sway a world to which his father's virtues shall have brought peace....
>
> The serpent shall perish, and the false poison plant shall perish;
> Assyrian spice shall spring up on every soil....

1. Broadcast by the B.B.C. in 1951 and published in *The Listener*. The translation quoted is that of the Loeb Library. The translation of Dante quoted here and elsewhere is that of the Temple Classics.

Such phrases have always seemed excessive, and the child who was [122] the subject of them never cut any great figure in the world. It has even been suggested that Virgil was pulling his friend's leg by this oriental hyperbole. Some scholars have thought that he was imitating, or taking off, the style of the Sibylline oracles. Some have conjectured that the poem is covertly addressed to Octavius, or even that it concerns the offspring of Antony and Cleopatra. A French scholar, Carcopino, gives good reason to believe that the poem contains allusions to Pythagorean doctrine. The mystery of the poem does not seem to have attracted any particular attention until the Christian Fathers got hold of it. The Virgin, the Golden Age, the Great Year, the parallel with the prophecies of Isaiah; the child *cara deum suboles* – 'dear offspring of the gods, great scion of Jupiter' – could only be the Christ himself, whose coming was foreseen by Virgil in the year 40 B.C. Lactantius and St Augustine believed this; so did the entire mediaeval Church and Dante; and even perhaps, in his own fashion, Victor Hugo.

3 It is possible that still other explanations may be found, and we already know more about the probabilities than the Christian Fathers did. We also know that Virgil, who was a man of great learning in his time, and, as Mr Jackson Knight has shown us, well informed in matters of folklore and antiquities, had at least indirect acquaintance with the religions and with the figurative language of the East. That would be sufficient in itself to account for any suggestion of Hebrew prophecy. Whether we consider the prediction of the Incarnation merely a coincidence will depend on what we mean by coincidence; whether we consider Virgil a Christian prophet will depend upon our interpretation of the word 'prophecy'. That Virgil himself was consciously concerned only with domestic affairs or with Roman politics I feel sure: I think that he would have been very much astonished by the career which his fourth Eclogue was to have. If a prophet were by definition a man who understood the full meaning of what he was saying, this would be for me the end of the matter. But if the word 'inspiration' is to have any meaning, it must mean just this, that the speaker or writer is uttering something which he does not wholly understand – or which he may even misinterpret when the inspiration has departed from him. This is certainly true of poetic inspiration: and there is more obvious reason for admiring Isaiah as a poet than for claiming Virgil as a prophet. A poet may believe that he is expressing only his private experience; his lines may be for him only a means of talking about himself without giving himself away; yet [123] for his readers what he has written may come to be the expression both of their own secret feelings and of the exultation or despair of a generation. He need not

know what his poetry will come to mean to others; and a prophet need not understand the meaning of his prophetic utterance.

4 We have a mental habit which makes it much easier for us to explain the miraculous in natural terms than to explain the natural in miraculous terms: yet the latter is as necessary as the former. A miracle which everybody accepted and believed in with no difficulty would be a strange miracle indeed; because what was miraculous for everybody would also seem natural to everybody. It seems to me that one can accept whatever explanation of the fourth *Eclogue*, by a scholar and historian, is the most plausible; because the scholars and historians can only be concerned with what Virgil *thought* he was doing. But, at the same time, if there is such a thing as inspiration – and we do go on using the word – then it is something which escapes historical research.

5 I have had to consider the fourth *Eclogue*, because it is so important in speaking of the history of Virgil's place in the Christian tradition that to avoid mention of it might lead to misunderstanding. And it is hardly possible to speak of it without indicating in what way one accepts, or rejects, the view that it prophesies the coming of Christ. I wanted only to make clear that the literal acceptance of this *Eclogue* as prophecy had much to do with the early admission of Virgil as suitable reading for Christians, and therefore opened the way for his influence in the Christian world. I do not regard this as simply an accident, or a mere curiosity of literature. But what really concerns me is the element in Virgil which gives him a significant, a unique place, at the end of the pre-Christian and at the beginning of the Christian world. He looks both ways; he makes a liaison between the old world and the new, and of his peculiar position we may take the fourth *Eclogue* as a symbol. In what respects, therefore, does the greatest of Roman poets anticipate the Christian world in a way in which the Greek poets do not? This question has been best answered by the late Theodor Haecker, in a book, published some years ago in an English translation under the title *Virgil the Father of the West*. I shall make use of Haecker's method.

6 Here I shall make a slight and perhaps trivial diversion. When I was a schoolboy, it was my lot to be introduced to the *Iliad* and to the *Aeneid* in the same year. I had, up to that point, found the [124] Greek language a much more exciting study than Latin. I still think it a much greater language: a language which has never been surpassed as a vehicle for the fullest range and the finest shades of thought and feeling. Yet I found myself at ease with Virgil as I was not at ease with Homer. It might have been rather different if we had started with the *Odyssey* instead of the *Iliad*; for when we came to read certain selected books of the *Odyssey* –

and I have never read more of the *Odyssey* in Greek than those selected books – I was much happier. My preference certainly did not, I am glad to say, mean that I thought Virgil the greater poet. That is the kind of error from which we are preserved in youth, simply because we are too natural to ask such an artificial question – artificial because, in whatever ways Virgil followed the procedure of Homer, he was not trying to do the same thing. One might just as reasonably try to rate the comparative 'greatness' of the *Odyssey* and James Joyce's *Ulysses*, simply because Joyce for quite different purposes used the framework of the *Odyssey*. The obstacle to my enjoyment of the *Iliad*, at that age, was the behaviour of the people Homer wrote about. The gods were as irresponsible, as much a prey to their passions, as devoid of public spirit and the sense of fair play, as the heroes. This was shocking. Furthermore, their sense of humour extended only to the crudest form of horseplay. Achilles was a ruffian; the only hero who could be commended for either conduct or judgement was Hector; and it seemed to me that this was Shakespeare's view also:

> If Helen then be wife to Sparta's king,
> As it is known she is, these moral laws
> Of nature and of nations speak aloud
> To have her back returned . . .

All this may seem to have been simply the caprice of a priggish little boy. I have modified my early opinions – the explanation I should now give is simply that I instinctively preferred the *world* of Virgil to the *world* of Homer – because it was a more civilised world of dignity, reason and order. When I say 'the world of Virgil', I mean what Virgil himself made of the world in which he lived. The Rome of the imperial era was coarse and beastly enough; in important respects far less civilised than Athens at its greatest. The Romans were less gifted than the Athenians for the arts, philosophy and pure science; and their language was more obdurate [125] to the expression of either poetry or abstract thought. Virgil made of Roman civilisation in his poetry something better than it really was. His sensibility is more nearly Christian than that of any other Roman or Greek poet: not like that of an early Christian perhaps, but like that of Christianity from the time at which we can say that a Christian civilisation had come into being. We cannot compare Homer and Virgil; but we can compare the civilisation which Homer accepted with the civilisation of Rome as refined by the sensibility of Virgil.

7 What, then, are the chief characteristics of Virgil which make him sympathetic to the Christian mind? I think that the most promising way

of giving some indication briefly, is to follow the procedure of Haecker and try to develop the significance of certain key words. Such words are *labor*, *pietas*, and *fatum*. The *Georgics* are, I think, essential to an understanding of Virgil's philosophy – using the word with the distinction that we do not mean quite the same thing when we speak of the philosophy of a poet, as when we speak of the philosophy of an abstract thinker. The *Georgics*, as a technical treatise on farming, are both difficult and dull. Most of us have neither the command of Latin necessary to read them with pleasure, nor any desire to remind ourselves of schooltime agonies. I shall only recommend them in the translation of Mr Day Lewis who has put them into modern verse. But they are a work to which their author devoted time, toil and genius. Why did he write them? It is not to be supposed that he was endeavouring to teach their business to the farmers of his native soil; or that he aimed simply to provide a useful handbook for townsmen eager to buy land and launch out as farmers. Nor is it likely that he was merely anxious to compile records, for the curiosity of later generations, of the methods of agriculture in his time. It is more likely that he hoped to remind absentee landowners, careless of their responsibilities and drawn by love of pleasure or love of politics to the metropolis, of the fundamental duty to cherish the land. Whatever his conscious motive, it seems clear to me that Virgil desired to affirm the dignity of agricultural labour, and the importance of good cultivation of the soil for the well-being of the state both materially and spiritually.

8 The fact that every major poetic form employed by Virgil has some precedent in Greek verse, must not be allowed to obscure the originality with which he recreated every form he used. There is I think no precedent for the *spirit* of the *Georgics*; and the [126] attitude towards the soil, and the labour of the soil, which is there expressed, is something that we ought to find particularly intelligible now, when urban agglomeration, the flight from the land, the pillage of the earth and the squandering of natural resources are beginning to attract attention. It was the Greeks who taught us the dignity of leisure; it is from them that we inherit the perception that the highest life is the life of contemplation. But this respect for leisure, with the Greeks, was accompanied by a contempt for the banausic occupations. Virgil perceived that agriculture is fundamental to civilisation, and he affirmed the dignity of manual labour. When the Christian monastic orders came into being, the contemplative life and the life of manual labour were first conjoined. These were no longer occupations for different classes of people, the one noble, the other inferior and suitable only for slaves or almost slaves. There was a great deal in the medieval world which was not Christian; and practice in the

lay world was very different from that of the religious orders at their best: but at least Christianity did establish the principle that action and contemplation, labour and prayer, are both essential to the life of the complete man. It is possible that the insight of Virgil was recognised by monks who read his works in their religious houses.

9 Furthermore, we need to keep this affirmation of the *Georgics* in mind when we read the *Aeneid*. There, Virgil is concerned with the *imperium romanum*, with the extension and justification of imperial rule. He set an ideal for Rome, and for empire in general, which was never realised in history; but the ideal of empire as Virgil sees it is a noble one. His devotion to Rome was founded on devotion to the land; to the particular region, to the particular village, and to the family in the village. To the reader of history this foundation of the general on the particular may seem chimerical; just as the union of the contemplative and the active life may seem to most people chimerical. For mostly these aims are envisaged as alternatives: we exalt the contemplative life, and disparage the active, or we exalt the active, and regard the contemplative with amused contempt if not with moral disapproval. And yet it may be the man who affirms the apparently incompatible who is right.

10 We come to the second word. It is a commonplace that the word *piety* is only a reduced, altered and specialised translation of *pietas*. We use it in two senses: in general, it suggests devout church-going [127], or at least church-going with the appearance of devoutness. In another sense, it is always preceded by the adjective 'filial', meaning correct behaviour toward a parent. When Virgil speaks, as he does, of *pius Aeneas*, we are apt to think of his care of his father, of his devotion to his father's memory, and of his touching encounter with his father on his descent into the nether regions. But the word *pietas* with Virgil has much wider associations of meaning: it implies an attitude towards the individual, towards the family, towards the region, and towards the imperial destiny of Rome. And finally Aeneas is 'pious' also in his respect towards the gods, and in his punctilious observance of rites and offerings. It is an attitude towards all these things, and therefore implies a unity and an order among them: it is in fact an attitude towards life.

11 Aeneas is therefore not simply a man endowed with a number of virtues, each of which is a kind of piety – so that to call him *pius* in general is merely to use a convenient collective term. Piety is one. These are aspects of piety in different contexts, and they all imply each other. In his devotion to his father he is not being just an admirable son. There is personal affection, without which filial piety would be imperfect; but personal affection is not piety. There is also devotion to his father as his

father, as his progenitor: this is piety as the acceptance of a bond which one has not chosen. The quality of affection is altered, and its importance deepened, when it becomes love *due* to the object. But this filial piety is also the recognition of a further bond, that with the gods, to whom such an attitude is pleasing: to fail in it would be to be guilty of impiety also towards the gods. The gods must therefore be gods worthy of this respect; and without gods, or a god, regarded in this way, filial piety must perish. For then it becomes no longer a *duty*; your feeling towards your father will be due merely to the fortunate accident of congeniality, or will be reduced to a sentiment of gratitude for care and consideration. Aeneas is pious towards the gods, and in no way does his piety appear more clearly than when the gods afflict him. He had a good deal to put up with from Juno; and even his mother Venus, as the benevolent instrument of his destiny, put him into one very awkward position. There is in Aeneas a virtue – an essential ingredient in his piety – which is an analogue and foreshadow of Christian humility. Aeneas is the antithesis, in important respects, of either Achilles or Odysseus. In so far as he is heroic, he is heroic as the original Displaced Person, the fugitive from a ruined city and an obliterated society, [128] of which the few other survivors except his own band languish as slaves of the Greeks. He was not to have, like Ulysses, marvellous and exciting adventures with such occasional erotic episodes as left no canker on the conscience of that wayfarer. He was not to return at last to the remembered hearth-fire, to find an exemplary wife awaiting him, to be reunited to his son, his dog and his servants. Aeneas's end is only a new beginning; and the whole point of the pilgrimage is something which will come to pass for future generations. His nearest likeness is Job, but his reward is not what Job's was, but is only in the accomplishment of his destiny. He suffers for himself, he acts only in obedience. He is, in fact, the prototype of a Christian hero. For he is, humbly, a man with a mission; and the mission is everything.

12 The *pietas* is in this way explicable only in terms of *fatum*. This is a word which constantly recurs in the *Aeneid*; a word charged with meaning, and perhaps with more meaning than Virgil himself knew. Our nearest word is 'destiny', and that is a word which means more than we can find any definitions for. It is a word which can have no meaning in a mechanical universe: if that which is wound up must run down, what destiny is there in that? Destiny is not necessitarianism, and it is not caprice: it is something essentially meaningful. Each man has his destiny, though some men are undoubtedly 'men of destiny' in a sense in which most men are not; and Aeneas is egregiously a man of destiny, since upon him the future of the Western World depends. But this is an

election which cannot be explained, a burden and responsibility rather than a reason for self-glorification. It merely happens to one man and not to others, to have the gifts necessary in some profound crisis, but he can take no credit to himself for the gifts and the responsibility assigned to him. Some men have had a deep conviction of their destiny, and in that conviction have prospered; but when they cease to act as an instrument, and think of themselves as the active source of what they do, their pride is punished by disaster. Aeneas is a man guided by the deepest conviction of destiny, but he is a humble man who knows that this destiny is something not to be desired and not to be avoided. Of what power is he the servant? Not of the gods, who are themselves merely instruments, and sometimes rebellious ones. The concept of destiny leaves us with a mystery, but it is a mystery not contrary to reason, for it implies that the world, and the course of human history, have meaning.

[129] **13** Nor does destiny relieve mankind of moral responsibility. Such, at least, is my reading of the episode of Dido. The love affair of Aeneas and Dido is arranged by Venus: neither of the lovers was free to abstain. Now Venus herself is not acting on a whim, or out of mischief. She is certainly proud of the destiny of her son, but her behaviour is not that of a doting mother: she is herself an instrument for the realisation of her son's destiny. Aeneas and Dido had to be united, and had to be separated. Aeneas did not demur; he was obedient to his fate. But he was certainly very unhappy about it, and I think that he felt that he was behaving shamefully. For why else should Virgil have contrived his meeting with the Shade of Dido in Hades, and the snub that he receives? When he sees Dido he tries to excuse himself for his betrayal. *Sed me iussa deum* – but I was under orders from the gods; it was a very unpleasant decision to have imposed upon me, and I am sorry that you took it so hard. She avoids his gaze and turns away, with a face as immobile as if it had been carved from flint or Marpesian rock. I have no doubt that Virgil, when he wrote these lines, was assuming the role of Aeneas and feeling very decidedly a worm. No, destiny like that of Aeneas does not make the man's life any easier: it is a very heavy cross to bear. And I do not think of any hero of antiquity who found himself in quite this inevitable and deplorable position. I think that the poet who could best have emulated Virgil's treatment of this situation was Racine: certainly the Christian poet who gave the furious Roxane the blasting line '*Rentre dans le Néant d'où je t'ai fait sortir*' could, if anyone, have found words for Dido on this occasion.

14 What then does this destiny, which no Homeric hero shares with Aeneas, mean? For Virgil's conscious mind, and for his contemporary readers, it means the *imperium romanum*. This in itself, as Virgil saw it, was a worthy justification of history. I think that he had few illusions and that he saw clearly both sides of every question – the case for the loser as well as the case for the winner. Nevertheless even those who have as little Latin as I must remember and thrill at the lines:

> His ego nec metas rerum, nec tempora pono:
> Imperium sine fine dedi . . .
> Tu regere imperio populos, Romane, memento
> (hae tibi erunt artes) pacique imponere morem,
> parcere subiectis et debellare superbos . . .

[130] I say that it was all the end of history that Virgil could be asked to find, and that it was a worthy end. And do you really think that Virgil was mistaken? You must remember that the Roman Empire was transformed into the Holy Roman Empire. What Virgil proposed to his contemporaries was the highest ideal even for an unholy Roman Empire, for any merely temporal empire. We are all, so far as we inherit the civilisation of Europe, still citizens of the Roman Empire, and time has not yet proved Virgil wrong when he wrote *nec tempora pono: imperium sine fine dedi*. But, of course, the Roman Empire which Virgil imagined and for which Aeneas worked out his destiny was not exactly the same as the Roman Empire of the legionaries, the pro-consuls and governors, the business men and speculators, the demagogues and generals. It was something greater, but something which exists because Virgil imagined it. It remains an ideal, but one which Virgil passed on to Christianity to develop and to cherish.

15 In the end, it seems to me that the place which Dante assigned to Virgil in the future life, and the role of guide and teacher as far as the barrier which Virgil was not allowed to pass, was not capable of passing, is an exact statement of Virgil's relation to the Christian world. We find the world of Virgil, compared to the world of Homer, to approximate to a Christian world, in the choice, order and relationship of its values. I have said that this implies no comparison between Homer the poet and Virgil the poet. Neither do I think that it is exactly a comparison between the worlds in which they lived, considered apart from the interpretation of these worlds which the poets have given us. It may be merely that we know more about the world of Virgil, and understand it better; and therefore see more clearly how much, in the Roman idea according to Virgil, is due to the shaping hand and the philosophical mind of Virgil himself. For, in the sense in which a poet is a philosopher (as distinct from the sense in which a great poet may embody a great philosophy

in great poetry) Virgil is the greatest philosopher of ancient Rome. It is not, therefore, simply that the civilisation in which Virgil lived is nearer to the civilisation of Christianity than is that of Homer; we can say that Virgil, among classical Latin poets or prose writers, is uniquely near to Christianity. There is a phrase which I have been trying to avoid, but which I now find myself obliged to use: *anima naturaliter Christiana*. Whether we apply it to Virgil is a matter of personal choice; but I am inclined to think that he just falls short: and that is why I said [131] just now that I think Dante has put Virgil in the right place. I will try to give the reason.

16 I think of another key word, besides *labor*, *pietas* and *fatum*, which I wish that I could illustrate from Virgil in the same way. What key word can one find in the *Divine Comedy* which is absent from the *Aeneid*? One word of course is *lume*, and all the words expressive of the spiritual significance of light. But this, I think, as used by Dante, has a meaning which belongs only to explicit Christianity, fused with a meaning which belongs to mystical experience. And Virgil is no mystic. The term which one can justifiably regret the lack of in Virgil is *amor*. It is, above all others, the key word for Dante. I do not mean that Virgil never uses it. *Amor* recurs in the *Eclogues* (*amor vincit omnia*). But the loves of the shepherds represent hardly more than a poetic convention. The use of the word *amor* in the *Eclogues* is not illuminated by meanings of the word in the *Aeneid* in the way in which, for example, we return to Paolo and Francesca with greater understanding of their passion after we have been taken through the circles of love in the *Paradiso*. Certainly, the love of Aeneas and Dido has great tragic force. There is tenderness and pathos enough in the *Aeneid*. But Love is never given, to my mind, the same significance as a principle of order in the human soul, in society and in the universe that *pietas* is given; and it is not Love that causes *fatum*, or moves the sun and the stars. Even for intensity of physical passion, Virgil is more tepid than some other Latin poets, and far below the rank of Catullus. If we are not chilled we at least feel ourselves, with Virgil, to be moving in a kind of emotional twilight. Virgil was, among all authors of classical antiquity, one for whom the world made sense, for whom it had order and dignity, and for whom, as for no one before his time except the Hebrew prophets, history had meaning. But he was denied the vision of the man who could say:

'Within its depths I saw ingathered, bound by love in one volume, the scattered leaves of all the universe.'

Legato con amor in un volume.

Variants from 1951:

Title [and *passim*] Virgil] Vergil

[Before para. 1:] Everyone knows of the importance of Vergil for St Augustine, and of the status conceded to him in the Christian tradition, culminating in his elevation by the greatest of all Christian poets to the position of guide through the first two stages of the *Divine Comedy*. Everyone knows that Vergil became, in the Middle Ages, an almost mythical figure, first as a prophet of the Incarnation, and then as a fabulous magician whose poem could be employed for purposes of divination. To elaborate on such matters would be the task of a scholar and historian, and that is the first reason for my avoiding this course: I should not be able to tell you anything that you did not already know. I do not propose to discuss the history of Vergilian studies, the story of his adoption by Christian writers, or his influences upon the Fathers of the Church, or his reputation during the Middle Ages. There is, however, another reason.

1 [Heading:] **Reasons for Esteem**
 [After 'Greek or Roman':] Sympathy is only one form of valuation.

2 Octavius] Octavian
 [Between 'attention' and 'until':] , from the point of view of its mystery,

3 more obvious reason] better reason still
 He need not know . . . prophetic utterance] [Not represented in 1951.]

5 consider] speak about
 in speaking of] in beginning
 his peculiar position] this peculiar station
 in a book, published] in a little book on Vergil, which was published

6 [Heading:] **'Easier' than Homer**
 [Between 'surpassed' and 'as':] , and perhaps not equalled,
 [Between 'Homer accepted' and 'with the civilisation':] – I do not mean the civilisation of the time of the Trojan wars, but that of the time at which the Homeric poems were put into shape –

7 [Heading:] **Key Words**
 as when we speak] and when we speak
 duty] duty of any people

9 it may be the man] it is the man
 is right] may be right

10 [Heading:] **Meaning of Piety**

Sir John Davies[1]

OPAP, 132–7.

Originally publ., unsigned, in *TLS*, 1297 (9 Dec. 1926), 906: Gallup C188a.

1 Chief Justice John Davies died on December 7, 1626. He left a number of poems, a philosophical treatise, 'Reason's Academy', some legal writings, and several long State Papers on Ireland. As a public servant he had a distinguished career; but very likely the poem which has preserved his memory, *Nosce Teipsum*, was what commended him to King James. Possibly James was more appreciative of learning than of poetical merit; but, in any case, he recognised merit in a poet who was, in some respects, as out of place in his own age as he is in ours.

2 Davies's shorter poems are usually graceful and occasionally lovely, but they are so completely eclipsed even by the modest reputation of *Nosce Teipsum* and *Orchestra* that they are never chosen as anthology pieces. *Nosce Teipsum*, by its gnomic utterance and its self-contained quatrains, lends itself to mutilation; but a stanza or two is all that has been anthologised. Probably all that most readers know of Davies is represented by the two stanzas in the *Oxford Book of English Verse*:

> I know my soul hath power to know all things,
> Yet she is blind and ignorant in all:
> I know I'm one of Nature's little kings,
> Yet to the least and vilest things am thrall.
>
> I know my life's a pain and but a span;
> I know my sense is mock'd in everything;
> And, to conclude, I know myself a Man –
> Which is a proud and yet a wretched thing.

3 Fine and complete as the two stanzas are they do not represent the poem, and no selection of stanzas can represent it. Davies is a [133] poet of fine lines, but he is more than that. He is not one of that second rank of poets who, here and there, echo the notes of the great. If there is, in *Orchestra*, a hint of the influence of Spenser, it is no more than the debt which many Elizabethans owe to that master of versification. And the plan, the versification, and the content of *Nosce Teipsum* are, in that age, highly original.

4 The poem of *Nosce Teipsum* is a long discussion in verse of the nature of the soul and its relation to the body. Davies's theories are not those of the later seventeenth-century philosophers, nor are they very good

---

1. Published in *The Times Literary Supplement* in 1926.

Aristotelianism. Davies is more concerned to prove that the soul is distinct from the body than to explain how such distinct entities can be united. The soul is a spirit, and, as such, has wit, will, reason and judgement. It does not appear as the 'form' of the body, and the word 'form' appears in the poem rather in the sense of 'representation' (*similitudo*). The soul is in the body as light is in the air – which disposes of the scholastic question whether the soul is more in one part of the body than another. Nor are the problems of sense perception difficult to resolve: Davies is not troubled by the 'reception of forms without matter'. His contribution to the science of acoustics is the explanation that sounds must pass through the 'turns and windings' of the ear:

> For should the voice directly strike the braine,
> It would astonish and confuse it much.

Whether or not Davies borrowed his theories – if they deserve the name of theories – from Nemesius or from some other Early Christian author, and whether he got them direct or secondhand, it is evident that we cannot take them very seriously. But the end of the sixteenth century was not a period of philosophic refinement in England – where, indeed, philosophy had visibly languished for a hundred years and more. Considering the place and the time, this philosophical poem by an eminent jurist is by no means a despicable production. In an age when philosophy, apart from theology, meant usually (and especially in verse) a collection of Senecan commonplaces, Davies's is an independent mind.

5 The merit and curiosity of the poem, however, reside in the perfection of the instrument to the end. In a language of remarkable clarity and austerity Davies succeeds in maintaining the poem consistently on the level of poetry; he never flies to hyperbole or bombast, and he never descends, as he easily might, to the [134] pedestrian and ludicrous. Certain odd lines and quatrains remain in the memory, as:

> But sith our life so fast away doth slide,
> As doth a hungry eagle through the wind,

(a simile which Alexander borrows for his *Julius Caesar*), or

> And if thou, like a child, didst feare before,
> Being in the darke, where thou didst nothing see;
> Now I have brought thee torch-light, fear no more;
> Now when thou diest, thou canst not hud-winkt be.

Davies has not had the credit for great felicity of phrase, but it may be observed that, when other poets have pilfered from him or have arrived independently at the same figure, it is usually Davies who has the best of it. Grosart compares the following two passages showing a simile used by Davies and by Pope:

> Much like a subtill spider, which doth sit
> In middle of her web, which spreadeth wide;
> If aught do touch the utmost thread of it,
> She feels it instantly on every side.

Pope:

> The spider's touch, how exquisitely fine,
> Feels at each thread, and lives along the line.

Davies's spider is the more alive, though he needs two more lines for her. Another instance is the well-known figure from the *Ancient Mariner*:

> Still as a slave before his lord,
>   The ocean hath no blast;
> His great bright eye most silently
>   Up to the Moon is cast –

where 'most' is a blemish. Davies has (in *Orchestra*):

> For loe the Sea that fleets about the Land,
>   And like a girdle clips her solide waist,
> Musicke and measure both doth understand;
>   For his great chrystall eye is always cast
> Up to the Moone, and on her fixèd fast;
>   And as she daunceth in her pallid spheere
> So daunceth he about his center heere.

[135] But the mastery of workmanship of *Nosce Teipsum* and its beauty are not to be appreciated by means of scattered quotations. Its effect is cumulative. Davies chose a difficult stanza, one in which it is almost impossible to avoid monotony. He embellishes it with none of the flowers of conceit of his own age or the next, and he has none of the antitheses or verbal wit with which the Augustans sustain their periods. His vocabulary is clear, choice and precise. His thought is, for an Elizabethan poet, amazingly coherent; there is nothing that is irrelevant to his main argument, no excursions or flights. And, although every quatrain is complete in itself, the sequence is never a 'string of pearls' (such as was fashionable in the next age, as in Crashaw's *Weeper*); the thought is continuous. Yet no stanza ever is identical in rhythm with another. The style appears plain, even bald, yet Davies's personal cadence is always there. Many critics have remarked the condensation of thought, the economy of

language, and the consistency of excellence; but some have fallen into the error of supposing that Davies's merit is of prose. Hallam, after praising the poem, says:

> If it reaches the heart of all, it is through the reason. But since strong argument in terse and correct style fails not to give us pleasure in prose, it seems strange that it should lose its effect when it gains the aid of regular metre to gratify the ear and assist the memory.

6 Hallam's criticism is topsy-turvy. Hallam's heart must have been peculiarly inaccessible, or his reason very easily touched. The argument is not strong; had Davies entered the ring of philosophical argument his contemporary, Cardinal Bellarmine, could have knocked him out in the first round. Davies had not a philosophical mind; he was primarily a poet, but with a gift for philosophical exposition. His appeal is, indeed, to what Hallam calls the heart, though we no longer employ that single organ as the vehicle of all poetic feeling. The excellence of the theory of body and soul which Davies expounded is, however, irrelevant. If some one had provided him with a better theory the poem might have been, in one aspect, a better one; in another aspect it does not matter a fig. The wonder is that Davies, in his place and time, could produce so coherent and respectable a theory as he did. No one, not even Gray, has surpassed Davies in the use of the quatrain which he employed for *Nosce Teipsum*; and no poem in any similar metre (compare *The Witch of Atlas*) is metrically superior to *Orchestra*. Even his little acrostic poems on the name of Queen Elizabeth are admirable in grace and melody. And with [136] this genius for versification, with a taste in language remarkably pure for his age, Davies has that strange gift, so rarely bestowed, for turning thought into feeling.

7 In the effort to 'place' Davies, who appears anomalous, critics have compared him on the one hand to the Senecals, to Chapman and Daniel and Greville, and on the other hand to Donne and the metaphysicals. Neither classification is quite exact. Davies's only direct debt as a poet seems to be to Spenser, the master of everybody. The type of his thought, and consequently the tone of his expression, separates him from the Senecals. His thought, as we have said, is inferior as philosophy, but it is coherent and free from eccentricity or pose. He thinks like a scholastic, though the quality of his thought would have shocked a scholastic. Chapman, Daniel and Greville, so far as they can be said to have thought at all, thought like Latin rhetoricians. Like the other dramatists, they imbibed from Seneca a philosophy which is essentially a theatrical pose. Hence their language, even when pure and restrained – and Daniel's is astonishingly pure and restrained – is always orotund and oratorical;

their verse is as if spoken in public, and their feelings as if felt in public. Davies's is the language and the tone of solitary meditation; he speaks like a man reasoning with himself in solitude, and he never raises his voice.

8 In the same way Davies may be said to have little in common with Donne. It is not merely Davies's restraint in the use of simile and metaphor. The verbal conceit, as used by Donne, implies a very different attitude towards ideas from that of Davies, perhaps a much more conscious one. Donne was ready to entertain almost any idea, to play with it, to follow it out of curiosity, to explore all its possibilities of affecting his sensibility. Davies is much more medieval; his capacity for belief is greater. He has but the one idea, which he pursues in all seriousness – a kind of seriousness rare in his age. Thought is not exploited for the sake of feeling, it is pursued for its own sake; and the feeling is a kind of by-product, though a by-product worth far more than the thought. The effect of the sequence of the poem is not to diversify or embellish the feeling: it is wholly to intensify. The variation is in the metrics.

9 There is only one parallel to *Nosce Teipsum*, and, though it is a daring one, it is not unfair to Davies. It is the several passages of exposition of the nature of the soul which occur in the middle of [137] the *Purgatorio*. To compare Davies with Dante may appear fantastic. But, after all, very few people read these parts of Dante, and fewer still get any pleasure out of them: in short, these passages are probably as little read or enjoyed as *Nosce Teipsum* itself. Of course they are vastly finer, for two quite different reasons: Dante was a vastly greater poet, and the philosophy which he expounds is infinitely more substantial and subtle:

> Esce di mano a lui, che la vagheggia
> > primo che sia, a giusa di fanciulla
> > che piangendo e ridendo pargoleggia,
>
> L'anima semplicetta, che sa nulla,
> > salvo che, mossa da lieto fattore,
> > volentier torna a cio che la trastulla.
>
> Di picciol bene in pria sente sapore;
> > quivi s'inganna, e retro ad esso corre,
> > se guida o fren non torce suo amore.[1]

---

1. From his hands who fondly loves her ere she is in being, there issues, after the fashion of a little child that sports, now weeping, now laughing, the simple, tender soul, who knoweth naught save that, sprung from a joyous maker, willingly she turneth to that which delights her. First she tastes the savour of a trifling good; there she is beguiled and runneth after it, if guide or curb turn not her love aside.

It is not in any way to put Davies on a level with Dante to say that anyone who can appreciate the beauty of such lines as these should be able to extract considerable pleasure from *Nosce Teipsum*.

Variants from 1926:
1   what commended him] his commendation to
2   has been anthologised] survives in this form
3   Davies is] If Davies is
    but he is more] he is more
4   Davies's is] Davies is
6   vehicle] receptacle
    [No translation of Dante in 1926.]

Milton I[1]

OPAP, 138–45.

Revised from *Essays and Studies by Members of the English Association*, 21 (2 July 1936), [32]–4, where the article is signed 'T. S. Eliot' (Gallup B28).

1 While it must be admitted that Milton is a very great poet indeed, it is something of a puzzle to decide in what his greatness consists. On analysis, the marks against him appear both more numerous and more significant than the marks to his credit. As a man, he is antipathetic. Either from the moralist's point of view, or from the theologian's point of view, or from the psychologist's point of view, or from that of the political philosopher, or judging by the ordinary standards of likeableness in human beings, Milton is unsatisfactory. The doubts which I have to express about him are more serious than these. His greatness as a poet has been sufficiently celebrated, though I think largely for the wrong reasons, and without the proper reservations. His misdeeds as a poet have been called attention to, as by Mr Ezra Pound, but usually in passing. What seems to me necessary is to assert at the same time his greatness – in that what he could do well he did better than anyone else has ever done – and the serious charges to be made against him, in respect of the deterioration – the peculiar kind of deterioration – to which he subjected the language.

2 Many people will agree that a man may be a great artist, and yet have a bad influence. There is more of Milton's influence in the badness of the bad verse of the eighteenth century than of anybody's else: he certainly did more harm than Dryden and Pope, and perhaps a good deal

---

1. Contributed to *Essays and Studies* of The English Association, Oxford University Press, 1936.

of the obloquy which has fallen on these two poets, especially the latter, because of their influence, ought to be transferred to Milton. But to put the matter simply in terms of 'bad influence' is not necessarily to bring a serious charge: because a good deal of the responsibility, when we state the problem in these terms, may devolve on the eighteenth-century poets themselves for being such bad poets that they were incapable of [139] being influenced except for ill. There is a good deal more to the charge against Milton than this; and it appears a good deal more serious if we affirm that Milton's poetry could *only* be an influence for the worse, upon any poet whatever. It is more serious, also, if we affirm that Milton's bad influence may be traced much farther than the eighteenth century, and much farther than upon bad poets: if we say that it was an influence against which we still have to struggle.

3 There is a large class of persons, including some who appear in print as critics, who regard any censure upon a 'great' poet as a breach of the peace, as an act of wanton iconoclasm, or even hoodlumism. The kind of derogatory criticism that I have to make upon Milton is not intended for such persons, who cannot understand that it is more important, in some vital respects, to be a *good* poet than to be a *great* poet; and of what I have to say I consider that the only jury of judgement is that of the ablest poetical practitioners of my own time.

4 The most important fact about Milton, for my purpose, is his blindness. I do not mean that to go blind in middle life is itself enough to determine the whole nature of a man's poetry. Blindness must be considered in conjunction with Milton's personality and character, and the peculiar education which he received. It must also be considered in connexion with his devotion to, and expertness in, the art of music. Had Milton been a man of very keen senses – I mean of *all* the five senses – his blindness would not have mattered so much. But for a man whose sensuousness, such as it was, had been withered early by book-learning, and whose gifts were naturally aural, it mattered a great deal. It would seem, indeed, to have helped him to concentrate on what he could do best.

5 At no period is the visual imagination conspicuous in Milton's poetry. It would be as well to have a few illustrations of what I mean by visual imagination. From *Macbeth*:

>   This guest of summer,
> The temple-haunting martlet, does approve
> By his loved mansionry that the heaven's breath
> Smells wooingly here: no jutty, frieze,
> Buttress, nor coign of vantage, but this bird

> Hath made his pendant bed and procreant cradle:
> Where they most breed and haunt, I have observed
> The air is delicate.

[140] It may be observed that such an image, as well as another familiar quotation from a little later in the same play,

> Light thickens, and the crow
> Makes wing to the rooky wood

not only offer something to the eye, but, so to speak, to the common sense. I mean that they convey the feeling of being in a particular place at a particular time. The comparison with Shakespeare offers another indication of the peculiarity of Milton. With Shakespeare, far more than with any other poet in English, the combinations of words offer perpetual novelty; they enlarge the meaning of the individual words joined: thus 'procreant cradle', 'rooky wood'. In comparison, Milton's images do not give this sense of particularity, nor are the separate words developed in significance. His language is, if one may use the term without disparagement, *artificial* and *conventional*.

> O'er the smooth enamel'd green . . .

> . . . paths of this drear wood
> The nodding horror of whose shady brows
> Threats the forlorn and wandering passenger.

('Shady brow' here is a diminution of the value of the two words from their use in the line from *Dr Faustus*

> Shadowing more beauty in their airy brows.)

The imagery in *L'Allegro* and *Il Penseroso* is all general:

> While the ploughman near at hand,
> Whistles o'er the furrowed land,
> And the milkmaid singeth blithe,
> And the mower whets his scythe,
> And every shepherd tells his tale,
> Under the hawthorn in the dale.

It is not a particular ploughman, milkmaid, and shepherd that Milton sees (as Wordsworth might see them); the sensuous effect of these verses is entirely on the ear, and is joined to the concepts of ploughman, milkmaid, and shepherd. Even in his most mature work, Milton does not infuse new life into the word, as Shakespeare does.

[141]   The sun to me is dark
And silent as the moon,
When she deserts the night
Hid in her vacant interlunar cave.

Here *interlunar* is certainly a stroke of genius, but is merely combined with 'vacant' and 'cave', rather than giving and receiving life from them. Thus it is not so unfair, as it might at first appear, to say that Milton writes English like a dead language. The criticism has been made with regard to his involved syntax. But a tortuous style, when its peculiarity is aimed at precision (as with Henry James), is not necessarily a dead one; only when the complication is dictated by a demand of verbal music, instead of by any demand of sense.

> Thrones, dominations, princedoms, virtues, powers,
> If these magnific titles yet remain
> Not merely titular, since by decree
> Another now hath to himself engrossed
> All power, and us eclipsed under the name
> Of King anointed, for whom all this haste
> Of midnight march, and hurried meeting here,
> This only to consult how we may best
> With what may be devised of honours new
> Receive him coming to receive from us
> Knee-tribute yet unpaid, prostration vile,
> Too much to one, but double how endured,
> To one and to his image now proclaimed?

With which compare:

> However, he didn't mind thinking that if Cissy should prove all that was likely enough their having a subject in common couldn't but practically conduce; though the moral of it all amounted rather to a portent, the one that Haughty, by the same token, had done least to reassure him against, of the extent to which the native jungle harboured the female specimen and to which its ostensible cover, the vast level of mixed growths stirred wavingly in whatever breeze, was apt to be identifiable but as an agitation of the latest redundant thing in ladies' hats.

This quotation, taken almost at random from *The Ivory Tower*, is not intended to represent Henry James at any hypothetical 'best', any more than the noble passage from *Paradise Lost* is [142] meant to be Milton's hypothetical worst. The question is the difference of intention, in the elaboration of styles both of which depart so far from lucid simplicity. The sound, of course, is never irrelevant, and the style of James certainly depends for its effect a good deal on the sound of a voice, James's own, painfully explaining. But the complication, with James, is due to a determination not to simplify, and in that simplification lose any of the real intricacies and by-paths of mental movement; whereas the complication of a Miltonic sentence is an active complication, a complication deliberately introduced into what was a previously simplified and abstract thought. The dark angel here is not *thinking* or conversing, but making a speech carefully prepared for him; and the arrangement is for the sake of musical value, not for significance. A straightforward utterance, as of a Homeric or Dantesque character, would make the speaker very much more real to us; but reality is no part of the intention. We have in fact to read such a passage not analytically, to get the poetic impression. I am not suggesting that Milton has no idea to convey which he regards as important: only that the syntax is determined by the musical significance, by the auditory imagination, rather than by the attempt to follow actual speech or thought. It is at least more nearly possible to distinguish the pleasure which arises from the *noise*, from the pleasure due to other elements, than with the verse of Shakespeare, in which the auditory imagination and the imagination of the other senses are more nearly fused, and fused together with the thought. The result with Milton is, in one sense of the word, *rhetoric*. That term is not intended to be derogatory. This kind of 'rhetoric' is not necessarily bad in its influence; but it may be considered bad in relation to the historical life of a language as a whole. I have said elsewhere that the living English which was Shakespeare's became split up into two components one of which was exploited by Milton and the other by Dryden. Of the two, I still think Dryden's development the healthier, because it was Dryden who preserved, so far as it was preserved at all, the tradition of conversational language in poetry: and I might add that it seems to me easier to get back to healthy language from Dryden than it is to get back to it from Milton. For what such a generalisation is worth, Milton's influence on the eighteenth century was much more deplorable than Dryden's.

6 If several very important reservations and exceptions are made, I think that it is not unprofitable to compare Milton's develop-[143]ment with that of James Joyce. The initial similarities are musical taste and abilities, followed by musical training, wide and curious knowledge, gift for acquiring languages, and remarkable powers of memory perhaps fortified by defective vision. The important difference is that Joyce's imagination is not naturally of so purely auditory a type as Milton's.

In his early work, and at least in part of *Ulysses*, there is visual and other imagination of the highest kind; and I may be mistaken in thinking that the later part of *Ulysses* shows a turning from the visible world to draw rather on the resources of phantasmagoria. In any case, one may suppose that the replenishment of visual imagery during later years has been insufficient; so that what I find in *Work in Progress* is an auditory imagination abnormally sharpened at the expense of the visual. There is still a little to be seen, and what there is to see is worth looking at. And I would repeat that with Joyce this development seems to me largely due to circumstances: whereas Milton may be said never to have seen anything. For Milton, therefore, the concentration on sound was wholly a benefit. Indeed, I find, in reading *Paradise Lost*, that I am happiest where there is least to visualise. The eye is not shocked in his twilit Hell as it is in the Garden of Eden, where I for one can get pleasure from the verse only by deliberate effort not to visualise Adam and Eve and their surroundings.

7 I am not suggesting any close parallel between the 'rhetoric' of Milton and the later style of Joyce. It is a different music; and Joyce always maintains some contact with the conversational tone. But it may prove to be equally a blind alley for the future development of the language.

8 A disadvantage of the rhetorical style appears to be, that a dislocation takes place, through the hypertrophy of the auditory imagination at the expense of the visual and tactile, so that the inner meaning is separated from the surface, and tends to become something occult, or at least without effect upon the reader until fully understood. To extract everything possible from *Paradise Lost*, it would seem necessary to read it in two different ways, first solely for the sound, and second for the sense. The full beauty of his long periods can hardly be enjoyed while we are wrestling with the meaning as well; and for the pleasure of the ear the meaning is hardly necessary, except in so far as certain key-words indicate the emotional tone of the passage. Now Shakespeare, or Dante, will bear innumerable readings, but at each reading all the ele-[144]ments of appreciation can be present. There is no interruption between the surface that these poets present to you and the core. While therefore, I cannot pretend to have penetrated to any 'secret' of these poets, I feel that such appreciation of their work as I am capable of points in the right direction; whereas I cannot feel that my appreciation of Milton leads anywhere outside of the mazes of sound. That, I feel, would be the matter for a separate study, like that of Blake's prophetic books; it might be well worth the trouble, but would have little to do with my interest in the poetry. So far as I perceive anything, it is a glimpse of a theology that I find in large part repellent, expressed through a mythology which would

have better been left in the Book of *Genesis*, upon which Milton has not improved. There seems to me to be a division, in Milton, between the philosopher or theologian and the poet; and, for the latter, I suspect also that this concentration upon the auditory imagination leads to at least an occasional levity. I can enjoy the roll of

> . . . Cambula, seat of Cathaian Can
> And Samarchand by Oxus, Temir's throne,
> To Paquin of Sinaean kings, and thence
> To Agra and Lahor of great Mogul
> Down to the golden Chersonese, or where
> The Persian in Ecbatan sate, or since
> In Hispahan, or where the Russian Ksar
> On Mosco, or the Sultan in Bizance,
> Turchestan-born . . . ,

and the rest of it, but I feel that this is not serious poetry, not poetry fully occupied about its business, but rather a solemn game. More often, admittedly, Milton uses proper names in moderation, to obtain the same effect of magnificence with them as does Marlowe – nowhere perhaps better than in the passage from *Lycidas*:

> Whether beyond the stormy Hebrides,
> Where thou perhaps under the whelming tide
> Visit'st the bottom of the monstrous world;
> Or whether thou to our moist vows deny'd
> Sleep'st by the fable of Bellerus old,
> Where the great vision of the guarded Mount
> Looks toward Namancos and Bayona's hold . . .

[145] than which for the single effect of grandeur of sound, there is nothing finer in poetry.

9 I make no attempt to appraise the 'greatness' of Milton in relation to poets who seem to me more comprehensive and better balanced; it has seemed to me more fruitful for the present to press the parallel between *Paradise Lost* and *Work in Progress*; and both Milton and Joyce are so exalted in their own kinds, in the whole of literature, that the only writers with whom to compare them are writers who have attempted something very different. Our views about Joyce, in any case, must remain at the present time tentative. But there are two attitudes both of which are necessary and right to adopt in considering the work of any poet. One is when we isolate him, when we try to understand the rules of his own game, adopt his own point of view: the other, perhaps less

usual, is when we measure him by outside standards, most pertinently by the standards of language and of something called Poetry, in our own language and in the whole history of European literature. It is from the second point of view that my objections to Milton are made: it is from this point of view that we can go so far as to say that, although his work realises superbly one important element in poetry, he may still be considered as having done damage to the English language from which it has not wholly recovered.

Variants from 1936:
Title A NOTE ON THE VERSE OF JOHN MILTON
1 has ever done] has ever done it
4 purpose] purposes
5 enamel'd] *enamelled*
in its influence] in itself, though likely to be bad in its influence
but it may be considered] and it may be considered
6 James Joyce] Mr. James Joyce
musical taste] musical tastes
Joyce's] Mr. Joyce's
Joyce] Mr. Joyce [*passim*]

Milton II[1]

OPAP, 146–61.

Originally a lecture delivered on 26 Mar. 1947. Publ. as 'Milton', Annual Lecture on a Master Mind, Henrietta Hertz Trust of the British Academy (1947): Gallup A 49. Repr. in *SR*, 56. 2 (Apr./June 1948), [185]–209 (Gallup C531), and in *Proceedings of the British Academy*, 33 (1951), [61]–79.

At the end of para. 16 'as the farthest possible remove' has been corrected to 'at the farthest possible remove'.

1 Samuel Johnson, addressing himself to examine Milton's versification, in the *Rambler* of Saturday, January 12, 1751, thought it necessary to excuse his temerity in writing upon a subject already so fully discussed. In justification of his essay this great critic and poet remarked: 'There are, in every age, new errors to be rectified, and new prejudices to be opposed'. I am obliged to phrase my own apology rather differently. The errors of our own times have been rectified by vigorous hands, and the prejudices opposed by commanding voices. Some of the errors and prejudices have been associated with my own name, and of these in particular I shall find

---

1. The Henrietta Hertz Lecture, delivered to the British Academy, 1947, and subsequently at the Frick Museum, New York.

myself impelled to speak; it will, I hope, be attributed to me for modesty rather than for conceit if I maintain that no one can correct an error with better authority than the person who has been held responsible for it. And there is, I think, another justification for my speaking about Milton, besides the singular one which I have just given. The champions of Milton in our time, with one notable exception, have been scholars and teachers. I have no claim to be either: I am aware that my only claim upon your attention, in speaking of Milton or of any other great poet, is by appeal to your curiosity, in the hope that you may care to know what a contemporary writer of verse thinks of one of his predecessors.

2 I believe that the scholar and the practitioner in the field of literary criticism should supplement each other's work. The criticism of the practitioner will be all the better, certainly, if he is not wholly destitute of scholarship; and the criticism of the scholar will be all the better if he has some experience of the difficulties of writing verse. But the orientation of the two critics is different. The scholar is more concerned with the understanding of the masterpiece in the environment of its author: with the world in which the author lived, the temper of his age, his intellectual [147] formation, the books which he had read, and the influences which had moulded him. The practitioner is concerned less with the author than with the poem; and with the poem in relation to his own age. He asks: Of what *use* is the poetry of this poet to poets writing to-day? Is it, or can it become, a living force in English poetry still unwritten? So we may say that the scholar's interest is in the permanent, the practitioner's in the immediate. The scholar can teach us where we should bestow our *admiration* and *respect*: the practitioner should be able, when he is the right poet talking about the right poet, to make an old masterpiece actual, give it contemporary importance, and persuade his audience that it is interesting, exciting, enjoyable, and *active*. I can give only one example of contemporary criticism of Milton, by a critic of the type to which I belong if I have any critical pretensions at all: that is the Introduction to Milton's *English Poems* in the 'World Classics' series, by the late Charles Williams. It is not a comprehensive essay; it is notable primarily because it provides the best prolegomenon to *Comus* which any modern reader could have; but what distinguishes it throughout (and the same is true of most of Williams's critical writing) is the author's warmth of feeling and his success in communicating it to the reader. In this, so far as I am aware, the essay of Williams is a solitary example.

3 I think it is useful, in such an examination as I propose to make, to keep in mind some critic of the past, of one's own type, by whom to measure one's opinions: a critic sufficiently remote in time, for his local errors

and prejudices to be not identical with one's own. That is why I began by quoting Samuel Johnson. It will hardly be contested that as a critic of poetry Johnson wrote as a practitioner and not as a scholar. Because he was a poet himself, and a good poet, what he wrote about poetry must be read with respect. And unless we know and appreciate Johnson's poetry we cannot judge either the merits or the limitations of his criticism. It is a pity that what the common reader to-day has read, or has remembered, or has seen quoted, are mostly those few statements of Johnson's from which later critics have vehemently dissented. But when Johnson held an opinion which seems to us wrong, we are never safe in dismissing it without inquiring why he was wrong; he had his own 'errors and prejudices', certainly, but for lack of examining them sympathetically we are always in danger of merely countering error with error and prejudice with prejudice. Now Johnson was, in his day, very much a modern: he [148] was concerned with how poetry should be written in his own time. The fact that he came towards the end, rather than the beginning of a style, the fact that his time was rapidly passing away, and that the canons of taste which he observed were about to fall into desuetude, does not diminish the interest of his criticism. Nor does the likelihood that the development of poetry in the next fifty years will take quite different directions from those which to me seem desirable to explore, deter me from asking the questions that Johnson implied: How should poetry be written now? and what place does the answer to this question give to Milton? And I think that the answers to these questions may be different now from the answers that were correct twenty-five years ago.

4 There is one prejudice against Milton, apparent on almost every page of Johnson's *Life of Milton*, which I imagine is still general: we, however, with a longer historical perspective, are in a better position than was Johnson to recognise it and to make allowance for it. This is a prejudice which I share myself: an antipathy towards Milton the man. Of this in itself I have nothing further to say: all that is necessary is to record one's awareness of it. But this prejudice is often involved with another, more obscure: and I do not think that Johnson had disengaged the two in his own mind. The fact is simply that the Civil War of the seventeenth century, in which Milton is a symbolic figure, has never been concluded. The Civil War is not ended: I question whether any serious civil war ever does end. Throughout that period English society was so convulsed and divided that the effects are still felt. Reading Johnson's essay one is always aware that Johnson was obstinately and passionately of another party. No other English poet, not Wordsworth, or Shelley, lived through or took sides in such momentous events as did Milton; of no other poet is it so difficult

to consider the poetry simply as poetry, without our theological and political dispositions, conscious and unconscious, inherited or acquired, making an unlawful entry. And the danger is all the greater because these emotions now take different vestures. It is now considered grotesque, on political grounds, to be of the party of King Charles; it is now, I believe, considered equally grotesque, on moral grounds, to be of the party of the Puritans; and to most persons to-day the religious views of both parties may seem equally remote. Nevertheless, the passions are unquenched, and if we are not very wide awake their smoke will obscure the glass through which we examine Milton's poetry. Something has been done, cer-[149]tainly, to persuade us that Milton was never really of any party, but disagreed with everyone. Mr Wilson Knight, in *Chariot of Wrath*, has argued that Milton was more a monarchist than a republican, and not in any modern sense a 'democrat', and Professor Saurat has produced evidence to show that Milton's theology was highly eccentric, and as scandalous to Protestants as to Catholics – that he was, in fact, a sort of Christadelphian, and perhaps not a very orthodox Christadelphian at that; while on the other hand Mr C. S. Lewis has opposed Professor Saurat by skillfully arguing that Milton, at least in *Paradise Lost*, can be acquitted of heresy even from a point of view so orthodox as that of Mr Lewis himself. On these questions I hold no opinion: it is probably beneficial to question the assumption that Milton was a sound Free Churchman and member of the Liberal Party; but I think that we still have to be on guard against an unconscious partisanship if we aim to attend to the poetry for the poetry's sake.

5 So much for our prejudices. I come next to the positive objection to Milton which has been raised in our own time, that is to say, the charge that he is an unwholesome influence. And from this I shall proceed to the permanent strictures of reproof (to employ a phrase of Johnson's) and, finally, to the grounds on which I consider him a great poet and one whom poets to-day might study with profit.

6 For a statement of the *generalised* belief in the unwholesomeness of Milton's influence I turn to Mr Middleton Murry's critique of Milton in his *Heaven and Earth* – a book which contains chapters of profound insight, interrupted by passages which seem to me intemperate. Mr Murry approaches Milton after his long and patient study of Keats; and it is through the eyes of Keats that he sees Milton.

> Keats [*Mr Murry writes*] as a poetic artist, second to none since Shakespeare, and Blake, as a prophet of spiritual values unique in our history, both passed substantially the same judgement on Milton: 'Life to him would be death to me.' And whatever may be

our verdict on the development of English poetry since Milton, we must admit the justice of Keats's opinion that Milton's magnificence led nowhere. 'English must be kept up,' said Keats. To be influenced beyond a certain point by Milton's art, he felt, dammed the creative flow of the English genius in and through itself. In saying this, I think, Keats voiced the very inmost of the English genius. To pass under the spell of Milton is to be con-[150]demned to imitate him. It is quite different with Shakespeare. Shakespeare baffles and liberates; Milton is perspicuous and constricts.

7 This is a very confident affirmation, and I criticise it with some diffidence because I cannot pretend to have devoted as much study to Keats, or to have as intimate understanding of his difficulties, as Mr Murry. But Mr Murry seems to me here to be trying to transform the predicament of a particular poet with a particular aim at a particular moment in time into a censure of timeless validity. He appears to assert that the liberative function of Shakespeare and the constrictive menace of Milton are permanent characteristics of these two poets. 'To be influenced beyond a certain point' by any one master is bad for any poet; and it does not matter whether that influence is Milton's or another's; and as we cannot anticipate where that point will come, we might be better advised to call it an *un*certain point. If it is not good to remain under the spell of Milton, is it good to remain under the spell of Shakespeare? It depends partly upon what genre of poetry you are trying to develop. Keats wanted to write an epic, and he found, as might be expected, that the time had not arrived at which another English epic, comparable in grandeur to *Paradise Lost*, could be written. He also tried his hand at writing plays: and one might argue that *King Stephen* was more blighted by Shakespeare than *Hyperion* by Milton. Certainly, *Hyperion* remains a magnificent fragment which one re-reads; and *King Stephen* is a play which we may have read once, but to which we never return for enjoyment. Milton made a great epic impossible for succeeding generations; Shakespeare made a great poetic drama impossible; such a situation is inevitable, and it persists until the language has so altered that there is no danger, because no possibility, of imitation. Anyone who tries to write poetic drama, even to-day, should know that half of his energy must be exhausted in the effort to escape from the constricting toils of Shakespeare: the moment his attention is relaxed, or his mind fatigued, he will lapse into bad Shakespearian verse. For a long time after an epic poet like Milton, or a dramatic poet like Shakespeare, nothing can be done. Yet the effort must be repeatedly made; for we can never know in advance when the moment is approaching at which a new epic, or a new

drama, will be possible; and when the moment does draw near it may be that the genius of an individual poet will perform the last mutation [151] of idiom and versification which will bring that new poetry into being.

8 I have referred to Mr Murry's view of the bad influence of Milton as generalised, because it is implicitly the whole personality of Milton that is in question: not specifically his beliefs, or his language or versification, but the beliefs as realised in that particular personality, and his poetry as the expression of it. By the *particular* view of Milton's influence as bad, I mean that view which attends to the language, the syntax, the versification, the imagery. I do not suggest that there is here a complete difference of subject matter: it is the difference of approach, the difference of the focus of interest, between the philosophical critic and the literary critic. An incapacity for the abstruse, and an interest in poetry which is primarily a technical interest, dispose my mind towards the more limited and perhaps more superficial task. Let us proceed to look at Milton's influence from this point of view, that of the writer of poetry in our own time.

9 The reproach against Milton, that his technical influence has been bad, appears to have been made by no one more positively than by myself. I find myself saying, as recently as 1936, that this charge against Milton

> appears a good deal more serious if we affirm that Milton's poetry could *only* be an influence for the worse, upon any poet whatever. It is more serious, also, if we affirm that Milton's bad influence may be traced much farther than the eighteenth century, and much farther than upon bad poets: if we say that it was an influence against which we still have to struggle.

10 In writing these sentences I failed to draw a threefold distinction, which now seems to me of some importance. There are three separate assertions implied. The first is, that an influence has been bad in the past: this is to assert that good poets, in the eighteenth or nineteenth century, would have written better if they had not submitted themselves to the influence of Milton. The second assertion is, that the contemporary situation is such that Milton is a master whom we should avoid. The third is, that the influence of Milton, or of any particular poet, can be *always* bad, and that we can predict that wherever it is found at any time in the future, however remote, it will be a bad influence. Now, the first and third of these assertions I am no longer prepared to make, because, detached from the second, they do not appear to me to have any meaning.

[152] 11 For the first, when we consider one great poet of the past, and one or more other poets, upon whom we say he has exerted a bad influence,

we must admit that the responsibility, if there be any, is rather with the poets who were influenced than with the poet whose work exerted the influence. We can, of course, show that certain tricks or mannerisms which the imitators display are due to conscious or unconscious imitation and emulation, but that is a reproach against their injudicious choice of a model and not against their model itself. And we can never prove that any particular poet would have written better poetry if he had escaped that influence. Even if we assert, what can only be a matter of faith, that Keats would have written a very great epic poem if Milton had not preceded him, is it sensible to pine for an unwritten masterpiece, in exchange for one which we possess and acknowledge? And as for the remote future, what can we affirm about the poetry that will be written then, except that we should probably be unable to understand or to enjoy it, and that therefore we can hold no opinion as to what 'good' and 'bad' influences will *mean* in that future? The only relation in which the question of influence, good and bad, is significant, is the relation to the immediate future. With that question I shall engage at the end. I wish first to mention another reproach against Milton, that represented by the phrase 'dissociation of sensibility'.

12 I remarked many years ago, in an essay on Dryden, that:

> In the seventeenth century a dissociation of sensibility set in, from which we have never recovered; and this dissociation, as is natural, was due to the influence of the two most powerful poets of the century, Milton and Dryden.

13 The longer passage from which this sentence is taken is quoted by Dr Tillyard in his *Milton*. Dr Tillyard makes the following comment:

> Speaking only of what in this passage concerns Milton, I would say that there is here a mixture of truth and falsehood. Some sort of dissociation of sensibility in Milton, not necessarily undesirable, has to be admitted; but that he was responsible for any such dissociation in others (at least till this general dissociation had inevitably set in) is untrue.

14 I believe that the general affirmation represented by the phrase 'dissociation of sensibility' (one of the two or three phrases of my coinage – like 'objective correlative' – which have had a success in the world astonishing to their author) retains some validity; [153] but I now incline to agree with Dr Tillyard that to lay the burden on the shoulders of Milton and Dryden was a mistake. If such a dissociation did take place, I suspect that the causes are too complex and too profound to justify our accounting for the change in terms of literary criticism. All we can say is,

that something like this did happen; that it had something to do with the Civil War; that it would even be unwise to say it was caused by the Civil War, but that it is a consequence of the same causes which brought about the Civil War; that we must seek the causes in Europe, not in England alone; and for what these causes were, we may dig and dig until we get to a depth at which words and concepts fail us.

15 Before proceeding to take up the case against Milton, as it stood for poets twenty-five years ago – the second, and only significant meaning of 'bad influence' – I think it would be best to consider what permanent strictures of reproof may be drawn: those censures which, when we make them, we must assume to be made by enduring laws of taste. The essence of the permanent censure of Milton is, I believe, to be found in Johnson's essay. This is not the place in which to examine certain particular and erroneous judgements of Johnson; to explain his condemnation of *Comus* and *Samson* as the application of dramatic canons which to us seem inapplicable; or to condone his dismissal of the versification of *Lycidas* by the specialisation, rather than the absence, of his sense of rhythm. Johnson's most important censure of Milton is contained in three paragraphs, which I must ask leave to quote in full.

> Throughout all his greater works [*says Johnson*] there prevails an uniform peculiarity of *diction*, a mode and cast of expression which bears little resemblance to that of any former writer; and which is so far removed from common use, that an unlearned reader, when he first opens the book, finds himself surprised by a new language.
>
> This novelty has been, by those who can find nothing wrong with Milton, imputed to his laborious endeavours after words suited to the grandeur of his ideas. *Our language*, says Addison, *sunk under him*. But the truth is, that both in prose and in verse, he had formed his style by a perverse and pedantic principle. He was desirous to use English words with a foreign idiom. This in all his prose is discovered and condemned; for there judgment operates freely, neither softened by the beauty, nor awed by the dignity of his thoughts; but such is the power of his poetry, that his call is obeyed without resistance, the reader feels himself in [154] captivity to a higher and nobler mind, and criticism sinks in admiration.
>
> Milton's style was not modified by his subject; what is shown with greater extent in *Paradise Lost* may be found in *Comus*. One source of his peculiarity was his familiarity with the Tuscan poets; the disposition of his words is, I think, frequently Italian; perhaps sometimes combined with other tongues. Of him at last, may be said what Jonson said of Spenser, that he *wrote no language*, but

has formed what Butler called a *Babylonish dialect*, in itself harsh and barbarous, but made by exalted genius and extensive learning the vehicle of so much instruction and so much pleasure, that, like other lovers, we find grace in its deformity.

16 This criticism seems to me substantially true: indeed, unless we accept it, I do not think we are in the way to appreciate the peculiar greatness of Milton. His style is not a *classic* style, in that it is not the elevation of a *common* style, by the final touch of genius, to greatness. It is, from the foundation, and in every particular, a personal style, not based upon common speech, or common prose, or direct communication of meaning. Of some great poetry one has difficulty in pronouncing just what it is, what infinitesimal touch, that has made all the difference from a plain statement which anyone could make; the slight transformation which, while it leaves a plain statement a plain statement, has always the maximal, never the minimal, alteration of ordinary language. Every distortion of construction, the foreign idiom, the use of a word in a foreign way or with the meaning of the foreign word from which it is derived rather than the accepted meaning in English, every idiosyncrasy is a particular act of violence which Milton has been the first to commit. There is no cliché, no poetic diction in the derogatory sense, but a perpetual sequence of original acts of lawlessness. Of all modern writers of verse, the nearest analogy seems to me to be Mallarmé, a much smaller poet, though still a great one. The personalities, the poetic theories of the two men could not have been more different; but in respect of the violence which they could do to language, and justify, there is a remote similarity. Milton's poetry is poetry at the farthest possible remove from prose; his prose seems to me too near to half-formed poetry to be a good prose. To say that the work of a poet is at the farthest possible remove from prose; his prose seems to me too near to half-formed poetry to be a good prose.

17 To say that the work of a poet is at the farthest possible remove from prose would once have struck me as condemnatory: it now seems to me simply, when we have to do with a Milton, the pre-[155]cision of its peculiar greatness. As a poet, Milton seems to me probably the greatest of all eccentrics. His work illustrates no general principles of good writing; the only principles of writing that it illustrates are such as are valid only for Milton himself to observe. There are two kinds of poet who can ordinarily be of use to other poets. There are those who suggest, to one or another of their successors, something which they have not done themselves, or who provoke a different way of doing the same thing: these are likely to be not the greatest, but smaller, imperfect poets with whom later poets discover an affinity. And there are the great poets

from whom we can learn negative rules: no poet can teach another to write well, but some great poets can teach others some of the things to avoid. They teach us what to avoid, by showing us what great poetry can do without – how *bare* it can be. Of these are Dante and Racine. But if we are ever to make use of Milton we must do so in quite a different way. Even a small poet can learn something from the study of Dante, or from the study of Chaucer: we must perhaps wait for a great poet before we find one who can profit from the study of Milton.

18 I repeat that the remoteness of Milton's verse from ordinary speech, his invention of his own poetic language, seems to me one of the marks of his greatness. Other marks are his sense of structure, both in the general design of *Paradise Lost* and *Samson*, and in his syntax; and finally, and not least, his inerrancy, conscious or unconscious, in writing so as to make the best display of his talents, and the best concealment of his weaknesses.

19 The appropriateness of the subject of *Samson* is too obvious to expatiate upon: it was probably the one dramatic story out of which Milton could have made a masterpiece. But the complete suitability of *Paradise Lost* has not, I think, been so often remarked. It was surely an intuitive perception of what he could not do, that arrested Milton's project of an epic on King Arthur. For one thing, he had little interest in, or understanding of, individual human beings. In *Paradise Lost* he was not called upon for any of that understanding which comes from an affectionate observation of men and women. But such an interest in human beings was not required – indeed its *absence* was a necessary condition – for the creation of his figures of Adam and Eve. These are not a man and woman such as any we know: if they were, they would not be Adam and Eve. They are the original *Man* and *Woman*, not types, but prototypes. They have the general characteristics of men and [156] women, such that we can recognise, in the temptation and the fall, the first motions of the faults and virtues, the abjection and the nobility, of all their descendants. They have ordinary humanity to the right degree, and yet are not, and should not be, ordinary mortals. Were they more particularised they would be false, and if Milton had been more interested in humanity, he could not have created them. Other critics have remarked upon the exactness, without defect or exaggeration, with which Moloch, Belial, and Mammon, in the second book, speak according to the particular sin which each represents. It would not be suitable that the infernal powers should have, in the human sense, characters, for a character is always mixed; but in the hands of an inferior manipulator, they might easily have been reduced to *humours*.

20 The appropriateness of the material of *Paradise Lost* to the genius and the limitations of Milton, is still more evident when we consider the visual imagery. I have already remarked, in a paper written some years ago, on Milton's weakness of visual observation, a weakness which I think was always present – the effect of his blindness may have been rather to strengthen the compensatory qualities than to increase a fault which was already present. Mr Wilson Knight, who has devoted close study to recurrent imagery in poetry, has called attention to Milton's propensity towards images of engineering and mechanics; to me it seems that Milton is at his best in imagery suggestive of vast size, limitless space, abysmal depth, and light and darkness. No theme and no setting, other than that which he chose in *Paradise Lost*, could have given him such scope for the kind of imagery in which he excelled, or made less demand upon those powers of visual imagination which were in him defective.

21 Most of the absurdities and inconsistencies to which Johnson calls attention, and which, so far as they can justly be isolated in this way, he properly condemns, will I think appear in a more correct proportion if we consider them in relation to this general judgement. I do not think that we should attempt to *see* very clearly any scene that Milton depicts: it should be accepted as a shifting phantasmagory. To complain, because we first find the arch-fiend 'chain'd on the burning lake', and in a minute or two see him making his way to the shore, is to expect a kind of consistency which the world to which Milton has introduced us does not require.

22 This limitation of visual power, like Milton's limited interest in [157] human beings, turns out to be not merely a negligible defect, but a positive virtue, when we visit Adam and Eve in Eden. Just as a higher degree of characterisation of Adam and Eve would have been unsuitable, so a more vivid picture of the earthly Paradise would have been less paradisiacal. For a greater definiteness, a more detailed account of flora and fauna, could only have assimilated Eden to the landscapes of earth with which we are familiar. As it is, the impression of Eden which we retain, is the most suitable, and is that which Milton was most qualified to give: the impression of *light* – a daylight and a starlight, a light of dawn and of dusk, the light which, remembered by a man in his blindness, has a supernatural glory unexperienced by men of normal vision.

23 We must, then, in reading *Paradise Lost*, not expect to see clearly; our sense of sight must be blurred, so that our *hearing* may become more acute. *Paradise Lost*, like *Finnegans Wake* (for I can think of no work which provides a more interesting parallel: two books by great blind musicians, each writing a language of his own based upon English) makes this peculiar demand for a readjustment of the reader's mode of

apprehension. The emphasis is on the sound, not the vision, upon the word, not the idea; and in the end it is the unique versification that is the most certain sign of Milton's intellectual mastership.

24 On the subject of Milton's versification, so far as I am aware, little enough has been written. We have Johnson's essay in the *Rambler*, which deserves more study than it has received, and we have a short treatise by Robert Bridges on *Milton's Prosody*. I speak of Bridges with respect, for no poet of our time has given such close attention to prosody as he. Bridges catalogues the systematic irregularities which give perpetual variety to Milton's verse, and I can find no fault with his analysis. But however interesting these analyses are, I do not think that it is by such means that we gain an appreciation of the peculiar rhythm of a poet. It seems to me also that Milton's verse is especially refractory to yielding up its secrets to examination of the single line. For his verse is not formed in this way. It is the period, the sentence and still more the paragraph, that is the unit of Milton's verse; and emphasis on the line structure is the minimum necessary to provide a counter-pattern to the period structure. It is only in the period that the wave-length of Milton's verse is to be found: it is his ability to give a perfect and unique pattern to every paragraph, [158] such that the full beauty of the line is found in its context, and his ability to work in larger musical units than any other poet – that is to me the most conclusive evidence of Milton's supreme mastery. The peculiar feeling, almost a physical sensation of a breathless leap, communicated by Milton's long periods, and by his alone, is impossible to procure from rhymed verse. Indeed, this mastery is more conclusive evidence of his intellectual power, than is his grasp of any *ideas* that he borrowed or invented. To be able to control so many words at once is the token of a mind of most exceptional energy.

25 It is interesting at this point to recall the general observations upon blank verse, which a consideration of *Paradise Lost* prompted Johnson to make towards the end of his essay.

> The music of the English heroic lines strikes the ear so faintly, that it is easily lost, unless all the syllables of every line co-operate together; this co-operation can only be obtained by the preservation of every verse unmingled with another as a distinct system of sounds; and this distinctness is obtained and preserved by the artifice of rhyme. The variety of pauses, so much boasted by the lovers of blank verse, changes the measures of an English poet to the periods of a declaimer; and there are only a few skilful and happy readers of Milton, who enable their audience to perceive where the lines end or begin. *Blank verse*, said an ingenious critic, *seems to be verse only to the eye.*

26 Some of my audience may recall that this last remark, in almost the same words, was often made, a literary generation ago, about the 'free verse' of the period: and even without this encouragement from Johnson it would have occurred to my mind to declare Milton to be the greatest master of free verse in our language. What is interesting about Johnson's paragraph, however, is that it represents the judgement of a man who had by no means a deaf ear, but simply a *specialised* ear, for verbal music. Within the limits of the poetry of his own period, Johnson is a very good judge of the relative merits of several poets as writers of blank verse. But on the whole, the blank verse of his age might more properly be called unrhymed verse; and nowhere is this difference more evident than in the verse of his own tragedy *Irene*: the phrasing is admirable, the style elevated and correct, but each line cries out for a companion to rhyme with it. Indeed, it is only with labour, or by occasional inspiration, or by submission to the influence of the older dramatists, that the blank verse of the nineteenth century [159] succeeds in making the absence of rhyme inevitable and right, with the rightness of Milton. Even Johnson admitted that he could not wish that Milton had been a rhymer. Nor did the nineteenth century succeed in giving to blank verse the flexibility which it needs if the tone of common speech, talking of the topics of common intercourse, is to be employed; so that when our more modern practitioners of blank verse do not touch the sublime, they frequently sink to the ridiculous. Milton perfected non-dramatic blank verse and at the same time imposed limitations, very hard to break, upon the use to which it may be put if its greatest musical possibilities are to be exploited.

27 I come at last to compare my own attitude, as that of a poetical practitioner perhaps typical of a generation twenty-five years ago, with my attitude to-day. I have thought it well to take matters in the order in which I have taken them to discuss first the censures and detractions which I believe to have permanent validity, and which were best made by Johnson, in order to make clearer the causes, and the justification, for hostility to Milton on the part of poets at a particular juncture. And I wished to make clear those excellences of Milton which particularly impress me, before explaining why I think that the study of his verse might at last be of benefit to poets.

28 I have on several occasions suggested, that the important changes in the idiom of English verse which are represented by the names of Dryden and Wordsworth, may be characterised as successful attempts to escape from a poetic idiom which had ceased to have a relation to contemporary speech. This is the sense of Wordsworth's Prefaces. By the

beginning of the present century another revolution in idiom – and such revolutions bring with them an alteration of metric, a new appeal to the ear – was due. It inevitably happens that the young poets engaged in such a revolution will exalt the merits of those poets of the past who offer them example and stimulation, and cry down the merits of poets who do not stand for the qualities which they are zealous to realise. This is not only inevitable, it is right. It is even right, and certainly inevitable, that their practice, still more influential than their critical pronouncements, should attract their own readers to the poets by whose work they have been influenced. Such influence has certainly contributed to the taste (if we can distinguish the *taste* from the *fashion*) for Donne. I do not think that any modern poet, unless in a fit of irresponsible peevishness, has ever denied [160] Milton's consummate powers. And it must be said that Milton's diction is not a poetic diction in the sense of being a debased currency: when he violates the English language he is imitating nobody, and he is inimitable. But Milton does, as I have said, represent poetry at the extreme limit from prose; and it was one of our tenets that verse should have the virtues of prose, that diction should become assimilated to cultivated contemporary speech, before aspiring to the elevation of poetry. Another tenet was that the subject-matter and the imagery of poetry should be extended to topics and objects related to the life of a modern man or woman; that we were to seek the non-poetic, to seek even material refractory to transmutation into poetry, and words and phrases which had not been used in poetry before. And the study of Milton could be of no help here: it was only a hindrance.

29 We cannot, in literature, any more than in the rest of life, live in a perpetual state of revolution. If every generation of poets made it their task to bring poetic diction up to date with the spoken language, poetry would fail in one of its most important obligations. For poetry should help, not only to refine the language of the time, but to prevent it from changing too rapidly: a development of language at too great a speed would be a development in the sense of a progressive deterioration, and that is our danger to-day. If the poetry of the rest of this century takes the line of development which seems to me, reviewing the progress of poetry through the last three centuries, the right course, it will discover new and more elaborate patterns of a diction now established. In this search it might have much to learn from Milton's extended verse structure; it might also avoid the danger of a *servitude* to colloquial speech and to current jargon. It might also learn that the music of verse is strongest in poetry which has a definite meaning expressed in the properest words. Poets might be led to admit that a knowledge of the literature of their own language, with a knowledge of the literature and the grammatical construction of other languages, is a very valuable part of the poet's equipment. And they might, as I have already hinted, devote some study to Milton as, outside the theatre, the greatest master in our language of freedom within form. A study of *Samson* should sharpen anyone's appreciation of the justified irregularity, and put him on guard against the pointless irregularity. In studying *Paradise Lost* we come to perceive that the verse is continuously animated by the departure from, and return to, the regular [161] measure; and that, in comparison with Milton, hardly any subsequent writer of blank verse appears to exercise any freedom at all. We can also be led to the reflection that a monotony of unscannable verse fatigues the attention even more quickly than a monotony of exact feet. In short, it now seems to me that poets are sufficiently liberated from Milton's reputation, to approach the study of his work without danger, and with profit to their poetry and to the English language.

Variants from 'Milton' (1947):

Title Milton

1 January 12,] 12 January

10 at any time] , at any time

13 **(end)** [Fn. in 1947:] On one point I should take issue with Dr. Tillyard. A little further on he quotes another phrase of mine, of earlier date: 'The Chinese Wall of Milton's blank verse.' He comments: 'It must have been an ineffective wall, for *Venice Preserved*, *All for Love* and similar plays in blank verse were not confined by it. They owe nothing to Milton's versification.' Of course not – these were *plays*, and I have long maintained that dramatic blank verse and non-dramatic blank verse are not the same thing. The Chinese Wall there, if it existed, was erected by Shakespeare.

15 as the application] by his applying

19 [Between 'prototypes' and 'They have the general':] : if they were not set apart from ordinary humanity they would not be Adam and Eve.

20 [at 'some years ago.', fn. in 1947:] In *Essays and Studies by Members of the English Association*, vol xxi, 1936. pp. 32 ff.

24 [at 'with his analysis.', fn. in 1947:] Beyond raising one question, in connexion with Bridges' account of Milton's use of recessive accent. It does not seem to me that such recession, as of *obscéne* to *óbscene* in the line
      Next Chemos, the obscene dread of Moab's sons
simply reverses the value of the two syllables: I should say that the second syllable retains something of its length, and the first something of its shortness, and that the surprise and variety are due to each syllable becoming *both* long and short. The effect is like that of a tide-rip, in which a peculiar type of wave is produced by the conflict of two opposing forces.

26 nineteenth century succeeds] *nineteenth* century succeeds
      sink to] approach

[**Between paras. 26 and 27:**] I now come to the point at which it is desirable to quote passages in illustration of what I have been saying about Milton's versification. It is best, I think, to take familiar passages rather than to seek originality by choosing those which have been less often drawn to our attention. The first is the Invocation which opens Book III of *Paradise Lost*:

> Hail holy light, offspring of Heaven first-borne,
> Or of th'Eternal Coeternal bean
> May I express thee unblam'd? Since God is light,
> And never but in unapproached light
> Dwelt from Eternitie, dwelt then in thee,
> Bright effluence of bright essence increate.
> Or hear'st thou rather pure Ethereal stream,
> Whose Fountain who shall tell? before the Sun,
> Before the Heavens thou wert, and at the voice
> Of God, as with a mantle didst invest
> The rising world of waters dark and deep,
> Won from the void and formless infinite.

This passage is compact of Miltonic philosophy, but for that I must refer you to such critics as Professor Saurat and Mr. Lewis. For my purpose, it illustrates, first, Milton's power in the use of imagery of light. Second, it illustrates the closeness of the structure. If we were to attempt to analyse the Miltonic music line by line, that music would be lost: the individual line is right, not merely in itself, not merely in relation to the lines immediately preceding and following, but in relation to every other line in the passage. To extract this passage of twelve lines is to mutilate it. I contrast with this passage the following. In what I have just read there is no divagation from the point; the next passage is chosen to show Milton's skill in extending a period by introducing imagery which tends to distract us from the real subject:

> Thus Satan talking to his neerest Mate
> With Head uplift above the wave, and Eyes
> That sparkling blaz'd, his other Parts besides
> Prone on the Flood, extended long and large
> Lay floating many a rood, in bulk as huge
> As whom the Fables name of monstrous size,
> *Titanian*, or *Earth-born*, that warr'd on *Jove*,
> *Briarios* or *Typhon*, whom the Den
> By ancient *Tarsus* held, or that Sea-beast
> *Leviathan*, whom God of all his works
> Created hugest that swim th'Ocean stream:
> Him haply slumbring on the *Norway* foam
> The pilot of some small night-foundered Skiff,[1]
> Deeming some Island, oft, as Sea-men tell,
> With fixed Anchor in his scaly rind
> Moors by his side under the Lee, while Night
> Invests the Sea, and wished Morn delayes:
> So stretcht out huge in length the Arch-fiend lay
> Chain'd on the burning Lake. . . .

[Footnote: The term *night-foundered*, which I presume to be of Milton's invention, seems unsuitable here. Dr Tillyard has called my attention to the use of the same adjective in *Comus*, i. 483:

> Either som one like us night-foundered here

where, although extravagant, it draws a permissible comparison between travellers lost in the night, and seafarers in extremity. But when, as here in *Paradise Lost*, it is transferred from the travellers on land to adventurers by sea, and not to the men but to their *skiff*, the literal meaning of *founder* immediately presents itself. A *foundered* skiff could not be *moored*, to a whale or to anything else.]

There are, as often with Milton, criticisms of detail which could be made. I am not too happy with eyes that both blaze and sparkle, unless Milton meant us to imagine a roaring fire ejecting sparks: and that is *too* fiery an image for even supernatural eyes. The fact that the lake was burning somewhat diminishes the effect of the fiery eyes; and it is difficult to imagine a burning lake in a scene where there was only darkness visible. But with this kind of inconsistency we are familiar in Milton. What I wish to call to your attention is the happy introduction of so much extraneous matter. Any writer, straining for images of hugeness, might have thought of the whale, but only Milton could have included the anecdote of the deluded seamen without our wanting to put a blue pencil through it. We *nearly* forget Satan in attending to the story of the whale; Milton recalls us just in time. Therefore the diversion strengthens, instead of weakening, the passage. Milton plays exactly the same trick a few lines further on, when he speaks of Satan's shield:

> the broad circumference
> Hung on his shoulders like the Moon, whose Orb
> Through Optic Glass the *Tuscan* Artist views
> At Ev'ning from the top of *Fesole*,
> Or in *Valdarno*, to descry new Lands,
> Rivers or Mountains in her spotty Globe.
> His Spear, to equal which the tallest pine
> Hewn on *Norwegian* hills, to be the Mast
> Of some great Ammiral, were but a wand. . . .

Here I think that the two sudden transitions, to the Tuscan astronomer and thence to the Norwegian pine, followed by the concentrated astonishing image of sea-power, are most felicitous. If I may put it in this way without being misunderstood, I find in such passages a kind of inspired *frivolity*, an enjoyment by the author in the exercise of his own virtuosity, which is a mark of the first rank of genius. Addison, whose opinion is quoted and confirmed by Johnson, said that *Paradise Lost* is 'universally and perpetually interesting'; the two critics found the source of this perpetual interest in the subject matter; but the assertion of Johnson that 'all mankind will, through all ages, bear the same relation to Adam and Eve, and must partake of that good and evil which extend to themselves', even when it commands the assent of the Christian believer, will not wholly account for the absorbed attention which I think any poetry lover to-day ought to be able to give to the poem from end to end. I find the reason more certainly in the extraordinary style which because of its perpetual variety compels us to curiosity to know what is coming next, and in the perpetual surprises of reference such as those I have just quoted.

It may be observed also, that Milton employs devices of eloquence and of word-play in which poets of his time were practised, which perpetually relieve the mind, and facilitate the declamation. Frequently the same word is happily repeated:

> My sentence is for open Warr: Of Wiles
> More unexpert, I boast not: then let those
> *Contrive* who *need*, or when they *need*, not now.
> For while they *sit contriving*, shall the rest,
> Millions that stand in Arms, and longing wait
> The Signal to ascend, *sit* lingring here
> Heav'ns fugitives . . . .[1]

[Footnote: It might, of course, be objected that 'millions that *stand* in arms' could not at the same time '*sit* lingring'.]

To give another instance:

> *Receive* him coming, to *receive* from us
> Knee-tribute still unpaid, prostration vile,
> Too much *to one*, but double now endur'd,
> *To one* and to his image now proclaim'd?

He also uses alliteration, and most effectively:

> Of midnight march, and hurried meeting here.

Of such devices, none is quite original; Milton's blank verse would not have been possible without developments which had taken place in the two generations preceding; but what Milton made from what he learned is unique. Some of these devices appear in the late plays in which Shakespeare returned to realize surprising possibilities of his earliest manner:

> 'Tis still a dream, or else such stuff as madmen
> Tongue, and brain not; either both, or nothing;
> Or senseless speaking, or a speaking such
> As sense cannot untie . . .
>
>   Nobly he yokes
> A smiling with a sigh, as if the sigh
> Was that it was, for not being such a smile;
> The smile mocking the sigh, that it would fly
> From so divine a temple to commix
> With winds that sailors rail at.

The long and involved sentence structure is conspicuously developed by Massinger, from whom Milton may have taken a hint. I quote again a passage from Massinger which I quoted long ago in an essay on that dramatist:

> What though my father
> Writ man before he was so, and confirm'd it,
> By numbering that day no part of his life
> In which he did not service to his country;
> Was he to be free therefore from the laws

> And ceremonious forms in your decrees?
> Or else because he did as much as man
> In those three memorable overthrows,
> At Granson, Morat, Nancy, where his master,
> The warlike Charalois, with whose misfortunes
> I bear his name, lost treasure, men and life,
> To be excused from payment of those sums
> Which (his own patrimony spent) his zeal
> To serve his country forced him to take up?

The talent expended upon such a construction was, of course, ill-applied to the theatre. The verse has got out of hand, for dramatic purposes; and its only possible future was through the genius of Milton.

28 cry down] depreciate
(if we can distinguish the *taste* from the *fashion*)] , if we can distinguish the *taste* from the *fashion*,

29 liberated from Milton's reputation] sufficiently removed from Milton, and sufficiently liberated from his reputation

Johnson as Critic and Poet[1]

OPAP, 162–92.

In the first para. of section II 'The Shropshire Lad' has been corrected to 'A Shropshire Lad'.

It is primarily with Johnson as a critic, as the author of *The Lives of the Poets*, that I am here concerned. But I shall have something to say of his poetry also; because I think that in studying the criticism of poetry, by a critic who is also a poet, we can only appreciate his criticism – its standards, its merits, and its limitations, in the light of the kind of poetry that he wrote himself. I consider Johnson one of the three greatest critics of poetry in English literature: the other two being Dryden and Coleridge. All of those men were poets, and with all of them, a study of their poetry is highly relevant to the study of their criticism, because each of them was interested in a particular kind of poetry.

If this relevance is less apparent in the case of Johnson, than with Dryden and Coleridge, it is for trivial reasons. A great deal of bibliography has accumulated about Johnson, yet relatively little has been written about his writings; his two long poems have been neglected; and as for *The Lives of the Poets*, few educated persons have read more than half a dozen of them, and of these half-dozen, what is remembered is chiefly the passages with which everyone disagrees. One reason for indifference to his criticism, is

---

1. The Ballard Matthews Lectures, delivered at University College, North Wales in 1944.

that he was not the initiator of any poetic movement: he was a secondary poet at the end of a movement which had been initiated by greater poets than he, and his poems represent a personal variation of a style which was well established. Dryden, and Coleridge in partnership with Wordsworth, represent for us something *new* in poetry in their time. What Dryden wrote about poetry is therefore more exciting than what Johnson wrote. In his critical essays, he was outlining laws of writing for two generations to come: Johnson's view is retrospective. Dryden, concerned with defending his own way of writing, proceeds from the general to the particular: [163] he affirms principles, and criticises particular poets only in illustration of his argument; Johnson, in the course of criticising the work of particular poets – and of poets whose work was ended – is led to generalisations. Their historical situations were quite different. It is not, in the long run, relevant to our judgement of an author's greatness, whether he comes at the beginning of an age or at the end; but we are inclined to favour unduly the former. Of Johnson's influence there is nothing to say; and we are always impressed by a reputation for influence, as influence is a form of power. But when the tide of influence, which a writer may set in motion for a generation or two, has come to its full, and another force has drawn the waters in a different direction, and when several tides have risen and fallen, great writers remain of equal potentiality of influence in the future. It remains to be seen whether the literary influence of Johnson, as, in political thought, the influence of his friend of the other party, Edmund Burke, does not merely await a generation which has not yet been born to receive it.

An obvious obstacle to our enjoyment in reading *The Lives of the Poets* as a whole – and we must read it as a whole if we are to appreciate the magnitude of Johnson's achievement – is that we have not read the works of many of the poets included, and no inducement of pleasure or profit can be offered us to do so. Some of his minor eighteenth-century poets I have read in order to understand why Johnson approved of them; some I have only glanced at; and there are a number, of whom Johnson's commendation is so mild or his treatment so perfunctory, that I have not bothered even to look them up. Nobody wants to read the verses of Stepney or Walsh; I hardly think that any PhD candidate would be encouraged by his advisers to devote his thesis to a study of the work of Christopher Pitt. Johnson's assertion that Yalden's poems 'deserve perusal' is no more convincing than a letter of introduction written for an importunate visitor whom the writer wants to get rid of. The student of the history of literary taste may be struck by Johnson's remark that 'perhaps no composition in our language has been oftener perused than Pomfret's *Choice*' and want to find out why. But the common reader will probably be more discontented by Johnson's omissions, than made curious by all his inclusions. Everyone knows that the collection represented the choice of a group of booksellers, or publishers, who presumably thought that the works of all these authors were saleable, and who certainly thought, with more evident reason, that prefaces by Dr [164] Johnson would go far to compensate for the want of copyright, in commending their edition to the public. We may be pretty sure that Johnson himself, though he did his best by everybody, would not have thought all of his authors worth including. Yet we know that Johnson had some liberty to add to the collection, for we are told that he suggested three of the poets, of one of whom, Sir Richard Blackmore, I shall have something more to say.

That the predecessors and contemporaries of Shakespeare, and the metaphysical poets before Cowley, were at that time unsaleable, would have been justification for the booksellers' vetoing any proposal by Johnson for their inclusion. But there is no evidence that Johnson wanted to include them; the evidence goes to show that his acquaintance with them was very limited, and that he was perfectly content to edit a library of poetry which began with Cowley and Milton. The very fine *Preface to Shakespeare* is a separate work, and shows no evidence of awareness of the need to estimate any poet in relation to his predecessors and contemporaries. Yet this very innocence of the historical and comparative methods which modern criticism takes for granted, contributes to the singular merit of this Preface; and the virtues of Shakespeare to which he calls attention, are mostly those in which Shakespeare was unique, which he did not share, even in degree, with the other dramatists.

This limitation of the area of English poetry is a positive characteristic of importance. It would be a capital error to attribute the narrow range of Johnson's interests solely to ignorance, or solely to lack of appreciation, or even to both. To say that his ignorance was due to lack of understanding, would probably be truer than to say that his lack of understanding was due to ignorance: but it is not so simple as that. If we censure an eighteenth-century critic for not having a modern, historical and comprehensive appreciation, we must ourselves adopt towards him, the attitude the lack of which we reprehend; we must not be narrow in accusing him of narrowness, or prejudiced in accusing him of prejudice. Johnson had a positive point of view which is not ours; a point of view which needs a vigorous effort of imagination to understand; but if we can grasp it, we shall see his ignorance or his insensibility in a different light. Walter Raleigh says of Johnson that

> he had read immensely for the *Dictionary*, but the knowledge of English literature which he had thus acquired was not always

serviceable for a different purpose. In some respects it was even a [165] hindrance. Johnson's *Dictionary* was intended primarily to furnish a standard of polite usage, suitable for the classic ideals of the new age. He was therefore obliged to forego the use of the lesser Elizabethans, whose authority no one acknowledged, and whose freedom and extravagance were enemies to his purpose.

To the poet and critic of the eighteenth century, the values of language and literature were more closely allied than they seem to the writers and to the reading public of to-day. Eccentricity or uncouthness was reprehensible: a poet was prized, not for his invention of an original form of speech, but by his contribution to a common language. It was observed by Johnson and by men of his time, that there had been progress in refinement and precision of language, as of refinement and decorum of manners; and both these attainments, being recent, were highly esteemed. Johnson is able to censure Dryden, for his bad manners and bad taste in controversy. New it is generally observable of mankind, that in the elation of success in some course which we have set ourselves, we can be oblivious of many things which we have been obliged to resign in the accomplishment of it. We do not take kindly to the thought that, in order to gain one thing, we may have to give up something else of value. With these lost values the path of history is strewn and always will be: and perhaps a purblindness to such values is a necessary qualification, for anyone who aspires to be a political and social reformer. The improvement of language, which the eighteenth century had achieved, was a genuine improvement: of the inevitable losses only a later generation could become aware.

Johnson, certainly, saw the body of English poetry from a point of view which took for granted a progress, a refinement of language and versification along definite lines; and which implied a confidence in the rightness and permanence of the style which had been achieved – a confidence so much stronger than any we can place in the style, or styles, of our own age that we can hardly see it as anything but a blemish upon his critical ability. The emphasis upon, the care for, the common style and the common rules, which Johnson exhibits, and which make him sometimes appear to measure great genius by the standards suitable only to smaller minds, may lead to an exaggeration of the value of pedestrian poetry which conforms, over that of work of individual genius which is less law-abiding. Yet the obtuseness which we are apt to attribute to Johnson is seldom apparent in his positive affirma-[166]tions, but chiefly by silence; and this silence is evidence, not of individual insensibility, but of an attitude which is difficult for us to assume. From Johnson's point of view, the English language of the previous age was not sufficiently advanced, it was still 'in its infancy'; the language with which earlier poets worked was too rough, for those poets to be treated on the same footing with those of a more polished age. Their work, when they were not of the very highest rank, was a subject of study more suitable for the antiquary than for the cultivated reading public. The sensibility of any period in the past is always likely to appear to be more limited than our own; for we are naturally much more aware of our ancestors' lack of awareness to those things of which we are aware, than we are of any lack in ourselves, of awareness to what they perceived and we do not. We may ask then whether there is not a capital distinction to be drawn between a limited sensibility – remembering that the longer extent of *history* of which we have knowledge, makes all minds of the past seem to us limited – and a defective sensibility; and accordingly ask whether Johnson, within his proper limits, is not a sensitive as well as a judicial critic; whether the virtues he commended in poetry do not always remain virtues, and whether the kinds of fault that he censured do not always remain faults and to be avoided.

Even if I have not yet succeeded in making my meaning very clear, I hope that I have done something to unsettle your minds, and to prepare for an investigation of the charge against Johnson of being insensitive to the music of verse. A modern reader remembers nothing more clearly, from a reading of *The Lives of the Poets*, than Johnson's remarks on the versification of Donne and of Milton's *Lycidas*. If we recall no other opinion of Johnson, we recall the following:

> The metaphysical poets were men of learning, and to show their learning was their whole endeavour: but unluckily resolving to show it in rhyme, instead of writing poetry they only wrote verses, and very often such verses as stood the trial of the finger better than of the ear; for the modulation was so imperfect that they were only found to be verses by counting the syllables.

Of the work of Cleveland, and some of the other minor metaphysicals, this judgement would be sound enough; but that Johnson included Donne in this censure, we can be sure from his observation that Ben Jonson resembled Donne 'more in the ruggedness of his lines than in the cast of his sentiments'. Nowadays we regard [167] Donne as a very accomplished craftsman indeed, as a versifier of signal virtuosity; and what Johnson denotes as 'ruggedness' strikes our ear as a very subtle music. But the judgement on *Lycidas*, as well known as the judgement on the metaphysical poets, equally outrages our sensibility. Johnson declares that in this poem 'the diction is harsh, the rhymes uncertain, and the numbers unpleasing'. With some other of Johnson's remarks about *Lycidas* we may find it possible to agree. If we think that an elegy requires the justification of unfeigned and cordial regret, we may find the poem frigid. The conjugation of Christian and classical imagery is in accord with a baroque taste which did not please the eighteenth century: and I must admit for myself that I have never felt happy in the spectacle of Fr Camus and St Peter marching in the same procession, like a couple of professors strolling down King's Parade on their way to hear the university sermon. But surely it is the musical virtue of the verse which clothes the absurdities in grandeur, and makes all acceptable. So we ask, was Johnson insensible to the music of verse? Had he, had the whole of his generation, defective hearing?

There is perhaps no more stubborn cause of extreme differences of opinion, between respectable critics of poetry, than a difference of ear: and by 'ear' for poetry I mean an immediate apprehension of two things which can be considered in abstraction from each other, but which produce their effect in unity: rhythm and diction. They imply each other: for the diction – the vocabulary and construction – will determine the rhythm, and the rhythms which a poet finds congenial will determine his diction. It is the immediate favourable impression of rhythm and diction which disposes us to accept a poem, encourages us to give it further attention and to discover other reasons for liking it. This immediacy may be lacking, in the reading of the poetry of one generation by another. Not until a literature has arrived at maturity – not, perhaps, until it has passed the moment of maturity and advanced far into later age, can critics perceive that rhythm and diction do not simply improve, or deteriorate, from one generation to another, but that there is also pure change, such that something is always being lost, as well as something being gained. In the perfection of any style it can be observed, as in the maturing of an individual, that some potentialities have been brought to fruition only by the surrender of others; indeed, part of our pleasure in early literature, as of the delight which we take in children, is in our consciousness of many [168] potentialities not all of which can be realised. In this respect, primitive literature can be richer than that which follows. A literature is different from a human life, in that it can return upon its own past, and develop some capacity which has been abandoned. We have seen in our own time, a renewed interest in Donne; and, after Donne, in earlier poets such as Skelton. A literature can also renew itself from the literature of another language. But the age in which Johnson lived, was not old enough to feel the need for such renewal: it had just arrived at its own maturity. Johnson could think of the literature of his age, as having attained the standard from which literature of the past could be judged. In a time like ours, in which novelty is often assumed to be the first requisite of poetry if it is to attract our attention, and in which the names of *pioneer* and *innovator* are among the titles most honoured, it is hard to apprehend this point of view. We easily see its absurdities, and marvel at the assurance with which Johnson could reprehend *Lycidas* for the absence of the merit which we find most conspicuous in it, and could dismiss Donne for the roughness of his diction. And when Johnson writes of Shakespeare, we are puzzled by Johnson's silence about the mastery of versification. Here there was no prejudice against a particular fashion of writing, as when he discusses the metaphysicals; no personal dislike of the man, as when he treats of Milton; but only the acutest observation, the highest esteem, the most just and generous praise: but he assigns to Shakespeare the very highest rank among poets, on every other ground than that of the beauty of rhythm and diction.

My point is that we should not consider this obtuseness, which to us is very strange, as a personal defect of Johnson which diminishes his stature as a critic. What is lacking is an historical sense which was not yet due to appear. Here is something which Johnson can teach us: for if we have arrived at this historical sense ourselves, our only course is to develop it further; and one of the ways in which we can develop it in ourselves is through an understanding of a critic in whom it is not apparent. Johnson fails to understand rhythm and diction which to him were archaic, not through lack of sensibility but through specialisation of sensibility. If the eighteenth century had admired the poetry of earlier times in the way in which we can admire it, the result would have been chaos: there would have been no eighteenth century as we know it. That age would not have had the conviction necessary for perfecting the [169] kinds of poetry that it did perfect. The deafness of Johnson's ear to some kinds of melody was the necessary condition for his sharpness of sensibility to verbal beauty of another kind. Within his range, within his time, Johnson had as fine an ear as anybody. Again and again, when he calls attention to beauties or to blemishes in the work of the poets of whom he writes, we must acknowledge that he is right, and that he is pointing out something that we might not have noticed independently. It may prove that his criteria are permanently relevant.

There is another consideration, in the problem of the difference between the sensibilities of one century and another, which is worth mention. That is the problem of the emphasis on sound or on sense. The greatest poetry, I think we may agree, passes the most severe examination in both subjects. But there is a great deal of good poetry, which establishes itself by a one-sided excellence. The modern inclination is to put up with some degree of incoherence of sense, to be tolerant of poets who do not know themselves exactly what they are trying to say, so long as the verse sounds well and presents striking and unusual imagery. There is, in fact, a certain merit in melodious raving, which can be a genuine contribution to literature, when it responds effectually to that permanent appetite of humanity for an occasional feast of drums and cymbals. We all want to get drunk now and again, whether we do or not: though an exclusive addiction to some kinds of poetry has dangers analogous to those of a steady reliance upon alcohol. Besides the poetry of sound – and, from one point of view, occupying an intermediate position between the poetry of sound and the poetry of sense – there is poetry which represents an attempt to extend the confines of the human consciousness and to report of things unknown, to express the inexpressible. But with this poetry I am not here concerned. Between the two extremes of *incantation* and *meaning* we are I think to-day more easily seduced by the music of the exhilaratingly meaningless, than contented with intelligence and wisdom set forth in pedestrian measures. The age of Johnson, and Johnson himself, were more inclined to the latter choice. Johnson could accept much as poetry, which seems to us merely competent and correct; we, on the other hand, are too ready to accept as poetry what is neither competent nor correct. We forgive much to sound and to image, he forgave much to sense. And to exceed in one direction or the other is to risk mistaking the ephemeral for the permanent. [170] Johnson sometimes made mistakes. I referred, a little earlier, to Sir Richard Blackmore.

Impressed by Johnson's assertion that Blackmore's *Creation* alone was a poem which 'would have transmitted him to posterity among the first favourites of the English Muse', and his statement that it was by his own recommendation that Blackmore was included in the library which he introduced, I read the poem with some curiosity. I came to the conclusion that Johnson's praise of this poem shows a grievous lapse in two directions. In the first place, the poem almost at once violates some excellent rules which Johnson himself, in treating of a greater poet, had laid down for the use of triplet and alexandrine in the rhymed couplet form. Instead of reserving the triplet (three lines rhyming together and alexandrine as the third line) for the conclusion of a period, where this termination can be very effective, Blackmore introduces a triplet almost at the start; and presently offers us an alexandrine as the second line of a couplet. What is much worse, the versification is sometimes no better than that of a schoolboy's exercise. But Johnson, like all good churchmen and all good Tories, abominated Hobbes – a notable atheist and totalitarian. He must have been blinded to defects which he would have reproved in Dryden or Pope, by the satisfaction he got from the following lines alluding to that philosopher:

> At length Britannia's soil, immortal dame!
> Brought forth a sage of celebrated name,
> Who with contempt on blest Religion trod,
> Mocked all her precepts, and renounced her God.

To apply the kind of minute criticism in which Johnson excelled, we may remark that the first line is bad grammar, because *dame* is grammatically in apposition to *soil* instead of to *Britannia*; and we may censure the second line by remarking that Hobbes's name was not celebrated until a long time after his birth. We should expect also, that the personification of Religion, as a helpless female stamped upon by Hobbes, would be too inelegant for Johnson's taste. I think that this is the kind of lapse which can most severely be censured in a critic – the lapse from his own standards of taste. And secondly, my reading of the poem led me to suspect that even on grounds of content Johnson should have rejected it. For Johnson – and it is a very important thing about him – was one of the most orthodox churchmen, as well as one of the most [171] devout Christians, of his day: and Blackmore seems to me to be expressing pure deism. I can only suppose that deism so permeated the atmosphere of the century that Johnson's nose failed to respond to its smell.

I want however to distinguish this species of error – the critic's failure to apply his own standards – from those apparent errors which spring from the principles of a particular mind at a particular time, and which no longer seem to us errors in the same sense, once we succeed in apprehending the point of view. Such will be found, and they will at first bewilder us, in Johnson's various remarks about writers of blank verse. For this kind of verse, he appears to give the highest place to Akenside, of whom he says, that 'in the general fabrication of his lines he is perhaps superior to any other writer of blank verse'. Even leaving out of account the blank verse of the great dramatic poets of a previous age – or the dramatic verse of Otway at his best – this seems at first an extravagant assertion.

Nowadays we use words so loosely that a writer's meaning may sometimes be concealed from us, simply because he has said exactly what he meant. To extract the meaning from Johnson's assertion about Akenside, we must first compare Akenside's versification with that of other blank verse writers of his century; we have also to compare what Johnson has said about the others, and with what he said about Milton's verse. In his essay on Milton, you will remember that Johnson confirms the words of Addison who said of Milton *the language sunk under him*. Johnson goes on to say that Milton 'had formed his style by a perverse and pedantic principle' and that 'he was desirous to use English words with a foreign idiom'. But, having made this criticism, he goes on to utter the highest praise: Milton 'was master of his language to its full extent'. And in mentioning the weakness of 'heroic' blank verse; particularly the difficulty, in speaking it, of preserving the metrical identity of each line; and finally, after saying everything that can be said against blank verse, he makes the handsome admission: 'I cannot prevail upon myself to wish that Milton had been a rhymer; for I cannot wish his work to be other than it is; yet, like other heroes, he is to be admired rather than imitated.' The acknowledgement of Milton's greatness as a versifier is unequivocal. But there are laws, for the use of words and the construction of sentences, which Milton defies. The lawbreaker should not be praised for his lawlessness; and a second-rate poet may be more law-[172]abiding than a poet of great genius. So, Akenside, 'in the general fabrication of his lines', may be more correct than Milton; and if we value correctness, in that respect superior.

I do not think that the history of blank verse since Milton's time altogether gives him the lie. 'The music of the English heroic lines strikes the ear so faintly,' says Johnson, 'that it is easily lost'. That is true: the alternative danger is a monotonous thumping, which ceases to have any music at all. What Johnson failed to remark is, that Milton made blank verse a successful medium for the heroic poem, by that very eccentricity which Johnson reproves.

Johnson did, however, see the verse of Milton as an exception. He admits that there are purposes for which blank verse remains the proper medium; though he does not trouble to define and particularise those purposes. Of Young's *Night Thoughts* he says:

> This is one of the few poems in which blank verse could not be changed for rhyme but with disadvantage. The wild diffusion of the sentiments, and the digressive sallies of imagination would have been compressed and restrained by confinement to rhyme.

His approval of the use of blank verse by Thomson in his *Seasons* expresses a similar approval:

> His is one of the works in which blank verse is properly used. Thomson's wide expansion of general views, and his enumeration of circumstantial varieties, would have been obstructed and embarrassed by the frequent intersections of the sense, which are necessary effects of rhyme.

Let us return to Akenside, the author upon whose blank verse Johnson has bestowed such high commendation: its context is this:

> In the general fabrication of his lines, he is perhaps superior to any other author of blank verse; his flow is smooth, and his pauses are musical; but the concatenation of his verse is too long continued, and the full close does not occur with sufficient frequency. The sense is carried on through a long intertexture of complicated clauses, and, as nothing is distinguished, nothing is remembered.
>
> The exemption [Johnson continues, generalising from his criticism of Akenside] which blank verse affords from the necessity of closing the sense with the couplet betrays luxuriant and active minds into such self-indulgence, that they pile image upon image, ornament upon ornament, and are not easily persuaded to close the sense at all. Blank verse will therefore, I fear, be too often found in description exuberant, in argument loquacious, and in narration tiresome.

[173] To say that the concatenation of Akenside's verse is too long continued, and that the sense is carried on through a long intertexture of complicated clauses, is a censure which is fully justified by our examination of Akenside's lines; though it is only fair to remark that this concatenation, these complicated clauses, were exactly what Milton was able to manipulate with conspicuous and solitary success. But the general observations on the dangers of blank verse are such as later writers in this form would have done well to ponder. And Johnson could not foresee that later poets would also be able to exhibit in the rhymed couplet, through their desire to extend the resources of this form beyond the rigid limits imposed by the best eighteenth-century verse, the same exuberance, the same loquacity, and the same tiresomeness that Johnson lists as the vices of blank verse. We have only to look at William Morris for examples.

Amongst all the poets whose works Johnson introduced, we can I think agree that Thomson and Young are the only ones who have left blank verse poems which are still more or less readable, and which are still of importance for the student of English poetry to read. In praising their versification, therefore, Johnson shows himself to be not unaware of how blank verse should be written. In qualification of his approval of Akenside's versification, it must be added that his praise of the poem which shows Akenside's moderate gifts at their best, *The Pleasures of Imagination* (or, *Pleasures of the Imagination*) is very faint indeed.

> The words are multiplied till the sense is hardly perceived; attention deserts the mind, and settles in the ear. The reader wanders through the gay diffusion, sometimes amazed, and sometimes delighted; but, after many turnings in the flowery labyrinth, comes out as he went in. He remarked little, and laid hold on nothing.

Which is as direct an intimation that the poetry is not worth reading, as Johnson cared to give. I have put myself to the mechanical operation of reading this poem through, yet I cannot say that I have read it; for, as Johnson foretold, 'attention deserted the mind'. So in effect I have read only passages. Yet I retain the impression that the sound is more melodious than that of the verses of either Thomson or Young, though these are much more substantial poets. His syllables are well disposed; his pauses, his sentence structures, are generally such as to give perpetual variety, without breaking down the metre altogether; and though he is always dull, he is seldom absurd. If you dip into Thomson's *Seasons*, you will constantly find delightful landscapes; but you will find also a frequent endeavour to elevate the humble, and embellish the matter-of-fact, which invites ridicule. Take for instance his humane exhortation to the angler:

> But let not on thy hook the tortur'd worm
> Convulsive, twist in agonising fold.

Akenside never says anything worth saying, but what is not worth saying he says well. The close of the third book of his poem (which is left unfinished in the middle of the fourth book) is good enough to quote:

> When at last
> The Sun and Nature's face again appear'd,
> Not far I found me; where the public path,
> Winding through cypress groves and swelling meads,
> From Cnossus to the cave of Jove ascends.
> Heedless I followed on; till soon the skirts
> Of Ida rose before me, and the vault
> Wide-opening pierced the mountain's rocky side.
> Entering within the threshold, on the ground
> I flung me, sad, faint, overworn with toil.

If you did not know who wrote these lines, you might attribute them to some better poet. But, as Johnson observes of the same writer's odes: 'to what use can the work be criticised that will not be read?' Yet I think we can now understand, and within limits accept, the assertion that 'in the general fabrication of his lines, (Akenside) is perhaps superior to any other writer of blank verse'.

I cannot help wondering how many blank verse poems of the nineteenth century will be perused by posterity with any greater excitement, than we now derive from those of Thomson, Young, or Cowper. There will remain *Hyperion*, *The Prelude* (which, however tedious in many places, has to be read entire), a few fine short pieces of Tennyson, some dramatic monologues of Browning. But in general, I think that the nineteenth-century poems which promise to remain permanently pleasurable, are poems in rhyme.

That Johnson regarded blank verse as more suitable for the theatre than rhyme, we may infer from his preference for *All for Love* among Dryden's heroic plays, and from his having chosen blank verse as the medium for his own tragedy *Irene*. That Johnson [175] failed to understand the peculiarities of *dramatic* blank verse is evident from this play: for we find the blank verse to be that of a writer who thought and felt in terms of the rhymed couplet. I have already observed, that in all of Johnson's high and just praise of Shakespeare as a dramatic poet, he speaks as if Shakespeare had written in a language of which the sense had been preserved, but of which the sound meant nothing to us: for there is not a word about the music of Shakespeare's verse. Johnson holds that blank verse is more suitable to the stage, simply because it is nearer to prose: in other words, people conversing do occasionally produce an unconscious iambic pentameter, but almost never fall into rhyme. I do not think that this judgement is altogether valid. If Johnson failed, on the one hand, to appreciate the special music of dramatic blank verse, he was also deceived in thinking that blank verse is necessarily the more conversational form. I remarked long ago, that Dryden seems to me to approximate more closely to the tones of conversation in his rhymed plays than he does in *All for Love*. Johnson's *Irene* has all the virtues which verse by Johnson should be expected to have; and for Johnson, who did not ordinarily labour at his writing, it appears a very painstaking piece of work. His verse has none of the dramatic qualities; it is correct, but correctness in such isolation becomes itself a fault. The play would be more readable to-day, if he had written it in rhyme; the whole would be more easily declaimed, and the good things more easily remembered; it would lose none of its excellence of structure, thought, vocabulary and figures of speech. What would be mellifluous in rhyme, is merely monotonous without it.

I have been occupied so far, primarily with the task of trying to reduce some of the obstacles to the appreciation of Johnson as a critic. Before closing, there remain two incidental opinions of Johnson which I must face, because otherwise I should expose myself to the charge of evading them. The first is Johnson's opinion of choral drama, which was unfavourable; the second is his attitude towards religious or devotional verse, which was condescending. I must therefore direct the jury on these two points.

> If *Paradise Regained* has been too much depreciated, *Samson Agonistes* has in requital been too much admired. It could only be

by long prejudice, and the bigotry of learning, that Milton preferred the ancient tragedies, with their encumbrance of a chorus, to the exhibitions of the French and English stages, and it is only by a blind confidence in the reputation of Milton, that a drama [176] can be praised in which the intermediate parts have neither cause nor consequence, neither hasten nor retard the catastrophe.

I may have occasion to remind you again, how emphatically Johnson was *modern* in his time: his preference of the French and English theatre to the Greek is only one example of this. I should wish to qualify his reproof of Milton, in the passage I have just quoted, by saying that I do not believe it was primarily long prejudice, or the bigotry of learning, which led Milton to write his play on the Greek model. I think that it was first of all a knowledge, conscious or unconscious, of what were his own gifts. He chose, in *Samson*, the one subject most suitable for him; and he took the Greek model because he was a poet, and not a dramatist, and in this form he could best exhibit his mastery and conceal his weaknesses. What is more odd, however, since Johnson holds up French as well as English drama for imitation, is that he makes no reference to the case, inconvenient for his thesis, of Racine's *Athalie*. Racine was a poet of the theatre, if there ever was one; in *Athalie* he employs the chorus; and *Athalie*, I think, is a very great play indeed. But, with this exception, Johnson was judging choral drama according to dramatic standards which I do not think that most of us apply to *Samson*. For many people, *Samson* is the most readable of Milton's major works: certainly, more readable than *Paradise Regained*. We can even enjoy *Samson*, as we can enjoy *Comus*, when it is performed. But I do not believe that anyone could enjoy them directly as drama: we need either to be pretty familiar with the text, or else have a very quick ear for the appreciation of verbal beauty. Otherwise, I do not think that the plot or the characterisation of either piece would long hold our attention.

I am inclined to believe that on the whole Johnson, if he is allowed to criticise *Samson* as drama, is right. I do not believe that he appreciated the dramatic force of the Greek conventions in their own place and time. Indeed, I doubt whether it was possible for anyone to do so in the undeveloped state of archeological knowledge in his time: certainly, our own understanding of the Greek plays as plays has been immensely extended by recent study and research. But the real question is whether the form of Greek drama can be naturalised for the modern world. And I suspect that the chief justification for Milton, as for some later poets, in imitating the Greek form of drama, is that the use of a chorus enables poets with no skill in the theatre, to make the most of their accomplishments, and thereby conceal some of their defects.

[177] Johnson's opinions on religious verse are most fully stated in his Life of Waller. It is there that he observes

> Let no pious ear be offended, if I advance, in opposition to many authorities, that poetical devotion cannot often please.... Contemplative piety, of the intercourse between God and the human soul, cannot be poetical....

These and other words might have been transposed into his Life of Watts, and are confirmed there by the following:

> His devotional poetry is, like that of others, unsatisfactory. The paucity of its topics enforces perpetual repetition, and the sanctity of the matter rejects the ornaments of figurative diction.

As a criticism of Watts, this is just enough. To a generation which has learned to admire the religious sonnets of Donne, the lyrics of George Herbert, Crashaw and Vaughan, it seems narrowly perverse. I think that we have to take account, not only of the limitations of the literary taste of his time, but of its religious limitations also. The two support each other here: for as it did not occur to the mind of Johnson that there were poetic values, in earlier periods, which had vanished during the perfecting of those of his own, so I do not think that it could occur to him that there was a religious sensibility which had disappeared also. Johnson's strictures are applicable to *most* of the religious verse that has been written since, as well as to that of his own time. What vitiates his condemnation, is the absence of any discrimination between the religious poetry of public worship, and the religious poetry of personal experience. In the hymn, the anthem, the sequence, the intrusion of personal experience would be impertinent; and perhaps for this reason the poetry of public worship is at its best in the impersonal eloquence of the Latin language. It is true that some devotional religious verse appears to be equally valid in both contexts. Some of George Herbert's poems are found in hymnals: yet I always feel them to be less satisfactory as hymns than those of Watts; for I am always aware of the personality of Herbert, and never conscious of any personality of Watts. But most of the devotional poetry of the eighteenth century has the merit neither of the one kind nor of the other. The reasons why good poetry in this kind was not written, and the reasons why Johnson could not recognise its possibility, have to do with the limitations of religious sensibility in that century. I say limitations, rather than lack of sensibility, for no one can read Johnson's *Prayers and Meditations* or Law's *Serious Call* without [178] acknowledging that this age also has its monuments of religious devotion.

II

I do not propose to discuss the poetry of the eighteenth century in general; or even to discuss Johnson's Lives of Dryden and Pope, except to extract from them some statements indicating Johnson's critical theory. I must say something of Johnson's poetry, on the principle which I have already affirmed, that we can only understand a poet's criticism of poetry in relation to the poetry which he writes. Of his shorter poems, we can only say of the most of them that they possess those two qualities which Johnson believed to be all that can be asked of short poems: neatness and elegance. One of them, 'Long expected one-and-twenty', might provide an interesting comparison, not to Johnson's disadvantage, with *A Shropshire Lad*: Housman's verse is also neat and elegant, but on the point of poetic diction, and on that of edification – two of Johnson's criteria, as we shall see – we might grant that Johnson's poem is superior. The only one, I think, of Johnson's short poems which is more than neat and elegant, the only one which does what no one before him could have done and which no successor could emulate, is the poem on the death of Dr Levett, the man 'obscurely wise and coarsely kind' – a poem unique in tenderness, piety and wisdom. The two poems on which Johnson's title as a poet must rest are *The Vanity of Human Wishes* and *London*. *London* has 364 lines, *The Vanity of Human Wishes* 263. Johnson was a meditative poet: he could not have expressed himself fully in a poem of less length; and being only a meditative poet, he did not have the resources for a poem of more ample scope.

London has fine lines and passages, but it does not seem to me successful as a whole. The setting, or prologue to the poem, is artificial. It is wearisome to have the invective against the metropolis presented as the speech of 'injur'd Thales' to a friend who is seeing him off at Greenwich, as he enters a wherry for the ship which will take him into voluntary exile in Pembrokeshire. There is, as elsewhere in the poem, a suspicion of falsity. Johnson wished to write a satire in the manner of Juvenal, in order to denounce the wickedness of London; but that Johnson should ever have contemplated leaving London for the remote promontory of St David's is so inconsistent with his character, and his confessed [179] sentiments in later life, that we cannot believe he ever meant it. He was the last man to have domiciled himself at St David's, or to have appreciated the beauties of that romantic spot when he got there.

> For who would leave, unbribed, Hibernia's land,
> Or change the rocks of Scotland for the Strand?

The answer is, Samuel Johnson, if anybody. These may seem carping objections. But they reinforce my doubt, whether Johnson was the right man for satire. Johnson was a moralist, and he lacked a certain divine levity which makes sparkle the lines of the two great English verse satirists. Indignation may make poetry, but it must be indignation recollected in tranquillity: in *London* I feel that a feigned indignation is presented, instead of a real indignation being recalled. In the satire of Dryden, as in a different way in that of Pope, the object satirised disappears in the poetry, is hardly more than the pretext for poetry. With Dryden, the man ridiculed becomes absurdly gigantic; and Pope's noxious insect becomes something beautiful and strange. In *London* the total effect is one of querulousness. The indictment of a whole city fails: it is incredible, even in the eighteenth century, that you could never go out at night without being set upon by boisterous drunkards, or sleep in your own house without danger of being killed by burglars. Johnson utters generalisations, and the generalisations are not true: what keeps the poem alive is the undercurrent of personal feeling, the bitterness of the hardships, slights, injuries and privations, really experienced by Johnson in his youth.

Johnson's mind tended towards the general reflection supported by instances. In a well known passage, Imlac, the preceptor of Rasselas, is made to observe that

> The business of a poet is to examine, not the individual, but the species; to remark general properties and large appearances; he does not number the streaks of the tulip, or describe the different shades in the verdure of the forest. He is to exhibit in his portraits of nature such prominent striking features, as recall the original to every mind; and must neglect the minuter discriminations, which one may have remarked, and another have neglected, for those characteristics which are alike obvious to vigilance and carelessness.

This disposition to the general affects even Johnson's regulations of poetic diction. 'It is a general rule of poetry,' he says in his [180] Life of Dryden, 'that all appropriated terms of art should be sunk in general impressions, because poetry is to speak an universal language. This rule is still stronger with regard to arts not liberal, and therefore far removed from common knowledge'; and he proceeds to reprimand Dryden for using technical terms of seamanship, most of which – such as *seam*, *mallet*, *tarpauling* – we should now consider unexceptionable. But with Johnson's ideas of poetic diction I am not yet concerned: I only wish to suggest that Johnson's rules for poetry were to some degree limited by the kind of poetry which he himself was able to write.

In *The Vanity of Human Wishes* Johnson found the perfect theme for his abilities. The idea, which is indicated by the title, was not new, and never had been. That is not necessary or even desirable for a poem of this sort: what is essential is that it should be an idea which the reader will not for a moment question. In this respect, as a meditative poem, *The Vanity of Human Wishes* is superior to Gray's *Elegy*; for the latter poem contains one or two ideas which are perhaps not very sound: the likelihood that the village churchyard, or any churchyard, contained the body of a potential Hampden, Milton or Cromwell is exceedingly small. Gray, of course, in this poem, is by no means purely meditative: what the *Elegy* gains by its description, by its evocation of the rural landscape of England, is all important. On the other hand, if Johnson had confined himself to the general, and not supported it with instances, there would be little left of *The Vanity of Human Wishes*. Of these, the passage on Charles of Sweden is the most quoted and the best sustained. These thirty-two lines compose a paragraph which is, in itself, quite perfect in form: the rising curve of ambition, the sudden calamity, and the slow decline and degradation through which we see the conqueror

> Compelled a needy supplicant to wait
> While ladies interpose and slaves debate,

culminating in

> a barren strand,
> A petty fortress, and a dubious hand.

But this passage is not one which preserves its full value when extracted: it requires both what precedes and what follows, and takes only its proper place in the complete poem.

Great poetry of the type of *The Vanity of Human Wishes* is rare; [181] and we cannot reproach Johnson for not writing more of it, when we consider how little of such poetry there is. Yet this type of poetry cannot rise to the highest rank. It is, by its nature, of rather loose construction; the idea is given at the start, and as it is one universally accepted, there can be but little development, only variations on the one theme. Johnson did not have the gift of structure. For a more elaborate construction – and structure I hold to be an important element of poetic composition – a variety of talents – descriptive, narrative and dramatic – are required. We do not ordinarily expect a very close structure of a poem in rhymed couplets, which often looks as if, but for what the author has to say, it might begin or end anywhere. But there is a poem, by a contemporary and friend of Johnson, which has a high degree of organisation. I place

The Deserted Village higher than any poem by Johnson or by Gray. In Goldsmith's poem, the art of transition is exemplified in perfection. If you examine it paragraph by paragraph, you will find always a shift just at the right moment, from the descriptive to the meditative, to the personal, to the meditative again, to the landscape with figures, to the delineation of individuals (the clergyman and the schoolmaster) with a skill and concision seldom equalled since Chaucer. These parts are properly proportioned. Finally, the idea is one which, while as acceptable as Johnson's, is more original and also prophetic:

> Ill fares the land, to hastening ills a prey,
> Where wealth accumulates, and men decay.

I have made this digression, because I do not think that Johnson shows great power of construction in his own poems, and because I do not think that he recognises the importance of considering structure in the valuation of a poem. I pass now to review those properties of a good poem, which Johnson both illustrates in his own verse and especially commends in the work of others.

Johnson attached importance to *originality*. Originality is one of those numerous terms the meaning of which may alter from generation to generation, and we must be careful to examine what it meant to Johnson. His use of the word is illustrated by the following passage from his Life of Thomson:

> As a writer, Thomson is entitled to one praise of the highest kind: his mode of thinking, and of expressing his thought, is original. His blank verse is no more the blank verse of Milton, or of any other poet, than the rhymes of Prior are the rhymes of Cowley. [182] His numbers, his pauses, his diction, are of his own growth, without transcription, without imitation. He thinks in a peculiar train, and he thinks always as a man of genius; he looks round on Nature and on Life with the eye which Nature bestows only upon a poet; the eye that distinguishes in everything presented to its view, whatever there is on which imagination can delight to be detained, and with a mind that at once comprehends the vast, and attends to the minute. The reader of *The Seasons* wonders that he never saw before what Thomson shows him, and that he never yet has felt what Thomson impresses.

Originality is found, here, in a 'mode of thinking and of expression'. But the thought itself does not have to be novel or difficult of apprehension and acceptance; it may be, and for Johnson most often is, the commonplace, or a thought which, when grasped, is so quickly admitted that the reader wonders that he never thought of it for himself. Originality does not require the rejection of convention. We have grown accustomed, during the last century and more, to such a riot of individual styles that we may forget that originality is as significant in a settled period as it is in one of constant change; we have become so accustomed to differences of poetic style recognisable by anybody, that we may be less sensitive to the finer variations within a form, which the mind and ear habituated to that form may perceive. But originality, when it becomes the only, or the most prized virtue of poetry, may cease to be a virtue at all; and when several poets, and their respective groups of admirers, cease to have in common any standards of versification, any identity of taste or of tenets of belief, criticism may decline to an advertisement of preference. The originality which Johnson approves, is an originality limited by the other qualities which he demands.

Johnson attached importance to *edification*. This term has become the object of derision, though what the term means may be something from which we can never escape. That poetry should teach wisdom or inculcate virtue, seems to most people a quite secondary, even an extraneous value; to some it even seems incompatible with the true function of poetry. But we must first observe, that Johnson, when his critical sense is alert, is never given to overrating a poem on the sole ground of its teaching a pure morality. He held that a poem should be interesting, and that it should give immediate pleasure. Indeed, I think he overstates this requirement, when he says, in his Life of Cowley:

> [183] Whatever professes to benefit by pleasing, must please at once. The pleasures of the mind imply something sudden and unexpected; that which elevates must also surprise. What is perceived by slow degrees may gratify us with the consciousness of improvement, but will never strike with the sense of pleasure.

I agree that a poem which makes no immediate impression, which in no way compels our attention, is not likely to arouse a thrill later. But Johnson does not seem to me to allow for the possibility of any development or expansion of enjoyment, and the gradual awareness to new beauties, to follow from better acquaintance; nor does he allow for the ripening of the reader and the development of his sensibility through deeper experience and more extensive knowledge. I did not, however, quote his sentence for the purpose of disagreement, but to indicate the strictness with which pleasure and edification are associated in Johnson's mind. He speaks of 'whatever professes to benefit by pleasing'; he says, 'that which elevates must always surprise.' The edification is not a separable addition to a poem, it is organically essential to it. We do not have *two* experiences, one of pleasure and one of edification: it is one experience which we analyse into constituents.

In judging the permanence of the principles of a critic belonging to an age very different from our own, we must constantly reinterpret his language according to our own situation. In the most generalised sense, I suppose that 'edification' means only that from good poetry, certainly from great poetry, we must derive some benefit as well as pleasure. If we identity 'edification' with the propagation of the moral ideas of Johnson's time – ideas which Christians may hold to be tainted with deism, and which others may find too Christian – we fail to see that it is merely our notions of edification that have changed. When Matthew Arnold said that poetry was a criticism of life, he was maintaining the standard of edification. Even the doctrine of 'art for art's sake' is only a variation under the guise of a protest; and in our time, the defence of poetry as a substitute for religion, and the attempt, not always successful or beneficial to poetry, to express or impose a social philosophy in verse, indicate that it is only the content of 'edification' that changes.

If, therefore, we allow to 'edification' all the elasticity of which the term is capable, it seems to come to no more than the assertion that poetry should have some serious value for the reader: a proposition which will not be denied and which is therefore hardly [184] worth affirming. Our only disagreement will be about the kind of content which we consider edifying. Our real difficulty with Johnson's view is rather different. We distinguish more clearly between the conscious intention of the writer, and the effect of the work. We distrust verse in which the author is deliberately aiming to instruct or to persuade. This distinction does not form one of the commonplaces of Johnson's thinking. He is, however, I believe, really concerned with the morality of the poem, and not with the moral designs of the poet.

> Bossu is of opinion (says Johnson in his Life of Milton) that the poet's first work is to find a moral, which his fable is afterwards to illustrate and establish. This seems to have been the process only of Milton; the moral of other poems is incidental and consequent; in Milton's only it is essential and intrinsic.

I think that this statement is true of Milton, though if Johnson had been better acquainted with Dante he might not have taken Milton as an unique example. It appears to show, however, that what interests Johnson is the edifying power of the poem, rather than the deliberate intention of the poet.

We are all, of course, influenced in our degree of attraction to any particular work of art, by our sympathy with, or antipathy towards, the ideas, as well as the personality of the author. We endeavour, and in our time must endeavour, to discount this attraction or repulsion, in order to arrive at a just valuation of the artistic merit. If we lived, like Johnson, in an age of relative unity and of generally accepted assumptions, we should probably be less concerned to make this effort. If we were agreed upon the nature of the world we live in, on the place of man in it and on his destiny; if we were agreed as to what we meant by wisdom, by the good life for the individual and for society, we should apply moral judgements to poetry as confidently as did Johnson. But in an age in which no two writers need agree about anything, an age in which we must constantly admit that a poet with a view of life which we believe to be mistaken, may write much better poetry than another whose view is the same as our own, we are forced to make this abstraction; and in making it, we are tempted to ignore, with unfortunate results, the moral value of poetry altogether. So that, of a poet's view of life, we incline to ask, not 'is it true?' but 'is it original?' And it is one of the theses maintained in this discussion of Johnson's criticism, that Johnson was in a position, as no critic of equal stature has been since, to write purely *literary* criticism, just [185] because he was able to assume that there was a general attitude towards life, and a common opinion as to the place of poetry in it.

I come next to Johnson's use of the term *poetic diction*. To most people nowadays, I imagine, 'poetic diction' means an idiom and a choice of words which are out of date, and which perhaps were never very good at their best. If we are temperate, we mean the use of idiom and vocabulary borrowed from poets of a different generation, idiom and vocabulary no longer suitable for poetry. If we are extreme, we mean that this idiom and vocabulary were always bad, even when they were fresh. Wordsworth, in his Preface, says: 'there will also be found in these volumes little of what is usually called poetic diction.' Johnson uses the term in a eulogistic sense. In the Life of Dryden he remarks:

> There was, therefore, before the time of Dryden no poetical diction, no system of words at once refined from the grossness of domestic use, and free from the harshness of terms appropriate to particular arts. Words too familiar, or too remote, defeat the purpose of a poet. From these sounds which we hear on small or on coarse occasions, we do not easily receive strong impressions, or delightful images; and words to which we are nearly strangers, whenever they occur, draw that attention to themselves which they should transmit to things.

We must bear in mind, with regard to vocabulary and construction, what I tried to put before more generally: that the notion of the language as perpetually in change is not one which had impressed itself upon the age of Johnson. He looked back some two centuries and marked in language, as in manners, a continuous improvement. As for the improvement which he noted, he was not deceived: but he had neither the awareness of anything lost, nor the apprehension of inevitable changes to come. Nor does Wordsworth himself evince any more consciousness of the constancy with which language must change, than was Johnson: what he thought he had established was a return to a diction of popular simplicity and rural purity. In his perception that the language of literature must not lose its connexion with the language of speech, Wordsworth was right; but his standard of the right poetic diction was no more relative than Johnson's. We, on the contrary, should be able to recognise that there should be, for every period, some standard of correct poetic diction, neither identical with, nor too remote from, current speech; and must concede that the right poetic diction, fifty years hence, will not be the same as that for [186] to-day. I mean that the vocabulary, the idiom, and the grammatical rules for poetry cannot be identical with those of prose. In the choice of words, Johnson's restriction remains true: that 'those sounds which we hear on small or on coarse occasions' are to be avoided – except, I must add, when it is the purpose of the poet to present something small or coarse; and that 'words to which we are nearly strangers, whenever they occur, draw that attention to themselves which they should transmit to things' – except I should add, when the word is the only word for that thing, or when it is the poet's purpose to draw attention to the word.

To criticise the poetic diction of eighteenth-century poetry is one thing, to criticise an eighteenth-century theory of poetic diction is another. We must remember that if there is no 'poetic diction' admitted, we have no standard for criticising good and bad writing in poetry: to deny that there is any right common style, is as dangerous as to insist that the poetic style of our time should be the same as that of the nineteenth century. Our modern vocabulary accommodates many comparatively new words which to Johnson would have sounded barbarous. We have been inventing, discovering, fashioning and theorising at a rate unknown to any earlier time, and a new word establishes itself much more quickly. No word is too new, if it is the only word for the purpose; no word is too archaic, if it is the only word for the purpose. And many occasions, which to Johnson would have seemed 'small' or 'coarse', seem to us fit occasions to be celebrated in verse. Johnson's view of poetic diction remains sound; but we have to use our own wits in the application of it.

That Johnson was alert to the vice of *mannerism*, appears from another passage in his Life of Dryden, a passage which should be taken to heart by everyone who aspires to write good verse:

> He who writes much will not easily escape a manner, such a recurrence of particular modes as may easily be noted. Dryden is always *another and the same*; he does not exhibit a second time the same elegancies in the same form, nor appears to have any art other than that of expressing with clearness what he thinks with vigour. His style could not easily be imitated, either seriously or ludicrously; for, being always equable and always varied, it has no prominent or discriminative characters.

I wished to draw particular attention to this point of poetic diction, because it is an essential standard of Johnson's criticism, and because I think that the absence of any common standard of poetic [187] diction is a weakness both of modern verse and of our criticism of it. And I deliberately took this up directly after touching upon his standard of *edification*. That poetry, when it illustrates some moral truth or inculcates some virtuous practice, is more to be commended than when it does not; and that poetry which recommends or insinuates bad principles, or leads into error, is to be condemned, is shown throughout in Johnson's treatment of his authors. Yet Johnson said, in praising Akenside's *Pleasures of Imagination*: 'with the philosophical or religious tenets of the author I have nothing to do; my business is with his poetry.' Johnson did not confuse his judgement of what an author was saying, with his judgement about the way in which he said it. Now I observe sometimes in contemporary criticism of poetry, and in the more ambitious reviewing of poetry, a confusion of these judgements. The standard of edification has been fractured into a variety of prejudices; with no common opinion as to what poetry ought to teach, the critic is not necessarily liberated from moral judgement, but will frequently declare a poem good or bad, according to his sympathy with, or antipathy from, the author's point of view. Not infrequently too, the critic's knowledge of the author's views will be derived from other sources than the particular poem presented for his criticism, and will influence his judgement upon that poem. And with the question whether a poem is well or ill written, whether it could be improved, whether the cadences are musical, whether the choice of words is fastidious and literate, whether the imagery is happily found and properly distributed, whether the syntax is correct and whether the violations of normal construction are justified: such questions are avoided as if they laid the questioner under suspicion of pedantry. The result is too often comment which is of no value to the author, except when, if favourable, it may be good advertisement; a criticism of the hustings, by which reviewers range themselves for or against a particular poet.

That there is to-day no definite standard of taste in poetry, is partly the result of conditions of society and historical origins, beyond our control and beyond our responsibility. The most, perhaps, that we can do, and that is worth the doing, is to learn to recognise the benefits to the writer and to his critic of *common style* in poetry. It is in fact only when a common style is recognised, from which the poet may not depart too far without censure, that the term 'poetic diction', in any but a derogatory sense, has meaning. When such standards for a common style exist, the author [188] who would achieve originality is compelled to attend to the finer shades of distinction. To be original within definite limits of propriety may require greater talent and labour, than when every man may write as he pleases, and when the first thing expected of him is to be different. To be obliged to work upon the finer shades is to be compelled to strive for precision and clarity: a good deal of what is blamed as wilful obscurity on the part of modern writers is the result of the lack of any common style, and the consequent difficulty of communication. Those conditions also favour the flowering of something for which Johnson's own verse, at its best, is eminent: *eloquence*. Eloquence is a virtue associated with great oratory: it should be distinguished from the baser, and far commoner type of political oratory, by the test of its appeal to the reason and to the sensibility, and its avoidance of appeal to the coarser and more inflammable passions, Eloquence is that which can stir the emotions of the intelligent and judicious. But, in poetry, not all poetry which does this is, in my use of the word, eloquent; poetry is eloquent, only if the poet is appealing to emotions which the intelligent and judicious can experience together – in other words, not to a single reader but to an audience. It is not an universal virtue in poetry; it is effective of some results and incompatible with the attainment of others; but most of the great poets have displayed it on occasion. It is related to that peculiar force in the poetry of Johnson and Goldsmith, as in the poetry of Dryden and Pope before them, which I may indicate by saying that every word and epithet goes straight to its mark. In comparison, much of later poetry has employed words rather for the sake of overtones, associations, and indefinite suggestiveness. The greatest poets have done this too; we must admit that we can err by exclusive attention to the one kind of use of words or to the other.

In the Life of Pope, Johnson defines, as illustrated in Pope's poetry, the three qualities which constitute poetic genius. He says significantly that Pope has these three qualities 'in proportions very nicely adjusted to each other'; which is a wholesome reminder that it is not separate qualities, but qualities in relation to each other, by which we must judge a poet – that, in fact, the perfection of their proportion is itself the final quality. He writes as follows:

He had *invention*, by which new trains of events are formed, and new scenes of imagery displayed, as in *The Rape of the Lock*, and [189] by which extrinsic and adventitious embellishments and illustrations are connected with a known subject, as in the *Essay on Criticism*. He had *imagination*, which strongly impresses on the writer's mind, and enables him to convey to the reader, the various forms of nature, incidents of life, and energies of passion, as in his *Eloisa*, *Windsor Forest*, and *Ethic Epistles*. He had *judgment*, which selects from life or nature what the present purpose requires, and by separating the essence of things from its concomitants, often makes the representation more powerful than the reality; and he had colours of language always before him, ready to decorate his matter with every grace of elegant expression, as when he accommodates his diction to the wonderful multiplicity of Homer's sentiments and descriptions.

The dangers of attempting to catalogue the faculties of the poet are of two kinds. These denominations may separate faculties which are only found together; and they may be taken too seriously, as final psychological or philosophical truth, when they are merely analyses of pragmatic validity, to be tested by their usefulness in helping us to weigh the merits of particular poets. It is prudent, not simply to choose the set of definitions which we find most congenial, or to assume that that one is most exact which is most recent; but to collate all those of respectable authority of different ages. We find that these have a great deal in common. Johnson follows Dryden in the use of the term *invention*, but puts it beside *imagination*, whereas Dryden had made *invention* a species of *imagination*, together with *fancy* and *elocution*; Johnson does not employ *elocution*, but introduces *judgement*. Coleridge concentrates upon *imagination*, in which he finds depths of meaning unsuspected by either Dryden or Johnson; and belittles fancy – with a sharpness of distinction between *fancy* and *imagination* which I find difficult to apply in practice. The changes in the meaning of words, and these changes of emphasis, are part of the history of our civilisation. A contemporary critic, engaged in the same task of analysis, would produce another, and more complicated account, which would probably be influenced by the study of sciences of more recent growth. The modern account would fit in better with our mental furniture, but would not necessarily be more true for this reason; because of the unsettled state of the sciences upon which it might draw, it might even be more inclined to stray from what is the true purpose of such discriminations, the help they afford in discerning the merits and defects of particular [190] pieces of poetry. The accounts of Dryden and Johnson, because these critics were concerned with literature as literature, and not with psychology or sociology, and because of their very simplicity, have enduring usefulness. The particular interest of Johnson's variation, I think, lies in his use of the term *judgement* – a reminder of the great importance of the critical faculty in creative composition.

> In the present age the poet – (I would wish to be understood as speaking generally, and without allusion to individual names) – seems to propose to himself as his main object, and as that which is the most characteristic of his art, new and striking images; with incidents that interest the affections or excite the curiosity. Both his characters and his descriptions, as much as possible, are specific and individual, even to a degree of portraiture. In his diction and metre, on the other hand, he is comparatively careless.

These words are not mine, but Coleridge's. They could well enough be applied to the present time; and on the other hand the principle maintained is one which I am sure Johnson would have approved. Similarly, Coleridge's observations on poetic diction, when compared with Johnson's, show a fundamental agreement on the difference between the use of language in verse and its use in prose. In an age like ours, lacking common standards, poets need to remind themselves that it is not sufficient to rely upon those gifts which are native to them, and which they exercise with ease, but that good poetry must exhibit several qualities in proportion, of which one is good sense. Their judgement should also be employed, in discovering for themselves the sources of their own strength and weakness; in curbing the exuberance of their force, and avoiding occasions on which they would display only their weakness. I remember once being told that a famous tennis player had said, that she was all the better for being naturally weak in certain strokes; for the effort to overcome her deficiency, and manoeuvre so that it should be least exposed, had greatly increased her resourcefulness. There is something here which poets might ponder.

A thorough examination of Johnson's criticism would require, first, a study of the eighteenth-century background; second, a study of Johnson himself, not as the subject of anecdote, but in his other works, and in his religious and political opinions; and, finally, a much more detailed study of his criticism of the greater of the poets who came under his observation: Shakespeare, Milton, Dryden, Pope, Gray. Such would be a work of more scholarship [191] than I profess. I only want to suggest to the student of English poetry and of the criticism of poetry that here is a subject which deserves much more serious investigation than it has yet received. And, in closing, I wish to sum up those points which seem to me to have particular relevance to the criticism of poetry in our own time.

In the first place, it is remarkable that Johnson's *Lives of the Poets* is the only monumental collection of critical studies of English poets in the language, with a coherence, as well as an amplitude, which no other English criticism can claim. It is worth while asking ourselves why no later work of criticism is of the same kind. Nineteenth-century criticism, when it has not belonged primarily to the category of scholarly research, the presentation of the ascertainable facts about one author or another, has tended to be something less purely *literary*. With Coleridge, criticism merges into philosophy and a theory of aesthetics; with Arnold, it merges into ethics and propaedeutics, and literature becomes a means towards the formation of character; in some critics, of whom Pater is a specimen, the subject-matter of criticism becomes a pretext of another kind. In our own day, the influence of psychology and of sociology upon literary criticism has been very noticeable. On the one hand, these influences of social disciplines have enlarged the field of the critic, and have affirmed, in a world which otherwise is inclined to depreciate the importance of literature, the relations of literature to life. But from another point of view this enrichment has also been an impoverishment, for the purely literary values, the appreciation of good writing for its own sake, have become submerged when literature is judged in the light of other considerations. That this has happened, must not be attributed either for approval or disparagement to individual critics. It is simply that the conditions under which literature is judged simply and naturally as literature and not another thing, no longer prevail. For such judgement of literature to be the normal and natural task of the critic, a settled society is necessary; a definite and limited public, in the midst of which there would be a smaller number of persons of taste and discrimination, with the same background of education and manners. It must be a society which believes in itself, a society in which the differences of religious and political views are not extreme. Only in such a society can the standard of a *common style* of good writing become established and unquestioned. That is the kind of society for which Johnson wrote. It is evidence of the change of society, accelerated in our own time, a change [192] which brings inevitably a change in the consciousness of the literary critic himself, that in attempting to explain, to myself and to my audience, the peculiar interest of Johnson's criticism, I am forced to put myself at a point of view so very different from his own, and intrude the suggestion of social background which has become the necessary concern of criticism.

The conclusion that no work comparable to *The Lives of the Poets* could be written to-day, should not lead us either to elevate Johnson to a pinnacle, and lament the decline of civility which makes such criticism impossible; nor should it on the other hand tempt us to treat these essays merely as a curiosity of no bearing upon our actual problems. Their first value is a value which all study of the past should have for us: that it should make us more conscious of what we are, and of our own limitations, and give us more understanding of the world in which we now live. Their secondary value is, that by studying them, and in so doing attempting to put ourselves at their author's point of view, we may recover some of the criteria of judgement which have been disappearing from the criticism of poetry. We do not need to accept all of Johnson's judgements, or agree with all his opinions, to extract this lesson. Nor do we need to overrate the poetry of that period of which the names of Dryden and Johnson may serve as boundaries. But amongst the varieties of chaos in which we find ourselves immersed today, one is a chaos of language, in which there are discoverable no standards of writing, and an increasing indifference to etymology and the history of the use of words. And of the responsibility of our poets and our critics, for the preservation of the language, we need to be repeatedly reminded.

Byron[1]

OPAP, 193–206.

A revision of 'Byron (1788–1824)' originally publ. in *From Anne to Victoria*. Essays by Various Hands, ed. Bonamy Dobrée (18 Feb. 1937), 601–19: Gallup B30.

Two corrections have been made to the text in *OPAP*: in fn. 1 'Ann' has been corrected to 'Anne', and in para. 30, instead of 'a solemn country', the 1937 reading, 'a solemn century', has been restored.

1 The facts of a large part of Byron's life have been well set forth, in the last few years, by Sir Harold Nicolson and Mr Quennell, who have also provided interpretations which accord with each other and which make the character of Byron more intelligible to the present generation. No such interpretation has yet been offered in our time for Byron's verse. In and out of universities, Wordsworth, Coleridge, Shelley and Keats have been discussed from various points of view: Byron and Scott have been left in peace. Yet Byron, at least, would seem the most nearly remote from the sympathies of every living critic: it would be interesting, therefore, if we could have half a dozen essays about him, to see what agreement could be reached. The present article is an attempt to start that ball rolling.

2 There are several initial difficulties. It is difficult to return critically to a poet whose poetry was – I suppose it was for many of our contemporaries,

---

1. Contributed to 'From Anne to Victoria', a collection of essays edited by Bonamy Dobrée. Published by Cassell & Co., 1937.

except those who are too young to have read any of the poetry of that period – the first boyhood enthusiasm. To be told anecdotes of one's own childhood by an elderly relative is usually tedious; and a return, after many years, to the poetry of Byron is accompanied by a similar gloom: images come before the mind, and the recollection of some verses in the manner of *Don Juan*, tinged with that disillusion and cynicism only possible at the age of sixteen, which appeared in a school periodical. There are more impersonal obstacles to overcome. The bulk of Byron's poetry is distressing, in proportion to its quality; one would suppose that he never destroyed anything. Yet bulk is inevitable in a poet of Byron's type; and the absence of the destructive element in his composition indicates the kind of interest, and the kind of lack of interest, that he took in poetry. We have come to expect poetry to be something very concentrated, something distilled; but [194] if Byron had distilled his verse, there would have been nothing whatever left. When we see exactly what he was doing, we can see that he did it as well as it can be done. With most of his shorter poems, one feels that he was doing something that Tom Moore could do as well or better; in his longer poems, he did something that no one else has ever equalled.

3 It is sometimes desirable to approach the work of a poet completely out of favour, by an unfamiliar avenue. If my avenue to Byron is a road that exists only for my own mind, I shall be corrected by other critics: it may at all events upset prejudice and encourage opinion to form itself anew. I therefore suggest considering Byron as a Scottish poet – I say 'Scottish', not 'Scots', since he wrote in English. The one poet of his time with whom he could be considered to be in competition, a poet of whom he spoke invariably with the highest respect, was Sir Walter Scott. I have always seen, or imagined that I saw, in busts of the two poets, a certain resemblance in the shape of the head. The comparison does honour to Byron, and when you examine the two faces, there is no further resemblance. Were one a person who liked to have busts about, a bust of Scott would be something one could live with. There is an air of nobility about that head, an air of magnanimity, and of that inner and perhaps unconscious serenity that belongs to great writers who are also great men. But Byron – that pudgy face suggesting a tendency to corpulence, that weakly sensual mouth, that restless triviality of expression, and worst of all that blind look of the self-conscious beauty; the bust of Byron is that of a man who was every inch the touring tragedian. Yet it was by being so thorough-going an actor that Byron arrived at a kind of knowledge: of the world outside, which he had to learn something about in order to play his role in it, and of that part of himself which was

his role. Superficial knowledge, of course: but accurate so far as it went.

4 Of a Scottish quality in Byron's poetry, I shall speak when I come to *Don Juan*. But there is a very important part of the Byronic make-up which may appropriately be mentioned before considering his poetry, for which I think his Scottish antecedence provided the material. That is his peculiar diabolism, his delight in posing as a damned creature – and in providing evidence for his damnation in a rather horrifying way. Now, the diabolism of Byron is very different from anything that the Romantic Agony (as Mr Praz calls it) produced in Catholic countries. And I do not [195] think it is easily derived from the comfortable compromise between Christianity and paganism arrived at in England and characteristically English. It could come only from the religious background of a people steeped in Calvinistic theology.

5 Byron's diabolism, if indeed it deserves the name, was of a mixed type. He shared, to some extent, Shelley's Promethean attitude, and the Romantic passion for Liberty; and this passion, which inspired his more political outbursts, combined with the image of himself as a man of action to bring about the Greek adventure. And his Promethean attitude merges into a Satanic (Miltonic) attitude. The romantic conception of Milton's Satan is semi-Promethean, and also contemplates Pride as a *virtue*. It would be difficult to say whether Byron was a proud man, or a man who liked to pose as a proud man – the possibility of the two attitudes being combined in the same person does not make them any less dissimilar in the abstract. Byron was certainly a vain man, in quite simple ways:

> I can't complain, whose ancestors are there,
>   Erneis, Radulphus – eight-and-forty manors
> (If that my memory doth not greatly err)
>   Were their reward for following Billy's banners. . . .

6 His sense of damnation was also mitigated by a touch of unreality: to a man so occupied with himself and with the figure he was cutting nothing outside could be altogether real. It is therefore impossible to make out of his diabolism anything coherent or rational. He was able to have it both ways, it seems; and to think of himself both as an individual isolated and superior to other men because of his own crimes, and as a naturally good and generous nature distorted by the crimes committed against it by others. It is this inconsistent creature that turns up as the Giaour, the Corsair, Lara, Manfred and Cain; only as Don Juan does he get nearer to the truth about himself. But in this strange composition of attitudes and beliefs the element that seems to me most real and deep is that of a perversion of the Calvinist faith of his mother's ancestors.

7   One reason for the neglect of Byron is, I think, that he has been admired for what are his most ambitious attempts to be poetic; and these attempts turn out, on examination, to be fake: nothing but sonorous affirmations of the commonplace with no depth of [196] significance. A good specimen of such imposture is the well-known stanza at the end of Canto XV of *Don Juan*:

> Between two worlds life hovers like a star,
>   'Twixt night and morn, upon the horizon's verge.
> How little do we know that which we are!
>   How less what we may be! The eternal surge
> Of time and tide rolls on, and bears afar
>   Our bubbles; as the old burst, new emerge,
> Lashed from the foam of ages; while the graves
> Of empire heave but like some passing waves.

verses which are not too good for the school magazine. Byron's real excellence is on a different level from this.

8   The qualities of narrative verse which are found in *Don Juan* are no less remarkable in the earlier tales. Before undertaking this essay I had not read these tales since the days of my schoolboy infatuation, and I approached them with apprehension. However absurd we find their view of life, they are, as tales, very well told. As a *tale-teller* we must rate Byron very high indeed: I can think of none other than Chaucer who has a greater readability, with the exception of Coleridge whom Byron abused and from whom Byron learned a great deal. And Coleridge never achieved a narrative of such length. Byron's plots, if they deserve that name, are extremely simple. What makes the tales interesting is first a torrential fluency of verse and a skill in varying it from time to time to avoid monotony; and second a genius for divagation. Digression, indeed, is one of the valuable arts of the story-teller. The effect of Byron's digressions is to keep us interested in the story-teller himself, and through this interest to interest us more in the story. On contemporary readers this interest must have been strong to the point of enchantment; for even still, once we submit ourselves to the point of reading a poem through, the attraction of the personality is powerful. Any few lines, if quoted in almost any company, will probably provide a momentary twitch of merriment:

> Her eye's dark charm 'twere vain to tell,
> But gaze on that of the Gazelle,
> It will assist thy fancy well;

> As large, as languishingly dark,
> But Soul beam'd forth in every spark. . . .

[197] but the poem as a whole can keep one's attention. *The Giaour* is a long poem, and the plot is very simple, though not always easy to follow. A Christian, presumably a Greek, has managed, by some means of which we are not told, to scrape acquaintance with a young woman who belonged to the harem, or was perhaps the favourite wife of a Moslem named Hassan. In the endeavour to escape with her Christian lover Leila is recaptured and killed; in due course the Christian with some of his friends ambushes and kills Hassan. We subsequently discover that the story of this vendetta – or part of it – is being told by the Giaour himself to an elderly priest, by way of making a confession. It is a singular kind of confession, because the Giaour seems anything but penitent, and makes quite clear that although he has sinned, it is not really by his own fault. He seems impelled rather by the same motive as the Ancient Mariner, than by any desire for absolution – which could hardly have been given: but the device has its use in providing a small complication to the story. As I have said, it is not altogether easy to discover what happened. The beginning is a long apostrophe to the vanished glory of Greece, a theme which Byron could vary with great skill. The Giaour makes a dramatic entrance:

> Who thundering comes on blackest steed,
> With slackened bit and hoof of speed?

and we are given a glimpse of him through a Moslem eye:

> Though young and pale, that sallow front
> Is scathed by fiery passion's brunt . . .

which is enough to tell us, that the Giaour is an interesting person, because he is Lord Byron himself, perhaps. Then there is a long passage about the desolation of Hassan's house, inhabited only by the spider, the bat, the owl, the wild dog and weeds; we infer that the poet has skipped on to the conclusion of the tale, and that we are to expect the Giaour to kill Hassan – which is of course what happens. Not Joseph Conrad could be more roundabout. Then a bundle is privily dropped into the water, and we expect it to be the body of Leila. Then follows a reflective passage meditating in succession on Beauty, the Mind, and Remorse. Leila turns up again, alive, for a moment, but this is another dislocation of the order of events. Then we witness the surprise of Hassan and his train – this may have been months or even years after Leila's [198] death – by the Giaour and his banditti, and there is no doubt but that Hassan is killed:

> Fall'n Hassan lies – his unclosed eye
> Yet lowering on his enemy. . . .

Then comes a delightful change of metre, as well as a sudden transition, just at the moment when it is needed:

> The browsing camels' bells are tinkling:
> His mother look'd from her lattice high –
>   She saw the dews of eve besprinkling
> The pasture green beneath her eye,
>   She saw the planets faintly twinkling:
> ''Tis twilight – sure his train is nigh.'

9 Then follows a sort of exequy for Hassan, evidently spoken by another Moslem. Now the Giaour reappears, nine years later, in a monastery, as we hear one of the monks answering an inquiry about his visitor's identity. In what capacity the Giaour has attached himself to the monastery is not clear; the monks seem to have accepted him without investigation, and his behaviour among them is very odd; but we are told that he has given the monastery a considerable sum of money for the privilege of staying there. The conclusion of the poem consists of the Giaour's confession to one of the monks. Why a Greek of that period should have been so oppressed with remorse (although wholly impenitent) for killing a Moslem in what he would have considered a fair fight, or why Leila should have been guilty in leaving a husband or master to whom she was presumably united without her consent, are questions that we cannot answer.

10 I have considered the Giaour in some detail in order to exhibit Byron's extraordinary ingenuity in story-telling. There is nothing straightforward about the telling of the simple tale; we are not told everything that we should like to know; and the behaviour of the protagonists is sometimes as unaccountable as their motives and feelings are confused. Yet the author not only gets away with it, but gets away with it *as narrative*. It is the same gift that Byron was to turn to better account in *Don Juan*; and the first reason why *Don Juan* is still readable is that it has the same narrative quality as the earlier tales.

11 It is, I think, worth noting, that Byron developed the verse *conte* considerably beyond Moore and Scott, if we are to see his [199] popularity as anything more than public caprice or the attraction of a cleverly exploited personality. These elements enter into it, certainly. But first of all, Byron's verse tales represent a more mature stage of this transient form than Scott's, as Scott's represents a more mature stage than Moore's. Moore's *Lalla Rookh* is a mere sequence of tales joined together by a ponderous

prose account of the circumstances of their narration (modelled upon the *Arabian Nights*). Scott perfected a straightforward story with the type of plot which he was to employ in his novels. Byron combined exoticism with actuality, and developed most effectively the use of *suspense*. I think also that the versification of Byron is the ablest: but in this kind of verse it is necessary to read at length if one is to form an impression, and relative merit cannot be shown by quotation. To identify every passage taken at random as being by Byron or Moore would be connoisseurship beyond my powers; but I think that anyone who has recently read Byron's tales would agree that the following passage could not be by him:

> And oh! to see the unburied heaps
> On which the lonely moonlight sleeps –
> The very vultures turn away,
> And sicken at so foul a prey!
> Only the fierce hyena stalks
> Throughout the city's desolate walks
> At midnight, and his carnage plies –
>   Woe to the half-dead wretch, who meets
> The glaring of those large blue eyes
>   Amid the darkness of the streets!

12 This is from *Lalla Rookh*, and was marked as if with approval by some reader of the London Library.

13 *Childe Harold* seems to me inferior to this group of poems (*The Giaour, The Bride of Abydos, The Corsair, Lara*, etc.). Time and time again, to be sure, Byron awakens fading interest by a purple passage, but Byron's purple passages are never good enough to do the work that is expected of them in *Childe Harold*:

> Stop! for thy tread is on an Empire's dust

is just what is wanted to revive interest, at that point; but the stanza that follows, on the Battle of Waterloo, seems to me quite false; and quite representative of the falsity in which Byron takes refuge whenever he *tries* to write poetry:

> [200] Stop! for thy tread is on an Empire's dust!
> An Earthquake's spoil is sepulchred below!
> Is the spot mark'd with no colossal bust?
> Nor column trophied for triumphal show?
> None; but the moral's truth tells simpler so,
> As the ground was before, so let it be; –
> How that red rain hath made the harvest grow!

> And is this all the world has gained by thee,
> Thou first and last of fields! king-making victory?

14 It is all the more difficult, in a period which has rather lost the appreciation of the kind of virtues to be found in Byron's poetry, to analyse accurately his faults and vices. Hence we fail to give credit to Byron for the instinctive art by which, in a poem like *Childe Harold*, and still more efficiently in *Beppo* or *Don Juan*, he avoids monotony by a dextrous turn from one subject to another. He has the cardinal virtue of being never dull. But, when we have admitted the existence of forgotten virtues, we still recognise a falsity in most of those passages which were formerly most admired. To what is this falsity due?

15 Whatever it is, in Byron's poetry, that is 'wrong', we should be mistaken in calling it rhetoric. Too many things have been collected under that name; and if we are going to think that we have accounted for Byron's verse by calling it 'rhetorical', then we are bound to avoid using that adjective about Milton and Dryden, about both of whom (in their very different kinds) we seem to be saying something that has meaning, when we speak of their 'rhetoric'. Their failures, when they fail, are of a higher kind than Byron's successes, when he succeeds. Each had a strongly individual idiom, and a sense of language; at their worst, they have an interest in the *word*. You can recognise them in the single line, and can say: here is a particular way of using the language. There is no such individuality in the line of Byron. If one looks at the few single lines, from the Waterloo passage in *Childe Harold*, which may pass for 'familiar quotations', you cannot say that any of them is great poetry:

> And all went merry as a marriage bell . . .
> On with the dance! let joy be unconfined. . . .

16 Of Byron one can say, as of no other English poet of his emi-[201]nence, that he added nothing to the language, that he discovered nothing in the sounds, and developed nothing in the meaning, of individual words. I cannot think of any other poet of his distinction who might so easily have been an accomplished foreigner writing English. The ordinary person talks English, but only a few people in every generation can write it; and upon this undeliberate collaboration between a great many people talking a living language and a very few people writing it, the continuance and maintenance of a language depends. Just as an artisan who can talk English beautifully while about his work or in a public bar, may compose a letter painfully written in a dead language bearing some resemblance to a newspaper leader, and decorated with words like 'maelstrom' and 'pandemonium': so does Byron write a dead or dying language.

17 This imperceptiveness of Byron to the English word – so that he has to use a great many words before we become aware of him – indicates for practical purposes a defective sensibility. I say 'for practical purposes' because I am concerned with the sensibility in his poetry, not with his private life; for if a writer has not the language in which to express feelings they might as well not exist. We do not even need to compare his account of Waterloo with that of Stendhal to feel the lack of minute particulars; but it is worth remarking that the prose sensibility of Stendhal, being sensibility, has some values of poetry that Byron completely misses. Byron did for the language very much what the leader writers of our journals are doing day by day. I think that this failure is much more important than the platitude of his intermittent philosophising. Every poet has uttered platitudes, every poet has said things that have been said before. It is not the weakness of the ideas, but the schoolboy command of the language, that makes his lines seem trite and his thought shallow.

18 *Mais que Hugo aussi était dans tout ce peuple.* The words of Péguy have kept drifting through my mind while I have been thinking of Byron:

> Non pas vers qui chantent dans la mémoire, mais vers qui dans la mémoire sonnent et retentissent comme une fanfare, vibrants, trépidants, sonnant comme une fanfare, sonnent comme une charge, tambour éternel, et qui battra dans les mémoires françaises longtemps après que les réglementaires tambours auront cessé de battre au front des régiments.

19 But Byron was not 'in *this* people', either of London or of Eng-[202]land, but in his mother's people, and the most stirring stanza of his Waterloo is this:

> And wild and high the 'Cameron's gathering' rose!
> The war-note of Lochiel, which Albyn's hills
> Have heard, and heard, too, have her Saxon foes: –
> How in the noon of night that pibroch thrills,
> Savage and shrill! But with the breath which fills
> Their mountain-pipe, so fill the mountaineers
> With the fierce native daring which instils
> The stirring memory of a thousand years,
> And Evan's, Donald's fame rings in each clansman's ears!

20 All things worked together to make *Don Juan* the greatest of Byron's poems. The stanza that he borrowed from the Italian was admirably

suited to enhance his merits and conceal his defects, just as on a horse or in the water he was more at ease than on foot. His ear was imperfect, and capable only of crude effects; and in this easy-going stanza, with its habitually feminine and occasionally triple endings, he seems always to be reminding us that he is not really trying very hard and yet producing something as good or better than that of the solemn poets who take their verse-making more seriously. And Byron really is at his best when he is not trying too hard to be poetic; when he tries to be poetic in a few lines he produces things like the stanza I have already quoted, beginning:

Between two worlds life hovers like a star.

21 But at a lower intensity he gets a surprising range of effect. His genius for digression, for wandering away from his subject (usually to talk about himself) and suddenly returning to it, is, in *Don Juan*, at the height of its power. The continual banter and mockery, which his stanza and his Italian model serve to keep constantly in his mind, serve as an admirable antacid to the highfalutin which in the earlier romances tends to upset the reader's stomach; and his social satire helps to keep him to the objective and has a sincerity that is at least plausible if not profound. The portrait of himself comes much nearer to honesty than any that appears in his earlier work. This is worth examining in some detail.

22 Charles Du Bos, in his admirable *Byron et le besoin de la fatalité*, quotes a long passage of self-portraiture from *Lara*. Du Bos [203] deserves full credit for recognising its importance; and Byron deserves all the credit that Du Bos gives him for having written it. This passage strikes me also as a masterpiece of self-analysis, but of a self that is largely a deliberate fabrication – a fabrication that is only completed in the actual writing of the lines. The reason why Byron understood this self so well, is that it is largely his own invention; and it is only the self that he invented that he understood perfectly. If I am correct, one cannot help feeling pity and horror at the spectacle of a man devoting such gigantic energy and persistence to such a useless and petty purpose; though at the same time we must feel sympathy and humility in reflecting that it is a vice to which most of us are addicted in a fitful and less persevering way; that is to say, Byron made a vocation out of what for most of us is an irregular weakness, and deserves a certain sad admiration for his degree of success. But in *Don Juan*, we get something much nearer to genuine self-revelation. For Juan, in spite of the brilliant qualities with which Byron invests him – so that he may hold his own among the English aristocracy – is not an heroic figure. There is nothing absurd about his presence of mind and courage during the shipwreck, or about his prowess in the Turkish wars: he exhibits a kind of physical courage and capacity

for heroism which we are quite willing to attribute to Byron himself. But in the accounts of his relations with women, he is not made to appear heroic or even dignified; and these impress us as having an ingredient of the genuine as well as of the make-believe.

23 It is noticeable – and this confirms, I think, the view of Byron held by Mr Peter Quennell – that in these love-episodes Juan always takes the passive role. Even Haidee, in spite of the innocence and ignorance of that child of nature, appears rather as the seducer than the seduced. That episode is the longest and most carefully elaborate of all the amorous passages, and I think it deserves pretty high marks. It is true that after Juan's earlier initiation by Donna Julia, we are hardly so credulous as to believe in the innocence attributed to him with Haidee; but this should not lead us to dismiss the description as false. The *innocence* of Juan is merely a substitute for the *passivity* of Byron; and if we restore the latter we can recognise in the account some authentic understanding of the human heart, and accept such lines as

> Alas! They were so young, so beautiful,
>   So lonely, loving, helpless, and the hour
> [204] Was that in which the heart is always full,
>   And having o'er itself no further power,
>   Prompts deeds eternity cannot annul. . . .

24 The lover of Donna Julia and of Haidee is just the man, we feel, to become subsequently the favourite of Catherine the Great – to introduce whom, one suspects, Byron had prepared himself by his eight months with the Countess of Oxford. And there remains, if not innocence, that strange passivity that has a curious resemblance to innocence.

25 Between the first and the second part of the poem, between Juan's adventures abroad and his adventures in England, there is a noticeable difference. In the first part the satire is incidental; the action is picaresque, and of the best kind. Byron's invention never fails. The shipwreck, an episode too well-known to quote, is something quite new and quite successful, even if it be somewhat overdone by the act of cannibalism in which it culminates. The last wild adventure occurs directly after Juan's arrival in England, when he is held up by footpads on the way to London; and here again, I think, in the obituary of the dead highwayman, is something new in English verse:

> He from the world had cut off a great man,
>   Who in his time had made heroic bustle.
> Who in a row like Tom could lead the van,

>   Booze in the ken, or at the spellken hustle?
>   Who queer a flat? Who (spite of Bow-street's ban)
>   On the high toby-spice so flash the muzzle?
>   Who on a lark, with black-eyed Sal (his blowing)
>   So prime, so swell, so nutty, and so knowing?

26 That is first rate. It is not a bit like Crabbe, but it is rather suggestive of Burns.

27 The last four cantos are, unless I am greatly mistaken, the most substantial of the poem. To satirise humanity in general requires either a more genial talent than Byron's, such as that of Rabelais, or else a more profoundly tortured one, such as Swift's. But in the latter part of *Don Juan* Byron is concerned with an English scene, in which for him there was for him nothing romantic left; he is concerned with a restricted field that he had known well, and for the satirising of which an acute animosity sharpened his powers of observation. His understanding may remain superficial, but it is precise. Quite [205] possibly he undertook something that he would have been unable to carry to a successful conclusion; possibly there was needed, to complete the story of that monstrous house-party, some high spirits, some capacity for laughter, with which Byron was not endowed. He might have found it impossible to deal with that remarkable personage Aurora Raby, the most serious character of his invention, within the frame of his satire. Having invented a character too serious, in a way too real for the world he knew, he might have been compelled to reduce her to the size of one of his ordinary romantic heroines. But Lord Henry and Lady Adeline Amundeville are persons exactly on the level of Byron's capacity for understanding; and they have a reality for which their author has perhaps not received due credit.

28 What puts the last cantos of *Don Juan* at the head of Byron's works is, I think, that the subject matter gave him at last an adequate object for a genuine emotion. The emotion is hatred of hypocrisy; and if it was reinforced by more personal and petty feelings, the feelings of a man who as a boy had known the humiliation of shabby lodgings with an eccentric mother, who at fifteen had been clumsy and unattractive and unable to dance with Mary Chaworth, who remained oddly alien among the society that he knew so well – this mixture of the origin of his attitude towards English society only gives it greater intensity. And the hypocrisy of the world that he satirised was at the opposite extreme from his own. Hypocrite, indeed, except in the original sense of the word, is hardly the term for Byron. He was an actor who devoted immense trouble to *becoming* a role that he adopted; his superficiality was something that he created for himself. It is difficult, in considering Byron's poetry, not to be drawn into an analysis of the man: but much more attention has already been devoted to the man than to the poetry, and I prefer, within the limits of such an essay as this, to keep the latter in the foreground. My point is that Byron's satire upon English society, in the latter part of *Don Juan*, is something for which I can find no parallel in English literature. He was right in making the hero of his house-party a Spaniard, for what Byron understands and dislikes about English society is very much what an intelligent foreigner in the same position would understand and dislike.

29 One cannot leave *Don Juan* without calling attention to another part of it which emphasises the difference between this poem and any other satire in English: the Dedicatory Verses. The Dedica-[206]tion to Southey seems to me one of the most exhilarating pieces of abuse in the language:

> Bob Southey! You're a poet – Poet Laureate,
> And representative of all the race;
> Although 'tis true that you turn'd out a Tory at
> Last, yours has lately been a common case;
> And now, my Epic Renegade! what are ye at? . . .

kept up without remission to the end of seventeen stanzas. This is not the satire of Dryden, still less of Pope; it is perhaps more like Hall or Marston, but they are bunglers in comparison. This is not indeed English satire at all; it is really a *flyting*, and closer in feeling and intention to the satire of Dunbar:

> Lene larbar, loungeour, baith lowsy in lisk and lonye;
>   Fy! skolderit skyn, thow art both skyre and skrumple;
> For he that rostit Lawrance had thy grunye,
>   And he that hid Sanct Johnis ene with ane womple,
>   And he that dang Sanct Augustine with ane rumple,
> Thy fowll front had, and he that Bartilmo flaid;
>   The gallowis gaipis eftit thy graceles gruntill,
> As thow wald for ane haggeis, hungry gled.

30 To some this parallel may seem questionable, but to me it has brought a keener enjoyment, and I think a juster appreciation of Byron than I had before. I do not pretend that Byron is Villon (nor, for other reasons, does Dunbar or Burns equal the French poet), but I have come to find in him certain qualities, besides his abundance, that are too uncommon in English poetry, as well as the absence of some vices that are too common.

And his own vices seem to have twin virtues that closely resemble them. With his charlatanism, he has also an unusual frankness; with his pose, he is also a *poète contumace* in a solemn century; with his humbug and self-deception he has also a reckless raffish honesty; he is at once a vulgar patrician and a dignified toss-pot; with all his bogus diabolism and his vanity of pretending to disreputability, he is genuinely superstitious and disreputable. I am speaking of the qualities and defects in his work, and important in estimating his work; not of the private life, with which I am not concerned.

Variants from 1937:

Title BYRON | (1788–1824)

1 Sir Harold Nicholson] Mr. Nicholson
   nearly remote] nearly equally remote
3 since he wrote in English] as a reminder that he wrote in English
   a poet of whom] and one of whom
   [Between 'Sir Walter Scott.' and 'I have always seen':] Possibly Byron, who must have thought of himself as an English poet, was the more Scotch of the two because of being unconscious of his true nationality.
4 of a people steeped in Calvinistic theology] provided by a nation which had been ruined by religion. It was a monstrosity, of course, for Scotland to bring forth; but it could come only from a people who took religion more seriously than the English.
5 Greek adventure.] Greek adventure, in which he could not be said to be wholly insincere.
6 own crimes] innate daring evil
   mother's ancestors] Scottish ancestors
8 [Between 'with apprehension.' and 'However absurd':] They are, however, extremely readable.
   than Chaucer] since Chaucer
   greater readability] equal readability
   a narrative] narratives
   a confession] his confession
   wild dog] wild-dog
   moment,] moment;
10 extraordinary ingenuity] extraordinary native ingenuity
13 *Lara*, etc.).] *Lara*, etc.) because of the slightness of the narrative
14 [Between 'faults and vices.' and 'Hence we fail':] We abominate the commonplace, we expect profundity – though often satisfied by the appearance without the reality – we are suspicious of anything immediately intelligible, we demand an insurgence of the unconscious, and we are patiently prepared to be bored.
15 rhetoric] *rhetoric*
16 talks English] *talks* English
19 but in his mother's people,] [Not represented in 1937.]

20 trying very hard and yet] trying very hard, and yet
27 acute animosity] acute personal animosity
30 does Dunbar or Burns] do Dunbar or Burns

Goethe as the Sage[1]

OPAP, 207–27.

Publ. as *Gedenkschrift zur Verleihung des Hansischen Goethe-Preises 1954 der gemeinnützingen Stiftung F.V.S. zu Hamburg durch die Universität Hamburg an Thomas Stearns Eliot* (Aug. 1955): Gallup B74. Revised in *OPAP*.

1 On the mantelpiece of my office room there has stood for some fifteen years and more, among portraits of literary friends, the facsimile of a drawing of Goethe in old age. The drawing is full of life – the work, one feels, not only of a gifted draughtsman but of an artist inspired by his subject.[2] Goethe stands with his hands clasped behind his back; the shoulders are bent and the posture stooping; but although the body may be weakened by infirmities, it is obviously still ruled by a vigorous mind. The eyes are large and luminous, the expression mischievous, both benign and mephistophelian: we are in the presence of a man who combines the vitality of youth with the wisdom of age. There was a moment, some years ago, when the picture was violently dislodged, together with its companions; but, as one would expect of Goethe, this portrait, serene, alert and critical, survived and ignored the incidents of that disturbed time.

2 This is the Goethe of the days of the conversations with Eckermann. It is Goethe the Sage: and as what I have to say here might almost be called a Discourse in Praise of Wisdom, this picture would form an appropriate frontispiece to my text. If one employs this word 'sage' with all the care and scruple it deserves, then one has in mind one of the rarest achievements of the human spirit. Poetic inspiration is none too common, but the true sage is rarer than the true poet; and when the two gifts, that of wisdom and that of poetic speech, are found in the same man, you have the great poet. It is poets of this kind who belong, not merely to their own people but to the world; it is only poets of this kind of whom one can think, not primarily as limited by their own language and nation, but as great Europeans.

---

1. An address delivered at Hamburg University on the occasion of the award of the Hanseatic Goethe Prize for 1954, in May 1955.

2. The artist, I am informed, was Maclise, then a young man on a visit to Weimar.

3 At first, I had wondered whether there remained anything to [208] say about Goethe which had not been better said already. When I came, however, to the point at which I had to choose a topic and outline my mode of treatment, I found myself bewildered by excess of possibilities – by the numberless aspects of Goethe, and the numberless contexts in which Goethe could be considered. In the end I was able to reduce my possible topics to two; but on further meditation, I discovered that the two were so closely connected in my mind as to form one problem which I must treat as a whole. The first problem was: what are the common characteristics of that select number of authors, of whom Goethe is one, who are Great Europeans? And the second was: what is the process by which one becomes reconciled to those great authors to whom in one's youth one was indifferent or antipathetic – not only why it takes place, but why it ought to take place; not only the process but the moral necessity of the process. In the course of this essay I shall be considering these two problems in turn; I hope that the reader may come to agree that the sub-title I had in mind – a Discourse in Praise of Wisdom – is not wholly unjustified.

4 In the development of taste and critical judgement in literature – a part or an aspect of the total process of coming to maturity – there are, according to my own experience, three important phases. In adolescence, I was swept with enthusiasm for one author after another, to whichever responded to the instinctive needs at my stage of development. At this enthusiastic stage the critical faculty is hardly awake, for there is no comparison of one author with another, no full awareness of the basis of the relationship between oneself and the author in whose work one is engrossed. Not only is there but little awareness of rank: there is no true understanding of greatness. This is a standard inaccessible to the immature mind: at that stage, there are only the writers by whom one is carried away and those who leave one cold. As one's reading is extended, and one becomes acquainted with an increasing variety of the best writers of prose and verse, at the same time acquiring greater experience of the world and stronger powers of reflection, one's taste becomes more comprehensive, one's passions calmer and one's understanding more profound. At this stage, we begin to develop that critical ability, that power of self-criticism, without which the poet will do no more than repeat himself to the end of his life. Yet, though we may at this stage enjoy, understand and appreciate an indefinite variety of artistic and philosophic genius, there will remain obstinate cases of authors of high [209] rank whom we continue to find antipathetic. So the third stage of development – of maturation so far as that process can be represented

by the history of our reading and study – is that at which we begin to enquire into the reasons for our failure to enjoy what has been found delightful by men, perhaps many generations of men, as well qualified or better qualified for appreciation than ourselves. In trying to understand why one has failed to appreciate rightly a particular author, one is seeking for light, not only about that author, but about oneself. The study of authors whose work one fails to enjoy can thus be a very valuable exercise, though it is one to which common sense imposes limits: for nobody has the time to study the work of all the great authors in whose work he takes no pleasure. This process of examination is not an effort to enjoy what one has failed to enjoy: it is an effort to understand that work, and to understand oneself in relation to it. The enjoyment will come, if it does come, only as a consequence of the understanding.

5 There are obvious reasons, in my own case, for difficulty with Goethe. For anyone like myself, who combines a Catholic cast of mind, a Calvinistic heritage, and a Puritanical temperament, Goethe does indeed present some obstacles to be surmounted. But my experience is, that recognition of the obstacles – a recognition requiring self-examination still more than examination of the author – while it does not make these obstacles disappear, can render them less important. Differences which are unexamined never emerge from the obscurity of prejudice: the better we understand our failure to appreciate an author, the nearer we come to appreciation – since understanding and sympathy are closely related. Without ever having denied Goethe's genius, without remaining unmoved by that part of his poetry most easily assimilated by a foreigner, I had, I fear, been irritated by him. In time, I came to understand that my quarrel with Goethe was – apart from some personal traits which now seem to me of diminished importance – primarily a quarrel with his age; for I had, over the years, found myself alienated from the major English poets of the nineteenth century, both of the Romantic Movement and of the Victorian period. I still enjoy particular poems; but with the exception of Coleridge – and Coleridge rather as philosopher and theologian and social thinker than as poet – I have more and more lost touch with their authors. Tennyson, Browning, Arnold, Meredith: their philosophy of life came to seem to me flimsy, their [210] religious foundations insecure. But I had had the experience of living through that poetry in my boyhood: that remained to me. I had been, for a time, very much moved by these poets: I felt, and feel, that I had learned from them what I was capable of learning and what they were capable of teaching me. With Goethe it is a different matter. As for the English poets to whom I have just alluded, I can imagine them as greater poets if they had held a different view of

life. But with Goethe, on the other hand, it seems right and necessary that he should have believed what he did, and behaved as he did. And antipathy overcome, when it is antipathy to any figure so great as that of Goethe, is an important liberation from a limitation of one's own mind.

6 It may seem egotistic frivolity for me to spend so much time on the mutations of my own attitude towards Goethe. I do so for two reasons. First, because the few scattered references to Goethe in my earlier critical essays are mostly grudging and denigratory; so that if I am to justify my present attitude, and avert all suspicion of insincerity, I must give some account of the evolution of my own mind. Second, because I think that the situation can be generalised in such a way as to be of value. I have said that, so far as my own development is typical, one's self-education begins, in adolescence, by being enraptured, invaded, carried away by one writer after another (I am thinking of course of one's education in poetry). Subsequently, one acquires a knowledge and enjoyment of a variety of work; one is influenced by minds of increasingly different character; one becomes more self-possessed; critical judgement develops; one is more conscious of what one is doing and of what is happening in one's explorations of the masterpieces of thought and imagination. After middle age, again, two further changes have come upon me. On the one hand, my literary predilections shrink: I wish to return more and more often to the work of fewer and fewer poets. And on the other hand, I find that there may be a few authors whom I have never really known, in the sense of intimacy and ease, with whom I must settle my account before I die.

7 I began, some years ago, to think that I must eventually make the effort to reconcile myself to Goethe: not primarily to repair an injustice done, for one has committed many such literary injustices without compunction, but because I should otherwise have neglected some opportunity of self-development, which it would be culpable to neglect. To entertain this feeling, is already an important [211] admission: it is, surely, the admission that Goethe is one of the Great Europeans. The reader will now see, I hope, how it is that the two subjects – the problem of reconciliation and the definition of the Great European – become so closely entangled in my mind that I could not consider one without touching on the other.

8 It seems to me that the safest approach to this definition, is to take a few men whose right to this title is universally admitted, and consider what they have in common. I shall first, however, lay down the limits within which my selection is made. In the first place, I shall limit myself to poets, because poetry is the department in which I am best qualified to appreciate greatness. In the second place, I shall exclude all Latin and Greek

poets. My reason for doing this is indicated by the title which Theodor Haecker gave to his essay on Virgil: *Vergil, Vater des Abendlandes*. The great poets of Greece and Rome, as well as the prophets of Israel, are ancestors of Europe, rather than Europeans in the medieval and modern sense. It is because of our common background, in the literatures of Greece, Rome, and Israel, that we can speak of 'European literature' at all: and the survival of European literature, I may mention in passing, depends on our continued veneration of our ancestors. As such, they are set apart from my present investigation. There are also modern poets, whose influence has been very important in countries and languages not their own, who are unsuitable for my purpose. In Byron we have a poet who was the poet of an Age, and for that Age the poet of all Europe. In Edgar Poe, America produced a poet who, largely through his influence on three French poets of three successive generations, may be considered European; but the exact place and rank of these two men is still, and perhaps always will be, the subject of controversy; and I wish to limit myself to men whose qualifications are undisputed.

9 What, to begin with, are our criteria? Two, surely, are *Permanence* and *Universality*. The European poet must not only be one who holds a certain position in history: his work must continue to give delight and benefit to successive generations. His influence is not a matter of historical record only; he will continue to be of value to every Age, and every Age will understand him differently and be compelled to assess his work afresh. And he must be as important to readers of his own race and language as to others: those of his own race and language will feel that he is wholly one of them, and indeed their representative abroad. To readers of [212] different nations and different ages he may mean many different things: but his importance no nation or generation will question. The history of what has been written about the work of such a man will be a part of the history of the European mind.

10 Obviously, one cannot draw up two lists, one of great poets who are great Europeans, the other of those who fail to qualify for this distinction. All we can do, I think, is to agree upon a minimal number, consider what common characteristics they have, and endeavour to approximate to a definition, by which we then proceed to measure other poets. Of three I do not think that there can be any doubt: they are Dante, Shakespeare and Goethe.

11 Here I must introduce a word of caution. I doubt whether we should call a poet a 'great European' unless he is also a great poet; but I think that we have to admit that there are great poets who are not Great Europeans. Indeed, I suspect that when we call any Man of Letters a Great European,

we are exceeding the limits of purely literary judgement – we are making an historical, a social, and an ethical valuation as well. Compare Goethe with a somewhat younger English contemporary, William Wordsworth. Wordsworth was surely a great poet, if the term has any meaning at all; at his best, his flight was much higher than that of Byron, and as high as that of Goethe. His influence was, moreover, decisive for English poetry at a certain moment: his name marks an epoch. Yet he will never mean to Europeans of other nationality, what he means to his own compatriots; nor can he mean to his own compatriots what Goethe means to them. Similarly – but here I speak with becoming diffidence – it seems to me possible to maintain that Hölderlin was at moments more inspired than Goethe: yet he also, can never be to the same degree a European figure. Into the possible account of the differences between the two kinds of poet, I do not propose to enter: I wish only, in this context, to remind you that if Dante, Shakespeare, and Goethe are incontestably European men, it is not merely because they are the greatest poets of their languages. They would not be great Europeans unless they were great poets, but their greatness as Europeans is something more complex, more comprehensive, than their superiority over other poets of their own language.

12 There is also the temptation, with Shakespeare and Goethe though not with Dante, to think of the two great mythical figures whom they created: Hamlet and Faust. Now, Hamlet and Faust have become European symbols. They have this in common with [213] Odysseus and Don Quixote, that each is very much of his own country, and yet the fellow-countryman of all of us. Who could be more Greek than Odysseus, more Spanish than Don Quixote, more English than Hamlet, or more German than Faust? Yet they have all entered into the composition of all of us, they have all helped – as is the function of such figures – to explain European man to himself. So we may be tempted to classify Shakespeare and Goethe as European men, simply because they have each created a European myth-hero. Yet the play of *Hamlet* and the drama of *Faust* are only parts of the structures built by Shakespeare and Goethe: parts which would be very much diminished if each were the only work of its author. What gives Shakespeare and Goethe their status is not any one masterpiece, but the total work of a lifetime. And on the other hand Cervantes is, for those of us who are not learned in Spanish literature, the man of one book: however great the book, this is not enough to give Cervantes a place with Dante, Shakespeare and Goethe. *Don Quixote* is unquestionably among that select number of books that satisfy the test of 'European literature': that is to say, books without a knowledge of which – in the sense of having not only read, but assimilated – no

man of European race can be truly educated. But we cannot say that it is necessary for the educated European to know Cervantes, in the sense in which we can say that the educated European must know Dante, Shakespeare and Goethe. As a man of one book, Cervantes is for us entirely in that book; he is, so to speak, Don Quixote understanding himself. What part of the work of Dante, Shakespeare or Goethe can we isolate and say that it gives us the essential Dante, Shakespeare or Goethe? It is not to belittle Cervantes simply to say that we cannot know him, as we can know these three other men. And I am not committing the error of separating the men from their writings, and idolising the men, though that, especially in the case of Goethe, where we have so much documentation about the man, as well as the immense body of his own work, is dangerously easy to do. I am speaking of the men as they exist in their writings, in the three worlds which they have created to remain forever part of the European experience.

13 I would say first, as something immediately obvious, that in the work of these three men we find three common characteristics: *Abundance, Amplitude,* and *Unity*. Abundance: they all wrote a good deal, and nothing that any of them wrote is negligible. By [214] Amplitude, I mean that each had a very wide range of interest, sympathy and understanding. There is a variety of interests, there is universal curiosity and a more comprehensive capacity than that of most men. Other men have had versatile talent, other men have had restless curiosity: what characterises the variety of interests and the curiosity of men like Dante, Shakespeare and Goethe is the fundamental Unity. This unity is hard to define, except by saying that what each of them gives us is Life itself, the World seen from a particular point of view of a particular European age and a particular man in that age.

14 I have no need to dilate upon the diversity of the interests and activities of Dante and Goethe. Shakespeare, it is true, confined himself, or was confined by circumstance, to the medium of the theatre; but when we consider the immense range of theme and character within that framework, the immense variety and development of his technique, his continuous attack on new problems, we must acknowledge at least that in this amplitude and abundance Shakespeare stands apart even from those few writers for the theatre who as dramatists and poets are his equals. As to Unity, I think that the unity of Dante's political, theological, moral and poetic aims is too evident to need demonstration. I would assert, from my own experience, that the unity of Shakespeare's work is such that you not only cannot understand the later plays unless you know the early plays: you cannot understand the early plays without knowing

the late ones. It is not so easy to detect the unity in Goethe's work. For one thing, it is more bewilderingly miscellaneous than that of either of the other men; for another thing, I must confess that there is so much of this vast work that I do not know, or know only superficially, that I am far from being the advocate best qualified to plead the case. I will say only then, that I believe sincerely that the better I knew his work – every volume of the most voluminous edition – the more certain I should be of its unity. The test is this: does every part of a man's work help us to understand the rest?

15 I shall risk affirming this belief at the point at which it is most likely to be questioned. For most of my life I had taken it for granted that Goethe's scientific theories – his speculations about the plant-type, about mineralogy and about colour – were no more than the amiable eccentricities of a man of abounding curiosity who had strayed into regions for which he was not equipped. Even now, I have made no attempt to read his writings on these [215] subjects. It was, first, that the unanimity of ridicule and the ease with which the learned in these matters appear to dismiss Goethe's views, impelled me to wonder whether Goethe may not have been right, or at least whether his critics might not be wrong. Then, only a few years ago I came upon a book in which Goethe's views were actually defended: *Man or Matter*, by Dr Ernst Lehrs. It is true that Dr Lehrs is a disciple of Rudolph Steiner, and I believe that Rudolph Steiner's science is considered very unorthodox; but that is not my affair. What Dr Lehrs did for me was to suggest that Goethe's scientific views somehow fitted with his imaginative work, that the same insight was struggling for expression in both, and that it is not reasonable to dismiss as utter nonsense in the field of scientific enquiry, what we accept as inspired wisdom in poetry. I shall return to this point presently in another context: but, at the risk of exposing myself to ridicule, I will say that in consequence of what Dr Lehrs has written about Goethe's science, I think I understand parts of *Faust*, such as the opening scene of Part II, better than before; and I now believe that Part II is a greater work than Part I – the contrary of what I had always been told by those more learned than myself.

16 It is at least certain that we must, in endeavouring to understand such men as the three I am talking about, try to enter into all of their interests. Literary criticism is an activity which must constantly define its own boundaries; also, it must constantly be going beyond them: the one invariable rule is, that when the literary critic exceeds his frontiers, he should do so in full consciousness of what he is doing. We cannot get very far with Dante, or Shakespeare, or Goethe, without touching upon theology, and philosophy, and ethics, and politics; and in the case

of Goethe penetrating, in a clandestine way and without 'legitimation papers', into the forbidden territory of science.

17 My argument or pleading up to this point has been purely negative. I have merely affirmed that in the work of Dante, Shakespeare and Goethe you find Abundance, Amplitude and Unity. Abundance and Amplitude patently, and Unity if you take the trouble to look for it. Having postulated that Dante, Shakespeare and Goethe were three great Europeans, it seems to follow that these characteristics must be found together in any other author before we can award him the same rank. It is possible, however, that an author might illustrate Abundance, Amplitude and Unity and yet fail to be a great European. I think there is a further positive [216] character to be considered. But before approaching the final problem, there is another term to be discussed: *Universality*.

18 So far as we can judge from our three exemplars, the European writer is no less emphatically a man of his own country, race and language than any of those lesser authors whose appeal is exclusively, or with few exceptions, to their own compatriots. One may even say that Dante, Shakespeare and Goethe are not only very Italian, very English, very German, but are also representative each of the particular region in which he was born. It is obvious, of course, that the sense in which they are local is no limitation of their appeal, though there is much about each to which only his fellow-countrymen can respond. They are local because of their concreteness: to be human is to belong to a particular region of the earth, and men of such genius are more conscious than other human beings. The European who belonged to no one country would be an abstract man – a blank face speaking every language with neither a native nor a foreign accent. And the poet is the least abstract of men, because he is the most bound by his own language: he cannot even afford to know another language equally well, because it is, for the poet, a lifetime's work to explore the resources of his own. The way in which he is attached to, dependent upon, and representative of his own people, is not, I should add, to be identified with patriotism (a conscious response to particular circumstances) though it be the kind of attachment out of which the noblest patriotism may spring. It is a kind of attachment which may even be in sharp contrast with the patriotic sentiment of many of the poet's compatriots.

19 Next, the European poet is not necessarily a poet whose work is easier to translate into another language than that of poets whose work has significance only to their fellow-countrymen. His work is more translatable, only in this way: that whereas in the translating of such a poet as Shakespeare, into another language, just as much of the original

significance is lost, as is lost when we translate a lesser poet, there is also more saved – for more was there. What can be translated? A story, a dramatic plot, the impression of a living character in action, an image, a proposition. What cannot be translated is the incantation, the music of the words, and that part of the meaning which is in the music. But here again, we have not got to the bottom of the matter; we have only attempted to indicate what makes a poet translatable, and not put our finger on the reason why Dante, Shakespeare and Goethe [217] can be said to belong, as we cannot with equal confidence say of any other poets, not only to their fellow-countrymen but to all Europeans.

20 We can, I think, accept without much difficulty the apparent paradox that the European poet is at the same time no less, but in a way rather more positively a man of his particular race, country, and local culture than is the poet appreciable only by his compatriots. We can at one and the same time feel that such a poet, to whatever nation he belongs, is our compatriot, and yet that he is a representative, one of the greatest representatives, of his own people. Such a man can help his fellow-countrymen to understand themselves, and help other people to understand, and to accept them. But the question of the way in which he is representative of his own age is somewhat more difficult. In what way is a man representative of his own age, and yet of permanent importance – not because of his 'representative' character, but in himself alone – for all subsequent ages?

21 As we should expect from the foregoing, just as a man can be a great poet, without being a 'European' poet, just as he can be representative of his people, and have interest for other peoples only in that capacity, so a man can be representative of his own time and be of importance to other times only as a help towards the understanding of his own age. But, as I tried to say earlier, we are interested in Dante, Shakespeare and Goethe not only in relation to their own country, language and race, but timelessly and directly: every educated European must ask the question, irrespective of his language, his citizenship, his heredity, and the age into which he was born, 'what have Dante, and Shakespeare and Goethe to say directly to me – and how shall I answer them?' It is this direct confrontation that is of ultimate importance. Now, if we take the word literally, the really 'representative' man of a period, like the representative man of a nation, is a man who is neither too big nor too small. I do not mean that he is *l'homme moyen sensuel*. But a man who was insignificant could only represent an insignificant period – and no period in history is so negligible as that; whereas the very exceptionality of a truly great man must make us suspect that he is not altogether 'representative'. I think that

if we could take our three poets as wholly representative of their ages, we should find that they were each limited by his age in a way in which they are not limited. In short, we take these men as representative, only to find them unrepresentative. [218] For a man can be unrepresentative, not only by being behind or ahead of his age, but by being above it. Certainly, we must not assume that such men as these share all the ideas of their age. They share the problems, they share the language in which the problems are discussed – but they may repudiate all the current solutions. And even when they lead a social or a public life, they have also more solitude than the majority of men. Their representative character, if representative they be, must be something that we feel but cannot altogether formulate.

22 There is a great deal we do not know about Dante the man, there is very little we do know about Shakespeare. About the life of Goethe a great deal is known. I am, I confess, not one of those who know very much. But the more I have learnt about Goethe, from his own work and from commentaries on it, the less I find it possible to identify him with his age. I find him sometimes in complete opposition to his age, so complete perhaps as to have been greatly misunderstood. He seems to me to have lived more fully and consciously on several levels than most other men. The Privy Councillor, the lion of a small court, the collector of prints, drawings and intaglios, was also the man who lay awake in anguish in Weimar, because an earthquake was taking place in Messina. After reading Dr Lehrs's book, to which I have alluded, and then re-reading certain passages of *Faust*, it came to me that 'Nature' to Wordsworth and to Goethe meant much the same thing, that it meant something which they had experienced – and which *I* had not experienced – and that they were both trying to express something that, even for men so exceptionally endowed with the gift of speech, was ultimately ineffable. Not so very long ago I was sent a postcard reproduction of a portrait of William Blake: it was a well-known drawing, with which I was quite familiar. But I happened to set it for a moment on my mantelpiece, beside the portrait of Goethe, and I thought I noticed a similar expression in their eyes. Only, Blake looked other-worldly: Goethe looked, at the moment when the artist had caught him, equally at home in both worlds. Blake also rejected some of the dominant opinions of his age. You see that I cannot get away from the Farbenlehre and the Ur-Pflanze. Is it simply a question of who was right, Goethe or the scientists? Or is it possible that Goethe was wrong only in thinking the scientists wrong, and the scientists wrong only in thinking Goethe wrong? Is it not possible that Goethe, without wholly knowing what he was doing, was to assert the claims of a [219] different type of consciousness from that which was to

dominate the nineteenth and twentieth centuries? If so, then Goethe is about as unrepresentative of his Age as a man of genius can be. And perhaps the time has come when we can say that there is something in favour of being able to see the universe as Goethe saw it, rather than as the scientists have seen it: now that the 'living garment of God' has become somewhat tattered from the results of scientific manipulation.

23 Certainly Goethe was of his age. We can hardly ignore or treat as accidental, the fact that Dante, Shakespeare and Goethe should have come to stand, each for a period in modern European history, in so far as a poet can occupy that role; and we remember Goethe's own words about the man and the moment. But we must remember, for one thing, that we tend to think of an Age in terms of the man whom we take as representative of it, and forget that equally a part of the man's significance may be his battle with his Age. I have merely been trying to introduce some cautious reservations into our use of the term 'representative', dangerous when applied to such men. The man who is a 'representative' of his people may be the severest critic of his people and an outcast from it; the man who is 'representative' of his time may be in opposition to the most widely-accepted beliefs of his time.

24 So far I have been engaged, first in recognising certain qualities in default of which we cannot admit a poet to this select company; and then in defining the sense in which 'representativeness', either of a place and a language, or of an age, may be considered characteristic. But we have yet to ask: what is the quality which survives translation? which transcends place and time, and is capable of arousing a direct response as of man to man, in readers of any place and any time? It must be also something which can be present in varying degrees – for obviously Dante, Shakespeare and Goethe are not the only 'European' poets. But it must be something capable of recognition by a great diversity of men: for the ultimate test of such a poet, as I have said at the beginning, is that no European who is quite ignorant of his work can be called educated – whether the poet's language is his own, or whether he has learnt that language by painful study, or whether he can only read a translation. For while complete ignorance of the language very narrowly limits one's appreciation of such a poet, it is no excuse whatever for complete ignorance of his work.

25 I am afraid that the word I am about to pronounce will strike [220] many an ear as an anticlimax to this exordium, for it is simply the word *Wisdom*. There is no word, however, more impossible to define, and no word more difficult to understand. To understand what Wisdom is, is to be wise oneself: and I have only the degree of understanding of Wisdom,

that can be attained by a man who knows that he is not wise, yet has reason to believe that he is wiser than he was twenty years ago. I say twenty years ago, because I am under the distressing necessity of quoting a sentence I printed in 1933. It is this:

> Of Goethe perhaps it is truer to say that he dabbled in both philosophy and poetry and made no great success of either; his true role was that of the man of the world and sage, a La Rochefoucauld, a La Bruyère, a Vauvenargues.

26 I have never re-read the passage in which this sentence is buried: I have always found the re-reading of my own prose writings too painful a task. I discovered this quotation not so very long ago in Mr Michael Hamburger's introduction to his edition and translation of the text of Hölderlin's poems: Mr Hamburger is my authority for attributing this sentence to myself. He quoted it, I need hardly say, with disapproval. It is an interesting sentence: interesting because it enunciates so many errors in so few words together with one truth: that Goethe was a sage. But the error to which I particularly wish to call attention, is the identification of wisdom with worldly wisdom. It does not diminish my admiration for La Rochefoucauld, to say that the wisdom of a 'man of the world' is a very limited wisdom indeed; but now, at least, I can no longer confound the two wisdoms. There is worldly wisdom, and there is spiritual wisdom. Wisdom which is merely the former may turn out in the end to be folly, if it ignores, or aspires to judge, those things which are beyond its understanding; wisdom which is purely spiritual wisdom may be of no help in affairs of this world. So I think that generally we mean, when we speak of a man as 'wise' and where the context does not show that we mean one kind of wisdom rather than another, that such a man has wisdom of a greater range than other men. And this we can say of Goethe. It may be that there are areas of wisdom that he did not penetrate: but I am more interested in trying to understand the wisdom he possessed, than in defining its limitations. When a man is a good deal wiser than oneself, one does not complain that he is no wiser than he is.

27 There may be observed another error in the sentence which I [221] quoted against myself, beyond the one I have just pointed out. It seems to suggest that wisdom is something expressible in wise sayings, aphorisms and maxims; and that the sum of such maxims and sayings, including those which a man has thought but never communicated, constitute his 'wisdom'. These may be tokens of wisdom, certainly; and to study the sayings of a sage can contribute towards the development of any wisdom of which the reader is capable. But wisdom is greater than any sum of

wise sayings, and Wisdom herself is greater than the actualisation of wisdom in any human soul.

> Wisdom shall praise herself,
> And shall glory in the midst of her people.
> In the congregation of the Most High shall she open her mouth,
> And triumph before His power.
>
> Ecclus. xxiii.

28 The wisdom of a human being resides as much in silence as in speech: and, says Philotheus of Sinai, 'men with a silent mind are very rarely found.'[1] Wisdom is a native gift of intuition, ripened and given application by experience, for understanding the nature of things, certainly of living things, most certainly of the human heart. In some men it may appear fitfully and occasionally, or once in a lifetime, in the rapture of a single experience beatific or awful: in a man like Goethe it appears to have been constant, steady and serene. But the wise man, in contrast to the merely worldly-wise on the one hand, and the man of some intense vision of the heights or the depths on the other, is one whose wisdom springs from spiritual sources, who has profited by experience to arrive at understanding, and who has acquired the charity that comes from understanding human beings in all their variety of temperament, character and circumstance. Such men hold the most diverse beliefs; they may even hold some tenets which we find abhorrent; but it is part of our own pursuit of wisdom, to try to understand them.

29 I believe then, that it is finally by virtue of the wisdom informing his work, that an author enters this category of 'great Europeans'; by virtue of his wisdom that he is the common countryman of all of us. He is not necessarily easy to understand; as I have said, he may present as many difficulties of interpretation as any other. But [222] the foreigner who has been reading Dante or Shakespeare or Goethe in translation, or who has been handicapped by imperfect knowledge of the language in reading the original, does not ask, as he may ask about many of our great poets, 'what is it that Italians, or Englishmen, or Germans, find to admire in this author?' I am far from suggesting that the wisdom of these poets is something distinct from the poetry, and that what the foreigner enjoys is the former without the latter. The wisdom is an essential element in making the poetry; and it is necessary to apprehend it as poetry in order to profit by it as wisdom. The foreign reader, in absorbing the wisdom, is being affected by the poetry as well. For it is the wisdom of poetry,

---

1. It is relevant to mention an essay by Josef Pieper: *Ueber das Schweigen Goethes* (Kösel-Verlag, München).

which would not be communicated at all, if it were not experienced by the reader as poetry.

30 There arises, at this point, a question which cannot be left unanswered: partly because I have raised it myself, in a somewhat different form, many years ago, and am no longer satisfied with my own account of it; and partly because it has recently been raised by a philosophical critic for whose opinions I have great respect, Professor Erich Heller of Cardiff. I refer to a recent book, *The Disinherited Mind*,[1] and particularly to a chapter on Rilke and Nietzsche. Professor Heller criticises, severely but without asperity, certain pronouncements of my own on *Thought and Belief in Poetry*, made many years ago. Some of what I said then I would not now defend, and some I should now be inclined to qualify or put differently: but with regard to other of my assertions, I am not too downcast by Professor Heller's censure, inasmuch as, by Dr Heller's own admission, I share these errors with Goethe himself. The question is as to the place of 'ideas' in poetry, and as to any 'philosophy' or system of beliefs held by the poet. Does the poet hold an 'idea' in the same way that a philosopher holds it; and when he expresses a particular 'philosophy' in his poetry, should he be expected to believe this philosophy, or may he legitimately treat it merely as suitable for a poem? And furthermore, is the reader's acceptance of the same philosophy a necessary condition for his full appreciation of the poem?

31 Now in so far as anything I have written on the subject in the past says or suggests that the poet need not believe a philosophical idea which he has chosen to embody in his verse, Professor Heller is, no doubt, quite right in contradicting me. For [223] such a suggestion would appear to be a justification of insincerity, and would annihilate all poetic values except those of technical accomplishment. To suggest that Lucretius deliberately chose to exploit for poetic purposes a cosmology which he thought to be false, or that Dante did not believe the philosophy drawn from Aristotle and the scholastics, which gave him the material for several fine cantos in the *Purgatorio*, would be to condemn the poems they wrote. But I think that Professor Heller oversimplifies the problem by generalising from the particular case that he is arguing: he is in this essay concerned to show that Rilke was not only deeply influenced by Nietzsche in his youth, but that the view of life revealed in Rilke's most mature poems is a kind of poetic equivalent of the philosophy of Nietzsche. And I am quite prepared to admit that in the case of the relation of Rilke to Nietzsche, Dr Heller makes out a very good case.

1. Published by Bowes & Bowes, Cambridge. A German edition has been published under the title of *Enterbter Geist* (Suhrkamp-Verlag).

32 To explore the problem of poetic belief versus philosophic belief, and the nature of the attitude (whether of belief or of *Annahme*) of the poet towards a philosophic system, would not only take us very far but would take us a long way from my subject: what is however pertinent to our investigation is the question of the belief called for from the reader of a poem. Dr Heller seems to me to imply that the reader himself must accept the philosophy of the poet, if he is to appreciate the poetry. It is, apparently, on this ground that Dr Heller censures the judgement of a brilliant critic, Hans Egon Holthusen, about Rilke. 'If the ideas (of Rilke) were all humbug,' says Dr Heller, 'or if, as Herr Holthusen says in his book about Rilke,[1] they were all wrong, in the sense of contradicting [224] that "intuitive logic" which tells us what is a true and what is a false picture of man, then the poetry would have little chance of being what he believes it to be: great poetry.'

33 Dr Heller goes so far as to say: 'there is no poetry left if we feel that the "ideas" are false to the point of being a distortion of the true image of man.' We are led, it seems, to this strange conclusion: that Herr Holthusen is suffering from a delusion when he imagines that he enjoys the poetry of Rilke, because for him there can be no poetry left. And on the other hand, Dr Heller himself is driven to accept an intolerable situation: that of a 'rift which has made it impossible for most Christians not to feel, or at least not to feel also as true many "truths" which are incompatible with the truth of their faith'. Which not only *appear* incompatible, mind you, but which *are* incompatible! But if we feel the truth of 'incompatible truths',

---

1. *Rilke*: by H. E. Holthusen. Bowes & Bowes, Cambridge, in an excellent series (*Studies in Modern European Literature and Thought*) edited by Dr Heller himself. Dr Heller does not quote, but the following paragraph from Herr Holthusen's essay must be the origin of his comment:

> Once abstracted from the concrete liveliness of their metaphorical language, from their aesthetic context, and regarded as philosophical doctrine, Rilke's 'ideas' are wrong. And this assertion is valid if we assume that there is an objectively valid criterion of distinction between 'right' and 'wrong' ideas, that there is a kind of intuitive logic governing groups of ideas in their agreement with the being of man, that, in brief, there exists an intellectual equilibrium enabling us to distinguish right ideas from wrong ones. The idea of 'my own death' is wrong because death cannot be conquered by monistic feeling; for death must always remain wholly other than ourselves, a conquest through that which is alien to us, an invasion of human reality by a reality that is more than human. The idea of love that abdicates from Possession is wrong: so is the idea of a glorification of the world: of creation without a creator, of immanence without transcendence: the metamorphosis of all transcendent realities into an imminent all-and-one: the dissolving of God into inwardness: the dissolving of His person into the most intense feeling: the naming of the Divine in terms of feeling – indeed the whole vocabulary of the 'unsayable' and 'invisible'. All these ideas are as wrong as the prophetic theses, of Nietzsche – the doctrine of the Eternal Recurrence, of the Superman – or 'satanism' of Baudelaire.

is not the feeling of truth wholly illusory? I find myself in agreement with Herr Holthusen: and indeed, if he is wrong and Dr Heller is right, then I can only enjoy the poetry of Rilke under a misunderstanding.

34 What I am aiming at, by a devious route, is the establishment of a distinction between the *philosophy* of a poet and his *wisdom*. Unless it is possible to draw such a distinction, then I am condemned to remain blind to the merits of some of the greatest poets. But first I must venture a theory of the relation between acceptance of the philosophy and enjoyment of the poetry.

35 It is best, I think, to keep in mind not the philosophy of a poet – for that may vary with his development – but the philosophy of what can be called a philosophical poem. There are three obvious examples: the *Bhagavadgita*, *De rerum naturae* of Lucretius, and the *Divine Comedy* of Dante. And the third of these has peculiar advantages for our purposes in that it is based upon theological doctrine which belongs to the Western World and which is still believed by a great many people. These three poems represent three views of the world in as sharp contradiction of each other as possible. Ignoring the other *differentiae* – the fact that the *Bhagavadgita* is the most remote from me in language and in culture, and that Dante is nearer to me in time than Lucretius, am I called upon to admit that as a Christian I can understand Dante's poem better than the others, though I ought to be able to understand it still better if I was a Roman Catholic? It seems to me that what I do, [225] when I approach a great poem such as the *Holy Song* of the Indian epic, or the poem of Lucretius, is not only, in Coleridge's words, to suspend my disbelief, but to try to put myself in the position of a believer. But this is only one of the two movements of my critical activity: the second movement is to detach myself again and to regard the poem from outside the belief. If the poem is remote from my own beliefs, then the effort of which I am the more conscious is the effort of identification: if the poem is very close to my own beliefs, the effort of which I am more conscious is the effort of detachment. With the *Divine Comedy*, I find a kind of equilibrium: it is rather with the poetic parts of the Bible, the prophets and most of all the Gospels, that I find the effort of detachment – that is, the effort to appreciate 'the Bible as literature' – and in the translations of our Authorised Version and of Martin Luther the Bible is a part of both our literatures – there, is the effort of detachment most difficult. With the *Duinese Elegies*, I admit, I find myself at the opposite extreme: I could be content to enjoy the verbal beauty, to be moved by the music of the verse; and I have to force myself to try to enter into thought which is for me both difficult and uncongenial.

36 You will observe that in this systole and diastole, this movement to and fro, of approach and withdrawal, or identification and distinction, I have been careful to avoid the terms *form* and *content*. The notion of appreciation of form without content, or of content ignoring form, is an illusion: if we ignore the content of a poem, we fail to appreciate the form; if we ignore the form, we have not grasped the content – for the meaning of a poem exists in the words of the poem and in those words only. Nor does what I have been talking about exhaust the content. We have not, in what I have just been saying, been concerned with the whole of the content: only with the content as philosophical system, as 'ideas' which can be formulated in other words, as a system of ideas to which there is always some possible alternative system for the reason to accept. This philosophical system must be tenable: a poem arising out of a religion which struck us as wholly vile, or out of a philosophy which seemed to us pure nonsense, simply would not appear to be a poem at all. Otherwise, when two readers of equal intelligence and sensibility approach a great poem, the one from the starting point of belief in the philosophy of the author, and the other from the starting point of some different philosophy, they should tend towards a point, which they may never quite reach, at [226] which the two appreciations correspond. Thus it is conceivable that Professor Heller and Herr Holthusen might almost arrive at the point of sharing their appreciation of Rilke.

37 I entered upon this analysis not for its own sake, but in order to reach the conclusion that there is something more in the greatest poetry than 'ideas' of a kind that we must either accept or reject, expressed in a form which makes the whole a work of art. Whether the 'philosophy' or the religious faith of Dante or Shakespeare or Goethe is acceptable to us or not (and indeed, with Shakespeare, the question of what his beliefs were has never been finally settled) there is the Wisdom that we can all accept. It is precisely for the sake of learning Wisdom that we must take the trouble to frequent these men; it is because they are wise men that we should try, if we find one of them uncongenial, to overcome our aversion or indifference. Of revealed religions, and of philosophical systems, we must believe that one is right and the others wrong. But wisdom is λόγος ζυνός, the same for all men everywhere. If it were not so, what profit could a European gain from the Upanishads, or the Buddhist Nikayas? Only some intellectual exercise, the satisfaction of a curiosity, or an interesting sensation like that of tasting some exotic oriental dish. I have said that Wisdom cannot really be defined. What is the Wisdom of Goethe? As I have suggested, Goethe's sayings, in prose or in verse, are merely illustrations of his wisdom. The best evidence of the wisdom

of a great writer, is the testimony of those who can say, after a long acquaintance with his works, 'I feel a wiser man because of the time that I have spent with him.' For wisdom is communicated on a deeper level than that of logical propositions; all language is inadequate, but probably the language of poetry is the language most capable of communicating wisdom. The wisdom of a great poet is concealed in his work; but in becoming aware of it we become ourselves more wise. That Goethe was one of the wisest of men I have long admitted; that he was a great lyric poet I have long since come to recognise; but that the wisdom and the poetry are inseparable, in poets of the highest rank, is something I have only come to perceive in becoming a little wiser myself. Thus I return to gaze at the features of the Goethe on my mantelpiece. I have named him and two others as the three poets who are incontestably great Europeans. But I should not like to close without reminding you that I think of these men as set apart, not in kind, but in degree; that there have been others, even within living memory, who [227] though of lower rank are of the same company; and that one measure of the survival of our European culture in the future, will be the ability of European peoples to continue to produce such poets. And if the time comes when the term 'European literature' ceases to have any meaning, then the literature of each of our nations and languages will wither away and perish also.

Variants from 1955:

Subtitle Address by T. S. Eliot | Hamburg, 1955

1   [No. fn. 2.]
    the picture] he
    its companions;] his mantelpiece companions,

2   say here] say today

[Between end of para. 2 and 'When I came, however,' in para. 3:]   Now, having presented this portrait of Goethe to your imagination, let me make my beginning proper. The honour of the Hanseatic Goethe Prize is a great one. It is not an honour to which any man of letters could be indifferent; but I confess that my gratification on receiving the announcement was mingled with apprehension and alarm: and that not solely for the obvious reason that many people would consider me an unworthy recipient of the Prize. I had for some years cherished the intention of making my peace with Goethe; but what I had in mind was a long period of reading and re-reading, of living with Goethe to see what would come of it; and here I was, so to speak, pointing a pistol at my own head by accepting the Goethe Prize. It is true that I was given every kindness and latitude, when, owing to illness, I saw no prospect of serious work for several months. I was even told that my address on this occasion need not be concerned with Goethe: so, if it is essentially about Goethe, you should know that I myself wished it to be so.

3   this essay] this hour

[Between 'in turn;' and 'come to agree':] I can only ask your patience until the end, in the hope that their unity may reveal itself. In that event you may also

5 diminished importance] very diminished importance
nineteenth century] Nineteenth Century

6 [Between 'frivolity' and 'to spend':] , on such an occasion as this,
my present attitude] this discourse
of course] primary [*for* primarily]
of work] of different works

10 [Between 'distinction.' and 'All we can do':] There is no borderline: there can be no comprehensive unanimity

11 their greatness as Europeans] their greatness

12 parts of] a part of
parts] a part
masterpiece, but] masterpiece, but,
on the other hand] , on the other hand,
without a knowledge of which] books without a knowledge of which
[Between 'understanding himself.' and 'It is not to belittle':] Dante cannot be in that way identified with even the whole of the Divine Comedy, or Shakespeare with any of his plays; and what part of Goethe's work can we isolate to say that it gives us the essential Goethe?

14 range of theme] range of themes
the later plays] the late plays
[Between 'the late ones.' and 'It is not so easy':] At each transit of the cycle you can understand each play better.

15 or at least whether] or at least
fitted with] fitted in with

17 [Between ' this point has' and 'been purely':] , you must observe,

19 a proposition] proposition

20 rather more positively] rather more, positively
appreciable only by] appreciable to
his own people] his own people also

22 About the life of Goethe a great deal is known] A great deal is known about the life of Goethe
commentaries on] expositions of
re-reading] re-read

23 [After 'beliefs of his time.':] When we call one of these men 'representative' we must take care not to be led astray by the word.

25 reason to believe] some faith

26 have never] never
so few words together with one truth: that Goethe was a sage.] in so few words. But the error] The error
in defining] to define

27 There may be observed] You may have observed
including] including, if you like,

28 The wisdom of] But wisdom in
being] being,
intense vision] intense but narrow vision
29 in making the poetry] in making the poetry poetry
31 Rilke's most mature poems] his most mature poems

Rudyard Kipling[1]

OPAP, 228–51.

Originally publ. as an introductory essay to *A Choice of Kipling's Verse* made by T. S. Eliot (11 Dec. 1941), 5–36. Signed 'T. S. Eliot' and dated '*26th September* 1941': Gallup B39. A condensed version of this was publ. in *Harper's*, 185. 2 (July 1942), [149]-57: Gallup C478.

1 There are several reasons for our not knowing Kipling's poems so well as we think we do. When a man is primarily known as a writer of prose fiction we are inclined – and usually, I think, justly – to regard his verse as a by-product. I am, I confess, always doubtful whether any man can so divide himself as to be able to make the most of two such very different forms of expression as poetry and imaginative prose. If I make an exception in the case of Kipling, it is not because I think he succeeded in making the division successfully, but because I think that, for reasons which it will be partly the purpose of this essay to put forward, his verse and his prose are inseparable; that we must finally judge him, not separately as a poet and as a writer of prose fiction, but as the inventor of a mixed form. So a knowledge of his prose is essential to the understanding of his verse, and a knowledge of his verse is essential to the understanding of his prose. In so far therefore as I concern myself here with his verse by itself, it is only with the aim of restoring it to its place afterwards and seeing the total work more clearly. In most studies of Kipling that I have read, the writers seem to me to have treated the verse as secondary, and in so doing to have evaded the question – which is, nevertheless, a question that everyone asks – whether Kipling's verse really is poetry; and, if not, what it is.

2 The starting point for Kipling's verse is the motive of the ballad-maker; and the modern ballad is a type of verse for the appreciation of which we are not provided with the proper critical tools. We are therefore inclined to dismiss the poems, by reference to poetic criteria which do not apply. It must therefore be our task to understand the type to which they belong,

---

1. The introduction to *A Choice of Kipling's Verse*, published by Faber & Faber in association with Methuen and Macmillan, in 1941, also in America by Doubleday.

before attempting to value them: we must consider what Kipling was trying to do [229] and what he was not trying to do. The task is the opposite of that with which we are ordinarily faced when attempting to defend contemporary verse. We expect to have to defend a poet against the charge of obscurity: we have to defend Kipling against the charge of excessive lucidity. We expect a poet to be reproached for lack of respect for the intelligence of the common man, or even for deliberately flouting the intelligence of the common man: we have to defend Kipling against the charge of being a 'journalist' appealing only to the commonest collective emotions. We expect a poet to be ridiculed because his verse does not appear to scan: we must defend Kipling against the charge of writing jingles. In short, people are exasperated by poetry which they do not understand, and contemptuous of poetry which they understand without effort; just as an audience is offended by a speaker who talks over its head, and by a speaker whom it suspects of talking down to it.

3 A further obstacle to the appreciation of many of Kipling's poems is their topicality, their occasional character, and their political associations. People are often inclined to disparage poetry which appears to have no bearing on the situation of to-day; but they are always inclined to ignore that which appears to bear only on the situation of yesterday. A political association may help to give poetry immediate attention: it is in spite of this association that the poetry will be read, if it is read, to-morrow. Poetry is condemned as 'political' when we disagree with the politics; and the majority of readers do not want either imperialism or socialism in verse. But the question is not what is ephemeral, but what is permanent: a poet who appears to be wholly out of touch with his age may still have something very important to say to it; and a poet who has treated problems of his time will not necessarily go out of date. Arnold's *Stanzas from the Grande Chartreuse* voice a moment of historic doubt, recorded by its most representative mind, a moment which has passed, which most of us have gone beyond in one direction or another: but it represents that moment forever.

4 We have therefore to try to find the permanent in Kipling's verse: but this is not simply to dissociate form from content. We must consider the content itself, the social and political attitude in its development; and, making an effort to detach ourselves from the assumptions of our own generation, enquire whether there is something more in Kipling than is expressed by Beerbohm's caricature of the Bank Holiday cornet virtuoso on the spree.

[230] I

5 In my selection of Kipling's verse I have found no place for the earliest published: to be precise, the selection begins from page 81 of the Collected Edition. The earlier work is juvenilia, but yet is work which, having been published in its time and had a success in its time, is essential reading for a full understanding of Kipling's progress. Most of it is what it was intended to be, light reading in an English newspaper in India: it exhibits that same precocious knowingness about the more superficial level of human weakness that is both effective and irritating in some of his early stories of India. It is obviously the work of a clever young man who might go far in journalism, but neither in feeling nor in rhythm does most of it give any hint that the author would ever write a memorable poem. It is unnecessary to say that it is not poetry: what is surprising and interesting is that it does not pretend to be poetry, that it is not the work of a youth whom anyone would suspect of any aspiration to write poetry. That he is gifted, that he is worth watching, is obvious when you know how young he is: but the gift appears to be only for the ephemeral, and the writer appears to aim at nothing higher.

6 There were, however, literary influences in the background. We have among his verse a pastiche of *Atalanta in Calydon* made for his own immediate purposes; we remember also that McIntosh Jellaluddin (who is introduced as falling over a camel foal while reciting *The Song of the Bower*) on one occasion recited the whole of *Atalanta* beating time with a bedstead leg. There was Kipling's family connection with Pre-Raphaelite society; and Kipling's debt to Swinburne is considerable. It is never an imitation: the vocabulary is different, the content is different, the rhythms are different. There is one early monologue which is much more closely imitated from Browning than anything is imitated from Swinburne: but it is in two poems extremely unlike Browning's in style – *McAndrew's Hymn* and *The 'Mary Gloster'* – that Browning's influence is most visible. Why is the influence of Swinburne and Browning so different from what you would expect? It is due, I think, to a difference of motive: what they wrote they intended to be poetry; Kipling was not trying to write poetry at all.

7 There have been many writers of verse who have not aimed at writing poetry: with the exception of a few writers of humorous verse, they are mostly quickly forgotten. The difference is that they [231] never did write poetry. Kipling does write poetry, but that is not what he is setting out to do. It is this peculiarity of intention that I have in mind in calling Kipling a 'ballad-writer' and it will take some time to make clear what I mean by that. For I am extending and also somewhat limiting the meaning of

the word 'ballad'. It is true that there is an unbroken thread of meaning connecting the various kinds of verse to which the term 'ballad' has been applied. In the narrative Border Ballad, the intention is to tell a story in what, at that stage of literature, is the natural form for a story which is intended to arouse emotion. The poetry of it is incidental and to some extent unconscious; the form is the short rhymed stanza. The attention of the reader is concentrated on the story and the characters; and the ballad must have a meaning immediately apprehensible by its auditors. Repeated hearings may confirm the first impressions, may repeat the effect, but full understanding should be conveyed at one hearing. The metrical form must be of a simple kind which will not call attention to itself, but repetitions and refrains may contribute an incantatory effect. There should be no metrical complications corresponding to subtleties of feeling that cannot be immediately responded to. At another stage of culture – as in Anglo-Saxon and in the elaborate forms of Welsh – poetry develops a conscious virtuosity, requiring a virtuosity of appreciation on the part of the audience: the forms impose upon the bard restrictions and obstacles in overcoming which he exhibits his skill. It must be remembered that this sophistication is not only present in what we call 'modern' literature or in the later stages of development of classical literatures such as those of Latin, Greek, Sanskrit, Persian, or Chinese: it is a stage sometimes reached in the poetry of peoples of lower cultures. And on the other hand, ballad verse is not simply a stage in historical development: the ballad persists and develops in its own way, and corresponds to a permanent level of enjoyment in literature. There is always a potential public for the ballad: but the social conditions of modern society make it difficult for the good ballad to be written. It is perhaps more difficult now than it was at the time when *Barrack Room Ballads* were written: for Kipling had at least the inspiration and refreshment of the living music-hall.

8 In order to produce the contemporary ballad, it is of no particular help to hold advanced social views, or to believe that the literature of the future must be 'popular' literature. The ballad [232] must be written for its own sake and for its own purposes. It would be a mistake, also, and a supercilious kind of mistake, to suppose that the audience for balladry consists of factory workers, mill hands, miners and agricultural labourers. It does contain people from these categories, but the composition of this audience has, I suspect, no relation to any social and economic stratification of society. The audience for the more highly developed, even for the more esoteric kinds of poetry is recruited from every level: often the uneducated find them easier to accept than do the half-educated. On the other hand, the audience for the ballad includes many who are,

according to the rules, highly educated; it includes many of the powerful, the learned, the highly specialised, the inheritors of prosperity. I do not mean to suggest that the two audiences ought to be, or must be, two worlds: but that there will be one audience capable only of what I may call ballad attention, and a smaller audience capable of enjoying both the ballad and the more difficult forms of poetry. Now it is to the ballad attention that Kipling addresses himself: but that does not mean that all of his poems appeal only on that level.

9 What is unusual about Kipling's ballads is his singleness of attention in attempting to convey no more to the simple minded than can be taken in on one reading or hearing. They are best when read aloud, and the ear requires no training to follow them easily. With this simplicity of purpose goes a consummate gift of word, phrase, and rhythm. There is no poet who is less open to the charge of repeating himself. In the ballad, the stanza must not be too long and the rhyme scheme must not be too complicated;[1] the stanza must be immediately apprehensible as a whole; a refrain can help to insist upon the identity within which a limited range of variation is possible. The variety of form which Kipling manages to devise for his ballads is remarkable: each is distinct, and perfectly fitted to the content and the mood which the poem has to convey. Nor is the versification too regular: there is the monotonous beat only when the monotonous is what is required; and the irregularities of scansion have a wide scope. One of the most interesting exercises in the combination of heavy beat and variation of pace found in 'Danny Deever', a poem which is technically (as well as in content) remarkable. The regular recurrence of the same end-words, which gain immensely by imperfect rhyme (*parade* [233] and *said*) gives the feeling of marching feet and the movement of men in disciplined formation – in a unity of movement which enhances the horror of the occasion and the sickness which seizes the men as individuals; and the slightly quickened pace of the final lines marks the change in movement and in music. There is no single word or phrase which calls too much attention to itself, or which is not there for the sake of the total effect; so that when the climax comes:

> 'What's that that whimpers over'ead?' said Files-on-Parade,
> 'It's Danny's soul that's passin' now,' the Colour-Sergeant said.

(the word *whimper* being exactly right) the atmosphere has been prepared for a complete suspension of disbelief.

---

1. Though Kipling could manage even so difficult a form as the sestina.

10 It would be misleading to imply that all of Kipling's poems, or at least all that matter, are 'ballads': there is a great variety of kinds. I mean only that the approach to the understanding of what he was trying to do, in all his varied verse, is through the ballad motive. The best introduction, for my present purpose, is to call attention to a dozen or so particular poems representing his different types. For the reader to whom the ballad approach to poetry is the most natural, there is no need to show that Kipling's verse reaches from time to time the intensity of 'poetry': for such readers it is more useful to discuss the content, the view of life, and to overcome the prejudices which they may entertain against any verse which has a different subject matter or a different point of view from that which they happen to accept: to detach it, furthermore, from irrelevant association with subsequent events and attitudes. That I shall attempt in the next section. In choosing the examples which follow here, I have in mind rather the reader who, if he believes that Kipling wrote 'political jingles', stresses the word *jingles* rather than the word *political*.

11 The first impression we may take from inspection of a number of the poems chosen to show the variety, is that this variety is suspiciously great. We may, that is, fail to see in it more than the virtuosity of a writer who could turn his hand to any form and matter at will: we may fail to discern any unity. We may be brought to admit that one poem after another does, in one way or another, have its 'poetic' moment, and yet believe that the moments are only accidental or illusory. It would be a mistake to assume that a few poems can be chosen which are 'poetry', and that the rest, by [234] implication, need not be read. A selection made in this way would be arbitrary, because there is no handful of poems which can be so isolated from the rest; it would be misleading because the significance of the 'poems' would be lost except with the background of the 'verse', just as the significance of the verse is missed except in the context of the prose. No part of Kipling's work, and no period of his work, is wholly appreciable without taking into account the others: and in the end, this work, which studied piecemeal appears to have no unity beyond the haphazard of external circumstances, comes to show a unity of a very complicated kind.

12 If, therefore, I call particular attention to 'Danny Deever' as a barrack-room ballad which somehow attains the intensity of poetry, it is not with the purpose of isolating it from the other ballads of the same type, but with the reminder that with Kipling you cannot draw a line beyond which some of the verse becomes 'poetry'; and that the poetry, when it comes, owes the gravity of its impact to being something over and above the bargain, something more than the writer undertook to

give you; and that the matter is never simply a pretext, an occasion for poetry. There are other poems in which the element of poetry is more difficult to put one's finger on, than in 'Danny Deever'. Two poems which belong together are *McAndrew's Hymn* and *The 'Mary Gloster'*. They are dramatic monologues, obviously, as I have said, owing something to Browning's invention, though metrically and intrinsically ballads. The popular verdict has chosen the first as the more memorable: I think that the popular verdict is right, but just what it is that raises *McAndrew's Hymn* above *The 'Mary Gloster'* is not easy to say. The rapacious old ship owner of the latter is not easily dismissed, and the presence of the silent son gives a dramatic quality absent from McAndrew's soliloquy. One poem is no less successful than the other. If the McAndrew poem is the more memorable, it is not because Kipling is more inspired by the contemplation of the success of failure than by that of the failure of success, but because there is greater poetry in the subject matter. It is McAndrew who creates the poetry of Steam, and Kipling who creates the poetry of McAndrew.

13 We sometimes speak as if the writer who is most consciously and painstakingly the 'craftsman' were the most remote from the interests of the ordinary reader, and as if the popular writer were the artless writer. But no writer has ever cared more for the craft of words than Kipling: a passion which gives him a prodigious [235] respect for the artist of any art and the craftsman of any craft,[1] and which is perhaps involved in his respect for Free Masonry. The problems of the literary artist constantly recur in his stories:[2] in *Wireless*, for instance, where the poor consumptive chemist's assistant is for a night identified with Keats at the moment of writing *The Eve of St Agnes*; in *The Finest Story in the World*, where Kipling takes the trouble to provide a very good poem, in rather free verse (the 'Song of the Galley Slaves') and a very bad poem in regular verse, to illustrate the difference between the poem which forces its way into the consciousness of the poet and the poem which the writer himself forces. The difference between the craft and the art of poetry is of course as difficult to determine as the difference between poetry and balladry. It will not help us to decide the place of Kipling in poetry: we can only say that Kipling's craftsmanship is more reliable than that of some

---

1. *The Bull that Thought* in the bull-ring 'raged enormously; he feigned defeat; he despaired in statuesque abandon, and thence flashed into fresh paroxysms of wrath – but always with the detachment of the true artist who knows that he is but the vessel of an emotion whence others, not he, must drink'.

2. In *Proofs of Holy Writ* (a story published in the *Sussex* edition only), Shakespeare and Jonson discuss a problem of choice of words put before them by one of the translators of the King James Bible.

greater poets, and that there is hardly any poem, even in the collected works, in which he fails to do what he has set out to do. The great poet's craft may sometimes fail him: but at his greatest moments he is doing what Kipling is usually doing on a lower plane – writing transparently, so that our attention is directed to the object and not to the medium. Such a result is not simply attained by absence of decoration – for even the absence of decoration may err in calling attention to itself – but by never using decoration for its own sake,[1] though, again, the apparently superfluous may be what is really important. Now one of the problems which arise concerning Kipling is related to that skill of craftsmanship which seems to enable him to pass from form to form, though always in an identifiable idiom, and from subject to subject, so that we are aware of no inner compulsion to write about this rather than that – a versatility which may make us suspect him of being no more than a performer. We look, in a poet as well as in a novelist, for what Henry James called the Figure in the Carpet. With the greatest of modern poets this Figure is perfectly manifest (for we can be sure of the existence of the Figure without perfectly [236] understanding it): I mention Yeats at this point because of the contrast between his development, which is very apparent in the way he writes, and Kipling's development, which is only apparent in what he writes about. We expect to feel, with a great writer, that he *had* to write about the subject he took, and in that way. With no writer of equal eminence to Kipling is this inner compulsion, this unity in variety more difficult to discern.

14 I pass from the earlier ballads to mention a second category of Kipling's verse: those poems which arise out of, or comment upon topical events. Some of these, such as 'The Truce of the Bear', in the form of an apologue, do not aim very high.[2] But to be able to write good verse to occasion is a very rare gift indeed: Kipling had the gift, and he took the obligation to employ it very seriously. Of this type of poem I should put 'Gehazi' – a poem inspired by the Marconi scandals – very high, as a passionate invective rising to real eloquence (and a poem which illustrates, incidentally, the important influence of Biblical imagery and the Authorised Version language upon his writing). The poems on Canada and Australia, and the exequy on King Edward VII, are excellent in their kind, though not very memorable individually. And the gift for occasional verse is allied to the gift for two other kinds of verse in which

---

1. The great speech of Enobarbus in *Antony and Cleopatra* is highly decorated, but the decoration has a purpose beyond its own beauty.

2. Though 'The Truce of the Bear' should be cited among the poems which evidence Kipling's political insight.

Kipling excelled: the epigram and the hymn. Good epigrams in English are very few; and the great hymn writer is very rare. Both are extremely objective types of verse: they can and should be charged with intense feeling, but it must be a feeling that can be completely shared. They are possible to a writer so impersonal as Kipling: and I should like the reader to look attentively at the *Epitaphs of the War*. I call Kipling a great hymn writer on the strength of 'Recessional'. It is a poem almost too well known to need to have the reader's attention called to it, except to point out that it is one of the poems in which something breaks through from a deeper level than that of the mind of the conscious observer of political and social affairs – something which has the true prophetic inspiration. Kipling might have been one of the most notable of hymn writers. The same gift of prophecy appears, on the political plane, in other poems, such as 'The Storm Cone', but nowhere with greater authority than in 'Recessional'.

15 It is impossible, however, to fit all of Kipling's poems into one or another of several distinct classes. There is the poem 'Gethse-[237]mane', which I do not think I understand,[1] and which is the more mysterious because of the author's having chosen to place it so early in his collected edition, since it bears the sub-heading '1914-1918'. And there are the poems of the later period.

16 The verse of the later period shows an even greater diversity than the early poems. The word 'experimentation' may be applied, and honourably applied, to the work of many poets who develop and change in maturity. As a man grows older, he may turn to new subject-matter, or he may treat the same material in a different way; as we age we both live in a different world, and become different men in the same world. The changes may be expressed by a change of rhythm, of imagery, of form: the true experimenter is not impelled by restless curiosity, or by desire for novelty, or the wish to surprise and astonish, but by the compulsion to find, in every new poem as in his earliest, the right form for feelings over the development of which he has, as a poet, no control. But just as, with Kipling, the term 'development' does not seem quite right, so neither does the term 'experimentation'. There is great variety, and there are some very remarkable innovations indeed, as in 'The Way Through The Woods' and in 'The Harp Song of the Dane Women':

> What is a woman that you forsake her,
> And the hearth-fire and the home-acre,
> To go with the old grey Widow-maker?

---

1. Though the death of his son must be the cause of its intensity.

and in the very fine 'Runes on Weland's Sword'. But there were equally original inventions earlier ('Danny Deever'); and there are too, among the later poems, some very fine ones cast in more conventional form, such as 'Cold Iron', 'The Land', 'The Children's Song'.

17 I confess therefore that the critical tools which we are accustomed to use in analysing and criticising poetry do not seem to work; I confess furthermore that introspection into my own processes affords no assistance – part of the fascination of this subject is in the exploration of a mind so different from one's own. I am accustomed to the search for form: but Kipling never seems to be searching for form, but only for a particular form for each poem. So we find in the poems an extraordinary variety, but no evident pattern – the connexion is to be established on some other level. Yet this is no display of empty virtuosity, and we can be sure that there is no ambition of either popular or esoteric success for its [238] own sake. The writer is not only serious, he has a vocation. He is completely ambidextrous, that is to say completely able to express himself in verse or prose: but his necessity for often expressing the same thing in a story and in a poem is a much deeper necessity than that merely to exhibit skill. I know of no writer of such great gifts for whom poetry seems to have been more purely an instrument. Most of us are interested in the form for its own sake – not apart from the content, but because we aim at making something which shall first of all *be*, something which in consequence will have the capability of exciting, within a limited range, a considerable variety of responses from different readers. For Kipling the poem is something which is intended to *act* – and for the most part his poems are intended to elicit the same response from all readers, and only the response which they can make in common. For other poets – at least, for some other poets – the poem may begin to shape itself in fragments of musical rhythm, and its structure will first appear in terms of something analogous to musical form; and such poets find it expedient to occupy their conscious mind with the craftsman's problems, leaving the deeper meaning to emerge from a lower level. It is a question then of what one chooses to be conscious of, and of how much of the meaning, in a poem, is conveyed direct to the intelligence and how much is conveyed indirectly by the musical impression upon the sensibility – always remembering that the use of the word 'musical' and of musical analogies, in discussing poetry, has its dangers if we do not constantly check its limitations: for the music of verse is inseparable from the meanings and associations of words. If I say then, that this musical concern is secondary and infrequent with Kipling, I am not implying any inferiority of craftsmanship, but rather a different order of values from that which we expect to determine the structure of poetry.

18 If we belong to the kind of critic who is accustomed to consider poems solely by the standards of the 'work of art' we may tend to dismiss Kipling's verse by standards which are not meant to apply. If, on the other hand, we are the biographical critic, interested primarily in the work as a revelation of the man, Kipling is the most elusive of subjects: no writer has been more reticent about himself, or given fewer openings for curiosity, for personal adoration or dislike.

19 The purely hypothetical reader who came upon this essay with no previous acquaintance with Kipling's verse, might perhaps [239] imagine that I had been briefed in the cause of some hopelessly second-rate writer, and that I was trying, as an exhibition of my ingenuity as an advocate, to secure some small remission of the penalty of oblivion. One might expect that a poet who appeared to communicate so little of his private ecstasies and despairs would be dull; one might expect that a poet who had given so much of his time to the service of the political imagination would be ephemeral; one might expect that a poet so constantly occupied with the appearances of things would be shallow. We know that he is not dull, because we have all, at one time or another, by one poem or another, been thrilled; we know that he is not ephemeral, because we remember so much of what we have read. As for shallowness, that is a charge which can only be brought by those who have continued to read him only with a boyish interest. At times Kipling is not merely possessed of penetration, but almost 'possessed' of a kind of second sight. It is a trifling curiosity in itself that he was reproved for having placed in defence of the Wall a Roman Legion which historians declared had never been near it, and which later discoveries proved to have indeed been stationed there: that is the sort of thing one comes to expect of Kipling. There are deeper and darker caverns into which he penetrated – whether through experience or through imagination does not matter: there are hints in *The End of the Passage*, and later in *The Woman in His Life* and *In the Same Boat*: oddly enough, these stories are foreshadowed by an early poem which I have not included, 'La Nuit Blanche', which introduces one image which reappears in *The End of the Passage*. Kipling knew something of the things which are underneath, and of the things which are beyond the frontier.[1]

1. Compare the description of the agony in *In the Same Boat* (a story the end of which is truer to the experience than is the end of *The Brushwood Boy*): 'Suppose you were a violin string – vibrating – and someone put his finger on you' with the image of the 'banjo string drawn tight' for the breaking wave in *The Finest Story in the World*. Compare also the story *A Matter of Fact* (of the submarine volcanic eruption which projects the sea-monster to the surface) with the opening passages of *Alice in Wonderland*: both depict external events which have exact nightmare correspondence to

20 I have not explained Kipling's verse or the permanent hold that it can have upon you. It will be enough if I can help to keep him out of the wrong pigeon-holes.[1] If the reader of this book denies [240] that Kipling is a great writer of verse, I hope at least that he will have found new reasons for his judgement, for the ordinary charges brought against him are either untrue or irrelevant. I have been using the term 'verse' with his own authority, for that is what he called it himself. There is poetry in it; but when he writes verse that is not poetry it is not because he has tried to write poetry and failed. He had another purpose, and one to which he adhered with integrity. It is expressed in the following poem (from *A Diversity of Creatures*):

THE FABULISTS
1914–1918

When all the world would keep a matter hid,
    Since Truth is seldom friend to any crowd,
Men write in fable as old Æsop did,
    Jesting at that which none will name aloud.
And this they needs must do, or it will fall
Unless they please they are not heard at all.

When desperate Folly daily laboureth
    To work confusion upon all we have,
When diligent Sloth demandeth Freedom's death,
    And banded Fear commandeth Honour's grave –
Even in that certain hour before the fall,
Unless men please they are not heard at all.

Needs must all please, yet some not all for need,
    Needs must all toil, yet some not all for gain,
But that men taking pleasure may heed,
    Whom present toil shall snatch from later pain.

---

some spiritual terror. *A Matter of Fact* is a better story than *In the Same Boat*, for the psychological explanation of the latter story comes as an anti-climax to the experience.

1. Dr J. H. Oldham has drawn my attention to the relevance of the chapter on 'Art and Magic' in that very remarkable book, *The Principles of Art*, by Professor R. G. Collingwood. Collingwood takes Kipling as an example of 'the artist as magician', and defines a magical art as 'an art which is representative and therefore evocative of emotion, and evokes of set purpose some emotions rather than others in order to discharge them into the affairs of practical life'. Professor Collingwood's contribution here seems to me extremely valuable; but while Kipling is a very good example of what he calls 'the artist as magician', I do not feel that 'the artist as magician' is a complete description of Kipling as a writer of verse.

Thus some have toiled, but their reward was small
Since, though they pleased, they were not heard at all.

This was the lock that lay upon our lips,
    This was the yoke that we have undergone,
Denying us all pleasant fellowships
    As in our time and generation.
[241] Our pleasures unpursued age past recall,
And for our pains – we are not heard at all.

What man hears aught except the groaning guns?
    What man heeds aught save what each instant brings?
When each man's life all imaged life outruns,
    What man shall pleasure in imaginings?
So it has fallen, as it was bound to fall,
We are not, nor we were not, heard at all.

II

21 I have expressed the view that the variety of Kipling's verse and its mutations from one period to another, cannot be accounted for, and given a unified pattern, by tracing development as we might with most poets. His development cannot be understood through his verse alone, because he was, as I said at the beginning, an integral prose-and-verse writer; and to understand changes we have to consider the prose and the verse together. Kipling appears first to be a writer of different phases and occupations, who in each phase is completely developed, who is never so committed to the pursuit of one verse form as to be prevented from moving to another. He is so different from other poets that the lazy critic is tempted merely to assert that he is not a poet at all, and leave it at that. The changes in his poetry, while they cannot be explained by any usual scheme of poetic development, can to some extent be explained by changes in his outward circumstances. I say 'to some extent', because Kipling, apparently merely the reflection of the world about him, is the most inscrutable of authors. An immense gift for using words, an amazing curiosity and power of observation with his mind and with all his senses, the mask of the entertainer, and beyond that a queer gift of second sight, of transmitting messages from elsewhere, a gift so disconcerting when we are made aware of it that thenceforth we are never sure when it is *not* present: all this makes Kipling a writer impossible wholly to understand and quite impossible to belittle.

22 Certainly an exceptional sensitiveness to environment is the first characteristic of Kipling that we notice; so that on one level, we may trace his course by external circumstances. What life would have made of such a man, had his birth, growth, maturity and age all taken place in one set of surroundings, is beyond speculation: as life directed, the result was to give him a peculiar [242] detachment and remoteness from all environment, a universal foreignness which is the reverse side of his strong feelings for India, for the Empire, for England and for Sussex, a remoteness as of an alarmingly intelligent visitor from another planet. He remains somehow alien and aloof from all with which he identifies himself. The reader who can get a little distance – but not deep enough – below the level of Kipling's popularity as a teller of tales and reciter of ballads, and who has a vague feeling of something further underneath, is apt to give the wrong explanation of his own discomfort. I have tried to disturb the belief that Kipling is a mere writer of jingles: we must now consider whether these 'jingles' are, in a denigratory sense, 'political'.

23 To have been born in India and to have spent the first remembered years there, is a circumstance of capital importance for a child of such impressionability. To have spent the years from seventeen to twenty-four earning his living there, is for a very precocious and observant young man an important experience also. The result is, it seems to me, that there are two strata in Kipling's appreciation of India, the stratum of the child and that of the young man. It was the latter who observed the British in India and wrote the rather cocky and acid tales of Delhi and Simla, but it was the former who loved the country and its people. In his Indian tales it is on the whole the Indian characters who have the greater reality, because they are treated with the understanding of love. It is Purun Bhagat, it is the four great Indian characters in *Kim* who are real: the Lama, Mahbub Ali, Hurree Chunder Mookerjee, and the wealthy widow from the North. As for the Britons, those with whom he is most sympathetic are those who have suffered or fallen – McIntosh Jellaludin has learned more than Strickland.[1] Kipling is of India in a different way from any other Englishman who has written, and in a different way from that of any particular Indian, who has a race, a creed, a local habitation and, if a Hindu, a caste. He might almost be called the first citizen of India. And his relation to India determines that about him which is the most important thing about a man, his religious attitude. It is an attitude of comprehensive tolerance.[2] He is not an unbeliever – on the contrary, he can accept all faiths: that of the Moslem, that of the Hindu, that of the Buddhist, Parsee or Jain, even (through [243] the historical imagination)

---

1. On the subject of Kipling's ethics, and the types of man which he holds up for respect, see a valuable essay by Mr Bonamy Dobrée in *The Lamp and the Lute*.
2. Not the tolerance of ignorance or indifference.

that of Mithra: if his understanding of Christianity is less affectionate, that is due to his Anglo-Saxon background – and no doubt he saw enough in India of clergy such as Mr Bennett in *Kim*.

24 To explain Kipling's feeling for the Empire, and his later feeling for Sussex, as merely the nostalgia of a man without a country, as the need for support felt by the man who does not belong, would be a mistake which would prevent us from understanding Kipling's peculiar contribution. To explain away his patriotic feeling in this way is only necessary for those who consider that such feeling is not a proper theme for verse. There are perhaps those who will admit to expression in poetry patriotism on the defensive: Shakespeare's Henry V is acceptable, in his otherwise embarrassing grandiloquence, because the French army was a good deal bigger than the English force, even though Henry's war could hardly be described as a defensive one. But if there is a prejudice against patriotic verse, there is a still stronger prejudice against imperial patriotism in verse. For too many people, an Empire has become something to apologise for, on the ground that it happened by accident, and with the addition that it is a temporary affair anyway and will eventually be absorbed into some universal world association: and patriotism itself is expected to be inarticulate. But we must accustom ourselves to recognising that for Kipling the Empire was not merely an idea, a good idea or a bad one; it was something the reality of which he felt. And in his expression of his feeling he was certainly not aiming at flattery of national, racial or imperial vanity, or attempting to propagate a political programme: he was aiming to communicate the awareness of something in existence of which he felt that most people were very imperfectly aware. It was an awareness of grandeur, certainly, but it was much more an awareness of responsibility.

25 There is the question of whether 'political' poetry is admissible; there is the question of the way in which Kipling's political poetry is political; there is the question of what his politics were; and finally, there remains the question of what we are to say of that considerable part of his work which cannot, by any stretch of the term, be called political at all.

26 It is pertinent to call attention to one other great English writer who put politics into verse – Dryden. The question whether Kipling was a poet is not unrelated to the question whether Dryden [244] was a poet. The author of *Absalom and Achitophel* was satirising a lost cause in retrospect, and he was on the successful side; the author of *The Hind and the Panther* was arguing a case in ecclesiastical politics; and both of these purposes were very different from that which Kipling set himself. Both of Dryden's poems are more political in their appeal to the reason

than any of Kipling's. But the two men had much in common. Both were masters of phrase, both employed rather simple rhythms with adroit variations; and by both the medium was employed to convey a simple forceful statement, rather than a musical pattern of emotional overtones. And (if it is possible to use these terms without confusion) they were both classical rather than romantic poets. They arrive at poetry through eloquence; for both, wisdom has the primacy over inspiration; and both are more concerned with the world about them than with their own joys and sorrows, and concerned with their own feelings in their likeness to those of other men rather than in their particularity. But I should not wish to press this likeness too far, or ignore the great differences: and if Kipling suffers in some respects by the comparison, it must be remembered that he has other qualities which do not enter into it at all.

27 Kipling certainly thought of verse as well as prose as a medium for a public purpose; and if we are to pass judgement upon his purpose, we must try to set ourselves in the historical situations in which his various work was written; and whether our prejudice be favourable or antagonistic, we must not look at his observations of one historical situation from the point of view of a later period. Also, we must consider his work as a whole, and the earlier years in the light of the later, and not exaggerate the importance of particular pieces or phrases which we may not like. Even these may be misinterpreted. Mr Edward Shanks, who has written the best book on Kipling that I have read (and whose chapter on 'The Prophet of Empire' resumes Kipling's political views admirably) says of the poem called 'Loot' (a soldier ballad describing the ways of extorting hidden treasure from natives): 'this is wholly detestable, and it makes the commentator on Kipling turn red when he endeavours to explain it.' This is to read an attitude into the poems which I had never suspected. I do not believe that in this poem he was commending the rapacity and greed of such irregularities, or condoning rapine. If we think this, we must also presume that 'The Ladies' was written to glorify miscellaneous miscegenation on the part of professional soldiers quartered in foreign lands. Kipling, [245] at the period to which these poems belong, undoubtedly felt that the professional ranker and his officers too were unappreciated by their peaceful countrymen at home, and that in the treatment of the soldier and the discharged soldier there was often less than social justice: but his concern was to make the soldier known, not to idealise him. He was exasperated by sentimentalism as well as by depreciation or neglect – and either attitude is liable to evoke the other.

28 I have said that in Kipling as a poet there is no development, but mutation; and that for the development we must look to changes in the environment and in the man himself. The first period is that of India; the second that of travel and of residence in America; the third is that of his settlement in Sussex. These divisions are obvious: what is not so obvious is the development of his view of empire, a view which expands and contracts at the same time. He had always been far from uncritical of the defects and wrongs of the British Empire, but held a firm belief in what it should and might be. In his later phase England and a particular corner of England become the centre of his vision. He is more concerned with the problem of the soundness of the *core* of empire; this core is something older, more natural and more permanent. But at the same time his vision takes a larger view, and he sees the Roman Empire and the place of England in it. The vision is almost that of an idea of empire laid up in heaven. And with all his geographical and historical imagination, no one was farther than he from interest in men in the mass, or the manipulation of men in the mass: his symbol was always a particular individual. The symbol had been, at one time, such men as Mulvaney or Strickland: it became Parnesius and Hobden. Technical mechanics do not lose their charm for him; wireless and aviation succeed steam, and in one of his most other-worldly stories – *They* – a considerable part is played by an early, and not very reliable, model of a motor car: but Parnesius and Hobden are more important than the machines. One is the defender of a civilisation (of a civilisation, not of civilisation in the abstract) against barbarism; the other represents the essential contact of the civilisation with the soil.

29 I have said that there is always something alien about Kipling, as of a visitor from another planet; and to some readers he may still seem alien in his identification of himself with Sussex. There is an element of *tour de force* in all his work, which makes some [246] readers uncomfortable: we are always suspicious of people who are too clever. Kipling is apt to arouse some of the same distrust as another great man who was alien in a very different way, and on a more worldly level – though he too had his vision of empire and his flashes of profound insight. Even those who admire Disraeli most may find themselves more at ease with Gladstone, whether they like the man and his politics or not. But Disraeli's foreignness was a comparatively simple matter. And undoubtedly the difference of early environment to which Kipling's foreignness is due gave him an understanding of the English countryside different from the understanding of a man born and brought up in it, and provoked in him thoughts about it which the natives would do well to heed.

30 It may well be unfortunate for a man's reputation that he should have great success early in life, with one work or with one type of work: for then his early work is what he is remembered by, and people (critics, sometimes, most of all) do not bother to revise their opinions in accordance with his later work. With Kipling, furthermore, a prejudice against the content may combine with a lack of understanding of the form to produce an inconsistent condemnation. On the ground of content, he is called a Tory; and on the ground of style, he is called a journalist. Neither of these terms, to be sure, need be held in anything but honour: but the former has come to acquire popular odium by a vulgar identification with a nastier name: to many people a critical attitude towards 'democracy' has come to imply a friendly attitude towards fascism – which, from a truly Tory point of view, is merely the extreme degradation of democracy. Similarly the term 'journalist', when applied to anyone not on the staff of a newspaper, has come to connote truckling to the popular taste of the moment. Kipling was not even a Tory, in the sense of one giving unquestioning loyalty to a political party: he can be called a Tory in a sense in which only a handful of writers together with a number of mostly inarticulate, obscure and uninfluential people are ever Tories in one generation. And as for being a journalist (in the sense mentioned above) we must keep in mind that the causes he espoused were not popular causes when he voiced them; that he did not aim to idealise either border warfare or the professional soldier; that his reflections on the Boer War are more admonitory than laudatory. It may be proposed that, as he dwelt upon the glory of empire, in so doing he helped to conceal its more seamy side: the commercialism, exploitation and neglect. No attentive reader of [247] Kipling can maintain, however, that he was unaware of the faults of British rule: it is simply that he believed the British Empire to be a good thing, that he wished to set before his readers an ideal of what it should be, but was acutely aware of the difficulty of even approximating to this ideal, and of the perpetual danger of falling away even from such standard as might be attained. I cannot find any justification for the charge that he held a doctrine of race superiority. He believed that the British have a greater aptitude for ruling than other people, and that they include a greater number of kindly, incorruptible and unselfseeking men capable of administration; and he knew that scepticism in this matter is less likely to lead to greater magnanimity than it is to lead to a relaxation of the sense of responsibility. But he cannot be accused of holding that any Briton, simply because of his British race, is necessarily in any way the superior or even the equal of any individual of another race. The types of men which he admires are unlimited by any prejudice; his maturest work on India, and his greatest book, is *Kim*.

31 The notion of Kipling as a popular entertainer is due to the fact that his works have been popular and that they entertain. However, it is permitted to express popular views of the moment in an unpopular style: it is not approved when a man holds unpopular views and expresses them in something very readable. I do not wish to argue longer over Kipling's early 'imperialism', because there is need to speak of the development of his views. It should be said at this point, before passing on, that Kipling is not a doctrinaire or a man with a programme. His opinions are not to be considered as the antithesis of those of H. G. Wells. Wells's imagination is one thing and his political opinions another: the latter changed but did not mature. But Kipling did not, even in the sense in which that activity can be ascribed to Wells, *think*: his aim, and his gift, is to make people see – for the first condition of right thought is right sensation: the first condition of understanding a foreign country is to smell it, as you smell India in *Kim*. If you have seen and felt truly, then if God has given you the power you may be able to think rightly.

32 The simplest summary of the change in Kipling, in his middle years, is 'the development of the imperial imagination into the historical imagination'. To this development his settling in Sussex must have contributed to no small degree: for he had the humility to subdue himself to his surroundings, and the freshness of vision of the stranger. My references here will be to stories [248] rather than to poems: that is because the later unit is a poem and a story together – or a story and two poems – combining to make a form which no one has used in the same way and in which no one is ever likely to excel him. When I speak of 'historical imagination' I do not assume that there is only one kind. Two different kinds are exemplified by Victor Hugo and Stendhal in their accounts of the battle of Waterloo. For the first it is the charge of the Old Guard, and the sunken road of Ohain; for the latter it is Fabrice's sudden awareness that the little pattering noise around him is caused by bullets. The historian of one kind is he who gives life to abstractions: the historian of another kind may imply a whole civilisation in the behaviour of a single individual. H. G. Wells can give an epic grandeur to the accumulation of an American fortune. Kipling's imagination dwells on the particular experience of the particular man, just as his India was realised in particular men. In *The Finest Story in the World* there appears the same passion for the exact detail that is given scope in his studies of machinery. The Greek galley is described from the point of view of the galley slave. The ship was 'the kind rowed with oars, and the sea spurts up through the oar-holes, and the men row sitting up to their knees in water. Then there's a bench running down between the two lines of oars, and an overseer with a whip walks up and down

the bench to make the men work. . . . There's a rope running overhead, looped to the upper deck, for the overseer to catch hold of when the ship rolls. When the overseer misses the rope once and falls among the rowers, remember the hero laughs at him and gets licked for it. He's chained to his oar, of course – the hero . . . with an iron band round his waist fixed to the bench he sits on, and a sort of handcuff on his left wrist chaining him to the oar. He's on the lower deck where the worst men are sent, and the only light comes from the hatchways and through the oar-holes. Can't you imagine the sunlight just squeezing through between the handle and the hole and wobbling about as the ship moves?'

33 The historical imagination may give us an awful awareness of the extent of time, or it may give us a dizzy sense of the nearness of the past. It may do both. Kipling, especially in *Puck of Pook's Hill* and *Rewards and Fairies*, aims I think to give at once a sense of the antiquity of England, of the number of generations and peoples who have laboured the soil and in turn been buried beneath it, and of the contemporaneity of the past. Having previously exhibited an imaginative grasp of space, and England in it, [249] he now proceeds to a similar achievement in time. The tales of English history need to be considered in relation to the later stories of contemporary Sussex, such as *An Habitation Enforced*, *My Son's Wife*, and *The Wish House*, together with *They* in one aspect of this curious story. Kipling's awareness and love of Sussex is a very different affair from the feeling of any other 'regional' writer of comparable fame, such as Thomas Hardy. It is not merely that he was highly conscious of what ought to be preserved, where Hardy is the chronicler of decay; or that he wrote of the Sussex which he found, where Hardy wrote of the Dorset that was already passing in his boyhood. It is, first, that the conscience of the 'fabulist' and the consciousness of the political and historical imagination are always at work. To think of Kipling as a writer who could turn his hand to any subject, who wrote of Sussex because he had exhausted his foreign and imperial material, or had satiated the public demand for it, or merely because he was a chameleon who took his colour from environment, would be to miss the mark completely: this later work is the continuation and consummation of the earlier. The second peculiarity of Kipling's Sussex stories I have already touched upon, the fact that he brings to his work the freshness of a mind and a sensibility developed and matured in quite different environment: he is discovering and reclaiming a lost inheritance. The American Chapins, in *A Habitation Enforced*, have a passive role: the protagonist in the story is the house and the life that it implies, with the profound implication that the countryman belongs to the land, the landlord to his tenants, the

farmer to his labourers and not the other way about. This is a deliberate reversal of the values of industrial society. The Chapins, indeed (except for the point of their coming from a country of industrialised mentality) are a kind of mask for Kipling himself. He is also behind the hero of a less successful story in the same group, *My Son's Wife*. (I call this story less successful because he seems to point his moral guide a little too directly, and because the contrast between the garrulous society of London – or suburban – intellectuals and the speechless solicitor's daughter who likes hunting is hammered with too great insistence. The contrast between a bucolic world in which the second-rate still participates in the good, and an intellectual world in which the second-rate is usually sham and always tiresome, is not quite fair. The animus which he displays against the latter suggests that he did not have his eye on the object: for we can judge only what we understand, and [250] must constantly dine with the opposition.) What is most important in these stories, and in *The Wish House*, and in *Friendly Brook*, is Kipling's vision of the people of the soil. It is not a Christian vision, but it is at least a pagan vision – a contradiction of the materialistic view: it is the insight into a harmony with nature which must be re-established if the truly Christian imagination is to be recovered by Christians. What he is trying to convey is, again, not a programme of agrarian reform, but a point of view unintelligible to the industrialised mind. Hence the artistic value of the *obviously* incredible element of the supernatural in *The Wish House*, which is exquisitely combined with the sordid realism of the women of the dialogue, the country bus, the suburban villa, and the cancer of the poor.

34 This hard and obscure story, *The Wish House*, has to be studied in relation to the two hard and obscure poems (not here included) which precede and follow it, and which would be still more hard and obscure without the story. We have gone a long way, at this stage, from the mere story-teller: a long way even from the man who felt it his duty to try to make certain things plain to his countrymen who would not see them. He could hardly have thought that many people in his own time or at any time would take the trouble to understand the parables, or even to appreciate the precision of observation, the calculating pains in selecting and combining elements, the choice of word and phrase, that were spent in their elaboration. He must have known that his own fame would get in the way, his reputation as a story-teller, his reputation as a 'Tory journalist', his reputation as a facile writer who could dash off something about what happened yesterday, his reputation even as a writer of books for children which children liked to read and hear read.

35 I return to the beginning. The late poems like the late stories with which they belong, are sometimes more obscure, because they are trying to express something more difficult than the early poems. They are the poems of a wiser and more mature writer. But they do not show any movement from 'verse' to 'poetry': they are just as instrumental as the early work, but now instruments for a matured purpose. Kipling could handle, from the beginning to the end, a considerable variety of metres and stanza forms with perfect competence; he introduces remarkable variations of his own; but as a poet he does not revolutionise. He is not one of those writers of whom one can say, that the *form* of English poetry will [251] always be different from what it would have been if they had not written. What fundamentally differentiates his 'verse' from 'poetry' is the subordination of musical interest. Many of the poems give, indeed, judged by the ear, an impression of the mood, some are directly onomatopoeic: there is a harmonics of poetry which not merely is beyond their range but would interfere with the intention. It is possible to argue exceptions; but I am speaking of his work as a whole, and I maintain that without understanding the purpose which animates his verse as a whole, one is not prepared to understand the exceptions.

36 I make no apology for having used the terms 'verse' and 'poetry' in a loose way: so that while I speak of Kipling's work as verse and not as poetry, I am still able to speak of individual compositions as poems, and also to maintain that there is 'poetry' in the 'verse'. Where terminology is loose, where we have not the vocabulary for distinctions which we feel, our only precision is found in being aware of the imperfections of our tools, and of the different senses in which we are using the same words. It should be clear that when I contrast 'verse' with 'poetry' I am not, *in this context*, implying a value judgement. I do not mean, here, by verse, the work of a man who would write poetry if he could: I mean by it something which does what 'poetry' could not do. The difference which would turn Kipling's verse into poetry, does not represent a failure or deficiency: he knew perfectly well what he was doing; and from his point of view more 'poetry' would interfere with his purpose. And I make the claim, that in speaking of Kipling we are entitled to say '*great* verse'. What other famous poets should be put into the category of great verse writers is a question which I do not here attempt to answer. That question is complicated by the fact that we should be dealing with matters as imprecise as the shape and size of a cloud or the beginning and end of a wave. But the writer whose work is *always* clearly verse, is not a great verse writer: if a writer is to be that, there must be some of his work of which we cannot say whether it is verse or poetry. And the poet who could not write 'verse' when verse was needed, would be without that sense of structure which is required to make a poem of any length readable. I would suggest also that we too easily assume that what is most valuable is also most rare, and vice versa. I can think of a number of poets who have written great poetry, only of a very few whom I should call great verse writers. And unless I am mistaken, Kipling's position in this class is not only high, but unique.

Variants from 1941:

1. New para. at 'When a man'
[Between 'imaginative prose.' and 'If I make an exception':] I am willing to pay due respect, for instance, to the poetry of George Meredith, of Thomas Hardy, of D. H. Lawrence as part of their *œuvre*, without conceding that it is as good as it might have been had they chosen to dedicate their whole lives to that form of art.

5. my selection of Kipling's verse] the selection which follows
earliest published] earliest of Kipling's published verse

7. the short rhymed stanza] short rhymed stanzas

9 fn. [after 'sestina.':] See p. 45.

13. 'Song of the Galley Slaves'] *Song of the Galley Slaves* in this volume
fn. 2 There is a tale not reprinted in his collected works, but of considerable interest from this point of view, in which Shakespeare and Jonson discuss a problem of choice of words put before them by one of the translators of the King James Bible. See also the poem on Shakespeare in this volume.

14. [No fn. 2.]

15. [No fn. 1.]

17. emerge from] emerge, if there, from

19. into which he penetrated] which he penetrated

23. [Between 'understanding of love.' and 'Purun':] One is not very loving between seventeen and twenty-four. But it is
   fn. 2 [after 'indifference.':] see *The Mark of the Beast*, which those who do not believe in the existence of the Beast probably consider a beastly story.

28. phase England] phase England,
corner of England become] corner of England, becomes

31. changed but did not] change but do not
even in the sense] in the sense
Wells, *think*] Mr. Wells, think

32. H. G. Wells] Mr. Wells
[Between 'American fortune' and 'Kipling's imagination':] : Mr. Lytton Strachey (to name a lesser figure) gave reality to the great by dilating upon their foibles.

33. *My Son's Wife*] *His Son's Wife*
My Son's Wife] *His Son's Wife*

34. obscure story, *The Wish House*, has to be] obscure story has to be
hear read] hear

[Additional para. at end:] Such reflections could be pursued indefinitely: but this essay is intended as an introduction: if it assists the reader to approach Kipling's verse with a fresh mind, and to regard it in a new light, and to read it as if for the first time, it will have served its purpose.

Yeats[1]

OPAP, 252–62.

Revised from 'The Poetry of W. B. Yeats', the First Annual Yeats Lecture, delivered to the Friends of the Irish Academy at the Abbey Theatre, June 1940, and publ. in *Purpose*, 12. 3/4 (July/Dec. 1940), 115–27: Gallup C457.

In para. 2 'mistery' has been corrected to 'mystery'; in 11, 'the later line;' to 'the later line,' and in 12, 'the *Green Helmet*' to '*The Green Helmet*'.

1 The generations of poetry in our age seem to cover a span of about twenty years. I do not mean that the best work of any poet is limited to twenty years: I mean that it is about that length of time before a new school or style of poetry appears. By the time, that is to say, that a man is fifty, he has behind him a kind of poetry written by men of seventy, and before him another kind written by men of thirty. That is my position at present, and if I live another twenty years I shall expect to see still another younger school of poetry. One's relation to Yeats, however, does not fit into this scheme. When I was a young man at the university, in America, just beginning to write verse, Yeats was already a considerable figure in the world of poetry, and his early period was well defined. I cannot remember that his poetry at that stage made any deep impression upon me. A very young man, who is himself stirred to write, is not primarily critical or even widely appreciative. He is looking for masters who will elicit his consciousness of what he wants to say himself, of the kind of poetry that is in him to write. The taste of an adolescent writer is intense, but narrow: it is determined by personal needs. The kind of poetry that I needed, to teach me the use of my own voice, did not exist in English at all; it was only to be found in French. For this reason the poetry of the young Yeats hardly existed for me until after my enthusiasm had been won by the poetry of the older Yeats; and by that time – I mean, from 1919 on – my own course of evolution was already determined. Hence, I find myself regarding him, from one point of view, as a contemporary and not a predecessor; and from another point of view, I can share the feelings of younger men, who came to know and admire him by that work from 1919 on, which was produced while they were adolescent.

---

1. The first annual Yeats Lecture, delivered to the Friends of the Irish Academy at the Abbey Theatre, Dublin, in 1940. Subsequently published in *Purpose*.

2 Certainly, for the younger poets of England and America, I am [253] sure that their admiration for Yeats's poetry has been wholly good. His idiom was too different for there to be any danger of imitation, his opinions too different to flatter and confirm their prejudices. It was good for them to have the spectacle of an unquestionably great living poet, whose style they were not tempted to echo and whose ideas opposed those in vogue among them. You will not see, in their writing, more than passing evidences of the impression he made, but the work, and the man himself as poet, have been of the greatest significance to them for all that. This may seem to contradict what I have been saying about the kind of poetry that a young poet chooses to admire. But I am really talking about something different. Yeats would not have this influence had he not become a great poet; but the influence of which I speak is due to the figure of the poet himself, to the integrity of his passion for his art and his craft which provided such an impulse for his extraordinary development. When he visited London he liked to meet and talk to younger poets. People have sometimes spoken of him as arrogant and overbearing. I never found him so; in his conversations with a younger writer I always felt that he offered terms of equality, as to a fellow worker, a practitioner of the same mystery. It was, I think, that, unlike many writers, he cared more for poetry than for his own reputation as a poet or his picture of himself as a poet. Art was greater than the artist: and this feeling he communicated to others; which was why younger men were never ill at ease in his company.

3 This, I am sure, was part of the secret of his ability, after becoming unquestionably the master, to remain always a contemporary. Another is the continual development of which I have spoken. This has become almost a commonplace of criticism of his work. But while it is often mentioned, its causes and its nature have not been often analysed. One reason, of course, was simply concentration and hard work. And behind that is character: I mean the special character of the artist as artist – that is, the force of character by which Dickens, having exhausted his first inspiration, was able in middle age to proceed to such a masterpiece, so different from his early work, as *Bleak House*. It is difficult and unwise to generalise about ways of composition – so many men, so many ways – but it is my experience that towards middle age a man has three choices: to stop writing altogether, to repeat himself with perhaps an increasing skill of virtuosity, or by taking thought to adapt himself to middle age and find a different [254] way of working. Why are the later long poems of Browning and Swinburne mostly unread? It is, I think, because one gets the essential Browning or Swinburne entire in earlier poems; and in

the later, one is reminded of the early freshness which they lack, without being made aware of any compensating new qualities. When a man is engaged in work of abstract thought – if there is such a thing as wholly abstract thought outside of the mathematical and the physical sciences – his mind can mature, while his emotions either remain the same or only atrophy, and it will not matter. But maturing as a poet means maturing as the whole man, experiencing new emotions appropriate to one's age, and with the same intensity as the emotions of youth.

4 One form, a perfect form, of development is that of Shakespeare, one of the few poets whose work of maturity is just as exciting as that of their early manhood. There is, I think, a difference between the development of Shakespeare and Yeats, which makes the latter case still more curious. With Shakespeare, one sees a slow, continuous development of mastery of his craft of verse, and the poetry of middle age seems implicit in that of early maturity. After the first few verbal exercises you say of each piece of work: 'This is the perfect expression of the sensibility of that stage of his development.' That a poet should develop at all, that he should find something new to say, and say it equally well, in middle age, has always something miraculous about it. But in the case of Yeats the kind of development seems to me different. I do not want to give the impression that I regard his earlier and his later work almost as if they had been written by two different men. Returning to his earlier poems after making a close acquaintance with the later, one sees, to begin with, that in technique there was a slow and continuous development of what is always the same medium and idiom. And when I say development, I do not mean that many of the early poems, for what they are, are not as beautifully written as they could be. There are some, such as 'Who Goes With Fergus?', which are as perfect of their kind as anything in the language. But the best, and the best known of them, have this limitation: that they are as satisfactory in isolation, as 'anthology pieces', as they are in the context of his other poems of the same period.

5 I am obviously using the term 'anthology piece' in a rather special sense. In any anthology, you find some poems which give you complete satisfaction and delight in themselves, such that you are [255] hardly curious who wrote them, hardly want to look further into the work of that poet. There are others, not necessarily so perfect or complete, which make you irresistibly curious to know more of that poet through his other work. Naturally, this distinction applies only to short poems, those in which a man has been able to put only a part of his mind, if it is a mind of any size. With some such you feel at once that the man who wrote them must have had a great deal more to say, in different contexts, of equal interest.

Now among all the poems in Yeats's earlier volumes I find only in a line here or there, that sense of a unique personality which makes one sit up in excitement and eagerness to learn more about the author's mind and feelings. The intensity of Yeats's own emotional experience hardly appears. We have sufficient evidence of the intensity of experience of his youth, but it is from the retrospections in some of his later work that we have our evidence.

6 I have, in early essays, extolled what I called impersonality in art, and it may seem that, in giving as a reason for the superiority of Yeats's later work the greater expression of personality in it, I am contradicting myself. It may be that I expressed myself badly, or that I had only an adolescent grasp of that idea – as I can never bear to re-read my own prose writings, I am willing to leave the point unsettled – but I think now, at least, that the truth of the matter is as follows. There are two forms of impersonality: that which is natural to the mere skilful craftsman, and that which is more and more achieved by the maturing artist. The first is that of what I have called the 'anthology piece', of a lyric by Lovelace or Suckling, or of Campion, a finer poet than either. The second impersonality is that of the poet who, out of intense and personal experience, is able to express a general truth; retaining all the particularity of his experience, to make of it a general symbol. And the strange thing is that Yeats, having been a great craftsman in the first kind, became a great poet in the second. It is not that he became a different man, for, as I have hinted, one feels sure that the intense experience of youth had been lived through – and indeed, without this early experience he could have never attained anything of the wisdom which appears in his later writing. But he had to wait for a later maturity to find expression of early experience; and this makes him, I think, a unique and especially interesting poet.

7 Consider the early poem which is in every anthology, 'When you are old and grey and full of sleep', or 'A Dream of Death' in the same [256] volume of 1893. They are beautiful poems, but only craftsman's work, because one does not feel present in them the particularity which must provide the material for the general truth. By the time of the volume of 1904 there is a development visible in a very lovely poem, 'The Folly of Being Comforted', and in 'Adam's Curse'; something is coming through, and in beginning to speak as a particular man he is beginning to speak for man. This is clearer still in the poem 'Peace', in the 1910 volume. But it is not fully evinced until the volume of 1914, in the violent and terrible epistle dedicatory of *Responsibilities*, with the great lines

> Pardon that for a barren passion's sake,
> Although I have come close on forty-nine. . . .

And the naming of his age in the poem is significant. More than half a lifetime to arrive at this freedom of speech. It is a triumph.

8   There was much also for Yeats to work out of himself, even in technique. To be a younger member of a group of poets, none of them certainly of anything like his stature, but further developed in their limited path, may arrest for a time a man's development of idiom. Then again, the weight of the pre-Raphaelite prestige must have been tremendous. The Yeats of the Celtic twilight – who seems to me to have been more the Yeats of the pre-Raphaelite twilight – uses Celtic folklore almost as William Morris uses Scandinavian folklore. His longer narrative poems bear the mark of Morris. Indeed, in the pre-Raphaelite phase, Yeats is by no means the least of the pre-Raphaelites. I may be mistaken, but the play, *The Shadowy Waters*, seems to me one of the most perfect expressions of the vague enchanted beauty of that school: yet it strikes me – this may be an impertinence on my part – as the western seas descried through the back window of a house in Kensington, an Irish myth for the Kelmscott Press; and when I try to visualise the speakers in the play, they have the great dim, dreamy eyes of the knights and ladies of Burne-Jones. I think that the phase in which he treated Irish legend in the manner of Rossetti or Morris is a phase of confusion. He did not master this legend until he made it a vehicle for his own creation of character – not, really, until he began to write the *Plays for Dancers*. The point is, that in becoming more Irish, not in subject-matter but in expression, he became at the same time universal.

9   The points that I particularly wish to make about Yeats's development are two. The first, on which I already touched, [257] is that to have accomplished what Yeats did in the middle and later years is a great and permanent example – which poets-to-come should study with reverence – of what I have called Character of the Artist: a kind of moral, as well as intellectual, excellence. The second point, which follows naturally after what I have said in criticism of the lack of complete emotional expression in his early work, is that Yeats is pre-eminently the poet of middle age. By this I am far from meaning that he is a poet only for middle-aged readers: the attitude towards him of younger poets who write in English, the world over, is enough evidence to the contrary. Now, in theory, there is no reason why a poet's inspiration or material should fail, in middle age or at any time before senility. For a man who is capable of experience finds himself in a different world in every decade of his life; as he sees it with different eyes, the material of his art is continually renewed. But in fact, very few poets have shown this capacity of adaptation to the years. It requires, indeed, an exceptional honesty and courage to face the change.

Most men either cling to the experiences of youth, so that their writing becomes an insincere mimicry of their earlier work, or they leave their passion behind, and write only from the head, with a hollow and wasted virtuosity. There is another and even worse temptation: that of becoming dignified, of becoming public figures with only a public existence – coat-racks hung with decorations and distinctions, doing, saying, and even thinking and feeling only what they believe the public expects of them. Yeats was not that kind of poet: and it is, perhaps, a reason why young men should find his later poetry more acceptable than older men easily can. For the young can see him as a poet who in his work remained in the best sense always young, who even in one sense became young as he aged. But the old, unless they are stirred to something of the honesty with oneself expressed in the poetry, will be shocked by such a revelation of what a man really is and remains. They will refuse to believe that *they* are like that.

> You think it horrible that lust and rage
> Should dance attendance upon my old age;
> They were not such a plague when I was young:
> What else have I to spur me into song?

These lines are very impressive and not very pleasant, and the sentiment has recently been criticised by an English critic whom I generally respect. But I think he misread them. I do not read them [258] as a personal confession of a man who differed from other men, but of a man who was essentially the same as most other men; the only difference is in the greater clarity, honesty and vigour. To what honest man, old enough, can these sentiments be entirely alien? They can be subdued and disciplined by religion, but who can say that they are dead? Only those to whom the maxim of La Rochfoucauld applies: 'Quand les vices nous quittent, nous nous flattons de la créance que c'est nous qui les quittons.' The tragedy of Yeats's epigram is all in the last line.

10 Similarly, the play *Purgatory* is not very pleasant, either. There are aspects of it which I do not like myself. I wish he had not given it this title, because I cannot accept a purgatory in which there is no hint, or at least no emphasis upon Purgation. But, apart from the extraordinary theatrical skill with which he has put so much action within the compass of a very short scene of but little movement, the play gives a masterly exposition of the emotions of an old man. I think that the epigram I have just quoted seems to me just as much to be taken in a dramatic sense as the play *Purgatory*. The lyric poet – and Yeats was always lyric, even when dramatic – can speak for every man, or for men very different

from himself; but to do this he must for the moment be able to identify himself with every man or other men; and it is only his imaginative power of becoming this that deceives some readers into thinking that he is speaking for and of himself alone – especially when they prefer not to be implicated.

11 I do not wish to emphasise this aspect only of Yeats's poetry of age. I would call attention to the beautiful poem in *The Winding Stair*, in memory of Eva Gore-Booth and Con Markiewicz, in which the picture at the beginning, of:

> Two girls in silk kimonos, both
> Beautiful, one a gazelle,

gets great intensity from the shock of the later line,

> When withered, old and skeleton gaunt,

and also to *Coole Park*, beginning

> I meditate upon a swallow's flight,
> Upon an aged woman and her house.

In such poems one feels that the most lively and desirable emotions of youth have been preserved to receive their full and due expression [259] in retrospect. For the interesting feelings of age are not just different feelings; they are feelings into which the feelings of youth are integrated.

12 Yeats's development in his dramatic poetry is as interesting as that in his lyrical poetry. I have spoken of him as having been a lyric poet – in a sense in which I should not think of myself, for instance, as lyric; and by this I mean rather a certain kind of selection of emotion rather than particular metrical forms. But there is no reason why a lyric poet should not also be a dramatic poet; and to me Yeats is the type of lyrical dramatist. It took him many years to evolve the dramatic form suited to his genius. When he first began to write plays, poetic drama meant plays written in blank verse. Now, blank verse has been a dead metre for a long time. It would be outside of my frame to go into all the reasons for that now: but it is obvious that a form which was handled so supremely well by Shakespeare has its disadvantages. If you are writing a play of the same type as Shakespeare's, the reminiscence is oppressive; if you are writing a play of a different type, it is distracting. Furthermore, as Shakespeare is so much greater than any dramatist who has followed him, blank verse can hardly be dissociated from the life of the sixteenth and seventeenth centuries: it can hardly catch the rhythms with which English is spoken nowadays. I think that if anything like regular blank verse is

ever to be re-established, it can be after a long departure from it, during the course of which it will have liberated itself from period associations. At the time of Yeats's early plays it was not possible to use anything else for a poetry play: that is not a criticism of Yeats himself, but an assertion that changes in verse forms come at one moment and not at another. His early verse-plays, including *The Green Helmet*, which is written in a kind of irregular rhymed fourteener, have a good deal of beauty in them, and, at least, they are the best verse-plays written in their time. And even in these one notices some development of irregularity in the metric. Yeats did not quite invent a new metre, but the blank verse of his later plays shows a great advance towards one; and what is most astonishing is the virtual abandonment of blank verse metre in *Purgatory*. One device used with great success in some of the later plays is the lyrical choral interlude. But another, and important, cause of improvement is the gradual purging out of poetical ornament. This, perhaps, is the most painful part of the labour, so far as the versification goes, of the modern poet who tries to write a play in [260] verse. The course of improvement is towards a greater and greater starkness. The beautiful line for its own sake is a luxury dangerous even for the poet who has made himself a virtuoso of the technique of the theatre. What is necessary is a beauty which shall not be in the line or the isolable passage, but woven into the dramatic texture itself; so that you can hardly say whether the lines give grandeur to the drama, or whether it is the drama which turns the words into poetry. (One of the most thrilling lines in *King Lear* is the simple:

>   Never, never, never, never, never

but, apart from a knowledge of the context, how can you say that it is poetry, or even competent verse?) Yeats's purification of his verse becomes much more evident in the four *Plays for Dancers* and in the two in the posthumous volume: those, in fact, in which he had found his right and final dramatic form.

13 It is in the first three of the *Plays for Dancers*, also, that he shows the internal, as contrasted with the external, way of handling Irish myth of which I have spoken earlier. In the earlier plays, as in the earlier poems, about legendary heroes and heroines, I feel that the characters are treated, with the respect that we pay to legend, as creatures of a different world from ours. In the later plays they are universal men and women. I should, perhaps, not include *The Dreaming of the Bones* quite in this category, because Dermot and Devorgilla are characters from modern history, not figures of pre-history; but I would remark in support of what I have been saying that in this play these two lovers have something of

the universality of Dante's Paolo and Francesca, and this the younger Yeats could not have given them. So with the Cuchulain of *The Hawk's Well*, the Cuchulain, Emer and Eithne of *The Only Jealousy of Emer*; the myth is not presented for its own sake, but as a vehicle for a situation of universal meaning.

14 I see at this point that I may have given the impression, contrary to my desire and my belief, that the poetry and the plays of Yeats's earlier period can be ignored in favour of his later work. You cannot divide the work of a great poet so sharply as that. Where there is the continuity of such a positive personality and such a single purpose, the later work cannot be understood, or properly enjoyed, without a study and appreciation of the earlier; and the later work again reflects light upon the earlier, and shows us beauty and significance not before perceived. We have also to [261] take account of the historical conditions. As I have said above, Yeats was born into the end of a literary movement, and an English movement at that: only those who have toiled with language know the labour and constancy required to free oneself from such influences – yet, on the other hand, once we are familiar with the older voice, we can hear its individual tones even in his earliest published verse. In my own time of youth there seemed to be no immediate great powers of poetry either to help or to hinder, either to learn from or to rebel against, yet I can understand the difficulty of the other situation, and the magnitude of the task. With the verse-play, on the other hand, the situation is reversed, because Yeats had nothing, and we have had Yeats. He started writing plays at a time when the prose-play of contemporary life seemed triumphant, with an indefinite future stretching before it; when the comedy of light farce dealt only with certain privileged strata of metropolitan life; and when the serious play tended to be an ephemeral tract on some transient social problem. We can begin to see now that even the imperfect early attempts he made are probably more permanent literature than the plays of Shaw; and that his dramatic work as a whole may prove a stronger defence against the successful urban Shaftesbury Avenue vulgarity which he opposed as stoutly as they. Just as, from the beginning, he made and thought his poetry in terms of speech and not in terms of print, so in the drama he always meant to write plays to be played and not merely to be read. He cared, I think, more for the theatre as an organ for the expression of the consciousness of a people, than as a means to his own fame or achievement; and I am convinced that it is only if you serve it in this spirit that you can hope to accomplish anything worth doing with it. Of course, he had some great advantages, the recital of which does not rob him of any of his glory: his colleagues, a people with a

natural and unspoilt gift for speech and for acting. It is impossible to disentangle what he did for the Irish theatre from what the Irish theatre did for him. From this point of advantage, the idea of the poetic drama was kept alive when everywhere else it had been driven underground. I do not know where our debt to him as a dramatist ends – and in time, it will not end until that drama itself ends. In his occasional writings on dramatic topics he has asserted certain principles to which we must hold fast: such as the primacy of the poet over the actor, and of the actor over the scene-painter; and the principle that the theatre, while it need not be [262] concerned only with 'the people' in the narrow Russian sense, must be for the people; that to be permanent it must concern itself with fundamental situations. Born into a world in which the doctrine of 'Art for Art's sake' was generally accepted, and living on into one in which art has been asked to be instrumental to social purposes, he held firmly to the right view which is between these, though not in any way a compromise between them, and showed that an artist, by serving his art with entire integrity, is at the same time rendering the greatest service he can to his own nation and to the whole world.

15 To be able to praise, it is not necessary to feel complete agreement; and I do not dissimulate the fact that there are aspects of Yeats's thought and feeling which to myself are unsympathetic. I say this only to indicate the limits which I have set to my criticism. The questions of difference, objection and protest arise in the field of doctrine, and these are vital questions. I have been concerned only with the poet and dramatist, so far as these can be isolated. In the long run they cannot be wholly isolated. A full and elaborate examination of the total work of Yeats must some day be undertaken; perhaps it will need a longer perspective. There are some poets whose poetry can be considered more or less in isolation, for experience and delight. There are others whose poetry, though giving equally experience and delight, has a larger historical importance. Yeats was one of the latter: he was one of those few whose history is the history of their own time, who are a part of the consciousness of an age which cannot be understood without them. This is a very high position to assign to him: but I believe that it is one which is secure.

Variants from 1940:

[Additional para. before para. 1:] The invitation to address you on this occasion and in this place was at the same time irresistible and terrifying. You have instituted an annual lecture in memory of the greatest poet of our time – certainly the greatest in this language, and so far as I am able to judge, in any language. This is the first lecture, and in a theatre for ever associated with his name, the centre of some of his most important activity. The responsibility which I have accepted is considerable. I have thought it fit, on the first of these annual ceremonies, to devote my words to the work of William Butler Yeats himself: that is what I should wish to do, and what I expect you would wish to hear. But even after taking this obvious decision, my subject left me a wide range of selection. The achievement of a great poet cannot be surveyed in an hour. There are many aspects of his work – cultural, political, religious – which can be better treated by a compatriot. In what way can a visitor like myself discuss Yeats's work with the greatest freshness and with the least impertinence? It seemed to me that a certain informality, and even personality, might be permitted if I was to consider a few aspects of his poetry from the point of view of his admirers and fellow practitioners outside of Ireland, and especially in England and America.

1 university,] university
2 opposed] contradicted
3 such a masterpiece] a masterpiece
5 has been able to put only] has only been able to put
6 as follows] this
   a later maturity] a late maturity
8 who seems to me to have been] who, begging your pardon, seems to me to have been
   the pre-Raphaelite phase] his pre-Raphaelite phase
   this may be an impertinence] and this is what may be an impertinence
9 doing, saying, and] doing, saying and
12 even in these] even in these,
13 could not have given them.] could not have done.
14 the plays of Shaw] the plays of Ibsen or of Shaw
   Shaftesbury Avenue vulgarity] Shaftesbury Avenue-vulgarity
14–15 [Between 'the whole world.' and 'The questions of difference':] I have come here to do honour to the memory of a great poet. It is a pleasure to me to praise him, and to have the privilege of doing so here and before this audience; and if I had not had the conviction of praising him in all sincerity I should not have come at all. But to be able to praise, it is not necessary to feel complete agreement; and I should not think it right to dissimulate the fact that there are aspects of his thought and feeling which to myself are unsympathetic. I say this not in order to express my own beliefs, which I shall leave in silence, but rather to indicate the limits which I have set to my criticism.

Preface

Preface (vii–ix) to *My Brother's Keeper: James Joyce's Early Years* by Stanislaus Joyce, ed. by Richard Ellmann.

Advance issue of Dec. 1957 of 375 copies for distribution gratis. Repr. in the first edn of 3 Feb. 1958, and in the edn publ. by Faber & Faber on 23 May 1958.
Gallup B77.

Curiosity about the private life of a public man may be of three kinds: the useful, the harmless, and the impertinent. It is useful, when the subject is a statesman, if the study of his private life contributes towards the understanding of his public actions; it is useful, when the subject is a man of letters, if the study throws light upon his published works. The line between curiosity which is legitimate and that which is merely harmless and between that which is merely harmless and that which is vulgarly impertinent, can never be precisely drawn. In the case of a writer, the usefulness of biographical information, for increasing our understanding and making possible a keener enjoyment or a more critical evaluation, will vary according to the type of which the writer is a representative, and the way in which he has exploited his own experience in his books. It is difficult to believe that greater knowledge of the private life of Shakespeare could much modify our judgement or enhance our enjoyment of his plays; no theory about the origin or mode of composition of the Homeric poems could alter our appreciation of them as poetry. With a writer like Goethe, on the other hand, our interest in the man is inseparable from our interest in the work; and we are impelled to supplement and correct what he tells us in various ways about himself, with information from outside sources; the more we know about the man, the better, we think, we may come to understand his poetry and his prose.

[viii] In the case of James Joyce we have a series of books, two of which at least are so autobiographical in appearance that further study of the man and his background seems not only suggested by our own inquisitiveness, but almost expected of us by the author himself. We want to know who are the originals of his characters, and what were the origins of his episodes, so that we may unravel the web of memory and invention and discover how far and in what ways the crude material has been transformed. Our interest extends, therefore, inevitably and justifiably, to Joyce's family, to his friends, and to every detail of the topography and the life of Dublin, the Dublin of his childhood, adolescence, and young manhood. What Joyce's brother Stanislaus has done for us is to make us acquainted with the family environment in which the two boys grew up, with details that no one else could have provided. We regret

that he died leaving the story unfinished: we shall never have, from any other source, the account of the middle years in Trieste which Stanislaus could have given us. But we are fortunate to have so full an account of boyhood and youth in Dublin, by the man who was observing and studying his brother, sedulously, admiringly, and jealously, as no one else ever observed or studied him.

It would be a mistake, however, to classify this book as merely a unique piece of documentation on the early life of one of the great writers of the century. *My Brother's Keeper* is also a remarkable exposition of the relationship between a famous man and a brother of whose existence the world remained unaware. Stanislaus himself, in this book, becomes as interesting to us as James. The brothers are so much alike and yet so different! James Joyce was devoted to his father, and to his father's memory; the attitude of Stanislaus was very different, as instanced by his report of the terrible scene at their mother's death-bed. Where James, in political and religious [ix] matters, was indifferent or merely mocking, Stanislaus manifests a sometimes appalling violence. I have read the book twice, and find myself fascinated and repelled by the personality of this positive, courageous, bitter man who was a prey to such mixed emotions of affection, admiration, and antagonism – a struggle in the course of which, as Mr Ellmann in his introduction points out, he saw his famous brother, at certain moments, with a startling lucidity of vision. I had thought that the book might be entitled *Memories of a Son and Brother* – with a difference. With another difference, *My Brother's Keeper* has a quality of candour which reminds me of Gosse's *Father and Son*. Possessed as he was by the subject matter of his memoir, Stanislaus Joyce, under the exasperation of this thorn in his flesh, became himself a writer, and the author of this one book which is worthy to occupy a permanent place on the bookshelf beside the works of his brother.

1958

[A special message about Ezra Pound]

Books and Art, 1. 5 (Feb. 1958), 59. Gallup C621.

Introduced by: 'T. S. ELIOT, O.M., in a special message to *Books and Art*, says:'.

It is appalling to think that a man who is perhaps the greatest poet of his generation, who has certainly had a great seminal influence on other poets, who has done so much to shape the poetry of our age, and who has in the past done so much for other writers, should end his life as an inmate of St Elizabeth's Hospital in Washington. As for his economic theories, they may be very sound; but political thinking needs to be supported by a profound understanding of human nature. Yet whatever follies of political judgement Pound may have committed in the past, the question of what he might say or do after his release is irrelevant to the question of justice in keeping him confined, especially if the term of his confinement has already exceeded the length of sentence upon others who have been tried and found guilty. I have no sympathy with Pound's racial prejudices, and among the people of my acquaintance who wish, as I do, that he might be released, I know no one who shares those views. I do not think that his views should be considered, in considering the question of his release. He is a poet of genius. He has been detained since 1944 and is now seventy-two. I should like to see him free to live out the rest of his life as he lived it before the late war.

[Report on Obscene Publications]

Report from the Select Committee on Obscene Publications Together With the Proceedings of the Committee, Minutes of Evidence and Appendices.
Contains, pp. 14–21, 'Minutes of Evidence Taken . . . Thursday, 30th January, 1958 . . . Mr. T. S. Eliot, O.M., D.Litt, and Mr. E. M. Forster, C.H., D.Litt., called in and examined.' Publ. 12 May 1858. Gallup B78.
Material supplementary to Eliot's own words has been added in order to establish context.

Chairman

110. We have invited you as two distinguished authors whom we thought could give us very representative views; we know that Mr Forster was interested in this question of law some years ago, and we value very much your advice and help. This Committee has been appointed to see if the law relating to obscene publications should be consolidated, and to make observations on the existing law and advise whether it should be amended. Perhaps the first question I should ask you is whether in your view the law relating to obscene publications should be consolidated? – (Mr *Forster*.) I am in favour of it being consolidated. (Mr *Eliot*.) I do not quite understand the term 'consolidated'.

111. At the moment there are a great number of Acts of Parliament dealing with it, and there is also, of course, the common law? – I am quite in favour of consolidating them and of the allusion in the Bill to the common law.

112. We have had before us the evidence of the Society of Authors which they gave to the Committee last Session. That was principally in support of the Bill introduced by Lord Lambton last Session, though in fact one of the witnesses at the hearing before us advised a new definition of obscenity. I think what I would like to ask you, Gentlemen, is this: do you think the existing law should be amended? – Do you mean, Sir, with regard to the definition of obscenity and widening the scope?

113. Yes? – I do very definitely. I do think that the law with respect to the exploitation of horror, cruelty or violence, whether or not related to any sexual context – it is often related to sexual context but sometimes the relation to sexual context is very obscure – should be clarified. I wholly applaud that addition myself. I do not know what Mr Forster thinks? (Mr *Forster*.) I entirely agree with Mr Eliot.

114. Could I ask both you Gentlemen whether you think the present law prevents the publication of works of literary merit that are not intended to corrupt? – (Mr *Eliot*.) One can speak best from one's experience. I have one book in mind about which Mr Forster can speak with more

authority than I can – I was involved somewhat in its defence, but he was involved much more than I, but my own experience, of course, has been not so much as publisher but as a literary man. I have not had anything to do with these matters in connection with my publishing firm. I mean the affair of James Joyce and *Ulysses*, of which I was a very interested observer as a friend and admirer of his. What particularly scandalised me at that time, so far as my memory goes, was the confiscation and destruction of the books printed in Paris when the book could not be printed in this country because the printers were all frightened of being involved. It should, in my opinion, have been printed in this country and its importation, if not printed in this country, should not have been stopped in that way arbitrarily.

115. How long ago was that incident? – That was in the early Twenties; I cannot give you the exact date but, speaking from memory, I should think it was about 1922. I have a copy of the first edition printed in Paris and I could check that date.

[. . .]

[16] 127. Yes? – (Mr *Eliot*.) If I may say so, I think that the question of the different formats with additions is hardly likely to arise in any work which is to be considered of literary merit, which would be published presumably by a reputable publisher in the first place and a reputable publisher would hardly produce an edition of that type, or license the production of an edition of that type, to be shown in certain types of shop. There is, of course, one form of pseudo-obscenity which is well-known nowadays, and that is to produce a cheap edition of a book which is not in itself offensive but with a jacket designed with a picture intended to invite purchase in the expectation of obscenity. I do not know how one can reach that form of obscenity. – (Mr *Forster*.) Was not that the case of *Boy*, a novel by Mr James Hanley which was first produced and put on general sale and was then reissued with a pornographic dust jacket? – (Mr *Eliot*.) That might happen, but I should think that was very exceptional. You would not find *Lady Chatterley's Lover* produced in that way in that type of shop.

Chairman

128. Are you suggesting, Mr Eliot, that a book of literary merit cannot be obscene? – No, I think a book of literary merit can be obscene but I think each case must be judged on its own merits. I think books of literary merit which are of some antiquity and fame seem to me to free themselves of the taint merely by the passage of time. That is a difficult point of view to defend, but I think we do feel it when we see

the rather absurd objections raised to well known works like *Boccaccio*.

129. Do you feel the power of depravity wears out in the course of time? – I should say that it did, yes, because the type of people who are likely to be depraved are people who want current reading. I do not think depravable people are likely to be depraved by the classics. There is something in the contemporaneity of pornographic literature. I am not really familiar with pornographic literature, but there are classics of pornographic literature which relatively are innocuous compared to what is put on the market as new. The tests in pornography, as in everything else, I imagine, change from age to age.

131. [Forster on Radclyffe Hall's *The Well of Loneliness*:] I wrote letters to the Press on the subject, but was not allowed to give evidence. I do not know if Mr Eliot was in it? – (Mr *Eliot*.) No; I was one of the signatories of a letter which I believe was never printed because the author found it not flattering enough to the work. I did read the book for the purpose of writing or not writing, and I felt it should have been permitted. The book was so dull very few people would have read it, and as a matter of fact I had great difficulty myself in getting through this 'labour of love', as you might call it.

[. . .]

[17] *Mr Renton*

133. May I ask Mr Eliot this? He has referred to works of literary merit and works which are not of literary merit and has said that the decision as to whether there is literary merit or not must depend on the circumstances of each case. – ? – (Mr *Eliot*.) May I amend that statement a little? I think, especially in view of the book we have just been talking about, the intention of the author is relevant. If the author intends it to be a work of literature, even if they fail, I think it puts it in a different category from that of the pornographic author who, as I understand it, is willing to sell to people with somewhat perverted tastes and who, although there may be no intention to deprave or corrupt, the person, is probably aware of and indifferent to the differences of depravity and corruption. But I should put in a separate category works which are obviously intended to be of literary merit. Obviously that leaves considerable border-line cases, because I do not think in these matters you can construct any net which will catch the fish you want and let the others go through; you either catch too many fish and do injustice to some, or you will not catch enough and do harm to the public.

134. If I may follow this up, let us assume for the moment that a court of law is faced with the need to make a decision as to whether or not a

book has in fact got literary merit, can you offer us any broad criterion as to how the court should decide whether there is literary merit or not? – I cannot, except by the court receiving expert evidence. Now, what is expert evidence in regard to literary or artistic merit? Obviously expert evidence is a definite thing with regard to the medical, legal or scientific character of a book, but as to the literary, artistic merit it will all depend on getting the opinion of the right people, and who can say absolutely who are the right people? Some distinguished authors, well-known authors, have been in my experience extremely prudish; others have been, perhaps too lax, but on the whole I think this would work well.

135. It might result in one side calling, for example, James Joyce, as an expert witness and the other side called one of the authors (whom you ought not to name) whom you regard as prudish? – Yes. I think cases might arise in which this would not completely solve the case, but I do not see how you could do better.

Viscount *Lambton*

136. If I may ask these two eminent literary figures this question; have either of you ever been restricted in your writing by the present law, and, secondly – and Mr Eliot may have answered this to a certain extent – have your printers ever suggested any changes in your work with regard to the present law as it now stands? – In my case I can answer no to both questions, due to the completely anodyne nature of my writings. When I mentioned printers I was thinking of the original attempt of the lady, a most excellent and extremely puritanical person who wanted to publish *Ulysses* in this country, and was prepared to take the consequences, but she could not get any printer to undertake it. They were afraid of the consequences for themselves.

137. So do you think in your experience that you can definitely say works of genuine literary merit have suffered from the constriction of the [18] present law? – This work of definite literary merit has suffered. It has suffered from restrictions which made printers timid, and it also has suffered from the arbitrary methods of the Customs.

[. . .]

138. [. . .] [Mr *Forster*.] Some authors – I will not say Mr Eliot or myself – are inhibited by the harsh and at present uncertain position of the law as regards obscenity, and I think that many of them wish to introduce scenes or phrases and hesitate to do so in case they get into trouble. (Mr *Eliot*) I should even add to that that in the present state of the law it seems to me possible for an author to appeal to the wrong emotions in such a way as to escape prosecution, whereas another author who is not

appealing to those but who is serious may be prosecuted. There again I think it is excellent that the words 'dominant effect' should be used of the whole work. There has been too much based on isolated extracts.

Mr *Elwyn Jones*

139. In view of what you have said, I take it you concede that even if a work was a work of literary merit or artistic merit, if its dominant effect was such as to be likely to deprave or corrupt or if it offended against a reasonable man's sense of decency, it should be the subject of prosecution; or would you say that it was saved by its quality as a work of literary or artistic merit? – It certainly will be safe with time, but as for the work in question I have not myself come across such a work. I should like to have an example in mind and cannot think of one.

140. I certainly cannot suggest one. – I dislike *Lady Chatterley's Lover*, but on different grounds from those on which it created a scandal.

141. If you were to make the concession I have suggested what troubles me about the proviso in Section 2 is this: is the magistrate not entitled to say, 'I have to decide whether the dominant effect of this book is to deprave or corrupt. If it does, it does not matter tuppence about literary or artistic merit'? Would you commend such an approach by a tribunal to the responsibility with which it is charged? – I can imagine possible cases in which I might be compelled to, but I should think they would be very rare because I think that the serious intention is on the whole incompatible with the likelihood of depraving and corrupting. I would not exclude the possibility of such a case, but I have not met with one.

Sir *Lancelot Joynson-Hicks*

142. I wonder if I could ask for a little further elaboration of the witnesses' views about this question of intention on the part of the author? If, as I rather understood at the beginning, the criterion of obscenity was generally to be accepted as its effect on the reader, what can the intention of the author have to do with it? – The intention of the author here is related to the public for whom it is designed, is it not? In this clause it is not made quite clear. – I do not see why there is a comma after 'intended' – whether the intention of the author alone is taken into account or the intention of the publisher and the distributor. They may have three different intentions.

143. You surely would not suggest that a greater offence is committed by an author who tries to write a book which is calculated to deprave and fails than by an author who unintentionally writes a book which does succeed in depraving? – I think on your premises one must agree, but

I think in these matters one has to think: do such cases arise, and how often? I do not think one can stay entirely in the domain of possibilities. One can always construct dilemmas, but I think that any Act has got [19] to be administered – it takes both intelligence and sensibility to conclude it.

144. The number of instances which have apparently been in your mind of books which are perhaps on the border-line are very few, are they not, perhaps half a dozen going over a period of thirty years? – I think the border-line cases are in my mind more under point *(b)* nowadays. I think it is possible that here again is a point where the literary merit is relevant. A second-rate author trying to write a masterpiece seriously may unconsciously put in pornographic matter or matter which is likely to deprave or corrupt. I do not think that would occur in the case of anything which I should myself respect as a work of literature.

[. . .]

146. [. . .] The question I want to ask is whether, in the light of the positions these gentlemen do hold, they would feel, in the interest of the public as a whole that it is better to run the risk of letting in more purely pornographic work to the exclusion of the possibility of some work which may or may not have literary merit, or whether every opportunity should be given to the publication of any work which can claim literary merit even at the risk of letting in more pornographic literature? – (Mr *Eliot.*) I think myself that everyone has a bias one way or the other, and it is just as well to admit it. My own bias, subject to revision through the consequences of any legislation, would be to run the risk of admitting too much rather than of excluding or suppressing works of general literary value. I know there is a risk either way and that is one I should be prepared to take, because one has to choose one or the other.

Mr *Roy Jenkins*

147. [. . .] [Mr *Forster.*] The point where I did not follow Mr Eliot was the business of the depravity wearing off. I feel it is rather a matter of people being ashamed of attacking the classics as they feel they might put their foot in it, whereas they are not ashamed of attacking something contemporary. There is a certain awe surrounding the classics. It is not so much that they become innocuous, I feel, but that there is a certain diffidence in approaching them. – (Mr *Eliot.*) One thing that seems to me relevant is that the classics – one refers to Martial, Aristophanes or Boccaccio – were written under very different conditions from which pornographic literature is written today. The fact that the whole temper of their age and place was different from that of our own age now seems to

me relevant. – (Mr *Forster.*) The public did not fuss so much. – (Mr *Eliot.*) I think many things they took for granted, and therefore these things did not deprave and corrupt in the same way. We would not suppress a Roman or Latin or Greek classic on the ground that it corrupted its readers at the time when it was contemporary. I should think it is very doubtful if any of the classics I have mentioned contributed to the corruption of the Athenians or Romans. It was all part of the fun!

150. Do you know of any contemporary work with any possible claim to literary merit, published by a reputable publisher and appearing in normal format, whether prosecuted or not prosecuted, which in your view would do harm to any reader? [Mr *Forster.*] – No, I cannot say I do. A novel by Mr Walter Baxter was prosecuted and got through finally. – (Mr *Eliot.*) Was not Lawrence's *The Rainbow* prosecuted? – (Mr *Forster.*) Yes, and I think it came out in a modified edition afterwards. – (Mr *Eliot.*) Was it altered? – (Mr *Forster.*) I think *The Rainbow* was altered. – (Mr *Eliot.*) I should not think that anything of Lawrence's I have read would be likely to corrupt.

Mr *Nicolson*

[. . .]

156. [. . .] you are anxious expert evidence should be admitted. What is therefore your objection to the setting up of such a board which would have no power of ultimate decision but only power of advising on these specific matters? – (Mr *Eliot.*) My objection is this: how should we trust the person who chooses a board to choose the right people? In each particular case the people offer themselves, but the idea of a permanent board makes me very apprehensive.

157. Would you be happier to leave the fate of one of your own books in the hands of an ordinary jury? – I do not like the idea of an ordinary jury, for that matter, on these things. I like the idea of the defence being able to call men of letters who would be prepared to defend the particular book in question. (Mr *Forster.*) I agree. (Mr *Eliot.*) And it is for the public opinion and for the opinion of the judge – somebody has got to decide whether those are the best qualified men of letters.

Sir *Spencer Summers*

158. [. . .] If the law is changed in such a way as to allow to be published a significant number of books which are now for some reason withheld from the public there is grave danger that the flood-gates might be open to practically anything; if, on the other hand, any changes in law made little or no difference and let two or three books through it would hardly

be worth making them. [. . .] How can one prevent that [21] happening whilst permitting some, to which exception is taken for their being withheld, to go through? – I think books will always be written with the aim just to escape whatever regulations there are, but I think that the provisions of this Bill do not seem to me to increase the risk of a flood of obscene publication in the least. I should have thought on the whole, reading this Bill, that especially in its widening of the context by Clause 20 (*b*) it was more likely to purify the air than to pollute it.

Sir *Lancelot Joynson-Hicks*

159. If that Bill were now law have you any idea how many books would be written in a year which are deliberately not written now because of the existing law? – I do not know anything about these unwritten masterpieces. I have never come across one; it has not been written. Nor do I know any author who has been prevented from writing. It may be simply that there are slight differences. Sometimes manuscripts are read by the publishers and submitted to legal opinion if there is any question of libel or obscene libel. [. . .] [Mr *Forster*.] I think it is so important that authors should have free minds and should not be worrying that they are going to be dropped on, and they will have much less cause for worrying if this Bill becomes law. (Mr *Eliot*.) I think they will have less worry about irresponsible prosecutions. In Clause 8 there is the provision that proceedings should only be taken with the consent of the Attorney-General, which seems to me important in that it is a centralisation of responsibility. (Mr *Forster*.) Excellent, yes. – (Mr *Eliot*.) That I entirely applaud. It is the piecemeal persecution here and there when a publisher does not know where it will come from, or if you get some eccentric common informer and ignorant or biassed magistrates, when you are in for trouble. This does not make it a matter of much greater responsibility in the prosecution of a book, and I think it should.

Mr *Renton*

160. Arising out of Mr Forster's last answer, at a time when there is a great deal of obscene literature and a great many people – I am not referring to authors necessarily – anxious to make profit from publishing obscene literature, does he think it is more important that a few authors should be given more freedom, or that the public should be more protected from obscene literature? – (Mr *Forster*.) You are speaking to an author, you see. I think it is more important authors should have more freedom, but I speak under my limitations. (Mr *Eliot*.) I should have thought – perhaps it is innocence on my part, being relatively unfamiliar with obscene literature – that really obscene literature is fairly easily identifiable to any person

of education, intelligence and some sensibility, but that any question, in any case, is a question of certain border-line cases one way or the other. Where there is a border-line, and I do not believe it is a very wide one, I think it should be in favour of laxity rather than of strictness, that is all. I should not like to see the publication, importation and display of really pornographic literature flourish. Apparently it flourishes anyway in an under-hand way. I should not like to see it tolerated any further.

Introduction

Introduction (vii–xxiv) to Paul Valéry, *The Art of Poetry*, translated by Denise Folliot. Signed 'T. S. ELIOT' at the end. Publ. 16 June 1958. Gallup B79. In the last para. 'we' has been inserted between 'which' and 'notice'.

Among the several motives which may impel a poet to write about poetry, we must not overlook those arising from necessity or obligation. A young poet may find himself writing essays on poets and poetry, simply because a young poet, if he has any talent for journalism at all, can earn more money by writing about other poets' poetry, than he can by selling his own. If he hopes that success in later years will free him from this kind of distraction, his hope is vain: he will merely, if successful, exchange one form of constraint for another. There is a banquet: he has to respond to the toast of 'Poetry', or to propose the health of some distinguished foreign visitor. There is a centenary to be commemorated, a tablet to be unveiled, or the birthday of some venerable poet to be honoured: it is necessary that a middle-aged poet should be present to drop the grain of incense, or fix, for the moment, a reputation. There is a young, unknown, and very promising poet to be assisted: the sale of his book will be promoted, or at least the reviewers will be more attentive, if some respected senior artisan will preface it. World conferences and congresses, European and local conferences and congresses, follow each other in endless succession: the public thirst for words about poetry, and for words from poets about almost anything – in contrast to its thirst for poetry itself – seems insatiable. In [viii] short, the compulsions and solicitations to a poet to write about poetry, and to talk about poetry, instead of writing poetry, begin early in life and continue to the end.

The life of Paul Valéry forms no exception to this rule. On the contrary: far from having purchased exemption by eminence, Valéry provides the most conspicuous confirmation of my words. He has said somewhere, that he never wrote prose except under some outside pressure or stimulus. This is surely an exaggeration: yet no poet has ever been more the victim of such molestations of fortune – to which, indeed, we owe some of his most remarkable prose, and without which we should have been deprived of much of what we know of a singularly fascinating mind. His situation in life was such that he arrived at the importunities of fame without altogether escaping the coercion of want. In his later years, he was saved from the possibility of financial embarrassment by being found a professorship at the Collège de France. There he earned his livelihood, long after the poetry which provides the solid foundation for his fame had been written, by lecturing to the public – on the Art of Poetry. His inaugural lecture, I have no doubt, drew a large and fashionable audience; but, because of the subtlety of the argument, and the indistinctness of his enunciation, it may have been difficult for the audience to follow. The irony of such a life as Valéry's is only fully apparent in retrospect.

The occasional character of most of Valéry's critical writing, of his *poétique*, must not however be allowed to suggest that there is anything perfunctory about it. He obviously enjoyed writing about poetry, still more about the process of writing poetry, and most of all about the process by which his own poetry got written. If the best of his poems are among the masterpieces, the best of his critical essays are among the most remarkable curiosities of French literature.

[ix] The writer whose critical essays have mostly been responses to particular situations is exposed, once the essays have been collected and published together, to a misunderstanding against which the prospective reader should be warned. In reading a volume of collected essays we are all, especially when approaching them for the first time, prone to expect a unity to which such work does not pretend. The essays contained in the present volume are some of them divided by many years from each other; and the other French texts were published in collections assembled chronologically rather than by subject matter. The student of the *poétique* of Valéry may start in the expectation of complete coherence; and when he does not find it, he may be tempted to complain of inconsistencies and to deride repetitions. Here and there, among Valéry's writings, you will find the same passage repeated almost verbatim, without apology or explanation. I do not myself object to this: I prefer to read critical essays in their original form, not reshaped at a later date into an artificial unity. Indeed, I regard repetitions and contradictions in a man's writing as valuable clues to the development of his thought. When I have, myself, occasion to write on some subject which I have treated in different circumstances in the past, I prefer to remain in ignorance of my opinion of twenty or thirty years ago, until I have committed to paper my opinion of today. Then, and not till then, I wish to refresh my memory. For if I find a contradiction, it is evidence that I have changed my mind; if there

is a repetition, it is the best possible evidence that I am of the same mind as ever. An unconscious repetition may be evidence of one's firmest convictions, or of one's most abiding interests.

I have thought it desirable to insist upon the occasional character of many of Valéry's essays; but I do not want to suggest that the choice of subject was always dictated by the [x] occasion, or that the results, even when the subject was imposed, are ever negligible. In the main, the subjects are obviously of his own choosing; and the occasion was only the necessary stimulus to provoke a train of thought. Even when the subject may have been indifferent, or the occasion unwelcome, Valéry was skilful enough to turn it to his own account, to direct it towards one of his dominant topics of meditation.

The direction which Valéry's meditations on poetry tended to take was no doubt suggested to him by an essay of Edgar Poe's; but what was for Poe merely the theme of one literary exercise among many, a *tour de force* perhaps, became for Valéry almost an excessive preoccupation. Valéry's *art poétique* is inspired by different motives, and directed to different ends, from those of any of the treatises, essays, or scattered dicta of other poets, with the single exception of Poe, from Horace to the present day. Apart from practical precepts which have been the fruit of experience, much of the best writing by poets about poetry has been written in defence of some new style or of some new attitude towards the material of poetry. Amongst such writings are the essays of Dryden, the prefaces of Wordsworth, and (in part) Coleridge's *Biographia Literaria*. Beside forensic and polemic criticism, there is the judicial: Samuel Johnson, in his *Lives of the Poets*, appears in the role of a judge, who has not himself chosen the persons to be tried in his court. Other poets have been moved to write criticism in revision of current opinion or traditional judgement, or to bring to light the work of some poet unjustly ignored, or to restore the reputation of some depreciated poet. Often, a poet is most effective as critic, when he writes about those poets whose work has influenced his own, or with whom he feels some affinity. And on the [xi] other hand, a poet may write with unusual understanding of some poet whom he admires and likes because that poet's work is utterly different from anything that he himself does or wants to do. In our time, Mr Ezra Pound combined several of these functions of the poet as critic: the training of young writers, the education of the public taste with regard to forgotten, undervalued, or unknown poets of the past in several languages, and the advertisement of those contemporary and younger writers whose work met with his approval.

Valéry's *poétique* fits nowhere in the foregoing classification. His appreciations of earlier poetry – for instance, the charming 'Concerning

Adonis' in this volume – are all too few; his appreciations of living poets, in his occasional prefaces, are most interesting when he wanders from his subject. He is not didactic, and so has little in common with Horace or Boileau or Pound. There are valuable hints to poets; but his motive is never primarily to guide the young, or to advance the claims of a new school of poetry, or to interpret and revalue the poetry of the past. There are valuable hints to readers; but Valéry is not primarily interested in teaching his readers anything. He is perpetually engaged in solving an insoluble puzzle – the puzzle of how poetry gets written; and the material upon which he works in his own poetry. In the end, the question is simply: how did I write *La Jeune Parque* (or *Le Cimetière marin*)? The questions with which he is concerned are questions which no poet of an earlier generation would have raised; they are questions that belong to the present self-conscious century. This gives to Valéry's thought a singular documentary value.

There are, of course, incidental observations which can be taken to heart by the young poet; there are observations which can help the reader towards understanding the nature [xii] of poetry. There are also, if I am not mistaken, observations dangerous for the young poet, and observations confusing for the reader. Before attempting to define Valéry's central interest, it seems proper to give a few instances of these incidental remarks of both kinds.

The insistence, in Valéry's poetics, upon the small part played, in the elaboration of a poem, by what he calls the *rêve* – what is ordinarily called the 'inspiration' – and upon the subsequent process of deliberate, conscious, arduous labour, is a most wholesome reminder to the young poet. It is corrective of that romantic attitude which, in employing the word 'inspiration', inclines consciously or unconsciously to regard the poet's role, in the composition of a poem, as mediumistic and irresponsible. Whenever we come across a poem (this has often happened to me in the course of reading manuscripts) which appears to have some original merit, but which has been turned out into the world in an unfinished state, or perhaps is only a kind of note of something which might provide the material of a good poem, we suspect that the author has depended too confidently upon his 'inspiration'; in other words, that he has shirked the labour of smelting what may have been payable ore. On the other hand, as any advice, literally and unintelligently applied, can lead to disastrous consequences, it is as well to point out that while the poet should regard no toil as too arduous and no application of time as too long, for bringing a poem as near perfection as his abilities will take it, he should also have enough power of self-criticism to know where to stop. As with the painting in Balzac's *Le Chef-d'oeuvre inconnu*, there may be a point beyond which every alteration the author makes will be for the worse. A short poem, or a passage of a long poem, may appear in its final form at once; or it may have to go through the transformations of a dozen drafts. And my own experience [xiii] is, that when the result is successful, nobody except the author himself will be able to distinguish between those passages which have undergone no alteration, and those which have been rewritten again and again. I think I understand what Valéry means when he says that a poem is never finished: at least, his words to this effect have a meaning for me. To me they mean that a poem is 'finished', or that I will never touch it again, when I am sure that I have exhausted my own resources, that the poem is as good as *I* can make *that* poem. It may be a bad poem: but nothing that I can do will make it better. Yet I cannot help thinking that, even if it is a good poem, I could have made a better poem of it – the same poem, but better – if I were a better poet.

A corollary, perhaps, of Valéry's emphasis upon the fundamental 'brainwork' (is not the phrase Dante Rossetti's?) is his insistence upon the value for the poet of the exercise of difficult and complicated rhyming stanza forms. No poet was ever more conscious of the benefit of working in strict forms, the advantage to be gained by imposing upon oneself limitations to overcome. Such exercises are, of course, of no use to the man who has nothing to say, except possibly that of helping him to appreciate the work of those poets who have used these forms well; but what they can teach the genuine poet, is the way in which form and content must come to terms. It is only by practising the sonnet, the sestina, or the villanelle, that we learn what sort of content can *not* be expressed in each of these forms; and it is only the poet who has developed this sense of fitness who is qualified to attempt 'free verse'. No one should write 'free verse' – or, at least, offer it for publication – until he has discovered for himself that free verse allows him no more freedom than any other verse.

Another important contribution by Valéry to the educa-[xiv]tion of the poet is his emphasis upon *structure*. Although a poem can be made out of a succession of felicitous verses, it must nevertheless be built. This law, like others, could be made too absolute, and lead us into absurdities as deplorable as those of some eighteenth-century critics. It need not oblige us to deny all merit to FitzGerald's *Rubáiyát*: for that poem does make a total impression which is not merely the sum of the impressions of the several quatrains; but it does, I think, justify us in affirming that *The Deserted Village* approximates to a perfection that we miss in the *Elegy Written in a Country Church-yard*.

Valéry's analogy, in the matter of structure, is Architecture. Elsewhere, as we shall see presently, he compares poetry to the Dance; and he always maintained that assimilation of Poetry to Music which was a Symbolist tenet. Between these analogies there is no contradiction, unless we are misled by the famous phrase of Walter Pater. For Music itself may be conceived as a striving towards an unattainable timelessness; and if the other arts may be thought of as yearning for duration, so Music may be thought of as yearning for the stillness of painting or sculpture. I speak as one with no technical training in music, but I find that I enjoy, and 'understand', a piece of music better for knowing it well, simply because I have at any moment during its performance a memory of the part that has preceded and a memory of the part that is still to come. Ideally, I should like to be able to hold the whole of a great symphony in my mind at once. The same is true, surely, of a great tragedy: the better we know it, the more fully we hold in mind, during the action, what has preceded and what is to come, the more intense is our experience. It is only in a detective thriller, or in some kinds of comedy and farce, that the *unexpected* is a contribution to, and even a necessary element of, our enjoyment.

[xv] I have considered Valéry's insistence upon hard work, upon study of prosodic and stanzaic form, and upon structure. There is, however, one direction in which Valéry's theory and practice take him, which seems to me not without its dangers. This direction is indicated, is even imposed, by the sharp distinction which he draws between poetry and prose. He supports this division by a very neat and persuasive analogy, *viz*.:

Poetry : Prose : Dancing : Walking (or Running)

Prose, Valéry maintains, is *instrumental*: its purpose is to convey a meaning, to impart information, to convince of a truth, to direct action; once its message has been apprehended, we dismiss the means by which it has been communicated. So with walking or running: our purpose is to get to a destination. The only value of our movement has been to achieve some end that we have set ourselves. But the purpose of the dance is the dance itself. Similarly with poetry: the poem is for its own sake – we enjoy a poem as we enjoy dancing; and as for the words, instead of looking *through* them, so to speak, we are looking *at* them. That is, as I have just remarked, persuasive; or rather, it illuminates like the flash of an empty cigarette lighter in the dark: if there is no fuel in the lighter, the momentary flash leaves a sense of darkness more impenetrable than before. It would be a quibble, to point out that dancing is sometimes purposive (the purpose of a war dance, I believe, is to rouse the dormant pugnacity of the dancers); for even if dancing is always pure delight in rhythmical movement, the analogy may be misleading. I think that much poetry will be found to have the instrumental value that Valéry reserves to prose, and that much prose gives us the kind of delight that Valéry holds to be solely within the [xvi] province of poetry. And if it is maintained that prose which gives that kind of delight *is* poetry, then I can only say that the distinction between poetry and prose has been completely obliterated, for it would seem that prose can be read as poetry, or poetry as prose, according to the whim of the reader.

I have never yet come across a final, comprehensive, and satisfactory account of the difference between poetry and prose. We can distinguish between prose and verse, and between verse and poetry; but the moment the intermediate term *verse* is suppressed, I do not believe that any meaningful distinction between prose and poetry is meaningful.

It is not however, this attempt to discover some essential difference between prose and poetry that seems to me dangerous, but a tendency, which is very much favoured by this account of prose and poetry, to approve a difference of vocabulary and idiom between poetry and prose. The words set free by Valéry from the restrictions of prose may tend to form a separate language. But the farther the idiom, vocabulary, and syntax of poetry depart from those of prose, the more artificial the language of poetry will become. When the written language remains fixed, while the spoken language, the vulgar speech, is undergoing changes, it must ultimately be replaced by a new written language, founded on current speech. Now the language of prose is ordinarily nearer to that of speech than is the language of poetry; so that if poetry arrogates the right to idiom, vocabulary, and syntax different from that of prose, it may eventually become so artificial as no longer to be able to convey living feeling and living thought. Speech on every level, from that of the least educated to that of the most cultivated, changes from generation to generation; and the *norm* for a poet's language is the way his contemporaries talk. In assimilating poetry to [xvii] music, Valéry has, it seems to me, failed to insist upon its relation to speech. The poet can improve, indeed it is his duty to try to improve, the language that he speaks and hears. The characters in a play can, and usually should, have a much greater mastery of language than their originals in life would have. But neither the poem nor the play can afford to ignore the necessity of persuading us that this is the language we should ourselves speak, if we spoke as well as we should like to speak. It is perhaps significant that Valéry should attach so much importance as he does to the achievement of Mallarmé, and nowhere (so far as I am aware) acknowledge any indebtedness to the discoveries of Laforgue and Corbière.

Those observations of Valéry, which should be taken to heart by poets, can also be pondered with profit by readers – not for direct understanding of poetry, but as a help to understanding the kind of preparation that the poet needs, and the nature of the labour that the poet undertakes. And especially pertinent for the reader of poetry – and for the critic of poetry – is his repeated insistence that poetry must first of all be *enjoyed*, if it is to be of any use at all; that it must be enjoyed as poetry, and not for any other reason; and that most of the rest of what is written, talked, and taught is philology, history, biography, sociology, psychology. He defends the privacy, even the anonymity, of the poet, and the independence of the poem when it has been written and dismissed by the poet. At this stage, the poet's interpretation of his poem is not required: what matters is what the poem means – in the sense in which a poem may be said to have 'meaning'. What the poet meant it to mean or what he thinks it means now that it is written, are questions not worth the asking.

So far, however, I have not approached the essential problem, which is that of the characteristics distinguishing [xviii] Valéry's *art poétique* from that of anyone else. His purpose is not to teach the writing of poetry or to improve the understanding of it; his purpose is not primarily to facilitate the understanding of his own poetry – though it will very soon strike the perception of the perceptive reader, that much of what he predicates of 'poetry' is applicable only to his own poetry. The best approach, I believe, is through a little essay, of very early date, included in this volume, entitled 'On Literary Technique'. The date is 1889, but this early credo gives a clue to his later development. What it announces is no less than a new style for poets, as well as a new style for poetry. The satanist, the dandy, the *poète maudit* have had their day: eleven years before the end of the nineteenth century Valéry invents the role which is to make him representative of the twentieth:

> . . . a totally new and modern conception of the poet. He is no longer the disheveled madman who writes a whole poem in the course of one feverish night; he is a cool scientist, almost an algebraist, in the service of a subtle dreamer. A hundred lines at the most will make up his longest poems. . . . He will take care not to hurl on to paper everything whispered to him in fortunate moments by the Muse of Free Association. On the contrary, everything he has imagined, felt, dreamed, and planned will be passed through a sieve, weighed, filtered, subjected to *form*, and condensed as much as possible so as to gain in power what it loses in length: a sonnet, for example, will be a true quintessence, a nutrient, a concentrated and distilled juice, reduced to fourteen lines, carefully *composed* with a view to a final and overwhelming effect.

We must remember that Valéry was a very young man when he wrote these enthusiastic words; but in making this allowance, we are all the more struck by the fact that this is essentially the point of view to which he was to adhere throughout [xix] his life. The association of the 'dreamer' and the 'algebraist', for example, was to remain unbroken. The loyalty to Poe ('a hundred lines at the most') was to endure to the end. But what is most impressive about the passage I have just quoted, is that it discloses, behind Valéry's Idea of Poetry, another and perhaps the controlling Idea – Valéry's Idea of the Poet. It is from the conception of the poet that he proceeds to the conception of poetry, and not the other way about. Now this Idea of the Poet was a prophetic one, prophetic not only of the mature Valéry, but of the ideals and the idols of the coming age. Looked at in this way, the 'cool scientist' is an alternative, rather than the antithesis to the 'dishevelled madman': a different mask for the same actor. Poe, to be sure, combined both roles: but it is only as the 'cool scientist' that Valéry sees him, 'mathematician, philosopher, and great writer'. True, Valéry wrote this credo during the time of des Esseintes and Dorian Gray. The mature Valéry would not have extolled, as he did in this same manifesto of 1889, 'the morbid search for the rarest pleasures'; nor would he have overworked the qualification 'too' ('we love the art of this age . . . too vibrant, too tense, too *musical*', etc). What is significant is not such phrases as these, but the introduction of such a substantive as 'nutrient' (*osmazôme*) and such a verb as 'distill' (*cohober*). In the year 1889, the young Valéry has already cast himself in the role which he was to play with such distinguished success during the years from 1917 (the publication of *La Jeune Parque*) to his death in 1945.

Valéry in fact invented, and was to impose upon his age, not so much a new conception of poetry as a new conception of the poet. The tower of ivory has been fitted up as a laboratory – a solitary laboratory, for Valéry never went so far as to advocate 'teamwork' in the writing of poetry. The [xx] poet is comparable to the mathematical physicist, or else to the biologist or chemist. He is to carry out the role of scientist as studiously as Sherlock Holmes did: this is the aspect of himself to which he calls the public's attention. Our picture of the poet is to be very like that of the austere, bespectacled man in a white coat, whose portrait appears in advertisements, weighing out or testing the drugs of which is compounded some medicine with an impressive name.

What I have said above is what I may call the primary aspect of Valéry's poetics. The secondary aspect is its relation to his own poetry. Everything that he says about the writing of poetry must be read, of course, with constant reference to the poetry that he wrote. No one, I think, will find these essays fully intelligible until he has read Valéry's most important poems. To some extent, I see his essays on poetry as a kind of defence and vindication of his own poems – a justification of their being the kind of poems they are, of their being as brief as they are, and of their being as few as they are. And to some extent the essays seem to me a kind of substitute for the poems he did not write. In one respect especially I find these essays very different from Poe's 'Philosophy of Composition', different and more genuine. I have never been able to believe that Poe's famous essay is an account of how 'The Raven' was written: if 'The Raven' was written with so much calculation, then it ought, as I have said elsewhere, to be better written than it is. But what for Poe was an ingenious exercise, was deadly earnest for Valéry, and from very early years. Therefore, one is ready to believe that Valéry's critical intelligence was active from the start, and that he had thought very deeply on how to write poetry before he composed either *La Jeune Parque* or *Le Cimetière marin*: and this, for me, gives to his notes on the writing of these poems, a value greater [xxi] than any I can attach to Poe's. Certainly, one feels that Valéry's theory and practice are faithful to each other: how far his practice was the application of the theory, and how far his theory is simply a correct account of his practice, is an unanswerable question. It is this unity of the two which gives his essays a perennial fascination.

Valéry's account of the genesis, maturation, and completion of a poem cannot fail to arouse responses both of assent and of dissent from other poets. There are moments when I feel that an experience of Valéry's has some correspondence with one of my own: when he has recorded some process which I recognise and of which he makes me for the first time fully conscious. It is not in the nature of things that there should be a point-for-point correspondence between the mental processes of any two poets. Not only do poems come into being in as many ways as there are poets; for the same poet, I believe, the process may vary from poem to poem. Every poem has its own embryological pattern: and only the poem of a Valéry is attended, throughout its gestation, by an illustrious medical specialist. Sometimes, I think, Valéry allowed himself to be carried away too far by his metaphors of the clinic and the laboratory, as in the following general statement about his labours preparatory to writing a poem:

> With every question, before making any deep examination of the content, I take a look at the language; I generally proceed like a surgeon who sterilises his hands and prepares the area to be operated on. This is what I call *cleaning up the verbal situation*. You must excuse this expression equating the words and forms of speech with the hands and instruments of a surgeon.

This passage I find very obscure; but it may be the fact that I cannot identify, under the disguise of this metaphor, any [xxii] experience of my own, that makes me suspect that 'cleaning up the verbal situation' is, in plain English, eyewash.

The questions I have left to the end are: Why are Valéry's essays worth reading, and with what expectation should we read them? These questions would be easier to answer if the essays could be fitted into any existing category, the usefulness of which is admitted. We do not turn to Valéry's *art poétique* in the hope of learning how to write poetry or how to read it. We do not even turn to it primarily for the light it throws on Valéry's poetry: certainly we can say as truly that if the prose throws light on the poems, the poems also illuminate the prose. I think that we read these essays, and I think people will continue to read them, because we find Valéry to be a singularly interesting, enigmatic, and disturbing author, a poet who has realised in his life and work one conception of the role of the poet so amply as to have acquired also a kind of mythological status. We read the essays because, as Valéry himself says, 'there is no theory that is not a fragment, carefully prepared, of some autobiography.' We could almost say that Valéry's essays form a part of his poetical works. We read them for their own sake, for the delight in following the subtleties of thought which moves like a trained dancer, and which has every resource of language at its command; for the pleasure of sudden illuminations even when they turn out to be *feux follets*; for the excitement of an activity which always seems on the point of catching the inapprehensible as the mind continues indefatigably to weave its fine logo-daedal web.

There is, in the mind and work of Valéry, a curious paradox. He presents himself to the reader, not only as a tireless explorer of the labyrinths of philosophic speculation, but also, under the aegis of Leonardo da Vinci, as a man of [xxiii] scientific temper, fascinated by the problems of method; a ranging and restless mind; a dilettante of science but a specialist in a science of his own invention – the science of poetry. Yet, when we peruse the list of titles of his essays, we find a remarkably limited subject matter, with no evidence of omnivorous reading, or of the varied interests of a Coleridge or a Goethe. He returns perpetually to the same insoluble problems. It would almost seem that the one object of his curiosity was – himself. He reminds us of Narcissus gazing into the pool, and partakes of the attraction and the mystery of Narcissus, the aloofness and frigidity of that spiritual celibate.

The one complaint which I am tempted to lodge against Valéry's poetics, is that it provides us with no criterion of *seriousness*. He is deeply concerned with the problem of process, of how the poem is made, but not with the question of how it is related to the rest of life in such a way as to give the reader the shock of feeling that the poem has been to him, not merely an experience, but a serious experience. And by 'experience' I mean here, not an isolable event, having its value solely in itself and not in relation to anything else, but something that has entered into and been fused with a multitude of other experiences in the formation of the person that the reader is developing into. I put it in this way, to avoid giving the misleading impression that I place the *seriousness* simply in the value of the materials out of which the poem is made. That would be to define one thing in terms of another kind of reality. The material of a poem is only *that* material after the poem has been made. How far the seriousness is in the subject treated, how far in the treatment to which the poet subjects it, how far in the intention of the poet, and how far it is in the poet below the level of conscious intention, we shall never agree upon with any poem that has [xxiv] ever been written. But in mentioning something of which we notice the absence in Valéry's poetics, I am not questioning the seriousness of his own finest poems. If some of Valéry's poems were not very serious poems indeed – if two of them at least, were not as likely to last as long as the French language – there could have been no interest for him in studying the process of their composition, and no delight for us in studying the result of his study.

[Lady Margaret Rhondda]

Memorial tribute for Lady Margaret Rhondda. *T&T*, 39 (26 July 1958), 911.
Not in Gallup but would be C624a.

Sir, – I hope and believe that the death of Viscountess Rhondda will not bring to an end so valuable a periodical as *Time and Tide*, but her death does seem to mark the end of an epoch. That phrase at least indicates something of the place she seemed to me to occupy. I have been a reader of *Time and Tide* for more years than I can remember; I had been impressed by the integrity and independence of mind of its Proprietor and Editor long before I had met Viscountess Rhondda herself.

Many who knew her will have spoken of her kindness, of her hospitality (which I remember both in Surrey and in London), of the wide scope of her interests, and of her passionate sense of public responsibility. I should like to recall one instance of her fairness and tolerance. There was no paper in which I felt more assurance that any serious letter of mine was likely to be accepted than *Time and Tide*. There was one occasion on which I felt impelled to protest against an undertaking which no one had publicly questioned. I do not think that Viscountess Rhondda agreed with me; the man whom this enterprise was designed to commemorate had been her friend; nevertheless she printed my letter and told me privately that she respected my motives in writing it. Among other excellences Viscountess Rhondda had the great and rare virtue of magnanimity.

I am, etc.,
T. S. ELIOT

T. S. Eliot Talks about his Poetry

Eliot introducing his poems at a reading he gave at Columbia University on 28 Apr. 1950. He was introduced by Lionel Trilling.
Columbia University Forum, 2. 1 (Fall 1958), 11–14. Gallup C626.

[12] Ladies and gentlemen: It is some three years since I have read any of my poems in New York. It is longer than I care to remember since I had the privilege of reading to Columbia University, and even then I don't think I had the additional glory of speaking to both Columbia and Barnard at once. It was so long ago, it occurs to me that perhaps I may have been reading then to the fathers or the mothers – or to the fathers *and* the mothers – of some of the present audience. At any rate, I should like to think that there are some of the present audience who have never heard me read before.

Now this isn't because of the comparative penury of my output of poetry. If you have heard me before, you may hear some of the same tunes again. I think on the whole that in one respect to have rather a small volume of poetry to choose from has a certain advantage; it gives me the hope that a large part of the audience will have read, and will be more or less familiar with, some of the things that I am reading. And I think that it's always interesting to hear an author read his own poem if you know it already and can compare his interpretation of it with your own.

To those who may hear poems that they've not read, I should like to say for their consolation that I myself can never understand a poem until I've read it to myself. All that I get from hearing a new poem is – I may say to myself, 'This sounds interesting, I would like to read it.' So I hope that I'll give that at least to those who may hear something unfamiliar.

But the chief reason why I hope that some out of this audience are hearing a few poems for the first time is not that I shall read the same poems I read before, it is that I shall make the same preliminary *remarks* that I have made before. There are certain things that I always say when

I give a reading, and anyone who has heard me already will have heard them before, and anyone who ever hears me again will hear them again. They've really been reduced to what seem to me the essentials.

I'd like to explain in the first place that when I read my poems, I read them in chronological order. They fall into certain definite periods, between which there are gaps indicating a sort of state of mental drought when I didn't expect to write anything ever again.

Then, as I always say, I read the best, I think, the poems that I've written most recently or which are at least remote from my present existence; so that I always believe that I read rather better toward the close of the evening than I do at the beginning. I've almost lost touch with the man I was when I wrote the early poems.

The other thing is that I occasionally make remarks in between poems or groups of poems. I do so for the purpose of separating one poem or one type of poem from another, and of giving you, the audience, an interval in which to rest and clear the previous poems away from your minds before you hear the next. I think that it can be extremely fatiguing and in the end make no effect at all if a man just reads his poems straight ahead without making any comment. So you are to take these comments merely [13] as necessary interruptions or intervals, and you need pay no more attention to them than they command from you.

Now, there's one other remark to make, and that is to compare direct poetry-reading like this with the gramophone record. I've made, as other poets have nowadays made, gramophone records of a large number of my poems, and I've taken some trouble over them, and I've learned a lot from doing so about enunciation. The question is, is there any advantage to a live reading – in which the author is standing in your presence reading to you – over a gramophone record? Well, there are two reasons, I think, why a reading is different from a gramophone record.

In the first place, when you're making a gramophone record, you are very much on edge to avoid slips. Your chief anxiety is not to do anything wrong, whereas when you're reading directly to an audience, you're not worrying so much about making slips or doing something wrong, but you're anxious to get something positively right. A gramophone record may have no mistakes in it, but at the same time the anxiety to avoid mistakes rather prevents one from expanding as one sometimes does in front of an appreciative audience. The other reason is that I've found it impossible to do recording for more than twenty minutes at a time because the strain is so great in recording that fatigue in the voice begins to show after that time. Therefore, a gramophone recording such as I make is made up of sections which are put together; having made the sections myself, I can often detect the joints where I left off one day and began another day, perhaps halfway through a poem. When one is reading to an audience one may make mistakes and they don't matter, but one has the opportunity of occasionally rising to one's very best, an opportunity one hasn't in recording.

Now, in a public reading my remarks in between poems become less and less necessary except as interruptions, because there are so many people nowadays who understand my poems better than I do and have explained them to other people, to the world, and to me. And sometimes my poems turn out to be much more unpleasant than I thought they were. But I'll try to say something here and there merely to give you a breathing space between poems.

Now, the first period of which I shall give specimens is the period up to, say, about 1914. That was a long time ago. I shall read you *The Love Song of J. Alfred Prufrock*. I wrote it a long time ago, and perhaps I don't read it as well as I would have done a long time ago, because I like some of my later poems better. However, I'll do my best by it because I know there are people who like it better than some of my later works. I shall read one other poem of the same period, *Rhapsody on a Windy Night*, which I don't think I've ever read to an audience, so that will be rather an experiment. But I'll begin with *Prufrock*.

[Reads *The Love Song of J. Alfred Prufrock*.]

There is one thing I might say about *Prufrock*. Some years ago a scholar wrote an article about it in a learned journal. He made a rather interesting discovery. He discovered something that I hadn't been aware of myself: that before writing *Prufrock*, I had been reading and had been very much influenced by Dostoevsky's *Crime and Punishment*. He produced parallel passages which quite convinced me – because I knew that I *had* been reading *Crime and Punishment*. Unfortunately, he went on to prove something which wasn't so. As the English translation of *Crime and Punishment* by Constance Garnett appeared in 1914, he inferred that *Prufrock* had been written in 1914. If he had written to ask the author, he would have been told – as he was later, having sent me an offprint of his article – that I had read *Crime and Punishment* in the French translation, which appeared, I think, in 1909 or 1910.

Rhapsody on a Windy Night. This was written in Paris in 1910 or 1911. I don't know very much about it now. If it needs any explanation, I must leave it to others to explain. But I don't think I've ever read it to an audience.

[Reads *Rhapsody on a Windy Night*.]

I can't explain that now . . . I recognise the geraniums; they were Jules Laforgue's geraniums, not mine, I'm afraid, originally.

Now the next period, which is, say, 1915 to 1919, includes several poems in quatrains, dealing with a man named Sweeney and other people. These poems were largely influenced by Ezra Pound's suggestion that one should study [14] Théophile Gautier and take a rest from *vers libre* in regular quatrains. Part of the outcome of this was the poem, which I shall read, called *The Hippopotamus*. This is a poem which I originally read, I remember, at a poetry reading for the benefit of some Red Cross affair with Sir Edmund Gosse in the chair, and he was profoundly shocked. On the other hand, the late Arnold Bennett liked it better than anything I'd written up to the time of his death, and kept asking me to write 'another Hippopotamus'.

Thirdly, it's the only poem of mine which I've any reason to suppose that James Joyce ever read. Once when I saw him in Paris he told me that he'd been to the Jardin des Plantes and had paid his respects to my friend The Hippopotamus. I imagine that he may have read this poem. However, it doesn't seem as shocking to anybody now, I think, as it did all those years ago; I think very few things remain as shocking.

[Reads *The Hippopotamus*.]

Of course, things do come back on one. A good many years later I became a churchwarden, and I often thought of those lines '. . . the True Church need never stir / To gather in its dividends', when we were wondering how to keep the church going on the collections, which weren't so good as one would have liked. So one lives and learns.

Now I'm going to try another experiment. We come to the third period and *The Waste Land*. I'm going to see if I can read *A Game of Chess*, although it seems to me that my cockney accent isn't quite good enough. On the other hand, I was encouraged the other day when someone told me that my recording of this seemed to them very good. Even if my cockney accent isn't good enough, I hope that I'll convey something by reading this which wouldn't otherwise transpire.

[Reads *A Game of Chess,* followed by *What the Thunder Said* from *The Waste Land.*]

At this point there is a rather important break in my work for several years; so before going on, I choose to read a poem of a very different sort, which comes from a later period still; in fact, which doesn't really belong to any particular period. It's from *The Book of Practical Cats*, and it's called *Growltiger's Last Stand*.

[Reads *Growltiger's Last Stand.*]

We now come to 1929 – *Fragment of an Agon*, which I don't often try. Again, I'm doing something I don't usually do. You'll just have to imagine the different speakers. I can't stop to indicate who is saying what, but Mr

Sweeney is saying most of what's of any importance. This was a work I never finished because it has to be spoken too quickly to be possible on the stage, to convey the sort of rhythm that I intended. It was much too fast for dialogue, really.

[Reads *Fragment of an Agon* and the fifth section of *Ash Wednesday*.]

I think I'll read two of the Ariel poems. I'd like to read one which came much later than any of the others, indeed later than any in my collected volume, which I wrote about three or four years ago, more or less to order.

[Reads *The Cultivation of Christmas Trees* and *Lines for an Old Man*.]

I should like to read one chorus from *Murder in the Cathedral*, and then I'm afraid I must read one whole Quartet. [Applause]. I will read the opening chorus to the second part of *Murder in the Cathedral*. This wasn't in the original production because it was thought that if the first part opened with a chorus, it would be more symmetrical if the second one did so. Then I should like to end, if I may, by reading the whole of *East Coker*, the second Quartet. All the last three Quartets are in a sense war poems – increasingly. *East Coker* belongs to the period of what we called the 'phony war'.

['Mr Eliot read the last two poems, thanked his audience for their attention, and received their applause.']

Bishop Bell

Postscript to an obituary notice for Bishop George Bell,
The Times, 14 Oct. 1958, 13. Gallup 626a.

I hope that it is not too late for a reader who has been abroad and who has just returned to England, to add a personal postscript to your obituary notice of Bishop Bell, and to Sir Charles Tennyson's tribute to his services to the arts.

On a summer afternoon in 1934, walking in the garden of his Palace, Dr Bell proposed to me that I should write the play for the next Canterbury Festival. I accepted the invitation and wrote *Murder in the Cathedral*. To Dr Bell's initiative (and subsequently to Mr Ashley Duke's enterprise in bringing the play to London) I owe my admission to the theatre.

I am only one among other artists and poets who have benefited from the patronage of Bishop Bell, and who have reason to remember him with gratitude and affection.

The Very Revd F. P. Harton

Supplement to John Betjeman's postscript to the obituary notice for
The Very Revd F. P. Harton. *The Times*, 14 Oct. 1958, 13.
Prefaced with 'Mr. T. S. Eliot writes: – '. Gallup 626b.

In supplementing your obituary notice of the late Dean of Wells, Mr John Betjeman – through whom I became acquainted with Dr Harton many years ago when he was vicar of Baulking – has written admirably of the Dean's personality and the impression he made on all who came in contact with him. I should like, however, to give a little more emphasis to the particular combination of scholarship with a deep understanding of ascetic theology and of the spiritual which is found in his writings. We owe him a debt of gratitude for *The Elements of the Spiritual Life* and it is greatly to be regretted that he did not live to complete the study of the work of Richard of Saint Victor with which he was occupied at the time of his death.

[Salutation]

Message to the Hungarian Writers' Association Abroad. *Iroldalmi Újág* (1 Nov. 1958), 2.
Prefaced by a translation into Hungarian headed 'ÜDVÖZLÉSEK [Salutation] |
T. S. Eliot'. Not in Gallup but would be C626b (thus rendering 'C626b' C626c).

I am very happy to send a message for the annual general meeting of the Hungarian Writers' Association Abroad, a message both to the writers who remain in Hungary and to those who have taken refuge in other countries. The plight of the literary artist (who of all men needs freedom of expression) under a repressive and alien regime is one with which all writers more happily placed should sympathise. But we who are writers in the western world must also sympathise very deeply with those literary artists who endeavour to express themselves in their own tongue while living in a foreign country. It is surely more difficult for the writer, than for the musician or the practitioner of one of the plastic arts, to keep alive his genius and his spirit when deprived from the nourishment of his native country: I am happy at least that you have periodicals in which to express yourselves and to communicate with each other and with others of your community who are from home.

Television is not Friendly Enough

City Press, 28 Nov. 1958, 12. Subheaded *'By T. S. ELIOT'*. A reply to a question printed as part of a special feature: Gallup. Gallup C628.

The sentence 'one of the strongest qualities of television is that the performers seem to move right into people's homes' irritates me very much. I am not a lover of television, and the prospect of the performers of a play 'moving right into my home' is one I do not welcome.

I much prefer moving out of my home and seeing them in flesh and blood in the theatre, rather than looking at a kind of photograph likely to give me a headache.

I do not agree with the statement that television has an intimacy and friendliness which the living theatre has lost. If the theatre has lost its intimacy and friendliness, when did it lose it?

DIFFERENT QUESTION

If it lost it when the Elizabethan stage was replaced by the proscenium stage, that is a different question altogether. The intimacy and friendliness lost by the proscenium stage is certainly not recaptured, in my experience, by television. In fact, I feel much more remote from a televised play than I do from any play at any West End theatre.

I should like to make it clear that I am not discussing the pros and cons of two types of theatre but the pros and cons of any type of theatre in which one sees the living actors over a theatre which merely gives one a kind of photographic reproduction.

[Eliot's choice of Books of the Year]

Sunday Times, 28 Dec. 1958, 6.
Eliot's choice is one of eight printed. Gallup C629.

I must remind your readers that it would be obviously unsuitable for me to include any book with the imprint of the publishing house of which I am a director; and that I pass over works (for example, of philosophy and theology) designed for a limited public. Under these restrictions, I have chosen three books out of those I have read among this year's publications.

Critical studies of the work of novelists are apt to be meaningless for readers who have not read the authors in question, and superfluous for those who have. Erich Heller's study of Thomas Mann is an exception.

I have not read Mann's novels, but I feel sure that those who have done so will understand Mann much better after reading *The Ironic German* (Secker & Warburg); and as for myself, I not only have learned a good deal about Mann, but (as with everything that Professor Heller writes) have profited by contact with the mind of Professor Heller.

The writing of Erich Kahler, to judge by *The Tower and the Abyss* (Cape), has this in common with that of Professor Heller, that whether one agrees with the author or not, what he writes must provoke fresh thinking on the part of any reader capable of that exertion. There have been many books written on 'the predicament of our age', some of which I have read, but none of which has impressed me more deeply. The author is concerned with a common danger which he discerns the world over, one which transcends political and ideological differences between East and West, a danger the portents of which are to be observed in America as well as in Russia, a danger the nature of which is indicated by his contrast between 'community' and 'collective'. In the former he finds the proper condition of Man, in the latter Man's transformation into something like the social insects. Few books in this field of thought since Ortega y Gasset's *The Revolt of the Masses* have stirred and disturbed my mind so deeply.

A book of a different category from either of the two mentioned above is *The Chequered Shade: Reflections on Obscurity in Poetry* by John Press (Oxford). The author has not only read and digested all the contemporary poetry against which the reproach of obscurity has been brought, but is thoroughly well equipped to draw parallels and contrasts with the obscurities of English poetry of the past. He quotes felicitously, has great critical acumen, and his style is agreeable; and on its own plane of discourse the book seems to me to say the last word on the subject of obscurity in poetry. I say 'on its own plane of discourse' having in mind the different approach to the study of contemporary poetry to be found in two chapters of Erich Kahler's book.

1959

[Edwin Muir]

The Times, 7 Jan. 1959, 14.
Gallup C630.

Your obituary of Edwin Muir does justice both to the man and to his work, and requires neither supplement nor correction. Nevertheless I hope that a personal tribute from an admirer will not be amiss. Muir's literary criticism had always seemed to me of the best of our time; after I came to know him I realised that it owed its excellence not only to his power of intellect and acuteness of sensibility but to those moral qualities which make us remember him, as you say justly, as 'in some ways almost a saintly man'.

It was more recently that I came to regard his poetry as ranking with the best poetry of our time. As a poet he began late; as a poet he was recognised late; but some of his finest work – perhaps his very finest work – was written when he was already over 60. His two most recent volumes of verse, *The Labyrinth* and *One Foot in Eden*, are, I think, those which contain more of his best work than any other; and the still more recent and as yet unpublished poems which I have seen show no falling off in quality. For this late development we are reminded of the later poetry of Yeats; and Muir had to struggle with bad health also: but in the one case as in the other (and Muir is by no means unworthy to be mentioned together with Yeats) we recognise a triumph of the human spirit.

Rudyard Kipling

<small>*Mercure de France*, 1145 (Jan. 1959), 5–15. Translated into French, as the headnote states, by Henri Fluchère. Not in Gallup but would be C630a.</small>

<small>Minor corrections have been made to the texts quoted by the translator.</small>

<small>The article 'The Unfading Genius of Rudyard Kipling', published in *Kipling Journal*, 26. 129 in Mar. 1959 (Gallup C632; *see below*, pp. 435–40), derives to some extent from this address but resembles it only very intermittently.</small>

L'Académie Septentrionale a reçu M. T. S. Eliot en remplacement de Rudyard Kipling. Il a été accueilli dans la Compagnie par M. Maurice Garçon.

On sait que l'oeuvre de Rudyard Kipling a été révélée aux lecteurs français par Le Mercure de France, *qui a publié presque tous ses ouvrages. C'est une raison de plus pour notre revue de se réjouir de pouvoir publier les deux discours prononcés à l'occasion de cette réception qui s'est déroulée le 4 octobre à Paris.*

Le discours de M. T. S. Eliot a été traduit par M. Henri Fluchère. – M. F.

Messieurs,

En me choisissant pour faire partie de l'Académie Septentrionale, vous m'avez fait un grand honneur, honneur d'une espèce particulièrement chère a mon coeur. L'idée d'une Culture Européenne, culture à laquelle chaque nation de l'Occident devrait payer sa contribution, est une idée que j'ai toujours caressée. Ainsi en est-il de l'idéal de l'homme de lettres dont les oeuvres deviennent l'héritage, non seulement de ses compatriotes et des peuples qui parlent sa langue, mais [6] du publique cultivé de chaque pays d'Europe: se trouver dans les rangs des écrivains de cet ordre, voilà l'idéal le plus élevé auquel poète, romancier ou philosophe puisse aspirer. Être invité, par conséquent, à représenter l'Angleterre à l'Académie Septentrionale est un honneur que je suis bien qualifié pour apprécier, méritais-je ou non de le recevoir. Et lorsque j'ai appris que j'avais été choisi pour occuper la place que Rudyard Kipling avait occupée, et qu'il m'écherrait de prononcer son éloge dans cette assemblée, j'ai ressenti de l'orgueil, et, d'une certaine façon, j'ai eu le sentiment de quelque chose d'inévitable.

J'aimerais expliquer pourquoi le nom de Rudyard Kipling a éveillé en moi ce sentiment de la fatalité et du devoir. Lorsque j'ai fait un choix des poèmes de Kipling publié en 1941 avec une longue présentation, le moment était bien choisi pour rappeler au publique anglais l'importance de Kipling et faire revivre une réputation qui s'était amenuisée sous l'influence des critiques libéraux, pour ne pas dire radicaux. L'étonnement fut cependant considérable dans le monde des lettres de voir un poète dont les vers étaient considérés comme le pôle opposé de ceux de Kipling se faire le champion de Kipling non seulement comme prosateur, mais comme versificateur, et même poète. Alors que ma poésie était d'abord apparue trop obscure et abstruse pour mériter la faveur populaire, celle de Kipling était depuis longtemps tenue pour trop simple, trop primitive, trop populaire, en vérité, trop proche des mauvais vers de la chanson de music-hall pour mériter autre chose que le mépris du critique difficile. On me soupçonna sinon d'insincérité, du moins de prendre un malin plaisir au paradoxe. Cependant les vers, aussi bien que les contes de Kipling, avaient déjà fait sur ma jeunesse une profonde impression.

C'était, bien sûr, le Kipling de la première heure, celui des *Ballades de la Chambrée* et des *Simples Contes des Collines*. Son influence est demeurée en moi, et s'est révélée à moi, comme il advient avec des influences de jeunesse, par d'étranges signes irrationnels. Le premier de mes poèmes à devenir célèbre s'appelle [7] *La Chanson d'Amour de J. Alfred Prufrock*. Dans le poème lui-même, on trouve l'influence de Laforgue, et aussi de Dostoiewski. Kipling ne se fait sentir que dans le titre: je suis sûr, en effet, qu'il ne serait pas appelé *La Chanson d'Amour* si n'avait pas existé le titre d'un poème de Kipling qui s'était obstinément implanté dans ma tête: *La Chanson d'Amour de Har Dyal*. Bien des années plus tard, j'écrivis un poème intitulé *Les Hommes Creux*. Là encore Kipling est dans le titre, et dans le titre seulement, car c'est un écho du titre de l'un de ces poèmes, *Les Hommes Brisés*.

Quinze ans plus tard (voici maintenant dix-neuf ans), j'ai été élu Fellow honoraire de Magdalene College à Cambridge, et mon prédécesseur dans cet honneur avait été Rudyard Kipling. Finalement, comme je viens de le dire, j'ai fait ce choix de poèmes pour lequel j'ai écrit une introduction. Et me voici à Paris, en train de succéder à Rudyard Kipling à une place d'honneur fort distinguée, et de célébrer ses mérites. Kipling m'a accompagné, d'une façon ou d'une autre, toute ma vie, et pourtant, je ne l'ai jamais rencontré, et je n'ai pas de raison de supposer qu'il ait jamais connu mon existence.

Il y a peut-être une autre raison à la déférence et à la sympathie que je ressens envers Kipling, raison qui donne une similitude, ou plutôt une analogie, entre ses antécédents et les miens. Kipling a passé sa première enfance aux Indes; il est allé à l'école en Angleterre; mais il est retourné aux Indes à l'âge de dix-sept ans. Pendant deux ans il a vécu en Amérique, où sa maison, Naulahka, se trouve encore. Plus tard, il s'est fixé en Angleterre, bien qu'il ait passé ses hivers sous le climat plus douce de l'Amérique du Sud. C'était un citoyen de l'Empire Britannique, longtemps avant de se naturaliser, pour ainsi parler, dans un coin particulier d'un comté particulier de l'Angleterre. La topographie de l'histoire de sa vie est en vérité différente de la mienne, et l'hérédité est également différente. Kipling était à moitié anglais et à moitié écossais des Hautes-terres, tandis que mon hérédité est complètement anglaise. Mais chez Kipling [8] comme chez moi, je découvre quelque chose du métèque. Le point de vue du métèque, à la fois dans les critiques qu'il adresse à son pays d'adoption, et dans son affection pour lui, reste différent de celui de l'indigène. Cela est évident dans quelques-uns des poèmes écrits après que Kipling se soit installé dans le Sussex. Par exemple, *Le rappel*:

> Sous leurs pieds dans l'herbe engagés
> S'attache et court notre charme prompt.
> Ils reviendront comme étrangers;
> Comme des fils, ils resteront.

(Je cite partout la traduction des *Poèmes Choisis* par M. Jules Castier.) Ici, Kipling a dans l'esprit le couple américain de l'histoire que le poème accompagne, couple qui s'installe en Angleterre pour devenir gentilshommes campagnards dans le village d'où la famille de la femme était partie pour l'Amérique. Pareillement, dans la *Chanson de Sir Richard*, le récitant du poème est un Chevalier normand, compagnon de Guillaume-le-Conquérant, qui s'est fixé en Angleterre:

> Ah, j'ai suivi mon Duc dès avant d'être amant,
> Pour prendre en Angleterr' fief, et rançon, et prix;
> Mais voilà que le jeu se retourne, à présent:
> L'Angleterre, à présent, c'est elle qui m'a pris.

Et il est clair que Sir Richard aussi n'est autre que Kipling lui-même.

Je crois que cette conscience qu'a Kipling d'être un peu étranger est présente à la fois dans les critiques, parfois sévères qu'il adresse à l'Angleterre, et dans son dévouement pour l'Angleterre. Peut-être cela pourrait même avoir quelque chose à faire avec la fascination et la répugnance que son oeuvre peut exercer. Je ne souhaite pas m'étendre sur cette caractéristique ici, je passerai plutôt à ces quatre aspects de Kipling dont je pense qu'il nous faut tenir compte si nous voulons le comprendre. Ce sont le Kipling journaliste, le Kipling artiste [9] littéraire, le Kipling moraliste, et, enfin, le Kipling chercheur religieux et prophète.

C'est comme journaliste, et tant que membre de la salle de rédaction d'un journal de langue anglaise aux Indes, que Kipling fit ses débuts. Ses premiers contes et ses premiers poèmes furent écrits pour un journal, et c'est dans les contes sur l'Inde et, surtout, relatifs à des Anglais aux Indes, que l'aspect journalistique de Kipling est le plus évident. Son premier métier est, peut-être, à l'origine de quelques-uns des vices de son style (il serait plus exact, aussi bien que plus gentil, de dire les faiblesses) qui irritent tant de lecteurs de ses contes de la vie hindoue et de la vie aux Indes: cette habileté d'un jeune homme qui prétend de se faire passer pour un homme du monde. D'autre part, l'entraînement de journaliste est sans doute à l'origine de quelques-unes des vertus du style de Kipling aussi bien. Peut-être faut-il lui attribuer le fait qu'il soit devenu un auteur de contes plutôt de romans, car *Kim*, livre écrit plus tard, qui est, je crois, sa plus grande oeuvre, n'a pas la structure d'un roman: l'intrigue n'y est rien que le prétexte pour brosser un incomparable tableau d'Inde et créer quatre ou cinq personnages inoubliables. Et le travail que Kipling devait faire pour son journal a bien pu aiguiser son pouvoir d'observation et son génie pour traduire en mots non seulement les images visuelles, mais les sons, les odeurs et les valeurs tactiles de l'Inde.

À mesure que nous remarquons moins dans l'oeuvre postérieure de Kipling ses qualités de journaliste, nous remarquons davantage celles de l'artiste. Feu André Chevrillon, dont l'ouvrage sur Kipling reste capital, et dont il faut traiter avec respect les opinions en ce sujet, dit de *Kim*, livre publié cinq ans après son retour en Angleterre, et dix ans après sa dernière visite aux Indes:

> L'art en est supérieur, mais c'est un art réfléchi, concerté. Quel contraste avec les puissances de rêve et de désir, les fougues d'imagination, l'impétuosité rectiligne de la *Lumière qui s'éteint*!

[10] Cette affirmation est sans doute vraie, mais, si elle est destinée à donner l'impression que les premières oeuvres de Kipling sont les meilleures, je ne puis y concourir. Je ne vois pas de déclin, mais plutôt un progrès dans les oeuvres que Kipling écrivit plus tard dans le Sussex. Là où se trouve moins de violence, et peut-être moins de force, il y a un gain en profondeur aussi bien qu'un progrès en habileté artistique.

Mais peut-être ai-je tort de dire progrès en habileté artistique. Peut-être est-ce simplement le fait que ces dons artistiques qui avaient toujours été consommés, et qui pouvaient être employés à une si grande diversité de sujets que plus d'une oeuvre, conte ou poème, considérée en soi peut produire l'effet d'un magnifique tour de force, peut-être n'est-ce pas l'habileté artistique qui se développe, mais simplement le sujet qui change. Il me suffit de comparer *À la Fin du Passage* ou *La Marque de la Bête* avec *La plus belle Histoire du Monde*; ou encore *L'Enfant de la Brousse* avec *Eux* et la *Maison du Désir* (je compare des histoires qui traitent toutes du surnaturel) pour voir que l'abandon de l'effet immédiat, spectaculaire et frappant est plus que justifié par le gain en profondeur. Les contes de la première période sont ceux qui révèlent le plus de richesses à une seconde ou une troisième lecture.

C'est le moraliste chez Kipling qui persiste à travers toute son oeuvre et donne de l'unité à son immense variété. Le moraliste du début est plus simplement un stoïque, l'homme qui fait sa tâche assignée: *Les Fils de Marthe*:

> Eux, ils ne prêchent point que leur Dieu les réveille
> Avant que les boulons se soient trop desserrés.
> Eux, ils n'enseignement point que Sa Pitié conseille
> De quitter leur travail aux instants désirés.
> Ainsi qu'aux chemins clairs, aux foules parsemées,
> Ils veillent au désert, et par les fonds obscurs,
> En garde, et vigilants le long de leur journées,
> Pour que les jours d'autrui soient nombreux plus sûrs.

[11] Le succès a perdu son prestige: c'est l'homme qui a fait son devoir sans être remarqué ni récompensé, qui est offert à notre admiration, et même l'homme dont la vie est un échec total et qui est tombé au plus bas (et l'on pourrait réunir toute une galerie de ces déchets humains parmi les personnages de Kipling) vaut mieux que celui qui s'est contenté de s'enricher égoïstement. Le moraliste est toujours présent, même dans ces contes comme ceux en *Livre de la Jungle* qui paraissent n'être superficiellement que de simples fantaisies pour amuser la jeunesse. Il se peut même que ce soit le moraliste chez Kipling qui ait paru déplaisant à ces intellectuels qui, dans ma jeunesse, l'ont déconsidéré. Il savait bien que la morale est rébarbative et qu'il faut la faire passer insidieusement ou, comme on dit dans le jargon contemporain, subliminairement. Dans ce remarquable poème intitulé *Les Fabulistes* que j'ai ailleurs cité in extenso, il rend la chose très explicite:

> Quand la Folie sans frein jours après jour travaille
> À confondre à jamais tout ce qui fit notre heur,
> Quand le Nonchaloir veut que Liberté défaille,
> Et que la Peur panique au tombeau met l'Honneur,
> Même à l'heure certaine où la chute survient,
> À moins qu'homme ne plaise, il n'est ouï en rien.

Kipling, comme je l'ai déjà suggéré, fut toujours fasciné par le surnaturel. À l'intérêt qu'il portait s'ajoutait un intérêt pour les machines et la technique ainsi qu'un don prophétique pour le progrès technique qui fait de lui l'égal de H. G. Wells dans la science-fiction. Comparer les deux hommes c'est énoncer la simplicité et même la naïveté de Wells et la grande complexité de Kipling. Kipling était, comme son oeuvre l'atteste, un homme d'une profonde sensibilité religieuse. Mais même son sentiment religieux est complexe ou ambivalent. Dans sa morale, il y a une forte dose de Puritanisme, et dans ce qu'il écrit au sujet de l'Inde, il apparaît clairement que l'Inde qu'il connaissait le mieux – Le Panjab de son enfance auquel il est retourné – c'est l'Inde musulmane, et non [12] pas l'Inde hindoue. C'est le type musulman – et l'Islam a bien des choses en commun avec le protestantisme, et pas seulement son iconoclastie – que Kipling trouve le plus sympathique: même si dans *Kim* il est aussi généreux et bien disposé envers l'agent secret bengali, Hurree Chunder Mookerjee, et envers le lama thibétain qu'il l'est envers Mahbub Ali, le maquignon pathan. Pourtant, et spécialement dans *Kim*, il montre une tolérance envers les dieux de toutes les religions et envers le non-dieu de Buddhism qui est plus caractéristique de la mentalité hindoue que de celle de l'Islam; et, dans le Christianisme lui-même, il montre plus de respect pour les catholiques que pour les protestants. Et j'ajoute que, contrairement, au protestantisme et à l'Islamisme, Kipling se découvre une inclination marquée pour le rituel. Je ne sais pas s'il était lui-même franc-maçon, mais il avait manifestement un goût très vif pour la franc-maçonnerie; et dans son oeuvre ultérieure, son intérêt semble s'être détourné de l'Empire Britannique pour aller vers la Ville Eternelle, comme dans *La Chanson Anglo-romaine*:

> Le père de mon père encor' n'y mit les yeux,
> Et moi, ne m'adviendra probablement, en somme,
> De contempler non plus ce plus sacré des lieux,
>   Le coeur même de Rome!

Ce n'est pas la mythologie de Rome, ce n'est certainement pas l'antique République, mais l'Empire à l'époque de sa plus grande expansion lorsque la Bretagne jusqu'au Mur de Hadrien était un province des confins; c'est l'empire Romain en tant que prototype de l'Empire qui répand la civilisation, la justice et l'ordre; et, parmi les religions, ce sont les religions à mystères, et en premier lieu, le culte de Mithra, tel que le connaissaient les légionnaires romains, qui s'empare de son imagination. Comme il arrive quelquefois aux Protestants qui ont perdu leur foi, ou chez qui la foi chrétienne n'est plus qu'un vestige, Kipling garde du Protestantisme comme une espèce de moralité stoïque; et il lui faut assouvir ce besoin qu'il a du rituel, de la forme de la céré-[13]monie qui n'est jamais tout à fait apaisée chez les sensitifs et les imaginatifs, en dehors de la Foi chrétienne.

Je ne saurais éluder de dire quelque chose des vues politiques de Kipling dans ma mesure où on les trouve dans ses oeuvres publiées. Je n'ai pas à m'occuper des opinions qu'il exprime par autres moyens, mais seulement de ce qu'il dit dans quelques-unes de ses histoires. Il ne faut pas oublier que Kipling n'était pas un homme de parti; il n'avait pas de part au jeu politique qui comporte toujours un côté sordide. Et il n'avait pas non plus – et voici qui est important – un esprit doué pour la pensée abstraite: sa pensée lui venait en images. Il n'était pas philosophe et il n'avait pas de philosophie politique en dehors du code simple et vigoureux qui constituait sa morale. Sa seule philosophie politique est celle qu'on trouve dans *Les dieux des en-têtes de cahiers*:

> À l'époq' du Carbonifèr', bombanc' promise grâce au sol:
> En dépouillant un Pierr' tout seul au grand profit, d' la mass'
>   des Paul.
> Avions d' l'argent à pleines mains n'trouvions rien pour notre
>   argent . . .
> Les Dieux des Cahiers nous on dit: "Si tu n'travaill's la mort
>   te reprend."

Mais il était quelque chose de plus rare qu'un philosophe – un prophète. Je veux dire par là que son esprit était intuitif, presque jusqu'au don de seconde vue, plutôt que ratiocinateur. Son génie, si je le comprends bien, gisait dans son pouvoir d'observation, de description et dans le don d'intuition.

Du pouvoir descriptif de Kipling, je ne peux guère ici parler, car on ne peut le montrer qu'avec des exemples, et la diversité des objets que Kipling a regardés et décrits – hommes et femmes, paysages, animaux et machines, choses de la nature et de l'art – est infinie. L'acuité de son observation et son pouvoir de description sont si grands qu'ils peuvent donner à quelques lecteurs l'impression qu'il n'a vue que la surface des [14] choses et que sa sensibilité manquait de profondeur. Mais c'est là une vue elle-même superficielle. Kipling ne s'intéressait pas, certes, à l'analyse raffiné des passions et des mobiles humains. Il préférait se confiner à quelques touches significatives et c'est en action qu'il voyait les êtres humains. Prenons garde, cela n'était pas dû à quelque lacune, mais au fait qu'il était un intuitif en non pas un intellectuel – raison de plus, peut-être, pour expliquer qu'il ait été mésestimé par les intellectuels d'une génération plus jeune. L'homme qui possède une vue prophétique est toujours condamné à se trouver dans la position désavantagée de Cassandre, car comment les gens ordinaires qui raisonnent peuvent-ils être sûrs qu'un prophète est réellement un prophète? Et si la prophétie est du genre sinistre, on peut toujours trouver des raisons plausibles pour croire à l'erreur agréable plutôt qu'à la dure vérité . . .

Les deux grandes guerres, Kipling les avait prévues. C'était dans l'attente de la guerre de 1914 qu'il écrivit son ode si noble à la France. Je me permets de citer quelques vers de la première strophe:

> Brisée à tous les coups de la fortune adverse,
> Soulevée au-dessus de tous les durs effrois[.]
> Par cette saine ardeur qui vivre nous déverse,
> Ce bouclier parfait qui garde le Gaulois . . .
> La première à poursuivre une vérité neuve
> Et l'ultime à laisser la Vérité qui meurt,
> France, qui doit aimer d'un amour sans épreuve
> Toute âme qui s'éprend d'une autre âme, sa soeur.

Déjà en 1932, année bien plus fatidique que la plupart ne s'en sont rendu compte, il prévoyait 1939 et il écrivit son avertissement *Le Cône des Tempêtes*:

> C'est encor pleine nuit, [et] nul astre qui point
> Ne nous saurait leurrer. L'aurore est encore loin.
> C'est la tempête, ici, depuis longtemps prévue,
> Lente á se déclarer, mais sûre en sa tenue.

1932! Kipling mourut en 1936, trois ans avant la tem-[15]pête. Il avait connu une vaste célébrité quand il était encore très jeune. Il vécut assez vieux pour se voir jugé d'après ses oeuvres de jeunesse, frappées d'immaturité et pour voir son oeuvre ultérieure et, à mon avis, encore plus belle, à la fois prose et vers, ignorée des intellectuels, quoique toujours lue par un large public. Il avait perdu son fils unique dans la première grande guerre, il avait reçu de grands honneurs et en avait refusé d'aussi grands. Il aimait la France et il pensait à la France et à l'Angleterre comme aux bastions les plus solides de la culture, dressés contre les influences qui se dirigeaient vers la détérioration, le totalitarisme et la discipline du chaos. Dans ses dernières années, il regardait l'avenir du monde avec de plus en plus d'appréhension. Il fut inhumé dans l'Abbaye de Westminster. Ceux qui portaient le drap funèbre étaient le Premier Ministre, un Amiral, un Général et le Maître d'un collège. Il fut, je crois, à tout prendre, le plus grand homme de lettres de l'Angleterre de son temps – un homme de lettres certainement unique dans son espèce, et, par conséquent, difficile à comparer avec tout autre.

The Art of Poetry I

T. S. ELIOT

Paris Review, 21 (Spring/Summer 1959) [47]–70. Gallup C631.

This is the first of a new series of interviews on the Art of Poetry which *The Paris Review* published along with its outstanding series on The Art of Fiction. Included in the latter collection were such authors as E. M. Forster, Thornton Wilder, William Faulkner, Ernest Hemingway, Alberto Moravia, François Mauriac, Henry Green, James Jones and others. Future issues would have interviews with Lawrence Durrell, W. Somerset Maugham, Kingsley Amis, André Malrau, and Jean Cocteau.

On p. 49 'Fitzgerald's' has been emended to 'FitzGerald's'.

The interview took place in New York, at the apartment of Mrs Louis Henry Cohn, of House of Books, Ltd, who is a friend of Mr and Mrs Eliot. The bookcases of the attractive living room contain a remarkable collection of modern authors. On a wall near the entrance hangs a drawing of Mr Eliot, done by his sister-in-law, Mrs Henry Ware Eliot. An inscribed wedding photograph of the Eliots stands in a silver frame on a table. Mrs Cohn and Mrs Eliot sat on a sofa at one end of the room, while Mr Eliot and the interviewer faced each other in the centre. The microphone of a tape recorder lay on the floor between them.

[48] Mr Eliot looked particularly well. He was visiting the United States briefly on his way back to London from a holiday in Nassau. He was tanned, and he seemed to have put on weight in the three years since the interviewer had seen him. Altogether, he looked younger and seemed jollier. He frequently glanced at Mrs Eliot during the interview, as if he were sharing with her an answer which he was not making.

The interviewer had talked with Mr Eliot previously in London. The small office at Faber and Faber, a few flights above Russell Square, displays a gallery of photographs on its walls: here is a large picture of Virginia Woolf, with an inset portrait of Pius XII; here are I. A. Richards, Paul Valéry, W. B. Yeats, Goethe, Marianne Moore, Charles Whibley, Djuna Barnes and others. Many young poets have stared at the faces there, during a talk with Mr Eliot. One of them has told a story which illustrates some of the unsuspected in Mr Eliot's conversation. After an hour of serious literary discussion, Mr Eliot paused to think if he had a final word of advice; the young poet, an American, was about to go up to Oxford as Mr Eliot had done forty years before. Then, as gravely as if he were recommending salvation, Mr Eliot advised the purchase of long woolen underwear because of Oxford's damp stone. Mr Eliot is able to be avuncular while he is quite aware of comic disproportion between manner and message.

Similar combinations modified many of the comments which are reported here, and the ironies of gesture are invisible on the page. At times, actually, the interview moved from the ironic and the mildly comic to the hilarious. The tape is punctuated by the head-back Boom Boom of Mr Eliot's laughter, particularly in response to mention of his early derogation of Ezra Pound, and to a question about the unpublished, and one gathers improper, King Bolo poems of his Harvard days.

[49] INTERVIEWER

Perhaps I can begin at the beginning. Do you remember the circumstances under which you began to write poetry in St Louis when you were a boy?

ELIOT

I began I think about the age of fourteen, under the inspiration of FitzGerald's *Omar Khayyám*, to write a number of very gloomy and atheistical and despairing quatrains in the same style, which fortunately I suppressed completely – so completely that they don't exist. I never showed them to anybody. The first poem that shows is one which appeared first in the *Smith Academy Record*, and later in *The Harvard Advocate*, which was written as an exercise for my English teacher and was an imitation of Ben Jonson. He thought it very good for a boy of fifteen or sixteen. Then I wrote a few at Harvard, just enough to qualify for election to an editorship on *The Harvard Advocate*, which I enjoyed. Then I had an outburst during my junior and senior years. I became much more prolific, under the influence first of Baudelaire and then of Jules Laforgue, whom I discovered I think in my Junior year at Harvard.

INTERVIEWER

Did anyone in particular introduce you to the French poets? Not Irving Babbitt, I suppose.

ELIOT

No, Babbitt would be the last person! The one poem that Babbitt always held up for admiration was Gray's *Elegy*. And that's a fine poem but I think this shows certain limitations on Babbitt's part, God bless him. I have advertised my source, I think; it's Arthur Symons's book on French poetry,[1] which I came across in the Harvard Union. In those days the Harvard Union was a meeting place for any undergraduate who chose to belong to it. They had a very nice little library, like the libraries in many Harvard houses now. I liked his quota-[50]tions and I went to a foreign

---

1. *The Symbolist Movement in Literature.*

book shop somewhere in Boston, (I've forgotten the name and I don't know whether it still exists) which specialised in French and German and other foreign books and found Laforgue, and other poets. I can't imagine why that bookshop should have had a few poets like Laforgue in stock. Goodness knows how long they'd had them or whether there were any other demands for them.

INTERVIEWER

When you were an undergraduate, were you aware of the dominating presence of any older poets? Today the poet in his youth is writing in the age of Eliot and Pound and Stevens. Can you remember your own sense of the literary times? I wonder if your situation may not have been extremely different.

ELIOT

I think it was rather an advantage not having any living poets in England or America in whom one took any particular interest. I don't know what it would be like but I think it would be a rather troublesome distraction to have such a lot of dominating presences, as you call them, about. Fortunately we weren't bothered by each other.

INTERVIEWER

Were you aware of people like Hardy or Robinson at all?

ELIOT

I was slightly aware of Robinson because I read an article about him in *The Atlantic Monthly* which quoted some of his poems, and that wasn't my cup of tea at all. Hardy was hardly known to be a poet at that time. One read his novels but his poetry only really became conspicuous to a later generation. Then there was Yeats but it was the early Yeats. It was too much Celtic twilight for me. There was really nothing except the people of the 90's who had all died of drink or suicide or one thing or another.

[51] INTERVIEWER

Did you and Conrad Aiken help each other with your poems, when you were co-editors of the *Advocate*?

ELIOT

We were friends but I don't think we influenced each other at all. When it came to foreign writers, he was more interested in Italian and Spanish, and I was all for the French.

INTERVIEWER

Were there any other friends who read your poems and helped you?

ELIOT

Well, yes. There was a man who was a friend of my brother's, a man named Thomas H. Thomas who lived in Cambridge and who saw some of my poems in *The Harvard Advocate*. He wrote me a most enthusiastic letter and cheered me up. And I wish I had his letters still. I was very grateful to him for giving me that encouragement.

INTERVIEWER

I understand that it was Conrad Aiken who introduced you and your work to Pound.

ELIOT

Yes it was. Aiken was a very generous friend. He tried to place some of my poems in London, one summer when he was over, with Harold Monro and others. Nobody would think of publishing them. He brought them back to me. Then in 1914, I think, we were both in London in the summer. He said, 'You go to Pound. Show him your poems.' He thought Pound might like them. Aiken liked them, though they were very different from his.

INTERVIEWER

Do you remember the circumstances of your first meeting with Pound?

[52] ELIOT

I think I went to call on him first. I think I made a good impression, in his little triangular sitting room in Kensington. He said 'Send me your poems.' And he wrote back, 'This is as good as anything I've seen. Come around and have a talk about them.' Then he pushed them on Harriet Monroe, which took a little time.

INTERVIEWER

In an article about your *Advocate* days, for the book in honour of your sixtieth birthday, Aiken quotes an early letter from England in which you refer to Pound's verse as 'touchingly incompetent'. I wonder when you changed your mind.

Eliot

Hah! *That* was a bit brash, wasn't it? Pound's verse was first shown me by an editor of *The Harvard Advocate*, W. G. Tinckom-Fernandez, who was a crony of mine and Conrad Aiken's and the other Signet[1] poets of the period. He showed me those little things of Elkin Mathews, *Exultations* and *Personae*.[2] He said, 'This is up your street; you ought to like this.' Well, I didn't, really. It seemed to me rather fancy old-fashioned romantic stuff, cloak and dagger kind of stuff. I wasn't very much impressed by it. When I went to see Pound, I was not particularly an admirer of his work, and though I now regard the work I saw then as very accomplished, I am certain that in his later work is to be found the grand stuff.

Interviewer

You have mentioned in print that Pound cut *The Waste Land* from a much larger poem into its present form. Were you benefited by his criticism of your poems in general? Did he cut other poems?

Eliot

Yes. At that period, yes. He was a marvelous critic [53] because he didn't try to turn you into an imitation of himself. He tried to see what you were trying to do.

Interviewer

Have you helped to rewrite any of your friends' poems? Ezra Pound's for instance?

Eliot

I can't think of any instances. Of course I have made innumerable suggestions on manuscripts of young poets in the last twenty-five years or so.

Interviewer

Does the manuscript of the original, uncut *Waste Land* exist?

Eliot

Don't ask me. That's one of the things I don't know. It's an unsolved mystery. I sold it to John Quinn. I also gave him a notebook of unpublished poems, because he had been kind to me in various affairs. That's the last I heard of them. Then he died and they didn't turn up at the sale.

1. Harvard's literary club.
2. Early books of Pound, published by Elkin Mathews in 1909.

INTERVIEWER

What sort of thing did Pound cut from *The Waste Land*? Did he cut whole sections?

ELIOT

Whole sections, yes. There was a long section about a shipwreck. I don't know what that had to do with anything else, but it was rather inspired by the Ulysses Canto in *The Inferno*, I think. Then there was another section which was an imitation *Rape of the Lock*. Pound said, 'It's no use trying to do something that somebody else has done as well as it can be done. Do something different.'

INTERVIEWER

Did the excisions change the intellectual structure of the poem?

[54] ELIOT

No. I think it was just as structureless, only in a more futile way, in the longer version.

INTERVIEWER

I have a question about the poem which is related to its composition. In *Thoughts After Lambeth* you denied the allegation of critics who said that you expressed 'the disillusionment of a generation,' in *The Waste Land*, or you denied that it was your intention. Now F. R. Leavis, I believe, has said that the poem exhibits no progression; yet on the other hand, more recent critics, writing after your later poetry, found *The Waste Land* Christian. I wonder if this was part of your intention.

ELIOT

No, it wasn't part of my conscious intention. I think that in *Thoughts After Lambeth*, I was speaking of intentions more in a negative than in a positive sense, to say what was not my intention. I wonder what an 'intention' means! One wants to get something off one's chest. One doesn't know quite what it is that one wants to get off the chest until one's got it off. But I couldn't apply the word 'intention' positively to any of my poems. Or to any poem.

INTERVIEWER

I have another question about you and Pound and your earlier career. I have read somewhere that you and Pound decided to write quatrains, in the late teens, because *vers libre* had gone far enough.

Eliot

I think that's something Pound said. And the suggestion of writing quatrains was his. He put me onto *Emaux et Camées*.[1]

Interviewer

I wonder about your ideas about the relation of form to [55] subject. Would you then have chosen the form before you knew quite what you were going to write in it?

Eliot

Yes, in a way. One studied originals. We studied Gautier's poems and then we thought, 'Have I anything to say in which this form will be useful?' And we experimented. The form gave the impetus to the content.

Interviewer

Why was *vers libre* the form you chose to use in your early poems?

Eliot

My early *vers libre*, of course, was started under the endeavour to practice the same form as Laforgue. This meant merely rhyming lines of irregular length, with the rhymes coming in irregular places. It wasn't quite so *libre* as much *vers*, especially the sort which Ezra called 'Amygism'.[2] Then, of course, there were things in the next phase which were freer, like 'Rhapsody on a Windy Night'. I don't know whether I had any sort of model or practice in mind when I did that. It just came that way.

Interviewer

Did you feel, possibly, that you were writing against something, more than from any model? Against the poet laureate perhaps?

Eliot

No, no, no. I don't think one was constantly trying to reject things, but just trying to find out what was right for oneself. One really ignored poet laureates as such, the Robert Bridges. I don't think good poetry can be produced in a kind of political attempt to overthrow some existing form. I think it just supersedes. People find a way in which they can say something. 'I can't say it that way, what way can I find [56] that will do?' One didn't really *bother* about the existing modes.

---

1. Poems by Théophile Gautier.
2. A reference to Amy Lowell, who captured and transformed imagism.

INTERVIEWER

I think it was after 'Prufrock' and before 'Gerontion' that you wrote the poems in French which appear in your *Collected Poems*. I wonder how you happened to write them. Have you written any since?

ELIOT

No, and I never shall. That was a very curious thing which I can't altogether explain. At that period I thought I'd dried up completely. I hadn't written anything for some time and was rather desperate. I started writing a few things in French and found I *could*, at that period. I think it was that when I was writing in French I didn't take the poems so seriously, and that, not taking them seriously, I wasn't so worried about not being able to write. I did these things as a sort of *tour de force* to see what I could do. That went one for some months. The best of them have been printed. I must say that Ezra Pound went through them, and Edmond Dulac, a Frenchman we knew in London, helped with them a bit. We left out some, and I suppose they disappeared completely. Then I suddenly began writing in English again and lost all desire to go on with French. I think it was just something that helped me get started again.

INTERVIEWER

Did you think all about becoming a French symbolist poet like the two Americans of the last century?

ELIOT

Stuart Merrill and Viele-Griffin. I only did that during the romantic year I spent in Paris after Harvard. I had at that time the idea of giving up English and trying to settle down and scrape along in Paris and gradually write French. But it would have been a foolish idea even if I'd been much more bilingual than I ever was, because, for one thing, I don't think that one can be a bilingual poet. I don't know of any [57] case in which a man wrote great or even fine poems equally well in two languages. I think one language must be the one you express yourself in in poetry, and you've got to give up the other for that purpose. And I think that the English language really has more resources in some respects than the French. I think, in other words, I've probably done better in English than I ever would have in French even if I'd become as proficient in French as the poets you mentioned.

INTERVIEWER

Can I ask you if you have any plans for poems now?

Eliot

No, I haven't any plans for anything at the moment, except that I think I would like, having just got rid of *The Elder Statesman*, (I only passed the final proofs just before we left London) to do a little prose writing of a critical sort. I never think more than one step ahead. Do I want to do another play or do I want to do more poems? I don't know until I find I want to do it.

Interviewer

Do you have any unfinished poems that you look at occasionally?

Eliot

I haven't much in that way, no. As a rule, with me an unfinished thing is a thing that might as well be rubbed out. It's better, if there's something good in it that I might make use of elsewhere, to leave it at the back of my mind than on paper in a drawer. If I leave it in a drawer it remains the same thing but if it's in the memory it becomes transformed into something else. As I have said before, *Burnt Norton* began with bits that had to be cut out of *Murder in the Cathedral*. I learned in *Murder in the Cathedral* that it's no use putting in nice lines that you think are good poetry if they don't get the action on at all. That was when Martin Browne was useful. He would say, 'There are very nice lines here, but they've nothing to do with what's going on on stage.'

[58] Interviewer

Are any of your minor poems actually sections cut out of longer works? There are two that sound like 'The Hollow Men'.

Eliot

Oh, those were the preliminary sketches. Those things were earlier. Others I published in periodicals but not in my collected poems. You don't want to say the same thing twice in one book.

Interviewer

You seem often to have written poems in sections. Did they begin as separate poems? I am thinking of *Ash Wednesday*, in particular.

Eliot

Yes, like 'The Hollow Men', it originated out of separate poems. As I recall, one or two early drafts of parts of *Ash Wednesday* appeared in *Commerce* and elsewhere. Then gradually I came to see it as a sequence.

That's one way in which my mind does seem to have worked throughout the years poetically – doing things separately and then seeing the possibility of fusing them together, altering them, and making a kind of whole of them.

INTERVIEWER

Do you write anything now in the vein of *Old Possum's Book of Practical Cats* or 'King Bolo'?

ELIOT

Those things do come from time to time! I keep a few notes of such verse, and there are one or two incomplete cats that probably will never be written. There's one about a glamour cat. It turned out too sad. This would never do. I can't make my children weep over a cat who's gone wrong. She had a very questionable career, did this cat. It wouldn't do for the audience of my previous volume of cats. I've never done any dogs. Of course dogs don't seem to lend themselves to verse quite so well, collectively, as cats. I may eventually [59] do an enlarged edition of my cats. That's more likely than another volume. I did add one poem, which was originally done as an advertisement for Faber and Faber. It seemed to be fairly successful. Oh yes, one wants to keep one's hand in, you know, in every type of poem, serious and frivolous and proper and improper. One doesn't want to lose one's skill.

INTERVIEWER

There's a good deal of interest now in the process of writing. I wonder if you could talk more about your actual habits in writing verse. I've heard you composed on the typewriter.

ELIOT

Partly on the typewriter. A great deal of my new play, *The Elder Statesman*, was produced in pencil and paper, very roughly. Then I typed it myself first before my wife got to work on it. In typing myself I make alterations, very considerable ones. But whether I write or type, composition of any length, a play for example, means for me regular hours, say ten to one. I found that three hours a day is about all I can do of actual composing. I could do polishing perhaps later. I sometimes found at first that I wanted to go on longer, but when I looked at the stuff the next day, what I'd done after the three hours were up was never satisfactory. It's much better to stop and think about something else quite different.

INTERVIEWER

Did you ever write any of your non-dramatic poems on schedule? Perhaps the *Four Quartets*?

ELIOT

Only 'occasional' verse. The *Quartets* were not on schedule. Of course the first one was written in '35, but the three which were written during the war were more in fits and starts. In 1939 if there hadn't been a war I would probably have tried to write another play. And I think it's a very good thing I didn't have the opportunity. From my personal point of view, the one good thing the war did was to prevent me [60] from writing another play too soon. I saw some of the things that were wrong with *Family Reunion*, but I think it was much better that any possible play was blocked for five years or so to get up a head of steam. The form of the *Quartets* fitted in very nicely to the conditions under which I was writing, or could write at all. I could write them in sections and I didn't have to have quite the same continuity; it didn't matter if a day or two elapsed when I did not write, as they frequently did, while I did war jobs.

INTERVIEWER

We have been mentioning your plays without talking about them. In *Poetry and Drama* you talked about your first plays. I wonder if you could tell us something about your intentions in *The Elder Statesman*.

ELIOT

I said something, I think, in *Poetry and Drama* about my ideal aims, which I never expect fully to realise. I started, really, from *The Family Reunion*, because *Murder in the Cathedral* is a period piece and something out of the ordinary. It is written in rather a special language, as you do when you're dealing with another period. It didn't solve any of the problems I was interested in. Later I thought that in *The Family Reunion* I was giving so much attention to the versification that I neglected the structure of the play. I think *The Family Reunion* is still the best of my plays in the way of poetry, although it's not very well constructed.

In *The Cocktail Party* and again in *The Confidential Clerk*, I went further in the way of structure. *The Cocktail Party* wasn't altogether satisfactory in that respect. It sometimes happens, disconcertingly, at any rate with a practitioner like myself, that it isn't always the things constructed most according to plan that are the most successful. People criticised the third act of *The Cocktail Party* as being rather an epilogue, so in *The Confidential Clerk* I wanted things to turn up in the third act which were fresh events. Of course, *The Confidential* [61] *Clerk* was so well constructed in some ways that people thought it was just meant to be farce.

I wanted to get to learn the technique of the theatre so well that I could then forget about it. I always feel it's not wise to violate rules until you know how to observe them.

I hope that *The Elder Statesman* goes further in getting more poetry in, at any rate, than *The Confidential Clerk* did. I don't feel that I've got to the point I aim at and I don't think I ever will, but I would like to feel I was getting a little nearer to it each time.

INTERVIEWER

Do you have a Greek model behind *The Elder Statesman*?

ELIOT

The play in the background is the *Oedipus at Colonus*. But I wouldn't like to refer to my Greek originals as models. I have always regarded them more as points of departure. That was one of the weaknesses of *The Family Reunion*; it was rather too close to the *Eumenides*. I tried to follow my original too literally and in that way led to confusion by mixing pre-Christian and post-Christian attitudes about matters of conscience and sin and guilt.

So in the subsequent three I have tried to take the Greek myth as a sort of springboard, you see. After all, what one gets essential and permanent, I think, in the old plays, is a situation. You can take the situation, rethink it in modern terms, develop your own characters from it, and let another plot develop out of that. Actually you get further and further away from the original. *The Cocktail Party* had to do with Alcestis simply because the question arose in my mind, what would the life of Admetus and Alcestis be, after she'd come back from the dead; I mean if there'd been a break like that, it couldn't go on just as before. Those two people were the centre of the thing when I started and the other characters only developed out of it. The character of Celia, who came to be really the most important character in the play, was originally an appendage to a domestic situation.

[62] INTERVIEWER

Do you still hold to the theory of levels in poetic drama (plot, character, diction, rhythm, meaning) which you put forward in 1932?

ELIOT

I am no longer very much interested in my own theories about poetic drama, especially those put forward before 1934. I have thought less about theories since I have given more time to writing for the theater.

INTERVIEWER

How does the writing of a play differ from the writing of poems?

ELIOT

I feel that they take quite different approaches. There is all the difference in the world between writing a play for an audience and writing a poem, in which you're writing primarily for yourself – although obviously you wouldn't be satisfied if the poem didn't mean something to other people afterward. With a poem you can say, 'I got my feeling into words for myself. I now have the equivalent in words for that much of what I have felt.' Also in a poem you're writing for your own voice, which is very important. You're thinking in terms of your own voice, whereas in a play from the beginning you have to realise that you're preparing something which is going into the hands of other people, unknown at the time you're writing it. Of course I won't say there aren't moments in a play when the two approaches may not converge, when I think ideally they *should*. Very often in Shakespeare they do, when he is writing a poem and thinking in terms of the theatre and the actors and the audience all at once. And the two things are one. That's wonderful when you can get that. With me it only happens at odd moments.

INTERVIEWER

Have you tried at all to control the speaking of your verse by the actors? To make it seem more like verse?

[63] ELIOT

I leave that primarily to the producer. The important thing is to have a producer who has the feeling of verse and who can guide them in just how emphatic to make the verse, just how far to depart from prose or how far to approach it. I only guide the actors if they ask me questions directly. Otherwise I think that they should get their advice through the producer. The important thing is to arrive at an agreement with him first, and then leave it to him.

INTERVIEWER

Do you feel that there's been a general tendency in your work, even in your poems, to move from a narrower to a larger audience?

ELIOT

I think that there are two elements in this. One is that I think that writing plays (that is *Murder in the Cathedral* and *The Family Reunion*) made a difference to the writing of the *Four Quartets*. I think that it led to a greater simplification of language and to speaking in a way which is more like conversing with your reader. I see the later *Quartets* as being much simpler and easier to understand than *The Waste Land* and *Ash Wednesday*. Sometimes the thing I'm trying to say, the subject matter, may be difficult, but it seems to me that I'm saying it in a simpler way.

The other element that enters into it, I think, is just experience and maturity. I think that in the early poems it was a question of not being able to – of having more to say than one knew how to say, and having something one wanted to put into words and rhythm which one didn't have the command of words and rhythm to put in a way immediately apprehensible.

That type of obscurity comes when the poet is still at the stage of learning how to use language. You have to say the thing the difficult way. The only alternative is not saying it at all, at that stage. By the time of *The Four Quartets*, I couldn't have written in the style of *The Waste Land*. In *The Waste* [64] *Land*, I wasn't even bothering whether I understood what I was saying. These things, however, become easier to people with time. You get used to having *The Waste Land*, or *Ulysses*, about.

INTERVIEWER

Do you feel that *The Four Quartets* are your best work?

ELIOT

Yes, and I'd like to feel that they get better as they go on. The second is better than the first, the third is better than the second, and the fourth is the best of all. At any rate, that's the way I flatter myself.

INTERVIEWER

This is a very general question, but I wonder if you could give advice to a young poet about what disciplines or attitudes he might cultivate to improve his art.

ELIOT

I think it's awfully dangerous to give general advice. I think the best one can do for a young poet is to criticise in detail a particular poem of his. Argue it with him if necessary; give him your opinion, and if there are any generalisations to be made, let him do them himself. I've found that different people have different ways of working and things come to them in different ways. You're never sure when you're uttering a statement that's generally valid for all poets or when it's something that only applies to yourself. I think nothing is worse than to try to form people in your own image.

INTERVIEWER

Do you think there's any possible generalisation to be made about the fact that all the better poets now, younger than you, seem to be teachers?

ELIOT

I don't know. I think the only generalisation that can be made of any value will be one which will be made a genera-tion later. All you can say at this point is that at different times there are different possibilities of making a living, or different limitations on making a living. Obviously a poet has got to find a way of making a living apart from his poetry. After all, artists do a great deal of teaching, and musicians too.

INTERVIEWER

Do you think that the optimal career for a poet would involve no work at all but writing and reading?

ELIOT

No, I think that would be – but there again one can only talk about oneself. It is very dangerous to give an optimal career for everybody, but I feel quite sure that if I'd started by having independent means, if I hadn't had to bother about earning a living and could have given all my time to poetry, it would have had a deadening influence on me.

INTERVIEWER

Why?

ELIOT

I think that for me it's been very useful to exercise other activities, such as working in a bank, or publishing even. And I think also that the difficulty of not having as much time as I would like has given me a greater pressure of concentration. I mean it has prevented me from writing too much. The danger, as a rule, of having nothing else to do is that one might write too much rather than concentrating and perfecting smaller amounts. That would be *my* danger.

INTERVIEWER

Do you consciously attempt, now, to keep up with the poetry that is being written by young men in England and America?

ELIOT

I don't now, not with any conscientiousness. I did at one time when I was reading little reviews and looking out for [66] new talent as a publisher. But as one gets older, one is not quite confident in one's own ability to distinguish new genius among younger men. You're always afraid that you are going as you have seen your elders go. At Faber and Faber now I have a younger colleague who reads poetry manuscripts. But even before that, when I came across new stuff that I thought had real merit, I would show it to younger friends whose critical judgement I trusted and get their opinion. But of course there is always the danger that there is merit where you don't see it. So I'd rather have younger people to look at things first. If they like it, they will show it to me, and see whether I like it too. When you get something that knocks over younger people of taste and judgement and older people as well, then that's likely to be something important. Sometimes there's a lot of resistance. I shouldn't like to feel that I was resisting, as my work was resisted when it was new, by people who thought that it was imposture of some kind or other.

INTERVIEWER

Do you feel that younger poets in general have repudiated the experimentalism of the early poetry of this century? Few poets now seem to be resisted the way you were resisted, but some older critics like Herbert Read believe that poetry after you has been a regression to out-dated modes. When you talked about Milton the second time, you spoke of the function of poetry as a retarder of change, as well as a maker of change, in language.

ELIOT

Yes, I don't think you want a revolution every ten years.

INTERVIEWER

But is it possible to think that there has been a counter-revolution rather than an exploration of new possibilities?

Eliot

No, I don't see anything that looks to me like a counter-revolution. After a period of getting away from the traditional [67] forms, comes a period of curiosity in making new experiments with traditional forms. This can produce very good work if what has happened in between has made a difference: when it's not merely going back, but taking up an old form, which has been out of use for a time, and making something new with it. That is not counter-revolution. Nor does mere regression deserve the name. There is a tendency in some quarters to revert to Georgian scenery and sentiments: and among the public there are always people who prefer mediocrity, and when they get it, say 'What a relief! Here's some real poetry again.' And there are also people who like poetry to be modern but for whom the really creative stuff is too strong – they need something diluted.

What seems to me the best of what I've seen in young poets is not reaction at all. I'm not going to mention any names, for I don't like to make public judgements about younger poets. The best stuff is a further development of a less revolutionary character than what appeared in earlier years of the century.

Interviewer

I have some unrelated questions that I'd like to end with. In 1945 you wrote 'a poet must take as his material his own language as it is actually spoken around him.' And later you wrote, 'the music of poetry, then, will be a music latent in the common speech of his time.' After the second remark, you disparaged 'standardised BBC English'. Now isn't one of the changes of the last fifty years, and perhaps even more of the last five years, the growing dominance of commercial speech through the means of communication? What you referred to as 'BBC English' has become immensely more powerful through the ITA and BBC television, not to speak of CBS, NBC, and ABC. Does this development make the problem of the poet and his relationship to common speech more difficult?

Eliot

You've raised a very good point there. I think you're right, it does make it more difficult.

[68] Interviewer

I wanted *you* to make the point.

Eliot

Yes, but you wanted the point to be *made*. So I'll take the responsibility of making it: I do think that where you have these modern means of communication and means of imposing the speech and idioms of a small number on the mass of people at large, it does complicate the problem very much. I don't know to what extent that goes for film speech, but obviously radio speech has done much more.

Interviewer

I wonder if there's a possibility that what you mean by common speech will disappear.

Eliot

That is a very gloomy prospect. But very likely indeed.

Interviewer

Are there other problems for a writer in our time which are unique? Does the prospect of human annihilation have any particular effect on the poet?

Eliot

I don't see why the prospect of human annihilation should affect the poet differently from men of other vocations. It will affect him as a human being, no doubt in proportion to his sensitiveness.

Interviewer

Another unrelated question: I can see why a man's criticism is better for his being a practising poet, better although subject to his own prejudices. But do you feel that writing criticism has helped you as a poet?

Eliot

In an indirect way it has helped me somehow as a poet – to [69] put down in writing my critical valuation of the poets who have influenced me and whom I admire. It is merely making an influence more conscious and more articulate. It's been a rather natural impulse. I think probably my best critical essays are essays on the poets who had influenced me, so to speak, long before I thought of writing essays about them. They're of more value, probably, than any of my more generalised remarks.

Interviewer

G. S. Fraser wonders, in an essay about the two of you, whether you ever met Yeats. From remarks in your talk about him, it would seem that you did. Could you tell us the circumstances?

Eliot

Of course I had met Yeats many times. Yeats was always very gracious when one met him and had the art of treating younger writers as if they were his equals and contemporaries. I can't remember any one particular occasion.

Interviewer

I have heard that you consider that your poetry belongs in the tradition of American literature. Could you tell us why?

Eliot

I'd say that my poetry has obviously more in common with my distinguished contemporaries in America, than with anything written in my generation in England. That I'm sure of.

Interviewer

Do you think there's a connection with the American past?

Eliot

Yes, but I couldn't put it any more definitely than that, you see. It wouldn't be what it is, and I imagine it wouldn't be so good; putting it as modestly as I can, it wouldn't be what it is [70] if I'd been born in England, and it wouldn't be what it is if I'd stayed in America. It's a combination of things. But in its sources, in its emotional springs, it comes from America.

Interviewer

One last thing. Seventeen years ago you said, 'No honest poet can ever feel quite sure of the permanent value of what he has written. He may have wasted his time and messed up his life for nothing.' Do you feel the same now, at seventy?

Eliot

There may be honest poets who do feel sure. I don't.

– DONALD HALL

Foreword

Foreword (vii–xii) to *Katherine Mansfield and other Literary Studies*
by J. Middleton Murry (1959). Publ. 19 Mar. 1959. Signed 'T. S. ELIOT'. Gallup B80.

I am not in every respect the person best qualified to introduce this book. The three essays here posthumously published are studies of three writers of prose fiction. With the exception of one article and two prefaces, and a very few pieces of literary journalism which remain uncollected, I have never attempted criticism of prose fiction: it follows that I have no special competence to criticise criticism of prose fiction. It is, therefore, of Middleton Murry as a literary critic in general that I shall speak; and I shall try to indicate the kind of literary criticism that he practised, and to indicate his eminence – I might say solitary eminence – in this kind of criticism in my generation.

There are several types of literary critic: I think that the most important distinction is between the writer whose criticism is a by-product of his creative activity, and the writer whose criticism is itself his creative act. I myself belong to the first of these two classes: my best criticism has to do with the writing of poetry, with poets who have influenced me, or from whose work I have learned something about the art of poetry, and with other writers, for example theologians or philosophers, who through their style have affected my sensibility and consequently have affected the content of my verse. However great the differences, my critical activity has been of the same nature as that of Ezra Pound; and it is in relation to my own poetry that my criticism must be viewed. Nor is this class, of writers whose literary criticism is a by-product of their creative activity, limited to poets writing about the art of poetry and novelists writing about the art of fiction. [viii] The literary criticism to be found in the writings of Wyndham Lewis is also a by-product of another activity: or, rather, is incidental to a polemic pursued in the course of philosophical and social studies. Middleton Murry, on the other hand, was a literary critic first and foremost. He had published poems, a verse play and several novels; and had achieved no great success in any of these forms. His originality – and he had indeed an original mind – went into his criticism, a kind of criticism which, in exploring the mind and soul of some creative writer, explored his own mind and soul also. His compositions in verse and in prose fiction may I think be ignored, except for the curious light they throw here and there upon the author; and his other writings, those concerned directly with theological, social or political matter, should be considered as by-products of a mind of which the primary activity was literary criticism.

I first met Murry by appointment at some meeting-place whence he was to conduct me to his home in Hampstead for dinner and for a discussion of his projects for *The Athenaeum*, a defunct weekly which was to be revived, as a review of arts and letters, under his editorship. I had heard of him in the circle of Lady Ottoline Morrell, where I had already on one occasion met Katherine Mansfield; but until he wrote to propose this meeting we had held no communication with each other. I do not know what he may have been told about me; what is important is that he had never seen any prose that I had written. He had read (no doubt having had it brought to his attention at Garsington) my first small book of verse, *Prufrock and Other Observations*, and it was entirely because of the impression this little book had made upon him that he invited me to become his assistant editor. With this invitation in view he had asked me to meet him. After our meeting, I sent him some copies of *The Egoist*, in the editing of which I had assisted Miss Harriet Weaver, so that he might judge of my abilities as a prose writer and journalist. It speaks of the man, however, that he had made up his mind that he wanted me with him in his editorial venture, without having seen any literary criticism of mine, and wholly on the strength of his approval of *Prufrock*. After a good deal of hesitation I declined; and I think that I was wise to do so, and to remain for some years more at my desk in the City. I did, however, become one of Murry's regular contributors, reviewing some book at length as often as three weeks out of four, during a considerable time. In this way we met often, and became friends – though I was never one of that inner group of which the storm centre was D. H. Lawrence. And in spite of extreme differences in certain areas of opinion (to which some of my effusions in *The Criterion* bear witness) we always remained friends, though meeting in later years very rarely indeed. Our last meeting, in December 1956, was a particularly happy one.

Some of Murry's best literary essays had already appeared in *The Times Literary Supplement* under the editorship of Bruce Richmond. It should be recorded here that it was in this periodical (then at its zenith) that a review by Murry of *La Jeune Parque* first told English readers of the importance of an unknown poet called Paul Valéry – a service which Valéry always remembered with gratitude. But Murry himself proved from the start of the new *Athenaeum* to be a first-rate editor: and it seems to me that the period when we had both *The Times Literary Supplement* under Richmond and *The Athenaeum* under Murry (we had also for a time *Arts and Letters* and *The Calendar*) was the high summer of literary journalism in London in my lifetime. To be a good editor requires a certain humility and tolerance as well as a positive personality: for the editor himself must give his paper its coherence and its purpose, while allowing the greatest possible freedom, within the limits of sanity and good sense to his chosen con-[x]tributors. And it is more difficult still to be a good editor when a man has, as Murry had, the vocation to be a literary critic himself.

A similar combination of contrasted qualities made Murry the kind of critic that he was. He could immerse himself in the work of one or another author the study of whose writings responded to his own need, and in so doing reveal his own mind. In a pamphlet which is the best introduction to Murry's literary criticism that we could wish to have, Mr Philip Mairet says: 'The subjects he selected and his treatment of them were determined by the subjective aims which moved him to become a critic – at least in his best work.'[1] He proceeds to quote (from *Discoveries*, 1924) the following statement by Murry himself:

> After all, I believe that criticism is a personal affair and that the less we critics try to disguise this from ourselves the better. On what attracts and excites and fascinates us and in pursuit of our own completion, in obedience, if you like, to our own secret rhythm which we also must have if our work is to be vital at all – on that alone we shall have something to say worth hearing.

'In pursuit of our own completion' – how well that indicates the motive of the literary critic by vocation! That Murry had the 'objective aims' of which Mr Mairet speaks, that he obeyed his own 'secret rhythm' in his own words, is as much as to say that Murry's literary criticism has a unity which is conferred by Murry himself. But we must not infer that his interests were narrow or his capacity for appreciation limited to those authors whose work fascinated him most. Readers unfamiliar with the scope of his criticism may associate Murry as a critic with his studies of Dostoievsky or of Keats, and, among contemporaries, with D. H. Lawrence and Katherine Mansfield, and may think of his mind as [xi] parasitic upon the minds of certain authors whose work he would have liked to emulate. Such a judgement, apart from its misunderstanding of the critical mind in general, would ignore the diversity of subject matter which Murry could appreciate and of authors whose merits he could recognise. I have mentioned his praise of Paul Valéry at a time when the genius of Valéry was not widely appreciated even in France. I remember the appearance in *The Athenaeum* of a very perceptive review by Murry of *Ulysses* at the time of publication of that book. I remember also that Ezra Pound (over a pseudonym) wrote a number of articles for *The Athenaeum*

---

1. *John Middleton Murry*, by Philip Mairet. Published for the British Council and the National Book League by Longmans Green & Co.

at Murry's invitation. Murry's knowledge and understanding of French literature and (in translation) of Russian fiction were considerable; he wrote well on Milton and Benjamin Constant; and in 1954 he produced a critical biography of Jonathan Swift which no student of Swift can afford to overlook.

Not all critics of literature can be comprehended in one or the other of the two classes of critic which I distinguished at the beginning: the critic whose criticism is a by-product of his creative work and the critic for whom criticism is a primary activity into which he may be said to put his creative gift (as Ste-Beuve put himself into *Port-Royal*). There is also the good journalist, he who can review with discernment current literature, but no assemblage of whose writings, because of the insignificance of the personality informing them, can be more than a miscellany; there is also the academic critic, the scholar whose study of a particular author or of a particular period, whose researches, discoveries and interpretations of fact can enlarge our understanding – and the borderline between scholar and critic is by no means clearly demarcated. But critics of literature of the kind to which Middleton Murry belonged are among the rarest. The three writers, essays on whom compose this book, have all [xii] their own importance: but they are also important to us because they were important to Murry, and because we are interested in what happened to Murry's mind and sensibility when they came in contact with literature that he found important.

The Unfading Genius of Rudyard Kipling

Kipling Journal, 26. 129 (Mar. 1959), 9–12. 'By T. S. Eliot, O.M.'
Gallup C632.

When I received the invitation to propose the toast at the annual luncheon of the Kipling Society, I felt no hesitation in accepting. It came to me like a decree of Destiny: a feeling which I think Kipling himself would have understood. I am often enough invited to speak, but the feeling to which I refer comes to me very seldom. It is a very different emotion from that of the mere inescapability of a task accepted only because one can find no plausible reason for declining. Nor, I hasten to add, does it mean that I considered myself either an authority on the subject, or in the least gifted as an after-dinner speaker. It is simply that I have come to have a feeling, almost a superstition, that it is a kind of obligation laid upon me to testify for Rudyard Kipling whenever the opportunity presents itself.

Rudyard Kipling, whom I never knew and never saw, and who probably never heard of me, has touched my life at sundry times and in divers manners. In 1939, I was elected to an Honorary Fellowship of Magdalene College, Cambridge, of which the previous incumbent had been Kipling. In 1941, I was invited to prepare a selection of Kipling's verse and to provide a long introduction. Two weeks ago I was in Paris, being introduced into a society called Académie Septentrionale, where I had to pronounce the *éloge* of my predecessor – Rudyard Kipling. And here I am today to perform a similar function.

All this might be dismissed as coincidence, or as a series in which one event led to another. But Kipling has accompanied me ever since boyhood, when I discovered the early verse – *Barrack Room Ballads* – and the early stories – *Plain Tales from the Hills*. There are boyhood enthusiasms which one outgrows; there are writers who impress one deeply at some time before or during adolescence and whose work one never re-reads in later life. But Kipling is different. Traces of Kipling appear in my own mature verse where no diligent scholarly sleuth has yet observed them, but which I am myself prepared to disclose. I once wrote a poem called *The Love Song of J. Alfred Prufrock*: I am convinced that it would never have been called 'Love Song' but for a title of Kipling's that stuck obstinately in my head: 'The Love Song of Har Dyal'. Many years later I wrote a poem called 'The Hollow Men': I could never have thought of this title but for Kipling's poem 'The Broken Men'. One of the broken men has turned up recently in my work, and may be seen at this time on the stage of the Cambridge Theatre. And I leave you to guess why a Persian cat I once possessed was dignified by the name of Mirza Murad Ali Beg.

[10] So much to explain to you my feeling of destiny. When I made the selection from Kipling's verse which I have already mentioned, in 1941, the moment was well chosen to remind the public of Kipling's importance, and to revive a reputation which had diminished under the influence of liberal, not to say radical critics. But it aroused considerable astonishment in the world of letters, that Kipling should be championed not only as a prose writer but as a writer of verse, by a poet whose verse was generally considered to be at the opposite pole from Kipling's. Whereas my poems had appeared too obscure and recondite to win popular approval, Kipling's had long been considered too simple, too crude, too popular, indeed too near the doggerel of the music hall song, to deserve from the fastidious critic anything but disdain. I was suspected, if not of insincerity, at least of a mischievous delight in paradox. Yet I think that the facts which I have just recounted should convince the present audience that this was not true.

There is perhaps a reason of a different order than any I have so far implied, for my regard for Kipling's work, a reason given by a similarity, or rather an analogy, between his background and mine. Kipling passed his early childhood in India; he was brought back to England for his schooling; he returned to India at the age of seventeen. Two years of his life were spent in America. Later, he settled in Sussex, but came to pass his winters in the more benign climate of South Africa. He had been a citizen of the British Empire, long before he naturalised himself, so to speak, in a particular part of a particular county of England. The topography of my own life history is very different from his, but our feeling about England springs from causes not wholly dissimilar. The word *metic* is perfectly good English, though to many people the French *metèque* may be more familiar. It does not apply perhaps in the strictest sense to either of us, since we come both from wholly British stock; but I think that Kipling's attitude to things English, like mine, was in some ways different from that of any native-born Briton. I feel this in some of the poems written after Kipling settled in Sussex. For example, 'The Recall':

> Under their feet in the grasses
> My clinging magic runs.
> They shall return as strangers,
> They shall remain as sons.

He is referring to the American couple of the story which this poem accompanies, who settle in England in the village from which the wife's family had gone to America: but I feel that he is writing out of his own experience. Similarly, in 'Sir Richard's Song' the speaker is a Norman knight, a follower of William the Conqueror, who has settled in England:

> I followed my Duke ere I was a lover,
>   To take from England fief and fee;
> But now this game is the other way over –
>   But now England hath taken me!

Sir Richard, too, I think, is Kipling himself.

[11] What is one to say, in a few minutes, about the amazing man of genius, every single piece of writing of whom, taken in isolation, can look like a brilliant *tour de force*; but whose work has nevertheless an undeniable unity? There are at least half a dozen aspects of Kipling upon which one would like to dilate: the journalist, the literary artist, the observer of men, of landscapes and countries and of machines also, the moralist, the curious seeker into the abnormal and paranormal, and the seer. To do justice to Kipling, to draw the portrait of the man in his writings, one would have to consider him under all of these aspects, and then show the

unity behind them. I can touch today only upon two aspects which seem to me of special importance: those of the moralist and the seer.

The moralist in Kipling appears constantly throughout his work: it is one of the elements which contribute to make unity of it. Often, it approximates to a kind of stoicism, in the popular use of that word: the man held up for admiration is the man who has done his allotted task, without the expectation of reward or concern with recognition. Thus the 'Sons of Martha':

> It is their care in all the ages to take the buffet and cushion
>   the shock.
> It is their care that the gear engages; it is their care that the
>   switches lock.
> It is their care that the wheels run truly; it is their care to
>   embark and entrain,
> Tally, transport, and deliver duly the Sons of Mary by land
>   and main.

In an essay written many years ago, which remains one of the best studies of Kipling that we have, Colonel Bonamy Dobrée pointed out how constantly worldly success is disparaged; and that even the man who is an utter failure in life (and a gallery of such human wreckage can be assembled from among Kipling's characters) may be a nobler figure than the man who has successfully feathered his own nest. The moralist is always present, even in those tales of *The Jungle Book* which are taken by many readers to be merely fantasies to amuse the very young. It may be the moralist in Kipling that is displeasing to those intellectuals who have belittled him in my time. He was well aware that the moral is unwelcome, and must be insinuated, or conveyed (as we say nowadays) subliminally. This is explicit in 'The Fabulists':

> When all the world would keep a matter hid,
>   Since Truth is seldom friend to any crowd,
> Men write in fable as old Aesop did,
>   Jesting at that which none will name aloud.
> And this they needs must do, or it will fall
>   Unless they please they are not heard at all.

It is only by keeping in mind Kipling the moralist and Kipling the seer that we can, I think, consider his politics. With his opinions, except as found in his published works, I am not concerned – only with his poems and his stories. Kipling was not a party man. Nor had he – and this is important – a mind gifted for abstract thought: he thought in images. He was not a philosopher, and his political philosophy is all in his firm and simple code of behaviour. What he has to say about politics may be summed up in 'The Gods of the Copy-Book Headings':

[12] In the Carboniferous Epoch we were promised abundance for all,
By robbing selected Peter to pay for collective Paul;
But, though we had plenty of money, there was nothing our money could buy,
And the Gods of the Copy-Book Headings said: *if you don't work you die.*

But Kipling was something rarer than a philosopher, he was a prophet. (Remember how long ago he wrote *The Man Who Was* and 'The Truce of the Bear'.) His mind was intuitive, rather than ratiocinative. His genius, if I understand it at all, lay in his powers of observation, description and intuition. That there is something a little *uncanny* in it all, even in his power of observation, is illustrated by an anecdote which I was told in Cambridge, and which may not be widely known. When he paid his first visit to Magdalene College, on being made an Honorary Fellow, he expressed a wish to view the Pepys Library and the manuscript of Pepys's diary. The College, knowing that Kipling was a man who asked questions, and whose questions were apt to be unexpected and unanswerable, had assembled all the available scholars learnèd about Pepys and his time. Kipling asked the one question for which they were unprepared: what was the formula for the ink that Pepys used? He observed that it was dissimilar to that of any manuscript of the period that he had seen. The matter was looked into later, and it was found that Pepys had used an ink made by a formula of his own invention. And we all know the story of the Roman Legion which he placed at Hadrian's Wall.

I suggest that the fact that Kipling was an intuitive and not an intellectual, may go to account for his being underrated by intellectuals who are not intuitives: He had a gift of prophecy, and he must have appreciated the frustration of Cassandra. He foresaw two wars. That of 1914 is foreshadowed in his 'Ode to France' written in 1913. And in 1932 he foresaw, in 'The Storm Cone', the storm that was to burst seven years later, three years after his death. In his last years he regarded the future of the world with more and more misgiving. He seems to me the greatest English man of letters of his generation. Before lifting my glass I should like to quote in full, as a reminder of the man, the short poem which concludes his volume of verse – a poem of which I should like to have been the author:

> If I have given you delight
> By aught that I have done,
> Let me lie quiet in that night
> Which shall be yours anon:
>
> And for the little, little span
> The dead are borne in mind,
> Seek not to question other than
> The books I leave behind.

Ladies and gentlemen, I give you The Unfading Genius of Rudyard Kipling.

ANNUAL LUNCHEON,
21 October, 1958

[Statement about *The New Leader*]

New York Times Book Review, 5 Apr. 1959, 16.
Not in Gallup but would be C632a.

The New Leader is one of the few weeklies I read most of with regularity. I find statements of fact not otherwise available to me; I find the point of view generally sympathetic; and when I disagree (as I inevitably do from time to time), it helps me to understand better some position different from my own.

The Panegyric by Mr T. S. Eliot

Obituary notice for Father Eric Cheetham, *S. Stephen's Magazine*, May 1959, [5–7].
Gallup C633.

Eliot had more briefly commemorated Fr Cheetham in *CT*, 139. 4856
(9 Mar. 1956), 12 (Gallup C603; *see above*, pp. 116–17).

It was in the autumn of 1933 that I first attended Mass at St Stephen's. I had returned from a year of lecturing in America; and while looking about for a more permanent abode, was stopping at a boarding house in Courtfield Gardens. I think that Father Cheetham came to dinner there one night, for he knew the lady who was the proprietor. In this way or some other, I became known to him as a new member of his congregation:

and not very long afterwards he offered me rooms, which had become vacant, in his presbytery in Grenville Place. My circumstances at the time were somewhat unusual, and I shall not forget the sympathy and understanding with which he responded to my explanation. I remained his Paying Guest for seven years, first in Grenville Place and then in Emperor's Gate, in a house of which he had rented the two top stories. We only parted in the summer of 1940: the furniture was stored, I retired to friends in the country and to my office in Bloomsbury, and Father Cheetham found shelter in what always seemed to me a characteristic choice of abode – the basement of the Albert Hall.

I begin with these personal details as offering my credentials for addressing you to-day on the occasion of the dedication of the statue of St Stephen which we have given to the church, members of his flock, present friends and absent friends, in memory of Eric Samuel Cheetham. There are others who have known him longer than I. I think of two who are probably here to-day. There must be many who have known him not so long as I, but who have known him in different contexts and seen other aspects of his character than those which I have seen. I only speak as one who lodged with him for seven years, and who was his Warden from 1934 – just twenty-five years ago – throughout the rest of his incumbency. It is characteristic of his ways that I was never elected formally, but merely appointed by him, no objections being raised at the Vestry. Years later, when I discovered this irregularity, I suggested to the Archdeacon that I should have an act of indemnity for everything that I had done in the capacity of Warden; but he thought it unnecessary. I only mention this trifling fact because it throws a tiny ray of light on the character of a man who was the most modest, the most diffident, the humblest-minded autocrat whom I have ever known.

Eric Cheetham came to St Stephen's, as curate to Lord Victor Seymour, in 1917. He was himself a son of Lancashire, and remained a Lancastrian, even to taking an occasional holiday at Blackpool. But after Chad's he went, I think, to an East End Parish before he came to us. It is not every young priest who can be equally successful in the East End and in Kensington. I know nothing of Fr Cheetham's earlier career; but I feel sure, from my knowledge of his character, that he would have been as distinguished and successful as a vicar in East London, as he was here.

Eric Cheetham possessed several gifts invaluable to a priest. To mention a small matter first – or what may seem a small matter – he had the gift of being able to edit a parish magazine – or to adapt a parish magazine to his peculiar talents. For his parish magazine was certainly original. How he found time to edit it – I was about to say write [6] it, I do not know. His own contributions were composed in a very individual style, in which dashes often seemed to do duty for more conventional punctuation marks. It reminded one of his conversation; and perhaps that was one reason for the magazine being read, as I believe it was, by many former parishioners who like to keep in touch with St Stephen's. Then again, he had a great love of the theatre, and had in him just enough, but not too much, of the showman. A moment ago I suggested that it seemed appropriate that he should have made his abode in the Albert Hall during the bombing: I was reminded of a pageant which he put on there, I think on behalf of the Mothers' Union, at rather short notice. It was an impressive pageant: and in such enterprises Fr Cheetham showed great resourcefulness – for he could, at a pinch, make bricks without straw. His theatrical gifts were always under his control; and his liturgical sense of accuracy and precision was combined with good taste and discretion. As a preacher, too, he was very effective: his sermons had a beginning, a middle and an end. They always gave the impression of having been thought out for that particular congregation and for that particular occasion; and one always had the feeling of being the man in the pew – the man or woman – to whom he was talking. With devotion to Catholic doctrine and Catholic observance, he combined true evangelical zeal. He had a strong sense of pastoral responsibility, and I suspect that he often helped those who were in need of help, in ways which exceeded the bounds of ordinary pastoral activity.

At the time of Fr Cheetham's resignation, when he was a very sick man with not long to live, I wrote an appreciation of his ministry in which I made some of the points that I have just repeated. In any such piece of writing, about a man whom one has known and loved, one is always most conscious, especially after the man is dead, of the things that one has failed to say. I can at least add a word now about Fr Cheetham's war service, at the time when he slept, so far as sleep was possible, in the depths of the Albert Hall. I don't think that Fr Cheetham was any more impassive or insensitive to danger than the rest of us; but he and Fr Alderson, who was then his curate, said their daily masses through the worst of the bombardment. This was not all: Fr Cheetham made himself, one might say, almost priest-in-charge of the Gloucester Road Tube Station platform, and gave much attention to the needs of the people – and their children – who came to spend their nights there. And here also I should mention that it is owing to his foresight and to his efforts in collecting contributions for this purpose, that we have a fund which enables us to supplement, in these difficult times, the stipend of Vicar and Assistant Clergy.

But a recital of gifts, accomplishments and achievements never can be enough in itself to account for the impression that such a man as

Fr Cheetham makes upon those who come in close contact with him. It can do everything, perhaps, but one thing – explain why the man was lovable and loved. When we really love a person, we love the weaknesses and foibles of that person. Eric Cheetham was very lovable, and was also, at times, extremely irritating; and one loved him the more for the irritation he caused. There was more than one occasion on which [7] my fellow warden and I, having gone by appointment to discuss some problem with him, were obliged finally to leave in a state of exhaustion and frustration, because Fr Cheetham had done all the talking and had not given us the opportunity to say what we had come to say or to ask the questions to which we needed answers. Again, there was in the man a mixture of shrewdness and simplicity, of business sense and confusion, of order and disorder. I suppose we all present some contradictions, to the eyes of those who know us best: in Eric Cheetham's case I think they were aggravated by the fact that he tried to do too many things and to respond to too many appeals. He pushed himself too hard, and his health, always uncertain because of early illnesses, suffered accordingly. We recognised in him qualities of integrity, generosity, and natural goodness developed by Christian discipline; we recognised the strength and depth of his faith: but in the end the quality of which one is most aware in people one loves is simply – their lovableness.

A generation or two passes, and the name of such a man means nothing to the world. Those who come to worship here after the lapse of time will know only that a man of that name was here as curate and vicar for thirty-nine years. May this figure of St Stephen, erected in his memory, at least remind the worshippers who will follow us that a priest named Eric Samuel Cheetham was loved and honoured in memory by all those who came under his care.

[Mr Ashley Dukes]

The Times, 7 May 1959, 18. Prefaced with 'Mr T. S. Eliot writes: – '.
Gallup C634.

I should like to add a note to your excellent obituary notice of Ashley Dukes. It was Dukes who, after seeing a performance of *Murder in the Cathedral* at the Canterbury Festival for which it was written, saw that the play had further possibilities, and brought the whole production to London. Owing to his enterprise a play designed for a special occasion and for a very brief run came to the notice of the general public.

[Address]

The new University Library at the University of Sheffield was opened by Eliot on 12 May 1959, the same day as he was awarded the degree of Doctor of Laws *honoris causa*. His remarks are introduced as *'Opening Address by Dr. T. S. Eliot, O.M.' University of Sheffield. Reprint from the 54th Annual Report* . . . [1960], 23–6.

Gallup (252–3) provides additional bibliographical information, but misplaces the address in 12 May 1958 as C625.

I appreciate very highly the honour of being invited to open this new library of Sheffield University. But experience has taught me that no kind of public speaking that I have practised (I have practised several) has ever prepared me to undertake a new kind. I experience always the same trepidation. I have opened in the past a church bazaar, I have opened an exhibition of posters, a bowling green; I have even opened a library, but it was a very small library in a building that served several other purposes. All that I have learned from my experience of opening things is that, after making my little address, I must not forget to declare the bazaar, the bowling green, the exhibition, or whatever it is, open. I have never opened a building of this great size, and I feel as if I had been temporarily made responsible for some vast mechanism or organism which I was quite incompetent to control. A university library, a great up-to-date library, is a very complex product of architecture and engineering; and I have read with astonishment the list of industries, represented by thirty-two sub-contractors and twenty suppliers, which have contributed to make this edifice what it is. And I do not even know what a 'fibrous plaster mullion casing' may be! When one considers the rate at which *necessary* books must be acquired by a university library (twenty years ago, I read, this collection was growing at the rate of 5,000 volumes a year – I don't know at what rate it is growing this year) one begins to understand something of the forethought, skill and industry that must go to the design and construction of the building to house the books so that the needs of readers and of staff may be met, and the books themselves cared for properly.

I have been using the word 'library' to refer to the building itself and to its organisation; and it is to celebrate the completion of this building and the beginning of its service to the University that I am here speaking to you to-day. But the same word means the building and the collection of books which it houses. It is only the building that can be 'new'. A library can never be new. New books must constantly be added; but a library is something which grows, which has grown and which must keep on growing. So I feel that it is right, on any occasion which marks a stage in a library's development – such as a generous gift of books or of funds, or, as to-day, the inauguration of a new building in which to house and from which to circulate the books – to honour the benefactors who started the collection, and those who toiled to improve and extend it. Among such honoured names here I find mentioned particularly at the beginning, after that of Edgar Allen himself, those of Professor Moore Smith, Sir Charles Firth and Professor Mayor of Cambridge, scholars of English Literature, of history and of Latin respectively. Sir Charles Firth, I understand, left [24] his private library to the University. And this leads me to a point which seems to me worth making: that the private, the personal library precedes the public library in the order of generation; and from there to another point: that the private and the public library complement each other and are both necessary for every educated man.

By *private* library I mean here primarily the collection of books which each man forms for himself, rather than the library which he may have inherited from his forebears. A library which is *merely* a heritage, one which the possessor does nothing to increase or improve, is a dead thing unless it is available to at least one person for knowledge or delight. Fortunate are those whose parents had a good library and encouraged their children to make use of it: the mere presence of shelves of good books, and the awareness of their importance to our elders, is an asset in childhood. But it is the library that a man forms for himself that matters most. Almost all of us, I suspect, when we visit for the first time the house of someone we know but slightly or not at all, if we find ourselves alone in a room, will slip to the bookcase to see what books are there; for the choice of books can tell us a good deal about their owner.

When I speak on the other hand of a *public* library, I mean here a library which is not the exclusive property of an individual, and which is open either to the whole public or to all those possessing certain qualifications – such as membership of the university to which the library belongs. I include the great national libraries, the university libraries, the municipal libraries; also the circulating subscription libraries, and certainly those libraries of great distinction and great public usefulness such as the London Library, the Leeds Library and the Liverpool Athenaeum. Some libraries have grown from a private library given as a bequest; most libraries have benefited from time to time by bequests of private libraries. The nucleus, I suppose, of a library should be, in any department, the books which a man interested in those subjects might be expected to buy for himself if he had unlimited financial resources, unlimited house room – and if the books were all available. It is true that no one would want, even had he the means of possessing it, a library of vast size; it is true that we go to a library for books which we need to consult but do not wish to possess. Of books which are merely tools, there are many which we need to consult only once; there are books of which only one paragraph may be necessary for our purpose.

On the other hand, one's private library does not consist only of books one wishes to re-read or to consult frequently. Apart from those books which one keeps because of one's relations with the writer or donor; apart from those books which remain on our shelves simply because we cannot make up our minds to dispose of them, or because we never find time for weeding them out, there are many books which we want to keep even when there is no likelihood of our ever re-reading them. I must, for instance, have my Shakespeare complete, because there is nothing of Shakespeare's which I may not want to re-read or to consult at any moment. But I also like to keep the complete plays of Ben Jonson, and those of Beaumont and Fletcher, though nothing is less likely than that I shall ever re-read more than one or two of their plays. There are books in my possession which I have never read from cover to cover; there are even books which I have bought and never read at all – to the profit of the bookseller though not to that of my education. Sometimes buying a book seems to do instead of reading it. But all the books that I have mentioned are appropriate to my [25] tastes and interests. Nothing in a private library should be purely accidental. That, of course, is a counsel of perfection which I can't say my own library illustrates, though my wife has done her best to weed out the waifs and strays and replace them by more desirable occupants. Finally, I like to own the *complete* works of a few writers: I have always maintained that every educated person ought to know the *entire* works of at least one author – let us say, for general readers, one of the great novelists. There is also a satisfaction in owning the complete works of a great writer, even if there is no likelihood of one's ever reading them all. Once or twice in my life I have been led astray by this desire, and I should like now to make a public confession. There was an occasion when I was a young American in London on my way to Oxford on a scholarship from Harvard. While in London I happened to stray, I do not know why or where, into a book auction room. I had never been in an auction room before, and I got rather carried away by the facility with which one could make oneself the owner of vast quantities of books at what seemed to be very low prices. So the result was that my bid had been accepted for a very large parcel of books, including the complete works of Voltaire in French. Now Voltaire, as you know, was one of the most industrious writers who ever lived, and his complete works occupy a good deal of space. For some reason I was not required to pay for them or take them away at the time. I left my name, I think, and was to go back the next day to remove the books. That gave me time to reflect overnight, and I thought: well, in the first place to carry these books about will cost me far more than the books themselves; in the second place, what shall I ever do with this vast number of volumes of Voltaire? Had I got to be saddled with this for the rest of my life? I should never be able to get rid of it. I am shamed to say I never went back and I had not paid for the books. I don't know whether they ever made any attempt to trace me or not. Perhaps I shall be traced now. I am glad to have relieved my conscience, by confession, of this perilous stuff.

I am here, however, not to talk about my own books or about those I have escaped possessing, but to open a great university library. You may well wonder how I can justify rattling on at such length about private libraries – about that collection of books which each of us, no matter how straitened his means or how narrow his living quarters, should form for himself. My excuse lies in the fact that the private library and the public library, as I have said, are necessary complements to each other. A man who owned *no private library at all*, or whose books consisted merely of tools, such as the books used in preparation for his examinations, would *not be an educated man*. And a man whose reading consisted only of the books that he had bought for himself would *not be an educated man either*. It is of inestimable value in our education to live for several years in propinquity to and with free use of a great university library. It is during these years, and by frequenting such a library, that we learn to assimilate thoroughly the contents of a few books and to taste discriminatingly a great many; we learn how to skim, which is very important, as well as how to read intensively. Reading intensively in the subjects of our election and discursively in the subjects of our curiosity, we ought, when young, to be curious about many things, as well as eager to master one. For if we do not indulge our curiosity during the formative years, we are in danger of becoming incurious – and uninteresting – persons later. The presence of an impressive library such as this should have a benign influence [26] upon those who, being members of the university to which it belongs – and I am proud to think that I too am now a member of this university – are free to make use of that library.

With such thoughts as these in mind, I am happy to have the privilege of opening this library, and I forthwith declare it open.

Preface

Eliot's Prefaces (pp. 9–13) to his translations of St-J. Perse's *Anabasis* as finally publ. on 22 May 1959 by Faber & Faber (Gallup A16).

I am by no means convinced that a poem like *Anabase* requires a preface at all. It is better to read such a poem six times, and dispense with a preface. But when a poem is presented in the form of a translation, people who have never heard of it are naturally inclined to demand some testimonial. So I give mine hereunder.

Anabase is already well known, not only in France, but in other countries of Europe. One of the best Introductions to the poem is that of the late Hugo von Hofmannsthal, which forms the preface to the German translation.[1] There is another by Valéry Larbaud, which forms the preface to the Russian translation.[2] And there was an informative note by Lucien Fabre in the *Nouvelles Littéraires*.[3]

For myself, once having had my attention drawn to the poem by a friend whose taste I trusted, there was no need for a preface. I did not need to be told, after one reading, that the word *anabasis* has no particular reference to Xenophon or the journey of the Ten Thousand, no particular reference to Asia Minor; and that no map of its migrations could be drawn up. Mr Perse is using the word *anabasis* in the same literal sense in which Xenophon himself used it. The poem is a series of images of migration, of conquest of vast spaces in Asiatic wastes, of destruction and foundation of cities and civilisations of any races or epochs of the ancient East.

I may, I trust, borrow from Mr Fabre two notions which may be of use to the English reader. The first is that any obscurity of the poem, on first readings, is due to the suppression of 'links in the chain', of explanatory and connecting matter, and not to incoherence, or to the love of cryptogram. [10] The justification of such abbreviation of method is that sequence of images coincides and concentrates into one intense impression of barbaric civilisation. The reader has to allow the images to fall into his memory successively without questioning the reasonableness of each at the moment; so that, at the end, a total effect is produced.

Such selection of a sequence of images and ideas has nothing chaotic about it. There is a logic of the imagination as well as a logic of concepts. People who do not appreciate poetry always find it difficult to distinguish between order and chaos in the arrangement of images; and

---

1. See page 84.
2. See page 80.
3. See page 88.

even those who are capable of appreciating poetry cannot depend upon first impressions. I was not convinced of Mr Perse's imaginative order until I had read the poem five or six times. And if, as I suggest, such an arrangement of imagery requires just as much 'fundamental brainwork' as the arrangement of an argument, it is to be expected that the reader of a poem should take at least as much trouble as a barrister reading an important decision on a complicated case.

I refer to this poem as a poem. It would be convenient if poetry were always verse – either accented, alliterative, or quantitative; but that is not true. Poetry may occur, within a definite limit on one side, at any point along a line of which the formal limits are 'verse' and 'prose'. Without offering any generalised theory about 'poetry', 'verse' and 'prose', I may suggest that a writer, by using, as does Mr Perse, certain exclusively poetic methods, is sometimes able to write poetry in what is called prose. Another writer can, by reversing the process, write great prose in verse. There are two very simple but insuperable difficulties in any definition of 'prose' and 'poetry'. One is that we have three terms where we need four: we have 'verse' and 'poetry' on the one side, and only 'prose' on the other. The other difficulty follows from the first: that the words imply a valuation in one context which they do not in another. 'Poetry' introduces a distinction between good verse and bad verse; but we have no one word to separate bad prose from good prose. As a matter of [11] fact, much bad prose is poetic prose; and only a very small part of bad verse is bad because it is prosaic.

But *Anabase* is poetry. Its sequences, its logic of imagery, are those of poetry and not of prose; and in consequence – at least the two matters are very closely allied – the *declamation*, the system of stresses and pauses, which is partially exhibited by the punctuation and spacing, is that of poetry and not of prose.

The second indication of Mr Fabre is one which I may borrow for the English reader: a tentative synopsis of the movement of the poem. It is a scheme which may give the reader a little guidance on his first reading; when he no longer needs it he will forget it. The ten divisions of the poem are headed as follows:

    i. Arrival of the conqueror on the site of the city he is to found.
    ii. Marking out of its boundary walls.
    iii. Consultation of the augurs.
    iv. Founding of the city.
    v. Longing for new worlds to conquer.
    vi. Plans for establishment and for filling the coffers.

    vii. Decision to undertake fresh expedition.
   viii. March through desert wastes.
    ix. Arrival at borders of a great land.
     x. Warrior-prince received with honours and celebrations. He rests for a spell but is soon yearning to be on his way again, this time with the navigator.

And I believe this is as much as I need to say about Perse's *Anabasis*. I believe that this is a piece of writing of the same importance as the later work of James Joyce, as valuable as *Anna Livia Plurabelle*. And this is a high estimate indeed.

I have two words to add, one about the author, the other about the translation. The author of this poem is, even in the most practical sense, an authority on the Far East; he has lived there, as well as in the tropics. As for the translation, it would not be even so satisfactory as it is, if the author had not [12] collaborated with me to such an extent as to be halftranslator. He has, I can testify, a sensitive and intimate knowledge of the English language, as well as a mastery of his own.

T. S. ELIOT

1930

[13] Note to Revised Edition

Since the last publication, nineteen years ago, of the text of *Anabase* together with my translation, this and other poems of the author have extended his reputation far beyond the bounds of his own country. St-John Perse is a name known to everyone, I think, who is seriously concerned with contemporary poetry in America. It has therefore seemed high time that the translation should be revised and corrected.

When this translation was made, St-John Perse was little known outside of France. The translator, perhaps for the reason that he was introducing the poem to the English-speaking public, was then concerned, here and there, less with rendering the exact sense of a phrase, than with coining some phrase in English which might have equivalent value; he may even have taken liberties in the interest of originality, and sometimes interposed his own idiom between author and reader. But (to revert to the first person) I have always refused to publish the translation except in this way, *en regard* with the French text. Its purpose is only to assist the Englishspeaking reader who wishes to approach the French text. The method of the author, his syntax and his rhythm, are original; his vocabulary includes some unusual words; and the translation may still serve its purpose. But at this stage it was felt that a greater fidelity to the exact meaning, a more literal translation, was what was needed. I have corrected not only my own licences, but several positive errors and mistakes. In this revision I have depended heavily upon the recommendations of the author, whose increasing mastery of English has enabled him to detect faults previously unobserved, and upon the assistance of Mr John Hayward, to whom also I wish to make acknowledgement.

T. S. ELIOT

1949

Note to the Third Edition

The alterations to the English text of this edition have been made by the author himself, and tend to make the translation more literal than in previous editions.

T. S. ELIOT

1958

A Note

Note on Allen Tate. *SR*, 67. 4 (Autumn 1959), [576].
'Homage to Allen Tate . . . in honor of his sixtieth birthday.' Gallup C635.

The tribute which I should have liked to pay to Allen Tate would have required my re-reading everything of his that I have ever read, and reading all of his published work that I have not read. For such an act of homage I have not had the time at my disposal. What can I say about him in the space of a paragraph, I reflected, which shall be something more than a simple salutation from an old friend?

Others, no doubt, will assess his achievements severally: his contributions to poetry, to prose fiction, to literary criticism and to social thinking. Considerable as is his accomplishment in each of these areas, the whole, I believe, is greater than the sum of its parts; and I think it will become clear at some future time that Allen Tate's eminence, among his contemporaries, consists in his uncommon combination of excellences. Literary critics have frequently been bad poets; good poets have frequently been political simpletons. Allen Tate is a good poet and a good literary critic who is distinguished for the sagacity of his social judgement and the consistency with which he has maintained the least popular of political attitudes – that of the sage. He believes in reason rather than enthusiasm, in wisdom rather than system; and he knows that many problems are insoluble and that in politics no solution is final. By avoiding the lethargy of the conservative, the flaccidity of the liberal, and the violence of the zealot, he succeeds in being a representative of the smallest of minorities, that of the intelligent who refuse to be described as 'intellectuals'. And what he has written, as a critic of society, is of much greater significance because of being said by a man who is also a good poet and a good critic of literature.

Countess Nora Wydenbruck

Obituary notice, *The Times*, 2 Sept. 1959, 14. Gallup C636.

Mr T. S. Eliot, O.M., writes:

Nora Wydenbruck was a gifted writer; but very exceptionally gifted as a translator both from English into German and from German into English. She was completely bilingual; and I imagine that her command of Italian was also secure. For the same translator to render successfully Rilke's *Duinese Elegies* into English and my *Four Quartets* into German is a feat of translation for which I know no parallel. Her versions of *The Cocktail Party* and *The Confidential Clerk* are those read and performed in German-speaking countries. I mourn her loss in this capacity, and, in common with her many friends in England, as a charming and gracious survivor of the *ancien régime* in Vienna.

[Greeting to the Staatstheater Kassel]

Das neue Staatstheater Kassel: Festschrift zur Eröffnung der neuen Häuser am 12. und 13. September 1959 (1959), [14]. The volume included an unattributed German translation. Not in Gallup but would be B81a.

I am happy in the knowledge that Kassel now possesses its new Staatstheater; I am proud that my latest play *The Elder Statesman* should be produced in this theatre in its first season; and I am grateful for the opportunity of sending a word of greeting to be included in the Festschrift which commemorates the opening of your Staatstheater.

The theatre has always been of first importance in my career as a writer. Among the English influences upon my development as a poet, the verse dramatists of the age of Shakespeare took first place: many of my early poems appear, in retrospect, to have been striving, so to speak, toward the condition of drama. And it has been my ambition, for the last twenty-five years, to bring back poetry to the stage, to accustom the public to plays written in verse but concerned with contemporary society and with characters talking in contemporary idiom. I have been aware, from the moment I began to write for the stage, that there were living dramatists with greater native talent for the theatre, writers of unerring instinct for theatrical effect, and of technical accomplishment which I could not hope to emulate. Nevertheless, I maintain that it is only in poetry that the deepest emotion and the finest states of feeling can be expressed; and that it is more possible for a poet, by enthusiasm and hard work, to become a playwright, than for a prose playwright to become a poet. This thought has been my solace and encouragement.

In my first play of modern life *The Family Reunion* (first produced 20 years ago) I was concerned primarily with developing a verse idiom suitable for the contemporary scene. In my next two plays, *The Cocktail Party* and *The Confidential Clerk*, I was struggling to acquire a greater mastery of dramatic construction, and the verse less often rises to become poetry. In *The Elder Statesman* I have, I think, a play simpler in plot than *The Confidential Clerk*, but in verse which is more often poetic than is that of the play which preceded it. I await with keenest interest the reaction of audiences in Germany. I am very proud that *The Elder Statesman* should be presented in Kassel in the same season with plays by two great poetic dramatists, one German and one Greek.

T. S. ELIOT
5th August, 1959.

[Address at Mary Institute]

An address delivered at the Mary Institute, St Louis, Missouri, on 11 Nov. 1959. Publ. in *From Mary to You*, Centennial Issue (Dec. 1959), 133–6. Gallup C637.

At the end of the address Eliot read *The Dry Salvages*, of which the first 14 lines are printed in the issue.

If you've read your programmes for this evening you will be acquainted with the reasons which have been put forward for doing me the honour of asking me to speak this evening. But you do not yet know all the reasons I have for accepting this honour, and I propose presently to say something about that and to tell you something of my early association with Mary Institute.

As for the name of Mary Institute, it always will seem to be a moot point in my family whether it was named for my little Aunt Mary or for little Mary Smith, or for both. Mary Smith was certainly the daughter of the benefactor, the friend of my grandfather whose generosity founded this school and the defunct Smith Academy from which I, myself, graduated. I don't think it greatly matters. I prefer to think that the school was named for both. They both died far too young ever to have been pupils of the school. I'm sure, however, that my grandfather, who foresaw the educational needs – foresaw and endeavoured to anticipate the educational needs – of the growing city, must in any case have meant the name of this school as well as the name of Smith Academy to perpetuate the memory of his two friends the Smiths who gave the funds for their foundation.

[134] Now I had four older sisters, all of whom attended Mary Institute; at least one cousin, I think, and other cousins who were here at one time or another who attended it. So it should be obvious that but for the difference of sex my brother and I would also have graduated from Mary Institute, I went, of course, like my brother to the fraternal-brotherly institution of Smith Academy. We were well taught and I was happy there.

The old Mary Institute – one of the old Mary Institutes, should I say – the Institute of which I have such close associations – stood at the corner of Beaumont Street and Locust Street. Now my family lived at 2635 Locust Street, next door. The schoolyard of Mary Institute seemed to me, as a child, of vast extent; but on going that way and endeavouring to decipher any traces of either our house or Mary Institute, I came to the conclusion that it must have been rather small, but it seemed to me very big. At any rate this schoolyard abutted on my father's property. There was at the front of our house a sort of picket fence which divided our front yard from the schoolyard. This picket fence merged a little later as it passed the wall of the house into a high brick wall which concealed our back garden from the schoolyard and also concealed the schoolyard from our back garden. There was a door in this wall and there was a key to this door. Now, when the young ladies had left the school in the afternoon and at the end of the week, I had access to the schoolyard and used it for my own purposes of play. When the girls had left in the afternoon, the schoolyard was mine for a playground, first of all under the supervision of my nurse and later for practising approach shots with a lofter, which was sometimes dangerous for the windows. They must have been very brief approach shots, but then I was a very small boy with a very small lofter, or mashie. At any rate, then, in the schoolyard I remember a mound on which stood a huge ailanthus tree. Oh, it seemed to me very big and round on this little mound. And I have a photograph of myself standing against this ailanthus tree at the age of seven or eight in the company of a crony of the same age, the crony who was later, I think, president of that International Exchange Bank in Zurich and was certainly first vice-president of the Chase-Manhattan Bank of New York. It's interesting to know that my boyhood friend and I both became bankers although he became so much more distinguished than myself. His name is Thomas H. McKittrick, Jr, but he was known to me at the time simply as Tom Kick.

But my use of the schoolyard isn't all. I had access to the gymnasium also. It was a very different looking gymnasium than this. It seemed vast to me then, but this is much vaster. But I remember that without a playmate I was able to use the swinging rings and the parallel bars and the Indian clubs which were pleasant to fling about. Occasionally one ventured further into the school, of course after all the girls and the teachers had left, wandering about the corridors smelling of chalk and ink and cedar pencils as school corridors do – or used to do in those days – and making quite free of it, making myself, in fact, quite at home in Mary Institute.

Then there was Uncle Henry. Uncle Henry Jones was the janitor. He was a romantic figure; he lived in a sort of basement flat under the Beaumont Street entrance. He was a romantic figure to me as a child, not only because he possessed a parrot which actually did a little talking but because he was reputed to have been a runaway slave and certainly had one mutilated ear. He is said to have been tracked by bloodhounds. But Uncle Henry Jones was a great friend of the family. In fact, his family were great friends of the family because his son Stephen, and in succession to Stephen his grandson Charlie, undertook in succession the duties of looking after the furnace, washing the sidewalk, cutting the grass, and so on – bringing in the coal and wood.

I've always been heretofore, or at least I had become at one time, rather careful about [135] anecdotes or stories which I remembered having been told as a child because some years ago I made a mistake and thought I had been told by my father that our grandmother in the early days used, when there wasn't enough meat about the place, to go out and shoot a wild turkey. I told this in good faith, put it in print in fact, thinking I had heard it from my father. Well, there were cries of derision and letters from my sisters and brother, all of whom were much older than myself that I was not in a position to argue with, saying this was not so and grandma had never shot a wild turkey. I'm sorry she didn't.

However, to return for a moment to Uncle Henry Jones, I consulted my sister about this and she can't give any opinion about it; so I can tell the story as I remember it, which was that Uncle Henry had two wives, not in succession but apparently married to them both at the same time, and that this was only discovered when suddenly a new Auntie was found in place of the old Auntie, and I understood that this was the first or more legitimate bride who had turned up to turn the other one out. This, at any rate, is the story which I believed, and I'm sure to me it only added to my awe and respect of Uncle Henry. Well, you know, either in spite of or perhaps because of this propinquity it's interesting that I remained extremely shy with girls. And, of course, when they were in the schoolyard I was always on the other side of the wall; and on one occasion I remember, when I ventured into the schoolyard a little too early when there were still a few on the premises and I saw them staring at me through a window, I took flight at once.

However, you will see that with this background and having frequented Mary Institute at the time and in the way I did, I consider myself in a sense to be an alumnus, I will say even the one and only alumnus of Mary Institute, and I hereby place my claim before you for your consideration; and, of course, that is not the reason, I am sure, that I was invited here this evening but it's one of the reasons why I accepted.

Six years ago I had the honour of speaking at the centennial at Washington University. I'm very happy to be here this evening to take part in the centennial of Mary Institute. I think that a centennial at any educational institution has a special significance. It not only celebrates the past but it expresses a confidence and faith in the future. It is a kind of expression of faith that for other generations than those who are here now there will be another centennial a hundred years hence.

Mary Institute has had to move west several times in its history. I'm very glad that it stopped at Beaumont Street during the period of my childhood. But it has moved and thriven and got bigger and more important as it has moved out, but now I hope that it will be able to remain where it is, and surely it looks so stable and certain that I feel sure that it will be here for an indefinite and very long future. It does seem to me of some importance that an educational institution should be able to stay in the same place. In education the subjects taught and the methods of teaching vary from one age to another. Even the meaning of the word *education* itself changes. You've only to look at the definitions and at the examples given of the use of the word *education* from the sixteenth to the twentieth century in the complete *Oxford Dictionary* to grasp the fact of the perpetually changing and developing meaning of the word.

But on two things good education must always depend, I think: first on the teachers, on their ability, their learning, their character – in short, on their vocation to teach – and second on the traditions of the particular school or college. Of course, there is a sentimental aspect to tradition and that's a good thing in itself. But there's a deeper value also than merely particular ways and pleasant customs or anecdotes of past teachers and past pupils. It's natural and right for alumnae and alumni to be proud of the history of the schools [136] in which they have been educated. The celebration of this centenary is, I feel, an assurance that Mary Institute has come of age and that her traditions are now well established. I give her my most cordial wishes and devout prayers for her future.

Now, Mr Beasley has suggested that I might end this evening by reading you one of my poems. I don't think I've ever read in St Louis. Whether he was merely prudent in thinking what is perfectly true, that my poems, whatever their merit, are certainly superior to my speechifying – that, at any rate, he knows what the poems are and that a poem would atone for a bad speech, I don't know. But I do propose presently to read one of my poems and read one which seems to me particularly appropriate for this time and place because it's about the river and the sea, the Mississippi and the Atlantic Ocean on the coast of New England, the two great natural forces which impressed my childhood imagination.

1960

Foreword

Foreword to Wyndham Lewis, *One-Way Song*, 7–10. Signed 'T. S. Eliot'.
Publ. 25 Feb. 1960. Gallup B82.

One-Way Song was first published in 1933, and has been long out of print. The text here is identical with that of the 1933 edition. The four poems and *envoi* appear to have been written at the same time: their unity of mood and of idiom is so manifest that we recognise them as constituting a single poem or poem-sequence.

The publishers' note on the jacket of the first edition is itself a good introduction. Composed in the style of editorial anonymity suitable to book-jackets, it yet bears signs which lead me to suspect (I was out of England at the time and had no hand in it) that the author supplied his publishers with material. For this reason I transcribe it in full:

> This considerable poem of two thousand lines is in fact a series of four pieces. *The Song of the Militant Romance* is a lyrical statement of the Romantic attitude in art. There is no counterbalancing statement of the Classical attitude. But in the body of the long succeeding piece, *If So the Man You Are*, a number of Boileau-like verses (and again here and there in the *One-Way Song* itself) effect, without comment, the necessary contrast. In *If So the Man You Are* it is mainly the portion given up to the apology and denunciation put into the mouth of 'The Enemy' (who comes on the stage to carry on for a while the argument) that these Boileau-like couplets are to be found.
>
> [8] Throughout this chain of poems the expression is dramatic: that is to say it is invariably a person, or a variety of persons, speaking. From time to time the personality of the Bailiff of the *Childermass* thrusts its way into the forefront of the *dramatis personae* and tinctures strongly the character of the verse.
>
> On the whole *One-Way Song*, as this group of poems is named, would probably come under the head of 'satiric verse': and to give an idea of the general nature of the performance, it would be said that, making allowance for the difference in scale, and in the style of art,

these verses proceed from the same impulse as that which produced *The Apes of God* or *The Wild Body*, and in part the *Childermass*. In manner, dramatisation, and technical intention, it belongs to that group of works.

This explanation anticipates a point which I wish to make more explicitly: that the poem cannot be fully understood without some knowledge of Wyndham Lewis's prose work. To those readers who take up this book with no acquaintance with Lewis's prose writings (and they are the readers to whom such a preface as this should primarily be addressed) I suggest reading next, *The Wild Body* for style and for powers of visual observation and description; the *Childermass*, for powers of visual imagination and fantastic invention; *Time and Western Man* for philosophical criticism; and *Paleface* or *The Writer and the Absolute* for polemical criticism of contemporary fiction. And the books I have just mentioned illustrate only a part of Lewis's activity as a writer. Mr E. W. F. Tomlin, in his useful brief study[1] of Lewis's work, discovers four main categories, but I should be inclined to find several more, putting the *Childermass* and *The Human Age* into a group apart, and the two finest of the novels, *The Revenge for Love* and *Self Condemned*, into another class by themselves.

The question for the reader to ask who reads *One-Way Song* without any knowledge of Lewis's other writings, is not 'Is this poetry?' The first question is simply: 'Does this writing attract or repel me?' After we have acquainted ourselves with a few of Lewis's prose books, we may return to *One-Way Song* and draw comparisons, finding perhaps some similarity to the work of the 'snarling satirists' of the Elizabethan age – an age of writers of a vigour, opulence of diction and careless abundance which make them congenial to the genius of Lewis.[2] If we then decide that *One-Way Song* is *verse* rather than *poetry*, we shall find that it belongs with that body of high-ranking verse which is more important than most minor poetry; and it would be only the very obtuse who could dismiss this verse as *doggerel*. You will have to admit that it has style; though it is to the prose writings that you must go if you are to discover in Lewis one of the permanent masters of style in the English language.

I have suggested that the question for the reader to ask is whether the style of *One-Way Song* attracts or repels us. From the very first page of

---

1. *Wyndham Lewis* by E. W. F. Tomlin. In the series 'Writers and their Work' published for the British Council by Longmans Green & Co.
2. In *The Lion and the Fox* (a study of the role of the hero in the plays of Shakespeare) Lewis makes some very acute observations on the work of that great poet and dramatist George Chapman.

any book of Lewis, no reader remains neutral: you are either attracted or repelled. Lewis is unto the 'intellectuals' a stumbling-[10]block, and unto the multitude foolishness. The latter indeed are still hardly aware of his name. The more respectable of the former, being unable to stomach his work, treat Lewis for the most part to an uneasy silence; the less respectable vociferate the cry of 'fascist!' – a term falsely applied to Lewis, but flung by the *massenmensch* at some who, like Lewis, choose to walk alone. If you have read some of Lewis's prose writing, and admired it, you will need no introduction to *One-Way Song*; if you read *One-Way Song*, and are attracted by Lewis's style, so different from that of any other living writer, then you have an introduction to the rest of his work.

The Influence of Landscape upon the Poet

Daedalus, Journal of the American Academy of Arts and Sciences, Proceedings, 89. 2 (Spring 1960), [420]–2. Followed by a reading of *The Dry Salvages* from *Four Quartets*. The text of the poem was printed on pp. 423–8. Gallup C639.

When I was informed of the time placed at my disposal for what I might have to say on this occasion, I was seized with apprehension. I most heartily wished to signify my appreciation of the honour which has been accorded to me by the Academy. Any allocution to that end should, I considered, be something quite new, fresh – even if not epoch-making. In any case, I do not keep a drawerful of unpublished lectures and sermons for repeated use, and when I have undertaken to deliver an address for the second time I have usually found it a painful experience: for I am sure to come across some passages of which I have forgotten the meaning, and others where I have come to disagree with my own opinions. I wished to write something quite new, and if possible worthy of the occasion; but I knew that between the time of the invitation, and my departure from England, I simply should not have the leisure. I was reminded of the time, many years ago, when I did deliver, in this country, the same lectures repeatedly in various universities: it was a way of getting about and seeing America and earning the money to do so. There was one occasion on which I had to prepare a new lecture at short notice, and a lecture which I never delivered again anywhere. I had undertaken to speak at a certain university – I prefer to forget where – and two days beforehand encountered a friend who said that he looked forward to hearing me on the subject of the great English letter writers. Startled, I returned to my rooms and looked up the correspondence: sure enough, the invitation was to deliver a lecture on a foundation dedicated to Great English Letter Writers. So I prepared a lecture of the right length, with some references to Letter Writers in it, the letters of Keats and D. H. Lawrence being fresh in my memory: I managed to take up a good deal of time, I remember, by expatiating on the subject of my own ignorance in general, with particular reference to [421] my ignorance of English Letter Writers. Whether the address was a success or not I do not know.

You may suspect from this anecdote that what I am saying now is merely an elaborate way of saying that I have nothing to say. Not so. I shall only talk briefly, it is true, and after that I propose to read to you one of my *Quartets*, but there is a relation between what I have to say and the poem I shall read. For my subject is simply 'The Influence of Landscape upon the Poet'. The association of ideas by which I came to the subject is somewhat as follows. This is the Emerson-Thoreau Award: it brings to mind Concord in particular and New England in general. Then I reflected that my honoured predecessor, the *doyen* of American poets to-day, was Robert Frost, distinctly in the mind of everyone a New England poet. Then I asked myself whether I had any title to be a New England poet – as is my elder contemporary Robert Frost, and as is my junior contemporary, Robert Lowell: and I think I have. Of course I know that the Academy is the American Academy; and just as the French Academy is not the Paris Academy, but draws its immortals from every region of France, so likewise the American Academy draws upon all the – I was about to say forty-eight but realise that I must now say fifty states: and let me extend my best wishes to Alaska for future representation here as well as in Washington. Nevertheless, this seems the occasion for me to stake my claim to a New England status. I am used to dealing with the question of whether I am, qua poet, American or English; and usually can escape by pointing out that whichever Wystan Auden is, I am the other: though seriously my poetry, like that of other poets, shows traces of every environment in which I have lived.

Now, when I speak of the influence of landscape, I am not thinking of Nature Poetry. Robert Frost is not definable as a Poet of Nature; his scope is much wider than that, and he is a poet of human nature as well as of flora, fauna, and landscape: but he is certainly a poet who has been deeply affected by the New England landscape. It is true that I am from Missouri, and that my father before me was born in St Louis. But Robert Frost was born in San Francisco, which is a good deal farther away from New England than is St Louis. He came East, according to that useful compendium, *The Oxford Companion to American Literature*, at the age of ten. Well, I came East too, at the age of seventeen, to a school not remote from Brookline; and as far back as I can remember and before, my family had spent every summer on the New England coast. So my personal landscape is a composite. In St Louis, my grandmother – as was very [422] natural – wanted to live on in the house that my grandfather had built; my father, from filial piety, did not wish to leave the house that he had built only a few steps away; and so it came to be that we lived on in a neighbourhood which had become shabby to a degree approaching slumminess, after all our friends and acquaintances had moved further west. And in my childhood, before the days of motor cars, people who lived in town stayed in town. So it was, that for nine months of the year my scenery was almost exclusively urban, and a good deal of it seedily, drably urban at that. My urban imagery was that of St Louis, upon which that of Paris and London have been superimposed. It was also, however, the Mississippi, as it passes between St Louis and East St Louis in Illinois: the Mississippi was the most powerful feature of Nature in that environment. My country landscape, on the other hand, is that of New England, of coastal New England, and New England from June to October. In St Louis I never tasted an oyster or a lobster – we were too far from the sea. In Massachusetts, the small boy who was a devoted bird watcher never saw his birds of the season when they were making their nests.

I am not maintaining that early impressions are the only ones that count. Far from it: later impressions come to cover them, and to fuse, in some sort, with them. English landscape has come to be as significant for me, and as emotionally charged, as New England landscape. I do believe, however, that the impressions made by English landscape upon myself are different from those made upon poets for whom it has been the environment of their childhood.

What I have been saying was, in its first intention, merely an elaboration of the simple 'Thank you'. But I hope that my words will shed some light upon the poem I am about to read; and also substantiate, to some degree, my claim to being, among other things, a New England poet. You will notice, however, that this poem begins where I began, with the Mississippi; and that it ends, where I and my wife expect to end, at the parish church of a tiny village in Somerset.

On Teaching the Appreciation of Poetry

Critic, 18. 5 (Apr./May 1960), 13–14, 78–80. Gallup C640.
Repr. in *Teachers College Record*, Dec. 1960, 215–21.

On p. 14 'Fitzgerald's' has been emended to 'FitzGerald's', and on p. 78
'*The Shropshire Lad*' has been corrected to '*A Shropshire Lad*'.

I hold no diploma, certificate, or other academic document to show that I am qualified to discuss this subject. I have never taught anybody of any age how to enjoy, understand, appreciate poetry, or how to speak it. I have known a great many poets, and innumerable people who wanted to be told they were poets. I have done some teaching, but I have never 'taught poetry'. My excuse for taking up this subject is of wholly different origin. I know that not only young people in colleges and universities, but secondary school children also, have to study, or at least acquaint themselves with, poems by living poets; and I know that my poems are among those studied, by two kinds of evidence. My play *Murder in the Cathedral* is a set book in some schools: there is an edition of the English text published in Germany with notes in German, and an edition published in Canada with notes in English. The fact that this play, and some of my other poems, are used in schools brings some welcome supplement to my income; and it also brings an increase in my correspondence, which is more or less welcome, though not all the letters get answered. These are letters from the children themselves, or, more precisely, the teenagers. They live mostly in Britain, the United States, and Germany, with a sprinkling from the nations of Asia. It is in a spirit of curiosity, therefore, that I approach the subject of the teaching of poetry: I should like to know more about these young people and about their teachers and the methods of teaching.

For some of my young correspondents seem to be misguided. Sometimes I have been assigned to them as a 'project', more often they have made the choice themselves – it is not always clear why. (There was one case, that of an Egyptian boy, who wanted to write a thesis about my work, and as none of my work was locally available and as he wanted to read it, asked me to send him all my books. That was very exceptional, however.) Very often the writers ask for information about myself, sometimes in the form of a questionnaire. I remember being asked by one child whether it was true that I only cared to associate with lords and bishops. Sometimes a photograph is asked for. Some young persons seem to want me to provide them with all the material for a potted biography, including mention of my interests, tastes and ways of amusing myself. Are these children studying poetry, or merely studying poets?

Very often they want explanations, either of a whole poem ('what does it mean') or of a particular line or phrase; and the kind of question they ask often suggests that their approach to that poem has been wrong, for they want the wrong kind of explanation, or ask questions which are simply unanswerable. Sometimes, but more rarely, they are avid for literary sources; which would seem to indicate that they have started too early on the road to Xanadu.

Now, when I was young, this sort of thing did not happen. I did study English at school, beginning, thank God, with grammar, and going on to 'rhetoric' – for which also I am grateful. And we had to read a number of set books of prose and verse – mostly in school editions which made them look peculiarly unappetising. But we never were made to read any literature which could be called contemporary. Tennyson could hardly be called 'contemporary' by the time I had to study some of the *Idylls of the King*. I must admit that at the turn of the twentieth century there were precious few great poets about, and still fewer whom the authorities would have considered suitable for our perusal. Swinburne would hardly have done, in those days; I don't know whether he has reached the school curriculum today. Yeats was still a minor poet of the 'Nineties. But even if Trumbull Stickney and George Cabot Lodge, two poets of whose work I remain ignorant to this day, had been famous, instead of merely respectable, I doubt if my school authorities would have set any of their poetry for us.

No. Not only were we not encouraged to take an interest in the poetry actually being written, but even had we been, I doubt whether we should have thought of entering into correspondence with the authors. Some of the juvenile correspondence I receive seems to be instigated by the teachers, but the greater part does not. Indeed, some of my letters, I suspect, are inspired by a desire to score off teacher, and the hope of getting some statement from the horse's mouth which will be a direct contradiction of what has been taught. (I [14] confess that this last type of letter is one which I sometimes take pleasure in answering – when teacher seems to me to have been wrong.) But my point is, that this pressure upon the poet from young people who have been compelled to read his work is a modern phenomenon. I don't believe that Tennyson and Browning, Longfellow and Whittier (to say nothing of Poe and Whitman, poets whose works we did not study) were embarrassed by juvenile correspondence choking up their letterboxes. The teaching of the contemporary literature, the introduction of the young to poetry by living poets, is something that came about in my time, without my being aware of what was happening. I have had other surprises of this kind. When I returned to give a course of lectures at Harvard in 1932, after seventeen years' absence from America, I looked out of my window and saw a bird which arrested my attention because it looked like a starling. As a boy I had been an eager bird-watcher, and I knew most of the resident and migratory birds of New England, and I knew no bird with that peculiar stumpy tail. On inquiry, I found that it *was* a starling: that bird had arrived and multiplied in America while I wasn't looking. The starling has come to stay, and so, I think, has the academic study of the work of living authors.

I do not wish to suggest that I deplore the introduction of the young, as part of their education, to the work of living authors – to the work of *some* living authors. Nor am I suggesting that I think that the methods of teaching are altogether wrong. All I aim to indicate is, that the teaching of contemporary poetry is a difficult task, and that contemporary poetry cannot be taught by exactly the same methods as are suitable for poetry of the past. And I mean by 'poetry of the past', the poetry of any period, as soon as that period has become a part of history. The teacher who aims at teaching pupils to appreciate contemporary poetry, to distinguish between the good and the bad, the genuine and the spurious, the original and the imitative, to enjoy the best and only the best, needs himself to have both enthusiasm and discrimination. He needs to be as well educated, as scholarly in his knowledge of the literature of the past, as the teacher who confines his tuition to the literature of the past; and he needs independent good taste.

I am not suggesting that to teach the curriculum as it was taught when I was a boy, we can dispense with enthusiasm and good taste. But that curriculum was limited to authors whose place had been pretty well fixed by the judgement of time. It included a couple of plays of Shakespeare, several of Milton's minor poems, and selections from standard English and American authors down to the latter part of the nineteenth century. These were authors of whose works, it could be assumed, no educated man should be wholly ignorant. And here, as I have already asserted, is the important difference: the poetry of the past is already a part of history. No man can be called educated if ignorant of the history of his own country, or his own race, or his own language: indeed we should know something of the history of civilisation, of the struggle of man to raise himself from savagery to the condition of the highest triumphs of the arts and sciences, of religion and morals. And our historical knowledge of any past age is incomplete unless we know something of the literature of that age. To enter imaginatively into the life of men in a past age we need everything we can learn from their literature, and particularly from their poetry, of the way they thought and felt. Thus, the teacher of the literature of the past may find his task to be primarily that of an historian, though he should also be a lover of that literature and have the capacity to communicate his feeling for it to his pupils. But the poetry of the present, the best of which *will become* a part of history, cannot be studied in exactly the same way as the poetry which is already history.

Let me at this point consider first the drawbacks to that school study of poetry of the past which ignores the fact that poetry is something which *goes on being written*, which is being written now while the pupils are sitting at their desks construing *L'Allegro* and *Il Penseroso*, and that the poet hopes that people will read it for enjoyment. And then let me consider the disadvantages of over-emphasis upon actuality which ignores the fact that much of the poetry written in the same language in the past is as good, and that some of it is better, than what is being written now.

The great weakness of the method by which I was introduced – academically introduced, I mean – to English poetry was that it did not help me to enjoy it. I think that many people have suffered in the same way from their introduction to the plays of Shakespeare: I took a dislike to *Julius Caesar* which lasted, I am sorry to say, until I saw the film of Marlon Brando and John Gielgud, and a dislike to *The Merchant of Venice* which persists to this day. Perhaps the fact that I had to memorise and declaim, in front of the class, Antony's oration and Portia's quality of mercy, and that I was a very poor declaimer, may have had something to do with it. But I also disliked *L'Allegro* and *Il Penseroso*: I am thankful that I did not have to study *Lycidas* in the same way. Coleridge's *Ancient Mariner* barely survived. I have no fault to find with our teacher. We had examinations to pass and it was his business to see that we should be able to answer the questions.

I do not know that there is any better way of studying English literature, at that stage; and it may be that a few plays and poems must be sacrificed, in order that we may learn that English literature exists, and that an orderly historical acquaintance with it is desirable. We also, I remember, had a history book of English literature to study, and had to learn something about the great writers of every period from the Age of Shakespeare to the end of the nineteenth century. The knowledge that we acquired served a purpose; and I do not believe that it would have served that purpose so well if the emphasis had been on appreciation, instead of on an orderly outline of literature and some information about the chief historical reputations. After all, how many boys and girls of thirteen or fourteen can appreciate Shakespeare or Milton? I didn't.

I think I have mentioned somewhere among my essays that my first experience of intense excitement from poetry came when I was fourteen, and came, not from anything put in my way by my work at school, but by happening to pick up at home a copy of FitzGerald's *Omar Khayyám*. And, at the risk of repeating myself, I will suggest that it is at or on the approach of puberty that a boy or girl may suddenly discover that poetry is capable of giving a kind of delight hitherto wholly unsuspected. Very likely this illumi-[78]nation will come as the sudden shock of a particular poem: a poem discovered by oneself, or presented by an older person or by one's teacher. But it will probably not be one of the poems that one has had to study, in a school text supported by notes (and for passing examinations the notes may be more important than the text!). I am not sorry that I was made to study certain things of Shakespeare and Milton in the way I have described. But the discovery of poetry is a different experience altogether, and the discovery may be more important than the poem through which we make the discovery. Our first 'discovery' of poetry – say at fourteen or fifteen or sixteen – may be through a poem of which, after our acquaintance is wider and our taste more developed, we cease to think very highly.

There are, in fact, some poems and some poets, whose function seems to be to awaken our capacity for enjoyment, to retire later on to a lower (but still, most often, honourable) place. The earlier poems of Byron, for instance, *A Shropshire Lad* of A. E. Housman; the poems of Rupert Brooke. The greatest poets are those whom we have to grow up to, and whose work we appreciate more fully as we mature. At sixteen I discovered (by reading a section of our history of English literature which we were not required to read) Thomson's *City of Dreadful Night*, and the poems of Ernest Dowson. Each was a new and vivid experience. But *The City of Dreadful Night* or Dowson's 'Impentitentia Ultima' would hardly, even today, be considered suitable for academic study at the age I have in mind. It is in fact necessary to choose works by the greater writers for us to study, at an age at which we are not yet mature enough to enjoy them.

Let me now consider the situation when our emphasis, in teaching children of the same ages, is on enjoyment rather than on information, and upon contemporary poets rather than upon a selection of the great classics. This offers the teacher greater liberty, but prepares for him greater pitfalls. That rough and ready valuation, ordinarily called 'the verdict of history', has not yet been passed, and the teacher must follow his own judgement as to what poets, and what poems, he should choose for initiating his pupils into the delights of poetry. There is plenty of contemporary poetry to serve the purpose. But opinion about the relative importance of living poets can vary widely, even among persons of taste; apart from the permanent chasm between those who lean towards what is called 'traditional' verse and those who prefer the 'experimental'. And the successful teacher, who teaches the poetry of his choice with enthusiasm, will be in danger of implanting his own personal tastes in the minds of his pupils, or (what is worse) teaching them to parrot opinions which they are too passive to share. But even if we postulate an ideal teacher of impeccable taste – and I have never known anyone incapable of going wrong at one time or another about living authors, and I include myself in this universal fallibility – that teacher could rouse enthusiasm but could do little to train taste and understanding. For without some knowledge of the poetry of the past, and enjoyment of what we know, we cannot really appreciate the poetry of the present.

The dangers of a concentration of interest upon contemporary poetry appears most clearly and painfully when the reader aspires to write poetry himself, or herself. I have never judged a poetry competition, but I have known those who have; and one friend who had on one occasion undertaken to read a great number of such contributions was appalled by the evidence of the meagreness of the contestants' knowledge of poetry of the past. Most aspirants had some acquaintance with the poetry of John Donne; a good many had read poems by Blake; and coming down to recent times, they were familiar with the work of Gerard Manley Hopkins and William Butler Yeats. There are would-be poets who write regular verse with, at best, dull metronomic accuracy: modern poetry is unknown to them. There are others who write 'free verse' with an ear untrained by the practice of regular verse: they have probably dieted solely on contemporary verse.

It is not however, for students who aspire to write poetry, but simply with those capable of becoming intelligent and sensitive readers, that I am chiefly concerned. I maintain that no one can go very far in the discerning enjoyment of poetry, who is incapable of enjoying poetry other than that of his own place and time. It is in fact a part of the function of education to help us to escape – not from our own time, for we are all bound by that – but from the intellectual and emotional limitations of our own time. It is a commonplace that we appreciate our home all the more fully and consciously after foreign travel; it is not such a commonplace, to assert that we can appreciate the poetry of our own time better for knowing and enjoying the best poetry of previous ages. We understand and appreciate our own language the better for having some command of a foreign language. Those whose knowledge of poetry in the English language extends no further than to the immediate precursors of the poetry of our time, such as Hopkins and Yeats, or whose knowledge of the past is limited to the poetry extolled by some persuasive critic of the day (like myself), are limited in their understanding of the poetry that they do know. If, as I believe, poetry plays an important part in the process of education, then these readers are uneducated.

You may think at this point that I have reached an *impasse*. On the one hand, the historical approach to English and American literature, with obligatory reading of a selection of classics, seems unlikely to awaken any appetite or curiosity that would lead to independent reading; nor does it present poetry and prose as living arts. On the other hand, the study of contemporary poetry, while it may be an immediate stimulant, may encourage a provincialism of taste – for provincialism in *time* is as deplorable as provincialism in *place* – which is the opposite of educative.

To me it seems that the two ways of approach to poetry should be combined, so that young people might be brought to see literature – and poetry especially – both in its historical aspect and in its actuality, as a permanent heritage and as something which is still going on, as a necessary part of knowledge and as something to be enjoyed. Here are involved two different, though related meanings of the word *understanding*. In the teaching of great litera-[79]ture of the past, understanding is primarily what ensues from a knowledge of historical and biographical facts, the conditions under which a masterpiece was written, the peculiarities of idiom and vocabulary which mark it as of a different age from ours, etc. In approaching a contemporary work, a poem by a living poet, our understanding is primarily a matter of insight. I know of one teacher who, without any preliminary explanation, played to her pupils a gramophone record of a poem by a living poet. She played it twice, and then told her girls to write down their feelings and impressions, to put in words as well as they could what this poem had meant to them. And I know that for one of her pupils at least – they were girls of fourteen – the impression that this poem made upon her opened the path to understanding not only of other poems of the same poet, but to poetry of earlier times, indeed to all poetry. And the teacher had not told the class that they were to admire this poem, still less what they were to admire about it; least of all had she given any hint as to what it was about or what it meant. She had chosen wisely and with taste, but had left the poem to do its own work.

This incident seems to me to suggest that at that age – from fourteen to sixteen, I should say – when the sensibility begins, if ever, to respond passionately to poetry, the poetry of our own age may be able to make a more immediate impact than that of earlier generations. It is not merely that there are no difficulties of style and idiom; not merely that there is less oppression by the mass of critical opinion. There is more than enough of the latter: and may I suggest in passing that the young should be encouraged to read poetry by living poets rather than books about contemporary poetry – that they should know and love certain poetry before they read *about* that poetry. I think that young people then recognise obscurely that the poet speaking to them is of their own time and that his sensibility and theirs have something in common.

I do not believe that the work of living poets should be taught formally. I do not believe that youngsters should take examinations in it. I think that the choice of poems to present to a class should represent the taste of the teacher, not be set by a board. Unless the teacher is a person who reads poetry for enjoyment, he or she cannot stimulate pupils to enjoy it. Nor should the young have a great deal of contemporary verse forced upon them: at this stage we are not concerned to equip young people with a familiarity with the names of all the living poets of reputation, but with starting them on the way to enjoying poetry.

I am assuming, of course, that the teacher who introduces them to modern poetry will be the same teacher who takes them through their annotated textbooks of the classics, and who wants them to pass their examinations on these texts with credit. Perhaps I am merely clamouring for the Ideal Teacher. But don't 'educationalists' sometimes forget, in their teaching about teaching, that the one essential for good teaching is the good teacher? The good teacher then will instruct his or her pupils well in the historical understanding of literature, and at the same time will lead those of them who have the capacity to see that the literature of the past, about which the educated person must be informed as a part of history, is also lit-[80]erature to be enjoyed, and that without enjoyment it is meaningless. The good teacher will make pupils aware that literature is a continuous activity, and that more literature is being made even while they are busy with that of the past. In introducing the pupils to modern poetry that the teacher likes, he will be reminding them of the essential part of enjoyment. For it doesn't matter so much, in my opinion, that the teacher's enthusiasm should be aroused by the very best contemporary poetry – in other words, the poetry of which I myself approve – as that the enthusiasm should be infectious. The pupils capable of developing good taste will eventually discover for themselves the better poetry, and as for the others it is probably better that they should like the second rate, the unoriginal, than that they should not like any poetry at all: the essential is to have the experience of enjoying *something*.

My Ideal Teacher, accordingly, will teach the prescribed classics of literature as history, as a part of history which every educated person should know something about, whether he likes it or not; and then should lead some of the pupils to enjoyment, and the rest at least to the point of recognising that there are other persons who do enjoy it. And he will introduce the pupils to contemporary poetry by exciting enjoyment:

enjoyment first, and understanding second. It may be only by reading such poetry to them as an extra-curricular activity, or it may be by a reading, or a gramophone record, and then asking the class to set down impressions and reactions. I think that such an introduction to poetry is justifiable even for those pupils who never come to show any love for poetry or any intelligent and sensitive appreciation of it. And the pupils who have some aptitude for enjoyment and understanding of what is good in literature (and as this is a question of degree, there can be no clear division between the sheep and the goats) will find that their knowledge of the great poetry which has had the approval of successive generations will sharpen their discrimination and refine their enjoyment of the poetry which is being written in their own time; and their enjoyment of the poetry written in their own time will help them towards enjoyment of the classics of literature. For our own poetry of today and that of our forefathers, the foundations upon which we build and without which our poetry would not be what it is, will eventually be seen as forming one harmonious whole.

Thomas Stearns Eliot

Autobiographical note, *Harvard College Class of 1910. Fiftieth Anniversary Report* (June 1960), 133–6. Gallup C642.

On p. 134 'All Souls' has been corrected to 'All Souls'; the superfluous comma has been removed from 'Norton, Professor'; Sadlers' Wells' has been corrected to 'Sadler's Wells'; and *Baverische Academie der Schone Kuenste* as been correted to *Bayerischen Akademie der Schönen Künste*. On pp. 134 and 136 'Psaltar' has been corrected to 'Psalter'. On p. 134 .

HOME ADDRESS: Faber & Faber, Ltd, 24, Russell Square, London, W.C. 1

OFFICE ADDRESS: Faber & Faber, Ltd, 24, Russell Square, W.C. 1.

OCCUPATION: Author and Publisher.

MARRIED: Vivienne Haigh Haigh-Wood, June 26, 1915, London (died 1947); Esmé Valerie Fletcher, January 10, 1957, London.

ACADEMIC DEGREES: A.B., Harvard; and A.M., 1910.

HONORARY DEGREES: D.Litt. (Oxford 1948); Litt.D. (Columbia 1933); Cambridge 1938; Bristol 1938; Leeds 1939; Harvard, Yale and Princeton 1947; Washington University 1953; Rome 1958; Sheffield 1959; LL.D. (Edinburgh 1937; St Andrews 1953); D. es L. (Paris, Aix-Marseille, Rennes); D.Phil. (Munich); D.Lit. (London).

DECORATIONS: Order of Merit, 1948; Officer, Légion d'Honneur; Orden pour le Mérite (W. Germany), 1959.

[134] OTHER DISTINCTIVE AWARDS: Nobel Prize for Literature, 1948; Honorary Fellow, Magdalene College, Cambridge, 1939; Honourable Fellow, Merton College, Oxford, 1949; Hanseatic Goethe Prize (Hamburg), 1954; Signet Society Medal; Dante Medal (Florence), 1959; Emerson-Thoreau Medal (American Academy of Arts and Sciences), 1959.

MEMBER OF: Athenaeum and Garrick Clubs, several dining clubs, the Burke Club (political); All Souls club (religious), the rest social; foreign member, Accademia dei Lincei (Rome); foreign member, *Bayerischen Akademie der Schönen Künste* (Munich); foreign member, American Institute of Arts and Letters (New York); Honourable Citizen of Dallas, Texas; Honourable Deputy Sheriff of Dallas County; Churchwarden, St Stephen's, South Kensington, 1934–1959; member of Archbishop of Canterbury's Commission for the Revision of the Psalter, 1958–.

OFFICES HELD: Director, Faber & Faber, Ltd; president of The London Library, 1952–; vice president of The Church Union, The English Speaking Union, the Religious Drama Society; ex-president of 'Books Across the Sea', the Classical Association (1943); the Virgil Society (1944); and of the Fédération Britannique des Comités d'Alliance Française; Clark Lecturer, Trinity College, Cambridge (1926); Charles Eliot Norton Professor of Poetry, Harvard (1932–33); Boutwood Lecturer, Corpus Christi College, Cambridge (1938).

PUBLICATIONS: My publications up to 1950 inclusive are listed in *T. S. Eliot: A Bibliography*, by Donald Gallup. My chief publications after that date are *The Confidential Clerk* (a play), 1954; *The Elder Statesman* (a play), 1959; and *On Poetry and Poets* (literary essays), 1957.

What the Secretary appears to be bent on extracting from his wretched classmates is a full-length autobiography. If he really wants everything he says he wants he should have provided a good deal more paper, but I'm glad he didn't. I don't see why I should again review my life 'since graduation': I did my best to oblige him in this respect 25 years ago, and that statement can stand, with two important qualifications – I now prefer claret to burgundy, and I prefer Inspector Maigret to Arsène Lupin. So I shall begin with 1933: that is a good date for me, as that is the year in which I broke into Show Business. In that year I was commissioned to write the text for a mammoth pageant to advertise the need for 45 new churches in the outer suburbs of London. The Pageant was produced at Sadler's Wells in the summer of 1934 with great success and so many amateur actors that the Clerkenwell Town Hall had to be adapted temporarily as a dressing room. The success of *The Rock* (that was the name of my pageant, but somebody else had decided on that name before it was written) led to my being invited to write a play for the [135] Canterbury Festival of 1935, and this was *Murder in the Cathedral*, which was subsequently brought to London and which has been turning up in all sorts of places ever since. My next play was not finished until the beginning of 1939. I cannot altogether account for my time during the intervening four years: there was an ecumenical religious conference at Oxford in 1937, in which I was involved; and in 1938 I was the guest of the Portuguese Government for three weeks as a *membro do jury* for the Camoens Prize. But all the while I was doing five days a week at my office, reading manuscripts, interviewing authors, dictating letters, and editing *The Criterion* as well as publishing books – the same routine as indicated in my previous report. I was responsible for a number of books, but chiefly for our poetry list, in which I take some pride. I also take pride in the thought of all the books which I persuaded my firm to decline – or most of them, for we all make mistakes now and then. So time did not hang heavy on my hands. However, in March, 1939, *The Family Reunion* was produced for a limited run. With only modest success; but since I have written more successful plays, some people have come to the opinion that *The Family Reunion* is the best.

And in that same year, 1939, I had *three* books published: something which had never happened before and is unlikely to happen again.

Then came the War, and one's life was too disturbed for play-writing. Instead, I wrote, in 1940, 1941 and 1942, three of my four 'quartets'. I was an Air Raid Warden until I found myself suffering so much from lack of sleep (not being of the stuff that heroes are made of) that I took up my abode with friends in Surrey, coming up to London in the middle of the week to sleep at my office and content my conscience with firewatching. My wartime activities included serving on the editorial board of *The Christian News-Letter*, which took me for some time to Oxford every two weeks; and two excursions for the British Council (there were to have been several others which never came off): I had five weeks in Stockholm in 1942, and a week in Paris in 1945. I remember that I had to deliver a lecture there on VE Day, with Paul Valéry taking the chair for me.

In the last few years I have taken my responsibilities as director of a publishing house more lightly. I appear at my office only [136] on three days of the week, and I write very few blurbs. My fifth play was produced last year; and the dinner party for the cast after the first performance became, at the stroke of midnight, a birthday party to celebrate my 70th birthday. I was presented by the company with a very fine leather cover which, I was told, was to hold the script of my next play which I have not yet begun to write. However, even when not engaged upon a play, I find no lack of occupation. I am much concerned with the problem of saving the London Library, threatened with ruin by the exactions of the Inland Revenue, and with the revision of the Psalter. I must admit that my wife makes me take life much more easily nowadays, and that I flourish under this regime.

You ask us to account to you for our 'satisfactions', our 'deep convictions' and our 'philosophy of life'. Well, it would be very difficult for me to recapitulate my convictions and my philosophy of life briefly enough to make my statement admissible to the Class Report. The books I have written may be taken as an expression of my philosophy of life: implicit in the poetry, explicit in some of the prose. But as for my satisfactions – the greatest, most complete and abiding satisfactions are those which spring from my marriage (on January 10th, 1957, at 6: 15 in the morning by special licence from the Archbishop of Canterbury in order to evade the Press) to Valerie Fletcher; and without the satisfaction of this happy marriage no achievement or honour could give me satisfaction at all.

[Tribute to Giuseppe Ungaretti]

As printed in *Il taccuino del vecchio, con testimonianze di amici stranieri del poeta*, by Giuseppe Ungaretti, ed. Leone Piccini (1960), 71. The volume included an Italian translation of Eliot's letter. Not in Gallup but would be B82b.

Dear Signor Piccioni,

I hear from our mutual friend Mr Bernard Wall that you are proposing to pay homage to Giuseppe Ungaretti on his seventieth birthday. I should like very much to add my word of tribute as one poet to another for what it is worth. I have always refused to speak of any living poet as a 'great poet' for I have held that greatness is something conferred on a poet by history and the evidence of greatness is his being able to speak to generations of his fellow countrymen long after he is dead. Nor amongst living poets did I care to assign rank, and that reserve is still more an obligation when considering poets writing in another language than one's own. But I do feel that Giuseppe Ungaretti is one of a very small number of genuine poets of my generation and is a worthy representative of Italian poetry to the rest of Europe and America. I wish to salute him fraternally on the occasion of his seventieth birthday.

I remain,
Yours very sincerely,
T. S. Eliot

[On the production of *The Confidential Clerk*]

Greeting on the production of *The Confidential Clerk* during Linz English Week. *Landestheater Linz*, [?Dec.] 1960, 103. Printed as a facsimile of the original MS, with German translation opposite on p. 102. Gallup C645.

I was pleased and proud to learn that my play *The Confidential Clerk* was to be performed at the Linz English Week. I never ask myself the question which of my plays I like the best, but I have definite feelings about my characters. By the time any play of mine is finished and produced, I have had to live with the personages in it for two or three years. *The Confidential Clerk* stands out for me among my plays, by the fact that I have always felt an affectionate sympathy with *all* the personages in it. I hope that the theatre-goers of the Linz English Week will regard these emissaries of mine with benevolence; and I should be happy if they could regard them also as friends.

With this hope they come to greet you – all seven of them.

T. S. Eliot

1961

Bruce Lyttelton Richmond

TLS, 3072 (13 Jan. 1961), [17]. Subheaded 'By T. S. Eliot'. Gallup C647.

It was Richard Aldington who took me to Bruce Richmond's office in Printing House Square, I believe at Richmond's request, probably in 1920. Aldington was at that time reviewing French literature regularly for *The Times Literary Supplement*, and Richmond knew of our acquaintance. Richmond had seen articles and reviews of mine in *The Athenaeum* (edited by Middleton Murry) in which they had been appearing for a year or more past. At that time I was still a clerk in Lloyds Bank: but whether my presentation at *The Times* took place in my lunchtime, or after bank hours, or on a Saturday afternoon, I cannot now remember. Nor do I remember what was said at this (for me) memorable meeting. There is still a picture of the scene in my mind: the chief figure a man with a kind of bird-like quality, a bird-like alertness of eye, body and mind. I remember his quickness to put the newcomer at ease; and the suggestion in his mien and movement of an underlying strength of character and tenacity of purpose, but to be summoned to the presence of the Editor of *The Times Literary Supplement* and to be invited to write for it was to have reached the top rung of the ladder of literary journalism: I was overawed, by *The Times* offices themselves, by the importance of the occasion, and in spite of the cordial warmth of the greeting, by the great editor himself.

* * *

For Bruce Richmond was a great editor. To him I owe a double debt, first for the work he gave me to do and for the discipline of writing for him, and second for illustrating, in his conduct of the weekly, what editorial standards should be – a lesson I tried to apply when I came to edit *The Criterion*. Richmond took a personal interest in the men and women who wrote for him: I remember many a pleasant luncheon as his guest, when his next suggestion for an article or review would be put forward: and incidentally I learnt to appreciate the merits of Russian Stout and Double Gloucester cheese. The province assigned to me in the *Literary Supplement* was Elizabethan and Jacobean poetry, but chiefly dramatic poetry. The result of our first meeting was my leading article on Ben

Jonson; and nearly all of my essays on the drama of that period – perhaps all of my best ones – started as suggestions by Richmond. A book was forthcoming to 'serve as a peg' for an article; a book for review was usually designated as 'my pigeon'. In this way, one gradually became an authority in the field allotted. But once a writer was established among his reviewers and leader-writers, Richmond was ready to let him make excursions outside of the original area. Thus, a chance remark in conversation revealed that I was an ardent admirer of Bishop Lancelot Andrewes, and I was at once commissioned to write the leader which appears among my collected essays.

* * *

One lesson that I learnt from writing for *The Times Literary Supplement* under Richmond was that of the discipline of anonymity. I had served my apprenticeship as a reviewer in *The Athenaeum* under Murry, but there all the articles and reviews were signed. I am firmly convinced that every young literary critic should learn to write for some periodical in which his contributions will be anonymous. Richmond did not hesitate to object or delete, and I had always to admit that he was right. I learnt to moderate my dislikes and crotchets, to write in a temperate and impartial way; I learnt that some things are permissible when they appear over one's name, which become tasteless eccentricity or unseemly violence when unsigned. The writer of the anonymous article or review must subdue himself to his editor – but the editor must be a man to whom the writer can subdue himself and preserve his self-respect. It is also necessary that the editor should read every word of what he prints; for he is much more deeply inculpated in what he prints anonymously, than in what he prints over the writer's name.

This brings me to my second point. I have said that it was from Bruce Richmond that I learnt editorial standards, and that I endeavoured to apply them in editing *The Criterion*. Of course it is far easier to edit a literary quarterly than to edit a literary weekly. But apart from this, there was one quality of Bruce Richmond as an editor which I could not emulate, and that is his own anonymity. His name never appeared; he wrote nothing; he did not give lectures or public addresses. Yet, and all the more because he remained in the background, he *was* the *Literary Supplement* in a way impossible to an editor who was primarily or even secondarily a writer. I believe Richmond kept his name out of *Who's Who* for years and was only obliged to yield to that moderate degree of publicity when his University made him a Doctor of Letters *honoris causa*.

Though I could not, and naturally would not, devote my life to *The Criterion* as Richmond devoted his to *The Times Literary Supplement*,

I did try to model my conduct on his to some respects. I learnt from him that it is the business of the editor to know his contributors personally, to keep in touch with them and to make suggestions to them. I tried to form a nucleus of writers (some of them, indeed, recruited from *The Times Literary Supplement*, and introduced to me by Richmond) on whom I could depend, differing from each other in many things, but not in love of literature and seriousness of purpose. And I learnt from Richmond that I must read every word of what was to appear in print – even though, in *The Criterion*, all contributions were signed or initialled.

* * *

It is a final tribute to Richmond's genius as an editor that some of his troupe of regular contributors (I am thinking of myself as well as of others) produced some of their most distinguished critical essays as leaders for the *Literary Supplement*. For Bruce Richmond we wanted to do our best. Good literary criticism requires good editors as well as good critics. And Bruce Richmond was a great editor: fortunate those critics who wrote for him.

Preface

John Davidson: A Selection of his Poems. Preface (xi–xii) by T. S. Eliot. Edited with an introduction by Maurice Lindsay. With an essay by Hugh McDiarmid. Subheaded 'T. S. ELIOT', and signed in facsimile at the end. Publ. 20 Mar. 1961. Gallup B83.

I feel a peculiar reverence, and acknowledge a particular debt, towards poets whose work impressed me deeply in my formative years between the ages of sixteen and twenty. Some were of an earlier age – the late sixteenth and early seventeenth centuries – some of another language; and of these, two were Scots: the author of *The City of Dreadful Night*, and the author of 'Thirty Bob a Week'. It is because I am given an opportunity of expressing, once again, my gratitude to John Davidson, that I write this preface.

I have, indeed, no other excuse. Mr Maurice Lindsay has provided the biographical account needed to introduce the work of John Davidson, and Mr Hugh McDiarmid has written at length of Davidson and of Davidson's significance in his own development. I cannot better the testimony of a fellow makar of Davidson. Modesty requires me to write briefly; but loyalty requires me to write.

What exactly is my debt to John Davidson I cannot tell, any more than I can describe the nature of my debt to James Thomson: I only know that the two debts differ from each other. Some may think, from what I have said on this subject before (Mr Lindsay has quoted my word which appeared in *The Saltire Review*), that the obligation to Davidson was merely for technical hints. Certainly, 'Thirty Bob a Week' seems to me the only poem in which Davidson freed himself completely from the poetic diction of English verse of his time (just as 'Non Sum Qualis Eram' seems to me the one poem in which, by a slight shift of rhythm, Ernest Dowson freed himself). But I am sure that I found inspiration in the content of the poem, and in the complete fitness of content [xii] and idiom: for I also had a good many dingy urban images to reveal. Davidson had a great theme, and also found an idiom which elicited the greatness of the theme, which endowed this thirty-bob-a-week clerk with a dignity that would not have appeared if a more conventional poetic diction had been employed. The personage that Davidson created in this poem has haunted me all my life, and the poem is to me a great poem for ever.

I do not wish, however, to give the impression that for me Davidson is the author of one poem only. Davidson wrote too much and sometimes tediously; and I am happy with this selection. Here are some lovely lyrics and ballads; 'The Runnable Stag' has run in my head for a good many years now; and I have a fellow feeling with the poet who could look with a poet's eye on the Isle of Dogs and Millwall Dock. To me, Davidson's blank verse is rather hard going. I allow for the fact that, as in the case of Thomas Hardy, I find the philosophy uncongenial. No matter: in everything that Davidson wrote I recognise a real man, to be treated not only with respect but with homage.

Obituary

SIR GEOFFREY FABER
A POET AMONG PUBLISHERS

The Times, 1 Apr. 1961, 12. Gallup C648.

Sir Geoffrey Faber, president of the publishing house that bears his name, died yesterday, aged 71. Geoffrey Cust Faber was born on August 23, 1889, at Malvern, and was the second son of the Rev. Henry Mitford Faber, a housemaster at Malvern College. His family, of Yorkshire origin, was associated with education and with the Church. His grandfather had been a Fellow of Magdalen College, and was a brother of Father Faber.

The first Headmaster of Malvern, Canon Arthur Faber, was a first cousin of his father's. His grandmother's family (Cust) was also clerical, and also of Yorkshire stock.

From Rugby Faber went up to Oxford with a scholarship at Christ Church, where he secured a First Class in Honour Mods. and a Second Class in Greats, and also took an active part in the O.U.D.S. After leaving Oxford he qualified himself for the Bar, but never took up practice. He was early attracted towards publishing – two of his Oxford friends, Michael Sadleir and John Heinemann, had preceded him into this profession – and accepted an appointment with the Oxford University Press at the beginning of 1913. He abandoned this post, and had not yet fixed on any other occupation, at the beginning of the war. After four years of service, he was demobilised in 1919 and in the same year was elected to a fellowship of All Souls College.

Faber's future field of activity was, however, not yet determined. His father's cousin, Mr David Faber, invited him to join the brewing firm of Strong and Company of Romsey; soon after this he married. But the brewery was not to provide a career. He abandoned this profession in 1923, shortly after having been appointed Estates Bursar of All Souls, and it was through his connexion with the college that the opportunity came for what was to be his life's work. The Scientific Press was the name of a publishing firm founded by Sir Henry Burdett, which specialised in medical publications, especially those designed for the use of trained nurses; it also published a highly successful weekly paper for trained nurses, *The Nursing Mirror*. Sir Henry Burdett's daughter had married Mr Maurice Gwyer (later Sir Maurice Gwyer and Lord Chief Justice of India) who was also a fellow of All Souls. The Scientific Press was a very profitable enterprise; the directors formed the design of enlarging the business, and employing some of the profits in general publishing. The Gwyers invited Faber to join the board and to become the chairman of a new company; and the Scientific Press was transformed into Faber and Gwyer Ltd, general publishers.

The new firm began business at the end of 1925, in the premises still occupied by its successor, Faber and Faber Ltd. Faber added two recruits of his own choosing: Mr R. H. I. de la Mare, and Mr T. S. Eliot. For the four years of its existence under this name, the business was only moderately successful; both the original directors and the new members were inexperienced in general publishing, and only a few outstanding successes gave hope of a successful future. In 1929 the majority shareholders were the Gwyers and Faber himself. The Gwyers were ready to liquidate the business; only Faber was determined to continue. *The Nursing Mirror* was disposed of on very advantageous terms; Mr and

Mrs Gwyer withdrew their interest; and Faber, with his own capital, transformed the firm of Faber and Gwyer into that of Faber and Faber.

Such a venture, at that moment, appeared a very risky one: but it demonstrated Faber's courage and tenacity of purpose in his chosen profession. His faith was gradually justified; and Faber himself steadily advanced to a position of high distinction in the publishing world. Through Sir Stanley Unwin, he became one of the publishers' representatives on the Joint Advisory Committee of Publishers and Booksellers, a position which he resigned in 1934 on joining the Council of the Publishers' Association. In 1937 he became treasurer of the Association; and in 1939, shortly before the outbreak of the 1939–45 War, he was made president.

The presidency of the Publishers' Association proved to be, under wartime conditions, a much more onerous position than could have been anticipated. At the very outset occurred a crisis of the first magnitude. At the beginning of the war, Sir Kingsley Wood, Chancellor of the Exchequer, imposed the purchase tax. Faber, and a few other persons of prescience, immediately appreciated the disastrous possibilities of the application of this tax to books. The consequences would have extended much farther than merely to those engaged in writing, printing, and publishing, as Faber was one of the first to see: the whole intellectual life of the nation might have been silenced, and its communication with that of America and the Dominions broken. Upon Faber, as president of the Publishers' Association, fell the chief responsibility of marshalling the forces of protest against the imposition of this tax There were others to help; and the Archbishop of Canterbury (Dr Cosmo Lang) lent his powerful support. The government was finally induced to exempt books from the purchase tax; the output of books in quantity and quality, during years when all business, especially in London, was carried out under immense difficulty, was the admiration of the world. This service alone would entitle Faber's name to perpetuity.

To be head of an important and expanding publishing firm, with responsibility for its policy and its finance, at the same time giving constant attention to many matters of detail; to be chairman of the Publishers' Association during several of its most difficult years; to be chairman of the National Book League during a formative period; to be responsible, as the Estates Bursar of a great college, for the administration of landed property scattered throughout England (all of which had periodically to be visited); to take an active interest in public affairs (as chairman of a committee, he wrote for the Conservative Party an admirable Report on Secondary Education); all these activities combined, at a difficult period in the nation's history, would seem to be more than enough for one man. They do not, however, exhaust Faber's interests or his record.

Apart from specialised writings such as the essays and addresses collected in a volume *A Publisher Speaking*, and other compositions directed towards a special public, such as an admirably written little book on the history of the All Souls Bursarship, Faber will be remembered especially first for *The Oxford Apostles*. This is a study of the Oxford Movement into which he was drawn by his interest in his great-uncle Father Faber, and is a book which will remain among the essential bibliography of that phase of Anglican history. Second, there is his monumental biography of Benjamin Jowett. This book was the fruit of years of study and reading, and *Jowett* must remain the standard biography of the great Master of Balliol. To the preparation of this book he gave endless care and the highest standard of scholarship. It was published in 1957: the work he devoted to this book may indeed have made too heavy demands upon his strength in the postwar years.

For those who knew him, however, his volume of collected poems *The Buried Stream* will remain the most intimate expression of the author's personality. It was indeed as a poet that he would have wished to distinguish himself; though his modesty and diffidence prevented him from estimating his own verse at its true value. in 1960 he formally resigned from the chairmanship of Faber and Faber Ltd, and was appointed to the newly created post of president.

Faber received his knighthood in the New Year honours of 1954. He married in 1919 Enid, one of the daughters of Sir Erle Richards (also fellow of All Souls); and leaves, besides his widow, two sons and a daughter.

Preface

Preface to *Hugo Von Hofmannsthal Poems and Verse Plays Bilingual Edition*, Bollingen Series XXXIII. 2, ed. Michael Hamburger, xi–xii. Signed 'T. S. ELIOT' at the end. Publ. 14 Apr. 1961. Gallup B84.

By music lovers the world over the name of Hugo von Hofmannsthal is identified as that of the author of the librettos of Richard Strauss's operas. To those visitors from America and England who have attended performances of *Jedermann* at Salzburg or elsewhere, Hofmannsthal is also known as a dramatist, though his other plays are little read, and seldom if ever performed, in English-speaking countries. But he was also a very fine poet, the less recognised as such abroad since the quantity of his lyric verse is small. Lastly, he wrote very distinguished prose. This volume contains a selection from Hofmannsthal's less-known work among his verse plays and lyric poetry.

I am tempted to contrast Hofmannsthal's verse plays with those of William Butler Yeats; and the inclusion here of several of them makes it possible for the English-speaking reader who knows no German to draw a comparison between the shorter plays of the two poets. Yeats in his early plays drew upon the pre-Christian folklore of Ireland; he used other sources in his *Plays for Dancers*; it is only in his short play on the Resurrection that he used Christian material (for apart from the name there is nothing Christian about his *Purgatory*). But the theme of the Resurrection play is one that Hofmannsthal would never have chosen. Yeats was very positively Irish and Protestant – his Christianity is what [xii] remained to him of a Protestant heritage. Hofmannsthal was equally positively Austrian and Catholic – his Christianity is that of a *practising* Catholic. (He was, I believe, a tertiary of the Franciscan Order.) I leave any further comparison of contrast to be developed by whoever will; my immediate purpose in linking the two names was to make the point that Hofmannsthal is worthy to stand with Yeats and with Claudel as one of the three men who did most, in the same age, to maintain and re-animate verse drama – in German, English, and French respectively.

Geoffrey Faber

The text of an address delivered at the memorial service for Sir Geoffrey Faber at St Giles-in-the-Fields on 10 May 1961. *Encounter*, 17. 1 (July 1961), 81–2. Signed *'T. S. Eliot'*. Repr. privately in 100 copies for distribution *gratis* in Dec. 1961 (Gallup A71). Gallup C653.

'All Souls'' has been corrected to 'All Souls' throughout.

The longer and the more intimately one has known a man, the more difficult it is to choose, in brief memorial phrases, the memories to evoke, the gifts and qualities to emphasise, and the achievements to celebrate. My association with Geoffrey Faber began thirty-five years ago: for nearly half my life, in business, in outside interests, in working hours and in social relaxation, I was constantly in his company. In any tribute that I can pay, however brief, I find myself inevitably recording something of my own life as well. Let me begin then by recalling the occasion of our first meeting, and one subsequent incident, both of which throw light upon his character.

In 1925 it was that I went, in some trepidation, to see Faber at his London home. For personal reasons, I had found it necessary to change my means of livelihood, and to seek a new position which should also give some assurance of permanence. Faber, on the other hand, was looking only for a writer with some reputation among the young, who could attract promising authors of the younger generation as well as of our own, towards the newly-founded firm of Faber and Gwyer. He wanted an informal adviser and, in fact, a 'talent scout'. My name had been suggested to him with warm commendation by my elder friend Charles Whibley, on an occasion when Whibley was a week-end guest at All Souls. I do not remember how it was, during that evening's conversation between Faber and myself, that our two designs became identical. I suspect that it was merely that we took to each other. However that may be, our meeting led to his inviting me to join his Board of Directors – not without his having difficulties to overcome. Vigorous championship, no doubt, on his part, and several testimonials from distinguished older authors, were needed to persuade his fellow-directors to accept, on those terms, a man of letters so obscure as myself. I had more reason to be grateful to Faber, at that time, than he ever knew. But the action was typical of him: once he had made up his mind about a man his confidence was unlimited. And thus he assembled round him – and more easily after Faber and Gwyer had become Faber and Faber – a happy and congenial team of colleagues.

My other illustration is an incident not generally known. We became friends very quickly. It was not so very long before he actually proposed me for a research fellowship at All Souls. Only those who are aware of Faber's intense devotion to the College will realise what a great honour he wished to do me, and what generous feeling inspired him. It was a distinction for which my qualifications were not obvious either to myself or to the College. I am happy to say that the College was spared the ignominy of electing an unscholarly member and I was spared the waste of energy involved in pretending to a scholarship which I did not possess. But I treasure the memory of Faber's generosity, his wish to take me into his beloved college as he had taken me into his business counsels, his home circle, and his personal friendship.

Faber was a man of varied interests and several occupations, and it may be said that he touched none than he did not adorn. First of all he was a poet: an admirer of George Meredith (I shall always remember one evening when he read *Love in the Valley* aloud), he had most in common with another poet whose name is forever associated with Oxford. Matthew Arnold was the poet with whom he had the closest affinity. To-day I shall not speak of his poetry except to remind you that we cannot understand Faber if we ignore the poet in him. Second, Faber, again like Arnold, was also a scholar – a Double First, and not (as stated in *The Times* obituary) a First in Mods and a Second in Greats. That he had also great practical abilities is shown, not only from his conduct of a growing publishing business, but from his work as Estates Bursar of All Souls. It has struck me that his knowledge of farm administration gained as Estates Bursar may have stood him in good stead when, as a country squire, he turned his attention to the breeding of pedigree cattle. Then there is a short but distinguished list of prose works. His *Oxford Apostles* was one of the two best books to appear in the year of the Centenary of the Oxford Movement; and his biography of *Benjamin Jowett*, over which he had toiled for years, is a monumental work which illustrates his indefatigable, conscientious maintenance of the highest standards of scholarship.

[82] During the last war I saw Faber every week, at first sharing in the middle of the week the Fabers' basement shelter, and later fire-watching with him at Russell Square; and I was privy to two of his wartime activities. The first was when, as President of the Publishers' Association, he organised the protest which obtained the remission of the purchase tax to be levied on books. The second was when he drafted the report on Secondary Schools as Chairman of a Committee appointed by the Minister of Education. At one time Faber had thought of standing for Parliament. He had the integrity, the constancy of purpose, and the firmness of principle of the Statesman, but not, perhaps, all the arts of the Politician.

It is chiefly, however, as Publisher and as Friend that I wish to-day to remember Geoffrey Faber. Any calling that Faber had accepted would have been, with him, the occupation of a gentleman; but for him that of Publisher most certainly was. He loved good books, and what he chiefly wanted as a publisher was to publish good books. If they were good enough, they were worth losing money on. And it was not only the books that he himself liked that he was glad to publish. Having chosen his colleagues, he trusted them, and was happy to publish any book that one of them thought good enough to be worth fighting for. And I shall not forget the patience and skill with which he conducted our weekly book committee. He endured our vagaries and our divagations; he was judicious in settling our arguments, and genially tolerant of the practical jokes and horse-play with which some of us, in the early days, would occasionally disorganise the meeting.

Geoffrey Faber was endowed with many talents which he employed happily and well. He was fortunate in many ways, fortunate especially in his marriage. His wife, I know, was his wise counsellor, even in publishing, particularly in the early days when we were learning to be publishers; the partaker of all his interests and his strong rock and his bulwark in his last painful years of illness. Our thoughts and our prayers to-day must be with her and with their family, as well as with him. I remember Geoffrey Faber in many situations, in peace and in war, in work and in play, on land and on sea, at home and abroad. I loved the man, and part of my own life is in the grave with him. May he rest in peace.

Talking Freely: T. S. Eliot and Tom Greenwell

Yorkshire Post, 29 and 30 Aug. 1961. Gallup C653b.
Eliot's answers were tape-recorded.

Greenwell: You believe, do you not, that the critic should criticise from a particular moral standpoint?
Eliot: I cannot dictate to other critics what their moral standpoints should be. It seems to me that a critic, just like every other human being, should have some moral standpoint. And I think it is very difficult to draw the line between purely literary criticism and criticism involving moral, religious, social or political views. You can only say that criticism, so far as it is literary criticism, is aimed primarily at the literary values of the work.

I should think it is almost impossible to isolate the literary value of a work?
Yes, I should agree with that. A critic's views and convictions are bound to affect his criticism. His criticism might be rather empty if they didn't.

I wonder if you could tell me what you think of poetry that contains whole prose passages; that of Marianne Moore, for instance.
It is well known that I have great admiration for the work of Marianne Moore.

Some of her poems contain whole prose passages from newspapers and periodicals.
Chiefly in the form of notes, and I was an earlier culprit as a note-writer. And I was preceded by Shelley with *Queen Mab*. As for incorporating prose passages, as quotations in the poem itself, Ezra Pound has done that successfully. And some years ago I wrote a poem called 'Triumphal March'. In it I included a list of war material, which was lifted directly from a book by a German General after the first war. I'm not sure it wasn't Von Ludendorff. This was war material given up in 1918. It was prose, certainly, but it came in very effectively for my purpose and, you know, I still think the poem is rather a good poem.

That is all right provided there is something rather more poetic than the prose that is quoted. But where the main substance . . .
Well, I should have to take each poem on its own merits, I'm afraid. I think it is justifiable in each case in which you can justify it.

True: I think it is justifiable to use anything provided the poet uses it, rather than takes advantage of it.
Yes, obviously, if the poet merely puts those things together, a sort of collage of bits, without contributing anything himself, which I was accused of doing in some of my early works because of quotations and references, then there is nothing new, nothing original. Nothing to hold the thing together.

Regarding quotations and references, I feel that in your early work you were not thinking of an audience when you wrote. Or, if you were, you wrote as Donne did, for an audience already familiar with your terms of reference, and found it necessary to make notes for people who were not familiar with your terms of reference.
I think my making notes was inspired by an accusation by a critic. In one of my early poems I used, without quotation marks, the line 'the army of unalterable law' from a poem by George Meredith, and this critic accused me of having shamelessly plagiarised, pinched, pilfered that line. Whereas, of course, the whole point was that the reader should recognise where it came from and contrast it with the spirit and meaning of my own poem.

So, I thought I don't want this to happen again: I'll give the references to my poetic quotations, which I did. At least I couldn't be accused of fraud. But I've given that up lately. In my later poems, there isn't so much quotation. There is a certain amount, but I did prefer not to use notes, myself – to leave that to the sort of readers who are interested to ferret out sources.

What do you feel to be the function of poetry?
The function of poetry is to give pleasure, and if you ask what kind of pleasure I can only say the kind of pleasure that poetry gives. But I think good poetry, in giving that kind of pleasure, is doing something for the reader beyond that pleasure. It isn't merely pleasure, it is an enhancement of life, an enlargement of our sensibility, and it is something which to those who enjoy it makes life more worth living.

But in your own works you don't strictly aim at being read for pleasure?
Don't I? Certainly not *strictly*!

I am sure you don't think primarily in terms of entertainment.
Well, in my non-dramatic poetry I think primarily in terms of something I want to say. And if I have said it satisfactorily to myself, that is the first thing. But, of course, poetry must entertain or it won't be read.

The fact that it entertains may be quite incidental.
It is necessary, surely?

But this is not the object?
A piece of music that no one wanted to hear would rather fail of its purpose, wouldn't it?

But the idea of entertaining the public is not the thing that stimulates you to write?
No, it's not organised like a Music Hall turn, certainly. I think that what stimulates me to write a poem is that I have something inside me that I want to get rid of. I have to get it out. it is almost a kind of defecation, if you like. But I don't know what it is that I want to get rid of, until I have got rid of it. In other words, I don't think one knows exactly what one wants to say until one has said it.

But that thing inside you is not the desire nor the need to entertain?
No, no, it isn't. But, at the same time, unless a poet feels that what he gets out is going to convey something, or mean something to others, then he hasn't really got it out. It's got to be in such a form that other people can take it. The impulse is to get rid of it but it has got to be, somehow or other, passed on even if to a very few people.

But you yourself don't make many concessions to the people who want to be entertained. Rather like Donne, perhaps.
I don't believe any good poet makes concessions in that way. Certainly not in non-dramatic poetry, because I think that is introducing another element into it which would be irrelevant.

In your poetry and plays do you try to put over some sort of religious message?
Oh, no. I am not really interested in messages in that way. If I had a message to convey, whether religious or non-religious, I would convey it just as I would send a telegram in the necessary words to communicate it. I wouldn't wrap it up in the drama. I leave it to other people to find the messages. People find all sorts of messages in Shakespeare, for instance. His plays are inexhaustible for the interpreters. Shakespeare provided rich material from which people can fabricate their own messages.

Which is, perhaps, really the prime function of art. To stimulate people into thinking and feeling for themselves.
It stimulates thought and it stimulates sensibility. Sensibility very often more than thought. But both.

Your own work in many people has bred some sort of feeling and even acceptance of a fatalistic approach – perhaps even a despairing approach – to religion.
Well, I am sorry about the despair. People have found in some of my early poems a note of despair, but taking my work as a whole, and I should wish it to be taken as a whole, I don't think that my later work is despairing at all. Quite the contrary.

I think there is always the suggestion, there, though, that you're rather disappointed to find that man is not capable, really capable, of better things.
Oh, no. There is no reason for being disappointed or for making anything of that. One has to see the limitations of humanity and its weaknesses, but it seems to be rather childish to go on being distressed by the obvious conditions of humanity.

This suggests acceptance of a lower state of man than one might wish for.
Well, we all do that, don't we? We all wish for a better state of man than we find. I don't see that I am any exception to the general run of human beings in that respect.

Are you yourself not, perhaps, a failed mystic?
I don't think I am a mystic at all, though I have always been much interested in mysticism. But I seem to remember that somewhere Yeats said, in answer to a question, that he wasn't a mystic but a poet. Rather implying that you couldn't be both. With me, certainly, the poetic impulse is stronger than the mystical impulse.

There have been poets whose poetic inspiration depended on some mystical insight, at one time or another, of an unsystematic kind. No doubt Wordsworth and Vaughan and Traherne and even Tennyson, I believe, had had some curious mystical experiences. But I can't think of any mystic who was also a fine poet, except Saint John of the Cross. A great many people of sensibility have had some more or less mystical experiences. That doesn't make them mystics. To be a mystic is a whole-time job – so is poetry.

I sometimes feel that that is why you settled for something less. This conception of suffering, the need for suffering, and the salvation that can come from suffering. Your idea that Baudelaire, for instance, through his suffering might have found beatitude. Your idea that Coleridge had failed as a religious person.

I don't remember saying anything of that sort. Coleridge certainly was a religious man, and has a very important piece in the history of religious thinking in the 19th Century. I believe some of his writings stimulated Cardinal Newman and Frederick Denison Maurice. But I am always in the process of revising my views of Coleridge in the light of further knowledge. When I wrote a postcard for the National Portrait Gallery of a portrait of Coleridge, I still accepted the idea of Coleridge which was propagated by Carlyle in his 'Life of Alexander Stirling'. The idea of Coleridge as a lazy man. But Coleridge was a man of infinite industry, far more industrious that I am myself. I certainly wouldn't accept the idea that Coleridge failed religiously.

You have previously suggested that.
Did I?

You once said of The Confidential Clerk *that the critics had found different meanings. Is that important to you? I mean, critics are still finding different meanings in Shakespeare. If a particular message were more important to you than the form, the art, or the message that you, the artist, are probably not even yourself aware of – I think this can very often happen as a message is an automatic thing – you would write unequivocal basic English prose?*

The message the author is unaware of is probably the most authentic, but I'd rather the critics found different meanings. So long as they find different meanings that's all right. People find different meanings in Shakespeare. If they all found the same meanings it would be rather dull. I'm always interested in the meanings that people find in my plays – *The Cocktail Party* especially – and am usually surprised by them, but it is always pleasant to find that what one has written has meant such a variety of things to different people.

In a play I am certainly not interested in the message. I try to think of an interesting situation, and sometimes it is a situation which has been treated in classical Greek drama, but then one thinks of the situation abstracted from the Greek environment, thinks what is the nearest equivalent to that situation in the modern world. The situation develops the characters and then I become interested in the characters. They become rather obsessive, as I imagine all dramatists and even novelists find.

One lives so long with one's characters that one is glad to have done with them.

[30 Aug. 1961] I can compare my feelings, when I have completely finished and done with a play, to that of somebody who has been travelling on the railways, on a long journey, in conversation with other travellers in the same carriage whom he found at first extremely interesting but is very glad to see the last of. As I said, one lives so long with one's characters that one is glad to have done with them.

Nevertheless, it is the characters that interest me. I noticed, for instance, in *The Cocktail Party*, that some people thought I had a rather low opinion of matrimony, and that I was holding up as the ideal a life of sacrifice and martyrdom. Taking a rather poor view of marriage, in fact. Not at all. I was interested in my two particular characters and I thought out the way in which they would quarrel with each other but I didn't mean them to be typical of all married couples. I was just interested in those two people, named Edward and Lavinia. They became very real to me. It is inventing characters and bringing them to life that is exciting.

The characters, rather than what they might represent?
Yes, if they are real they will represent things to other people, no doubt.

What is your feeling about religious drama?
Religious drama means to me a very specialised form of drama. It is drama that is appropriate for production in churches, in church halls or in connection with raising money for churches. It is drama which has a religious subject treated in a Christian way. That is a very definite department of drama. It's not what I'm primarily interested in myself.

My first opportunities for writing for the stage were connected with religious drama and when I was invited by Bishop Bell of Chichester to write a play for the Canterbury Festival, it naturally occurred to me to take the story of St Thomas Becket as it would be appropriate to the place. But I am more interested in drama which has no conscious aim at anybody, but which is just an ordinary play written by a believing Christian – there should be Christian assumptions in the background as there are with Corneille and Racine.

Of course, Racine did write two definitely religious dramas, *Athalie* and *Esther*[,] but in *Berenice*, for instance he is writing as a Christian, but not as a propagandist. His faith is implicit. That is the way I should like to write plays myself: in so far as I am a Christian what I write will be Christian but not pulpit oratory.

It is perhaps even more difficult for Christian propaganda to be art, because it is too obvious. There is much propaganda that is art because people don't realise that it is propaganda. This is why a great deal of Left Wing propaganda manages to come over as art. There is not that sales resistance to the message. But do you feel that great works are possible from a non-Christian?

I am certainly not prepared to say that only a Christian can produce a great work of art. Other religions, Buddhism for instance, have produced great art. I feel that a great work of art must have an inspiration which verges on religious insight.

There can even be great religion behind it, of course, which cannot be given any label at all, either Christian or Buddhist or Hindu or what have we. There may be that tremendous religious feeling behind it that cannot really be defined, except perhaps in broadly mystical terms.

There might. I think I should like to judge, anyway, every case on its own merits. I would certainly not make a ruling that a work of art must propagate such or such beliefs. I mean, that's more like some very Left Wing or Nazi intolerance.

You said that H. G. Wells's writing propagated a belief that the value of the present lies in its service to the future and nowhere else. Does this mean that you believe that the present has a right to look after itself now and again? Perhaps even at the expense of posterity?

I don't remember in what context I wrote the sentence to which you refer. I will take your word for it that I did say it, and there is indeed something familiar about the remark. But it certainly doesn't mean that the present should look after itself at the expense of posterity. No, on the contrary, I feel very much affected in my thinking by three books about the waste of resources and our indifference to the welfare of future generations.

I am thinking of two books by the Earl of Portsmouth – Viscount Lymington he was when he wrote them – and a book by the late Michael Roberts, called *The Estate of Man*: both of which call attention to the way in which the natural resources of the world are being squandered. No, I only meant that human values are in the present as well as in the future, that the human beings who are living today are just as valuable, just as important as those to come after us. I don't want to sacrifice the future to the present, but I don't want to sacrifice the present to the future as I see it, so to speak. It is for other future. I don't want the present to be selfishly indifferent to the future. Far from it: we must assert the rights of the living people of every generation, while it's here, to life, liberty and the pursuit of happiness.

There was a phrase about the consolation of religion being 'pie in the sky'. But for some of the prophets of an earthly paradise it's pie in the future, but no pie for the living. What do the Tibetans think about that, I wonder, under their present rulers? It was curious about H. G. Wells because he had marvellous imagination, he wrote some wonderful stuff, but his science fiction doesn't give one a very happy view of things, does it? *Wars of the Worlds* – all sorts of horrors to come. *The Time Machine* is a fearful, though a wonderful, imaginative piece. It is a great story, but it's most depressing about the future.

Well, this is simply because he was forced through intellectual probing to accept science, but he didn't want to believe in science. He wanted desperately to find something over and about it. His imagination was limited by his fear of the easy abuse of the imagination.

There is much that I respect about H. G. Wells. He seems to me a tragic figure in the sense in which Bernard Shaw was not a tragic figure. Shaw seems complacent. I don't think Wells was, in his later years.

Wells really did feel rather deeply.

I am not talking about them as men. Which was the nicer man I don't know. I didn't know either of them; but Wells, I think, had more imagination and I think that *The Country of the Blind* is one of the greatest short stories ever written. A terrible story.

There is almost enough in that to postpone all judgements and stop all decisions. To make us bury our heads in the corner and feel that we can never know the truth about anything. That story troubles me tremendously. The King's new clothes –

Oh, Hans Christian Andersen – yes, another rather frightening writer. Not suitable for children. Curious.

Well the King's new clothes is certainly very adult and the message is very like the message of The Country of the Blind. *The more this intellectual stuff catches on – the more do people become aware of the limited scope of intellect. They reach a point where they feel that it's quite impossible to discover objective truth, yet anything short of that is considered a letdown. Have you ever felt yourself part of a Movement?*

No – no. I don't know anything about Movements. There was something called the Imagist Movement in London, but that was rather before I came there. I have been associated with other poets, contemporary poets whose poetry I liked as everyone knows, but I was never aware of partaking in a Movement. If there is a movement one may be in it and not see it, so to speak. It is for other people looking back in perspective, to see a Movement.

What do you hope to have achieved?

To achieve? I don't know, one never knows what position one will occupy a generation or two hence. All one can say is that one will have, perhaps, a certain historical place in the literary history of our period. You know, one always likes to think that one's last work is one's best so far – and that one will do something slightly better in the next one. What I should like to do – I should like to write some poems that would give my wife as much delight as the poems which I have already written have given her.

That's a worthy goal. What plans have you at the moment?
Well, I am trying to write a very long essay on George Herbert. Then, when that's done, I shall try to think about another play, because one always wants to write just one more play, you know? Once you have been bitten by the theatre you want to do just one more play.

Have you any theme in mind?
No. I haven't yet. I'll just lie fallow for a bit, I think.

You seem to be rather withdrawn at times. You don't much care for publicity or the hurly-burly of the literary scene – although, by Jove, you have been up to your neck in it for years.
Well, I don't know – I'm not anxious to appear in the public eye, or to take part in anything except things I know about.

I remember when I had occasion to ask if you still felt the same way about Hamlet *now as you did in 1929, your reply was 'Well I haven't really thought about it since.' I thought that a very good reply, especially as your judgement on* Hamlet *has produced from the pens of many critics during the past 30 years, more words than are contained in the play! But do you feel, basically, that once something is done it is not really worth while trying to explain to people why it was done, or trying to go over old ground and perhaps even making excuses for early mistakes.*
Well, every critical statement represents a particular moment in the critic's life and is conditioned too by the context – in a wide as well as a narrow sense – in which it was written.

Preface

Preface to an Exhibition Catalogue for E. McKnight Kauffer, from a t.s. in the Chapin Library of Rare Books and Manuscripts, Williams College, Williamstown, MA, written before 27 Sept. 1961. Signed 'T. S. Eliot' in holograph.

Included here, though not published, on Eliot's understanding that the preface would be published. Not in Gallup but would be C653c.

Some years ago I was invited to open a retrospective exhibition of the poster art of McKnight Kauffer, arranged at the Victoria and Albert Museum, a little after his death. As advance publicity for that exhibition I made my one and only appearance on television; but when the time for the exhibition arrived I found myself in a clinic, and was obliged to tape-record my opening speech for delivery, so to speak, *in absentia*.

The present occasion is the first, however, on which I have ever written an introduction to the catalogue of an exhibition of the work of an artist.

I do this with diffidence, as I cannot claim to possess the authority as an art critic which is expected of the author of a printed preface. It is something, perhaps, that Kauffer was a friend of mine for whom I felt a warm affection. Kauffer had many friends, and I cannot conceive of anyone knowing him well without becoming very much attached to him. But I think that he and I felt that our relationship was particularly brotherly. People remarked on our likeness, and I remember with delighted amusement that three hall porters, in the apartment-house in New York where he lived, took it for granted, independently of each other and on seeing me for the first time, that I was indeed his brother. I felt very much flattered, for Kauffer was not only handsome and distinguished in appearance, but always beautifully dressed and knew how to wear his clothes.

All this is quite irrelevant. What is more relevant is the fact that he designed for me the cover illustrations for several of my 'Ariel' poems, and the jacket for the American edition of my *Four Quartets*. I feel competent to give high praise to his mastery and the art of illustration, and his mastery of poster art. In the former branch of art he was brilliant: in the latter he was supreme.

I forget how many years it was ago that a design of a rooster, crowing at sunrise, appeared on the London hoardings to draw our attention to Eno's Fruit Salt. That rooster, announcing the break of day, also announced the dawn of a new era of poster art in England. It showed, to those who had the sensibility to recognise it, that a real artist was at work, and that a design of genuine artistic merit could be also highly effective as advertising. This advertisement was followed by others still more daring and equally effective. A few more advertisers of taste recognised the possibilities; and the work of other artists of distinction began to appear in public places. But in my opinion McKnight Kauffer was not only a pioneer in this work, but remains unequalled for his poster designs. The period during which he was active in poster work, and which ended with his return to America, was one in which poster art in England was in its high summer. This we owed to Kauffer more than to any other artist.

For Kauffer's poster art I am only saying what is of common agreement. As for his work as an illustrator, I can testify not only by my having chosen him for so much of my own work, but by calling attention to one of his last achievements before his death: his illustrations to an edition of the works of Edgar Allan Poe, including the two terrifying portraits of Poe. It is very exceptional for an artist to be able to enlarge our understanding of a poet: I cannot think of any similar instance. My assurance on his point gives me, as a poet, my credentials for praising an artist[.]

Miss Harriet Weaver

Obituary notice, included in a t.s. letter to the Editor of *The Times* dated 16 Oct. 1961. Not printed. It forms the entire substance of the letter, and is included here as a self-contained obituary notice that Eliot intended should be printed. Not in Gallup but would be C653c. *See also* Gallup C656, *below*, pp. 501–2.

Miss Harriet Weaver, whose death at the age of 85 is announced in your issue of Oct. 16th, was so modest and self-effacing a woman that her generous patronage of men of letters was hardly known except to those who benefited by it. And of these persons, I am the only survivor at this time in a position to speak of her. As proprietor of the Egoist Press, she was the first publisher of Joyce's *Portrait of the Artist as a Young Man*, of Wyndham Lewis's first novel *Tarr*, of poems by Miss Marianne Moore, and of my own first book of poems *Prufrock and Other Observations*. She also issued a fortnightly paper *The Egoist*: I succeeded Mr Richard Aldington as assistant editor for the last year or two of its existence.

In her publishing ventures, Miss Weaver was guided by the counsel of Mr Ezra Pound, himself the first champion and impresario of the writings of Joyce, Lewis and myself. But Miss Weaver's support, once given, remained steadfast. Her great disappointment was her failure to persuade any printer in this country to print *Ulysses*; her subsequent generosity to James Joyce, and her solicitude for his welfare and that of his family, knew no bounds.

My book of *Selected Essays*, first published by Fabers' in 1932, is dedicated to this good, kind, courageous and lovable woman to whom I owe the publication of my first book.

Mögen Sie Picasso?

Contribution to a symposium in honour of Picasso's eightieth birthday. *Frankfurter Allgemeine Zeitung* . . ., 245 (21 Oct. 1961), Supplement, [1–2]. Gallup C 654.

Ich danke Ihnen für Ihr Schreiben vom 22. August und für die schmeichelhafte Einladung, an einem Symposion über Picassos Werk teilzunehmen. Jedoch habe ich mir nie Kunstkritik in der Öffentlichkeit erlaubt, weil ich mich nicht berechtigt fühle, in diesen Dingen mitzusprechen. Ich weiß, daß Picasso ein großer Maler ist, aber ich habe Vorbehalte gegenüber einem beträchtlichen Teil seines Werkes und seiner vermutlichen Auswirkung. Allerdings war ich von der Schönheit der 'Gaukler' ('Les Saltimbanques'), die ich vor einigen Jahren in der Art Gallery in Chicago sah, einfach überwältigt. Es gibt einige wirklich [2] großartige Gemälde, die einen völlig überraschen, wenn man sie zum erstenmal sieht, selbst dann, wenn man sie oft in Reproduktionen gesehen hat.

A Note of Introduction

An introduction to David Jones's *In Parenthesis*. Publ. in
In Parenthesis seinnyessit e gledyf ym penn mameu David Jones, vii–viii.
Subheaded 'by T. S. Eliot'. Publ. Dec. 1961. Gallup B85.

In Parenthesis was first published in London in 1937. I am proud to share the responsibility for that first publication. On reading the book in typescript I was deeply moved. I then regarded it, and still regard it, as a work of genius.

A work of literary art which uses the language in a new way or for a new purpose, does not call for many words from the introducer. All that one can say amounts only to pointing towards the book, and affirming its importance and permanence as a work of art. The aim of the introducer should be to arouse the curiosity of a possible new reader. To attempt to explain, in such a note as this, is futile. Here is a book about the experiences of one soldier in the War of 1914–18. It is also a book about War, and about many other things also, such as Roman Britain, the Arthurian Legend, and divers matters which are given association by the mind of the writer. And as for the writer himself, he is a Londoner of Welsh and English descent. He is decidedly a Briton. He is also a Roman Catholic, and he is a painter who has painted some beautiful pictures and designed some beautiful lettering. All these facts about him are important. Some of them appear in his own Preface to this book; some the reader may discover in the course of reading.

When *In Parenthesis* is widely enough known – as it will be in time – it will no doubt undergo the same sort of detective analysis and exegesis as the later work of James Joyce and the *Cantos* of Ezra Pound. It is true that *In Parenthesis* and David Jones's later and equally remarkable work *The Anathemata*, are provided by the author with notes; but author's notes (as is illustrated by *The Waste Land*) are no prophylactic against interpretation and dissection: they merely provide the serious researcher with more material to interpret and dissect. The work of David Jones has some [viii] affinity with that of James Joyce (both men seem to me to have the Celtic ear for the music of words) and with the later work of Ezra Pound, and with my own. I stress the affinity, as any possible influence seems to me slight and of no importance. David Jones is a representative of the same literary generation as Joyce and Pound and myself, if four men born between 1882 and 1895 can be regarded as of the same literary generation. David Jones is the youngest, and the tardiest to publish. The lives of all of us were altered by that War, but David Jones is the only one to have fought in it.

Those who read *In Parenthesis* for the first time, need to know nothing more than this and what the author tells us in his own Preface, except that *In Parenthesis* and *The Anathemata* have been greatly admired by a number of writers whose opinions usually command attention. The commentaries, as I have said, will follow in time. Good commentaries can be very helpful: but to study even the best commentary on a work of literary art is likely to be a waste of time unless we have first read and been excited by the text commented upon even without understanding it. For that thrill of excitement from our first reading of a work of creative literature which we do not understand is the beginning of understanding, and if *In Parenthesis* does not excite us before we have understood it, no commentary will reveal to us its secret. And the second step is to get used to the book, to live with it and make it familiar to us. Understanding begins in the sensibility: we must have the experience before we attempt to explore the sources of the work itself.

1962

[Interview]

Interview with T. S. Eliot. Donald Carroll, interviewer.
Quagga, 2. 1 ([1st quarter?] 1962), 31–3. Gallup C655.

A headnote explains that only the first of the eight questions was answered at interview. Eliot sent in the remaining answers.

Certainly the most striking characteristic of the present milieu in America is the fact that most of our young poets are to be found in the colleges and universities, usually conducting courses in the mechanics of poetry. Is this likely to result in an excessive concern with stylistics to the impoverishment of language?
I have no evidence that teaching has had an adverse effect on anyone's poetry. However, it does lead to an excessive writing *about* poetry. Now I have no individual in mind here. But I think *a priori* it would be a bad thing for a young poet to teach poetry. I've always advised young poets going into literary journalism *not* to review poetry. For the same reason I've advised young poets not to go into publishing. In other words, they shouldn't read too much of what others are doing. My poetic formation was already determined – I was thirty-seven – when I entered publishing. I'm glad I wasn't a youngster.

[32] *Is the development of a prose style important to an individual's poetic development?*
I don't know how one would go about developing a prose style as one would develop one's muscles, but I think that it is important that prose which a poet writes should be good prose. In other words, there are prose virtues and poetic virtues in common. Pound once said something about the desirability of verse being as well written as good prose.

Would you still direct young poets in their reading to the Elizabethans and the French Symbolists? In view of the developments of the last forty years is there another period which you think deserves renewed attention?
I would not direct young poets to any particular reading in that way. I should certainly hope that they will learn enough Italian to read Dante, who can do them no harm and can do a great deal of good, but I directed

myself to reading the Elizabethans and Symbolists and I should hope that young poets would direct themselves rather than ask their elders for directions.

Are such disciplines as grammar and logic declining and, as a result, taking rhetoric with them?
I am certainly under the impression that grammar and what was called in my boyhood rhetoric are nowadays neglected. Instead of teaching children creative writing I would like to see them learning how to express themselves clearly and grammatically and economically.

Do you believe, as some writers have suggested, that our young poets today are too talented – that is, sophisticated in technique yet self-conscious in vocabulary?
I have no belief about young poets as a crowd. It is of course possible to have talent without genius.

[33] *Is the jettisoning of classical education in the United States likely to have a sterilising effect on American literature? If so, how can it be avoided?*
I think that the abandonment of the teaching of Latin and Greek is most deplorable. Without Latin it is impossible to understand one's own language; without Latin and Greek one fails to understand a great deal of modern literature. The only way to avoid jettisoning classical education is to keep it up.

Should a small poetry magazine restrict itself to publishing one particular mode of verse or, say, one particular cast of poets; or can it afford the luxury of an eclectic editorial policy?
I should say that the policy of a poetry magazine depends on who edit it, but that it can easily be too narrow or too comprehensive.

What is the primary function of the little magazine?
As for the function of a little magazine, I think that it provides an opportunity for unknown young authors, and an opportunity to publish material which is extremely limited or too new in kind to be acceptable to the magazines which depend on large circulation.

Miss Harriet Weaver

'Notes & Topics', *Encounter*, 18. 1 (Jan. 1962), 101. Signed *'T. S. Eliot'*. Gallup C656. Gallup: 'written originally in shorter form as a letter to the London *Times*, but not published there': *See above*, p. 496.

Miss Harriet Shaw Weaver, whose death at the age of eighty-five was announced in *The Times* of October 16th, was so modest and self-effacing a woman that her generous patronage of men of letters was hardly known beyond the circle of those who benefited by it. And of these persons, now that James Joyce and Wyndham Lewis are dead, there is no writer living who owes her as great a debt of gratitude as I do. On reading the announcement of her death, I immediately wrote a letter to *The Times*, which was not published. So I hope you will allow me the space to offer my tribute at somewhat greater length.

As proprietor of The Egoist Press, Miss Weaver was the first publisher of Joyce's *Portrait of the Artist as a Young Man*, of Wyndham Lewis's first novel *Tarr*, of poems by Miss Marianne Moore, and of my own first book of poems *Prufrock and Other Observations*. In these publishing ventures, she was guided by the counsel of Ezra Pound, himself the first champion and impresario of Joyce, Lewis, Marianne Moore, and myself. But Miss Weaver's support, once given, remained steadfast. Her great disappointment was her failure to persuade any printer in this country to take the risk of printing *Ulysses*; her subsequent generosity to James Joyce, and her solicitude for his welfare and that of his family, knew no bounds. I presume that she possessed ample means, but she lived very frugally: I imagine that her publishing usually showed a deficit; and the money that she devoted to the cause of literature must have amounted to a substantial part of her fortune.

Miss Weaver also published a fortnightly periodical, which began as *The New Freewoman*, but which in my time and to the end was called *The Egoist*. I succeeded Richard Aldington as assistant editor for the last year or two of its existence. Aldington had gone off to the war, and Pound nominated me to be his successor. As editor-in-chief, Miss Weaver limited her control to publishing instalments of a philosophical work by her friend Miss Dora Marsden. An instalment occupied the first half of each issue; and the assistant editor was allowed to fill up the remaining pages with whatever matter he liked or could obtain. I deeply regret my folly in throwing away my file copies many years ago, and I cannot now remember how I filled the pages at my disposal. Two or three of my own early essays appeared there, notably 'Tradition and the Individual Talent'; and at least once I filled a column with Letters to the Editor – of my own composition, and under fictitious names. I also enjoyed the use of the office, a small room in some building in the Adelphi, occasionally visited, I believe, by a charwoman. It was all great fun, my first experience of editorship.

In 1932 I dedicated my *Selected Essays* to this good, kind, unassuming, courageous, and lovable woman, to whom I owe so much. What other publisher in 1917 (the Hogarth Press was not yet in existence) would, I wonder, have taken *Prufrock*?

Notes Towards the Definition of Culture

Notes Towards the Definition of Culture was publ. in a new British edn by Faber & Faber on 23 Mar. 1962. Originally publ. by Faber on 5 Nov. 1948. Gallup A51.

The 1962 edn had a new Preface. Section II of the Appendix contained revisions to versions printed in 1946 and 1953, but in the interests of keeping the Appendix intact the revisions are recorded with the 1948 text. (*See* Vol. 3, pp. 710–14, in the present edition.)

[7] Preface to the 1962 Edition

These 'Notes' began to take shape towards the end of the Second World War. When it was suggested that they should be reprinted in 'paper back' form, I re-read them for the first time for some years, expecting that I should have to qualify some of the opinions expressed herein. I found to my surprise that I had nothing to retract, and nothing upon which I was disposed to enlarge. One footnote, on p. 70, I have re-written: it may still be that I have tried to say too much too briefly, and that the notion needs further elaboration. Here and there I have tried to improve a sentence without altering the sense. I owe to a friend, the late Richard Jennings, the correction of a spelling which gives a false etymology (*autarchy* corrected to *autarky* on p. 116).

I have lately had occasion to review my literary criticism over forty years and account for developments and changes of opinion, and I propose one day to submit my social criticism to the same examination. For as a man matures, and acquires greater experience of the world, the years may be expected to bring about even greater changes in his views on social and political matters than in his tastes and opinions in the field of literature. I should not now, for instance, call myself a 'royalist' *tout court*, as I once did: I would say that I am in favour of retaining the monarchy in every country in which a monarchy still exists. But that question, as well as others on which my views, or the way in which I would express my views, have changed, or developed, is not touched upon in the present essay.

T.S.E.
October, 1961.

[Memorial Tribute for Mrs Violet Schiff]

The Times, 9 July 1962, 18. Headed 'Mr. T. S. Eliot writes:'.
Gallup C659.

The death of Violet Schiff, after a long illness, will cause great grief to relatives and to many friends, among whom I and my wife are proud to be numbered. I write, however, not only to express a personal sorrow but because of my memories of Violet and her husband, the late Sydney Schiff, in the world of art and letters 40 years ago. In the 1920s the Schiffs' hospitality, generosity, and encouragement meant much to a number of young artists and writers of whom I was one. The Schiffs' acquaintance was cosmopolitan, and their interests embraced all the arts. At their house I met, for example, Delius and Arthur Symons, and the first Viscountess Rothermere, who founded *The Criterion* under my editorship. Middleton Murry and Katherine Mansfield knew their house, and Wyndham Lewis and Charles Scott-Moncrieff, and many others.

When I married in 1957, Violet Schiff welcomed me and my wife, whom she took to her heart at once. She was already an invalid and could not be persuaded to pay visits, but was always happy to receive her friends. Her mind was as active as ever, and her interest in people and in the arts was undiminished. It was, indeed, in her last years when she was house-bound and, I suspect, often in pain, that her qualities impressed me most deeply: the vigour of her speech, the animation of her face, and the warmth of her sympathy. Hers was a sympathy which made one feel that she understood much more than had been, or could be, put into words: that she was aware of, and responded to, that which could not be spoken. In consequence of this sensitiveness she could regard people with a gentle, clear-sighted charity.

I write primarily to pay homage to a beloved friend, but also in the hope that some future chronicler of the history of art and letters in our time may give to Sydney and Violet Schiff the place which is their due.

[Interview with T. S. Eliot]

Grantite Review, 24. 3 (Election 1962), 16–20. Gallup C662.

On p. 17 a printer's error 'washstand' for 'wasteland' was corrected by pasting in a cancel slip. On p. 19 'crime of sin' has been corrected to 'crime or sin'.

Could you enlarge on your view that the work of art should stand by itself? Does the finished work when it is read have necessarily to be connected with the author?

I think that to take a work of art simply as the starting point of an enquiry about the author, his background and private life and all that has led up to his producing this work of art – I think this is a mistaken attitude. I don't mean that the author's background and history have nothing to do with the work of art – which is of course not independent of the author's personality. But in order to enjoy and appreciate the work of art, one needs only that work of art itself. Kipling – a poet whose work I very much admire – put some verses at the end of his collected works, which are very much to the point. Here they are:

> If I have given you delight
>   By aught that I have done,
> Let me lie quiet in that night
>   Which shall be yours anon:
> And for the little, little span
>   The dead are borne in mind,
> Seek not to question other than
>   The books I leave behind.

I put these lines also at the end of the selection of his poems which I made some years ago.

To enjoy that lovely lyric of Shelley beginning 'Art thou pale for loneliness' we don't need to ask who was Shelley and what was he like. The lyrics of Shakespeare are beautiful in themselves, but also they have a dramatic value, each coming where it does in the play. You don't get all the delight they are capable of giving you, unless you read the plays in which they occur. Look at *Cymbeline*, for instance. And you don't really know any one play of Shakespeare fully until you have read them all. It is I think true of all major poets that you need to read a great deal of their work. In some cases, *all*.

We have read that you have said that there is room for the Romantic in life but not in letters. Could you expand this?

I don't remember where and when I said this – it rings a bell in my mind – it must have been a good many years ago. But I'm not so much interested in the classical-romantic distinction as I once was. You can find the romantic wherever you look for it and the classical in the best of the romantic. To tell the truth, the discussion rather bores me now.

Do you agree with the publication of Rose Macaulay's letters?
I could answer this question better if I had read the letters. But one cannot always read books just to decide whether they ought to be read or not. After the newspaper discussion, and especially after reading what Rebecca West [17] said about them, I felt repugnance. I did not want to violate Rose Macaulay's privacy.

Prufrock. Did the person you had in mind represent the age, or is he a character from the Waste Land?
I could not have answered that question at all when I wrote *Prufrock*. It was partly a dramatic creation of a man of about 40 I should say, and partly an expression of feeling of my own through this dim imaginary figure. In the theatre, for instance, I always feel that dramatic characters who seem living creations have something of the author in them. Sometimes, as W. B. Yeats would have said, it is the anti-mask: something which is not only different, but the opposite of the author as he is. Take two characters of Shakespeare. I think that Iago is alive, and Richard III a dummy: a splendidly dramatic dummy, to be sure, who speaks lines written by Shakespeare – a great privilege for a dummy – and a good role for some good actors. And I think of Shakespeare as a delightful man, but I think that he put something that he suppressed in himself into Iago. And a dramatist might put something of him – or her – self into a character of the other sex, too. Richard III is a pure villain, and pure villainy is one kind of purity in which it is hard to believe. Even the Devil is a fallen Angel.

There has been a good deal of nonsense written about the name *Prufrock*. Someone discovered that there had been a shop in St Louis, Missouri, where I spent my boyhood up to the age of 16, which bore the name Prufrock. Then the question arose whether as a boy I had ever had occasion to pass down the street in which the shop was found. And someone else has discovered symbolism in the name which allied it to *Touchstone*! But I chose the name because it sounded to me very very prosaic. I have taken names often because they sounded to me euphonious – like Sweeney or Rabinovitch.

How much do you think Pound owes to Hopkins?
Nothing at all. Remember that Pound and I had both written a great deal before we ever heard of Hopkins. I remember glancing at the first edition of Hopkins on the table of Roger Fry the art critic, who was interested. I did not read Hopkins until the edition came out which was prefaced

by Charles Williams. I don't know whether Pound has ever read him at all. Hopkins became known just in time to influence poets like Auden, Spender and Day Lewis. Anybody who was young enough could hardly escape his influence. Day Lewis most, I think; but he seems to me closer to Thomas Hardy. There again was a poet whose influence came later than any that could influence Pound or me. When I was 18 or 19, I read Hardy's novels; but I did not know of him as a poet until years later. He had written novels, I believe, because one can't make a living on poetry alone. But, speaking of money[,] that Russian poet who was over here as the guest, I believe, of the British Council told me that there were over 1,500 professional poets in Russia. (Whether this was his ground for maintaining, as he appeared from a newspaper interview to have done, that Russian poetry today was the best in the world, I don't know.) When I asked what he meant [18] by 'professional poet', for the term was new to me, he said that they earned their living by their poetry. He admitted, however, that only about fifty of them were good poets. I said that I have never heard of so many good poets in any one country at one time (including China, I had in mind) but whether this got through to him, as we talked through an interpreter, I do not know. I was told that the only language he knew except Russian was Spanish.

When you first read Yeats did you value his work and do you value it now?
Well, when I first read Yeats, it was in the early days when he was writing Celtic Twilight stuff: Deirdre and Cuchulan and all that. He seemed to me then merely a minor member of the Nineties Group of poets (Dowson and Johnson were the best). Yeats, you see, was rather a late developer. His first poems that excited me appeared in 1916 or 1917. And then he went from strength to strength; and some of his best work was his last. That's a wonderful achievement. I admire his later poems very much indeed. And he read them well: but when he read aloud from English poets, in the chant and the brogue that suited his own – well, Blake sounded rather odd.

Do you feel that this scientific age presents greater problems of communication?
This age, whether you call it scientific, or technological, or anything else, does present problems of communication. But I have never worried about communication in my poems, only in my plays. Communication is obviously easier – and this applies especially in the theatre – the more the dramatist, the actors and the audience have beliefs and standards in common. In an essay called *The Three Voices of Poetry* I made the point that in a poem the author may be, so to speak, talking to himself:

at least, he is really writing something to be spoken by his own voice. In a play, the author, whether he is writing in verse or prose – is writing something which some producer will take and train some actor to speak to an audience: the author may not know when he is writing, who the producer will be, who the actors will be, or who the audience will be: he must try to write something that can survive handling by any producer and any actors who want to perform that play, and for any audience that will want to see it.

. . . Of course, I often find other people's poems very obscure, but my own seem to me quite clear and simple. But I think that the practice of writing for the theatre has made me write more simply in my later poems. When I was writing my first play, Mr Martin Browne, the producer, advised me to strike out some lines which were very good in themselves, because they did not pertain to the character of the speaker in the play, or because they did not advance the action. I think the discipline of writing for the stage does make for clarity.

The Ariel Poems; *do these reflect a search for faith?*
I was already a practising member of the Church of England when I wrote them. Faber & Faber published every year for several years a series of short new poems by well known living poets, which were illustrated by some well-known artist and sold as a kind of Christmas Card. Hence *Journey of the* [19] *Magi*. I was asked to produce a poem for the season and so I chose that subject. Later, I chose other subjects, year by year, with no seasonal association. We brought the series to an end, and I kept the title for those of my poems which had been written in this way.

Do you feel that a period of doubt is essential to the gaining of faith?
Any belief about the universe requires faith, whether religious belief or not. There can be simple faith without any antecedent doubt, but it can only be the faith of very simple people. There are of course many people who hold no beliefs about the universe at all; but they are simply people who don't think at all. But for people of intellect I think that doubt is inevitable. Pascal had a very sceptical mind and he was a spiritual descendant of Montaigne. The doubter is a man who takes the problem of his faith seriously. Any religious faith is in a way incredible, but a materialistic or anti-religious attitude involves believing something else equally incredible.

Many people find the Four Quartets *hard to understand, could you attempt a brief explanation?*
No, I cannot explain the *Four Quartets*. Any attempt on my part to explain would merely be saying something else. One can say that *Little Gidding* is a patriotic poem – it was written during the dark days of

1942 – but that is only one aspect of it. It was after writing the first two that I saw the pattern required four in all. I associated them with the four elements: air, earth, water and fire, in that order.

Your plays seem to have connections with Greek Drama. Does the death of the 'Elder Statesman' resemble the transfiguration of Oedipus?
Yes, of course it is based on *Oedipus at Colonus*. What I have done in all my plays after *Murder in the Cathedral* has been to look for a permanent human situation, in some Greek drama, and develop it freely in our world of today. Thus *The Cocktail Party* was based on Euripides' *Alcestis*: the return of the wife who had died. The other characters were added; the husband and wife situation was Euripides. In the *Elder Statesman* I did not want to make my protagonist guilty of the most heinous crimes: the patricide and incest of the Greek dramatist. It was more effective, for my purpose, to take some lesser crime or sin, some act of cowardice, which would be humiliating for the transgressor to think of, and which he would keep out of mind as long as he could.

The Dean of Westminster in an interview with Ludovic Kennedy remarked that this is a post-Christian era. Would you comment on this?
Christians are certainly in a minority, and in a small minority, when one considers that the majority of people, in most of their activity, are able to ignore the Christian Faith – though some of them might be annoyed if they were proclaimed to be non-Christian. One reason why I could not interest myself in the recent discussion about Sir Charles Snow and Dr Leavis is that I believe – and I wrote an essay which seeks to make the point – that culture springs up with and in the practice of a religion: the major cultures have been in the past so [20] closely involved with the major religions as to be the other aspect of the religion. Neither Sir Charles Snow nor Dr Leavis appears to take that view.

A number of people have remarked that you joined the establishment when you became an Anglican. How would you answer these critics?
Let other people think what they choose to think. If the suggestion is that I was seeking social status, like a man who wanted to get into a good club, I observed many years ago that one advantage of living in a post-Christian age was that no one could say one had become a Christian for respectability's sake. Several years ago an M.P. said to me: 'I have seen you described recently as a member of the Establishment, together with the Archbishop of Canterbury.' I asked him where he had read that. He said: 'In *The Queen*.'

Has the poet a moral duty to his readers, did your views on this change when you became a Christian?

The poet has the same moral obligations as any other man; but they are his moral duties as a human being. A man could be a very good poet, and yet fail conspicuously in his moral obligations and responsibilities. When one is writing a poem, one may not be thinking about one's moral duties. One just has something inside that one wants to get out, and the only way to get it out and at the same time to find out what it is that one wants to get out, is to find the words for it. If you are a poet, you will come to know when you have found the words and when you haven't.

Peter Sellers: What do you think of him?
Peter Sellers is certainly very versatile. I admired very much his work in *I'm All Right Jack*. And I have a gramophone record in which he does a surprising variety of turns.

Would you agree that nationalism is outdated?
The extreme of nationalism is ridiculous and so is the extreme of internationalism. At the present time we can observe the extremes of both. I say 'ridiculous', but I must say also 'deplorable'. The Russians seem to encourage both.

Are you interested in politics?
I am interested in politics just as every thinking person must be; but I am one of those who would much prefer not to have to think about politics. Politics do not interest me in the way in which they interest politicians.

Who is your favourite composer?
Of living composers, I admire Stravinsky. I liked Bartok. Of the classics, I find the Austrians – Haydn, Mozart and Schubert – very sympathetic. Beethoven is terrific, but I do not feel on quite such intimate terms with his music as with that of those three Austrians!

[Tribute to Victoria Ocampo]

As printed from Eliot's letter in *Testimonios sobre Victoria Ocampo* (1962), 94.
Not in Gallup but would be C663a.

... I would be glad to be recorded as one who recognised the place occupied by Victoria Ocampo in the literary world, for her services to literature and culture in the Argentine Republic and in South America generally. I know the distinction of *Sur* and have had the pleasure of meeting Victoria Ocampo on several occasions when she visited this country. I am glad to place myself on record as one of those who recognised her international services to literature.

T. S. Eliot
London, June 1962.

[Memorial Tribute for Sylvia Beach]

The Times, 13 Oct. 1962, 10. Gallup C664.

Repr. in *Mercure de France*, 349 (Aug./Sept. 1963), [9]–10, with French translation, 11–12, and in Dec. 1963 as *Sylvia Beach (1887–1962)*: Gallup B88.

I made the acquaintance of Sylvia Beach, and at the same time of her friend Adrienne Monnier, on a visit to Paris early in the nineteen twenties, and thereafter saw them frequently during that decade. Only the scattered survivors of the Franco-Anglo-American literary world of Paris of that period, and a few others like myself who made frequent excursions across the Channel, know how important a part these two women played in the artistic and intellectual life of those years. To Adrienne Monnier, with *Navire d'Argent*, I owe the introduction of my verse to French readers; and so I became a visitor to her bookshop and to that of Shakespeare and Company. A guest of Mlle Monnier, or a guest of Miss Beach, would meet men of the *Nouvelle Revue Française* or of the group associated with *Commerce*: Gide, Schlumberger, Valéry, Fargue, Larbaud and Groethuysen are among those I encountered there. I dined with Sylvia Beach for the last time two years before the last war; I remember that Gide and Schlumberger were there also.

I did not see either Sylvia Beach or Adrienne Monnier again until 1945, when I was sent to Paris after the evacuation only a few days before VE Day. I found them at Adrienne's and gave them the tea and the soap which I had brought for them from England. They told me that I was their first visitor from this side of the Channel.

Some of us in England, who appreciated the service which Sylvia, at her *librairie*, had rendered to contemporary English and American literature in France, would have liked to see Shakespeare and Company put on its feet again. But the British Council was powerless to help, as Sylvia was an American citizen; and the Americans had no organisation comparable to the British Council. Nor were the auspices for such an undertaking so propitious as they had been 25 years before. Nor, I suspect, did Sylvia, after the hardships she had endured, and the imprisonment she had suffered, have the resiliency or the physical strength to resume her former role.

No tribute to Sylvia Beach would do her justice that did not stress her services to James Joyce. But for two generous and devoted women – Harriet Weaver and Sylvia Beach – I do not know how Joyce could have survived or how his works could have got published. In the early thirties Joyce discovered that for reasons connected with the legality of his testamentary disposition he needed to spend a period of two or three consecutive months in England. Being the man he was, he rented, for his brief sojourn, an unfurnished flat: a dreary little flat, for which he then proceeded to buy some still drearier necessary pieces of furniture. (How he eventually disposed of flat and furniture I do not remember.) It then transpired that he had no bank account: it was Sylvia who acted as his banker. When he needed money he wrote to Sylvia, who promptly sent a banker's draft, which he would then give to me to cash for him at my bank. What the financial arrangement may have been between those two, or what accounts were kept, I never knew.

In 1960 Sylvia Beach came to London, at the time of the publication of her book. She passed through London again this summer on her way to and from Dublin, but my wife and I were out of town and missed her. The last glimpse we had of her was on the television screen being interviewed by Mr Malcolm Muggeridge. And very delightfully she talked; and very charming she appeared, gay and youthful for her age. It was all the greater shock to read of her death the other day. A brave, generous and very lovable woman.

T. S. ELIOT

George Herbert

Publ. on 26 Nov. 1962 for The British Council and the National Book League by Longmans, Green & Co. Writers and Their Work series, No. 152, 7–39. Gallup A73.

I

The family background of a man of genius is always of interest. It may show evidence of powers which blaze forth in one member, or it may show no promise of superiority of any kind. Or it may, like that of George Herbert, show distinction of a very different order. There is a further reason for knowing something of the ancestry of George Herbert: it is of interest to us because it was important to him.

The family of Herbert was, and still is, notable among the British aristocracy. I say British rather than English, because one branch of the family, that to which the poet belonged, had established itself in Wales and had intermarried with Welsh landed families. The Herberts lay claim to being of Norman-French origin, and to having been land-holders since the Norman conquest. At the time of the Wars of the Roses the Herberts of Wales had supported the Yorkist cause; but after the battle of Bosworth they transferred their allegiance to the new monarch, the Lancastrian Henry Tudor, himself a Welshman on his father's side, who ascended the throne as Henry VII. Under the new dynasty the Herberts continued to flourish. Henry VII was determined to exert in Wales the same authority that he enjoyed in England – a control to which the local chieftains of Wales were not accustomed. Among those Welshmen of position and authority who supported and advanced King Henry's law and order in Wales was Sir Richard Herbert of Montgomery Castle. Montgomery lies in North Wales; in the South another Herbert was (and is) Earl of Pembroke; and still another branch of the family is represented by the Earl of Carnarvon.

George Herbert's ancestors and kinsmen were active both in the service of the King and in local affairs. Their rank was among the highest. Several of the family were distinguished for their courage, their prowess in war and duel and [8] their astonishing feats of arms. An exceptional race, but giving no indication of literary tastes and ability before the time of George Herbert and his brother Edward. That two poets, brothers, should appear in a family so conspicuous for warlike deeds, administrative gifts and attendance at Court, can only be accounted for by the fact that their mother, the wife of Sir Richard Herbert of Montgomery, was a woman of literary tastes and of strong character and of exceptional gifts of mind as well as beauty and charm. She was Magdalen, daughter and heiress of Sir Richard Newport, a wealthy landowner in Shropshire.

George Herbert was born in 1593. Three years later his father died, leaving the mother with ten children, seven boys and three girls. Edward was the eldest son; the younger sons would have, of course, to make their own way in life – presumably, as other Herberts had done, in the wars or in some public service – but Lady Herbert's standards were high and she was determined to give them all a good education. The eldest, Edward, the other poet of the family and the heir to the estates, was thirteen and already an undergraduate at Oxford when his father died. At fifteen Edward was married off to an heiress (a Herbert of another branch) but continued at Oxford, where his mother moved her family to be near him and to supervise his education. There she made friends, and even held a kind of salon, among the more brilliant of the learned dons.

It is worth while to say something of Edward Herbert, the eldest brother, not merely to mention his poetry but to point the striking contrast between the two gifted brothers. Edward was ambitious to live abroad, to enjoy court life in foreign capitals and to engage in rather dilettante diplomacy; and to this end he learned French, Italian and Spanish. He seems to have been a man of great physical strength, and was noted for his address at sports and success in love-making: in short, he was a man of abounding vitality. He was later raised to the peerage as Lord Herbert of Cherbury, by which name he is known as author of at least two very [9] fine poems familiar to readers of anthologies. He was not only a poet, but something of a philosopher, and entertained distinctly heretical views in religious matters. On the other hand, John Donne spoke well of him, and Ben Jonson was a friend and correspondent. For he enjoyed the society of men of letters, among whom he moved as an equal as well as among the courtiers of Europe and among ladies and gentlemen of fashion. In Edward the characteristic traits of the Herberts and some of the particular traits of Magdalen Herbert, his mother, appear to have been combined. In George, of frailer constitution and contemplative mind, we seem to find more of Magdalen; yet he was as proudly conscious of being a Herbert as any other Herbert, and at one period had the family inclination to life in the world of public affairs.

By far the most important for our study of George Herbert, of the men of letters and the scholars who delighted in the company of Magdalen Herbert, was John Donne. He was enough older in years to have the admiration of the younger man and to influence him: he was enough beneath Lady Herbert in rank to be almost a protégé. The friendship between Donne and Lady Herbert is commemorated in one of Donne's best known and most loved poems 'The Autumnal', in which is found the couplet which every lover of Donne's poetry knows by heart:

> No Spring, nor Summer Beauty hath such grace
> As I have seen in one autumnal face.

To the influence of Donne's poetry upon that of Herbert we shall return presently. Meanwhile it is in place to provide a brief survey of Herbert's life and a sketch of his character.

At the age of twelve George Herbert was sent to Westminster School, where he became proficient in the usual disciplines of Latin and Greek, and gained also – what is equally important for mention here – an advanced practice in music: not only in the choral singing for which that famous school was well known because of its associa-[10]tion with the services in Westminster Abbey, but also with a difficult instrument – the lute. If we remember Herbert's knowledge of music, and his skill at the instrument, we appreciate all the better his mastery of lyric verse. From Westminster he went on to Trinity College, Cambridge, being one of three boys of Westminster School who were given scholarships to that College at that time.

At Westminster School Herbert had an exemplary record. The relation of the school to the Abbey had also familiarised him with the church offices, in which the boys took part. (Their close attention to the sermon was ensured by the requirement that they should afterwards compose a summary of it in Latin.) At the university Herbert was equally forward; sober and staid in his conduct and diligent in his studies, he was given particular attention by the Master. It was said of him, however, that he was careful to be well, even expensively dressed; and that his attitude towards his fellow undergraduates of lower social position was distant, if not supercilious. Even Isaac Walton (his most nearly contemporary biographer) who tends to emphasise Herbert's saintliness, admits that Herbert, at this stage of his life, was very much aware of the consideration which he thought due to his exalted birth.

At the age of twenty-three Herbert was made a Fellow of his own college of Trinity. He began by instructing the younger undergraduates in Greek grammar; later he taught rhetoric and the rules of oratory. His health was never good; and the climate of Cambridge was somewhat harsh for a young man of frail constitution. His income as Fellow and Tutor was eked out by a small allowance from his brother Edward (the head of the family) and occasionally by gifts from his step-father. For his mother had, in middle age, married again, and was now the wife of Sir John Danvers. But Herbert's poor health meant doctors' bills and occasional absences from Cambridge; as a learned scholar of an active and curious mind he needed constantly to purchase books, and books were expensive, especially those which had to [11] be imported from the continent. He therefore sought to improve his finances, and at the same time attain a position of considerable dignity, by obtaining appointment as Public Orator to the University.

Herbert had not yet formed the design of passing his life as a country parson. Indeed, the post of Public Orator was one which would bring him into the great world and even into contact with the court of James I. He achieved his aim; and during his tenure of this office acquired an extensive acquaintance, which his family connections and his own wide sympathies helped to enlarge. He greatly admired Sir Francis Bacon, a man of a type of mind very different from his own; another elder friend with whom he was on affectionate terms was the saintly Bishop Lancelot Andrewes. Nor did a wide divergence of religious attitude and belief diminish the warm regard between him and his elder brother Edward.

A Fellow of a College was expected to take holy orders in the Church of England within seven years of his appointment, or resign his Fellowship. Herbert was, like his mother, a practising and devout Anglican, but at this time his ambition looked toward the world of Court and Government. His violent attack, in the form of a Latin thesis, upon the Puritan position in the person of one of its most outrageous zealots, Andrew Melville, was his only sortie into religious controversy; though undoubtedly wholly sincere, Herbert probably aimed at winning the approval of King James. He would certainly have liked public office, but had neither the wiles of ingratiation, nor the means or the wish to buy his way in. His next step was to become Member of Parliament for Montgomery – an election which came to him almost as a matter of course as a member of the Herbert family. But this period of his life was not marked by success: two great noblemen of whose patronage he felt assured died, and the death of King James himself, in the following year, seems to have left him with little hope of a Secretaryship of State.

[12] It was necessary to review this much of Herbert's early life to make the point that Herbert, though from childhood a pious member of the Anglican Church, and a vigorous opponent of the Puritans and the Calvinists, felt no strong vocation to the priesthood until his thirty-first year. There were at least four persons in his life who may, by precept or example, have influenced him to this decision. His mother, to whom he was devotedly attached, was, we know, a woman not only of strong character, but of great piety. Two friends much older than himself have already been mentioned: Dr John Donne and Bishop Andrewes. And finally, there was his dear friend Nicholas Ferrar of Little Gidding, an exemplar of High Churchmanship. whose domestic life approached that of a religious community. To Ferrar it was that he consigned, upon his death, the manuscript collection of verse upon which his fame is founded, the collection *The Temple* which we should not know had Ferrar not chosen to publish it; this he did in the same year in which Herbert died.[1]

---

1. Four editions of *The Temple* appeared within three years of its first publication; its popularity continued to the end of the century. In the eighteenth century Herbert's poems were generally disparaged: Cowper, for instance, though he found in them a strain of piety which he admired, regarded them as 'gothick and uncouth', and this was the universal opinion of that age. The restoration of Herbert's reputation was begun by Coleridge who, in a letter to William Collins, dated 6th December 1818, writes: '. . . I find more substantial comfort now in pious George Herbert's "Temple" which I used to read to amuse myself with his quaintness – in short, only to laugh at – than in all the poetry since the poems of Milton. If you have not read Herbert, I can recommend the book to you confidently. The poem entitled "The Flower" is especially affecting; and, to me, such a phrase as "and relish versing" expresses a sincerity, a reality, which I would unwillingly exchange for the more dignified "and once more love the Muse", &c. And

[13] Herbert's mother died in 1626. George Herbert was for a time a guest in the house of his step-father's elder brother, Lord Danvers, and in 1629, having already taken holy orders, he married Jane Danvers, the daughter of a cousin of Lord Danvers. It was a happy marriage. Six years after Herbert's death, his widow married Sir Robert Cook. In her widowhood, Isaac Walton says:

> ...She continued mourning, till time and conversation had so moderated her sorrows, that she became the happy wife of Sir Robert Cook of Highnam in the County of Gloucester, Knight. And though he put a high value on the excellent accomplishments of her mind and body; and was so like Mr Herbert, as not to govern like a Master, but as an affectionate Husband; yet she would even to him take occasion to mention the name of Mr George Herbert, and say that name must live in her memory, till she put off mortality.

George Herbert died of consumption at the age of forty. For the last ten years of his life he had been rector of the parish of Bemerton in Wiltshire. That he was an exemplary parish priest, strict in his own observances and a loving and generous shepherd of his flock, there is ample testimony. And we should bear in mind that, at the time when Herbert lived, it was most unusual that a man of George Herbert's social position should take orders and be content to devote himself to the spiritual and material needs of a small parish of humble folk in a rural village. From Walton's *Life* I must quote one anecdote:

> In another walk to *Salisbury*, he saw a poor man, with a poorer horse, that was fall'n under his Load; they were both in distress, and needed present help; which Mr *Herbert* perceiving, put off his Canonical Coat, and help'd the poor man to unload, and after, to lead his horse: The poor man blest him for it: and he blest the poor man; and was so like the *good Samaritan* that he gave him money to refresh both him and his horse; and told him, *That if he lov'd himself, he should be merciful to his Beast*. Thus he left the poor man, and at his coming to his musical friends at *Salisbury*, they began to wonder that Mr *George Herbert* which [14] us'd to be so trim and clean, came into the company so soyl'd and discompos'd;

---

so, with many other of Herbert's homely phrases.' (*Letters*, Vol. IV, edited by Earl Leslie Griggs, 1959).

Writing to Lady Beaumont in 1826, Coleridge says: 'My dear old friend Charles Lamb and I differ widely (and in point of taste and moral feeling this is a rare occurrence) in our estimate and liking of George Herbert's sacred poems. He greatly prefers Quarles – nay he dislikes Herbert.' (*The Letters of Charles Lamb*, edited by E. V. Lucas, Vol. I, 1935).

but he told them the occasion. And when one of the company told him, *He had disparag'd himself by so dirty an employment*; his answer was, *That the thought of what he had done, would prove Musick to him at Midnight; and that the omission of it would have upbraided and made discord in his Conscience, whensoever he should pass by that place; for, if I be bound to pray for all that be in distress, I am sure that I am bound so far as it is in my power to practise what I pray for. And though I do not willingly pass it is in my power to practise what I pray for. And though I do not wish for the like occasion every day, yet let me tell you, I would not willingly pass one day of my life without comforting a sad soul, or shewing mercy; and I praise God for this occasion*: And now let's tune our instruments.

In this context is worth mention a prose treatise of Herbert's entitled *A Priest to the Temple Or the Country Parson His Character, etc.* In this treatise he sets forth the duties and responsibilities of the country parson to God, to his flock, and to himself; and from what we know of Herbert we can be sure that he practised, and always strove to practise, what he here prescribes to other priests. The story of the poor man and his horse is all the more touching when we read that the Parson's apparel should be

> plaine, but reverend, and clean, without spots, or dust, or smell; the purity of his mind breaking out, and dilating it selfe even to his body, cloaths, and habitation.

We are told elsewhere in the same treatise that a priest who serves as domestic chaplain to some great person is not to be

> over-submissive, and base, but to keep up with the Lord and Lady of the house, and to preserve a boldness with them and all, even so farre as reproofe to their very face, when occasion calls, but season-ably and discreetly.

The pride of birth natural to Herbert is transformed into [15] the dignity of the servant of God. The parson, he continues, should be a man of wide reading: Herbert mentions the Church Fathers and the Scholastics, and tells us that the parson should be attentive to later writers also. The parson must give careful attention to his sermon, taking due account of the needs and capacities of his parishioners, and keeping their attention by persuading them that his sermon is addressed to this particular congregation and to one and all of them. And he should, especially when visiting the sick, or otherwise afflicted, persuade them to particular confession, 'labouring to make them understand the great good use of this antient and pious ordinance'.

We are not to presume, however, that George Herbert was naturally of a meek and mild disposition. He was, on the contrary, somewhat haughty; proud of his descent and social position; and, like others of his family, of a quick temper. In his poems we can find ample evidence of his spiritual struggles, of self-examination and self-criticism, and of the cost at which he acquired godliness.

> I struck the board, and cry'd, No more.
>   I will abroad.
>   What? shall I ever sigh and pine?
> My lines and life are free; free as the rode,
>   Loose as the winde, as large as store.
>   Shall I be still in suit?
>   Have I no harvest but a thorn
>   To let me bloud, and not restore
> What I have lost with cordiall fruit?
>   Sure there was wine
> Before my sighs did drie it: there was corn
>   Before my tears did drown it.
>   Is the yeare onely lost to me?
>   Have I no bayes to crown it?
> No flowers, no garlands gay? all blasted?
>   All wasted?
>   Not so, my heart: but there is fruit
>   And thou hast hands.
> [16]   Recover all thy sigh-blown age
> On double pleasures: leave thy cold dispute
> Of what is fit and not. Forsake thy cage,
>   Thy rope of sands,
> Which pettie thoughts have made, and made to thee
>   Good cable, to enforce and draw,
>   And be thy law,
> Whilst thou didst wink and wouldst not see.
>   Away; take heed;
>   I will abroad.
> Call in thy deaths head there: tie up thy fears.
>   He that forbears
>   To suit and serve his need
>   Deserves his load.
> But as I rav'd and grew more fierce and wilde
>   At every word,

> Me thought I heard one calling, *Child*!
>   And I reply'd, *My Lord*.
>
> ('The Collar')

To think of Herbert as the poet of a placid and comfortable easy piety is to misunderstand utterly the man and his poems. Yet such was the impression of Herbert and of the Church of England given by the critic who wrote the introduction to the World's Classics edition of Herbert's poems in 1907. For this writer, the Church of England, in Herbert's day as well as in his own, is typified by a peaceful country churchyard in the late afternoon:

> Here, as the cattle wind homeward in the evening light, the benign, white-haired parson stands at his gate to greet the cowherd, and the village chimes call the labourers to evensong. For these contented spirits, happily removed from the stress and din of contending creeds and clashing dogmas, the message of the gospel tells of divine approval for work well done . . . And among these typical spirits, beacons of a quiet hope, no figure stands out so brightly or more memorably than George Herbert.

This rustic scene belongs to the world of Tennyson and Dickens; but no more to the world of George Herbert than [17] to our world today. It is well that the latest World's Classics edition (the text based on that established by F. E. Hutchinson) has a new introduction by a learned and sensitive critic, Miss Helen Gardner. The earlier introduction gave a false picture both of Herbert and his poetry, and of the Church itself in an age of bitter religious conflict and passionate theology: it is worth quoting in order to point out how false a picture this is.

II

The poems on which George Herbert's reputation is based are those constituting the collection called *The Temple*. About *The Temple* there are two points to be made. The first is that we cannot date the poems exactly. Some of them may be the product of careful re-writing. We cannot take them as being necessarily in chronological order: they have another order, that in which Herbert wished them to be read. *The Temple* is, in fact, a structure, and one which may have been worked over and elaborated, perhaps at intervals of time, before it reached its final form. We cannot judge Herbert, or savour fully his genius and his art, by any selection to be found in an anthology; we must study *The Temple* as a whole.

To understand Shakespeare we must acquaint ourselves with all of his plays; to understand Herbert we must acquaint ourselves with all of *The Temple*. Herbert is, of course, a much slighter poet than Shakespeare; nevertheless he may justly be called a major poet. Yet even in anthologies he has for the most part been underrated. In Sir Arthur Quiller-Couch's *Oxford Book of English Verse*, which was for many years unchallenged in its representative character, George Herbert was allotted five pages – the same number as Bishop King and much less than Robert Herrick, the latter of whom, most critics of today would agree, is a poet of very much slighter gifts. For poetic range Herbert was [18] commonly considered more limited than Donne; and for intensity he was compared unfavourably with Crashaw. This is the view even of Professor Grierson, to whom we are greatly indebted for his championship of Donne and those poets whose names are associated with that of Donne.

And here we must exercise caution in our interpretation of the phrase 'the school of Donne'. The present writer once contemplated writing a book under that title; and lately the title has been used by a distinguished younger critic for a study covering the same ground. The phrase is legitimate and useful to designate that generation of men younger than Donne whose work is obviously influenced by him, but we must not take it as implying that those poets who experienced his influence were for that reason lesser poets. (Professor Grierson, indeed, seems to consider Andrew Marvell the greatest, greater even than Donne.) That Herbert learned directly from Donne is self-evident. But to think of 'the school of Donne', otherwise 'the metaphysical poets', as Donne's inferiors, or to try to range them on a scale of greatness, would be to lose our way. What is important is to apprehend the particular virtue, the unique flavour of each one. Comparing them with any other group of poets at any other period, we observe the characteristics which they share: when we compare them with each other, their differences emerge clearly.

Let us compare a poem by Donne with a poem by Herbert; and as Herbert's poetry deals always with religious matter, we shall compare two religious sonnets. First, Donne:

> Batter my heart, three person'd God; for, you
> As yet but knocke, breathe, shine, and seeke to mend;
> That I may rise, and stand, o'erthrow mee, and bend
> Your force, to breake, blowe, burn and make me new.
> I, like a usurpt towne to 'another due,
> Labour to 'admit you, but Oh, to no end,
> Reason your viceroy in mee, mee should defend,
> But is captiv'd, and proves weake or untrue.

[19] Yet dearely 'I love you, and would be loved faine,
But am betroth'd unto your enemie:
Divorce mee, 'untie, or break that knot againe;
Take mee to you, imprison mee, for I
Except you 'enthrall mee, never shall be free,
Nor ever chast, except you ravish mee.

And here is George Herbert:

PRAYER (I)

Prayer the Churches banquet, Angels age,
    Gods breath in man returning to his birth,
    The soul in paraphrase, heart in pilgrimage,
The Christian plummet sounding heav'n and earth;
Engine against th' Almightie, sinners towre,
    Reversed thunder, Christ-side-piercing spear,
    The six daies world transposing in an houre,
A kinde of tune, which all things heare and fear,
Softnesse, and peace, and joy, and love, and blisse,
    Exalted Manna, gladnesse of the best,
    Heaven in ordinarie, man well drest,
The milkie way, the bird of Paradise,
    Church-bels beyond the starres heard, the souls bloud,
    The land of spices; something understood.

The difference that I wish to emphasise is not that between the violence of Donne and the gentle imagery of Herbert, but rather a difference between the dominance of intellect over sensibility and the dominance of sensibility over intellect. Both men were highly intellectual, both men had very keen sensibility: but in Donne thought seems in control of feeling, and in Herbert feeling seems in control of thought. Both men were learned, both men were accustomed to preaching – but not to the same type of congregation. In Donne's religious verse, as in his sermons, there is much more of the *orator*: whereas Herbert, for all that he had been successful as Public Orator at Cambridge University, has a much more intimate tone of speech. We do not know what Herbert's sermons were like; but we can conjecture that [20] in addressing his little congregation of rustics, all of whom he knew personally, and many of whom must have received both spiritual and material comfort from him and from his wife, he adopted a more homely style. Donne was accustomed to addressing large congregations (one is tempted to call them 'audiences') out of doors at Paul's Cross, Herbert only the local congregation of a village church.

The difference which I have in mind is indicated even by the last two lines of each sonnet. Donne's

> ... for I
> Except you 'enthrall me, never shall be free,
> Nor ever chast, except you ravish mee.

is, in the best sense, *wit*. Herbert's

> Church-bels beyond the starres heard, the souls bloud,
> The land of spices, something understood

is the kind of poetry which, like

> magic casements, opening on the foam
> Of perilous seas, in faery lands forlorn

may be called *magical*.

Of all the poets who may be said to belong to 'the school of Donne', Herbert is the only one whose whole source of inspiration was his religious faith. Most of the poetry upon which rests the reputation of Donne is love poetry, and his religious verse is of a later period in his life; his reputation, and his influence upon other poets would have been as great had he written no religious poetry at all. Richard Crashaw, who had himself frequented the community of Nicholas Ferrar at Little Gidding before his conversion to the Church of Rome, might still have been a notable poet had he written no religious verse – even though his devotional poems are his finest. Herbert, before becoming Rector of Bemerton, had never been a recluse: he had, in his short life, [21] wide acquaintance in the great world, and he enjoyed a happy marriage. Yet it was only in the Faith, in hunger and thirst after godliness, in his self-questioning and his religious meditation, that he was inspired as a poet. If there is another example since his time of a poetic genius so dedicated to God, it is that of Gerard Hopkins. We are certainly justified in presuming that no other subject-matter than that to which he confined himself could have elicited great poetry from George Herbert. Whether we regard this as a limitation, or as the sign of solitary greatness, of a unique contribution to English poetry, will depend upon our sensibility to the themes of which he writes.

It would, however, be a gross error to assume that Herbert's poems are of value only for Christians – or, still more narrowly, only for members of his own church. For the practising Christian, it is true, they may be aids to devotion. When I claim a place for Herbert among those poets whose work every lover of English poetry should read and every student of English poetry should study, irrespective of religious belief or unbelief, I am not thinking primarily of the exquisite craftsmanship, the extraordinary metrical virtuosity, or the verbal felicities, but of the *content* of the poems which make up *The Temple*. These poems form a record of a spiritual struggle which should touch the feeling, and enlarge the understanding of those readers also who hold no religious belief and find themselves unmoved by religious emotion. Professor L. C. Knights, in an essay on George Herbert in his *Explorations*, both expresses this doubt on the part of the non-Christian and dispels it:

> Even Dr Hutchinson, whose superbly edited and annotated edition of the Complete Works is not likely to be superseded ... remarks that 'if to-day there is a less general sympathy with Herbert's religion, the beauty and sincerity of its expression are appreciated by those who do not share it'. True, but there is much more than the 'expression' that we appreciate, as I shall try to show. Herbert's poetry is an integral part of the great English tradition.

[22] Whether the religious poems of Donne show greater profundity of thought, and greater intensity of passion, is a question which every reader will answer according to his own feelings. My point here is that *The Temple* is not to be regarded simply as a collection of poems, but (as I have said) as a record of the spiritual struggles of a man of intellectual power and emotional intensity who gave much toil to perfecting his verses. As such, it should be a document of interest to all those who are curious to understand their fellow men; and as such, I regard it as a more important document than all of Donne's *religious* poems taken together.

On the other hand, I find Herbert to be closer in spirit to Donne than is any other of 'the school of Donne'. As the personal bond, through Lady Herbert, was much closer, this seems only natural. Other powerful literary influences formed the manner of Crashaw, the Roman Catholic convert: the Italian poet Marino and the Spanish poet Gongora, and, we are told,[1] the Jesuit poets who wrote in Latin. Vaughan and Traherne were poets of mystical experience; each appears to have experienced early in life some mystical illumination which inspires his poetry. And the other important poet of the 'metaphysical' school, Andrew Marvell, is a master of secular and religious poetry equally. In my attempt to indicate the affinity of Herbert to Donne, and also the difference between them, I have spoken earlier of a 'balance' between the intellect and the sensibility. But equally well, (for one has recourse to diverse and even mutually contradictory metaphors and images to express the inexpressible) we can speak of a 'fusion' of intellect and sensibility in different proportions.

---

1. By Mario Praz, whose *Seicentismo e marinismo in Inghilterra* is essential for the study of Crashaw in particular.

In the work of a later generation of 'metaphysicals' – notably Cleveland, Benlowes and Cowley – we encounter a kind of emotional drought, and a verbal ingenuity which, having no great depth of feeling to work upon, tends towards corruption of language, [23] and merits the censure which Samuel Johnson applies indiscriminately to all the 'school of Donne'.

To return to the import of *The Temple* for all perceptive readers whether they share Herbert's faith or no. Professor Knights quotes with approval Dr Hutchinson's description of the poems as

> colloquies of the soul with God or self-communings which seek to bring order into that complex personality of his which he analyses so unsparingly.

but goes on to make a qualification which seems to me very important. Dr Hutchinson believes that Herbert's principal temptation was *ambition*. We need not deny that Herbert had been, like many other men, ambitious; we know that he had a hot temper; we know that he liked fine clothes and fine company, and would have been pleased by preferment at Court. But beside the struggle to abandon thought of the attractions offered to worldly ambition, Professor Knights finds 'a dejection of spirit that tended to make him regard his own life, the life he was actually leading, as worthless and unprofitable'. Mr Knights attributes the cause partly to ill-health, but still more to a *more ingrained distrust*. It was perhaps distrust of himself, or fear of testing his powers among more confident men, that drove him to the shelter of an obscure parsonage. He had, Mr Knights suggests, to rid himself of the torturing sense of frustration and impotence and accept the validity of his own experience. If this is so, Herbert's weakness became the source of his greatest power, for the result was *The Temple*.

I have called upon Mr Knights's testimony in evidence that Herbert is not a poet whose work is significant only for Christian readers; that *The Temple* is not to be taken as simply a devotional handbook of meditation for the faithful, but as the personal record of a man very conscious of weakness and failure, a man of intellect and sensibility who hungered and thirsted after righteousness. And that by its *content*, as well as because of its technical accomplish-[24]ment, it is a work of importance for every lover of poetry. This is not, however, to suggest that it is unprofitable for us to study the text for closer understanding, to acquaint ourselves with the liturgy of the Church, and identify the Biblical allusions. One long poem which has been subjected to close examination is *The Sacrifice*. There are sixty-three stanzas of three lines each, sixty-one of which have the refrain 'Was ever grief like Mine?' I mention this poem, which is a very fine one, and not so familiar as are some of the shorter and more lyrical pieces, because it has been carefully studied by Professor William Empson in his *Seven Types of Ambiguity*, and by Miss Rosamund Tuve in her *A Reading of George Herbert*. The lines are to be taken as spoken by Christ upon the Cross. We need, of course, enough acquaintance with the New Testament to recognise references to the Passion. But we are also better prepared if we recognise the Lamentations of Jeremiah, and the Reproaches in the Mass of the Presanctified which is celebrated on Good Friday.

> *Celebrant*: I led thee forth out of Egypt, drowning Pharaoh in the Red Sea: and thou hast delivered me up unto the chief priests.
> *Deacon & Subdeacon*: O my people, what I have done unto thee, or wherein have I wearied thee? Testify against me.

It is interesting to note that Mr Empson and Miss Tuve differ in their interpretation of the following stanza:

> *O all ye who passe by, behold and see*;
> Man stole the fruit, and I must climbe the tree;
> The tree of life to all, but onely me:
> >   Was ever grief like mine?

Mr Empson comments: 'He climbs the tree to repay what was stolen, as if he were putting the apple back'; and develops this explanation at some length. Upon this interpretation Miss Tuve observes rather tartly: 'All (Mr Empson's) rabbits roll out of one small hat – the fact that [25] Herbert uses the time-honoured "climb" for the ascent of the Cross, and uses the word "must", to indicate a far deeper necessity than that which faces a small boy under a big tree'. Certainly, the image of *replacing* the apple which has been plucked is too ludicrous to be entertained for a moment. It is obvious that Christ 'climbs' or is 'lifted up' on the Cross in atonement for the sin of Adam and Eve; the verb 'climb' being used traditionally to indicate the *voluntary* nature of the sacrifice for the sins of the world. Herbert was, assuredly, familiar with the imagery used by the pre-Reformation Church. It is likely also that Donne, learned in the works of the scholastics, and also in the writings of such Roman theologians contemporary with himself as Cardinal Bellarmine, set a standard of scholarship which Herbert followed.

To cite such an instance as this, however, is not to suggest that the lover of poetry needs to prepare himself with theological and liturgical knowledge *before* approaching Herbert's poetry. That would be to put the cart before the horse. With the appreciation of Herbert's poems, as with all poetry, enjoyment is the beginning as well as the end. We must enjoy the poetry before we attempt to penetrate the poet's mind; we must enjoy it before we understand it, if the attempt to understand it is to be worth the trouble. We begin by enjoying poems, and lines in poems, which make an immediate impression; only gradually, as we familiarise ourselves with the whole work, do we appreciate *The Temple* as a coherent sequence of poems setting down the fluctuations of emotion between despair and bliss, between agitation and serenity, and the discipline of suffering which leads to peace of spirit.

The relation of enjoyment to belief – the question whether a poem has more to give us if we share the beliefs of its author, is one which has never been answered satisfactorily: the present writer has made some attempt to contribute to the solution of the problem, and remains dissatisfied with his attempts. But one thing is certain: that even if a reader enjoys a poem more fully when he shares the beliefs of the [26] author, he will miss a great deal of possible enjoyment and of valuable experience if he does not seek the fullest understanding possible of poetry in reading which he must 'suspend his disbelief'. (The present writer is very thankful for having had the opportunity to study the *Bhagavad Gītā* and the religious and philosophical beliefs so different from his own, with which the *Bhagavad Gītā* is informed.)

Some of the poems in *The Temple* express moods of anguish and sense of defeat or failure:

> At first thou gav'st me milk and sweetnesses;
> > I had my wish and way:
> My dayes were straw'd with flow'rs and happinesse;
> > There was no moneth but May.
> But with my yeares sorrow did twist and grow,
> And made a partie unawares for wo. . . .
>
> Yet, though thou troublest me, I must be meek;
> > In weaknesse must be stout.
> Well, I will change the service, and go seek
> > Some other master out.
> Ah my deare God! though I am clean forgot,
> Let me not love thee, if I love thee not.

The foregoing lines are from the first of five poems all of which bear the title 'Affliction'. In the first of two poems both of which are entitled 'The Temper', he speaks of his fluctuations of faith and feeling:

> How should I praise thee, Lord! how should my rymes
> > Gladly engrave thy love in steel,
> > If what my soul doth feel sometimes,
> > > My soul might ever feel!

The great danger, for the poet who would write religious verse, is that of setting down what he would like to feel rather than be faithful to the expression of what he really feels. Of such pious insincerity Herbert is never guilty. We [27] need not look too narrowly for a steady progress in Herbert's religious life, in an attempt to discover a chronological order. He falls, and rises again. Also, he was accustomed to working over his poems; they may have circulated in manuscript among his intimates during his lifetime. What we can confidently believe is that every poem in the book is true to the poet's experience. In some poems there is a more joyous note, as in 'Whitsunday':

> Listen sweet Dove unto my song,
> And spread thy golden wings in me;
> Hatching my tender heart so long,
> Till it get wing, and flie away with thee. . . .
>
> Lord, though we change, thou art the same;
> The same sweet God of love and light:
> Restore this day, for thy great name,
> Unto his ancient and miraculous right.

In 'The Flower' we hear the note of serenity, almost of beatitude, and of thankfulness for God's blessings:

> How fresh, O Lord, how sweet and clean
> Are thy returns! ev'n as the flowers in spring;
> To which, besides their own demean,
> The late-past frost tributes of pleasure bring.
> Grief melts away
> Like snow in May,
> As if there were no such cold thing.
>
> . . . .
>
> And now in age I bud again,
> After so many deaths I live and write;
> I once more smell the dew and rain,
> And relish versing: O my onely light,
> It cannot be
> That I am he
> On whom thy tempests fell all night.[1]

---

1. A. Alvarez in *The School of Donne* says justly of this stanza: 'This is, I suppose, the most perfect and most vivid stanza in the whole of Herbert's work. But it is, in every sense, so natural that its originality is easily missed.' (See also Coleridge on this poem: footnote to p. 10.)

[28] I cannot resist the thought that in this last stanza – itself a miracle of phrasing – the imagery, so apposite to express the achievement of faith which it records, is taken from the experience of the man of delicate physical health who had known much illness. It is on this note of joy in convalescence of the spirit in surrender to God, that the life of discipline of this haughty and irascible Herbert finds conclusion: *In His will is our peace.*

III

Of all the 'school of Donne' Herbert is the closest to the old Master. Two other fine poets of the group might just as well be said to belong to the 'school of Herbert'. The debt of Vaughan to Herbert can be shown by quotation; Herbert's most recent and authoritative editor, Dr F. E. Hutchinson, says: 'There is no example in English literature of one poet adopting another's work so extensively.' As for Crashaw, he undoubtedly admired Herbert. Nevertheless, in spite of a continuity of influence and inspiration, we must remember that these four poets, who form a constellation of religious genius unparalleled in English poetry, are all highly individual, and very different from each other.

The resemblances and differences between Donne and Herbert are peculiarly fascinating. I have suggested earlier that the difference between the poetry of Donne and Herbert shows some parallel to the difference between their careers in the Church. Donne the Dean of St Paul's, whose sermons drew crowds in the City of London; Herbert the shepherd of a little flock of rustics, to whom he laboured to explain the meaning of the rites of the Church, the significance of Holy Days, in language that they could understand. There are, however, lines which might have come from either, where we seem to hear the same voice – Herbert echoing the idiom or reflecting the imagery of Donne. There is at least one poem of Herbert's in which he plays with extended metaphor in the manner of Donne. [29] It is 'Obedience' where he uses legal terms almost throughout:

> My God, if writings may
> Convey a Lordship any way
> Whither the buyer and the seller please;
> Let it not thee displease,
> If this poore paper do as much as they.

. . . .

> He that will passe his land,
>   As I have mine, may set his hand
> And heart unto this Deed, when he hath read;
>   And make the purchase spread
> To both our goods, if he to it will stand.

Such elaboration is not typical of Herbert. But there is *wit* like that of Donne in 'The Quip'. One feels obliged to quote the whole poem:

> The merrie world did on a day
> With his train-bands and mates agree
> To meet together, where I lay,
> And all in sport to geere at me.
>
> First, Beautie crept into a rose,
> Which when I pluckt not, Sir, said she,
> Tell me, I pray, Whose hands are those?
> *But thou shalt answer, Lord, for me.*
>
> Then Money came, and clinking still,
> What tune is this, poore man? said he:
> I heard in Musick you had skill.
> *But thou shalt answer, Lord, for me.*
>
> Then came brave Glorie puffing by
> In silks that whistled, who but he?
> He scarce allow'd me half an eie.
> *But thou shalt answer, Lord, for me.*
>
> Then came quick Wit and Conversation,
> And he would needs a comfort be,
> And, to be short, make an Oration.
> *But thou shalt answer, Lord, for me.*
>
> [30] Yet when the houre of thy designe
> To answer these fine things shall come;
> Speak not at large; say, I am thine:
> And then they have their answer home.

Professor Knights observes very shrewdly: 'the personifications here have nothing in common with Spenser's allegorical figures or with the capitalised abstractions of the eighteenth century: "brave Glorie puffing by in silks that whistled" might have come straight from *The Pilgrim's Progress*.' How audible are these silks 'that whistled'! 'Puffing' is equally apt: the same principle is used, to produce another but equally striking effect, elsewhere:

> Sometimes Death, puffing at the doore,
> Blows all the dust about the floore.
> ('The Church Floore')

Herbert is a master of the simple everyday word in the right place, and charges it with concentrated meaning, as in 'Redemption', one of the poems known to all readers of anthologies:

> Having been tenant long to a rich Lord,
>   Not thriving, I resolved to be bold,
>   And make a suit unto him, to afford
> A new small-rented lease, and cancell th'old.
> In heaven at his manour I him sought:
>   They told me there, that he was lately gone
>   About some land, which he had dearly bought
> Long since on earth, to take possession,
> I straight return'd, and knowing his great birth,
>   Sought him accordingly in great resorts;
>   In cities, theatres, gardens, parks, and courts:
> At length I heard a ragged noise and mirth
>   Of theeves and murderers: there I him espied,
>   Who straight, *Your suit is granted*, said, & died.

The phrase 'ragged noise and mirth' gives us, in four words, the picture of the scene to which Herbert wishes to introduce us.

[31] There are many lines which remind us of Donne:

> What though my bodie run to dust?
> Faith cleaves unto it, counting ev'ry grain
> With an exact and most particular trust,
>   Reserving all for flesh again.
> ('Faith')

>   My God, what is a heart?
> Silver, or gold, or precious stone,
> Or starre, or rainbow, or a part
> Of all these things, or all of them in one?
> ('Mattens')

>   ... learn here thy stemme
> And true descent; that when thou shalt grow fat,
> And wanton in thy cravings, thou mayst know
> That flesh is but the glasse, which holds the dust

> That measures all our time; which also shall
> Be crumbled into dust. . . .
> 					('Church-monuments')

> Lord, how can man preach thy eternall word?
> 			He is a brittle crazie glasse: . . .
> 					('The Windows')

> My bent thoughts, like a brittle bow,
> 			Did flie asunder: . . .
> 					('Deniall')

Herbert must have learned from Donne the cunning use of both the learned and the common word, to give the sudden shock of surprise and delight.

> But man is close, reserv'd, and dark to thee:
> 			When thou demandest but a heart,
> 				He cavils instantly.
> 			In his poore cabinet of bone
> 				Sinnes have their box apart,
> Defrauding thee, who gavest two for one.
> 					('Ungratefulnesse')

[32]
> 		The fleet Astronomer can bore,
> And thred the sphere with his quick-piercing minde:
> He views their stations, walks from doore to doore,
> 			Surveys, as if he had design'd
> To make a purchase there: he sees their dances,
> 				And knoweth long before
> Both their full-ey'd aspects, and secret glances.
> 					('Vanitie')

> My thoughts are all a case of knives . . .
> 					('Affliction IV')

The following lines are very reminiscent of Donne:

> 			How soon doth man decay!
> When clothes are taken from a chest of sweets
> 			To swaddle infants, whose young breath
> 				Scarce knows the way;
> 			Those clouts are little winding sheets,
> Which do consigne and send them unto death
> 					('Mortification')

Here and there one can believe that Herbert has unconsciously used a word, or a rhythm of Donne, in a very different context from that of the original, as perhaps in the first line of 'The Discharge':

> Busie enquiring heart, what wouldst thou know?

Donne begins 'The Sunne Rising' with the line

> Busie old foole, unruly Sunne . . .

If Herbert's line be an echo and not a mere coincidence – the reader must form his own opinion – it is all the more interesting because of the difference in subject matter between the two poems. If Herbert, in writing a poem of religious *mortification*, could echo a poem of Donne which is an *aubade* of the lover's complaint that day should come so [33] soon, it suggests that the literary influence of the elder man upon the younger was profound indeed.

Herbert's metrical forms, however, are both original and varied. To have invented and perfected so many variations in the form of lyrical verse is evidence of native genius, hard work and a passion for perfection. Two of his poems are such as would be considered, if written by a poet today, merely elegant trifles: 'The Altar' and 'Easter Wings'. In each, there is a disposition to longer and shorter lines so printed that the poem has a shape, the one of an altar and the other of a pair of wings. Such a diversion, if employed frequently, would be tedious, distracting and trying to the eyesight and we must be glad that Herbert did not try to make further use of these devices: yet it is evidence of Herbert's care for workmanship, his restless exploration of variety, and a kind of gaiety of spirit, a joy in composition which engages our delighted sympathy. The exquisite variations of form in the other poems of *The Temple* show a resourcefulness of invention which seems inexhaustible, and for which I know no parallel in English poetry. Here, we can only quote a stanza from each of a brief selection to suggest the astonishing variety:

> O my chief good,
> How shall I measure out thy bloud?
> How shall I count what thee befell.
>   And each grief tell?
>   ('Good Friday')

> O blessed bodie! Whither are thou thrown?
> No lodging for thee, but a cold hard stone?
> So many hearts on earth, and yet not one
>   Receive thee?
>   ('Sepulchre')

Poems in such measures as these, and more obviously *The Sacrifice*, which we have quoted earlier, seem to indicate an ear trained by the music of liturgy.

[34]   Rise, heart; thy Lord is risen. Sing his praise
                    Without delays,
      Who takes thee by the hand, that thou likewise
                    With him mayst rise:
      That, as his death calcined thee to dust,
      His life may make thee gold, and much more, just.
                    ('Easter')

The slow movement of the last line quoted above has something of the movement of the exquisite line which ends Donne's 'Nocturnall upon S. Lucies Day':

Bothe the yeares, and the dayes deep midnight is.

Somewhat similar to the movement of 'Good Friday' (quoted above) is:

            Since, Lord, to thee
         A narrow way and little gate
      Is all the passage, on my infancie
            Thou didst lay hold, and antedate
                My faith in me.
                    ('Holy Baptisme I')

Close enough to the form of 'Holy Baptisme' for its difference to be all the more striking is

         Lord, I confesse my sinne is great;
         Great is my sinne. Oh! gently treat
      With thy quick flow'r, thy momentarie bloom;
            Whose life still pressing
            Is one undressing,
         A steadie aiming at a tombe.
                    ('Repentance')

The next quotation has a solemn liturgical movement suited to the subject-matter and the title:

[35]   O Do not use me
         After my sinnes! look not on my desert,
         But on thy glorie! then thou wilt reform
         And not refuse me: for thou onely art

> The mightie God, but I a sillie worm;
> O do not bruise me!
>
> ('Sighs and Grones')

Herbert knows the effect of denying a rhyme where it is expected:

> When my devotions could not pierce
> Thy silent eares;
> Then was my heart broken, as was my verse:
> My breast was full of fears
> And disorder:
>
> ('Deniall')

The roughness of the metre of the line

> Then was my heart broken, as was my verse

is exactly what is wanted to convey the meaning of the words. The following stanza has an apparent artlessness and conversational informality which only a great artist could achieve:

> Lord, let the Angels praise thy name.
> Man is a foolish thing, a foolish thing,
> Folly and Sinne play all his game.
> His house still burns, and yet he still doth sing,
> *Man is but grasse,*
> *He knows it, fill the glasse.*
>
> ('Miserie')

The next poem to be quoted is one of several poems of Herbert which, while being, like all the rest of his work, personal, have been set to music and sung as hymns:

> King of Glorie, King of Peace,
> I will love thee:
> And that love may never cease,
> I will move thee.
>
> ('Praise II')

[36] The same masterly simplicity is visible in:

> Throw away thy rod,
> Throw away thy wrath;
> O my God,
> Take the gentle path.
>
> ('Discipline')

I wish to end by giving in full the poem which, significantly, I think, ends *The Temple*. It is named 'Love III', and indicates the serenity finally attained by this proud and humble man:

> Love bade me welcome: yet my soul drew back,
>   Guiltie of dust and sinne.
> But quick-ey'd Love, observing me grow slack
>   From my first entrance in,
> Drew nearer to me, sweetly questioning,
>   If I lack'd any thing.
>
> A guest, I answer'd, worthy to be here:
>   Love said, You shall be he.
> I the unkinde, ungratefull? Ah, my deare,
>   I cannot look on thee.
> Love took my hand, and smiling did reply,
>   Who made the eyes but I?
>
> Truth Lord, but I have marr'd them: let my shame
>   Go where it doth deserve.
> And know you not, sayes Love, who bore the blame?
>   My deare, then I will serve.
> You must sit down, sayes Love, and taste my meat:
>   So I did sit and eat.

[37] George Herbert
A Select Bibliography

(Place of publication London, unless otherwise stated)

Bibliography:

A HERBERT BIBLIOGRAPHY, by G. H. Palmer; Cambridge, Mass. (1911)
– a privately printed catalogue of the compiler's collection of books by and about Herbert. Useful but incomplete.
A BIBLIOGRAPHY OF STUDIES IN METAPHYSICAL POETRY, 1939–1960. compiled by L. E. Berry; Wisconsin (1964c).

Collected Editions:

THE WORKS, with Preface by W. Pickering and Notes by S. T. Coleridge. 2 vols. (1835–6).
THE COMPLETE WORKS, ed. A. B. Grosart. 3 vols. (1874)
– textually most unreliable, but the first edition to make use of the Williams MS.

THE ENGLISH WORKS NEWLY ARRANGED, ed. G. H. Palmer. 3 vols. (1905–1907)
– an important edition, notwithstanding some editorial liberties and speculations.
WORKS, ed. F. E. Hutchinson; Oxford (1941)
– the definitive edition in the Oxford English Texts Series. The World's Classics reprint, 1961, has a valuable introduction by H. Gardner.

Selections:
SELECTED POEMS OF GEORGE HERBERT, ed. D. Brown (1960).
THE LATIN POETRY OF GEORGE HERBERT: A BILINGUAL EDITION, translated by M. M. McCloskey and P. R. Murphy; Athens, Ohio (1964).
SELECT HYMNS TAKEN OUT OF MR HERBERT'S TEMPLE (1967).

Separate Works:
THE TEMPLE, SACRED POEMS AND PRIVATE EJACULATIONS; Cambridge (1633)
– 13 editions were published before 1709 but none thereafter until 1799. The Nonesuch Press edition (1927) ed. F. Meynell (with a bibliographical note by G. Keynes) is based on the Bodleian MS (Tanner 307) which was the copy licensed in 1633 for the printer by the Cambridge Vice-Chancellor and his assessors.
[38] WITTS RECREATIONS. WITH A THOUSAND OUTLANDISH PROVERBS SELECTED BY MR G. H. (1640)
– the proverbs attributed to Herbert were published separately in 1651 as *Jacula Prudentum*.
HERBERT'S REMAINS (1652)
– contains most of *A Priest to the Temple* and *Jacula Prudentum*.
A PRIEST TO THE TEMPLE, OR, THE COUNTREY PARSON HIS CHARACTER, AND RULE OF HOLY LIFE (1671)
– a selection, ed. G. M. Forbes, was published in 1949.
Herbert contributed Latin and Greek poems to the following memorial collections:
Epicedium Cantabrigiense, in Obitum Henrici Principis Walliae. Cambridge, 1612 (2 Latin poems); *Lacrymae Cantabrigienses, in Obitum Reginae Annae.* Cambridge, 1619 (1 Latin poem); *True Copies of the Latine Orations, made at Cambridge on the 25 and 27 of Februarie last past,* 1623 (1 Latin oration with English translation); *Oratio qua Principis Caroli Reditum ex Hispaniis Celebravit Georgius Herbert.* Cambridge, 1623 (1 Latin oration); *Memoriae Francisci, Baronis de Verulamio, Sacrum,* 1626 (1 Latin

poem); *A Sermon of Commemorations of the Lady Danvers by John Donne. Together with other Commemorations of her, called Parentalia by her Sonne, G. Herbert*, 1627 (19 Latin and Greek Poems).

Some Critical and Biographical Studies:
>THE LIFE OF MR GEORGE HERBERT, by I. Walton (1670)
>– reprinted in Walton's *Lives*, 1670 (World's Classics edition, 1923).
>THE LIFE OF LORD HERBERT OF CHERBURY (1764)
>– Edited by H. Walpole. See also Lord Herbert's *Poems*, ed. Moore Smith; Oxford, 1923.
>BIOGRAPHIA LITERARIA, by S. T. Coleridge (1817)
>– chapters xix and xx.
>METAPHYSICAL POEMS AND LYRICS OF THE SEVENTEENTH CENTURY, ed. with an introduction by H. Grierson; Oxford (1921).
>SEICENTISMO E MARINISMO IN INGHILTERRA, by M. Praz; Florence (1925).
>A CONCORDANCE TO THE ENGLISH POEMS, by C. Mann; Boston, Mass. (1927).
>SEVEN TYPES OF AMBIGUITY, by W. Empson (1930).
>THE DONNE TRADITION, by G. Williamson; Cambridge, Mass. (1930).
>[39] FOUR METAPHYSICAL POETS, by J. Bennett; Cambridge (1934)
>– revised, 1953. Reissued, 1959, with new section of Herbert, as *Five Metaphysical Poets*.
>THE METAPHYSICAL POETS, by J. B. Leishman; Oxford (1934).
>STUDIES IN SEVENTEENTH CENTURY IMAGERY, by M. Praz (1939)
>– revised and enlarged edition, 1964.
>EXPLORATIONS: STUDIES IN LITERARY CRITICISM, by L. C. Knights (1946)
>– contains his essay on Herbert first printed in *Scrutiny*, 1933.
>A READING OF GEORGE HERBERT, by R. Tuve; Chicago (1952)
>– revised edition, 1965.
>GEORGE HERBERT, by M. Bottrall (1954).
>GEORGE HERBERT, by J. H. Summers; Cambridge, Mass. (1954).
>TWO GENTLE MEN, by M. Chute; New York (1959)
>– biographies of Herbert and Herrick. English edition, 1960.
>THE SCHOOL OF DONNE. by A. Alvarez (1961).
>POETRY AND THE FOUNTAIN OF LIGHT: Observations on the Conflict between Christian and Classical Traditions in Seventeenth Century Poetry, by H. R. Swardson (1962).

[The Common Market]

Contribution to 'Going into Europe': A Symposium.
Encounter, 19. 6 (Dec. 1962), 65. Gallup C667.

On the precise terms which Britain can accept, or on which Britain can be accepted into the Common Market, I do not consider myself competent to pronounce. There are obviously economic, political, and legal problems to be solved. Nor does this seem to me a matter to be decided by a plebiscite. Nor does it seem to me that it should be an issue between political parties.

You seek to obtain the views of 'writers, scholars, and intellectuals generally'. I am neither a scholar not an intellectual generally; but, as a writer, I believe that all that any member of these three categories can offer of value is a statement of his personal bias for or against our joining, prior to any consideration of the possible terms.

I have always been strongly in favour of close cultural relations with the countries of Western Europe. For this reason my personal bias is in favour of Britain's entering into the Common Market. And I have not been impressed by the emotional appeals of some of those who maintain that to take this course would be a betrayal of our obligations to the Commonwealth.

T. S. Eliot on the Language of *The New English Bible*

Sunday Telegraph, 98 (16 Dec. 1962), 7. Gallup C668.
Repr. in *The New English Bible Reviewed*, ed. Dennis Nineham (1965), 96–101,
and in *Contemporary Controversy: Readings for Composition and Discussion*,
ed. Morris Freedman and Paul B. Davis (1966), 113–17.

There are three points of view from which any translation of the Bible may be examined: that of doctrine, that of accuracy of translation, and that of English prose style. In what follows I am concerned only with the question of style.

The translation of the Bible undertaken over 350 years ago at the suggestion of King James I was made by the best scholars in the kingdom. It was a revision of previous translations; the task was parcelled out between six committees, and a general committee spent over two years in revising the work of the six.

In the preparation of the *New English Bible*, of which only the New Testament has been completed and published, an equally careful procedure has been followed. There have been four 'panels', of which one has been responsible for the New Testament, and another is responsible for 'the literary revision of the whole'.

Again, the committees have been enlisted from among the best scholars in the kingdom, and, this time, with complete freedom of choice; for denominational considerations have played no part.

Errors Of Taste

The age covered by the reigns of Elizabeth I and James I was richer in writers of genius than is our own, and we should not expect a translation made in our time to be a masterpiece of our literature or, as was the Authorised Version of 1611, an exemplar of English prose for successive generations of writers.

We are, however, entitled to expect from a panel chosen from among the most distinguished scholars of our day at least a work of dignified mediocrity. When we find that we are offered something far below that modest level, something which astonishes in its combination of the vulgar, the trivial, and the pedantic, we ask in alarm: 'What is happening to the English language?'

I shall give a few quotations in illustration, before examining the principles of translation adopted by the translators, as set forth in the Introduction: principles which seem to me to take us some way towards understanding the frequent errors of taste in the translation itself.

The translation of a passage may be subjected to criticism on several grounds. I can illustrate this very well by examining a sentence in St Matthew (hereinafter referred to as 'Matthew', in conformity with the *New English Bible*) the earlier version of which will be a familiar quotation to many even of those who are ignorant of the Scriptures: 'Do not feed your pearls to pigs.'

We notice, first, the substitution of 'pigs' for 'swine'. The *Complete Oxford Dictionary* says that 'swine' is now 'literary' but does not say that it is obsolete. I presume, therefore, that in substituting 'pigs' for 'swine' the translators were trying to choose a word nearer to common speech, even if at the sacrifice of dignity.

I should have thought, however, that the word 'swine' would be understood, not only by countryfolk who may have heard of 'swine fever', but even by the urban public, since it is still applied, I believe, to human beings as a term of abuse.

Next, I should have thought that the sentence would be more in accord with English usage if the direct and indirect objects were transposed, thus: 'Do not feed pigs upon your pearls.' To make 'pearls' the direct object is, if I am not mistaken, an Americanism, and my belief is confirmed, rather than dispelled, by the examples of this usage given in the *Oxford English Dictionary*.

The most unfortunate result, however, is that the substitution of 'feed' for 'cast' makes the figure of speech ludicrous. There is all the difference in the world between saying that pigs do not *appreciate* the value of pearls, and saying, what the youngest and the most illiterate among us know, that they cannot be *nourished* on pearls.

Too Literal

This is not the only instance in which a figure of speech, or illustration, has been ruined; though in some other places rather by literalness, as 'no man can be slave to two masters', which ceases to carry any admonition, and becomes merely a flat statement about the conditions of slavery.

'Or how can you say to your brother, "Let me take the speck out of your eye", when all the time there is that plank in your own?' may be literally accurate but will certainly, if it is read in church, raise a giggle among the choirboys. As for the house built on sand, 'down it fell with a great crash!'.

As for clarity, I find some passages more puzzling in the *New English Bible* than in the Authorised Version. Surely others besides myself will take no comfort from being told, as the first beatitude: 'How blest are those who know that they are poor.' (The translator of Luke is more nearly in accord with the Authorised Version here.)

And the unlearned, on being told that 'a man who divorces his wife must give her a note of dismissal', will marvel at the apparent facility with which the Hebrews could get rid of their wives. 'Bill of divorcement', even though it gives no clear notion of the process required by Jewish law, at least sounds ceremonious.

The foregoing examples are all taken from 'the Gospel according to Matthew', an Evangelist who seems to have been especially unlucky in his translator. The other Gospels, however, conform to the same style (or absence of style) in their monotonous inferiority of phrasing.

I wish nevertheless to quote one brief passage in order to give the translator of 'Luke' his due (Luke iii. 14–15). To the soldiers who ask what they should do John the Baptist replies: 'No bullying; no blackmail; make do with your pay!'

I admit gladly that lapses of taste are less offensive when committed against a 'Letter' – that is to say, against what we have known heretofore as an 'Epistle' – than when committed against a Gospel. And there is much more justification, I will even say *need*, for modern translations of the Epistles than for modern translations of the Gospels.

A Difficult Writer

Some years ago Dr J. H. Oldham lent me the translation of St Paul's Epistles made by Gerald Warre Cornish (who fell in action, I believe, in the first World War). It struck me as admirable and very useful. To imagine, however, that a modern translation can make St Paul's meaning clear is an exaggeration: what it can make clear is what the familiarity of the Authorised Version may disguise from us – the fact that St Paul is a difficult writer.

A modern translation makes it easier for us to get to grips with the thought of St Paul: it does not relieve us of the necessity of using our own minds, any more than can a translation of Kant's *Critique of Pure Reason*.

And if the translations of Paul in the *New English Bible* did not offend our taste with Boeotian absurdities similar to those in the translations of the Gospels (e.g. Paul 'formulated the charge' that Jews and Greeks alike are all under the power of sin) they might take a respectable place among modern translations.

I do not propose to prolong my inventory of verbal infelicities in the *New English Bible*. *The Times Literary Supplement* of March 24, 1961, had an excellent article on 'Language in the New Bible'; and the Trinitarian Bible Society has issued, as a leaflet, a useful list of specimens of bad taste, compiled by the Rev. Terence H. Brown and available at the price of one penny.

Translators' Aims

The instances I have given will suffice to prepare the way for an examination of the principles which the translators have set before themselves. These find their statement in the Introduction. I do not think that this Introduction has yet received enough attention.

According to the Introduction, the translators have set before themselves several aims: fidelity to what the author wrote; clarity; finer shades of idiom (than in the Authorised Version); to say in our own native idiom what they believed the author to be saying in his; and contemporaneity.

We are told that the language of the Authorised Version is 'even more definitely archaic, and less generally understood, than it was 80 years ago' (when the Revised Version was prepared) '*for the rate of change in English usage has accelerated*'.

I put this clause in italics, because it seems to me significant – and ominous. The English usage of 80 years ago, we are told, is out of date. And if the rate of change has accelerated, is it not likely to continue the acceleration? What is likely to be the fate of the *New English Bible* 80 years hence?

We are then told that for a version more modern than that of 1881 'an attempt should be made consistently to use the idiom of contemporary English to convey the meaning of the Greek'. This requirement of contemporaneity is emphasised at the end of the same paragraph: 'The present translators have been *enjoined* (italics mine) to replace Greek constructions and idioms by those of contemporary English.'

Change for Worse

No attempt is made to substantiate the assertion that the rate of change of English usage has accelerated, or to inform us in what respects English usage is changing. It does not seem to have occurred to the mind of the anonymous author of this Introduction that change can sometimes be for the worse, and that it is as much our business to attempt to arrest deterioration and combat corruption of our language, as to accept change.

Nor are we given any definition of 'contemporaneity'. Is it to be found in the writing of the best contemporary writers of English prose, and if so, who are they and who is to decide who they are? Or is it to be found in colloquial speech, and if so at what level of literacy?

Will the readers who find 'sweated all day in the blazing sun' suits them better than 'borne the burden and heat of the day' be the same as those who find 'extirpate' more 'contemporary' than 'destroy'?

When we turn to the description on the jacket we find that the aim was 'to be in style neither traditional nor modernistic'. If style is to be contemporary without being modernistic, the words 'contemporary' and 'modernistic' should be carefully defined.

For Whose Use?

At the time when the *New English Bible* was published, it seems that Dr Dodd appeared in a television programme and explained the purposes for which it was designed. As I did not hear him on that occasion, I quote from the article in *The Times Literary Supplement* to which I referred earlier:

> In a helpful television programme . . . Dr Dodd, the director of the enterprise, told viewers whom the new Bible was intended for: it was, he said, for people who do not go to church, for a rising generation less well educated than formerly in classical and literary traditions, and for churchgoers so well accustomed to the language of the Authorized Version that they may have come to find it soothing rather than meaningful.

So long as the *New English Bible* was used only for private reading, it would be merely a symptom of the decay of the English language in the middle of the 20th century. But the more it is adopted for religious services the more it will become an active agent of decadence.

There may be Ministers of the Gospel who do not realise that the music of the phrase, of the paragraph, of the period is an essential constituent of good English prose, and who fail to understand that the life of a reading of Gospel and Epistle in the liturgy is in this music of the spoken word.

The first appearance of the *New English Bible* in churches has, I believe, been in the reading of the Epistle for the day. Nothing will be gained, for the new version will be just as hard to grasp, when read in church, as the Authorised Version, and it will lack the verbal beauty of the Authorised Version.

To understand any version we must study it at home, or under direction. And if use of the *New English Bible* 'Letters' in churches is followed by adoption of the *New English Bible* Gospels, must we not look forward to the day when the Collects of Cranmer are revised for use in Anglican churches, to make them conform to 'contemporary English'?

It is good that those who aspire to write good English prose or verse should be prepared by the study of Greek and Latin. It would also be good if those who have the authority to translate a dead language could show understanding and appreciation of their own.

1963

[The Festival of Poetry]

Untitled message in the Souvenir Programme of the Festival of Poetry. *Festival of Poetry 1963 Director Patric Dickinson Souvenir Programme*, [9–10]. Signed in facsimile at the end. Publ. July 1963. Gallup B86.

For the last thirty-eight years I have been concerned with the publication of poetry, and during that time I have, I believe, acquired as much knowledge of the public for poetry, and of the market for the work of new poets, as anyone still active in the world of letters. Interest in poetry, and in the work of younger poets, is certainly more widespread than it was in the twenties. Poetry prizes get more attention, and, owing to the wireless as well as to public poetry readings, many more people have become accustomed to the sound of verse. But it remains true, that the number of people capable of appreciating the new and unusual – capable of distinguishing between the significant and the negligible – and, what is more, with confidence in their own taste – remains very small. The reputation of a poet spreads very slowly: a younger generation may never realise that some poet now famous is their eyes, may have waited for years before his work was known to more than a very small audience, and that it may have had to be fought for by a very few enthusiasts.

In the early stages a poet may have had the advantage of two supports: the 'little magazine' and the 'little publisher'. By the latter, I mean the small press which confines itself to the publication of new poets still unknown – the press which, owing perhaps to the devotion of one generous person, is on the lookout for new talent and is prepared to back it at a loss. Little magazines and little publishers come and go, but it would be a sad day when they vanished altogether. For the larger public capable of enjoying the work of young poets needs some assurance, not necessarily of notable success, but at least of the approval of critics in high places.

[10] It was with such reflections in mind that I welcomed the foundation of the Poetry Book Society and became one of its original directors. It is with such reflections in mind that, having taken no part in the conduct of the Society for some years, I am happy to associate myself with its Festival by attesting my enduring interest in the cause for which it was founded.

[*The Tower* by Hugo von Hofmannsthal]

Note on *The Tower* by Hugo von Hofmannsthal. *Hugo von Hofmannsthal Selected Plays and Libretti*, edited and introduced by Michael Hamburger, lxxiii–lxxiv. Signed '*T. S. ELIOT*' at the end. Publ. 29 Oct. 1963. Gallup B87.

The longest and much the most important single piece in the present collection is the difficult and little-known *The Tower*; and to this strange play I wish to call special attention. I doubt whether this play can be called a 'success', but if not, it is at least a failure grander and more impressive than many successes. In a postscript to an edition of the German text of the play,[1] Herr Gerhard Meyer-Sichting tells us that the poet spent nearly ten years – from 1918 to 1927, the last years of his life – in writing and rewriting this play. *The Tower* is written in prose; but here also I speak of Hofmannsthal as 'the poet', for the play is essentially poetic drama. I do not know whether it has ever been presented on the stage; but the latter part, with the episodes of the Gipsy and the King of the Children, becomes so phantasmagoric that one can only imagine its representation in terms of a dream-film such as Jean Cocteau might devise. The plot is suggested by Calderón's *Life is a Dream*; but Calderón's play is for Hofmannsthal hardly more than a point of departure; two plays could hardly be more different in spirit and intention than these of the Spaniard and the Austrian. Hofmannsthal was well practised in the craft of the theatre, and if *The Tower* is unplayable, we must attribute this not to failure of [lxxiv] skill but to the fact that what the author wished here to express exceeded the limits within which the man of the theatre must work. For the surface meaning, the real or apparent reason for human behaviour which must be immediately apprehensible by the audience if a play is to hold their interest, Hofmannsthal cares less and less as the play proceeds. He seems to have loaded this play, in symbolism which perhaps has more than one level of significance, with all the burden of his feelings about the catastrophe of the Europe to which he belonged, the Europe which went down in the wreck of empires between 1914 and 1918. As Herr Meyer-Sichting justly says, there is much in the play which cannot be 'understood', but only 'intuited'.[2] The play expresses not only the author's suffering during those years that remained to him, but also his ultimate Christian hope. I find it interesting to compare the message

---

1. *Der Turm* (Frankfurt a/M: S. Fischer Verlag, 1952).
2. He is speaking specifically of the episodes of the Gipsy and the King of the Children. His words are: 'beide Vorgänge sollten nicht "gedeutet" werden. Man kann sie nur ahnen, nicht "verstehen".' I give the quotation in full, as my 'intuit' is rather a free translation of *ahnen*.

of *The Tower*, so far as I have succeeded in grasping it, with that of the masterly essay which Paul Valéry wrote in 1919, called *La Crise de l'esprit*: an essay which, because so much of its prophecy has already come to pass, is more terrifying since the second World War than it was at the date of its first publication. Both men were poets; both had their formation and first practised their art in the world before 1914; both lived on – the French poet eighteen years after the death of the Austrian – into a waning civilisation. Perhaps the hope of the one and the despair of the other were each in its own realm justified.

[Obituary Notice for Louis MacNeice]

The Times, 5 Sept. 1963, 14. Headed 'Mr T. S. Eliot, O.M., writes:'. Gallup C672.

There is little that I can add to the encomiums of Louis MacNeice which have already appeared in the press, except the expression of my own grief and shock. The grief one must feel at the death of a poet of genius, younger than oneself, and the shock of his unexpected death just as my firm had ready for publication a new volume of his verse.

MacNeice was one of several brilliant poets who were up at Oxford at the same time, and whose names were at first always associated, but the difference between whose gifts shows more and more clearly with the lapse of time. MacNeice in particular stands apart. If the term 'poet's poet' means a poet whose virtuosity can be appreciated only by other poets, it may be applied to MacNeice. But if it were taken to imply that his work cannot be enjoyed by the larger public of poetry readers, the term would be misleading. He had the Irishman's unfailing ear for the music of verse, and he never published a line that is not good reading. I am very proud of having published the first volume he had to offer after coming down from the university.

As for the radio plays, no other poet, with the exception of the author of *Under Milk Wood*, has written works as haunting as MacNeice.

[Anti-Semitism in Russia]

To the Director of the 92nd Street Young Men's and Young Women's Hebrew Association.

Tradition: A Journal of Orthodox Jewish Thought, 5. 2 (Fall 1963), 317–18.
Originally submitted by Eliot for a pamphlet that remained unpublished.
Not in Gallup but would be C672a.

17 February 1953

Dear Dr Kolodney,

As one of the poets who have enjoyed the hospitality of the Poetry Center, I cannot fail to respond to your request of the 12th instant. But a mere expression of agreement with 'a public stand against the present anti-semitic policy of the Soviet Government' is not enough – for what decent individual could decline to support such a protest? One ought, I think, to say a little more than that.

[318] The only striking difference between the present anti-Semitism in Russia, and the anti-Semitism of Hitler's Germany, seems to me this: that the Russians have learned from the mistakes of the Germans, and are much shrewder propagandists. The Nazis persecuted Jews for being Jews, and thereby incurred at once the antipathy of all civilised people. The Russians refrain from any overt doctrine of racial superiority, which would too flatly contradict their supposed principles, and interfere with their foreign policy. Just as they have condemned and destroyed their more important Christian victims, not on the ground of their being Christians, but always on some pretext of treason or civil crime, so the Jews who are condemned to death – or worse – are condemned on some other ground, than that of being Jews. But it comes to the same thing in the end.

In all anti-Semitic movements there is a similar pattern of *policy* and *hysteria*. The hysteria of the crowd is aroused by deliberate calculations. But there is an element of hysteria in the calculation itself. True anti-Semitism – as distinguished from anti-Semitism in Arab countries, which has much more of the nature of ordinary racial, nationalistic and religious conflict – is a movement *within* a country, of a government against Jews who are its own citizens. It is a symptom of profound difficulty, disorder, and maladjustment in the economy and in the spiritual life of that nation; and is exploited by rulers as a desperate remedy which only aggravates, in the end, the malady of which it is a symptom. This reflection provides a more rational ground for the belief which I hold anyway, that any government which persecutes and stigmatises any body of its own nationals – and most notably the Jews – will in the end have to pay the full penalty for so doing; and the unfortunate people whom it rules will have to make expiation for having such a government.

Yours sincerely,
T. S. Eliot

Elizabethan Dramatists

Revised dedication page and Preface to *Essays on Elizabethan Drama* (1956 edn) in *Elizabethan Dramatists* (Dec. 1963).

Preface

ED, 5–8.

Revised from the Preface of the 1956 edn. In the opening sentence 're-read' has been altered to 'reread' (the form used twice in para. 2, and consistently in 1956).

1 Before choosing the essays which appear in this book, I naturally reread all of my published papers to which the title 'Elizabethan Dramatists' is applicable. At most of them I had not looked, I suspect, since their previous publication, and the result of this fresh examination surprised me.

2 Two of the essays were concerned with Shakespeare: *Shaskespeare and the Stoicism of Seneca* and *Hamlet and His Problems*. A third was entitled *Four Elizabethan Dramatists* with the somewhat pretentious subtitle 'Preface to an Unwritten Book'. All three of these essays on re-examination embarrassed me by their callowness, and by a facility of unqualified assertion which verges, here and there, on impudence. The *Hamlet*, of course, had been kept afloat all these years by the success of the phrase 'objective correlative' – a phrase which, I am now told, is not even my own but was first used by Washington Alston. These three essays were the first to be reread; and when I had read them I turned with trepidation to reread my essays on Shakespeare's contemporaries. I was astonished to find that these essays struck me as very good indeed.

3 What is the reason for my forming such different judgements on different essays? I believe that the explanation is at least partly to be found in the fact that Shakespeare is so much greater than any of his contemporaries. About Marlowe, or Ford, or even Ben Jonson, it is possible for a young man (and I was a very young man, [6] or an immature

youngish man, when I wrote these essays) to have something to say with which he will still find himself in agreement thirty years or more later. It may even be that a youthful sensibility is the most desirable qualification for writing about these minor poets and dramatists. Mature wisdom, and much experience of men and books, is perhaps unnecessary for the appreciation of their work. But, for the understanding of Shakespeare, a lifetime is not too long; and of Shakespeare, the development of one's opinions may be the measure of one's development in wisdom.

4 However this may be, I have rejected these three essays in compiling this book. Instead, I have included *Seneca in Elizabethan Translation*, which seems to me to deserve its place as the first essay in Elizabethan drama. Even in this essay there is a reference to Shakespeare which may be too confident: my opinion of *Titus Andronicus* remains unchanged, but I would not now assert with such assurance that Shakespeare had *no* hand in any play with which his name has been traditionally associated. However, my interest in this essay is only to vindicate Seneca from the charge of being responsible for the horrors of the Elizabethan and Jacobean theatre. And, like the other essays, *Seneca in Elizabethan Translation* contains some good quotations. And that perhaps is another reason why it is easier to write about the minor dramatists than about Shakespeare; an essay about one of them can be worth reading for the quotations alone. Quotations from Shakespeare are too well known; it is not enough to quote well; the critic must have something to say worth saying about his quotations from Shakespeare.

5 I call the attention of students of Elizabethan drama [7] to the fact that the date of each essay is given in the Table of Contents. This is a practice I like to observe in printing any collection of essays; but it is peculiarly important where the critical judgements may depend on the conclusions of current scholarship. It may well be that later scholarly research has disproved assumptions which I then accepted. On the other hand, if in discussing any dramatist I have ignored any work of scholarship with which I should have been acquainted when I wrote about him, I shall expect my criticism to be marked down accordingly.

6 On the whole, I think that these essays do provide a helpful introduction to the study of the poetic drama of the age of Elizabeth I and James I, and to the very interesting differentia of temperament and technique between the dramatists. There are two conspicuous omissions. I do not so much regret the absence of an essay on the work of John Webster: a great deal has been written on this subject, two of his plays are very well known and are from time to time performed, and I have alluded constantly to Webster in discussing other dramatists. But I very much

regret the fact that I did not, during that period of my life at which these essays were written, have occasion to write about the work of that very great poet and dramatist, George Chapman. It is too late now: to attempt to repair such a gap, after many years' neglect, would be almost as futile as to attempt to remove the blemishes (of which one is aware) in one's early poems. The most remarkable appreciation of Chapman in my time (works of scholarship apart) is to be found in *The Lion and the Fox* by Wyndham Lewis.

7 I owe a debt of gratitude to Charles Whibley, who [8] commissioned *Seneca in Elizabethan Translation* as an introduction to these translations in his Tudor Translation Series; and more than to anyone else to Sir Bruce Lyttelton Richmond, at whose behest seven of these nine essays were written for the *Times Literary Supplement*.

T.S.E.
June 1962

Variants from the 1956 edn

v No dedication in 1963] IN MEMORIAM | DONALD BRACE

1 When it was suggested that I should make, for inclusion in the Harvest series, a selection of essays from the selection of my essays published under the title of *Selected Essays*, my first thought was to reprint a small selection published many years ago in England, called *Elizabethan Essays*. With this aim in view, it seemed prudent to reread these essays, at most of which I had not looked, I suspect, since I read the proof for that book. The result was somewhat surprising.

4 essay in Elizabethan drama] "essay in Elizabethan drama"
['Even in this essay . . . Jacobean theatre':] [Not represented in *1956*.]
And, like] Like
the minor dramatists] minor Elizabethan and Jacobean drama
essay about one of them] essay
to say worth saying] worth saying

7 I have included one essay, that on John Marston, which was written just too late for inclusion in *Elizabethan Essays*. I have dedicated the present book to the friend and publisher who introduced *Selected Essays* to the American reader in 1932; but I should like to express a debt of gratitude also to the late Charles Whibley, who commissioned *Seneca in Elizabethan Translation* as an introduction in the Tudor Translation Series; and to Sir Bruce Lyttelton Richmond, at whose behest, when he was editor of *The Times Literary Supplement*, I wrote most of the essays on individual dramatists.

June 1962] *December 1955*

1964

Ulysses, Order, and Myth

Review of *Ulysses* by James Joyce (Shakespeare and Company, Paris), 1922.
Limited edn. Now with 1964 Postscript.

Originally publ. in *Dial*, 75. 5 (Nov. 1923), [480]-3. Signed 'T. S. Eliot'. Gallup C147.
In Jan. 1964 Eliot added the Postscript to accompany the reprinting as 'Myth and
Literary Criticism' in *The Modern Tradition: Backgrounds of Modern Literature*,
ed. Richard Ellmann and Charles Feidelson, Jr (1965), 661.

A hyphen has been removed from the title *Self Condemned* in the Postscript.

Mr Joyce's book has been out long enough for no more general expression of praise, or expostulation with its detractors, to be necessary; and it has not been out long enough for any attempt at a complete measurement of its place and significance to be possible. All that one can usefully do at this time, and it is a great deal to do, for such a book, is to elucidate any aspect of the book – and the number of aspects is indefinite – which has not yet been fixed. I hold this book to be the most important expression which the present age has found; it is a book to which we are all indebted, and from which none of us can escape. These are postulates for anything that I have to say about it, and I have no wish to waste the reader's time by elaborating my eulogies; it has given me all the surprise, delight, and terror that I can require, and I will leave it at that.

Amongst all the criticisms I have seen of the book, I have seen nothing – unless we except, in its way, M. Valery Larbaud's valuable paper which is rather an Introduction than a criticism – which seemed to me to appreciate the significance of the method employed – the parallel to the *Odyssey*, and the use of appropriate styles and symbols to each division. Yet one might expect this to be the first peculiarity to attract attention; but it has been treated as an amusing dodge, or scaffolding erected by the author for the purpose of disposing his realistic tale, of no interest in the completed structure. The criticism which Mr Aldington directed upon *Ulysses* several years ago seems to me to fail by this oversight – but, as Mr Aldington wrote before the complete work had appeared, fails more honourably than the attempts of those who had the whole book before them. Mr Aldington treated Mr Joyce as a prophet of chaos; and wailed at the flood of Dadaism which his prescient eye [481] saw bursting forth at the tap of the magician's rod. Of course, the influence which Mr Joyce's book may have is from my point of view an irrelevance. A very great book may have a very bad influence indeed; and a mediocre book may be in the event most salutary. The next generation is responsible for its own soul; a man of genius is responsible to his peers, not to a studio-full of uneducated and undisciplined coxcombs. Still, Mr Aldington's pathetic solicitude for the half-witted seems to me to carry certain implications about the nature of the book itself to which I cannot assent; and this is the important issue. He finds the book, if I understand him, to be an invitation to chaos, and an expression of feelings which are perverse, partial, and a distortion of reality. But unless I quote Mr Aldington's words I am likely to falsify. 'I say, moreover,' he says,[1] 'that when Mr Joyce, with his marvelous gifts, uses them to disgust us with mankind, he is doing something which is false and a libel on humanity.' It is somewhat similar to the opinion of the urbane Thackeray upon Swift. 'As for the moral, I think it horrible, shameful, unmanly, blasphemous: and giant and great as this Dean is, I say we should hoot him.' (This, of the conclusion of the 'Voyage to the Houyhnhnms' – which seems to me one of the greatest triumphs that the human soul has ever achieved. – It is true that Thackeray later pays Swift one of the finest tributes that a man has ever given or received: 'So great a man he seems to me that thinking of him is like thinking of an empire falling.' And Mr Aldington, in his time, is almost equally generous.)

Whether it is possible to libel humanity (in distinction to libel in the usual sense, which is libeling an individual or a group in contrast with the rest of humanity) is a question for philosophical societies to discuss; but of course if *Ulysses* were a 'libel' it would simply be a forged document, a powerful fraud, which would never have extracted from Mr Aldington a moment's attention. I do not wish to linger over this point: the interesting question is that begged by Mr Aldington when he refers to Mr Joyce's 'great *undisciplined* talent'.

I think that Mr Aldington and I are more or less agreed as to what we want in principle, and agreed to call it classicism. It is because of this agreement that I have chosen Mr Aldington to at-[482]tack on the present issue. We are agreed as to what we want, but not as to how to get it, or as to what contemporary writing exhibits a tendency in that direction. We agree, I hope, that 'classicism' is not an alternative to 'romanticism', as of political parties, Conservative and Liberal, Republican and Democrat, on a 'turn-the-rascals-out' platform. It is a goal toward which all good literature strives, so far as it is good, according to the possibilities of

---

1. *English Review*, April 1921.

its place and time. One can be 'classical', in a sense, by turning away from nine-tenths of the material which lies at hand, and selecting only mummified stuff from a museum – like some contemporary writers, about whom one could say some nasty things in this connexion, if it were worth while (Mr Aldington is not one of them). Or one can be classical in tendency by doing the best one can with the material at hand. The confusion springs from the fact that the term is applied to literature and to the whole complex of interests and modes of behaviour and society of which literature is a part; and it has not the same bearing in both applications. It is much easier to be a classicist in literary criticism than in creative art – because in criticism you are responsible only for what you want, and in creation you are responsible for what you can do with material which you must simply accept. And in this material I include the emotions and feelings of the writer himself, which, for that writer, are simply material which he must accept – not virtues to be enlarged or vices to be diminished. The question, then, about Mr Joyce, is: how much living material does he deal with, and how does he deal with it: deal with, not as a legislator or exhorter, but as an artist?

It is here that Mr Joyce's parallel use of the *Odyssey* has a great importance. It has the importance of a scientific discovery. No one else has built a novel upon such a foundation before: it has never before been necessary. I am not begging the question in calling *Ulysses* a 'novel'; and if you call it an epic it will not matter. If it is not a novel, that is simply because the novel is a form which will no longer serve; it is because the novel, instead of being a form, was simply the expression of an age which had not sufficiently lost all form to feel the need of something stricter. Mr Joyce has written one novel – the *Portrait*; Mr Wyndham Lewis has written one novel – *Tarr*. I do not suppose that either of them will ever write another 'novel'. The novel ended with [483] Flaubert and with James. It is, I think, because Mr Joyce and Mr Lewis, being 'in advance' of their time, felt a conscious or probably unconscious dissatisfaction with the form, that their novels are more formless than those of a dozen clever writers who are unaware of its obsolescence.

In using myth, in manipulating a continuous parallel between contemporaneity and antiquity, Mr Joyce is pursuing a method which others must pursue after him. They will not be imitators, any more than the scientist who uses the discoveries of an Einstein in pursuing his own, independent, further investigations. It is simply a way of controlling, of ordering, of giving a shape and a significance to the immense panorama of futility and anarchy which is contemporary history. It is a method already adumbrated by Mr Yeats, and of the need for which I believe Mr Yeats to have been the first contemporary to be conscious. It is a method for which the horoscope is auspicious. Psychology (such as it is, and whether our reaction to it be comic or serious), ethnology, and *The Golden Bough* have concurred to make possible what was impossible even a few years ago. Instead of narrative method, we may now use the mythical method. It is, I seriously believe, a step toward making the modern world possible for art, toward that order and form which Mr Aldington so earnestly desires. And only those who have won their own discipline in secret and without aid, in a world which offers very little assistance to that end, can be of any use in furthering this advance.

[Postscript]

In rereading, for the first time after many years, this expression of my critical opinion, I am unfavourably impressed by the overconfidence in my own views and the intemperance with which I expressed them. The sentence beginning 'the next generation is responsible for its own soul' strikes me as both pompous and silly. And Wyndham Lewis, before he died, wrote two books, *The Revenge for Love* and *Self Condemned*, which are not only far superior to *Tarr* but which are definitely 'novels'. To say that the novel ended with Flaubert and James was possibly an echo of Ezra Pound and is certainly absurd. To say that other writers must follow the procedure of *Ulysses* is equally absurd. But I disagree as much now as I did then with the words quoted from Mr Aldington writing in the *English Review* in 1921.

JANUARY 1964   T. S. E.

Knowledge and Experience in the Philosophy of F. H. Bradley

Knowledge and Experience in the Philosophy of F. H. Bradley was publ. on 31 Jan. 1964. Gallup A75.

Contents: 'Preface' by T.S.E.; I. 'On our Knowledge of Immediate Experience'; II. 'On the Distinction of "Real" and "Ideal"'; III. 'The Psychologist's Treatment of Knowledge'; IV. 'The Epistemologist's Theory of Knowledge'; V. 'The Epistemologist's Theory of Knowledge (continued)'; VI. 'Solipsism'; VII. 'Conclusion'; 'Notes'; Appendix I 'The Development of Leibniz's Monadism'; Appendix II 'Leibniz's Monadism and Bradley's Finite Centres'; 'Selected Bibliography' and 'Index' (both by Anne C. Bolgan, who edited the volume).

[7] TO MY WIFE
who urged me to publish
this essay

Preface

KEPB, 9–11.

From October 1911 until June 1914 I was a student in the Harvard Graduate School as a candidate for the degree of Doctor of Philosophy. This degree was to be attained in three stages: at the end of the second year by Preliminary Examinations in which one was tested in all the branches of philosophy which one had studied, and in the ability to translate French and German philosophical work into English; later by the presentation of a dissertation on a subject approved by the heads of the department; and finally a *viva*, in which the aspirant defended his thesis and was again tested for his command of logic, psychology and the history of philosophy.

The dissertation which is here published for the first time, was prepared during those years and during a year in which, thanks to the award of a Sheldon Travelling Fellowship by Harvard University, I was at Merton College as a pupil of Harold Joachim, the disciple of Bradley who was closest to the master. To Harold Joachim I owe a great deal: the discipline of a close study of the Greek text of the *Posterior Analytics*, and, through his criticism of my weekly papers, an understanding of what I wanted to say and of how to say it. On going down from Oxford in 1915 I made the decision to stay in England, and had to seek a source of livelihood. From the autumn of 1915 until the end of 1916 I earned my living as a schoolmaster. I did not, however, abandon immediately the intention of fulfilling the conditions for the doctor's degree. Harvard had made it possible for me to go to Oxford for a year; and this return at least I owed to Harvard. So, amongst my other labours, I completed the first draft of my dissertation, and despatched it across the Atlantic for the judgement of the Harvard Department of Philosophy. In April 1916, when this work was completed, I was a junior master at the Highgate Junior School.

[10] So much for the origins of this study of the theory of knowledge according to the philosophy of Francis Herbert Bradley. I did not return to Harvard to complete the requirements for the doctor's degree, and I did not see that University again for seventeen years after I had left it. Nor did I give any further thought to this dissertation after learning that it had been officially approved. A few years ago Professor Hugh Kenner of California in his book *The Invisible Poet* drew attention to it in a chapter on my debt to Bradley. My curiosity, however, was first stimulated by a visit from Professor Anne Bolgan of the University of Alaska, who had read the script in the Harvard University archives, and had obtained, with my permission, a photostatic copy. She had also seen there the carbon copy of a letter to me from Professor J. H. Woods written shortly after my dissertation had been presented, in which he said that Josiah Royce, the *doyen* of American philosophers, had spoken of it 'as the work of an expert'. Mr William Jackson, curator of the Houghton Library at Harvard, supplied me with a photostatic copy of the text (the original typescript being, of course, the property of the University).

To Professor Bolgan, who has made a close study of this essay, I am deeply indebted. She has read the present text and made important corrections and suggestions; she has most painstakingly edited the text. We have endeavoured, however, only to remove such errors and blemishes as appear to have been due to carelessness or haste. She has also checked my references (as far as is now possible) and has prepared a select bibliography, the index, and valuable notes.

I wish also to thank Mr Peter Heath of the University of St Andrews, for translating the passages quoted from German authors.

Forty-six years after my academic philosophising came to an end, I find myself unable to think in the terminology of this essay. Indeed, I do not pretend to understand it. As philosophising, it may appear to most modern philosophers to be quaintly antiquated. I can present this book only as a curiosity of biographical interest, which shows, as my wife observed at once, how closely [11] my own prose style was formed on that of Bradley and how little it has changed in all these years. It was she who urged me to publish it; and to her I dedicate it.

There is evidently a page or so missing from chapter VI: the gap occurs after the last sentence of the paragraph which here ends at the top of page 146. What may at first appear more serious is the loss of one or several pages of the conclusion of the essay. The last page of the typescript ends with an unfinished sentence: *For if all objectivity and all knowledge is relative. . . .* I have omitted this exasperating clause: it is suitable that a dissertation on the work of Francis Herbert Bradley should end with the words 'the Absolute'. Mr Jackson tells me that these pages were missing when the script came into his care. This does not seem to me to matter: the argument, for what it is worth, is there.

But at Professor Bolgan's suggestion I have appended, as partial compensation for the loss of the concluding page or pages, two essays which I wrote in 1916, and which appeared in *The Monist*, a philosophical periodical published in Chicago. It was Philip Jourdain, the British correspondent of that journal (to whom, I remember, I had been introduced by Bertrand Russell) who kindly commissioned these articles. They appeared in a number devoted to the celebration of the bi-centenary of the death of Leibniz.

The original title of this dissertation was *Experience and the Objects of Knowledge in the Philosophy of F . H. Bradley* with the sub-title *A thesis submitted in partial fulfilment of the requirements for candidates for the doctorate of philosophy in philosophy at Harvard University*.

T.S.E.

[15] Chapter I
On Our Knowledge of Immediate Experience
KEPB, 15–31.

It is not my intention in the present paper to cover the whole field of epistemology, or even to hint at the existence of many questions of which my subject seems to demand some discussion. The formation of general ideas, the theory of judgement and inference, probability and the validity of knowledge, fall outside the scope of my attempt. And the problem of error will seem to receive very slight treatment. In the present chapter I wish to take up Bradley's doctrine of 'immediate experience' as the starting point of knowledge. Then the rest of the essay will occupy itself with the development of subject and object out of immediate experience, with the question of independence, and with the precise meaning of the term 'objectivity'.

Bradley uses the term 'experience' and the term 'feeling' almost interchangeably, both in *Appearance* and in the essay 'On Our Knowledge of Immediate Experience'[1] which is the most important *locus* for my present

---

1. In *Essays on Truth and Reality* (referred to as *Truth and Reality* in subsequent notes). [Anne C. Bolgan's editorial endnotes are rendered as fns. and identified as hers, not

chapter. In the use of these terms we must observe the greatest caution. We must be on guard, in the first place, against identifying experience with consciousness, or against considering experience as the adjective of a subject. We must not confuse immediate experience with sensation, we must not think of it as a sort of panorama passing before a reviewer, and we must avoid thinking of it as the content or substance of a mind. And 'feeling' we must remember, is a term of very wide application, so that in some of its quite legitimate uses it is cer-[16]tainly not identical with 'experience'. We must accustom ourselves to 'feeling' which is not the feeling of psychologists, though it is in a way continuous with psychological feeling. And when we are told (*Appearance*, p. 406) that feeling is 'the immediate unity of a finite psychical centre' we are not to understand that feeling is merely the feeling *of* a mind or consciousness. 'It means for me, first, the general condition before distinctions and relations have been developed, and where as yet neither any subject nor object exists. And it means, in the second place, anything which is present at any stage of mental life, in so far as that is only present and simply is. In this latter sense we may say that everything actual, no matter what, must be felt; but we do not call it feeling except so far as we take it as failing to be more.' (*Appearance*, pp. 406–7.)

Keeping these quotations in mind, we turn at once to the words with which the whole theory is summed up in the essay to which I have referred. Experience, we are told, 'is not a stage which shows itself at the beginning and then disappears, but it remains at the bottom throughout as fundamental. And further, remaining, it contains in itself every development which in a sense transcends it. Nor does it merely contain all developments, but in its own way it acts as their judge.'[1] In these words we have expressed the whole difference between Bradley's view of experience and those of certain other contemporary philosophers. For, in the first place, immediate experience is not at any stage of consciousness merely a presentation which can be isolated from other elements also present or subsequent in consciousness. It is not 'sense-data' or sensations, it is not a stream of feeling which, as merely felt, is an attribute of the subject side only and must in some way be 'related' to an external world. And it is not, lastly, more pure or more immediate in the animal or the infant mind than in the mind of the mathematician engaged upon a problem. Whether there is a stage at which experience is merely immediate, Bradley says, we have agreed to leave doubtful. But here, I feel sure, he has understated his case, and we may assert positively that there is

Eliot's.]
1. Bradley, *Essays on Truth and Reality*, 161. [Bolgan.]

indeed no such stage. This point is worthy of some elucidation.

[17] We are forced, in building up our theory of knowledge, to postulate something given upon which knowledge is founded. And we are forced to a certain extent to consider this construction as something which takes place in time. We think, on the one hand, of material presented to our notice at every moment, and of the whole situation in knowing as a complex with this datum as one of the constituents. And we think also of the development of consciousness in biological evolution as a development of knowledge. And if there is any problem of knowledge at all, neither of these points of view is irrelevant. But we are apt to confuse the two: from the genetic point of view, all of the stages are actualities, whereas the various steps in knowing described in an actual piece of knowing in the mind of an adult man are abstractions, not known as separate objects of attention. They all exist at the same time; there is no priority in our experience of one element or another. When we turn to inspect a lower stage of mind, child or animal, or our own when it is least active, we do not find one or another of these elements into which we analyse the developed consciousness, but we find them all at a lower stage. We do not find feeling without thought, or presentation without reflection: we find both feeling and thought, presentation, redintegration and abstraction, all at a lower stage. And if this is the case, such study of primitive consciousness seems futile; for we find in our own knowing exactly the same constituents, in a clearer and more apprehensible form.

But on the other hand, if all the same constituents were present in every case of knowing, if none were omitted in error, or if none had any temporal precedence over another, all analyses of knowing would be equally tenable. There would be no practical difference: for when there are no bones, anybody can carve a goose. If we did not think that at some moments our consciousness is nearer to 'pure' experience than at others, if we did not think of 'sense-datum' as prior to 'object', if we did not feel that 'act' or 'content', or 'immanent' and 'transcendent' object were not as independent of each other, as capable of entering into different contexts as a table and a chair, the fact of their difference would be a perfect [18] example of useless knowledge. In the philosophy of Bradley we shall find this difficulty in an aggravated form, although a form no more fatal, I think, than the form which it may take in any other philosophy. There is immediate experience, contrasted with ideal construction; which is prior, and in some sense, certainly, prior in time, to the ideal construction. But we go on to find that no actual experience could be merely immediate, for if it were, we should certainly know nothing about it; and also that the line between the experienced, or the given, and the constructed can nowhere be clearly drawn. Then we discover that the difference in no instance holds good outside of a relative and fluctuating point of view. Experience alone is real, but everything can be experienced. And although immediate experience is the foundation and the goal of our knowing, yet no experience is only immediate. There is no absolute point of view from which real and ideal can be finally separated and labelled. All of our terms turn out to be unreal abstractions; but we can defend them, and give them a kind of reality and validity (the only validity which they can possess or can need) by showing that they express the theory of knowledge which is implicit in all our practical activity. And therefore we allow ourselves to hold both that a lower stage of mere feeling is irrelevant and that knowledge is based upon and developed out of feeling.

We may say, then, on turning our attention to lower levels of being, that what we find is not a subtraction, but a general impoverishment. The animal may be as Mr Bradley says 'immersed in practice'; but this is by no means the same thing as immersion in feeling. The animal acts; and any feeling which is acted upon so far goes beyond mere presentation. No stage can be so low as to be mere feeling; and on the other hand man surely feels more than the animal. There is no greater mistake than to think that feeling and thought are exclusive – that those beings which think most and best are not also those capable of the most feeling.

Although there is no stage of life which is more nearly immediate experience than another, and although we are unacquainted with any element in our experience which we can single out as immedi-[19]ate; although we cannot know immediate experience directly as an object, we can yet arrive at it by inference, and even conclude that it is the starting point of our knowing, since it is only in immediate experience that knowledge and its object are one. The fact that we can to a certain extent make an object of it, while at the same time it is not an object among others, not a term which can be in relation to anything else: this throws our explanation into the greatest embarrassment. We are forced to use terms drawn out of it, to handle it as an adjective of either subject or object side, as *my* experience, or as the experienced world. The monistic account is apt to take the first course, pluralism the second. But whether we say 'the world is my experience' or (James, *Essays in Radical Empiricism*, p. 27) that experience 'is made of *that*, of just what appears, of space, of intensity, of flatness, brownness, heaviness, or what not', we have been in either case guilty of importing meanings which hold good only *within* experience. We have no right, except in the most provisional way, to speak of *my* experience, since the I is a construction out of experience, an abstraction from it; and the *thats*, the browns and hards and flats, are equally ideal constructions from experience, as ideal as atoms. An *élan vital* or 'flux' is equally abstracted from experience, for it is only in departing from immediate experience that we are aware of such a process. In short, we can only discuss experience from one side and then from the other, correcting these partial views. This preface is necessary if we are to understand Bradley's use of such terms as 'feeling', 'psychical' or 'spiritual', all of which *seem* to emphasise the subject side of experience.

The real, we are told, is felt. 'To find reality we must betake ourselves to feeling. It is the real, which there appears which is the subject of all predicates.' We must be careful not to identify reality with feeling, either *my* feeling, or collective feeling, or an impersonal current of feeling. Feeling is to be taken (*Appearance*, p. 419) 'as a sort of confusion, and as a nebula which would grow distinct on closer scrutiny'. That of which it is a confusion, and into which it can be analysed, is (*Appearance*, p. 405) 'speaking broadly . . . two great modes, perception and thought on the [20] one side, and will and desire on the other side. Then there is the aesthetic attitude . . . and . . . pleasure and pain'. Feeling is 'the general state of the total soul not yet at all differentiated into any of the preceding special aspects'. And again it is 'any particular state so far as internally that has undistinguished unity'. Thus immediate experience seems to be in one aspect a condition of the conscious subject. The real appears in feeling, and feeling is 'the general state of the total soul' though we find elsewhere that the soul is itself not real. And even this statement does not tell us that feeling is reality, or even that feeling is real. Feeling is not (*Appearance*, p. 407) a 'consistent aspect of reality' although reality is that which we encounter in feeling or perception.

The reasons for denying that feeling is consistently real are briefly as follows. *Mere* feeling is something which could find no place in a world of objects. It is, in a sense, an abstraction from any actual situation. We have, or seem to have at the start a 'confusion' of feeling, out of which subject and object emerge. We stand before a beautiful painting, and if we are sufficiently carried away, our feeling is a whole which is not, in a sense, *our* feeling, since the painting, which is an object independent of us, is quite as truly a constituent as our consciousness or our soul. The feeling is neither here nor anywhere: the painting is in the room, and my 'feelings' about the picture are in my 'mind'. If this whole of feeling were complete and satisfactory it would not expand into object, and subject with feelings about the object; there would, in fact, be no consciousness. But in order that it should be feeling at all, it must be conscious, but so far as it is conscious it ceases to be merely feeling. Feeling therefore is an aspect, and an inconsistent aspect, in knowing; it is not a separate and isolable phase. On the one hand, feeling is an abstraction from anything actual; on the other hand the objects into which feeling is differentiated have a kind of union which they do not themselves account for; they fuse into each other and stand out upon a background which is merely felt, and from which they are continually requiring supplementation. In order that these developments – thought, will, pleasure and pain, objects – may be possible, feeling [21] must have been given; and when these developments have arrived, feeling has expanded and altered so as to include them. (*Truth and Reality*, p. 175: 'At every moment my state, whatever else it is, is a whole of which I am immediately aware. It is an experienced non-relational unity of many in one.') This is what we mean by saying that feeling is self-transcendent.

Now it is easy to fall into the error of imagining that this self-transcendence of feeling is an event only in the history of souls, and not in the history of the external world. It is hard to disabuse ourselves of the prejudice that feeling is something subjective and private, and that it affects only what feels, not what is felt. The reason for this is not far to seek. Feeling itself is properly speaking neither subjective nor objective, but its development into an articulate whole of terms and relations seems to affect the conscious subject, but not the objects of which the subject is conscious. I have the familiar sensation of red, which develops into a bull in a field; and this may well be an important event to me, affecting my course across the field, without making any impression upon the bull. The only reality which feelings can have, it is thought, is in a consciousness; we do not think of the external world as dependent upon feeling, unless we go so far as to say that it is dependent upon being felt – unless, that is, we think of it as the adjective of some transcendental self. On one side the history of the world is the history of my experience, on the other my experience itself is largely ideal, and requires the existence of much which falls outside of itself. Experience is certainly more real than anything else, but any experience demands reference to something real which lies outside of *that* experience.

We may express the difficulty briefly in this way. In feeling the subject and the object are one. The object becomes an object by its felt continuity with other feelings which fall outside of the finite centre, and the subject becomes a subject by its felt continuity with a core of feeling which is not related to the object. But the point at which a line may be drawn is always a question for partial and practical interests to decide. Everything, from one point of view, is subjective; and everything, from another point of [22] view, is objective; and there is no *absolute* point of view from which a decision may be pronounced. Hence any history of the process must be only relatively true: it must be a history of the object side, postulating the subject, or a history of the subject side, postulating the object side. For feeling, in which the two are one, has no history; it is, as such, outside of time altogether, inasmuch as there is no further point of view from which it can be inspected. In time, there are the two sides, subject and object, neither of which is really stable, independent, the measure of the other. In order to consider how the one came to be as it is, we are forced to attribute an artificial absoluteness to the other. We observe, first, the development of mind in an environment which *ex hypothesi* is not dependent upon mind; and second, in order to conceive the development of the world, in the science of geology, let us say, we have to present it as it would have looked had we, with *our* bodies and our nervous systems, been there to see it. To say that the world really was as we describe it, a million years ago, is a statement which overlooks the development of mind. To say that mind, in its beginnings in child or aborigine or animal, really was as we describe it, is to commit oneself to a relative truth of the same sort. In the same way in our theory of knowledge, when we leave the moment of immediate experience, we are forced to present our account either as the history of mind in its environment, or as the history of the world as it appears to mind.

What I have said is in defence of the use of the word 'feeling'. In describing immediate experience we must use terms which offer a surreptitious suggestion of subject or object. If we say presentation, we think of a subject to which the presentation is present as an object. And if we say feeling, we think of it as the feeling of a subject about an object. And this is only to make of feeling another kind of object, a kind of object which will be discussed in a later chapter. Nevertheless we can arrive at this metaphysical use of the term feeling in its psychological and current use, and show that 'feelings', which are real objects in a world of objects, are different from other objects, are feelings, because of their participation in the nature of feeling in this other sense. The feeling [23] which is an object is feeling shrunk and impoverished, though in a sense expanded and developed as well: shrunk because it is now the object of consciousness, narrower instead of wider than consciousness; expanded because in becoming an object it has developed relations which lead it beyond itself.

Although I speak of 'feelings' as shrunk and impoverished, I do not admit that every feeling was at any stage the whole content of consciousness. The majority of feelings have never succeeded in invading our minds to such an extent as completely to fill it; they have from first to last some objectivity. I do not mean that they are any the less intense for this, or that they disappear under attention. A toothache, or a violent passion, is not necessarily diminished by our knowledge of its causes, its character, its importance or insignificance. To say that one part of the mind suffers and another part reflects upon the suffering is perhaps to talk in fictions. But we know that those highly-organised beings who are able to objectify their passions, and as passive spectators to contemplate their joys and torments, are also those who suffer and enjoy the most keenly. And most of us are able to give a name to some of our feelings, to recognise in a vague way love and hate, envy and admiration, when they arise in our own minds. This naming of feelings, while it may give a very imperfect clue to their nature, is nevertheless of the greatest importance. It is obvious that we can no more explain a passion to a person who has never experienced it than we can explain light to the blind. But it should be obvious also that we can explain the passion equally well: it is no more 'subjective', because some persons have never experienced it, than light is subjective because the blind cannot see. We can explain it by its relations; by its effect upon the heart-beat, its toxic alterations of the system, by its effects in conduct and social intercourse. Without these relations, which give the feeling its whatness, the feeling could not be said to exist. Over and above all relations, it is true, the feeling must be a *that*, merely there; although strictly speaking not anywhere or at any time. But this aspect of mere existence does not distinguish feeling specifically from any other object. No object is exhausted [24] by its relations, and this aspect of mere existence, in all objects as well as feelings, is what we call immediate experience. This aspect of immediacy, of bare existence, is a character of even the most restricted feelings, though they may be at every moment the object of consciousness as well.

We find our feelings, accordingly, on the one side to be of the same nature as immediate experience, and on the other to present no radical difference from other objects. We do not call the furniture of our rooms 'feelings' (unless we mean the mere presence of appearances in our mind) and our ordinary speech declares that two people may share the same feeling as well as regard the same object. Yet we persist in believing that about feelings there is something private, that we cannot 'know' them from the outside; although we are compelled to admit that often an observer understands a feeling better than does the person who experiences it. So far as feelings are objects at all, they exist on the same footing as other objects: they are equally public, they are equally independent of consciousness, they are known and are themselves not knowing. And so far as feelings are merely felt, they are neither subjective nor objective. Let us assume, for the moment, that my experience may consist of one single feeling, and that there is one object before me which I either love or hate. Adhering to my own point of view, in which the feeling is *merely* felt (i.e., I am not conscious of it), the feeling cannot be subjective, for it cannot be said to exist at all. For whom will my feeling be subjective? For the dispassionate observer, who seeing the same object without the same feeling, subtracts my feeling from the object, to make of it a separate and independent entity existing in my mind. In other words, what is subjective is the whole world – the whole world as it is for me – which, because it is (for me) the whole world, cannot be contrasted with anything else 'objective'; and equally truly nothing is subjective. There is no reason, so long as the one feeling lasts and pervades consciousness, why I should cut off part of the total content and call it the object, reserving the rest to myself under the name of feeling. It is only in social behaviour, in the conflict and readjustment of finite centres, [25] that feelings and things are torn apart. And after this separation they leave dim and drifting edges, and tend to coalesce.

We must maintain, then, that in any cognition there is never more than a practical separation between the object and that which apprehends it. The object stands out, if you will, against a background of experience; and although it has relations which fall outside of our experience, it is likewise an abstraction from experience, continually capable of subtraction or addition. 'The object before me is unstable and it moves so as to satisfy me . . . I insist that in addition to other influences (whose working I admit), the object is moved also by that which is merely felt. There are connections of content now actually present in feeling, and these are able to jar with the object before me. And they are able further to correct that object by supplementation from themselves.'[1]

With the status of the feeling become objective I shall be occupied in a later chapter; it is here only necessary to insist on the validity of the continuous transition by which feeling becomes object and object becomes feeling. One important case of this transition is sense-deception. The resolution of contradictions of sense may be found in a process of assimilation of feeling to a new object, or in assimilation of object to feeling. In the case of the stick in water, for example, the real object for the psychologist may include not only the 'real' stick but an instance of refraction. That the object in the illusion is quite as real as the 'real' object is a truth to which the new realism has well called attention. The new object and the false, we may add, are continuous, and the new object has been constructed by adding to the old object elements which were first experienced and not contemplated.

We are not here concerned with the absolute objective criterion for the permanence and independence of any special class of objects; it is enough if we can make clear that we have no immediate distinction between object and feeling. It may accordingly be said that the real situation is an experience which can never be wholly defined as an object nor wholly

1. Bradley, *Essays on Truth and Reality*, 170. [Bolgan.]

enjoyed as a feeling, but in which any of the observed constituents may take on the one or the other aspect. The further question is this: to what extent can we [26] say that identity persists in such a change: to what extent may we say that the felt feeling and the observed feeling are the *same*? With the general question of identity we are not here concerned. But between the special case of identity of which I speak and identity in the usual sense there is a striking difference. The latter is identity of objects (points of attention). This case is not the identity of two feelings both objectified. It is the identity of something which is an object with something which is not. When the difference is noted the very statement of the question will I think provide the answer. There is, between the felt and the objectified feeling, a continuity which is not interrupted by any objective difference; and so far as there is no perceived difference we may assume the two to be the same.

This rather subtle question, which really belongs to a later part of the discussion, is worth some little detail here. In considering how far feeling may be an object (and may be known) we may ask whether our conclusions will have a bearing upon experimental psychology. We may say that if psychology sets up a sharp factual line of demarcation between processes and things, and yet proposes to investigate the former as objects of science, it is committed to a contradiction.[1] Introspection can give us only terms, and not processes. In the same way as the mathematical representation of motion is and is not the same as the motion represented, so the object in psychology is and is not the same as the process. And it is only when psychology pretends to deal with something more 'subjective' or more philosophic than the subject-matter of any other science that its pretensions lead it astray.

Yet to say that we have no knowledge of the process, of feeling and the transition from the merely felt to the objectified would be even more a vagary. The transition is not saltatory. It is neither wholly unconscious nor capricious, but is more or less a willed change. The attention to the feeling presupposes that there is such an object present, and that the attention has not manufactured the object (*Truth and Reality*, pp. 162 ff.). So that in [27] attending to a sensation or feeling any change of which we are aware besides the change felt in attending may be attributed to the sensation or feeling and held to be independent of the attention; and if we are aware of no other change than the attention, we may consider that any other change is meaningless.

The more fundamental aspect of the question, however, is this (*Truth and Reality*, p. 169):

---

1. See Joachim, *Mind* 69, January 1909, and G. E. Moore and Dawes Hicks in *Proc. Arist. Soc* 1909–10, on the subject-matter of psychology.

In any emotion one part of that emotion consists already of objects, of perceptions and ideas before my mind. And, the whole emotion being one, the special group of feeling is united with these objects before my mind, united with them integrally and directly though not objectively. . . . For when the object-part of our emotion is enlarged by further perception or idea, the agreement or disagreement with what is felt is not merely general and suffused, but is located through the object in one special felt group. And this special connexion and continuity with the object explains, I think, how we are able further to transform what is observed by the addition of elements from what is felt. There are features in feeling (this is the point) which already in a sense belong to and are one with their object, since the emotion contains and unites both its aspects.

The error, then, would consist in any sharp division between enjoyment and contemplation, either in general or at any particular moment, or in treating the distinction of feeling and object as a possible *scientific* distinction. Science may make the distinction between feeling of object and object of feeling, but it cannot make a distinction between feeling and object as such. And now we are in a better position to inquire into the situation (in order not to say relation) of feeling, thought and object in experience. It will be recognised, first, that experience is non-relational. Relations can hold only between terms, and these terms can exist only against the background of an experience which is not itself a term. The objectified feeling of psychology does not exist apart from the rest of feeling which is merely felt, no matter how negligible that rest of feeling may appear. But within experience we always find relations, and in this sense we may say that non-relational experience does not exist. These relations, however, are [28] not experience, and while they are experienced and therefore real, they are not real as relations. Yet, just as relations, they seem to be essential to reality. In this way a contradiction has 'broken out'. 'Feeling has a content, and this content is not consistent within itself. . . .'[1] This situation it is which prompts us to pass on by new construction to a larger felt whole in which the same puzzling terms and relations appear. No experience is self-consistent, because of the ideal aspects with which it is shot through. Yet these ideal aspects are likewise real, and themselves issue from a felt background.

We may now go on to consider the place of consciousness in experience. In order to understand Bradley's answer to this problem we must keep in mind two different and apparently contradictory aspects of the situation.

---

1. Bradley, *Appearance and Reality*, 407 [Bolgan].

Experience, we have been told, is not co-extensive with consciousness, but is wider. 'There is an immediate feeling, a knowing and being in one, with which knowledge begins' (*Truth and Reality*, p. 159). Feeling is more than either object or subject, since in a way it includes both. On the other hand, we must remember that the conscious subject, as a construction, falls partly outside of any whole of feeling. 'The finite content is necessarily determined from the outside.'[1] We must therefore expect to find consciousness to be both something immediately given and something which would not be in the immediate experience unless it also extended beyond it. Consciousness is not an entity, but an aspect, and an inconsistent aspect, of reality. Experience, we may assert, both begins and ends in something which is not conscious. And that this 'not conscious' is not what we call 'unconscious' should be sufficiently obvious. For what we term unconscious is simply an element *in* experience which arises in *contrast* to other elements in experience. It refers either to certain supposed mental entities which guide or influence our conscious actions. And I need not point out that this use of the term is of very doubtful value. Undoubtedly our mental life is directed by many influences of which we are not conscious, and undoubtedly there is no clear line to be drawn between that of which we are conscious and that which as 'feeling' [29] melts imperceptibly into a physiological background. But so far as this fringe is contrasted with that which is actually conscious, it is merely an object in our world like any other. And the 'unconscious' conceived merely as external objects is only the unfeeling; it is the other side of experience and not the whole. The unconscious, in short, denotes something within experience, as the conscious does, and neither of these terms will represent the whole.

At the beginning then consciousness and its object are one. So far we are in agreement with at least two schools of contemporary philosophy.[2] We can say with James (*Radical Empiricism*, p. 23) 'the instant field of the present is ... only virtually or potentially either subject or object'. Confining ourselves to this instant field (which we must remember is only an abstraction) we grant that no division can be found between an awareness and that of which it is aware. We cannot allow Mr Russell's supposition of a 'consciousness' which might merely exist for a moment and experience a sensation of red. The 'red' would simply be a 'neutral entity' which might be taken as mental or physical according to context, but where there is no context there is neither mental nor physical. What James calls the context is that of which Bradley speaks when he says that

1. Bradley, *Appearance and Reality*, 407. [Bolgan.]
2. And in opposition to Russell and Moore.

the finite content is 'determined from the outside'. This determination from the outside is unending. In the first place, there is my present physical constitution, which determines the experience without being an element in it, and there is my whole past, conceived either as the history of my body or as the sequence of my conscious experiences, so far as I can detach them from the objects in the experience, and consider them only as adjectives of myself. And secondly, there are the nature and the connections of the object, which fall outside of the present moment of experience, and are discovered on closer scrutiny. As we develop subject and object side, they seem to approximate independence, for the object is certainly independent of this knower, and the knower independent of any particular object: on the one side we get souls or selves, on the other the physical universe. That [30] objects are dependent upon consciousness, or consciousness upon objects, we most resolutely deny. Consciousness, we shall find, is reducible to relations between objects, and objects we shall find to be reducible to relations between different states of consciousness; and neither point of view is more nearly ultimate than the other. But if we attempt to put the world together again, after having divided it into consciousness and objects, we are condemned to failure. We cannot create experience out of entities which are independent of experience. Nor could we be conscious at all unless these ideal connections somehow entered into the experience, breaking up its immediate unity. Yet the original unity – the 'neutral entity' – though transcended, remains, and is never analysed away. In our perception of the red flower the original mere red, in which awareness and awared are one, persists.

We can assert much more than seems implied in the last sentence. It is not merely 'in my experience' that the moment of identity is essential. My existence is dependent upon my experience of red in the flower, and the existence of the flower is dependent upon its unity in feeling (as red) with me. Whatever relations the flower may afterwards be discovered to have, its nature must be such that its being under these conditions experienced as red will be essential to the whole account of it. The real flower, we can say, will be the sum of its effects – its actual effects upon other entities – and this sum must form a system, must somehow hang together. And if we attribute to the flower any other reality besides these effects, which are actual only in experiences, we are thrown back upon what it is for itself – i.e., upon its experience of itself. And here we only face the old difficulties of subject and object over again in the form of pan-psychism. To carry the problem to this point may be possible. Neither attacking nor defending the pan-psychist view, I consider it negligible. For if the existence of subject or object is always relative, then the point to which we elaborate this relativity is a matter of indifference.

Thus we are led to the conclusion that the only independent reality is immediate experience or feeling. And we have seen that [31] to think of feeling as subjective, as the mere adjective of a subject, is only a common prejudice. So far as it is feeling and nothing more, it is self-sufficient and demands no further supplementation. 'My' feeling is certainly in a sense mine. But this is because and in so far as I *am* the feeling. I do not in consequence know (in the sense of understand) my own feeling better than does an outsider. If it be objected that I must have a feeling in order to understand it, the same may be said of every other object in the world.

Immediate experience, we have seen, is a timeless unity which is not as such present either any*where* or to any*one*. It is only in the world of objects that we have time and space and selves. By the failure of any experience to be merely immediate, by its lack of harmony and cohesion, we find ourselves as conscious souls in a world of objects. We are led to the conception of an all-inclusive experience outside of which nothing shall fall. If anyone object that mere experience at the beginning and complete experience at the end are hypothetical limits, I can say not a word in refutation for this would be just the reverse side of what opinions I hold. And if anyone assert that immediate experience, at either the beginning or end of our journey, is annihilation and utter night, I cordially agree. That Mr Bradley himself would accept this interpretation of his (*Truth and Reality*, p. 188) 'positive non-distinguished non-relational whole' is not to be presumed. But the ultimate nature of the Absolute does not come within the scope of the present paper. It is with some of the intermediate steps that the following chapters are concerned.

Chapter II
On the Distinction of 'Real' and 'Ideal'
KEPB, 32–56.

The conclusion of the preceding chapter has been that reality as we may know it, the ultimate criterion which gives meaning to our judgements of existence, is so far as it appears at all, our experience, yet an experience which only to a certain extent – from a certain necessary but untenable point of view – is 'ours'. As a development and in support of this conclusion, we are driven to question the status of those elements within experience which exist only by virtue of their reference to other elements which are, in that reference, real, and we shall come to the conclusion that the apparently fundamental separation between the real and the ideal is but tentative and provisional, a moment in a process. This conclusion is nothing new; it is no novelty even in the essay which I shall chiefly quote, that on 'Floating Ideas and the Imaginary'[1] (*Mind,* October 1906); it is familiar to students of Hegel. I can only plead that I seem to find it constantly neglected or misinterpreted. Accordingly, after a general statement of the theory, I shall attempt to make the position clearer by criticism of such systems as would do without this theory, and shall try to show its full importance in the thought of Mr Bradley. Afterwards I shall attempt to point out some undeveloped consequences for the theory of objects, in regard to unreal and imaginary objects, 'intended' objects, and process (act) as object. The whole discussion, needless to say, is bound up very closely with that of perception and judgement, which will immediately follow.

[33] The theory, in its general terms, is stated in *Appearance,* Chapter XXIV.

> There is a view which takes, or attempts to take, sense-perception as the one known reality. And there is a view which endeavours, on the other side, to consider appearance in time as something indifferent .... We have seen that the separation of the real into idea and existence is a division admissible only within the world of appearance .... In order to be fact at all, each presentation must exhibit ideality .... But the union in all perception of thought with sense, the co-presence everywhere in all appearances of fact with ideality – this is the one foundation of truth.

And further, 'when an idea qualifies the universe, how can it be excluded from reality' (*Appearance,* pp. 334–5).

The ordinary view of the relation of real and ideal I take to be this. We are given in 'experience' something called fact which is real because independent, and independent because real. This fact is not necessarily fact of sense perception, or of physical reality, but the fact may be itself an idea from an external point of view, an idea placed in reality. And the objection that a fact is always an objective, and not simply a *that,* does not in the popular view militate against its independence. The fact may appear with its fullest development of definition, with innumerable stipulations of relationship, yet we 'apprehend' it as independent, and proceed to erect between it and its percipient an abstraction called thought, the existence of which is its reference to reality. And popular epistemology then asks us to accept the elaborated and sophisticated object as 'real', and yet to maintain the proviso that all the positive qualifications which make it just what it is are products of the 'activity of thought'. In other words, the popular theory of knowledge, from which

---

1. Reprinted in *Truth and Reality.*

our philosophies spring, is realistic and nominalistic at the same time. That this is a just description I think there will be little question; and whatever direction our solutions take, I doubt whether we ever wholly escape the crude antithesis.

Now there are several ways in which this difficulty is escaped or evaded. The simplest is that of sensation and thought, or, as in the Kantian philosophy, the distinction between an external reality [34] from which we receive material, and the formative activity of consciousness. This distinction – ultimately that between activity and passivity – will serve to classify a vast number of systems, both idealistic and realistic; for I am not satisfied merely that the distinction should be finally transcended, but wish to enquire into its validity as a starting point. So that a conational psychology such as that of Mr Alexander, or of Lipps – any psychology which deals with 'processes' as its subject-matter – will fall into a class with such an idealism as was recently advocated by Professor Adams.[1] And the second attitude is that of psychologists such as Stout, who would make a sharp distinction between content and object, and between psychical and physical object.[2] This I believe is the more usual attitude in psychology. And again there is the view of those who would reduce everything to object and immediate apprehension, reducing the 'activity' of thought to a minimum, as Meinong, Russell, or Miss Wodehouse.

These views it will be necessary to criticise, but without some elaboration of the point of view from which these criticisms will be made, what I have to say may appear inconsequent and negative. The common complaint, accordingly, lodged against all these views, is that it does not matter from what point of view or with what data you start, you will, if you do not stop arbitrarily, come to one conclusion; and whether or no psychology has the right to stop, whether psychology is independent of metaphysics, will be one of the questions involved. And, according to this view, activity and passivity, immediacy and mediation, acquaintance and description, will be transcended in the process of completion of our knowledge. In the words of Mr Bosanquet:[3] 'we shall ... meet, with uncompromising resistance, the attempt to take any form of immediateness, understood as excluding mediation, for an absolute and reliable datum, whether in the form of an object of simple apprehension, called by the name of fact, or in the form of an indeterminate creative impulse called by the name of life, or in [35] the form of a subject of experience, impervious and isolated, called by the name of "self"'.

1. *Philos. Rev.*, 1913.
2. See his controversy with Mr Joseph.
3. *Prin. of Indiv. and Value*, p. 13.

The first point to be made is that the difference between real and ideal is in a sense an ideal difference. It is created within a limited sphere of meaning and recognisable only within that sphere. If we would recognise a difference between reality and its attributes, we must have become aware of the fact of error, and of alterations of content in relation to the same intended object. We become aware that we have intended a reality, that we have, within our experience, delimited a field as real; that we have brought this field into relation with ourselves: and in error and in alterations of content we come to consider meaning as another reality beside that which it intends. This discovery must be qualified in two ways. First, the reality which we have intended is an ideal construction. It is not reality as a whole, but the radiation from a particular and indefinable point; a field of quite uncertain extent, assumed and selected. And second, the idea with which this reality is qualified is itself real, though of a reality which we cannot possibly define; for, though its existence as a fact is another thing from its meaning, yet its meaning is inextricably involved in its existence as a fact. The idea is something real, or it could not be even ideal; and on the other hand the reality to which it refers is an ideal reality, cut off, in a sense, and isolated; for the attribution of an idea to reality as such is not within our power. On the other hand, the reality intended tends to identify itself with the content of the idea; and on the other hand this content pretends to identify itself with reality. Without the ideal aspect of the real the distinction would be impossible. And unless the idea were itself real it would be unable to relate itself to reality.

But how, it will be said, will these statements be reconciled with the previous assertions that reality is experience? You have first defined reality as experience, and have then declared experience to be indefinable: you now pretend that we have always before us an ideal fragment which we call reality, and of which we predicate the ideal. Are not the two statements hopelessly at variance? If the [36] first statement about reality is true, how can the second reality be real in any sense; and have we not rather a wholly imaginary world of imaginary predications completely cut off, as far as our knowledge and acquaintance goes, from the reality upon which you have insisted?

In order to reply to this objection, in which the whole realistic position is implied, it will be necessary to dispose of a difficult prejudice. The real and the ideal (including the unreal) are not two separate groups of objects. Nor, as we shall see, can they be distinguished as object and 'process' or 'act'. Neither the absolute real nor the absolute ideal can as such enter into discourse; it is only when two entities 'take of each other', so to speak, that either of them can be real or ideal. Reality is simply that which is intended and the ideal is that which intends; and ultimately – for we have no reason to stop – the intending is the totality of intending, and the intended is the whole of reality. This whole of reality, of course, will as discussed present both real and ideal aspects; but this differentiation in what should be simple will fall outside of our metaphysics (*Appearance*, p. 352). It is inclusive with reference to our system, and that is all that we require.[1]

The division of real and ideal into two groups of objects is an action of a natural and inevitable tendency. As we shall later urge, an object is simply that to which we attend, and we cannot attend to process or idea without making it to that extent an object. But, just as no object is wholly object, so we can, by constant correction and discretion, to some degree handle idea without reducing it wholly to object. In the first place, we must remember that the distinction of real and ideal is one that does not arise until the ideal is recognised as having a reality of its own, apart (in a sense) from its meaning; and yet as preserving its identity in this new aspect. Without the '*Mitmensch*' (fellow man) and our introjection the question of ideality would never arise. It is easy to mistake the issue here, and to say that the idea is simply not recognised. We [37] can imagine a solitary autochthon, yet gifted with reason and, if you like, with some power of expression, making judgements, quite unaware of their ideal relation to the reality intended. And for this hermit, as a centre of experience, these judgements will simply not come into question – the question as to their existence will be one to which there is no answer, either affirmative or negative. And this is everywhere the case, that until the ideal is recognised as real, it is not even ideal. And I use the word 'recognise' with this in view: the idea as idea (as meaning) is neither existent nor nonexistent, and could we consistently keep to this internal view it would not be real. It will be said, I know, that the externality of the idea is implied in its internality. But this implication exists only for a point of view which contains both points of view.

With these considerations in mind, let us return to the discussion of the relation of Reality as subject, to reality as the fragment to which predicates are assigned.[2] In any case of judgement or perception something is assumed to be real, and this something is a background of

---

1. 'Wherever the idea can be merely *one aspect* [italics mine] of a single presentation, there we can say that the ideal content exists, and is an actual event.' *Appearance*, p. 352.

2. 'It would be impossible that any man should have a world, the various provinces of which were quite rationally connected, or appeared always in system. . . . He means, from time to time, by reality some one region of the Real, which habitually he fails to distinguish and define.' *Appearance*, p. 325.

indefinite extent continuous with the content which is asserted of it. The background has ideal characteristics which are rather felt than predicated, and which are capable of indefinite transmutation in a more and more inclusive view. This provisional reality has, on the one hand, the character of an ideal construction, for it is a sphere in which our ideal activity has been exercising itself; and on the other hand it is apart from the particular idea at the moment and under the aspect of predication. It is, in contrast with that idea, *accepted*; and the ideal aspect of it is for the occasion negligible, in contrast with the particular idea with which we are engaged. Thus, of course, an idea may justly be predicated of an ideal world; and our interpretation of the character of Ivanhoe may qualify the assumed reality of the story just as truly as the story itself, as a story, qualifies reality. The ideal world of the story qualifies reality – in what way, we are ultimately in ignorance – and [38] through this world our conception of the character of Ivanhoe is attached to reality. The question of imaginary and unreal objects belongs to a later part of the discussion. There is however one objection likely to be raised at this point, related to that question. The objection is this: the assertion that reality is always the subject is in apparent conflict with the fact of judgements in which reality is a predicate. In the judgement 'X is real' is reality the subject? The answer is this: In this judgement the subject is not a presentation which we call real or leave in the void. It is already largely placed and determined. It is already predicated of a world which has two spheres, and the question is: through which of the two it shall be related to the whole. The titular subject is already real, and the adjectival reality is only the assertion of one sphere in which it belongs. Yet in the course of the assertion the nature of the subject has altered. If the reality which we assert is the reality of ghosts, then the ghost as potential subject, previous to the judgement, is not the same ghost as that with which we emerge. The latter is a real ghost; and how can we say that the content of a real ghost is not different from that of an imagined or merely presented ghost? The subject, then, cannot have been the ghost, and the predicate cannot have been reality; for, on the one hand, the subject of a judgement cannot be altered by the judgement, and on the other hand, the predicate must add something to our knowledge – and we knew already that the ghost was in some sense real.

With the connection between the predication inside the proposition and the predication referring to the subject outside the judgement I shall be concerned later. I must call attention here, however, to the fact that the idea which is predicated of reality is not the content of a single word. The statement that ghosts are real is not, as we have seen, the predicating ghosts of reality. An idea is never given in a single word ('only in the sentence does the word first acquire actual life and being'[1]) when that word is an element in a judgement and not in itself the expression of a judgement. [39] The fact that words are always used in the expression of ideas, and are remembered and placed by attachment to a more or less indefinite group of ideas in which they have been used, may lead us to regard ideas as the meaning of words. Now there is a decided difference. ('The isolated substantive name lacks the positing therein of a subject, and hence it cannot be presented here, at the locus of perception, as a living source of multifarious activity. . . . It will be seen that the meanings of isolated words must be so presented, as if nothing in perception corresponded to them; they are founded purely on the articulate sounds we make, and in this alone possess a basis for their existence.'[2]) A word, it is true, may mean or stand for, an idea. But there will never obtain an identity between the meaning of the word as concept, and the meaning of the word as idea. As an idea it is predicated of reality, assigned a place in a system – more or less complete – which is assumed as real. But the concept – greenness, or triangularity – does not as such qualify reality at all. It is, in itself, neither real nor unreal. The meaning of a concept always exceeds the idea, and is of virtually indefinite extension. When we predicate the reality of ghosts, for example, we qualify reality, an ideal reality abstracted from the whole, by the idea of *real* ghosts; and this idea includes, on one side, much more than the word or concept ghost. The ghost conceived as real is a special kind of content with characteristics continuous with those of the fragment of reality in which he is set; the idea, from one point of view apart from the world and attached to it, yet contains already the character of the world, a world, as I said before, which shows by the very fact that that idea can be attached to it that it is somehow prepared for the reception of that idea.

In this way I make the distinction between concept and idea. [40] The idea is the total content which we mean about reality in any particular presentation. It is not purely or even primarily psychological, for its meaning is essential (and meaning, as I shall have occasion to consider later, does not as such form an object for psychology); and furthermore,

---

1. See Jerusalem, *Urteilsfunction*, p. 28: 'Das Wort, . . . gewinne erst im Satze wirkliches Leben und Sein. . . .' and *passim*, for relation of word to idea.

2. Gerber, *Sprache u. Erkennen*, pp. 102–3, is clear as to the unpresentability (*Unvorstellbarkeit*) of the word: 'Es fehlt dem isolierten nomen substantivum dies, dass in ihm ein Subjekt gesetzt ist, und so kann es nicht hier, an dem wahrgenommenen Orte vorgestellt werden als lebendige Quelle mehrfacher Thätigkeit, . . . Man sieht, dass die Bedeutungen der isolierten Wörter so vorgestellt werden müssen, wie ihnen in der Wahrnehmung nichts entspricht; sie gründen sich lediglich auf unsere Sprachlaute und haben nur an diesen den Boden für ihr Dasein.' – I fail to find, however, a clear distinction between concept and idea on the one hand, and idea and image on the other.

its meaning partially coincides with the reality which it intends. Nor is the idea purely a logical entity, since it always, in the end, comes to occupy a particular place in a real world. The concept, on the other hand, while it may in a sense – loosely, as I think – be called ideal, is not to be confounded with the ideality of the idea, and indeed in contrast with the idea had much better be called real.[1] The concept, in the first place, is extra-mental; it exceeds all actual and possible content, or definition. Nothing can secure you against the possibility that new experience may add to the meaning by extending the use. And properly speaking, a concept cannot be defined at all, for to define it is to restrict it to a definite circle of ideas. So far as it is thus identified with these ideas it ceases to be a concept; so far as it is present and practical, it is used to stand for a (not wholly definite) group of ideas. In this way we come mistakenly to identify the concept with one or several of its related ideas – to consider it as appearance as well as reality. And it is true that reality exists only through its appearances. It is only in some sense in ideas that concepts exist; and, in a sense, the pointing of the ideas at the concept constitutes the reality of the concept; its reality consists of the self-transcendence of ideas.

I am not confident that these definitions are valid ones, but they attempt to avoid Bradley's confusion of concepts with ideas, and Moore's confusion of ideas with concepts. Moore's criticisms of the passages in Bradley have however a certain force. 'Now to Mr [41] Bradley's argument that "the idea in judgment is the universal meaning" I have nothing to add.' But he says further, 'I shall in future use the term "concept" for what Mr Bradley calls a "universal meaning"; since the term "idea" is plainly full of ambiguities, whereas "concept" and its German equivalent *Begrijf* have been more nearly appropriated to the use in question.' This concept he substitutes for idea in such a use as the following: '. . . that the "idea used in judgment" is not a part of the content of our ideas, nor produced by any action of our minds, and that hence truth and falsehood are not dependent on the relation of *our* ideas to reality' where the idea used in judgement is properly an idea and not a concept.[2] Both Bradley

---

1. Professor Hoernlé ('Image, Idea, and Meaning,' p. 90) makes the following distinction between the real and the ideal: '1. In the first place, the contrast between idea and reality is taken to be a contrast between present reality and something which in some sense or another is "not present". Thus the past and the future are usually said to be "ideal" as against the reality of present experience; and again in volition we have the opposition between my present state and an idea of change, the "realization" of which would satisfy me. 2. Secondly, reality as contrasted with idea, is more particularly identified with sense perception.' – But I do not find this classification adequate; and it makes no place for the concept.

2. The three quotations here are from Moore, 'The Nature of Judgment', 177. [Bolgan.]

and Moore make but one distinction – that between a *psychical* idea and a *logical* idea. Russell (*Problems*, p. 99) makes a similar distinction: in 'the sense in which it denotes the *object* of an act of thought, whiteness is an "idea". Hence, if the ambiguity is not guarded against, we may come to think that whiteness is an "Idea" in the other sense, i.e. an act of thought; and thus we come to think that whiteness is mental.'

Bosanquet (*Essentials*, p. 74) hardly differs: '"Idea" has two principal meanings. *(a)* A psychical presentation and *(b)* An identical reference.'

It should be immediately evident that the idea in Bradley's judgement is a very different thing from the concept in Moore's. We do not in judgement, certainly, simply predicate of reality the content, or part of the content, of a so-called 'mental state'. So far we are all in accord. In 'Caesar crossed the Rubicon' the idea is just as 'external' as the reality of which it is predicated. But the idea in question is not a concept, but something of indefinite complexity. Caesar's crossing the Rubicon (the objective) has, as we consider it, elements which attach it more and more in one way or another to the real. The movement is not simply the movement of an idea toward reality; but the real comes to join itself, by presenting ideal aspects which are also real, to the self-realising idea. The idea was never at any moment of the process detached and 'floating'. In being an idea at all, it must mean to be real; it is [42] no more mental than the reality to which it is attached; its ideality consists in its meaning, and cannot be considered as a quality or mark by which it may be distinguished from the real. Hence, in the judgement above instanced the idea is the whole reality meant – and I shall try to show later, the whole meaning is ultimately the whole of reality.

It is at once apparent that neither of the definitions used by Bosanquet is adequate for idea in this sense. This is rather what idealists are accustomed to call 'ideal content'. Content is as equivocal a word as any, but I cannot see that any distinction is introduced by using 'ideal content' instead of idea. The idea predicated of reality is not part of any 'content'[1] nor is it composed of simpler ideas. It is meaningless, I think, to speak of the 'content' of the idea: is the content anything but the idea itself? For so far as the content is discrepant with the idea, I cannot see that it is the content of *that* idea.

There are here several issues:

1. the relation of idea to mental content
2. the relation of idea to image

---

1. Bosanquet, *Logic*, I, p. 44; 'I . . . shall follow Mr Bradley in using "idea" for a fixed content or logical meaning, not for the psychical images which pass through the mind and never recur. . . .'

3. the relation of idea to concept and speech
4. the relation of idea to identical reference

Let us consider the last question first. I wish to distinguish idea from 3 and from 4, and 3 and 4 from each other. Fixed reference is thus manipulated by Bosanquet (*Logic*, I, p. 69): '... the idea, as used in judgment, is a general signification, or in other words, a fixed reference. And because fixed, it is limited; limited to portions of content which serve as indices of the reference, and are compatible with psychical accompaniments that vary with the series of images.'

The essence of an idea, for Bosanquet, seems to be that it should refer to something (*Essentials*, p. 75: the identity which two people mean to mean when they say 'Saint Paul's Cathedral' is the idea). What, in this case, is the idea? It is hardly the actual [43] object meant – the object is that to which the idea refers. It is not the word or sound 'Cathedral', nor is it the intention of the two people to refer to the same thing; it is the fact of their reference to the same thing. And '... the content of this reference *is* the object of our thought.[1] Now the idea, in this sense, can hardly be the idea which is predicated of reality. It is (*Essentials*, pp. 78–9) a 'concrete habit or tendency', a 'selective rule', and again it is a thing ('mental unit or image') which stands for something else.[2]

The idea predicated of reality cannot be either a 'mental presentation' or a conation, nor can it be simply a meaning – for a meaning always means to be something more than a meaning. It is not certainly a compound of simpler elements. Bradley is clear on this point (*Logic*, p. 12):

> We may say ... that all (judgments) have but one (idea). We take an ideal content, a complex totality of qualities and relations, and we then introduce divisions and distinctions, and we call these products separate ideas with relations between them. And this is quite unobjectionable. But what is objectionable, is our then proceeding to deny that the whole before our mind is a single idea.... The relations between the ideas are themselves ideal.... And the whole in which they subsist is ideal, and so one idea.

There is here a fixed reference in the sense that the idea aims to be (though any expression one can use will remain a metaphor) a reality, and the latter, as real, is independent of its relations. The fixity of the

---

1. Bosanquet, *The Essentials of Logic*, 75. [Bolgan.]
2. Mr Bosanquet says (*Essentials*, p. 79) 'Mere mental facts, occurrences in my mental history, taken as such, cannot enter into judgment'. But I should ask whether the so-called mental facts are mental at all, and whether they do not enter into judgement just as do any other 'non-mental' facts.

reference is not the character of fixity of meaning which the words have in language, nor is its fixity due to a composition of these fixities. It is not as if I took a number of sentence elements which have each an identity of reference and compounded them into a whole which has an identity by virtue of the ingredient identities. The idea, though largely dependent for its existence upon the forms of its expression, must yet not be confused with these forms. The idea is that reality which I intend, and the identity is only the [44] assumption of *one* world; it is not the characteristic of it as idea, but as world.

The idea, and its predication of reality, may exist previous to the articulation of language. It is not true that language is simply a development of our ideas; it is a development of reality as well. The idea is developed from within, as language shows a richness of content and intricacy of connections which it assumes to have been really there, but which are as well an enrichment of the reality grasped. Wherever there is an appreciation of a presentation and a relating of it to the subject's world there is an idea and a judgement: and this is practically universal. The sea-anemone which accepts or rejects a proffered morsel is thereby relating an idea to the sea-anemone's world. The fixity is simply this reference to a definite place in the world – a world which is built up from the subject's point of view. This, for the subject, is the only world, but it is not a solipsistic world, for it is not contrasted with any other possible world.

These remarks have been directed against such an interpretation of Bosanquet's definition as would infer that the idea, as idea, detached from its reality, need mean the same thing for various subjects. 'Saint Paul's' might retain its full fixity of meaning for me if everyone else meant by the same term, let us say 'Notre-Dame'. There would, of course, be contradiction in my world which I should have to rectify in one way or another; but the social consilience goes toward the construction of our world and not toward the definition of idea.

It is in this sense, then, that idea involves identical reference. The inquiry brings us consequently to the relation of idea to its articulated content and to the concept. The idea in predication is not necessarily of definite extent; it may be extended or narrowed or analysed. We are familiar with the objection 'but you imply much more than this' – or 'but you mean no more than' – and sometimes are immediately aware of an expansion or contraction of our idea. And again the idea may be analysed into component ideas. In the example which Bradley has given (*Logic*, pp. 12–13) we may first have an idea *wolf-eating-lamb*, and from this we separ-[45]ate the ideas, let us say, of *wolf*, of *lamb*, and perhaps further, of *eating*. And this fact would at first seem to controvert what I have said, above (p. 38), for we seem to have an idea for each word. I should reiterate the distinction between word as concept and word as idea. There may be, in a sense, degrees of ideality and conceptuality. In all judgement, even of the simplest sort, there is involved recognition. The actual idea judged, it is true, is unique, or the judgement would not be made, but the judgement is made only through universal connections. In the cruder perception, *wolf-eating-lamb,* these connections are few and indistinct; in the developed knowledge we notice elements in this one idea which can be isolated through their relation to elements in other judgements, and which attain the status of ideas by bringing these relations with them to the particular case, so that the result is that a complex of connections is present in the particular perception or judgement, and besides being evoked by the idea, tends itself to become an idea and be judged about. And for this idea the one word (*wolf,* if you like) may stand. Yet it is a mutilation of connections to say that the one word stands for this 'idea'. For it does so only by virtue of its close connection with a number of more primary ideas. The *wolf* has become a reality perceived or judged, on a higher plane, as *wolf-eating-lamb* was in cruder knowledge; and this evolution of the idea can go on to the degree of abstraction upon which we find it practicable to live. This, then, is an idea 'of higher order', composed out of lower ideas and capable of entering as an ingredient in more particular ideas which are predicated of reality. The ideas of higher order are themselves less frequently predicated, for obvious reasons; their existence usually implies their assumption as ideal elements of reality (*Kraftcentra*). And these ideas of higher order, in their turn upon a higher plane, may be elements, rather felt than judged, in judgements of higher order, which in their own way are like the primitive judgements attributing a total situation to reality.[1]

[46] We have marked briefly the steps in the development of general ideas. And we find that the generality of an idea is a matter of degree; every perception involves some degree of recognition and the operation of a universal. Accordingly we must now ask, what is the difference between such a general idea and a concept? I define concept (see pp. 39–40) as that which a word denotes, and idea (or general idea) as that to which a word refers in reality, this reference being contingent. And a concept, as I have said (p. 40) is a thing-in-itself; it can be suggested, rather than defined, through more and more general ideas, but is at no point to be identified with these ideas. The concept it is of which the

---

1. These levels of idea and judgement correspond, of course, to the levels of experience referred to in the essay of Bradley, used above ('On Our Knowledge of Immediate Experience').

word is properly the sign or symbol. I am in partial agreement with Sigwart (I, p. 42): 'Words are generally held to be signs of Concepts. But a Concept in the logical sense is a work of art, produced by a conscious elaboration of our ideas in which its characteristics are analysed and its definition fixed, and it is the work of logic to help us to attain to the ideal state in which words represent such Concepts.' Of course I should be unwilling to admit that a concept is a 'work of art' or that it is in any way *created* by thought, or that greenness, triangularity, or to the right of, is '*produced by* a conscious elaboration of our ideas'. There is no meaning, so far as I can see, in saying either that the concept is created or that it is 'eternal'. In a sense, concepts are omnipresent, and in a sense, they are never known at all. We have, in the simplest case in which a concept appears, an intuitive knowledge of it (if one likes to talk of intuition), and on the other hand as I say, beyond intuitive 'knowledge' we know the concept only through ideas – through its appearances. And we must not confuse the development of the language with development in concepts; for it would, I think, be more apt to say that the development of language is the history of our exploration of the world of concepts. The goal of language is in this sense unattainable, for it is simply that of a complete vocabulary of concepts, each independent of the rest; and all of which, by their various combinations, would give complete and final knowledge – which would, of course, be knowledge without a knower.

[47] If this be true, how are we to estimate Mr Moore's assertion that 'a proposition is composed of concepts'? He accepts Bradley's statement that the idea in judgement is the universal meaning; but we have interpreted this universal meaning and Bosanquet's 'fixed' or 'identical' reference as an ideal reality in the form of universal connections; and not as the concept. Mr Moore postulates the ultimate vocabulary of which I have spoken. Once given this vocabulary of concepts, it would be quite true to say, as Moore does say (*Mind* 1899, p. 182), 'the world is formed of concepts. These are the only objects of knowledge. A thing becomes intelligible first when it is analysed into its constituent concepts.' For it is true that the concept is reality and the idea appearance, and I should almost agree that the concept is the only object of knowledge. But I defy Mr Moore to show a case of a concept which is actually known; and if he presents cases of such, I am certain that he has taken the shadow for the substance, the idea for the concept. It is true that existence (for which we substitute here *reality*) is itself a concept and true that we can define reality only by a reference to truth – for this only means that our only criterion for the degree of reality of a given appearance is the criterion of consistency and inclusiveness; it certainly does not mean that because

reality is a concept it is known. What collateral can Mr Moore put up on behalf of such 'knowledge'?

We have thus seen in what way an idea is an identical reference and in what way it is related to the concept: the idea may precede the articulate thought, and likewise the concept may be said as an existent to precede thought, although its existence is not known of until late in the development of language. I turn accordingly to consider the relation of idea to image and mental presentation, and to the aspect of idea as a mental sign or symbol. And here I find serious difficulties with Mr Bradley's views, difficulties which may be due to my own obtuseness, but in which I seem to find my objection supported by the objections of Mr Moore and Mr Hoernle. 'For logical purposes ideas are symbols, and they are nothing but symbols (*Logic*, p. 3).... A symbol has 1. existence; 2. content. By a sign we understand any sort of fact which is [48] used with a meaning. The meaning may be part of the original content, or it may have been discovered or even added by a further extension.... P. 4: A sign is any fact that has a meaning, and meaning consists of a part of the content, original or acquired, cut off, fixed by the mind, and considered apart from the existence of the sign.'[1]

In what sense is an idea a sign? This seems a most treacherous statement. A sign has its existence beside its content, and it is just this separate existence – the fact that the sign might be misinterpreted or simply not recognised as a sign at all, which makes it a sign and not an identity. Take some of the examples of sign which Bradley mentions. A flower may become the sign or symbol of an emotion; the fox is the symbol of cunning. The meaning of these signs consists in a 'part of the content (original let us concede in the case of the fox, acquired in the case of the flower) cut off and considered apart'. Now does an idea refer to reality as

---

1. Mr Eliot's quotations from pages 3 and 4 of Bradley's *The Principles of Logic* are slightly inaccurate and some connecting sentences which clarify the idea considerably have been omitted. The passage, with the relevant parts added, reads as follows:

> For logical purposes ideas are symbols, and they are nothing but symbols. And, at the risk of commonplace, before I go on, I must try to say what a symbol is.
>
> In all that is we can distinguish two sides, (i) existence and (ii) content. In other words we perceive both *that* it is and *what* it is. But in anything that is a symbol we have also a third side, its signification, or that which it means....
>
> But there is a class of facts which possess an other and additional third side. They have a meaning; and by a sign we understand any sort of fact which is used with a meaning. The meaning may be part of the original content, or it may have been discovered and even added by a further extension. Still this makes no difference. Take anything which can stand for anything else, and you have a sign. Beside its own private existence and content it has this third aspect.... A sign is any fact that has a meaning, and meaning consists of a part of the content (original or acquired), cut off, fixed by the mind, and considered apart from the existence of the sign. [Bolgan.]

fox refers to cunning? The quality to which the fox or the flower refers is something known or knowable otherwise than through the fox or the flower. And this is the case even when the sign is not fox in general, but as, let us say, when a withered flower is the sign of a particular moment in our history. The flower may be the only reminder we have of this moment, but it is in fact because of its essential heterogeneity with the event that it is able to replace itself and us with it, in the past. A flower may be the sign of an idea, but how can an idea be the *sign* of a reality? Such a view would surely lead us to a representational theory of knowledge.

The idea certainly has a sort of existence apart from the reality to which it refers, but the apartness is of a special sort and may easily be misunderstood. There may or may not be a mental content beside the meaning, but Mr Hoernle is certainly right in holding the meaning to be no part of this content (*op. cit.*, p. 74): 'We have nothing to qualify reality with except the contents of our minds, our imagery, which we "divorce" and "cut loose" from its existence in the mind so as to weave a garment for reality out of it.' The meaning is the idea, and the idea may be continuous with or in a sense dependent upon 'mental content', [49] but so far as it is idea, is distinct therefrom. We must ask then (1) in what way idea is not that which it means, and (2) in what way it is not the 'mental' images and conditions.

The contrast between meaning and reality is not so apparent when the reality intended is a present sense perception as in some other cases. In memory, for example, or anticipation, there may be the consciousness of an intended reality and of a present meaning which are not co-existent in time. The reality is there, and the 'mental state' here. And inasmuch as this present state may omit the greater part of what was present to the reality which is remembered, and may likewise add or distort, we are accustomed to form in imagination the notion of a perfect idea of the past experience identical in content with the experience itself, and differing only in that it is present as a memory instead of past as an experience. The effort of memory, in this case, would be to identify itself with the past experience, and the completion of the process would be hallucination. This I suppose is the natural view – based upon comparison of cases of greater and less success in recollection – but it is simply a tissue of contradiction. It assumes, in the first place, that memory is always of images, whereas it is frequently of objectives, which may tend, it is true, to reinstate the imaginal conditions of the experience, but which may be independent of these conditions both for appearance and for certitude. And it may assume in the second place, a reinstatement of objects in a way which implies a point of view which was never actual. What we attend to in perception is one group of objects; what we attend to in memory is a different group: not, as in perception, the object as in itself it really is, but its image. Not that there are two distinct entities, the object and its image – the difference is not one of physical objects, but of intended objects. In perception we intend the object; in recollection we intend a complex which is composed of image and feeling. We do not intend to remember simply the object, but the object as we remember it. And this new object is much more *the experience* than *the past object*, for we try to remember how we felt toward the past object.

[50] It will be said: this feeling-object which we intend is simply a moment in the reinstatement of the total situation, the consummation of which operation would be the presence of the object as object and of the feeling as feeling. To recall feeling we are often told, is merely to live it over; it cannot be known or remembered, but only felt. And to this objection we can retort that hallucination is not the satisfaction and consummation of memory, but its disease. And so far as the feeling is merely felt, so far as the situation is merely lived over again, it is not a case of memory at all. We are attempting to recall, let us say, a public address which we have heard. If memory were simply a restoration of the past, we might expect to recall first the words or fragment of the sentences which the speaker uttered, rather than the sense which we extracted therefrom. For these sounds which he uttered take precedence in time of the meaning; the meaning, to use Meinong's phrase, is a *zeitverteilter Gegenstand*, and the fact that we recall the meaning, in most cases, before we recall the actual words, would imply that the past presents itself in a different time-order than that of the objective time in which the events are held to have taken place. Now in most cases the meaning is what we want; if we had to live through the whole speech again to re-extract the meaning, we should find it very inconvenient. And the meaning can hardly be said to exist in time as the spoken words exist. Furthermore, the meaning intended in attention to the speaker is not the same as the meaning intended in recollection. In hearing we aim at the meaning of the speaker – in memory we aim at the meaning which we drew from his words. And the same distinction holds good, though it is less apparent, even with the speaker's words: for we intend in the one case the words as spoken, in relation to the speaker, and we intend in the other the words as we heard them. And the words in this aspect, were never an actual object of perception; they have their existence only in memory. The past which we aim at is the experience of an ideal individual, who should have been both internal and external to ourselves, who should have both known and experienced the past to which *in a very loose sense* our memory may be said to 'refer'.

[51] In short, it appears that the past in the sense in which it is supposed to be recalled, in popular psychology, simply never existed; the past lived

over is not memory, and the past remembered was never lived. But it will again be objected, if there is not a partial identity, and the possibility of degrees of identity, between the idea and an objective past reality, how is the idea to be distinguished from an idea of imagination? And it may be answered that there is an identity – not the sort of identity which we find between two objects, but that which can be found between two aspects. The past as lived and the past as remembered are in fact one and the same in intention, although in fact there is no reason to say either that they are the same or different. In order to make either statement, one would have to show a point of fact to which both refer, or one to which one refers and the other does not; and this identical viewpoint does not occur. You either live the past, and then it is present, or you remember it, and then it is not the same past as you once lived: the difference is not between two objects, but between two points of view. Two points of view may intend the same thing without there being any 'thing' which is the same. The sameness is a function of the two points of view. But there may, as we have seen, be a certain amount of discrepancy without any impeachment of memory, as when we 'remember' as the statement of a speaker what is actually a present inference from what we heard.[1]

[52] The identity in question is an ideal identity, a relation which exists only in relation with other (in fact, with all the other) identities in the series: it is an identity supported, if you like the phrase, by the will. You have a past experience and a present memory and, if these were all that existed, even they would not exist for they would constitute two utterly

---

1. My remarks on the memory-image are I think thoroughly in accord with the conclusions of Titchener; but for me differences are essential which for Titchener appear to be only accidental (*Text-book of Psychology*, Part II, pp. 418–19). 'Is it not something of a paradox that the memory-image should be thus variable and instable? At first thought, yes: because we are ready to accept, from popular psychology, the notion that an image is a memory-image of itself, in its own right; and if that were the case, the image must of necessity copy or reproduce the perception. On reflection, no: because the image is, after all, made into a memory-image by the feeling of familiarity. So there is no reason in the world why it should copy the original experience. All it has to do – if we may ourselves talk a popular psychology – is to mean that experience (the meaning is given as the context of associated ideas and attitude) and to be recognized as meaning it. Suppose for a moment that memory-images were just weaker copies of the earlier perceptions, and nothing less or more: our mental life would, so far as we can imagine it, be an inextricable confusion of photographically accurate records. It is, in reality, because the image breaks up, because nervous impressions are telescoped, short-circuited, inter-changed, suppressed, that memory, as we have memory, is at all possible. The remark has often been made that, if we did not forget, we could not remember. That is true. But we may go even farther and say that, if the mental image could not decay [cf. Hobbes] it could not either be the conscious vehicle of memory.'

My claim is that it is a bad metaphor to speak of the change from percept to memory-image as a decay. There is an alteration, not only in fullness and order, but in content. There are two essentially different points of view.

disparate worlds. But you have also an experience b and a memory B, and so on, and when you have the two alphabets given and only then you have some standard for comparison. The reference of each memory is not given separately, but you are, in a sense, given the whole series first. You cannot say simply 'A is identical with a', but you say 'A is identical with a, with regard to the identity of B with b' and vice versa.[1]

The idea, if the foregoing remarks have any cogency, is not a glass through which we descry a past reality, but the idea of a past reality is itself the object, an object which is not past in the sense of a past object of experience, and which is not present in the sense of a present object. It may appear a paradoxical statement, but it is not altogether untrue to say that the object of a memory is the memory itself: meaning only that we must distinguish between the object of the memory and the object of our attention when we remember. In memory, consequently, there is no more divorce between idea and reality than in any other kind of apprehension; the reality is our memory of a past experience, the idea is the reality in so far as we find the idea satisfactory; and when the idea fails to satisfy, we identify it with some other reality of memory or imagination. And the more or less figurative expression 'some other reality' must not mislead us: the operation consists simply in recognising the idea for what it already is. How much this qualification explains is a question which introduces us to the dangerous problem of error, and this problem I shall [53] have to postpone till I have gathered in several other floating embarrassments. I should like now to offer some remarks on the relation of idea and reality when the reality is an anticipated event and when it is an imaginary event or object.

It is obvious that an image located in the future cannot intend the real event, and the theory which possessed some plausibility in the case of memory cannot here apply. In remembering, we have seen, we have a memory which with respect to other memories refers to a particular reality. In the case of an idea located in the future, there is no such correspondence to be found, for the anticipated event may never realise itself. Ideas of anticipation, accordingly, occupy a place between ideas of memory and ideas of imagination. Such ideas may vary in two ways: in the degree of their realisation, and in the degree of their connection with the present. This connection, again, may vary in two ways: the idea may be associated with the present, and spring therefrom, either in virtue of its probability or in virtue of its interest. And here is a line of

---

1. In the original typescript, this sentence reads: 'You cannot say simply " is identical with a", but you say " is identical with a, with regard to the identity of B with b" and vice versa.' The sense, however, clearly requires the insertion of the capital letter A in the spaces left open and they have therefore been added to the 1916 text. [Bolgan.]

demarcation between anticipation and imagination: a purely imaginary event can never really be set in the future, for such a disposition of ideas implies a continuity with the real existence of the subject, and a 'future' which has not such continuity is no future at all, but might as well be called past. An author can imagine, if you like, what 'might' happen to his characters in the sequel, but such events are either such as the author can imagine himself making to happen, or such as he imagines the characters themselves as anticipating or such as he accepts or rejects. And if I present to myself the figure of a centaur or dryad as existing 'in the future', I do one of two things. I either throw myself direct into a visionary world, which I proceed to qualify by the term 'future', or I qualify present reality and the idea of centaur so as to make the latter to me a real possibility. And the imaginary here mentioned is not as future imaginary; it is the real future of an imaginary present. An anticipated idea, then, cannot be wholly imaginary, and on the other hand it cannot essentially refer to an event which becomes actual. These observations seem so obvious that I must apologise for offering them.

[54] As to the degree of realisation, it is not in principle involved. For we have seen that the degree of 'identity' between the memory and its intended real experience is not a question; and here, from the point of view of the idea, we are concerned only with possibility and interest. Though the difference of principle between ideas of the future and ideas of imagination is clear, yet the difference of fact is often hard to determine. We must of course consider an idea as possible, but we may so consider it with a greater or less degree of evidence, as we are moved by interest (including of course fear) or by knowledge: an idea which may appear to an outsider a pure imagination, possesses fatality for one crazed by fear or passion. It has frequently been said that we never desire what we think absolutely inapprehensible: it is however true that some of our sharpest agonies are those in which the object of desire is regarded as both possible and imaginary, in which in fact the *aspro martiro* is due to the irony of the contrast: the mistress exists as possessed in the real world of anticipation of the disappointed lover, while present reality is forcing itself in upon him with the conviction that this possession is imaginary. Images of future satisfaction to which we looked forward with confidence, we are constantly compelled to consign to the limbo of imagination; and we frequently forget that they were not imaginary in their genesis. The principle of the idea of anticipation, in short, I take to be this. The present as experience is as we have seen (Chapter I) indefinable and in this sense unknown, but its character, and ultimately its existence depend upon the internal qualification of real by ideal; and in this sense the present is ideal construction, and an ideal construction in which ideal

constructions of the past and future are integral. These ideas do not qualify a real past and future, for there is no real past or future for them to qualify; past and future are as such themselves ideal constructions. Ideas of the past are true, not by correspondence with a real past, but by their coherence with each other and ultimately with the present moment; an idea of the past is true, we have found, by virtue of relations among ideas. Similarly, an idea of the future is not applied to the real complex which shall [55] represent the realisation or falsification of this idea. The present of ideal construction, the present of meaning and not simply of psychical or physical process, is really a span which includes my present ideas of past and future. The reality of the future is a present reality, and it is this present future-reality of which our ideas of anticipation are predicated, and with which they are identified. 'She must weep or she will die' is a statement *not* about the *real future* (which would be a contradiction) but about the *real future*.[1] We are not to say that one of these ideas is realised and the other left floating 'like Mahomet's coffin'[2]; there is really but one idea, and that is predicated of a present future with which it is identical. The reality is immanent to the idea, or else the idea is not the idea of that reality.

If the last statement is true at all, it is true of the ideas of imagination as well as of any other. I shall state very briefly what I take to be the principle here involved, leaving the full discussion of the existence of unreal objects to a later chapter, in connection with the theories of Meinong. If I figure to myself the character of a personage of fiction, it is not true to say that there is no real object to which the idea means to 'correspond'. The distinction between real and unreal is practically useful but metaphysically baseless and indefensible. The character of fiction is imperfectly real because it is imperfectly ideal. And the round square, so far as it is idea (and I do not mean image) is also real. It is not unreal, for there is no reality to which it should correspond and does not. If there were to be such a reality, one would have to have an idea of it – and this idea which you call unreal is the only idea of it which you can present. The detailed discussion of this point I shall take up in connection with the problem of content, object, act, and presentation. The complete idea is the reality, and it is not until the idea realises itself, and thus becomes really ideal, that we can really trace its ideal connections. When the poet says

> I lived with shadows for my company

---

1. This sentence makes sense if we alter the final phrase to read: '. . . but about the present future.'
2. The phrase is Bradley's. See *Essays on Truth and Reality,* 40 [Bolgan].

she is announcing at once the defect and the superiority of the world she lived in. The defect, in that it was vaguer, less of an [56] idea, than the world of others; the superiority, in that the shadows pointed toward a reality, which, if it had been realised, would have been in some respects, higher type of reality than the ordinary world – compared to which the ordinary world would be less real, and which the ordinary world might be said to 'mean'.[1]

The question in what sense an idea is 'meaning', may now be resolved. I accept Bradley's definition of a judgement as the predication of an idea of reality, and I agree that this idea is one whole. And in the article to which I have frequently referred ('Floating Ideas') he has laid down the general doctrine of the relation of real and ideal. But I maintain that for metaphysical purposes at least (*Logic*, p. 3) the notion of idea as symbol is quite inadequate. An idea is not a symbol as a fox is of cunning, or an anchor of hope. You cannot so isolate existence and meaning, in the case of ideas. And to say that an idea is an identical reference is only partially true. There is however a sense in which it may be said that idea is meaning. We may say, in one way, that every idea means itself; its ideality consists in its 'pointing toward' its realisation, or (we have found it to be the same thing) toward its own idealisation. Hence an idea as contrasted with reality, is something which cannot be grasped – for it can only be described in terms of that reality – in which case you have the reality and not the idea; or it must be described in terms of some other reality – in which case it has lost its meaning, and is no longer the same idea. The existence of idea, then, in contrast with the real, is only in the process, eluding our pains; for as soon as you touch it, you find that the whole world resolves itself into ideas – or into reals. The idea is, as idea, Act; and how far Act can be made an object, together with its relation to content, presentation, and object (*Inhalt, Vorstellung*,[2] *Gegenstand*) will form the subject of the ensuing chapter.

---

1. Mr Eliot's meaning here is easily clarified if we read the passage as follows:

    The defect, in that it was vaguer, less of an idea, than the world of others; the superiority, in that the shadows pointed toward a reality, which, if it had been realized, would have been in some respects a higher type of reality than that of the ordinary world. Compared to it, the ordinary world would be less real, and that which the ordinary world might be said to 'mean'. [Bolgan.]

2. Should I apologise for the fact that my use of 'idea' does not correspond with that of any author with whom I am acquainted? I have tried to show in the foregoing that *idea* should not be used indifferently with *concept* or with *image,* and *presentation* has a rather different use from either.

Chapter III
The Psychologist's Treatment of Knowledge
KEPB, 57–83.

The conclusion derived from the two preceding sections has been that within the whole which is experience and is reality there is a distinction of real and ideal (within which is included the distinction of real and unreal): a distinction which turns out to be appearance and not real, inasmuch as the real is largely ideal, and the ideal is also real; a distinction, however, which in a sense supports reality.[1] For it is by this distinction that the word reality contains any meaning. We have found that reality is in a sense dependent upon thought, upon a relative point of view, for its existence; for ultimately the world is completely real or completely ideal, and ideality and reality turn out to be the same. And we found that the ideal can never be set over against the real absolutely, but tends to run, either forward or back, into the real which it intends, or the real out of which it may be said to be made: for both these reals are after all nothing but itself at another stage of development. It will be evident that the problem of error, in such a theory, becomes a very clamorous one. To approach this problem we must examine more narrowly the various moments of the process of apprehending an object: and inquire whether the distinction of real and ideal, as we have found its general principle, corresponds to the distinction of object and act, or of object and presentation. The nature of mental 'activity' and the operation of categories must be discussed. And the [58] question, much agitated in recent years[2] of the subject-matter of psychology, must be agitated again.

The distinction between real and ideal in psychology takes several forms. On the one hand, it may be said, is external reality, and on the other mental content, which is ideal in so far as it intends that reality and has reality of its own as well; and which, under the aspect of that reality of its own, can be studied by the psychologist. Or we may deny the possibility of a valid distinction between content and external reality, and distinguish only between object and act or conation. Or we may deny activity to consciousness altogether, and assemble existents in one complex or another. Or we may say that reality consists of elements

---

1. Mr Bradley does not commit himself to the assertion that non-relational experience is impossible, but it is implicit in his position. This, of course, is not in conflict with the other assertion that all experience is in the end non-relational.

2. I refer to the articles in *Mind* by Bradley, Prichard, Joseph, Stout, and Joachim; to the articles in the *Proc. Arist. Soc.* and in the *British Journal of Psychology* by Alexander; and articles in the *Proc. Arist. Soc.* by Stout, Hicks and Dumville. I shall also refer to writings of Meinong, Messer and Lipps (especially the latter's *Inhalt und Gegenstand*).

of sensation, the rest being ideal construction. Or there is the view of Mr Bradley, for whom everything is in a way psychical, and for whom therefore the distinction between object and act is not identical with that between an internal and an external reality but is reducible to the problem of knowing one's own mind.

The questions involved are these: in an act of apprehension is there a part which is strictly mental and a part which is strictly external? and even if the distinction can be made, can it be made sharply enough to give us a class of objects which can form a separate science, psychology? and the ultimate question is: is there a problem of the possibility of knowledge as well as that of the morphology and structure of knowledge?

There are two terms of psychology, which imply unexamined assumptions, and one of which at least has undergone the fire of recent realism: 'mental content', and 'psychical process'. The first is an assumption still of the majority of psychologists. The presentation of an external object may or may not 'agree' with that object, but in the cases where we assume a complete agreement or identity, the presentation is like a point at which the [59] circumferences of two circles are in contact: the one point may be taken twice over in two diverging contexts. Thus Miss Wodehouse declares (p. 13) that content has one context, while object has another. The one is continuous with mental history, the other with external or physical. And Witasek states the theory in a more extreme way (which Miss Wodehouse would probably not accept) when he says (p. 3): 'a stone die is hard and cold, grey and heavy and angular: the presentation thereof, the thought or memory of the die, has none of these characteristics, and cannot have them – it merely itself contains, over again, the presentation of hard and cold and so on. . . . My *inner picture* . . . of the tree . . . is known only to myself.'[1] Hofler is saying the same thing when he makes the distinction: 'Physical phenomena are presented as spatial, and indeed in extended fashion, as located at a place; all mental phenomena are *unspatial*.'[2] Stout (*Manual*, p. 58) says: 'If I perceive a triangle, my perception is not triangular – it is not made up of lines and angles.' And the same view is implied by Titchener, when he says (*Text-book*, p. 37): 'The psychologist seeks, first of all, to analyse *mental experience* [italics mine] into its simplest components.'

---

1. 'Ein steinerner Würfel ist hart und kalt, grau und schwer und eckig; die Vorstellung von ihm, der Gedanke, die Erinnerung an ihn, hat nichts von diesen Eigenschaften, und kann nichts davon haben – sie enthält nur selber wiederum die Vorstellung von hart und kalt und anderem. . . . [M]ein *inneres Bild* [italics mine] vom Baume . . . das kenne ich allein. . . .'

2. 'Physische Erscheinungen werden als räumlich und zwar, 1. als ausgedehnt, 2. als an einem Orte befindlich vorgestellt; alle psychische Erscheinungen sind *unräumlich*.'

This assumption that references or meanings can be handled in the same way as the objects to which they refer, an assumption which so far as I can find, it is hardly thought necessary to defend, is an assumption which I believe to have very slight foundation.[1]

[60] I wish to consider several typical instances of the theory, and point out the untenable postulates upon which it rests. I would then discuss certain ambiguities in the position of Mr Bradley in this matter, and sketch a theory which appears to me more consistent with his metaphysical views. And first I should like to offer a tentative definition of Fact. A fact, I would submit, is a point of attention which has only one aspect, or which can be treated under one aspect. A fact, then, is an ideal construction, and has its existence within a more or less variable sphere of practical or scientific interest. It is not a judgement simply, but an objective asserted ('it is a fact that'); it contains an internal judging and an external recognising of the validity of the judgement. Thus when I say 'Velasquez painted this portrait of Philip II' there is as yet no fact expressed; when I say 'it is a fact that V., etc.', or 'it is true that – ' or 'I know that – ' I am concerned with fact. There is a sphere of historical Reality which is taken for granted, a sphere existing in such a way that the judgement referred to must be either right or wrong, and this sphere we will call 'matter of fact'. And if this judgement is made upon the ground of internal evidence, there may be as well a sphere of aesthetic values taken for granted. Facts are not merely found in the world and laid together like bricks, but every fact has in a sense its place prepared for it before it arrives, and without the implication of a system in which it

---

1. As I am in this discussion particularly indebted to Mr Prichard I will ask permission to quote at some length from *Kant's Theory of Knowledge*, pp. 125-6: '[T]he tendency to think that the only object or, at least, the only direct object of the mind is something mental still requires explanation. It seems due to a tendency to treat self-consciousness as similar to consciousness of the world. When in reflection we turn our attention away from the world to the activity by which we come to know it, we tend to think of our knowledge of the world as a reality to be apprehended similar to the world which we apprehended prior to reflection. We thereby implicitly treat this knowledge as something which, like the world, merely *is* and is not the knowledge of any thing; in other words, we imply that, so far from being knowledge, i.e. the knowing of a reality, it is, precisely that which we distinguish from knowledge, viz. a reality to be known, although – since knowledge must be mental – we imply that it is a reality of the special kind called mental. But if the knowledge upon which we reflect is thus treated as consisting in a mental reality which merely *is*, it is implied that in this knowledge the world is not, at any rate directly, object of the mind, for *ex hypothesi* a reality which merely *is* and is not the knowledge of anything has no object . . . . The root of the mistake lies in the initial supposition – which, it may be noted, *seems to underlie the whole treatment of knowledge by empirical psychology* [italics mine] – that knowledge can be treated as a reality to be apprehended, in the way in which any reality which is not knowledge is a reality to be apprehended.'

belongs the fact is not a fact at all. The ideality essential to fact means a particular point of view, and means the exclusion of other aspects of the same point [61] of attention. There is a sense, then, in which any science – natural or social – is *a priori*: in that it satisfies the needs of a particular point of view, a point of view which may be said to be more original than any of the facts that are referred to that science. The development of a science would thus be rather organic than mechanical; there is a fitness of the various facts for each other, with that instinctive selection and exclusion which is a characteristic of human personality at its highest. Thus the character of a science, like the character of a man, may be said both to be already present at the moment of conception, and on the other hand to develop at every moment into something new and unforeseen. But it will have, from its crudest beginnings, a character to which (though it may belie all our verbal definitions) it will always remain consistent.

Accordingly we may well look, without seeking to formulate narrowly, for the traits of psychology's maturity in the features of infancy. And I have been unable to discover, in the first place, that any scientific individuality is possible as 'reference or meaning', or that you can conjure up one by the magic word 'presentation'. The presentation, I shall argue, is identical with the object from the point of view of the experiencing subject, and from this point of view you have, in metaphysics, no appeal. If we come to find anything more real (as common sense tells us that we must) our criterion will not be an arbitrary division of experience and an arbitrary neglect of the individual, but a theory of degrees of reality. And it is only this arbitrary division which gives us the puzzles of immanent and transcendent object, of unreal and imaginary.

'Whatever constituents of our total experience at any moment,' says Stout (*Manual*, p. 57), 'directly determine the nature of the object as it is perceived or thought of at that moment, belong to the cognitive side of our nature, and are called *presentations*.' I do not know in the first place exactly what limits Mr Stout feels justified in setting to the 'total experience at any moment'; for this definition would surely not exclude physiological process or logical category. Does he mean the 'content of consciousness'? But a so-called [62] content of consciousness is not, any more than the world of knowledge, a mere collection of entities in which being and being known is identical; so far as they refer to their objects they are not themselves known, and so far as they are made objects of knowledge they no longer refer to objects.[1] The sensation of red, as cognitive, is not a presentation, but awareness of a red object, an object which is not in any case mental. What do we mean when we turn our attention from a red

---

1. As has been ably pointed out by Mr Prichard and I believe by Professor Cook Wilson.

object to a sensation red? We are, I think, simply diverting attention from a variously determined object to a uniquely determined one. The so-called real object is in Mr Stout's words 'circumscribed and directed by a plexus of visual and other presentations'.[1] He should either say, I think, that the object *is* this plexus, or admit that even a single sensation circumscribes and directs an object. I cannot see why two or more sensations should give us the object when one does not. For Mr Stout admits that the object may really be presented. 'We may say, if we choose, that the object itself is *presented*, but we must not say that it is a presentation; and when we say that it is presented, it is better to say that it is presented *to* consciousness, than that it is presented *in* consciousness' (*An. Psych.*, I, p. 47). I fail to discern the difference; even if consciousness could have perceptions both outside and inside, I do not know how it would succeed in distinguishing one kind from the other. The difference is simply this: a 'red object' is an object which is otherwise known than by the quality red; it is an object which has been given a determined place in an order. The sensation is an object which has not yet thus been placed. It is incorrect, then, to say that we can have sensations of redness; redness is a concept; or to say that we have sensations of red. The sensation is of a red *something*, a red spot or area. And the discovery that the cause of the sensation is a pathological irritation does not affect the objectivity of the sensation in the least. The red 'that' was there, and the fact that the object cannot be further defined and verified does not make it any the less object.

[63] The distinction between object and presentation can be made, as we have seen, in another way: the perception of a triangle, says Stout, is not triangular; the idea of a stone, says Witasek, is not hard and grey. This statement I believe to be in a sense false, and in a sense mere juggling with words. You argue that because idea and object are different, the idea cannot have the physical qualities of the object, and the fact that the idea cannot have these qualities goes to show that there is an 'idea' different from the object. The confusion of course is between reference and existence: the idea is conceived to have an existence apart from its object. This existence, as I have attempted to show in the preceding chapter, is simply the fact of its reference. This fact (which is an objective) cannot be said to be triangular or grey (though it may be hard) – but the fact thus isolated is not the idea; the fact of the reference of the idea must not lead us to speak of the idea as a fact; the idea is only matter of fact. And indeed we may say that the idea is an *abstraction from itself* – for the whole idea is (and yet cannot be) the reality, the idea, and the fact of reference of the idea.

1. Stout, *A Manual of Psychology*, 60. [Bolgan.]

When we say, then[,] that the idea or the perception of a triangle is not triangular, we mean only the fatuity, that the fact of reference is not triangular. And as I have attempted to show in the preceding chapter, the idea (and the perception) is always in a sense identical with the reality which it intends. There can be for a perception, as we have seen, an indeterminate object; there can as well be a mistaken object, and in this way, when the same perception seems to be transferred from one object to another, we are tempted to say that the perception exists and is an object itself apart from any intended object. We have all had the experience of remarking a large bird in the distance, and discovering that it is a small insect a foot or two away. Here we say was a perception which has attached to two different objects. It is not so. There are two different perceptions, the second more consistent with a 'world', but no more closely attached to an object presented *to* consciousness than is the first. There cannot, that is, be a perception of an object if the object perceived is not really [64] there. And when you attempt to consider this 'presentation' apart from any prejudice as to the nature of reality you are committed to a contradiction. You must treat the perception either as an illusion or as true. Apart from one or the other of these two points of view the perception simply does not exist. Any attempt to separate percept from object merely doubles the object. A perception cannot be an object for psychology in the sense in which Mr Stout would have it, because it involves two irresoluble points of view.

I confess that I am confused rather than enlightened by Mr Stout's rejoinder to Mr Prichard (*Mind*, April 1907). He says: 'For Psychology, the *esse* of the facts with which it deals is *percipi* in the sense that it considers things only in so far as they are at any moment known, or in so far as they come to be known ... to an individual mind, and so enter into further relations both to the knowing mind, and to each other.' The fallacy of this statement, if I read it rightly, is as follows. The *esse* of no fact can be *percipi*. Now is psychology really considering 'things only in so far as they are at any moment known ... to an individual mind'? For so far as they are known to an individual mind they *are* simply, and that's an end of it. And if as psychologists, we inquire into the nature of things as known to another individual mind, we are doing much more than we think: we are abstracting from them one kind of reality which they had for this mind, and substituting therefor another kind – namely, their reality as related to this mind. In Mr Stout's well-known instance, the man enjoying a cigar, there are, following out his definition, three cigars present:

1. The cigar known to the smoker.
2. The (cigar known to the smoker) as known to the psychologist.
3. The cigar known to the psychologist, in the role of private citizen.

Now if we content ourselves with being psychologists and not epistemologists, we have no warrant for identifying these three cigars. And Mr Stout not only insists upon the different points of [65] view (the experiences of individual minds) but holds the inconsistent belief that psychology can exhibit the construction of the external world – that it can first abstract wholly from reality, and then piece reality together out of the abstractions.

Again, Mr Stout's beliefs in regard to the nature of sensations are far from clear. In the reply to Mr Prichard he says (*ibid.*, p. 241): 'What we [himself and Dr Ward] refer to when we speak of sensation is something apprehended as distinct from the act of apprehension.... Sensations ... are ... objects or, as Ward would say, "presentations".' This seems clear enough, though we may be disconcerted in referring back to the preceding page to find that a presentation, as the word is used by Dr Ward, is 'whatever is known *qua* known, whether directly or indirectly'. There is an ambiguity about the phrase 'known *qua* known'. It may mean: 1. from the point of view of the knower; 2. from the point of view of an observer regarding the knower in the act of knowing. Now on turning to Stout's article 'Are Presentations Mental or Physical? A Reply to Professor Alexander' (*Proc. Arist. Soc.*, 1908–9, a year later than the reply to Prichard), we find stated on page 245: 'Sensations ... cannot be merely objects if they are capable of entering into the constitution of properly subjective states.' And on page 246: 'Can Retentiveness be explained if presentations are Physical?' And referring to the *Manual*, we find that (p. 119) 'It is better to restrict the term *sensation* to the special form of consciousness which accompanies the actual operation of stimulus'. I do not know what a 'special form of consciousness' is; the phrase is at best hardly luminous. And when I find the author in one and the same article (*Mind*, p. 241, April 1907) stating that a sensation is an object, and later suggesting (*ibid.*, p. 242) that an (external) object may be made up of sensations, as a plant is of root, stem, leaves, etc., I conclude that I know neither what is sensation nor what is object.

The confusion results, I think, not so much from there not being several realities to correspond to the several terms, as from the use of terms in a plural marriage to mean several things indifferently: and to the fact that there are not distinct classes of *objects* to [66] correspond to the several (real) distinctions. The former difficulty is peculiar to Mr Stout; the latter is a general difficulty of the subject-matter, and is apparent in a psychologist of a very different school, Professor Alexander. Mr Alexander is equally certain that a field of the psychical may be sharply distinguished from the non-psychical, though he draws the line elsewhere. In several remarkable articles, and notably that 'On Sensations and Images' (*Proc. Arist. Soc.*, 1909–10) he has maintained a conational psychology. (*Proc. Arist. Soc.*, 1908–9): '. . . mind consists of conations, affection being treated as a modality of conation.' And in the article just cited: 'The sentience is mental, but it is held not to vary in quality. The *sensum*, which I shall commonly call sensation, is non-mental.' Similarly (p. 13): 'the imaging is mental, the image physical.' In the attention to a green object, the object of our attention 'may be merely the sensation green' (p. 1).[1]

In contrast to the theory of Mr Stout, such a view has manifest conveniences. It enables us, in the first place, to do away with the equivocal 'presentation' which we have found such a source of embarrassment. Where Stout vacillates between feeling and object, the two are here sharply discriminated. The difficulties of unreal objects, of presentations which present nothing, are apparently avoided. Yet I think that the ultimate objections are much the same after all. In the first place, consider the status of sensation. Mr Alexander appears to assume, like almost everybody else, that we may have a consciousness which is in the strictest sense the consciousness of a sensation, and of nothing else. I have argued (*supra*, p. 62) that a 'sensation of colour' is a loose expression for a perception of a coloured something, and when we think of a colour, it is of a thing not otherwise conditioned than by that colour that we think. Similarly, in the case of a cutaneous pain-sensation, it is of an object conditioned only by that pain-sensation that we think. The sensation, I maintain, is always a way of being conscious of an object, and as we become conscious of this consciousness, it may result in an added determination either of the object or of the self. Hence, on my view, a conscious-[67]ness of red is on the one hand a red consciousness and on the other hand the consciousness of a red object.

Otherwise, I think, Mr Alexander will find the same difficulty in constructing an object out of sensations as does Mr Stout. A sensation is certainly an object in the sense that it is the object to which it refers; but

---

1. The first sentence quoted from Alexander in this paragraph is from page 6 of 'Mental Activity in Willing and in Idea', whereas the remaining three quotations are from pages 7, 13, and 1 respectively of 'On Sensations and Images'. The first of these three quotations should begin with the sentence, 'I stated roundly that mind consisted of conations . . .', and the second, according to the original, should read as follows: 'The imaging of an external or physical thing is of course mental. What is here maintained is that the image itself is non-mental, or external, or I am prepared to say physical.' [Bolgan.]

when we are aware of an object, the sensations through which we come into contact with it do not persist alongside it as independent objects, as on the ultra-objective theory I should expect them to. We seem to find a fallacy which can be attacked thus: *The object of attention and the qualities or conditions of this object cannot be equally objective from the point of view for which they exist as such.*

In a sensation, that is, there are two verbal moments, the -ing and the -ed, which can be discriminated when together but cannot be treated apart. The evidence that they can be discriminated for certain practical purposes is simply this, that when we speak of a sensation, in our quotidian vocabulary we can with perfect propriety have *emphasis* on either the active or the objective aspect, never meaning wholly one or the other in isolation. Sensation-in-itself is in the language of Bradley 'feeling' or experience as more original than consciousness; but sensation in itself is not as such capable of being an object of attention (Chapter I). Sensation and perception, on the theory I have just outlined, are different in concept but in existence different only in degree. Sensation as known is always some degree of crude perception:[1] the moment we speak of 'having a sensation' we have stepped into the theory of knowledge, have posited a self and consequently an external world; it is still sensation, however, in that it is rather a feeling of a peculiar relation than a characterisation of either subject or object.

The situation of the separate sensations, then, with regard to the developed object, is this: the sensations cannot be objects on the same plane as the developed object, since it is to this object, and not as before, to themselves (as by the vagueness of their reference they may loosely be said to do) that they refer. They are the ways of being conscious – the *content* – of this object, [68] and in a sense the total experience may be said to be, on a higher plane, a fuller sensation of a remoter object (and so on). In other words, there is a constant transcendence of object into reference, and the absolutely objective is nowhere found. This, I think, furnishes a pertinent criticism of Mr Alexander. In a world so objective as that of Mr Alexander one cannot have a genuine object presented to one. ('On Sensation and Images', p. 15): 'Fully realise that perceiving a thing means that mind and the thing are together in the same sense as the table and the floor are together, and you understand that the imagination of the table means that the mind and the table are together; but the table in its imagined form, with imperfections and added elements.' I do not

---

1. The sense here requires the deletion of the word 'is' and the insertion of the word 'involves'. The sentence would then read: 'Sensation as known always involves some degree of crude perception.' [Bolgan.]

see how they can be together unless it is admitted that the object is only the compound of sensations – a position which may lead to Berkeley, and certainly leads to nominalism; (*Con. Psych.*, p. 253)[1]: '... a thing as perceived contains besides sensory elements other elements present to the mind only in ideal form.... But the ideal elements are themselves objective and non-mental. They exhibit their true relation to the sensory elements in the course of the perceptual process itself.' I do not think that we ought to say that a thing is made up of sensory elements and ideas, as a pastry is made up of the right ingredients and good cooking. I do not think that it is true that we can or do attend to both sorts of elements at the same time in the same way. It is true, if you like, that the ideal elements are non-mental, but their relation with the real elements is one of mutual reference and implication; and in a world composed solely of objects I can find no room for implication. The picture which certain masses of colour 'imply' is just as 'objective' as the colour-sensations, but not objective in the same way; the cognition of the picture means a transition to a different plane of reality. The colour-masses have thus transcended themselves, and ceased to be simply objects.

This introduces us to Mr Alexander's theory of the subject-matter of psychology. Over against sensation the properly mental element is conation. (*Con. Psych.*, p. 243): 'the subject, as given in enjoyment and therefore in the only form in which it enters into [69] psychology is nothing but the continuous tissue of its acts of conation or attention.' Psychology 'will describe how differently it *feels* or *is enjoyed* when we sense or perceive or will or the like.' Now my difficulty as I have already said, is in understanding what is left when you abstract from a mental state its reference; or what comes to the same thing, what reference is left when you have only the reference. 'In watching a ball which one is trying to catch, the perceptive conation whose object is the approaching ball is that complex of visual and anticipatory tactual conations which issue in movements of the eyes and more particularly of the hands' (*Con. Psych.*, p. 248). I cannot find anything here, once the non-mental or objective elements are abstracted, upon which I can lay my finger. I can see material for psycho-physics, but Mr Alexander insists that psycho-physics is a different field (*ibid.*, p. 248 ff.). I can only understand conation, so far as we may be said to be conscious of it at the moment, and Mr Alexander's conation goes far beyond this point, inasmuch as it is everywhere present – the subject in psychology is a 'continuous tissue' of its acts of conation.

---

1. This reference, as are all those to *Con. Psych.*, is to Alexander, 'Foundations and Sketch-plan of a Conational Psychology.' [Bolgan.]

There is no reason for regarding conation as ultimate even from a psychological point of view, unless we are ready to accept a psychology of faculty. And I can see no reason for making will more original than thought. (*ibid.*, p. 263): '... [T]he act of judgment is maintained to be literally an act of will.' The proposition which is the *cognitum* of the judgement is the object willed. It is as possible to state will in intellectual terms, and to say (what I do not believe to be any truer) that will is the self-realisation of an idea. The conation, I am ready to admit, exists, but only in a certain context: only with on one side a self to which the conation is attached (but which is never identified with that conation) and on the other side with a real world (real from the point of view of this self, which is all the reality required) which the conation intends. For in willing (and in desiring (Messer) which is another form of conation) some reality is already posited; and in desire the object desired is recognised as somehow real (Bradley). Thus it cannot be wholly true that (*ibid.*, p. 265) '... it is in willing that [70] objects ... become known *as* real. ...' And in this relation the conation ceases to be merely a conation.

I cannot help thinking that Mr Alexander's conation tends to find its full reality in physiological process, much as its author may himself deprecate this conclusion. 'There is,' he says (*ibid.*, p. 252), 'good reason for believing that these differences [in conation] are really of a spatial character, really are differences *of the locality and direction of the physiological processes* [italics mine] and that that locality and direction are actually enjoyed.' If what we 'enjoy' is the physiological process, then either this process is the object of the enjoyment – which is impossible, as the enjoyment refers to an entity of which we are conscious; or the process *is* the enjoyment – in which case nothing remains surely but to study the process itself. And the tendency toward physiology becomes still more natural if we mean to treat affections (*Proc. Arist. Soc.*, 1908–9, p. 6) 'as a modality of conation'. The necessity for so considering them appears only when we have made conation so substantial as to isolate it from the intended reality, and the consequence is to make the tertiary qualities aesthetic, and entirely subjective. Now I am prepared to argue that affections are just as objective *if* objectivity is to be absolute and not in any sense a matter of degree – as are sensations. Why should anger be any less objective than pain-sensation? Can we not contemplate our affections as well as our sensations? And if it be said that affections are essentially *wahrnehmungsflüchtig* (perceptually elusive), in contrast to sensation I reply that it appears to me everywhere a matter of degree. And finally I seem to discover that Mr Alexander, like Mr Stout, instead of recognising everywhere differences of degree, has erected sharp bounds and everywhere transgressed them. One of the bounds is this:

'we contemplate objects, we enjoy our states.'[1] We are then told that 'the fundamental fact of experience informs us that mind is but one thing together with external things . . .' and on the next page that panpsychism overlooks 'the fundamental difference of mind and things which is expressed by saying that the one is enjoyed and the others contemplated' ('The method of metaphysics', pp. 4 and 5).

[71] An equally interesting and more satisfactory demarcation of the field of psychology is that of Lipps (*Inhalt und Gegenstand*). In this essay, in which I find very little to question, Lipps makes the claim that things, and not merely sensations, are given to us. (p. 512): 'A person who sees things . . . is not seeing sensations, or presentations, or perceptions, or experiences. . . .' (p.513): '. . . sensation . . . is a determination of myself. . . . At the same time the sensing is . . . also, in a manner, a determination of (for example) the blue or red.' There is a relative distinction into 1. Myself; 2. My sensing; 3. That which is sensed, or the content of sensation. What we are conscious of is *object* (p. 520: 'To think something, or think of something, is to have something as an object');[2] an object which is conditioned by our knowledge of it, because it is *our* object; but which is real, and not mere *Erscheinung* (appearance) – which is, *qua* our object, independent of us. The sensation is at once a *Bestimmung* (determination) of the object and of the *Ich* (the self), a relation between the two which conditions whichever you direct your attention toward.

The *Ich* and its objects then form metaphysically one whole, a whole from which we can abstract in either direction. Qualities in relation to external points of attention give us the realities of practice and natural science; in relation to (*in Beziehung auf*) the *Ich* they give the subject-matter of psychology. Mental states, Lipps insists, have no independent existence: there are simply relations which in our reference constitute the external or objective and in another reference constitute the psychical. *Eigenschaften* (characteristics) in themselves are not objects, not capable of being made a point of attention; they can only be experienced with respect to a point of attention. While normative science – logic, ethics, aesthetics – is 'lyrisch', psychology is 'episch' – gives not *Ausdruck* (expression), but *Bericht* (report). Normative [72] science is the expression

---

1. The reference is to a passage from page 3 of Alexander, 'The Method of Metaphysics and the Categories' wherein he says: 'I propose to say that the mind is enjoyed and its objects contemplated.' [Bolgan.]

2. (p. 512) 'Wer Dinge sieht . . . sieht nicht Empfindungen oder Vorstellungen oder Perzeptionen oder experiences. . . .' (p. 513): '. . die Empfindung . . . eine Bestimmung meiner ist . . . Zugleich ist das Empfinden . . . in gewissem Sinne auch eine Bestimmung des Blau oder Rot. . . .' There is a relative distinction into: 1. Ich; 2. mein Empfinden; 3. das Empfundene oder der Empfindungsinhalt. What we are conscious of is *object* (p. 520: Etwas denken, an etwas denken, dies heisst etwas zum Gegenstande haben).

of the *ueberindividuelles Ich,* which is in a sense the realisation of the limited *Ich.* (p. 663): (The 'supra-individual self') 'is in us, but we are not identical with it. Indeed, so far as we are not, we *ought* to be so. This ought is the call, which is an expression both of the *presence* of this self in us, and of our own *limitations.*' As for empirical psychology, (p. 654)

> it does not, indeed, replace the processes in consciousness, which experience declares to 'belong' to the soul, by other conscious processes. But to the occurrence of such processes it adds a variety of determinations, which are of another nature, and so cannot figure in immediate experience: such as stimuli, associations, memory-traces, capacities, character-traits and dispositions. It thereby creates, upon causal principles, a world of the mentally or psychically real, which absolutely transcends, and is thus wholly beyond comparison with, what is given in the immediate experience of the self.[1]

This theory has a certain resemblance to that of Ward for whom the subject-matter of psychology does not consist in any particular group of entities, but in the 'whole choir of heaven and earth' from a certain point of view. But there are aspects of Lipps's theory which leads us toward the conclusion that this point of view does not exist. Can *Empfinden* (sensing) be turned inside out and applied to the *Ich* in the same way as to the thing? I am inclined to think that there is a confusion here. I cannot see why, on the ground of the threefold division *Ich – Empfinden – Empfundene* (self – sensing – sensed) and the characterisation, which seems to me admirable, of *Empfinden* as a *Bestimmung* (determina-[73]tion) of both *Ich* and object, any further determination of the status of sensation should be necessary. This one situation is that which it always occupies. I am not, in experience of a colour, treating the sensation as a qualification of the blue or red any more than of myself. However I express myself, I mean only that the sensation is there as a relation between myself and the object, a relation which is internal and goes to make up both self and object. And if you propose to detach this sensation any further from the

---

1. (The 'ueberindividuelles ich') 'ist in uns, aber wir sind es doch nicht. Eben, soweit wir es nicht sind, sollen wir es sein. Dies Sollen ist die Forderung; und diese ist der Ausdruck zugleich für das Dasein jenes Ich in uns, und für unsere Schranke.' As for empirical psychology (p. 654): 'Sie ersetzt freilich nicht die Bewusstseinserlebnisse, die nach Aussage jener Erfahrung an der Seele "haften", durch andere Bewusstseinserlebnisse. Aber sie fügt zu dem Haben Bewusstseinserlebnissen allerlei Bestimmungen, die nichts dergleichen sind, und darum in der unmittelbaren Erfahrung nicht vorkommen können. So die Reize, die Assoziationen, die Gedächtnispueren, die Anlagen, Charaktereigenschaften, Dispositionen. Sie baut so dem Kausalgesetze gemäss eine Welt des seelischen oder des psychischen Realen auf, die dem in der unmittelbaren Icherfahrung Gegebenen absolut transzendent, ja damit völlig unvergleichlich ist.'

object and make it a determination solely of the self, then you put it in an entirely false situation. Lipps has already said that the object is really given to us, and the *Ich* really given to us, and that the sensations are not separate objects which stand between us and the object. Now the aim of natural science, I suppose, is simply to dispose of the various appearances which are found to be determinations of the *Ich* and of the real object so far as they are found to have the relation to the subject which they were supposed to have only to the thing – or rather, so far as they are found to have relations and to be distinguishable in thought from the thing. The goal of science, consequently, would be a system of terms in relation, of terms the nature of each of which would be constituted by its place in the system; which would be completely definable by their position, and which would have no characteristics which could be isolated from the system. Every empirical discipline, of course, uses terms the explanation of which would fall outside of that system in which they are explanatory; terms which we require a fresh point of view to analyse.

The attitude of science, then, involves the constitution of a larger and larger limbo of appearance – a larger field of reality which is referred to the subjective side of experience. Economics is appearance for the biologist, biology for the chemist. Similarly, social psychology is appearance to the individual psychologist. It is when we ask what the simple terms of individual psychology are that I am at a loss.

For the relation of appearances (the appearances which condition both self and object) to an ultimate external reality is not the province of any one science to decide, inasmuch as fields of [74] discourse are objective or subjective in different contexts, and as things are non-mental in various ways, so they can be mental in various ways, and if the subject-matter of psychology is to be appearance in relation to the self, we have not one science, but a whole universe of sciences, corresponding to the self as found expressed in the structure of social civilisation, in its works of science, in the laws of thought, in image or in sensation.

I think, then, that Lipps has been deceived into conclusions which are inconsistent with his own admirable division of mental and physical, by the tacit assumption that in the sciences other than psychology we abstract from the psychical aspect. The psychical aspect, he has shown himself, is always present: wherever there is the *Ich*, there is a continuity between the *Ich* and its object; not only in the case of perception, but in every case of knowledge. In science we have only abstracted from *one or several spheres of mental reality* – and from physical reality at the same time. We have then done in every science what Lipps asks us to do specially in the case of psychology – considered a field of reality as a condition and expression of the self.

What, if this be true, has Lipps in mind as the field of psychology? Simply, I think, the old chimera, 'states of consciousness', meanings torn from their reference. You have first a mind essentially related to a world. In order to study the mind, you abstract it from the world – but abstract the world with it, and double the world to get a *real* world. You then assert that the first world simply exists as presentation, and that reference is to *your* world, and not to the subject's. And all this comes from the fallacy of treating a difference of aspects as a difference of things.

We meet, however[,] with definitions which make no distinction between mental and non-mental. Thus Miss Wodehouse's (p. 13) content is as objective as object; psychology does not expand the contents of the object but limits them 'because it is interested in their shape' (p. 20). This is an important, and radically different, definition, of the subject-matter of psychology; the external world and the mental world are of exactly the same stuff, and are *ultimately identical, but as experienced are both fragments.* [75] The world examined by the psychologist is the world which is the content of consciousness in relation to the various elements in the constitution of the subject which condition it; and these elements, I should suppose, may be either that part of the external world which has previously been content of that consciousness, or the physiological and psycho-physical conditions. On the one hand the content is continuous with the whole external universe (p. 21) and on the other hand with the history of that subject. In the latter relation it is the subject-matter of psychology: psychology, accordingly, deals rather with the personal than with the 'psychical'.

This division would seem to give us two clear groups of objects. But I am not convinced that the connections of content may not be reduced to connections of the real world on the one hand and to physiological connections on the other. Memory content must be considered as connected according to the reality remembered and *in the same way as the reality remembered*: that is, the laws which hold of the reality hold of the memory connections in their reference; the laws of the physical world hold of ideas of that world so far as those ideas are real ideas. And so far as those ideas are not real, as from being a specification they are merely a tendency, and from a tendency merely an undifferentiated feeling, the idea is dissolved into physiological conditions. So far as the idea is real, we have seen above, it is not idea; and so far as it is not real it is not idea. This is equally true of ideas of imagination or of ideas of memory. It is not true that the ideas of a great poet are in any sense arbitrary: certainly in the sense in which imagination is capricious, the ideas of a lunatic or an imbecile are more 'imaginative' than those of a poet. In really great imaginative work the connections are felt to be bound by as logical necessity as any connections to be found anywhere; the apparent irrelevance is due to the fact that terms are used with more or other than their normal meaning, and to those who do not thoroughly penetrate their significance the relation between the aesthetic expansion and the objects expressed is not visible.

But it is no wise true that the connections of content are [76] subjective and peculiarly subject-matter for psychology. They are personal if you like, but a work of imagination is never simply personal. So far as we consider it as *only* personal – i.e. significant only to the author – we explain it not as imagination but as the product of pathological conditions. Thus we are tempted to explain a poem of Mallarmé as we explain dreams, as due to morbid physiological activity. And if it is said that this radical separation would do away with all criticism, we may point out that criticism – involving the circumstances under which a work was produced – is other than psychology in that it includes at every point a reference to a real world with which the other is compared: a procedure which in psychology is inadmissible.

It is sufficient for the purpose of this chapter to have argued that a 'psychological event' can not be torn from its context and be set in a context of other purely psychological events: the problem of the relation of an idea to the real world from the point of view of epistemology must be taken up later. The theory of the idea which I have proposed, and which I believe to be substantially in harmony with Mr Bradley's metaphysics, implies to this point only that the idea, as you try to grasp it as an object, either identifies itself with the reality or melts back in the other direction into a different reality, the reality of its physiological basis. Ideas in relation with the nervous system on the one hand, and with the intended reality on the other, may have a certain existence in epistemology, but have no pretension to a purely 'psychological' existence. And here I find myself in conflict with much that Mr Bradley has had to say on the subject of psychology, especially in his articles on Active Attention, on the Definition of Will, and on a Defence of Phenomenalism in Psychology.[1] The first two articles are explanatory – they substitute for data of immediacy universal connections; we may therefore inquire what these data are. The last article defends a view very similar to those which I have been attacking.

'Psychology,' says Bradley (p. 28),[2] 'is to be concerned with psychical events, and such an event is whatever is immediately experienced, either as

---

1. All three of these articles have been reprinted in Bradley's *Collected Essays*, volume II. For the reader's convenience, therefore, Mr Eliot's references have been transposed to this more generally used and easily accessible volume. [Bolgan.]

2. *Collected Essays* II, 366. [Bolgan.]

a whole or as an integral aspect of a whole, [77] and is not for the purpose in hand taken otherwise than as an adjective happening to and qualifying a particular soul. These facts are events because they happen in time, each with a place in the order of the "real world" in general. . . . [T]he meaning of one soul or subject, . . . must be fixed arbitrarily.' (p. 35)[1]: 'You can only explain events . . . by the laws of their happening, and it does not matter for your purpose, so long as these laws work, whether they possess ultimate truth or are more or less fictitious and false.' The difficulty which I find with such a definition lies in the definition of event. Psychical event, it is said, is immediately experienced (distinct from experience). And the question I raise is whether in our conscious life anything is immediately experienced except experience itself. And in the second place the event taken as happening to that particular soul is not the same event from the point of view of that soul, for from the latter point of view the event does not 'qualify' the soul, but qualifies external reality. And if from another point of view, then what is the event? Till you have 'the laws of their happening' how can you be said to have the event? An event, I should suppose, is a *what* – a *that* somehow interpreted, for you must single out some one aspect, you must occupy some point of view not internal to the event, before there is anything of which there can be a law.

Mr Bradley's position involves a parallelism between knowledge as the reality which it intends and knowledge as event in the soul (p. 30).[2] 'To say that ideas and judgements do not happen at a certain time, and that in this sense they fail to be occurrences, seems clearly contrary to fact. . . .'[3] '[T]he idea or the judgement, . . . is assuredly a psychical event. . . . A truth, we may say, is no truth at all unless it happens in a soul and is thus an event which appears in time.'[4] This seems to me to involve a confusion of the psychological point of view with the metaphysical. From the latter standpoint this statement is correct; from the former it seems palpably false. A truth as truth must of course *appear* independent of the soul as experienced in the perception of that truth, and its oneness with the soul (as truth) is a matter of metaphysical unity and not relative to its happening 'in' a soul. A truth as such [78] is quite independent of finite soul, and we may say that it is the finitude of truth which constitutes the finite soul. So far then, as it is an event it is not a truth or a judgement at all. And so far as we are conscious of it as an event it is not in the same

1. *Collected Essays* II, 375. [Bolgan.]
2. *Collected Essays* II, 368. [Bolgan.]
3. *Collected Essays* II, 369 [Bolgan.]
4. *Collected Essays* II, 370 [Bolgan.]

sense the 'truth' that we are conscious of. In knowledge then the event of knowledge is not something that enters into consciousness.

It is certainly not from the point of view of the subject that the idea or judgement is an event, and from the subject's viewpoint the only laws of happening are the laws of the world of which he is conscious, while from the outsider's point of view, the only laws are laws which lie beyond the consciousness of the subject. But, it will be said, the subject is conscious of previous ideas and judgements as events in his own career: if he were conscious of them merely as realities apprehended, he would not be aware of his past at all, for it would not be *his* past, but the past of the world. We are constantly passing, that is to say, from the judgement as reality to the judgement as a qualification of ourselves – a view which my own account of memory is obliged to support. I again offer, however, the theory of identity there presented, and emphasise the fact that memory is an elaborate and artificial product, which can be treated from the point of view of psychophysics as subject to laws – though only so far as it is not memory – which serves a practical need, and does not pretend to give anything which was ever as such actual. As in memory of an external reality we may have an image which refers to a reality, so in recollection of our own judgement we assert an objective (*that* we judged so and so), an assertion which refers to the judgement as an event but which constitutes it as an event in the act of assertion. For a reference, as I have suggested in several passages, does not everywhere imply the existence of that to which it refers, outside of the reference itself.

Let us say, then[,] that in memory and in the observation of the actions of others we have reference to events which are never as such actual. Have we not here a consistent enough point of view to determine a subject-matter? I would offer two objections. In the first place, these events as psychic phenomena have no laws. [79] For internally, their relations among themselves are determined only by the real world from the point of view of the subject, and externally by the real world from the point of view of the subject, and externally by the real world from somebody else's point of view[1]; while their mid-way reality is at once greater and less than such as science can grasp. And in the second place the soul is not something definite to which phenomena can be attached all on the same plane, but varies with the meaning which each phenomenon has for it. In order to know what a particular event is, you must know the soul to which it

---

1. The sense here requires the omission of the entire third line, and of the first word in the fourth line as well. The sentence would then read:

   For internally, their relations among themselves are determined only by the real world from the point of view of the subject, and externally by the real world from some body else's point of view. . . . [Bolgan.]

occurs, and the soul exists only in the events which occur to it; so that the soul is, in fact, the whole world of its experience at any moment, while both soul and event transcend that moment. The soul is its whole past so far as that past enters into the present, and it is the past as implied in the present. (*Appearance*, p. 275): 'But at any one time . . . the soul is the present *datum* of psychical fact, plus its actual past and its conditional future.' But I cannot feel satisfied with the statement (*Mind*, 33, p. 29)[1] that 'The soul . . . *is* the dispositions which it has acquired'. 'In saying that the soul has a disposition of a certain kind, we take the present and past psychical facts as the subject, and we predicate of this subject other psychical facts, which we think it may become.' (*Appearance*, p. 276). Now I question whether it is ever a 'psychical' fact which we take as the subject in a disposition. Men are avaricious, generous, vicious, or self-sacrificing, and these qualities I suppose are dispositions. But avarice and generosity are not psychical events but social interpretations of behaviour, behaviour involving the whole organism. What is in the mind of the avaricious or generous man is not avarice or generosity, but a real world qualified in a certain way, and these qualifications are interpreted or introspected as subjective, conditioned by a disposition. But to be 'subjective' is not to be mental, and to be a disposition is ultimately to be a disposition of the whole organism – so that I can see no difference between psychical and physical disposition. For disposition must rest upon something which is actual and this must be a physical structure.

[80] What then as to the doctrine of Mr Bradley (*op. cit.*, *Mind*, p. 41),[2] that an emotion can be attended to? I believe this doctrine to be correct. For on the theory which I have outlined above, pleasure as pure feeling is an abstraction, and in reality is always partially objective: the emotion is really part of the object, and is ultimately just as objective. Hence when the object, or complex of objects, is recalled, the pleasure is recalled in the same way, and is naturally recalled on the object side rather than on the subject side: though it tends (*op. cit.*, *Mind*, p. 44)[3] to instate itself as an active pleasure.[4]

As to the theory of attention and the theory of will[5] I think that they illustrate in detail the objections that I have raised in general. Will, we are told, is the self-realisation of an idea; and this explanation I protest against as metaphysics and not psychology. I cannot feel, with regard to

1. *Collected Essays* II, 368. [Bolgan.]
2. *Collected Essays* II, 382. [Bolgan.]
3. *Collected Essays* II, 385. [Bolgan.]
4. Cf. T.P. Nunn, *Proc. Arist. Soc.*, 1909–10, p. 192.
5. 'Active Attention', *Mind*, 1902, No. 41. 'Definition of Will', *Mind*, Nos. 44, 46, 49.

an explanation of a faculty which explains it by reference to something which falls outside of consciousness, that such is a psychological explanation. Mr Bradley is concerned with will only in operation: 'With will taken in its full sense I agree that psychology cannot concern itself' (i.e., will as 'standing tendency').[1] And with will as I am aware of will I cannot concede that this definition has anything to do. '[B]ecause I am aware of the idea as itself making the change . . . I am aware also that this change is the work of myself.'[2] But the idea has to be my idea. 'Provided . . . that the idea has remained qualified in my mind as the act of another, it cannot in its proper character, and as such, realize itself in my person.'[3] The fact that the idea has to be my idea seems to give away the whole case; for so far as it is *my* idea it is already willed.

So far as will is not felt, I cannot see any reason for using the concept at all; and so far as it is felt, it requires no explanation and can find none. Mr Bradley's account might be a true account of what goes on when we think that there is will; but in order to be a true account it would have to justify its point of view. Ideas, [81] as I have claimed, are not objects, but occupy a half-way stage between existence and meaning. From a purely external point of view there is no will; and to find will in any phenomenon requires a certain empathy; we observe a man's actions and place ourselves partly but not wholly in his position; or we act, and place ourselves partly in the position of an outsider. And this doubleness of aspect is in fact the justification for the use of the term. Another person, and in its degree another *thing,* is not for us simply an object; there is always, I believe, a felt continuity between the object and oneself. The only error lies in regarding this community as due to the common possession of a character which belongs to both subject and object as such, and belongs to each independently. This character is then treated as a thing. But will is not a character of consciousness purely, and it is not at all a character of things as such; it arises only in a conflict, and is in the primitive mind cognised as a character of object as naturally as of subject; so that it is only by a certain degree of abstraction that we come to think of ourselves as willing and of objects as moved by 'forces' – an expression which simply indicates the degree of objectification which we have succeeded in establishing. For these reasons I am inclined to regard will as indefinable and as offering no problem. If we are to have a psychology we must postulate a faculty of will, though we hold will to be finally mere appearance. And such psychology, I think, will be not a

---

1. *Collected Essays* II, 484. [Bolgan.]
2. *Collected Essays* II, 520. [Bolgan.]
3. *Collected Essays* II, 497. [Bolgan.]

scientific but a philosophical discipline. For science deals with objects or with the relations of objects; and will, we have said, belongs to a place half-way between object and subject.

Attention likewise belongs in the class of half-objects. 'Popular psychology,' says Titchener (*Psychology of Feeling and Attention*, p. 181), 'regards attention, indifferently, as faculty and as manifestation of faculty.' Here, I suggest, popular psychology is right, for popular psychology (in this sense) is the only psychology that there is. And I believe that Bradley's theory of attention, like Titchener's, is merely an attempt to reduce attention to something else without knowing what that something is. What can we have, in an account of attention, but a description of physio-[82]logical conditions and a description of the realities apprehended? And there is only attention, I submit, when the conditions and the reality apprehended are confused. That this interfusion is everywhere found does not alter the case. For it is only as felt that the two are confused, and when we turn this feeling into an object the two elements fall apart: 'We cannot attend to several disconnected objects at once; we organize them into a single object' ('Active Attention', p. 21).[1] This I believe to be true, but what does it mean? That the world, so far as it is a world at all, tends to organise itself into an articulate whole. The real is the organised. And this statement is metaphysics, so if it comes to us as a novelty it is not psychology. From a psychological point of view, things perceived are connected so far as they are perceived to be connected. If we contemplate several objects, and recognise them as disconnected, they *are* disconnected except for metaphysics, and that is the complete statement of the case. 'But is there then,' says Mr Joseph (*Mind*, 1911),

> no such thing as psychology . . . [I]f I were asked what it really is, I should say, not a science, but a collection of more or less detached inquiries, of the result of which philosophy must take account. There are for example inquiries into 'double personality' and kindred puzzles, which must affect any theory of the real nature of the individual soul or self; there are experiments about association-time, reaction-time, etc., which help to explain why one man's mind works quicker than another's, but no more throw light on the nature of thinking than the determination of the duration of the crotchet explains the beauty of music. [T]here are more definitely

---

1. These sentences are not to be found in the article cited but, in this same article, Bradley does make a statement closely similar to the one quoted. It reads:

> There is in attention never more than one object, the several 'objects' being diverse aspects of or features within this. *Collected Essays* II, 431. [Bolgan.]

psycho-physical investigations, *e.g.*, into brain-localisation which may have therapeutic value, and of course any facts about the relation of what is mental to what is cerebral are important to a theory of the soul, as of a knower belonging somehow to the same whole with the known.

I can subscribe to most of this statement. There is certainly an important field for psycho-physics and the study of behaviour, and there are even certain processes where introspection is not without value. But this knowledge, I insist, is knowledge either of physiology, biology, or of the external world, and implies both a [83] real known external world and a real nervous system: for we are not to say that there is a mental content which is mental. There is, in this sense, nothing mental, and there is certainly no such thing as consciousness if consciousness is to be an object or something independent of the objects which it has. There are simply 'points of view', objects, and half-objects. Science deals only with objects; psychology, in the sense of rational or faculty psychology, may deal with half-objects, and metaphysics alone with the subject, or point of view.

Chapter IV
The Epistemologist's Theory of Knowledge
KEPB, 84–111.

'And there can be really no such science as the theory of cognition.'
(*Appearance*, p. 65)

It has been the conclusion of the foregoing chapter that no distinct province of mental objects exists as the field of psychology; that no definition can anywhere be found to throw the mental on one side and the physical on the other; that we can never construct the external world from the mental, for the external is already implied in the mental. The difference between mental and real, or in the excellent terms of Mr Alexander between the personal and the objective, is one of practical convenience and varies at every moment; so that the terms content and presentation do not stand for objects of a science but for aspects of an object. We go on to ask, naturally, whether the terms with which the epistemologist deals are any more substantial. The distinctions of *immanent* and *transcendent* object, the terms *real* and *unreal* object, *a priori* and *a posteriori* knowledge, *phenomenon* and *reality, passive apprehension* and the *activity of consciousness*; these are all terms which have a certain significance in practical knowledge. But whether thought has more than a practical validity, whether there is any reality for thought to reach and whether thought reaches it – the absolute validity of knowledge – is the problem of the theory of knowledge. There are evidently three divisions of the question: the problem of the genesis of knowledge, of the structure of knowledge, and of the possibility of knowledge. It is, I believe, the position of all sound idealism, and I believe is the position of Mr Bradley, that the only real problem is the second. For it may be said, in criticism [85] of the first problem, that it does not deal with objects of *knowledge*, and in criticism of the third, that there are no *objects* of knowledge, when the object is treated as a hard and fast reality.

The present chapter is to consider the claims of the third problem, and I will only touch very briefly on the question of the 'growth of knowledge'. While the problem is by no means a negligible one, it can never occupy a place of priority in the theory of knowledge, and the reason is simply this. We are all agreed that the knowledge of the world possessed by man is superior to that possessed by the ape, and that the knowledge of the European is superior to that of the savage, but there remains in this knowledge a *somehow* which is not resolved unless by a theory which is not the outcome of any 'genetic' research. There is recognised in the history which we consider a growth, but it is a growth of 'knowledge' only in the vague or practical sense of the world. In evolution or in the development of the child there is a systematic alteration of values, with an outer expansion and an inner elaboration of content, which we find to be continuous with the values and the content of our own experience. But this alteration is a growth of knowledge only if knowledge is already assumed; and if we make no assumptions about the validity of our own knowledge the growth which we trace is not the growth of knowledge at all, but is the history only of adaptation, if you like, to environment. And in such an account, of course, our knowledge of the environment to which we see the organism adapting itself is taken not as absolute but as relative: we assume only a system of relations such that our knowledge will not be falsified on the plane on which it is knowledge. Nothing, then, is so far known as to the nature of knowledge.

The basis of structural psychology, as we have seen, resolves itself into physiology; and while physiology is by no means irrelevant to the problem of knowledge, its contribution is always indirect. Knowledge being given, physiology can suggest the limitations and give some of the conditions of truth and error; it gives us the background against which knowledge is set and into [86] which it tends to fade. And we are obliged to believe that in a final account the knowledge which we think to possess and the conditions of it will be necessary to explain and complete each other. Meanwhile physiology gives an account, not of our knowledge as knowledge, but under some other aspect. And so long as we have no ultimate and complete knowledge the study of these aspects will remain relevant to epistemology. The intended object is ultimate reality. But in knowing as we experience it the aspect which is knowing is continuous with the other aspects and can never be definitely separated from them at any point. So far as it is knowing, there is no problem and, if there be a problem – of which I am very doubtful – it is constituted by the relation of knowing to the other aspects. Epistemology, therefore, is simply the process by which what is at first knowledge is absorbed into another aspect: knowing becomes known, an activity becomes an object, and the process can be repeated *ad infinitum.*

It is claimed, however, that epistemology occupies a position of unique authority and constitutes a distinct science apart from psychology, physiology, logic, or biology. Epistemology makes the claim of both scientific certainty and metaphysical ultimacy. And it is, I believe, to be repudiated by both scientist and metaphysician; by the first because the external criteria of his science do not concern him, and by the second because he is engaged in the construction of a system, and must place himself at an external point of view from which the wholly internal aspect of knowledge disappears. In a metaphysic such as Mr Bradley's, certainly, there can be no place for a theory of knowledge, for the terms which such a discipline must use have not the requisite substantiality. The problem, it may be remarked, has two parts which are not infrequently confused: the problem of the knowledge of the objects or truths which we do know, and the problem of knowledge in general. In the first we assume the existence of knowledge and inquire into its conditions; in the second we assume nothing and inquire into the possibility of knowledge. And the fact that the two are perhaps never treated wholly independently must not lead us to think that they are not two independent problems. In [87] epistemology we attempt to describe a relation between the knower and the known, to give a description which shall leave both as we find them – which shall, that is, describe an experience which shall still be recognisable after the description; but we ask also the very different question of the validity and meaning of the noetic experience, and this question can only be answered in terms which leave the original experience unrecognisable.

The philosopher who attempts to answer either of these questions must, I believe, be either a dualistic realist or a 'criticist' (which is ultimately the same thing) for I do not propose to classify Kant as anything but a dualistic realist. He assumes that there is a real world, a world of realities of one sort or at most two; he then inquires how we come to know this world. And as a result of this sharp and quite dogmatic division he burdens himself with all the trouble of unreal and imaginary objects, and with the problem of error. I shall first state briefly the criticism of such a 'real world' from the point of view of *Appearance and Reality,* and elucidate it further by criticism of such analyses of the act of knowledge as those of Meinong and Messer.

There is a dilemma which may be said to be given at the start. Either the external world is presented always as it is, and is never more or other than what is given; or else there is a describable relation between our knowing and that which is known. And if we accept the first alternative, it is said, we are left with no real world at all, for anything and everything incongruous and inconsistent, will be equally real, and in no significant sense will it constitute a 'world'. We are then to assume one real world independent of our knowledge of it, surround consciousness with an opaque veil of 'subjectivity' and ask in what form and in what way reality penetrates this integument. We assume no acquaintance with objects except as presented, but the epistemologist makes it his task to prove that there is a relation between knowledge and its object which is not simply that of knowledge.

Mr Russell (*Mind*, 1904. 'Meinong's Theory of Complexes and Assumptions, III') gives a list of five theories of knowledge which is suggestive.

[88]   1. '[K]nowledge does not differ from what is known ...
2. We may admit the distinction of content and object, but hold that the latter is merely immanent.
3. We may hold that the object is immanent when false, transcendent when true.
4. We may hold that when a judgement is false there is no object; but when true, there is a transcendent object.
5. We may hold that the object is always transcendent.'

The first of these is that which Mr Russell attributes to idealism, though to what idealism he refers I am unable to discover. I contend that every one of these accounts is ultimately meaningless, owing to the confusion of the practical with the metaphysical points of view. The last four all accept the distinction of content and object, though upon what grounds I am at a loss to say. 'When we consider the presentation of something simple, say redness, it is evident that the presentation and the object are distinct' (Russell, *ibid.*, p. 514). But in the first place (Chapter III, p. 62) it is not quite correct to say that redness is a presentation, and furthermore I cannot find any evidence offered for the distinctness of presentation and object. But (Russell, *ibid.*, p. 207):

> The content of a presentation exists when the presentation exists, but the object need not exist – it may be self-contradictory, it may be something which happens not to be a fact, such as a golden mountain, it may be essentially incapable of existence as for instance equality, it may be physical, not psychical, or it may be something which did exist or will exist, but does not exist at present. What is called the existence of an object in presentation is really not existence at all: it may be called pseudo-existence. . . . The content tends to be ignored in favour of the object; there are no natural designations for contents, which have to be named and distinguished by their objects.

Such a theory of content and object is evidently based upon the assumption of a world of real and independent objects: it assumes that the typical case of apprehension is that of a physical object; it forces our apprehension of 'ideal' objects into the same mould, [89] and it ends in the paradox that we may refer to an object when no object is present. It appears to assume also that there may be objects which are – in fact that the typical object is – merely existent, and do not to some extent subsist as well.

I wish to recall the criticism which I directed upon 'content' in the preceding chapter. From the argument there offered it would appear that the golden mountain is as real and objective as any thing else. If it were merely content the content would be the object, and we should have to account for our error in mistaking the one for the other. But it could not be even content unless it intended to be object. So far as the idea 'golden mountain' is a real idea, so far is it a real object. I will not however, pursue these comments farther until I have outlined the view of a 'real world' which these four theories mentioned by Mr Russell seem to overlook. There is a real world, corresponding to that intended by these theories, which is neither identical with Bradley's Reality nor incompatible with it. And I may be at some pains to suggest what is essentially indefinable, what this real world is; why it is tempting as a starting-point for epistemology, why it is unreal inside a metaphysical system, yet presupposed by every system. I have agreed heartily to the views of Professor Alexander and Dr Nunn in regard to the reality of all objects. But it is evident that in practice this doctrine is hopelessly untrue. We are forced to assume that some objects are real and others simply unreal; it is only in refined practice that we find degree of reality to any extent useful, and we never, I think, dispense with the blunt 'real' and 'unreal' altogether. For without the unreal, as without the element of negation, you cannot have a world of finite experience at all. Such a world involves selection and emphasis, and we cannot too frequently be told that the world of practice is supported by interest and valuation. But our interests and our values, we shall be told vary from moment to moment. So does the real world, according to that fragment of it which happens to be the focus of our attention. Against the background of practical reality that is, are various systems both social and scientific, which are so to speak lived together in a coherence which cannot be formulated.

[90] The process by which this world is constructed has of course two aspects. On the one hand the selection of certain experiences as real and the rejection of others builds up the world, and on the other hand the assumption of a real world gives a standard for such choice; the external world is thus doubly supported in its externality. Thus the distinction between that content which is merely personal and that which is objective is *not* a distinction between two classes of object absolutely, but a distinction valid only so long as we support one point of view – that of practical interest in the difference. There is a real world, if you like, which is full of contradictions, and it is our attempt to organise this world which gives the belief in a completely organised world, an hypothesis which we proceed to treat as an actuality – whence the question how and how far we come into contact with this world of absolute order.

The principle involved in the question of immanent and transcendent objects I believe to be this: a reality intended need not be in itself actual, though its actuality be presupposed in the reality of the intention. We intend, from our divers limited points of view, a single real world, and we forget that metaphysically this real world is only real so far as it finds realisation through these points of view. It is not my purpose at this point to expound the doctrine of points of view, which will belong properly under the head of Solipsism, but only to sketch the outlines of the position from which Epistemology is criticised. I repeat then that the objective world is only actual in one or other point of view, but that each point of view intends to be, not a point of view, but the world one and impersonal, and in this double aspect, according to which reality is on the one hand given and on the other hand merely symbolised, I find what may be called in a way the transcendence of the object and the justification for the distinction between content and object. But it must be remarked that such a distinction has only practical validity, and does not hold where a particular content has not been already selected as real. It is not true to say that some objects are immanent and some transcendent by virtue of any characteristic which can be found in them *as* [91] *objects,* for all objects are equally immanent and equally transcendent. The criterion of reality, therefore, is to be found, not in the relation of the object to the subject, but in the directness with which the object is relatable to the intended world – for it is not always the same sphere of reality to which we refer our objects. So that the reality of the object does not lie in the object itself, but in the extent of the relations which the object possesses without significant falsification of itself. These relations are all different points of view upon the object – i.e. they relate different aspects to a single point of reference: in this process of relation the object itself is altered, for what was at first the object pure and simple becomes the object under a single aspect. And a point of view, it may here be remarked, need not be considered as identical with one human consciousness; so that we may be said to move from one point of view to another when we determine an object by another relation. If this be true, then the movement between one 'finite centre' and another will not differ in kind from that inside of one consciousness, and will consist in the constitution of a real world by ideal references of many aspects.

In this case, the 'real world' of epistemology (to be distinguished from the Reality of metaphysics) will be an essentially indefinite world of identical references of an indefinite number of points of view, particularly those of other civilised adults with whom we come in contact, but quite possibly extending to all finite centres with which we can establish an identical reference. In the light of this view, and recalling the account of idea which I have laboured to express in the first three chapters several of the distinctions of Meinong appear to me elaborate superfluities. I would choose as an example his distinction of *Inhalt* (content) and *Gegenstand* (object) with reference to *Pseudoexistenz* (pseudoexistence). It is meaningless, Meinong says,[1] to speak of an object as existent only 'in der Vorstellung' ('in presentation'). 'An Object that exists only "in my presentation", simply does not exist at all . . .: We may now summarise as follows: existence, for the knower, is, viewed from the standpoint of the Object, a pseudo-[92]existence, and it remains only to establish what, in such cases, the actual existent is, which is thus in the strict sense perceived.'[2] We must clearly distinguish, he says, the *Inhalt* of a *Vorstellung* (presentation) from its *Gegenstand*.

> If I think first of red and then of green, it naturally cannot be the same, or a precisely similar presentation, whereby I first apprehend the one object and then the other. But that which respectively distinguishes these two presentations, so that the first is appropriated to the one

1. *Erfahrungsgrundlagen unseres Wissens*, p. 56.
2. '[E]in Objekt, das nur "in meiner Vostellung" existiert, eigentlich gar nicht existiert . . . : Man kann jetzt kurz sagen: die Existenz, die er erkennt, ist, vom Standpunkte der Objekte besehen, eine Pseudoexistenz, und es bleibt nur festzustellen, was in solchen Fällen das wirklich Existente, das also im strengen Sinne Wahrgenommene ist.'

object and the second to the other, is their content. Clearly, the object apprehended in a presentation cannot possibly exist; but still less, then, can the content, whereby it is apprehended. The latter is a constituent of the presentation, and cannot be absent, or the presentation itself would be absent too.[1]

A good deal depends, of course, on the use of the word *Vorstellung* and I have been unable to find – admitting, however, that I find Meinong an exceedingly difficult author – that the meaning of this very obscure word is anywhere defined; and I have occasion to complain, indeed, that just those words are taken for granted which have the most need of new or revised definitions. What, in the quotation just given, is the difference of *Vorstellung* but the difference of object? Both *Vorstellung* and *Inhalt* seem here identical with object. For the 'idea' here in question is not a logical idea, not the idea which we predicate of reality; the idea in this sense would be for Meinong identical with the object, since there is no question of predicating the *Vorstellung* of red of the real red. The idea here is the psychologist's idea, which is for the psychologist an aspect of the object [93] in mental context. I have already protested against amputating this aspect for the purpose of a 'special science'; but to graft the member on again after it is dead seems to me even more gratuitous. In the sense in which there are two ideas (red and green) there are not at the same time two objects, for we have substituted the ideas for the objects. And when we proceed to talk of the 'content' of an idea we are simply making a devious return to the object. It is not true, I have contended, to say that an idea has an object, for idea *is* (not *has*) a reference to an object. So far as the idea is real it is the object, so far as the idea is unreal the object is unreal or indeterminate.

The distinction between idea and content of idea may be accounted for perhaps in connection with Meinong's analysis of *Ausdruck* (expression) and *Bedeutung* (meaning).[2] 'Thus anyone who utters, say, the word "sun", normally gives *expression* also, whether he wants to or not, to the fact that a certain presentation, either of perception or imagination, is occurring in him. The nature of this presentation is determined initially

---

[1] 'Denke ich das eine Mal an Rot das andere Mal an Grün, so kann es natürlich nicht dieselbe resp. eine genau gleiche Vorstellung sein, vermöge deren ich einmal diesen, einmal jenen Gegenstand erfasse. Das aber, worin diese beiden Vorstellungen jedenfalls verschieden sind, wodurch die eine diesem, die andere jenem Gegenstande zugeordnet ist, das ist ihr Inhalt. Bekanntlich muss der Gegenstand, den eine Vorstellung erfasst, durchaus nicht existieren; um so gewisser aber der Inhalt, durch den sie ihn erfasst. Er ist ein Stück an der Vorstellung, das nicht fehlen kann, ohne das die Vorstellung selbst fehlt.' (*ibid.*, 57.)

[2] See U. *Annahmen*, 2te Aufl., p. 24 ff.

by what is presented therein, namely its object, and this object is in fact what is meant by the word "sun".'[1]

It would appear from this passage that we express the idea, but mean the object. This being admitted, it is well to ask whether the object, in the case of an unreal object, is merely the content of the idea: and we find, I think, the psychologist's error of treating two points of view as if they were one. The idea in question refers merely to the judgement made by the hearer to the effect that the speaker has 'an idea of' certain objects; but the object apprehended by the hearer is an object which from the point of view of the speaker does not exist. The speaker can only mean; and even if he means his own 'state of consciousness' what is really active is a meaning which is not meant. The idea, furthermore, which is [94] apprehended is only a half-object: it exists, that is, as an object only by our half putting ourselves in the place of the speaker and half contemplating him as an object. The distinction, consequently, between *Ausdruck* and *Bedeutung* must[2] be drawn too closely. For no expression is even expression unless we attribute it meaning, and meaning cannot be merely contemplated, but must be *erlebt* (experienced). Hence even in the case of error – Pseudoexistenz – the object must be transcendent or there is no object at all: and in this I am in accord with Mr Russell.

The occasion for the distinction of immanent and transcendent objects is obviously the fact of error. No object can, we find, be merely immanent, for the reason that so far as an object is an object it will have relations which transcend it, transcend the perception; relations which constitute it, but which ultimately transform and absorb it. The poorer an object is in relations, the less it is object; and the limiting case of pseudoexistence is an object with no relations – this would be the only purely imaginary object, and would of course not be an object at all, but a feeling, which as such, would have its relations of another sort. Mr Russell's declaration that all objects are transcendent, however[,] seems to provoke only new difficulties. (p. 515)[3]: 'It is not maintained, of course, that the object must *exist;* that would be to maintain that a certain specific proposition

---

1. 'Wer also etwa das Wort "Sonne" ausspricht, bringt dadurch normalerweise, gleichviel ob er es auch will oder nicht, zum *Ausdruck*, dass sich eine bestimmte Vorstellung, es kann natürlich so gut Wahrnehmung's wie Einbildungsvorstellung sein, in ihm zuträgt. Was für eine Vostellung das ist, bestimmt sich zunächst nach dem, was durch vorgestellt wird, also ihrem Gegenstande, und dieser Gegenstand ist eben das, was das Wort "Sonne" bedeutet.' (*ibid.*, 25.)
2. The sense here requires the insertion of the word 'not'. The sentence would then read:
   The distinction, consequently, between *Ausdruck* and *Bedeutung* must not be drawn too closely. [Bolgan.]
3. Russell, 'Meinong's Theory of Complexes and Assumptions (III),' 515. [Bolgan.]

must hold of the object, whereas all that seems essential is that there should *be* such an object; and the assertion of being, if not analytic, is yet more nearly so than any other assertion.' The content, Mr Russell tells us, implies the object and the relation of the content to object. This seems very much like my theorem (p. 90), that a reality intended need not be itself actual though its reality be presupposed in the reality of the intention, but it leaves to the transcendence of the object, as Mr Russell states it, only a formal value, through its insinuation of the distinction between existence and being; a distinction which implies that Mr Russell means no more by transcendence than Meinong does by immanence. So that Mr Russell's theory appears to end in bankruptcy, [95] inasmuch as we are left without a criterion for either truth or judgement or reality of object.

Meinong's theory of perception is complicated, as I suggested above, by the division which he draws between real and ideal objects, between *inferiora* and *superiora*. Mr Russell classifies *superiora* as follows: relations (including likeness, differences, and the complexes formed of terms related by a relation), and the kind of objects (which we may call plurals) of which numbers other than 0 and 1 can be asserted. The difficulty which I find with this account is that it would seem possible for virtually any object to be either inferior or superior: a melody, for example, is superior and composed of tones as its *inferiora*; but the simple tone is composed of vibrations, and is in fact as absolutely a 'zeitverteiltes Gegenstand' as is the melody. Furthermore, it is by no means clear what the relation of a *superius* to its *inferiora* is. A melody, as Mr Russell observes, is not a fifth note; what is added is the relation – but 'rightly related' to the constituents! Now it may be asked whether a relation to its terms, whether the relation is apprehended as an object in the same way as the object, and whether in any complex there are two *superiora*, the relation uniting, and the whole complex.[1] And finally I would ask (and this is the only essential question) whether the division really corresponds to the objects with which we actually come into contact.

It is only with great trepidation that I venture to interpret so obscure an author as Alexis von Meinong. But I am interested to note my own impression that the ideal object (which is always an object of higher order) tends to the foreground of certainty, while the real object drops into the obscurity of a noumenon. So, toward the end of the book

---

1. Mr Eliot's meaning here is easily clarified if we alter the passage to read:
   Now it may be asked whether a relation to its terms is apprehended as an object in the same way as is the object, and whether in any complex there are not two *superiora* – the relation uniting, and the whole complex. [Bolgan.]

Über die Erfahrungsgrundlagen (*On the Empirical Foundations of Our Knowledge*) the author is apparently more and more cautious in attributing characters to the real object. (p. 93): The object O is divided into o ('das Dingmoment', the factor of thinghood) and o´ ('die Gesamtheit der "im äusseren Aspekte gegebenen Eigenschaften",' the totality of characteristics presented to outward view). In respect of o, the [96] chalk is hardly to be distinguished from the inkstand; to be sure, the perceptual presentation of the former offers us one o´ for the purpose, and that of the latter another: but these are precisely those sensible qualities, for whose real presence we have no evidence.' (*ibid.*, p. 94): The phenomenal determinations o'_1, o'_2 are paralleled, in fact, by noumenal determinations $\bar{o}_1$ and $\bar{o}_2$, of which it is evident, indeed, that the very same relations of comparison hold between them as between the o´s; wherein lies implicit at the same time a claim in any case self-evident, namely that the substantial factor o, guaranteed to us by the good evidence already validated, does not exist, as it were, in unnatural, or indeed impossible, isolation, but that the existent does in fact consist of things having characteristics.'[1]

This is, if you like, knowledge of an external reality, but it is knowledge of a very critical sort indeed. The *superiora* become *Erkenntnisinstrument* ('instruments of knowledge'), and while the 'aspects' furnish evidence, not for themselves but for the objects (or perceptions?) of which they are aspects, yet it is the aspect which is presented. The thing is known, but only through appearances which exist as references to the thing, and do not necessarily give evidence for their own existence. This seems to me essentially the position of the critical philosophy: the thing is known through its appearances, but as soon as the distinction is made appearance and thing fall apart, and appearance replaces thing as a point of attention.

The distinction between inferior and superior objects, on the whole, strikes me as thoroughly critical. To treat things, not as moments of objectivity, but as ultimate lumps which can be [97] grasped after all

---

1. 'Die Kreide unterscheidet sich vom Tintenfass schwerlich in betreff des o; dafür bietet uns die Wahrnehmungsvorstellung der ersteren freilich ein o´1, die des letzteren ein o´2: aber das sind ja eben jene sensiblen Qualitäten, für deren Dasein wir keine Evidenz haben.' (p. 94): 'Den phanomenalen Bestimmungen o'_1, o'_2 etc. stehen vielmehr noumenale Bestimmungen $\bar{o}'_1, \bar{o}'_2$ etc. gegenüber, von denen eben evident ist, dass zwischen ihnen die nämlichen Vergleichungsrelationen gelten wie zwischen den o´, worin zugleich die allerdings selbstverständliche Behauptung beschlossen liegt, dass das substantielle Moment o, das uns durch die bereits geltend gemachte gute Evidenz gesichert ist, nicht etwa in unnatürlicher oder eigentlich unmöglicher Isoliertheit existiert, sondern dass das Existierende doch jedenfalls Dinge mit Eigenschaften sind.'

relations[1] have been stripped away, seems to be the attempt of both Meinong and Kant. To treat ideal relations as 'superior' objects, somehow built upon the real objects, and in a sense dependent upon them (Russell, *op. cit.*, p. 207 ff.)[2] is a step toward making relations into categories. For it appears (unless I misinterpret) that the ideal relations are more certainly known than the real, being (in Meinong's sense) *a priori*, and the objects of 'inner perception' are more certainly known than those of outer perception. (*op. cit.*, p. 99)[3]: 'Thus in dealing with ideal objects, there is no need at all to disclaim the influence of subjectivity; but so far as the evidence is not still to seek, this leads merely to a sort of selection among the equally available *superiora*, whose totality the intrinsically limited intellect cannot attempt to assess. But this subjectivity in no way compromises the validity of what we are able to know *a priori*, once we obtain it. Thus things-in-themselves are like, unlike, etc.'[4]

But it would appear that this likeness among objects is a matter of inference and not of direct acquaintance. We do not know reality in substance, we know it in relation: we know, that is, a relation among content which cannot be falsified when carried over to the thing, inasmuch as the content is only content with reference to the thing, so that the relation is not directly known of the content as such. The profoundest obscurity enfolds the notion of *Adäquatheit* (adequateness), an ideal relation between the object of the idea and reality (*Annahmen*, p. 263). If *Wirklichkeit* (actuality) is real, then in the apprehension of an ideal object (cf. *ibid.*, p. 265) I do not see what the relation of *Adäquatheit* between the ideal object apprehended and the 'real' ideal object can be, for there cannot be two sets of ideal objects, [98] and the ideal relation between the ideal object apprehended and the real object can be nothing more than a relation of identity. In this case the *Adäquatheit* must be between the real content of an idea and a real complex, which would mean that in knowledge we do not apprehend relations but a specific case of relation, and that the complex of terms related is not ideal but real, and that the relation of aspect to thing is always a real relation.

1. 'For a thing to exist it must possess identity. . . . and further this identity is ideal.' *Appearance*, p. 61.

2. Russell, 'Meinong's Theory of Complexes and Assumptions (I),' 207. [Bolgan.]

3. Meinong, *Uber die Erfahrungsgrundlagen unseres Wissens*, 99–100. [Bolgan.]

4. 'So wird man in betreff idealer Gegenstände den Einfluss der Subjectivität durchaus nicht in Abrede zu stellen brauchen; diese führt aber, soweit die Evidenz nicht ausbleibt, nur zu einer Art Auswahl unter den gleichsam verfügbaren Superioren, deren Gesamtheit der durch seine Natur begrenzte Intellekt zu ermessen gar nicht versuchen kann. Aber die Gültigkeit dessen, was wir, so wie wir einmal beschaffen sind, a priori zu erkennen vermögen, wird durch diese Subjectivität in keiner Weise in Frage gestellt. Die Dinge an sich sind also gleich, ungleich etc.'

We are here in full cry after the familiar *ignis fatuus* of epistemology, the search for terms, which persist in dissolving into relations. The reliance upon 'inner perception' is I think only another case of retreat to a relation as more secure than a thing. It is evidently the conclusion of the preceding chapter that there is properly no such thing as internal perception, and that in any case it provides no more certain knowledge than outer perception, but perhaps less, and certainly later. There is surely no more evidence in memory[1] than in perception, whether it be the memory of a feeling, desire, or perception. To pass from the subject to the content of a perception is not in general to pass from the less to the more certain. For as we have seen, every perception has an object, and whether that object is 'real' or not depends simply on the number and kind of relations which, in a particular context, we may for practical purposes demand: reality is a convention. To fall back on the content is simply to assert a quasi-object: there was an experience, as if. . . . To make an object of the content is to attend to something quite as uncertain in evidence as any other object. The content objectified, that is, is something which was never as such experienced; because the I which attends to the content is a wider, more developed I than the I which first experienced the content. So that the content is not in any exact sense a part of the self, and is subject to exactly the same conditions of evidence as any other object. There will be, then, evidence for object and evidence for content, but not necessarily stronger for one than for the other, and in most cases, I am inclined to believe, stronger for object than for content.

I have already raised objections to the drawing and quartering of reality into real and ideal objects: this objection I should now like to amplify. I seem to find here some confusion as to just what is implied by the word *object*: and I cannot but feel that the distinction of real and ideal, inferior and superior objects, is a clumsy substitute for the notion of degrees of truth and reality. It is admitted (Russell, *op. cit.*, p. 352)[2] that the division between objects and objectives is not altogether sharp (cf. 'black-board' and 'the blackness of the board'). May we not then fairly inquire whether there can be found a single case of an object which cannot be treated as an objective? or indeed of an objective which cannot be treated as an object? Even the perception of the familiar epistemologist's table can be treated as the assertion *that* certain experiences are given – the table being only

---

1. Bradley, *Mind*, April 1899, p. 160: 'Our justification for regarding memory as in general accurate is briefly this, that by taking such a course we are best able to order and harmonize our world. There is in the end no other actual or possible criterion of fact and truth, and the search for a final fact and for an absolute datum is everywhere the pursuit of a mere *ignis fatuus*.'

2. Russell, 'Meinong's Theory of Complexes and Assumptions (II), 352. [Bolgan.]

the condensed aspect of the objective asserted. And as Meinong affirms that a perception is also an *Existenzurteil* (existential judgement), so any judgement involves as well the perception of the judgement (i.e., the perception of its correctness).

The object has not yet been exactly defined. An object is as such a point of attention, and thus anything and everything to which we may be said to direct attention is an object.

But the objects among which we live are much more than this; here we have abstracted from everything about a thing which could localise it either in a 'subjective' or in an 'objective' world. The element of objectivity is the capacity of anything to be, or to be considered as (the distinction will explain itself later) a point of attention, but the point of attention is of course only an abstraction. It is only as the point of attention becomes qualified – becomes a *what* – that it is even a *that*; a number of characteristics, none of which is essential to its objectivity, and none of which is objective in the sense of being an object, nevertheless constitute *its* objectivity: its *thatness* is in direct ratio to its *whatness*. And the thing, in order to be a thing even, must be capable of entering into a kind of existence in which it is not a [100] thing. I do not argue that a thing ceases to be a thing when it ceases to be a point of attention: this is I believe supposed to be the point of view of subjective idealism. For I do not recognise the validity of the question. There is an identity which persists, an identity due to which the objectivity is not annihilated, but rendered meaningless. The thing does not cease to exist, it exists in other ways, ways which are not thinghood, but can only be expressed or suggested in terms of thinghood. And without the potentiality of these other forms of existence the thing would not even be a thing: *existence, I mean to say, is not identical with thinghood*. The world is not made up of things, nor of things and 'other things'; but existence is capable of appearing more or less under the aspect of thinghood. The account which I offer is, I know, anything but lucid! I can only plead in excuse that the point is one of the most difficult in the theory of knowledge. But one of the consequences, which will perhaps go to make the matter more intelligible, is that there are no objects of strictly lower order, and no objects of strictly higher order. What Meinong has in mind are two aspects of existence which when contemplated, are both objects, but so far as they are objects, are of the same order. The only alternative, I insist, is to assume that the lower objects alone are objects, and the higher, categories, that only 'real' things exist, and that in point of fact there are no real things, but only things in themselves, i.e. hypothetical limits. And from this point of view Meinong has, as I intimated, only a step to take to Kant.

The whole question is, as Mr Russell suggests, closely bound up with the theory of time. Meinong maintains that the objects of lower order may be directly perceived. But it is surely evident that so far as an object has meaning it is not an object of this sort. For meaning involves relations; at least (we need) the relation of identity[1] through which a universality of function is recognised through a diversity of situation.

[101] And I do not see how you can make the distinction between *superiora* and *inferiora* at all unless you claim the existence and the perceptibility of *inferiora* apart from *superiora*. Surely the whole construction falls to the ground once you admit their inseparability. For in this case there not only is no logical priority, but the one is so dependent for its existence upon the other that the two are only discriminated aspects of the same moment of objectivity, and we may say that in a sense neither of the two is the object we know.

The 'object which we know' is however only a certain aspect. We encounter a difficulty in the fact that we are forced to use the same term 'object' for more than one aspect. For it is clear that the slightest consideration of the nature of an object analyses ideal from real elements. Any description must bring to light elements which subsist rather than exist, and some elements are chosen as existents simply with reference to others that do not: none can be said to be in itself purely existent. You cannot get a world of real things by joining together a number of subsistents with a number of existents, for it turns out that there is nothing in the world which is wholly in time – there are, that is, no pure *thats*. No object, it is implied, is merely an object; for the real presence of ideal elements in the simplest and most objective of objects implies a kinship between that object and all other objects in which that idea element is exemplified; the mere identity of an object with itself constitutes a relation between that object and all other objects. So that the curious dualism of Mr Russell (*Problems*, pp. 99–100) which has much in common with obvious, though I can hardly think correct, interpretations of Plato, will not hold good of a world which is always partially in time, but never wholly in time, with respect to any of its elements.

What constitutes a real object, accordingly, is the practical need or occasion. We may treat, that is, an object of attention as a term or as a complex as occasion demands, and it is only a question of practice to what point, under analysis, it remains the same object. And it will

---

1. 'For a thing to exist it must possess identity; and identity seems a possession with a character at best doubtful. If it is merely ideal, the thing itself can hardly be real. . . . And this identical content is called ideal because it transcends given existence. Existence is given only in presentation, and, on the other hand, the thing is a thing only if its existence goes beyond the now, and extends into the past.' *Appearance*, pp. 61–2.

always be a question on your hands just what it is that persists in time. Ordinarily there is no difficulty, [102] for the object is not *bestimmt*; it fluctuates as occasion demands, and as elements in it are treated as real or as ideal, but as the terms are analysed into relations, it appears finally that nothing is in time except time itself. This point of view, however, is of course only a limit, and is never reached.

So much for the 'existence' of 'real' objects. It will be said on the other side that there are objects which are purely ideal: relations, such as identity and difference, and the objects of pure mathematics. To this also I must object. We *intend* ideal objects, just as we *intend* real ones, and in practice the difference in intention is difference in reality. But I do not see how, in a critical examination of first principles, such a distinction can maintain itself absolutely. The objection is as follows. The existent and the subsistent are two aspects of reality which are intended but never actually grasped, and the difference between them is not the difference between two classes of object, for *in so far as* they are objects they are of the same sort; the difference is *extra-objective*. What for example do we attend to when we make an object of the relation 'difference'. So far as it is an object, it is not a relation; it is something corresponding to that relation in the world of objects: not as a correspondence of two separate entities, but by continuous transition. And this *object* is subject to all the difficulties of the existent object in reversed order. As a relation it is a relation of terms; as an object it is a simple term or a complex of terms again related. It will not do to say that the relation is apprehended in a case of itself; that the relation difference is grasped through the difference of a specific content, red and green. For this is to admit that the true object is the complex (*a*) red-different-from-green, or (*b*) difference-of-green-from-red. (*a*) and (*b*) are evidently the same object in one sense and different objects in another. The practical attention is in the same direction, but there is a difference of emphasis: one cannot say absolutely that the objects are the same. So far as we regard it as the same (*a*) will represent the tendency in the direction of existence, and (*b*) the tendency in the direction of subsistence: but red-and-green on the one hand and difference on the other [103] will never be actualised. We do not need to refute the protest that difference is not different, and that whiteness is not white, in order to reach this conclusion. For we mean only that neither subsistence nor existence can be real, and that what is intended in the act of attending to an object is always something real.

The last point needs some elucidation. An abstraction, it is here argued, is not merely *as such* an object of attention. The abstraction has an individual existence, though not independent of that from which it is abstracted, and it is this individual existence which is the object so far as there is an object. If there is given in primary experience a real object A from which we abstract the superior ideal object *a*, then *a* is at once something more and something less than A. It is less in that it is intended to be merely a subsistent aspect of A, and more in that it has an existence of its own, with conditions to a large degree independent of A. And in this way it is also in a sense less than itself, in that being a subsistent, it is limited as well by conditions of existence. This leads to the consideration of the relation of symbol to that which it symbolises.[1]

I mean here by symbol both what Mr Peirce calls by that name and what he calls an eicon; excluding the index.[2] Symbol, I mean, in the sense of the real (or rather objective) end of a continuity which terminates at one end in an *intended existent* or *subsistent* and at the other end in an object (*erfassbar*, apprehensible) which must have both existent and subsistent aspects. Now in any use of a word which symbolises an abstraction the actual object of attention, I submit, is exceedingly variable: there is not simply one determinate object in various contexts, but the object varies with the context. Thus, in any use of an abstract term, we may distinguish between the logical meaning, which is an intended object, and the real meaning, which is a part of the experience and not an object real or intended. For the intended object we always substitute to [104] perhaps a greater or a less degree the present symbol. It must be emphasised, however, that there is properly speaking, no relation between the symbol and that which it symbolises, because they are continuous. The reality without the symbol would never be known, and we cannot say that it would even exist (or subsist); but on the other hand the symbol furnishes proof of the reality, inasmuch as without the reality it would not be that symbol: i.e. there would be an identity left which would for our purposes be irrelevant. The word 'relation' would not be the word 'relation' without the reality 'relation' which is not in itself an object; for no word can exist without a meaning, and if the word 'relation' did not have the meaning 'relation' it would have to have some other meaning. You cannot, that is to say, determine two realities, the word and its meaning: the word (here the existent) is continuous with the meaning (here subsistent). It consequently transpires that neither the word alone

---

1. 'No abstraction (whatever its origin) is in the end defensible. For they are none of them quite true, and with each the amount of possible error must remain unknown. The truth asserted is not, and cannot be, taken as real by itself. The background is ignored because it is assumed to make no difference . . . But an assumption of this kind obviously goes beyond our knowledge.' *Appearance*, p. 478.

2. The reference is to Peirce, *Collected Papers* Volume II, Book II, Chapter 3, 'The Icon, Index, and Symbol', 156–73. [Bolgan.]

(for there is no word alone) is the object, for the logical meaning (which is an abstraction and cannot be grasped without the word) nor the total of word and meaning, for there is no total; word and meaning being continuous, and the continuity not an object.[1,2]

The (true) object, then, is never a mere universal, nor a mere particular, nor a complex composed of universals and particulars. It was known, I should suppose, by Plato, that universals and particulars cannot be in any meaningful sense related, inasmuch as they are not separate existences. And so I cannot find any more satisfaction in the account of Mr Russell than in that of Meinong. [105] For Mr Russell, as for Meinong, universals or particulars may be known by direct acquaintance. But whereas for Meinong both seem to be treated as direct objects, Russell's acquaintance certainly refers to another kind of knowledge than that of objects. Thus acquaintance is defined as 'direct cognitive relation to that object. . . .'[3] The cognitive relation here is presentation. Sense-data, universals, and perhaps the self are thus known. Now whatever may be said of universals, neither sense-data nor the self are known primitively by what is commonly called presentation, i.e. presentation as an object: for we are surely somehow 'acquainted' with sense-data and the self in the practical apprehensions of objects long before we make objects (presentations) of the sense-data themselves.

The theory of Meinong starts from the postulate of the reality of objects – everything that is real is an object. Mr Russell starts apparently from the reality of universals and sense-data, and from these elements

---

1. The following passage appears to have some appropriateness: 'We must attach *some* meaning to the words we use, if we are to speak significantly and not utter mere noise; and the meaning we attach to our words must be something with which we are acquainted. Thus when, for example, we make a statement about Julius Caesar, it is plain that Julius Caesar himself is not before our minds, since we are not acquainted with him. We have in mind some *description* of Julius Caesar: . . . "the founder of the Roman Empire", or, perhaps, merely "the man whose name was *Julius Caesar*". (In this last description, *Julius Caesar* is a noise or shape with which we are acquainted.) Thus our statement does not mean quite what it seems to mean, but means something involving, instead of Julius Caesar, some description of him composed wholly of particulars and universals with which we are acquainted.' Russell, *Problems*, pp. 58–9. But I find the notion of acquaintance completely unsatisfactory.

2. Mr Eliot's meaning here is easily clarified if we alter the passage to read:

   It consequently transpires that neither the word alone is the object (for there is no word alone), nor the logical meaning (which is an abstraction and cannot be grasped without the word), nor the total of word and meaning (for there is no total – word and meaning being continuous, and the continuity not an object). [Bolgan.]

3. 'Knowledge by Acquaintance and Knowledge by Description,' *Proc. Arist. Soc.*, 1910–11.

late in the order of knowledge[1] he builds up the external world. 'We have acquaintance,' says Mr Russell, in a passage which strikingly recalls Locke (*Problems*, pp. 51–2), 'in sensation with the data of the outer senses,[2] and in introspection with the data of what may be called the inner sense – thoughts, feelings, desires, etc. . . . In addition to our acquaintance with particular existing things, we also have acquaintance with what we shall call *universals,* that is to say, general ideas, such as *whiteness, diversity, brotherhood,* and so on.' Inasmuch as we are stated (*ibid.,* p. 52) not to be acquainted with physical objects it may be inferred that we are not acquainted with anything in its character of *object,* but only in the felt whole of experience; with the interesting consequence that objects are not directly known but inferred, and that anything which is named is so far not [106] among our acquaintance. And here again we encounter an interesting rapprochement of realism to Kantianism. The entities (to use as non-committal a term as possible) which we know (by acquaintance) are not objects but means by which we apprehend objects, while the object is directly quite beyond the span of our knowledge. There are, on this interpretation, 'no such things' as objects, there are only experiences. 'All names of places – London, England, Europe, the Earth, the Solar System – similarly involve, when used, descriptions which start from some one or more particulars with which we are acquainted. I suspect that even the Universe, as considered by metaphysics, involves such a connection with particulars.[3] In logic, on the contrary, where we are concerned not merely with what does exist, but with whatever might or could exist or be, no reference to actual particulars is involved.' (*Problems*, p. 56). In making a statement about something known only by description, Mr Russell says, we may *intend* to make the statements about the *object* itself – but we never do so (*ibid.,* p. 56). To know an object is simply to know that there is that object: we know only an objective which asserts an existence; and to say that we have direct acquaintance with that objective is not to make the object any more real.

Apparently another person may be an intended object, but can be a real object only to the person himself – and a person is not an object to himself, because he is directly acquainted with himself, and acquaintance

---

1. Cf. '. . . [L]a mentalité des sociétés inférieures . . . comporte bien des représentations abstraites, et des représentations générales; mais ni cette abstraction, ni cette généralité ne sont celles de nos concepts.' Lévy-Bruhl, *Les Fonctions Mentales*, p. 137.

2. Cf. Nettleship, *Remains*, I, pp. 176–7.

3. Cf. the idealistic doctrine of the essential connection of the universe with the moment of perception.

is not a subject-object relation.[1] The world thus appears as an ideal construction of descriptions linked to the physiological and to the logical system.

What then is the relation of universals and particulars in the world of objects? 'A thing, of the every-day sort is constituted by a bundle of sensible qualities belonging to various senses, but sup-[107]posed all to co-exist in one continuous portion of space.'[2,3] It is apparently by a sort of projection of sense-data (not, it must be remembered, themselves objects) that we obtain the reality (or the illusion?) of a thing. This is, incidentally, very near to Berkeley, nearer certainly than Mr Russell's interpretation of Berkeley.[4] But it is, from a slightly different point of view, very near to Kant. You have the data of sense united by logic, and this determination of the manifold is for a subject, since the data of sense are real only in acquaintance, and acquaintance means the enjoyment by a subject. It would appear that the thing, which is always an object of higher order (as there are properly no objects of lower order for Mr Russell) is a logical construction, composed of two sorts of material, sense-data and universals, both of which are if you like objective, but hardly objective in the same sense in which objects are objective. Consequently, on this interpretation of Mr Russell's theory, one cannot say with Meinong that objects are either existent or subsistent, or are compounds of both ingredients, for the only entities which are purely existent are those of sense and introspection, and the only entities which are purely subsistent are universals.[5]

---

1. It is true that in the article cited on page 105, acquaintance is defined as 'direct cognitive relation to that object'. But the whole account of acquaintance, both in this article and in the *Problems* seems to me to point directly to enjoyment and not to contemplation, and I cannot help feeling that one of the obscurities of Mr Russell's position lies in treating as objects what are at the same time meant not to be objects.

2. 'Relations of Universals and Particulars', *Proc. Arist. Soc.*, 1911–12, pp. 6–7. [Bolgan.]

3. The passage quoted is from pages 7–8 of Russell's 'On the Relations of Universals and Particulars' but is quoted in a slightly inaccurate way. It should read as follows:
   If, on the other hand, we consider what may be called 'real' space, *i.e.* the inferred space containing the 'real' objects which we suppose to be the cause of our perceptions, then we no longer know what is the nature of the qualities, if any, which exist in this 'real' space, and it is natural to replace the bundle of qualities by a collection of pieces of matter having whatever characteristics the science of the moment may prescribe.

4. Cf. 'The ideas of sight and touch make two species, entirely distinct and heterogeneous'. . . . (*Prin. of Human Knowledge*, XLIV) with 'If we talk of *one* space we substitute for the perceived sense data a collection of pieces of matter having whatever qualities the science of the moment may prescribe.' 'Universals and Particulars', p. 7.

5. It is true that Mr Russell speaks elsewhere as if we were directly acquainted with things. (*Problems*, p. 136): '[we may know] . . . by means of *acquaintance* with the

It is interesting to note, furthermore, how uncertain the *evidence* for the existence of objects becomes when we begin by assuming them absolutely, and on this theory. The only things that we know by acquaintance 'are neither true nor false': sense-data (*Problems*, p. 113), universals, and the objects of inner perception.[1] The latter, as I intimated, are so far as known by [108] acquaintance not objects – so far as they are objects they are subject to all the conditions of outer perceptions. The universals also are assuredly neither true nor false, inasmuch as you do not have falsehood without an existence proposition.

Whiteness and brotherhood are it is true *a priori* (in the sense defined by Meinong, which is ultimately the sense of Kant as well) but they are not knowledge, nor are they known. We *experience* universals, and we *experience* particulars, but knowledge is always of *objects,* in which both are elements. And this is as true of the objects of mathematics, I submit, as of anything else: the actual object is always composed of existent and of subsistent elements, and is defined (practically) as an existent or as a subsistent object by the tendency of its use. Numbers, considered as merely subsistent, have no true or false combinations, for they are not known. They are simply *erlebt* (experienced) in the contemplation of objects to which they apply; 2 plus 2 = 4 is thus neither true nor false; but when we add four real objects together, we know (as objects), that two of the objects with two of the objects makes four objects, and we experience by acquaintance the 2 plus 2 = 4. We can of course abstract the numbers simply and determine them by a moment of objectivity; but what we have then is not the number in itself but an object corresponding to it. For how should objects apply to objects, as numbers apply to things? Numbers are not objects; nor, as I shall try to point out later, is number strictly a category.

The question then from the point of view of Mr Russell's philosophy, is how we proceed from acquaintance with entities which are neither real nor unreal to a knowledge of real objects which is true or false. 'We agreed provisionally that physical objects cannot be quite like our sense-data, but may be regarded as *causing* our sensations' (*Problems*, p. 30). Space, moreoever, is an *assumption* (*ibid.*, pp. 30, 31). Time consists in an order of before and after, but we cannot apparently be sure that the time-order which events seem to have is the same as the

---

complex fact itself, which may (in a large sense) be called perception, though it is by no means confined to objects of the senses.' But I do not see how, according to the passage quoted earlier, we can be directly acquainted with anything that is strictly true or false of the real world.

1. Cf. Locke's Essay, Bk. II, Ch. I, Para. 19, 'Consciousness is the perception of what passes in a man's own mind.'

time-order which they do have (*ibid.*, p. 32). In regard to the characters of objects, secondary qualities are not characters of physical objects [109] (*ibid.*, p. 35), but in an experience of red and blue, we may 'reasonably presume' (*ibid.*, p. 34) that a difference in the object corresponds to the difference of red and blue. 'Thus we find that, although the *relations* of physical objects have all sorts of knowable properties, derived from their correspondence with the relations of sense-data, the physical objects themselves remain unknown in their intrinsic nature, so far at least as can be discovered by means of the senses' (*ibid.*, p. 34). This seems very near to *Funktionsbegriff* (functional conception). The thing, if it *is* any more than a function of these relations is the merest assumption of popular prejudice. And these difficulties of a dualistic realism come from the standpoint of epistemology – of assuming that there is a real world outside of our knowledge and asking how we may know it.

Another difficulty of this point of view is the problem of time in knowledge and in reality. Knowledge of a universal, if a universal could be an object, would be knowledge of an object which is not in time, and the knowledge consequently would be out of time. For we attend to something, and if our attention is a temporal process the object can hardly fail to persist in time. But on the other hand, if existent objects are wholly in time, the very persistence of our attention upon them will involve the holding together of various moments of sensation by a common meaning, and that meaning will not be within the time to which it refers. I have tried to indicate one way of escape from this dilemma, in asserting the relativity of the subsistent and the existent, and pointing out the fact that a real object always has existent and subsistent elements. And this is substantially the conclusion of Mr Russell from one point of view, if as several passages imply the object is a sort of projection composed of universals and particulars known by acquaintance. But there is a further difficulty in the apprehension of these composite entities: 'And as with space, the qualitative content – which is not merely temporal, and apart from which the terms related would have no character – presents an insoluble problem. How to combine this in unity with the time which it fills, and again how to establish [110] each aspect apart, are both beyond our resources. And time so far, like space, has turned out to be appearance.' (*Appearance*, p. 34).

Just what is the meaning of simultaneity of perceiving and perceived? When I perceive an object, is there any meaning in the statement that the object is 'there' at the same time that my perception is 'there'? If we make this assertion, and affirm that the object is composed of sense-data which are strictly in time and universals (relations) which are not in time, we face the question: what time is it that the object exists in?

'It must not be supposed,' says Mr Russell, 'that the various states of different physical objects have the same time-order as the sense-data which constitute the perceptions of those objects' (*Problems*, p. 33). We thus have two time-orders which are not reducible to each other, or the possibility of a continuum of various time-orders from the immediate order of experience *sensa* to the object itself, which, so far as it is *that* object, is not in time at all. And reality seems to fluctuate between these two impossible limits. Impossible, because on the one hand that which is purely in time cannot be said to exist at all. To exist it must be a *what*, and to be a *what* is to have (internal) ideal relations to other *whats*, relations which are not in time. And on the other hand, the object of perception cannot be consistent with itself as an object, because so far as it is that object, it is timeless; and so far as it changes, it never was that object, but a remoter object which is capable of persisting through the two states of itself: any object which is wholly real is independent of time, and after any noticed change that which it was previously is to be regarded as an appearance. The time-order then will vary according to what we take as the object – the 'real' sun, for example, or the perceived sun. The two are, if you like, the same sense-data in different relations, and for two objects to exist at the same time means an alliance by the same ideal relation. What does it mean to say that my character and the ten o'clock train, or the reputation of Herbert Spencer and his volume which lies on my table, or my table and the electrons exist at the same time? There is no exact meaning, and the statement [111] has meaning only so far as we refer both to a single world, in which we vaguely feel that they are reconciled by experience; they are held together, that is, by a feeling of their *identical reference*, though that to which they refer does not exist.

This explanation (if it deserve the name) is the only escape that I can find from the time difficulty in perception. There is no time difficulty, because perception isn't in time; but there are several time-orders, and the collision occurs only when we arbitrarily assume that one is real and that there is a separate order of perception which must somehow correspond to it. But in a dualistic realism, the time difficulty appears very serious indeed, and real time seems to be as much an inference as is real space. So here again I suspect that we approach very close to criticism. For the real time and real space are demanded only by the way the problem has been set: a real (physical) world is assumed, then when we come to ask how we know this world, it appears that all we are sure of is data and forms of immediate experience, out of which the physical world is constructed – as a consequence of which the 'objectivity' of the external world becomes otiose or meaningless.

Chapter V
The Epistemologist's Theory of Knowledge

continued

KEPB, 112–40.

I should now like to discuss some points in connection with unreal objects, and the theories of Meinong and Russell, indicating the realistic assumptions which underlie their solutions, and which alone create the problem. This will serve as an introduction to the larger question of denoting, meaning and context.

There are two questions here involved: that of the existence of unreal objects, and that of the truth or falsity of statements about unreal objects. And again, in the case of unreal objects, there are objects of hallucination, objects of imagination, and objects denoted, but apparently neither believed in nor assumed (the round square). It is chiefly with the last that these two authors are engaged. With regard to all of these types of object I would recall what I have said of the relations of real and ideal, and would urge the following contention: the problem is wholly factitious, and owes its origin to the false assumption of epistemology – the assumption that there is one world of external reality which is consistent and complete: an assumption which is not only ungrounded but in some sense certainly false. Reality contains irreducible contradictions and irreconcilable points of view. How this statement is consistent with a monistic metaphysic I shall endeavour to show in another place.

I wish to touch upon the facts of visual hallucination first, because, while the problem is essentially the same as that dealt with by Meinong and Russell, it appears in a more readily [113] apprehensible form, and because it has by some been reduced to a different explanation from that of unreal objects in judgement, whereas I believe the hallucination to be in virtually the same position as the round square; both are non-existent, and both are intended objects. Both assert their reality, though perhaps in a difference of degree. Professor Holt says (*The New Realism*, p. 306) in stating the claim of an hypothetical opponent : '. . . not the distorted image as such, but the distorted image which *asserts itself to be*, or which *the realist asserts to be the real object* – . . . this is the crux for realism.' This appears to involve a *petitio principii*: it is not admitted that there is a 'distorted image as such'. In the case of the stick in water (which is quite distinct from the phenomena of hallucination) there is if you please 'distorted image as such'; if, that is, you abstract the stick under normal conditions and choose to call that the stick. But here you have only a case of completion of partial aspects of the same object; you say, for example, that it is one and the same object which you intend under two aspects, and the two aspects, when added together, give an object which is essentially continuous with each aspect in its meaning. And this, I think, constitutes the difference between so-called sense illusion and hallucination: the difference of direction of self completion of the object as first presented. In this sense the assertion of Professor Holt is essentially correct; if it is interpreted as meaning that there is nothing in the immediate presentation of the object to determine its reality or unreality; it is I believe mistaken so far as it means that there is in an absolute sense a given object which is not internally related to its own completion. And the degree to which this claim (as it may be called) is realised without practical falsification of the first presentation is the degree of truth of the first presentation. The stick under water is continuous with the stick out of water, in a way in which an hallucination is not; for the latter can complete itself only backward, i.e., the experience has its relations in the direction of neural process, not in the direction which the image intends. It is by this capacity of indefinite self-completion, and not by any ear-marks, that we judge the reality of a presentation; [114] but without this capacity, or the claim, we could not have even a presentation.

The reality of an hallucination is not, in the first place, judged merely by vividness or precision. Vividness, in the ordinary sense, is no more a condition of hallucination than is the liveliness of an idea the condition of belief. An hallucination simply cannot be as vivid as a normal waking impression without fulfilling all the conditions of such impression. There is no question of mere brightness of mental image, in the way in which a well made photograph is brighter than a short exposure. For brightness in this sense is a wholly objective matter; when we look at a dim photograph our impression is as precise and clear as when we examine a very sharp photograph. You cannot, that is, define the strength of an hallucination by the supposed objective clearness of a presentation which is really 'there'; you cannot say that the hallucination has all the characteristics of a reality except the third dimension, for example. Such an explanation leaves us wondering why we do not have the hallucination of reality – as well as the 'illusion' – when we contemplate a picture. And it is perhaps in point to offer this one remark on tridimensionality. Three dimensions exist wherever three dimensions are implied. Now in the contemplation of a picture our attitude may I think be analysed into two: we contemplate the reality referred to by the lines and tones, and, we contemplate the lines and tones themselves. A picture is analogous to any of the common figures of optical illusion; the meaning (or reference) of the picture corresponds to the illusory direction of the lines, and the actual arrangements of paint to the 'real' directions. In point of fact the apparent direction of the lines is just as objective as the real direction; the apparent direction is the 'meaning' of the figure. So the tridimensionality of the picture is just as real as the onedimensionality of the surface: so far as it is a picture, so far as it refers to three dimensions, it has three dimensions. An hallucination, also, has three dimensions for the point of view of the hallucinated is the *only* point of view; whereas in the case of a picture there is another point of view which is recognised at the same time. An hallucination is therefore wholly [115] unlike a picture, in that there is one point of view from which it is real, and another from which it does not exist at all; though from the point of view of an outsider it may be what I have previously denominated an intended half-object; i.e., we intend something which from our point of view is wholly inexistent. In order to acknowledge the existence of hallucinations we have partially to concede their truth.[1]

No comparison with normal experience, according to the considerations above, can give an account of the plausibility of an hallucination, for so far as it exists it has all the features of the real world, and it exists so far as it is believed in. The principle upon which I insist is of course the unity and continuity of feeling and objectivity, the fact that, as dwelt upon in the first chapter, the two are only discriminated aspects in the whole of experience. Take, for instance, a child frightened by a bogey. The child 'thinks it sees' a bear. The meaning of this phrase is by no means self-evident, for we have, I believe, no criterion for saying that the child does or does not see a bear. Such an illusion may be much more, or much less, than a cinematograph bear; Pierre Janet gives examples, from among his hystericals, of the sensation of touch and weight as well. But in a commonplace hallucination (cf. William James in his cabin) the moment of perception is usually I believe very slight indeed, though – and this is an important point – we can never say that it is altogether

---

1. This paragraph is only the detailed examination of a point which falls under the general doctrine here stated: 'Error is without any question a dangerous subject, and the chief difficulty is as follows: We cannot, on the one hand, accept anything between non-existence and reality, while, on the other hand, error obstinately refuses to be either. It persistently attempts to maintain a third position, which appears nowhere to exist, and yet somehow is occupied. In false appearance there is something attributed to the real which does not belong to it. But if the appearance is not real, then it is not false appearance because it is nothing. On the other hand, if it is false, it must therefore be true reality, for it is something which is. And this dilemma at first sight seems insoluble. Or, to put it otherwise, an appearance, which is, must fall somewhere. But error, because it is false, cannot belong to the Absolute; and again, it cannot appertain to the finite subject, because that with all its contents cannot fall outside the Absolute; at least, if it did, it would be nothing. And so error has no home, it has no place in existence; and yet, for all that, it exists. And for this reason it has occasioned much doubt and difficulty.' *Appearance*, pp. 164–5.

[116] absent. In the case of the frightened child, I am not prepared to support the James-Lange theory, but I do not see any priority of image over emotion, or vice versa. There is, if you like, a tendency for emotion to objectify itself,[1] but the implication is surely mutual, for feeling and image react upon one another inextricably, and the two aspects are so closely related, that you cannot say that the relation is casual.

It is therefore not altogether true or altogether false to say that the child sees a bear. For to take one group of relations of the word 'bear', and say that this group and no other shall constitute the meaning, is not only unwarranted but impossible. The child does not know just what it means when it says 'bear', nor do we know what it means; it does not know just what it has perceived when it has been frightened by a 'bear', nor do we know what it has perceived. For as the difference between real bear and illusory bear is a difference of fullness of relations, and is *not* the sort of difference which subsists between two classes of objects, so the one word must cover both reality and error. The only case in which it is possible in any sense to say that a perception is 'mistaken' is when there is actually before us an object closely enough resembling the object of the erroneous perception to justify our saying that it was this object which we perceived and from which we made false inferences; so that the degree of error which we recognise is in inverse ratio to the degree of similarity between the first and the second perception. The error is thus error because we are able in practice to assume that it was the true object that we perceived the whole time. In practice, that is to say, you can credit the possibility of a false inference from a truly apprehended premiss; but in theory you cannot say that the premiss is truly apprehended in one case and not in the other, for you have no right to say that it is the same premiss. The premiss (here the perception from which we infer) is only *that* premiss with reference to what follows, and in this sense, every inference is a true inference. For in metaphysics there is no concatenation of inferences, but there is a starting-point which expands itself and [117] can neither be arrested nor analysed, for the process is not one simply of addition, but of inner development, so that the starting-point itself is altered, and you cannot say absolutely what the starting-point was. When we take these facts into consideration, we find that it is only relatively that we can declare an erroneous object to have been inferred from a true perception. The real object was 'there', and in a practical sense it was that to which the perception referred, but the solution, in which we account for a true and a false perception by summing them up under an identical reference, is essentially a *practical* solution, inasmuch as it involves an

---

1. Cf. Lipps, *Vom Fühlen, Wollen, und Denken*, p. 70.

interpretation of a point of view which we do not accept, that of the error, and an interpretation is essentially unverifiable.

The error is an error then, because we compare it to a cognate reality. It differs from hallucination in that in the latter case there is no cognate reality. The difference is of course of degree only, for we do compare the differences of an identity with respect to hallucination: the room as it really is versus the room plus the spectre, and the fact that it is the same room gives us warrant for affirming error. We only say that an object is unreal with respect to something else which we declare to have been affirmed at the same time and which continues to be real, while the other does not. Now an hallucination has a greater degree of substantiality than an error, because of its greater independence; there is, strictly speaking, nothing to contrast it with except its own unreality. An hallucination, therefore, is not a 'mistake', for it is not attached to the real world in the direction of objectivity; it cannot be interpreted as referring to any object which is actually 'there'. It is attached to the real world, but its real relations are in the direction of physiological foundation, and this involves a much more radical change of point of view than mere error.

We have seen that the hallucination does not differ from the real object by defect of any specific qualities (weight, solidity, internality, etc.) for such a question belongs wholly to another dimension. It does not differ by contrast with some other (real) object which we are said (really) to intend. Reality, we find, is not [118] to be defined by anything in the immediate content.[1] There is a common form of reconciliation, however, which possesses a high degree of persuasiveness, and which does indeed explain unreal objects of perception in a limited way. The error, the hallucination, and the reality, will all be equally real in themselves, and perhaps ultimately harmonious; but we are in practice concerned only with a very restricted field of reality, a field no more real from the absolute point of view than any of the fragments which we exclude from it. We assume a complex *a-b-c-d,* and we exclude *x-B* fragments of a different alphabet, because we prefer the alphabet of which we have the more letters. The so-called hallucination is real and true when properly understood; when stating an error we really meant a truth. It is only because we have arbitrarily separated one portion of reality from the rest, a separation necessary for experience from finite centres, that we are obliged to relegate the rest to unreality. The world as we are acquainted with it from this limited point of view is an artificial construction, and, our point of view not being large enough to grasp the whole, we consider

---

1. See Nettleship, *Remains*, I, p. 188, '[T]here is no way of testing the truth or falsehood of an experience except by going beyond it. . . .'

the rest simply as the debris of our own slight structure. This is perhaps a doctrine of certain idealisms; and it is, so far as I understand, the doctrine of Professor Holt, who says (*op. cit.*, p. 357): 'The ... content (i.e., an image) simply is, and is in itself neither true nor false.' The idealist asserts, 'We have at first A, which possesses the qualities *c* and *b*, inconsistent adjectives which collide; and we go on to produce harmony by making a distinction within this subject. That was not really mere A, but either a complex within A, or (rather here) a wider whole in which A is included. The real subject is A+D; and this subject contains the contradiction made harmless by division, since A is *c* and D is *b*.' (*Appearance*, p. 170).

These two statements seem to me substantially the same. One asserts that the content simply is; the other that the transmuted content is the same content as the first. Both assert, I believe, in [119] the case of hallucination, that there is a real object present which is interpreted in two different ways, true or false. But we have seen that there is no choice but whether the object be real or nonexistent. If the real subject is not A but A+D, yet on the other hand the subject to which both *c* and *b* referred is A simply, and (for an idealist at least) the quality which refers to a different subject is a different quality; while for Professor Holt there is in illusory experience a real contradiction, and yet (*The New Realism*, p. 366) '... by reality we seem to mean the thing most remote from contradiction.'

No account of error in terms of 'dissolution' can ultimately satisfy, though its only justification is its ultimacy (*Appearance*, pp. 170–1). Such an account is ostensibly idealistic, since its criterion is coherence, and ultimate coherence is postulated, so that no purely 'unreal' objects are to be left over, as in a realistic world; but it is compelled to make assumptions of simple correspondence. 'Let us suppose the reality to be $X (a\ b\ c\ d\ e\ f\ g\ldots)$ and that we are able only to get partial views of this reality.'[1] But in metaphysics it is only by a euphemism that such a partial view is a view of *that* object, rather than a complete view of a different object; and the self-completion of the view involves the affirmation of another reality to which the reality apprehended fails to conform. You may say that the partial view or the hallucination implies its own self-contradiction and transcendence. But in the 'transcendence' of error, I insist, the error, as a real object, is not got rid of. An object is not transcended, though a point of view is; and it is only as we consider the hallucination not as an object, but as an element in a point of view, that it can be said to be 'transcended', 'transmuted', or 'dissolved'. Such a theory as that here outlined by Mr Bradley or by Professor Holt appears

---

1. Bradley, *Appearance and Reality*, 170. [Bolgan.]

unsatisfactory in that the unreality is merely pushed back and not done away with. What we thought was the object was not the object. But we have seen that an object is an object so far as it is thought to be so. The alteration from error to truth is not a change in the object, but a change in the whole situation, and the object, so far as it is an object, must be admitted to persist as a real object [120] in history. The illusion which I have lived through is no more unreal than is Julius Caesar unreal because he is dead. If the world is as essentially connected as idealists would often have us think, the unreal object must still persist and influence reality.[1]

The situation in regard to hallucinations and in regard to erroneous judgements is not essentially different. The one asserts the existence of an unreal object, and the other the subsistence of an unreal objective; and the line between object and objective, and between existence and subsistence, cannot as we have seen be sharply drawn. Something is asserted to be, which is not; though in order to assert the being of an object we must in some way perceive it. 'The problem of error cannot be solved by an enlarged scheme of relations. . . . For there is a positive sense and a specific character which marks each appearance, and this will still fall outside' (*Appearance*, p. 172). We can thus approach to no solution so long as we regard the world as made up of objects.

We must conclude then that the difference between hallucination and reality is not the difference between an unreal object and a real one. All objects are real, and the unreality is not of them *qua* objects, but because of certain other relations into which (in their reality otherwise than as objects) they fail to enter. An hallucination, we are constantly tempted to forget, is not an object, but a sphere of reality; its existence is internal as well as external. The contradictions which we have to reconcile are not two objects, for objects in themselves cannot contradict each other (this is in agreement, I believe, with Mr Holt) but two points of view, although I should maintain (as against Mr Holt) that the object is inseparable from the point of view.[2] The hallucination is a whole world of feeling, and the object is simply that world so far as objectified, You cannot, therefore, compare the two objects [121] directly, but only through the media of the two points of view of error and truth (though the two viewpoints are in themselves as objective as you please). We are unable to say, however,

---

1. Cf. Joachim, *Nature of Truth*, pp. 144–5: 'For precisely that feature in error, which at the time robs it of its sting for the erring person (viz. his untroubled confidence in the truth of his judgement), constitutes the distinctive character of error and its power for mischief. And this feature is never annulled and never converted into an element of the fuller knowledge. The triumphant development of astronomy has neither annulled nor absorbed the persecution of Galileo. . . .'

2. Though two points of view may intend the same object. See later.

that one point of view is right and the other wrong, for we thus imply an element of identity, or of identical reference; the assertion of one point of view against another must be made from a third point of view, which somehow contains the first and second. And yet it must be noticed (for I see no way to avoid this hair-splitting) that it is only from the third point of view that the first two are therein contained. For as soon as we have realised that we have reached a third point of view we are already at a fourth, in which the first and second reassert themselves once more. So that it is only so long as we can support a particular point of view (and this involves not recognising it as such) that we can believe that the contradiction between truth and error is superseded. To this matter I shall recur later. The chief result that I would emphasise here is that an hallucination involves much more than the assertion of contradictory objects; it involves a change in the subject as well. The *I* who saw the ghost is not the *I* who had the attack of indigestion. In a change of viewpoint, there is [in] some sense at least a total change, and I shall ask in another place just what sort of identity persists.

With imaginary objects we come to a class which is frequently, under the name of assumptions, distinguished sharply from objects of belief, both true and erroneous. I cannot feel that this distinction is needed. On the basis of the previous discussion, it should appear that any object is real in so far as it is attended to, and that when we assert an error or hallucination, we attend not to the object itself but to the experience. When I think of the golden mountain, I think of something which is to that extent real, i.e., what we call its unreality will appear from subsequent relations and not from the immediate presentations. There is, upon this view, nothing which we may call mere presentation. When we speak of presentation, (see my third chapter) we refer to something which was never actually presented, the 'content'; what is presented is really the object, and this is not presented as [122] a presentation, but as real. Undoubtedly it will be objected that we do think of objects as unreal. To this point I shall recur later; here I shall only recall what was said about the object of hallucination; in referring to a past hallucination the direct object is an experience, the indirect object the hallucinatory object. As the imaginary object does not differ essentially from this indirect object, I shall pass to it through a consideration of the object of a past hallucination.

I said that the direct object is an erroneous experience. But this is a real object only to a slight extent, and at the first analysis appears to be an intended object. For it splits into two parts, like other psychological objects: the physiological part and the real part. On the one hand we intend what 'really went on'; if it is certain 'ideas' in the 'mind' then these ideas (Chapter II) dissolve into the physiological process; and nothing 'went on' which cannot be described by the neurologist. On the other hand we intend the object intended by the patient, and this is on our part a true case of assumption as far as it is successful. When we intend an intention, that is to say, we intend something which is real in our world in combination with something which is not real in our world. But the experience as a whole *is* real in our world; other men's experiences are realities with which we come into contact, and which are continually influencing us. Here then, we have cases in which an assumption forms part of a reality: in which an assumption is real not simply as a real assumption (i.e., the fact that we made the assumption is true), but we have to make the assumption in order to apprehend an object which we know to be real. In cases like this we seem to confront a feature of the assumption neglected by Meinong. For the object of the hallucination is not assumed in the way in which objects which we do not know to exist are assumed; the object here is known not to exist. We cannot intend the intention of an object without intending the object itself; this is what I have called the indirect object when the direct object is an experience. And where the experience is an assumption and not an hallucination the matter is still further complicated. Another man 'assumes' the golden mountain; [123] I intend this experience as an object. I ought theoretically to be able to assume the assumption without committing myself to any attitude toward the golden mountain on my own account; but I find that I am obliged to make an indirect object of the mountain, intend it not only *through* the intention of the assumption, but directly. This immediacy holds true even if the object is something of which I know nothing, and the name of which has no meaning for me. I still *intend* the same object. Here again, in order to apprehend a reality (someone's making an assumption) I am forced to make an assumption myself. According to the account which I have given of psychology, in fact, we make assumptions in the apprehension of a large number of real objects.

I infer from these facts that assumption is not a simple act, but that the term may be made to cover every act from acceptance to rejection; and that the apprehension of an object known to be imaginary does not differ essentially from the apprehension of any other object, unless we have hocus-pocussed an external reality to which ideas are to 'conform'. Can we, in reading a novel, simply assume the characters and the situations? On the contrary, I seem to find that we either accept them as real, (with hallucination as the limiting case) or consider them as *meanings*, as a criticism of reality from the author's point of view. Actually, I think that if we did not vacillate between these two extremes (one of which alone would give the 'photographic' novel and the other the arid 'pièce à thèse') a novel would mean very little to us. The characters and the situations are all 'imaginary', but is there any one act which so apprehends them, cut off and 'floating'? In order to be imaginary, they must be contrasted with something which is real. There must, furthermore, be specific points of resemblance and difference: for the type of reality with which the imaginary object is contrasted must be a type to which the latter pretends to belong. Now so far as merely the imaginary object intends such a reality and falls short, it is not an object of any kind real or imaginary, but falls under what I have said previously of 'mere idea'. If the character in fiction is an imaginary object, it must be by virtue of something more than its being imaginary, i.e. merely [124] intending to be a reality which it is not. It must be, as I said, contrasted with this reality; to be contrasted it must be more than a pure reference; it must have in fact another aspect in which it has a reality of its own distinct from its reference. The fiction is thus more than a fiction: it is a *real* fiction.

We thus analyse the intended object of fiction into its reference and its reality. The reality in its turn is not a simple object but an intended object, for it includes everything from the antecedents of the character in the author's mind, to the symbols which express the character on paper. We may mean the character as a presentation to the author's mind; but a figure in fiction may and often does have an existence for us distinct from what is merely our interpretation of what the author 'had in mind'. Frequently we feel more confidence in our own interpretation of the character than in any account of the genesis and meaning which the author may give himself. This is not always mere accident; no really 'vital' character in fiction is altogether a conscious construction of the author. On the contrary, it may be a sort of parasitic growth upon the author's personality, developing by internal necessity as much as by external addition. So that we come to feel that the point of view from which the author criticises is not wholly internal to the point of view from which he created the character. Of course this difference should not be insisted upon, for the author may shift from a creative to a critical point of view and back at any moment.[1] Now a character which is 'lived through', which is real to us not merely by suggesting 'that sort of person' but by its independent cogency, is to the extent of its success real. Treating it as imaginary involves a change of viewpoint. Besides this reality, the character has other relations which are inconsistent with

---

1. The combination of criticism and creation is found perhaps in such writers as Molière and Stendhal: whilst the characters of Balzac and Dostoevsky are much more nearly lived through simply.

reality. It belongs in other contexts, has relations which are incompatible with its reality. Its unreality, therefore, is not in itself, but in relations extending far beyond itself; its reality is its reference, and its unreality as that to which it refers is its [125] reality as an 'imaginary' object. And, on the other hand, as an imaginary object it is just as real as anything; it is as a real object that it is imaginary.

An imaginary object has thus two main aspects: its intention to be real and its reality as an intention. As the former it is limited by its paucity of relations; as the latter it exists by virtue of its relations. There is, strictly speaking, no imaginary objective: we attend to a complex which comprehends two points of view – a real object with few relations and an intended object which consists of its relations. When we speak of the character as a fiction we mean a relation between an object real from one point of view and certain entities (ultimately physical) which are real from another point of view. The imaginary object, it will follow, is a highly complex ideal construction. It exists as such only from a third point of view which includes the two just mentioned; but these two also are in the closest dependence upon one another. For the real relations of the intended object (the mental and physical conditions which attended the genesis and realisation of that character of fiction) would not be such as they are without the intention to realise a fiction.

At this point I must introduce another complication. The author himself may attend to his fiction not merely as an intended reality (i.e. he may not be and in reality I suppose never is conscious of his fiction from the point of view from which it is real). He may be conscious of the continual *va-et-vient* of ideas in the process of realisation; the intended reality shifts and changes as he deserts one outcome for another; and he may be conscious furthermore of the effort to express felt emotions and abstract ideas by 'clothing them in flesh and blood'. So that I do not believe that the author in process of composition is ever, in practice, occupied with a single point of view; or that in practice any moment ever exists when one point of view is in exclusive possession. But the 'imaginary object' has all these relations and in fact *is* these relations.

Finally, I do not see any possibility of saying that the imaginary object either subsists or exists. For when we think of the character [126] in fiction, we go on to think of some aspect in the complex. Becky Sharp exists in the time-order of *Vanity Fair*, but this time-order does not itself exist. Becky exists as an event in the life of Thackeray, and as an event in the life of every reader in the same way that every real person exists as an event in the life of every other real person with whom he comes in contact. But the object denoted by the word Becky does not exist, for it is simply the identical reference of several points of view.

If the evidence which I have offered has any relevance, it should appear that assumption or entertainment is by no means a simple act like acceptance or rejection. The object is not a simple object. There is a simple object which is real in the same way in which an hallucination is real, but this object is only part of the object of the assumption. The chief advantage which this theory pretends to offer over Meinong's is its greater consistency with Bradley's views on floating ideas. The *Annahme*, as I understand it, is such a floating idea. If reality is all of a piece, as the epistemologist believes, then the imaginary must be cut off and floating 'like Mahomet's coffin' between earth and sky. In the theory which I outline, the distinction of objective and subjective, external reality and mental, is unnecessary. Whatever is gathered together in consciousness equally is, and is real or unreal only in relation.

A third class of objects is that of unreal objects. These differ from the two foregoing in that they are neither believed in nor partially believed in, but are intended objects of 'denoting phrases which denote nothing'. In the other two classes there always is an object, although in the case of assumptions the object[1] dissolves into entities which are not themselves objects but do not fail to exist. We might say that in an assumption the object is real, but is not an object, and that in the intention of an unreal object the object is an object but is not real. The question is, in the words of Mr Russell, whether 'any grammatically correct denoting phrase stands for an *object*'. ('On denoting', *Mind*, 1905, p. 482).

[127] The difficulty with Meinong's view, according to Mr Russell, is that such an object may infringe the law of contradiction. The present King of France will both exist and not exist, the round square will be round and not round. The fallacy of this criticism lies, I believe, in treating existence as being for metaphysics as well as for formal logic, a simple predicate.[2] To say that the present King of France both exists and not exists is no more false than to say that my typewriter both exists and not exists inasmuch as it now exists for me who am looking at it, and not for Mr Russell who is looking at something else. In other words, in asserting existence of any object, we denote existence but do not mean it; and yet, we do mean to denote, and this meaning to denote is an essential part of the denoting.

The difficulty is greatly enhanced by the fact that in the use of any phrase we cannot always be sure to what extent we are meaning the

---

1. Making a sharp distinction between the object of the assumption and the object of the belief which is one of the points of view entering into the assumption.

2. From the point of view taken in this paper, of course, any simple judgement of existence will always be partially false. But this is not precisely the argument used here.

denotation or meaning the meaning, and how far we are denoting the denotation or denoting the meaning. For practical purposes the phrase 'the present King of France' denotes a real object but has no meaning; but this will not do for us, because any denoting phrase which can be used in a proposition means to have meaning, and is therefore not meaningless, and also a phrase cannot denote without likewise having meaning. While we may say, according to Mr Russell, that

(1) 'The present King of France' is a denoting phrase,

we may not say

(2) The present King of France is bald.

It is possible, however, to deny the admissibility of the first of the two propositions, for it implies the partial maintenance of two points of view. I do not see how we can refer to the meaning of a phrase without referring also to its denotation.

Proposition (1) is about 'the present King', but would not be a proposition unless we assumed at one moment the existence of the present King. For if we *know* that 'the present King' denotes [128] nothing, then it isn't denoting; and if we say that it means to denote, then we have transported ourselves to a point of view internal to the meaning, and actually mention the present King of France. In logic, perhaps, but not in metaphysic, a denoting phrase may denote nothing. Somehow, obscurely, the object denoted is acknowledged existence. It is non-existent according to the practical standards which recognise no degrees between existence and non-existence; but for metaphysics, it cannot be denied practical reality without being admitted to some more attenuated but (if you like) equally real reality.

And notice that the contrast is not at all that between the solid reality and the idea. This is to confuse denotation with meaning. 'Chimeras do not exist.'[1] This proposition does not say: Ideal chimeras do not exist. The chimeras to which existence is denied are not the chimeras 'in my head' but the real chimeras. But surely, it will be objected, we do not say: Real chimeras are unreal! Yet that is in my opinion, just what, from the point of view of metaphysics, we do say, and any other statement would be meaningless. The explanation so far as there is one, is simply this. The phrase, 'real chimeras' can be taken in two ways: (1) the chimeras which are actually experienced; (2) chimeras which are 'real'. The word 'real' has

---

1. The passage referred to in Bradley's *The Principles of Logic*, 115 reads as follows:

    Let us take such a denial as 'Chimaeras are nonexistent'. 'Chimaera' is here ostensibly the subject, but is really the predicate. [Bolgan.]

in (1) meaning, and in (2) denotation. On the other hand in order to have meaning in (1), it must denote something which in experience is actually judged to be real in sense (2), and in order to have denotation in (2) it must have meaning in actual experience. By substituting alternately we get

> Chimeras such as are experienced, are not real.
>
> Real chimeras (i.e., such as would satisfy all the conditions of reality) are not experienced – not met with in experience.

Here by denying the predication of denotation of meaning and vice versa we seem to escape contradiction. But the evasion is only momentary. For the phrase 'chimeras such as are experienced' denotes real chimeras, and the phrase 'real chimeras' means [129] chimeras which are actually experienced. Can we say that the non-existent chimeras are real chimeras in denotation and imaginary chimeras in meaning? We have some idea of that to which we deny existence, and the idea, we have seen above, is so far as it is ideal as well the reality which it intends, and we must say similarly of the denoting phrase, that so far as it denotes it denotes a real object.

What has been said of the status of ideas, in a previous chapter, will thus apply to a certain extent to denoting phrases. In each there is the moment of objectivity, so that it implies its own fulfilment in reality, as an object of practical experience. Idea and phrase both denote realities, but the realities which they denote are so far as idea or phrase denotes, identical with the idea or the phrase. It is a mistake, I think, to treat the word as something which barely points to the object, a sign-post which you leave behind on the road. The word 'chimera' or the idea 'chimera' is the beginning of the reality chimera and is absolutely continuous with it, and the 'present King of France' is already partially real. The phrase directs your attention to an object but the object is an object because it is also that object, because the mere hypothetical moment of objectivity is qualified by the characters of the phrase, which are real properties at once of the phrase and of the object. Just as the idea refers to itself, so the denoting phrase denotes itself. But just as an idea is not a thing, and our difficulties arise from trying to treat it as a thing, so a denoting phrase is not a thing. It is not simply *that,* for a mere *that* (which is in fact only a theoretical limit) does not refer to something else; reference is a kind of activity, original or delegated. Like an idea, a word or phrase has existence outside of its objectivity, and a denoting phrase in particular resembles an idea in having an existence which straddles so to speak two moments of objectivity; the one moment being simply those marks or sounds which denote, and the other the object denoted.

This is the only way that I can discover to get over the metaphysical difficulties of unreal objects: to a very large extent we are not dealing with objects at all, and it is only when we try to press [130] an exact meaning that we find language forcing untenable theories upon us. The denoting phrase is not an object, and existence is a complex notion. What we denote when we *denote the denoting phrase* is not the phrase as such, for that is an activity rather than an object, but rather the tendency toward objectification in the direction toward us; that is, the 'word', the written sign, or the *vox et praeterea nihil*. But this object itself is an abstraction and not real, for when you have stripped it of its power, its reference, it is no longer that object, but something quite unrelated to the denoting. It would thus appear that in denoting the object is no more than a moment of objectivity, and that in thinking of a denoting phrase we mean an object which dissolves into two sub-objects and a relation. And this analysis is a falsification, for one object cannot, as we have said, refer to another without being more than an object, and the sub-objects, abstracted from the reference, disappear.

The usefulness of this account will not be at first evident but it may go a little way toward solving the difficulties raised by other explanations. The difficulty of Meinong's theory that there are unreal objects is, as Mr Russell points out, the fact that such objects violate the law of contradiction; and the difficulty of Mr Russell's theory is the contradiction of phrases denoting which yet denote nothing – a pure mystery. The position of Meinong is untenable, I think, only so long as we assume that although objects may exist in various ways, they can exist only in one degree. While it is true that the round square is both square and round, it is not true to say that it is both round and not round, although square may imply, in other contexts, not-round. This is to confuse two planes of reality; so far as the object exists at all it is both square and round, but the squareness and roundness which it has are the squareness and roundness of that degree of reality; the object is not present upon that level of reality upon which square and round are contradictory, though it is none the less, *qua* object, real. Objects exist for us in two ways: As we *intend* an object, the intended object is so far real, and as we experience an object, it realises itself, and comes to require a [131] certain degree of fullness of relations before it considers itself an object. The ordinary objects (by which we set our standard of reality for the intended objects denoted by the symbols which denote those ordinary or usual objects) are objects of the second sort. But we are accustomed to handle and use them by symbols which merely denote them; we forget that their reality is as much in their meaning as in their denotation, and we take it for granted that they simply are. Nor is this belief error – the matter is much more complicated than that! *As* objects, it is true that they simply are: but unfortunately, in order to be objects, they must be much more; they must be continuous with experience, and continuous with it in a rich and full way. Now commonly we do not treat unreal objects as objects *simpliciter*: the common-sense solution is to treat our 'real' objects *simpliciter*, and our unreal or imaginary objects as more immediately continuous with experience. Yet when we come to *préciser* we find ourselves reversing the procedure for we discover that it was just this continuity with experience, this fullness of relation, which gave us what we call our real objects, and just the discontinuity, the mere intention, which gave us our unreal objects. The 'unreal' object, *qua* object, is just the bare intention, the object-moment; whereas the 'real' object *is* real because it has so much to draw upon; because if removed it would, we feel, leave so much more of a void in our experience. And yet this unlimited credit is not the object itself; for it is not as such objective. So we are forced to conclude that one object is more real than another – more of an object – by virtue of non-object relations.[1] Both real object and unreal object are, *qua* objects, equally real; when, both, so to speak, are at the fovea. It is only when we cease to consider either simply as an object, that one appears to be real and the other unreal.

We may say, then, that the unreal object, although it exists, does not violate the law of contradiction.[2] While it is, broadly speaking, true that the present King of France both exists and [132] does not exist, it is not true in the same sense; for 'exists', as we have seen, is not a simple predicate. I suppose that it will be objected, to this assertion, that any judgement of existence would be rendered a tautology, for it could no more than declare that an object has the sort of existence that it has. Such an objection would in my opinion hold good only if the sorts of existence were cut off from each other like inches along a yard-stick. When we say exists, we mean a degree of existence to be determined by the context, and when we state the subject, we do not need to know the precise degree of reality which it is to have. In other words, a substantive in isolation is not yet even a substantive, for its degree of quality is quite unknown. Which states no more than that a substantive in complete isolation does not exist; for it would be a symbol that symbolised nothing, and hence would not be a symbol at all, but another reality (i.e., certain marks on paper, etc.).

It is essential to the doctrine which I have sketched that the symbol or sign be not arbitrarily amputated from the object which it symbolises, as

---

1. Ultimately, it must be remembered, there are not even relations.
2. And I am tempted, by the way, to regard as a dead letter a law which cannot be violated. Is not this law as useless as the vermiform appendix?

for practical purposes, it is isolated (see p. 90). No symbol, I maintain, is ever a mere symbol, but is continuous with that which it symbolises. Without words, no objects. The object, purely experienced and not denominated, is not yet an object, because it is only a bundle of particular perceptions; in order to be an object it must present identity in difference throughout a span of time. Now of course I do not pretend that there are no objects for the higher animals, or even for the lower; the difference is in one aspect only of degree. But we may say that in any knowledge prior to speech the object is not so much an identity recognised as such as it is a similar way of acting; the identity is rather lived out than known. What we are here concerned with is the explicit recognition of an object as such, and I do not believe that this occurs without the beginnings of speech. We may say if we like that the dog sees the cat and knows it as a cat, though it does not know its name, and I have no objection to this way of speaking loosely. But when we ask in what this knowledge consists, we can only point to a form of behaviour. [133] Our only way of showing that we are attending to an object[1] is to show that it and ourself are independent entities, and to do this we must have names. So that the point at which behaviour changes into mental life is essentially indefinite; it is a question of interpretation whether an expression which is repeated at the approach of the same object (as a cat may have a peculiar way of acting at the approach of a dog) is behaviour or language.[2] In either case, I insist, it is continuous with the object; in the first case because we have no object (except from the point of view of the observer, which must not be confused with that of the patient under examination), and in the second case because it is language which gives us objects rather than mere 'passions'. Or at least we have no objects without language.

I know that it will be objected that I am here confusing the genetic with the structural standpoint; and in reply I can only urge, that I have found the two organically related, and that I cannot admit that metaphysics may analyse and find truth in one part of the analysis, discarding the other. The object, you will say, is now known as independent of the word, though like enough without words we might not have come to know objects. It is true, I reply, that when we mean an object with a word we mean the object and not the word, and we might mean the same

---

1. This is not to say that the *phenomena* of attention are not observable among animals, but that such phenomena need not be in every aspect interpreted as those of *attention*.
2. The sense requires the insertion of the word 'there' between 'dog' and 'is'. The sentence would then read:

> [I]t is a question of interpretation whether in expression which is repeated at the approach of the same object (as a cat may have a peculiar way of acting at the approach of a dog), there is behaviour or language. [Bolgan.]

object by a different word, though I think that you quite underestimate the closeness with which particular words are woven into our reality. But the object which we denote in this sense is the object *qua* object, and not the bundle of experiences which the object means. The object *qua* object would not exist without this bundle of experiences, but the bundle would not be a bundle unless it were held together by the moment of objectivity which is realised in the name. I am very far from meaning that it is the act of naming which makes the object, for the activity does not proceed from one side more than from another. Objects cannot arise without names, and names never spring up without objects, ready to be [134] applied to the first objects to which they seem appropriate. Nor do I mean that the object did not exist until it was known, but only that it has not the character of objectivity until it is known as an object.

The name is not the object, certainly. We may say more truly that it is a category through which one grasps the object (if anyone has a taste for categories), but even this will not state the case correctly, if the category is conceived as something subjective, contrasted with the object. I should prefer to speak of the name as the moment of denotation; it is not that which is denoted, obviously, or merely a convenient means for denoting something which exists in complete independence of the name. It denotes an object which is not itself, and yet, when we ask just what this object is which is denoted, we have nothing to point to but the name. We do not denote any qualities of the object, as such; we do not, that is, denote any definition which could be given of the object; we denote not its *whatness* but its *thatness*. And we must not forget that even 'that' is a name; if I ask you to what you refer, you may simply point to the object and say 'that'; you mean, if you like, a certain bundle of perceptions, but unless what you mean has this name 'that' it is not an object. The simplest thing that a thing can be is to be 'that', is to be merely object; and we are not denoting 'that', and it is not object, until we have these two words at our disposal. Try to think of what anything would be if you refrained from naming it altogether, and it will dissolve into sensations which are not objects; and it will not be that particular object which it is, until you have found the right name for it.

This relationship of thing and name has interesting aspects on the other side. If we cannot say that we have that object until we have that name, since each name is a different way of organising a set of experiences, so on the other hand we have not really got that name until we have the right object. It is evident that a name is not a name unless it is the name of something, that the feeling of a meaning, if ever so faint, will just make the difference between a name and a mere *Laut-complex*. Now just as an object which we [135] cannot name is as yet only the adumbration of that object, so the name of which the object is not as yet distinct is only the adumbration of that name; we sometimes find ourselves guilty of using very specific names when for all that we know the name is equivalent merely to 'object'. Yet the name implies particularity. As we may fancy, if we like, objects wandering about waiting to be met with and be named (like the animals in the Garden of Eden), so we may fancy names wandering about in our heads waiting for objects. But such is an hypothetical limit which is never reached. Now as imaginary objects and imaginary spheres of reality are not 'in our heads', any more than the 'real' world is, names may be names of real objects in imaginary spheres. 'The present King of France' is not the name for anything in the 'real' world – but in the real world the 'present King of France' is not a name at all: supposing that there were such a real world cut off from all imaginary worlds, 'the present King of France' would be a mere noise – in the real world.

This, however[,] is a digression. Though we cannot say that we have either name or object (to recur to the beginning of the last paragraph) until we have the complete object for that name or the complete name for that object, yet the point at which this mystic marriage occurs is not exactly determinable. This should make a little clearer my observations on the child's imaginary bear (p. 115). The child means 'bear', we may say, without really knowing what bear means; yet so far as it has reacted to the bogey in the same way as it would to a real bear, the name 'bear' in the child's mind has a real bear to back it up. The name has terminated in an experience, and as even the word 'chimera' terminates in an experience in so far as the word is admitted to have a meaning, and not merely itself to *be,* the word has a real object.

The discussion of real and unreal objects will proceed with eternal fruitlessness so long as we maintain the belief that there is one consistent world of the real and that the rest is illusory. Nor do we advance a step farther by affirming that everything is real, for this alteration merely crams all the unreality into thought [136] which was formerly in perception, and in nowise resolves the question. The whole difficulty, I believe, arises from taking existence as a simple concept. Whereas, I have tried to show, we can never extricate the denotation of 'real' from its meaning. The process of development of a real world, as we are apt to forget in our theories, works in two directions; we have not first a real world to which we add our imaginings, nor have we a real world out of which we select *our* 'real' world, but the real and the unreal develop side by side. If we think of the world not as ready made – the world, that is, of meaning for us – but as constructed, or constructing itself, (for I am careful not to talk of the creative activity of mind, a phrase meaningless in metaphysics) at every moment, and never more than an approximate construction, a construction essentially practical in its nature: then the difficulties of real and unreal disappear. Theories of knowledge usually assume that there is one consistent real world, in which everything is real and equally real, and that it is our business to find it. They do this largely, I suppose, because common sense does the same thing, not realising that the denotations of real and unreal may hold good for a practical point of view and not for a metaphysical. While the real world of epistemology is hard and fast, its *whatness* and its *thatness* inseparably geminated, the real world of practice is essentially vague, unprecise, swarming with what are, from a metaphysical point of view, insoluble contradictions. We forget that what has grown up from a purely practical attitude cannot be explained by a purely theoretical. The real and the unreal are, from the outside point of view which we attempt to take as epistemologists, equally real, and our consequent troubles are due to the fact that these contrasts arose and have their meaning, only from the internal point of view which we have abandoned in seeking an explanation.

We can never, I mean, wholly explain the practical world from a theoretical point of view, because this world is what it is by reason of the practical point of view and the world which we try to explain is a world spread out upon a table – simply *there*! The plight into which we put ourselves is however inevitable, for the [137] theoretical point of view is the inevitable outgrowth of the practical. We arrive at objects, as I have tried to show, by meaning objects; sensations organise themselves around a (logical) point of attention and the world of feeling is transmogrified into a world of self and object. We thus have an object which is constituted by the denoting, though what we denote has an existence as an object only because it is also not an object, for *qua* object it is merely the denoting, the projection of shadow of the intention; as *real* object it is not object, but a whole of experiences which cluster round the point of denotation.[1] Now in practice do we use the complex meaning or only the denotation? I do not see any final answer to this question. For a theoretical account of the practical attitude would be a description from an outside point of view; and a 'practical' account would give merely the theory of our practice. A theory of practice or a practice of theory would be equally beside the mark: the first inevitably would reduce everything to meaning and the second would reduce everything to denoting. So far as objects are objects, we always intend to denote them, of course; but in practice, they are only objects partially or occasionally, and we cannot decide to what extent.

---

1. Not always, or even usually, a 'bundle of sensations'. All the associations and ideal relations are here meant.

Practice, and this is the difficulty (though all our difficulties are perhaps one in different forms) is shot through with theory, and theory with practice. The hypothetical transition from sensation to subject-object, which I have attempted to outline, is a speculative activity. The assumption of a real world is a theory; nothing, in fact, is merely found. And the distinction between theory and practice can nowhere be positively drawn; whether we are setting up an assumption 'for our own ends' or purely from the love of speculation, is everywhere matter for a relative distinction. In general we may say, nevertheless, that the sharper and more complete the lines, the more theoretical the account; and in this way, when we attempt to define practice we get a theory, and a theory may incorporate itself into our practice. Hence our theory will be found full of practical motives and [138] practical consequences, and our practice will be found to be largely based upon speculation.

To return, after this long digression, to our objects, I conclude that we can never give an exact description or explanation of the relations of the real and the unreal. For we have no difficulty with the matter at all until we begin to think (yet this thinking was forced upon us originally by the practical difficulties of illusion). Practically, as I said before, we use 'real' in two senses, and thus skip, within the practical, between practical and theoretical points of view. 'Chimeras do not exist.' A theoretical account of this might be, I said, 'real chimeras are not real'. This might be the theoretical account of what we really say, or the theory which we practise, or the theoretical account of the theory that we practise. Or we might give either of the alternatives which I offered earlier. But in every judgement there arises the contrast between reality and unreality.[1] A contrast which from a point of view (outside the sphere of interest of that judgement) is unjustified in the form in which it presents itself, and always means something different. But in the end these accounts are simply interpretations which have greater or less utility. 'Chimeras do not exist.' If we understand this it needs no explanation, if not we can find none. 'The King of France is bald.' This is true or false or meaningless according to its context and bearing. That the theory needs working out in great detail I cannot see. It would be tying knots in the east wind. We have secured, I think, a general principle, and have seen why it neither demands nor admits complete elaboration.

What I have been saying may seem to have no direct bearing upon the metaphysics of Mr Bradley, but the whole position taken here throughout the discussion of the epistemological attitude has been in support of

---

1. So that we may not too perversely say that judgement is the predication of an ideal content of Unreality.

this metaphysic. For from this point of view the problem of knowledge does not exist; the distinction between inner and outer, which makes the epistemologist's capital, cannot stand. We have seen that the word 'idea' does not [139] refer to something ('thing') which intervenes between the object and the percipient, but is a stage in the process of realisation of a world. The object so far as there is an object is presented to the knower without mediation of category or other psychological apparatus. Knowledge, that is to say, cannot be defined in terms of anything else; and so far as there is any problem, it has its origin in the fact that knowing is not simply knowing, but has another aspect. And why this is, I have to some extent attempted to show. We tend to think of objects – of things – as being objects under any and every condition: if they are not objects when they are not known, then the only alternative, we think, is that they disappear altogether. But we have seen that even within experience objects could not be objects unless they were much more; and their objectivity, their being denoted, is only a moment of their reality; a moment which we say metaphorically is supported by an act of the will, although I should never admit that the situation was due to the subject side any more than to the object side, or that the notion of activity was ultimately possible in any sense.

The real world, if the real world means the world of real objects, is thus something with which we are in immediate contact, and indeed quite real – as real as you like – though varying and unprecise. Its 'relation' to the knower is however not here in question, inasmuch as knowledge is not a relation. The real world is not inside or outside; it is not presented in consciousness or to consciousness as a particular grouping of entities, for as presented it is not in or to consciousness at all: it simply is. There is no meaning, I think, in saying that in knowing consciousness is either active or passive, or that there is an 'awareness' beyond the mere psycho-physiological phenomena of attention; or that consciousness 'is' its object or is different from its object. But knowing, we have found, is only part of a larger process of experience, and the point at which we have real knowing is never precisely determinable. There is always, in our experience, a real world 'external' in a restricted sense, for there is always, in any existence worthy of us, a real object of attention, and so far as there is, the object [140] is directly known but not directly experienced; for the object, to be an object, is always meant to be something more than its abstracted qualities, and to be directly known cannot be directly experienced.[1] But the object as object

---

1. 'Sugar is obviously not mere whiteness, mere hardness, and mere sweetness; for its reality lies somehow in its unity. But if, on the other hand, we inquire what there can

cannot be self-supporting. Its objectivity is merely externality, and nothing in reality can be merely external, but must possess being 'for' itself. Yet to mean it as an object means to mean it as more than an object, as something *ultimately* real. And in this way every object leads us far beyond itself to an ultimate reality: this is the justification for our metaphysics.

The objects which are apprehended by every finite centre are as apprehended real. The question arises, how the worlds of these various centres may be said to form one world; inasmuch as there is no 'objective' criterion for reality in the sense of an external solid world to which our individual presentations should conform. The real world, I have insisted, consists in the common meaning and 'identical reference' of various finite centres. This leads to a question, cardinal in the philosophy of Mr Bradley; the question of finite centres and solipsism.

Chapter VI
Solipsism

KEPB, 141–52.

It should be evident why the conclusions already reached demand an examination of Solipsism; but I will briefly recount them. We have seen that there is no other object than that which appears, and its appearance as an object gives it, in an absolute sense, all that objectively it could possibly mean. If you are willing to make the abstraction of a world appearing to one finite centre alone, then we may say that nothing in this world is false or erroneous, but is what it is and as it is. And outside of the objectivity of objects appearing to finite centres, there is no objectivity at all, for we have found that objectivity and thinghood are aspects under which reality appears; true but partial aspects; and that the reality of a 'thing' (we are here painfully hampered by language) is in no wise limited to its thinghood. But beyond the objective worlds of a number of finite centres, each having its own objects, there is no objective world. Thus we confront the question: how do we yoke our divers worlds to draw together? how can we issue from the circle described about each point of view? and since I can know no point of view but my own, how can I

---

be in the thing beside its several qualities, we are baffled once more. We can discover no real unity existing outside these qualities, or, again, existing within them.' *Appearance*, p. 16.

know that there are other points of view, or admitting their existence, how can I take any account of them?[1]

Solipsism has been one of the dramatic properties of most philosophical entertainers. Yet we cannot discard it without recognising that it rests upon a truth. '[T]hough my experience is not the whole world, yet that world appears in my experience, and, so far as it exists there, it *is* my state of mind. . . . And so, in the [142] end, to know the Universe, we must fall back upon our personal experience and sensation'.[2] This doctrine I should like to develop in something of detail, with regard to real objects. And in doing this I must summon in the theory of points of view upon which I have relied before. Obviously, by the conclusions at which I have arrived, it is true to say that the real world is real because and in so far as it appears to a finite centre, and yet it has in each appearance to mean to be more – to be real, that is, only so far as it is not an appearance to a finite centre. From a point of view completely detached, reality would contain nothing but finite centres and their several presentations; but from the point of view of each centre, there is an objective world upon which several points of view are trained, and to which they all refer. And it is just the confusion of these two truths which gives the stuffed solipsism of the philosophers. I have tried to show that there can be no truth or error without a presentation and discrimination of two points of view; that the external world is a construction by the selection and combination of various presentations to various viewpoints: and that the selection which makes reality is in turn made possible by the belief in reality: unless we assumed the existence of a world of truth we could not explain the genesis of error, and unless we had presentations of error as well as of truth we could not make that construction which is the real world. But taking the various experience-centres as real, we may inquire, with reference to this manifold, in what consists the reality of the one world which they all suppose.

Every finite centre, we may lay down, intends an 'objective' world; and the genesis of this intention is an obscure and difficult matter. We cannot say anything on the subject which will be more than an interpretation; but I offer this as a provisional account, admitting that any account that expresses itself as a temporal sequence can be only very provisional indeed. The first objects, we may say, with which we come into contact

---

1. The controversy between Brunetière and France is rather instructive, showing a muddling of the question by two men who are not philosophers, but have each his own personal solution in practice.
2. Bradley, *Appearance and Reality*, 229. [Bolgan.]

are half-objects,[1] they are other finite centres, not attended to directly as objects, [143] but are interpretations of recognised resistances and felt divergences. We come to interpret our own experience as the attention to a world of objects, as we feel obscurely an identity between the experiences of other centres and our own. And it is this identity which gradually shapes itself into the external world. There are two (or more) worlds each continuous with a self, and yet running in the other direction – *somehow* – into an identity. Thus in adjusting our behaviour to that of others and in co-operating with them we come to intend an identical world.

We ask then naturally, in what the identity consists, beyond the 'identical reference'. Yet while the question is natural, I cannot admit that it is legitimate. And I should like to recall various passages in which I have spoken of 'identical reference', especially in connection with memory. It appeared there that an element of identity might be present, without our being able to isolate it as an actuality. The relation found to obtain between an experience and our recollection of it was not a relation of mere resemblance, but involved a common reference to a third reality, which was known simply as *the* reality which both intended. A reference to an identity, it was laid down, *is* the identity, in the sense in which a word *is* that which it denotes. An identity is intended, and it could not have been intended, we say, unless it was there; but its being 'there' consists simply in the intention, and has no other meaning. What do we mean when we say that two people see 'the same' object? We think loosely that the identity consists in the fact that when one looks at the object from the same angle as the other, the two images before the two minds are the same. We compare two prints of the same negative and find them identical. But there is evidently a difference between the two cases (a difference which is ultimately, however, one of degree) in that the difference between the two points of view is a difference, if we choose to consider it so, of two whole worlds; the identity is of two realities which cannot possibly be set side by side and compared. All identity is ideal ... 'in this sense that it involves the self-transcendence of that which is identical' (*Appearance*, p. 526). And this fact, that identity in the [144] content of two minds is an identity of ideal meaning may cause us to ask if even in the simplest case of comparison the identity is not equally ideal. All identities which two objects may present, though simply of colour or of form, involve a self-transcendence on the part of the particulars. This means, of course, only that we have no knowledge of mere particulars. But it means also that the identity between one man's world and another's

---

1. But of course they are not apprehended as such. There is a felt conflict and difference between centres, and this breaks up the unity of our expression.

does not consist, as we readily are led to believe, in one world which is the world of right perception, and which is, apart from being known, exactly what it is when we know it.

This fact, furthermore, ought to be self-evident. Identity, we have learned, is nowhere bare identity, but must be identity in diversity. If we are hit on the head with the same club, the club is only 'the same' because it has appeared in two different contexts. There are two different experiences, and the sameness is quite ideal. We do, of course, partially put ourselves at the point of view of the man who hit us, and partially at each other's points of view; and it is the interweaving of these viewpoints which gives us the objective club. There is no one club, no one world, without a diversity of points of view for it to be one to. The 'real' turns out everywhere to be ideal – but is none the less real for that. Point to anything as 'independent' of a finite centre, and you find that what is independent is merely the moment of objectivity – and this is ideal.

When I say that there is one world because one world is intended, I have still stated only half of the case; for any explanation in terms of 'because' (a term made necessary by the weakness of human conceiving) can be only misleading unless we turn it about the other way as well. Let us say, therefore, that we are able to intend one world because our points of view are essentially akin.[1] For it is not as if the isolated individuals had contributed each a share and entered into partnership to provide a public world. The selves, on the contrary, find themselves from the start in common dependence upon one indifferent Nature. Nature assumes, inevitably, a different aspect to each point of view; no two finite centres, we may say, apprehend the same Nature, yet each centre has pressed upon it the fact that from the one Nature it with all its neighbours sprang. To claim that this is inconsistent with the isolation of our monads is to confuse the genetic and the structural standpoints. My mind, that is, I must treat as both absolute and derived; absolute, in that it is a point of view from which I cannot possibly escape (to which indeed I am bound so closely that the word escape is without meaning); derived, in that I am able, by virtue of the continuity of mind with the non-mental, to trace in some way its origin, with that of other minds, from an indifferent material.

---

1. '... the foundation of it all is this, that no phase in a particular consciousness is merely a phase of the apparent subject, but it is always and essentially a member of a further whole of experience, which passes through and unites the states of many consciousnesses, but is not exhausted in any, nor in all of them, as states, taken together. It is true that my state of mind is mine, and yours is yours; but not only do I experience in mine what you experience in yours – that would be consistent with the total independence of the two minds – but I experience it differently from you, in such a way that there is a systematic relation between the two contents experienced, and neither is intelligible or complete without the other.' Bosanquet, *Prin. of Ind. and Value*, p. 315.

Biologically, we see minds in a common medium, and treating minds thus as objects, we conclude their content to be similar just as we find their physical structure and their environment similar. And from this point of view we talk about the one 'external' world and the various 'mental contents' referring to it. For minds may be intended objects; and their objectivity is continuous with their subjectivity, the mental continuous with the merely mechanistic. But we must remember that no view is original or ultimate: when we inquire into the real world, however, we mean the world from the viewpoints of finite centres as subjects only; we mean the real world for us now, not from the point of view of some further developed mind tracing its ancestors and the world they lived in.

The world, we may insist, is neither one nor many except as that one or many has meaning in experience, and it is either one or many according as we contemplate it altogether as an object, talking still, if you will, of minds, but meaning rather the phenomena which mind presents to an observer: or as we treat the world as finite centres and their experiences. From the first point of view the world is *a priori* one; from the second point of view [146] the world is *a priori* many; and I am convinced that this is the only form in which monism or pluralism can appear. And the two views are so far from antagonistic as to be complementary. The self, we find, seems to depend upon a world which in turn depends upon it; and nowhere, I repeat, can we find anything original or ultimate. And the self depends as well upon other selves; it is not given as a direct experience, but is an interpretation of experience by interaction with other selves (see *Appearance*, p. 219). The self is a construction, and yet the[1]

The doctrine of finite centres appears in an interesting light when compared with the theories of Leibniz, with which it has very striking affinities. Compare, for example, the celebrated paragraph of the *Monadology*, 57: 'And as the same town, looked at from various sides, appears quite different and becomes as it were numerous in aspects; even so, as a result of the infinite number of simple substances, it is as if there were so many different universes, which, nevertheless, are nothing but aspects (*perspectives*) of a single universe, according to the special point of view of each monad.' (Latta's ed., p. 248).

---

1. Page 186 of the original typescript ends with this dangling phrase. Page 187 then follows immediately with the new paragraph beginning 'The doctrine of finite centres . . .,' and continues exactly as given here on page 146. Some material, intervening between these two paragraphs, has obviously been removed. The only other difficulty of this same nature arises at the end of the very last page of the presently existing typescript where, again, the page ends with an incompleted sentence. In both cases, the argument being formulated is identical with that which Mr Eliot goes on to develop in his *Monist* articles – more especially the second one entitled 'Leibniz's Monads and Bradley's Finite Centres.' [Bolgan.]

It is easy to raise objections to Leibniz's form of statement, but I think that his aim becomes more intelligible in the light of our 'finite centres'. Leibniz appears to have made the error, it is true, of identifying a point of view with a felt unit, or self.[1] And for Leibniz the internal view of the world was ultimate. But the assertion that 'the monads have no windows' in no wise entangles him in solipsism, for it means (or may be taken to mean) what Mr Bradley means in saying that our knowledge of other finite centres is only through physical appearance within our own world. When an event occurs within my world it occurs to me, but I would not be I apart from the event; it is from the beginning coloured by my personality, as my personality is coloured by it. A theory of internal relations is thus implicit; and perhaps a recognition of the continuity of terms and relations contributed to the doctrine [147] of monads. If anything could appear as really acting upon and altering the self, the latter would take the place merely of one object among others, and so far as it is subject, we can conceive it as having aspects, but not relations. And when we qualify our world by the recognition of another's it is not his world as it is in reality, but his world as it affects us that enters into our world. We arrive at the belief in other finite selves in a sense by inference, though on the other hand it is assumed that these other selves exist, or they could not be phenomenally represented in our world. To say that I can know only my own states, accordingly, is in no wise the foundation of solipsism, unless it were possible that I should know my states as my states, and as nothing else, which would be a palpable contradiction. What I know is my own state simply as the real aspect (knowledge as object) seems to take precedence of the ideal aspect (knowledge as meaning). The statement that 'monads have no windows', therefore, means only that the objectivity of one's world is ideal; and that the reality is experience.

And the pre-established harmony is unnecessary if we recognise that the monads are not wholly distinct, and that the subjective self is continuous with the self as object. A monad was for Leibniz, I believe, something real in the way in which a physical organism is real: he imagined the monads, that is, on this analogy, and identified the monad with the phenomenal soul. Now for Bradley the finite centre, (or what I call the point of view), is not identical with the soul. We may think provisionally of finite centres as the units of soul life; units, however, whose limits cannot be drawn with any precision. For we vary by passing from one point of view to

---

[1]. 'Finite centres of feeling, while they last, are (so far as we know) not directly pervious to one another. But . . . a self is not the same as such a centre of experience.' *Appearance*, p. 464.

another or as I have tried to suggest, by occupying more than one point of view at the same time, an attitude which gives us our assumptions, our half-objects, our figments of imagination; we vary by self-transcendence. The point of view (or finite centre) has for its object one consistent world, and accordingly no finite centre can be self-sufficient, for the life of a soul does not consist in the contemplation of one consistent world but in the painful task of unifying (to a greater or less extent) jarring and incompatible ones, and passing, when possible, [148] from two or more discordant viewpoints to a higher which shall somehow include and transmute them. The soul is so far from being a monad that we have not only to interpret other souls to ourself but to interpret ourself to ourself. Wherever a point of view may be distinguished, I say, there a point of view is. And whereas we may change our point of view, it is better not to say that the point of view has changed. For if there is a noticeable change, you have no identity of which to predicate the change. The point of view, we may say, is as such purely ideal; it can hardly be said to possess existence.

The doctrine here set forth must not however be construed as a psychical atomism, or anything of that sort; the finite centres (as I understand the matter) are not all of one size or shape, but vary with the context. Thus, while one soul may experience within itself many finite centres, the soul itself may be considered in a loose sense as a finite centre. The more of a personality it is, the more harmonious and self-contained, the more definitely it is said to possess a 'point of view', a point of view toward the social world. Wherever, in short, there is a unity of consciousness, this unity may be spoken of as a finite centre. Yet neither the term 'soul' nor the term 'self' is ever identical with the term 'finite centre'. 'Then from immediate experience' (at any level) 'the self emerges, and is set apart by a distinction' (p. 464).[1] To realise that a point of view is a point of view is already to have transcended it: what was merely a picture in two dimensions (if you please) becomes a real landscape with an infinity of aspects as the 'what' disengages itself from the 'that'. The 'what' continues to be recognised as a true qualification of the 'that', but is as well a qualification of the apprehending consciousness, and the real object results from the abstraction and comparison of the various points of view.

What constitutes the difference, therefore, between two points of view, is the difference which each is capable of making to the other. There could be no such thing, we may say, as a single finite centre, for every experience implies the existence of something independent of the

---

1. Bradley, *Appearance and Reality*, 464. [Bolgan.]

experience, something capable, therefore, of [149] being experienced differently, and the recognition of this fact is already the transition to another point of view. Treating the experience as the reality, we may say (*ibid.*, p. 464) that 'Finite centres of feeling, while they last, are . . . not directly pervious to one another.' So far as experiences go, we may be said in a sense to live each in a different world. But 'world' in this sense, is not the world with which solipsism is concerned; each centre of experience is unique, but is unique only with reference to a common meaning. Two points of view, in consequence, can be said to differ only so far as they intend the same object, though the object, we have seen, is only such with reference to a point of view.

Two points of view take cognisance of each other, I suppose, by each making a half-object of the other. Strictly speaking, a point of view taking note of another is no longer the same, but a third, centre of feeling; yet it is something different from a centre of feeling: more properly a self, a 'construction based on, and itself transcending, immediate experience'.[1] Everywhere, we must constantly remind ourselves, the difference is one of degree; and when one finite centre affects another merely as an alteration in its experience, and is not consciously recognised as another centre, we can hardly say that there is a self. And inasmuch as the finite centre is an experience, while the self is one aspect in that experience, and again contains and harmonises several experiences, we may say that the self is both less and more than such a centre, and is ideal. For this reason it is more correct to say that a self passes from one point of view to another, than to say that one point of view takes cognisance of another. But a finite centre may be made an intended object by a self, and thus enter into another finite centre, though not as such. Thus we may continue to say that finite centres are impervious. Identity we find to be everywhere ideal, while finite centres are real. When we ask what, finally, in the finite centre is the common property of several finite centres, intending the same object, the answer is: nothing – 'really', everything – 'ideally', and in practice there may be a greater or less amount of community. We may schematise it crudely thus: [150]

---

1. Bradley, *Appearance and Reality*, 465. [Bolgan.]

In Theory	Really	a	All unique, but
		b	All may be an intended object in another finite centre.
	Ideally	c	The intended object in each centre is public. Whatever is made an object is public.
In Practice	Really	d	Two finite centres may be judged from a third point of view to resemble each other
	Ideally	e	As much is public as is not discernibly different.

Note that in *(d)* the resemblance is predicated on the ground of behaviour; it is predicated not of the centres as such, but inferred from ideal identity of object when we observe two organisms behaving in the same way toward what from our point of view is the same object for each. Similarly we may infer the resemblance of a centre of feeling in another self to one of our own, though the two experiences as such have no relation to each other, not even the relation of difference.

The reflection of the world in finite centres, of a world which is real only as it appears in those centres, is a form of monadism which, as we find, by no means implies a 'pluralistic universe'. These centres are not things, and to speak of them as 'independent' or 'isolated' is more misleading than illuminating. When we speak of such isolated centres we mean always souls. A centre of experience, however, is always 'below, or else wider than and above, the distinction' (*Appearance*, p. 468) of self and not-self. A soul, or a self (though the two terms are not everywhere equivalent (see *ibid*., p. 464, note)) is always the 'creature of an intellectual construction';[1] it is never simply given, but depends upon a transcendence of immediacy. And a doctrine of solipsism would have to show that myself and my states were immediately given, and other selves inferred. But just because what is given is not my self but my world, the question is meaningless. The process of the genesis [151] of the self and of other selves is ultimately perhaps unknowable, since there is no 'because' which we can assign. There are reasons for believing that externality was recognised as force or as spirit before it was apprehended in the form of objects; as the primitive life, furthermore, is immersed in practice and incapable of the degree of speculative interest necessary for the constitution of an object. On the other hand we may say that we know other finite centres only through the mediation of objects. 'The immediate experiences of finite beings cannot, as such, come together.... A direct connexion between souls we cannot say is impossible, but on the other hand, we find no

---

1. Bradley, *Appearance and Reality*, 468. [Bolgan.]

good reason for supposing it to exist. . . . We may assume then that souls do not influence each other except through their bodies.' (*Appearance*, pp. 303–4).

The issue here hangs only on the exact meaning which we are to attribute to the word 'knowledge'. We become acquainted with the existence of other souls, we may say, through the influence which they exert upon the content of our experience, but we only become acquainted with that content as content through the postulation of foreign activities influencing it, so that we are led to distinguish a 'what' and a 'that'. But the question at what point either becomes explicit is essentially unanswerable. We can only say that the self, the other selves, and the objects do in this process become more precise, and clear. And we can say that we have no knowledge of other souls except through their bodies, because it is only thus that we can enter into their world.

On the other hand, as we need to be reminded, we have no direct (immediate) knowledge of anything: the 'immediately given' is the bag of gold at the end of the rainbow. Knowledge is invariably a matter of degree: you cannot put your finger upon even the simplest datum and say 'this we know'. In the growth and construction of the world we live in, there is no one stage, and no one aspect, which you can take as the foundation. Radical empiricists assume that we have an 'immediate' knowledge of a mysterious flux, and criticists assume that we know sense-data, or universals, immediately, as we do not know objects or other [152] selves. But where we are first interested in knowing, there is the first thing known; and in this way we may say (if we choose to employ this language) that that of which we have immediate knowledge is the external world, for without externality there is no knowledge. The platform of knowing, in fact, is the assertion of something to be known, something independent of me so far as that knowing is concerned. No absolute assertion about the object's dependence or independence is made or implied. Hence if the object is only my state both object and I must be strangely transmuted, for I only know myself in contrast to a world. And it will be equally true to say that I am only a state of my objects. But, it will be objected, if knowledge of objects belongs to a world which is admittedly a construction, should not we return to the primitive experience to find reality? Or are you not tacitly affirming that the world in which we find ourselves now is the real world, and is the process of which you speak not a process in knowledge rather than a process in reality? This question introduces us to the relation of thought and reality, and the doctrine of degrees of truth, with which I intend to close.

Chapter VII
Conclusion

KEPB, 153-69.

The task of this concluding chapter is merely to weave together the conclusions of the other chapters and present them if possible as a coherent whole; and to touch as well upon certain consequences which have not as yet appeared. We may draw, I believe, certain inferences as to the nature of reality which will forbid us to accept either an idealistic or a realistic philosophy at its full value. But I believe that all of the conclusions that I have reached are in substantial agreement with *Appearance and Reality*, though I have been compelled to reject certain theories, logical and psychological, which appear in the *Principles* and elsewhere. Out of absolute idealism we retain what I consider its most important doctrines, Degrees of Truth and Reality and the Internality of Relations; we reject the reliance upon 'consciousness' or 'the work of the mind' as a principle of explanation. With regard to objects, I have reached the conclusion that all objects are non-mental; and with regard to mental activity, I conclude that we find only physiological activity or logical activity, both independent of, and more fundamental than what we call the activity of mind. But the materialism, which (as exemplified particularly in the work of Mr Bosanquet) from one point of view may very justly be said to lie at the basis of idealism, presents only one aspect of the situation. If the aim of my examination of structural psychology was to demonstrate that the more accurately and scientifically one pursues the traces of mentality in the 'mind' of the individual, the less one finds; so on the other hand my examination of the epistemologist's world has been an attempt to prove that the more closely one scrutinises the 'external world', and the more eagerly and positively one plucks at it, the less there [154] is to see and touch. Cut off a 'mental' and a 'physical' world, dissect and classify the phenomena of each: the mental resolves into a curious and intricate mechanism, and the physical reveals itself as a mental construct. If you will find the mechanical anywhere, you will find it in the workings of mind; and to inspect living mind, you must look nowhere but in the world outside. Such is the general doctrine to which my theory of objects points.

There are other conclusions bound up with this doctrine. As to the problem of knowledge, we have found that it does not exist. Knowledge, that is to say, is not a relation, and cannot be explained by any analysis. We do not say, however, that in knowing the 'mind' comes into immediate and direct contact with the object, for we find that such an assertion has no great meaning, for there is no 'mind' for the object to be brought into contact with, and with the physical organism the object known may or may not be in direct contact. And to say that the object is dependent on or independent of the knower – this again I think is a statement of no great importance, though of the two alternatives I think that it is perhaps truer to say that the object is independent. For *qua* known, the object is simply there, and has no relation to the knower whatever, and the knower, *qua* knower, is not a part of the world which he knows: he does not exist.

This bare and hypothetical knowledge, I admit, is only a part of what serves our use. We do not, in point of fact, simply know: we make tentative and hardly formulated theories of knowledge in practice, theories which go to make up our real knowledge. And again there is much in that which we call knowledge which is not knowing in what narrowly speaking is the only legitimate sense. It is these two disturbing factors which complicate and indeed create the problem. The point is worthy of great elaboration, and even in so sketchy a discussion as the present may occupy us for several moments. What I mean is this. Theoretically, that which we know is merely spread out before us for pure contemplation, and the subject, the I, or the self, is no more consciously present than is the inter-cellular action. But I do not say that such a condition is or was ever realised in practice; indeed, such [155] knowledge would hardly be of any profit. The real situation is rather that we have as I have tried to show in the first chapter a felt whole in which there are moments of knowledge: the objects are constantly shifting, and new transpositions of objectivity and feeling constantly developing. We perceive an object, we will say, and then perceive it in a special relation to our body. In our practical relations with objects we find it convenient and even essential to consider the object's relation to ourself as itself an object; in many cases this is what is important. This self may be primarily the body, but the body is in felt continuity with the spiritual self. And in cases where the presence of the self is an important part in the meaning of the knowledge, a sort of theory of knowledge is at work. It is this sort of knowing, I presume, that induces us to think of knowing as a relation. There is a relation between the object and the self: a relation which is theoretical and not merely actual, in the sense that the self as a term capable of relation with other terms is a construction. And this self which is objectified and related is continuous and felt to be continuous with the self which is subject and not an element in that which is known. As it is metaphysics which has produced the self so it is epistemology, we may say, which has produced knowledge. It is perhaps epistemology (though I offer this only as a suggestion, and to make clearer the sort of thing that I mean) that has given us the fine arts; for what was at first expression and behaviour may have developed under the complications of self-consciousness, as we became aware of ourselves as reacting aesthetically to the object.

In any case, we are constantly developing and rectifying our perceptions by comparison with other perceptions; we are constantly on the lookout for error, and our recognition and allowances for error already nominate us as epistemologists; for this means that we have a tentative working theory of our relation to the external world. It is thus, to a certain extent, a theory of knowledge that gives us an external world, but a theory which cannot hold beyond a certain range of practice. Theory and practice are, we find, inextricable: for without theory we should [156] not have our present practice, and without the practice in which it finds its application the theory would be meaningless.

No theory of knowledge, consequently, can establish itself on a firm foundation by defining the sort of relation that knowing is, for knowing is not a relation; in order to give any account of knowing we must bring in the terms which are related, and these terms are only provisionally definable. We can only define the thing as known and the knower as knowing, and yet both things and knower imply a transcendence of these limitations, a transcendence which has no end. And it is only so far as our knowledge is invalid or incomplete that research into the nature of knowing can bear any fruit, for when we believe our knowledge to be correct and sufficient we can do no more than describe the physical relations between our body and the object apprehended. In any analysis of knowledge, knowing is assumed; we can to a certain extent explain false knowing in terms of true knowing, but we cannot explain true knowing in terms of anything else.

While we cannot, it thus appears, 'know knowing', what we can do is to describe in a general way the process of transition and development which takes place when there is an organism which is a part of the world and yet is capable to a certain degree of contemplating the world. Knowing, we have said, is inextricably intertwined with processes which are not knowing; knowing, furthermore, is only an aspect in a continuous reality. We can to a certain extent describe the rise and decay of objects. And this is not because the object is essentially dependent upon consciousness, for I do not know what such a phrase would mean: but because consciousness and its object are both only evanescent aspects in reality. When we think what knowing really means in our experience,[1] how essentially relative its meaning is, for it can never escape from the

---

1. The sense here requires the insertion of the words 'we find'. The passage would then read:

ultimate limits of its own meaning; and even when it consciously intends to be unconditionally true, that unconditionality is within these bounds and no statement can claim to be true except when it has meaning. So that while we make no attempt to explain knowledge, we can I think offer a limited insight into its nature by indicating the fringe through [157] which it passes into something else, and by indicating the stages of the process which we call degrees of truth.

My first step, in accordance with this plan, was to attempt to suggest the reality out of which subject and object are sorted, and upon which as background they have their meaning. Our first step is to discover what experience is not, and why it is essentially indefinable. We saw that within experience there presented themselves the two aspects of ideality and reality, but that this distinction did not correpond to a division among objects: for a thing is real or ideal only in relation. We found that what we call the 'real' in experience is largely ideal, and that what we call 'ideal' is largely real, and that Reality itself would not be reality without its appearances. The ideal and the real, the mental and the non-mental, the active and the passive, these are terms which apply only to *appearance*; which take their meaning from narrow and practical contexts.

In seeking for the object of knowledge, then, we need no investigation into the process of knowing or the nature of an external world. It is not true that we deny the existence of an external world, for anyone who pursues this path of inquiry will come to the conclusion that this question is ultimately meaningless. But demanding at the start what it is that we know for most certain (and this method deserves the name of empiricism as much as anything does) we find that we are certain of everything, – relatively, and of nothing, – positively, and that no knowledge will survive analysis. The virtue of metaphysical analysis is in showing the destructibility of everything, since analysis gives us something equally real, and for some purposes more real, than that which is analysed. In analysing knowledge, we merely educe the fact that knowledge is composed of ingredients which are themselves neither known nor cognitive, but which melt into the whole which we call experience.[1] The analysis of the object, from this point of view, reveals the fact that in asking what the object [158]

When we think what knowing really means in our experience, we find how essentially relative its meaning is, for it can never escape from the ultimate limits of its own meaning. . . . [Bolgan.]

1. 'For while the This cannot be brought into the unity of knowledge, it is unquestionably a part of reality. And so the failure of knowledge to bring it into unity with itself involves that the part of the object which *is* brought into unity with the subject is only an abstraction from the full object. . . . The result is that we know objects, so to speak, from the outside. . . .' McTaggart, *Heg. Dialectic*, p. 222.

is we merely turn in a circle. The object is not its qualities, for these are simply enjoyed with respect to the object; the object as such, it transpires, is merely the point of *attention;* that which an electron, a Balkan league, my table, whiteness, have in common as objects is just the *moment of objectivity.* The objecthood of an object, it appears, is the fact that we intend it as an object: it is the attending that makes the object, and yet we may say with equal truth that if there were no object we could not attend. The fact that an object is an object, in this light, appears to be the least fact about it, and its reality is due to the experiences which cluster around it: an object is real, we may say, in proportion to its relations outside of its objectivity.

I should be asked, no doubt, whether an object ceases to be an object on ceasing to be known. This question I feel justified in refusing to answer, since I cannot feel that anyone who understands what I have meant by objectivity will ask it. For practical purposes, undoubtedly, we may think of objects as objects when they are not objects to anyone, or I may think of an object as an object when it is the object of your attention and not of mine: but in general to think of an object is (not to *think* of it as my object, but) to make an object of it. The object, I mean to say, is none the less *real* when I am not attending to it, but it is no longer object. For all that 'object' means is a connection of certain experiences with a moment of objectivity, of experiences which would not exist as what they are unless connected in *that* way with *that* point of attention (moment of objectivity), and of a point of attention which would not be without those qualities, for those qualities essentially refer to it, and *it* is only the fact of their intended reference. The object is a complex of experiences with a reference, and the reference itself is an experience. But we cannot say that it is *my* experience, for I am only I in relation to objects. The object thus resolves itself into experience. But this by no means implies that the object does not persist outside of my experience, or that another subject may not know the same object. For in making this last statement we have so shifted the stage properties that 'object' no longer means exactly the same thing. [159] This should have been made clear by the discussion of solipsism. Wherever I intend an object, there an object is; wherever two people intend the same object, there an identical object is; and wherever we together intend the existence of an object outside of our knowledge, there an object does exist outside of our knowledge; but we must not forget that in all three of these cases we have theory as well as practice. From one point of view we know that the object exists; but from another point of view this is mere hypothesis: we have a certain latitude, that is, as to what we shall take for granted, and we may put ourselves at the individual or the social point of view, as we please; but we must not forget that unless we make allowance at the start for the equality of their claims to validity we shall be left with a most uncomfortable hiatus, for we can never deduce the one from the other.

It is difficult to tell when we are assigning to a word only such precision and *portée* as is justified in practice, and when we are going beyond use into pure speculation which will make no difference to our practice. We may easily be overawed by language, and attribute to it more philosophic prestige than it really deserves. The word 'object' means a certain type of experience and the theories involved in that experience: theories which lose their meaning beyond a certain point. The only way in which we can handle reality intellectually is to turn it into objects, and the justification of this operation is that the world we live in has been built in this way. At the same time we are forced to admit that the construction is not always completely successful. While we can to a certain extent treat relations as if they were terms, we find with such entities as ideas that to treat them so is almost a step backward rather than a step forward, inasmuch as we can only apprehend their reality by putting ourselves in the place of an obscure world and abandoning a clear and scientific one. There is left psycho-physics and rational psychology. There have developed, I mean to say, certain objects which I have denominated half-objects, having much of the character of objects without being wholly apprehensible. Their nature is that they do not belong to any point of view, but depend for their existence [160] upon our apprehending two points of view at once, and pursuing neither. Thus the 'mental' would have no place in a 'real' world such as the scientist intends, and the real world would consist in the relations of points whose entire existence was relation: whose reality consisted in their external relations. And it is obvious that such a view is in its way quite as tenable as any other: a theory which reduces reality to mathematical relations of simples is continuous with our ordinary tendency toward objectification, and hence is not less 'true' in the usual sense, than any other; inasmuch as objectification is the creation of a new world, and the assertion that the two worlds are the same is an act of faith, only to be contrasted with another act of faith to the effect that the two are not the same.

The fundamental difficulty is this. When we attend to an object we do not know precisely what it is that we denote or that we mean. In any case of ocular error this fact is patent, and is more than suggested by the discussions of the *Theaetetus*. When I mistake one object for another, I can say loosely that the real object was the object which I 'really' saw, and upon the sight of which I made a mistaken inference. But you never can tell at precisely what point the mistake occurred; how much that is to say was received unaltered from without and how much was constructed from within. We have come upon this *impasse* in theorising upon bears: far as the object is experienced as *that* object so far it *is* that object, and the rectification is a matter of further experience, through which the illusory object and the real object are bound together in an (ideal) identity of meaning in a practical world. It is, in fact, this real world, which is not metaphysically the real world, that unites the false and the true in a common reference, and thus makes the false false and the true true. Now there is precisely the same difficulty when we explain an appearance by a reality: when we appear only to be revealing the reality of the appearance we may be said to be only presenting another appearance, and the greater the dissimilarity that we find between the two the more certainly our construction falls apart into two worlds.

[161] The object of attention, in the first place, has not certain definite limits: its 'that' and its 'what' exhibit a degree of looseness in practice. The object can be the same object though its description more or less vary, and the same description can preserve itself through an indefinite variation of the attention. We never can say, actually, to exactly what we are attending; it is never the hypothetical point and it is to a large extent the ideal synthesis of data by meaning which constitutes the point of attention. I look at a bottle, and the point to which I attend is the bottle; though not necessarily the real bottle, for there may be perhaps no real bottle there; so that we may say the real point of attention is the intended object. In this sense, attention is the intention to attend. The attention is not in practice attention to a point, but to a *that* which is a *that* because it has a single meaning. A *that* which we did not qualify as a *what* would not be even a mere *that*. On the other hand the two aspects of the real object, the *thatness* and the *whatness*, are always distinct because of their difference in meaning; so that we say, in different senses, that we attend to the object which is *that* and *what*, and that we attend literally to the *that* alone. Inasmuch as the *that* is the point of reference of its common qualities, its persistence depends upon our recognition of the community of meaning of the qualities, and this community of meaning is ultimately practical. It is ultimately in every case a question of practice how far any group of qualities constitutes one object, and metaphysics depends upon our ability and good-will to grasp appearance and reality as one. And this limitation is as true of one sort of metaphysic as of another.

Regarding the matter from this light, we must to a certain extent put our theories to the pragmatic test. An account of reality, or of any field of it, which has the appearance of going to the point of substituting a new type of objects for the old will be a true theory and not merely a new world, if it is capable of making an actual practical difference in our attitude toward the old, or toward some already accepted object, so that there may be an identity uniting differences of quality. It is obvious that it is this [162] felt identity between appearance and reality that will constitute explanation, and that the identity is a fragile and insecure thing. Adhering to a strictly common-sense view (which may be defined, I presume, as that which insists on the reality of the more primary objects) the theories of speculative physics seem perhaps as chimerical and uncalled-for as those of metaphysics. There is however considerable difference. A science is such because it is able to deal with objects which are all of one type; and the aim of each science is to reduce reality (so far as reality comes within the purview of that science) to one type of object, and the ultimate type of object I should suppose (acknowledging my incompetence to speak) to be points in mathematical relation. But physical theories (so far as I can pretend to be informed, from popular accounts), are apt to end in mystery, inasmuch as the final object is often not an object at all; if the ultimate is some kind of energy or motion it is not an object but at most a half-object, since it possesses some internality. At this point a theory would become metaphysical, passing from one type of object to another; and two types can only be held together by an act of faith.

It is not within my present purpose or capacity to schematise the various types of object and their relations. Chapters II and III were devoted to one of the most important classes, that of the half-objects of psychology. Chapter IV endeavoured to set forth the ideality of all objects, and the relativity of the distinction between 'real' objects and 'ideal' objects; finally,[1] with the difference between real and unreal objects, and the analysis of imaginary objects and assumptions. The fifth chapter was engaged upon the object as the object of one and as the object of several knowers; the resolution, on the one hand, of the object into experience, and its maintenance as identical reference. We have thus distinguished broadly several types; things, half-objects, double objects, and objects of reference. Half-objects are such as exist, like ideas, only from an internal-external point of view; double objects are such as exist as objects from two points of view, like mental images, hallucinations and objects in fiction, which have a reality in their own space and time, and a different [163] reality in our space and time.[2] Objects of reference are such as unreal objects, where the reality of the object consists in

---

1. The sense here requires the insertion of the words 'it dealt'. The passage would then read:

    [F]inally, it dealt with the difference between real and unreal objects, and with the analysis of imaginary objects and assumptions. [Bolgan.]

2. This depends, of course, upon the continuity of symbol and symbolised.

barely more than the object's being intended (and perhaps 'sensations' and categories, which are supposed to be enjoyed and not contemplated, belong in this class: for the being of such objects consists in their not being objects). All these types, and 'universals' and 'particulars' as well, may be reduced, in a certain aspect, to things;[1] for things are the lowest order, so to speak; and on the other hand the thing is analysable into intended objects (qualities) and the intention (or moment of objectivity). But every transformation of type involves a leap which science cannot take, and which metaphysics must take. It involves an *interpretation,* a transmigration from one world to another, and such a pilgrimage involves an act of faith.

In a transformation of object-type there is a change of point of view; in a metaphysical theory there is an attempt to bind together all points of view in one.

And this, I think, should show us why the notion of truth, literal truth, has so little direct application to philosophic theory. A philosophy can and must be worked out with the greatest rigour and discipline in the details, but can ultimately be founded on nothing but faith: and this is the reason, I suspect, why the novelties in philosophy are only in elaboration, and never in fundamentals. There are two uses of the word truth, as we are apt to forget in philosophising: the truth or error of the metaphysician does not concern the historian in any literal sense. The historian sets out in search of truth from a different gate. And of course the only real truth is the whole truth. I have called attention to the real world (Chapter V), as the felt background against which we project our theories, and with reference to which our speculations have their use. We all recognise the world as the same 'that'; it is when we attempt to describe it that our worlds fall apart, for as we have seen, the same 'that' can only persist through a limited range of whatness. But just as we all admit the world to be the same world, though we cannot specify in precisely what respects, for there are no precise respects, so we feel that there are truths valid for this world, though we do not know what these truths are; and it is with this sort that the refined and subtilised common sense which is Critical Taste occupies itself. The true critic is a scrupulous avoider of formulae; he refrains from statements which pretend to be literally true; he finds fact nowhere and approximation always. His truths are truths of experience rather than of calculation.

Even these lived truths are partial and fragmentary, for the finest tact after all can give us only an interpretation, and every interpretation, along perhaps with some utterly contradictory interpretation, has to be taken

---

1. These can of course be double half-objects as well.

up and reinterpreted by every thinking mind and by every civilisation. This is the significance of the late Samuel Butler's epigram to the effect that the whole duty of man was to serve both God and Mammon: for both God and Mammon are interpretations of the world and have to be reinterpreted. It is this sort of interpretation (which formally consists I believe in transformations of object-type) that the historian, the literary critic, and the metaphysician are engaged with. Yet the difference between interpretation and description remains probably a question of degree. When the objects dealt with are close enough to the physical foundations of our existence to be in practice identical for all individuals, so that only one point of view is involved, we get truths which are equally true for everyone; and to what extent differences of opinion are tenable, and how deep into the body of a science these differences may sink, are questions which each science must work out for itself.... And if you wish to say that only those truths which can be demonstrated can be called true, I will acquiesce, for I am as good a materialist[1] as anybody; but though materialist, I would point out what a little way such truths bring us. For materialism itself is only an interpretation, and we cannot assert that all the types [165] of object which we meet are reducible to this one type of thing. Any assertion about the *world*, or any *ultimate* statement about any *object in* the world, will inevitably be an interpretation. It is a valuation and an assignment of meaning. The things of which we are collectively certain, we may say our common formulae, are certainly not true. What makes a real world is difference of opinion.[2] I remember a phrase of Eucken's, a phrase which had a certain *entrain* about it: *es gibt keine Privatwahrheiten* (there are no private truths). I do not recall the context, and am not concerned with the meaning which the phrase had there; but I should reverse the decision, and say: All significant truths are private truths. As they become public they cease to become truths; they become facts, or at best, part of the public character; or at worst, catchwords.

If these reflections are meant to be taken seriously, I shall be told, what excuse is there for a philosophy of the absolute? a philosophy which transforms objects to the drastic extent of transforming them all into one, and then declaring that this is no object at all? Such a question, though natural, would show I think a complete ignorance of the nature of the 'dialectic process'. The fact that we can think only in terms of

---

1. 'For how instructive and how amusing to observe in each case the conflict of sensation with imported and foreign experience. Perhaps no truth after all could be half so rich and half so true as the result of this wild discord – to one who sees from the centre.' *Appearance*, p. 172.

2. The materialism advocated is in substance, I think, the materialism of Mr Bosanquet.

things does not compel us to the conclusion that reality consists of things. We have found from the first that the thing is thoroughly relative, that it exists only in a context of experience, of experience with which it is continuous. From first to last reality is experience, but experience would not (so far as we know) be possible without attention and the moment of objectivity. We are able to distinguish a growth in clearness of the object, a detachment and independence which it seems to have in greater degree in relation to the higher forms of life: so that we can say, from our point of view, that subject and object emerge from a state of feeling. We can I think say this truly from our point of view. At the same time we must remember that in saying anything about types of consciousness different from our own, we are making statements [166] about worlds which are different from ours, though continuous. Truth on our level is a different thing from truth for the jellyfish, and there must certainly be analogies for truth and error in jellyfish life. So that what in one aspect is a development of the real world is from another aspect a new world. And yet the statement that there is such a development will be true so far as it goes.

And we have the right to say that the world is a construction. Not to say that it is *my* construction, for in that way 'I' am as much 'my' construction as the world is; but to use the word as best we can without implying any active agent: the world is a construction out of finite centres. Any particular datum can be certain only with regard to what is built upon it, not in itself: and every experience contains the principle of its own self-transcendence. Every experience is a paradox in that it means to be absolute, and yet is relative; in that it somehow always goes beyond itself and yet never escapes itself. The simple error of mistaking one man for another illustrates this well enough. There is an ideal identity which persists between experiences and rectifies our judgements; and it is this identity, together with the transcendence, which gives us degrees of truth. This theory simply asserts that a reality, a *that*, may persist under different conditions of *whatness*, though the *that* be indefinable, i.e. though we do not know what *that* it is that has persisted. We never know, in any assertion, just what, or how much, we are asserting.[1] We denote a *that* which as like as not turns out not to be the *that* that we thought it was; it continues to be the same *that* but with very different qualities: and the truth in question is found by continually analysing the given and widening its relations. Knowledge means a greater control over the material, and this control can only be given by increasing and developing

---

1. 'No judgment is ever entirely severed from a larger background of meaning, though the background may be relatively obscure except at that portion of itself which is thrown into relief and formulated as *this* judgment.' Joachim, *Nature of Truth*, p. 113.

the content. Whether we say that this is a new world or not is a matter of practical convenience. But we do *intend* it to be the same, and we feel that it is the reality which we failed at first to [167] grasp. The cruder and vaguer, or more limited, is somehow contained and explained in the wider and more precise, and this feeling of identity is all that is needed for the postulation of identity.[1] No judgement is limited to the matter in hand: you affirm that something is something else; and in the simple analytic judgement of sense you posit a 'that' to deny it. The judgement which you make is true only within the range of your experience; for it is the use you make of it that determines its meaning. And furthermore no judgement is true until you understand it; and you never wholly understand it, because 'understanding' experience means merely knowing how to use it; so that what we actually know of a judgement is not its truth but its utility (and truth never *is* utility). That at which we aim is the real as such; and the real as such is not an object.

Thus the process toward the theoretical goal returns upon itself. We aim at a real thing: but everything is real as experience, and as thing everything is ideal. When we define an experience, we substitute the definition for the experience, and then experience the definition; though the original experience may have been itself a definition: but the experiencing is quite another thing from the defining. You start, or pretend to start, from experience – from any experience – and build your theory. You begin with truths which everyone will accept, perhaps, and you find connections which no one else has discovered. In the process, reality has changed, in one sense; for the world of your theory is certainly a very different world from the world from which you began. To the builder of the system, the identity binding together the appearance and the reality is evident; to anyone outside of the system it is not evident. To the builder the process is the process of reality, for thought and reality are one; to a critic, the process is perhaps only the process of the builder's thought. From the critic's standpoint the metaphysician's world may be real only as the child's bogey is real. The one thinks of reality in terms of his [168] system; the other thinks of the system in terms of the indefinite social reality. There occurs, in short, just what is sure to occur in a world in which subject and predicate are not one. Metaphysical systems are condemned to go up like a rocket and come down like a stick. The question can always be asked of the closest-woven theory: is this the reality of *my* world of appearance? and if I do not recognise the identity,

---

1. 'The sciences of botany, of the physiology of the senses, of the physical conditions of colour, &c. – these may be said to absorb and to preserve the "truth" of such judgements as "this tree is green".' *Ibid.*, pp. 112–13.

then it is not. It will not do to say that my denial reasserts, unless I see that it does. For a metaphysics to be accepted, good-will is essential. Two men must *intend* the same object, and *both* men must admit that the object intended is the same.

We are forced to the assumption that truth is one, and to the assumption that reality is one. But dissension rises when we ask the question: what one? Our system has pretended to be about the world of those who do not accept it as much as about the world of those who do. And the world, as we have seen, exists only as it is found in the experiences of finite centres, experiences so mad and strange that they will be boiled away before you boil them down to one homogeneous mass. Thus calamity menaces our theory whether it be a theory of coherence or of correspondence. If of correspondence, where can you say that there exists the world to correspond? For such a world would be susceptible to all the criticisms which we have directed against the objects within the world. And if of coherence, it serves us no better; for what is it that coheres? Ideas, we shall be told, and not realities; and the whole structure is a faquir's show for a penny.

In part, I believe, these objections are trivial and in part mistaken. The notion of correspondence, as applied here, exhibits merely a case of the seduction of psychology. There is no question of correspondence (I have tried to show), there is no mere 'idea', except ideally in practice, when we find an 'objective' world because we have other people's 'ideas' which clash and conflict with our own. How can the notion of correspondence apply in metaphysics until we have a social metaphysical background as we have a social background for our non-metaphysical theories? And this will never be. So long as our descriptions and explanations [169] can vary so greatly and yet make so little practical difference, how can we say that our theories have that intended identical reference which is the objective criterion for truth and error? And on the other hand our theories make all the difference in the world, because the truth has to be *my* truth before it can be true at all. This is because an 'objective' truth is a relative truth: all that we care about is how it works; it makes no difference whether a thing really is green or blue, so long as everyone behaves toward it on the belief that it is green or blue. But a metaphysical doctrine pretends to be '*true*' simply, and none of our pragmatic tests will apply. The notion of correspondence will not do, for it has no meaning here. The notion of consistency fails in the same way, if it is not merely 'ideas' that we are examining, but reality. The Absolute, we find, does not fall within any of the classes of objects: it is neither real nor unreal nor imaginary. But I do not think that supersubtle defence is necessary. A metaphysic may be accepted or rejected without our assuming that from the practical point of view it is either true or false. The point is that the world of practical verification has no definite frontiers, and that it is the business of philosophy to keep the frontiers open. If I have insisted on the practical (pragmatic?) in the constitution and meaning of objects, it is because the practical is a practical metaphysic. And this emphasis upon practice – upon the relativity and the instrumentality of knowledge – is what impels us toward the Absolute.[1]

Appendix I
The Development of Leibniz's Monadism[2]
KEPB, 177–97.

The study of *Monadology* may be comprised in three stages. In the first we isolate the work; with no other aid than the philosophical counters which itself employs, we attempt to draw its fantastic world around us and find it real. Perhaps we supplement it by searching in other works of Leibniz for elucidations of points which are not clear; but in any case we take the *Monadology* as a creed and test our possibilities of belief. No philosophy can be understood without this preliminary effort to accept it on its own terms; but its true value can never be extracted solely in that way. The perfected or the summarised form of any system is the starting point, not the terminus of study. We must effect a radical restatement, find in it motives and problems which are ours, giving it the dignity of a place in the history of science when we withdraw from it the sanctity of a religion. In losing the consistency of a closed system, it gains the consistency of reason, is attached to something larger than itself. Russell and Couturat have accomplished this revaluation for Leibniz. But beside the leading motive, the reason of a philosophy, there are other strata both below and above: prejudices, traditions, suggestions, motives which imperfectly assimilate to the central motive, all of which combine to give to the system the form which it has. The present essay is merely a preface to the investigation of these forces.

There are influences of suggestion, influences of tradition, personal influences, and, moreover, there is more than one conscious [178] interest. Among influences of the first sort upon Leibniz (none of them of the highest importance) I should class a variety of authors whose contributions to

---

1. The unfinished sentence 'For if all objectivity and all knowledge is relative' with which the last page of original typescript ends has been omitted here. See Mr Eliot's *Preface* and Note 44. [Bolgan.]

2. Reprinted from *The Monist* XXVI (October 1916) 534–56. Translations have been added for this edition.

Leibniz are more verbal than profound. Leibniz' reading was wide beyond any point of selection, and he appears to have derived some entertainment from such philosophers as Giordano Bruno, Maimonides, and the Averrhoists.[1] Bruno is a classic example of influence in the most superficial sense. It is not certain, nor is it important, at what period Leibniz became acquainted with Bruno's works. For the probability that Leibniz was struck by the figurative language, that Bruno may have been in the background when Leibniz wrote some of his more imaginative passages, there is evidence enough. For the probability that Bruno affected Leibniz' thought, there is no evidence whatever. What we have is a statement which bears strong superficial resemblances to the statement of Leibniz; the arguments, such as they are, the steps which lead up to the statement, are not similar. Leibniz' arguments are sufficiently strong not to demand support from the fact that there were monadologists before Leibniz. To his imagination we may concede plagiarism. But it is with the sources of his thought, not with the sources of his imagery, that we are concerned.

The other sources mentioned may be dismissed in the same way. It is interesting, perhaps, but not valuable, to observe that Leibniz read with appreciation a book by Maimonides. And though he never couples the names of Spinoza and Maimonides together, the notes which he made upon this book single out just the points of resemblance to the *Theologico-politicus* – the first work of Spinoza that he read. He was interested in Hebrew and Arabic studies. Bossuet sends to him for a translation of the Talmud. He announces to Bossuet a translation of the Koran. A dialogue of 1676 shows that he knew, through Maimonides, the doctrines of the Averrhoists and of a certain Jewish sect, the Motekallem. In 1687, while traveling in Bavaria, he undertook [179] some study of the Kabbala, and perhaps noticed the theory of emanation from an infinite being which consists in an indivisible point – and the microcosm is said to be a familiar idea in Jewish philosophy. These studies, rather shallow it is true, illustrate Leibniz' insatiable curiosity toward every sort of theological hocus-pocus. Monadism was probably a satisfaction of this side of Leibniz' mind, as well as the outcome of his logical and metaphysical thought.

Of influences of suggestion, there is only one which may have been of the first importance – the influence of Plato, to be treated later. The main influences which directed Leibniz are of three kinds: the scholastic Aristotelian tradition in which he was brought up, the very early stimulus of a personal teacher toward a mathematical conception of the universe,

---

1. For Bruno, see H. Brunnhofer: *G. Brunos Lehre vom Kleinsten*. For Maimonides, see Foucher de Careil: *Leibniz, la philosophie juive*; Rubin: *Erkenntnistheorie Maimons*.

and Leibniz' temporary adhesion to atomism. His chief motives, more or less corresponding to this classification, were theological, logical, and physical.

Merz expresses the conventional opinion in saying that the *De principio individui* 'bears testimony to the young author's extensive knowledge of scholastic learning as well as to his dexterity in handling their dialectical methods.'[1] I am incompetent to impugn the scholastic erudition of young Leibniz, but a perusal of this document impels me to exclaim with Kabitz, 'as if the copious citation of passages from scholastic compendia proved any "astonishing" learning on the part of Leibniz; as if he could not obtain these quotations just as well second-hand!'[2] The treatise is very short and very dull. Two or three passages in it are often quoted. 'Pono igitur: omne individuum sua tota entitate individuatur';[3] and 'Sed si omnis intellectus creatus tolleretur, illa relatio periret, et tamen res individuarentur, ergo tunc se ipsis.'[4] The principle of individuation is not mental, nor is it [180] negative. Though Leibniz documents this work with such names as Occam, Scotus, Aquinas, Suarez, Molina, Zabarella, what the thesis shows is not extent of learning or originality of thought. It shows that there was a certain body of inheritance which pointed in a certain direction. It shows a scholastic point of view from which Leibniz never really escaped, and which he never wholly rejected.[5] In the light of these quotations is to be interpreted not only monadism, but the materialistic atomism which for a time engaged his attention. At this early period, and indeed throughout his life, there is little evidence of direct adaptations from Aristotle. But here as always one finds the acceptance of the problem of substance, transmitted from Aristotle through the form which the school had given it. In some ways diametrically in opposition with Aristotle, this scholastic view of substance which Leibniz held is yet an Aristotelian inheritance. This point is of capital importance.

It appears that Leibniz abandoned his study of the philosophers of the church when he felt called, at a very early age, 'to adopt the mechanical

---

1. Merz, p. 15.

2. Kabitz, *Die Philosophie des jungen Leibniz*, p. 50.

3. 'I propose therefore that every individual thing is made individual by its own whole being.'

4. 'But if every intellect in creation were taken away, that relationship would perish; yet even so things would be made individual, and therefore in that event by themselves.'

5. Nolen, *Quid L. Aristoteli debuerit*, p. 27, quotes Leibniz as follows: 'Mea doctrina de substantia composita videtur esse ipsa doctrina scholae peripateticae. Nisi quod ille monadas non agnovit.' ('My doctrine of substance seems to be derived from the doctrine of substance of the peripatetic school, except that the latter was ignorant of monads.')

view of nature....'[1] But there was never a complete renunciation, and Leibniz, who seldom spoke ill of a dead philosopher, always praises the schoolmen. The change was a transition and not an apostasy. In 1663, at Jena, while pursuing his studies in jurisprudence, he fell under the influence of Weigel. Weigel was acquainted with the work of Copernicus, Kepler, and Galileo. Kabitz says that 'the fundamental conception of Leibniz' system according to which the universe is an harmonic, mathematico-logical related whole ... became a firm conviction with Leibniz through Weigel, before he was acquainted with the work of Hobbes.'[2] Bisterfeld of Leyden is another mathematician admired by Leibniz in his youth, and his influence is supposed to be visible in the *Arte Combinatoria*. The idea of a harmony [181] of a universe of individual substances is present in other writings of Leibniz' adolescence.

Leibniz' scholastic training in metaphysics under Thomasius was followed by that period in which, as he says, 'when I had freed myself from the yoke of Aristotle [by which he means the attenuated scholasticism of his day], I took to the void and the atoms, for that is the view which best satisfies the imagination.'[3] This may have been about 1666.[4] It is easy to see from the *De principio individui* (written, according to his own chronology, when he had already fallen under the influence of Gassendi) that this liberation was merely a development of extreme nominalism in the currents of his time. In 1676 he can still write, 'Ego magis magisque persuasus sum de corporibus insecabilibus ... simplicissima esse debent ac proinde sphaerica,' but goes on to say 'Nullus enim locus est tam parvus quin fingi possit esse in eo sphaeram ipso minorem. Ponamus hoc ita esse, nullus erit locus assignabilis vacuus. Et tamen Mundus erit plenus, unde intelligitur quantitatem inassignabilem esse aliquid.'[5] The atomism survives in 1676, although the void is abandoned, and the influence of his mathematical work is visible (this was just at the end of the period in Paris, when he was corresponding with Newton through the medium of Oldenburg). In this year occurred also his visit to London and to the Hague.

1. Merz, p. 15.
2. Kabitz, *op. cit.*, p. 112.
3. Latta, p. 300.
4. See Kabitz, p. 53.
5. Couturat, 1903, p. 10. ('I am more and more convinced about indivisible particles ... they must be very simple and therefore spherical. For there is no place so small that it would be impossible to imagine in it a sphere smaller than itself. We therefore propose the following: no assignable place shall be empty. And yet the Universe shall be full, from which it is understood that an unassignable quantity is still something.')

In the next period of his life, when he had for some years been occupied chiefly with mathematical matters, falls the elaboration of his argument against Descartes's theory of matter – Descartes, who had been partly responsible for Leibniz' tendency toward a mechanical view. The unsatisfactory character of the views of Descartes and of Gassendi had, it is true, been pointed out by Leibniz several years before. In this later period, besides physics and pure mathematics, a third scientific interest may be noted. He [182] refers often to Swammerdam, Leeuwenhoek, and Malpighi, and it is evident that he felt a genuine enthusiasm for the progress of biology, aside from the support which certain theories lent to his doctrine of preformation. But as his interest in biology is apparently subsequent to the observable beginnings of monadism, these theories were rather a confirmation than a stimulus.

To these philosophical and scientific occupations must be joined another which was no less important. This is his perfectly genuine passion for theology. Developed perhaps out of his early training, this theology, in a mind which never lost an interest it had once taken up, remained a powerful influence throughout his life. His solicitude for the orthodoxy of his philosophy was not merely policy or timidity; his theological disputations are not merely a cover for logical problems. Leibniz' theological motive is responsible for much of the psychology of his monads; it took deep root in his system, though not altogether without disturbance of the soil. The only two interpretations of Leibniz which are of any importance, that of Dillmann[1] and the superior interpretation of Russell and Couturat, minimise the significance of this motive.

'Ma métaphysique est toute mathématique, pour dire ainsi, ou la pourroit devenir,' Leibniz writes to the Marquis de l'Hôpital (Dec. 27, 1694). And Russell says in speaking of the subject-object relation, 'the whole doctrine depends, throughout, upon this purely logical tenet.'[2] Strictly speaking, this assertion is perfectly justified. For a historical account, it is insufficient. Leibniz puts his problems into logical form, and often converts them slyly into logical problems, but his prejudices are not always prejudices of logic. The value of Leibniz' logic is to a certain extent separable from the value of his philosophy. The view of the nature of substance with which he starts is due to a logical problem. But there is no logical descent from pluralism to the view that the ego is substance. Leibniz' view of substance is derived from Aristotle but his *theory* of substance is different: it is Aristotle's theory filtered through scholasticism and tinctured by atomism and theology.

1. *Neue Darstellung der Leibnizischen Monadenlehre.*
2. Russell, p. 49.

When we father the problem of substance upon Aristotle, we [183] must remember that it was a problem which he never succeeded in resolving, or pretended to have resolved. The chief inheritance of modern philosophy from his doctrine is the proposition that 'substance is that which is not predicated of a subject, but of which all else is predicated' (*Metaphysica Z* 1029a 8–9). Aristotle recognises that there are various senses in which we may use the term, and various substances besides the sensible substances, which have matter. In one sense, the composite of form and matter (e.g., animals and plants) is substance; in another sense substance is 'the form by which the matter is some definite thing' (1041b 8). And again the substratum (1028b 36–37) is that of which everything is predicated. Matter certainly is not substance, because matter has neither limit nor the potency of limit by separation (see Δ 1017b 1–8). And again the universal is more substantial than the particulars (H1042a 13–15). Wherever Aristotle pursues the concept of substance, it eludes him. These tentative definitions, assumed for dialetic purposes, are abandoned in favour of that of 1041b 27–3l. This bears, it is true, very striking resemblances to the substance of Leibniz. As to the meaning of form and the relation of formal to efficient and final cause, Aristotle remains difficult and vague, while for Leibniz the formal and efficient causes in the case of substance are identical.

There is another and very serious difficulty in the theory of Aristotle. From one of Aristotle's points of view only the individual should be real, from the other only the specific. The form is always ἄτομον (indivisible); thought analyses and resynthesizes its constituents to give the λόγος τοῦ τί ἦν εἶναι (the reason for a thing being what it is). Of the subject, either the whole or a part of the definition can be affirmed: thus we can define Socrates *qua* man as ζῷον δίπουν λογικόν (a rational two-footed animal). But predications of particular individuals belong to the attributive, not to the definitory, type of judgement. In this type of judgement the predicate affirmed, although it belongs to the subject, is not a constituent of the subject's essential nature. As the essential nature of Socrates is man, anything which is not contained in the form of man in general will be attributive only and not definitory, inasmuch as it might have been otherwise. For Aristotle, not all [184] predicates are contained in their subjects. Hence there can be no definition of individuals of a species (1039b 27–30). The substance must be individual, in order to be the subject; it must be a 'this'. But the 'this' cannot be composed of universals, because no number of 'suches' will constitute a 'this', and on the other hand it cannot be composed of other substances. We thus get two opposed views: the substance is the form of the species, in which case it breaks loose from the concrete thing and gives rise to the same difficulties which Aristotle censured in Plato; or the substance is the individual thing, in which case there is no definition and no knowledge. One view is in harmony with Aristotle's methodology, the other with his theory of elementary cognition.[1]

Aristotle is here betrayed by his representation theory – the exact correspondence between constituents of propositions and constituents of things; although in other contexts he is an epistemological monist. The same incoherence appears in his account of the soul. Is the substance the compound of matter and form, or the form alone?

It was the Aristotelian problem of substance, affected by scholasticism, that Leibniz took upon his shoulders at the beginning of his career. Later in life he observes that he has been re-reading Aristotle, and that he finds much of value in him. The extent of his acquaintance with the text may be left in doubt. It is probable that he had little or no direct knowledge, that he abandoned the study of the history of philosophy almost altogether for some years, and the fresh approach to Aristotle did not produce much effect upon his subsequent work. The interest lies in Leibniz' saturation which the Aristotelian tradition – in spite of a momentary peevishness against the degenerate scholasticism in which he had been brought up – and in the compound to which the contact of this training with the speculations of contemporary science give rise. To this particular problem the drawing of parallels and the estimating of borrowings – conscious and uncon-[185]scious – is irrelevant. Nor are we here concerned with the question whether 'this seemingly fantastic system could be deduced from a few simple premisses.'[2] The question is the actual genesis of the system. If, at the age of fifteen, Leibniz inclined to the view that substances are particular individuals and that relations exist only in the mind; if we can see that his transition to atomic materialism follows quite easily from this; if we find that his further development depended upon the way in which his scientific researches and his theological prejudices – largely an inheritance from his early training – played into each other; then we shall conclude that his metaphysics and his scientific achievements – logical and mathematical – are two different values.

What is curious about Leibniz' mind is the existence of two distinct currents. As a scientist he has a clear and consistent development. Every step is justified and coherent from this point of view alone. His metaphysics is carefully built upon his scientific evolution. On the other

---

1. In *An. post.* Book II (Chap. XIX) 100*a* 15–17 we are told how the knowledge of the universals arises through experience of particulars. 'First principles' are arrived at by induction. What is not made clear is the status of the particulars after scientific knowledge is established.

2. Russell, p. viii.

side is a strong devotion to theology. His study of Descartes marks a stage in the development of both. Descartes's theory of matter, and Descartes's theory of self-consciousness both had their effect upon him. And it is always the same mind working, clear and cold, the mind of a doctor of the church. He is nearer to the Middle Ages, nearer to Greece, and yet nearer to us, than are men like Fichte and Hegel.

We have seen that there is a very great difference between the Aristotelian theory of substance and the nominalism deriving from it with which Leibniz starts. Both in the *Metaphysica* and in the *De anima*, it is true, Aristotle leaves the answer somewhat ambiguous. When he discusses the substance of organic beings we are apt to think that each individual is a substance – that the form of each body is an individual – one form for Socrates, and another for Callias. It is difficult to avoid this conclusion, but in general, for Aristotle as well as for Plato, whatever was merely individual was perishable and incapable of being a subject of knowledge. But if we say, with Burnet[1] that 'Plato found reality, whether intelligible or sensible, in the combination of matter and form and [186] not in either separately', and take the same view of Aristotle, yet we cannot say that they found it in each individual as a world apart. This is an instance of the differences between Leibniz and the Greeks. In Leibniz we find the genesis of a psychological point of view; ideas tend to become particular mental facts, attributes of particular substances. If the form or principle of Aristotle were different in each man, this form would be Leibniz' soul. For the Greek the human was the typically human, individual differences were not of scientific interest; for the modern philosopher individual differences were of absorbing importance.

We may now trace the two currents which are imperfectly united in the monad. Leibniz approaches the problem of substance primarily as a physicist. 'Leibniz does not begin with the problem, what is the substance of the body, what is its origin, but from this: how the principle of the body itself may be conceived.'[2] To those readers – there are still a few – who know Leibniz only through the *Monadology,* the steps to the conclusion will remain unknown. Unless we appreciate the original question we shall be unable to understand his solution of the problem of body and soul, and of the problem of our knowledge of external objects. He never asked the question, 'do physical bodies exist?' but always, 'what is the principle which makes physical bodies intelligible?' The answer is found in his reaction to Cartesianism. And at this point, while the problem of energy was engaging his attention, he read some of the dialogues of Plato,

---

1. *Greek Philosophy*, pp. 331-2.
2. Dillman, p. 63.

and was confirmed in his conclusions especially by certain parts of the *Sophist*. What we get is on the one hand an explanation of the principle of matter, and on the other an idealistic metaphysic, largely influenced by Descartes, based upon self-consciousness. The latter aspect has of course been more exploited than the former.

Leibniz' account of physical matter is a much more scientific, but in some respects much cruder, explanation than Aristotle's. For Aristotle's account is fundamentally a relativistic one, i.e., 'matter' has various meanings in relation to shifting points of view which form a series but are not themselves defined. There [187] are meanings in various contexts, but no absolute meaning; and the series of points of view, the series of contexts, has no absolute meaning either. One misses the whole point of Aristotle's theory if one regards matter as a 'thing'. It is – whether as primitive matter, as the four elements, or as any compounds (I mean συνθέσεις (syntheses, compositions) not μίξεις (mixtures)) of any degree of complexity formed out of these – one side of a contrast in the mind (or imposed upon the mind) though this mind is no more absolutely definable than matter itself. (Hence Aristotle is neither an idealist, in the modern sense, nor a pragmatist.) *Materia prima* is not simply negative nor is it positive in any apprehensible way. It is simply the furthest possible extension of meaning of a concept which has arisen out of practical complexes. The next stage in the conception of matter, it will be recollected, is that of a subject possessing two out of two pairs of opposites (wet-dry, hot-cold). The *materia prima* is not *actual,* because it has no predicates; the smallest number of predicates which an actual existent can have is two. That is, whatever is merely hot, or merely dry, is not a substance but is identical with the quality itself; but whatever is hot and wet, or cold and dry, is a substance different from its predicates. These elements – the possible combinations of four qualities – are capable of transmutation into one another in a cycle which occurs in the exchange of qualities (the hot-dry becomes hot-wet, the hot-wet becomes wet-cold, etc.). The third stage of matter is that of the stable compounds of the four elements held together in various proportions. This progress is not a chemical theory in the modern sense; it is a series of points of view. The formal cause is therefore identical with the thing itself, and whether the form is there is a question of what we regard as the thing. The lump of marble is a σωρός (pile, heap) of higher compounds of the four elements – or it is a statue. One must keep in mind the two apparently inconsistent propositions: (1) there are no forms of individuals,[1] (2) the form and the matter compose one whole.

---

1. Except of course eternal and unique individuals, like the moon, which is the only individual of its species. And for later theology, the angels.

[188] Aristotle is too keen a metaphysician to start from a naive view of matter or from a one-sided spiritualism. To a certain extent Leibniz keeps this middle ground too. But his metaphysics tends to fall apart, as the result of his inherited nominalism, and the fissure between his scientific and his theological interests. Starting as a physicist, Leibniz naturally assumes that matter is not a relative term but that it is (if it exists at all, of which he has no doubt) something absolute. The substantiality of matter consists then (after his defection from Cartesianism) in the concept of force. Force is not conceived as something behind matter, which could be actual without matter. But neither is it a 'form' in quite the Aristotelian sense. The 'real and animated point' of the *Système nouveau* is from an Aristotelian point of view merely another individual, or a form of an individual. It is purely and simply a physical explanation. It involves no theory of knowledge, because it does not take into account the point of view of an observer; it is a contrast not between matter and form, but between a particular substance and its states.

Leibniz' distinction between *materia prima* and *materia secunda* (of bodies) is superficially Aristotelian. But it is really only a distinction between two ways in which matter may be considered for the purposes of the physicist. It is a distinction of uses and not of contexts. 'Matter' is not a relative term. The ancient distinction between matter and form does not correspond to the modern distinction, since Descartes, of matter and spirit. And the dichotomy is as strongly marked in Leibniz as in Descartes. His solution of the difficulty marks the wide gulf that separates modern from ancient philosophy. For Aristotle matter and form were always relative, but never identical. For Leibniz matter and spirit are absolute reals, but are really (as for Spinoza) the same thing. The difference for Leibniz is that between internal and external aspects. *Materia prima* is not a stage, it is an external aspect, and even for physics he finds this aspect insufficient. He is therefore led gradually into a metaphysical conception. But from this metaphysical account of the nature of the physical universe to his doctrine of souls there is really no legitimate inference.

[189] The theory of forces, as the substances of which material changes are the states, is not the theory of the soul which derives from his more theological interest. It is, as we have said, simply an analysis of the physical universe. Had Leibniz been quite consistent he would have gone on to explain organic and conscious activity on a strictly physical basis. This he did accomplish in some measure. His doctrine of expression[1] is an account of perception consistent with a purely physical and

---

1. See Letter to Arnauld, Oct. 6, 1687.

mathematical point of view. But his transmigration[1] of human souls is muddled by the identification of soul, in the sense of personality, with the animated point; of the core of feeling of the self with the force of which it is predicated. From his physical point of view he cannot arrive at self-consciousness, so that his doctrine of force has two grounds – the theory of dynamics and the *feeling* of activity. If we refuse to consider self-consciousness a simple and single act, if making an object of oneself merely means the detachment and observation of particular states by other states, then the 'force' slips out of our hands altogether. It remains 'internal', it is true, in contrast with primary matter, but its internality is not a character of self-consciousness. And in this event the whole theory becomes completely naturalistic. Something is the subject, but it is not the *I* which I know, or which anybody knows. And there then remains no reason why we should longer maintain a plurality of subjects. Force becomes one. Against such a conclusion Leibniz was set, (1) because it ceases to have any value for physics, and (2) because it interferes with our claim for personal immortality. Theology and physics join forces (so to speak) to rob metaphysics of its due.

Hence two curious difficulties arise. An animated force, a monad, tends to become an animated atom. The monad exerts its activity at a point in space and time. Artefacts, as for Aristotle, are merely groups of monads without a dominant monad. Organic bodies are groups with a dominant monad. In the latter case, in [190] the case of a human being, in what sense is my body *mine,* since it is also the bodies of other monads? The dominant monad should be the form of the body, instead of which it bears a strong resemblance to a larger or more powerful cell, and the soul would have to be located, like Descartes's, in a particular place. Russell, in contrasting Leibniz' two conflicting theories says of the second view: 'in the other theory, mind and body together make one substance, making a true unity.'[2] So they ought to do. If the mind cannot make the body into a *unum per se,* instead of a mere aggregate, the original physical theory has advanced to a point at which mind and body fall apart. The second view appears to descend from Aristotle.[3] The first appears to descend from atomism. From neither philosophy does Leibniz ever shake himself quite free.

---

1. Leibniz of course explicitly repudiates any 'transmigration' of monads. But when he comes to the human soul its adventures seem to be tantamount to this.
2. Russell, p. 150.
3. Leibniz actually says (letter to Arnauld, July 14, 1686): 'The soul is nevertheless the form of the body.'

There is, from the physical side, a sense in which the monad is truly immortal. Force is indestructible, and will continue in various manifestations. But force in this sense is entirely impersonal. We cannot conceive of its persistence except by associating it with particular particles of matter. Leibniz is led by his difficulties almost to the point of either denying the existence of matter altogether, or else setting up a sort of matter which will be something real besides monads.

The second objection is connected with the generation and destruction of life. For Aristotle some account of generation and destruction is rendered possible by his provisional distinction between efficient and formal causes. Aristotle was not embarrassed by a belief in personal immortality, and his philosophy confines itself with fair success to an examination of the actual, the present life. But Leibniz' force is indestructible in a different sense from Aristotle's form.[1] It persists in time as a particular existence. The monad which is myself must have previously existed; it must have [191] been one of the monads composing the body of father or mother.[2] This theory has the disadvantages of practically denying the independence of mind from body and of separating monadhood from selfhood. It substitutes biological behaviour for conscious activity.

Commencing with an analysis of the nature of matter, Leibniz is led to the view of a universe consisting of centres of force. From this point of view the human soul is merely one of these forces, and its activity should be reducible to physical laws. Under the influence of an Aristotelian doctrine of substance, he comes to conclusions which are not at all Aristotelian, by his nominalistic assumption that substances are particulars. From a materialistic atomism he is led to a spiritualistic atomism. In this he shows again an important difference between the ancient and the modern world. It is illustrated in the prejudice of Aristotle against the differences between individuals of the same species which he ascribes to the perverse and unaccountable influence of matter. To the Greek, this variety of points of view would seem a positive evil; as a theory of knowledge, it would seem a refuge of scepticism; to Leibniz and the modern world, it enhances the interest of life. And yet the view of Leibniz comes, *via* nominalism, out of Aristotle himself.

From the point of view of physics we have a consistent explanation which represents a great advance upon crude materialism. But it is difficult to retain the separate forces unless we conceive of matter as a

1. Aristotle and Plato, I am inclined to believe, owe their success in navigating between the particular and the universal, the concrete and the abstract, largely to the fact that 'forms', 'species', had to the Greek mind not exactly the same meaning as for us. They were concrete without being particular.
2. Russell, p. 154.

positive principle of individuation. Not that the doctrine of activity and passivity is wholly unsatisfactory.[1] Its effect is to reduce causality to function. And but for the Aristotelian influence, it might possibly have done so. Instead of monads we might then have had atomic particulars. But Leibniz sometimes confuses the mathematico-physical and the historical points of view. It is true that the future of the monad should be theoreti-[192]cally predictable. But Leibniz leaves the basis of prediction uncertain. Without recourse to mysticism, the reasons why a monad should pass from the unconscious to the conscious state, why one of the monads composing the body of father or mother should suddenly be elected to domination over a new body of monads, remain unsolved. We have seen that the notion of soul or spirit is not to be reached by the theory of monads as an explanation of the principle of matter. If it is part of Leibniz' inheritance we may inquire just what Aristotle's view of the soul was.

Leibniz' theory of soul is, like that of Descartes, derived from scholasticism. It is very remote from that of either Plato, Aristotle, or Plotinus. For the Greeks, even for Plotinus, the soul is a substance in a sense which does not include personal immortality. For Aristotle there is no continuity between the stages of soul, between vegetable, animal, and human life. And the definition of monads as 'points of view' is, so far as I can see, entirely modern.

For Aristotle, according to his own explicit statement, there is no 'soul' in general. As the species of figure to figure in general, so are the souls of various species of animal to 'soul' in general.[2] In the higher grades of soul the same functions persist, but in a form altered by the nature of the whole. The organs of different species are related by analogy – as root is to plant, so mouth is to animal, but mouth is not a development of root. The *De anima* is not so much a psychological as a biological treatise. We find in the animal the τροφή (nourishment) and αὔξησις (growth) of the plant, but completely altered in the addition of a new faculty – αἴσθησις (perception). And these faculties are not sharp dividing lines, but in the ascending scale are used more and more loosely.[3] The natural species are immutable, and the difference does not consist in addition or subtraction of faculty.

1. There are implicitly two views of activity and passivity. According to one, causality is a useful way of treating natural phenomena. According to the other, there is true activity in clear perception, true passivity in confused. This illustrates the mixture of motives.

2. *De Anima*, Book II, 414b, 20 ff.

3. Cf. Book II, 413b, 12-13; 414a, 31 ff; and Book III, 432a, 15 ff. Motion, according to 413b, 13, is not a fourth species of the soul besides θρεπτικόν, αἰσθητικόν, διανοητικόν (the principles of growth, perception, and thought).

There is a suggestion, but only a suggestion, of the doctrine of Aristotle in the three classes of monads. Even the lowest class of [193] monad has appetition.[1] The second has feeling (sentiment) which is something more than αἴσθησις (perception) and includes φαντασία (imagination) and perhaps διάνοια (thought). The soul of man only has self-consciousness, a knowledge of eternal and necessary truths – νοῦς (mind). It seems very probable that this scheme was suggested by Aristotle[2] but there is a profound difference. The classification of Aristotle is on the basis of biological functions. These are functions of the organism as a whole, a complex substance. Plants are not ζῷα (animals), and have no appetition. Aristotle makes much of the distinction between beings which are attached to a single place and those which move about. For Leibniz the distinction is not biological, but psychological, and is everywhere a difference of degree. The lower monads, if they had clearer perceptions, would rise in the scale. It is not a limitation of the body, but a limitation of the nature of the monad itself which establishes differences. For Leibniz the series is a continuum; for Aristotle it is not. For Leibniz desire characterises mind; for Aristotle desire is always of the complex organism; the function of mind is solely the apprehension of the eternal and necessary truths and principles.

There is another point upon which Leibniz may have drawn his inspiration from Aristotle, and that is the 'common sense'. 'The ideas which are said to come from more than one sense, like those of space, figure, motion, rest, are rather from common sense, that is from the mind itself, for they are ideas of the pure understanding, but they are related to the external, and the senses make us perceive them.'[3] Leibniz' theory appears to be a transition between Aristotle and Kant. What Aristotle says is this: 'The above [i.e., colour, sound, etc.] are called qualities which belong to the respective senses; the perceptions common to all are motion, rest, number, figure, magnitude. These are not *propria* of any, but are common to all.'[4] Whereas Leibniz stuffs these κοινά (common qualities) into the mind, Aristotle goes no farther than to say [194] that they are perceived κατὰ συμβεβηκός (accidentally) by all the senses. There is not, as is sometimes thought, a 'common sense' which apprehends them, as

---

1. *Monadology*, 19.

2. And, in passing, it seems possible that the theory of Leibniz may have supplied a hint for the romantic evolutionism of Diderot.

3. Russell, p. 163.

4. *De Anima*, Book II, 418a, 17 ff.

the eye perceives colour.[1] What is interesting in the present context is the cautious empiricism of Aristotle's theory, contrasted with the more daring but less sound speculations of Leibniz.

The question of the relation of mind to matter is handled by Leibniz differently from either Aristotle or Spinoza. I am inclined to think that it was conceived quite independently of Spinoza. Leibniz attacks Spinoza fiercely on the ground of Spinoza's naturalism, and for his disbelief in free-will and immortality.[2] He perceives, quite correctly, that Spinoza's view of the relation of mind and body leads to a materialistic epiphenominalism. 'With Spinoza the reason does not possess ideas, it is an idea.' He insists that the mind and the body are not the same thing, any more than the principle of action and the principle of passion are the same thing. But he inclines to believe that the difference between mind and matter is a difference of degree, that in all created monads there is materiality. (There seems to be a relation between *materia prima* of monads and *materia prima* of matter.) Now this suggests the Aristotelian relativity of matter and form; for Aristotle the higher substances are more 'formed', the percentage of crude matter seems to decrease. There is no matter and no form in an absolute sense (except the form of God, who is rather a disturbing factor). But whereas for Aristotle matter exists only in contrast with form, and formed matter may be the matter for a higher form, for Leibniz matter really exists independently of spirit, but is really spirit.

Leibniz' use of the term 'entelechy' is not identical with that of Aristotle. The monad is called entelechy apparently because it is complete in itself, complete in the sense of self-sufficient; while the entelechy of Aristotle is the *completion* or actuality of something. In the *De anima* the soul is called the first entelechy of body. [195] To be strictly consistent, Aristotle should perhaps have held that soul is the second entelechy, since he maintains that it is only actual when it energises; but he is merely trying to distinguish between the form and its operation.[3] Entelechy means that the body would not be a human body without the soul. It is difficult, it is true, not to think of the soul as something added to the body (as to Galatea) or else to identify soul with the (living) body. Soul is to body as cutting is to the axe: realising itself in its actions, and not completely real when abstracted from what it does. In the light of Aristotle's elaborate

---

1. Zabarella, probably the greatest of all Aristotelian commentators, is very positive on this point.

2. See Foucher de Careil: *Réfutation inédite de Spinoza par Leibniz*.

3. See *De anima*, Book II, 412a, 28, where δυνάμει ζωὴν ἔχοντος means having 'the potentiality of functioning', not 'the potentiality of soul'. The above distinction between form and operation was pointed out by Zabarella.

critique of earlier theories of the soul, his view is seen as an attempt to get away from the abstractions of materialism or of spiritualism with which we begin. For Aristotle reality is here and now; and the true nature of mind is found in the activity which it exercises. Attempt to analyse the mind, as a thing, and it is nothing. It is an operation. Aristotle's psychology therefore starts with psycho-physics, and ascends to speculative reason. It is only then that we perceive what mind is, and in retrospect find that it was present in the simplest sensation.

The word entelechy as used by Leibniz loses the meaning which it had for Aristotle. It becomes figurative and unimportant. Leibniz appears at first less a dichotomist than either Aristotle or Descartes. In effect, the breach between mind and matter becomes far wider than in the system of Aristotle. In order that mind may persist at all times as something distinct from the body, appeal is made to the subconscious, – a parallelism even more mystifying than that of Spinoza. With Leibniz the relation of mind and matter is closer, the relation of body and soul more remote, than with Aristotle. The weakness in Leibniz' theory of body and soul may be due to two causes. On the one hand his theological bias made separation of body and soul essential; and on the other hand it was necessary, for his more strictly philosophical argument, that the monads should persist after the compound substances, the bodies, which are their points of view. It [196] is required both by his theory of substance, and by his demand for a mathematical metaphysic. The causal series which is the monad should apparently have no last term.[1] Perception (in Leibniz' general statement of expression) requires that every series should be similar both to every other series and to the series of series.[2] The same theory which demands unconscious perception seems to demand also a series which shall not terminate in time. Supposing that the destruction of individual monads shall leave the total, as an infinite number, undiminished, nevertheless the monad as a substance will have to shut up shop, and we shall be left with a number of relations relating nothing. Some sort of persistence is necessary for the system, though not the personal immortality which Leibniz is interested in supporting. It is evident that with the possibility of changes of 'points of view' the meaning of prediction becomes hopelessly attenuated. Every moment will see a new universe. At every moment there will be a new series of series; but continuity makes necessary a point of view from which there shall be a permanent series of series of series.

---

1. See Russell: 'Recent work on the philosophy of Leibniz', *Mind*, Vol. XII (1903) pp. 199–200.
2. See *ibid.*, p. 199.

Leibniz' theory of mind and matter, of body and soul, is in some ways the subtlest that has ever been devised. Matter is an arrested moment of mind, 'mind without memory'.[1] By state is not meant feeling, but the monad at any instant of time.[2] In many ways it is superior to that of Aristotle. When he turns to preformation, to the *vinculum substantiale*, to the immortality of the soul, we feel a certain repulsion; for with all the curious fables of the *Timaeus* or the *Physics* and Aristotle's history of animals, we know that Aristotle and Plato were somehow more secure, better balanced, and less superstitious than the man who was in power of intellect their equal.

There are two other points in monadism which direct attention to the Greeks. These are the theory of innate ideas and the theory [197] of substance as force expressed in the 'Sophist'. So far as the question of indebtedness goes I think that the answer is clear enough. The views which Leibniz held were urged upon him by his own premises. He undoubtedly read Plato at a time when his own theory was not yet crystallised, but he cannot be said to have borrowed. He may be given full credit for having restored to life in a new form the doctrines of Plato and Aristotle. The monad is a reincarnation of the form which is the formal cause of Aristotle. But it is also more and less. The outstanding difference is that he sets out from an investigation of *physical* force, and his monads tend to become atomic centres of force, particular existences. Hence a tendency to psychologism, to maintain that ideas always find their home in particular minds, that they have a psychological as well as a logical existence. Leibniz on this side opened the way for modern idealism. To his anticipations of modern logic of a school opposed to absolute idealism, it is unnecessary for me to point. No philosophy contains more various possibilities of development, no philosophy unites more various influences. That he did not always unite them successfully – that he never quite reconciled modern physics, medieval theology, and Greek substance – is not to be reproved when we consider the magnitude of his task and the magnitude of his accomplishment.

---

1. Quoted from *Theoria motus abstracti*, 1671 by Latta, p. 230 n. Compare the Bergsonian theory of matter as consciousness 'running down'.
2. Cf. 'only indivisible monads and their states are absolutely real'.

Appendix II
Leibniz's Monads and Bradley's Finite Centres[1]
KEPB, 198–207.

No philosopher is more fantastic than Leibniz in presentation, few have been less intelligently interpreted. At first sight, none is less satisfactory. Yet Leibniz remains to the end disquieting and dangerous. He represents no one tradition, no one civilisation; he is allied to no social or literary tendency; his thought cannot be summed up or placed. Spinoza represents a definite emotional attitude; suggestive as he is, his value can be rated. Descartes is a classic, and is dead. *Candide* is a classic: Voltaire was a wise man, and not dangerous. Rousseau is not a classic, nor was he a wise man; he has proved an eternal source of mischief and inspiration. Reviewing the strange opinions, almost childish in *naiveté*, of birth and death, of body and soul, of the relation between vegetable and animal, of activity and passivity – together with the pitiful efforts at orthodoxy and the cautious ethics of this German diplomat, together with his extraordinary facility of scientific insight, one is disconcerted at the end. His orthodoxy is more alarming than others' revolution, his fantastic guesses more enduring than others' rationality.

Beside the work of Russell and of Couturat I have found only one author of assistance in attempting to appreciate the thought of Leibniz. In Bradley's *Appearance and Reality* I seemed to find features strikingly similar to those of monadism. So that re-reading Leibniz I cannot help thinking that he was the first to express, perhaps half unconsciously, one of those fundamental varieties of [199] view which perpetually recur as novelties. With his motives, logical and otherwise, I am not here concerned. I only wish to point out, and leave for consideration, certain analogies.

That monadism begins with Leibniz I think will be conceded. It is characteristic of the man that everything about his monads, except the one essential point which makes them his own, he may have borrowed from an author with whom he was certainly acquainted. Bruno's theory has everything in common with that of Leibniz except this one point. A kind of pre-established harmony, the continuity of animal and vegetable and of organic and inorganic, the representation of the whole in the part, even the words *monadum monas* (the monad of monads): these points

---

1. Reprinted from *The Monist* XXVI (October 1916) 566–76. Translations have been added for this edition.

of identity one finds.[1] But the monad of Bruno has this difference: it has windows. And it is just the impenetrability of the Leibnizian monads which constitutes their originality and which seems to justify our finding a likeness between Leibniz and Bradley. In any case, there is no philosopher with whom the problem of sources is less important than with Leibniz. The fact that he could receive stimulation from such various sources and remain so independent of the thought of his own time[2] indicates both the robustness and the sensitiveness of genius. He had studied Thomas, and probably with great care the *Metaphysics* and the *De anima,* but he was not an Aristotelian; he was probably profoundly struck by the passage *Sophistes* 247e, but any one who has read his panegyric of the *Phaedo*[3] will probably agree that his praise is more the approval of posterity than the inter-[200]pretation of discipleship. Leibniz' originality is in direct, not inverse ratio to his erudition.

More than multiplicity of influences, perhaps the multiplicity of motives and the very occasional reasons for some of Leibniz' writings, make him a bewildering and sometimes ludicrous writer. The complication of his interests in physics, his interests in logic, and his equally genuine interest in theology, make his views a jungle of apparent contradictions and irrelevancies. His theory of physical energy, for example, leads to an unsound metaphysical theory of activity, and his solicitude for the preservation of human immortality leads to a view which is only an excrescence upon monadism,[4] and which is in every way less valuable than Aristotle's. Thus there are features of the theory which are inessential. When we confine our attention to the resemblances between Leibniz' and Bradley's views, we will find I think that they cover everything essential. These are (1) complete isolation of monads from each other; (2) sceptical theory of knowledge, relativistic theory of space,

---

1. See H. Brunnhofer, *G. Bruno's Lehre vom Kleinsten als die Quelle der praestabilierten Harmonie von Leibniz* (Leipsic, 1890), pp. 59–63, for quotations, e.g. from *De Triplici Minimo*: 'Deus est monadum monas.' Also from *Spaccio della bestia trionfante*: 'In ogni uomo, in ciascuno individuo si contempla un mondo, un universo.' Brunnhofer even traces the window metaphor back to the Song of Solomon: 'Prospiciens per fenestras'.

2. At least he affirms his independence. In 1679 he writes to Malebranche that, as when he began to meditate he was not imbued with Cartesian opinions, he was led to 'entrer dans les choses par une autre porte et decouvrir de nouveaux pays'. He is also inclined to speak rather slightingly of Spinoza. See Wendt, *Die Entwickelung der Leibnizischen Monadenlehre bis zum Jahre 1695* (Berlin, 1886). The germs of monadism appear as early as 1663.

3. *Discourse on Metaphysics,* Chapter XXVI.

4. It leads Leibniz almost to the admission that persistence in the case of the lower types of monad is meaningless. Cf. *Discourse,* XXXIV.

time, and relations, a form of anti-intellectualism in both writers; from which follows (3) the indestructibility of the monads; (4) the important doctrine of 'expression'.[1] Certain distinctions of Bradley's, as the (relative) distinction between finite centres and selves, are also implicit in Leibniz. The relation of soul and body, the possibility of panpsychism, the knowledge of soul by soul, are problems which come to closely similar solutions in the two philosophies.

I suggest that from the 'pluralism' of Leibniz there is only a step to the 'absolute zero' of Bradley, and that Bradley's Absolute dissolves at a touch into its constituents.

In the first place, Leibniz' theory of degrees of perfection among monads approximates to a theory of degrees of reality. Mr Russell has pointed out how easy a step it would have been for Leibniz to have made reality the subject of all predicates. The world consists of simple substances and their states. The subject [201] is never, even from a timeless point of view, merely equivalent to the sum of its states; it is incapable of exhaustion by any addition of predicates. The question with which Leibniz attempted to cope in his first thesis, and the question which he was never able satisfactorily to settle, was what makes a real subject, what the principle of individuation is. Nowhere in the correspondence with Arnauld do we find a trustworthy mark of differentiation between substantial and accidental unities. If everything which can have predicates, everything which can be an object of attention, is a substance, the whole theory falls to the ground; but if this is not the case, we shall either be obliged to make reality the subject of all predicates, or we shall be forced to distinguish, as do some idealists, between judgements and pseudo-judgements, and the logical basis for monadism fails. If we cannot find by inspection an obvious and indubitable token of difference between the substantial and the accidental, we shall in the end find substantiality only in reality itself; or, what comes to the same thing, we shall find degrees of substantiality everywhere. In the latter case substance becomes relative to finite and changing points of view, and in the end again we must seek refuge in the one substance, or resign ourselves to find no refuge at all.

This omnipresence of substance, in degree, comes very near at times to being Leibniz' true doctrine. 'One thing expresses another, in my use of the term,' he says, 'when there is a constant and regulated relation between what can be said of the one and of the other.... Expression is common to all forms, and is a class of which ordinary perception, animal feeling, and intellectual knowledge are species.... Now, such expression is found everywhere, because all substances sympathize with

---

1. See Letter to Arnauld, Oct. 6, 1687.

one another and receive some proportional change corresponding to the slightest motion in the whole universe'; and further in the same letter 'you object that I admit substantial forms only in the case of animated bodies – a position which I do not, however, remember to have taken.'[1] We remark also that the lowest monads are in no very significant sense persistent: '[T]he result from a moral or practical [202] standpoint is the same as if we said that they perished in each case, and we can indeed say it from the physical standpoint in the same way that we say bodies perish in their dissolution.'[2] The permanence of these monads seems to assert itself in order to save a theory.

There is indeed a point of view, necessary even in the severest monism, from which everything, so far as it is an object, so far as it can be assigned predicates, is equally real. But if we recognise the relativity of the point of view for which reality is merely the fact of being an object from that point of view, then the only criterion of reality will be completeness and cohesion. Suppose that some of the objects from a point of view are not direct objects (things), but other points of view, then there is no phenomenal test of their reality, *qua* points of view. So far as we cannot treat them as things, the only objective criterion of the reality will be their perfection. In any system in which degrees of reality play a part, reality may be defined in terms of value, and value in terms of reality.

Leibniz does not succeed in establishing the reality of several substances. On the other hand, just as Leibniz' pluralism is ultimately based upon faith, so Bradley's universe, actual only in finite centres, is only by an act of faith unified. Upon inspection, it falls away into the isolated finite experiences out of which it is put together. Like monads they aim at being one; each expanded to completion, to the full reality latent within it, would be identical with the whole universe. But in so doing it would lose the actuality, the here and now, which is essential to the small reality which it actually achieves. The Absolute responds only to an imaginary demand of thought, and satisfies only an imaginary demand of feeling. Pretending to be something which makes finite centres cohere, it turns out to be merely the assertion that they do. And this assertion is only true so far as we here and now find it to be so.

It is as difficult for Bradley as for Leibniz to maintain that there is any world at all, to find any objects for these mirrors to mirror. [203] The world of both is ideal construction. The distinction between 'ideal' and 'real' is present to Leibniz as well as to Bradley. The former's theory of

---

1. To Arnauld, Oct. 6, 1687.
2. *Discourse on Metaphysics*, Chapter XXXIV.

space is, like the latter's, relativistic, even qualitative.[1] Relations are the work of the mind.[2] Time exists only from finite points of view. Nothing is real, except experience present in finite centres. The world, for Bradley, is simply the *intending* of a world by several souls or centres.

> The world is such that we can make the same intellectual construction. We can, more or less, set up a scheme, in which every one has a place, a system constant and orderly, and in which the relations apprehended by each percipient coincide.... Our inner worlds, I may be told, are divided from each other, but the outer world of experience is common to all; and it is by standing on this basis that we are able to communicate. Such a statement would be incorrect. My external sensations are no less private to myself than are my thoughts or my feelings. In either case my experience falls within my own circle, a circle closed on the outside; and, with all its elements alike, every sphere is opaque to the others which surround it. With regard to communicability, there is in fact not any difference of kind, but only of degree.... [I]t is not true that our physical experiences have unity, in any sense which is inapplicable to the worlds we call internal.... In brief, regarded as an existence which appears in a soul, the whole world for each is peculiar and private to that soul.... No experience can lie open to inspection from outside; no direct guarantee of identity is possible.... The real identity of ideal content, by which all souls live and move, cannot work in common save by the path of external appearance.[3]

Perhaps this is only a statement of a usual idealistic position, but never has it been put in a form so extreme. A writer to whose words Mr Bradley would probably subscribe, Professor Bosanquet, formulates the orthodox view: '[N]o phase in a particular con-[204]sciousness is merely a phase of the apparent subject, but it is always and essentially a member of a further whole of experience, which passes through and unites the states of many consciousnesses....'[4] This view Mr Bradley also holds. But he more often emphasises the other aspect. Each finite centre is, 'while it lasts', the whole world. The world of practice, the world of objects, is constructed out of the ideal identities intended by various souls.

---

1. See *Appearance*, p. 32; Letter to Arnauld, April 30, 1687.
2. 'And as regards space and time Leibniz always endeavoured to reduce them to attributes of the substances in them. Thus Leibniz is forced ... to the Kantian theory that relations, though veritable, are the work of the mind.' Russell, p. 14.
3. *Appearance*, p. 304 ff.
4. *Principle of Individuality and Value,* p. 315.

For Bradley, I take it, an object is a common intention of several souls, cut out (as in a sense are the souls themselves) from immediate experience. The genesis of the common world can only be described by admitted fictions, since in the end there is no question of its origin in time: on the one hand our experiences are similar because they are of the same objects, and on the other hand the objects are only 'intellectual constructions' out of various and quite independent experiences. So, on the one hand, my experience is in principle essentially public. My emotions may be better understood by others than by myself; as my oculist knows my eyes. And on the other hand everything, the whole world, is private to myself. Internal and external are thus not adjectives applied to different contents within the same world; they are different points of view.

I will pass now to another consideration. Is the finite centre or the soul the counterpart to the monad? It is very difficult to keep the meanings of 'soul', 'finite centre', and 'self' quite distinct. All are more or less provisional and relative. A self is an ideal and largely a practical construction, one's own self as much as that of others. My self 'remains intimately one thing with that finite centre within which my universe appears. Other selves on the contrary are for me ideal objects. . . .'[1] The self is a construction in space and time. It is an object among others, a self among others, and could not exist save in a common world. The soul (as in the passage quoted at length) is almost the same as finite centre. The soul, considered as finite centre,[2] cannot be acted [205] upon by other entities, since a finite centre is a universe in itself. 'If you confine your attention to the soul as a soul, then every possible experience is no more than that which happens in and to this soul. You have to do with psychical events which qualify the soul, and in the end these events, so far as you are true to your idea, are merely states of the soul. Such a conception is for certain purposes legitimate and necessary. . . .'[3] Change, accordingly, cannot be due to any agency outside of these states themselves; it can only be, 'in every state of a substance, some element or quality in virtue of which that state is not permanent, but tends to pass into the next state. This element is what Leibniz means by activity.'[4]

The soul only differs from the finite centre in being considered as something not identical with its states. The finite centre, so far as I can pretend to understand it, *is* immediate experience. It is not in time, though

---

1. *Truth and Reality*, p. 418.
2. 'A soul is a finite centre viewed as an object existing in time with a before and after of itself', ibid., p. 414.
3. ibid., p. 415.
4. Russell, p. 45.

we are more or less forced to think of it under temporal conditions. 'It comes to itself as all the world and not as one world among others. And it has properly no duration through which it lasts. It can contain a lapse and a before and after, but these are subordinate.'[1] The finite centre in a sense contains its own past and future. 'It has, or it contains, a character, and on that character its own past and future depend.'[2] This is more clearly the case with the soul. But it would be untrue to go on and declare that the soul 'bears traces' of everything that happens to it. It would be a mistake to go on, holding this view of the soul, and distinguish between various grades of soul according to faculty. This would be to confuse the soul which is a whole world, to which nothing comes except as its own attribute and adjective, with the soul which can be described by its way of acting upon an environment. In this way Leibniz thrusts himself into a nest of difficulties. The concepts of centre, of soul, and of self and personality must be kept distinct. The point of view from which each soul is a world in itself must not be confused with the point of view from which each soul is only the function of a [206] physical organism, a unity perhaps only partial, capable of alteration, development, having a history and a structure, a beginning and apparently an end. And yet these two souls are the same. And if the two points of view are irreconcilable, yet on the other hand neither would exist without the other, and they melt into each other by a process which we cannot grasp. If we insist upon thinking of the soul as something *wholly* isolated, as *merely* a substance with states, then it is hopeless to attempt to arrive at the conception of other souls. For if there are other souls, we must think of our own soul as more intimately attached to its own body than to the rest of its environment; we detach and idealise some of its states. We thus pass to the point of view from which the soul is the entelechy of its body. It is this transition from one point of view to another which is known to Mr Bradley's readers as transcendence. It is the failure to deal adequately with transcendence, or even to recognise the true nature of the problem, which makes Leibniz appear so fantastic, and puts him sometimes to such awkward shifts.

Thus Leibniz, while he makes the soul the entelechy of the body, is forced to have recourse to the theory of the dominant monad. Now I contend that if one recognises two points of view, which are irreconcilable and yet melt into each other, this theory is quite superfluous. It is really an attempt to preserve the reality of the external world at the same time that it is denied, which is perhaps the attempt of all pan-psychism: to substitute

---

1. *Truth and Reality*, p. 410
2. *ibid.*, p. 411.

for two concepts which have at least a relative validity in practice – consciousness and matter – one which is less useful and consequently less significant – animated matter. So far as my body is merely an adjective of my soul, I suppose that it needs no outside explanation; and so far as it possesses an independent reality, it is quite unnecessary to say that this is because it is compounded of elements which are adjectives of other souls or monads. Leibniz has here done no more than to add to the concepts of psychical and physical a third and otiose concept.

The monad in fact combines, or attempts to combine, several points of view in one. Because Leibniz tries to run these different [207] aspects together, and at the same time refuses to recognise that the independence and isolation of the monads is only a relative and partial aspect, he lets himself in for the most unnecessary of his mysteries – the pre-established harmony. Bradley turns the Absolute to account for the same purpose. 'The one Absolute' knows itself and realises itself in and through finite centres. 'For rejecting a higher experience,' Mr Bradley says, 'in which appearances are transformed, I can find no reason....'[1] But what we do know is that we are able to pass from one point of view to another, that we are compelled to do so, and that the different aspects more or less hang together. For rejecting a higher experience there may be no reason. But that this higher experience explains the lower is at least open to doubt.

Mr Bradley's monadism is in some ways a great advance beyond Leibniz'. Its technical excellence is impeccable. It unquestionably presents clearness where in Leibniz we find confusion. I am not sure that the ultimate puzzle is any more frankly faced, or that divine intervention plays any smaller part. Mr Bradley is a much more skilful, a much more finished philosopher than Leibniz. He has the melancholy grace, the languid mastery, of the late product. He has expounded one type of philosophy with such consummate ability that it will probably not survive him. In Leibniz there are possibilities. He has the permanence of the pre-Socratics, of all imperfect things.

---

1. *Truth and Reality*, p. 613.

[A Tribute to Wilfred Owen]
FROM MR T. S. ELIOT (O.M.)
(Poet, scholar and dramatist. Nobel Prize Winner.)

A Tribute to Wilfred Owen, compiled by T. J. Walsh, 28.
Privately printed Mar. 1964, and made available to persons interested in return for a donation of 5s. to the Wilfred Owen Library Fund. Gallup B89.

I am sorry that I cannot at present afford the time to write anything for you about the poems of Wilfred Owen. I should have to refresh my memory of these poems before doing so. But there is one poem of his at least, 'Strange Meeting', which is of permanent value and, I think, will never be forgotten, and which is not only one of the most moving pieces of verse inspired by the war of 1914–18, but also a technical achievement of great originality.

A Note on Translation
Arena, 19 (Apr. 1964), 102–3. Gallup C673.
On p. 103 'poetry writing in other languages' has been emended to 'poetry written in other languages'.

I can judge the merit of George Seferis, so to speak, from his translations of my own choruses into Greek which seem to be magnificent, and I am delighted that he should translate the whole of my play, *Murder in the Cathedral*.

Of course, it is easier to read translations of my own work. I can follow them easily in modern Greek because I have studied Ancient Greek as a lad in America and at Oxford, and because I have been very pleased with such works as I have seen in his translations. His choral work is magnificent and I have always longed to see it – at least the choruses – put in modern Greek by a modern Greek poet of distinction, and I couldn't ask for anyone better or more distinguished [103] than Seferis. I don't know his poetry yet, only very slightly. I can, of course, read his translations of my poetry because I know the poetry so well. Of course, all my knowledge of modern Greek was gained in a commercial way. I gained it some years ago when I was working in the city of London because I wanted to be able to read company reports and the reports of the Greek Banks, and that is why I know what I do know of modern Greek. But I feel an affinity with him and I should say there must be some resemblance between the poetry . . . but, of course, in a way it is more difficult for an author to see his resemblances, the resemblance of his work to that of poetry written in other languages, than it is for a third person. I have often been told that I have much in common with the genially Italian poet, Montale, and I read some of his poetry with great pleasure. But as for the resemblance ... but I think that is for an outsider to notice. I should think that as to whether Seferis was a great poet – I said somewhere long ago that a greatness is something you can't obtain, for a contemporary that is something which is conferred or at least shown by time and a man's reputation. What you can say about a contemporary poet is that his poetry is genuine, that it is authentic. I am convinced from reading my own choruses in his translations that his poetry is authentic, that it is a genuine poetry. Now I don't think that a translation of poetry into every language can really convey the spirit of the poetry. It is so wedded to, it is so much in the language in which it is written that I have never seen for instance any translations of the poetry in foreign languages that I do know, for instance Goethe or Dante, or the French poets I know particularly well, which really conveyed the spirit of the original. It is so much the spirit of the language in which it is written.

In an interview with M. Phocas

Edwin Muir: 1887–1959

An Appreciation by T. S. Eliot, O.M.

Publ. in *Listener*, 71. 1835 (28 May 1964), 872: Gallup C674. Revised as 'Preface' to *Selected Poems: Edwin Muir* (1965): Gallup B90. *See below*, pp. 719–21.

[Tribute to Georg Svensson on his 60th Birthday]

Published in holograph facsimile by Swedish publishing firm Albert Bonniers Förlag in the single volume of tributes to Svensson on the occasion of his 60th birthday (11 Oct. 1964).

Not in Gallup but would be B89a.

Georg Svensson is one of those friends whom I have known so long that I cannot remember when I first met them. No doubt it was in London, before my memorable visit to Sweden in 1942, and at Faber and Faber's as the representative of Bonniers. But this I do know: that neither Fabers, nor I personally, nor England, has a better friend in Stockholm than Georg Svensson. I send him now my cordial and affectionate regards. At sixty years, he is still a youngster in my eyes. May he continue to flourish for many years to come, and to knit the bonds between the two countries.

T. S. Eliot

A Conversation with T. S. Eliot

'A Conversation with T. S. Eliot' [by Leslie Paul], *KR*, 27. 1 (Winter [1964/]1965), [11]–21. Part of an interview taken down on tape in 1958. Gallup C676.

On page 15 *'Notes towards the Definition of a Culture'* in Paul's question has been corrected (twice) to *'Notes Towards the Definition of Culture'*.

I have always been interested in the great and lively sweep of T. S. Eliot's ideas and interests, and usually take the opportunity to discuss them with him on the too-rare occasions when we meet. His political ideas, for instance – aristocratic and theocratic in a time barren of political ideas – I think fascinating and seminal and too little pursued. In 1958, I arranged with the European Service of the BBC a discussion with Eliot that would cover many of his ideas and activities. I hoped to draw out the whole politico-literary, and Christian, man. We talked in our shirt-sleeves in the board room of Faber and Faber on the hottest London day I can remember. The first part of our conversation, mostly about Dr Erich Kahler's The Tower and the Abyss, *is lost forever because the technicians were so interested that they omitted to switch on the tape, and we were wise enough not to attempt to repeat a spontaneous discussion. Fortunately, the omission was soon discovered, but it accounts for the seeming abruptness of my first question. For reasons that are now obscure to both Eliot and myself, the conversation was not published at the time.* – L. P.

Leslie Paul: The first question I want to ask you is really a political one. In *The Idea of a Christian Society*, which you wrote almost twenty years ago, you said, I think, that the choice before us was between the formation of a new Christian culture and the acceptance of a pagan one. Do you still feel that this is the choice before us?

[12] *T. S. Eliot*: Well, I don't know whether or not I'd use those exact words. I think I should prefer now to say a new or renewed Christian society rather than 'culture', but I never remember exactly quotations from my own works – neither can I identify them. However, in any case,

I no longer feel that the most likely alternative is a pagan culture. I shouldn't use that phrase any longer. You see, we've had since I wrote – or it was going on then – the attempt in Hitler's reign to foster a Germanic culture, and that, if it wasn't altogether an attempt to suppress Christian culture, was at least an attempt to bypass it.

Paul: A deliberately pagan one.

Eliot: Yes. A conscious attempt to be pagan. Well, the doctrines of this non-Christian pan-Germanism appear to us ridiculous, I think, if we read their pronouncements nowadays. They're merely ludicrous. There's still going on today, of course, the attempt of Communism to foster a kind of religion of humanity . . .

Paul: That's not pagan?

Eliot: I think the real paganism is something which arises naturally, like the culture among primitive peoples. And, of course, the religion of humanity turns out often to be a religion of inhumanity. But it is an attempt to replace the religious emotions by a kind of deification of an abstract humanity. We need a new word rather than 'pagan', but even so what I'm attempting to get at is this: that what we notice about the emotions aroused by either Nazism or Communism, emotions which attempt to replace religious emotion, is that they can only be kept alive – kept hot – by presenting always the image of an enemy; an enemy and an earthly god, I think. Well, the earthly god is inseparable somehow from the enemy. He only remains in the position of a god so long and there is an enemy.

Paul: You're speaking of Stalin or Hitler?

Eliot: Yes. Now, I don't think that either of these religions should properly be called pagan, but if you do call them pagan then we must say that they're inferior as religions to genuine primitive pagan religion. And I don't think that [13] they can survive. That is my point. The religious fervour can't last as time more and more shows the speciousness of the doctrines. Supposing Communism became so fully established that there was no longer any enemy of it remaining – though possibly the enemy would always have to be invented – if there was no enemy remaining, there would be no religion left. It would merely become another regime of some people controlling others, with no fervour about it at all. In short, I don't believe that any religion can survive which is not a religion of the supernatural and of life after death in some form.

Paul: That means goodbye to Auguste Comte? – and all the ideas of a sort of religion of humanity?

Eliot: Yes. It's very instructive to study Comte and to see how rather pathetic it looks nowadays – this ambitious attempt to do something which cannot be done by direct human willing.

Paul: I see that. It has the pathos of some sort of faded fashion now, doesn't it? Well, there's a question that's begun to perturb me very much. It is not so much this business of a new pagan culture but rather what I would like to call a 'cultureless culture' – on the lines of the 'foodless food' which I think Orwell spoke about.

Eliot: Yes, exactly.

Paul: What I really mean by that, I suppose, is this mass entertainment culture which is absolutely, as far as I can see, without any values at all – and yet is getting hold of the world. I think that it seems to be part of a whole process of spiritual drying-up, as if man no longer possessed or even wanted to possess any kind of spiritual inwardness, as though the whole business of inwardness or spirituality just bored him stiff. . . . Well, you're the poet of *The Waste Land* and what you have to say about this ought to be important.

Eliot: I do think that what you are pointing to is exactly what seems to me to be happening. One sees so many signs in literature and in the theatre of absence of values. The only values expressed in many plays and novels are, I suppose, the values indicated by their absence. I think that a good deal of what's happening now was foreshadowed long ago. You [14] know Ortega y Gasset's remarkable book, *The Revolt of the Masses*? It was published in the '20s but it is certainly worth rereading now. There's a deterioration, it seems to me, in the quality of amusement as it becomes more mass entertainment and as the media for mass entertainment become more highly developed. The cinema first; now, television. It's profitable to appeal to the largest audience and therefore to the lowest common denominator. I think that the end of a purely materialistic civilisation with all its technical achievements and its mass amusements is – if, of course, there's no actual destruction by explosives – simply boredom. A people without religion will in the end find that it has nothing to live for. I did touch on this problem a good many years ago in an essay I wrote on the death of a great music-hall artist, Marie Lloyd.

Paul: But what about nihilism?

Eliot: I don't think nihilism can be kept up indefinitely. What is the source of refreshment in nihilism? One generation can find satisfaction in expressing nihilism, but where does the next generation go on from there?

Paul: Nihilism against boredom hasn't much meaning, has it? You must have nihilism against some established order, some set of values, or there's nothing to destroy – you can't find anything to strike at.

Eliot: Quite so. Nihilism would have been impossible without the things that nihilism condemned. If the objects of nihilist attack disappear, there is nothing left. Nihilism itself disappears with them.

Paul: Nihilism itself becomes boredom. Well, the awareness of this spreading of a spiritual desert has been acute in all your plays and many of your poems. I would go back to 'The Hollow Men' as well as *The Waste Land*, and to some of the choruses in *Murder in the Cathedral*. To me, you have been very much the poet who saw this desolation coming. Do you feel that, looking back?

Eliot: I think that you are perhaps exaggerating the conscious element in it when you say 'saw it coming'. I never venture to interpret my own poetry, and I would hesitate to make myself a prophet. In any case, you see, the prophetic [15] element in poetry very often is unconscious in the poet himself. He may be prophesying without knowing it. What he absorbs from the atmosphere is not altogether conscious in him.

Paul: Still, if the reader sees this prophecy, I think he is entitled to say it is there.

Eliot: Sometimes, as Godfrey Benn said once in a very interesting essay, the poet is aware only when he starts a poem of something inside him that needs to come out and be shaped. He doesn't know what it is, but his poem, the poem he eventually makes, is a release for him. It may at the same time be expressing the hopes or the fears, the anxiety or the faith, which he shares unconsciously with the rest of humanity or with the rest of his people.

Paul: All the same, although you are a poet you are also a prophet, you know, because *The Idea of a Christian Society* and *Notes Towards the Definition of Culture* have been efforts – at least, I see them as efforts – to put into ordinary, workaday language some of the ideas there in your poetry. There's a question I'd like to ask: in *The Idea of a Christian Society* you spoke about a Christian élite, a kind of clerisy, like Coleridge's clerisy, as a means of salvation. But in *Notes Towards the Definition of Culture* you seem to me to put more hope in the class structure of society. I won't say *the* class structure because that sounds like the present one. But a society with *a* class structure. This is an age in which even to appear to approve of class is regarded as a bit outrageous. So I'd like to know whether you still stand by this position today?

Eliot: First of all, as far as the two essays are concerned, they are not dealing with quite the same problem – or, alternatively, if it's the same problem they are not approaching it from the same point of view. The Christian élite which I spoke about in *The Idea of a Christian Society* is an élite which may be drawn from all classes and from all cultural strata. In that, I wasn't so concerned with the question of class or classless society.

Paul: But I thought you had moved from one position to the other?

[16] *Eliot*: Well, in the second essay I was considering more the actual class structure. I think now that the problem of a class or classless society is one of the permanent problems of humanity, because all abstract statements are unsatisfactory.

Paul: Thinking of class as an abstraction?

Eliot: Perhaps I can express it as a kind of paradox: whenever one contemplates a stratified class society one is emotionally moved toward classlessness, and whenever one contemplates an actual, existing classless society – if there is anything of the sort – one sees the faults of that and is moved emotionally toward a class structure. In these matters one is contrasting something actual and observed with an idea or ideal preferable to the actuality one sees – because in practice every society is very imperfect, and every society commits injustices of one kind or another. But today it seems to me more important to argue the case for a class society because the general accepted idea is one of equalitarianism. And when one considers the classless society, even so far as it has adumbrated itself in the present situation of the world – its mediocrity, its reduction of human beings to the mass . . .

Paul: And this boredom, listlessness, too . . .

Eliot: That comes later. But the reduction which Plato foresaw, the reduction to a mass ready to be controlled, manipulated, by a dictator or an oligarchy – observing all those things one is emotionally disposed toward a class society.

Paul: Yes, as a protection against the Hitlers and the Stalins, *and* the Khrushchevs.

Eliot: But, on the other hand, one might say in general that any healthy – of course, the word 'healthy' may be begging the question – but shall we say any healthy classless society will tend to form itself into classes? On the other hand, any healthy class society will tend to facilitate the transition from one class to another. It will be flexible; it will somewhat blur the outlines of its classes. A very rigid class distinction is petrifaction. So when I defend a class society it is because its merits should be emphasised at the present time.

Paul: But what was in my mind, I see now, in linking the clerisy with the class was the idea that the clerisy was of [17] people dedicated in some way to service to society, irrespective of reward. And the idea of a class structure is that it enables society to be held together in a way which is difficult to describe but which creates a nation because such a class is prepared to serve without reward. It is this idea, which is not really present in democracy, that privileges in society should go along with responsibilities, that interests me.

Eliot: The fault, the evil, in a class society is when privilege exists without responsibility and duty. The evil of the classless society is that it tends to equalise the responsibility, to atomise it into responsibility of the whole population – and therefore everyone becomes equally irresponsible.

Paul: I'd like to now change the conversation and go on to the arts. I want to ask you about the position of the writer or the artist in contemporary society. One problem seems to me roughly this: there don't appear to be any accepted norms any more, any standards and values, for the arts. Another problem is the divorce which has occurred between the poet and the people. The poet has become a poet writing for himself or just for a very few people. There's no longer anybody writing for the masses as Tennyson was, or Kipling was. And then there's the financial problem young writers must face if they are to try and get established. I don't know whether you feel prepared to speak about that? Do you see a way forward?

Eliot: There are so many questions involved here, and some of them go so deep, that it is awfully difficult to deal with them all in any brief form. For instance, the arts are sometimes accused of obscurity and preciosity – of being remote from the people. But is it altogether that the artist is leaving the people or that the people are leaving the artist? This is all bound up with the problem in our minds of cultureless culture. Then I think there's a special problem for the dramatist (I can't speak for the novelist): we have a rather unsettled state of society – and the dramatist ought to know exactly whom he is writing for . . .

Paul: Or what the society is he's writing about? You mean that society isn't moving in any direction that can even possibly be understood or conceived?

[18] *Eliot*: Then there are the practical economic questions which I think are less, or should be less, severe for the poet than for other writers, or for

the painter, sculptor, or musician, because the poet can get a part-time job; he can earn his living in other ways.

Paul: Not always.

Eliot: He ought to be able to get a job somewhere that will keep him alive. I know that doesn't invariably work, but then poets always have had difficulties at one time or another. I just say that I know some poets who manage to earn their living in one way and write poetry as well.

Paul: Such as schoolmastering or broadcasting?

Eliot: And there is this further difficulty, which is perhaps more acute in some countries than others: the problem of publication for poetry. The cost of producing books goes up all the time.

Paul: You're speaking now as a publisher?

Eliot: I'm speaking now as a publisher, and I know what I'm talking about there. It's interesting to find that the number of the élite of the public, the people who are interested enough to buy works by new, modern names, and little-known writers, or to patronise rather superior magazines, remains more or less constant, however the population goes up.

Paul: Yes, that's very strange.

Eliot: The costs of publication go up, but our readers do not go up in proportion. Therefore, it is much more difficult to get poetry published, especially by unknown poets. It really depends on a small number of people in the publishing world discerning the best and seeing that it gets published.

Paul: What about your own poetry? We've had a series of brilliant plays from you, and I myself feel that they've done something quite unique for the English theatre. But in pure poetry we've had nothing since the very deeply moving, philosophical *Four Quartets*. What about that? Are they really your last words?

Eliot: I never make rash vows or acts of renunciation. I only know what to do next; I can't think ahead of that. But I can tell you this much, that in the past my poems and my [19] plays were somewhat sandwiched together. For instance, the first of my *Quartets* is *Burnt Norton*: the inspiration for that was certain lines which were cut out of the beginning of *Murder in the Cathedral*. The lines are not identically reproduced, but essentially they are the same. This was my first actual play, of course, and the producer pointed out to me that the lines were strictly irrelevant to the action and didn't get things forward. Well, those lines led to *Burnt Norton*. After that, my next production was *The Family Reunion*. When I saw it produced I thought there were certain obvious faults of construction and I wanted to sit down and write immediately another play free from those faults. Well, then the war came and I had other duties and things to do, and I was here and there, so I turned to writing the other three *Quartets*, and they occupied the war years very well. I was able in the conditions in which I was living to write poems of that type and length. When the war was over I wanted to turn again to write the play which I had planned to write in 1939, and since then – since 1948 – I've written three plays.

Paul: Do you feel that you've written the play – or plays – that you wanted to write in 1939?

Eliot: I hope that, altogether, the plays are better than what I would have written then. I think that a certain suspension was good for me.

Paul: In that case, we may hope that a certain suspension will produce more poems.

Eliot: I hope so, too. But I can't look as far ahead as that. I just wait to see what I am impelled to do next.

Paul: Do you feel that in the *Quartets* and in the plays you succeeded in a personal prosody? You were always interested in forging a loose, flexible, and accentual line instead of a heroic line. I thought you feared the gigantic shadow of Shakespeare over poetic drama. Have you laid that ghost, do you think?

Eliot: Well, in a sense, it's the shadow of Shakespeare, but it's also the shadow of non-dramatic blank verse since Shakespeare. It's a shadow of *Paradise Lost*, of Wordsworth's *Excursion*; it's the shadow of Tennyson and Browning – of all [20] the people who have written blank verse. It's very difficult to write blank verse which is both good poetry and sounds like people talking . . .

Paul: – Which is realistic?

Eliot: Therefore, I felt it was necessary to find a metric which was as far removed as possible from the iambic pentameter. That's what I hammered out for myself in *The Family Reunion* and have used since. You asked if it was a personal prosody: it may be too personal a prosody. What I mean is that I should like – my ambition would have been – to start a prosody which would be an impersonal one, so to speak, useful to other dramatists – poetic dramatists – coming after me.

Paul: A *public* prosody.

Eliot: I don't know whether what I've done is a personal prosody or to any degree a public one. On the other hand, there's this: it may be that the norm of English versification is iambic pentameter, but that the only way to refresh it from one time to another will be to get away from it in a curve which will gradually return – having freed itself from the stiffness of previous generations. It may mean future verse dramatists will be able to go back to the iambic pentameter as a fresh instrument. And if I have helped in bringing that about I should be very happy, beyond the grave.

Paul: One last question. I think you once said in *The New English Weekly* that *The Waste Land* as published was as revised by the hand of Ezra Pound. Now, is there ever likely to be a chance that we may see the original? If you will publish the original, that will be most exciting.

Eliot: It was more a question of excisions, as I remember, than of revisions. He cut out a lot of dead matter. I think that the poem as originally written was about twice the length. It contained some stanzas in imitation of Pope, and Ezra said to me, 'Pope's done that so well that you'd better not try to compete with him.' – Which was sound advice. And there was also a long passage about a shipwreck which I think was inspired by the Ulysses canto in Dante's *Inferno*. At any rate, he reduced it in length. Well, the fate of that manuscript or typescript with his blue-pencilings on it is one of the [21] permanent – so far as I know – minor mysteries of literature. It was bought by a man named John Quinn in New York who was a patron of art and letters. He bought the manuscript from me. I don't remember what he paid for it, but I'm sure he was generous. It went to him. I gave him out of gratitude for other things he'd done for me another manuscript – a manuscript book of early poems of mine, certain few of which have been printed but most of which remain unprinted. Years later, John Quinn died. There was a sale of his collection of manuscripts as well as of his works of art. Neither of these items appeared in the sale. We don't know, nobody knows, what became of them. Or who was responsible for their disappearance. Perhaps someday they will turn up. Perhaps not.

Paul: I think what we'd better suggest is that there should be a Rockefeller fellowship for the search for *The Waste Land*. And I think, having proposed this, I'd be entitled to apply for it.

Eliot: You know, I'm in two minds about that search. I should like it to be found as evidence of what Ezra himself called his maieutic abilities – evidence of what he did for me in criticising my script. On the other hand, for my own reputation, and for that of *The Waste Land* itself, I'm rather glad that it has disappeared.

1965

[Eliot Interviewed by T. S. Matthews]

Mademoiselle, 61 (May 1965), 68.
Not in Gallup but would be C677a.

The following remarks of T. S. Eliot were made during an interview I had with him, in his small top-floor office overlooking Russell Square, in 1958. The text was shown to him and he made several corrections and additions which have been included.

How did you happen to live in England?

ELIOT: At 26, one still doesn't look very far ahead. I'd had a year at Oxford, on a travelling scholarship from Harvard, and intended to teach philosophy. I read Aristotle at Oxford with Professor Joachim. Through Conrad Aiken, I met Ezra Pound, and sent him some unpublished poems; Pound was very enthusiastic, and got *Prufrock* published. That tipped the balance. Pound encouraged me to stay in England; then I got married, and eventually became a British subject.

In spite of your British nationality, you are still widely regarded as an American. How do you think of yourself?

ELIOT: In certain contexts as American, in others as British. I feel that this is my home, but I like to revisit the United States as often as I can, and see my friends and relations. There is a certain feeling for landscape which one never loses. And there is something in my poetry which wouldn't be there but for my American background.

If you could influence the future of America, in what ways would you like to see it changed?

ELIOT: I'm rather a regionalist by temperament, and I don't like to see different parts of the country tending to become uniform. I don't like to see, for instance, an increasing uniformity in speech.

If you could save only one of your poems from oblivion, which would you choose?

ELIOT: I think an author is apt to be biased – and if I say *Little Gidding*, that is perhaps because it is the most recent of my poems. It is not a compliment to a poet to be enthusiastic about what he did a long time ago. That one was very consciously worked over, and I think the best of the *Quartets*.

Do you agree that there are no great poets, only good ones and bad ones?

ELIOT: Greatness is something conferred by time. All you can say about your contemporaries is whether they're genuine and original or not.

Which of your plays do you regard as the best?

ELIOT: There is no one play that I'm quite satisfied with. *Family Reunion* had a satisfactory idiom, and its characters talked poetry, but it was not a well-constructed play. I think *The Confidential Clerk* the best-constructed of my plays, according to theatrical standards. I don't suppose I shall ever achieve my aim of combining the best poetry with the best theatre.

Do you regret any of your published poems, 'The Hippopotamus', for example?

ELIOT: There is no published poem of mine that I should wish to withdraw. I see no reason for being ashamed of 'The Hippopotamus'. Certainly I wouldn't have written it ten years later. It shocked Edmund Gosse – but I know it was a favourite of Arnold Bennett's. I don't often read 'The Hollow Men' when I give readings; it's not bad but I think its mood is rather too despairing. I might more easily regret some statements that I've made. There is one small book of lectures, *After Strange Gods*, which I let go out of print.

What do you think of Ezra Pound as a poet?

ELIOT: It's difficult to say. It's a delicate point to express a *judgement* about any living contemporary. He is certainly the greatest craftsman of verse of our time. A poet's poet. His work has been of inestimable value to a younger generation of poets – technically, in the way of cleaning up language. His poetry and everything he says *about* poetry ought to be studied by poets for generations to come. He has written some great poetry, though I shouldn't care to specify the *Cantos* as a whole.

Have you a one-sentence theory of poetry – like Wordsworth's 'emotion recollected in tranquillity'?

ELIOT: There are so many kinds of poem that one definition doesn't apply to all. I like Wordsworth's definition, except that I don't think it's necessarily only emotion that's recollected: I think that it may be a composite variety of disparate experiences which are fused into a whole – the wholeness of which is inexplicable. It is almost impossible to think of poetry as a whole and make a generalisation from it. But a poem should be able to move us before we understand it.

I once heard you say, apropos Sherlock Holmes's rebuke to Watson ('Cut out the poetry, Watson!'), that you had been trying to do that all your life.

Eliot: Yes, I meant 'Get down to the bones, have nothing superfluous.' I learnt that from Dante too. My aim has been the maximum emotional effect with the minimum verbal decoration.

Do you expect to write much more?

Eliot: I don't expect one thing or another. There have been periods in my life when I felt I had nothing more to say, and would never write again. I had that feeling in 1932; then in 1933 I was asked to write *The Rock*, and in the following year *Murder in the Cathedral* – which led to *Burnt Norton*, using some lines which had appeared in the play. In the last ten years or so, my only urge has been to the theatre. I hope I shall write more poems, but I shall know when I have to. I never want to write a poem until there is something uncomfortable inside me, of the sort that can only be expelled by putting it into words.

Editor's Note: *T. S. Matthews, a former editor of* Time *magazine, who now lives in London, had had a long friendship with the late Mr Eliot.*

Thomas Stearns Eliot

Autobiographical note, *Harvard College Class of 1910. Fifty-fifth Anniversary Report* (June 1965), 52. An editorial note states that Eliot sent in the report in late December 1964. Gallup C677b.

Since the last Report I have had to spend more time in a warmer climate (Caribbean) as I suffer from emphysema and find an English winter increasingly hard to endure. But my wife takes the most wonderful care of me and I enjoy being at home as much as possible. I published *Collected Poems of 1909–1962* in 1963, and have a volume of essays coming out next year. In September I received the Presidential Medal of Freedom from the American Ambassador in London as I was unable to attend the ceremony in Washington.

Preface

Preface to *Selected Poems: Edwin Muir*, 9–11. Publ. 15 July 1965.
Signed 'T. S. Eliot' at the end. Gallup B90.

Revised from 'Edwin Muir: 1887–1959 An Appreciation . . .',
Listener, 71. 1835 (28 May 1964), 872 (Gallup C674).

1 As my correspondence files indicate, it was only in the last years of Edwin Muir's life, when he brought his later poems to me for publication, that I saw much of him, and I cannot say that I ever came to know him really intimately. He was a reserved, reticent man, not fluent in conversation. Yet his personality made a deep impression upon me, and especially the impression of one very rare and precious quality. There have been other encounters in my life with men who have left me with the impression of this particular quality, including several men whom I have never come to know well. They have been those men of whom I should say, without hesitation, that they were men of complete *integrity*. And as I have grown older, I have come to realise how rare this quality is. That utter honesty with oneself and with the world is no more common among men of letters than among men of other occupations. I stress this unmistakable integrity, because I came to recognise it in Edwin Muir's work as well as in the man himself. The work and the man are one: his autobiography, and the lecture on Orcadian folk poetry, which is the first of his Norton lectures at Harvard, help us to understand his own poetry. And I cannot believe that Edwin Muir ever uttered one disingenuous word in speech, or committed one disingenuous word to print.

2 I do not remember when, or in what context, we first met. I seem to remember him, in earlier days, as a contributor to the *New Age*. It would have been characteristic of Orage, in whose papers so many notable writers made their appearance, to discover this shy man of genius. But I must admit that in my youth I gave little heed to Muir's poetry. His poetry was not of the kind which I was trying to write myself, and it was not until after my own lines of development were well established that it began to appeal to me. How much of this late appeal was due to the maturing of Muir's power, and how much to the maturing [10] of my own taste, I cannot tell. A young poet is apt to be indifferent to the work of a contemporary who is following a different path from his own. But when I came to study the volume of his *Collected Poems*, before publication, I was struck, as I had not been before, by the power of his early work. Yet, on the other hand, it is still his late work which seems to me the most remarkable.

3 In my earlier years, or rather in the second phase of my development, I went through a period of concentrating my attention on experiment in metric and language. It may be that to focus my conscious mind in this way helped to release my imagination. For some poets, perhaps, this experiment with forms of verse and with varieties of expression may remain a permanent preoccupation. I do not believe that technique was ever a primary concern with Edwin. He was first and foremost deeply concerned with what he had to say – and by that I do not mean that his purpose was ever didactic or that he was striving to convey a 'message'. But under the pressure of emotional intensity, and possessed by his vision, he found, almost unconsciously, the right, the inevitable way of saying what he wanted to say.

4 Kathleen Raine wrote a review of Edwin Muir's *Collected Poems* in *The New Statesman* for April 23, 1960 which I hope she will reprint in some volume of essays, and which I can say little to supplement. But I should like to add this one thought: Edwin Muir will remain among the poets who have added glory to the English language. He is also one of the poets of whom Scotland should always be proud. But there is, furthermore, it seems to me, something essential which is neither English nor Scottish, but Orcadian. There is the sensibility of the remote islander, the boy from a simple primitive offshore community who then was plunged into the sordid horror of industrialism in Glasgow, who struggled to understand the modern world of the metropolis in London, and finally the realities of central Europe in Prague where he and his wife – to whom together we owe our knowledge of Kafka – saw the Iron Curtain fall and where they saw their friends gradually finding it safer to avoid their company. And all of this experience is somehow concentrated into that great, that terrifying, poem of the atomic age – 'The Horses'.

The poems in this selection were all taken from *The Collected Poems of Edwin Muir* – 1921–1958 – edited after Muir's death by Willa Muir and J. C. Hall (Faber and Faber, 2nd edition 1964). I found the task more difficult than I had suspected. The poems in that book are of such uniformly high quality that any selection must appear arbitrary – I must therefore caution the reader against the assumption that I offer them as the *best* of Muir: such a choice is impossible. I have only endeavoured to make a selection representative of all aspects of his work. [11]

Variants from 1964:

Title Edwin Muir: 1887–1959 An Appreciation by T. S. Eliot, O.M.
1 As my correspondence files indicate, it was only] It was only
   integrity] integrity

2 [Heading]: **Shy man of genius**
   New Age] *New English Weekly*
3 , almost unconsciously,] almost unconsciously
   inevitable] inevitable,
4 1960] 1960,
   volume of essays,] volume of essays
   Horses'] Horses'[1]
   [Fn. 1]: This poem was first published in *The Listener* and is reprinted by courtesy of Messrs Faber and Faber.
   ['The Horses' is quoted in full in 1964.]
   [After 'The Horses' is quoted]: – *From One Foot in Eden (Third Programme)*
   [Last para. not represented in 1964.]

[Tribute to Aldous Huxley]

Aldous Huxley 1894–1963: A Memorial Volume, ed. Julian Huxley, 30–2.
Headed 'T. S. Eliot'. Publ. 14 Oct. 1965. Gallup B91.

My earliest memory of Aldous Huxley dates from 1914 or 1915. I spent that academic year at Merton College, on a travelling scholarship from Harvard. The last able-bodied British undergraduates were passing from the O.T.C. to the trenches, and beyond the Rhodes scholars from America and the Commonwealth there were hardly any left except those who, like Aldous, were wholly unfit for military service. But one enterprising undergraduate, whose identity has vanished from my memory, organised a 'Nineties Club' – surely the final tribute to that literary epoch! – and those convened for the first meeting assembled on the lawn of one of the colleges: I believe that it was Balliol, Aldous's own college. The convener, I remember, had sought to enliven the occasion by sporting a red ribbon on his pince-nez eyeglasses. I do not remember that Aldous was very active in this society, but I remember his being pointed out to me on that occasion.

It was only after Oxford that I met Aldous Huxley: that meeting was at Garsington, where we were to meet from time to time as guests of Lady Ottoline Morrell. To her I had been introduced by Bertrand Russell; and it is her house and some of her frequent guests who appear, under the thinnest of disguises, in *Crome Yellow*. My own standing in that society had been established by my first volume of verse (a book which might never have seen publication but for the enthusiastic support of Ezra Pound, to whom I had taken it on the advice of Conrad Aiken). My prestige was such that Aldous submitted for my opinion his own book of verse, *Leda and Other Poems*: I am afraid that I was unable to show any enthusiasm for his verse. After this attempt he wisely confined himself to the essay and that variety of fiction which he came to make his own.

I remember Aldous next after his marriage to Maria Nys, when they were living in a basement flat – crammed of course with books – in the Westbourne Grove area. Middleton Murry, [31] whose editorial flair approached genius, was running *The Athenaeum*, and for him Aldous wrote a weekly column of a kind that he could do to perfection. His reading was immense, his taste impeccable, and his ear acute – I remember his pointing out to me once that the metre of Tennyson's 'Catullus' was identical with that of Edward Lear's 'Yonghy-Bonghy-Bo'. And I was delighted to find that in his last brief book, *Literature and Science*, he quotes a line of Mallarmé which had impressed me so deeply that I paraphrased it in *Little Gidding*: *donner un sens plus pur aux mots de la tribu.*

There is one anecdote of Aldous which I am sure that I remember more clearly than does anyone else, because the situation was highly embarrassing for myself. We were both among the guests invited to speak after a dinner of the Poetry Circle of a ladies' club. We spoke in order of seniority, culminating with Dean Inge. The speakers had all been assigned topics in advance, and a list of the speakers and their topics was conspicuously displayed on the tables. Aldous had already risen to speak when I glanced at the list, and saw to my horror that my topic, on which I had so carefully prepared myself, had been assigned to someone else, and the subject billed to me was entirely different. It was difficult enough to make conversation with two ladies neither of whom I knew, and to compose a new speech at the same time. But Aldous was embarked on what promised to be a speech of some length, and I was hopeful. However, the room was close and airless, and Aldous had unwisely started to smoke a large cigar. He had just alluded to Creon, and I hoped that he was good for five more learned and witty minutes, when he jack-knifed on to the table. Two or three male guests carried him out to another room, and I was called upon to fill the gap. It was my first after-dinner speech: a baptism of fire. Mercifully, I have no recollection of anything I said.

(I have another reason to remember that dinner. One of my neighbours subsequently invited me to dine at her house; and to her I owe my introduction to the Tarot pack, which I turned to account in *The Waste Land*. I pay this tardy tribute of thanks. But I should not like my present reader to draw the inference [32] that this lady was the original of my Madame Sosostris – a wholly fictitious character!)

After Aldous and Maria had transferred themselves to California I did not see him for many years. A few years ago my wife and I met him at the flat of an old friend of both of us. We had both become widowers and remarried since Aldous had left England and found a climate kinder to his frail health, and our wives met for the first time. Aldous was charming and interesting as ever: he had lately been to Brazil, and discoursed informatively about his visit. The Huxleys did not remain long in England, and that was my last sight of this gentle and lovable man. His place in English literature is unique and is certainly assured.

To Criticize the Critic and other writings

To Criticize the Critic and other writings was publ. by Faber & Faber on 11 Nov. 1965. Gallup A76.

Contents: 'Note' by Valerie Eliot; 'To Criticize the Critic' (1961); 'From Poe to Valéry' (1948); 'American Literature and the American Language' (1953); 'The Aims of Education' 1. Can 'Education' be Defined? 2. The Interrelation of Aims 3. The Conflict between Aims 4. The Issue of Religion (1950; i.e. 1950–1); 'What Dante Means to Me' (1950); 'The Literature of Politics' (1955); 'The Classics and the Man of Letters' (1942); 'Ezra Pound: His Metric and Poetry' (1917; i.e. 1918); 'Reflections on Vers Libre' (1917).

[7] Note

Illness prevented my husband from revising 'To Criticize the Critic' and 'The Aims of Education' which are printed here exactly as he left them. Had he lived he would have incorporated further reflections into the former and written a similar review of his sociological writings. After delivering the Education lectures in Chicago he put them aside with the intention of expanding them into a book when the opportunity arose, but it never did.

In response to many requests he promised that 'Ezra Pound: His Metric and Poetry' and 'Reflections on *Vers Libre*' should be included in this collection.

V[alerie]. E[liot].

To Criticize the Critic[1]

TCTC, 11–26.

Of what use, or uses, is literary criticism, is a question worth asking again and again, even if we find no answer satisfactory. Criticism may be, what F. H. Bradley said of metaphysics, 'the finding of bad reasons for what we believe upon instinct, but to find these reasons is no less an instinct.' But as I propose to talk about my own criticism my choice of subject needs to be further defended. In casting an eye over my own literary criticism of the last forty-odd years, I hope that I may be able to draw some conclusions, some plausible generalisations of wider validity, or – what is still more worth while – stimulate other minds to do so; also I hope I may provoke other critics to make similar confessions. My justification must be that there is no other critic, living or dead, about whose work I am so well informed as I am about my own. I know more about the genesis of my essays and reviews than about those of any other critic; I know the chronology, the circumstances under which each essay was written and the motive for writing it, and about all those changes of attitude, taste, interest and belief which the years bring to pass. For the work of those masters of English criticism whom I regard with most reverence such full information is not available to me. I am thinking especially of Samuel Johnson and of Coleridge, and not ignoring Dryden and Arnold. But at this point I should distinguish between the several types of literary critic, in order to remind you that generalisations drawn from the study of the work of a critic of one type may not be applicable to that of others.

First of all among those types of critics other than mine, I should put down the Professional Critic – the writer whose literary criticism is his chief, perhaps his only title to fame. This critic [12] might also be called the Super-Reviewer, for he has often been the official critic for some magazine or newspaper, and the occasion for each of his contributions the publication of some new book. The exemplar of this kind of criticism is of course the French critic Sainte-Beuve, who was the author of two important books, *Port-Royal* and *Chateaubriand et ses amis*, but the bulk of whose work consists in volume after volume of collected essays which had previously appeared week by week in the *feuilleton* of a newspaper. The Professional Critic may be, as Sainte-Beuve certainly was, a *failed* creative writer; and in the case of Sainte-Beuve it is certainly worth while to look at his poems, if one can come by them, as an aid to understanding why he wrote better about authors of the past than about

---

1. The sixth Convocation Lecture delivered at the University of Leeds in July 1961.

his contemporaries. The Professional Critic however is not *necessarily* a failed poet, dramatist or novelist: so far as I know, my old friend in America, Paul Elmer More, whose Shelburne Essays have something of the monumental appearance of the *Causeries du lundi*, attempted no creative writing. Another old friend of mine who was a Professional Critic, of both books and theatre, Desmond MacCarthy, confined his literary activity to his weekly article or review and employed his leisure in delightful conversation instead of devoting it to the books he never wrote. And Edmund Gosse – a different case again: for it is not his industry as a critic, but one book of autobiography which is already a classic – *Father and Son* – that will perpetuate his name.

Second, I name the Critic with Gusto. This critic is not called to the seat of judgement; he is rather the advocate of the authors whose work he expounds, authors who are sometimes the forgotten or unduly despised. He calls our attention to such writers, helps us to see the merit which we had overlooked and to find charm where we had expected only boredom. Of such was George Saintsbury, an erudite and genial man with an insatiable appetite for the second-rate, and a flair for discovering the excellence which is often to be found in the second-rate. Who but Saintsbury, in writing a book on the French Novel, would give far more pages to Paul de Kock than to Flaubert? There was also my old friend Charles Whibley: for example, read him on Sir [13] Thomas Urquhart or on Petronius. There was also Quiller-Couch, who must have taught many of those who attended his lectures at Cambridge, to find fresh sources of delight in English literature.

Third, the Academic and the Theoretical. I mention these two together, as they can overlap; but this category is perhaps too comprehensive, since it ranges from the purely scholarly, like W. P. Ker, who could illuminate an author of one age or language by an unexpected parallel with some author of another age or another language, to the philosophical critic, such as I. A. Richards and his disciple the philosophical critic William Empson. Mr Richards and Mr Empson are also poets, but I do not regard their work as a by-product of their poetry. And where are we to place other contemporaries, such as L.C. Knights or Wilson Knight, except as men who have combined teaching with original critical work? And another critic of importance, Dr F. R. Leavis, who may be called the Critic as Moralist? The critic who is also tenant of an academic post is likely to have made a special study of one period or one author but to call him a Specialist Critic would seem a kind of abridgment of his right to examine whatever literature he pleases.

And finally we come to the critic whose criticism may be said to be a by-product of his creative activity. Particularly, the critic who is also a poet. Shall we say, the poet who has written some literary criticism? The condition of entrance into this category is that the candidate should be primarily known for his poetry, but that his criticism should be distinguished for its own sake, and not merely for any light it may throw upon its author's verse. And here I put Samuel Johnson, and Coleridge; and Dryden and Racine in their prefaces; and Matthew Arnold with reservations; and it is into this company that I must shyly intrude. I hope you need by now no further assurance that it was not laziness that impelled me to turn to my own writings for my material. It most certainly was not vanity: for when I first applied myself to the required reading for this address, it was so long since I had read many of my essays that I approached them with apprehension rather than with hopeful expectations. [14]

I am happy to say that I did not find quite so much to be ashamed of as I had feared. There are, to be sure, statements with which I no longer agree; there are views which I maintain with less firmness of conviction than when I first expressed them, or which I maintain only with important reservations; there are statements the meaning of which I no longer understand. There may be areas in which my knowledge has increased; there are areas in which my knowledge has evaporated. On re-reading my essay on Pascal, for instance, I was astonished at the extent of the information I seem to have possessed when I wrote it. And there are some matters in which I have simply lost interest, so that, if asked whether I still hold the same belief, I could only say 'I don't know' or 'I don't care'. There are errors of judgement, and, what I regret more, there are errors of tone: the occasional note of arrogance, of vehemence, of cocksureness or rudeness, the braggadocio of the mild-mannered man safely entrenched behind his typewriter. Yet I must acknowledge my relationship to the man who made those statements, and in spite of all these exceptions, I continue to identify myself with the author.

Even in saying that, however, I think of a qualification. I find myself constantly irritated by having my words, perhaps written thirty or forty years ago, quoted as if I had uttered them yesterday. One very intelligent expositor of my work, who regarded it, furthermore, with a very favourable eye, discussed my critical writings some years ago as if I had, at the outset of my career as a literary critic, sketched out the design for a massive critical structure, and spent the rest of my life filling in the details. When I publish a collection of essays, or whenever I allow an essay to be re-published elsewhere, I make a point of indicating the original date of publication, as a reminder to the reader of the distance of time that separates the author when he wrote it from the author as he is today. But rare is the writer who, quoting me, says 'this is what

Mr Eliot thought (or felt) in 1933' (or whatever the date was). Every writer is accustomed to seeing his words quoted out of context, in such a way as to put an unintended construction upon them, by not over-scrupulous controversialists. But the quotation of pronouncements of many years ago, as if [15] they had been made yesterday, is still more frequent, because it is most often wholly without malice. I will give one instance of a statement which has continued to dog its author long after it has ceased, in his opinion, to be a satisfactory statement of his beliefs. It is a sentence from the preface to a small collection of essays entitled *For Lancelot Andrewes*, to the effect that I was a classicist in literature, a royalist in politics, and an Anglo-Catholic in religion. I ought to have foreseen that so quotable a sentence would follow me through life as Shelley tells us his thoughts followed him:

> And his own thoughts, along that rugged way,
> Pursued, like raging hounds, their father and their prey.

The sentence in question was provoked by a personal experience. My old teacher and master, Irving Babbitt, to whom I owe so much, stopped in London on his way back to Harvard from Paris, where he had been lecturing, and he and Mrs Babbitt dined with me. I had not seen Babbitt for some years, and I felt obliged to acquaint him with a fact as yet unknown to my small circle of readers (for this was I think in the year 1927) that I had recently been baptised and confirmed in the Church of England. I knew that it would come as a shock to him to learn that any disciple of his had so turned his coat, though he had already had what must have been a much greater shock when his close friend and ally Paul Elmer More defected from Humanism to Christianity. But all Babbitt said was: 'I think you should come out into the open.' I may have been a little nettled by this remark; the quotable sentence turned up in the preface to the book of essays I had in preparation, swung into orbit, and has been circling my little world ever since. Well, my religious beliefs are unchanged, and I am strongly in favour of the maintenance of the monarchy in all countries which have a monarchy; as for Classicism and Romanticism, I find that the terms have no longer the importance to me that they once had. But even if my statement of belief needed no qualification at all after the passage of the years, I should not be inclined to express it in quite this way.

So far as I can judge, from references, quotations and reprints in anthologies, it is my earlier essays which have made the deeper [16] impression. I attribute this to two causes. The first is the dogmatism of youth. When we are young we see issues sharply defined: as we age we tend to make more reservations, to qualify our positive assertions, to introduce more parentheses. We see objections to our own views, we regard the enemy with greater tolerance and even sometimes with sympathy. When we are young, we are confident in our opinions, sure that we possess the whole truth; we are enthusiastic, or indignant. And readers, even mature readers, are attracted to a writer who is quite sure of himself. The second reason for the enduring popularity of some of my early criticism is less easily apprehended, especially by readers of a younger generation. It is that in my earlier criticism, both in my general affirmations about poetry and in writing about authors who had influenced me, I was implicitly defending the sort of poetry that I and my friends wrote. This gave my essays a kind of urgency, the warmth of appeal of the advocate, which my later, more detached and I hope more judicial essays cannot claim. I was in reaction, not only against Georgian poetry, but against Georgian criticism; I was writing in a context which the reader of today has either forgotten, or has never experienced.

In a lecture on Johnson's *Lives of the Poets*, published in one of my collections of essays and addresses,[1] I made the point that in appraising the judgements of any critic of a past age, one needed to see him in the context of that age, to try to place oneself at his point of view. This is a difficult effort for the imagination; one, indeed, in which we cannot hope for more than partial success. We cannot discount the influence upon our formation of the creative writing and critical writing of the intervening generations, or the inevitable modifications of taste, or our greater knowledge and understanding of the literature preceding that of the age which we are trying to understand. Yet merely to make that effort of imagination, and to have these difficulties in mind, is worth our while. In reviewing my own early criticism, I am struck by the degree to which it was conditioned by the state of literature at the time at which it was written, as well as by the stage of maturity at which I had arrived, by the influences to which I [17] had been exposed, and by the occasion of each essay. I cannot myself bring to mind all these circumstances, reconstruct all the conditions under which I wrote: how much less can any future critic of my work have knowledge of them, or, if he has knowledge have understanding, or if he has both knowledge and understanding, find my essays of the same interest that they had for those who read them sympathetically when they first appeared? No literary criticism can for a future generation excite more than curiosity, unless it continues to be of use in itself to future generations, to have intrinsic value out of its historical context. But if any part of it does have this timeless value, then we shall appreciate that value all the more precisely if we also attempt to

---

1. *On Poetry and Poets* (Faber & Faber, 1957).

put ourselves at the point of view of the writer and his first readers. To study the criticism of Johnson or of Coleridge in this way is undoubtedly rewarding.

I can divide my own critical writing roughly into three periods. There was first the period of *The Egoist*, that remarkable bi-weekly edited and published by Miss Harriet Weaver. Richard Aldington had been sub-editor, and when he was called up for military service in the First World War Ezra Pound nominated me to Miss Weaver to fill his place. In *The Egoist* appeared an essay called *Tradition and the Individual Talent*, which still enjoys immense popularity among those editors who prepare anthological text-books for American college students. There were then two influences which are not so incongruous as might at first sight appear: that of Irving Babbitt and that of Ezra Pound. The influence of Pound at that time may be detected in references to Remy de Gourmont, in my papers on Henry James, an author whom Pound much admired, but for whom my own enthusiasm has somewhat flagged, and sundry allusions to authors, such as Gavin Douglas, whose work I hardly knew. The influence of Babbitt (with an infusion later of T. E. Hulme and of the more literary essays of Charles Maurras) is apparent in my recurrent theme of Classicism versus Romanticism. In my second period, after 1918, when *The Egoist* had come to an end, I was writing essays and reviews for two editors in whom I was fortunate, for they both gave me always the right books to review: Middleton Murry [18] in the short-lived *Athenaeum*, and Bruce Richmond in *The Times Literary Supplement*. Most of my contributions remain buried in the files of these two papers, but the best, and they are among the best of my essays, are reprinted in my collections. My third period has been, for one reason or another, one of public lectures and addresses rather than of articles and reviews.

And here I wish to draw what seems to me an important line of demarcation between the essays of generalisation (such as *Tradition and the Individual Talent*) and appreciations of individual authors. It is those in the latter category which seem to me to have the best chance of retaining some value for future readers: and I wonder whether this assertion does not itself imply a generalisation applicable to other critics of my type. But I must draw a distinction here too. Several years ago my New York publishers brought out a paper-back selection of my essays on Elizabethan and Jacobean drama. I made the selection myself, and wrote a preface explaining my choice. I found that the essays with which I was still pleased were those on the contemporaries of Shakespeare, not those on Shakespeare himself. It was from these minor dramatists that I, in my own poetic formation, had learned my lessons; it was by them, and not by Shakespeare, that my imagination had been stimulated, my sense of rhythm trained, and my emotions fed. I had read them at the age at which they were best suited to my temperament and stage of development, and had read them with passionate delight long before I had any thought, or any opportunity of writing about them. At the period in which the stirrings of desire to write verse were becoming insistent, these were the men whom I took as my tutors. Just as the modern poet who influenced me was not Baudelaire but Jules Laforgue, so the dramatic poets were Marlowe and Webster and Tourneur and Middleton and Ford, not Shakespeare. A poet of the supreme greatness of Shakespeare can hardly influence, he can only be imitated: and the difference between influence and imitation is that influence can fecundate, whereas imitation – especially unconscious imitation – can only sterilize. (But when I came to attempt one brief imitation of Dante I was fifty-five years old and knew exactly what I was doing.) Besides, imitation of a [19] writer in a foreign language can often be profitable – because we cannot succeed.

So much for those of my essays in literary criticism which I think have the best chance of survival, in the sense that they are those which have, I believe, the best chance of giving pleasure, and possibly enlarging the understanding, on the part of future readers, of the authors criticised. Now what of the generalisations, and the phrases which have flourished, such as 'dissociation of sensibility' and 'objective correlative'? I think also of an article on 'the function of criticism' written for *The Criterion*. I am not sure, at this distance of time, how valid are the two phrases I have just cited: I am always at a loss what to say, when earnest scholars, or schoolchildren, write to ask me for an explanation. The term 'objective correlative' occurs in an essay on *Hamlet and his Problems* in which I was perhaps not altogether guiltless of trailing my coat: I was at that time hand-in-glove with that gallant controversialist, J. M. Robertson, in his critical studies of Tudor and Stuart drama. But whatever the future of these phrases, and even if I am unable to defend them now with any forensic plausibility, I think they have been useful in their time. They have been accepted, they have been rejected, they may soon go out of fashion completely: but they have served their turn as stimuli to the critical thinking of others. And literary criticism, as I hinted at the beginning, is an instinctive activity of the civilised mind. But I prophesy that if my phrases are given consideration, a century hence, it will be only in their historical context, by scholars interested in the mind of my generation.

What I wish to suggest, however, is that these phrases may be accounted for as being conceptual symbols for emotional preferences. Thus, the emphasis on tradition came about, I believe, as a result of my reaction against poetry, in the English language, of the nineteenth and early twentieth centuries, and my passion for the poetry, both dramatic and lyric, of the late sixteenth and early seventeenth centuries. The 'objective correlative' in the essay on *Hamlet* may stand for my bias towards the more mature plays of Shakespeare – *Timon, Antony and Cleopatra, Coriolanus* notably – and towards those late plays of Shakespeare about which Mr [20] Wilson Knight has written illuminatingly. And the 'dissociation of sensibility' may represent my devotion to Donne and the metaphysical poets, and my reaction against Milton.

It seems to me, in fact, that these concepts, these generalisations, had their origin in my sensibility. They arise from my feeling of kinship with one poet or with one kind of poetry rather than another. I ought not to claim that what I am now saying holds good of other types of critic than mine, or even of other critics of the type to which I myself belong – that is, of poets who have also written critical essays. But about any writer in the field of aesthetics I always incline to ask: 'what literary works, paintings, sculpture, architecture and music does this theorist really enjoy?' We can, of course – and this is a danger to which the philosophical critic of art may be exposed – adopt a theory and then persuade ourselves that we like the works of art that fit into that theory. But I am sure that my own theorising has been epiphenomenal of my tastes, and that in so far as it is valid, it springs from direct experience of those authors who have profoundly influenced my own writing. I am aware, of course, that my 'objective correlative' and my 'dissociation of sensibility' must be attached or defended on their own level of abstraction, and that I have done no more than indicate what I believe to have been their genesis. I am also aware that in accounting for them in this way I am now making a generalisation about my generalisations. But I am certain of one thing: that I have written best about writers who have influenced my own poetry. And I say 'writers' and not only 'poets', because I include F. H. Bradley, whose works – I might say whose personality as manifested in his works – affected me profoundly; and Bishop Lancelot Andrewes, from one of whose sermons on the Nativity I lifted several lines of my *Journey of the Magi* and of whose prose there may be a faint reflection in the sermon in *Murder in the Cathedral*. I include, in fact, any writers whether of verse or prose, whose style has strongly affected my own. I have hope that such essays of mine on individual writers who have influenced me, may retain some value even for a future generation which will reject or ridicule my theories. I spent three years, when young, in the study of philosophy. What remains to me [21] of these studies? The style of three philosophers: Bradley's English, Spinoza's Latin and Plato's Greek.

It is in relation to essays on individual poets that I come to consider the question: how far can the critic alter public taste for one or another poet or one or another period of literature of the past? Have I myself, for example, been to any degree responsible for arousing interest and promoting appreciation of the early dramatists or of the metaphysical poets? I should say, hardly at all – as critic. We must distinguish of course between *taste* and *fashion*. Fashion, the love of change for its own sake, the desire for something new, is very transient; *taste* is something that springs from a deeper source. In a language in which great poetry has been written for many generations, as it has in ours, each generation will vary in its preferences among the classics of that language. Some writers of the past will respond to the taste of the living generations more nearly than to others; some periods of the past may have a closer affinity to our own age than others. To a young reader, or a critic of crude taste, the authors whom his generation favours may seem to be better than those fancied by the previous generation; the more conscious critic may recognize that they are simply more congenial, but not necessarily of greater merit. It is one function of the critic to assist the literate public of his day to recognise its affinity with one poet, or with one type of poetry, or one age of poetry, rather than with another.

The critic, however, cannot create a taste. I have sometimes been credited with starting the vogue for Donne and other metaphysical poets, as well as the minor Elizabethan and Jacobean dramatists. But I did not discover any of these poets. Coleridge, and Browning in turn, admired Donne; and as for the early dramatists, there is Lamb, and the enthusiastic tributes of Swinburne are by no means without critical merit. In our own time, John Donne has lacked no publicity: Gosse's *Life and Letters*, in two volumes, appeared in 1899. I remember being introduced to Donne's poetry when I was a Freshman at Harvard by Professor Briggs, an ardent admirer; Grierson's edition of the Poems, in two volumes, was published in 1912; and it was Grierson's *Metaphysical Poetry*, sent me to review, that gave me my first [22] occasion to write about Donne. I think that if I wrote well about the metaphysical poets, it was because they were poets who had inspired me. And if I can be said to have had any influence whatever in promoting a wider interest in them, it was simply because no previous poet who had praised these poets had been so deeply influenced by them as I had been. As the taste for my own poetry spread, so did the taste for the poets to whom I owed the greatest debt and about whom I had written. Their poetry, and mine, were congenial to that age. I sometimes wonder whether that age is not coming to an end.

It is true that I owed, and have always acknowledged, an equally great debt to certain French poets of the late nineteenth century, about whom I have never written. I have written about Baudelaire, but nothing about Jules Laforgue, to whom I owe more than to any one poet in any language, or about Tristan Corbière, to whom I owe something also. The reason, I believe, is that no one commissioned me to do so. For these early essays were all written for money, which I needed, and the occasion was always a new book about an author, a new edition of his works, or an anniversary.

The question of the extent to which a critic may influence the taste of his time I have answered, speaking for myself alone, by saying that I do not believe that my own criticism has had, or could have had, any influence whatever apart from my own poems. Let me turn now to the question: how far, and in what ways do the critic's own tastes and views alter in the course of his lifetime? To what extent do such changes indicate greater maturity, when do they indicate decay, and when must we consider them merely as changes – neither for better nor for worse? For myself, again, I find that my opinion of poets whose work influenced me in my formative stage remains unchanged, and I abate nothing of the praise I have given them. True, they do not now give me that intense excitement and sense of enlargement and liberation which comes from a discovery which is also a discovery of oneself: but that is an experience which can only happen once. And indeed it is to other poets than these that I am likely to turn now for pure delight. I turn more often the pages [23] of Mallarmé than of Laforgue, those of George Herbert than those of Donne, of Shakespeare than of his contemporaries and epigoni. This does not necessarily involve a judgement of relative greatness: it is merely that what has best responded to my need in middle and later age is different from the nourishment I needed in my youth. So great is Shakespeare, however, that a lifetime is hardly enough for growing up to appreciate him. There is one poet, however, who impressed me profoundly when I was twenty-two and with only a rudimentary acquaintance with his language started to puzzle out his lines, one poet who remains the comfort and amazement of my age, although my knowledge of his language remains rudimentary. I was never more than an inferior classical scholar: the poet I speak of is Dante. In my youth, I think that Dante's astonishing economy and directness of language – his arrow that goes unerringly to the centre of the target – provided for me a wholesome corrective to the extravagances of the Elizabethan, Jacobean and Caroline authors in whom I also delighted.

Perhaps what I want to say now is true of all literary criticism. I am sure that it is true of mine, that it is at its best when I have been writing of authors whom I have wholeheartedly admired. And my next best are of authors whom I greatly admire, but only with qualifications with which other critics may disagree. I do not ask to be reassured about my essays on minor Elizabethan dramatists, but am always interested to hear what other critics of poetry think, for instance, about what I have written on

Tennyson or Byron. As for criticism of negligible authors, it can hardly be of permanent interest, because people will cease to be interested in the writers criticised. And censure of a great writer – or a writer whose works have had the test of time – is likely to be influenced by other than literary considerations. The personality of Milton, as well as some of his politics and theology, was obviously antipathetic to Samuel Johnson, as it is to me. (But when I wrote my first essay on Milton, I was considering his poetry as poetry and in relation to what I conceived to be the needs of my own time; and when I wrote my second essay on Milton I did not intend it to be, what Desmond MacCarthy and others took [24] it to be, a recantation of my earlier opinion, but a development in view of the fact that there was no longer any likelihood of his being imitated, and that therefore he could profitably be studied. This reference to Milton is parenthetical.) I do not regret what I have written about Milton: but when an author's mind is so antipathetic to my own as was that of Thomas Hardy, I wonder whether it might not have been better never to have written about him at all.

Perhaps my judgement is less assured about writers who are contemporary or nearly so, than about writers of the past. Yet my valuation of the work of those poets contemporary with me, and of those poets younger than myself with whom I feel an affinity, remains unchanged. There is however one contemporary figure about whom my mind will, I fear, always waver between dislike, exasperation, boredom and admiration. That is D. H. Lawrence.

My opinions of D. H. Lawrence seem to form a tissue of praise and execration. The more vehement of my ejaculations of dislike are preserved, like flies in amber, or like wasps in honey, by the diligence of Dr Leavis; but between two passages which he quotes, one published in 1927 and the other in 1933, I find that in 1931 I was wagging my finger rather pompously at the bishops who had assembled at the Lambeth Conference, and reproaching them for 'missing an opportunity for dissociating themselves from the condemnation of two very serious and improving writers' – namely, Mr James Joyce and Mr D. H. Lawrence. I cannot account for such apparent contradictions. Last year, in the *Lady Chatterley* case, I expressed my readiness to appear as a witness for the defence. Perhaps the counsel for the defence were well advised not to put me into the witness box, as it might have been rather difficult to make my views clear to a jury by that form of inquisition, and a really wily prosecutor might have tied me up in knots. I felt then, as I feel now, that the prosecution of such a book – a book of most serious and highly moral *intention* – was a deplorable blunder, the consequences of which would be most unfortunate whatever the verdict, and give the book a kind of vogue which would have been abhorrent to the author. But [25] my antipathy to the author remains, on the ground of what seems to me egotism, a strain of cruelty, and a failing in common with Thomas Hardy – the lack of a sense of humour.

My particular reason for referring to my response to the work of Lawrence is that it is well to remind ourselves, in discussing the subject of literary criticism, that we cannot escape personal bias, and that there are other standards besides that of 'literary merit', which cannot be excluded. It was noticeable, in the Chatterley case, that some witnesses for the defence defended the book for the moral intentions of the author rather than on the ground of its being important as a work of literature.

In most of what I have been saying today, however, I have endeavored to confine myself to that part of my own critical prose which is most nearly definable as '*literary* criticism'. May I sum up the conclusions to which I have come, after re-reading all of my writing which can be covered by that designation? I have found that my best work falls within rather narrow limits, my best essays being, in my opinion, those concerned with writers who had influenced me in my poetry; naturally the majority of these writers were poets. And it is that part of my criticism concerned with writers towards whom I felt gratitude and whom I could praise wholeheartedly, which is the part in which I continue to feel most confidence as the years pass. And as for the phrases of generalisation which have been so often quoted, I am convinced that their force comes from the fact that they are attempts to summarise, in conceptual form, direct and intense experience of the poetry that I have found most congenial.

It is risky, and perhaps presumptuous, for me to generalize from my own experience, even about critics of my own type – that is, writers who are primarily creative but reflect upon their own vocation and upon the work of other practitioners. I am, I admit, much more interested in what other poets have written about poetry than in what critics who are not poets have said about it. I have suggested also that it is impossible to fence off *literary* criticism from criticism on other grounds, and that moral, religious and social judgements cannot be wholly excluded. That they can, and that literary merit can be estimated in complete [26] isolation, is the illusion of those who believe that literary merit alone can justify the publication of a book which could otherwise be condemned on moral grounds. But the nearest we get to pure literary criticism is the criticism of artists writing about their own art; and for this I turn to Johnson, Wordsworth and Coleridge. (Paul Valéry is a special case.) In other types of criticism, the historian, the philosopher, the moralist, the sociologist, the grammarian may play a large part; but in so far as literary criticism is purely literary, I believe that the criticism of artists writing about their own art is of greater intensity, and carries more authority, though the area of the artist's competence may be much narrower. I feel that I myself have spoken with authority (if the phrase itself does not suggest arrogance) only about those authors – poets and a very few prose writers – who have influenced me; that on poets who have not influenced me I still deserve serious consideration; and that on authors whose work I dislike my views may – to say the least – be highly disputable. And I should remind you again, in closing, that I have directed attention on my literary criticism *qua* literary, and that a study in respect of my religious, social, political or moral beliefs, and of that large part of my prose writing which is directly concerned with these beliefs would be quite another exercise in self-examination. But I hope that what I have said today may suggest reasons why, as the critic grows older, his critical writings may be less fired by enthusiasm, but informed by wider interest and, one hopes, by greater wisdom and humility.

From Poe to Valéry

TCTC, 27–42.
Repr. from the original edn of 1948 (Gallup A52).
See Vol. 3, pp. 721–34 in the present edition.

American Literature and the American Language[1]

TCTC, 43–60.

Slightly revised from *American Literature and the American Language*, an Address Delivered at Washington University on June 9, 1953, With an Appendix. Prepared by the Department of English St Louis, Missouri, Washington University: Gallup A62.

1 It is almost exactly forty-eight years ago that I made my first appearance on a public platform before a large audience. This was at the graduation exercises of the Class of 1905 of Smith Academy, an offshoot of this University; and my part in the ceremony was to deliver the valedictory poem of the year. I was informed afterwards, by one of my teachers, that the poem itself was excellent, as such poems go, but that my delivery was very bad indeed. Since then I have made some progress in elocution, and I have been more often criticised for the content of my speeches than for my manner of delivery; but I knew that today I should experience something like the trepidation which I well remember feeling on that evening so long

---

1. An address delivered at Washington University, St Louis, Missouri, on June 9th, 1953.

ago. When I sat down to prepare my notes for this address, I found myself distracted by so many memories of my early years, that I was tempted either to talk about nothing else, or to pass them all over in silence. The first alternative would have produced something too personal and autobiographic for the dignity of this occasion; the second would have meant the suppression of feelings which I do not wish to suppress. I shall therefore, before proceeding to my subject, say something to indicate what it means to me to be here in St Louis and to be speaking at Washington University in the hundredth year since its foundation; and I trust that a preamble somewhat longer than usual will not be amiss.

2 It is the fact that this is the centennial year of the University that gives me the excuse, as well as the stronger urge, to allude to my own upbringing. The early history of this University which [44] my grandfather served with tireless devotion until his death, is inextricably involved for me in family and personal history. I never knew my grandfather: he died a year before my birth. But I was brought up to be very much aware of him: so much so, that as a child I thought of him as still the head of the family – a ruler for whom *in absentia* my grandmother stood as vicegerent. The standard of conduct was that which my grandfather had set; our moral judgements, our decisions between duty and self-indulgence, were taken as if, like Moses, he had brought down the tables of the Law, any deviation from which would be sinful. Not the least of these laws, which included injunctions still more than prohibitions, was the law of Public Service: it is no doubt owing to the impress of this law upon my infant mind that, like other members of my family, I have felt, ever since I passed beyond my early irresponsible years, an uncomfortable and very inconvenient obligation to serve upon committees. This original Law of Public Service operated especially in three areas: the Church, the City, and the University. The Church meant, for us, the Unitarian Church of the Messiah, then situated in Locust Street, a few blocks west of my father's house and my grandmother's house; the City was St Louis – the utmost outskirts of which touched on Forest Park, terminus of the Olive Street streetcars, and to me, as a child, the beginning of the Wild West; the University was Washington University, then housed in a modest building in lower Washington Avenue. These were the symbols of Religion, the Community and Education: and I think it is a very good beginning for any child, to be brought up to reverence such institutions, and to be taught that personal and selfish aims should be subordinated to the general good which they represent.

3 Unlike my father, my uncles, my brother, and several of my cousins, I was never enrolled as an undergraduate in Washington University, but

was sent to another institution with which also there were family associations. But the earlier part – and I believe, the most important part – of my education is what I received in that preparatory department of the University which was named Smith Academy. My memories of Smith Academy are on the [45] whole happy ones; and when, many years ago, I learned that the school had come to an end, I felt that a link with the past had been painfully broken. It was a good school. There one was taught, as is now increasingly rare everywhere, what I consider the essentials: Latin and Greek, together with Greek and Roman history, English and American history, elementary mathematics, French and German. Also English! I am happy to remember that in those days English composition was still called *Rhetoric*. Lest you infer that the curriculum was incredibly primitive, I will add that there was a laboratory, in which physical and chemical experiments were performed successfully by the more adroit. As I failed to pass my entrance examination in physics, you will not be surprised that I have forgotten the name of the master who taught it. But I remember other names of good teachers, my gratitude to whom I take this opportunity of recording: Mr Jackson in Latin, Mr Robinson in Greek, Mr Rowe – though I was not one of his good pupils – in mathematics, Madame Jouvet-Kauffmann and Miss Chandler in French and German respectively, Mr Hatch, who taught English, commended warmly my first poem, written as a class exercise, at the same time asking me suspiciously if I had had any help in writing it. Mr Jeffries I think taught modern history; our ancient history was taught by the Greek and Latin masters. Well! so far as I am educated, I must pay my first tribute to Smith Academy; if I had not been well taught there, I should have been unable to profit elsewhere. And so far as I am badly educated, that is attributable to laziness and caprice. And before passing from the subject of Smith Academy, I wish to say that I remember it as a good school also because of the boys who were there with me: it seems that, for a school of small numbers, we were a well-mixed variety of local types.

4 Many other memories have invaded my mind, since I received the invitation to speak to you today; but I think these are enough to serve as a token of my thoughts and feelings. I am very well satisfied with having been born in St Louis: in fact I think I was fortunate to have been born here, rather than in Boston, or New York, or London.

[46] 5 The title I have chosen for this address seems to indicate that I have two subjects. Why am I talking about both: 'American literature', and 'the American language'? First, because they are related, and second because they must be distinguished. It is profitable to clear our minds about the meaning of the term 'the American language' before proceeding to talk

of American literature. As I have a reputation for affecting pedantic precision, a reputation I should not like to lose, I will add that I shall not ask 'what is literature?' However various may be people's notions as to what printed matter is literature and what is not, such differences of taste and judgement do not affect my problem.

6 My attention was recently called to this question of the differences between the English and American language, on receiving a copy of a new American dictionary. It appeared to me an excellent dictionary of its size, and likely to be useful in England as well as in this country; and to those interested in the making of dictionaries and the problems arising in the definition of words, I commend also a pamphlet by one of the editors, Mr David B. Guralnik, which struck me as very sound sense. But I was puzzled by the sub-title: it is called a dictionary 'of the American language'. Perhaps I am unconsciously bi-lingual, so that whichever language I hear or read seems to me my own; but certainly the vast majority of the words in this dictionary are words belonging to both America and England, and having the same meaning in both. And the definitions seemed to me to be written in English too. True, the spelling, where English and American usage differ, was the American spelling: but this presents no difficulty in England, where various editions of the work of Noah Webster (a famous lexicographer who I believe married my great-aunt) are in current use. And about spelling, I do not believe in hard and fast rules, and least of all in the hard and fast rules of champions of simplified spelling, such as the late Bernard Shaw. I hold that a word is something more than the noise it makes: it is also the way it looks on the page. I am averse to simplified spelling which destroys all traces of a word's origin and history. But I think, for example, that the English would do well to omit, from a word like 'labour', the superfluous U, which appears to be [47] merely an etymological error. As to whether 'centre' should be spelt 'centre' or 'center', that seems to me a matter of indifference. There is much to be said for the American spelling 'catalog'; on the other hand I distrust simplifications of spelling that tend to alter pronunciation, as, for example, the shortening of 'programme' to 'program', which throws the stress onto the first syllable. And I think that the advocates of a systematic simplified spelling – such as those who recently introduced a Bill in Parliament – overlook the fact that in attempting to fix spelling phonetically, they are also attempting to fix pronunciation: and both pronunciation and spelling, in both England and America, must inevitably change from age to age under the pressure of usage and convenience.

7 Apart from the differences of spelling and pronunciation, the only other important difference which I discovered between this dictionary and the standard dictionaries in England, is that a number of words are included, which have not yet found their way into the latter. I was gratified, for instance, to find *grifter* and *shill*, two words which I first encountered in a fascinating book about one specialised area of the American vocabulary, called *The Big Con*. And about such words as *grifter* and *shill* I am willing to risk a prediction. Either they will disappear from the American vocabulary, to be replaced by newer and shinier words with the same meaning, or, if they become permanently settled, as Dr Guralnik expects, they will find their way into the English vocabulary as well, and eventually into a supplement to the great Oxford dictionary. They will first appear in the vocabulary of that very large section of British society whose speech is constantly enriched from the films, and will make their way through the tabloid press to *The Times*, in *The Times* proceeding from the levity of the fourth editorial article to the solemnity of the first editorial article; and so their dictionary status in Britain will be assured. Many new words, of course, are ephemeral; and as Dr Guralnik, in the essay to which I have referred, ruefully admits, a lexicographer may make the mistake of admitting a word to his dictionary just as it is on the point of going out of fashion: a mistake not unlike that of buying shares in a company [48] just before its compulsory liquidation. Words can even disappear, and come into currency again after a period of seclusion. When I was a small boy, in this city, I was reproved by my family for using the vulgar phrase 'O.K.'. Then there was a period during which it seemed to have expired; but at some subsequent date it came to life again, and twenty-odd years ago swept like a tidal wave over England, to establish itself in English speech. As for its respectability here, I hold the most convincing piece of evidence yet: it occurs in a cable I received from Professor Cardwell.

8 Apart from some differences of spelling, pronunciation and vocabulary, there are between English and American a number of differences of idiom, for the most part reciprocally intelligible; there are also a few dangerous idioms, the same phrases with totally different meanings – in some cases leading to awkward misunderstanding and embarrassment. The sum total of these differences, however, does not seem to me to go so far as to justify us in speaking of English and American as different languages; the differences are no greater than between English as spoken in England and as spoken in Ireland, and negligible compared to the difference between English and Lowland Scots. But we must carry the question further, and ask: is it probable that speech in England and speech

in America are developing in such a way that we can predict the eventual division into two languages, so distinct that each country will provide one more foreign language for the school curriculum of the other?

9 Perhaps we can draw some conclusions from the transformations of languages in the past. The obvious examples, of course, are the decline of Latin and its transmutation into the several Romance languages; and the development from Sanskrit, through Pali, of the modern Indian languages Bengali, Mahratti and Gujarati. I make no pretence of being a philologist; but even to a person untrained in that science there is a striking parallel between the relation of Italian to Latin, and the relation of Pali to Sanskrit. It would at first sight seem within the bounds of possibility, that in the course of time American speech and writing might come to differ as much from present-day English, as Italian and Bengali differ from Latin and Sanskrit.

[49] 10 The question has, of course, no bearing on the literature of today; and far from presenting a pleasing prospect to a living author, it is one which he must shudder to contemplate. Even if we refrain from calling our works 'immortal', we all of us like to believe that what we write will go on being read for a very long time indeed. We cannot relish the thought that our poems and plays and novels will, at best, be preserved only in texts heavily annotated by learned scholars, who will dispute the meaning of many passages and will be completely in the dark as to how our beautiful lines should be pronounced. Most of us, we know, have a pretty good chance of oblivion anyway; but to those of us who succeed in dying in advance of our reputations, the assurance of a time when our writings will only be grappled with by two or three graduate students in Middle Anglo-American 42 B is very distasteful. As it would not have pleased a late Latin poet in Southern Gaul to be told by a soothsayer that his language, over which he took so much trouble, would in a few centuries be replaced by something more up-to-date.

11 We must also face the possibility, if we can draw any conclusions from the metamorphosis of Latin, of a long period of time during which everything written in our language will be arid, pedantic and imitative. It is, of course, a necessary condition for the continuance of a literature, that the language should be in constant change. If it is changing it is alive; and if it does not change, then new writers have no escape from imitating classics of their literature without hope of producing anything so good. But when a change occurs such as that which led to the supersession of Latin by French, Italian, Spanish and Portuguese, the new languages have to grow up from the roots of the old, that is, from the common speech of uneducated people, and for a long time will be crude and capable of

expressing only a narrow range of simple thoughts and feelings. The old culture had to decline, before the new cultures could develop. And for the development of a new and crude language into a great language, how much is not due to the happy accident of a few writers of great genius, such as Dante or Shakespeare?

12 Is the parallel with Latin and Sanskrit, however, valid? Is such [50] a transformation, for better or worse, of English into two distinct languages on the two sides of the Atlantic likely to take place? I think that the circumstances nowadays are very different. If such a transformation should occur, it will be due to social, political and economic changes very different from anything that is happening now, and on such a vast scale that we cannot even imagine them. There is, I suspect, behind the thinking of such students of language as Mr Mencken (whose monumental book on the American language is a philologist's picnic) a mistaken assimilation of language to politics. Such prophets seem to be issuing a kind of linguistic Declaration of Independence, an act of emancipation of American from English. But these patriotic spirits may be overlooking the other side of the picture.

13 In October last occurred an event which, while not as spectacular as the descent of Col. Lindbergh at Le Bourget in 'The Spirit of St Louis', is equally remarkable in its kind. For the first time, apparently, an American robin, well named *Turdus migratorius*, crossed the Atlantic under its own power, 'favoured' according to the report, by 'a period of strong westerly weather'. This enterprising bird was also intelligent, for it chose to alight on Lundy Island, off the coast of Devon, which happens to be a bird sanctuary. Of course even birds, nowadays, are not allowed to travel without undergoing official inquisition, so our robin was trapped, photographed, and released; and, I hope, provided with a ration book. It is interesting to speculate on the future of this pilgrim. Either he (or she, for the sex is not stated) will be followed by another of the opposite sex, in which event we may expect that England will soon be populated by American robins; or else our lone pioneer must make the best of it, and breed with the English thrush, who is not *migratorius* but *musicus*. In the latter event, the English must look out for a new species of thrush, with a faint red spot on the male breast in springtime; a species which, being a blend of *migratorius* and *musicus*, should become known as the troubadour-bird, or organ-grinder.

14 Now, if the American robin can perform such feats, what cannot the American language do? Favoured by very strong westerly weather, of course. Unless you yourselves draw a [51] linguistic iron curtain (and I think Hollywood, to say nothing of the proprietors of *Time*, *Life*, *The*

New Yorker and other periodicals, would object to that) you cannot keep the American language out of England. However fast the American language moves, there will be always behind it the pattering of feet: the feet of the great British public eager for a new word or phrase. The feet may sometimes be a long way behind, but they are tireless. In the long run, I don't see how you can keep the American language to yourselves. Britain is of course eager also to export, though baffled by tariff walls; but it seems that at present the current of language flows from west to east. The last war strengthened the flow in that direction; and people from Land's End to John o' Groats are nourished on American films, the speech of which they understand, I have been told, a good deal better than the American public understand that of British films. It may be, that this west-east current will be the stronger for a long time to come: but, whatever happens, I believe that there will always be a movement in one direction or the other. So that, against the influences towards the development of separate languages, there will always be other influences tending towards fusion.

15 It has seemed to me worth while to get this question of language out of the way before attempting to say what I mean by American Literature: as I believe that we are now justified in speaking of what has never, I think, been found before, two literatures in the same language.

16 When, however, I assert that the term 'American literature' has for me a clear and distinct meaning, I do not believe that this meaning is wholly definable; and I shall try to explain in what respect I think it is undesirable to try to define it. Like many other terms, the term 'American literature' has altered and developed its meaning in the course of time. It means something different for us today from what it could have meant a hundred years ago. It has a much fuller meaning now than it could have had then. By this I do not mean that American literature of the nineteenth century is less deserving of the name than American literature of the twentieth. I mean that the phrase could not mean quite the same thing to the writers of a century ago that it means to us; [52] that it is only in retrospect that their Americanness is fully visible. At the beginning, to speak of 'American literature' would have been only to establish a geographical distinction: Jonathan Edwards could hardly have understood what the term means today. Early American literature, without the achievements of later writers, would merely be literature written in English by men born or living in America. Washington Irving is less distinctively American than Fenimore Cooper. I suspect that the Leatherstocking novels, to a contemporary English reader, must have appeared to depict, not a new and different society, but the adventures

of English pioneers in new and undeveloped country; just as I suppose they still have, for English boys, much the same fascination as good tales of adventure of early life in British dominions and colonies anywhere. (Cooper has suffered, like Walter Scott, from being read in early youth, and by many people never read again: it remained for D. H. Lawrence, who discovered Cooper later in life, to write probably the most brilliant of critical essays on him.) The English reader of the day, certainly, would hardly have recognised in Natty Bumppo, a new kind of man: it is only in retrospect that such differences are visible.

17 The literature of nineteenth century New England, however, is patently marked by something more than the several personalities of its authors: it has its own particular *civilised* landscape and the ethos of a local society of English origin with its own distinct traits. It remains representative of New England, rather than of America: and Longfellow, Whittier, Bryant, Emerson, Thoreau – and even the last of the pure New Englanders, Robert Frost – yield more of themselves, I believe, to people of New England origin than to others; they have, in addition to their qualities of wider appeal, a peculiar nostalgic charm for New Englanders settled elsewhere. And as for the writer who to me is the greatest among them, Nathaniel Hawthorne, it seems to me that there is something in Hawthorne that can best be appreciated by the reader with Calvinism in his bones and witch-hanging (*not* witch-hunting) on his conscience. So the landmarks I have chosen for the identification of American literature are not found in New England. I am [53] aware that my choice may appear arbitrary; but in making such wide generalisations one must always take the risk. The three authors of my choice are Poe, Whitman, and Mark Twain.

18 I must hasten to explain what I do *not* mean. I do not imply that these writers are necessarily greater than others whom I have mentioned or could mention. Nor am I suggesting that these three men were individually 'more American' than others. Nor am I suggesting that American literature today *derives* from these three. Nor am I assuming that from a study of these three writers one could arrive at a formula of Americanism in literature. What their common American characteristics may be, is something I should consider it folly to attempt to define; and in seeking for their common qualities, one might easily overlook the essence of each.

19 I wish to emphasise the point that I am not concerned, in making such a selection, with questions of *influence*. A comparison of Poe and Whitman is illuminating. Amongst American poets, it is undoubtedly Poe and Whitman who have enjoyed the highest reputation abroad, both

in English-speaking lands and in countries where they are known in translation. What is remarkable about the posthumous history of Poe is the fact that his influence in France, on and through the intermediary of three great French poets, has been immense; and that his influence in America and in England has been negligible. I cannot think of any good poet, here or in England, who has been sensibly influenced by Poe – except perhaps Edward Lear. How is it that Poe can be chosen as a distinctively American author, when there is so little evidence that any American poet since Poe has written any differently than he would have written if Poe had never lived?

20 To Walt Whitman, on the other hand, a great influence on modern poetry has been attributed. I wonder if this has not been exaggerated. In this respect he reminds me of Gerard Manley Hopkins – a lesser poet than Whitman, but also a remarkable innovator in style. Whitman and Hopkins, I think, both found an idiom and a metric perfectly suited for what they had to say; and very doubtfully adaptable to what anyone else has to say. One reason why such writers as Whitman and Hopkins attract [54] imitators, is that in their less inspired verse they tend – as a writer with a highly idiosyncratic idiom may be tempted to do – to imitate themselves; and it is a man's imitation of himself, rather than his best work, that is most catching and most easily imitated. A true disciple is impressed by what his master has to say, and *consequently* by his way of saying it; an imitator – I might say, a borrower – is impressed chiefly by the way the master said it. If he manages to mimic his master well enough, he may succeed even in disguising from himself the fact that he has nothing to say.

21 It is possible, on the other hand, that the influence of Mark Twain may prove to have been considerable. If so, it is for this reason: that Twain, at least in *Huckleberry Finn*, reveals himself to be one of those writers, of whom there are not a great many in any literature, who have discovered a new way of writing, valid not only for themselves but for others. I should place him, in this respect, even with Dryden and Swift, as one of those rare writers who have brought their language up to date, and in so doing, 'purified the dialect of the tribe'. In this respect I should put him above Hawthorne: though no finer a stylist, and in obvious ways a less profound explorer of the human soul. Superficially, Twain is equally local, strongly local. Yet the Salem of Hawthorne remains a town with a particular tradition, which could not be anywhere but where it is; whereas the Mississippi of Mark Twain is not only the river known to those who voyage on it or live beside it, but the universal river of human life – more universal, indeed, than the Congo of Joseph Conrad.

For Twain's readers anywhere, the Mississippi is *the* river. There is in Twain, I think, a great unconscious depth, which gives to *Huckleberry Finn* this symbolic value: a symbolism all the more powerful for being uncalculated and unconscious.

22 Here we arrive at two characteristics which I think must be found together, in any author whom I should single out as one of the landmarks of a national literature: the strong local flavor combined with unconscious universality. We must not suppose that the former can always be identified on superficial examination. What is identifiably local about Poe? Apart from *The Gold Bug* and a few other prose pieces, there is little in the work of Poe [55] that appears to be based on the landscapes and the types of human being that he knew. His favourite settings are imaginary romantic places: a Paris or a Venice which he had never visited. It is very puzzling; but then Poe remains an enigma, a stumbling-block for the critic. Perhaps Poe's local quality is due simply to the fact that he never had the opportunity to travel, and that when he wrote about Europe, it was a Europe with which he had no direct acquaintance. A cosmopolitan experience might have done Poe more harm than good; for cosmopolitanism can be the enemy of universality – it may dissipate attention in superficial familiarity with the streets, the cafés and some of the local dialect of a number of foreign capitals; whereas universality can never come except through writing about what one knows thoroughly. Dostoevski is none the less universal for having stopped in Russia. Perhaps all that one can say of Poe is that his was a type of imagination that created its own dream world; that anyone's dream world is conditioned by the world in which he lives; and that the real world behind Poe's fancy was the world of the Baltimore and Richmond and Philadelphia that he knew.

23 You will have noticed that the three authors on whom I am concentrating my attention are three of those who have enjoyed the greatest reputation abroad. It is possible for foreigners to be mistaken about contemporary writers: I know that the contemporary English estimate of the importance of some French writer, or the contemporary French estimate of the importance of some English writer, can be grotesque. But I think that when enough time has elapsed the continued appreciation of foreigners is likely to indicate that an author does combine the local with the universal. The foreigner may at first be attracted by the differences: an author is found interesting because he is so unlike anything in the foreigner's own literature. But a vogue due to novel differences will soon fade out; it will not survive unless the foreign reader recognises, perhaps unconsciously, identity as well as difference. When we read a novel of

Dostoevski, or see a play by Tche[k]hov, for the first time, I think that we are fascinated by the odd way in which Russians behave; later, we come to recognise that theirs is merely an odd way of expressing thoughts and [56] feelings which we all share. And, though it is only too easy for a writer to be local without being universal, I doubt whether a poet or novelist can be universal without being local too. Who could be more Greek than Odysseus? Or more German than Faust? Or more Spanish than Don Quixote? Or more American than Huck Finn? Yet each one of them is a kind of archetype in the mythology of all men everywhere.

24 Having got to this point, let me now suggest that a national literature comes to consciousness at the stage at which any young writer must be aware of several generations of writers behind him, in his own country and language, and amongst these generations several writers generally acknowledged to be of the great. The importance of this background for the young writer is incalculable. It is not necessary that this background should provide him with models for imitation. The young writer, certainly, should not be consciously bending his talent to conform to any supposed American or other tradition. The writers of the past, especially of the immediate past, in one's own place and language may be valuable to the young writer simply as something definite to rebel against. He will recognise the common ancestry: but he needn't necessarily *like* his relatives. For models to imitate, or for styles from which to learn, he may more profitably go to writers of another country and another language, or of a remoter age. Some of my strongest impulse to original development, in early years, has come from thinking: 'here is a man who has said something, long ago or in another language, which somehow corresponds to what I want to say now; let me see if I can't do what he has done, in my own language – in the language of my own place and time.'

25 Such considerations should put us all on guard against an attitude of narrow national pride in our literature. Especially against asking questions such as 'is this new writer truly American or not? Does his work conform to the standards of America, to our definitions of what constitutes Americanism in literature?' It is obvious that such a critical censorship could only stifle originality. The cry has so often been raised about new writers: 'This isn't English!' or 'This isn't French!' or whatever the language [57] may be. Also, there is always the danger of overvaluing the local product just because it is local; and of unconsciously judging our own writers by less exacting standards than those we apply to writers of other nations. We are, in every country, always exposed to that danger. And to narrow your admission to subject matter or to style already accepted, would be to affirm that what is American has been

settled once and for all. A living literature is always in process of change; contemporaneous living literatures are always, through one or more authors, changing each other; and the literature written in America in future generations will, you may be sure, render obsolete any formulations of 'what is American' based on the work of writers up to and including those now writing.

26 From time to time there occurs some revolution, or sudden mutation of form and content in literature. Then, some way of writing which has been practised for a generation or more, is found by a few people to be out of date, and no longer to respond to contemporary modes of thought, feeling and speech. A new kind of writing appears, to be greeted at first with disdain and derision; we hear that the tradition has been flouted, and that chaos has come. After a time it appears that the new way of writing is not destructive but re-creative. It is not that we have repudiated the past, as the obstinate enemies – and also the stupidest supporters – of any new movement like to believe; but that we have enlarged our conception of the past; and that in the light of what is new we see the past in a new pattern. We might now consider such a revolution as that which has taken place in poetry, both in England and America, during the last forty years.

27 In talking about such an event, one must mention names. So, in order to be quite fair, I explain that I choose names as typical illustrations, that the poets mentioned are not necessarily valued in the order in which their names will occur, and that they are not all necessarily superior to all of the poets who are not mentioned. Furthermore, in any such literary revolution there is an overlap: some of the poets who continue to write in what is usually called a 'more traditional' manner are first-rate in their kind, and by the [58] verdict of history may prove to be more highly prized than many of the poets who have written in newer ways.

28 In the first decade of the century the situation was unusual. I cannot think of a single living poet, in either England or America, then at the height of his powers, whose work was capable of pointing the way to a young poet conscious of the desire for a new idiom. It was the tail-end of the Victorian era. Our sympathies, I think, went out to those who are known as the English poets of the nineties, who were all, with one exception, dead. The exception was W. B. Yeats, who was younger, more robust, and of more temperate habits than the poets of the Rhymers' Club with whom he had associated in his youth. And Yeats himself had not found his personal speech; he was a late developer; when he emerged as a great modern poet, about 1917, we had already reached a point such that he appeared not as a precursor but as an elder and venerated

contemporary. What the poets of the nineties had bequeathed to us besides the new tone of a few poems by Ernest Dowson, John Davidson and Arthur Symons, was the assurance that there was something to be learned from the French poets of the Symbolist Movement – and most of them were dead, too.

29 I do not propose to define the change that came about; I am merely tracing its course. Such a transformation as we have experienced in this century cannot be altogether attributed to one group of poets, still less to one individual. As so often happens in the fields of science, when a new discovery is made, it has been preceded by a number of scattered investigators who have happened to be groping, each at first in ignorance of the efforts of the others, in the same direction. In retrospect, it is often impossible to attribute the discovery to the genius of one scientist alone. The *point de repère* usually and conveniently taken, as the starting-point of modern poetry, is the group denominated 'imagists' in London about 1910. I was not there. It was an Anglo-American group: literary history has not settled the question, and perhaps never will, whether imagism itself, or the name for it, was invented by the American Ezra Pound or the Englishman T. E. Hulme. The poets in the group seem to have been drawn together by a com-[59]mon attraction towards modern poetry in French, and a common interest in exploring the possibilities of development through study of the poetry of other ages and languages. If imagism became more quickly and widely known in America than in England, that was largely because of the zealous, though sometimes misguided activity of Amy Lowell, who assumed the role of Advertising Manager for a movement which, on the whole, is chiefly important because of the stimulus it gave to later developments.

30 I think it is just to say that the pioneers of twentieth century poetry were more conspicuously the Americans than the English, both in number and in quality. Why this should have been must remain a matter for conjecture. I do not believe that it is attributable to the fact that so many more Britons were killed in the first war: the most remarkable of the British poets killed in that war whose work has been published, is in my opinion the late Isaac Rosenberg, who was outside the movement. Perhaps the young Americans of that age were less oppressed by the weight of the Victorian tradition, more open to new influences and more ready for experiment. (So far as my observation goes, I should say in general, of contemporary verse, that the most dangerous tendency of American versifiers is towards eccentricity and formlessness, whereas that of English versifiers is rather towards conventionality and reversion to the Victorian type.) But, looking at my own generation, the names

that come immediately to mind are those of Ezra Pound, W. C. Williams, Wallace Stevens – and you may take pride in one who is a St Louisan by birth: Miss Marianne Moore. Even of a somewhat younger generation, the names of Americans come to my mind most readily: Cummings, Hart Crane, Ransom, Tate. And I am choosing names only from among those whose work places them among the more radical experimenters: among poets of an intermediate type of technique the names of distinction are as numerous here as in England. And this is a new thing. In the nineteenth century, Poe and Whitman stand out as solitary international figures: in the last forty years, for the first time, there has been assembled a *body* of American poetry which has made its total impression in England and in Europe.

[60] 31 I am merely stating what seem to me cold facts. During the thirties the tide seemed to be turning the other way: the representative figure of that decade is W. H. Auden, though there are other British poets of the same generation whose best work will I believe prove equally permanent. Now, I do not know whether Auden is to be considered as an English or as an American poet: his career has been useful to me in providing me with an answer to the same question when asked about myself, for I can say: 'whichever Auden is, I suppose I must be the other'. Today there are several interesting younger poets in both countries, and England has acquired some valuable recruits from Wales. But my point in making this hurried review is simply this. In my time, there have been influences in both directions, and I think, to the mutual profit of literature on both sides of the Atlantic. But English and American poetry do not in consequence tend to become merged into one common international type, even though the poetry of today on one side of the ocean may show a closer kinship with poetry on the other side, than either does with that of an earlier generation. I do not think that a satisfactory statement of what constitutes the difference between an English and an American 'tradition' in poetry could be arrived at: because the moment you produce your definition, and the neater the definition is, the more surely some poet will turn up who doesn't fit into it at all, but who is nevertheless definitely either English or American. And the tradition itself, as I have said long ago, is altered by every new writer of genius. The difference will remain undefined, but it will remain; and this is I think as it should be: for it is because they are different that English and American poetry can help each other, and contribute towards the endless renovation of both.

Variants from 1953:

1   ago] ago,

2 centennial year of the University] centennial year of the University, Community] Community,

13 *Turdus*] turdus

The Aims of Education[1]
1. Can 'Education' be Defined?

TCTC, 61–77.

Revised from 'The Aims of Education. I. Can "Education" Be Defined?, *Measure*, 2. 1 (Dec. 1950), [3]–16 (Gallup C557).

1 A well-known divine, in a recent volume[2] devoted to the sort of problems with which I shall be here concerned, has pronounced a judgement which I have tried to take to heart. 'It is,' he says, 'unfortunately true that most educators do not sufficiently ignore literary dabblers but are, rather, unduly impressed by them.' He had preceded this harsh warning, to be sure, by a sentence which is less disturbing; he had just remarked: 'If the physical scientists, the religionists, the naturalists, the artists, and the students of human contacts could unite to bestow upon them [i.e., the literary dabblers] the privilege of talking exclusively to one another, and could turn jointly to the reconsideration of what constitutes true education to the restoration of sound thinking based upon adequate experience, there would be less confusion of mind in educational circles and more of that mutually helpful cooperation which properly exists between those who, by various methods and by complementary avenues, are seeking the one Truth.' I am not sure whether, in the present context, I am to be regarded as an artist or as a literary dabbler. Between helpful contribution and ignorant interference there may be a very narrow line indeed; and I must accept the risk if I am to say anything at all.

2 Education is a subject on which we all feel that we have something to say. We have all been educated, more or less; and we have, most of us, complaints to make about the defects of our own education; and we all like to blame our educators, or the [62] system within which they were compelled to work, for our failure to educate ourselves. And the literary dabbler has sometimes dabbled in teaching as well. I have been a schoolmaster, at a grammar school for one term, and for a year at a school for little boys; for three years of my life I conducted an Adult

---

1. The text of lectures delivered at the University of Chicago in November 1950. Printed in *Measure* (December 1950, Spring, Summer and Fall, 1951).

2. Bernard Iddings Bell, *Crisis in Education* (New York, McGraw-Hill Book Company, 1949).

Education class once a week; at one time I was an Assistant in Philosophy taking weekly tutorial groups, and at a much later age I was responsible for a course for undergraduates in the subject – God forgive me – of Contemporary English Literature. I do not include the various series of public lectures which I have given at universities, because no one has to pass an examination on such lectures, and therefore they are no part of education. And I mention my nominal qualifications only to affirm that in my opinion they are, for my present task, no qualifications at all.

3 A couple of years ago I produced a book called *Notes Towards the Definition of Culture* – a title which some readers declared to be pretentious and pedantic, and others declared to be evidence of mock-modesty. In this book I included, perhaps somewhat irrelevantly, a chapter treating a selection of what I believed to be current fallacies of educational theory. The chapter could not pretend to any unity or structure other than that of enumeration, and perhaps its chief function was to appease the feeling of irritation with a good deal of nonsense that had been talked and written in England during the war years. Having relieved the emotions with which my mind – or my liver – was charged, I felt much better; and thought that I should never be impelled to return to this subject. But, unfortunately, this chapter caught the eye of a very distinguished educator,[1] who, after a few polite commendations, exposed me publicly as the author of a mass of contradictions; and, in effect, called upon me to produce something more coherent or make my apology. Well, this is an attempt to do a little of both.

4 I immediately recognised one fault: that while, in the earlier and I hope better composed part of the book, I had attempted to distinguish between at least three different though closely related [63] meanings which the word *culture* has in different contexts, I had used the word *education* without bothering to analyse it in the same way. Yet it is immediately obvious that the word *education* means something different, to begin with when we are talking of what is offered and when we are talking of what is *received*; when we are talking of education as something done to people and when we mean what they do for themselves. We may mean the machine, or we may mean the contact of an apt pupil with the right teacher.

5 Here I must make an excursion. I have already exposed my willingness to risk the reputation of a literary dabbler in Education; I must risk that of a literary dabbler in semantics and semasiology. This is a still more forbidden preserve than Education; but the world is now so full of

---

1. Robert M. Hutchins, 'T. S. Eliot on Education', *Measure*, I (Winter 1950).

highly specialised subjects, the landscape is so completely divided into prohibited areas, with notice boards warning us that we must keep out, or that trespassers will be prosecuted, or simply to Beware of the Bull, that the literary dabbler is goaded to recklessness. So shall I mark off what I have to say on this subject – and abandon it later if it exposes me to too much derision – by entitling it 'Notes towards the Definition of Runcibility', or 'MacTaggart Refuted'.

6 The late John MacTaggart Ellis MacTaggart was a philosopher at Trinity College, Cambridge, who enjoyed a considerable reputation in his day. I have never read any of his works, but I believe that he was an Hegelian; an exponent of a philosophy now out of favour, except in the form of Dialectical Materialism. But it is said to have been Mr MacTaggart who offered the explanation that the word *runcible* means *tortoise-shell*. He based this interpretation upon two loci, one in *The Owl and the Pussycat*, and the other in *The Pobble Who Has No Toes*. You will remember that the Owl and the Pussycat ate their wedding feast with a runcible spoon; and that the Pobble's Aunt Jobiska had a runcible cat with crimson whiskers. Recognising that tortoise-shell spoons are sometimes made, and that tortoise-shell cats sometimes occur, MacTaggart affirmed that *tortoise-shell* was the only adjective applicable to both cats and spoons. Now, the question whether there is or is not any other adjective in the language applicable [64] to both cats and spoons is one I do not raise: I am ready to accept MacTaggart's findings on this point. Nor do I rest my objection on his inadequate knowledge of the works of Edward Lear; I mean, on the fact that in another poem Lear describes himself as going forth 'in a runcible hat'. It would be easy for any disciple of MacTaggart to get round that with a footnote suggesting that Lear was an eccentric – which can hardly be denied – and that anyone like Lear might well have worn the shell of a tortoise as a hat: pointing out, incidentally, the similarity of shape between the shell of a tortoise and the academic headdress of doctors of letters at some English Universities. No, I maintain that MacTaggart's method was wrong from the start.

7 It is a commonplace that the same word may develop two meanings which have no relation to each other except that of derivation from one root. Compare the verb *évincer* in French, meaning 'to eject, to dispossess', with the word *evince* in English, meaning nowadays 'to display, exhibit, manifest'. They both meant originally 'conquer' – they both started, that is, faithful to the meaning of the Latin from which they were formed. The modern use of the French verb is primarily legal. But the English verb has an interesting history. In the early sixteenth century,

when it still meant 'overcome, prevail over', it meant also 'convince' – overcoming in argument (of course, 'convince' retains the significance of victory), and to 'confute'. A little later, it appears as 'constrain, extort'; at the same time it could mean 'establish' or 'vindicate'. Towards the end of the eighteenth century it appears to make a sudden leap into meaning 'to make evident or manifest.' This leap is not so puzzling as it might seem, when we look at the quotation illustrating this meaning in the Oxford English Dictionary, taken from the *Voyages of Captain Cook* (1790): 'Their pacific disposition is thoroughly evinced, from their friendly reception of all strangers.' Here the meaning of 1790, 'to make evident or manifest', is not very remote from one meaning of 1610: 'to prove by argument or evidence'. And 'to make evident or manifest' gives an easy transition to the use from the early nineteenth century to the present day, that of 'display, exhibit, manifest'. Thus, the transition of a [65] word from one meaning to another may be easy, natural, and certainly in the history of *evince*, reasonable; each transition may be so imperceptible that the authors – and, we must not forget, the unremembered speakers – responsible for it may be unaware that they are committing any novelty: and yet it is a long way from the Latin verb *evincere*, to conquer, and the English verbs *exhibit* or *manifest*, which come from different roots. And there is a wide gulf between the meaning today of the English *evince* and the French *évincer*.

8 There is an obvious utility in acquainting ourselves with the history of important words, because without this understanding we are always reading modern meanings into the older texts of English literature. It is as necessary as it is to know, for example, that *suspenders* in England hold up socks, and that in America they support *pants*, which are held up in England by *braces*, and are not called *pants*, because that term is reserved for the garment underneath the American pants. But besides the variations of meaning of the same word in the same place at different times, and at the same time in different places, there is the still more important variation of meaning of the same word at the same time in the same place. Before proceeding farther, I want to suggest that this wobbliness of words is not something to be deplored. We should not try to pin a word down to one meaning, which it should have at all times, in all places, and for everybody. Of course there must be many words in a language which are relatively at least fixed always to one meaning. To say nothing of scientific terms, there are many substantives which name concrete objects and must have meant essentially the same thing throughout the history of the language: such as those two words which used to be employed by philosophers when they were considering

whether anything existed or not – namely, *table* and *chair*. But there are also many words which *must* change their meaning, because it is their changes in meaning that keep a language *alive*, or rather, that indicate that the language *is* alive. If they did not change, it would mean either that we were living exactly the same life as our ancestors (the rate of change in the meanings of words in the language of a primitive tribe I should [66] expect, other things being equal, to be very slow) or else that our language was no longer adequate to our needs – in which case, the more progressive language of some neighbour might supplant it.

9 Related to the change of meaning of words from one generation to another, are the variations of meaning which they may come to have at the same time, and it is these variations with which I am here concerned. When two words from the same root have acquired such diverse meanings in two different languages as *évincer* and *evince*, they are virtually two different words. The confusion would be intolerable if *evince* in English meant *both* 'to dispossess' and 'to manifest'. But there are many words which we must use in slightly different senses in different contexts; and the difference in meaning, though slight, may be very important. A great many of our confusions in thought arise from not observing that we are using the same word in several senses.

10 Now to come back for a moment to the word *runcible*. It is a nonsense word, but I think we can learn something about 'sense words' from examining nonsense words. Lewis Carroll's 'portmanteau' words, like *slithy*, *gimble*, and *wabe*, are not pure nonsense words, for he defined their meaning: neither is Edward Lear's *spongetaneous*. But *runcible*, so far as I can discover, is a pure nonsense word: being such, it has no root. It cannot be defined. But I should deny that there was no relationship between his three uses of the same word. The rightness of the word, in each of these uses, the fact that it satisfies us as applicable to objects so different as a cat, a spoon, and a hat, is something that our sensibility acknowledges: we also feel that in each use there is a different shade of meaning. It is the nonsense shadow of the kind of word with which I am concerned, and so it cannot mean *tortoise-shell*. And incidentally, Lear was a poet; so, if he had meant *tortoise-shell*, he would probably have said *tortoise-shell*.

11 The word I am after, of course, is *education*. In the book in which I indiscreetly committed myself to a chapter of notes on education, I made, as I have just said, some effort to distinguish three senses in which we use the word *culture*: meaning something a little different when we are speaking of the individual, the group, [67] or the society as a whole. I maintained that it would not do to have three different words, or even

to say always 'culture A, B, or C', because these meanings interpenetrate each other and give significance to each other; but that we must be constantly on guard not to make statements about one category which are applicable only to another. It is possible that I have done so myself, even in chapters in which I was trying to distinguish. We can hardly avoid occasionally misleading our readers, for it is more than we can do always to avoid misleading ourselves. And we must remember that the meaning of a word is never wholly represented by its definition, that is, by other words; and that there is an implicit unity between all the meanings of a word like 'culture' which cannot be wholly confined within a definition: this is the unity which we feel in going through the several definitions of the word in current use.

12 What I did not do, however, was to analyse the several meanings of 'education'. I do not think that any of the authors whose statements I was calling into question had done so either; but that is no excuse. Like the authors whom I criticised, I let it be assumed that 'education' had one meaning only.

13 Some light on the complexity of the meaning of the word can be found by examining, as we did with *evince*, the history of the word. I return to the O.E.D. The word *education* follows a pretty straight course, except for including the training of animals, and for one technical application to the training of silkworms. It is first applied to the teaching of the very young: in fact, the first illustration given, dating from 1540, speaks of the education of infants one year old. It then proceeds to the training of young persons with reference to the station they are to occupy in life: that is, to the fixed group. (Early treatises on education, of course, were concerned with preparing young gentlemen for life at court.) It proceeds next to 'the systematic instruction, schooling or training given to the young in preparation for the work of life'; also 'the whole course of scholastic instruction which a person has received': that is to say, the word develops along with schools and colleges; but it still has frequently a professional connotation – legal, for example, or medical. Finally, it becomes 'culture, or [68] development of powers, formation of character, as contrasted with the imparting of mere knowledge or skill'. And it is at this stage that we begin to get into difficulties over the meaning of the word in different contexts.

14 As time goes on, and a language ages, it becomes more difficult to find out what words mean, and whether they are meaning the same thing to different people. And when we use the *word* 'education', we are probably using it either so comprehensively that in consequence of meaning everything, it denotes nothing, or else we have at the back of our

minds one particular meaning. We may, for instance, be thinking of the 'educated man'. But the highest type of educated man is not simply a man who has been through the best educational institutions; he is, to begin with, more educable than most, and is one who has done much to educate himself since he ceased to be a pupil. We may mean by the educated man, one who is very highly trained and highly proficient in some very narrow specialty; or we may mean a man who has had a good 'all-round education' – which we then may proceed to sketch out, though we seldom agree as to what education is all-round, admitting that no one person has the time, even if he has the capacities, to be educated 'all-round'. When we think of the individual, we are apt, I believe, and rightly, to be stressing what the man does for himself, rather than what is done to him. And the perfectly educated man, like the perfectly cultured man, does not exist; and the kind of perfection in question differs according to the environment. It is easier to think in terms of the group. In earlier times, of which there remain vestiges, it was the *social* group; in our time it is more importantly the technical group. So long as you are concerned merely with a small group of the same social rank, the question of the purpose or meaning of education hardly arises. For the fact that all of the pupils have much the same background, have nominally the same religious alliance, and will proceed to later activities within the same group, means that a great deal of 'education' in the widest sense can be taken for granted or ignored. And where a technical education is concerned, its aim is clear, its success or failure can be measured; the only question is at what age to begin. [69] The students will, no doubt, come from very different backgrounds, and will eventually scatter, to lead, apart from their professional activities, very different lives; but the question of what they should be taught, and in what order, is a manageable one. The real difficulty arises when the word *education* is taken in its most recent meaning, 'culture, or development of powers, formation of character'. For the meaning in relation to a social or professional group is distinguished by all the things that it is not; whereas in the widest sense, education covers the whole of life for the whole of society.

15 I am not objecting to this developed meaning of the word. I think it was inevitable with the development of society in magnitude, in complexity, and in organisation, and with the pressure so evident in our own time, towards the conscious direction and centralisation of more and more of life. But we have been forced into meaning all this by education, in an age when, being more conscious of our culture, we are more doubtful of it; and in an age when there are divergent views as to how character should be formed. And there is the increasing danger, that in applying

this definition to the purposes of our educational institutions, we expect them to do for society what society ought to do for itself. And 'culture, development of powers, formation of character', provide an especially hard task to be set before our educational institutions of the present day. These institutions are, in all countries, so vast; they bring together students of such different types; they have so many departments; they are at the same time so highly organised and so formless. We can easily aim at more, and accomplish less, than our grandparents and great-grandparents did.

16 I should like to return to the list of the three ends of education suggested by Dr C. E. M. Joad, which I criticized briefly in my book, because they seem to me as good as any three that I have seen given. They are:

> To enable a boy or girl to make his or her living.
> To equip him to play his part as a citizen of a democracy.
> To enable him to develop all the latent powers and faculties
>   of his nature and so enjoy a good life.

[70] 17 These make up, in fact, the professional, the social, and the individual aspects of education, in terms in which Dr Joad sees them. The first, the training for a livelihood, is certainly a permanent part of education. But it is, of course, to be interpreted in connection with the second and third. The livelihood has to fit in with the needs and requirements of society; it has also to be the sort of living for which the individual is best fitted by tastes and capacities. What is implied is a good society: for it is well known that in most societies some highly important activities are underpaid or even discouraged. A good society, as well as a decent individual, is also implied by the third end, that of 'developing the latent powers'. For some of the latent powers might be evil, and the development of the individual's powers is not solely for his enjoyment of life: some of them should be beneficial, and the rest harmless to society.

18 So we get to the next question, what sort of society should it be? I am not happy to say simply 'in a democracy' as do Dr Joad and others. In the first place, this is a statement to which every politician nowadays in every country would subscribe; and when everybody agrees on using the same word to describe totally different institutions, it becomes suspect. In the second place, as the word always suggests to everybody the particular kind of democracy in which he lives, the next step is to say 'my democracy is more democratic than your democracy'; whereas it seems to me that each democratic country has to fashion a democracy which will differ in some respects from those of others, but may be equally 'democratic'.

Next, a democracy worthy of the name seems to me a democracy of human beings, not simply of formal systems; much depends upon the citizens and those whom they choose to represent them. There may be a lack of accord between the formal institutions and the ethos of the particular people that operates them; and for this reason, and because of corruption amongst those who make politics a profession, or indifference or ignorance or prejudice or ill-regulated emotion amongst the public, a democracy can sometimes work very badly.

19 We all agree on the affirmation that a democracy is the best possible aim for society; and the widest definition of democracy [71] that *I* can find, is a society in which the maximum of responsibility is combined with the maximum of individual liberty. But we cannot leave it at that. For one thing, the concept of 'responsibility' seems to imply that of 'freedom'; and vice versa. One becomes responsible not simply by having tasks imposed which one cannot escape; for an individual to be truly responsible he must be free to shirk his responsibilities; and no one can be said to be truly 'a free man' who is 'irresponsible' – that is, at the mercy of his whims or appetites – a man who takes no responsibility for himself.

20 I should make it quite clear that I accept Dr Joad's assertion that one of the aims of education should be to equip its products to play their parts as citizens of a democracy. When I say I accept it, I mean that any other assertion which contradicted it *within the same area of discourse* would be false. Such an assertion would be, for instance, that 'one of the aims of education should be to equip its products to play their parts as citizens of an anti-democracy', or 'it is not the business of education to form good citizens'. What I want to recognise is simply, that a definition of one term is likely to involve the use of undefined defining terms. Now, this seems to be inevitable; it is a permanent condition of language and of thought. A definition is sufficient, when, for the purpose of using the defined term correctly, we do not need a further definition of the defining terms. It is inadequate and dangerous, when we extend the meaning of the defining terms to what was not in the intention of the definer – because there is always this limitation to definition, that it is made by somebody, and is apprehended by somebody. There are areas of exact thought in which it does not matter who the definer was; but here we are not in one of those happy scientific paradises.

21 Now, in the assertion under examination, I think that it is necessary to assume that we mean the essence of democracy – that we are not selecting one meaning rather than another. It must mean all that I have suggested a few minutes ago: not merely a form of government, but a common ethos, a common way of responding emotionally, even common

standards of conduct in private life. But the reader of such a definition is apt to respond [72] to the word 'democracy' merely with a few shreds of impressions of conventions, elections, going to vote, and the like. If he proceeds to something more articulate, he may proceed to define democracy, either in a way that suggests to some readers that he doesn't mean democracy at all, or else in a way that leaves them unsatisfied. Dr Edward Leen, an Irish theologian, in an interesting and commendable book *What is Education?*, says: 'It is agreed that a certain acceptable meaning can be given to the statement that youth must be educated for democracy, provided we are clear as to what democracy means.' He then goes on to tell us what he means. 'Democracy rightly understood,' he says, 'is nothing less than aristocracy'. He should, I think, have said 'aristocracy rightly understood', because he goes on to give his own meaning to 'aristocracy'. He means 'an aristocracy of worth, not an aristocracy of accident'. The admission to it, he says, is not by money or by birth, but by the personal, moral, and intellectual effort.

22 Now for one thing, this is not the common meaning of 'aristocracy', and I am rather suspicious of attempts to change the common meaning by violence. But, for another, Dr Leen has, it seems to me, merely pushed the problem a stage farther away without helping us to get there; for the problem of how to get the best men as rulers is one which remains to be solved. And furthermore, it does not seem to me ideally democratic, for it at least may suggest that society is sharply divisible into rulers and ruled; he has, it seems to me, limited his view of democracy to the political aspect.

23 It is beginning to appear that a formal definition of education, and a generalised statement of its purpose, is not to be easily come by. The statement 'to equip boys and girls to play their part in a democracy' is evidently only a secondary purpose, unless we choose to restrict very narrowly the meaning of 'education'. For it is obvious that if this is an essential part of education, many of the greatest sages and scholars of the past cannot be called educated; and we must say this even of the fathers of democracy. As a secondary purpose, it must be accepted only with full awareness of its limitations and dangers. The chief danger is that, in a democratic society, education may come to be interpreted as [73] *educational adaptation to environment.* Surely, no one is educated to play his part in a democracy, if he has merely been adapted to the particular routine of democracy in which he finds himself; he must be educated to criticise his own democracy, to measure it against what democracy should be, and to recognise the differences between what is proper and workable in one democracy and what is proper and workable

in another. He must be adapted to it, certainly: for without being adapted to it, he cannot play a part in it, he can hardly survive in it. But he must not be completely adapted to it in the form in which he finds it around him; for that would be to train a generation to be completely incapable of any change or improvement, unable to make discoveries or experiments, or to adapt itself to those changes which go on perpetually without anyone's having deliberately intended to bring them about. So 'education for democracy' is not so simple a matter as it sounds when we first hear it.

24 We have seen that 'training to earn a livelihood', which is one of the purposes of education, means training in a particular society: a livelihood is made in quite different ways in different societies, and even in the best societies some of the ways of making a livelihood are far from praiseworthy. And the third purpose of education, 'to enable us to develop all the latent powers and faculties of our nature and so enjoy a good life', also has its full meaning only within the bounds of a particular society. If we mean by 'a good life' the kind of life which that society considers good, we are committed to a programme of complete adaptation; if we mean by it, a good life independent of the social limitations of place and time, we must have some other standard of goodness. And the development of *all* our latent powers (even if we confine ourselves to powers for *good*) is limited by the livelihood we have to earn, and the society in which we earn it. So it would seem that education must be partly a process of adaptation to our society as it is; partly a preparation for the sort of society we want it to become; and at the same time we are aware that education, and our responsibility towards those we educate, are not comprehended by our conception of our society as it is, however modified by what we aspire that it should be. What education [74] would we design, for instance, for an individual destined to become a permanent Robinson Crusoe? It would have to be pretty comprehensive, certainly, in practical skills: there is very little in the way of applied science that would come amiss; but his education would have to include, surely, some mental discipline, in the way of furnishing him with the mental and spiritual resources with which that hero was so well equipped, for enduring solitude. What education, on the other hand, would we design for pupils who we knew would have to live in a thoroughly *bad* society? Bad, not merely corrupt as all societies are, but organised towards evil? Our educators, fortunately, do not have to devise curricula for these situations; but unless our definition of education can give an answer to these two questions, it is not a complete definition.

25 I do not suggest that we ought to try to give a complete definition; I suggest only that it is well to recognise the incompleteness of any

definition that we give. The meaning of a word like 'education' is, to begin with, more than the sum of the meanings given in the dictionary, meanings which are no more than an account of the uses to which a word has been put by writers throughout several centuries. But, when a language is alive, such words will constantly be used in new contexts; they acquire new associations and lose some of the old ones; and every great writer contributes something to the meaning of the key words which he uses, those which are characteristic of his personal style. Some of these uses of the word die with him, others enter into the common language. The process of enrichment of the meaning of a word cannot go on indefinitely, without some uses of it becoming obsolete and forgotten: partly because our minds cannot contain them all, even if we are acquainted with them through our study of literature, and partly because an indefinite extension of meaning would lead to ambiguity and confusion. It is one of the advantages of the study of a dead language that it is more manageable, that the words in it have come to the limit of their meaning: there they are in the texts, and their meaning can be no more than what the authors, during the time in which that language flourished, have given them. We do not want our language to become a [75] dead language; yet we are always trying, and indeed must try, however vainly, if we are to think at all, to fix a permanent meaning for every word.

26 We all mean, by education, some training of the mind and generally of the body also – so that we can include training for sport as well as for skills directed to some further purpose. But we can have no clear or useful idea of what education is, unless we have some notion of what this training is *for*. Thus we come to inquire what is the purpose of education, and here we get deeply into the area of conflict. We can, as I have said, produce definitions which are valid within a limited but unstable context, as when we speak of 'training to play our parts as citizens of a democracy'. It is fortunate that there are areas of discourse within which we can agree that some of the words we use do not need to be defined, inasmuch as we are using the word in the same way – whatever that way is. But there is a point beyond which we become aware that the same proposition means something different to two people both accepting it – this happens very often in treaties and other political negotiations; and then we have to try to define one or more words which we had been employing under the impression that they meant the same thing to both of us. Just as dogma may not have to be asserted until a heresy has appeared to provoke it, so a word may not need to be defined until we discover that two or more people are using it with a difference of meaning.

27 I do not suggest for a moment that we should abandon the attempt to define the purpose of education (and the definition of the purpose is an inevitable step from the definition of the word itself). If we see a new and mysterious machine, I think that the first question we ask is, 'What is that machine *for*?' and afterwards we ask, 'How does it do it?' But the moment we ask about the purpose of anything, we may be involving ourselves in asking about the purpose of everything. If we define education, we are led to ask 'What is Man?'; and if we define the purpose of education, we are committed to the question 'What is Man for?' Every definition of the purpose of education, therefore, implies some concealed, or rather implicit philosophy or theology. [76] In choosing one definition rather than another, we are attracted to the one because it fits in better with our answer to the question 'What is Man for?' We may not know what our own answer is, because it may not be fully conscious, and may be wholly unconscious; our answer is not always in our minds, but in the unconscious assumptions upon which we conduct the whole of our lives. The man who has made the definition which you accept or reject, wholly or in part, may be more aware or less aware of the implication of his definition than you are: at the moment when he makes the definition, and at the moment of your reaction to it, probably neither of you is aware of all that is beyond the margin of the field of discourse.

28 It might appear from what I have just been saying – if anything appears at all – that we ought to drop the question 'What is education for?' and proceed to the question 'What is Man for?' I do not know much about Man, but I am sure that our minds do not and cannot work in that way. We cannot discuss ultimate problems in a vacuum; the whole of our mind, sensibility, and experience of life must be brought to bear upon them; part of our experience has been obtained in dealing with these secondary problems in their more limited contexts; and it is these secondary problems which provide us with the reasons for attacking the primary ones. Furthermore, the secondary problem is more nearly and obviously related to the practical questions which arise every day, and which have to be dealt with immediately in some fashion if we are to carry on at all. Nor do I deplore the fact that so many and various accounts of the purpose of education are given. We must go on inventing new ones. Each answer is a clue to what education means to somebody; an incentive to finding out what it means for oneself. If it meant exactly the same thing to everybody, the world would be a very dead place indeed; so we have no reason to deplore the fact, if we find the meaning of education as elusive as the meaning of the word *runcible*. [77]

Variants from 1950:

2   schoolmaster, at a grammar school] master at a grammar school
4   to begin with] to begin with,
7   Oxford English Dictionary} O. E. D.
21 *Education?*, says] *Education?* says
    [Between '"Nothing less than aristocracy'." and 'He means':] He should, I think, have said 'aristocracy rightly understood,' because he goes on to give his own meaning to 'aristocracy.'

The Aims of Education
2. The Interrelation of Aims

TCTC, 78–92.

Revised from 'The Aims of Education. 2. The Interrelation of Aims', *Measure*, 2. 2 (Spring 1951), [191]–203 (Gallup C561).

In the fn. to para. 17 'reveil' has been corrected to 'réveil'.

1 So far, we have accepted as the most convenient starting point Dr Joad's list of the three aims of education: the professional, or, in the humblest way of putting it, training to earn a living; the social, or, in Dr Joad's way of putting it, preparation for citizenship; and the individual, or, in Matthew Arnold's way of putting it, the pursuit of perfection. But we cannot define education as merely the sum of these three activities; for if the term 'education' is to cover all three and not be wholly applicable to any one of them separately, we must appreciate some relationship, or rather some mutual implication, between them, such that each, while it may still be called education, is not the whole of education by itself. We recognise that the choice of a livelihood is limited, first, by the capacities of the individual; and second, by the kinds of activity favoured or discouraged by the society in which the individual finds himself, or in other words, the kinds of thing that people are prepared to pay a man to do. The choice of a livelihood involves some adaptation to the social milieu, although some men are willing to earn a very modest living in order to pursue a vocation which seems more worth while to them than it does to their neighbours. Furthermore, we observe that there are some ways of earning a living which are not in themselves commendable, and which we should not train people for: parasitical activities, which feed, at best, on the follies, and, at worst, on the vices of mankind. And this raises the question of moral criteria; so that the formula of earning a living is doubly inadequate, and we are led to both of the other aims on our list. Or, if we start from the formula 'training for citizenship', that implies

training to make a living; or, in a wider sense, (including those persons, a few of whom still exist, who are able to live on unearned income), training in some useful activity. We can [78] stretch the term 'useful' very wide so as to include activities which to the great majority of mankind seem quite useless; but I think we must agree that the man who is, according to *every* standard of measurement, completely useless to society, is hardly a successful product of education. And I think we must agree that the best citizens are likely to be those who develop 'the latent powers and faculties of their nature'; or at least that any society which does not endeavour to make possible the development of the latent powers and faculties of those who have the best latent powers and faculties to develop has a very narrow and mediocre conception of citizenship, and will not be a society worth educating people for. Finally, the development of the latent powers and faculties depends upon the pursuit of the right activities, including the best occupation for a livelihood that the individual can find; and depends also upon the individual's finding himself in a society in which his powers and faculties can be nourished and can bear fruit. So each one of these aims of education leads to a process which can in the right context be called 'education', though we cannot define education by any one of them alone. And each one of these paths leads inevitably to moral judgements and decisions which take us beyond the limits within which we should like to confine 'education' if the subject is to be manageable.

2 The danger of the list, as a mere list, is that we cannot long retain all three of the items in equal balance in our minds, once we start trying to educate people. This is not only because, in consequence of attending to one, we are apt to overlook the others; it may be also that in practice the three aims happen sometimes to be incompatible, and we are forced to emphasise one rather than the other. And when we find we have gone too far to one extreme, the natural reaction is to go too far to the other.

3 When I first revisited universities, after the end of the war, I was told that the new generation – both of those whose higher education had been interrupted or deferred, and of those a few years younger coming straight from their schools – was much more serious than that which I had known in the thirties, and than [79] that of undergraduates in my own time. I am speaking of universities in England, in America, and on the continent of Europe. And indeed, ocular evidence appeared to confirm this. On every quadrangle of campus, and in the streets of university towns, I saw earnest faces with concentrated expressions, of young people who seemed to be always in transit from lecture to lecture, from tutorial to their rooms, from their rooms to the library. It was suggested to me that the anxiety visible on every face was the anxiety about a future livelihood.

They were anxious to learn, to learn as much as possible in the shortest time, in order to qualify themselves for the jobs which they were out to get as soon as they had their diplomas in their hands. Now it seems to me that in my time we were far less concerned, during the earlier academic years at least, with what we were going to do afterwards. There were, of course, the minority who, unlike myself, had revealed a distinct bent, in scholarship or in some particular field of science, and were so devoted to their subjects that they looked forward already to a higher degree and to a lifetime of teaching the subject of their interest. But I do not think that even these were oppressed by the thought that they might have any difficulty in getting a job: they might not find a very good place to start with, but the future was open. They looked forward rather to earning a livelihood through their mastery of the subject they were interested in; but not so many of them were concerned simply with taking a degree as a necessary condition of getting a job of some kind they knew not what.

4 Now I am aware that many of my contemporaries left college having gained only the advantage of being three or four years older when they came to look for a job than they would have been had they not gone there. One profited, of course, from friendships, from extra-curricular activities, and from associating with men of one's own generation from various parts of America. But I am not at the moment concerned with incidental benefits, but with the formal tuition. And on the wrong side of the balance sheet, I must put the unrestraint of the free elective system as practised in my time. By passing examinations in a certain number of wholly unrelated subjects one could, in three or four years, [80] obtain the certificate of education – the diploma of bachelor of arts. The only limitation was that you could not follow two courses in the same year if their lecture hours coincided. I knew one man whose principle of choice of courses was that the lectures should all fall on Tuesdays and Thursdays, with no lecture on Saturday: thus, he was free to spend four days a week in New York. I should add that he did not follow even this course of study with sufficient application to qualify him for a degree, though he made a passing acquaintance with the appreciation of music, and with housing problems in mining communities. I am not, however, so much concerned with the effect of this system of education upon the idler, as with its effect upon the young man like myself, with a good deal of ill-regulated curiosity in out-of-the-way subjects, who took, for instance, a perverse pleasure in dabbling with late Latin and Greek authors without having mastered the real classics. It is not the system of education promoted by those educators of the late nineteenth century whose notions had been developed in Germany that I am defending; what I regret is the

disappearance of a state of mind among undergraduates themselves. Those who were fundamentally serious minded, and not triflers, were able to pursue their studies for their own sake, simply because they cared for them. The change came from economic, social and perhaps political developments in the last forty years, which have been much accelerated in this decade; and, if conditions are the same today, one cannot urge students to abandon an attitude which has been forced upon them by circumstances. I only wish to make the point that while the three aims of education formulated by Dr Joad are complementary to each other, they can also interfere with each other. This may become a little more intelligible if I suggest that the aim which a man sets before himself, in training himself to earn a living, and the aim he sets before himself, in working to develop and cultivate his mind and sensibility, are different in kind. The first is an aim in pursuing which you can keep consciously in mind both the end and the means. You decide on the general field in which you wish to find employment, and then follow the course of instruction laid down, or generally accepted as suitable [81] preparation for that employment. But for that cultivation of powers and faculties which tends to make us educated men, apart from our professional occupations, disinterestedness is necessary: you have to pursue studies for their own sake, for the love of truth, or wisdom, or at least curiosity, ignoring any practical advantages which may come to you from mastering them.

5 Of course, I have oversimplified this problem. If a man is to excel in any profession, he must love the activity for its own sake; and its usefulness to society, and the financial and other rewards that it brings him, are merely justifications of it. Most of us, at least, find it necessary to persuade ourselves that the work we do is of some importance. But, on the other hand, the man who is narrowly concentrated in his own particular work is not wholly an educated man; he may be not only uncultivated, but in outside affairs an utter simpleton. Most of us have to sacrifice possibilities of educating ourselves beyond some point simply because we have not the time for it if we are to get our work done. On the other hand, the man who does not concentrate on work of his own, but pursues his education in various directions, will be only a dilettante. In the world there is room for both the narrow specialist and the dilettante. But the fact that there are different aptitudes and functions in a world in which we have to be tolerant of others does not solve the educational problem. And it seems to me that often, in our attempt to balance special training with general culture, we incline to methods of education which produce men and women highly trained in some narrow interest of science or scholarship, and smatterers in everything else; we tend to put them through a course

of study which attempts to combine the technical institute with the young ladies' finishing school. For if 'training to earn a living' and the 'development of all the latent powers and faculties' are treated simply as two unrelated disciplines to which every pupil must be subjected, the latter will be no more than useful as a kind of recreation. When we see that we perform our specialised work all the more intelligently because of seeing it in relation to the work of all sorts of other people, living and dead, who have devoted themselves to quite other types of work than our own, we are on our way to solving [82] for ourselves – this means finding the right compromise for ourselves – the puzzle of the balance between those activities in which we participate, and those of which we can only hope to be an appreciative spectator.

6 Perhaps I can give this discussion more appearance of reality, or at least provide light relief in the way of something more apprehensible, by asking 'What sort of education should a poet have?' I don't think any parents have ever brought a child up with a view to his becoming a poet; some parents have brought up their children to be criminals; but for good and loving parents a poet is almost the last thing they could want their child to be, unless they thought it was the only way of saving him from becoming a criminal. I suppose that poets, during their tender years, usually show an interest in language and expression, and give some indication of a bent for the study of languages rather than science. This is not always true; I have known men who in childhood seemed to their parents to give promise of becoming Humphry Davys or Clerk Maxwells, and suddenly shifted their interest to literature at fifteen or sixteen. Certainly, the fact that a child writes verses is no indication whatever that he will become a poet. Nearly everybody has written verses: a wise parent should not discourage the habit, but should attach no specific significance to it. But if the young poet is of the usual kind, he will probably excel in languages, particularly his own; and is likely to be of the type which flourishes on Latin and Greek. Certainly, the poet in later life ought to be equipped with a good knowledge of Latin and Greek literature, make himself fluent in one modern language besides his own, and have a reading knowledge of several others. How few of us, however, satisfy that qualification: I certainly do not. But what else should he study, from the point at which it is evident at least that a literary education is the most suitable for him? In the first place, he usually has to make his living, and poetry is conspicuously the occupation by which no one can expect to make a living. For most men, there is the conflict between the claims of the occupation which they make their chief concern in life, and the claims of 'the latent powers and faculties'. But the poet has a

threefold problem to solve: he must earn a [83] living, he must practise and perfect himself in writing, and he must cultivate other interests as well. He must do the last, not merely in order to exercise latent powers, in order to become a cultivated man; but because he must have these other interests in order to have something to write about. Almost no form of knowledge comes amiss (besides, of course, the knowledge of as much of the best poetry in several languages as he can assimilate) because without other intellectual interests his experience of men and women will be very limited. The condition is that everything should be grist that comes to his mill; that he should have a lively curiosity in what men have thought and done, and be interested in these things for their own sake. He is perpetually engaged in solving the problem that every man must solve for himself, that of relating every human activity to his own; and he cannot tell how much, or what, of the subjects he investigates will be directly useful to him as a poet. But his poetry will inevitably be affected by his studies and interests, and the more he can assimilate the better. And finally, he has the problem of procuring a livelihood: he has sometimes to choose between a dull routine which provides little or no food for his mind, or an active and interesting one which leaves him very little time and energy. For some, this livelihood can be found in various forms of journalistic or paraliterary occupation; in teaching and lecturing. For others, something as remote as possible from their literary interests is desirable: something which uses none of the kind of energy that goes into poetry, and which brings them in contact with worlds far removed from those of literary and artistic circles. One cannot generalise about how a poet should earn his living in this or in any conceivable society. But the worst thing for him, perhaps, from every point of view, would be to do nothing and care about nothing, except writing poetry.

7 So far, we have seen that earning a living and cultivating one's latent powers are not altogether easy to reconcile, and I have cited the special case of the poet, who wants to write poetry as well as earn a living and cultivate his latent powers. We may now ask whether the process of equipment to play one's part as a citizen may present any possible impediment to either of the [84] other aims of education. It all depends on the content which we give to the idea of citizenship, and the means which we take to equip people for it. I think that the idea of the 'good citizen' is a moral concept; if so, we should expect the good citizen to be simply the good man manifesting his goodness in the social context. But we can still, I think, speak of a man as a good citizen whom we may regard as in some respect or other not a good man. A man may be devoted to interests of his country, his region, or his city; he may sacrifice pleasure, comfort,

popularity, in the public interest; wear out his energies in toiling for the public good; and yet be in private life vicious and dishonorable. To what extent can we call such a man a good citizen? It is strange, to me, that this elementary question, that of the relation of good citizenship to goodness, of public to private virtue, has not received the attention of writers on education such as Dr Joad. Possibly the cultivation of virtue is regarded generally as the responsibility – the only responsibility – which educators leave to the parents. But the question of how far a bad man can be a good citizen is an interesting one in itself, and one about which Socrates, if he were alive today, would not fail to have something to say. For Dr Joad, at least, it is clear that the ethical problem is one to be passed over, and that for him education in citizenship is education in applying intelligence to public affairs.

8 This becomes clear when he tells us of what Education in Citizenship should consist. First, those things which seem to him obvious. A child should be taught history, constitutional history (including instruction in how he is governed and how his governors are elected, and the structure of local as well as national government); biology and physiology, so that he may be made free (that is Dr Joad's phrase) of the main facts, including the sexual facts, relating to the working of his own body; geography, and international affairs. This is a formidable programme for any child; and it is entirely training of the mind. I dare say that a knowledge of the main facts relating to the working of his own body might induce a child to brush his teeth morning and evening, if he were so rational a child as Dr Joad must have been: most of us learn the habit first, and the reason for it later. There [85] are perhaps a good many other things that the child could learn, merely in order to be a good citizen: jujitsu, to cope with burglars and footpads; first aid, in order to save the victims (for the Good Samaritan, from what little we know about him, seems to have had the makings of a good citizen). But my main comment on Dr Joad's list of accomplishments is not that it is all simply book-learning, but that it omits any mention of training in moral behaviour and feeling. One would think that the good citizen was simply the well-informed citizen; but I am not convinced that a child, who in Dr Joad's words, 'carries at the back of his mind a political map of the modern world', will be better qualified to distinguish between good government and bad. Dr Joad not only ignores what is generally called 'private' in favour of 'public' morality – thus ignoring the question whether we can ultimately draw any distinction between private and public morality; even his public morality appears to be merely a matter of being well-informed, and being trained to reason correctly.

9 Some of you may already have thought that I am devoting too much attention to Dr Joad, who wrote a popular and very readable book called *About Education*. You may even have suspected that I have done this because his is the only book on the subject that I have read. You would somewhat exaggerate my illiteracy if you thought this: I have chosen Dr Joad, partly because he puts a typical point of view so well – the point of view of the middle-brow intellectual who was reared on G. B. Shaw and H. G. Wells – for Dr Joad is not very much younger than myself – and partly because his attitude towards education is implicit in statements sometimes made by more qualified educators. In a list of the aims of education by an authority whose name carries very much more weight in these matters than Dr Joad's, I read that 'every man has a function as a man'. With this I do not disagree: every safety razor has a function as a safety razor. I then read, 'every man has a function as a citizen or subject of the society in which he lives.' With man's function as a man I shall try to cope later. Meanwhile, I may say that I do not see how his function as a citizen can be separated from his function as a man. I think the latter is the more important, but for reasons [86] which I must postpone giving. But I return to my previous question, whether the really good citizen must not be also a good man; with the qualification that in certain contexts we are entitled to say that so-and-so is a 'good citizen', without committing ourselves to the assertion that he is a 'good man'. When it comes to training a young person, or, as Dr Joad says, a child, to be a good citizen, I still think that it is important first to train him to become a good man.

10 There are incidental questions which we may ask. Democracy is the best form of society: on that we are all agreed. The chief point on which we do not agree is, as I have said before, what is a democracy. Most of us agree that democracy is of the parliamentary sort: that is, there are two parties, one in, one out, and neither party should be too long in or out. The government of our nation is, of course, rather more democratic when the party which we support is in, than when the other party is. I have been told that 'the function of the citizen of a democracy is to rule in turn for the good life of the whole'. Certainly, both parties, whether we call them Republican and Democrat, or Conservative and Labour, rule, when in office, for the good life of the whole: though none of them, when out of office, is likely to admit that the nation is being ruled for the good life of the whole. Certainly, in a democracy, every man should know how to rule and be ruled. To be wholly ruler, to be wholly ruled, is to lose humanity: and, in fact, the humblest worker needs to keep his own offspring in order, while the most powerful despot may be dominated,

if by no constitutional powers, by wife, or mistress, or friends. The essential of a democracy is that there is no *total* rule: for total rule means that somebody is in control of affairs about some of which he is totally incompetent. In a democracy, scientists and scholars and artists should rule in their own spheres: it is not a democracy when a symphony can be deviationist, or a melancholy poem about an unhappy love affair defeatist and decadent, or a biological theory subversive.

11 It seems to me that we may raise the question, how far good citizenship can be an aim of a curriculum of education. To a large extent, surely, it must be the product of a training which is not [87] consciously aimed at anything so comprehensive, and at the same time so narrowly defined as citizenship. The habits of accepting authority, of being able to exercise responsible freedom, of being able to exercise authority when compelled to assume it, are acquired unconsciously in early years. If parents are public-spirited people whose interests are not selfishly limited to themselves and their family, children will learn from their example (for the unconscious influence of parents is much more influential than their precepts) that they have a duty towards their neighbours, involving the assumption of responsibility and the exercise of self-control. And in so far as their mental capacities permit, they will learn that this duty involves not merely habitual responses, but thinking and making deliberate choices. In a school, they will learn adaptation to a larger community; and in a college, develop their public sense further in societies and voluntary activities.

12 Now when it is said that 'in a democracy the good man and the good citizen are identical', I do not disagree, but I should prefer to put it more generally and say simply, 'the good man and the good citizen are identical'. For the former proposition seems to imply another to this effect: 'in a state of society which is not a democracy one cannot be both a good man and a good citizen'. Now, under an evil system of government, the good man may sometimes realize his good citizenship by opposing that government. He will not, from the point of view of his rulers, be a good citizen; but then, from their point of view, he will not be a good man either. If good citizenship implies goodness, then there is something universal about good citizenship. Of course, we can say that the Christians martyred in the Roman persecutions were bad citizens; and from the point of view of their persecutors no doubt they were. Perhaps we may say, however, that in a democracy the good man has the greatest opportunity to exercise his goodness in citizenship; and the bad man the greatest opportunity to exercise his badness – or perhaps rather that in a democracy a greater number of good men, and a greater number

of bad men, have this opportunity. This gives us a kind of definition of democracy, as the kind of society which offers these opportunities; [88] but observe also that while we arrive at our definition of democracy by the aid of the term 'citizenship', we are also implying a definition of good citizenship in terms of democracy.

13 I am afraid that when we pass from the term 'good man' to the term 'good citizen' we are insensibly passing from one shade of meaning of 'good' to another. But the test of the degree of difference is not found within the proposition itself, but in the further conclusions we draw: the difference may not appear until we have gone quite a long way. Similarly in the sentence 'since in a democracy all men are rulers, all men must have the education that rulers must have'. Now we see what this means, and we do not disagree; but I think that there are here two different shades of meaning of the word 'rulers'. An eminent British civil servant, a couple of years ago, gave a broadcast talk to explain UNESCO to his fellow-citizens, and said that UNESCO was a 'world club'. Now, one sees what he meant to convey; yet I could not help making the comment that a club was by definition an organisation of which some people were not members: if everybody in the world were a member, it would cease to be a club. The difficulty here is not so extreme. But even though we agree that all men are rulers, we must not overlook differences in kind and degree of rule. If we think of any particular type of rulers, we can see that some of them need an education differing from that of other men: a judge of the Supreme Court is one kind of ruler, the conductor of an orchestra is another; and they have both had very specialised training, as well as special native aptitudes, to qualify them for the exercise of rule.

14 The difficulty, and the source of danger, is the application of the general statement about the aims of education, with which everyone can agree, to more concrete problems. From the general statement about education for citizenship we may pass, through the narrowing of the meaning to *political* activity, and through the narrowing of the meaning of education to what can be taught in classes and from books, to the putting of courses in citizenship into our curricula. I do not say that this is altogether a bad thing, though much could be transmitted by the intelligent teaching of history. It may even be necessary; but when it is, we should try [89] to be quite clear as to why it is. It may be necessary as a palliative of conditions beyond the scope or control of the educational system. In so far as it is an attempt to educate the social conscience, to inculcate virtues, it is trying to supply a training which should be given by the family and the social environment, and is needed because the family and the social environment are not what they should be. In

so far as it is the imparting of necessary or desirable knowledge and information, it may imply that the conduct of our society has become so complicated, the problems so interrelated, that it is beginning to make claims on the ordinary citizen greater than he can bear. For example, in earlier times foreign policy was the concern of only a very few persons in any nation; and it was only in relations with one foreign nation at a time – and with many foreign countries not at all – that the issues were so grave that it behooved every educated citizen to inform himself. Now we are all constantly concerned with what happens everywhere. The Spanish-American War was, it seemed at the time, nobody's business but that of the United States and Spain: nowadays, a war anywhere, even if of apparently small dimensions, is a matter of concern to everybody everywhere. I do not wish to pursue this minor question, but only to point the issue. By 'education for citizenship' we may mean training in the essential faculties which are necessary both in the conduct of one's personal affairs and in forming an opinion about public policy: the ability to reason, to weigh evidence, and to decide how much one needs to know in order to make up one's mind, and the ability to perceive the fundamental moral differences of right and wrong and apply them. And, so far as these things can be taught, they can be inculcated through the study of history. But we may also mean courses of study in all the manifold social problems of contemporary life: in political theory, in public finance, in economics, in municipal government, or in the whole field now covered by sociology, several very vital questions arise. At what age should these studies be begun? And how much time should be given to them at each stage? I do not believe that you can teach these things, beyond a point, to those who are not going to be individually concerned with them; because most of us cannot study very deeply any subject which does not concern us as individuals, which concerns us only as *members*. I do not mean that nobody should be deeply concerned with these matters: that would be absurd. But those who are deeply concerned with them, and justifiably concentrate their attention on them, are those who are going to make their living thereby, and what is more important, to express themselves by making active contributions. That is, the subjects to which we can profitably give the most attention are those in which we hope to excel. The desire to vote always for the right candidate cannot become the ambition of a lifetime.

15 Education for citizenship, then, seems to mean first of all the developing of social conscience; and I have already suggested that 'social' conscience can only be a development of 'conscience': the moment we talk about 'social conscience' and forget conscience, we are in moral danger – just as

'social justice' must be based upon 'justice'. The separation in our minds which results simply from dwelling constantly upon the adjective 'social' may lead to crimes as well as errors. In the name of social justice we can excuse, or justify to ourselves, or simply ignore, injustice: in the name of social conscience we can do the same by conscience. The same sort of substitutions can occur with the word 'democracy'. 'Social democracy' sounds at first a phrase to which no one could object; but the denotation can be so manipulated that it can be made to point to something which to most of us, I think, may be anything but 'democratic'.

16 What I hope has emerged from this wild-goose chase is that our list of three aims of education – the professional, the social and the development of all the latent powers and faculties – is one in which each aim is implicated with the others, and also that each one may be pursued in such a way as to interfere with the others. This is due to the applications we make of each of three undisputed propositions; and to the fact that in each step of the inferences we make, we may be applying narrower and questionable definitions of a word which in the original proposition did not need to be defined. I have so far said least about the incorrect inferences we may draw from 'the development of the latent powers and faculties' or, if we are not merely thinking of hobbies and recreations, what Arnold called the 'pursuit of perfection'. I once knew a man who, being of independent means, planned a comprehensive humanistic education for himself. I am not quite sure to what studies he applied himself at an American university, but they did not include Latin and Greek, because he deferred these until he should get to Oxford or Cambridge, where he thought he would have them at their best; or modern languages and literatures, because he intended, after Oxford or Cambridge, to spend a year or two at universities in France, Germany, and Italy in turn. An extensive course of travel was to crown this culture. Needless to say he never completed the programme. The pursuit of perfection, or of comprehensive culture, is not enough, because it is a by-product of our desire to *do* something. To perfect oneself, so far as one can, and in the ways in which one is perfectible, may be a duty, but only in relation to some aim beyond oneself. To this point I shall return later.

17 I propose to turn now to the question of the general presuppositions, assumptions, or conscious social and political theories upon which any theory of education must be based. In closing, however, I should like to quote a contemporary French writer, Gustave Thibon; from his introduction to that very profound and original book *La Pesanteur et la grâce* by Simone Weil. It is the thought of Simone Weil which he is expounding:

The soul devoted to the pursuit of the absolutely good meets in this world with insoluble contradictions. 'Our life is impossibility, absurdity. Everything that we will is contradicted by the conditions or by the consequences attached to it. That is because we are ourselves contradiction, being merely creatures . . .' If, for example, you have innumerable children: that tends to bring about overpopulation and war (the typical case is Japan). If you improve the material conditions of the people: you risk spiritual deterioration. If you devote yourself utterly to some person – you cease to exist for that person. Only imaginary goods imply no contradiction: the girl who desires a large family, the social reformer who dreams of the happiness of the people – such individuals do not encounter any obstacle so long as they refrain from [92] action. They sail along happily in a good which is absolute, but fictitious: to stumble against reality is the signal for waking up. This contradiction, the mark of our wretchedness and our greatness, is something that we must accept in all its bitterness.[1]

Variants from 1951:

1 sum] *sum*

4 economic, social and perhaps political] economic, social, and political

11 defined as citizenship] defined, as citizenship
people whose interests] people, whose interests

13 a 'world club'] "a world club"

16 the social and the development] the social, and the development

[No break for para. 17 in *1951*.]

---

1. 'L'âme attachée à la poursuite du bien pur se heurte ici-bas à d'irréductibles contradictions. "Notre vie est impossibilité, absurdité. Chaque chose que nous voulons est contradictoire avec les conditions ou les conséquences qui y sont attachées. C'est que nous sommes nous-mêmes contradiction, étant des créatures . . ." Ayez par exemple des enfants sans compter: vous favorisez la surpopulation et la guerre (le cas du Japon est typique à cet égard); améliorez le sort matériel du peuple: vous risquez d'altérer son âme: dévouez-vous entièrement à quelqu'un: vous cessez d'exister pour lui, etc. Seul le bien imaginaire ne comporte pas de contradiction: la jeune fille qui désire une nombreuse postérité, le réformateur social qui rêve le bonheur du peuple, etc. ne se heurtent à aucun obstacle tant qu'ils ne passent pas à l'action: ils voguent à pleine voile dans un bien pur, mais fictif; le choc contre le réel est le signal du réveil. Cette contradiction, signe de notre misère et de notre grandeur, nous devons l'accepter dans toute son amertume." Thibon, quoting Weil, in his preface to *La Pesanteur et la grâce* (Paris, Plon, 1950, pp. xx–xxi).

The Aims of Education

3. The Conflict between Aims

TCTC, 93–107.

Revised from 'The Aims of Education. 3. The Conflict between Aims', *Measure*, 2. 3 (Summer 1951), [285]–97 (Gallup C562).

1 We have already observed that the term 'education' has become more difficult of definition as a result of social changes in the last three or four hundred years. We may distinguish four important phases. In the first, we were concerned only with the training of a small minority for certain learned professions. In the second, with the refinement of culture, we were concerned with the education of the gentleman, or of the *honnête homme*; and at the same time, with the supply of the rudiments of literacy to a humbler stratum of society. During the nineteenth century, the minds of educators were largely occupied with the problem of extending the benefits, or supposed benefits, of education as then understood, to an increasing number of the population. The problem was apparently simple: men still thought that they knew what education was – it was what a part of the community had been receiving; and so long as this education could be supplied to increasing numbers, educators felt that they were on the right road. But today we realise that we have come near enough to the end of expansion to be faced with a wholly new problem. It is parallel to the end of geographical expansion. In the nineteenth century, the United States was still pushing westward; European nations were still staking claims for themselves in colonial empire.

2 Now the area of geographical expansion is over – at least, by the methods employed in the previous century. In the nineteenth century, there seemed also to be only the problem of educating more of the members of society. But now we are at a stage at which we are not simply trying to educate more people – we are already committed to providing everybody with something called education. We are coming to the end of our educational frontier. Long ago we decided that everybody must be taught to [94] read, write and cipher; and so long as there were large numbers who could not read, write, or cipher, we did not need to look too closely into the question of what education meant. Every stage of development of our society presents us not only with new, but with more difficult problems, as well as with the same problems in more difficult forms: for we have now to cope with a new illiteracy, and a much more difficult illiteracy to overcome – namely, the illiteracy of that part of the population which has had its elementary schooling but has

become illiterate through lack of occasion to use what it has been taught. This secondary illiteracy is a new phenomenon. It is aggravated by the effects of radio and cinema, and by the replacement, in popular periodicals, of words by pictures. I am convinced that readers in England – readers of *anything* – can be classified partly according to the size of type to which they can give attention. One can say that the educated man is one who can read the reports of Parliamentary debates, and the reports of important law cases, from beginning to end – skipping intelligently, of course. There is a large number who can read a few paragraphs, if the type is large enough. There is an increasing proportion of the population which can read only headlines of any part of a newspaper not concerned with sport or crime.

3 This is a kind of parenthesis, illustrative of the fact that even illiteracy – even analphabetism – is not a problem that can be finished with and written off. My point is that now that we are committed to giving everybody formal instruction, everything must be called into question and examined – the forms, the subject matter, the methods, the purposes. So we have always new problems, and the old ones in new forms.

4 What happens in our thinking about education is, of course, only a special instance of what is happening to human consciousness. In the world today we find ourselves more and more trying consciously to manipulate what had been left to take its own course – that is, our area of conscious manipulation becomes bigger and bigger. A problem comes into existence through our ability to become aware of it; the awareness shapes the problem; and once we are conscious of a problem, we cannot dismiss it from [95] consciousness; we find ourselves under obligation to try to find an answer.

5 By an 'educational system' – whether we are considering a particular institution, or the general organisation of instruction in which we can distinguish national characteristics – we mean something which is a compound of *growth* and *construction*. I accept the view which refers to 'the relativity of educational theory and practice to a prevailing order,' and I agree with Professor Adolf Lowe when he says:

> ... no system of education can be truly appreciated or criticized except against the background of the social order in which it operates. The reason for this is that education always serves a social purpose, even if both teacher and pupil are unaware of the fact and experience the educational contact as an entirely spontaneous undertaking. Actually at each stage, from elementary to university education, powerful social forces are at work, moulding the

maturing individual according to a pattern, thus aiming at creating a definite human type.[1]

I have only two comments to make on this quotation: first, that the 'powerful social forces' may be *more* or *less* conscious; and may consist of the influence of a dominant class, or of a prevailing attitude towards life of the society as a whole, or they may be concentrated, in a totalitarian regime, in the deliberate aims of the leaders of a political party. Second, we must recognise that the system of education in every country is the product of history, and reflects the history, and responds to the temperament, of that people. In so far as a system of education is something shaped by the conscious aims of a few men – whether these men are organising the education of their own people, or creating a system for some more backward race – there is always a grave danger of borrowing or imposing something which does not fit the ethos, the way of life, the habits of thought and feeling of that people. In America we have seen different aims and methods promoted by educators biased by an enthusiasm for German, or French, or English systems of education, respectively – educators who were [96] sometimes themselves partly educated in one or other of these countries. The intellectual formation of a man like President Eliot of Harvard, himself partly the product of the German system, led, I think, to an exaggerated application of German methods. On the other hand, I think it is very likely that the model of English institutions in India, and of Western educational methods in the East in general, was too hurriedly and confidently imposed. But the confusion of the imitation of various European systems in America, and of Western – including American – methods in the East, is now in danger of becoming more general, as every part of the world becomes more aware of every other; as the concentration of wealth and power shifts from one nation to another; and as a greater uniformity of culture seems likely to result from the pressure of one civilisation upon another.

6 In the changes of which I have been speaking, in the continual enlargement of the area of human planning, it is apparent that we are living in an age in which *construction* has priority over *growth*. This is a development which we must accept. We have not time to wait, or to leave things to be fought out between various natural forces. We live in an age when towns have to be designed, when we have to have regulations about the type of building, the height of building, and the uses to which building may be put, in every city area. And in such an age we also find ourselves

---

1. Lowe, *The Universities in Transformation* (Christian News Letter Books No. 9, London, Macmillan).

obliged to be more conscious about what we are doing in our educational institutions. Only we must remember that being more conscious about everything is a very great strain, for it imposes a greater and greater responsibility upon fewer and fewer people. The psychological and physiological strain upon the member of a government cabinet today, the strain of being head of a government, or even secretary of state or foreign minister, is almost greater than any human being should be asked to bear.

7 We must be prepared then, so far ahead as we can descry anything, for a tendency to universal standardisation in education everywhere. When, a couple of years ago, it was announced that an agreement had been reached for standardisation of nuts and bolts between Britain and the United States, so that we should [97] be able to buy a nut in one country and fit it to a screw in the other, the announcement appeared in very small print, but it struck me as the most important news of the day. It was also a portent. And the other thing for which we must be prepared is greater and greater intervention and control of education by the State. And when I say 'the State,' I do not mean Illinois or any other state – I mean the central government in every country. It has been formally a fact in certain European countries; but in all countries I think that the State is likely to find itself more obliged to pay the piper, and therefore more impelled to call the tune.

8 There are obvious material reasons for this. Educational institutions, especially the big universities, become more and more expensive to run. They become bigger, they need always more buildings, more staff, and their maintenance involves a higher and higher proportion of administrative and financial work. They need bigger and bigger libraries and museums; more and better laboratories; and scientific equipment becomes more and more elaborate and costly. At the same time, the endowments bring diminishing returns, and the private sources from which new endowments flowed are running dry. In the end, perhaps bankruptcy might lead to the universities' having to be taken over by the State or closed down. But on the other hand, the central governments become more and more interested in what the universities do. (I am, I ought to say, thinking of conditions in Britain: how far these observations apply to conditions in America is for you to judge. The British government, owing to the great expansion of the Civil Service, is a very large employer of labour: the requirements of the Civil Service become more varied and specialised, and must be satisfied by recruits from all the universities.) Also, every government today is more and more concerned with the advances of science in such ways as the governments find needful. If the universities

are not equipped to pursue the kind of research, and provide men trained in the specialties that the governments require, then the universities must be provided with the funds – and directed in the use of them.

9 Nobody dislikes totalitarian government more than I do; but [98] it is not enough merely to hate it, or to concentrate our detestation upon its uglier manifestations elsewhere. We must at least recognise the existence of pressures which are modifying society everywhere, if only in order to be alert to counteract them and to accept nothing that we can do without. Not all men are moved by unscrupulous love of power, or by fanatical ideology: men sometimes find themselves in a position where they have to assume more power than they want – or in a position in which the assumption of power may plausibly seem to be the only way of meeting some crisis or relieving some intolerable situation. And if it comes to seem more and more important for the centralised State to control every branch of instruction, to exercise the ultimate control, then the 'social purpose' of education will come to be identified with the 'social purpose' of the head of the department of State responsible for education.

10 I have been following a rather torturous course to lead to a question which really started me on it. In what I wrote about education several years ago, a critic finds an inconsistency. He says, 'Mr Eliot's chief complaint of other writers on education is that they seek to use the schools to achieve social purposes they have at heart. Then he falls into the pit he has digged for others: he wants to use the schools to advance social purposes of his own.' Now, I do not think that anybody can think seriously about education who is devoid of social purposes of his own; and I am sure that these social purposes will guide him towards some of his conclusions about education. For anyone who denies that education should have a social purpose will be omitting something without which it is not education. But I think that anyone who considers education in relation to social purpose should try to be quite clear as to what social purposes guide his own theory of education; which are peculiar to himself, or to a group whose views are not shared by some other group; which he believes to apply to the society to which he and his sympathisers belong; and which, if any, apply to every society.

11 What I have been saying before, therefore, was intended to elicit the fact that the meaning of the term 'social purpose' is subject to a good deal of variation. In a liberal democracy it should [99] mean something discernible in the mind and temperament of the people as a whole, something arising out of its common ethos, which finds expression through a variety of intellectual leaders holding varied and sometimes conflicting opinions. In a totalitarian society, it may mean something formulated in the brains

of a few persons in power, deduced from a particular political-social theory, and imposed by every means of compulsion and indoctrination, so that it may in time become integrated into the common ethos. This is a very different kind of social purpose. In a liberal society every writer on the subject will have some social purpose of his own; something he wishes to retain, restore, or introduce through the means of education. Therefore he should know himself how far his assumptions are his own, and how far he is justified in assuming that they are shared by all intelligent men of good will. He should, in short, examine his premises.

12 Now as education, it has been agreed, has several aims, the social purposes have to be guarded from interfering with the other aims; and also, we have to allow for the possibility that we may have several social purposes which have to be reconciled to each other. I remind you of the sage words of Gustave Thibon and Simone Weil, which I have already quoted. I shall take as an illustration 'the ideal of equality of opportunity,' because my previous reservations on the applicability of that ideal seem to have provoked especially strong dissent. This ideal certainly expresses a social purpose, and is equally applicable to other things than education: education is merely one of the benefits to which men and women should ideally have equal opportunity. This ideal has two very strong grounds of appeal, which must be distinguished. One is that ability is wasted, of which society has need, through our failing to recognise and train it. This is a utilitarian argument; it has force, but of a very different kind from the second. This is, that it is not just that any person should be prevented, by our failure to educate him, from the full development of his latent powers and faculties. The second seems to me the more universal and compelling, because it is a *moral* ground. Now on this ground at least, the assertion that every child should have equal opportunity for education is one which nobody will [100] deny. The only difficulty comes when we proceed, from cherishing this ideal, to attempt to realise it; and when we give it priority, in our educational schemes, over other ideals of education.

13 If we pursued the ideal of equality of opportunity rigorously we should, it seems to me, have to see to it that no educational institution was superior to any other professing to supply the same grade of education. We should certainly have to see to it that no institution gave a better education simply because it could charge higher fees, and select its pupils for any other reason than intellectual promise. To what extent do the pupils at expensive private schools get a better education? What is it that their parents are paying for? I know that the motives from which affluent parents choose a school are often motives which have nothing to do with

education. There is the desire that their children should mix with other children of the same economic status and social type; there is also the calculation that their children will make the sort of friends who will be 'useful' to them in later life; there is also the simple snobbism attached to the name of a particular school or university. But there are better reasons than these: there is the attraction of a foundation with traditions, and a long list of distinguished alumni. And there is the best reason of all, especially for the private school – for it is in school days that this reason is the most cogent: the parents know that their child will be a member of a small group, that he will be taught in a class of fifteen or twenty instead of in a class of forty or fifty. Anyone who has ever tried to teach young children knows that the larger your class is, beyond fifteen or twenty, the less you can teach.

14 It is certainly desirable that every school in the country should have enough accommodation, and enough teachers, to be able to teach children in smaller groups. I thought, in 1944, that the Education Act of that year – an attempt, certainly, to improve state education – put the wrong things first. Instead of extending immediately the years of compulsory education, and thus adding to the number of pupils, we should in my opinion have aimed first at the supply of more teachers and accommodation for those [101] already in the state-supported or -aided schools; and undertaken to give better teaching than we do, to those under fourteen. But when will we, in any country, provide the money for this reform? Again, before we train more teachers, we ought to consider whether we are paying our present teachers adequately. I have never worked in a coal mine, or a uranium mine, or in a herring trawler; but I know from experience that working in a bank from 9:15 to 5:30, and once in four weeks the whole of Saturday, with two weeks' holiday a year, was a rest cure compared to teaching in a school.

15 I am told that 'no American advocate of equality of opportunity would argue that the rich should be forbidden to set up schools of their own, which might turn out to be superior to those supported by the State.' This is advocacy of a limited equality, an equality qualified by a good deal of inequality. If the schools established by the rich for the rich turn out to be better schools (though I do not believe this is altogether true) then what becomes of equality of opportunity? And how can we limit our equality to an equal opportunity to get a good education? If one child has better opportunities in life than another, merely because his parents are richer, will not many people regard this situation as unjust? It would seem that inequality in education is merely a special instance of inequality in general, and if we affirm a principle in one area are we not

driven to accept it in all? Certainly, some English advocates of equality in education would go much further than, as I am told, American advocates do: they would abolish the private school and the privately endowed institution, or bring them all into the state system.

16 The usefulness of the phrase 'equality of opportunity' is confused by the various meanings which we attach to the word 'opportunity' – it means different things to different people, and different things to the same people at different moments, often without our knowing it. That everyone should, as far as we can make it possible, be able to pursue the activity for which he is best fitted, is an aim which we can all applaud. One has sometimes observed the son of people in well-to-do circumstances, admirably qualified by talent and temperament to be a first-rate garage [102] mechanic, yet never having the opportunity to become one. Pressure of family and environment, the acquirement of tastes incompatible with the occupation for which he is best fitted, and perhaps also a defective education, usually stand in his way. I am afraid that to most people at most times 'opportunity' means a good many other things than the opportunity to develop the latent powers and capacities: it means opportunity to make money, to acquire a higher social status, to have power over others. For some young women, opportunity means opportunity to get a screen test; and only a small number of those who crave this opportunity deserve it. In short, opportunity is an empty term unless we can answer the question 'opportunity for what?'

17 It would seem, then, that most of the time, when we talk of 'equality of opportunity,' we either do not know what we mean, or do not mean what we stay, or else are driven to conclusions from which most people would shrink. It is avoiding the issue if we assume vaguely that 'inequality' means only the injustice of overprivileged and underprivileged social classes. It may happen that a child at a state school finds a teacher who will elicit his aptitude for a particular subject, and that a child at an expensive private school has just the wrong teacher. But what about overprivileged and underprivileged areas in the same country? A poor state or country may not be able to provide such good equipment or teachers, such good libraries or laboratories, as a richer one. Should not that inequality be redressed also? Thus the claim of equality of opportunity, if pressed to its logical conclusion, seems to me to lead inescapably to a universal and exclusive state system of education, to the cost of which the richer parts of the country, like the richer individuals, will contribute proportionately, but from which they will derive only the same educational returns as their poorer neighbours. And next, is it just that the citizens of a wealthy or advanced nation should have greater opportunity for education than

those of a backward one? Unless we maintain that some races or peoples are superior to others we seem to be forced toward the goal of a world system of education. And finally, if we are to have complete equality of opportunity in education, it seems to follow that we must have a uniform system [103] for grading the intelligence of pupils, so that each shall receive just the kind and amount of education to which his gifts entitle him.

18 If, as I have suggested, the thoroughgoing application of the principle of equality of opportunity (reinforced by the other pressures of which I have spoken) tends towards increased control by the State, then the State will have something to say about opportunity. It will find itself limiting opportunity to those vocations which serve the ends of the State as conceived by those who happen to control the State. I am not suggesting that it would, in a Western democracy, reach the point of direction of labour; but by offering greater inducements and advantages and facilities in one direction rather than another, it might tend to limit education to the kinds of training which served the immediate purposes of the State.

19 The idea of equal opportunity, it would seem, has to be considered in relation to each of the three aims of education from which we started; and it might be that in this connection, also, one aim would be pursued in such a way as to interfere with another. The difficulty arises from the fact that we cannot, in practice, wholly separate one from another. There have been, no doubt, men who were animated by curiosity and the thirst for knowledge, to such a degree as to be able to pursue their studies quite apart from their actual calling in life. There have been Spinozas who, in order to be free to exercise a wholly unremunerative activity and one not regarded by the world as particularly useful, have been content to earn a modest livelihood by grinding lenses. There have been other men, in humble positions, in whom the speculative or contemplative motive has been so strong that they found happiness in this double life. On the other hand, there have been men so completely limited in interest to the duties of their occupation that they have seemed to be hardly more than machines. Most men escape from this only by way of recreations and hobbies, ordinarily of a rather trivial nature. The ideal is a life in which one's livelihood, one's function as a citizen, and one's self-development all fit into and enhance each other. For most of us, the full pursuit of any of these aims must interfere with another; [104] and we are obliged, at best, to make almost day-to-day calculations and decisions between the several claims. We are all limited, by circumstances if not by capacities. To get anything you want you find you have to sacrifice something else that you want; and in getting it, you find that you have to accept other things that you do not want. Yet we must maintain that a man is not

educated if he is merely trained to a trade or profession; that he has to play his part as a citizen; and that, as a citizen, to be something more than a voting machine, and, as a worker, to be something more than a working machine, he must be trained and developed to something more than citizenship and work. And we find that the principle of 'equal opportunity' is meaningless – that is, susceptible of being interpreted by everybody in terms of what he *desires*, instead of what he ought to desire – unless we answer the question 'opportunity for what?'

20 There are obviously some 'opportunities' which ought to be available to everyone. Every man should have the opportunity of earning a livelihood in reasonable and decent conditions; of marrying and rearing a family who will also have the same opportunity; of rest and recreation, and so forth. You will observe that this sentence is made up of terms which will have different meanings in different social contexts: it is necessarily vague. But when we proceed beyond material necessities we get into a region of values. And so the assertion of 'equal opportunity' leads us gradually to the point at which we must know what we mean by 'the good life'. The question 'What is education?' or the question 'What is the aim of education?' leads us to this point. Now it is unlikely that we shall all agree on an answer to the final question, 'What is Man?' Therefore, what we mean in practice by 'education' will be the highest common factor of what enough educated people mean by it. So you may say that 'education' is likely to mean, in practice, a compromise between what different people mean by it.

21 I hope that it is by now clear that I do not complain of other writers that 'they seek to use the schools to achieve social purposes which they have at heart.' When we talk about education, we cannot stop at education as if it were a field which we could [105] close off; an area in which we could come to agreement whatever our differences of philosophy. We must have a social purpose in education, we must be prepared to make clear to ourselves and to our hearers what our social purpose is. But the social purpose itself should not spring from a prejudice, an emotional bias in favour of equality or hierarchy, a bias in favour of freedom or of order. Nor is the social purpose in itself enough, for it does not take account of the whole nature of man.

22 We have seen that, just as we are led, the moment we begin to think seriously about education, to think about citizenship, so thinking about citizenship leads us to something beyond citizenship; for the good citizen in the end turns out to be the good man; and that leads wherever the whole problem of ethics is going to take us. Now a view of education such as Dr Joad's, which suggests that training for citizenship and training for

the development of one's latent powers and faculties can be carried on in separate departments, may seem clear enough about the discipline for citizenship, but offers no general prescription for the development, or we may say 'the improvement' of man as man. As citizens, men must hold certain principles in common, and must agree on certain social habits; the fact of having to get on with other people imposes some discipline. But in the question of the development of latent powers, this view does not proceed to maintain that there are certain latent powers for good, and certain latent powers for evil, in man as man; it suggests rather, that each man has latent powers and faculties peculiar to himself, illustrated by the various ways in which men spend their leisure time. It is perfectly true that some men have an aptitude for and take enjoyment in doing their own repairs about the house; whereas others are much better advised to send for a plumber, a carpenter, or an electrician. I have no doubt that when Dr Joad talks of latent powers and faculties, he is thinking of higher powers and faculties than those of the handy man. Nevertheless, he is leaving the area of latent powers and faculties uncontrolled. The danger of separation between the social and the private life – which has the corollary that the only criterion of morals is whether one's [106] conduct is harmful to one's neighbours, and that every man should be free to do as he likes with *himself* – is that the social code, the code of citizenship, will become more and more constrictive, more and more exercising a pressure towards *conformity*; and that this public servitude to society will be compensated by extreme licence in whatever conduct is supposed to be none of society's business.

23 It is true that in a society organised on this principle the social may prove in the end to encroach more and more upon the private. In a society organised to carry out this principle, the rules of matrimony and sexual relations may be, at first, much relaxed. But then it may be found that this relaxation has undesirable social consequences – that it affects the birth rate unfavourably, in a nation which finds that it needs more workmen and soldiers; or that it has an unfortunate effect upon the children, who may begin to show psychological aberrations, or may grow up to be less desirable citizens than the government wants them to be: and then private life will be interfered with in the name of society. People may be ordered to have larger families, or to have no families at all, according to whether they are judged to be suitable breeders of future citizens. Thus the individual may find his privacy, his opportunity for exercising his moral freedom and responsibility gradually taken away from him in the name of society.

24 The restoration of a kind of order in people's private lives, however, when it is made in the name of a social purpose only, furthers the reduction of men to machines, and is the opposite from the development of their humanity. The assumption that you can have areas of control, and areas of complete freedom, must lead either to a suffocating uniformity of order, or to chaos. The actual degree of freedom or control may differ between one area and another. We are all more willing to submit to regulation of our public than of our private behaviour, and gradually, with the increasing complexity of modern civilization, we are prepared to submit to more and more regulations in the public interest. There are still people who object to being vaccinated, but few people now resent being isolated when they have typhoid [107] fever. Most people recognise that the state of their drains is a matter in which they have a duty to their neighbours; though not everybody recognises that he has the same duty in respect to the noise of his radio set. In a flat, one expects to have less freedom in many petty details of life than in a solitary cottage in the country. On the other hand, people in England since the war have objected, and they have my sympathy, to being forbidden to set up a tool shed in a country garden without a licence from the government, or being forced to employ a workman to do what they are capable of doing themselves. Fortunately, we do not yet submit to universal regulation in the public interest; and fortunately, we are still capable of being shocked by private behaviour, even when it does not appear to injure anyone but the culprit himself. And so long as we are capable of resenting control, and of being shocked by other people's private lives, we are still human. We are, at least, recognising that man is something more than merely a social animal: that there should be limitations to social control. And by being shocked (when it is something more than a prejudice that is shocked) we are recognising, however dimly, that there is some law of behaviour which is something more than a duty to the State.

25 What, then, should we mean by the development of the individual's latent powers and faculties, if we go further than Dr Joad, and consider the individual, not as if he were a seed out of a packet with no name on it, which we plant and tend out of curiosity to see what it will become, and what sort of flower or fruit it will bear; but as a seed of a known plant which has been cultivated for many generations – a plant about which we know what its flower or fruit ought to be, if it receives the right nurture and grows to perfection? How are we to try to educate good men, seeing that the idea of the good citizen implies the good man? Are we to be content with a rough-and-ready description of the good citizen, leaving everybody to define goodness according to his own taste and fancy? As you may have feared, this question raises for me the final question, that of the relation of education to religion.

Variants from 1951:

[No break for para. 2 in *1951*.]

2   read, write and cipher] read, write, and cipher

8   (I am, I ought to say] I am, I ought to say
    from all the universities.)] from all the universities.

13 affluent parents] most affluent parents

24 flat] apartment house
    or being forced] or to being forced

The Aims of Education

4. The Issue of Religion

TCTC, 108–24.

Revised from 'The Aims of Education. 4. The Issue of Religion',
Measure, 2. 4 (Fall 1951), [362]–75 (Gallup C564).

1 We have, so far, arrived (I hope) at the conclusion that there is a reciprocal implication between education for citizenship, or as a social being, and the development of the latent powers of the individual, or the improvement of 'man as man'. A man cannot be altogether a good citizen unless he is also a good man; and the wholly good man must also be a good citizen – at least in the sense that he is one who cares for the good of his neighbours. The distinction, and the relationship, are similar to that between work and play. There is something wrong when a man gets no enjoyment from his work; and to play any game properly you have to work at it.

2 Even, however, if we recognise the mutual implication of citizenship and individual development, we still lack a standard by which to measure one or the other. We therefore incline to take either as the standard for the other in different contexts. In one context, citizenship is undefined; we take for granted that whatever it means, we all understand it; and our notion of individual development will be adapted to the undefined citizenship. In another context, we may do exactly the reverse. The limitation to one point of view will tend to make us either authoritarians, placing strict limitations upon the exercise of individual choice or caprice; the limitation to the other point of view will make us libertarians, holding, as some people have, that the best government is that which governs the least. The latter will tend to believe that human

beings are naturally good, and that left to themselves they will flower into good citizens; the former that you can make them good by enforcing good laws – or else, that the residue of a human being's behaviour, beyond what can be controlled by legislation, does not matter. And in this contest it is likely to be the authoritarians who will win, because authority [109] is a short cut to dealing with abuses and injustices; and the contexts in which we are members of a mass are more compulsive than those in which we are individuals. In the latter, we stand alone; and it is easier to submit to an authority with which we identify ourselves than to tolerate nonconformity in others.

3 Although we may at this point agree that citizenship and individual development imply each other, we lack an outside standard by which citizenship and individual development can both be measured; for the measurement by each other leaves us in a vicious circle of illusory definition, defining each in turn in terms of the other. We have found that 'the improvement of man as man' is an empty phrase, unless we can agree about what is improvement; and that we cannot agree about this unless we find a common answer to the question 'What is Man?' Now we cannot expect to agree to one answer to this question; for with this question, our differences will turn out in the end to be religious differences; and it does not matter whether you are a 'religious person' or not, or whether you expressly repudiate everything that you call 'a religion'; there will be some sort of religious attitude – even if you call it a nonreligious attitude – implied in your answer.

4 There are two questions which have to be distinguished: that of the place of religion in education, and that of the place of education in religion. The first is the question with which we are more familiar. To the question of the place of religion in education, there are several answers. The most important seem to be the following:

    1. Where the State itself professes allegiance to a particular religion, or religious denomination, this religion may be affirmed, and taught, in all the educational institutions controlled by the State; and the teaching will be in conformity with the doctrines of this religion. Private institutions, for those who profess another religion or branch of the same religion, and for those who object to all religious teaching, may under such a system be either tolerated or suppressed: but as the [110] suppression of every form of religious teaching except that of the official religion of the State seems to me unchristian, I am not concerned with this extreme. (All educational foundations might be religious, and none specially favoured by the State. As this would be an

accidental situation, implying that the State itself should take no responsibility for education, it is a purely hypothetical situation which need not concern us.)

2. The complete separation of religious instruction from instruction in other subjects. This means that in schools and colleges no religious beliefs would be taken for granted or inculcated. Religious instruction would be reserved for the home, the Sunday school, and of course the theological training college.

3. The imparting in schools of such religious instruction as represents the common belief of the greatest part of the local society, leaving the doctrines of any particular denomination to be taught by the parents and their church. This is more or less the intention of the Education Act of 1944: it is, of course, qualified by concessions to those parents who wish their children excused from this religious instruction, either on the ground of wanting more specific doctrine or that of another religion, or of objecting to religious teaching of any kind.

4. A mixed system, in which no religion is taught in the State schools, but in which the adherents of any religion may set up denominational schools for their own children.

These are, I believe, the chief ways of dealing with the problem of religion in education. They are all, unfortunately, unsatisfactory.

5 We may group together the first and the second of these systems as being based on a principle, and the third and fourth as based on expediency. In drawing this distinction I am not making any value judgment: an inconsistent method may work better than a consistent one. I am merely saying that the expedient systems are not logically defensible. If the denominational school embodies the correct theory of the relation of religion to education, then it is deplorable that the greater part of the population [111] should be deprived of its advantages; if the secular school embodies the correct theory, then it is questionable whether the denominational school should not be, to put it mildly, discouraged. (Of course, in practice, they are not so different as all that: education in secular schools does not necessarily quench religious faith in its products, and the pupils who have been educated in denominational schools frequently disencumber themselves of such religious education as they have received, very soon after they go out into the world.) Not only cannot both systems be right; the denominations cannot all be right either. Nor can the supporter of the schools of his church be altogether satisfied with his privileges. For he must be aware that his schools are tolerated by outsiders because they represent too small a minority to be

worth suppressing, or because they represent too powerful a minority to suppress. He must be aware also that the costs of equipping a modern university are so great that his own church cannot supply itself with enough to go round, and that great numbers of young people will proceed from their church schools into a very different atmosphere: in England, certainly, there is no great university in which the religious foundation is anything but vestigial.

6 The introduction into state-provided schools of such religious instruction as can be agreed upon as representing the common beliefs of the largest Christian sects is an experiment of the Education Act of 1944. This is a compromise between teaching the tenets of one particular denomination, and leaving religious education altogether to parents and Sunday schools. What its effect may be remains to be seen. Behind it, however, there is a remarkable theory of which its promoters were no doubt unaware. It is implicitly an assertion that 'Christianity' is simply what all Christians believe in common, and that this is what is essential; that the differences are unimportant; and that it is possible to be a satisfactory Christian without belonging to any church. In this way the State may be initiating a theological doctrine of its own, in contradiction to all the churches. Children are to be taught in schools all that is necessary to be a Christian; leaving to the parents the option of teaching them what is neces-[112]sary to be Episcopalian, Methodist, Presbyterian, Congregationalist or Baptist – just as they may have private lessons in piano or violin. That is the theory. The *tendency* would be, if it went to the whole length of that unlikely course, for the several churches to be supplanted by a new State Christianity. For the implication of teaching only a part of Christianity is that that is the only part which matters.

7 So much for the third and fourth methods. I have said that the first and second are defensible in principle. The first, that in which all State schools will teach the tenets of a particular religion and communion, is possible only under one of two conditions. Either the nation must be homogeneous in religion, so that the official religion of the State is that of the vast majority of individual citizens, or else a dictatorial government must impose its own doctrines on the mass of society – or at least impose a conformity of outward profession – by discipline, inoculation, or fraud. For such despotism there is nothing to be said. The former is possible only in a few countries, and even in these it presents dangers so grave that it may become as unsatisfactory as any other. It may lead to the control of the Church by the State, or to the control of the State by the Church: two situations between which there may not be much to choose.

But it has one striking advantage in theory at least. From my point of view, it does not matter in this particular context whether the Church established in education is a national Church with a national head, or an international Church with an international head. If a National Church, then it should have a hierarchy independent of the State, and prepared if necessary to oppose the State; but where the hierarchy is itself composed of clerics appointed by the State, we have to rely on the State not to appoint men who will be subservient to it. In either case, an authoritative and independent church is desirable for meeting the difficulty which I raised earlier in connection with the third of our 'aims of education'. I said that the second aim, 'training for citizenship', was directed by the meaning of citizenship represented by an outside authority, in relation to which the individual has defined rights, responsibilities, and duties of submission; and that the third aim, 'develop latent [113] powers', or 'improve man as man', was left to every individual, or at least to every educator, to interpret as he pleases. It is the province of our religious teachers to instruct us in our latent powers and tell us which are good and which are bad, and to give a definite meaning to the improvement of 'man as man'. We need a Church capable of conflict with the State as well as of co-operation with it. We need a Church to protect us from the State, and to define the limits of our rights, responsibilities, and duties of submission in relation to our rights, and to our responsibilities and duties to ourselves and towards God. And, owing to human fallibility, we may sometimes need the State to protect us against the Church. Too close identification of the two can lead to oppression from which there is no escape.

8 The system in which instruction in schools and colleges is purely secular, leaving religious instruction to parents and voluntary Sunday schools, appears at first to be the antithesis of that which I have just been discussing. It achieves consistency by attempting to leave out the third aim of education, or at least by limiting the meaning of 'latent powers' to 'capacities for everything except spiritual life', and the meaning of 'the improvement of man as man' to 'the improvement of man as the highest of the apes, or as *homo faber et ludens*' – but not as a son of God. But the assertion that a man's religion is his private affair, that from the point of view of society it is irrelevant, may turn out in the end to lead to a situation very favourable to the establishment of a religion, or a substitute for religion, by the State. The religious sense, and the sense of community, cannot be finally divorced from each other. They are first formed, certainly, in the family; and when they are defective in the family, the defect cannot be supplied by the school and the university. But on the

other hand, the contrast between a community life in which religion has no place, and a family life for which it is reserved, cannot be long endured; and the weakening of the social side of religion in the outside world will tend to weaken it in the family also; and the weakening of the religious bond between members of the same household, beginning at that early age at which we first think that we are thinking for ourselves, will leave the family reduced [114] to the insecure bond of affection and sentiment. Thus, when religion comes to be more and more an individual matter, and is no longer a family tie; when it becomes a matter of voluntary association on one day a week when the weather is neither too good nor too bad, and of a traditional and more and more meaningless verbiage in the pulpit and at times upon the political platform; when it ceases to inform the whole of life; then a vacuum is discovered, and the beliefs in religion will be gradually supplanted by a belief in the State. That part of the social life which is independent of the State will be diminished to the more trivial. The necessity will appear for a common belief in *something* to fill the place of religion in the community; and the liberals will find themselves surrendering more and more of the individual freedom which was the basis of their doctrine.

9 Let me return for a moment to the terms in which I put the first of my alternatives; that is,

> where the State itself professes allegiance to a particular religion or religious denomination, this religion may be affirmed, and taught, in all the educational institutions controlled by the State; and the teaching will be in conformity with the doctrines of this religion.

Now there are obvious practical difficulties here, the first of which is that such a system is patently out of the question in any actual English-speaking country. We have a bias in favour of freedom: and we are not racially or religiously sufficiently homogeneous. But where such homogeneity is found, there are incidental dangers to the spiritual life of a people upon which I shall not dilate. The more general dangers are three: that the State shall control the Church, or fashion its own Church; that the Church shall control the State; or that the citizen shall think of himself as owing allegiance, on the same plane, to two States. For the term 'religion' is just as slippery as 'education', or 'democracy', or a host of other terms: we tend to mean one thing in one context and another in another, and to think that because we use the same word we are indicating the same thing. When we talk of Church and State we are contrasting two institutions, and the Church [115] is something more, and something different from a secular institution. We are ignoring the religious aspect of the Church; and religion, just because it comprehends everything, cannot be compared with anything.

10 There is another complication which I must introduce at this point. You may remember that I started by criticizing the three aims of education which I took over, as a point of departure, from Dr Joad. I suggested that whereas 'education for citizenship' might come to mean something too precise and restricted to the standards of the moment, education for 'the development of latent powers' was dangerously vague; and that it was for another authority than the State to instruct us in the cultivation and discipline of moral, intellectual, and spiritual powers with which the State was not concerned. An excessive interference and control by the State, in the answer to the question 'What is a good citizen?' and a State regulation of the discipline calculated to produce good citizens, would produce only *conformity*. An excessive interference and control by a Church, in the answer to the question 'What is a good man?' might also produce mere conformity. For there are many aspects of the good life, both for the individual and for society, with which the Church is not directly concerned. The direct question to which the church of any religion must provide an answer is 'What is necessary for salvation?' Several churches, at various times and places, have been so sure that nothing was necessary *but* salvation, that a good deal of harm has come of it: for instance, the destruction of the Library of Alexandria by the Moslem invaders, the spoliation of shrines and casting down of images in the Protestant Reformation, and the use of torture and appalling forms of death as a deterrent to heresy. On the other hand, in past ages the churches of all countries have been the centres for the arts; the religions of Europe and Asia have provided the motive for the greatest works of art of these continents; and the civilisations of Europe and Asia would be inconceivable without their religious basis. Yet civilisation, and the development of higher forms of culture, can only be considered, from the religious point of view, as by-products. The fact that we do not get them except through belief in a [116] religion does not imply that any church, or any minister of religion, is necessarily competent to pronounce in all questions of art – as inspection of some modern religious edifices will attest.

11 It should by now be apparent why I suggested beforehand, in turning to the question of the place of religion in education, that all of the possibilities I listed were unsatisfactory. It is at least clear that in a society in which the population is not of only one religion, or, within one religion, is divided into sects – and this is the kind of society for which we have to legislate in English-speaking countries – one or another compromise

must be practised, and each society or community must find out for itself which kind of compromise is least unsatisfactory for its own religion. So that in such countries any theory of education which the framer designs to be realisable must stop short at the point beyond which religious differences cannot be ignored. Unless we can get complete agreement about religious truth – that is, the ultimate truth about Man – we must not expect to be able to agree upon an ideal system of education which can be put into practice. Many situations in life have to be dealt with by compromise, and we must not repine over this misfortune of the human condition. But I think that it is very important, when we are forced by circumstances to stop short of the proper terminus of our speculations, to be aware of what we are doing; in respect to the present subject matter, not to pretend that a theory of education can be complete which excludes the ultimate religious problems – and I have said that 'What is Man?' is one of these – and which attempts to delimit for the theory of education an area within which religion can be ignored.

12 I am now, I hope, in a position to remark that the inquiry into 'the place of religious teaching in education' with which I have been occupying myself for some minutes is really unimportant for the purposes which I set myself in these discourses. Only, it is a problem which has to be inquired into first, before we can see how and why it is unimportant in this context. In my 'aims of education' it is not the place of religion in education, but the place of education in religion, that is the vital issue. I began with stating three aims of education on which I hoped that we should [117] all agree, and then attempted to show first that each of these aims was involved in the others, and that each both extended and qualified the meaning of the others. I tried to show, after this, that the pursuit of the meaning of these three aims leads us beyond the frontiers of the area which we should like to fence off as that of education, and forces us into the difficult territory of social and political philosophy, ethics, and finally metaphysics and theology. So that until we all come to agree in our theology, our agreement on educational questions can only be an agreement on what is possible and desirable for a particular society under the peculiar conditions of its place, time, and composition. And in our theoretical discussion of education we should try to make clear to ourselves and to others what philosophy is behind our opinions.

13 I do not want to leave you with the impression that I think we should postpone our discussions of education, or our attempts to improve present systems and correct their faults, until we have come to an agreement on ultimate problems. Nor do I presume that if we all came to hold the same philosophical and religious views we should suddenly all find ourselves

in agreement as to how to run our schools and universities. We should simply have got to a point at which the possibilities of confusion and misunderstanding and conflict would be minimised. There would remain many questions to which philosophy and theology could give no direct answer, or to which they would give a variety of possible answers; and there would still be a vast field for that disagreement, argument, and experiment which are necessary for activity and improvement.

14 Let me now, as I draw to a close, try to sum up the several conclusions to which I have come on the way. First, that 'good citizenship' cannot be wholly limited to the definition of it provided by a government, or the doctrines of any particular political philosophy. Second, that the question 'What is the development of latent powers of the individual?' or the question 'How is man as man to be improved?' cannot be answered without reference to theology, although much is included in 'improvement' which is not immediately in the province of theology. So, [118] while we have found that we must consult our political philosophers for the elucidation they can give of our second aim of education, and that we must consult our theologians for help in elucidating the third, and our theologians who are also political philosophers for whatever they have to say on both questions together, we find that none of them covers the whole area to which each aim applies, and we are forced to reopen the question.

15 We have found that the two aims imply each other, just as both are implied in the first. We can say that we agree that every human being should, ideally, be educated to do the best of which he is capable by his neighbours and himself. He should, furthermore, be educated to be able to decide between conflicting claims: for we are, in practice, often faced with the necessity for sacrificing self-interest – not selfishness, but a high self-interest – to social claims, or of sacrificing social obligations to the needs of our own essential self. There are the claims represented by the State, and the claims represented by the Church; but there are, furthermore, the claims represented by our own being. If I feel ready to write a poem, and I therefore decline to address a meeting on behalf of some good cause, or prepare a paper for an important weekend conference, what is the outcome? If the poem turns out to be a good one, I feel justified; if it is a failure, I feel guilty. The success is always uncertain; and as for the failure, I am thinking of instances in which one could have been certain, in sacrificing the writing of the poem, of being engaged otherwise in doing something at least moderately useful. And if it is difficult to decide for ourselves, it is often impossible to judge for others. Was Thoreau a good citizen when he retired to Walden? Many a man has pursued a

course which seemed folly to his family, or which appeared antisocial, or which meant pain and sacrifice for others, and we denounce him or praise him afterwards according to results which could never have been predicted. So I think we must allow a place after all to individual choice in 'the development of latent powers', although with all the qualifications with which we have now loaded the phrase.

16 There is, however, another lane up which I must chase a hare [119] before coming to my conclusion. So far, our aims have been for the individual: to train him to become the best that he is capable of becoming. We have been concerned only with the present, not with the past or the future. Now I suggest that one aim of education should be concerned with another obligation besides that towards the persons to be taught. If we consider only the latter, our curriculum may vary with every wind of doctrine; our notions of what is a good way of earning a living, of what is good citizenship, and of what is good individual development, may be at the mercy of the prevailing mood of one generation, or the caprice of individual educators. It should be an aim of education to maintain the continuity of our culture – and neither continuity, nor a respect for the past, implies standing still. More than ever, we should look to education today to preserve us from the error of pure contemporaneity. We look to institutions of education to maintain a knowledge and understanding of the past. And the past has to be reinterpreted for each generation, for each generation brings its own prejudices and fresh misunderstandings. All this may be comprehended in the term history; but history includes the study of the great dead languages and of the past of modern languages, including our own. Particularly, indeed, our own; for we need to understand the way in which our words have been used in the past, how they have developed and altered their meanings, in order to understand how we are using them ourselves. And to preserve the wisdom of the past, we need to value it for its own sake, not simply to defend it on the ground of its usefulness. To support religion on the ground of its usefulness is obvious error; for the question, of what use is man to God, is more important than the question, of what use is God to man; and there is an analogy – though I admit the danger of drawing such an analogy with temporal affairs – in our relation to our culture. For if we estimate the wisdom and experience and art of the past only in terms of its usefulness to us, we are in danger of limiting the meaning of 'usefulness', and of limiting the meaning of 'us' to those who are now alive. What I wish to maintain is a point of view from which it appears more important – if we have to choose, and perhaps we do have to choose – that a small [120] number of people should be educated well, and others left with only a

rudimentary education, than that everybody should receive a share of an inferior quality of education, whereby we delude ourselves into thinking that whatever there can be the most of, must be the best. And what I plead for is what Matthew Arnold spoke of as 'the knowledge of the best that has been thought and said in the world' (and, I might add, the best that has been done in the world, and that has been created in the arts in the world); that this knowledge of history, in the widest sense, should not be reserved to a small body of experts – reserved to them and parcelled out among them – but that it should be the common possession of those who have passed through the higher grades of nonspecialised education; that it might well form, for most of them, the foundation for many of the more modern studies which now tend to be substituted for it.

17 We may now, having taken account of the aims of education and pursued the definition as far as we could, proceed to inquire what is the use of the sort of conclusion we arrive at. We find that we have given no definition of education, that in fact education does not appear to be definable. The most that we can do is to list a number of the things that education might be expected to do, and try to show that each of these, if it is to be called education, must imply the rest. They are several of the purposes which education has been made to serve; we have been able to arrive at definitions, of a sort, of some of these purposes; and although we cannot define education *simpliciter*, our awareness of the mutual implication of its several purposes gives us a feeling of an identity of the word which is similar to the feeling I have professed to have of identity among the several uses of the word *runcible*. We must continue, however, to speak of 'education' when we mean one of several possible uses of the word; and this felt identity is what makes it impossible for us to substitute, for the sake of clarity, several different words.

18 The final question is, 'What is the use of such inquiries: that is, does it make any difference to education in practice whether we speculate about the meaning of the word or not?' Men have been training their children ever since they were men, and indeed [121] before it: I do not know at what precise point in the scale of living creatures the training of the young may be said to begin. The content of education and its form have varied according to the organisation of the society in and for which the young have been trained; a long tradition and many educational institutions preceded the time at which the question 'What is education?' needed to be asked. Or rather, we ask the question about the purpose of an activity at some time after we have begun to practise it; and we have found that the question has to be asked again and again, because the activity itself alters from generation to generation. But the machinery of education,

which has now become vast and complicated almost the world over, has to be kept going all the time. Many changes and developments are due to accidents, to response to local and immediate circumstances; some are due to the deliberate purpose of individual educators – right or wrong; some to the influence of a book, such as Rousseau's *Emile* (and Rousseau was a literary dabbler like myself); some to political theory or theological doctrine; some to wisdom, some to folly, and some to circumstances beyond our control. But when we set out to define education, what are we trying to do? We are not trying to compose a lexical definition – that is, the customary use of a word. We are attempting to isolate the common element in a great number of kinds of training, pursued for different ends, in very different civilisations. We are attempting, that is, to devise a master key for a number of different locks. But we are also attempting to find a stipulative definition: we are not merely trying to say what the word education means – that is, has meant to those people whom we consider qualified to use it – but what true education should be. We are aiming at a real rather than a nominal definition, and are in effect trying to persuade people to accept a definition of our own. But our motive for attempting a definition may spring from our objection to the practice of education which we have endured or observed, or to the theories of other people of what education is. Since I have insisted on the fact that behind every theory of education we find, implicit or explicit, philosophical and theological, as well as sociological premises, it might be thought the question is one only for [122] philosophers, and not for those engaged in teaching and the administration of educational institutions. But the latter have a fund of experience, and, if they are wise men, a store of wisdom, about education, which only those who have actually made teaching their vocation can have. It seems to me that it is the task of educators to think and to write about education, but to clarify for themselves the social, philosophical and theological presuppositions which underlie their generalisations; and it is for the pure theoretician, the philosopher or theologian, to refer his theories to the educator – the man who has had experience of the difficulties of teaching anybody anything. It is, incidentally, for the legislator, when he is moved by aught but political expediency, to consult both, as well as to do a little thinking for himself.

19 It is obvious that no lexical definition of education can answer the question 'What is education?' since all that a dictionary can do is tell us the principal ways in which the word has been used in the past, and up to the date at which the lexicographer compiled his account of the word, by those writers whose authority he respects. While we are aware of a relation

among these several definitions of the uses of the word, we seem unable to get any one primary definition, which all these secondary definitions will imply. The definition we are seeking is one which involves judgements of value; it will therefore be one upon which we cannot all agree, so cannot possibly be a definition in the dictionary sense. (Incidentally, people have been very far from agreeing upon a definition of the word 'definition.') As for the list of aims, whether it be of three or more, and whether we introduce subdivisions or not, there are several qualifications to be made. It is always possible that one or more of the purposes listed by a writer may be wrong, or wholly unacceptable to others; it is possible that what is in fact the same purpose may be expressed by different writers in quite different terms; and it is always possible that the list ought to be longer. We all try, of course, to reduce it to as few as possible: that is one of the rules of the game. But just as the meaning of the word education has developed in the past, and may be expected to develop and change further in the future, so it is possible that in some future and unpredictable [123] situation the purposes of education will have to be formulated anew, and also that new purposes may appear which cannot be reduced to terms of those already recognised.

20 It may be observed, also, that the more clear and distinct we make our ideas on the subject, the less is the likelihood of agreement on what these aims or purposes are. The more definite your views, the fewer people will be found to accept them. Most people will accept the assertion that education involves some kind of moral training; fewer will accept the assertion that it involves religious training; and of those who accept the principle of religious training, fewer still will agree on how far it should go and how dogmatic it should be. We may agree that the educational question can be satisfactorily answered 'when we get our metaphysics, ethics, psychology, theology and politics straight enough to think straight about it.' But this is a date, I suspect, at the other end of infinity. The prospect of the sages of any one of these disciplines agreeing amongst themselves seems remote; the prospect of the practitioners of these several disciplines agreeing with each other, and upon the relative contributions of their sciences to the perfecting of education, seems remoter still.

21 We are all, in fact, trying to persuade other people: that is, we appeal to their emotions, and often indeed to their prejudices, as well as to their reason; and the best we can do is to see that *as well as* (to our reason) does not become *instead of* (to our reason). We can at least *try* to understand our own motives, passions, and prejudices, so as to be conscious of what we are doing when we appeal to those of others. This is very difficult, because our own prejudice and emotional bias always seems to

us so rational. We are perpetually engaged in pointing out the extent to which other people's reasoning is deflected by their sentiments. I am quite aware that I have been trying to persuade, though I may not be quite sure of what. But although I should be discouraged if nobody agreed with anything I have said, I should be thoroughly alarmed if everybody agreed; because a statement upon which everyone can agree, in the discussion of topics such as these, is pretty certain not to mean much. I hope, however, that my main [124] motive has been to unsettle your minds, rather than to impose a theory; and while I have gone on defining, I have not been thinking of convincing, though you may have been thinking of your next cocktail party.

Variants from 1951:
- 4 Education Act] British Education Act
- 6 Education Act] British Education Act
- 8 beliefs in religion] belief in religion
- 9 affirmed] assumed
- 10 Dr Joad] Dr C. E. M. Joad
- 15 turns out to be] turns out

What Dante Means to Me

TCTC, 125–35.

Repr. from 'What Dante Means to Me', a talk given by Eliot at the Italian Institute, London, on 4 July 1950 and publ. in *Italian News*, 2 (July 1950), 13–18. (Gallup C554). See Vol. 3, pp. 803–11, in the present edition.

The Literature of Politics

TCTC, 136–44.

Repr. from a lecture delivered at a Conservative Political Centre Literary Luncheon on 19 Apr. 1955 at the Overseas League, London. Originally published in June 1955: Gallup A67. *See above*, pp. 107–14.

The Classics and the Man of Letters[1]

TCTC, 145–61.

Revised from 'The Classics and the Man of Letters', The Presidential Address delivered to the Classical Association, 15 Apr. 1942; publ. 13 Aug. 1942: Gallup A40.

1 Not very long ago, an eminent author, in the course of expressing his views about the future of education after this war, went a little out of his way to declare that in the new order there would still be a place for Greek. He qualified this concession, however, by explaining that the study of Greek was a field of scholarship of equal dignity with Egyptology, and several other specialised studies which he named, and that the opportunity to pursue these studies should, in any liberal society, be provided for the few who were particularly drawn to them. I read this in one of the periodicals which are found in the waiting-rooms of certain experts in applied science; and having neglected to make a note of the passage before being summoned to my professional appointment, I cannot quote chapter and verse, and therefore withhold the name of the author. But this statement, made without irony and wholly in a spirit of enlightened generosity, started the train of thought which I propose to continue here. I am grateful to the writer for having suggested to my mind the only possible role in which I can present myself on this occasion. In my earlier years I obtained, partly by subtlety, partly by effrontery, and partly by accident, a reputation amongst the credulous for learning and scholarship, of which (having no further use for it) I have since tried to disembarrass myself. Better to confess one's weaknesses, when they are certain to be revealed sooner or later, than to leave them to be exposed by posterity: though it is, I have discovered, easier in our times to acquire an undeserved reputation for learning than to get rid of it: but that is neither here nor there. My point is that if I made those claims for the classics which [146] can only be supported by the erudition of the scholar, or those which can only be pleaded by what we now call the education*ist*, I might jeopardise the cause: for there are far better scholars than I, who attach less importance to the study of Latin and Greek than I do, and there are teachers who can demonstrate the impracticability of the studies which I should like to promote. But if I present the defence of the classics merely from the point of view of the man of letters, I am on safer ground: and I think you will agree that the claim to be a man of letters is, after all, a modest pretension. I must, however, begin by explaining why I have used this rather indefinite term, and what I mean by it.

1. The Presidential Address to the Classical Association at Cambridge on April 15th, 1942.

2 If I were more specific, and spoke of 'the poet', 'the novelist', 'the dramatist', or 'the critic', I should suggest to your minds a number of particular considerations which would distract your attention from the view of literature as a whole which I wish to keep before us in the present context. Take, for instance, the term 'poet' and the objections which it would immediately evoke. We are commonly inclined to assume that the creation of literature, and poetry especially, depends simply upon the unpredictable appearance from time to time of writers of genius; that genius cannot be brought into the world at will, and that when it does appear it is likely to break every rule, that no system of education can foster it, and no system of education can stifle it. If we look at literature as merely a succession of great writers, instead of looking at the literature of one European language as something which forms a significant whole in itself, and a significant part in the literature of Europe, this is the view we are likely to take. Taking this view, we look at each great writer by himself; and looking at him by himself, we are unlikely to believe that he would have been a great writer, or an inferior writer, if he had had a different kind of education. The defects of a great writer's background are inextricably confused with its advantages; just as the shortcomings of his character are indissolubly associated with his shining virtues, and his material difficulties with his success. Can we regret, for instance, that François Villon did not choose to mix with more respectable society, or that Robert Burns did not have the same schooling [147] as Dr Johnson? The life of a man of genius, viewed in relation to his writing, comes to take a pattern of inevitability, and even his disabilities will seem to have stood him in good stead.

3 This way of looking at a great poet or novelist or dramatist, is half of the truth: it is what we find when we look at one writer after another, without balancing this point of view by the imaginative grasp of a national literature as a whole. I wanted to make it clear that I do not pretend that a classical education is essential for the writer of genius: and unless I can suggest to your minds that a great literature is more than the sum of a number of great writers, that it has a character of its own, much of my contention will be misunderstood. It is because I do not want to concentrate your attention upon the man of genius that I have used the term 'man of letters'. This includes men of the second or third, or lower ranks as well as the greatest; and these secondary writers provide collectively, and individually in varying degrees, an important part of the environment of the great writer, as well as his first audience, his first appreciators, his first critical correctors – and perhaps his first detractors. The continuity of a literature is essential to its greatness; it is very largely

the function of secondary writers to preserve this continuity, and to provide a body of writings which is not necessarily read by posterity, but which plays a great part in forming the link between those writers who continue to be read. This continuity is largely unconscious, and only visible in historical retrospect: I need only refer you for evidence to the monumental, though brief, essay by Professor R. W. Chambers on *The Continuity of English Prose*. And it is within this continuity, and within this environment, that, for my present purpose, individual authors have to be considered. When we look at them in this way, we can see that, among the great, even some of the most formal and correct have been also innovators and even rebels, and that even some of the most revolutionary have carried on the work of those from whose influence they rebelled.

4 It would be easy, indeed, to muster an army of great names, of men who have become great writers with very little educational advantage. Bunyan and Abraham Lincoln are only two among [148] the names more frequently cited. These men, and others, learned how to use the English language very largely from the English Bible: and it is the tritest commonplace that a knowledge of the Bible, Shakespeare, and Bunyan (I might add the Book of Common Prayer) could teach a man of genius, or a man of first-rate ability short of genius, all that he needs in order to write English well. But I would remark first, that it is by no means irrelevant that the translators of that English Bible were great scholars in their time as well as great stylists; and we have to ask, not merely what had Shakespeare and Bunyan read, but what had the English authors read whose works nourished Shakespeare and Bunyan? And I would remark next, that the education given to Shakespeare, or Bunyan, or Lincoln, would be about the most difficult kind to get today. It would be much more reasonable to expect to find a poet with the learning of a Ben Jonson or a Milton than either a poet or prose writer who had had the advantages of Shakespeare or Bunyan. No schoolmaster could afford the reputation of sending his pupils forth as ill-furnished as these men were. And there is too much to read for anybody to be expected to master, and to believe in, a few authors; apart from the fact that out of school there is every pressure to write badly, to talk incoherently, and to think confusedly.

5 It should be apparent at this point, that our primary concern in considering the education of the man of letters, is not the amount of learning which a man acquires, the number of years during which he is subjected to the educational process, or the degree of scholastic distinction which he attains: what is of prime importance is the type of education within which his schooling falls. The most instructive contrast of degree of education

within the same type is provided by Shakespeare and Milton, our two greatest poets. We can say of Shakespeare, that never has a man turned so little knowledge to such great account: we must couple Milton with Dante, in saying that never has a poet possessed of such great learning so completely justified the acquisition of it. Shakespeare's education, what he had of it, belongs in the same tradition as that of Milton: it was essentially a classical education. The significance of a type of education may [149] lie almost as much in what it omits as in what it includes. Shakespeare's classical knowledge appears to have been derived largely from translations. But he lived in a world in which the wisdom of the ancients was respected, and their poetry admired and enjoyed; he was less well educated than many of his colleagues, but this was education of the same kind – and it is almost more important, for a man of letters, that his associates should be well educated than that he should be well educated himself. The standards and the values were there; and Shakespeare himself had that ability, which is not native to everyone, to extract the utmost possible from translations. In these two advantages he had what mattered most.

6 If Shakespeare's knowledge was fragmentary and second-hand, that of Milton was comprehensive and direct. A lesser poet, with the learning and tastes of Milton, would have been in danger of becoming a mere pedant in verse. An understanding of Milton's poetry requires some acquaintance with several subjects none of which are very much in favour today; a knowledge of the Bible, not necessarily in Hebrew and Greek, but certainly in English; a knowledge of classical literature, mythology and history of Latin syntax and versification and of Christian theology. Some knowledge of Latin is necessary, not only for understanding what Milton is talking about, but much more for understanding his style and his music. It is not that Milton's vocabulary is excessively weighted with Latin words: there was more of that in the previous century. An acquaintance with Latin is necessary if we are to understand, and to accept, the involutions of his sentence structure, and if we are to hear the complete music of his verse. The present generation may miss, what we cannot expect from Milton, the colloquial style, the sound of the conversational voice, the range of mood and emotion which requires a more homely diction for its expression; it may sometimes find his syntax tortured. Milton has been reproached, and there is some truth behind the reproach, for writing English like a dead language: I think it was Landor who said so, and Landor is a critic to be treated with respect. Milton's was certainly a style fatal to imitators: that is just as true of the style of James Joyce, and the influence of a great [150] writer upon other writers can neither add to nor detract from his title to honour. The point is that Milton's Latinism is essential to his greatness,

and that I have only chosen him as the extreme example of English poetry in general. You may write English poetry without knowing any Latin; I am not so sure whether without Latin you can wholly understand it. I believe, and have said elsewhere, that the rich possibilities of English verse – possibilities still unexhausted – owe much to the variety of racial strains bringing in a variety of speech and verse rhythms; and that English verse also owes much to the fact that Greek for three hundred years, and Latin for longer than that, have gone to its formation. And what I have said of verse can be applied to prose also, though perhaps with less compulsion: can we really enter into the style of Clarendon unless we have at least a smattering of Tacitus, or the style of Gibbon unless we have some awareness of the immense power upon him of the classical and post-classical chroniclers, the patristic and post-patristic theologians, who provided him with his material?

7 If a classical education is the background for English literature in the past, we are justified in affirming not merely that a good knowledge of Latin (if not of Greek) should be expected of those who teach English literature, but that some knowledge of Latin should be expected of those who study it. This is not quite the direction, however, which I propose to pursue. I am not here concerned with the teaching of literature, but with teaching only in relation to those who are going to write it. For many generations the classics provided the basis of the education of the people from whom the majority of our men of letters have sprung: which is far from saying that the majority of our men of letters have been recruited from any limited social class. This common basis of education has, I believe, had a great part in giving English letters of the past that unity which gives us the right to say that we have not only produced a succession of great writers, but a literature, and a literature which is a distinguished part of a recognisable entity called European Literature. We are then justified in inquiring what is likely to happen, to our language and our literature, when the connection between the classics and our [151] own literature is completely broken, when the classical scholar is as completely specialised as the Egyptologist, and when the poet or the critic whose mind and taste have been exercised on Latin and Greek literature will be more exceptional than the dramatist who has prepared himself for his task in the theatre by a close study of optical, electrical, and acoustical physics? You have the option of welcoming the change as the dawn of emancipation, or of deploring it as the twilight of literature; but at least you must agree that we might expect it to mark some great difference between the literature of the past and that of the future – perhaps so great as to be the transition from an old language to a new one.

8 In the past twenty years I have observed what seems to me a deterioration in the middle literary stratum, and notably in the standards and the scholarship which are wanted for literary criticism. Lest you judge too hastily that this complaint is merely the creak of rheumatic middle age, I will quote a representative of a younger literary generation than my own, Mr Michael Roberts:

> By the summer of 1939 there were only two serious literary papers in England: an admirable quarterly called *Scrutiny*, with a small circulation, and the *Times Literary Supplement*, which like the more serious libraries, had fewer readers in 1938 than in 1922. The notion of the quality became submerged in the idea that 'it's all a matter of taste', and the untutored taste of the individual was tempered only by the fear of being excessively eccentric or excessively conventional. One ingenious publisher succeeded in making the best of both worlds by advertising 'A Novel for a Few People. 20th Thousand.'

9 The reasons for such a decline are no doubt complex, and I am not going to suggest that this is all due to the neglect of classical studies, or that a revival of these studies would be enough to stem the current. But the disappearance of any common background of instruction, any common body of literary and historical knowledge, any common acquaintance with the foundations of English literature, has probably made it easier for writers to comply with the pressure of tendencies for which they were not [152] responsible. One function of criticism – I am not thinking of the great critics or the classics of criticism, but rather of the hebdomadary reviewer, formerly anonymous, who has now more often the publicity of signature, though seldom the satisfaction of higher pay – one function of criticism is to act as a kind of cog regulating the rate of change of literary taste. When the cog sticks, and the reviewers remain fast in the taste of a previous generation, the machine needs to be ruthlessly dismantled and reassembled; when it slips, and the reviewer accepts novelty as a sufficient criterion of excellence, the machine needs to be stopped and tightened up. The effect of either fault in the machine is to cause a division between those who see no good in anything that is new, and those who see no good in anything else: the antiquation of the old, and the eccentricity and even charlatanism of the new, are both thereby accelerated. The effect of this failure of criticism is to place the serious writer in a dilemma: either to write for too large a public or to write for too small a public. And the curious result of either choice, is to place a premium on the ephemeral. The novelty of a work of imagination which is only popular, and has nothing really new in it, soon wears off: for a later generation will prefer the original to the copy, when both belong to the past. And the novelty

of anything that is merely new produces only a momentary shock: the same work will not produce the same shock twice, but must be followed by something newer.

10 The charge has been brought against the more original literature of our time, that it has been written for a small and exclusive audience – an audience not small and exclusive because it was the best, but because (so it has been alleged) it consisted of perverse, eccentric, or anti-social people with their snobbish parasites. This appears to be an accusation which the most dissimilar groups can concur in bringing: the conservative who regard anything new as anarchic, and the radical who regard anything they do not understand as undemocratic. With the political passions enlisted for the support of these judgements, I am not here concerned. My point is that this is a consequence, not of individual aberrancy – though it creates a situation in which the sham can easily pass, for [153] a time and with some readers, as genuine – but of social disintegration: in the literary aspect, of critical decay. It arises from the lack of continuous communication of the artist, with his friends and fellow artists and the small number of keen amateurs of the arts, with a larger public educated in the same way; of taste cultivated upon the literature of the past but ready to accept what is good in the present when that is brought to their notice, and so with the world at large. If an author's first discriminating readers are themselves isolated from the larger world, their influence upon him may be unbalanced: their taste is in danger of yielding to their group prejudice and fancy, and they may easily succumb to the temptation of overvaluing the achievement of their members and favourite authors.

11 It is one thing to pass these strictures upon the present condition of literature, or to voice forebodings of its diminished future, and quite another to put forward positive suggestions about the type of education most profitable for the man of letters, and the way in which it could be fitted into the general educational scheme. In concern with education we are attentive to the problems of the child and the adolescent; very largely to the average or the mediocre child; very largely to the child whose educational opportunities have heretofore been meagre. When we think of the larger pattern we are apt to think (quite rightly) in terms of the production of good citizens. The question I leave with you is the question whether we think the maintenance of the greatness of our literature a matter of sufficient importance to be taken account of, in our educational planning, at all? and even if we agree about its importance, whether education can take any responsibility for it? The answer may be, No. But the question must be asked, and the answer must not be a hasty answer. The right answer can only come after some very hard

thinking, and thinking with very wide scope, by many people. I would not dissimulate the difficulty. The problem of training an adequate supply of good scientists, in various departments, is one very much with us; it is, I imagine, one much more readily capable of solution than is my problem. But I do not think that it would seem so much more soluble, were it not that we all recognise, [154] under the pressure of material evidence, its necessity; and I think that agreement on the importance of a problem makes the solution of it much more likely.

12 I can see that the proper training of a man with the scientific bent, even now when the ramifications of the sciences are so extensive and the knowledge to be assimilated in any branch of science so vast, is more readily susceptible of precise determination. So, for that matter, is the training for any other art than that of letters. The painter, the sculptor, the architect, the musician, though they may have more difficulty in scraping a living, or in combining the pursuit of their art with an unrelated stipendiary job, all have a much more definite technique to master than that of the writer. Their essential training is more technical; the subjects which they must learn are more clearly indicated; and they do not need that varied general culture without which the man of letters is ill-equipped. Another difference, not unconnected with the foregoing, is that literary ability does not, with any certainty, manifest itself so early, or with such precise confidence of its goal, as does a bent towards another art. A desire to express oneself in verse is (or so my experience inclines me to believe) a trait of the majority of Anglo-Saxons of both sexes at some stage of their development: it may persist long after the lack of vocation is patent to everyone except the authors themselves. When a schoolboy composes good verses, we are justified in expecting that he will, in later life, excel in some pursuit or other – but that pursuit may take him very far from poetry or letters – it may lead toward the bar or the episcopal bench. The truly literary mind is likely to develop slowly; it needs a more comprehensive and more varied diet, a more miscellaneous knowledge of facts, a greater experience of men and of ideas, than the kind required for the practice of the other arts. It therefore presents a more baffling educational problem. In saying this, I am not arrogating any preeminence for that art of letters itself: I am merely pointing out a difference in the preparation.

13 I should like to make clear at this point that there are several arguments in favour of the classical education with which, however cogent and sufficient, I am not here concerned. Into the [155] question whether all children, whatever their destination, should be taught elementary Latin, and perhaps Greek – the question whether it is desirable, and then whether it

is practicable – I shall not venture. I would only remark that the question of the age up to which all children should have the same education, and the question of the common element in all education up to a later stage, is a very important one even from the point of view of the man of letters: for upon this depends the possibility of a general audience, the possibility both of the author's being able to communicate with people in all walks of life, and of their being able to understand each other. I would also observe in passing, that to postpone the introduction to Latin to the age at which a boy appears to be more gifted for languages than for other studies is to postpone it too long – apart from my belief that it would be most desirable for everyone to possess some knowledge of Latin even if none of Greek. I am not here interested, however, in the advocacy of the study of these two languages as 'mental discipline'. I think that the defence of any study purely as 'discipline' in the modern sense can be maintained too obstinately: I have, for instance, heard compulsory chapel defended, by an unbeliever, on the ground that it was good for boys to have a duty which they disliked so much. The defence of 'discipline' in the abstract, the belief that any 'mental discipline' carried out in the right way and far enough will produce an abstract 'educated man', seems to have some relation to the egalitarian tendencies of the nineteenth century which extended to subjects of study the same ideal of equality held for the human beings who might study them. A *disciple*, at any rate, is surely a willing pupil, and one who attaches himself to a master voluntarily, because he believes in the value of the subject which the master professes and believes that that master is qualified to give him the initiation he wants. Discipleship, that is, starts by a valuation – by the desire to attain to some particular knowledge or proficiency, not by the desire for training in the abstract followed by the judgement that this subject of study will provide it. For my purpose it is the value of the subject that is in question, not the incidental and necessary 'discipline' by which its command is attained. And as I am not [156] considering discipline in the abstract, so I am not considering 'education' in the abstract, or the somewhat barren question of the definition of the abstract 'educated man'.

14 For my purposes, also, the distinction between 'vocational' and 'cultural' education is of little use: apart from the disadvantage that 'vocational' is apt to connote merely a salary and a pension, and 'cultural' to connote an 'education for leisure' which is either a refined hedonism or a skill to practise harmless hobbies. The writer, *qua* writer, seldom draws a salary, and he has no problem of occupying a supposed leisure. Everything may be grist to his mill, and the more knowledge of every kind that he can assimilate the better: the serious distinction, for him, is between the subjects which he should be taught, and the subjects which he should acquire by himself. His business is communication through language: when he is an imaginative writer, he is engaged in the most difficult form of communication, where precision is of the utmost importance, a precision which cannot be given beforehand but has to be found in every new phrase. In order to understand language in the way in which the man of letters should understand it, we must know the various purposes for which language has been used; and that involves some knowledge of the subjects for the communication of which men have used language in the past: notably of history, for you cannot understand the literature of the past without some knowledge of the conditions under which it was written, and the sort of people who wrote it; of logic, for that is an investigation of the anatomy of thought in language; of philosophy, for that is the attempt to use language in the most abstract way possible.

15 Into this already formidable programme we have to introduce at some stage at least one modern foreign language as well as our own language and the classics. It should be a major language with a parallel development to our own, and with a flourishing contemporary literature; for we are greatly helped to develop objectivity of taste if we can appreciate the work of foreign authors, living in the same world as ourselves, and expressing their vision of it in another great language. The possession of several foreign languages is of course better than of one alone; but it is impossible [157] to understand the language, the literature, and the people of more than one foreign country equally well. In our time, the most important foreign language for the man of letters, has been French: and I need not remind you that for French a knowledge of Latin is still more important, and a knowledge of Greek hardly less important, than for English. For a man of very exceptional linguistic ability, who was not already sunk beneath the burden of the acquirements I recommend, I believe that an acquaintance with some great and more remote language might be a very valuable addition; Hebrew suggests itself, but both for extreme difference of structure and intellectual dignity a very good choice would be Chinese: but to mention this is to scan the very horizon of possibility.

16 All these branches of learning have to be acquired through teachers; and there does not appear to be much space left in the curriculum for scientific subjects. I am assuming however that my excellent man of letters will have had (what I did not attain) enough training at school in the language of mathematics not to be completely baffled when he attempts, by himself, to understand the general significance of some scientific discovery. The only reason of universal applicability, why he could not

acquire more detailed scientific knowledge in his formal education, is the very obvious one that there was not time: for I have allowed for some hours to be spent in eating, sleeping, social ritual, conviviality, worship, athletic activities, and physical training. It is most desirable that he should be able, throughout his life, to take an interest in subjects in which he has not been trained; for, as I have suggested, to a person of some power of imagination almost anything can be of use. It is sometimes suggested that the wonders of science provide nourishment for the imagination. I am sure they can; but I think a distinction should be drawn between the imagination of a great scientist, arriving at a discovery on the basis of observed phenomena, the significance of which has escaped other equally well trained and informed scientists, and the imagination of a Lucretius, or even a Shelley, informing their scientific knowledge with an emotional life with which the scientist, as such, has no concern.

[158] 17 I have not, as you see, been urging the claims of the 'cultural' or general, education against specialised; for in its way, the education of the man of letters must be itself specialised and 'vocational'. But we have to face one more difficulty. I have made clear that I am not attempting to legislate for the man of genius, but for the environment of men of letters into which he will be born or find his way. But on the other hand you cannot draw a sharp line between the man of letters and his audience, between the critic in print and the critic in conversation. Nobody suffers more from being limited to the society of his own profession than does the writer: it is still worse when his audience is composed chiefly of other writers or would-be writers. He needs a small public of substantially the same education as himself, as well as the same tastes; a larger public with some common background with him; and finally he should have something in common with everyone who has intelligence and sensibility and can read his language. The problem of the survival of English literature, therefore, brings us to the problem of the need for unity in education, the need for some unification which will not be to the detriment of any of the branches of learning and investigation, scientific or humanistic. The problem, so much greater than any problem of administration, organisation, or curricular devices, because it is a spiritual problem, because its solution involves not merely planning, but *growing* a pattern of values, is so vast a problem that it is not one for the educational specialist alone, but for all who are concerned with the structure of society. It is one with which I have no more to do here than to show my awareness of it. My only contribution is to proclaim that the future of English Literature will be deeply affected by the way in which we solve or fail to solve this problem.

18 My particular thesis has been that the maintenance of classical education is essential to the maintenance of the continuity of English Literature. How, and by what adaptation to the necessary, the desirable, and the inevitable, the place for the classics in education is to be found is not a subject on which I have the right to claim your attention. But I am sure that this is one important line of defence of the classics. The standards of the highest scholarship have to be kept up, and the work of research honoured: [159] it is necessary that the prestige of the great scholars should not be allowed to dwindle. That there will continue to be a place for the great scholar – without whom the whole fabric of classical education crumbles – I do not doubt: what is less certain is that in the future he will be discovered young enough to be given the proper training; and that he will be allowed any greater role than that of preparing a few younger men to carry on his work, without prospect of wider influence. The second group is that of non-professional scholarship and of scholarship in other fields in which an accurate knowledge of the classical languages is, or should be required; it includes not only the theologians and the historians, but the clergy and ministry, the teachers of modern language and literature, and the literary critics. For the last of these, certainly, it should hardly be enough that he should have spent some years at school in acquiring languages, if he never afterwards opens a text: he must have the literature accessible and operative in his taste and judgement; he must be able to enjoy it. But the maintenance of these types of scholarship is not enough or even possible unless some knowledge of the civilisations of Greece and Rome, some respect for their achievements, some understanding of their historical relation to our own, and some acquaintance with their literature and their wisdom *in translation* can be cultivated among a very much larger number of people: among those who (like myself) have not remembered enough to read the originals with ease, and among those who have never studied the languages at all. A limited preserve of scholarship will be ineffectual unless a much wider respect for, and appreciation of the relevance of, the subject-matter of this scholarship can be disseminated amongst those who will never be given the first-hand knowledge.

19 My assertions about the dependence of English Literature upon the Latin and Greek literatures, will, I am aware, have no persuasive influence whatever upon several classes of people. There are those who do not believe that literature is a matter of any great importance, and those who, while conceding a certain value to the literature of the past, do not consider it of great importance that English Literature should continue to take a front rank. There are those who acknowledge the importance of

literature, but do [160] not believe that one type of education or another will make much difference to its further survival. There are those who, immersed perhaps in the immense difficulties of providing some sort of education or other to the whole of the nation, consider this extra problem less urgent, or complain that they have so many other things to think of that it is more than can be coped with. And finally, there are those who want so new a world that they even welcome the prospect of a breach of continuity. And in many minds, no doubt, all of these attitudes can co-exist in a half-formed state; now one, now another, presenting itself in consciousness.

20 To attempt to confute all these objections would be an impertinence in the present company, and some of them come much more within the province of those who have had life-long experience of the classroom and the council chamber. My appeal can only address itself to those who already accept the contention that the preservation of a living literature is more than a matter of interest only to amateurs of verse and readers of novels; and who see in it the preservation of developed speech, and of civilisation against barbarism. They will be those also who appreciate the need, if the present chaos is ever to be reduced to order, of something more than an administrative or an economic unification – the need of a cultural unification in diversity of Europe; and who believe that a new unity can only grow on the old roots: the Christian Faith, and the classical languages which Europeans inherit in common. These roots are, I think, inextricably intertwined. I should not care to risk the heresy, upon which some religious-political writers have appeared to verge, of regarding Christianity as a European, rather than a universal Faith: I do not wish to be accused of inventing a new heresy to the effect that salvation depends upon getting a first in classics. But the culture of Europe, such as it is, is a Christian culture; and conversely, the traditional religious faith of Europe, including Britain, cannot preserve its intellectual vigour unless a high standard of Latin and Greek scholarship is maintained amongst its teachers. But these considerations are beyond the mandate which I have assumed for this occasion. And I do not wish to leave you with the impression that I am asking too much of formal education, either in the [161] sphere of religion or in that of literature: I am quite aware that an educational system cannot of itself bring about either great faith or great literature: it is truer to say that our education is not so much the generator of our culture as the offspring of it. But those who care for the preservation, the extension, and the advancement of our culture cannot fail to interest themselves, however unqualified they may be to pass judgement, in our classical heritage.

Variants from 1942:

1 rid of it: but that] rid of it. But that
2 at will, and that] at will, that
3 a body of writings] a body of writing
  even some of the most formal] some of the most formal
  even some of the most revolutionary] some of the most revolutionary
4 too much to read] too much to read,
5 important, for a man of letters,] important, for a great writer,
6 the learning and tastes] the learning and the tastes
  none of which are] none of which is
  mythology and history of Latin syntax] mythology, and history, of Latin syntax
  You may write English poetry without knowing any Latin] Without knowing any Latin you may write English poetry
8 worlds by advertising] worlds, by advertising
10 ; of taste cultivated] (of taste cultivated
   their notice,] their notice)
12 they must learn] they must study
15 the literature, and the people] the literature and the people
   language for the man of letters,] language, for the man of letters,
16 athletic activities, and physical training] athletic activities and physical training
   has escaped] had escaped
18 the desirable, and the inevitable] the desirable and the inevitable
20 the extension, and] the extension and

Ezra Pound: His Metric and Poetry

TCTC, 162–82.

Reprinted (not altogether accurately) from the first edn (Jan. 1918): Gallup A2.
See Vol. 1, pp. 133–50, in the present edition.

Reflections on Vers Libre

TCTC, 183–[9].

Reprinted from *NS*, 8. 204 (3 Mar. 1917), 518–19 (Gallup C39).
See Vol. 1, pp. 53–8, in the present edition.

In the last sentence at the end of the penultimate para. 'Any' replaces the original 'And'. I have treated this as an error rather than a sole revision.

[Memoir of Richard Aldington]

Richard Aldington: An Intimate Portrait, ed. Alister Kershaw, 24–5. Publ. 20 Dec. 1965.
The contribution is headed '*T. S. Eliot*'. Gallup B92.

I met Richard first in 1917, just at the time when he was being drafted into the Army and I took over the assistant editorship of the *Egoist* from him. After the war I saw quite a lot of him. We were on very friendly terms and when I started the *Criterion* in 1921 he became my assistant editor at a very modest salary. (I, myself, took no salary at all because I was on the staff of Lloyds Bank and it was forbidden for members of the Bank staff to have other regular paid employment.) I think that in those years we exchanged quite a long correspondence and I visited him at least once when he was living with a lady, whose name I have forgotten, at Aldermaston – a village which was still very rural and had not acquired its recent associations. Richard was very sensitive, not to say touchy, in some ways and I am afraid that with good intentions, but clumsy lack of imagination, I hurt his feelings once or twice very deeply indeed. After that, I saw nothing of him and he wrote a cruel and unkind lampoon of me and [25] of my wife who died some years later, and of friends of mine such as Lady Ottoline Morrell and Virginia Woolf. But then he was living, I think, in France and his attacks on other authors, the two Lawrences and Norman Douglas, were more direct in books about those writers. But that quarrel had since subsided and I exchanged letters with him a few years before his death. He had heard that a number of my letters to him were in the possession of a certain American university and wrote to me to explain that this was by no wish of his own, but that the letters had been in a box which he had left in charge of a man who he supposed to be a friend and who later denied having any such box in his possession. I have no reason to doubt his word and have nothing left but feelings of friendliness and regard.

I hope this brief communication is better than nothing. We were on the same side for a long time and I was the first to give offence, although unintentionally, which made a breach between us.

1966

A Tribute To Mario Praz

Friendship's Garland: Essays Presented to Mario Praz on his Seventieth Birthday,
ed. Vittorio Gabrieli, vol. 1 p. [3]. Publ. 30 May 1966 as *Storia e letteratura*, 106–7.
Signed T. S. Eliot'. Gallup B93.

My first acquaintance with the work of Mario Praz came when, many years ago, the *Times Literary Supplement* sent me for review his *Secentismo e Marinismo in Inghilterra*. I immediately recognised these essays – and especially his masterly study of Crashaw – as among the best that I had ever read in that field. His knowledge of the poetry of that period in four languages – English, Italian, Spanish and Latin – was encyclopedic, and, fortified by his own judgement and good taste, makes that book essential reading for any reading of the English 'metaphysical poets'.

Had I any suitable unpublished essay to offer, I would gladly give it now in tribute to a great scholar. I tender these few words in testimony to my gratitude and admiration, not wishing my name to be absent from the roster of men of letters who, as well as more learned scholars of the period, owe him homage.

A Note on *The Criterion* By T. S. Eliot

Printed in the folder issued in Aug. 1966 to publicise the reprint of *The Criterion*,
and written specifically for the folder. Repr. as 'PREFACE' to the collected edn
publ. on 14 June 1967. Gallup E20, B94.

The Criterion, which I edited throughout the whole of the seventeen years during which it appeared, was founded by (Lilian) Lady Rothermere at the end of 1921: in the first number appeared *The Waste Land*. At that time I was on the staff of Lloyds Bank, a position which precluded my accepting any salary: but a small salary was paid to Richard Aldington as assistant editor, and to my faithful secretary Irene Fassett, who accompanied me when I joined the staff of Faber & Gwyer. For a time *The Criterion* appeared under the joint auspices of Lady Rothermere and that firm, which became Faber & Faber. It continued to be published by Faber & Faber until 1939, when war became imminent: the prospect for a quarterly of very limited appeal was so unpromising, that we decided to bring the magazine to an end.

When starting *The Criterion*, I wished to include representatives of both older and younger generations, and opened with a contribution from that genial *doyen* of English letters, George Saintsbury. G. K. Chesterton was also a generous contributor. I am proud to have introduced to English readers the work of Marcel Proust. I am proud of having published work by D. H. Lawrence, and by Wyndham Lewis, James Joyce and Ezra Pound. I am proud of having published the work of some of the younger English poets, such as Auden, Spender and MacNeice. Throughout I had always two aims in view: to present to English readers, by essays and short stories, the work of important new foreign writers, and to offer longer and more deliberate reviews than was possible in magazines of more frequent appearance. I think that both of my aims were realised, and that the seventeen volumes of *The Criterion* constitute a valuable record of the thought of that period between two wars.

Index of Article Titles

This index covers all four volumes in the present edition. Various publications listed here have similar or identical titles or may have appeared more than once in different versions. Publication dates are employed to help distinguish these; articles published separately and as chapters within books are listed both within the book entries and under their own titles.

The *Action Française*, M. Maurras and Mr Ward	Vol. I, page 714
An Address (1952)	IV 63
[Address] (1959)	IV 444
[Address at Mary Institute]	IV 453
Address By T. S. Eliot, '06	II 768
After Strange Gods	II 781
Preface	II 781
I	II 783
II	II 784
III	II 795
Appendix	II 803
The Age of Dryden (*UPUC* 1933)	II 709
[The Aims of Education. 1] (1950)	III 835
The Aims of Education. 2. The Interrelation of Aims (1951)	IV 16
The Aims of Education. 3. The Conflict between Aims (1951)	IV 17
The Aims of Education. 4. The Issue of Religion (1950)	IV 18
The Aims of Education 1 (*TCTC* 1965)	IV 751
The Aims of Education 2 (*TCTC* 1965)	IV 764
The Aims of Education 3 (*TCTC* 1965)	IV 777
The Aims of Education 4 (*TCTC* 1965)	IV 789
The Aims of Poetic Drama (1949)	III 771
The Aims of Poetic Drama (1949)	III 780
An American Critic	I 23
American Critics	II 3
American Literature	I 217
[American Literature and the American Language] (1953)	IV 78
American Literature and the American Language (*TCTC* 1965)	IV 736
American Prose	I 513
Andrew Marvell (1921)	I 358
Andrew Marvell (1923)	I 415
Andrew Marvell (*SE* 1932)	II 492
An Anglican Platonist	III 209
[Anti-Semitism in Russia]	IV 547

Apology for the Countess of Pembroke (1932)	II 655
Apology for the Countess of Pembroke (*UPUC* 1933)	II 700
Appendix (*ASG* 1934)	II 803
Appendix (*ICS* 1939)	III 316
Appendix (*ICS* 1939)	III 316
Appendix I: The Development of Leibniz's Monadism (*KEPB* 1964)	IV 680
Appendix II: Leibniz's Monads and Bradley's Finite Centres (*KEPB* 1964)	IV 697
Appendix The Unity of European Culture (*NTDC* 1948)	III 706
The Approach to James Joyce	III 476
Archbishop Bramhall	I 628
Arnold and Pater (1930)	II 176
Arnold and Pater (*SE* 1932)	II 564
The Art of Poetry I	IV 413
[*The Ascent of Olympus* by Rendel Harris]	I 200
Audiences, Producers, Plays, Poets	III 64
Augustan Age Tories	I 788
The Author of 'The Burning Babe'	I 504
The Ballet	I 468
Baudelaire (*SE* 1932)	II 554
[*Baudelaire and the Symbolists* by Peter Quennell]	II 102
Baudelaire in our Time (*FLA* 1928)	I 800
The Beating of a Drum	I 419
Ben Jonson (1919)	I 266
Ben Jonson (*SE* 1932)	II 389
Bergson	I 33
Beyle and Balzac	I 229
The Birds of Prey	I 3
Bishop Bell	IV 400
[Books by W. J. Perry]	I 448
Books of the Quarter	I 519
[Books of the Year]	IV 97
Books of the Year Chosen by Eminent Contemporaries	III 838
The Borderline of Prose	I 67
Bradley's *Ethical Studies*	I 678
[*Brahmadarsanam* by Sri Ananda Acharya]	I 165
A Brief Introduction to the Method of Paul Valéry	I 454
A Brief Treatise on the Criticism of Poetry	I 279
[Brief über Ernst Robert Curtius]	IV 119
Britain and America	III 529
Bruce Lyttelton Richmond	IV 476
Building up the Christian World	II 272
Byron (1788–1824) (1937)	III 162
Byron (*OPAP* 1957)	IV 305
[*The Canary Murder Case* by S. S. Van Dine]	I 667

INDEX OF ARTICLE TITLES • 823

Catholicism and International Order (1933)	II 672
Catholicism and International Order (*EAM* 1936)	III 82
Charles Péguy	I 41
Charles Whibley (*SE* 1932)	II 613
Charles Whibley: A Memoir	II 242
Charleston, Hey! Hey!	I 569
Chaucer's 'Troilus'	I 510
[Christian Amnesty]	III 579
The Christian Conception of Education	III 417
The Christian News-Letter (1940)	III 352, III 357, III 362
The Christian News-Letter (1941)	III 395
The Christian News-Letter (1942)	III 436
[*A Christian Sociology for To-day*]	II 839
Christianity and Communism	II 247
Christopher Marlowe (*SE* 1932)	II 366
The Church as Action	III 129
The Church's Message to the World	III 162
Civilization: 1928 Model	I 771
The Class and the Élite (1945)	III 553
The Class and the Elite (*NTDC* 1948)	III 645
The Classics and the Man of Letters (1942)	III 441
The Classics and the Man of Letters (*TCTC* 1965)	IV 803
Classics in English	I 47
The Comedy of Humours	I 267
[Commemoration of Irving Babbitt]	III 401
[Comment on a Lecture by Van Wyck Brooks]	III 434
[A Comment on James Thurber]	IV 17
A Commentary (1924)	I 439, I 444, I 449
A Commentary (1925)	I 459, I 465
A Commentary (1926)	I 493, I 497, I 517
A Commentary (1927)	I 544, I 588, I 615, I 621, I 630, I 638, I 654, I 672, I 674
A Commentary (1928)	I 681, I 698, I 713, I 740, I 767, I 812
A Commentary (1929)	II 16, II 38, II 67
A Commentary (1930)	II 84, II 139, II 161, II 177
A Commentary (1931)	II 186, II 192, II 203, II 216
A Commentary (1932)	II 236, II 267, II 278, II 650
A Commentary (1933)	II 656, II 660, II 667, II 674
A Commentary (1934)	II 774, II 829, II 833, II 845

824 • INDEX OF ARTICLE TITLES

A Commentary (1935)	III 3, III 30, III 49, III 57
A Commentary (1936)	III 66, III 132, III 137, III 145
A Commentary (1937)	III 155, III 168, III 192, III 205
A Commentary (1938)	III 216, III 232, III 237, III 243
A Commentary (1939)	III 262, III 265, III 268
A Commentary (1940)	III 383
Comments by T. S. Eliot	IV 90
Comments on T. S. Eliot's New Play *The Cocktail Party*	III 790
[The Common Market]	IV 538
Concerning 'Intuition'	I 640
Conclusion (*UPUC* 1933)	II 759
Conclusion (*KEPB* 1964)	IV 667
[*Conscience and Christ* by Hastings Rashdall]	I 35
Contemporanea	I 174
Contemporary English Prose	I 411
A Contemporary Thomist	I 113
[Contribution to journal on 'Das Theater ist unersetzlich' ('The theatre is irreplaceable')]	IV 100
A Conversation with T. S. Eliot	IV 707
Correspondence	I 108
Countess Nora Wydenbruck	IV 452
Creative Criticism	I 509
[The Criterion]	I 394
Critical	II 665
Criticism in England	I 233
Cultural Diversity and European Unity (1945)	III 541
Cultural Diversity and European Unity (1946)	III 562
Cultural Forces in the Human Order by T. S. Eliot	III 540
Culture and Anarchy	I 703
Culture and Politics	III 584
Cyril Tourneur (1930)	II 185
Cyril Tourneur (*SE* 1932)	II 417
Dainty Devices	I 735
Dante (*SW* 1920)	I 344
Dante (*SE* 1932)	II 448
Dante as a 'Spiritual Leader'	I 297
Das schöpferische Recht des Regisseurs (The creative right of directors)	IV 125
Découverte de Paris	IV 60
Des Organes Publics et Privés de la Cooperation Intellectuelle	III 489
[*A Defence of Idealism* by May Sinclair]	I 97
The Development of Leibniz's Monadism (1916)	I 41

The Development of Leibniz's Monadism (*KEPB* 1964)	IV 680
The Devotional Poets of the Seventeenth Century	II 133
A Dialogue on Poetic Drama (1928)	I 737
A Dialogue on Dramatic Poetry (*SE* 1932)	II 309
Diderot	I 59
Disjecta Membra	I 160
Dr Charles Harris	III 144
Donne in our Time	II 227
Dossier on *Murder in the Cathedral*	IV 54
Dramatis Personae	I 404
'A Dream within a Dream'	III 464
Dryden the Critic (*JDPDC* 1932)	II 641
Dryden the Dramatist (*JDPDC* 1932)	II 632
Dryden the Poet (*JDPDC* 1932)	II 624
The Duchess of Malfi at The Lyric: and Poetic Drama	I 274
The Duchess of Malfy	III 411
Durkheim	I 30
The Early Novel	II 63
[Editorial Notes]	III 261
Education in a Christian Society	III 333
The Education of Taste	I 237
[Edwin Muir] (1959)	IV 404
Edwin Muir: 1887–1959 (1964)	IV 706
Eeldrop and Appleplex, I	I 61
Eeldrop and Appleplex, II	I 89
[*Egoists* by James Huneker]	I 10
[*The Elementary Forms of the Religious Life* by Émile Durkheim]	I 130
[*Elements of Folk Psychology* by Wilhelm Wundt] (1917)	I 51
[*Elements of Folk Psychology* by Wilhelm Wundt] (1918)	I 131
[Eliot interviewed by T. S. Matthews]	IV 716
[Eliot's choice of Books of the Year]	IV 402
Elizabeth and Essex	I 835
Elizabethan Dramatists	IV 548
The Elizabethan Grub Street	II 28
Elizabethan Travellers' Tales	II 53
An Emotional Unity	I 700
English Satire	I 473
The English Situation	III 339
The English Tradition	III 373
English Verse Satire	I 499
Epigrams of an Elizabethan Courtier	I 577
The Epistemologist's Theory of Knowledge (*KEPB* 1964)	IV 612
The Epistemologist's Theory of Knowledge *continued* (*KEPB* 1964)	IV 635
Essays Ancient & Modern	III 71
Preface	III 71

Religion and Literature	III 72
Catholicism and International Order	III 82
The *Pensées* of Pascal	III 94
Modern Education and the Classics	III 106
In Memoriam	III 113
[*Essays of a Catholic Layman in England* by Hilaire Belloc]	II 215
Essays on Elizabethan Drama	IV 121
Euripides and Gilbert Murray: A Performance at the Holborn Empire	I 279
Euripides and Professor Murray (*SE* 1932)	II 323
Experiment in Criticism	II 71
An Extempore Exhumation	I 763
[*Extraits d'un Journal* by Charles du Bos]	II 48
Ezra Pound (1946)	III 574
Ezra Pound (1950)	III 824
Ezra Pound: His Metric and Poetry (1918)	I 133
Ezra Pound: His Metric and Poetry (*TCTC* 1965)	IV 816
[*Fashion in Literature* by E. E. Kellett]	II 222
Fr Cheetham Retires from Gloucester Road	IV 116
[The Festival of Poetry]	IV 544
For Lancelot Andrewes: Essays on Style and Order	I 791
Preface	I 791
Niccolo Machiavelli	I 792
Baudelaire in our Time	I 800
A Note on Richard Crashaw	I 807
A Foreign Mind	I 244
Foreword (1951)	IV 9
Foreword (1952)	IV 56
Foreword (1956)	IV 121
Foreword (1959)	IV 432
Foreword (1960)	IV 458
Foreword to the English Edition	IV 76
A Forgotten Utopia	I 92
Four Elizabethan Dramatists (*SE* 1932)	II 359
Four Elizabethan Dramatists. I A Preface (1924)	I 435
[*Four Quartets*]	III 587
Francis Herbert Bradley (*SE* 1932)	II 575
[*The Free Society* by John Middleton Murry]	III 605
[*The French Renascence* by Charles Sarolea]	I 25
Freud's Illusions	I 832
From Poe to Valéry (1948)	III 721
From Poe to Valéry (*TCTC* 1965)	IV 736
[From *Revelation*, ed. Baillie and Martin]	III 173
From T. S. Eliot	II 655
The Frontiers of Criticism (1956)	IV 119
The Frontiers of Criticism (*OPAP* 1957)	IV 221

INDEX OF ARTICLE TITLES

Full Employment and the Responsibility of Christians	III 534
The Function of Criticism (1923)	I 417
The Function of Criticism (SE 1932)	II 292
Fustel de Coulanges	I 816
The Future of Poetic Drama	III 246
A Game at Chesse	II 104
The Genesis of Philosophic Prose	II 33
Gentlemen and Seamen	I 8
Geoffrey Faber	IV 483
George Herbert	IV 511
I	IV 511
II	IV 519
III	IV 528
George Herbert A Select Bibliography	IV 535
Giordano Bruno	I 45
[*God* by J. Middleton Murry]	II 99
'Goethe as the Sage' (1955)	IV 115
Goethe as the Sage (OPAP 1957)	IV 319
The Golden Ass of Apuleius	I 775
Gordon Craig's Socratic Dialogues	IV 103
Grammar and Usage	I 559
The Great Layman	III 409
[*The Greene Murder Case* by S. S. Van Dine]	I 774
[Greeting to the Asociacíon de Artistas Aficionados]	IV 76
[Greeting to the Staatstheater Kassel]	IV 452
[*Group Theories of Religion and the Individual* by Clement C. J. Webb] (1916)	I 29
[*Group Theories of Religion and the Individual* by Clement C. J. Webb] (1916)	I 37
Hamlet (SE 1932)	II 384
Hamlet and his Problems	I 255
The Hawthorne Aspect	I 184
Homage to John Dryden	I 453
Preface	I 454
Homage to Wilkie Collins	I 562
Homage to Wyndham Lewis 1884–1957	IV 126
Hooker, Hobbes and Others	I 527
Hopousia	III 349
Housman on Poetry	II 678
The Humanism of Irving Babbitt (1928)	I 760
The Humanism of Irving Babbitt (SE 1932)	II 596
Humanist, Artist, and Scientist	I 257
A Humanist Theory of Value	II 87

The Idea of a Christian Society (1939)	III 268
The Idea of a Christian Society (1939)	III 270
Preface	III 270
The Idea of a Christian Society I	III 271
II	III 281
III	III 293
IV	III 299
Notes	III 303
Appendix	III 316
Appendix	III 316
The Idea of a Literary Review	I 484
The Idealism of Julien Benda	I 749
If I Were a Dean	II 199
Imperfect Critics: Swinburne As Critic (SW 1920)	I 315
The Importance of Wyndham Lewis	IV 126
In Memoriam (1930)	II 143
In Memoriam (EAM 1936)	III 113
In Memory of Henry James	I 116
In Praise of Kipling's Verse	III 436
In Sincerity and Earnestness: New Britain as I See It	II 840
The Influence of Landscape upon the Poet	IV 460
The Influence of Ovid	I 502
Inquiry into the Spirit and Language of Night	III 231
[Interview]	IV 499
[Interview with T. S. Eliot]	IV 504
Introduction (SW 1920)	I 302
Introduction (1926)	I 489
Introduction (1928)	I 708
Introduction (1930)	II 164
Introduction (1930)	II 176
Introduction (1931)	II 216
Introduction (UPUC 1933)	II 686
Introduction (1935)	III 35
Introduction (1936)	III 70
Introduction (1937)	III 167
Introduction (1944)	III 517
Introduction (1948)	III 609
Introduction (NTDC 1948)	III 617
Introduction (1948)	III 721
Introduction (1950)	III 798
Introduction (1950)	III 816
Introduction (1954)	IV 83
Introduction (1958)	IV 384
Introduction: 1928 (1949)	III 749
Introduction by T. S. Eliot (1928)	I 812
Introduction By T. S. Eliot (1952)	IV 31

INDEX OF ARTICLE TITLES

Introduction to Goethe	II 5
Introductory Essay	II 171
Introductory Note	III 444
Isolated Superiority	I 691
Israfel	I 613
An Italian Critic on Donne and Crashaw	I 475
John Bramhall (SE 1932)	II 528
John Donne	I 407
John Dryden (1921)	I 374
John Dryden (1930)	II 154
John Dryden (SE 1932)	II 503
John Dryden I, II and III	II 199
John Dryden The Poet the Dramatist the Critic	II 624
Dryden the Poet	II 624
Dryden the Dramatist	II 632
Dryden the Critic	II 641
John Dryden's Tragedies	III 467
John Ford (1932)	II 278
John Ford (SE 1932)	II 426
John Marston (1934)	II 842
John Marston (1934)	II 852
John Maynard Keynes	III 554
John Webster	I 694
Johnson as Critic and Poet (OPAP 1957)	IV 277
Kipling Redivivus	I 220
Knowledge and Experience in the Philosophy of F. H. Bradley	IV 555
Preface	IV 555
On Our Knowledge of Immediate Experience	IV 557
On the Distinction of 'Real' and 'Ideal'	IV 570
The Psychologist's Treatment of Knowledge	IV 591
The Epistemologist's Theory of Knowledge	IV 612
The Epistemologist's Theory of Knowledge *continued*	IV 635
Solipsism	IV 657
Conclusion	IV 667
Appendix I: The Development of Leibniz's Monadism	IV 680
Appendix II: Leibniz's Monads and Bradley's Finite Centres	IV 697
[*La guerra eterna e il dramma del' esistenza* by Antonio Aliotta]	I 164
[Lady Margaret Rhondda]	IV 395
Lambeth and Education. The Report Criticised	III 761
L'amitié Franco-Britannique	IV 74
Lancelot Andrewes (1926)	I 517
Lancelot Andrewes (SE 1932)	II 518
Last Words	III 256

The Latin Tradition	II 14
A Lay Theologian	III 322
Le Morte Darthur	II 805
'Le salut de trois grands poètes: Londres: T. S. Eliot'	IV 100
Leadership and Letters	III 736
Leçon de Valéry (1946)	III 554
'Leçon de Valéry' (1947)	III 580
Leibniz's Monads and Bradley's Finite Centres (1916)	I 41
Leibniz's Monads and Bradley's Finite Centres (*KEPB* 1964)	IV 697
Les Lettres Anglaises	I 608
The Lesson of Baudelaire	I 357
The Letters of J. B. Yeats	I 72
[*Letters of Mrs Gaskell and Charles Eliot Norton*]	II 672
Lettre d'Angleterre	I 385
Lettres Étrangères (1922)	I 398
Lettres Étrangères (1923)	I 426
The Lion and the Fox	III 212
Literature	IV 79
Literature, Science, and Dogma	I 579
Literature and the American Courts	I 150
Literature and the Modern World	III 24
The Literature of Fascism	I 824
The Literature of Politics (1955)	IV 107
The Literature of Politics (*TCTC* 1965)	IV 802
The Local Flavour	I 278
London Letter (1921)	I 364, I 369, I 374, I 377
London Letter (1922)	I 382, I 392, I 395, I 398
['Lotze, Bradley, and Bosanquet' by Agnes Cuming]	I 104
M. Bourget's Last Novel	I 83
Man and Society	III 346
The Man of Letters and the Future of Europe	III 522
The Man who was King	I 5
[*A Manual of Modern Scholastic Philosophy* by Cardinal Mercier]	I 102
Marianne Moore	I 431
Marie Lloyd (*SE* 1932)	II 584
Marivaux	I 205
Massinger	I 529
Matthew Arnold (*UPUC* 1933)	II 737
['The Meaning of the Universe' by C. E. Hooper]	I 103
Medieval Philosophy	I 539
[Memoir of Richard Aldington]	IV 817
[Memorial Tribute for Mrs Violet Schiff]	IV 503
[Memorial Tribute for Sylvia Beach]	IV 510

[*Mens Creatrix* by William Temple]	I 75
'The Merry Masque of Our Lady in London Town'	I 840
A Message	IV 88
[Message from T. S. Eliot]	IV 30
[Message to *Merkur*]	III 839
Message to the Anglo-Catholic Congress in London	II 160
The Metaphysical Poets (1921)	I 381
The Metaphysical Poets (*SE* 1932)	II 484
The Method of Mr Pound	I 262
Milton (1947)	III 588
Milton (1948)	III 605
Milton I (*OPAP* 1957)	IV 252
Milton II (*OPAP* 1957)	IV 259
The Minor Metaphysicals	II 149
Miss Harriet Weaver (1961)	IV 496
Miss Harriet Weaver (1962)	IV 501
[Mr Ashley Dukes]	IV 443
Mr Barnes and Mr Rowse	II 41
Mr Charles Williams	III 540
Mr Chesterton (and Stevenson)	I 679
Mr Doughty's Epic	I 25
Mr Harold Monro: A Poet and his Ideal	II 254
Mr Leacock Serious	I 27
Mr Lee Masters	I 44
Mr Lucas's Webster	I 746
Mr Middleton Murry's Synthesis	I 662
Mr Murry's Shakespeare	III 141
Mr P. E. More's Essays	II 11
Mr Reckitt, Mr Tomlin and the Crisis	III 162
[*Mr Shaw and 'The Maid'* by J. M. Robertson]	I 495
Mrs Runcie's Pudding	IV 98
The Modern Dilemma	II 680
Modern Education and the Classics (*EAM* 1936)	III 106
The Modern Mind (*UPUC* 1933)	II 747
Modern Tendencies in Poetry	I 287
Mögen Sie Picasso?	IV 496
More and Tudor Drama	I 532
Murmuring of Innumerable Bees	I 256
The Music of Poetry (1942)	III 434
The Music of Poetry (*OPAP* 1957)	IV 145
Mystic and Politician as Poet	II 143
[*The Mystical Doctrine of St John of the Cross*]	II 839
The Mysticism of Blake	I 651
The Naked Man	I 279
The Nature of Cultural Relations	III 459

The Need for Poetic Drama	III 150
The New Elizabethans and the Old	I 210
New Philosophers	I 180
Niccolo Machiavelli (1469–1527) (1927)	I 621
Niccolo Machiavelli (*FLA* 1928)	I 792
Nightwood	III 173
The Noh and the Image	I 80
A Note (1959)	IV 451
Note (*TCTC* 1965)	IV 723
A Note by T. S. Eliot	III 167
A Note of Introduction	IV 497
A Note on Culture and Politics (*NTDC* 1948)	III 686
A Note on Ezra Pound	I 192
A Note on *In Parenthesis* and *The Anathemata*	IV 101
A Note on Intelligence and Intuition	I 656
A note on *Monstre Gai* by Wyndham Lewis	IV 93
A Note on Poetry and Belief	I 565
A Note on Richard Crashaw (*FLA* 1928)	I 807
A Note on *The Criterion* By T. S. Eliot	IV 818
A Note on the Verse of John Milton	III 137
A Note on Translation	IV 705
A Note on Two Odes of Cowley	III 221
Note sur Mallarmé et Poe	I 525
Notes (1923)	I 410
Notes (1923)	I 418
Notes (*ICS* 1939)	III 303
Notes . . . from T. S. Eliot	III 835
Notes on Education and Culture: and Conclusion (*NTDC* 1948)	III 695
Notes on the Way [I]	III 6
Notes on the Way [II]	III 9
Notes on the Way [III]	III 14
Notes on the Way [IV]	III 19
Notes Towards the Definition of Culture (1943)	III 447
I	III 447
II	III 450
III	III 453
IV	III 456
Notes Towards the Definition of Culture (1948)	III 616
Preface	III 616
Introduction	III 617
The Three Senses of 'Culture'	III 623
The Class and the Elite	III 645
Unity and Diversity: The Region	III 662
Unity and Diversity: Sect and Cult	III 674
A Note on Culture and Politics	III 686
Notes on Education and Culture: and Conclusion	III 695

  Appendix The Unity of European Culture   III 706
Notes Towards the Definition of Culture (1962)   IV 502
  Preface to the 1962 Edition   IV 502

Obituary   IV 479
[Obituary Notice for Louis MacNeice]   IV 546
Observations   I 169
The Old Comedy   I 301
On a Recent Piece of Criticism   III 227
On Christianity and a Useful Life . . .   III 250
[On G. K. Chesterton]   III 136
On Our Knowledge of Immediate Experience (KEPB 1964)   IV 557
On Poetry (1947)   III 588
On Poetry and Poets   IV 134
  Preface   IV 134
  I. On Poets   IV 135
   The Social Function of Poetry   IV 135
   The Music of Poetry   IV 145
   What Is Minor Poetry?   IV 158
   What is a Classic?   IV 172
   Poetry and Drama   IV 189
   The Three Voices of Poetry   IV 208
   The Frontiers of Criticism   IV 221
  II. On Poets   IV 236
   Virgil and the Christian World   IV 236
   Sir John Davies   IV 247
   Milton I   IV 252
   Milton II   IV 259
   Johnson as Critic and Poet   IV 277
   Byron   IV 305
   Goethe as the Sage   IV 319
   Rudyard Kipling   IV 339
   Yeats   IV 362
On Reading Einstein   II 179
On Teaching the Appreciation of Poetry   IV 463
On the Distinction of 'Real' and 'Ideal' (KEPB 1964)   IV 570
On the Eve: A Dialogue   I 462
[On the production of *The Confidential Clerk*]   IV 475
Orage: Memories   II 864
'Our Culture'   III 595
[*Outlines of Jainism* by Jagmanderlal Jaini]   I 168
[*The Oxford Handbook of Religious Knowledge*]   II 838
The Oxford Jonson   I 757

The Panegyric by Mr T. S. Eliot   IV 440
Parnassus Biceps   I 667

Paul Elmer More	III 159
[Paul Elmer More, *Selected Shelburne Essays*]	III 70
The *Pensées* of Pascal (*EAM* 1936)	III 94
The Perfect Critic [I] (1920)	I 301
The Perfect Critic [II] (1920)	I 301
The Perfect Critic (*SW* 1920)	I 307
Personality and Demonic Possession	II 780
Philip Massinger (1920)	I 300
Philip Massinger (*SE* 1932)	II 435
[*Philosophy & War* by Émile Boutroux]	I 40
[*The Philosophy of Nietzsche* by A. Wolf]	I 20
The Phoenix Nest	I 568
Plague Pamphlets	I 506
Planning and Religion	III 470
[*The Playgoer's Handbook to the English Renaissance Drama* by Agnes Mure Mackenzie]	I 637
Plays of Ben Jonson	I 628
[*The Poems English Latin and Greek of Richard Crashaw* ed. L. C. Martin]	I 731
'Poet and Saint . . .'	I 608
The Poetic Drama	I 297
Poetry and Drama (1951)	IV 8
Poetry and Drama (1951)	IV 12
Poetry and Drama (*OPAP* 1957)	IV 189
Poetry and Film	IV 6
Poetry and Propaganda	II 107
Poetry and Religion	I 548
Poetry and Religion [II]	I 590
Poetry and the Schools	IV 124
Poetry by T. S. Eliot	III 833
[Poetry Collections and Commentary]	I 111
The Poetry of W. B. Yeats	III 349
Poets' Borrowings	I 731
The Point of View	I 8
Political Theorists	I 623
A Popular Shakespeare	I 488
Popular Theologians	I 602
A Portrait of Michael Roberts	III 795
The Possibility of a Poetic Drama (1920)	I 301
The Possibility of a Poetic Drama (*SW* 1920)	I 333
The Post-Georgians	I 214
The Preacher as Artist	I 270
A Prediction in Regard to Three English Authors	I 435
Preface (*HJD* 1924)	I 454
Preface (1928)	I 778
Preface (*FLA* 1928)	I 791

Preface (1929)	II 66
Preface (1931)	II 224
Preface (1932)	II 242
Preface (*UPUC* 1933)	II 685
Preface (*ASG* 1934)	II 781
Preface (*EAM* 1936)	III 71
Preface (*ICS* 1939)	III 270
Preface (1942)	III 426
Preface (1946)	III 558
Preface (*NTDC* 1948)	III 616
Preface (1950)	III 811
Preface (1951)	IV 10, IV 17, IV 18
Preface (1952)	IV 48
Preface (1954)	IV 92
Preface (*OPAP* 1957)	IV 134
Preface (1957)	IV 373
Preface (1959)	IV 448
Preface (1961)	IV 478
Preface (1961)	IV 482
Preface (1961)	IV 494
Preface (*ED* 1963)	IV 548
Preface (*KEPB* 1964)	IV 555
Preface (1965)	IV 719
Preface by T. S. Eliot	III 368
[*Preface to a Christian Sociology* by C. E. Hudson]	III 123
A Preface to Modern Literature	I 422
Preface to the 1928 Edition	I 737
Preface to the 1962 Edition (*NTDC* 1962)	IV 502
[Prefatory Note on James Joyce]	III 779
President Wilson	I 65
[Prizewinners]	I 398
The Problem of Education	II 842
The Problems of the Shakespeare Sonnets	I 574
Professional, Or . . .	I 162
Professor H. H. Joachim	III 242
Professor Karl Mannheim	III 583
Prólogo del autor para la edición española	III 574
Prologue to an Essay on Criticism (1928)	I 683
Prologue to an Essay on Criticism (1928)	I 721
Prose and Verse	I 358
The Prose of the Preacher	II 48
[*The Prospects of Humanism* by Lawrence Hyde]	II 202
The Psychologist's Treatment of Knowledge (*KEPB* 1964)	IV 591
Publishers' Preface	I 780
The Publishing of Poetry	IV 68

Recent British Periodical Literature in Ethics	I 123
Recent Detective Fiction	I 618
Records of the Class	I 473
[*The Reef of Stars* by H. de Vere Stacpoole]	I 50
Reflections on Contemporary Poetry. I.	I 86
Reflections on Contemporary Poetry [II]	I 98
Reflections on Contemporary Poetry [III]	I 105
Reflections on Contemporary Poetry [IV]	I 241
Reflections on the Unity of European Culture	III 554
Reflections on the Unity of European Culture (II) (1946)	III 561
Reflections on the Unity of European Culture (II) (1953)	IV 79
Reflections on the Unity of European Culture (III)	III 561
Reflections on *Vers Libre* (1917)	I 53
Reflections on Vers Libre (*TCTC* 1965)	IV 816
[*Reflections on Violence* by Georges Sorel]	I 77
Religion and Literature (1935)	III 30
Religion and Literature (*EAM* 1936)	III 72
[*Religion and Philosophy* by R. G. Collingwood]	I 76
Religion and Science: A Phantom Dilemma	II 256
[*Religion and Science* by J. T. Merz]	I 39
[*Religion and Science* by John Theodore Merz]	I 166
Religion without Humanism	II 117
Religious Drama: Medieval and Modern	III 195
Religious Drama and the Church	II 849
Rencontre	I 470
A Reply to Mr Ward	I 743
[Report on Obscene Publications]	IV 376
Reunion: Construction or Destruction	III 514
Reunion by Destruction	III 494
'Rhetoric' And Poetic Drama (*SE* 1932)	II 301
Rhyme and Reason	II 128
Richard Edwards	I 649
A Romantic Patrician	I 220
The Romantic Englishman, the Comic Spirit, and the Function Of Criticism	I 355
The Romantic Generation, If It Existed	I 248
[Rudyard Kipling] (1941)	III 411
Rudyard Kipling (*OPAP* 1957)	IV 339
Rudyard Kipling (1959)	IV 405
The Sacred Wood: Essays on Poetry and Criticism	I 302
Introduction	I 302
The Perfect Critic	I 307
Imperfect Critics: Swinburne As Critic	I 315
The Possibility of a Poetic Drama	I 333

INDEX OF ARTICLE TITLES • 837

Swinburne as Poet	I 340
Dante	I 344
[The Saddest Word]	IV 99
[Salutation]	IV 401
[Samuel Taylor Coleridge, 1772–1834]	II 829
Saving the Future	III 125
A Sceptical Patrician	I 225
A Scholar's Essays	I 670
['Schopenhauer and Individuality' by Bertram M. Laing]	I 104
Scylla and Charybdis	IV 35
The Search for Moral Sanction	II 261
Second Message to the Anglo-Catholic Congress	II 160
Second Thoughts about Humanism (1929)	II 23
Second Thoughts about Humanism (1929)	II 66
Second Thoughts about Humanism (SE 1932)	II 604
Selected Essays 1917–1932	II 284
Tradition and the Individual Talent	II 285
The Function of Criticism	II 292
'Rhetoric' And Poetic Drama	II 301
A Dialogue on Dramatic Poetry	II 309
Euripides and Professor Murray	II 323
Seneca in Elizabethan Translation	II 327
Four Elizabethan Dramatists	II 359
Christopher Marlowe	II 366
Shakespeare and the Stoicism of Seneca	II 373
Hamlet	II 384
Ben Jonson	II 389
Thomas Middleton	II 400
Thomas Heywood	II 408
Cyril Tourneur	II 417
John Ford	II 426
Philip Massinger	II 435
Dante	II 448
The Metaphysical Poets	II 484
Andrew Marvell	II 492
John Dryden	II 503
William Blake	II 513
Swinburne as Poet	II 518
Lancelot Andrewes	II 518
John Bramhall	II 528
Thoughts after Lambeth	II 535
Baudelaire	II 554
Arnold and Pater	II 564
Francis Herbert Bradley	II 575
Marie Lloyd	II 584
Wilkie Collins and Dickens	II 588

    The Humanism of Irving Babbitt   II 596
    Second Thoughts about Humanism   II 604
    Charles Whibley   II 613
Seneca in Elizabethan Translation (1927)   I 649
Seneca in Elizabethan Translation (*SE* 1932)   II 327
A Sermon   III 598
Seventeenth-Century Preachers   I 765
Shakespeare and Montaigne   I 477
Shakespeare and the Stoicism of Seneca (1927)   I 654
Shakespeare and the Stoicism of Seneca (*SE* 1932)   II 373
Shakespeare Criticism   II 819
Shelley and Keats (*UPUC* 1933)   II 727
Short Notices (1918)   I 173
Short Notices (1918)   I 183
Short Reviews   I 121
Shorter Notices   I 177
Should There Be a Censorship of Books?   III 51
The Significance of Charles Williams   III 575
The Silurist   I 645
Sir John Davies (1926)   I 534
Sir John Davies (*OPAP* 1957)   IV 247
Sir John Denham   I 760
[*Social Adaptation* by L. M. Bristol]   I 29
The Social Function of Poetry (1943)   III 480
The Social Function of Poetry (1945)   III 541
The Social Function of Poetry (*OPAP* 1957)   IV 135
Solipsism (*KEPB* 1964)   IV 657
Some Notes on the Blank Verse of Christopher Marlowe   I 255
Some Thoughts on Braille   IV 60
[*Son of Woman* by John Middleton Murry]   II 209
The Sources of Chapman   I 572
[A special message about Ezra Pound]   IV 375
[Speech at the Nobel Banquet]   III 719
[Speech to the BBC Governors]   IV 131
Spinoza   I 586
The Spoken Word   IV 12
Stage Studies   I 676
[Statement about *The New Leader*]   IV 440
[Statement on the Award of the Nobel Prize]   III 719
Stendhal the Romantic   I 534
The Story of the Pageant   II 832
Studies in Contemporary Criticism (1918)   I 197
Studies in Contemporary Criticism (1918)   I 201
Studies in Sanctity. VIII. George Herbert   II 244
A Study Of Marlowe   I 583
[*The Study of Religions* by Stanley A. Cook]   I 79

Style and Thought	I 157
A Sub-Pagan Society?	III 324
Swinburne	I 279
Swinburne and the Elizabethans	I 255
Swinburne as Poet (SW 1920)	I 340
Swinburne as Poet (SE 1932)	II 518
[T. S. Eliot] (1927)	I 544
[T. S. Eliot] (1942)	III 417
[T. S. Eliot] (1943)	III 446
T. S. Eliot Answers Questions	III 775
T. S. Eliot Nous Dit	III 794
T. S. Eliot on Poetry in Wartime	III 442
T. S. Eliot on the Language of *The New English Bible*	IV 538
T. S. Eliot Talks about his Poetry	IV 396
A Tale of a Whale	I 4
Talk on Dante	III 803
Talking Freely: T. S. Eliot and Tom Greenwell	IV 486
Tarr	I 190
Television is not Friendly Enough	IV 402
[*Theism and Humanism* by A. J. Balfour]	I 15
Thinking in Verse	II 122
[*Thomas Hardy* by H. C. Duffin]	I 22
Thomas Heywood (1931)	II 216
Thomas Heywood (SE 1932)	II 408
Thomas Middleton (1927)	I 621
Thomas Middleton (SE 1932)	II 400
Thomas Stearns Eliot (1917)	I 53
Thomas Stearns Eliot (1921)	I 354
Thomas Stearns Eliot (1935)	III 40
Thomas Stearns Eliot (1940)	III 346
Thomas Stearns Eliot (1950)	III 803
Thomas Stearns Eliot (1960)	IV 471
Thomas Stearns Eliot (1965)	IV 718
Thomas Stearns Eliot Gratulation	IV 79
'Those Who need Privacy and Those Whose Need is Company'	IV 27
Thoughts After Lambeth (1931)	II 192
Thoughts after Lambeth (SE 1932)	II 535
[Three Books by Eugene O'Neill]	I 496
The Three Provincialities (1922)	I 382
The Three Provincialities (1922) (1951)	IV 3
Three Questions	I 391
Three Reformers	I 784
The Three Senses of 'Culture' (NTDC 1948)	III 623
The Three Voices of Poetry (1953)	IV 82
The Three Voices of Poetry (OPAP 1957)	IV 208

840 • INDEX OF ARTICLE TITLES

To Criticize the Critic (*TCTC* 1965)	IV 724
To Criticize the Critic and other writings	IV 723
Note	IV 723
To Criticize the Critic	IV 724
From Poe to Valéry	IV 736
American Literature and the American Language	IV 736
The Aims of Education 1	IV 751
The Aims of Education 2	IV 764
The Aims of Education 3	IV 777
The Aims of Education 4	IV 789
What Dante Means to Me	IV 802
The Literature of Politics	IV 802
The Classics and the Man of Letters	IV 803
Ezra Pound: His Metric and Poetry	IV 816
Reflections on Vers Libre	IV 816
[To Ezra Pound on his Seventieth Birthday] (1955)	IV 115
[To Ezra Pound on his Seventieth Birthday] (1956)	IV 118
To the Reader	III 521
[*Totem* by Harold Stovin]	III 69
Towards a Christian Britain (1941)	III 390
Towards a Christian Britain (1941)	III 403
[*The Tower* by Hugo von Hofmannsthal]	IV 545
Tradition and Experiment in Present-Day Literature	II 71
Tradition and Orthodoxy	II 809
Tradition and the Individual Talent [I] (1919)	I 255
Tradition and the Individual Talent [II & III] (1919)	I 266
Tradition and the Individual Talent (*SE* 1932)	II 285
A Tribute	IV 91
[Tribute to Aldous Huxley]	IV 721
[Tribute to Ananda K. Coomaraswamy]	III 734
[Tribute to Artur Lundkvist]	IV 118
[Tribute to August Strindberg]	III 735
[Tribute to Charles Maurras]	III 602
[Tribute to Georg Svensson on his 60th Birthday]	IV 706
[Tribute to Giuseppe Ungaretti]	IV 474
[Tribute to John Davidson]	IV 130
[Tribute to Luigi Pirandello]	IV 68
A Tribute To Mario Praz	IV 818
[Tribute to Sir Hugh Walpole]	III 393
[Tribute to Victoria Ocampo]	IV 509
[A Tribute to Wilfred Owen]	IV 705
The Tudor Biographers	II 59
The Tudor Translators	II 23
Turbervile's Ovid	II 8
Turgenev	I 109
The Twelfth Century	I 635

Twenty-One Answers	III 594
Two Studies in Dante	I 781
The Two Unfinished Novels	I 119
[*The Ultimate Belief* by A. Clutton-Brock]	I 39
Ulysses, Order, and Myth (1923)	I 422
Ulysses, Order, and Myth (1964)	IV 551
Un Feuillet Unique	III 802
The Unfading Genius of Rudyard Kipling	IV 435
Unity and Diversity: Sect and Cult (*NTDC* 1948)	III 674
Unity and Diversity: The Region (*NTDC* 1948)	III 662
The Unity of European Culture (*NTDC* 1948)	III 706
[*Union Portraits* by Gamaliel Bradford]	I 61
The Use of Poetry and the Use of Criticism	II 685
Preface	II 685
Introduction	II 686
Apology for the Countess of Pembroke	II 700
The Age of Dryden	II 709
Wordsworth and Coleridge	II 716
Shelley and Keats	II 727
Matthew Arnold	II 737
The Modern Mind	II 747
Conclusion	II 760
The Value and Use of Cathedrals in England To-Day	IV 19
Vergil and the Christian World	IV 19
Verse Pleasant and Unpleasant	I 152
The Very Revd F. P. Harton	IV 401
A Victorian Sculptor	I 155
Views and Reviews [I]	III 43
Views and Reviews [II]	III 46
Views and Reviews [III]	III 55
Views and Reviews [IV]	III 61
Views and Reviews (1940)	III 328, III 331, III 386
Views and Reviews (1941)	III 393
Virgil and the Christian World (*OPAP* 1957)	IV 236
Virginia Woolf	III 390
The Voice of His Time	III 428
Wanley and Chapman	I 479
War-Paint and Feathers	I 260
Was There a Scottish Literature?	I 251
What Dante Means to Me (*TCTC* 1965)	IV 802
What Does the Church Stand For?	II 862
What France Means to You	III 519
What India is Thinking about To-day	I 12

What is a Classic? (1944)	III 521
What is a Classic? (1945)	III 534
What is a Classic? (*OPAP* 1957)	IV 172
What is Minor Poetry? (1944)	III 533
What Is Minor Poetry? (*OPAP* 1957)	IV 158
Whether Rostand Had Something About Him	I 251
Whitman and Tennyson	I 541
Why Mr Russell is a Christian	I 632
Why Rural Verse?	I 471
Wilkie Collins and Dickens (1927)	I 635
Wilkie Collins and Dickens (*SE* 1932)	II 588
William Blake (*SE* 1932)	II 513
William James on Immortality	I 95
[*The Wine of the Puritans* by Van Wyck Brooks]	I 7
[*With Americans of Past and Present Days* by J. J. Jusserand]	I 49
[*The Women of Trachis*: A Symposium]	IV 99
Wordsworth and Coleridge (*UPUC* 1933)	II 716
[Works by Conan Doyle and A. K. Green]	II 19
[*The World as Imagination* by E. D. Fawcett]	I 179
The Writer as Artist	III 369
The Writings of Charles Williams	III 598
Wyndham Lewis	IV 127
The Year's Poetry	III 141
Yeats (*OPAP* 1957)	IV 362